Assessing Learners with Special Needs

An Applied Approach

SIXTH EDITION

Assessing Learners with Special Needs

An Applied Approach

Terry Overton
University of Texas–Brownsville

Merrill
is an imprint of

Upper Saddle River, New Jersey
Columbus, Ohio

Library of Congress Cataloging in Publication Data

Overton, Terry.
　Assessing learners with special needs: an applied approach/Terry Overton. —6th ed.
　　p. cm
　Includes bibliographical references and indexes.
　ISBN-13: 978-0-13-159957-4
　ISBN-10: 0-13-159957-7
　1. Educational tests and measurements—United States 2. Special education—United States.
3. Behavioral assessment of children—United States. I. Title.
　LB30451.094 2009
　371.9—dc22　　　　　　　　　　　　　　　　2008000325

Vice President and Executive Publisher: Jeffery W. Johnston
Executive Editor: Ann Castel Davis
Editorial Assistant: Penny Burleson
Senior Managing Editor: Pamela D. Bennett
Production Editor: Sheryl Glicker Langner
Production Coordination: Roxanne Klaas, S4Carlisle
Design Coordinator: Diane C. Lorenzo
Photo Coordinator: Monica Merkel
Cover Designer: Diane Y. Ernsberger
Cover art: Superstock
Production Manager: Laura Messerly
Director of Marketing: Quinn Perkson
Marketing Manager: Erica DeLuca
Marketing Coordinator: Brian Mounts

This book was set in Bookman by S4Carlisle. It was printed and bound by Edwards Brothers, Inc. The cover was printed by Phoenix Color Corp.

Chapter Opening Photo Credits: Scott Cunningham/Merrill, pp. 2, 42, 358; Lori Whitley/Merrill, p. 102; Linda Kauffman/Merrill, p. 164; Copyright © 2008 by The Riverside Publishing Company. Photograph as seen on page 14 of The Riverside Publishing Company 2008 Clinical and Special Needs Catalog reproduced with permission of the publisher. All rights reserved. p. 130; Barbara Schwartz/Merrill, p. 200; Patrick White/Merrill, p. 250; David Young–Wolff/Photo Edit Inc., p. 316; Anne Vega/Merrill, p. 404; Maria B. Vonada/Merrill, p. 453.

Pearson® is a registered trademark of Pearson plc
Merrill® is a registered trademark of Pearson Education, Inc.

Pearson Education Ltd., London
Pearson Education Singapore, Pte. Ltd.
Pearson Education Canada, Inc.
Pearson Education—Japan

Pearson Education Australia PtY., Limited
Pearson Education North Asia, Ltd., Hong Kong
Pearson Educación de Mexico, S.A. de C.V.
Pearson Education Malaysia, Pte. Ltd.
Pearson Education Upper Saddle River, New Jersey

Merrill
is an imprint of

10 9 8 7 6 5 4 3 2 1
ISBN 13: 978-0-13-159957-4
ISBN 10:　　0-13-159957-7

For my Family

And a special thanks to the wonderful people at the University of Texas–Brownsville

The process of monitoring and assessing students within the general education environment who have academic and behavioral challenges continues to change as a result of changes in federal regulations and discovery of evidence-based practices. The sixth edition of *Assessing Learners with Special Needs: An Applied Approach* was written to reflect these changes in the assessment process.

Like earlier editions, the primary focus of this text is to provide students with a practical approach for learning about the complex procedures of the assessment process. The sixth edition incorporates the latest revision of IDEA, the Individuals with Disabilities Education Improvement Act, or IDEA 2004 and the regulations that govern public schools. This edition includes the following changes:

- An emphasis on progress monitoring, including progress monitoring applied to the acquisition of knowledge and skills presented in this text
- Changes within the assessment process according to the regulations of IDEA 2004
- Increased number of case studies throughout the text and inclusion of exercises in the text
- Expanded chapter on special considerations including assessment of Autism Spectrum Disorders
- Increased emphasis and coverage of curriculum-based assessment
- Increased consideration of students from culturally and linguistically diverse backgrounds in the assessment process

This text presents complex concepts in a step-by-step manner and provides students with practice exercises for each step. Students also have portions of assessment instruments, protocols, and scoring tables provided as part of their practice exercises. Students will participate in the educational decision-making process using data from classroom observations, curriculum-based assessment, functional behavioral assessment, and data from norm-referenced assessment.

This text is divided into four parts. Part 1, "Introduction to Assessment," introduces students to the basic concepts in assessment and types of assessment. This part also presents the legal issues of assessment in IDEA 2004 and ethical concerns of assessment.

Part 2, "Technical Prerequisites of Understanding Assessment," addresses the topics of descriptive statistics, reliability, and validity.

Part 3, "Assessing Students," presents the mechanics of both informal and formal assessment. Students practice curriculum-based assessment, behavioral assessment, and norm-referenced assessment.

Part 4, "Interpretation of Assessment Results," discusses interpretation of data for classroom interventions, eligibility decisions, and educational planning. Numerous case studies are included in this section.

SPECIAL FEATURES OF THE SIXTH EDITION

Each chapter contains the following special features to help facilitate a better understanding of chapter content.

Key Terms and Chapter Focus: Each chapter begins with a listing of Key Terms and a Chapter Focus. These Key Terms are defined in the margin at the point in the chapter where they are presented. The Chapter Focus serves as an advance organizer for readers to better prepare them for the concepts presented in the chapter.

Check Your Understanding: These exercises provide an opportunity for readers to monitor their progress in the learning and assessment process. These activities are included in the text with answers online on the Companion Website.

Monitor Your Progress: At the end of each Part of the text, students will monitor their progress as they master the material presented. Students first complete a baseline assessment and learn how to plot their scores against an aim line.

More Practice: These activities, available on the Companion Website, provide the reader with additional opportunities to analyze and apply new knowledge to different circumstances and situations.

Read More About: Occasionally there are assessment topics on which readers may want more information. In these circumstances, additional articles and topical information are available on the Companion Website.

Chapter Summary: The summary provides an overview of the important points covered in the chapter.

Think Ahead Exercises: These end-of-chapter exercises enable readers to gauge their understanding of the chapter as a whole. Answers to these exercises are available in the Appendix or on the Companion Website.

SUPPLEMENTS

The sixth edition has an enhanced supplement support package, including a Companion Website, an Instructor's Manual with Test Items, PowerPoint slides, and a computerized test bank and assessment software (TestGen®). All of these items were developed exclusively for this text by the author.

COMPANION WEBSITE

Located at *http://www.prenhall.com/overton,* the Companion Website for this text includes a wealth of resources for both professors and students. The Syllabus Manager™ enables professors to create and maintain the class syllabus online while also allowing the student access to the syllabus at any time from any computer on the Internet. The student portion of the website helps students gauge their understanding of chapter content through the use of online chapter reviews, resources for assessment, Web links, additional activities, case studies, and interactive self-assessments.

ONLINE INSTRUCTOR'S MANUAL WITH TEST ITEMS

The Instructor's Manual (also available online at the Instructor Resource Center, described below) is organized by chapter and contains chapter lecture outlines, classroom activities, and test items (including multiple choice, true/false, short answer, and essay questions).

ONLINE POWERPOINT SLIDES

The transparencies—available in PowerPoint slide format at the Instructor Resources Center, described below, highlight key concepts, summarize content, and illustrate figures and charts from the text.

INSTRUCTOR RESOURCE CENTER

The Instructor Resource Center at *www.prenhall.com* has a variety of print and media resources available in downloadable, digital format—all in one location. As a registered faculty member, you can access and download pass-code protected resource files, course management content, and other premium online content directly to your computer.

Digital resources available for *Assessing Learners with Special Needs: An Applied Approach,* Sixth Edition, include:

• Text-specific PowerPoint® Lectures
• An online version of the Instructor's Manual

To access these items online, go to *www.prenhall.com* and click on the **Instructor Support** button and then go to the **Download Supplements** section. Here you will be able to log in or complete a one-time registration for a user name and password. If you have any questions regarding this process or the materials available online, please contact your local Pearson sales representative.

ACKNOWLEDGMENTS

I would like to express my sincere gratitude to the many students and colleagues at the University of Texas–Brownsville for your support during this project. A special thanks to Dr. Roman Garcia de Alba, Dr. Steve Chamberlain, and Dr. Mary Curtis for their encouragement during this process.

I would also like to thank the following reviewers of the sixth edition: Elaine Beason, Texas A & M University—Texarkana; Dorota Celinski, Roosevelt University; Barbara Hong, Texas A & M International University; Margaret T. McLane, The College of St. Rose; Roberta Strosnider, Towson University.

BRIEF CONTENTS

CONTENTS

Note: Every effort has been made to provide accurate and current Internet
information in this book. However, the Internet and Information on it are
constantly changing, so it is inevitable that some of the Internet addresses
listed in this textbook will change.

Introduction to Assessment

CHAPTER 1

An Introduction

CHAPTER 2

Law, Ethics, and Issues

An Introduction

testing
assessment
Individuals with Disabilities
    Education Act
No Child Left Behind Act
Individuals with Disabilities
    Education Improvement Act
disproportionality
overrepresentation
prereferral intervention
    strategies
early intervening services
response to intervention (RTI)
core academic subjects
teacher assistance team
overidentification
problem-solving model
informal assessment
curriculum-based assessment
curriculum-based measurement
criterion-related assessment
criterion-referenced tests
performance assessment

portfolio assessment
dynamic assessment
error analysis
checklists
high-stakes testing
adequate yearly progress
alternative assessments
individualized education program
    (IEP)
ecological assessment
environmental assessment
individual assessment plan
screening
*Standards for Educational and
    Psychological Testing*
norm-referenced tests
standardized tests
individualized education program
    (IEP) team
eligibility meeting
alternative planning
Individual Family Service Plan
    (IFSP)

CHAPTER FOCUS

This introductory chapter presents an overview of the assessment process in general education in today's educational environment, reflecting current emphasis on inclusion and accountability in education for all children. The evaluation of student progress in general education occurs regularly. Teachers employ a problem-solving process incorporating intervention strategies in the classroom setting as well as screening and assessment of students who, even with appropriate interventions, require additional support in their classroom setting. Various types of assessment are presented along with considerations of assessment of the child as a whole.

CEC KNOWLEDGE AND SKILLS STANDARDS

The student completing this chapter will understand the knowledge and skills included in the following CEC Knowledge and Skills Standards from Standard 8: Assessment:

CC8K1—Basic terminology used in assessment

CC8K2—Legal provisions and ethical principles regarding the assessment of individuals

GC8K1—Specialized terminology used in the assessment of individuals with disabilities

GC8K2—Laws and policies regarding referral and placement procedures for individuals with disabilities

GC8K4—Procedures for use with individuals who may be at risk for disabilities

ASSESSMENT: A NECESSARY PART OF TEACHING

testing A method to determine a student's ability to complete certain tasks or demonstrate mastery of a skill or knowledge of content.

assessment The process of gathering information to monitor progress and make educational decisions if necessary.

Testing is one method of evaluating progress and determining student outcomes and individual student needs. Testing, however, is only one form of assessment. **Assessment** includes many formal and informal methods of evaluating student progress and behavior.

Assessment happens every day in every classroom for the purpose of informing the teacher about needed instructional interventions. A teacher observes the behaviors of a student solving math problems. The teacher then checks the student's answers and determines the student's ability to solve that particular type of math problem. If the student made mistakes, the teacher determines the types of errors and decides what steps must be taken to correct the miscalculations. This is one type of assessment. The teacher observes behavior, gathers information about the student, and makes instructional changes according to the information obtained.

MONITOR YOUR PROGRESS

In an effort to experience progress monitoring during this course, students are encouraged to turn to the pre-test at the end of this chapter before reading any further. This pre-test will be used as a measure to determine your progress as you work through the text. You will also learn how to plot an aim line and determine if your progress is consistent with the aim line or if you need additional study interventions to maintain your progress. At the end of each part or section of this text, you will find another probe of your skill development. Each score can be plotted along the aim line to monitor your progress. Good luck!

In the routine assessment of students, behavior is observed, progress is monitored and evaluated, and interventions are planned. With effective interventions that are based on scientific research, few students will require additional assessment or special support services. Some students, however, do not respond to intensive interventions and may continue to have academic difficulties. These students may require additional assessment and evaluation for possible special education support. The very best assessment practices, however, must adhere to legal mandates, ethical standards, and basic principles of measurement. Teachers and other educational personnel have a professional responsibility to be accountable for each decision about assessment. Therefore, knowledge of the fundamentals of assessment and the various types of assessment is necessary.

The process of assessment plays an important role in the determination of student outcomes. The **Individuals with Disabilities Education Act** of 1997 Amendments, **No Child Left Behind Act** of 2001, and the **Individuals with Disabilities Education Improvement Act** of 2004 place more emphasis on the assessment of all students for measuring attainment of educational standards within the general curriculum (*Federal Register*, 1999; *Federal Register*, 2006; Individuals with Disabilities Education Improvement Act of 2004 Conference Committee Report, 2004 as cited in IDEA 2004; PL 107-110, 2002; Ysseldyke, Nelson, & House, 2000). The effectiveness of earlier special education programs has also been debated in the literature, and such discussions have contributed to the current inclusion movement of students with disabilities in the general education curriculum and setting (Detterman & Thompson, 1997; Detterman & Thompson, 1998; Keogh, Forness, & MacMillan, 1998; Symons & Warren, 1998). Although the percentage of students receiving special education support continues to increase, so has the percentage of students in those programs graduating with regular high school diplomas (U.S. Department of Education, 2000, 2004). The rate has increased from 43.5% of all students with disabilities graduating from high school in 1993–94 to 51.1% in 2001–2002 (U.S. Department of Education, 2004). It is concerning that even with the increasing numbers of students with special needs graduating with diplomas, nearly half of the students receiving special education support services do not. This underscores the need for more emphasis on the accountability of serving special education students and their ability to progress in the general education curriculum. Table 1.1 presents the national data on students within disability categories who graduated with a general education diploma.

Educational accountability efforts include improving education and achievement for all students, and especially improving the educational outcomes for culturally, linguistically, and ethnically diverse students, who continue to be represented in disproportionate numbers in several categories of special education (*Federal Register*, 2006; U.S. Department of Education, 1999, 2000). Federal regulations specifically target additional procedures and funding, to address the disproportionate numbers of students of various ethnic groups who are found eligible for special education, when this may be the result of other cultural factors. The regulations also address students who may be denied services due to cultural or linguistic differences. When students from various ethnic or linguistically different groups are under- or overrepresented in special educ

---

Individuals with Disabilities Education Act Passed in 1990 to give new name to PL 94-142.

No Child Left Behind Act Law of 2001 that holds general education accountable for all students' academic achievement.

Individuals with Disabilities Education Improvement Act The reauthorization and amendments of IDEA.

Table 1.1   Students ages 14 and older with disabilities who graduated with a standard diploma[a]: 1993–94[b] through 2001–02[b].

Disability	1993–94	1994–95	1995–96	1996–97	1997–98	1998–99[c]	1999–2000	2000–01	2001–02
	Percent								
Specific learning disabilities	49.1	47.7	48.2	48.8	51.0	51.9	51.6	53.6	56.9
Speech/language impairments	42.9	41.7	42.2	44.8	48.1	51.2	53.2	52.3	55.7
Mental retardation	35.0	33.8	34.0	33.0	34.3	36.0	34.4	35.0	37.8
Serious emotional disturbance	27.0	26.0	25.1	25.9	27.4	29.2	28.6	28.9	32.1
Multiple disabilities	36.1	31.4	35.3	35.4	39.0	41.0	42.3	41.6	45.2
Hearing impairments	61.9	58.2	58.8	61.8	62.3	60.9	61.4	60.3	66.9
Orthopedic impairments	56.7	54.1	53.6	54.9	57.9	53.9	51.5	57.4	56.4
Other health impairments	54.6	52.6	53.0	53.1	56.8	55.0	56.5	56.1	59.2
Visual impairments	63.5	63.7	65.0	64.3	65.1	67.6	66.4	65.9	70.8
Autism	33.7	35.5	36.4	35.9	38.7	40.5	40.8	42.1	51.1
Deaf-blindness[d]	34.7	30.0	39.5	39.4	67.7	48.3	37.4	41.2	49.1
Traumatic brain injury	54.6	51.7	54.0	57.3	58.2	60.6	56.8	57.5	64.4
All disabilities	43.5	42.1	42.4	43.0	45.3	46.5	46.1	47.6	51.1

Source: U.S. Department of Education, Office of Special Education Programs, Data Analysis System (DANS). Table 4-1 in vol 2. These data are for the 50 States, DC, Puerto Rico, and the four outlying areas.

[a]The percentage of students with disabilities who exited school with a regular high school diploma and the percentage who exit school by dropping out are performance indicators used by OSEP to measure progress in improving results for students with disabilities. The appropriate method for calculating graduation and dropout rates depends on the question to be answered and is limited by the data available. For reporting under the *Government Performance and Results Act* (GPRA), OSEP calculates the graduation rate by dividing the number of students age 14 and older who graduated with a regular high school diploma by the number of students in the same age group who are known to have left school (i.e., graduated with a regular high school diploma, received a certificate-of-completion, reached the maximum age for services, died moved and are not known to be continuing in an education program or dropped out). These calculations are presented here.

[b]Data are based on a cumulative 12-month count.

[c]Two large states appear to have underreported dropouts in 1988–99. As a result, the graduation rate is somewhat inflated that year.

[d]Percentage is based on fewer than 200 students exiting school.

disproportionality
When students of a specific ethnic group are at risk for overidentification or are at risk for underrepresentation in special education.

services, it is called **disproportionality**. When too many students are found to be eligible from a specific ethnic group, it is known as **overrepresentation** of that group. For example, American Indian/Alaska Native students were 2.89 times more likely to receive special education and related services for developmental delay than any other group (U.S. Department of Education, 2006). Further explanation of disproportionality is provided in Chapter 2.

On January 8, 2002, the No Child Left Behind Act of 2001 was enacted (PL 107-110, 2002). This legislation further emphasized

overrepresentation
When the percentage of students of a culturally different group is greater than the percentage of individuals of that group in the LEA.

the accountability that educators must implement in the education of all children. Accountability in this sense means statewide assessment of all students to measure their performance against standards of achievement. Assessment of students with disabilities is based on the same principles as assessment of students in general education. Students with disabilities are required to take statewide exams or alternative exams to measure their progress within the general education curriculum. Teachers and other educational personnel must make decisions about the types of evaluations and tests and any accommodations that might be needed for statewide assessments in order to include students receiving special education support in accountability measures (*Federal Register*, 2006).

Inclusion of students with disabilities within the context of the general education classroom setting, as a mode of service delivery, has increased to more than 48% and will continue to increase due to the IDEA 2004 emphasis on general curriculum (U.S. Department of Education, 2004; *Federal Register*, 2006) and the accountability standards of No Child Left Behind (PL 107-110, 2002). This increase of students with disabilities in the general education environment results in common expectations for educational standards and common assessment (U.S. Department of Education, 1999, PL 107-110, 2002; *Federal Register*, 2006).

In November of 2004, the Individuals with Disabilities Education Improvement Act was completed by the congressional conference committee and sent to President Bush for approval. It was signed into law on December 3, 2004. This law reauthorized the original IDEA and aligned it with the No Child Left Behind Act of 2002. In the 2004 Individuals with Disabilities Improvement Act, known as IDEA 2004, additional emphasis was placed on setting high standards of achievement for students with disabilities. These high standards should reflect the general education curriculum and must be assessed by statewide assessment of all students. Like the No Child Left Behind Act, IDEA 2004 requires that school systems and state education agencies collect data to document student achievement. This most recent reauthorization of the original IDEA places higher standards of accountability on teachers and schools to ensure student achievement. The Rules and Regulations that govern state educational systems and local school systems was completed and reported in the *Federal Register* in 2006. Additional aspects of the law and the assessment requirements are presented in Chapter 2.

HISTORICAL AND CONTEMPORARY MODELS OF ASSESSMENT

Since the original public law was implemented in 1975, the typical process of assessment has included identification of specific deficits within a student that appeared to be the cause of the student's

Figure 1.1   The traditional model of assessment.

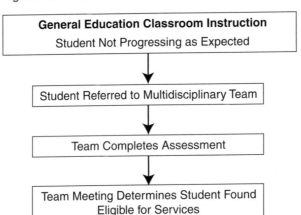

difficulty in the general education curriculum. The historical assessment model meant that when a general education teacher noticed that a student was having difficulty in the classroom, a referral was made to a multidisciplinary team. The multidisciplinary team, comprised of assessment personnel such as a school psychologist, speech clinician, and educational testing specialist, then evaluated the student. The Traditional Model of Assessment is presented in Figure 1.1. The team members and the child's parents then determined if the student met criteria for one of the categories of special education (McNamara & Hollinger, 2003). These categories are presented in Figure 1.2.

Research studies found varying referral practices and subsequently professionals in the field have recommended reform in the referral process. Research suggests referral practices in the past were inconsistent and may have been contributing to bias in the referral, assessment, and eligibility process. For example, studies found that males are referred more frequently and that students with a previous history of difficulties tend to be referred more often (Del'Homme, Kasari, Forness, & Bagley, 1996); female teachers referred students with behavioral problems more frequently than did male teachers (McIntyre, 1988); teachers referred students with learning and behavioral problems more often than those with behavioral problems alone (Soodak & Podell, 1993); and teacher referrals were global in nature and contained subjective rather than objective information in more than half the cases (Reschly, 1986; Ysseldyke, Christenson, Pianta, & Algozzine, 1983). According to research, a teacher's decision to refer may be influenced by the student's having a sibling who has had school problems as well as by the referring teacher's tolerance for certain student behaviors; the teacher with a low tolerance for particular behaviors may more readily refer students exhibiting those behaviors (Thurlow, Christenson, & Ysseldyke, 1983).

Figure 1.2 Disabilities defined in IDEA for which students are eligible for special education services.

Autism	A developmental disability significantly affecting verbal and nonverbal communication and social interaction, generally evident before age three, that adversely affects a child's educational performance. Other characteristics often associated with autism are engagement in repetitive activities and stereotyped movements, resistance change in daily routines, and unusual responses to sensory experiences. Autism does not apply if a child's educational performance is adversely affected primarily because the child has an emotional disturbance. A child who manifests the characteristics of autism after age three could be identified as having autism if other criteria are met.
Deaf-blindness	Concomitant hearing and visual impairments, the combination of which causes such severe communication and other developmental and educational needs that they cannot be accommodated in special education programs solely for children with deafness or children with blindness.
Deafness	A hearing impairment that is so severe that the child is impaired in processing linguistic information through hearing, with or without amplification that adversely affects a child's educational performance.
Emotional disturbance	A conditioning exhibiting one or more of the following characteristics over a long period of time and to a marked degree that adversely affects a child's educational performance: (A) An inability to learn that cannot be explained by intellectual, sensory, or health factors (B) An inability to build or maintain satisfactory interpersonal relationships with peers and teachers (C) Inappropriate types of behaviors or feelings under normal circumstances (D) A general pervasive mood of unhappiness or depression (E) A tendency to develop physical symptoms of fears associated with personal or school problems Emotional disturbance includes schizophrenia. The term does not apply to children who are socially maladjusted, unless it can be determined that they met other criteria for emotional disturbance.
Hearing impairment	An impairment in hearing, whether permanent or fluctuating, that adversely affects a child's educational performance but that is not included under the definition of deafness.
Mental retardation	Significantly subaverage general intellectual functioning existing concurrently with deficits in adaptive behavior and manifested during the developmental period that adversely affects educational performance.
Multiple disabilities	Concomitant impairments (such as mental retardation-blindness or mental retardation-orthopedic impairment), the combination of which causes such severe educational needs that they cannot be accommodated in special education programs solely for one of the impairments. Multiple disabilities does not include deaf-blindness.

Figure 1.2 continued.

Orthopedic impairment	Severe orhopedic impairment that adversely affects a child's educational performance. The term includes impairments caused by congenital anomaly, impairments caused by disease (e.g., poliomyelitis, bone tuberculosis) and impairments from other causes (e.g., cerebral palsy, amputations, and fractures or burns that cause contractures).
Other health impairment	Having limited strength, vitality, or alertness, including a heightened alertness to environmental stimuli, that results in limited alertness with respect to the educational environment that is due to chronic or acute health problems such as asthma, attention deficit disorder or attention deficit hyperactivity disorder, diabetes, epilepsy, a hear condition, hempophilia, lead poisoning, leukemia, nephritis, rheumatic fever, sickle cell anemia, and Tourette's syndrome, and adversely affects a child's educational performance.
Specific learning disability	A disorder in one or more of the basic psychological processes involved in understanding or using language, spoken or written, that may manifest itself in the imperfect ability to listen, speak, read, write, spell, or do mathematical calculations, including conditions such as perceptual disabilities, brain injury, minimal brain dysfunction, dyslexia, and developmental aphasia.
Speech or language impairment	A communication disorder, such as stuttering, impaired articulation, a language impairment, or a voice impairment, that adversely affects a child's educational performance.
Traumatic brain injury	An acquired injury to the brain caused by an external force, resulting in total or partial functional disability or psychosocial impairment, or both, that adversely affects a child's educational performance. Traumatic brain injury applies to open or closed head injuries resulting in impairments in one or more areas such as cognition, language, memory, attention, reasoning, abstract thinking, judgment, problem-solving, sensory, perceptual, and motor abilities; psychosocial behavior, physical functions; information processing and speech. Traumatic brain injury does not apply to brain injuries that are congenital or degenerative, or to brain injuries induced by brain trauma.
Visual impairment including blindness	An impairment in vision that, even with correction, adversely affects a child's educational performance. The term includes both partial sight and blindness.

Another study found that the characteristics of referred students may vary with student age (Harvey, 1991). Males were referred more frequently than female students at all grade levels. In the primary grade levels, younger students (for grade level) were referred more frequently than students who had birth dates farther from the school admission cutoff date (October 31). Students who were referred in the third grade or later had birth dates distributed evenly throughout the year, which suggests that students in the primary grades exhibited developmental differences rather than true learning or behavioral difficulties. Andrews, Wisnieswski, and Mulick (1997) found that students were referred at a higher rate if their height and weight were greater than average for their grade and gender. This study also found that more African-American students were referred for developmental disability services than Caucasian students and that males were referred more frequently for behavioral problems than females (Andrews et al., 1997).

Early research indicated that nationwide more than 90% of the students referred for evaluation were tested. Of those tested, 73% were subsequently found eligible for services in special education (Algozzine, Christenson, & Ysseldyke, 1982). More recently, Del'Homme et al., 1996 found that 63% of the students in their study who were referred subsequently received special education services. Students who are referred are highly likely to complete the evaluation process and receive special education services. In another study, 54% of the students referred for assessment were determined to be eligible (Fugate, Clarizio, & Phillips, 1993). Alternative practices, such as **prereferral interventions**, emerged (Graden, Casey, & Bonstrom, 1985; Graden, Casey, & Christenson, 1985). These interventions were intended to address bias in the referral process and prevent unnecessary additional assessment. By implementing intervention strategies, it was determined that the referral and evaluation rates decreased.

EARLY INTERVENING SERVICES

The inconsistent practices of the historic referral and assessment model resulted in the increasing rates of children referred for assessment and subsequently served in special education. The 2004 Individuals with Disabilities Improvement Act to IDEA began with Congressional Findings, which list areas that the Act is seeking to improve, including the use of prereferral interventions or **early intervening services**. The goal of increasing the use of early intervening services is to address the student's needs within the general education classroom and prevent additional assessment. Congress stated:

> Over 30 years of research and experience has demonstrated that the education of children with disabilities can be made more effective by providing incentives for whole school approaches and pre-referral intervention to reduce the need to label children as disabled in order to address their learning needs. (Individuals with Disabilities Education Improvement Act, 2004)

New regulations, that outline the practices expected in IDEA 2004, require school systems to provide methods of intervention for children who are at risk of having academic or behavioral difficulty. These interventions are addressed in the regulations as early intervening services. Particular emphasis is given to students in kindergarten through third grade and students who may be represented

prereferral intervention strategies Methods used by teachers and other team members to observe and modify student behaviors, learning environment, and/or teaching methods before making a formal referral.

early intervening services Evidence-based methods for addressing needs of students at risk for learning or behavioral disabilities or students who have exited from such services.

Anne Vega/Merrill

response to intervention (RTI) Application of learning or behavioral interventions and measurement of student's response to such interventions.

disproportionally; however, all students K–12 may receive these services. Early intervening services include those available to all children in the general education curriculum, such as general teaching methods, remedial instruction, and tutoring. In addition, schools are expected to use research-based methods for intervention and to document these efforts. These efforts may be included as part of the school's **response to intervention** methods, or **RTI** methods, for documenting possible learning and behavioral problems. Specific methods for data collection for response to intervention are included in the chapters on informal assessment (Chapters 6 and 7).

THREE-TIER MODEL OF INTERVENTION

core academic subjects In IDEA regulations, this includes English, reading or language arts, mathematics, science, foreign languages, civics and government, economics, arts, history, and geography.

One model that has been employed for both academic and behavioral interventions is a three-tier model. This model illustrates that the progress in **core academic subjects** of all children within the school setting should be monitored routinely. Their progress is monitored through standard methods such as statewide accountability assessment, teacher-made tests, and general educational performance in class. For students who have difficulty on these measures when compared to their peers, they are considered to be at risk of academic or behavioral problems and they then receive tier-two interventions, such as remedial assistance or tutoring. Using research-based strategies, the students receive interventions over a period of time and these efforts are documented. If these efforts fail, the teacher may request assistance through the **teacher assistance team** who recommends that the student receive intensive

teacher assistance team A team of various professionals who assist the teacher in designing interventions for students who are not making progress.

interventions, designed specifically to address the area of weakness or difficulty. If the child continues to struggle, the child may be referred for consideration of an evaluation for possible special education eligibility. The three-tier model is presented in Figure 1.3.

Functional assessment of academic performance problems has been suggested as a method of targeting difficulties and implementing specific intervention strategies (Daly, Witt, Martens, & Dool, 1997). This procedure provides hypotheses for the teacher to test through the use of classroom instructional interventions (see Figure 1.4). Once classroom teachers have documented the area of difficulty, they can systematically implement strategies for correction. Ideally, the intervention strategies will decrease referrals by resolving some students' learning or behavioral problems within the general education classroom (Nelson, Smith, Taylor, Dodd, & Reavis, 1992).

Strategies that may be selected to determine the area of academic or behavioral difficulty include observation by objective persons, informal assessment techniques, curriculum modifications, environmental (classroom) modifications, and consultation with the parents and other members of the multidisciplinary team.

Figure 1.3 A three-tier model.

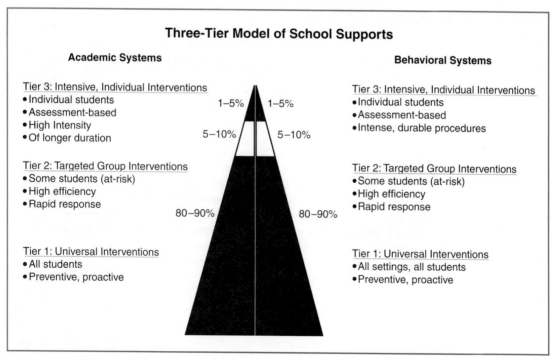

Source: Adapted from: Batsche, G. et al. (2005). *Response to intervention: Policy considerations and implementation.* Alexandria, VA: National Association of State Directors of Special Education. Retrieved from the National Association of State Directors of Special Education website *http://www.nasdse.org/documents/RtIAnAdministratorsPerspective1-06.pdf*

Figure 1.4 Academic interventions identified by the presumed function of the behavior.

Reasonable Hypotheses	*Possible Interventions*
The student is not motivated to respond to the instructional demands	Increase interest in curricular activities: 1. Provide incentives for using the skill 2. Teach the skill in the context of using the skill 3. Provide choices of activities
Insufficient active student responding in curricular materials	Increase active student responding: 1. Estimate current rate of active responding and increase rate during allocated time
Insufficient prompting and feedback for active responding	Increase rate of complete learning trials: 1. Response cards 2. Choral responding 3. Flash card intervention with praise/error correction 4. Peer tutoring
Student displays poor accuracy in target skill(s)	Increase modeling and error correction: 1. Reading passages to student 2. Use cover-copy-compare 3. Have student repeatedly practice correct response in context for errors
Student displays poor fluency in target skill(s)	Increase practice, drill, or incentives: 1. Have the student repeatedly read passages 2. Offer incentives for beating the last score
Student does not generalize use of the skill to the natural setting or to other materials/settings	Instruct the student to generalize use of the skill: 1. Teach multiple examples of use of the skill 2. Teach use of the skill in the natural setting 3. "Capture" natural incentives 4. Teach self-monitoring
The instructional demands do not promote mastery of the curricular objective	Change instructional materials to match the curricular objective: 1. Specify the curricular objective and identify activities that promote use of the skill in the context in which it is generally used
Student's skill level is poorly matched to the difficulty of the instructional materials	Increase student responding using better matched instructional levels: 1. Identify student's accuracy and fluency across instructional materials and use instructional materials that promote a high rate of responding

Source: School Psychology Review, 26 (4), 558. Copyright 1997 by the National Association of School Psychologists. Reprinted by permission of the publisher.

Although effective prereferral strategies have been found to reduce the number of referrals for assessment, one study found that general education teachers had only a vague understanding of specific strategies and how to implement them (Wilson, Gutkin, Hagen, & Oats, 1998). In this study, the participating teachers viewed the prereferral process as a step in the referral process rather than an intervention to prevent assessment. Another investigation of referral practices across the United States found that state requirements varied, practices were inconsistent, and many interventions did not involve actual teaching interventions to improve academic progress (Truscott, Cohen, Sams, Sanborn, & Frank, 2005). These studies illustrate the problems encountered in the referral process and have influenced a move toward more comprehensive and detailed intervention strategies such as the evidence-based practices implemented through RTI.

overidentification
Describes the phenomenon of identifying students who seem to be eligible for special education services but who are actually not disabled.

The more frequent use of better interventions is a step forward in the prevention of unnecessary evaluation and the possibility of misdiagnosis and **overidentification** of special education students. Halgren and Clarizio (1993) found that 38% of the students in special education were either reclassified or terminated from special education. This indicates a need for more specific identification of the learning or behavioral problems through referral and initial assessment.

Valles (1998) suggested that teacher training in special and general education may be needed to prevent inappropriate referrals of minority and bilingual students. Gopaul-McNicol and Thomas-Presswood (1998) caution that teachers of students whose primary language is not English often consider bilingual education or English as a Second Language (ESL) classes as prereferral interventions. In a study of the referral and assessment practices of Asian-American students, it was found that prereferral interventions were limited and did not reflect the approaches needed that may have assisted with language development (Poon-McBrayer & Garcia, 2000). In this study, these students were referred for evaluations when language interventions may have resolved the difficulties. Teachers of students with cultural and linguistic differences should employ prereferral intervention strategies that promote language acquisition in addition to ESL or bilingual curriculum. In one study, the RTI model was applied to English Language Learners (ELL) who were at risk of reading disabilities (Linan-Thompson, Vaughn, Prater, & Cirino, 2006). In this study, students whose primary language was Spanish, received intensive interventions using evidence-based practices and made significant gains therefore avoiding the need for special education referral.

Providing consulting services to general education teachers could help resolve student problems before referral (Zins, Graden, & Ponti, 1989). Serna, Forness, and Nielsen (1998) suggest that systemic changes in referral practices are needed at the preservice level of teacher training. This type of intervention would place team members in a consulting role for a large part of their service time and decrease the time they spent testing. Fuchs (1991) found that several features need to exist in the practice of prereferral interventions. The following list is adapted from this study:

1. Prereferral intervention should be included in the job descriptions of those persons responsible for implementation. This includes both professional and paraprofessional staff.
2. A consultant or team should serve to guide the prereferral effort.
3. All staff involved should receive adequate training in the prereferral strategies.
4. The consultation effort should be efficient and exhibit desired outcomes.
5. Consultants should define the problem behavior, set goals for students and teachers, collect data, and evaluate effectiveness.
6. Interventions should be agreeable to both consultants and teachers.
7. Strategies should be implemented as designed.
8. Data should be collected at multiple intervals. (p. 263)

The prereferral team or teacher assistant team members work together to determine what strategies might be effective for specific behavioral or academic challenges. It is important that the team uses effective problem-solving as they make these decisions. One study found that the team decision-making was influenced by having more specific data collected by the teacher and that parent input was also important in the decision-making process (Etscheidt & Knesting, 2007). It was also found that the interventions were more likely to be implemented with integrity when the interventions seemed reasonable and were judged likely to be acceptable interventions.

CONTEMPORARY MODEL OF ASSESSMENT

problem-solving model Strategies for intervention that identify problem, hypothesis for intervention, and measurement of those interventions, to meet student's needs.

Difficulties with the traditional approach to referral and assessment led educators to look for more effective methods. The goal of the contemporary model of assessment is to resolve the academic or behavioral challenges experienced by the student. This **problem-solving model** emphasizes finding a solution rather than determining eligibility or finding a special education placement. The contemporary model is presented in Figure 1.5. As noted in the

Figure 1.5 The contemporary assessment model.

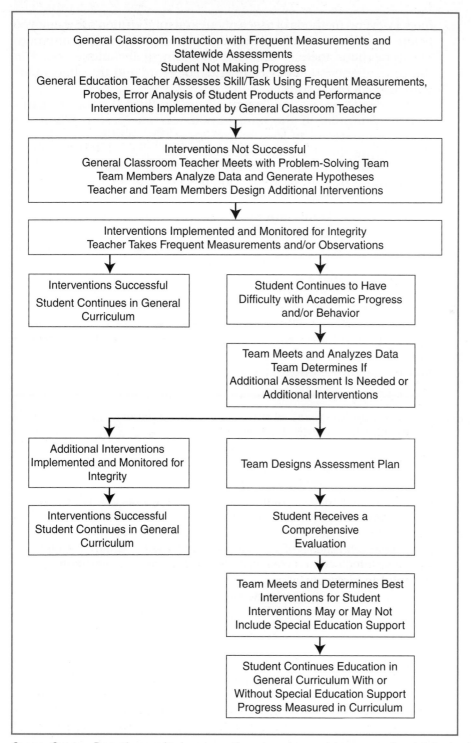

General Classroom Instruction with Frequent Measurements and
Statewide Assessments
Student Not Making Progress
General Education Teacher Assesses Skill/Task Using Frequent Measurements,
Probes, Error Analysis of Student Products and Performance
Interventions Implemented by General Classroom Teacher

Interventions Not Successful
General Classroom Teacher Meets with Problem-Solving Team
Team Members Analyze Data and Generate Hypotheses
Teacher and Team Members Design Additional Interventions

Interventions Implemented and Monitored for Integrity
Teacher Takes Frequent Measurements and/or Observations

Interventions Successful
Student Continues in General
Curriculum

Student Continues to Have
Difficulty with Academic Progress
and/or Behavior

Team Meets and Analyzes Data
Team Determines If
Additional Assessment Is Needed or
Additional Interventions

Additional Interventions
Implemented and Monitored for
Integrity

Team Designs Assessment Plan

Interventions Successful
Student Continues in General
Curriculum

Student Receives a
Comprehensive
Evaluation

Team Meets and Determines Best
Interventions for Student
Interventions May or May Not
Include Special Education Support

Student Continues Education in
General Curriculum With or
Without Special Education Support
Progress Measured in Curriculum

Source: Overton, Promoting academic success through environmental assessment . . . in interview in
Sch/Clinic, 39, 149–150. Copyright 2004 by PRO–ED, Inc. Reprinted by permission of publisher.

model, several methods of assessment and intervention are employed before consideration of a referral and comprehensive evaluation. These methods include informal assessment techniques used in the general education environment. The team and the child's parents discuss the results.

Interventions are implemented and additional data are gathered to determine if the intervention was successful. When the interventions result in less improvement than had been expected, the team meets to discuss additional strategies or interventions. When a student is referred, it is only to assist in finding a solution or appropriate intervention. The intervention may or may not include special education support.

The **Check Your Understanding** exercises included with this text provide an opportunity for you to monitor your own progress in learning the assessment process. Complete the activity for Chapter 1 included here. Additional exercises are provided on the Companion Website of this text at *www.prenhall.com/overton*.

Case Study

Jaime entered kindergarten three months after his family moved into the school district. He had not attended preschool, and his mother had little time to devote to preacademic skills. Jaime lives

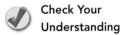

Check Your Understanding

Check your knowledge of the trends and foundations of assessment by completing Activity 1.1 below.

Activity 1.1

Answer the following questions.

1. According to the Traditional Assessment Model, what usually happened when a student was referred to a multidisciplinary team?

2. Research studies of the referral and assessment process found many indications of bias in the process. What are some examples of this bias?

3. Under the 2004 IDEA, the emphasis shifted from the traditional model with prereferral strategies to early intervening services. Why did the 2004 IDEA include this change?

Apply Your Knowledge

Read the case study to begin thinking about how to look for solutions for the student's difficulties. Refer to the Contemporary Assessment Model to list possible steps in the problem-solving process. _____
_____
_____

with his mother, father, and three older siblings. Jaime had experiences around other children in his extended family; however, Jaime had no experience in a structured learning environment. Within the first few weeks of school, Jaime's kindergarten teacher, Mrs. Johnson, began activities to teach phonemic awareness. Mrs. Johnson frequently measured her students' progress using curriculum-based measurement. During this assessment, Mrs. Johnson noted that Jaime was not progressing as expected.

informal assessment
Nonstandardized methods of evaluating progress, such as interviews, observations, and teacher-made tests.

1. According to the Contemporary Assessment Model, what steps have been taken by Mrs. Johnson?
2. List the steps that should happen before Mrs. Johnson consults with the problem-solving team.
3. What other information may be helpful in determining interventions?

For **MORE PRACTICE**, visit the Companion Website at *www.prenhall.com/overton* to analyze additional difficulties with the traditional referral process.

EVALUATING STUDENT PROGRESS IN THE CLASSROOM

curriculum-based assessment Using the content from the currently used curriculum to assess student progress.

curriculum-based measurement Frequent measurement comparing student's actual progress with expected rate of progress.

criterion-related assessment When items of an assessment instrument are related to meeting objectives or passing skill mastery objectives.

criterion-referenced tests Tests designed to accompany and measure a set of criteria or skill-mastery criteria.

Teachers use several methods to assess student progress in the classroom. Teacher-made tests, quizzes, and other **informal assessment** are used in an attempt to discover how the student is progressing. The teacher may develop assessments directly from curriculum materials. This type of assessment is **curriculum-based assessment**. Curriculum-based assessment is commonly used to measure a student's performance within the specific classroom curriculum.

Teachers may first notice that a student is having difficulty progressing as expected by taking frequent measurements of the student's classroom performance. These frequent measurements using the curriculum that is being taught are called **curriculum-based measurements**. Research supports curriculum-based measurement as an effective method of monitoring the progress of both general and special education students (Deno, 2003; Fuchs, Deno, & Mirkin, 1984; Fuchs, Fuchs, Hamlett, Phillips, & Bentz, 1994). This method is presented in detail in Chapter 5.

When students are tested for mastery of a skill or an objective, the assessment is called **criterion-related assessment**, and tests of this type may be labeled **criterion-referenced tests**. Criterion-referenced tests compare the performance of a student to a given criterion.

Another type of assessment used in the classroom requires students to create a product that demonstrates their skills or competency; the assessment of their creation is called **performance**

performance assessment When a student is required to create a product to demonstrate knowledge.

portfolio assessment Evaluating student progress, strengths, and weaknesses using a collection of different measurements and work samples.

dynamic assessment Assessment in which the examiner prompts or interacts with the student to determine the student's potential to learn a skill.

error analysis Using a student's errors to analyze specific learning problems.

checklists Lists of skills developmentally sequenced and used to monitor student progress.

high-stakes testing Accountability assessment of state or district standards, which may be used for funding or accreditation decisions.

adequate yearly progress The criterion set for schools based upon high stakes testing results.

alternative assessments Assessment methods for students with disabilities, designed to measure progress in the general curriculum.

assessment. The assessment of a collection of various types of products or assessments collected over time that demonstrate student progress is known as **portfolio assessment**. When the assessment process includes interaction or teaching and prompting to determine a student's potential to learn a skill, the teacher has used the technique known as **dynamic assessment**. In dynamic assessment, the teacher assesses the student's ability or capacity to learn a new skill rather than testing for mastery of the skill.

Learning how the student performs tasks may also provide insight into the nature of the academic or behavioral difficulty. Observing the steps a student takes to solve a problem or complete a task can benefit the teacher as well as the student. The teacher may ask the student to verbalize the steps taken while reading a paragraph for content or while solving a math equation. The teacher can then note the types or patterns of errors the student made during the process. This type of analysis is known as **error analysis** (e.g., $7 \times 3 = 10$; the student added rather than multiplied the numbers). Teachers also develop **checklists** to identify students who have mastered skills, tasks, or developmental expectations appropriate to their grade level. Checklists can be found in some commercial materials or school curriculum guides. Placement in the specific curriculum within the general education classroom may be based on a student's performance on skills listed on these commercial checklists or on other curriculum-based assessment results.

Current reform movements in special education and general education emphasize the changing role of assessment in special education (U.S. Congress, 1993; U.S. Department of Education, 1997). The result of this trend is the encouragement of nontraditional methods of assessment and the inclusion of students with disabilities in statewide accountability and competency testing (IDEA Amendments, 1997). Including students with disabilities in district and statewide assessment, or **high-stakes testing**, is necessary to determine the effectiveness of educational programs (Ysseldyke et al., 1998). These statewide assessments are used to monitor progress of individual schools and school systems. In the No Child Left Behind Act of 2001, schools are required to show **adequate yearly progress**, or AYP, in order to demonstrate that students are mastering the curriculum in the general classroom (PL 107-110, 2002). The AYP is measured using the results of the statewide assessments. Students with disabilities who are determined unable to participate in these statewide assessments are to be tested using **alternative assessments** to measure attainment of standards. Teachers will be required to use a variety of assessment techniques to assess student competency and demonstrate mastery of educational goals and objectives.

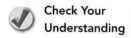

Check Your Understanding

Check your knowledge of the different types of assessment presented in the previous section by completing Activity 1.2 below.

Activity 1.2

Use the terms provided to answer the questions below.

> assessment
> error analysis
> alternate assessments
> curriculum-based assessment
> performance assessment
> high-stakes testing
> criterion-related assessment
> checklist
> portfolio assessment
> criterion-referenced tests
> dynamic assessment

1. A teacher wants to determine why a student who can multiply single-digit numbers cannot multiply double-digit numbers. The teacher asks the student to verbally describe the steps she is using in the process of multiplying double-digit numbers. This is _____.

2. The spelling series used in one classroom contains tests that are directly tied to the spelling curriculum. When the teacher uses these tests, _____ is being used.

3. A teacher collects class work, quizzes, book reports, and writing assignments to determine the students' strengths and weaknesses in language arts. This is known as _____.

4. When a teacher assesses a student's potential to learn a new math skill by prompting or cuing the student, _____ has been used.

5. For a teacher to determine a student's understanding of the solar system, the student is required to create a project that demonstrates the Earth's position relative to designated planets. This is _____.

6. A classroom teacher along with a team of other educational professionals determined that John, who has multiple disabilities, is not able to participate in the statewide assessment. The team develops _____ to assess John's attainment of educational goals.

7. A student is not progressing as the teacher believes he should for his age expectancy. The teacher uses teacher-made tests, observation, and criterion-referenced tests to gather information about the student. This teacher is using different methods of _____ to discover why the student is not making progress.

8. To determine whether a student has mastered a specific skill or objective, the teacher uses _____.

9. A first-grade student has difficulty with fine motor skills. The teacher is concerned that the student may not have the developmental ability to learn manuscript handwriting. The handwriting series lists skills a student must master before writing letters. Using this device, the teacher has employed a _____.

10. Assessment devices in a school's language arts series provide skills and objectives for each level of English, creative writing, and literature. These are _____.

11. Each year the Mulberry Elementary School tests students to determine which students have mastered state curriculum standards. This testing is known as _____.

Apply Your Knowledge

Analyze the following sentences written by Roberto. Identify the spelling errors.

1. The yellow kat is very big.

2. The oshun has big waves.

3. The kan was bent.

Your error analysis is that Roberto. . . . _____

_____

_____

individualized education program (IEP) A written plan of educational interventions designed for each student who receives special education.

ecological assessment Method of assessing a student's total environment to determine what factors are contributing to learning or behavioral problems.

environmental assessment Method of assessing the student's classroom environment.

In the past, a student was referred for testing, evaluated by team members, and, if determined eligible for special education services, given an **individualized education program** (IEP) and placed in a special education setting. Although these steps were reported nationally as those most commonly followed in the evaluation process (Ysseldyke & Thurlow, 1983), they do not include the step of prereferral intervention.

A prereferral model proposed by Graden, Casey, and Christenson (1985), however, includes "identifying, defining, and clarifying the problem, analyzing the components of the classroom ecology that affect the problem, designing and implementing interventions, and evaluating intervention effectiveness" (p. 383). As Graden and colleagues have written, this type of prereferral intervention looks at many variables surrounding the student's educational performance rather than assuming first that the difficulty is with the student. This type of assessment, called **ecological assessment** or **environmental assessment**, reflects a major trend toward considering the environment and assessing students in their natural environment (Overton, 2003; Reschly, 1986). One type of environmental assessment is presented in Figure 1.6.

Figure 1.6 Assessing the academic environment.

Assessment of Academic Environment

Name of Student _____

Class: _____

Duration of observation: _____ minutes.

Check all that are observed during this observational period.

Physical Environmental Factors

_____ Seating: Individual student desks

_____ Seating: Group tables

_____ Seating: Student desks grouped in pairs or groups of four

_____ Material organized for quick student access and use

_____ Target student's materials organized

Classroom Behavioral Structure

_____ Classroom expectations (rules) posted

_____ Verbal praise for effort of students

_____ Verbal praise for target student

_____ Quiet redirection for target student when needed

_____ Inconsequential minor behaviors are ignored

_____ Transitions were smooth

_____ Time lapse to begin task less than 3 minutes (for class)

_____ Time lapse to begin task less than 3 minutes (for target student)

_____ Time lapse to begin task 5 minutes or more (for class)

_____ Time lapse to begin task 5 minutes or more (for target student)

_____ Noise level consistent with task demands

_____ Classwide behavior plan used

Classroom Teacher's Instructional Behaviors

_____ Task expectations explained verbally

_____ Task expectations explained visually (on board, etc.)

_____ Task modeled by teacher

_____ Cognitive strategies modeled by teacher first (thinking aloud)

Teacher–Students Interactions

_____ Academic behavior/responses shaped by teacher for all students

_____ Teacher used proximity as a monitoring technique for all students

_____ Teacher used proximity for reinforcement technique for all students

_____ Teacher used one-on-one instruction to clarify task for all students

Teacher–Target Student Interactions

_____ Academic behavior/responses shaped by teacher for target student

_____ Teacher used proximity as a monitoring technique for target student

_____ Teacher used proximity for reinforcement technique for target student

_____ Teacher used one-on-one instruction to clarify for target student

Figure 1.6   continued.

Classroom Academic Structure
_____ Anticipatory set for lesson/activity
_____ Task completed by group first before individuals are expected to
complete task
_____ Academic behavior/responses modeled/assisted by peers
_____ Expected response or task made by pairs, groups, or teams
_____ Expected response made by individual students
_____ Tasks, instructions were structured and clear to students
_____ Tasks, instructions were unclear to target student
_____ A variety of teaching methods (direct instruction, media,
manipulatives) used
Extended Learning Experiences
          Advanced organizers used; cues, prompts, presented to class
_____ Homework assignment appropriate (at independent level, not
emerging skill level)
_____ Homework instructions are clear
_____ Homework assignment is displayed in consistent place in room
(board, etc.)
_____ Students use daily planner or other technique for homework/
classwork
_____ Homework assignment is planned for reinforcement of skill rather
than extension of work not completed during class
Other concerns of academic environment:

Source: From "Promoting Academic Success through Environmental Assessment" by Terry Overton, *Intervention in School and Clinic* vol. *39*, no. 3, pp. 149–150. Copyright 2004 by PRO–ED, Inc. Adapted with permission.

Messick (1984) proposed a two-phase assessment strategy that emphasizes prereferral assessment of the student's learning environment. The information needed during Messick's first phase includes*

1. Evidence that the school is using programs and curricula shown to be effective not just for students in general but for the various ethnic, linguistic, and socioeconomic groups actually served by the school in question.

2. Evidence that the students in question have been adequately exposed to the curriculum by virtue of not having missed too many lessons because of absence or disciplinary

---

*From Assessment in context: Appraising student performance in relation to instructional quality, by S. Messick (1984). *Educational Researcher. 13*, p. 5. Copyright 1984 by American Educational Research Association. Reprinted by permission of the publisher.

exclusion from class and that the teacher has implemented the curriculum effectively.

3. Objective evidence that the child has not learned what was taught.

4. Evidence that systematic efforts were or are being made to identify the learning difficulty and to take corrective instructional action, such as introducing remedial approaches, changing the curriculum materials, or trying a new teacher.

It is no longer considered acceptable to refer students who have difficulty in the general classroom without interventions unless they appear to be experiencing severe learning or behavioral problems or are in danger of harming themselves or others. Prereferral or early intervention strategies have had positive effects. In schools where a prereferral intervention model was implemented, consultation services increased within the general education classroom, and both testing and educational placements decreased significantly (Graden, Casey, & Bonstrom, 1985). In a study by Chalfant and Psyh (1989), the inappropriate referral rate decreased to 63% and interventions were successful in approximately 88% of the cases. Recent studies have found success in preventing inappropriate referrals by employing a problem-solving model throughout the assessment process (McNamara & Hollinger, 2003; VanDerHeyden, Witt, & Naquin, 2003). The problem-solving method requires the team to determine an effecive solution for the student's academic or behavioral difficulties. As part of this problem-solving strategy, a prereferral checklist may be used by the intervention team to clarify the target areas of difficulty and generate hypotheses for interventions. An example of a prereferral checklist is presented in Figure 1.7.

DESIGNING AN ASSESSMENT PLAN

When the team members determine that a comprehensive assessment will be needed in order to determine effective interventions, an assessment plan must be constructed. Federal law mandates that evaluation measures used during the assessment process are those measures specifically designed to assess areas of concern (IDEA Amendments of 1997). (The specific laws pertaining to the education of individuals with disabilities are discussed in Chapter 2.) Through the use of appropriate early intervention strategies, the referring teacher is able to pinpoint specific areas of difficulty, and the assessment team can then design an appropriate assessment plan. The team must determine which instruments will be administered and which special education professionals are needed to complete the assessment. Federal law also requires that the instruments selected have been validated for the purpose of intended use.

Figure 1.7 A prereferral checklist to determine whether all necessary interventions have been attempted.

Prereferral Checklist

Name of Student _____

Concerned Teacher _____

Briefly describe area of difficulty:

1. Curriculum evaluation:

    _____ Material is appropriate for age and/or grade level.

    _____ Instructions are presented clearly.

    _____ Expected method of response is within the student's capability.

    _____ Readability of material is appropriate.

    _____ Prerequisite skills have been mastered.

    _____ Format of materials is easily understood by students of same age and/or grade level.

    _____ Frequent and various methods of evaluation are employed.

    _____ Tasks are appropriate in length.

    _____ Pace of material is appropriate for age and/or grade level.

2. Learning environment:

    _____ Methods of presentation are appropriate for age and/or grade levels.

    _____ Tasks are presented in appropriate sequence.

    _____ Expected level of response is appropriate for age and/or grade level.

    _____ Physical facilities are conducive to learning.

3. Social environment:

    _____ Student does not experience noticeable conflicts with peers.

    _____ Student appears to have adequate relationships with peers.

    _____ Parent conference reveals no current conflicts or concerns within the home.

    _____ Social development appears average for age expectancy.

4. Student's physical condition:

    _____ Student's height and weight appear to be within average range of expectancy for age and/or grade level.

    _____ Student has no signs of visual or hearing difficulties (asks teacher to repeat instructions, squints, holds papers close to face to read).

    _____ Student has had vision and hearing checked by school nurse or other health official.

    _____ Student has not experienced long-term illness or serious injury.

_____ School attendance is average or better.

_____ Student appears attentive and alert during instruction.

_____ Student appears to have adequate motor skills.

_____ Student appears to have adequate communication skills.

5. Intervention procedures (changes in teaching strategies that have been attempted):

_____ Consultant has observed student:

Setting	Date	Comments
1.		
2.		
3.		

_____ Educational and curriculum changes were made:

Change	Date	Comments
1.		
2.		
3.		

_____ Behavioral and social changes were made:

Change	Date	Comments
1.		
2.		
3.		

_____ Parent conferences were held:

Date	Comments
1.	
2.	
3.	

_____ Additional documentation is attached.

individual assessment plan A plan that lists the specific tests and procedures to be used for a student who has been screened and needs further assessment.

For example, if the student has been referred for problems with reading comprehension, the appropriate assessment instrument would be one of good technical quality that has been designed to measure reading problems—specifically, reading comprehension skills. In addition to requiring selection of the appropriate tests, the law mandates that persons administering the tests be adequately trained to administer those specific tests and that more than a single instrument be used to determine eligibility for special services. To meet these mandates, the educator must design an **individual assessment plan** for each student. Maxam, Boyer-Stephens, and

Alff (1986) recommended that each evaluation team follow these specific steps in preparing an assessment plan:*

screening A review of records and student's school achievement to determine what interventions or additional assessment are needed.

1. Review all of the **screening** information in each of the seven areas (health, vision, hearing, speech and language skills, intellectual, academic, prevocational/vocational).

2. Determine what area(s) need further evaluation.

3. Determine the specific data-collection procedures to use (interviews, observation of behavior, informal or formal techniques, standardized tests).

4. Determine persons responsible for administering the selected procedures. These persons must be trained or certified if the assessment instrument calls for specific qualifications.

In addition to federal mandates and recommendations from professionals in the field of special education, the professional organizations of the American Psychological Association, the American Educational Research Association, and the National Council on Measurement in Education have produced the ***Standards for Educational and Psychological Testing*** (1999), which clearly defines acceptable professional and ethical standards for individuals who test children in schools. (Several of these standards are included in later chapters of this text.) The APA *Standards* (1999) emphasize the importance of using tests for the purpose intended by the test producer and place ethical responsibility for correct use and interpretation on the person administering and scoring tests in the educational setting. Other professional organizations, such as the Council for Exceptional Children and the National Association of School Psychologists, have ethics and standards about assessment. These are presented in Chapter 2.

Standards for Educational and Psychological Testing Professional and ethical standards that suggest minimum criteria for assessing students.

A student who has been referred for an initial evaluation may be found eligible for services according to the definitions of the various disabling conditions defined in federal law. (Refer to Figure 1.2.)

For **MORE PRACTICE** on distinguishing the definitions of the disability categories included in IDEA, visit the Companion Website at *www.prenhall.com/overton.*

THE COMPREHENSIVE EVALUATION

When a student has not had success in a learning environment after several prereferral strategies have been applied, a formal

*From *Assessment: A key to appropriate program placement* (Report No. CE 045 407, pp. 11–13) by S. Maxam, A. Boyer-Stephens, and M. Alff, 1986, Columbia, MO: University of Missouri, Columbia, Department of Special Education and Department of Practical Arts and Vocational-Technical Education. (ERIC Document Reproduction Service No. ED 275 835.) Copyright 1986 by the authors. Reprinted by permission.

norm-referenced tests Tests designed to compare individual students with national averages, or norms of expectancy.

standardized tests Tests developed with specific standard administration, scoring, and interpretation procedures that must be followed precisely to obtain optimum results.

referral is made. The team may then make a decision to recommend a comprehensive evaluation or perhaps a new educational intervention or alternative, such as a change in classroom teachers. If the committee recommends a comprehensive evaluation, the assessment plan is designed.

The types of assessment that may be used in a comprehensive evaluation are varied, depending upon the student's needs. Some instruments used are **norm-referenced tests** or assessment devices. These instruments have been developed to determine how a student performs on tasks when compared with students of the same age or grade level. These tests are also **standardized tests**. This means that the tests were developed with very structured and specific instructions, formats, scoring, and interpretation procedures. These specifics, written in the test manual, must be followed to ensure that the tests are used in the manner set forth by the test developers. Refer to Table 1.2 to compare the various types of tests used in assessing learners.

Table 1.2   Various types of assessment.

Type of Assessment	Purpose of Assessment	Who Administers Assessment	When Assessment Is Used
Ecological Assessment	To determine classroom environmental influences or contributions to learning	Teacher or Intervention Team member such as special education teacher	Any time students appear to have learning or behavioral difficulties
Norm-Referenced Tests	To compare a specific student's ability with that of same-age students in national sample	Group tests—by teachers, Individual tests—by teachers, school psychologists, educational diagnosticians, other members of IEP team	When achievement or ability needs to be assessed for annual, triennial, or initial evaluations
Standardized Tests	Tests given with specific instructions and procedures—often are also norm-referenced	Teachers, members of Intervention/IEP teams, such as school psychologists or educational diagnosticians	When achievement or ability need to be assessed for annual, triennial, or initial evaluations
Error Analysis	To determine a pattern of errors or specific type of errors	Teachers, other personnel working with student	Can be used daily or on any type of assessment at any time
Curriculum-Based Assessment	To determine how student is performing using actual content of curriculum	Teachers	To measure mastery of curriculum (chapter tests, etc.)

Table 1.2   continued.

Type of Assessment	Purpose of Assessment	Who Administers Assessment	When Assessment Is Used
Curriculum-Based Measurement	To measure progress of a specific skill against an aim line	Teacher	Daily or several times each week
Dynamic Assessment	To determine if student has potential to learn a new skill	Teacher, other members of Intervention or IEP team	Can be used daily, weekly, or as part of a formal evaluation
Portfolio Assessment	To evaluate progress over time in specific area	Teachers, members of Intervention or IEP team	Over a specific period of time or specific academic unit or chapters
Criterion-Referenced Tests	To assess a student's progress in skill mastery against specific standards	Teachers, members of Intervention or IEP team	To determine if student has mastered skill at end of unit or end of time period
Criterion-Related Tests	To assess student's progress on items that are similar to objectives or standards	Teachers, members of Intervention or IEP team	Same as criterion referenced tests
Checklists, Rating Scales, Observations	To determine student's skill level or behavioral functioning	Teacher, members of Intervention or IEP team	Curriculum placement determination or behavioral screening

individualized education program (IEP) team The team specified in the IDEA amendments to make decisions about special education eligibility and interventions.

eligibility meeting A conference held after a preplacement evaluation to determine if a student is eligible for services.

In addition to standardized norm-referenced tests, team members use informal methods such as classroom observations, interviews with teachers and parents, and criterion-referenced instruments. A team of designated professionals and the parents of the student make up the **individualized education program (IEP) team**. The team reviews the results from the assessments in the eligibility meeting. This meeting will determine what educational changes may be necessary to provide the best instruction for the student.

During the **eligibility meeting**, the IEP team may determine that the student is eligible for special education services based on the information collected through the evaluation process. If the student is eligible, an IEP, or individual education program, must be written for the student. If, however, the student is not eligible for special education services, **alternative planning** should be considered, including educational intervention suggestions for the student. Alternative planning may include a plan for accommodations in the general classroom setting under Section 504. This law (presented in Chapter 2) requires that students who have disabilities or needs but who are not eligible to receive services under IDEA must

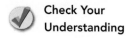
Check Your
Understanding

Check your knowledge of the referral process presented in the previous section by completing Activity 1.3 below.

Activity 1.3

Using the information provided in Table 1.2, determine the type(s) of assessment that may need to be included in a comprehensive assessment plan.

1. If a teacher wants to determine the types of mistakes a student is making on written expression tasks such as sentence writing, the teacher may use _____.

2. IEP team members are concerned that a student may be functioning within the range of mental retardation. In order to determine where the student's abilities are compared with other students his age, the team members determine that _____ should be included on the assessment plan.

3. The Teacher Assistance Team of a middle school receives a referral regarding a student who seems to have behavioral difficulty in only one of his classes during the day. In order to determine what is happening in this one classroom, the team decides that an _____ should be conducted.

4. In order to measure student progress against a standard set for all students in the same grade, _____ tests may be used.

5. When a teacher is concerned about a student's mastery of a specific math skill, the teacher may decide to use several measures, including _____.

alternative planning A plan designed for educational intervention when a student has been found not eligible for special education services.

Individual Family Service Plan (IFSP) A plan designed for children ages 3 and younger that addresses the child's strengths and needs as well as the family's needs.

have accommodations for their needs or disabilities in the regular classroom setting. A 504 accommodation plan is designed to implement those accommodations. A sample 504 accommodation plan is presented in Figure 1.8.

When the referred child is 3 years of age or younger and eligibility for services has been determined, the law requires that an **Individual Family Service Plan (IFSP)** be developed by the team members and parents. The IFSP differs from the IEP in that the family's needs as well as the child's needs are addressed.

For **MORE PRACTICE** on distinguishing between the IEP, Section 504 Plans, and IFSPs, visit the Companion Website at *www.prenhall.com/overton.*

ASSESSING THE WHOLE CHILD: CULTURAL CONSIDERATIONS

The 1997 IDEA Amendments (presented in Chapter 2) required that state educational systems report the frequency of occurrence of disabilities and the race/ethnicity of students with disabilities. The first

Figure 1.8   Sample 504 plan.

---

504 Accommodation Plan

Name of Student _____ Date _____

1. Describe the concern for this student s achievement in the classroom setting: _____

2. Describe or attach the existing documentation for the disability or concern (if documentation exists). _____

3. Describe how this affects the student's major life activities. _____
_____

4. The Child Study Team/504 Team has reviewed the case and recommends the following checked accommodations:

Physical Characteristics of Classroom or Other Environment

_____ Seat student near teacher.

_____ Teacher to stand near student when instructions are provided.

_____ Separate student from distractors (other students, air-conditioning or heating units, doorway).

Presentation of Instruction

_____ Student to work with a peer during seatwork time.

_____ Monitor instructions for understanding.

_____ Student to repeat all instructions back to teacher.

_____ Provide a peer tutor.

_____ Provide a homework helper.

_____ All written instructions require accompanying oral instructions.

_____ Teacher to check student's written work during working time to monitor for understanding.

_____ Student may use tape recorder during lessons.

---

reported results of this accounting are found in the *Twenty-Second Annual Report to Congress on the Implementation of the Individuals with Disabilities Education Act* (U.S. Department of Education, 2000). As reported in the literature for several years, particular groups of students from cultural and linguistically diverse backgrounds were found to be overrepresented in some categories of disabilities (see Table 1.3).

It has been observed that the disproportionate rate of occurrence of some students from various ethnic and cultural backgrounds happens in the disability categories that rely heavily on "clinical judgment," such as students with learning disabilities, students within the range of mild mental retardation, and students with emotional disturbances (Harry & Anderson, 1995). Fujiura

Assignments

—— Student requires reduced workload.

—— Student requires extended time for assignments.

—— Student requires reduced stimuli on page.

—— Student requires that work be completed in steps.

—— Student requires frequent breaks during work.

—— Student requires use of tape recorder for oral responses.

—— Student requires lower level reading/math problems.

—— No penalty for handwriting errors.

—— No penalty for spelling errors.

—— No penalty for grammatical errors.

Additional Accommodations for Medical Concerns (List)

_____

_____

Additional Accommodations for Behavioral Concerns (List)

_____

_____

Additional Resources for Parents (List)

_____

_____

Participating Committee Members

_____

_____

_____

_____

and Yamaki (2000) reported troubling patterns indicating that students from homes that fall in the range of poverty and that structurally include a single parent, are at increased risk for disabilities. Although there may be increased risks involved in environments that lack resources and support for single parents, the educational assessment of students from various cultural and linguistic backgrounds must be completed cautiously, fairly, and from the perspective of the child as a whole. Educators must keep the individual child's cultural, ethnic, and linguistic background in the forefront during the evaluation process.

Concern over the disproportionate rate of children from various ethnic and cultural groups being represented in special education categories resulted in directives to state educational agencies in

Table 1.3 Percentage of ethnic groups in special education.

Disability	American Indian	Asian/Pacific Islander	Black (non-Hispanic)	Hispanic	White (non-Hispanic)
Specific Learning Disabilities	1.4	1.4	18.3	15.8	63.0
Speech and Language Impairments	1.2	2.4	16.5	11.6	68.3
Mental Retardation	1.1	1.7	34.3	8.9	54.1
Emotional Disturbance	1.1	1.0	26.4	9.8	61.6
Multiple Disabilities	1.4	2.3	19.3	10.9	66.1
Hearing Impairments	1.4	4.6	16.8	16.3	66.0
Orthopedic Impairments	.8	3.0	14.6	14.4	67.2
Other Health Impairments	1.0	1.3	14.1	7.8	75.8
Visual Impairments	1.3	3.0	14.8	11.4	69.5
Autism	.7	4.7	20.9	9.4	64.4
Deaf-Blindness	1.8	11.3	11.5	12.1	63.3
Traumatic Brain Injury	1.6	2.3	15.9	10.0	70.2
Developmental Delay	.5	1.1	33.7	4.0	60.8
All Disabilities	1.3	1.7	20.2	13.2	63.6
Resident Population	1.0	3.8	14.8	14.2	66.2

Source: U.S. Department of Education (2001). *Twenty-Second Annual Report to Congress on the Implementation of the Individuals with Disabilities Education Act.* Washington, DC: Author.

IDEA 2004. The new version of IDEA includes specific mandates to states to make certain that policies and procedures are in place to prevent the disproportionate representation of ethnic groups in special education. The new requirements are discussed further in Chapter 2.

Portes (1996) posed the question, "What is it about culture and ethnicity that accounts for significant differences in response to the schooling process and its outcomes?" (p. 351). Portes further reasons that it is not fixed characteristics of students but more likely the learned behaviors and identities associated with school. An

Figure 1.9   Student progress monitoring graph.

Number Correct						Percent Correct
20	20	20	20	20	20	100%
19	19	19	19	19	19	95%
18	18	18	18	18	18	90%
17	17	17	17	17	17	85%
16	16	16	16	16	16	80%
15	15	15	15	15	15	75%
14	14	14	14	14	14	70%
13	13	13	13	13	13	65%
12	12	12	12	12	12	60%
11	11	11	11	11	11	55%
10	10	10	10	10	10	50%
9	9	9	9	9	9	45%
8	8	8	8	8	8	40%
7	7	7	7	7	7	35%
6	6	6	6	6	6	30%
5	5	5	5	5	5	25%
4	4	4	4	4	4	20%
3	3	3	3	3	3	15%
2	2	2	2	2	2	10%
1	1	1	1	1	1	5%
Your Possible Scores	**Pre-Test**	**End of Part I**	**End of Part II**	**End of Part III**	**End of Text**	

How does this graph work? Suppose you score a 10 on your pre-test or you answered 50% of the items correct. Circle that score as your baseline. If you would like to get 100% of the items correct, draw a straight line from the first score of 10 to the final % correct column score of 100%. This represents your goal line or your aim line. As you progress throughout the text, the more you study the material, the greater the chance that your scores will be along the goal line until you reach the 100% mark. See Figure 1.10 for this example. You will learn more about this process in the Curriculum-Based Measurement section of the text in Chapter 6.

example of such learned behaviors was described by Marsh and Cornell (2001), who found that minority students' experiences of school played a more important role in the likelihood of exhibiting at-risk behaviors than ethnicity. Educators must continue to strive for methods of assessment that are fair to all students. Burnette (1998) suggested the following strategies for improving accuracy in the assessment process in order to reduce disproportionate representation of minorities in special education:*

- Ensure that the staff knows requirements and criteria for referral and is kept abreast of current research affecting the process.

Reducing the disproportionate representation of minority students in special education. ERIC/OSEP Digest E566. March 1998.

- Check that the student's general education program uses instructional strategies appropriate for the individual, has been adjusted to address the student's area of difficulty, includes ongoing communication with the student's family, and reflects a culturally responsive learning environment.
- Involve families in the decision to refer to special education in ways that are sensitive to the family's cultural background.
- Use only tests and procedures that are technically acceptable and culturally and linguistically appropriate.
- Testing personnel should have had training in conducting these particular assessments and interpreting the results in a culturally responsive manner.
- Personnel who understand how racial, ethnic, and other factors influence student performance should be included in the eligibility decision.

Figure 1.10   Example of student progress graph: Baseline score of 50, goal 100%.

Number Correct						Percent Correct
20	20	20	20	20	20	100%
19	19	19	19	19	19	95%
18	18	18	18	18	18	90%
17	17	17	17	17	17	85%
16	16	16	16	16	16	80%
15	15	15	15	15	15	75%
14	14	14	14	14	14	70%
13	13	13	13	13	13	65%
12	12	12	12	12	12	60%
11	11	11	11	11	11	55%
10	10	10	10	10	10	50%
9	9	9	9	9	9	45%
8	8	8	8	8	8	40%
7	7	7	7	7	7	35%
6	6	6	6	6	6	30%
5	5	5	5	5	5	25%
4	4	4	4	4	4	20%
3	3	3	3	3	3	15%
2	2	2	2	2	2	10%
1	1	1	1	1	1	5%
Your Possible Scores	**Pre-Test**	**End of Part I**	**End of Part II**	**End of Part III**	**End of Text**	

- When eligibility is first established, a set of firm standards for the student's progress and readiness to exit special education should be recorded.

The early writings of Vygotsky concerning special education students' development and assessment cautioned professionals to be certain that the disability was not in "the imagination of the investigators" (Vygotsky, 1993, p. 38). Vygotsky also emphasized that the qualitative aspect of assessment in determining strengths and weaknesses is important rather than the concern only for quantifiable deficits in children. Vygotsky reminded educators that children with disabilities should be viewed in light of their developmental processes in their various environments (Gindis, 1999; Vygotsky, 1993).

The way the student adapts to his or her environment, including culture and school, has a profound impact on the student's ability to have a successful school experience. Today the IDEA Amendments call for educational equity and reform as well as emphasize the use of a variety of early intervening services and assessment techniques that will be useful in educational planning rather than assessment only for determining eligibility. The remaining chapters of this text present educators with both formal and informal assessment and evaluation procedures to be used in educational planning and intervention.

To **READ MORE ABOUT** early intervention and minority overrepresentation, visit the Companion Website at *www.prenhall.com/ overton.*

CHAPTER SUMMARY

Assessment includes many types of evaluation of student progress. Assessment is necessary to monitor achievement, measure achievement of statewide curriculum standards, screen students who may require comprehensive evaluations to determine eligibility for services for disabilities, and to determine when programs need to be modified. Assessment must consider the student's cultural, linguistic, and ethnic background during the process. Assessment must view the student as a whole. The Traditional Assessment Model has been found to be problematic. Educators are now supporting a Contemporary Assessment Model that emphasizes intervention and problem solving.

THINK AHEAD

The steps of the evaluation process are structured by both federal and state laws. The federal mandates are presented in Chapter 2. Why do you think it is necessary to have laws that regulate the assessment process in education?

EXERCISES

Part I

Select the correct terms and write them in the blank spaces provided in each of the following statements:

a. assessment
b. testing
c. curriculum-based assessment
d. error analysis
e. informal assessment
f. prereferral intervention strategies
g. individual assessment plan
h. norm-referenced test
i. performance assessment
j. eligibility meeting

k. early intervention services
l. checklist
m. continuous assessment
n. overidentification
o. APA *Standards*
p. screening
q. IEP
r. alternative planning
s. standardized tests
t. IFSP
u. dynamic assessment
v. disproportionality

_____ 1. Concerns regarding the _____ of students from diverse ethnic and cultural backgrounds emphasize the need for collecting assessment data in a variety of ways.

_____ 2. In order to assess all areas to obtain a view of the whole child, the _____ is designed for each individual student.

_____ 3. When a teacher wants to determine how a student solved a problem incorrectly, the teacher completes a(n) _____.

_____ 4. When a child from a different linguistic background is assessed by providing cues or prompts, a form of _____ has been employed.

_____ 5. As a result of the _____, an IEP or an alternative plan would be developed for a student.

_____ 6. _____ must be given in a specific manner as stated by the publisher, whereas informal tests include a variety of methods and strategies for collecting data.

_____ 7. If _____ prove to be unsuccessful, the team may conclude that the student requires additional assessment to determine if additional services are needed.

_____ 8. A test that compares a student's performance with a national sample of students of the same age or grade is known as a _____.

_____ 9. A student found to be eligible for services who is between the ages of 6 and 21 will have a personalized IEP written, whereas a(n) _____ will be designed for a student younger than school age.

_____10. Teachers who design assessment instruments from classroom materials are using _____ .

Part II

Answer the following questions:

1. One way to document that strategies have been attempted before referral is to use a

   _____

2. Why are statewide tests called high-stakes tests?

   _____

3. How might high-stakes testing improve the education of all students?

   _____

4. The 2004 Amendments to IDEA emphasize that more than 30 years of research indicates that the education of children with disabilities can be made more effective by

   _____

5. Summarize the best-practice procedures that include early intervening services and RTI and when an appropriate referral for special education may be made.

   _____

Answers to these questions can be found in the Appendix of this text or you may also complete these questions and receive immediate feedback on your answers by going to the Think Ahead module in Chapter 1 of the Companion Website.

COURSE PRE-TEST

Take this test before you read Chapter 1. You will begin to see your progress in the course when you take your next test at the end of Chapter 2. You will take a test to monitor progress at the end of each of the 4 parts of the text. Your instructor has the correct responses or you may check your responses on the Companion Website at *www.prenhall.com/overton*. After checking your responses, post on the graph at the end of the test. Each time you take a progress test, post the number of correct answers on the graph. Good Luck!

Pre-Test

Select the best answer from the terms below. Some of these terms may be used more than once.

a. dynamic assessment	e. disproportionality
b. criterion-referenced tests	f. mediation
c. ecological assessment	g. negatively-skewed distribution
d. standard scores	

h. estimated true score

i. ADOS

j. measures of central tendency

k. UNIT

l. Vineland-II

m. latency recording

n. impartial due process hearing

o. overrepresentation

p. interresponse time

_____ 1. Considered the best assessment for determining students who may have a pervasive developmental disorder.

_____ 2. These include, among others, the numerical representation for the average of scores.

_____ 3. The visual representation when more scores are located above the mean.

_____ 4. A measure of intelligence that may be more fair for students who are ELL.

_____ 5. These are determined during the norming process and follow normal distribution theory.

_____ 6. Tests designed to accompany a set of skills.

_____ 7. Assessing the learning environment.

_____ 8. When students from a specific group are under- or over-represented in specific eligibility categories.

_____ 9. Assesses how a student functions across environments or settings.

_____10. Measure of time between the presentation of a stimulus and a response.

Fill in the Blanks

11. _____ is an event that occurs before the target behavior but is removed from the actual environment in which the behavior occurs.

12. The purpose of this test is to assess the cognitive abilities of children ages 3–18 applying both a theory of fluid/crystallized intelligence factors and mental processing factors.

13. When writing test reports the analysis of the comprehensive results are included in the _____ section.

14. On the UNIT, the _____ subtest uses a pencil and paper to measure reasoning and planful behavior.

15. The purpose of assessment is to _____.

16. _____ are norm-referenced measures of student achievement and retention of learned information.

17. _____ is noted by a vertical line on the student data graph.

18. _____ requires a calculation using the student's obtained score, the mean, and the reliability coefficient.

19. _____ will provide a different distribution of scores than the distribution of obtained scores.

20. The K-TEA-II provides an _____ that may be useful in determining student needs.

Laws, Ethics, and Issues

Public Law 94-142
IDEA
IDEA Amendments of 1997
compliance
PL 99-457
IDEA 2004
due process
initial evaluation
comprehensive educational evaluation
informed consent
surrogate parent
consent form
parents' rights booklet
nondiscriminatory assessment
IDEA regulations
special education services

related services
grade equivalent
age equivalent
standard scores
annual goals
least restrictive environment
transition services
procedural safeguards
mediation
independent educational evaluation
impartial due process hearing
impartial hearing officer
Section 504 of the Rehabilitation Act of 1973
minority overrepresentation

CHAPTER FOCUS

This chapter includes the laws and ethical standards governing the use and interpretation of tests used in determining eligibility for special education services. The revisions in the federal regulations are a specific focus. Procedures for implementation of test results for educational interventions and issues of assessment are also included.

CEC KNOWLEDGE AND SKILLS STANDARDS

The student completing this chapter will understand the knowledge and skills included in the following CEC Knowledge and Skills Standards from Standard 8: Assessment:

CC8K1—Legal provisions and ethical principles regarding assessment of individuals

GC8K1—Specialized terminology used in the assessment of individuals with disabilities

CC8S6—Use of assessment information in making eligibility, program, and placement decisions for individuals with exceptional learning needs, including those from culturally and/or linguistically diverse backgrounds.

FROM CEC STANDARD 1: FOUNDATIONS:

CC1K4—Rights and responsibilities of students, parents, teachers and other professionals, and schools related to exceptional learning needs.

THE LAW: PUBLIC LAW 94-142 AND IDEA

Public Law 94-142 Education for All Handicapped Children Act of 1975; guarantees the right to a free and appropriate education in the least restrictive environment; renamed IDEA in 1990.

IDEA Individuals with Disabilities Education Act, passed in 1990 to give new name to PL 94-142.

IDEA Amendments of 1997 Passed in 1997, these amendments make several changes to the original law.

compliance To be operating within the federal regulations, within the confines of the law.

During the 1970s, substantial legal changes for persons with disabilities occurred. Much of the pressure for these changes came from parents and professionals. Another influential source affecting the language of the law was litigation in the civil court system. In 1975, the Education for All Handicapped Children Act, referred to as **Public Law 94-142**, was passed and two years later, the regulations were completed (Education of the Handicapped Act [EHA], 1975; *Federal Register*, 1977). In 1990, under PL 101-476, the act was renamed the Individuals with Disabilities Education Act, or **IDEA**. The regulations were written in 1992 (*Federal Register*, 1992). IDEA contains several major provisions guaranteeing the right to education for persons ages 3 to 21 with disabilities that require special services in the United States. The law grants the right to a free appropriate public education in the least restrictive environment. Many of IDEA's provisions concern the process of assessment. The law mandates that state education agencies (SEAs) ensure that proper assessment procedures are followed (*Federal Register*, 1992).

In 1997, IDEA was amended by the 105th Congress and is referred to as the **Individuals with Disabilities Education Act Amendments of 1997**. Although the original law has been in effect for two decades, professional educators must continue to monitor **compliance** with the mandates within each local education agency (LEA). Informed teachers and parents are the best safeguards for compliance in every school. Even several years after the law was enacted, one study revealed that only 28% of special educators felt they knew special education law (Silver, 1987). Congress noted continued difficulties with the implementation of the original law in the findings section of the law and stated that special education efforts should strive to ensure that students receive an appropriate education and that the rights of children and their parents are protected. The primary goals of Congress in passing the 1997 Amendments were summarized by Yell, Drasgow, and Ford (2000) and are presented in Table 2.1.

In 1999, the final regulations of the 1997 Amendments were published. The regulations governing assessment, titled Procedures for Evaluation and Determination of Eligibility (*Federal Register*, 1999), include changes to the original regulations of 1977 as well as sections that remain unchanged. The 1997 Amendments to IDEA and sections of the final regulations are incorporated in the following sections of this chapter.

Table 2.1   Congressional goals in passing IDEA 1997.

Major Goal	Explanation
Increasing parental participation	Parents must be more fully involved in the special education process through involvement in evaluation, program planning, and placement decisions.
Ensuring student access to the general curriculum	Students with disabilities have opportunity to be involved in the general curriculum and be educated with their nondisabled peers.
Decreasing inappropriate labeling	State education agencies give increased attention to racial, ethnic, and linguistic diversity to prevent inappropriate identification and mislabeling.
Using mediation to resolve disputes	Parents and educators are encouraged to work out their differences using nonadversarial means.
Improving educational results	Unnecessary paperwork requirements reduced to free teachers to focus on teaching and learning. Accountability mechanisms are incorporated in IDEA 97 (e.g., measurable annual goals).
Increasing school safety	IDEA 97 now includes disciplinary requirements.

Source: Copyright (as applicable) by the National Association of School Psychologists, Bethesda, MD. Reprinted with permission of the publisher. www.nasponline.org.

PL 99-457 IDEA amendments that extend services for special-needs children through infancy and preschool years.

In 1986 the Education for the Handicapped Act Amendments, **PL 99-457**, were passed. The final regulations, written in 1993 (*Federal Register*, 1993), were developed to promote early intervention for preschool children and infants with special needs or developmental delays. Additional changes were added in the 1997 Amendments of IDEA. Specific issues concerning PL 99-457 and the assessment of preschool children are discussed in Chapter 10.

In 2004, the Individuals with Disabilities Education Improvement Act was signed into law. This law was designed to address the portions of IDEA that needed improvement and to align this legislation with the No Child Left Behind Act of 2002. The changes included in this improvement act focused on:

- accountability of achievement by students with disabilities
- reduction of paperwork for educators and other professionals
- reduction of the noninstructional time spent by teachers (time spent completing paper work and attending meetings)
- providing additional means to resolve disagreements between schools and parents
- increasing early intervention activities and aligning this effort with No Child Left Behind

- improving teacher quality
- mandating efforts by state education agencies to decrease disproportionality of ethnic and culture representations in special education
- improvement of discipline policies of earlier legislation.

The changes in this act were based largely on the Congressional Findings listed before the actual legislation of 2004. To **READ MORE ABOUT** the Congressional Findings, visit the Companion Website at *www.prenhall.com/overton*.

Once a bill such as the Individuals with Disabilities Education Improvement Act has been signed by the president and becomes a law, the regulations are written which are the legal guidelines for implementing the law. It may take several months to two years to write the regulations. For example, when the original IDEA was passed as PL 94-142 in 1975, the regulations were not completed until 1977. More than one year after IDEA was signed into law, the final regulations were released. This chapter contains sections of the law that directly affect the assessment of children and youth of school age. The IDEA and **IDEA 2004** topics presented in this chapter are listed in Table 2.2.

IDEA 2004 Law that reauthorized and improved the 1997 Individuals with Disabilities Education Act (IDEA).

Table 2.2   IDEA topics presented in Chapter 2.

- Early intervening services
- Initial evaluations
- Parental consent
- Procedural safeguards
- Nondiscriminatory assessment
- Disproportionality of ethnic and cultural groups
- Determining needed evaluation data
- Evaluating children with specific learning disabilities
- Meeting the needs of persons with ADHD
- Multidisciplinary team evaluations
- The IEP team
- IDEA regular education teacher requirements
- Determining eligibility
- Parent participation
- Developing the IEP
- Considerations of special factors
- Transition services
- Due process
- Impartial due process hearings

IDEA AND ASSESSMENT

due process The
right to a hearing to
settle disputes; a
protection for
children with
disabilities and their
families.

initial evaluation
A comprehensive
evaluation before
receiving special
education services.

IDEA is a federal law containing mandates to promote fair, objective assessment practices and **due process** procedures, the foundations for legal recourse when parents or schools disagree with evaluation or placement recommendations. Teachers not only should be aware of the law but also should strive to maintain compliance in testing students, recommending placement, and developing IEPs. Teachers can help their local education agencies comply by following guidelines, meeting time lines, and correctly performing educational functions specified in the law. The first topics presented are the early intervening services that should be implemented prior to a referral for the **initial evaluation**, or the first evaluation of a student to determine if special education services are needed.

INITIAL EVALUATIONS

The provisions of IDEA as amended by the recent improvement act are presented throughout this chapter. The main section presented is Section 614 which concerns evaluations, parental consent, and reevaluations.

§614(a) Evaluations, Parental Consent, and Reevaluations—

(1) Initial Evaluations—
    (A) IN GENERAL—A State educational agency, other state agency, or local education agency shall conduct a full and individual initial evaluation in accordance with this paragraph and subsection (b) before the initial provision of special education and related services to a child with a disability under this part.
    (B) REQUEST FOR INITIAL EVALUATION—Consistent with subparagraph (D), either a parent of a child, or a State agency or local educational agency may initiate a request for an initial evaluation to determine if the child is a child with a disability.
    (C) PROCEDURES—
        (i) IN GENERAL—Such initial evaluation shall consist of procedures—
            (I) to determine whether a child is a child with a disability (as defined in section 602) within 60 days of receiving parental consent for the evaluation, or, if the State established a timeframe within which the evaluation must be conducted, within such timeframe, and
            (II) to determine the educational needs of such child.

Before a student can receive special education services in a general education classroom or in a special education setting, the members of the multidisciplinary team must complete a comprehensive individual evaluation of the student's needs. This evaluation should reflect consideration of the specific academic, behavioral, communicative, cognitive, motor, and sensory areas of concern. This **comprehensive educational evaluation** must be completed before eligibility can be determined. The IDEA 2004 requires that this comprehensive evaluation be completed within a specific timeframe of 60 days from the date that the parent signs a consent form for the evaluation. Additional specifications are presented in the law that address how the timeframe may be adjusted when a child transfers to a different school after the parent has signed the consent form. In addition, the law allows for flexibility of the timeframe if the parents do not produce the child for the evaluation or if the parents refuse to consent to the evaluation.

comprehensive educational evaluation A complete assessment in all areas of suspected disability.

PARENTAL CONSENT

The initial preplacement evaluation and subsequent reevaluations cannot take place without parental **informed consent**.

informed consent Parents are informed of rights in their native language and agree in writing to procedures for the child; consent may be revoked at any time.

§614(a) Evaluations, Parental Consent, and Reevaluations—

  (D) PARENTAL CONSENT
    (i) IN GENERAL—
       (I) CONSENT FOR INITIAL EVALUATION—The agency proposing to conduct an initial evaluation to determine if the child qualifies as a child with a disability as defined in section 602 shall obtain informed consent from the parent of such child before conducting the evaluation. Parental consent for evaluation shall not be construed as consent for placement for receipt of special education and related services.
      (II) CONSENT FOR SERVICES—An agency that is responsible for making a free appropriate public education available to a child with a disability under this part shall seek to obtain informed consent from the parent of such child before providing special education and related services to the child.
    (ii) ABSENCE OF CONSENT—
       (I) FOR INITIAL EVALUATION—If the parent of such child does not provide consent for an initial evaluation under clause (i)(I), or the parent fails to respond to a request to provide the consent, the local education agency may pursue the initial evaluation of the child by utilizing the procedures described in section 615, except to the extent inconsistent with State law relating to such parental consent.
      (II) FOR SERVICES—If the parent of such child refuses to consent to services under clause (i)(II), the local educational agency shall not provide special education and related services to the child by utilizing the procedures described in section 615.

surrogate parent Person appointed by the court system to be legally responsible for a child's education.

According to federal regulations, parental consent means that the parent, guardian, or **surrogate parent** has been fully informed of all educational activities to which he or she is being asked to consent. When a parent gives consent for an initial evaluation, for example, this means that the parent has been fully informed of the evaluation procedures and told why the school personnel believe these measures are necessary and that the parent has agreed to the evaluation.

Informed consent means that the parent has been informed in his or her native language or mode of communication. If the parent does not speak English, the information must be conveyed verbally or in writing in the parent's native language. In areas where languages other than English are prevalent, education agencies often employ bilingual personnel to translate assessment and placement information as necessary. Additionally, many state education agencies provide **consent forms** and **parents' rights booklets** in languages other than English. IDEA's statement regarding mode of communication sends a clear message that parents with visual or hearing impairments must be accommodated. The education agency must make every effort to provide sign interpreters for parents with hearing impairments who sign to communicate and large-type or Braille materials for parents with visual impairments who read in this fashion.

consent form Written permission form that grants permission for evaluation or placement.

parents' rights booklet Used to convey rights and procedural safeguards to parents.

IDEA 2004 includes provisions for allowing school systems to pursue the evaluation of a student without the parental consent if the school system follows the due process procedures within the law. In addition, this law states that parental consent for evaluation is not to be considered as consent for receiving special education services. Should parents refuse services that have been found to be necessary following the evaluation, the school system is not held responsible for the provision of such services.

The 2004 law addresses obtaining consent from parents when their child is a ward of the state in which they live. Local school systems must attempt to locate the parents and obtain consent for the evaluation and the receipt of services. However, if the parents cannot be found, the school can complete an initial evaluation without parental consent.

Parents must be notified of any action proposed by the local school regarding initial evaluations and options considered by IEP teams. These are among the many procedural safeguards provided to parents under the federal law. The law includes requirements of when parents should receive notice of their rights.

§615. Procedural Safeguards

(d) PROCEDURAL SAFEGUARDS NOTICE
    (1) IN GENERAL—
        (A) COPY TO PARENTS—A copy of the procedural safeguards available to the parents of a child with a

disability shall be given to the parents only 1 time a year, except that a copy also shall be given to the parents—

    (i) upon initial referral or parental request for evaluation;

    (ii) upon the first occurrence of the filing of a complaint under subsection (b)(6); and

    (iii) upon request by a parent

(B) INTERNET WEBSITE—A local educational agency may place a current copy of the procedural safeguards notice on its Internet website if such a website exists.

Within the procedural safeguards information, the law requires that parents be informed of the procedures and safeguards for obtaining an initial evaluation, the requirement of prior notice before actions can be taken, information about parental informed consent, how to obtain student records and who has access to those records, and the process to follow when parents have complaints as well as the methods to resolve complaints.

Parental consent must be obtained before the school releases any student records to a third party. If, for example, the school personnel want the records to be mailed to a psychologist in private practice, the parents must consent in writing to the school to release the records and must know exactly which records are to be mailed and to whom.

Federal law requires that school personnel inform the parents before assessment and before placement that their consent is considered mandatory and may be revoked at any time. Therefore, if the parents had previously agreed to a placement for their child in a special education resource room for 1 hour per day and it is later recommended that the student receive services 3 hours per day, the parents may revoke their consent to approve special education services if they believe it to be in the best interest of their child. Should the parents revoke their consent, they are guaranteed the rights of due process. The school personnel are granted the same rights of due process and may decide to file a complaint against the parents. (Due process is discussed in more depth later in this chapter.)

The Check Your Understanding exercises included with this text provide opportunity for you to monitor your own progress in learning the assessment process. Complete this activity in Chapter 2. Additional exercises are provided on the Companion Website for this text at *www.prenhall.com/overton*.

NONDISCRIMINATORY ASSESSMENT

nondiscriminatory assessment Fair and objective testing practices for students from all cultural and linguistic backgrounds.

Many of the requirements that guide professionals in the assessment process are concerned with fair testing practice. The regulations presented on **nondiscriminatory assessment** address the issue of nondiscriminatory assessment consistent with the original

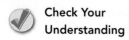

Check Your Understanding

Check your knowledge of procedures for initial evaluations by completing Activity 2.1 below.

Activity 2.1

Use the requirements that concern initial evaluation and informed consent to complete this activity. Choose from the phrases listed to answer the questions that follow the phrases:

> initial evaluation
> native language
> parents' rights booklet
> due process
> voluntary informed consent
> informed of activities
> mode of communication
> comprehensive evaluation
> revoke consent
> release of records
> reevaluation

1. The consent given by parents indicates that the parents have been _____ that the school personnel feel assessment procedures are necessary and in the child's best interest.

2. In compliance with IDEA, many parents are informed of their legal rights and responsibilities through the use of a _____.

3. A teacher would not be allowed to give a student's records to another interested party. Before the _____, the parents must consent in writing and receive an explanation of who would receive which records.

4. When parents decide that they no longer agree with a school placement or services for their child, they may _____, and if necessary, they may begin _____ procedures.

5. It is the responsibility of school personnel to provide information to parents in their _____ or using the _____ to comply with the federal law.

Apply Your Knowledge

Explain how the requirements regarding release of records affect the day-to-day life of a teacher (including a student teacher) working with special-needs students. _____

_____

_____

regulations. The regulations of 1999 add a statement regarding the assessment of students with limited English proficiency:

§614(b) Evaluation Procedures

(2) CONDUCT OF EVALUATION—In conducting the evaluation the local education agency shall—

  (A) use a variety of assessment tools and strategies to gather relevant functional, developmental, and academic information,

including information provided by the parent, that may assist in determining—
  (i) whether the child is a child with a disability; and
  (ii) the content of the child's individualized education program, including information related to enabling the child to be involved in and progress in the general education curriculum, or, for preschool children, to participate in appropriate activities;
(B) not use any single measure or assessment as the sole criterion for determining whether a child is a child with a disability or determining an appropriate educational program for the child; and
(C) use technically sound instruments that may assess the relative contribution of cognitive and behavioral factors in addition to physical or developmental factors.

This section of the law requires that multiple measures be used to obtain an accurate view of the child to determine if the child has a disability. It further states that the results of these evaluations are to be used to determine the content of the child's individualized educational program. This underscores that the purpose of the evaluation is to provide meaningful information that will assist in designing a program of intervention rather than simply evaluating a child to determine if the child is eligible for services. In addition, the law requires that the instruments used must be technically sound or, in other words, validated for such purposes.

IDEA includes the following additional requirements for evaluation of children to determine if they require special education support.

(3) ADDITIONAL REQUIREMENTS—Each local education agency shall ensure that—
  (A) assessments and other evaluation materials used to assess a child under this section—
    (i)   are selected and administered so as not to be discriminatory on a racial or cultural basis;
    (ii) are provided and administered in the language and form most likely to yield accurate information on what the child knows and can do academically, developmentally, and functionally, unless it is not feasible to so provide or administer;
    (iii) are used for purposes for which the assessments or measures are valid and reliable;
    (iv) are administered by trained and knowledgeable personnel; and
    (v)   are administered in accordance with any instructions provided by the producer of such assessments
  (B) the child is assessed in all areas of suspected disability
  (C) assessment tools and strategies that provide relevant information that directly assists persons in determining the educational needs of the child are provided; and

> (D) assessments of children with disabilities who transfer from 1 school district to another school district in the same academic year are coordinated with such children's prior and subsequent schools, as necessary and as expeditiously as possible, to ensure prompt completion of full evaluations

Nondiscriminatory assessment is mandated in the federal law to ensure fairness and objectivity in testing. This section requires that the instruments or techniques used in the assessment process are not racially or culturally biased. This section of the law sets forth the minimum criteria for nondiscriminatory assessment practice in special education. This section requires that the mode of communication used by the student be used in the assessment process. Like the communication standards written for parental consent, this section requires that school personnel find and use such appropriate methods as sign language or Braille if necessary to assess the individual's ability in the most fair and objective manner.

The assessment of students with limited proficiency or emerging proficiency in English is especially difficult. The law requires that assessment personnel make certain that the instruments employed in the assessment of students who have not mastered English, assess skills and abilities other than English skills.

The Act of 2004 clearly indicates that additional measures or strategies other than "tests," as well as parental input, should be considered in the evaluation process. This input should be incorporated in the eligibility decision and in educational interventions for the student. Moreover, information gathered should be for the purpose of enabling the student to participate in the general education curriculum. The assessment information is then to be used to determine if the child is eligible for special education services by meeting the criteria described in the definitions of special education (see Chapter 1). In addition, if the student is determined to be eligible for services, the assessment information gathered must be directly related to the components of the student's individualized educational program. This regulation is included as part of the emphasis that all assessment and subsequent evaluations be conducted with the goal of providing functional information that will be of benefit to the student.

In addition to using tests validated for the purpose for which they will be used, schools must ensure that tests are administered by trained personnel in the manner specified by the test producer. Much information regarding the training of personnel and administration of specific tests can be found in the individual test manuals, which the team member should study thoroughly before administration. Examples of errors made by professionals who do not comply with this section include administering tests or sections of a test to a group of students when the test was designed for individual administration, giving instructions to students in writing when the manual specifies oral presentation, or allowing 2 minutes for a test item when the test manual states that the time allowed is 90 seconds. When an examiner fails to follow directions specified by the developer of a standardized test, the results may lead to inaccurate interpretations and poor recommendations. In this regard, the testing has been unfair to the student.

The best and most consistent practice for using standardized instruments in the assessment of students for consideration of special services is to follow specific instructions provided for administration in a standardized manner. There are times, however, when the best practice for determining an *estimate* of the student's ability may require adaptation of the standardized administration. For example, it may be necessary when assessing a very young child who has a high level of anxiety or a child with limited cognitive ability to request that the parent or primary care-taker remain in the room, perhaps with the child sitting on the parent's lap. The parent in such situations may assist with some of the assessment items (such as providing translations if the young child has difficulty with articulation). In such cases, the 1999 regulations require that the modifications be explained in the written evaluation report. In such situations, an estimate of the child's ability has been obtained. This would require that additional measures, both standardized and nonstandardized, be incorporated into the assessment before making a decision about the student's eligibility.

The assessment of a student must include multiple measures designed for evaluating specific educational needs rather than using a single instrument. The law indicates that no single instrument should be used to determine eligibility. Before the passage of the original law (PL 94-142), numerous students were unfairly discriminated against because of conclusions based on a single IQ score. Often this resulted in very restrictive placement settings, such as institutions or self-contained classrooms, rather than more appropriate educational interventions. In addition to the federal mandates, court cases, such as *Larry P. v. Riles* (1984), have had a significant impact on discriminatory testing practices. This case and others are presented in Chapter 9.

Assessment can be discriminatory in other ways. The law mandates that the instruments used to assess one skill or area do not discriminate or unduly penalize a student because of an existing impairment. For example, a student with speech articulation problems who is referred for reading difficulties should not be penalized on a test that requires the student to pronounce nonsense syllables. The student in this case may have incorrectly pronounced sounds because of the speech condition, and the mispronunciations might be counted as reading errors. The reading scores obtained may be substantially lower than the student's actual reading ability because the misarticulations sounded like mispronunciations, or decoding errors, of the nonsense words.

The law also requires that students are assessed in all areas of suspected disability and that sensory, motor, and emotional areas should be included when appropriate. IDEA requires assessment personnel to consider all possible areas of need, even areas that are not typically thought to be associated or linked with the specific disability category. For example, it may not be uncommon for some students with specific learning disabilities to have difficulties in more than one academic area (e.g., spelling, writing, reading). Assessment personnel must also consider other areas that may require additional evaluation, such as emotional or motor areas. If these areas are determined to require educational interventions, these must be addressed through special education or related services (e.g., counseling or occupational therapy).

It is also required that the tests or instruments employed be psychometrically adequate. Test consumers are therefore required to have an understanding of general testing principles and the accuracy with which inferences about student's cognitive, academic, and behavioral functioning can be made using such instruments.

The law encourages the use of a variety of assessment devices and requires the participation of several professionals in the decision-making process. Using several varied assessment materials helps professionals to establish a more holistic view of the student. The professional expertise provided by a multidisciplinary team aids in promoting fair and objective assessment. It is necessary to involve many different professionals to assess all factors, such as vision, emotion, and language, that may need to be evaluated to reach the best educational decision.

These sections include the requirement to assess the student in all areas of suspected disability. In many cases, a referred student is known to have academic difficulty, but the disability might be due to many factors. The best way to determine whether the student truly has a disability, and if so, what type of disability, is to assess all of the suspected areas. For example, a referred student who demonstrated immature social skills and inappropriate behavior also demonstrated developmental and learning problems. When the referral information was submitted, background information was too limited to determine whether the student was having emotional problems or specific learning problems or possibly was subaverage in intellectual ability. In cases such as this, the law mandates that all areas be assessed to determine whether a disability exists. In this particular case, the young student was found to have a mild hearing impairment and subsequently had developed some behavioral problems. Appropriate audiological and educational interventions prevented further

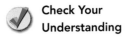

Check Your Understanding

Check your knowledge of fair assessment practices by completing Activity 2.2 below.

Activity 2.2

Read the following statements to determine whether they represent fair testing practice and then circle the appropriate answer. If the statement is unfair, write a statement explaining how to correct the situation. If you think the statement is fair, explain why you think so.

1. A screening test may be used to make placement decisions about a student who was referred for special education services.

    _____ Fair _____ Unfair

    Comments: _____.

2. Individuals who administer tests in the Woodlake local education agency are thoroughly trained to use each new instrument through school inservice sessions and graduate courses.

    _____ Fair _____ Unfair

    Comments: _____.

3. A special education teacher is asked to test a student who speaks only Japanese. The teacher cannot find a test in that language, so he observes the student in the classroom setting and recommends that the student be placed in special education.

    _____ Fair _____ Unfair

    Comments: _____.

4. A special education teacher is asked to give an educational test to a student from a minority culture. The test has been validated and proven to be culturally nondiscriminatory.

    _____ Fair _____ Unfair

    Comments: _____.

5. A student is referred for an evaluation for possible eligibility for special education. The student has cerebral palsy, and the team member has no knowledge of this disorder. The team member asks the physical therapist to give advice on how to administer the test and requests that the therapist attend and assist during the evaluation. The team member also requests the assistance of the school psychologist to determine how the adaptations affect the psychometrics of the test administration. The team member documents all changes in the reevaluation report.

    _____ Fair _____ Unfair

    Comments: _____.

6. A team decides to use the latest IQ score to make a decision regarding a change in eligibility for a student. The team agreed that no additional testing or data were necessary.

    _____ Fair _____ Unfair

    Comments: _____.

Apply Your Knowledge

According to legal requirements, list the possible circumstances in which you would be required to ask for consultative guidance from other professionals during the assessment process. _____

_____

_____

behavioral problems from developing and helped to remediate academic skills.

Other discriminatory test practices concerned with test bias, examiner bias, for example, are presented in the section "Research and Issues Concerning IDEA" later in this chapter. The IDEA Improvement Act of 2004 includes additional specific statements regarding the initial assessment and reevaluation of students that require the consideration of additional data. These regulations concern data that may exist from previous assessments completed by the classroom teacher as well as additional data provided by the parents and other sources.

DETERMINING NEEDED EVALUATION DATA

§614(c) Additional Requirements for Evaluation and Reevaluations—

(1) REVIEW OF EXISTING EVALUATION DATA—As part of an initial evaluation (if appropriate) and as part of any reevaluation under this section, the IEP Team and other qualified professionals, as appropriate, shall—

  (A) review existing evaluation data on the child, including—

    (i) evaluations and information provided by the parents of the child:

    (ii) current classroom-based, local, or State assessments, and classroom-based observations; and

    (iii) observations by teachers and related service providers: and

  (B) on the basis of that review, and input from the child's parents, identify what additional data, if any, are needed to determine—

    (i) whether the child is a child with a disability as defined in section 602(3), and the educational needs of the child, or, in case of a reevaluation of a child, whether the child continues to have such a disability and such educational needs;

    (ii) the present levels of academic achievement and related developmental needs of the child;

    (iii) whether the child needs special education and related services, or, in the case of a reevaluation of a child, whether the child continues to need special education and related services; and

(iv) whether any additions or modifications to the special education and related services are needed to enable the child to meet the measurable annual goals set out in the individualized education program of the child and to participate, as appropriate, in the general education curriculum.

The amendments of IDEA call on professionals and parents alike to determine what data may be needed to obtain the most accurate picture of the child's current ability and educational needs. The law requires that the services are designed to assist the student in meeting the measurable goals of the IEP, and, again, the law requires that the student should participate in the general curriculum unless there is data to indicate that this would not be appropriate. For example, the student might require a specifically different test for statewide accountability of the general education curriculum and would also require a curriculum that would be different than that expected of age and grade peers.

These requirements indicate that the IEP team may review data from a variety of sources and, in the case of reevaluation, may determine that enough data exist to support continued eligibility. In such cases, the student would not be subjected to additional testing to complete the review for continued placement unless the parents request that their child be reevaluated. The student's progress is to be reviewed, although this does not necessarily involve substantial formal testing procedures. The reevaluation may consist of the testing considered to be necessary to determine the student's current educational or behavioral functioning. For example, a student who excels in math but has a specific reading disability may not require a reevaluation of math skills.

Additional regulations specify that the IEP team may conduct the review of the existing data without a meeting. Following the review, if additional data are needed, the public agency shall go about administering tests and other instruments in order to obtain the needed data. In the case of reevaluations, if additional data are not needed, the parents are to be notified by the team that no additional data are needed. Parents are also to be informed of the reasoning for the decision and that they have the right to request an assessment. Should the parents request additional assessment, the team is then required to complete the testing before determining that the child should continue receiving special education support.

EVALUATING CHILDREN WITH SPECIFIC LEARNING DISABILITIES

The federal law includes not only the definition for learning disabilities (see Chapter 1) but it also includes guidelines to assist in the determination of learning disabilities. Until the reauthorization of IDEA 2004, the law stated that a learning disability was indicated when a child had a significant discrepancy between cognitive ability and academic achievement. Using the significant discrepancy model meant that a student would likely struggle for several years during the elementary years, until a significant discrepancy could be determined. Research indicates that students could benefit from intervention during the early years and the new law reflects this research. The 2004 Amendments state:

§614(b)

(6) SPECIFIC LEARNING DISABILITIES

    (A) IN GENERAL—Notwithstanding section 607(b), when determining whether a child has a specific learning disability as defined in section 602, a local education agency shall not be required to take into consideration whether a child has a severe discrepancy between achievement and intellectual ability in oral expression, listening comprehension, written expression, basic reading skill, reading comprehension, mathematical calculation, or mathematical reasoning.

    (B) ADDITIONAL AUTHORITY—In determining whether a child has a specific learning disability, a local education agency may use a process that determines if the child responds to scientific, research-based intervention as a part of the evaluation procedures described in paragraphs (2) and (3).

According to these statements about the determination of specific learning disabilities, the IEP Team may consider data that includes formal assessments and measures of various abilities, however, it is no longer necessary to determine that a discrepancy exists between cognitive ability and achievement before a student can receive services under this category. Additionally, other assessment models, such as a response to intervention, may be used when the school employs research-based interventions as part of the assessment process. As stated in Chapter 1, in the Contemporary Assessment Model and applying early intervening services, the team may use interventions and should those interventions not result in expected progress, this may be regarded as evidence to be used in an eligibility decision. The team may then determine other data that may be needed.

MEETING THE NEEDS OF PERSONS WITH ATTENTION DISORDERS

When PL 94-142 was revised, attention disorders were studied by the U.S. Department of Education (U.S. Department of Education, 1991) for possible addition as a new disability category to IDEA. The decision was made that attention disorders (such as attention deficit disorder, or ADD) did not need a separate category because students with these disorders were already served, for the most part, in settings for students with learning or behavioral disabilities.

If the criteria for either specific learning disabilities or emotional disturbance were not met, the student could be served in an appropriate setting under the category of Other Health Impairment "in instances where the ADD is a chronic or acute health problem that results in limited alertness, which adversely affects educational performance" (U.S. Department of Education, 1991, p. 3). The terms *attention deficit disorder* and *attention deficit hyperactivity disorder* (ADHD) are included among those listed in the definition of the category of Other Health Impairment (§ 300.7(c)(9)(i), IDEA, 1997).

In cases where the attention disorder does not significantly impair the student's ability to function in the regular classroom, the student may be served within the regular classroom under the provisions of Section 504 of the Rehabilitation Act of 1973 (discussed later in this chapter). This law requires that students be given reasonable accommodations for their disability in the general education environment.

Students with attention disorders must undergo a comprehensive evaluation by a multidisciplinary team to determine whether they are eligible for services and, if so, whether they would be better served by the provisions of IDEA or of Section 504.

IEP TEAM EVALUATION

IDEA regulations
Governing document that explains IDEA in operational terms.

To decrease the possibility of subjective and discriminatory assessment, **IDEA regulations** mandate that the comprehensive evaluation be conducted by the members of a multidisciplinary IEP team. As stated in the federal requirements, each student must be assessed in a variety of areas by a team made up of professionals from various disciplines according to the individual's needs. All areas of suspected disability are assessed. If the team has determined during screening and has specified in the assessment plan that the student needs further evaluation in speech, language, reading, and social/behavioral skills, then a speech-language clinician, a special education teacher or educational diagnostician, and a school psychologist will be members of the assessment team. The team may obtain additional information from the parents, classroom teacher, school nurse, school counselor, principal, and other school personnel. Figure 2.1 describes the responsibilities of the various members who might be on the IEP team.

In compliance with the nondiscriminatory section of the law, team members employ several types of assessment and collect different types of data. Team members select instruments for their validity, technical adequacy, cultural fairness, and objectivity. Because the law requires that a variety of methods be used in

Figure 2.1   IEP Team: Who's who?

Team members include, in addition to the child's parents, the following:

Team Member	Responsibilities
School nurse	Initial vision and hearing screens, checks medical records, refers health problems to other medical professionals.
Special education teacher	Consultant to regular classroom teacher during prereferral process; administers educational tests, observes in other classrooms, helps with screening and recommends IEP goals, writes objectives, and suggests educational interventions.
Special education supervisor	May advise all activities of special education teacher, may provide direct services, guides placement decisions, recommends services.
Educational diagnostician	Administers norm-referenced and criterion-referenced tests, observes student in educational setting, makes suggestions for IEP goals and objectives.
School psychologist	Administers individual intelligence tests, observes student in classroom, administers projective instruments and personality inventories; may be under supervision of a doctoral-level psychologist.
Occupational therapist	Evaluates fine motor and self-help skills, recommends therapies, may provide direct services or consultant services, may help obtain equipment for student needs.
Physical therapist	Evaluates gross motor functioning and self-help skills, living skills, and job-related skills necessary for optimum achievement of student; may provide direct services or consultant services.
Behavioral consultant	Specialist in behavior management and crisis intervention; may provide direct services or consultant services.
School counselor	May serve as objective observer in prereferral stage, may provide direct group or individual counseling, may schedule students and help with planning of student school schedules.

continued.

Figure 2.1   continued.

Team Member	Responsibilities
Speech-language clinician	Evaluates speech-language development, may refer for hearing problems, may provide direct therapy or consultant services for classroom teachers.
Audiologist	Evaluates hearing for possible impairments, may refer students for medical problems, may help obtain hearing aids.
Physician's assistant	Evaluates physical condition of student and may provide physical exams for students of a local education agency, refers medical problems to physicians or appropriate therapists, school social worker, or visiting teacher.
Home-school coordinator; school social worker or visiting teacher	Works directly with family; may hold conferences, conduct interviews, and administer adaptive behavior scales based on parent interviews; may serve as case manager.
Regular education teacher	Works with the special education team, student, and parents to develop an environment that is appropriate and as much like that of general education students as possible; implements prereferral intervention strategies.

assessment, the team should make use of additional classroom observations, informal assessment measures, and parent interviews. Additional data provided by outside sources or from previous assessment should also be considered.

The IDEA amendments specify that an IEP team comprises specific individuals who reach a decision regarding the student's eligibility for services and possible interventions. Each member of the IEP team contributes carefully documented information to the decision-making process.

§ 614(d) (1) (B) Individualized Education Program Team—

The term 'individualized education program team' or 'IEP Team' means a group of individuals composed of—

  (i) the parents of a child with a disability
  (ii) not less than 1 regular education teacher of such child (if the child is, or may be participating in the regular education environment);
  (iii) not less than 1 special education teacher, or where appropriate, not less than 1 special education provider of such child;
  (iv) a representative of the local educational agency who—

(I) is qualified to provide, or supervise the provision of, specially designed instruction to meet the unique needs of children with disabilities;

(II) is knowledgeable about the general education curriculum; and

(III) is knowledgeable about the availability of resources of the local educational agency;

(v) an individual who can interpret the instructional implications of evaluation results, who may be a member of a team described in clauses (ii) through (vi)

(vi) at the discretion of the parent or the agency, other individuals who have knowledge or special expertise regarding the child, including related services personnel as appropriate; and

(vii) whenever appropriate; the child with a disability

The amendments require that at a minimum, the IEP team should include the child's parents, a general education teacher (if the child is or may be participating in the general education environment), a special education teacher, a supervisor of special education services who is knowledgeable about general curriculum and local resources, and someone who is able to interpret the instructional implications of evaluation results. In many cases, one person may fulfill more than one role on the IEP team. The school or parent may invite others as long as they have knowledge of the child or the services that will be provided. Together, the IEP team and other professionals, as appropriate, determine eligibility based on federal and state criteria.

IEP Team Member Attendance   The federal law and subsequent regulations written for IDEA required that the specific team members attend all IEP team meetings. In addition, all team members were required to attend the complete meeting even though they may not have had new information to contribute. In an effort to clarify the team members' participation and to decrease the amount of time that teachers spend away from classroom instruction, new statements were included in IDEA 2004 regarding attendance. The law includes the following statements.

§ 614(d) (1) (C) IEP Team Attendance—

(i) ATTENDANCE NOT NECESSARY—A member of the IEP Team shall not be required to attend an IEP meeting, in whole or in part, if the parent of a child with a disability and the local education agency agree that the attendance of such member is not necessary because the member's area of the curriculum or related services is not being modified or discussed in the meeting.

(ii) EXCUSAL—A member of the IEP Team may be excused from attending an IEP meeting in whole or in part when the meeting involves a modification to or discussion of the member's area of the curriculum or related services, if—

(I) the parent and the local educational agency consent to the excusal; and

(II) the member submits, in writing to the parent and the IEP Team, input into the development of the IEP prior to the meeting.

(iii) WRITTEN AGREEMENT AND CONSENT REQUIRED—A parent's agreement under clause (i) and consent under (ii) shall be in writing.

These statements indicate that a member is not required to attend if there is no information being presented from that member either in written form or during the discussion by the Team. If the member is contributing to the meeting and cannot attend, with the parent's and school's consent, the member may submit the contribution in written form. As stated, the parental consent for either excusal or nonattendance must be given in writing.

These sections of the law provide guidance about how to involve general education teachers in the IEP process and encourage the child's teachers to contribute to the review and revision of the program.

DETERMINING ELIGIBILITY

IDEA 2004 Amendments include definitions and some fairly global criteria for determining eligibility for services for students with the following disabilities: autism, deaf-blindness, deafness, hearing impairment, mental retardation, multiple disabilities, orthopedic impairment, emotional disturbance, specific learning disability, speech or language impairment, traumatic brain injury, and visual impairment, including blindness. Most states have more specific criteria for determining eligibility for services, and many have different names for the conditions stated in the law. For example, some states use the term *perceptual disability* rather than *learning disability*, or *mental handicap* rather than *mental retardation*.

special education services Services not provided by regular education but necessary to enable an individual with disabilities to achieve in school.

During the eligibility meeting, all members should, objectively and professionally, contribute data, including informal observations. The decision to provide the student with special education services or to continue in a regular classroom without special education interventions should be based on data presented during the eligibility meeting. Parents are to be active participants in the eligibility meeting. School personnel should strive to make parents feel comfortable in the meeting and should welcome and carefully consider all of their comments and any additional data they submit. If the student has been found eligible for services, the team discusses educational interventions and specific **special education services** and **related services**. The federal requirements recommend that students are educated, as much as possible, with general education

related services Those services related to special education but not part of the educational setting, such as transporation and therapies.

students. Related services are those determined by the IEP Team to be necessary for the child to benefit from the instructional goals of the IEP. Examples of related services include psychological services, early identification of children with disabilities, and therapeutic recreation. The 2004 regulations specifically added the related services of interpreting for students who are deaf or hard of hearing and services of the school nurse.

The improvement act of 2004 includes statements regarding when a student cannot be found eligible for services. These are stated in the following section.

§614(b)

(4) *Determination of Eligibility and Educational Need*—Upon completion of the administration of assessments and other evaluation measures:

(A) the determination of whether the child is a child with a disability as defined in section 602(3) and the educational needs of the child shall be made by a team of qualified professionals and the parent of the child in accordance with paragraph (5); and

(B) copy of the evaluation report and the documentation of determination of eligibility shall be given to the parent.

(5) *Special Rule for Eligibility Determination*—In making a determination of eligibility under paragraph (4)(A), a child shall not be determined to be a child with a disability if the determinant factor for such determination is—

(A) lack of appropriate instruction in reading, including in the essential components of reading instruction (as defined in section 1208(3) of the Elementary and Secondary Education Act of 1965);

(B) lack of instruction in math; or

(C) limited English proficiency.

These sections state that the parent must be given a written copy of how the eligibility determination was made by the IEP Team.

This special rule for determining eligibility is aimed at preventing students from becoming eligible for special education solely on the basis of no instruction or limited instruction in reading or math. The special rule regarding appropriate instruction references the Elementary and Secondary Education Act. This reference links the Individuals with Disabilities Education Improvement Act with the No Child Left Behind Act for the definition of essential reading components. In this law, the essential components of reading are listed as:

Phonemic awareness

Phonics

Vocabulary development

Reading fluency, including oral reading skills; and

Reading comprehension strategies
[PL 107-110.§ 103(3)]

Students may not be found eligible solely on the basis of having limited English proficiency. In other words, students who have had these experiences must have other causative factors that result in the need for special education or related services. For example, a student may have had little or inappropriate instruction in math and be found eligible for services because of a reading disability if that has been documented through the evaluation.

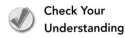

Check Your Understanding

Check your knowledge of the appropriate team member for consultation and assistance by completing Activity 2.3 below.

Activity 2.3

Determine who is the appropriate team member(s) to address the following problems and provide suggestions for interventions.

1. A student in class has been rubbing his eyes frequently, holds his books very close to his face, and seems to have difficulty seeing some printed words. You should request the assistance of _____.

2. A young student in first grade has difficulty holding her pencil correctly, using scissors, and coloring in class. You notice that this student has marked difficulty when compared to the other students in class. You tried several procedures to help her learn how to use these tools, but she continues to have difficulty. You decide to refer the child to _____.

3. Mr. Powers has a student in his class who seems to have difficulty staying awake. From time to time the student appears to be in a daze. Mr. Powers does not know if the child has a physical, emotional, or even drug-related problem. He asks you to help because "you know what to do with these types of problems." You advise Mr. Powers to contact _____.

4. Ms. Stewart has a third grade student who just doesn't seem to be learning. She tells you she has "tried everything" including changing to an easier textbook. She feels certain that the student has a learning disability. What might be some of the suggestions you can provide for Ms. Stewart? _____.

5. Miss Morales has a young male student who exhibits aggressive behaviors in class. She expresses concern that this student may harm himself or others. Your advice to Miss Morales is to _____.

Apply Your Knowledge

Whom should you contact when you are not certain of the type of learning or behavioral challenge a student exhibits or if you are uncertain of who the appropriate related services personnel would be for a specific type of difficulty? _____

_____

_____

PARENT PARTICIPATION

Every effort should be made to accommodate the parents so that they may attend all conferences pertaining to their child's education. The federal requirements emphasize the importance of parental attendance.

The importance of parent involvement was underscored in the provisions of PL 99-457. The amendments require that the intervention plan, called the Individual Family Service Plan (IFSP), be designed to include the family members. As mentioned in Chapter 1, the IFSP identifies family needs relating to the child's development that, when met, will increase the likelihood of successful intervention. The legislation emphasizes the family and the child with the disability (Turnbull, 1990).

The IDEA Amendments of 1997 and the IDEA Amendments of 2004 further stressed the importance of parent participation by including the parents on the IEP team and by encouraging parents to submit additional information to be used during the eligibility and planning process. These regulations also require that the parent be given a copy of the evaluation report as well as the documentation of eligibility upon completion of the administration of tests and other evaluation materials.

grade equivalent Grade score assigned to a mean raw score of a group during norming process.

IDEA 2004 added provisions for parents to be involved in the educational planning process of their child without having to convene the whole IEP Team for changes in the educational program. This new law allows for amendments to the child's program to be made if the parent and the school personnel, such as the child's general education or special education teacher, agree.

DEVELOPING THE INDIVIDUALIZED EDUCATION PROGRAM

age equivalent Age score assigned to a mean raw score of a group during norming process.

standard scores Scores calculated during norming process of a test follow normal distribution theory.

annual goals Long-term goals for educational intervention.

Every student receiving special education services must have an individualized education program or plan (IEP) that is written in compliance with the requirements of IDEA. Current levels of educational performance may include scores such as **grade equivalents**, **age equivalents**, and/or **standard scores**. In addition, present level-of-performance information should include classroom performance measures and classroom behavior. Measurable long-term goals, or **annual goals**, must be included in the IEP. Every area in which special education services are provided must have an annual goal.

The IDEA Amendments of 2004 stated requirements for the IEP team to incorporate in the IEP. These requirements, presented in the following section, indicate what should be included in the written individual educational program, a plan for instructional intervention.

§614(d) Individualized Education Programs—

(1) DEFINITIONS—In this title:

   (A) INDIVIDUALIZED EDUCATION PROGRAM—

      (i) IN GENERAL—The term 'individualized education program' or 'IEP' means a written statement for each child with a disability that is developed, reviewed, and revised in accordance with this section and that includes—

         (I) a statement of the child's present level of academic achievement and functional performance, including—

           (aa) how the child's disability affects the child's involvement and progress in the general education curriculum;

           (bb) for preschool children, as appropriate, how the disability affects the child's participation in appropriate activities; and

           (cc) for children with disabilities who take alternate assessments aligned to alternate achievement standards, a description of benchmarks or short-term objective;

        (II) a statement of measurable annual goals, including academic and functional goals, designed to—

           (aa) meet the child's needs that result from the child's disability to enable the child to be involved in and make progress in the general education curriculum; and

           (bb) meet each of the child's other educational needs that result from the child's disability;

        (III) a description of how the child's progress toward meeting the annual goals described in subclause (II) will be

Scott Cunningham/Merrill

measured and when periodic reports on the progress the child is making toward meeting the annual goals (such as through the use of quarterly or other periodic reports, concurrent with the issuance of report cards) will be provided

(IV) a statement of the special education and related services and supplementary aids and services, based on peer reviewed research to the extent practicable, to be provided to the child, or on behalf of the child, and a statement of the program modifications or supports for the school personnel that will be provided for the child—

    (aa) to advance appropriately toward attaining annual goals

    (bb) to be involved in and make progress in the general education curriculum in accordance with subclause (I) and to participate in extracurricular and other nonacademic activities; and

    (cc) to be educated and participate with other children with disabilities and nondisabled children in the activities described in this subparagraph

(V) an explanation of the extent, if any, to which the child will not participate with nondisabled children in the regular class and in the activities described in subclause (IV)(cc);

(VI) (aa) a statement of any individual appropriate accommodations that are necessary to measure the academic achievement and functional performance of the child on State and districtwide assessments consistent with section 621(a)(16)(A); and

    (bb) if the IEP Team determines that the child shall take an alternate assessment on a particular State or districtwide assessment of student achievement, a statement of why—

        (AA) the child cannot participate in the regular assessment and

        (BB) the particular alternate assessment selected is appropriate for the child;

(VII) the projected date for the beginning of service and modifications described in subclause (IV) and the anticipated frequency, location, and duration of those services and modifications. . . .

    The first requirement is that the IEP team include a statement of the student's current functioning and, most important, how the child's disability affects the child's ability to be involved with general education students. Since the 1997 Amendments it is assumed that students with disabilities will be educated with their nondisabled peers unless the IEP team provides reasons why this is not appropriate for the specific student (Huefner, 2000). The earlier regulations stated a preference for educating students in the general education environment; however, the language included since the 1997 Amendments is stronger. These IEP requirements focus on inclusion of the student with disabilities within the mainstream environment and with general education students for education and other activities outside the educational setting. This part of IDEA is known as the provision of educational services in the **least restrictive environment** (LRE, discussed further later in the chapter).

least restrictive environment The environment determined to be the most like that of nondisabled peers.

Several court cases have resulted in interpreting the least restrictive environment requirement of the child's IEP. The movement toward inclusion as a method of providing the least restrictive environment has been found to be appropriate in some situations and not in others. Yell (1995) has offered a method that may assist IEP teams in making the determination of the appropriate educational environment that is based on the results of current interpretation within the judicial system. This method is shown in Figure 2.2.

Figure 2.2 Determination of the least restrictive environment.

School district decisions should be based on formative data collected throughout the LRE process.

1. Has the school taken steps to maintain the child in the general education classroom?
   - What supplementary aids and services were used?
   - What interventions were attempted?
   - How many interventions were attempted?
2. Benefits of placement in general education with supplementary aids and services versus special education.
   - Academic benefits
   - Nonacademic benefits
3. What are the effects of the education on other students?
   - If the student is disruptive, is the education of the other students adversely affected?
   - Does the student require an inordinate amount of attention from the teacher, thereby adversely affecting the education of others?
4. If a student is being educated in a setting other than the general education classroom, are integrated experiences available with able-bodied peers to the maximum extent possible?
   - In what academic settings is the student integrated with able-bodied peers?
   - In what nonacademic settings is the student integrated with able-bodied peers?
5. Is the entire continuum of alternative services available from which to choose an appropriate environment?

Source: From Least restrictive environment, inclusion, and students with disabilities: A legal analysis, by M. L. Yell, 1995, *Journal of Special Education, 28*, 389–404. Copyright by PRO–ED, Inc. Adapted by permission.

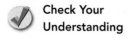

Check Your Understanding

Check your knowledge of the least restrictive environment and other requirements of IDEA by completing Activity 2.4 below.

Activity 2.4

As a special education teacher in Achievement Elementary School you are a member of the IEP team. The team is meeting to review the assessment results of a student who meets the eligibility criteria for mild mental retardation. One of the team members believes that this student should be placed in a self-contained special education setting for a majority of the school day. Explain your concerns about the environment and offer solutions.

Apply Your Knowledge

If the student in this scenario requires interventions in a special education setting, what would the team be required to include in the student's IEP? _____

_____

_____

The team must consider the extent to which the student can participate in statewide assessments. The level of participation in these assessments and any accommodations required must be stated in the IEP. It is clear that meeting the student's needs within the least restrictive environment is a goal of the Amendments of 1997 and 2004.

The 2004 Amendments add a component to the IEP that represents further alignment with the No Child Left Behind Act. In the No Child Left Behind Act, there is an emphasis on using research-based interventions and instructional methodology when addressing instruction in the early grades, especially in reading and math. In the most recent reauthorization of IDEA (2004), the IEP should include, to the extent practical, educational programming and strategies, that are based on peer-reviewed research. This represents the movement in educational reform to use instructional time wisely by incorporating teaching strategies that are supported by research in scholarly educational and psychological journals. The use of such strategies will increase the likelihood that students will make the progress expected each year. Making adequate progress in educational achievement is at the core of accountability in education. The statements regarding the IEP requirements of statewide assessment are tied to this movement of accountability in the education of students with disabilities.

The final regulations of IDEA 2004 included the definition of scientifically based research by stating that it is the same definition as that of the definition included in NCLB (also known as the Elementary and Secondary Education Act). To read more about this definition, visit the Companion Website at *www.prenhall.com/overton*.

As the Team considers the student's individual program, the 2004 Amendments require that the Team use the following guidelines to develop the IEP.

§614(d) (3) Development of the IEP—

(A) IN GENERAL—In developing each child's IEP, the IEP Team, subject to subparagraph (C), shall consider—
   (i) the strengths of the child;
   (ii) the concerns of the parents for enhancing the education of their child;
   (iii) the results of the initial evaluation or most recent evaluation of the child; and
   (iv) the academic, developmental, and functional needs of the child.

The IDEA amendments include a section of considerations for students with special factors or conditions. These considerations are presented in the following paragraphs.

§614(d) (3) (B) Consideration of Special Factors —The IEP Team shall:

(i) in the case of the child whose behavior impedes the child's learning or that of others, consider the use of positive behavioral interventions and supports, and other strategies to address that behavior;
(ii) in case of a child with limited English proficiency, consider the language needs of the child as such needs relate to the child's IEP;
(iii) in the case of the child who is blind or visually impaired, provide for instruction in Braille and the use of Braille unless the IEP Team determines, after evaluation of the child's reading and writing skills, needs, and appropriate reading and writing media (including an evaluation of the child's future needs for instruction in Braille or the use of Braille), that instruction in Braille of the use of Braille is not appropriate for the child;
(iv) consider the communication needs of the child, and in the case of a child who is deaf or hard of hearing, consider the child's language and communication needs, opportunities for direct communications with peers and professional personnel in the child's language and communication mode, academic level, and a full range of needs, including opportunities for direct instruction in the child's language and communication mode; and
(v) consider whether the child needs assistive technology devices and services.

Each of these requirements mandates the IEP team to consider specific needs of individuals, such as students with limited English proficiency and students with various disabilities. These specific needs, which have been determined through effective assessment, should be addressed in the IEP and progress monitored and reviewed, at least annually, by the IEP Team.

For **MORE PRACTICE** with IEP requirements, visit the Companion Website at *www.prenhall.com/overton*.

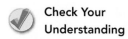

Check Your Understanding

Check your knowledge of comparing IDEA and Section 504 by completing Activity 2.5 below.

Activity 2.5

Refer to pages 68–70 of your text. Read the following descriptions of students and determine how their needs might best be served. Distinguish between which students fall under IDEA and which students can be served through Section 504.

1. Lorenzo was born with cerebral palsy and requires the use of a wheelchair. He is able to use a computer for word processing and completes all of his assignments using either his laptop or his computer at home. Lorenzo's most recent statewide assessments indicate that he is at or above the level expected in all academic areas. Lorenzo can be served _____.

2. Marilu has been found to have attention deficit disorder. She requires medication but her medication is time released and she does not need to take a dose at school. Marilu requires additional time to complete her assignments and performs best when she can sit near the teacher. Her report indicates that her grades are within the average range with the exception of math which is above average. Marilu can be served _____.

3. Randal has had signs of depression for the past several months. His parents decided to seek the assistance of an outside psychologist for counseling. Randal began to improve and he is now participating with his friends and playing team sports. His grades continue to decline and his reading skills are significantly below his peers. Because of his difficulty reading, his content subject grades began to fall as well. He was assessed and was found to have a significant reading disability. Randal can be served _____.

Apply Your Knowledge

A key component of a student meeting the eligibility requirements for a category of special education is that in addition to an existing condition, the condition or disability must also _____
_____
_____

TRANSITION SERVICES

In the section addressing the content of the IEP, the law addresses the needs of students who are nearing the age when they may make the transition to adult life.

§614(d) (1) (A) (i) (VIII) *beginning not later than the first IEP to be in effect when the child is 16, and updated annually thereafter—*

(aa) appropriate measurable postsecondary goals based upon age appropriate transition assessments related to training, education, employment, and where appropriate, independent living skills;

(bb) the transition services (including courses of study) needed to assist the child in reaching those goals; and

(cc) beginning not later than 1 year before the child reaches the age of majority under State law, a statement that the child has been informed of the child's rights under this title, if any, that will transfer to the child on reaching the age of majority under section 615(m).

transition services
Services designed to help students make the transition from high school to postsecondary education or work environment.

IDEA stressed the importance of **transition services** to prepare students 16 years or older for a work or postsecondary environment. Where appropriate in educational planning, younger students may also be eligible for such services. The law underscores the importance of early planning and decisions by all members affected, including the student. The planning for the needed transition begins by age 16 or younger, if appropriate.

The IDEA Amendments emphasized transition services to a greater extent than did other regulations. They also extended the rights to the student at the age of majority according to individual

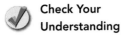

Check Your Understanding

Check your knowledge of the legal requirements of Individuals with Disabilities Education Improvement Act of 2004 by completing Activity 2.6 below.

Activity 2.6

After reviewing the legal requirements of IDEA 2004, complete the following.

1. IDEA 2004 requires that the IEP Team members participate in the team meetings. Under certain circumstances, some members of the IEP Team may be excused from attending the meeting. Explain when this is allowed and what must happen in order for this to be allowed.

2. Is it possible that a professional from an outside agency can determine that a child has a disability and the child should subsequently receive special education support?

3. A second-grade student recently enrolled in your school. The student is a recent immigrant from Mexico. Your school determines that the child had not previously been enrolled in school in Mexico due to his parents' lack of funds and due to a lack of transportation to school. The student's mother has recently obtained citizenship. Once the child began to attend your school, it was determined that the child could not read in English or Spanish. Can the student be referred for an evaluation for special education services?

4. Mrs. Lorenzo met with her son's teacher. They determined that her son might require an additional session of support time in the resource room which would increase the amount of time from two thirty-minute sessions per week to three thirty-minute sessions. In order to make this change to the IEP, will the Team need to be convened?

state laws. The age of majority is the age at which a child is no longer considered to be a minor (in many states, the age is 18). School personnel are responsible for communicating to the student that the rights under the law are now in the hands of the student rather than the parents. Moreover, the law requires that the student be informed of the transfer of rights a year before the student reaches the age of majority.

The 2004 Amendments add more specificity regarding the transitional assessment and appropriate annual goals. The statements stress that the postsecondary goals be measurable and that the goals should be based upon specific assessment in areas of education, employment, and daily living skills as appropriate.

DUE PROCESS

procedural safeguards Provisions of IDEA designed to protect students and parents in the special education process.

IDEA was influenced to a large degree by parent organizations and court cases involving individuals with disabilities and their right to education. When schools implement the provisions of the law, occasionally differences arise between the schools providing the service and the parents of the student with the disability. Therefore, IDEA contains provisions for parents and schools to resolve their differences. These provisions are called due process provisions.

The **procedural safeguards** are inherent throughout the portions of the law concerned with assessment. For example, parental informed consent is considered a procedural safeguard designed to prevent assessment and placement of students without parents' knowledge. Parents may withdraw their consent at any time. Other provisions promote fairness in the decision-making process. Included in these provisions are the parents' right to examine all educational records and the right to seek an independent educational evaluation as well as the right to a hearing to resolve differences.

mediation Process of settling a dispute between parents and schools without a full third-party hearing.

The IDEA Amendments of 1997 include a significant addition in the area of due process. The amendments provide new sections for promoting **mediation** as a method to resolve disagreements between parents and their local school agency. The requirements mandate local education agencies to provide mediation at no cost to the parents. The mediation process is voluntary on the part of the school and the parents. This process cannot be used by a local education agency to delay parental rights to a hearing or to deny any other rights provided in the regulations. The mediation process is to be conducted by qualified and impartial trained mediators who are included on a list maintained by each state.

IDEA 2004 adds a requirement for a resolution session to be held with the parents and the school personnel within 15 days of the filing of a complaint. This session is a step to resolve the complaint so that a formal hearing can be avoided. During this session, the school may not have an attorney present unless the parents are accompanied by their attorney. This is an opportunity for the school to resolve the issue in a timely manner. This resolution session may be waived if the parents and school personnel all agree in writing to do so. The parents may choose to waive the resolution meeting and to schedule a mediation meeting according to the 2004 Amendments.

independent educational evaluation
Comprehensive evaluation provided by a qualified independent evaluator.

The parents of a student who has been evaluated by school personnel may disagree with the results obtained during the assessment process. Should this occur, the parents have the right to obtain an independent evaluation by an outside examiner. The **independent educational evaluation** is provided by a qualified professional not employed by the local education agency. Should the independent evaluation results differ from the evaluation results obtained by school personnel, the school must pay for the evaluation. The exception to this is if the school initiates an impartial due process hearing to resolve the different results and the hearing officer finds in favor of the school. In this case, the parents would be responsible for paying for the independent evaluation. If, however, the hearing finds in favor of the parents, the school is responsible for payment.

IMPARTIAL DUE PROCESS HEARING

impartial due process hearing A hearing by an impartial officer that is held to resolve differences between a school and parents of a student with disabilities.

impartial hearing officer Person qualified to hear disputes between schools and parents; not an employee of school agency.

The parents and school are provided with procedures for filing complaints and requesting an **impartial due process hearing**. In a third-party hearing, the parents and the school may individually explain their side of the disagreement before an **impartial hearing officer**, a person qualified to hear the case. In some states, third-party hearing officers are lawyers; in other states, the hearing officers are special education professionals, such as college faculty who teach special education courses to prepare teachers.

Parents should be advised before the hearing that although counsel (an attorney) is not required for the hearing, they do have the right to secure counsel as well as experts to give testimony. After hearing each side of the complaint, the hearing officer reaches a decision. A finding in favor of the parents requires the school to comply with the ruling or appeal to a state-level hearing. In turn, if favor is found with the school, the parents must comply. If the parents do not wish to comply, they may be able to request a state-level hearing or file an appeal with a civil court.

While the school and parents are involved with due process and hearing procedures, the student remains in the classroom setting in which she was placed before the complaint was filed. This requirement has been called the stay-put provision.

SECTION 504

Section 504 of the Rehabilitation Act of 1973 A civil rights law that includes protection from discrimination and reasonable accommodations.

Section 504 of the Rehabilitation Act of 1973 includes many of the same concepts, such as procedural safeguards and evaluation, as those in IDEA. The law extends beyond the categories listed in IDEA and beyond the public school environment. This law is a civil rights law, and its purpose is to prevent discrimination against individuals with disabilities in programs receiving federal financial assistance. Students with disabilities are protected from discrimination in schools receiving federal financial assistance under Section 504, whether or not they are protected by IDEA. The law extends the educational regulations to include postsecondary environments, such as colleges and universities. It is used to address the situation of people with chronic health conditions in the public education setting who may not be addressed through IDEA, such as students with ADHD who do not need full special education support because of other significant learning disabilities.

Some notable differences exist between IDEA and Section 504 that were summarized by Yell (1997). These differences are presented in Table 2.3.

Table 2.3 Differences between IDEA and 504.

Component	IDEA	Section 504
Purpose of law	• Provides federal funding to states to assist in education of students with disabilities • Substantive requirements attached to funding	• Civil rights law • Protects persons with disabilities from discrimination in programs or services that receive federal financial assistance • Requires reasonable accommodations to ensure nondiscrimination
Who is protected?	• Categorical approach • Thirteen disability categories • Disability must adversely impact educational performance	• Functional approach • Students (a) having a mental or physical impairment that affects a major life activity, (b) with a record of such an impairment, or (c) who are regarded as having such an impairment • Protects students in general and special education
FAPE	• Special education and related services that are provided at public expense, meet state requirements, and are provided in conformity with the IEP • Substantive standard is educational benefit	• General or special education and related aids and services • Requires a written education plan • Substantive standard is equivalency

continued.

Table 2.3   continued.

Component	IDEA	Section 504
LRE	• Student must be educated with peers without disabilities to the maximum extent appropriate • Removal from integrated settings only when supplementary aids and services are not successful • Districts must have a continuum of placement available	• School must ensure that the students are educated with their peers without disabilities
Evaluation and placement	• Protection in evaluation procedures • Requires consent prior to initial evaluation and placement • Evaluation and placement decisions have to be made by a multidisciplinary team • Requires evaluation of progress toward IEP goals annually and reevaluation at least every 3 years	• Does not require consent; requires notice only • Requires periodic reevaluation • Reevaluation is required before a significant change in placement
Procedural safeguards	• Comprehensive and detailed notice requirements • Provides for independent evaluations • No grievance procedure • Impartial due process hearing	• General notice requirements • Grievance procedure • Impartial due process hearing
Funding	• Provides for federal funding to assist in the education of students with disabilities	• No federal funding
Enforcement	• U.S. Office of Special Education Programs (OSEP) (can cut off IDEA funds) • Complaints can be filed with state's department of education	• Compliance monitoring by state educational agency (SEA) • Complaint can be filed with Office of Civil Rights (OCR) (can cut off all federal funding)

Source: From *The law and special education*, by M. L. Yell, 1997, Upper Saddle River, NJ: Prentice Hall. Copyright by Prentice Hall.

For the purposes of assessment and educational planning, Section 504 seeks to meet the needs of students according to how students' conditions affect their functioning within life activities. This places the emphasis of assessment and program planning on a student's current functioning within that activity and calls for reasonable accommodations. For a college student with a specific learning disability, for example, the reasonable accommodations may include taking exams in a quiet room with extended time because of attention deficit disorder or waiving a foreign language requirement because of a specific learning disability in written language.

RESEARCH AND ISSUES CONCERNING IDEA

IDEA states that each school agency shall actively take steps to ensure that parents participate in the IEP process in several ways. First, the parents must agree by informed consent before the initial evaluation and before receiving special education services. The 1997 amendments added the provision that parents must consent prior to the reevaluation. The parents also participate in the decision-making process regarding eligibility. Following the eligibility determination, the parents are to participate in the development of the IEP. Legally, parents have the right to participate in the evaluation and IEP processes, and schools are mandated by the regulations to involve parents.

Informed consent is one of the first ways to ensure parental involvement and procedural safeguards. Informed consent is compounded by issues such as parental literacy, parental comprehension of the meaning of legal terminology, and the time professionals spend with parents explaining testing and special education. Parents' rights materials may be made more difficult to understand because of their use of highly specialized vocabulary. According to an early study involving observation and analysis of interactions in IEP conferences, parents' rights were merely "glossed over in the majority of conferences" (Goldstein, Strickland, Turnbull, & Curry, 1980, p. 283). This suggests that sufficient time may not be allotted to discussing issues of central concern to parents. Recent changes in the 1997 Amendments are designed to promote genuine parental involvement in educational assessment and planning.

Katsiyannis (1994) reviewed decisions and reports from the Office of Civil Rights (OCR) concerned with the question of procedural safeguards and parental involvement. Katsiyannis stated that the OCR found that the typical sequence of the referral/screening process denied procedural safeguards at the prereferral stage. Furthermore, parents should be informed of procedural safeguards at the time that the student is screened to determine whether additional assessment will be conducted. Educators should keep in mind that the new regulations stress parental involvement during all stages of the assessment and planning process. These regulations provide the minimum guidelines for professionals; best practice dictates that parents should be involved throughout their child's education (Sheridan, Cowan, & Eagle, 2000).

The provision granted to parents in the IEP process is active participation in the IEP conference by contributing to the formulation of objectives and long-term goals for their children. In the past, in traditional IEP conferences, parents were found to be passive and to attend merely to receive information (Barnett, Zins, & Wise, 1984; Brantlinger, 1987; Goldstein et al., 1980; Goldstein & Turnbull, 1982; Vaughn, Bos, Harrell, & Lasky, 1988; Weber & Stoneman, 1986). Parents are now considered to be equal team members in the IEP process.

An area of additional concern involves working with parents of culturally, linguistically, or environmentally diverse backgrounds. Professionals should make certain that materials and concepts presented are at the appropriate level. Special education or legal concepts are complex for many persons who are not familiar with the vocabulary and process. For persons who do not speak English as a primary language, legal terms and specialized concepts may be difficult even though materials are presented in the individual's native language. These concepts may be different from educational concepts of their original culture. Salend and Taylor (1993) suggested that the parents' level of acculturation be considered, noting that children may become acculturated much more quickly than their parents. In addition, Salend and Taylor have reminded educators to consider the family's history of discrimination and the family structure, since these factors may have an impact on the family's interactions with school personnel. Educational professionals should make every effort to be certain that all parents are familiar with the special education process, services available, and their expected role during the assessment and IEP processes.

Parents and educators working together will benefit the student's educational program. Establishing a positive relationship with parents requires educators to work with parents in a collaborative manner. Sheridan et al. provided a list of actions that may enhance the collaborative nature of the relationship (2000). These actions are presented in Table 2.4.

ISSUES OF NONDISCRIMINATORY ASSESSMENT

minority overrepresentation
When the percentage of a culturally different group is greater in special education classes than in the local education agency.

Perhaps no other area in the field of psychoeducational assessment has received more attention than that of nondiscriminatory assessment. Much of the research and controversial issues center around the overrepresentation of minority students in special education classes. **Minority overrepresentation** is found to occur when the percentage of minority students enrolled in particular special education classes is larger than the percentage of minority students enrolled in the local education agency. In other words, if classes for mildly disabled students were made up of 28% minority students yet only 12% of the local education agency was made up of minorities, the local education agency's special education classes would have an overrepresentation of minority students.

Table 2.4 Actions reflective of collaborative relationships.

1. Listening to one another's perspective.
2. Viewing differences as a strength.
3. Remaining focused on a mutual interest (e.g., assessment and planning for student needs).
4. Sharing information about the child, the home, the school system, and problems encountered in the system.
5. Asking for ideas and opinions about the child, problems, goals, and potential solutions.
6. Respecting the skill and knowledge of each other related to the student, the disability, and contextual considerations.
7. Planning together to address parents', teachers', and students' needs.
8. Making joint decisions about the child's educational program and goals.
9. Sharing resources to work toward goal attainment.
10. Providing a common message to the student about schoolwork and behavior.
11. Demonstrating willingness to address conflict.
12. Refraining from finding fault, and committing to sharing successes.

Source: Copyright (as applicable) by the National Association of School Psychologists, Bethesda, MD. Reprinted with permission of the publisher. www.nasponline.org.

The U.S. Department of Education reported that minority over-representation in special education continues to be problematic (U.S. Department of Education, 1997). Analyzing data from the Office of Civil Rights, the U.S. Department of Education reported that although African Americans account for 16% of the total population in schools, 32% of the students in settings for persons with mild mental retardation and 29% of the students diagnosed as having moderate mental retardation are African American. In addition to these classifications, African Americans account for 24% of the students within the category of emotional disturbance and 18% of students served as having specific learning disabilities. Concerns expressed in the *Nineteenth Annual Report to Congress on the Implementation of IDEA* (U.S. Department of Education, 1997) include minority students being placed into more segregated classroom settings and restrictive curricula, which results in lower achievement.

A study examining the relationship between state financial resources and special education categories reported that states with higher numbers of children who are considered living in poverty had lower percentages of students categorized as learning disabled, and states with more financial resources had a higher percentage of students with learning disabilities (McLaughlin & Owings, 1992). Sherman concluded that risk of experiencing developmental delays, emotional disturbance, or learning disabilities increased by 2.4% if the child comes from a family experiencing poverty (Sherman, 1994).

Children experiencing poverty are more likely to have health problems, developmental problems, and low achievement, which will require special education support (U.S. Department of Education, 1997).

Much of the blame for the overrepresentation of minorities in special education has been attributed to referral and evaluation practices. The amount of attention given to the assessment process may be due in part to IDEA's emphasis on nondiscriminatory assessment. The law clearly states that educational agencies should use evaluation procedures that are not racially or culturally discriminatory. This can have many implications when assessing students who have linguistic differences and those who may come from culturally different backgrounds or deprived environments. The following list of problems of bias in assessment is adapted from Reynolds, Lowe, and Saenz (1999):

1. Inappropriate content. Students from minority populations may lack exposure to certain items on the assessment instrument.

2. Inappropriate standardization samples. Ethnic minorities were not represented in the normative sample at the time of development of the instrument.

3. Examiner and language. White, English-speaking examiners may intimidate students of color and students from different linguistic backgrounds.

4. Inequitable social consequences. Because of discriminatory assessment practices, minority students may be relegated to lower educational placements, which may ultimately result in lower-paying jobs.

5. Measurement of different constructs. White test developers designed instruments assumed to measure academic or cognitive ability for all students. When used with minority students, however, the instruments may measure only the degree to which the minority students have been able to absorb white middle-class culture.

6. Different predictive validity. Instruments designed to predict the educational or academic outcome or potential for white students might not do so for minority students.

7. Qualitatively distinct minority and majority aptitude and achievement. This suggests that persons from various ethnic groups are qualitatively different and therefore tests designed to measure aptitude in one group cannot adequately measure the aptitude of another group. (Reynolds, Lowe, & Saenz, 1999, pp. 556–557)

Additional problems in biased assessment include overinterpretation of test results. This means that an examiner may report to have assessed a trait, attribute, or characteristic that the instrument is not designed to measure (Flaugher, 1978). For example, an examiner may report a cognitive ability level or a behavioral trait based on the results of a student's academic achievement test. The assessment is inaccurate because the test was designed to measure academic achievement only.

Another problem that may arise in assessment is that of testing students whose dominant language is not English. Although some instruments are published in languages other than English, such as Spanish, the translations may result in different conceptual meanings and influence test performance and test results (Fradd & Hallman, 1983). Lopez (1995) recommended that norm-referenced instruments should not be used with bilingual students. Lopez provides several reasons for this recommendation:

1. Norms are usually limited to small samples of minority children.
2. Norming procedures routinely exclude students with limited English proficiency.
3. Test items tap information that minority children may not be familiar with due to their linguistically and culturally different backgrounds.
4. Testing formats do not allow examiners the opportunity to provide feedback or to probe into the children's quality of responses.
5. The tests' scoring systems arbitrarily decide what are the correct responses based on majority culture paradigms.
6. The standardized testing procedures assume that the children have appropriate test-taking skills (Lopez, 1995, p. 1113).

IDEA mandates that the evaluation of students for possible special education services must involve the use of tests that have been validated for the purpose for which they are used. Regardless of these legal and professional guidelines, most norm-referenced tests used in schools are not diagnostic in nature but rather measure expected academic achievement or intellectual functioning. The developmental process of many instruments gives little attention to validity studies with disabled populations. Fuchs, Fuchs, Benowitz, and Barringer (1987) called for discontinuing use of tests with no validation data on disabled populations if those tests are used for diagnosis and placement of students with disabilities. The movement toward restructuring education and the way that special education services are delivered has resulted in a call for the use of more varieties of tests that measure the student's knowledge and skills as they relate to the curriculum

(IDEA Amendments of 1997; Lipsky & Gartner, 1997; U.S. Department of Education, 1997). The use of these devices will require additional research regarding validity, reliability, and generalizability (Burger & Burger, 1994). The regulations that guide the assessment process call for careful selection of assessment instruments and state that the purpose of the assessment is to determine educational needs.

The IDEA regulations contain language requiring that at a minimum, professionals be trained in assessment and, more specifically, that training or expertise is available to enable the examiner to evaluate students with disabilities. Past research has shown that some professionals responsible for the evaluation of students with disabilities lacked competence in test selection, scoring, and interpretations (Bennett, 1981; Bennett & Shepherd, 1982; McNutt & Mandelbaum, 1980; Ysseldyke & Thurlow, 1983). Valles (1998) advocated improving teacher training at the preservice level to decrease the likelihood that minorities are inaccurately diagnosed.

Of all of the controversial areas in nondiscriminatory assessment, the most controversial area remains that of IQ testing for the purpose of determining eligibility for services under the diagnostic category of mental retardation. One professional in the field (Jackson, 1975) called for banning the use of IQ tests. Some state and local education agencies, either by litigation or voluntarily, have discontinued the use of IQ tests with minority students. Evidence indicates, however, that IQ scores continue to be the most influential test score variable in the decision-making process (Sapp, Chissom, & Horton, 1984). MacMillan and Forness (1998) argue that IQ testing may only be peripheral in placement rather than the determining factor. In their study, they concluded that the use of IQ scores may in fact prevent some students from eligibility who may truly be in need of support services. The trend in assessment to use more functional measures than traditional assessment may be the result of assessment practices viewed as biased.

IDEA and the 1997 Amendments require that other data, such as comments from parents and teachers and adaptive behavior measures, be considered in the decision-making process. In calling for a complete reconceptualization of special education and the assessment process, Lipsky and Gartner (1997) posed the following questions:

> Why must children suspected of having a disability undergo a costly, lengthy, and intrusive process in order to receive public education services similar to ones that their peers without disabilities receive without such procedures?
>
> Why must parents of children with disabilities be denied opportunities available to parents of children without disabilities to choose the neighborhood school, or "magnet" or "school of choice" programs?

Why must children be certified to enter a special education system if all children are entitled to a free and appropriate education that prepares them effectively to participate in and contribute to the society of which they are a part?

Why must parents and their children in need of special education services lose substantial free-choice opportunities to gain procedural rights?

Are the gains worth the cost? (pp. 28–29)

These questions raise important issues for consideration. In attempting to provide appropriate services that are designed to meet the individual student's needs, it seems that the system may have become cumbersome and may even be unfair for some families. Patton (1998) suggested that the current system is unfair to African-American families because of the disproportionate numbers of children from these families placed in special education because of inaccurate diagnoses. Patton further stated that the current practices are not sensitive to minority cultures and behaviors. Others have called for a redirection of special education efforts in assessment and classification, particularly in applying these procedures to students who have emotional and behavioral disorders (Ruehl, 1998; Smith, 1997). These issues need additional investigation as schools implement the IDEA Amendments, with an emphasis on education of students with special needs in the regular classroom setting.

Disproportionality The research indicating that students who are from different ethnic, cultural, or linguistic backgrounds was influential in the revisions of IDEA. One method included in the IDEA 2004 regulations is through early intervening services. Through early intervening services, students, especially students in the targeted various groups from ethnic or culturally diverse backgrounds, can receive interventions that may prevent their placement in special education.

The regulations of IDEA 2004 include specific methods that states must follow to be accountable for making efforts to reduce disproportionality. State education agencies are mandated to collect and report data on the following: types of impairments of students identified as eligible to receive services, placement or educational environments of students, the incidents of disciplinary actions, the duration of disciplinary incidents, including suspensions and expulsions of students who are served under special education. All of these data are to be reported and when specific data indicate problematic disproportionality, the state educational agency is mandated to review the data and, if necessary, revise the methods and policies for identification and placement of students in special education.

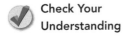 Check Your
Understanding

THE MULTIDISCIPLINARY TEAM AND THE DECISION-MAKING PROCESS

The regulations call for a variety of professionals and the parents of the student to be involved in the assessment and IEP processes. The decision-making process is to include all members of the IEP multidisciplinary team as another method of increasing accuracy of decisions. In a review of analogue research, Huebner (1991) determined that often teacher perceptions disproportionately influence the Team's decision. This results in inaccurate decision making and may be considered a form of bias in the assessment process. School psychologists, as members of the IEP multidisciplinary team, may rely on clinical judgment to make eligibility decisions and fail to consistently consider information across cases; such practices, too, may lead to errors in the decision-making process (Ward, Ward, & Clark, 1991).

In other studies, inconsistencies in decisions about eligibility made by teams have been found specifically in determining eligibility of mild disabilities, such as learning disabilities (Bocian, Beebe, MacMillan, & Gresham, 1999; MacMillan, Gresham, & Bocian, 1998). These researchers concluded that various forms of evidence, such as behaviors observed by teachers, may have weighed heavily in the decision-making process. Gresham, MacMillan, and Bocian (1998) postulated that eligibility decisions may be based on educational need more than actual legal criteria for students with mild disabilities.

LEAST RESTRICTIVE ENVIRONMENT

IDEA is designed to provide special education support services in the least restrictive environment. In many cases, this means that a student will be served within the general education classroom setting. Macready (1991) proposed that when a decision is made to place a student in an environment other than the general education setting, it should be viewed conceptually as a "foster placement rather than as a placement for adoption" (p. 151). The regulations of IDEA 1997 emphasize that students with disabilities should be educated within the general education environment unless there are justifiable reasons for the student to be educated in a special education setting.

Decisions about appropriate educational environments should be made carefully. Morsink and Lenk (1992) suggested that each decision be made on an individual basis and that the teacher's training and effectiveness in instruction and all environmental factors, such as the impact on other students or limiting environmental factors, be considered. Morsink and Lenk warned that a proposed placement, seen at first as the least restrictive environment, may indeed be an inappropriate environment when these factors are not considered to be favorable.

The provision of least restrictive environment may be implemented in various ways in different states and local education agencies. One study of six states found that finances, parent advocacy, categorically based systems, and varying layers of organizational structure all influenced the way that the least restrictive environment provision was implemented (Hasazi, Johnston, Liggett, & Schattman, 1994). This study found that these variables were complex and interconnected.

The research conducted by the U.S. Department of Education indicates that there has been an increasing trend to serve students in the general education classroom environment for most of the school day (1999). Figure 2.3 illustrates this trend.

The implementation of least restrictive environment and, more specifically, inclusion has been interpreted through litigation in several state and federal courts (Kubicek, 1994; Lipsky & Gartner, 1997; Yell, 1997). In summary, the courts have interpreted that the least restrictive environment decision must first consider placement in a regular education environment with additional supplementary aids if needed. If this arrangement will be equal or better for the student than the special education setting, the student should be placed within the general education environment. The student's academic and nonacademic benefits must be considered in the decision. This includes consideration of the benefits of social interaction in nonacademic activities and environments. The IEP team must also review the effect that the student will have on the teacher in terms

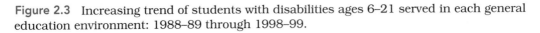

Figure 2.3 Increasing trend of students with disabilities ages 6–21 served in each general education environment: 1988–89 through 1998–99.

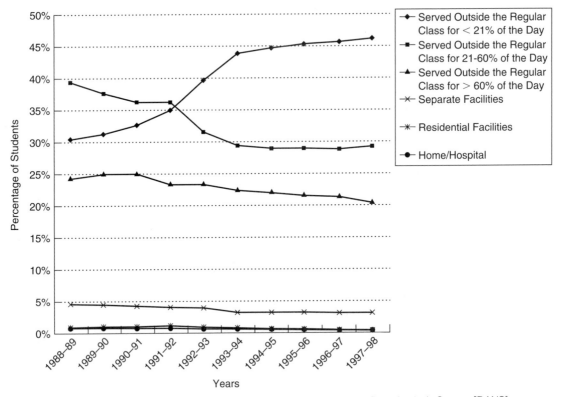

Source: U.S. Department of Education, Office of Special Education Programs, Data Analysis System [DANS], in *To assure the free appropriate public education of all children with disabilities,* 2000.

of time and attention required and the effect the student may have on the other students in the general classroom. If the educational services required for the student can be provided better and the education is considered superior in the segregated setting, the student may be placed in a special education environment. For additional review, please refer to Lipsky and Gartner (1997) and Yell (1997).

Research has produced interesting results regarding inclusion in general education settings. One study that surveyed secondary students found that more students expressed a desire for a pull-out program for meeting their educational needs but enjoyed inclusion for the social aspects (Klinger, Vaughn, Schumm, Cohen, & Forgan, 1998). Some of the students in this study stated that the general education environment was simply too noisy. Bennett, Lee, and Lueke (1998) state that inclusion decisions should consider the parents' expectations. Their research found that several factors, such as the parents' view of inclusion, may have an impact on the parents' desire to have their child served in a general education setting. Another study of general education teachers' perceptions of inclusion found that more teachers were willing to include students with mild disabilities in the general education setting (Scruggs & Mastropieri, 1996). In this study, only one-third of the teachers believed that they had enough time and training to adequately serve students with disabilities in their general education class-rooms. It is clear that placement decisions are complex.

IMPARTIAL HEARINGS

The procedural safeguards provided through due process seek to involve the parents in all stages of the IEP process rather than only during third-party hearings. Due process provisions specify at least 36 grounds for either schools or parents to seek a hearing (Turn-bull, Turnbull, & Strickland, 1979). If abused, the process could re-sult in chaos in the operation of school systems. The years since the law was enacted have witnessed a great deal of interpretation of un-certain issues through the judicial system (Turnbull, 1986).

Due process may be discriminatory because its cost may pro-hibit some families from following this procedure. The cost may in-volve both financial and human resources. The remaining problems are best summed up by Turnbull (1986):

> Problems remain. The greatest one seems to be the cost of due process. Cost consists of three elements: (1) the actual financial cost of the hearings; preparing for them, hiring attorneys and expert witnesses, paying for the documents required for evidence, and pursuing an ap-peal; (2) the emotional and psychic cost—the enormous energy and stress involved in a hearing and its appeal; and (3) the cost that con-sists of time spent and perhaps lost, when the child may (or may not) be receiving an appropriate education. (p. 192)

Because the financial cost may be so burdensome, educators are concerned that due process in IDEA may become yet another vehicle that increases rather than decreases discriminatory prac-tices. Budoff and Orenstein (1981) found that upper-middle-class parents were overrepresented in due process hearings and recom-mended using mediation without counsel as an alternative to the expensive hearing process. The 1997 Amendments that provide specific guidelines for mediation may result in more timely and eco-nomical resolutions. Engiles, Fromme, LeResche, and Moses (1999) suggested that there are strategies that schools and personnel can implement to increase participation in mediation of parents of culturally and linguistically diverse backgrounds. These authors included strategies, at the system level as well as the practitioner level, to involve parents in mediation. Engiles et al. remind educa-tors that some persons from various cultures do not believe that they should be involved in educational decisions, and others may not welcome the involvement of school personnel in family or personal matters. Increasing parental involvement and communication between parents and schools from the prereferral stage through the decision-making stage may decrease the need for both mediation and third-party hearings.

The difficulties with the hearing process were likely the influence in changing the 2004 Amendments to include a new resolution session. This allows the school another opportunity to resolve the issues in a more timely manner that will not require the costly and lengthy process often associated with hearings.

Should parents or schools exhaust the hearing process without satisfaction, the right remains for either party to take the case through the civil court system. IDEA continues to be interpreted through the judicial system.

ETHICS AND STANDARDS

In addition to the legal requirements of the process of assessment and planning in special and general education, ethical standards for practice have been established by professional organizations. In special education, standards of practice and policies have been set forth by the Council for Exceptional Children. The National Association of School Psychologists has established standards and ethics for professionals in the school psychology field. And the American Educational Research Association, the American Psychological Association, and the National Council on Measurement in Education have established the *Standards for Educational and Psychological Testing* (1999). These professional groups have policies regarding the education and assessment of students from culturally and linguistically diverse backgrounds.

Although professionals in the field of education and educational psychology are required by law to follow the regulations and federal mandates, the standards and ethics are established by professional groups to encourage professionalism and best practice. Sections of the standards, codes, and policies that are relevant to assessment and special education are included in the following pages.

The *Standards of Practice* set out by the Council for Exceptional Children (CEC) are similar to the federal regulations governing assessment, use of goals and objectives for planning, record keeping and confidentiality, and decision-making practices. The standards relevant to assessment are presented in Figure 2.4.

The policies of CEC for students from various ethnic groups and migrant students are designed to assist in decreasing the overrepresentation of minority students receiving special education support. These policies emphasize nondiscriminatory assessment

Figure 2.4   CEC standards for professional practice relevant to the assessment and planning process.

- Use assessment instruments and procedures that do not discriminate against persons with exceptionalities on the basis of race, color, creed, sex, national origin, age, political practices, family or social background, sexual orientation, or exceptionality.
- Base grading, promotion, graduation, and/or movement out of the program on the individual goals and objectives for individuals with exceptionalities.
- Provide accurate program data to administrators, colleagues, and parents, based on efficient and objective record keeping practices, for the purpose of decision making.
- Maintain confidentiality of information except when information is released under specific conditions of written consent and statutory confidentiality requirements.

Source: CEC policies for delivery of services: Ethnic and multicultural groups. *CEC Policy Manual*, Section Three, part 1, pp. 6, 20–21. Reprinted with permission.

practice, consideration of language dominance, and understanding of cultural heritage. The policy on migrant students calls on educational professionals to understand that the assessment and programming procedures used for stationary students are not appropriate for migrant students. It further points out that the frequent disruptions in education affect the students' lives in both educational and social areas. This CEC statement also reminds professional educators that the eligibility requirements and other special education considerations often differ from state to state. The CEC policy statements are presented in Figures 2.5 and 2.6.

In 2000, the National Association of School Psychologists revised the *Professional Conduct Manual*, which includes sections that cover all areas of practice for psychologists working within the school setting. The general principles for assessment and intervention and reporting data and conference results are presented in Figure 2.7. The principles are consistent with the legal requirements for assessment and the evaluation process.

The *Standards for Educational and Psychological Testing* also contain standards for all areas of testing and are consistent with the federal regulations. For example, the standards include language regarding using multiple measures for reaching decisions about the individual's functioning, following standardized administration procedures, and confidentiality of test results and test instruments. Selected standards are presented in Figure 2.8.

Figure 2.5   CEC policy on ethnic and multicultural groups relevant to the assessment and planning process.

Preamble

The Council believes that all policy statements previously adopted by CEC related to children with and without exceptionalities, as well as children with gifts and talents, are relevant and applicable to both minority and nonminority individuals. In order to highlight concerns of special interest to members of ethnic and multicultural groups, the following policy statements have been developed. (Chapter 08, Para. 1)

Ethnicity and Exceptionality

The Council recognizes the special and unique needs of members of ethnic and multicultural groups and pledges its full support toward promoting all efforts which will help to bring them into full and equitable participation and membership in the total society. (Chapter 08, Para. 2)

Identification, Testing, and Placement

The Council supports the following statements related to the identification, testing, and placement of children from ethnic and multicultural groups who are also exceptional.

a. Child-find procedures should identify children by ethnicity as well as type and severity of exceptionality or degree of giftedness.

b. Program service reporting procedures should identify children by ethnicity as well as exceptionality or degree of giftedness.

c. All testing and evaluation materials and methods used for the classification and placement of children from ethnic and multicultural groups should be selected and administered so as not to be racially or culturally discriminatory.

d. Children with exceptionalities who are members of ethnic and multicultural groups should be tested in their dominant language by examiners who are fluent in that language and familiar with the cultural heritage of the children being tested.

e. Communication of test results with parents of children from ethnic and multicultural groups should be done in the dominant language of those parents and conducted by persons involved in the testing or familiar with the particular exceptionality, fluent in that language, and familiar with the cultural heritage of those parents.

Source: CEC policies for delivery of services: Ethnic and multicultural groups. *CEC Policy Manual*, Section Three, part 1, pp. 6, 20–21. Reprinted with permission.

Figure 2.6 CEC policy on migrant students relevant to the assessment and planning process.

Preamble

Exceptional students who are mobile due to their parents' migrant employment, experience reduced opportunities for an appropriate education and a reduced likelihood of completing their education. Child-find and identification policies and practices, designed for a stationary population, are inadequate for children who move frequently. Incomplete, delayed, or inadequate transfer of records seriously impedes educational continuity. Interstate/provincial differences in special education eligibility requirements, programs and resources, minimum competency testing, and graduation requirements result in repetition of processing formalities, gaps in instruction, delays in the resumption of services, an inability to accumulate credits for graduation, and other serious inequities. In addition to the disruption of learning, mobility disrupts health care, training, teacher-student rapport, and personal relationships.

Source: CEC policies for delivery of services: Ethnic and multicultural groups. *CEC Policy Manual*, Section Three, part 1, pp. 6, 20–21. Reprinted with permission.

Figure 2.7 Selected principles from the National Association of School Psychologists *Professional Conduct Manual.*

C) Assessment and Intervention

1. School psychologists maintain the highest standard for educational and psychological assessment and direct and indirect interventions.
   a. In conducting psychological, educational, or behavioral evaluations or in providing therapy, counseling, or consultation services, due consideration is given to individual integrity and individual differences.
   b. School psychologists respect differences in age, gender, sexual orientation, and socioeconomic, cultural, and ethnic backgrounds. They select and use appropriate assessment or treatment procedures, techniques, and strategies. Decision-making related to assessment and subsequent interventions is primarily data-based.
2. School psychologists are knowledgeable about the validity and reliability of their instruments and techniques, choosing those that have up-to-date standardization data and are applicable and appropriate for the benefit of the child.
3. School psychologists use multiple assessment methods such as observations, background information, and information from other professionals, to reach comprehensive conclusions.
4. School psychologists use assessment techniques, counseling and therapy procedures, consultation techniques, and other direct and indirect service methods that the profession considers to be responsible, research-based practice.

---

continued.

Figure 2.7 continued.

5. School psychologists do not condone the use of psychological or educational assessment techniques, or the misuse of the information these techniques provide, by unqualified persons in any way, including teaching, sponsorship, or supervision.

6. School psychologists develop interventions that are appropriate to the presenting problems and are consistent with data collected. They modify or terminate the treatment plan when the data indicate the plan is not achieving the desired goals.

7. School psychologists use current assessment and intervention strategies that assist in the promotion of mental health in the children they serve.

D) Reporting Data and Conference Results

1. School psychologists ascertain that information about children and other clients reaches only authorized persons.
   a. School psychologists adequately interpret information so that the recipient can better help the child or other clients.
   b. School psychologists assist agency recipients to establish procedures to properly safeguard confidential material.

2. School psychologists communicate findings and recommendations in language readily understood by the intended recipient. These communications describe potential consequences associated with the proposals.

3. School psychologists prepare written reports in such form and style that the recipient of the report will be able to assist the child or other clients. Reports should emphasize recommendations and interpretations; unedited computer-generated reports, preprinted "check-off" or "fill-in-the-blank" reports, and reports that present only test scores or global statements regarding eligibility for special education without specific recommendations for intervention are seldom useful. Reports should include an appraisal of the degree of confidence that could be assigned to the information. Alterations of previously released reports should be done only by the original author.

4. School psychologists review all of their written documents for accuracy, signing them only when correct. Interns and practicum students are clearly identified as such, and their work is co-signed by the supervising school psychologist. In situations in which more than one professional participated in the data collection and reporting process, school psychologists assure that sources of data are clearly identified in the written report.

5. School psychologists comply with all laws, regulations, and policies pertaining to the adequate storage and disposal of records to maintain appropriate confidentiality of information.

Source: Copyright (as applicable) by the National Association of School Psychologists, Bethesda, MD. Reprinted with permission of the publisher. www.nasponline.org.

Figure 2.8 Selected standards from the *Standards for Educational and Psychological Testing.*

Standard	
5.1	Test administrators should follow carefully the standardized procedures for administration and scoring specified by the test developer, unless the situation or a test taker's disability dictates that an exception should be made. (p. 63)
5.7	Test users have the responsibility of protecting the security of test materials at all times. (p. 64)
10.1	In testing individuals with disabilities, test developers, test administrators, and test users should take steps to ensure that the test score inferences accurately reflect the intended construct rather than any disabilities and their associated characteristics extraneous to the intent of the measurement. (p. 106)
10.12	In testing individuals with disabilities for diagnostic and intervention purposes, the test should not be used as the sole indicator of the test taker's functioning. Instead, multiple sources of information should be used. (p. 108)
11.3	Responsibility for test use should be assumed by or delegated only to those individuals who have the training, professional credentials, and experience necessary to handle this responsibility. Any special qualifications for test administration or interpretation specified in the test manual should be met. (p. 114)
11.20	In educational, clinical, and counseling settings, a test taker's score should not be interpreted in isolation; collateral information that may lead to alternative explanations for the examinee's test performance should be considered. (p. 117)
12.11	Professionals and others who have access to test materials and test results should ensure the confidentiality of the test results and testing materials consistent with legal and professional ethics requirements. (pp. 132–133)
13.10	Those responsible for educational testing programs should ensure that the individuals who administer and score the test(s) are proficient in the appropriate test administration procedures and scoring procedures and that they understand the importance of adhering to the directions provided by the test developer. (p. 147)
13.13	Those responsible for educational testing programs should ensure that the individuals who interpret the test results to make decisions within the school context are qualified to do so or are assisted by and consult with persons who are so qualified. (p. 148)

Source: Copyright 1999 by the American Educational Research Association, The American Psychological Association, and the National Council on Measurement in Education. Reproduced with permission of the publisher.

CHAPTER SUMMARY

For more than 25 years federal laws have been in place to provide all students having special needs with a free and appropriate education. In order to receive special education support, assessment and planning procedures, as set out in the regulations, must be completed. The laws continue to be revised and strive to provide all students with appropriate education within the general education environment. Improvements in the laws focus on increasing parental involvement and including more considerations for students from culturally and linguistically diverse backgrounds. Ethics and policies of professional organizations encourage educators and assessment personnel to consistently use best practices in assessment and planning procedures.

THINK AHEAD

The procedures used to understand the results of a student's performance on test instruments involve basic statistical methods (presented in Chapter 3). Do you think tests using the same numerical scales can easily be compared?

EXERCISES

Part I

Match the following terms with the statements below.

a. Public Law 94-142
b. IDEA
c. IDEA Amendments of 1997
d. compliance
e. PL 99-457
f. due process
g. initial evaluation
h. comprehensive educational evaluation
i. informed consent
j. surrogate parent
k. consent form
l. parents' rights booklet
m. nondiscriminatory assessment
n. special education services
o. related services
p. grade equivalent
q. standard scores
r. annual goals
s. Individuals with Disabilities Educational Improvement Act
t. least restrictive environment
u. transition services
v. procedural safeguards
w. mediation
x. independent educational evaluation
y. impartial due process hearing
z. impartial hearing officer
aa. Section 504 of the Rehabilitation Act of 1973
bb. minority overrepresentation
cc. resolution session

_____ 1. Mary, a student receiving special education services, also needs the _____ of occupational therapy and speech therapy in order to benefit from her appropriate educational plan.

_____ 2. During the screening by educational professionals, it is determined that a student has significant educational needs and is therefore referred for a(n) _____.

_____ 3. The 2004 Amendments encourage parents and educational personnel to participate in a _____ to resolve disagreements.

_____ 4. A school system that meets appropriate timelines and follows all state and federal regulations is said to be in _____.

_____ 5. Parents who have a preschool-aged child with special needs may find assistance in obtaining educational services for their child through the federal regulations of _____.

_____ 6. In a specific school system, the ethnicity of the population was determined to include 17% of persons of Hispanic origin, yet more than 22% of the students receiving services for learning disabilities were of Hispanic origin. This system may have _____ of persons of Hispanic origin within the category of learning disabilities.

_____ 7. A fifth-grade student was recently assessed and was found not eligible to receive special education support. His parents decided that they disagreed with the assessment and therefore requested information to obtain a(n) _____.

_____ 8. During a meeting of the child study team, the members determined that the prereferral intervention strategies employed with a third-grade student were not successful in remediating reading difficulties. The members must now obtain _____ in order to begin the assessment process.

_____ 9. Initially, the federal law that mandated a free and appropriate public education for all children with disabilities was called the Education for All Handicapped Children Act. In 1990, this was renamed _____.

_____10. A major principle of IDEA is that all evaluation measures used during the assessment process should yield similar results for children regardless of their ethnicity. This principle is known as _____.

_____11. In December 2004, President Bush signed the _____.

Part II

Answer the following questions.

1. What were the sources of pressure that resulted in substantial legal changes in the 1970s?

2. The Individuals with Disabilities Education Improvement Act of 2004 requires that IEPs include what type of information regarding statewide assessments?

_____

_____

_____

3. When must parents be given their due process rights according to the 2004 Amendments?

_____

_____

_____

4. List the provisions for nondiscriminatory assessment according to the federal law.

_____

_____

_____

Part III

Summarize the research findings.

1. Summarize the research findings on the IEP Team decision-making process.

   _____

2. Explain how the research regarding third-party hearings may have had an impact on the changes concerning mediation and resolution sessions in the 2004 Amendments.

   _____

3. Summarize the difficulties of assessing students from culturally and linguistically diverse backgrounds.

   _____

   _____

   _____

Answers to these questions can be found in the Appendix of this text or you may also complete these questions and receive immediate feedback on your answers by going to the Think Ahead module in Chapter 2 of the Companion Website.

COURSE PROGRESS MONITORING ASSESSMENT

See how you are doing in the course after the conclusion of chapters in Part I by completing the following assessment. When you are finished, check your answers with your instructor or on the

Companion Website at *www.prenhall.com/overton.* Once you have your score, return to Figure 1.9, Student Progress Monitoring Graph in Chapter 1 and plot your progress.

Progress Monitoring Assessment

Select the best answer. Some of these terms may be used more than once.

a. early intervening services
b. RTI
c. norm-referenced tests
d. standardized tests
e. diagnostic tests
f. IDEA 2004
g. IDEA 1997
h. IDEA regulations

i. variance
j. derived score
k. basal score
l. field test
m. KBIT
n. WISC-IV
o. phonemic synthesis
p. phonemic awareness

_____ 1. This federal law included strategies to closely align with the No Child Left Behind Act and specifically addresses accountability.

_____ 2. Comprehension of individual sounds that make up words.

_____ 3. The two subtests that make up this measure are Vocabulary and Matrices.

_____ 4. The initial administration of an instrument to a sample population.

_____ 5. These instruments may provide additional information used for specific academic or other weaknesses.

_____ 6. This test includes a working memory index, perceptual reasoning index, and a processing speed index as well as verbal measures.

_____ 7. One component of this federal legislation was improving teacher quality.

_____ 8. These instruments provide comparisons with students the same age across the United States.

_____ 9. These instruments are structured to ensure that all students are administered the items in the same manner so that comparisons can be made more reliably.

_____10. These instruments provide comparisons with groups who are representative of the student population across the United States.

Fill in the Blanks

11. In an effort to encourage parents and schools to resolve their disagreements, _____ included mediation.

12. _____ is the type of validity that indicates a measure has items that are representative across the possible items in the domain.

13. _____ validity and _____ validity are differentiated by time.

14. The formula of SD $\sqrt{1-r}$ is how to determine _____.

15. _____ is a behavioral measure that indicates how students in a class view each other.

16. _____ is a computerized assessment of a student's ability to sustain attention across time.

17. The _____ is a measure of preschool students' language development that is based on a two-dimensional language model.

18. A criterion-related measure of self-help skills, prespeech, and speech development, general knowledge, social and emotional development, reading readiness, manuscript writing, and beginning math is the _____.

19. _____ is a form that indicates that the parents understand the testing procedures and that they are granting permission to the school to assess their child.

20. _____ are included at the end of the assessment report.

Technical Prerequisites of Understanding Assessment

CHAPTER 3

Descriptive Statistics

CHAPTER 4

Reliability and Validity

CHAPTER 5

An Introduction to Norm-Referenced Assessment

Descriptive Statistics

raw score	frequency polygon
norm-referenced tests	median
nominal scale	mean
ordinal scale	standard deviation
interval scale	variability
ratio scale	measures of dispersion
derived scores	variance
standard scores	range
descriptive statistics	skewed
measures of central tendency	positively skewed
normal distribution	negatively skewed
frequency distribution	percentile ranks
mode	z scores
bimodal distribution	stanines
multimodal distribution	deciles

CHAPTER FOCUS

This chapter presents the basic statistical concepts needed to interpret information from standardized assessment.

CEC KNOWLEDGE AND SKILLS STANDARDS

The student completing this chapter will understand the knowledge and skills included in the following CEC Knowledge and Skills Standards from Standard 8: Assessment:

CC8K1—Basic terminology used in assessment

CC8S5—Interpret information from formal and informal assessments.

WHY IS MEASUREMENT IMPORTANT?

Psychoeducational assessment using standardized instruments historically has been applied in the educational decision-making process. To properly use standardized instruments, one must understand test-selection criteria, basic principles of measurement, administration techniques, and scoring procedures. Careful interpretation of test results relies on these abilities. Thus, research that questions the assessment competence of special educators and other professionals is frightening because the educational future of so many individuals is at risk.

Of concern are studies indicating typical types of mistakes made by professionals in the field: Professionals identified students as eligible for services when test scores were within the average range and relied instead on referral information to make decisions (Algozzine & Ysseldyke, 1981). Data presented during educational planning conferences played little, if any, part in the team members' decisions (Ysseldyke, Algozzine, Richey, & Graden, 1982). Professionals continued to select poor-quality instruments when better tests were available (Davis & Shepard, 1983; Ysseldyke, Algozzine, Regan, & Potter, 1980).

Research by Huebner (1988, 1989) indicated that professionals made errors in the diagnosis of learning disabilities more frequently when scores were reported in percentiles. This reflects inadequate understanding of data interpretation.

Eaves (1985) cited common errors made by professionals during the assessment process. Some of the test examiners' most common errors, adapted from Eaves's research, include:

1. Using instruments in the assessment process solely because those instruments are stipulated by school administrators.

2. Regularly using instruments for purposes other than those for which tests have been validated.

3. Taking the recommended use at face value.

4. Using the quickest instruments available even though those instruments may not assess the areas of concern.

5. Using currently popular instruments for assessment.

6. Failing to establish effective rapport with the examinee.

7. Failing to document behaviors of the examinee during assessment that may be of diagnostic value.

8. Failing to adhere to standardized administration rules, which may include
   a. Failing to follow starting rules.
   b. Failing to follow basal and ceiling rules.
   c. Omitting actual incorrect responses on the protocol, which could aid in error analysis and diagnosis.
   d. Failing to determine actual chronological age or grade placement.

9. Making various scoring errors, such as
   a. Making simple counting errors.
   b. Making simple subtraction errors.
   c. Counting items above the ceiling as correct or items below the basal as incorrect.
   d. Entering the wrong norm table, row, or column to obtain a derived score.

  e. Extensively using developmental scores when inappro-
     priate.
  f. Showing lack of knowledge regarding alternative mea-
     sures of performance.
10. Ineffectively interpreting assessment results for educa-
    tional program use. (pp. 26–27)

The occurrence of such errors illustrates why educators need a basic understanding of the measurement principles used in assessment. McLoughlin (1985) advocated training special educators to the level of superior practice rather than meeting only minimum competencies of psychoeducational assessment. The *Standards for Educational and Psychological Testing* (AERA, APA, & NCME, 1999) warn that when special educators have little or no training in the basic principles of measurement, assessment instruments could be misused.

Much of the foundation of good practice in psychoeducational assessment lies in a thorough understanding of test reliability and validity as well as basic measurement principles. Borg, Worthen, and Valcarce (1986) found that most teachers believe that understanding basic principles of measurement is an important aspect of classroom teaching and evaluation. Yet research has shown that professionals who were believed to be specialists in working with students with learning problems were able to correctly answer only 50% of the items on a test of measurement principles (Bennett & Shepherd, 1982). As a result, this chapter is designed to promote the development of a basic understanding of general principles of measurement and the application of those principles.

GETTING MEANING FROM NUMBERS

raw score The first score obtained in testing; usually represents the number of items correct.

Any teacher who scores a test, either published or teacher-made, will subtract the number of items a student missed from the number of items presented to the student. This number, known as the **raw score**, is of little value to the teacher unless a frame of reference exists for that number. The frame of reference might be comparing the number of items the student answered correctly with the number the student answered correctly the previous day (e.g., Monday, 5 out of 10 responses correct; Tuesday, 6 out of 10 responses correct; etc.). The frame of reference might be a national sample of students the same age who attempted the same items in the same manner on a **norm-referenced** standardized test. In all cases, teachers must clearly understand what can and cannot be inferred from numerical data gathered on small samples of behavior known as *tests*.

norm-referenced tests Tests designed to compare an individual student's scores with national averages.

The techniques used to obtain raw scores are discussed in Chapter 5. Raw scores are used to obtain the other scores presented in this chapter.

REVIEW OF NUMERICAL SCALES

nominal scale
Numerical scale that uses numbers for the purpose of identification.

ordinal scale
Numerical scale in which numbers are used for ranking.

Numbers can denote different meanings from different scales. The scale that has the least meaning for educational measurement purposes is the **nominal scale**. The nominal scale consists of numbers used only for identification purposes, such as student ID numbers or the numbers on race cars. These numbers cannot be used in mathematical operations. For example, if race cars were labeled with letters of the alphabet rather than with numerals, it would make no difference in the outcome of the race. Numbers on a nominal scale function like names.

When numbers are used to rank the order of objects or items, those numbers are said to be on the **ordinal scale**. An ordinal scale is used to rank the order of the winners in a science fair. The winner has the first rank, or number 1, the runner-up has the second rank, or number 2, and so on. In this scale, the numbers have the quality of identification and indicate greater or lesser quality. The ordinal scale, however, does not have the quality of using equidistant units. For example, suppose the winners of a bike race were ranked as they came in, with the winner ranked as first, the runner-up as

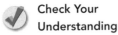 **Check Your Understanding**

Check your knowledge of the different types of numerical scales presented in the previous section by completing Activity 3.1 below.

Activity 3.1

Use the following terms to complete the sentences and answer the questions.

A. nominal scale   C. ordinal scale

B. interval scale   D. ratio scale

1. Measuring with a thermometer is an example of using numbers on the _____ scale.

2. Which scale(s) can be added and subtracted but not multiplied? _____

3. The ribbons awarded in a painting contest illustrate which scale? _____

4. Numbers pinned on the shirts of runners in a marathon are numbers used on the _____ scale.

5. The _____ scale has a true meaning of absolute zero.

Apply Your Knowledge

Which of the numerical scales is used to determine your semester GPA? _____

_____

_____

second, and the third bike rider as third. The distance between the winner and the second-place bike rider might be 9 seconds, and the difference between the second- and third-place bike riders might be 30 seconds. Although the numbers do rank the bike riders, they do not represent equidistant units.

interval scale A scale that uses numbers for ranking in which numerical units are equidistant.

Numbers that are used for identification that rank greater or lesser quality or amount and that are equidistant are numbers used on an **interval scale**. An example is the scale used in measuring temperature. The degrees on the thermometer can be added or subtracted—a reading of 38°F is 10° less than a reading of 48°F. The interval scale does not have an absolute-zero quality. For example, zero degrees does not indicate that there is no temperature. The numbers used on an interval scale also cannot be used in other mathematical operations, such as multiplication. Is a reading of 100°F really four times as hot as 25°F? An interval scale used in assessment is the IQ scale. IQ numbers are equidistant, but they do not possess additional numerical properties. A person with an IQ of 66 cannot be called two-thirds as smart as a person with an IQ of 99.

ratio scale Numerical scale with quality of equidistant units and absolute zero.

When numbers on a scale are equidistant from each other and have a true meaning of absolute zero, they can be used in all mathematical operations. This **ratio scale** allows for direct comparisons and mathematical manipulations.

When scoring tests and interpreting data, it is important to understand which numerical scale the numbers represent and to realize the properties and limitations of that scale. Understanding what test scores represent may decrease errors such as attributing more meaning to a particular score than should be allowed by the nature of the numerical scale.

DESCRIPTIVE STATISTICS

When assessing a student's behavior or performance for the purpose of educational intervention, it is often necessary to determine the amount of difference or deviance that the student exhibits in a particular area from the expected level for the age or grade. By looking at how much difference exists in samples of behavior, educational decision makers and parents can appropriately plan interventions. As previously mentioned, obtaining a raw score will not help with educational planning unless the evaluator has a frame of reference for that score. A raw score may have meaning when compared with previous student performance, or a raw score may be used to gain information from another set of scores called **derived scores**. Derived scores may be scores such as percentile ranks, **standard scores**, grade equivalents, age equivalents, or language quotients. Many derived scores obtain meaning from large sets of data or large samples of scores. By observing how a large sample of students the

derived scores Scores obtained by using a raw score and expectancy tables.

standard scores Derived scores that represent equal units; also known as *linear scores.*

same age or grade level performed on the same tasks, it becomes possible to compare a particular student with the large group to see if that student performed as well as the group, better than the group, or not as well as the group.

Large sets of data are organized and understood through methods known as **descriptive statistics**. As the name implies, these are statistical operations that help educators understand and describe sets of data.

descriptive statistics Statistics used to organize and describe data.

MEASURES OF CENTRAL TENDENCY

measures of central tendency Statistical methods for observing how data cluster around the mean.

One way to organize and describe data is to see how the data fall together, or cluster. This type of statistics is called **measures of central tendency**. Measures of central tendency are methods to determine how scores cluster—that is, how they are distributed around a numerical representation of the average score.

normal distribution A symmetrical distribution with a single numerical representation for the mean, median, and mode.

One common type of distribution used in assessment is called a **normal distribution**. A normal distribution has particular qualities that, when understood, help with the interpretation of assessment data. A normal distribution hypothetically represents the way test scores would fall if a particular test is given to every single student of the same age or grade in the population for whom the test was designed. If educators could administer an instrument in this way and obtain a normal distribution, the scores would fall in the shape of a bell curve, as shown in Figure 3.1.

In a graph of a normal distribution of scores, a very large number of the students tested are represented by all of the scores in the middle, or the "hump" part, of the curve. Because fewer students obtain extremely high or low scores, their scores are plotted or represented on the extreme ends of the curve. It is assumed that the same number of students obtained the higher scores as obtained the lower scores. The distribution is symmetric, or equal, on either side of the vertical line. The normal distribution is discussed throughout the text. One method of interpreting norm-referenced tests is to assume the principles of normal distribution theory and employ the measures of central tendency.

Figure 3.1   Normal distribution of scores, shown by the bell curve.

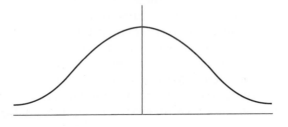

AVERAGE PERFORMANCE

frequency distribution Method of determining how many times each score occurs in a set of data.

Although educators are familiar with the average grade of C on a letter-grading system (interval scale), the numerical ranking of the C grade might be 70 to 79 in one school and 76 to 84 in another. If the educator does not understand the numerical meaning of *average* for a student, the letter grade of C has little value. The educator must know how the other students performed and what type of performance or score indicates average, what score is considered excellent, and what score is considered poor. To determine this, the teacher must determine what is considered average for that specific set of data.

One way to look at a set of data is to rank the scores from highest to lowest. This helps the teacher see how the group performed. After ranking the data in this fashion, it is helpful to complete a **frequency distribution** by counting how frequently each score occurred. Here is an example of 39 test scores, which the teacher ranked and then counted to record frequency:

DATA SET A

Score	Tally	Frequency
100	|	1
99	|	1
98	||	2
94	||	2
90	̶ǀ̶ǀ̶ǀ̶ǀ̶ǀ ||	5
89	̶ǀ̶ǀ̶ǀ̶ǀ̶ǀ || ||	7
88	̶ǀ̶ǀ̶ǀ̶ǀ̶ǀ || ̶ǀ̶ǀ̶ǀ̶ǀ̶ǀ ||	10
82	̶ǀ̶ǀ̶ǀ̶ǀ̶ǀ || |	6
75	||	2
74	|	1
68	|	1
60	|	1

mode The most frequently occurring score in a set of scores.

By arranging the data in this order and tallying the frequency of each score, the teacher can determine a trend in the performance of the class.

bimodal distribution A distribution that has two most frequently occurring scores.

Another way to look at the data is to determine the most frequently occurring score, or the **mode**. The mode can give the teacher an idea of how the group performed because it indicates the score or performance that occurred the most number of times. The mode for data set A was 88 because it occurred 10 times. In data set B (Activity 3.2), the mode was 70.

multimodal distribution A distribution with three or more modes.

Some sets of data have two modes or two most frequently occurring scores. This type of distribution of scores is known as a **bimodal distribution**. A distribution with three or more modes is called a **multimodal distribution**.

frequency polygon A graphic representation of how often each score occurs in a set of data.

A clear representation of the distribution of a set of data can be illustrated graphically with a **frequency polygon**. A frequency

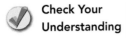
Check Your Understanding

Check your knowledge of the descriptive statistics presented in the previous section by completing Activity 3.2 below.

Activity 3.2

Refer to page 109 in your text. Place the following set of data in rank order and complete a frequency count.

Data Set B

92, 98, 100, 98, 92, 83, 73, 96, 90, 61, 70, 89, 87, 70, 85, 70, 66, 85, 62, 82

Score	Tally	Frequency	Score	Tally	Frequency
_____			_____		
_____			_____		
_____			_____		
_____			_____		
_____			_____		
_____			_____		
_____			_____		
_____			_____		

Apply Your Knowledge

Which of the numerical scales can be rank ordered?

_____

_____

_____

polygon is a graph with test scores represented on the horizontal axis and the number of occurrences, or frequencies, represented on the vertical axis, as shown for data set A in Figure 3.2.

The data that have been rank ordered and for which a mode or modes have been determined give the teacher some idea of how the students performed as a group. Another method of determining how the group performed is to find the middlemost score, or the **median**. After the data have been rank ordered, the teacher can merely count halfway down the list of scores; however, each score must be listed each time it occurs. For example, here is a rank-ordered set of data for which the median has been determined:

median The middle most score in a set of data.

100	79
97	79
89	79
85	68
85	62
78	60

78   median score

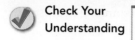
Check your knowledge of the descriptive statistics presented in the previous section by completing Activity 3.3 below.

Activity 3.3

Refer to page 109 in your text. Rank order the following set of data, complete a frequency count, and determine the mode.

Data Set C

62, 63, 51, 42, 78, 81, 81, 63, 75, 92, 94, 77, 63, 75, 96, 88, 60, 50, 49, 74

Score	**Tally**	**Frequency**	**Score**	**Tally**	**Frequency**
____			____		
____			____		
____			____		
____			____		
____			____		
____			____		
____			____		
____			____		

The mode is _____

Apply Your Knowledge

What do you think it would mean to the teacher if the data of three sets of exams were distributed so that the mode always occurred at the high end of the scores? _____
_____
_____

Figure 3.2   Frequency polygon for data set A.

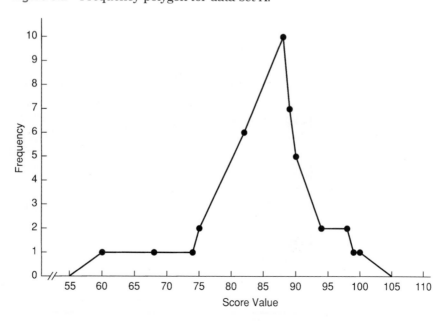

The median score has 50% of the data listed above it and 50% of the data listed below it. In this example, six of the scores are listed above 78 and six are listed below the median. Notice that although 78 is the median, it is not the mode for this set of data. In a normal distribution, which is distributed symmetrically, the median and the mode are represented by the same number.

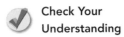 Check Your Understanding

Check your knowledge of the descriptive statistics presented in the previous section by completing Activity 3.4 below.

Activity 3.4

Rank order the data, complete a frequency count, and make a frequency polygon.

Data Set D

50, 52, 68, 67, 51, 89, 88, 76, 76, 88, 88, 68, 90, 91, 98, 69, 89, 88, 76, 76, 82, 85, 72, 85, 88, 76, 94, 82

Score	Tally	Frequency	Score	Tally	Frequency
_____			_____		
_____			_____		
_____			_____		
_____			_____		
_____			_____		
_____			_____		
_____			_____		
_____			_____		

Draw the frequency polygon here:

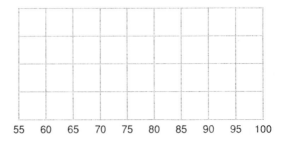

Apply Your Knowledge

What type of distribution did you plot using data set D? _____
_____
_____

In a set of data with an even number of scores, the median is the middlemost score even though the score may not actually exist in that set of data. For example,

100
96
95
90
85
83
82
80
78
77

The scores 85 and 83 occur in the middle of this distribution; therefore, the median is 84, even though 84 is not one of the scores.

Although the mode and median indicate how a group performed, these measures of central tendency do not accurately describe the

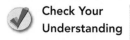

Check Your Understanding

Check your knowledge of the descriptive statistics presented in the previous section by completing Activity 3.5 below.

Activity 3.5

Find the median for the following sets of data.

Data Set E	Data Set F
100	88
99	88
96	88
88	86
84	80
83	76
82	75
79	74
76	70
75	68
70	
62	
60	

Median: _____   Median: _____

Apply Your Knowledge

Data set E has a higher median. Did the students represented by data set E perform significantly better than the students represented by data set F? Why or why not? Explain your answer. _____
_____
_____

mean Arithmetic average of a set of data.

average, or typical, performance. One of the best measures of average performance is the arithmetic average, or **mean**, of the group of scores. The mean is calculated as a simple average: Add the scores and divide by the number of scores in the set of data. For example:

90

80

75

60

70

65

80

100

80

80
___

$780 \div 10 = 78$

The sum of the scores is 780. There are 10 scores in the set of data. Therefore, the sum, 780, is divided by the number of scores, 10. The average, or typical, score for this set of data is 78, which represents the arithmetic average.

Often teachers choose to use the mean score to represent the average score on a particular test or assignment. If this score seems to represent the typical performance on the specific test, the teacher may assign a letter grade of C to the numerical representation of the mean score. However, as discussed next, extremely high or low scores can render the mean misrepresentative of the average performance of the class.

Using measures of central tendency is one way teachers can determine which score represents an average performance for a particular group on a particular measure. This aids the teacher in monitoring student progress and knowing when a student is performing well above or well below the norm or average of the group.

The mean can be affected by an extreme score, especially if the group is composed of only a few students. A very high score can raise the mean, whereas a very low score can lower the mean. For this reason, the teacher may wish to omit an extreme score before averaging the data. If scores seem to be widely dispersed, or scattered, using measures of central tendency may not be in the students' best interests. Moreover, such scatter may suggest that the teacher needs to qualitatively evaluate the students' performance and other factors such as teaching methods.

In research and test development, it is necessary to strive for and understand the normal distribution. Because of the symmetrical quality of the normal curve, the mean, median, and mode are all

Check Your Understanding

Check your knowledge of the measures of central tendency presented in the previous section by completing Activity 3.6 below.

Activity 3.6

Find the mean, median, and mode for each set of data.

Data Set G

90, 86, 80, 87, 86, 82, 87, 92

Mean: _____   Median: _____   Mode: _____

Data Set H

41, 42, 45, 42, 46, 47, 48, 47, 41, 41

Mean: _____   Median: _____   Mode: _____

Apply Your Knowledge

Using the mean, median, and mode you obtained for data sets G and H, can you determine which group of students performed in a more similar manner as a group? Explain your answer. _____

_____

_____

standard deviation A unit of measurement that represents the typical amount that a score can be expected to vary from the mean in a given set of data.

variability Describes how scores vary.

represented by the same number. For example, on tests measuring intelligence, the mean IQ is 100. One hundred is also the middlemost score (median) and the most frequently occurring score (mode). In fact, more than 68% of all of the IQ scores will cluster within 1 **standard deviation**, or one determined typical unit, above and below the score of 100. The statistic known as standard deviation is very important in special education assessment when the use of tests that compare an individual student with a norm-referenced group is necessary. Finding the standard deviation is one method of calculating difference in scores, or **variability** of scores, known as dispersion.

MEASURES OF DISPERSION

measures of dispersion Statistical methods for observing how data spread from the mean.

variance Describes the total amount that a group of scores varies in a set of data.

Because special educators must determine the degree or amount of difference exhibited by individuals in behaviors, skills, or traits, they must employ methods of calculating difference from the average or expected score. Just as measures of central tendency are used to see how sets of data cluster together around an average score, **measures of dispersion** are used to calculate how scores are spread from the mean.

The way that scores in a set of data are spread apart is known as the variability of the scores, or how much the scores vary from each other. When scores fall very close together and are not widely spread apart, the data are described as not having much variability, or **variance**.

Compare the following two sets of data:

Data Set I		Data Set J	
100	75	98	75
98	75	96	75
95	75	87	75
91	72	78	75
88	70	75	72
87	69	75	72
82	68	75	72
80	67	75	72
75	51	75	72
75	50	75	72

range The distance between the highest and lowest scores in a data set.

An easy way to get an idea about the spread is to find the **range** of scores. The range is calculated by subtracting the lowest score from the highest score.

Set I   **Set J**

$100 - 50 = 50$ $98 - 72 = 26$

The range for set J is about half that of set I. It appears that set I has more variability than set J. Look at the sets of data again. Both sets have the same median and the same mode, yet they are very different in terms of variability. When the means are calculated, it seems that the data are very similar. Set I has a mean of 77.15, and set J has a mean of 77.05. By using only measures of central tendency, the teacher may think that the students in both of these classes performed in a very similar manner on this test. Yet one set of data has approximately twice the spread, or variability of scores. In educational testing, it is necessary to determine the deviation from the mean in order to have a clearer picture of how students in groups such as these performed. By calculating the variance and the standard deviation, the teacher can find out the typical amount of difference from the mean. By knowing these typical or standard deviations from the mean, the teacher will be able to find out which scores are a significant distance from the average score.

To find the standard deviation of a set of scores, the variance must first be calculated. The variance can be described as the degree or amount of variability or dispersion in a set of scores. Looking at data sets I and J, one could probably assume that set I would have a larger variance than J.

Four steps are involved in calculating the variance:

Step 1 To calculate the amount of distance of each score from the mean, subtract the mean for the set of data from each score.

Step 2 Find the square of each of the difference scores found in Step 1 (multiply each difference score by itself).

Step 3 Find the total of all of the squared score differences. This is called the sum of squares.

Step 4 Calculate the average of the sum of squares by dividing the total by the number of scores.

Step 1: Difference	Step 2: Multiply by Itself	Squared
$100 - 77.15 = 22.85$	$22.85 \times 22.85 =$	522.1225
$98 - 77.15 = 20.85$	$20.85 \times 20.85 =$	434.7225
$95 - 77.15 = 17.85$	$17.85 \times 17.85 =$	318.6225
$91 - 77.15 = 13.85$	$13.85 \times 13.85 =$	191.8225

Step 1: Difference	Step 2: Multiply by Itself	Squared
$88 - 77.15 = 10.85$	$10.85 \times 10.85 =$	117.7225
$87 - 77.15 = 9.85$	$9.85 \times 9.85 =$	97.0225
$82 - 77.15 = 4.85$	$4.85 \times 4.85 =$	23.5225
$80 - 77.15 = 2.85$	$2.85 \times 2.85 =$	8.1225
$75 - 77.15 = -2.15$	$-2.15 \times -2.15 =$	4.6225
$75 - 77.15 = -2.15$	$-2.15 \times -2.15 =$	4.6225
$75 - 77.15 = -2.15$	$-2.15 \times -2.15 =$	4.6225
$75 - 77.15 = -2.15$	$-2.15 \times -2.15 =$	4.6225
$75 - 77.15 = -2.15$	$-2.15 \times -2.15 =$	4.6225
$72 - 77.15 = -5.15$	$-5.15 \times -5.15 =$	26.5225
$70 - 77.15 = -7.15$	$-7.15 \times -7.15 =$	51.1225
$69 - 77.15 = -8.15$	$-8.15 \times -8.15 =$	66.4225
$68 - 77.15 = -9.15$	$-9.15 \times -9.15 =$	83.7225
$67 - 77.15 = -10.15$	$-10.15 \times -10.15 =$	103.0225
$51 - 77.15 = -26.15$	$-26.15 \times -26.15 =$	683.8225
$50 - 77.15 = -27.15$	$-27.15 \times -27.15 =$	737.1225

Step 3: Sum of Squares: 3,488.55

Step 4: Divide the Sum of Squares by the Number of Scores

$$3,488.55 \div 20 = 174.4275$$

Therefore, the variance for data set I = 174.4275.

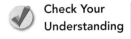

**Check Your
Understanding**

Check your knowledge of the measures of dispersion presented in the previous section by completing Activity 3.7 below.

Activity 3.7

Calculate the variance for data set J and compare with data set I.

Data Set J	Step 1: Difference	Step 2: Multiply by Itself	Squared
98 − 77.05 =			
96 − 77.05 =			
87 − 77.05 =			
78 − 77.05 =			
75 − 77.05 =			
75 − 77.05 =			
75 − 77.05 =			
75 − 77.05 =			
75 − 77.05 =			
75 − 77.05 =			
75 − 77.05 =			
75 − 77.05 =			
75 − 77.05 =			
75 − 77.05 =			
72 − 77.05 =			
72 − 77.05 =			
72 − 77.05 =			
72 − 77.05 =			
72 − 77.05 =			
72 − 77.05 =			

Step 3: Sum of Squares: _____

Step 4: Divide the Sum of Squares by the Number of Scores. Which set of data, J or I, has the larger variance? _____

Apply Your Knowledge

Data sets I and J have means that are very similar. Why do you think there is such a large difference between the variance of I and the variance of J? _____
_____
_____

STANDARD DEVIATION

Once the variance has been calculated, only one more step is needed to calculate the standard deviation. The standard deviation helps the teacher determine how much distance from the mean is typical and how much is considered significant.

Figure 3.3   Distribution for data set I.

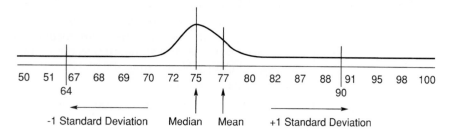

The standard deviation of a set of data is the square root of the variance.

Standard Deviation = $\sqrt{\text{Variance}}$

Because the variance for data sets I and J has already been calculated, merely enter each number on a calculator and hit the square root button. If a calculator is not available, use the square root tables located in most introductory statistics textbooks.

The square root of the variance for data set I is 13.21. Therefore, any test score that is more than 1 standard deviation above or below the mean score, either 13.21 above the mean or 13.21 below the mean, is considered significant. Look at data set I. The test scores that are more than 1 standard deviation above the mean (77.15) are 100, 98, 95, and 91. The scores that are more than 1 standard deviation below the mean are 51 and 50. These scores represent the extremes for this distribution and may well receive the extreme grades for the class: A's and F's. Figure 3.3 illustrates the distribution of scores in data set I.

Look at data set J. To locate significantly different scores, find those that are 1 or more standard deviations away from the mean of 77.05. Which scores are considered to be a significant distance from the mean?

STANDARD DEVIATION AND THE NORMAL DISTRIBUTION

In a normal distribution, the standard deviations represent the percentages of scores shown on the bell curve in Figure 3.4. More than 68% of the scores fall within 1 standard deviation above or below the mean. A normal distribution is symmetrical and has the same number representing the mean, median, and mode. Notice that approximately 95% of the scores are found within 2 standard deviations above and below the mean (Figure 3.4). To clarify the significance of standard deviation, it is helpful to remember that one criterion for the diagnosis of mental retardation is an IQ score of more than 2 standard deviations below the mean. The criterion of

Check Your Understanding

Check your knowledge of the measures of dispersion presented in the previous section by completing Activity 3.8 below.

Activity 3.8

Using the following sets of data, complete a frequency count and a frequency polygon; calculate the mean, median, and mode; calculate the range, variance, and standard deviation; and list the scores that are a significant distance from the mean.

Ms. Jones's Class Data

95, 82, 76, 75, 62, 100, 32, 15, 100, 98, 99, 86, 70, 26, 21, 26, 82

Frequency count:_____

Draw the frequency polygon of the data.

15 20 25 30 35 40 45 50 55 60 65 70 75 80 85 90 95 100

Mean: _____   Median: _____   Mode:_____

Range: _____   Variance: _____   Standard deviation: _____

Test scores that are a significant distance from the mean are

_____

Mrs. Smith's Class Data

76, 75, 83, 92, 85, 69, 88, 87, 88, 88, 88, 88, 77, 78, 78, 95, 98

Frequency count:_____

Draw the frequency polygon of the data.

65 70 75 80 85 90 95 100

Mean: _____   Median: _____   Mode:_____
Range: _____   Variance: _____   Standard deviation: _____
Test scores that are a significant distance from the mean are

_____

Apply Your Knowledge

Using the information you obtained through your calculations, what can you say about the performance of the students in Ms. Jones's class compared with the performance of the students in Mrs. Smith's class?

_____
_____
_____

Figure 3.4 Percentages of population that fall within standard deviation units in a normal distribution.

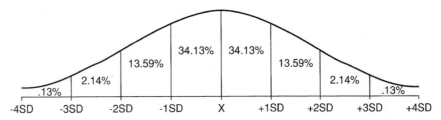

2 standard deviations above the mean is often used to determine that a student is within the gifted range. Using a standard deviation of 15 IQ points, an individual with an IQ of 70 or less and a subaverage adaptive behavior scale score might be classified as being within the range of mental retardation, whereas an individual with an IQ of 130 or more may be classified as gifted. The American Association on Mental Retardation (AAMR) classification system allows additional flexibility by adding 5 points to the minimum requirement; that is, the student within the 70–75 IQ range may also be found eligible for services under the category of mental retardation if there are additional supporting data.

MEAN DIFFERENCES

Test results such as those discussed in the preceding section should be interpreted with caution. Many tests that have been used historically to diagnose disabilities such as mental retardation have been shown to exhibit *mean differences*. A specific cultural or linguistic group may have a different mean or average score than that reported for most of the population; this is a mean difference. Accordingly, minority students should not be judged by an acceptable average for a different population. This issue is elaborated on in Chapter 9, "Measures of Intelligence and Adaptive Behavior."

SKEWED DISTRIBUTIONS

skewed Describes a distribution that has either more positively distributed scores or more negatively distributed scores.

When small samples of populations are tested or when a fairly restricted population is tested, the results may not be distributed in a normal curve. Distributions can be **skewed** in a positive or negative direction. When many of the scores are below the mean, the distribution is said to be **positively skewed** and will resemble the distribution in Figure 3.5. Notice that the most frequently occurring scores (mode) are located below the mean.

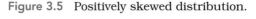

Figure 3.5   Positively skewed distribution.

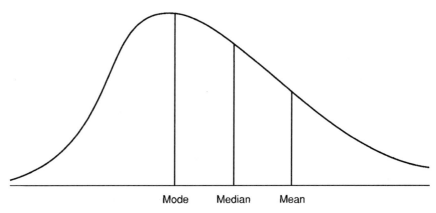

Figure 3.6   Negatively skewed distribution.

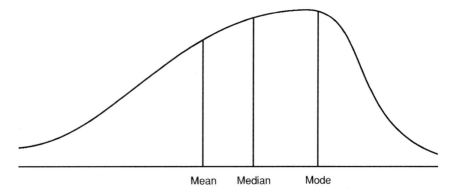

positively skewed
Describes a
distribution in which
more of the scores fall
below the mean.

**negatively
skewed** Describes a
distribution in which
more of the scores fall
above the mean.

When a large number of the scores occur above the mean, the distribution is said to be **negatively skewed**, as shown in Figure 3.6. Notice that the mode and median scores are located above the mean.

Figures 3.5 and 3.6 illustrate different ways that groups of scores fall, cluster, and are dispersed. As already discussed, extreme scores can change the appearance of a set of scores. Often, when working with scores from teacher-made tests, one or two scores can be so extreme that they influence the way the data are described. That is, the scores may influence or pull the mean in one direction. Consider the following examples:

Ms. Brown	Ms. Blue
100	100
92	92
86	86
80	80

78	78
78	78
78	78
75	75
74	74
72	6
813 ÷ 10 = 81.3	745 ÷ 10 = 74.5

The sets of data are very similar except for the one extreme low score. The greater the number of scores in the class, the less influence an extreme score has on the set of data. In small classes like those often found in special education settings, the mean of the class performance is more likely to be influenced by an extreme score. If Ms. Brown and Ms. Blue each had a class objective stating that the class would pass the test with an average score of 80, Ms. Brown's class would have passed the objective, but Ms. Blue's class would not have. When the extreme score is omitted, the average for Ms. Blue's class is 82.1, which meets the class objective.

When selecting norm–referenced tests, special educators must take care to read the test manual and determine the size of the sample used in the norming process. Tests developed using larger samples are thought to result in scores that are more representative of the majority population.

TYPES OF SCORES

percentile ranks
Scores that express the percentage of students who scored as well as or lower than a given student's score.

z scores Derived scores that are expressed in standard deviation units.

Percentile ranks and **z scores** provide additional ways of looking at data. Using percentile ranks is a method of ranking each score on the continuum of the normal distribution. The extreme scores are ranked at the top and bottom, and very few people obtain scores at the extreme ends. Percentiles range from the 99.9th percentile to less than the 1st percentile. A person who scores at the extremely high end of a test may be ranked near the 99th percentile. This means that she scored as well as or better than 99% of the students the same age or grade who took the same test. A person who scores around the average, say 100 on an IQ test, would be ranked in the middle, or the 50th percentile. A person who scores in the top fourth would be above the 75th percentile; in other words, the student scored as well as or better than 75% of the students in that particular age group. The various percentile ranks and their location on a normal distribution are illustrated in Figure 3.7.

Some have argued that using a percentile rank may not convey information that is as meaningful as other types of scores, such as z scores (May & Nicewander, 1994, 1997). deGruijter (1997) argued that May and Nicewander were faulty in their reasoning regarding percentile ranks and stated that percentile ranks are not inferior indicators of ability.

Figure 3.7   Relationship of percentiles and normal distribution.

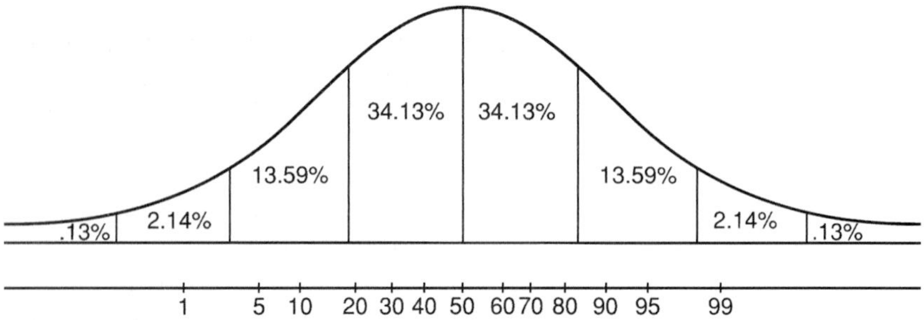

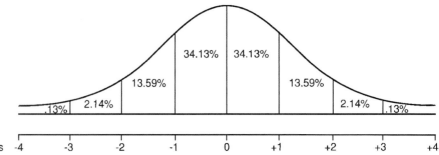

Source: From *Assessing special students* (3rd ed., p. 63) by J. McLoughlin and R. Lewis, 1990, Upper Saddle River, NJ: Merrill/Prentice Hall. Copyright 1990 by Prentice Hall. Adapted with permission.

Figure 3.8   Relationship of *z* scores and the normal distribution.

Source: From *Assessing special students* (3rd ed., p. 63) by J. McLoughlin and R. Lewis, 1990, Upper Saddle River, NJ: Merrill/Prentice Hall. Copyright 1990 by Prentice Hall. Adapted with permission.

Some tests use *T* scores to interpret test performance. *T* scores have an average or mean of 50 and standard deviation of 10. One standard deviation above the mean would be expressed as a *T* score of 60, and 40 would represent 1 standard deviation below the mean.

Another type of score used to describe the data in a normal distribution is called a *z* score. A *z* score indicates where a score is located in terms of standard deviation units. The mean is expressed as 0, 1 standard deviation above the mean is expressed as +1, 2 standard deviations above as +2, and so on, as illustrated in Figure 3.8. Standard deviation units below the mean are expressed as negative numbers. For example, a score that is 1 standard deviation below the mean is expressed using *z* scores as −1, and a score that is 2 standard deviations below is expressed as −2. Conversely, +1 is 1 standard deviation above the mean, and +2 is 2 standard deviations above the mean.

stanines A method of reporting scores that divide data into 9 groups and scores are reported as 1 through 9 with a mean of 5.

deciles A method of reporting scores that divides data into 10 groups with each group representing 10% of the obtained scores.

Stanines are used to report many group achievement test scores. Stanines divide the scores into 9 groups of scores and are reported as 1 through 9 with a mean of 5. The standard deviation unit of stanines is 2. This indicates that students who fall between the 3rd and 7th stanines are within the range expected for their age or grade group.

Deciles are scores that are reported in 10 groups ranging from a score of 10 for the lowest grouping to 100 for the highest group of scores. Each grouping represents 10% of the obtained scores.

Case Study for Score Interpretation: Percentile Ranks

Mr. Garza received a report from the school counselor regarding a student whom he had referred for an assessment of self-esteem. The student, Jorge, completed a norm-referenced questionnaire that assessed his own feelings and self-confidence about school, his peers, and his family. When the counselor met with Mr. Garza, the following scores were reported:

Self–Confidence with Peer Relationships	5th percentile rank
Self–Confidence with Family Relationships	95th percentile rank
Self–Confidence in Ability at School	12th percentile rank

In this case, self-confidence is something that is valued or consistent with better behavior and higher achievement. In other words, the more confidence a student reports, the better he may be able to function in school, with peers, and with family relationships. For Jorge, he answered in a manner that indicates he was ranked at the 5th percentile in self-confidence with peers. This means that about 95% of the students his age reported feeling more confident about their peer relationships. According to the responses made by the student, how confident is he about his ability to get along within his family? How confident is he in his ability to perform at school?

Because self-confidence is something that is valued, higher percentile ranks indicate that the student has confidence while lower percentile ranks indicate that he is not very confident about his ability.

When we assess behaviors that are impacting learning in a negative way, such as distractibility or signs of depression, for example, we want the percentile ranks to be lower. In other words, a percentile rank of 15 indicates that about 85% of the students in the sample displayed more behaviors that are consistent with distractibility or depression.

When assessing characteristics that are predictors of higher school achievement, such as IQ, we look for higher percentile ranks to indicate higher ability. A student who performed in a manner that resulted in a percentile rank of 90 indicates that the student performed better than about 90% of the students in the norm sample.

For **MORE PRACTICE** in calculating scores and applying test scores to cases, visit the Companion Website at *www.prenhall.com/overton.*

THINK AHEAD

Now that you know how to compare students' scores with each other, you will read about how to compare tests. You will learn how to determine whether tests are reliable and valid. Do you think a test must be both reliable and valid to obtain information about a student's abilities?

EXERCISES

Part I

Match these terms with the statements that follow.

a. nominal scale
b. positively skewed
c. measures of central tendency
d. frequency distribution
e. bimodal distribution
f. ordinal scale
g. multimodal
h. frequency polygon
i. measures of dispersion
j. negatively skewed

k. standard deviation
l. ratio scale
m. interval scale
n. mode
o. range
p. rank order
q. median
r. descriptive statistics
s. mean
t. normal distribution

_____ 1. In this set of data, what measures of central tendency are represented by the number 77: 65, 66, 82, 95, 77?

_____ 2. If the heights of all fifth-grade elementary students in one large city were measured, in what manner would the resulting data be displayed?

_____ 3. The following set of data is interesting because it is _____?
22, 47, 88, 62, 65, 22, 63, 89, 55, 74, 88, 99, 44, 65, 100.

_____ 4. In a university, all students are given a new student identification number upon registration. These numbers are on what scale?

_____ 5. All fourth-grade students in a Little City School were asked to participate in a reading contest to see which students could read the most books in a 3-month period. At the end of the 3 months, the winners were determined.

The 10 students who read the most books were awarded prizes. On the final day of the contest, the students anxiously looked at the list where the names were in _____ from the highest number of books read to the fewest.

_____ 6. The mean, median, and mode make up _____.

_____ 7. A seventh-grade prealgebra class completed the first test of the new school year. Here are the data resulting from the first test: 100, 99, 95, 90, 89, 85, 84, 82, 81, 80, 79, 78, 77, 76, 70, 68, 65, 62, 60, 59, 55. For this set of data, what does the number 45 represent?

_____ 8. The following set of data has what type of distribution: 88, 33, 78, 56, 44, 37, 90, 99, 76, 78, 77, 62, 90?

_____ 9. A set of data has a symmetrical distribution of scores with the mean, median, and mode represented by the number 82. This set of data represents a _____.

_____10. What term describes when a set of data has a mean that is less than the most frequently occurring scores?

Part II

Rank order the following data; complete a frequency distribution and a frequency polygon; calculate the mean, median, and mode; and find the range, variance, and standard deviation. Identify scores that are significantly above or below the mean.

Data

85, 85, 99, 63, 60, 97, 96, 95, 58, 70, 72, 92, 89, 87, 74, 74, 74, 85, 84, 78, 84, 78, 84, 78, 86, 82, 79, 81, 80, 86

_____	_____
_____	_____
_____	_____
_____	_____
_____	_____
_____	_____
_____	_____
_____	_____
_____	_____
_____	_____
_____	_____
_____	_____
_____	_____
_____	_____
_____	_____

Mean: _____   Median: _____   Mode: _____

Range: _____   Variance: _____   Standard deviation: _____

Scores that are a significant distance from the mean are

_____

Draw the frequency polygon here:

Figure 3.9 Relationships among different types of scores in a normal distribution.

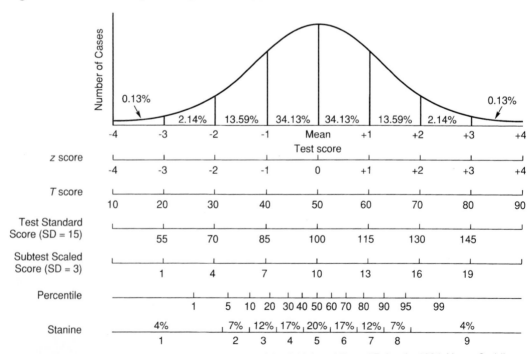

Use the normal distribution shown in Figure 3.9 to answer the following questions. You may need to use a ruler or straightedge, placed on the figure vertically, to identify the answers.

1. What percentage of the scores would fall between the z scores of -2.0 and $+2.0$? _____

2. What percentile rank would be assigned to the z score of 0? _____

3. What percentile rank would represent a person who scored at the z score of $+3.0$? _____

4. Approximately what percentile rank would be assigned for the IQ score of 70? _____

5. Approximately how many people would be expected to fall in the IQ range represented by the z scores of $+3.0$ to $+4.0$? _____

Companion
Website

Answers to these questions can be found in the Appendix of this text or you may also complete these questions and receive immediate feedback on your answers by going to the Think Ahead module in Chapter 3 of the Companion Website.

Reliability and Validity

KEY TERMS

reliability
correlation
correlation coefficient
scattergram
Pearson's *r*
internal consistency
test-retest reliability
equivalent forms reliability
alternate forms reliability
split-half reliability
Kuder–Richardson (K–R) 20
coefficient alpha
interrater reliability
true score

standard error of measurement
obtained score
confidence interval
estimated true score
validity
criterion-related validity
concurrent validity
predictive validity
content validity
presentation format
response mode
construct validity
validity of test use

CHAPTER FOCUS

This chapter presents reliability and validity of test instruments. You will learn the various methods of researching reliability and validity and which methods are appropriate for specific types of tests.

CEC KNOWLEDGE AND SKILLS STANDARDS

The student completing this chapter will understand the knowledge and skills included in the following CEC Knowledge and Skills Standards from Standard 8: Assessment:

CC8K1—Basic terminology used in assessment

CC8S5—Interpret information from formal and informal assessments

RELIABILITY AND VALIDITY IN ASSESSMENT

It is important for educators to feel that the assessment methods used in teaching are providing accurate information. Usually, inferences are made from test data. In each school district, these inferences and subsequent interpretations of test results may change or set the educational future of hundreds of students each school year. An understanding of the concepts of reliability and validity aids the educator in determining test accuracy and dependability as well as how much faith can be placed in the use of instruments in the decision-making process.

reliability The dependability or consistency of an instrument across time or items.

Reliability in assessment refers to the confidence that can be placed in an instrument to yield the same score for the same student if the test were administered more than once and to the degree with which a skill or trait is measured consistently across items of a test. Teachers administering tests of any type, formal or informal, must be aware that error will be present to some degree during test administration. Statistical methods for estimating the probable amount of error and the degree of reliability allow professionals to select instruments with the lowest estimate of error and the greatest degree of reliability. Because educators use assessment as a basis for educational intervention and placement decisions, the most technically adequate instruments are preferred.

CORRELATION

correlation A statistical method of observing the degree of relationship between two sets of data on two variables.

One concept important to the understanding of reliability in assessment is **correlation**. Correlation is a method of determining the degree of relationship between two variables. Reliability is determined by the degree of relationship between the administration of an instrument and some other variable (including a repeated administration of the same instrument). The greater the degree of the relationship, the more reliable the instrument.

Correlation is a statistical procedure calculated to measure the relationship between two variables. The two variables might be two administrations of the same test, administration of equivalent forms of the same test, administration of one test and school achievement, or variables such as amount of time spent studying and final exam grades. In short, correlation is a method of determining whether two variables are associated with each other and, if so, how much.

correlation coefficient The expression of a relationship between two variables.

There are three types of correlations between variables: positive, negative, and no relationship. The degree of relationship between two variables is expressed by a **correlation coefficient** (r). The correlation coefficient will be a number between $+1.00$ and -1.00. A -1.00 or $+1.00$ indicates a perfect degree of correlation. In reality, perfect correlations are extremely rare. A correlation coefficient of 0 indicates no relationship.

The closer to $+1.00$ the coefficient, the stronger the degree of the relationship. Hence, an r of .78 represents a stronger relationship than .65. When relationships are expressed by coefficients, the positive or negative sign does not indicate the strength of a relationship, but indicates the direction of the relationship. Therefore, r values of $-.78$ and $+.78$ are of equal strength.

POSITIVE CORRELATION

Variables that have a positive relationship are those that move in the same direction. For example, this means that when test scores representing one variable in a set are high, scores representing the other variable also are high, and when the scores on one variable are low, scores on the other variable are low. Look at the following list of scores. Students who made high scores on a reading ability test (mean = 100) also had fairly high classroom reading grades at the end of the 6-week reporting period. Therefore, the data appear to show a positive relationship between the ability measured on the reading test (variable Y) and the student's performance in the reading curriculum in the classroom (variable X).

	Scores on the Reading Ability Test (Variable Y)	Reading Grade at End of 6 Weeks (Variable X)
John	109	B+
Ralph	120	A+
Sue	88	C−
Mary	95	B+
George	116	A−
Fred	78	D−
Kristy	140	A+
Jake	135	A
Jason	138	A
Betty	95	B−
Jamie	85	C+

scattergram Graphic representation of a correlation.

To better understand this positive relationship, the scores on these two variables can be plotted on a **scattergram** (Figure 4.1). Each student is represented by a single dot on the graph. The scattergram shows clearly that as the score on one variable increased, so did the score on the other variable.

When plotting correlations on a scattergram, the closer the dots approximate a straight line, the nearer to perfect the correlation. Hence, a strong relationship will appear more linear. Figure 4.2 illustrates a perfect positive correlation (straight line) for the small set of data shown here.

	Test 1 (Variable Y)	Test 2 (Variable X)
George	100	100
Bill	95	95
Mary	87	87
Sue	76	76

Figure 4.1 Scattergram showing relationship between scores on reading ability test and reading grade for 6 weeks.

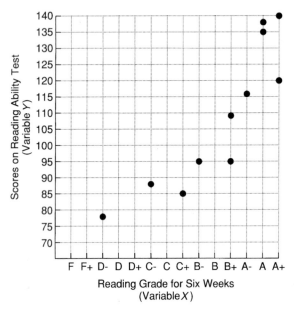

Figure 4.2 Scattergram showing a perfect positive correlation.

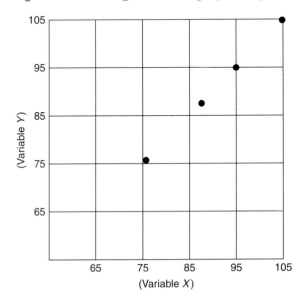

Examples of other variables that would be expected to have a positive relationship are number of days present in class and semester grade, number of chapters studied and final exam grade, and number of alcoholic drinks consumed and mistakes on a fine-motor test.

NEGATIVE CORRELATION

A negative correlation occurs when high scores on one variable are associated with low scores on the other variable. Examples of probable negative correlations are number of days absent and test grades, number of hours spent at parties and test grades, and number of hours missed from work and amount of hourly paycheck.

When the strength of a relationship is weak, the scattergram will not appear to have a distinct line. The less linear the scattergram, the weaker the correlation. Figure 4.3 illustrates scattergrams representing weak positive and weak negative relationships.

NO CORRELATION

When data from two variables are not associated or have no relationship, the $r = .00$. No correlation will be represented on a scattergram, with no linear direction either positive or negative. Figure 4.4 illustrates a scattergram of variables with no relationship.

Figure 4.3 Scattergrams showing (a) weak positive and (b) weak negative relationships.

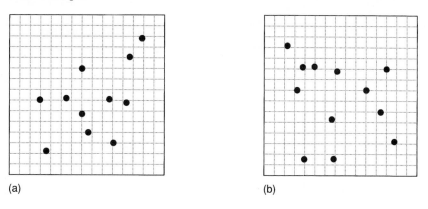

(a)   (b)

Figure 4.4 Scattergram showing no relationship.

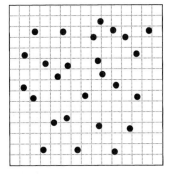

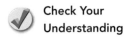

**Check Your
Understanding**

Check your knowledge of positive correlation by completing Activity 4.1 below.

Activity 4.1

The following sets of data are scores on a mathematics ability test and grade-level achievement in math for fifth graders. Plot the scores on the scattergram shown here.

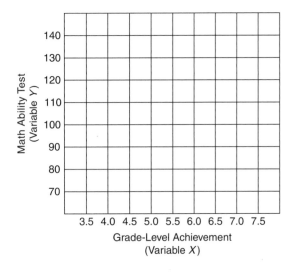

	Mathematics Ability Test Score (Variable Y)	**Grade-Level Achievement (Variable X)**
Wendy	115	6.5
Mary	102	5.5
Brad	141	7.4
Randy	92	4.7
Jamie	106	5.8
George	88	3.9

Apply Your Knowledge

Explain why this scattergram represents a positive correlation. _____
_____
_____

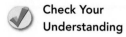

Check Your Understanding

Check your knowledge of negative correlation by completing Activity 4.2 below.

Activity 4.2

Here is an example of a negative correlation between two variables Plot the scores on the scattergram.

	Test 1 (Variable Y)	Test 2 (Variable X)
Heather	116	40
Ryan	118	38
Brent	130	20
William	125	21
Kellie	112	35
Stacy	122	19
Marsha	126	23
Lawrence	110	45
Allen	127	18
Aaron	100	55
Jeff	120	27
Sharon	122	25
Michael	112	43
James	105	50
Thomas	117	33

METHODS OF MEASURING RELIABILITY

A teacher who administers a mathematics ability test to a student on a particular day and obtains a standard score of 110 (mean = 100) might feel quite confident that the student has ability in math

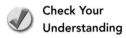
Check Your Understanding

Check your ability to distinguish between positive, negative, or no correlation by completing Activity 4.3 below.

Activity 4.3

Complete the scattergrams using the following sets of data. Determine whether the scattergrams illustrate positive, negative, or no correlation.

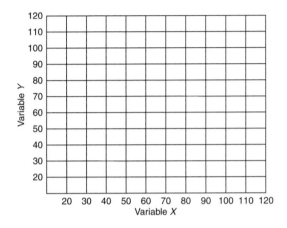

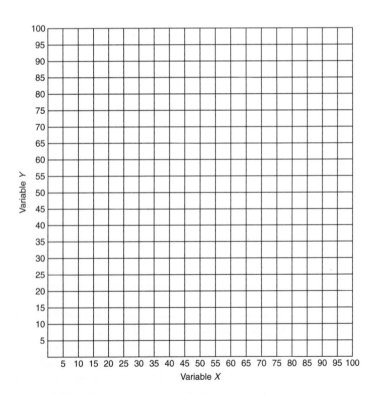

Variable Y	Variable X
100	110
96	94
86	91
67	72
77	85

Correlation appears to be

_____

Variable Y	Variable X
6	87
56	98
4	80
10	85
40	84
30	20
20	40
50	20

Correlation appears to be

_____

Apply Your Knowledge

Explain the concept of correlations: positive, negative, and no correlation.

_____

_____

_____

above expectancy for the age level. Imagine that a teacher recommended a change in the student's educational placement based on the results of that particular math test and later discovered that the math test was not reliable. Educators must be able to have confidence that test instruments used will yield similar results when administered at different times. Professionals must know the degree with which they can rely on a specific instrument.

Different methods can be used to measure the reliability of test instruments. The reliability statistics are calculated using correlational methods. One correlational method used is the Pearson's Product Moment correlation, known as **Pearson's *r*.** Pearson's *r* is a commonly used formula for data on an interval or a ratio scale, although other methods are used as well. The correlational studies of the reliability of tests involve checking the reliability of a test over time or the reliability of items within the

Pearson's *r*
A statistical formula for determining strength and direction of correlations.

internal consistency The consistency of the items on an instrument to measure a skill, trait, or domain.

test, known as **internal consistency**. For such studies, the procedures of test-retest, equivalent forms, split-half, and statistical methods called Kuder–Richardson formulas may be used.

TEST-RETEST RELIABILITY

One way to determine the reliability of a test is to measure the correlation of test scores obtained during one administration with the scores obtained on a repeated administration. The assumption of **test-retest reliability** is that the trait being measured is one that is stable over time. Therefore, if the trait being measured remained constant, the readministration of the instrument would result in scores very similar to the first scores, and thus the correlation between the two administrations would be positive.

test-retest reliability Study that employs the readministration of a single instrument to check for consistency across time.

Many of the traits measured in psychoeducational assessment are variable and respond to influencing factors or changes over time, such as instruction or student maturity. The readministration of an instrument for reliability studies should therefore be completed within a fairly short time period in an effort to control the influencing variables that occur naturally in the educational environment of children and youth. Typically, the longer the interval between test administrations, the more chance of variation in the obtained scores. Conversely, the shorter the interval between the two test administrations, the less likelihood that students will be influenced by time-related factors (experience, education, etc.). The difficulty with readministering the same instrument within a short period of time is that the student may remember items on the test. This *practice effect* most likely would cause the scores obtained on the second administration to be higher than the original scores, which would influence the correlation. The shorter the interval between administrations, the greater the possibility of practice effect; the longer the interval, the greater the influence of time variables.

The disadvantages of test-retest methods for checking test reliability have led to the use of other methods.

EQUIVALENT FORMS RELIABILITY

equivalent forms reliability Consistency of a test to measure some domain, traits, or skill using like forms of the same instrument.

To control for the influence of time-related and practice-effect variables of test-retest methods, test developers may choose to use **equivalent forms reliability**, also called **alternate forms reliability**. In this method, two forms of the same instrument are used. The items are matched for difficulty on each test. For example, if three items for phonetic attack of consonant blends are included on one version of a reading test, three items of the same nature must be included at the same level on the alternate form of the test. During the reliability study, each student is administered both forms, and the scores obtained on one form of the test are then paired with the

alternate forms reliability Synonymous term for equivalent forms reliability.

scores obtained on the equivalent form. The following are scores obtained on equivalent forms of a hypothetical reading test:

The Best-Ever Diagnostic Reading Test (x = 100)*

	Form 1	Form 2
John	82	85
Sue	76	78
Bill	89	87
Randy	54	56
Sally	106	112
Sara	115	109

*x = mean of sample.

This positive correlation indicates a fairly high reliability using equivalent forms reliability. In reality, an equivalent forms reliability study would involve a much larger sample of students. If this example had been an equivalent forms study using a large national sample, the educator could assume that both forms of the Best-Ever Reading Diagnostic Test are measuring the tested trait with some consistency.

If the test developer of the Best-Ever Reading Diagnostic Test also wanted the test to measure the stability of the trait over time, the manual would recommend that an interval of time pass between the administration of each form of the test. In using equivalent forms for measuring the stability over time, the reliability coefficient usually will not be as high as in the case of administering the same form of a test a second time. In the case of administering equivalent forms over a period of time, the influence of time-related variables will decrease the reliability coefficient as well as the practice effect that occurs in a test-retest reliability study of the same instrument.

Several published achievement and diagnostic tests that are used in special education consist of two equivalent forms. The advantage of this format is that it provides the educator with two tests of the same difficulty level that can be administered within a short time frame without the influence of practice effect. Often, local educational agencies practice a policy of administering one of the equivalent forms before writing short-term objectives for the year and administering the second form following educational interventions near the end of the school year. Educators administer the second form of the test to determine whether the educational objectives were achieved.

split-half reliability A method of checking the consistency across items by halving a test and administering two half-forms of same test.

INTERNAL CONSISTENCY MEASURES

Several methods allow a test developer to determine the reliability of the items on a single test using one administration of the test. These methods include **split-half reliability**, Kuder–Richardson (K–R) 20, and coefficient alpha.

Split-Half Reliability Test developers rely often on the split-half method of determining reliability because of its ease of use. This method uses the items available on the instrument, splits the test in half, and correlates the two halves of the test. Because most tests have the items arranged sequentially, from the easiest items at the beginning of the test to the most difficult items at the end, the tests are typically split by pulling every other item, which in essence results in two equivalent half-forms of the test. Because this type of reliability study can be performed in a single administration of the instrument, split-half reliability studies are often completed even though other types of reliability studies are used in the test development. Although this method establishes reliability of one half of the test with the other half, it does not establish the reliability of the entire test. Because reliability tends to increase with the number of items on the test, using split-half reliability may result in a lower reliability coefficient than that calculated by another method for the entire test (Mehrens & Lehmann, 1978). In this case, the reliability may be statistically adjusted to account for the variance in length (Mehrens & Lehmann, 1978).

Kuder–Richardson 20 and Coefficient Alpha As the name implies, internal consistency reliability methods are used to determine how much alike items are to other items on a test. An advantage of this type of reliability study is that a single test administration is required. This reflects the unidimensionality in measuring a trait rather than the multidimensionality (Walsh & Betz, 1985).

Kuder–Richardson (K–R) 20 A formula used to check consistency across items of an instrument with right/wrong responses.

Internal consistency is computed statistically by using either the **K–R 20** formula for items scored only right or wrong or the coefficient alpha formula for items when more than 1 point is earned for a correct response (Mehrens & Lehmann, 1978).

When a high correlation coefficient is expressed by an internal consistency formula such as K–R 20 or **coefficient alpha**, the educator can be confident that the items on the instrument measure the trait or skill with some consistency. These methods measure the consistency of the items but not the consistency or dependability of the instrument across time, as do the test-retest method or using equivalent forms in separate test administrations.

coefficient alpha A formula used to check consistency across terms of an instrument with responses with varying credit.

INTERRATER RELIABILITY

Many of the educational and diagnostic tests used in special education are standardized with very specific administration, scoring, and interpretation instructions. Tests with a great deal of structure reduce the amount of influence that individual examiners may have on the results of the test. Some tests, specifically tests that allow the examiner to make judgments about student performance, have a greater possibility of influence by test examiners. In other words,

interrater reliability The consistency of a test to measure a skill, trait, or domain across examiners.

there may be more of a chance that a score would vary from one examiner to another if the same student were tested by different examiners. On tests such as this, it is important to check the **interrater reliability**, or interscorer reliability. This can be accomplished by administering the test and then having an objective scorer also score the test results. The results of the tests scored by the examiner are then correlated with the results obtained by the objective scorer to determine how much variability exists between the test scores. This information is especially important when tests with a great deal of subjectivity are used in making educational decisions.

Case Study for Reliability

Mrs. Smith received a new student in her fifth-grade class. In the student's records were educational testing data. Because of difficulty in reading, the student had been assessed in her previous school using a brief screening reading test that assessed all reading levels by using a simple list of most common words. The student's scores did not indicate any reading difficulty, yet Mrs. Smith noticed that the student was struggling with the fifth-grade reader.

One aspect of technically reliable academic instruments is the number of items and the representativeness of the domain being assessed. In this case, the student was assessed with a very short instrument that did not adequately assess the domain of skills that comprise fifth-grade-level reading, such as comprehension, decoding, recognition, oral fluency, and silent reading fluency. Mrs. Smith decided to assess the student using a comprehensive reading test that measured all aspects of reading expected of a student in the fifth-grade. This administration indicated that the student was actually able to complete most reading tasks successfully at the third-grade reading level. This comprehensive reading test was more predictive of the student's actual instructional level of reading.

WHICH TYPE OF RELIABILITY IS THE BEST?

Different types of reliability studies are used to measure consistency over time, consistency of the items on a test, and consistency of the test scored by different examiners. An educator selects assessment instruments for specific purposes according to the child's educational needs. The reliability studies and information in the test manual concerning reliability of the instrument are important considerations for the educator when determining which test is best for a particular student. An educator should select the instrument that has a high degree of reliability related to the purpose of assessment. An adequate reliability coefficient would be .60 or greater, and a high degree of reliability would be above .80. For example, if the

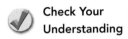

Check Your Understanding

Check your understanding of the different methods of studying reliability by completing Activity 4.4 below.

Activity 4.4

Select the appropriate reliability study for the purposes described (more than one answer may be correct).

A. split-half reliability

B. equivalent forms, separate administration times

C. K–R 20

D. interrater reliability

E. test-retest reliability

F. coefficient alpha

G. equivalent times, same administration time

_____ 1. Educator is concerned with item reliability, items are scored as right and wrong.

_____ 2. Educator wants to administer the same test twice to measure achievement objectives.

_____ 3. Examiner is concerned with consistency of trait over time.

_____ 4. Educator is concerned with item consistency, items scored with different point values for correct responses.

_____ 5. Examiner wants to administer a test that allows for examiner judgment.

Apply Your Knowledge

Explain the difference between internal reliability and other types of reliability. _____

_____

_____

examiner is interested in measuring a trait over time, the examiner should select an instrument in which the reliability or consistency over time had been studied. If the examiner is more concerned with the instrument's ability to determine student behavior using an instrument that allowed for a great degree of examiner judgment, the examiner should check the instrument's interrater reliability.

RELIABILITY FOR DIFFERENT GROUPS

The calculation of the reliability coefficient is a group statistic and can be influenced by the makeup of the group. The best test development and the manuals accompanying those tests will include information regarding the reliability of a test with different age or grade levels and even the reliability of a test with populations who differ on demographic variables such as cultural or linguistic backgrounds. The information in Table 4.1 illustrates how reliability may vary across different age groups.

Table 4.1 Split-half reliability coefficients, by age, for subtest, area, and total-test raw scores from the fall and spring standardization programs.

Subtest/Composite	Program (Fall/Spring)	Age					
		5	6	7	8	9	10
1. Numeration	F	.73	.82	.85	.90	.81	.85
	S	.51	.82	.89	.88	.89	.81
2. Rational Numbers	F	—	.24	.71	.68	.88	.89
	S	—	.27	.42	.86	.82	.86
3. Geometry	F	.63	.81	.79	.77	.82	.80
	S	.80	.81	.76	.77	.80	.75
4. Addition	F	.63	.65	.79	.84	.78	.40
	S	.58	.78	.84	.82	.84	.66
5. Subtraction	F	.25	.68	.64	.85	.89	.86
	S	.30	.70	.85	.90	.92	.85
6. Multiplication	F	.23	.41	.11	.76	.89	.90
	S	.07	.67	.68	.91	.93	.89
7. Division	F	.55	.49	.52	.51	.82	.86
	S	.18	.34	.53	.77	.80	.84
8. Mental Computation	F	—	.78	.68	.80	.85	.88
	S	—	.65	.67	.78	.78	.90
9. Measurement	F	.77	.89	.57	.77	.76	.77
	S	.92	.84	.85	.87	.84	.70
10. Time and Money	F	.50	.61	.73	.89	.87	.93
	S	.38	.70	.84	.89	.92	.86
11. Estimation	F	.44	.43	.50	.74	.86	.72
	S	.59	.50	.53	.85	.76	.84
12. Interpreting Data	F	.41	.86	.81	.80	.88	.85
	S	.32	.79	.83	.85	.88	.87
13. Problem Solving	F	.36	.60	.73	.71	.82	.86
	S	.55	.60	.77	.76	.87	.92
Basic Concepts Area[a]	F	.78	.87	.89	.91	.92	.93
	S	.82	.88	.87	.92	.92	.92
Operations Area[a]	F	.66	.86	.87	.93	.96	.96
	S	.73	.88	.92	.96	.96	.96
Applications Area[a]	F	.82	.91	.89	.94	.96	.96
	S	.88	.90	.93	.96	.96	.96
TOTAL TEST[a]	F	.90	.95	.95	.97	.98	.98
	S	.92	.95	.97	.98	.98	.98

[a]Reliability coefficients for the areas and the total test were computed by using Guilford's (1954, p. 393) formula for estimating the reliability of composite scores.
Source: From *KeyMath—Revised: A Diagnostic Inventory of Essential Mathematics, Manual. Forms A and B* (p. 67) by A. Connolly, 1988, Circle Pines, MN: American Guidance Service. Copyright 1988 by American Guidance Service. Reprinted by permission.

STANDARD ERROR OF MEASUREMENT

In all psychoeducational assessment, there is a basic underlying assumption: Error exists. Errors in testing may result from situational factors such as a poor testing environment or the health or emotions of the student, or errors may occur due to inaccuracies within the test instrument. Error should be considered when tests are administered, scored, and interpreted. Because tests are small samples of behavior observed at a given time, many variables can affect the assessment process and cause variance in test scores. This variance is called error because it influences test results. Professionals need to know that all tests contain error and that a single test score may not accurately reflect the student's **true score**. Salvia and Ysseldyke (1988a) stated, "A true score is a hypothetical value that represents a person's score when the entire domain of items is assessed at all possible times, by all appropriate testers" (p. 369). The following basic formula should be remembered when interpreting scores:

true score The
student's actual
score.

Obtained score = True score + Error

Conversely,

Obtained score − True score = Error

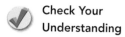

**Check Your
Understanding**

Check your ability to interpret the data presented in Table 4.1 by answering the questions in Activity 4.5 below.

Activity 4.5

Refer to your text, Table 4.1 to answer the following questions.

1. What type of reliability is reported in Table 4.1?

2. Look at the reliability reported for age 7. Using fall statistics, compare the reliability coefficient obtained on the Numeration subtest with the reliability coefficient obtained on the Estimation subtest. On which subtest did 7-year-olds perform with more consistency?

3. Compare the reliability coefficient obtained by 9-year-olds on the Estimation subtests with the reliability coefficient obtained by 7-year-olds on the same subtest. Which age group performed with more consistency or reliability?

Apply Your Knowledge

Explain why the reliability of an instrument may vary across age groups. _____

_____

_____

standard error of measurement The amount of error determined to exist using a specific instrument, calculated using the instrument's standard deviation and reliability.

obtained score The observed score of a student on a particular test on a given day.

True score is never actually known; therefore, a range of possible scores is calculated. The error is called the **standard error of measurement**, and an instrument with a large standard error of measurement would be less desirable than an instrument with a small standard error of measurement.

To estimate the amount of error present in an individual **obtained score**, the standard error of measurement must be obtained and applied to each score. The standard deviation and the reliability coefficient of the instrument are used to calculate the standard error of measurement. The following formula will enable the educator to determine the standard error of measurement when it has not been provided by the test developer in the test manual.

$$SEM = SD\sqrt{1-r}$$

where SEM = the standard error of measurement

SD = the standard deviation of the norm group of scores obtained during development of the instrument

r = the reliability coefficient

Figure 4.5 uses this formula to calculate the standard error of measurement for an instrument with a given standard deviation of 3 and a reliability coefficient of .78. The manual for this test would probably report the SEM as 1.4. Knowing the SEM allows the teacher to calculate a range of scores for a particular student, thus providing a better estimate of the student's true ability. Using the SEM of 1.4, the teacher adds and subtracts 1.4 to the obtained score. If the obtained score is 9 (mean = 10), the teacher adds and subtracts the SEM to the obtained score of 9:

$$9 + 1.4 = 10.4$$

$$9 - 1.4 = 7.6$$

The range of possible true scores for this student is 7.6 to 10.4.

Figure 4.5   Calculating the standard error of measurement (SEM) for an instrument with a standard deviation of 3.

$$SEM = 3\sqrt{1 - .78}$$
$$SEM = 3\sqrt{.22}$$
$$SEM = 3 \times .4690415$$
$$SEM = 1.4071245$$

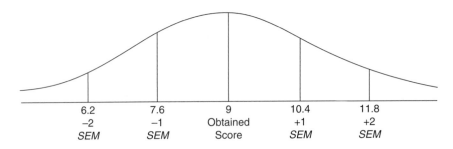

6.2	7.6	9	10.4	11.8
−2	−1	Obtained	+1	+2
SEM	*SEM*	Score	*SEM*	*SEM*

Thought to represent a range of deviations from an individual's obtained score, the standard error of measurement is based on the normal distribution theory. In other words, by using the standard error of measurement, one can determine the typical deviation for an individual's obtained score as if that person had been administered the same test an infinite number of times. When plotted, the scores form a bell curve, or a normal distribution, with the obtained score representing the mean, median, and mode. As with normal distributions, the range of ±1 standard error of measurement of the obtained score will occur approximately 68% of the times that the student takes the test. This is known as a **confidence interval** because the score obtained within that range can be thought to represent the true score with 68% accuracy. In the previous example, for instance, the student would score between 7.6 and 10.4 about 68% of the time.

If the teacher wanted 95% confidence that the true score was contained within a range, the band would be extended to ±2 standard errors of measurement of the obtained score. For the example, the extended range would be 6.2 to 11.8. The teacher can assume, with 95% confidence, that the student's true score is within this range.

As seen in Activity 4.6, a test with better reliability will have less error. The best tests for educational use are those with high reliability and a smaller standard error of measurement.

confidence interval The range of scores for an obtained score determined by adding and subtracting standard error of measurement units.

Applying Standard Error of Measurement   Williams and Zimmerman (1984) stated that whereas test validity remains the most important consideration in test selection, using the standard error of measurement to judge the test's quality is more important than reliability.

Williams and Zimmerman pointed out that reliability is a group statistic easily influenced by the variability of the group on whom it was calculated.

Sabers, Feldt, and Reschly (1988) observed that some, perhaps many, testing practitioners fail to consider possible test error when interpreting test results of a student being evaluated for special education services. The range of error and the range of a student's

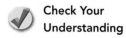
Check Your Understanding

Check your accuracy in calculating standard error of measurement by completing Activity 4.6 below.

Activity 4.6

Use the formula to determine the standard error of measurement with the given standard deviations and reliability coefficients.

$$SEM = SD \sqrt{1 - .r}$$

1. $SD = 5$ $.r = .67$ $SEM = $ _____
2. $SD = 15$ $.r = .82$ $SEM = $ _____
3. $SD = 7$ $.r = .73$ $SEM = $ _____
4. $SD = 7$ $.r = .98$ $SEM = $ _____
5. $SD = 15$ $.r = .98$ $SEM = $ _____

Notice the influence of the standard deviation and the reliability coefficient on the standard error of measurement. Compare the *SEMs* in problems 3 and 4, which have the same standard deviation but different reliability coefficients. Now compare the *SEMs* in problems 4 and 5, which have the same reliability coefficient but different standard deviations.

6. What happens to the standard error of measurement as the reliability increases? _____

7. What happens to the standard error of measurement as the standard deviation increases? _____

Apply Your Knowledge

How might a test with a large *SEM* result in an inaccurate evaluation of a student's abilities? _____

score may vary substantially, which may change the interpretation of the score for placement purposes.

In addition to knowing the standard error of measurement for an assessment instrument, it is important to know that the standard error of measurement will actually vary by age or grade level and by subtests. A test may contain less error for certain age or grade groupings than for other groupings. This information will be provided in the technical section of a good test manual.

Table 4.2 is from the *KeyMath—Revised* (Connolly, 1988) technical data section of the examiner's manual. The standard errors of measurement for the individual subtests are low and fairly consistent. There are some differences, however, in the standard errors of measurement on some subtests at different levels.

Table 4.2 Standard errors of measurement, by age, for scaled scores and standard scores from the fall and spring standardization programs.

Subtest/Composite	Program (Fall/Spring)	Age 5	6	7	8	9	10	11	12
1. Numeration	F	1.3	1.2	1.0	1.0	1.1	1.1	1.2	1.1
	S	1.7	1.1	1.0	1.0	1.0	1.2	1.1	1.0
2. Rational Numbers	F	—	—	—	—	1.2	1.0	1.0	1.0
	S	—	—	—	1.1	1.3	1.1	1.0	0.8
3. Geometry	F	1.5	1.3	1.4	1.4	1.2	1.2	1.3	1.1
	S	1.2	1.2	1.3	1.3	1.4	1.3	1.3	1.1
4. Addition	F	1.6	1.4	1.4	1.3	1.4	1.7	1.5	1.3
	S	1.8	1.4	1.3	1.4	1.4	1.5	1.3	1.3
5. Subtraction	F	—	1.6	1.5	1.3	1.1	1.1	1.5	1.3
	S	—	1.5	1.3	1.3	1.0	1.1	1.0	1.1
6. Multiplication	F	—	—	—	1.4	1.2	0.9	1.2	1.4
	S	—	—	—	1.0	1.1	1.2	1.1	1.1
7. Division	F	—	—	1.8	1.9	1.6	1.1	1.2	1.0
	S	—	—	2.0	1.6	1.4	1.2	1.1	1.0
8. Mental Computation	F	—	—	—	1.4	1.2	1.1	1.2	1.0
	S	—	—	1.7	1.3	1.2	1.1	1.1	0.9
9. Measurement	F	1.3	1.1	1.5	1.3	1.3	1.2	1.1	1.1
	S	1.2	1.1	1.2	1.1	1.1	1.3	1.1	0.9
10. Time and Money	F	—	1.6	1.3	1.1	1.0	1.0	1.0	1.0
	S	—	1.5	1.2	1.0	0.9	1.0	0.9	0.9
11. Estimation	F	—	1.7	1.8	1.4	1.3	1.3	1.2	1.0
	S	—	1.7	1.7	1.3	1.3	1.2	1.2	1.0
12. Interpreting Data	F	—	—	1.4	1.3	1.1	1.1	1.1	1.1
	S	—	—	1.3	1.2	1.1	1.1	1.1	1.0
13. Problem Solving	F	—	—	1.8	1.6	1.3	1.1	1.2	0.9
	S	—	—	1.6	1.4	1.2	1.1	1.1	0.9
14. Basic Concepts Area	F	5.8	5.3	4.8	4.7	4.0	3.7	3.9	3.3
	S	5.5	4.8	4.8	4.0	4.2	3.9	3.7	3.0
15. Operations Area	F	7.7	5.0	4.8	4.0	3.5	3.0	3.7	3.1
	S	7.1	5.0	4.3	3.5	3.2	3.3	2.9	2.7
16. Applications Area	F	5.8	4.1	4.3	3.6	3.1	2.8	3.0	2.6
	S	5.3	4.4	3.9	3.0	2.9	2.9	2.7	2.3
TOTAL TEST	F	4.1	3.0	2.9	2.5	2.2	1.9	2.2	1.8
	S	3.8	3.0	2.7	2.1	2.1	2.0	1.8	1.6

Source: From *KeyMath—Revised: A Diagnostic Inventory of Essential Mathematics, Manual. Forms A and B* (p. 72) by A. Connolly, 1988, Circle Pines, MN: American Guidance Service. Copyright 1988 by American Guidance Service. Reprinted by permission.

Consider the standard error of measurement for the Division subtest at ages 7 and 12 in the spring (S row). The standard error of measurement for age 7 is 2.0, but for age 12 it is 1.0. The larger standard error of measurement reported for age 7 is probably due to variation in the performance of students who may or may not have been introduced to division as part of the school curriculum. Most 12-year-olds, on the other hand, have probably practiced division in class for several years, and the sample of students tested may have performed with more consistency during the test development.

Given the two standard errors of measurement for the Division subtest at these ages, if a 7-year-old obtained a scaled score (a type of standard score) of 9 on this test ($x = 10$), the examiner could determine with 68% confidence that the true score lies between 7 and 11 and with 95% confidence that the true score lies between 5 and 13. The same scaled score obtained by a 12-year-old would range between 8 and 10 for a 68% confidence interval and between 7 and 11 for 95% confidence. This smaller range of scores is due to less error at this age on this particular subtest.

Consideration of SEMs when interpreting scores for students who are referred for a special education evaluation is even more important because a student's scores on various assessments are often compared with each other to determine if significant weaknesses exist. Standard 2.3 of the *Standards for Educational and*

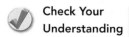

Check Your Understanding

Check your ability to use a SEM table to interpret test performance by completing Activity 4.7 below.

Activity 4.7

Use Table 4.2 to locate the standard error of measurement for the following situations.

1. The standard error of measurement for a 7-year-old who was administered the Problem Solving subtest in the fall is?_____

2. A 12-year-old's standard error of measurement for Problem-Solving if the test was administered in the fall is?_____

3. Using the standard error of measurement found in problems 1 and 2, calculate the ranges for each age level if the obtained scores were both 7. Calculate the ranges for both 68% and 95% confidence intervals._____

Apply Your Knowledge

When comparing the concepts of a normal distribution and the SEM, the SEM units are distributed around the _____ and the standard deviation units are evenly distributed around the _____.

Psychological Testing addresses the importance of considering SEMs when comparing scores:

> When test interpretation emphasizes differences between two observed scores of an individual or two averages of a group, reliability data, including standard errors, should be provided for such differences (1999, p. 32).

This is important because the differences found for one individual on two different measures may not be significant differences when the SEMs are applied. For example, historically students have been found eligible for special education services for specific learning disabilities because there were significant differences between an obtained IQ score and an academic achievement score. Look at the example below for Leonardo:

IQ score: 103

Reading Achievement Score: 88

The difference between these two scores is 15. In some school systems, the difference of 15 points may be considered significant and Leonardo could be found eligible for services for a learning disability. However, look at the range of scores when the SEMs are applied:

IQ score: 103; SEM 3 Range of Scores: 100–106

Reading Achievement Score: 88; SEM 7 Range of Scores: 81–95

In this example, basing a decision on the performance of this student on these two tests cannot be conclusive because the differences, when considering the range of scores, may not be significant. The student's true scores may actually be 100 on the IQ test and 95 on the Reading Achievement test, or a difference of only 5 points. This would indicate additional data would be needed to determine if the student required special education support. In practice, however, SEMs may not be considered when making decisions for eligibility. When the SEMs are not considered, the student may not receive accurate evaluation.

ESTIMATED TRUE SCORES

estimated true score A method of calculating the amount of error correlated with the distance of the score from the mean of the group.

Another method for approximating a student's true score is called the **estimated true score**. This calculation is founded in theory and research that the farther from a test mean a particular student's score is, the greater the chance for error within the obtained score. Chance errors are correlated with obtained scores (Salvia & Ysseldyke, 1988b). This means that as the score increases away from the mean, the chance for error increases. As scores regress toward the mean, the chance for error decreases. Therefore, if all the obtained scores are plotted on a distribution and all the values

Figure 4.6   Comparison of obtained and true scores.

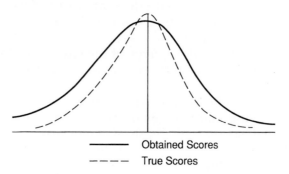

————— Obtained Scores

– – – – True Scores

of error are plotted on a distribution, the comparison would appear like that in Figure 4.6. Note that the true scores are located closer to the mean with less spread, or variability. The formula for estimated true score (Nunnally, 1967, p. 220) is

Estimated true score $= M + r(X - M)$

where M = mean of group of which person is a member
r = reliability coefficient
X = obtained score

This formula enables the examiner to estimate a possible true score. Because of the correlation of error with obtained scores, the true score is always assumed to be nearer to the mean than the obtained score. Therefore, if the obtained score is 120 (mean = 100), the estimated true score will be less than 120. Conversely, if the obtained score is 65, the true score will be greater than 65.

Using the formula for estimated true score, the calculation for an obtained score of 115 with an r of .78 and a mean of 100 would be as follows:

Estimated true score $= 100 + .78(115 - 100)$

$= 100 + .78(15)$

$= 100 + .11.7$

$= 111.7$

In this example, 111.7 is closer to the mean of 100 than 115.

Following is an example where the obtained score is less than the estimated true score:

Obtained score $= 64$, Mean $= 100$, $r = .74$

Estimated true score $= 100 + .74(64 - 100)$

$= 100 + .74(-36)$

$= 100 - 26.64$

$= 73.36$

The estimated true score can then be used to establish a range of scores by using the standard error of measurement for the estimated true score. Assume that the standard error of measurement for the estimated true score of 111.7 is 4.5. The range of scores ±1 standard error of measurement for 111.7 would be 107.2 to 116.2 for 68% confidence and 102.7 to 120.7 for 95% confidence.

The use of estimated true scores to calculate bands of confidence using standard error of measurement rather than using obtained scores has received some attention in the literature (Cahan, 1989; Feldt, Sabers, & Reschly, 1988; Sabers et al., 1988; Salvia & Ysseldyke, 1988a, 1988b). Whether using estimated true scores to calculate the range of possible scores or obtained scores to calculate the range of scores, several important points must be remembered. All test scores contain error. Error must be considered when interpreting test scores. The best practice, whether using estimated true scores or obtained scores, will employ the use of age- or grade-appropriate reliability coefficients and standard errors of measurement for the tests or subtests in question. When the norming process provides comparisons based on demographic variables, it is best to use the appropriate normative comparison.

TEST VALIDITY

To review, reliability refers to the dependability of the assessment instrument. The questions of concern for reliability are (a) Will students obtain similar scores if given the test a second time? (b) If the test is halved, will the administration of each half result in similar scores for the same student? (c) If different forms are available, will the administration of each form yield similar scores for the same student? (d) Will the administration of each item reliably measure the same trait or skill for the same student?

validity The quality of a test; the degree to which an instrument measures what it was designed to measure.

Validity is concerned not with repeated dependable results, but rather with the degree of good results for the purpose of the test. In other words, does the test actually measure what it is supposed to measure? If the educator wants to assess multiplication skills, will the test provide the educator with a valid indication of the student's math ability? Several methods can be used to determine the degree to which the instrument measures what the test developers intended the test to measure. Some methods are better than others, and some of the methods are more easily understood. When selecting assessment instruments, the educator should carefully consider the validity information.

CRITERION-RELATED VALIDITY

criterion-related validity Statistical method of comparing an instrument's ability to measure a skill, trait, or domain with an existing instrument or other criterion.

Criterion-related validity is a method for determining the validity of an instrument by comparing its scores with other criteria known to be indicators of the same trait or skill that the test developer wishes to measure. The test is compared with another criterion. The two main types of criterion-related validity are differentiated by time factors.

concurrent validity A comparison of one instrument with another within a short period of time.

Concurrent Validity **Concurrent validity** studies are conducted within a small time frame. The instrument in question is administered, and shortly thereafter an additional device is used, typically a similar test. Because the data are collected within a short time period, often the same day, this type of validity study is called concurrent validity. The data from both devices are correlated to see whether the instrument in question has significant concurrent criterion-related validity. The correlation coefficient obtained is called the *validity coefficient*. As with reliability coefficients, the nearer the coefficient is to ±1.00, the greater the strength of the relationship. Therefore, when the students in the sample obtain similar scores on both instruments, the instrument in question is said to be measuring the same trait or a degree or component of the same trait with some accuracy.

Suppose the newly developed Best in the World Math Test was administered to a sample of students, and shortly thereafter the Good Old Terrific Math Test was administered to the same sample. The validity coefficient obtained was .83. The educator selecting the Best in the World Math Test would have some confidence that it would measure, to some degree, the same traits or skills measured by the Good Old Terrific Math Test. Such studies are helpful in determining whether new tests and revised tests are measuring with some degree of accuracy the same skills as those measured by older, more researched instruments. Studies may compare other criteria as well, such as teacher ratings or motor performance of a like task. As expected, when comparing unlike instruments or criteria, these would probably not correlate highly. A test measuring creativity would probably not have a high validity coefficient with an advanced algebra test, but the algebra test would probably correlate better with a test measuring advanced trigonometry.

predictive validity A measure of how well an instrument can predict performance on some other variable.

Predictive Validity **Predictive validity** is a measure of a specific instrument's ability to predict performance on some other measure or criterion at a later date.

Common examples of tests that predict a student's ability are a screening test to predict success in first grade, a Scholastic Aptitude Test (SAT) to predict success in college, a Graduate Record Exam (GRE) to predict success in graduate school, and an academic potential or academic aptitude test to predict success in school. Much of psychoeducational assessment conducted in schools concerns using test results to predict future success or failure in a particular educational setting. Therefore, when this type of testing is carried out, it is important that the educator selects an instrument with good predictive validity research. Using a test to predict which students should enroll in basic math and which should enroll in advanced algebra will not be in the students' best interests if the predictive validity of the instrument is poor.

CONTENT VALIDITY

content validity
Occurs when the items contained within the test are representative of the content purported to be measured.

Professionals may assume that instruments reflecting a particular content in the name of the test or subtest have **content validity**. In many cases, this is not true. For example, on the Wide Range Achievement Test—Revision 3 (Wilkinson, 1993), the subtest Reading does not actually measure reading ability. It measures only one aspect of reading: word recognition. A teacher might use the score obtained on the subtest to place a student, believing that the student will be able to comprehend reading material at a particular level. In fact, the student may be able to recognize only a few words from that reading level. This subtest has inadequate content validity for measuring overall reading ability.

For a test to have good content validity, it must contain the content in a representative fashion. For example, a math achievement test that has only 10 addition and subtraction problems and no other math operations has not adequately represented the content of the domain of math. A good representation of content will include several items from each domain, level, and skill being measured.

Some of the variables of content validity may influence the manner in which results are obtained and can contribute to bias in testing. These variables may conflict with the nondiscriminatory test practice regulations of IDEA and the APA *Standards* (1985). These variables include **presentation format** and **response mode**.

presentation format The method by which items of an instrument are presented to a student.

response mode The method required for the examinee to answer items of an instrument.

1. *Presentation format.* Are the items presented in the best manner to assess the skill or trait? Requiring a student to silently read math problems and supply a verbal response could result in test bias if the student is unable to read at the level presented. The content being assessed may be math applications or reasoning, but the reading required to complete the task has reduced the instrument's ability to assess math skills for this particular student. Therefore, the content validity has been threatened, and the results obtained may unduly discriminate against the student.

2. *Response mode.* Like presentation format, the response mode may interfere with the test's ability to assess skills that are unrelated to the response mode. If the test was

designed to assess reading ability but required the student to respond in writing, the test would discriminate against a student who had a motor impairment that made writing difficult or impossible. Unless the response mode is adapted, the targeted skill—reading ability—will not be fairly or adequately measured.

Content validity is a primary concern in the development of new instruments. The test developers may adjust, omit, or add items during the field-testing stage. These changes are incorporated into a developmental version of the test that is administered to samples of students.

CONSTRUCT VALIDITY

construct validity
The ability of an instrument to measure psychological constructs.

Establishing **construct validity** for a new instrument may be more difficult than establishing content validity. *Construct*, in psychoeducational assessment, is a term used to describe a psychological trait, personality trait, psychological concept, attribute, or theoretical characteristic. To establish construct validity, the construct must be clearly defined. Constructs are usually abstract concepts, such as intelligence and creativity, that can be observed and measured by some type of instrument. Construct validity may be more difficult to measure than content because constructs are hypothetical and even seem invisible. Creativity is not seen, but the products of that trait may be observed, such as in writing or painting.

In establishing the construct validity of an instrument, the validity study may involve another measure that has been researched previously and has been shown to be a good indicator of the construct or of some degree or component of the construct. This is, of course, comparing the instrument to some other criterion, which is criterion-related validity. (Don't get confused!) Often in test development, the validity studies may involve several types of criterion-related validity to establish different types of validity. Anastasi (1988) listed the following types of studies that are considered when establishing a test's construct validity:

1. *Developmental changes.* Instruments that measure traits that are expected to change with development should have these changes reflected in the scores if the changeable trait is being measured (such as academic achievement).

2. *Correlations with other tests.* New tests are compared with existing instruments that have been found valid for the construct being measured.

3. *Factor analysis.* This statistical method determines how much particular test items cluster, which illustrates measurement of like constructs.

4. *Internal consistency.* Statistical methods can determine the degree with which individual items appear to be measuring the same constructs in the same manner or direction.

5. *Convergent and discriminant validation.* Tests should correlate highly with other instruments measuring the same construct but should not correlate with instruments measuring very different constructs.

6. *Experimental interventions.* Tests designed to measure traits, skills, or constructs that can be influenced by interventions (such as teaching) should have the intervention reflected by changes in pretest and posttest scores. (pp. 153–159)

Table 4.3 illustrates how construct validity is applied.

VALIDITY OF TESTS VERSUS VALIDITY OF TEST USE

Professionals in special education and in the judicial system have understood for quite some time that test validity and **validity of test use** for a particular instrument are two separate issues (Cole, 1981). Tests may be used inappropriately even though

validity of test use The appropriate use of a specific instrument.

Table 4.3   The Gray Oral Reading Tests. Applying construct validity to a reading instrument.

1. Because reading ability is developmental in nature, performance on the GORT-4 should be strongly correlated to chronological age.

2. Because the GORT-4 subtests measure various aspects of oral reading ability, they should correlate with each other.

3. Because reading is a type of language, the GORT-4 should correlate significantly with spoken language abilities.

4. Because reading is the receptive form of written language, the GORT-4 should correlate with tests that measure expressive written language.

5. Because reading is a cognitive ability, the GORT-4 should correlate with measures of intelligence or aptitude.

6. Because the GORT-4 measures reading, it should correlate with measures of automatized naming.

7. Because the GORT-4 measures reading, the results should differentiate between groups of people known to be average and those known to be low average or below average in reading ability.

8. Because the GORT-4 measures reading, changes in scores should occur over time due to reading instruction.

9. Because the items of a particular subtest measure similar traits, the items of each subtest should be highly correlated with the total score of that subtest.

Source: From *Gray Oral Reading Tests—4: Examiner's Manual.* By J. L. Wiederholt & B. R. Bryant, 2001. Copyright: Pro-Ed., Austin, Texas. Reprinted with permission.

they are valid instruments (Cole, 1981). The results obtained in testing may also be used in an invalid manner by placing children inappropriately or inaccurately predicting educational futures (Heller, Holtzman, & Messick, 1982).

Some validity-related issues contribute to bias in the assessment process and subsequently to the invalid use of the test instruments. Content, even though it may validly represent the domain of skills or traits being assessed, may discriminate against different groups. *Item bias*, a term used when an item is answered incorrectly a disproportionate number of times by one group compared to another group, may exist even though the test appears to represent the content domain. An examiner who continues to use an instrument found to contain bias may be practicing discriminatory assessment, which is failure to comply with IDEA.

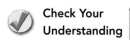

Check Your Understanding

Check your ability to understand the concepts of reliability and validity applied to actual research data on a specific achievement test by completing Activity 4.8 below.

Activity 4.8

The Best Achievement Test ever was recently completed and is now on sale. You are trying to determine if the test would be appropriate for elementary age students. The tables below are samples of what is provided in the test manual. Review the tables and answer the questions below.

Grade	Standard Error of Measurement	Test-Retest Score Reliability	Concurrent Criterion-Related Validity	Split-Half Reliability Coefficients
Grade K	6.27	.71	.65	.67
Grade 1	5.276	.79	.83	.75
Grade 2	4.98	.80	.82	.80
Grade 3	4.82	.81	.84	.81
Grade 4	4.80	.80	.83	.82
Grade 5	4.82	.81	.82	.83

1. Based on this information, in which grades would you feel that the test would yield more reliable results? Why? _____

2. Would you consider purchasing this instrument? _____

3. Explain how the concurrent criterion-related validity would have been determined? _____

_____

Predictive validity may contribute to test bias by predicting accurately for one group and not another. Educators should select and administer instruments only after careful study of the reliability and validity research contained in test manuals.

RELIABILITY VERSUS VALIDITY

A test may be reliable; that is, it may measure a trait with about the same degree of accuracy time after time. The reliability does not guarantee that the trait is measured in a valid or accurate manner. A test may be consistent and reliable but not valid. It is important that a test has had thorough research studies in both reliability and validity.

THINK AHEAD

The concepts presented in this chapter will be applied in the remaining chapters of the text. How do you think these concepts help professionals evaluate instruments?

EXERCISES

Part I

Match the following terms with the correct definitions.

a. reliability
b. validity
c. internal consistency
d. correlation coefficient
e. coefficient alpha
f. scattergram
g. estimated true score
h. Pearson's r
i. interrater reliability
j. test-retest reliability
k. equivalent forms reliability

l. true score
m. predictive validity
n. criterion-related validity
o. positive correlation
p. K–R 20
q. validity of test use
r. negative correlation
s. confidence interval
t. split-half reliability
u. standard error of measurement

_____ 1. A new academic achievement test assesses elementary-age students' math ability. The test developers found, however, that students in the research group who took the test two times had scores that were quite different upon the second test administration, which was conducted 2 weeks after the initial administration. It was determined that the test did not have acceptable _____.

_____ 2. A new test was designed to measure the self-concept of students at middle-school age. The test required students to use essay-type responses to answer three questions regarding their feelings about their own self-concept. Two assessment professionals were comparing the students' responses and how these responses were scored by the professionals. On this type of instrument, it is important that the _____ is acceptable.

_____ 3. In studying the relationship between the scores of the administration of one test administration with the second administration of the test, the number .89 represents the _____.

_____ 4. One would expect that the number of classes a college student attends in a specific course and the final exam grade in that course would have a _____.

_____ 5. In order to have a better understanding of a student's true abilities, the concept of _____ must be understood and applied to obtained scores.

_____ 6. The number of times a student moves during elementary school may likely have a _____ to the student's achievement scores in elementary school.

_____ 7. A test instrument may have good reliability; however, that does not guarantee that the test has _____.

_____ 8. On a teacher-made test of math, the following items were included: two single-digit addition problems, one single-digit subtraction problem, four problems of multiplication of fractions, and one problem of converting decimals to fractions. This test does not appear to have good _____.

_____ 9. A college student failed the first test of the new semester. The student hoped that the first test did not have strong _____ about performance on the final exam.

_____ 10. No matter how many times a student may be tested, the student's _____ may never be determined.

Part II

Complete the following sentences and solve the problem.

1. The score obtained during the assessment of a student may not be the score, because all testing situations are subject to chance _____.

2. A closer estimation of the student's best performance can be calculated by using the _____ score.

3. A range of possible scores can then be determined by using the _____ for the specific test.

4. The smaller the standard error of measurement, the more _____ the test.

5. When calculating the range of possible scores, it is best to use the appropriate standard error of measurement for the student's _____ provided in the test manual.

6. The larger the standard error of measurement, the less _____ the test.

7. Use the following set of data to determine the mean, median, mode, range, variance, standard deviation, standard error of measurement, and possible range for each score assuming 68% confidence. The reliability coefficient is .85.

Data: 50, 75, 31, 77, 65, 81, 90, 92, 76, 74, 88

Mean: _____   Median: _____   Mode: _____

Range: _____   Variance: _____   Standard deviation: _____

Standard error of measurement: _____

Obtained Score: **Range of True Scores:**

  a. 50   From ____ to ____

  b. 75   From ____ to ____

  c. 31   From ____ to ____

  d. 77   From ____ to ____

  e. 65   From ____ to ____

  f. 81   From ____ to ____

  g. 90   From ____ to ____

  h. 92   From ____ to ____

  i. 76   From ____ to ____

  j. 74   From ____ to ____

  k. 88   From ____ to ____

Companion
Website

Answers to these questions can be found in the Appendix of this text or you may also complete these questions and receive immediate feedback on your answers by going to the Think Ahead module in Chapter 4 of the Companion Website.

An Introduction to Norm-Referenced Assessment

KEY TERMS

domain   chronological age
item pool   test manual
developmental version   protocol
field test   raw score
norm-referenced test   basal
sample   ceiling
norm group   accommodations
interpolation   assistive technology

CHAPTER FOCUS

This chapter presents the basic mechanics of test design and test administration that the examiner needs to know before administering norm-referenced tests. Following a description of test construction, various techniques for completing test protocols and administering instruments are explained. Both individual norm-referenced testing and statewide high-stakes accountability assessment are discussed.

Norm-referenced assessment is the method that compares a student with the age or grade-level expectancies of a norm group. It is the standard method used in placement and classification decisions. The degree or amount of deviance from the expected norm is an important factor in determining whether a student meets the eligibility requirements necessary to receive special education services (Shapiro, 1996).

CEC KNOWLEDGE AND SKILLS STANDARDS

The student completing this chapter will understand the knowledge and skills included in the following CEC Knowledge and Skills Standards from Standard 8: Assessment:

CC8K1—Basic terminology used in assessment

CC8K4—Use and limitations of assessment instruments

CC8K5—National, state, or provincial, and local accommodations and modifications

CC8S9—Develop or modify individual assessment strategies

CC8S5—Interpret information from formal and informal assessments

GC8S3—Select, adapt, and modify assessments to accommodate the unique abilities and needs of individual with disabilities

GC8S4—Assess reliable methods of response of individuals who lack typical communication and performance

HOW NORM-REFERENCED TESTS ARE CONSTRUCTED

domain An area of cognitive development or ability thought to be evidenced by certain behaviors or skills.

item pool A large collection of test items thought to effectively represent a particular domain or content area.

developmental version The experimental edition of a test that is field-tested and revised before publication.

field test The procedure of trying out a test by administering it to a sample population.

norm-referenced test A test designed to yield average performance scores, which may be used for comparing individual student performances.

sample A small group of people thought to represent the population for whom the test was designed.

norm group A large number of people who are administered a test to establish comparative data of average performances.

Test developers who wish to develop an instrument to assess an educational **domain**, behavioral trait, cognitive ability, motor ability, or language ability, to name a few areas, will establish an item pool of test items. An **item pool** is a representation of items believed to thoroughly assess the given area. The items are gathered from several sources. For example, developers may use published educational materials, information from educational experts in the field, published curriculum guides, and information from educational research to collect items for the initial item pool for an educational domain. These items are carefully scrutinized for appropriateness, wording, content, mode of response required, and developmental level. The items are sequentially arranged according to difficulty. The developers consult with professionals with expertise in the test's content area and, after thorough analysis of the items, administer a **developmental version** to a small group as a **field test**. During the field-testing stage, the test is administered by professionals in the appropriate discipline (education, psychology, speech-language, etc.). The professionals involved in the study critique the test items, presentation format, response mode requirements, administration procedures, and the actual test materials. At this time, revisions may be made, and the developmental version is then ready to be administered to a large sample of the population for whom it was designed. The steps of test construction are illustrated in Figure 5.1.

A **norm-referenced test** is designed to provide the teacher with the capability of comparing the performance of one student with the average performance of other students in the country who are of the same age or grade level. Since it is not practical or possible to test every student of that same age or grade level, a **sample** of students is selected as the comparison group, or **norm group**. In the norming process, the test is administered to a representative sample of students from across the country. A good representation will include a large number of students, usually a few thousand students, who represent diverse groups. Ideally, samples of students from all cultures and linguistic backgrounds who represent the diverse students for whom the test was developed will be included in the norming process. The norming process should also include students with various disabilities.

The development of a norm-referenced test and the establishment of comparison performances usually occur in the following manner. The items of the test, which are sequentially arranged in the order of difficulty, are administered to the sample population. The performance of each age group and each grade group is analyzed. The average performance of the 6-year-olds, 7-year-olds,

Figure 5.1 Steps in test development.

1. Domain, theoretical basis of test defined. This includes support for construct as well as defining what the domain is not.
2. Exploration of item pool. Experts in the field and other sources of possible items are used to begin collecting items.
3. Developmental version of test or subtests.
4. Field-based research using developmental version of test or subtests.
5. Research on developmental versions analyzed.
6. Changes made to developmental versions based on results of analyses.
7. Standardization version prepared.
8. Sampling procedures to establish how and where persons in sample will be recruited.
9. Testing coordinators located at relevant testing sites representing preferred norm sample.
10. Standardization research begins. Tests are administered at testing sites.
11. Data collected and returned to test developer.
12. Data analyzed for establishing norms, reliability, validity.
13. Test prepared for final version, packaging, protocols, manual.
14. Test available for purchase.

8-year-olds, and so on is determined. The test results are analyzed by grade groups as well, determining the average performance of first graders, second graders, and so on. The analysis of the test results might resemble Table 5.1.

The average number correct in Table 5.1 represents the arithmetic average number of items successfully answered by the age or grade group of students who made up the norming sample. Because these figures will later be used to compare other students' performances on the same instrument, it is imperative that the sample of students be representative of the students who will later be assessed. Comparing a student to a norm sample of students who are very different from the student will not be an objective or fair comparison. Factors such as socioeconomic, cultural, or linguistic background; existing disabilities; and emotional environment are variables that may influence a student's performance. The student should be compared with other students with similar backgrounds and of the same age or grade level.

The data displayed in Table 5.1 illustrate the mean performance of students in a particular age or grade group. Although the data represent an average score for each age or grade group, test developers often analyze the data further. For example, the average

Table 5.1   Analysis of results from the Absolutely Wonderful Academic Achievement Test.

Grade	Average Number of Items Correct	Age	Average Number of Items Correct
K	11	5	9
1	14	6	13
2	20	7	21
3	28	8	27
4	38	9	40
5	51	10	49
6	65	11	65
7	78	12	79
8	87	13	88
9	98	14	97
10	112	15	111
11	129	16	130
12	135	17	137

performance of typical students at various times throughout the school year may be determined. To provide this information, the most accurate norming process would include nine additional administrations of the test, one for each month of the school year. This is usually not practical or possible in most instances of test development. Therefore, to obtain an average expected score for each month of the school year, the test developer usually calculates the scores using data obtained in the original administration through a process known as **interpolation**, or further dividing the existing data (Anastasi & Urbina, 1998).

Suppose that the test developer of the Absolutely Wonderful Academic Achievement Test actually administered the test to the sample group during the middle of the school year. To determine the average performance of students throughout the school year, from the first month of the school year through the last month, the test developer further divides the correct items of each group. In the data in Table 5.1, the average performance of second graders in the sample group is 20, the average performance of third graders is 28, and the average performance of fourth graders is 38. These scores might be further divided and listed in the test manual on a table similar to Table 5.2.

The obtained scores also might be further divided by age groups so that each month of a **chronological age** is represented. The scores for age 11 might be displayed in a table similar to Table 5.3.

It is important to notice that age scores are written with a dash or hyphen, whereas grade scores are expressed with a decimal.

interpolation The process of dividing existing data into smaller units for establishing tables of developmental scores.

chronological age The numerical representation of a student's age, expressed in years, months, and days.

Table 5.2   Interpolated grade equivalents for corresponding raw scores.

Number of Items Correct	Grade
17	2.0
17	2.1
18	2.2
18	2.3
19	2.4
20	2.5
20	2.6
21	2.7
22	2.8
23	2.9
24	3.0
25	3.1
26	3.2
27	3.3
27	3.4
28	3.5
29	3.6
30	3.7
31	3.8
32	3.9
33	4.0
34	4.1
35	4.2
36	4.3
37	4.4
38	4.5
39	4.6
40	4.7
42	4.8
43	4.9

Table 5.3   Interpolated age equivalents for corresponding raw scores.

Average Number of Items Correct	Age Equivalents
57	11–0
58	11–1
60	11–2
61	11–3
62	11–4
63	11–5
65	11–6
66	11–7
68	11–8
69	11–9
70	11–10
71	11–11
72	12–0

This is because grade scores are based on a 10-month school year and can be expressed by using decimals, whereas age scores are based on a 12-month calendar year and therefore should not be expressed using decimals. For example, 11–4 represents an age of 11 years and 4 months, but 11.4 represents the grade score of the 4th month of the 11th grade. If the scores are expressed incorrectly, a difference of about 6 grades or 5 years could be incorrectly interpreted.

BASIC STEPS IN TEST ADMINISTRATION

test manual
A manual that accompanies a test instrument and contains instructions for administration and norm tables.

When administering a norm-referenced standardized test, it is important to remember that the test developer specified the instructions for the examiner and the examinee. The **test manual** contains much information, which the examiner must read thoroughly and understand before administering the test. The examiner should practice administering all sections of the test many times before using the test with a student. The first few attempts of practice administration should be supervised by someone who has had experience with the instrument. Legally, according to IDEA, any individual test administration should be completed in the manner set forth by the test developer and should be administered by trained personnel. Both legal regulations and standards and codes of ethics hold testing personnel responsible for accurate and fair assessment.

protocol The response sheet or record form used by the examiner to record the student's answers.

The examiner should carefully carry out the mechanics of test administration. The first few steps are simple, although careless errors can occur and may make a difference in the decisions made regarding a student's educational future. The **protocol** of a standardized test is the form used during the test administration and for scoring and interpreting test results.

BEGINNING TESTING

The following suggestions will help you, the examiner, establish a positive testing environment and increase the probability that the student will feel comfortable and therefore perform better in the testing situation.

1. Establish familiarity with the student before the first day of testing. Several meetings in different situations with relaxed verbal exchange are recommended. You may wish to participate in an activity with the student and informally observe behavior and language skills.

2. When the student meets with you on test day, spend several minutes in friendly conversation before beginning the test. Do not begin testing until the student seems to feel at ease with you.

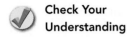

Check Your Understanding

Check your ability to use developmental score tables by completing Activity 5.1 below.

Activity 5.1

Refer to the tables in your text and answer the following questions.

1. In Table 5.1, what was the average score of the sample group of students in grade 7? _____

2. According to Table 5.1, what was the average number of correct items of the sample group of students who were 16 years of age? _____

3. What was the average number of correct items of the sample group of students who were 6 years of age? _____

4. Why did students who were in first grade have an average number of 14 correct responses while students in grade 6 had an average of 65 correct responses? _____

5. According to the information provided in Table 5.2, what was the average number of correct responses for students in the third month of grade 3? _____

6. Were students in the sample tested during the third month of the third grade? _____ By what means was the average for each month of the school year determined? _____

7. According to the information provided in Table 5.3, what was the average number of correct responses for students of the chronological age 11–2? _____

8. Write the meaning of these expressions:

    4.1 means _____
    4–1 means _____
    3.3 means _____
    6–7 means _____
    10.8 means _____

Apply Your Knowledge

Write an explanation for a parent that clarifies the difference between a grade-equivalent score and the grade level of academic functioning. _____
_____
_____

3. Explain why the testing has been suggested at the level of understanding that is appropriate for the student's age and developmental level. It is important that the student understand that the testing session is important, although the child should not feel threatened by the test. Examples of explanations include the following:

    • To see how you work (solve) math problems.
    • To see how we can help you achieve in school.

- To help you make better progress in school.
- [Or if the student has revealed specific weaknesses] To see how we can help you with your spelling [or English, or science, etc.] skills.

4. Give a brief introduction about the test, such as: "Today we will complete some activities that are like your other school work. There are some math problems and reading passages like you have in class," or, "This will help us learn how you think in school," or "This will show us the best ways for you to . . . (learn, read, work math problems)."

5. Begin testing in a calm manner. Be certain that all instructions are followed carefully.

During test administration, the student may ask questions or give answers that are very close to the correct response. On many tests, clear instructions are given that tell the examiner when to prompt for an answer or when to query for a response. Some items on certain tests may not be repeated. Some items are timed. The best guarantee for accurate assessment techniques is for the examiner to become very familiar with the test manual. General guidelines for test administration, suggested by McLoughlin and Lewis (2001), are presented in Figure 5.2.

Figure 5.2   General guidelines for test administration.

Test administration is a skill, and testers must learn how to react to typical student comments and questions. The following general guidelines apply to the majority of standardized tests.

STUDENT REQUESTS FOR REPETITION OF TEST ITEMS

Students often ask the tester to repeat a question. This is usually permissible as long as the item is repeated verbatim and in its entirety. However, repetition of memory items measuring the student's ability to recall information is not allowed.

ASKING STUDENTS TO REPEAT RESPONSES

Sometimes the tester must ask the student to repeat a response. Perhaps the tester did not hear what the student said, or the student's speech is difficult to understand. However, the tester should make every effort to see or hear the student's first answer. The student may refuse to repeat a response or, thinking that the request for repetition means the first response was unsatisfactory, answer differently.

STUDENT MODIFICATION OF RESPONSES

When students give one response, then change their minds and give a different one, the tester should accept the last response, even if the modification comes after the tester has moved to another item. However, some tests specify that only the first response may be accepted for scoring.

CONFIRMING AND CORRECTING STUDENT RESPONSES

The tester may not in any way—verbal or nonverbal—inform a student whether a response is correct. Correct responses may not be confirmed; wrong responses may not be corrected. This rule is critical for professionals who both teach and test, because their first inclination is to reinforce correct answers.

Figure 5.2   continued.

REINFORCING STUDENT WORK BEHAVIOR

Although testers cannot praise students for their performance on specific test items, good work behavior can and should be rewarded. Appropriate comments are "You're working hard" and "I like the way you're trying to answer every question." Students should be praised between test items or subtests to ensure that reinforcement is not linked to specific responses.

ENCOURAGING STUDENTS TO RESPOND

When students fail to respond to a test item, the tester can encourage them to give an answer. Students sometimes say nothing when presented with a difficult item, or they may comment, "I don't know" or "I can't do that one." The tester should repeat the item and say, "Give it a try" or "You can take a guess." The aim is to encourage the student to attempt all test items.

QUESTIONING STUDENTS

Questioning is permitted on many tests. If in the judgment of the tester the response given by the student is neither correct nor incorrect, the tester repeats the student's answer in a questioning tone and says, "Tell me more about that." This prompts the student to explain so that the response can be scored. However, clearly wrong answers should not be questioned.

COACHING

Coaching differs from encouragement and questioning in that it helps a student arrive at an answer. The tester must *never* coach the student. Coaching invalidates the student's response; test norms are based on the assumption that students will respond without examiner assistance. Testers must be very careful to avoid coaching.

ADMINISTRATION OF TIMED ITEMS

Some tests include timed items; the student must reply within a certain period to receive credit. In general, the time period begins when the tester finishes presentation of the item. A watch or clock should be used to time student performance.

Source: From *Assessing Special Students* (5th ed., p. 87 by J. McLoughlin and R. Lewis, 2001, Upper Saddle River, NJ: Merrill/Prentice Hall. Copyright by Prentice Hall. Reprinted by permission).

As stated in professional ethics and IDEA, tests must be given in the manner set forth by the test developer and adapting tests must be done by professionals with expertise in the specific area being assessed who are cognizant of the psychometric changes that will result.

CALCULATING CHRONOLOGICAL AGE

Many tests have protocols that provide space for calculating the student's chronological age on the day that the test is administered. It is imperative that this calculation is correct because the chronological age may be used to determine the correct norm tables used for interpreting the test results.

The chronological age is calculated by writing the test date first and then subtracting the date of birth. The dates are written in the

Figure 5.3   Calculation of chronological age for a student who is 8 years, 6 months old.

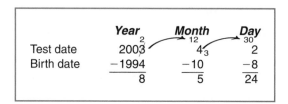

order of year, month, and day. In performing the calculation, remember that each of the columns represents a different numerical system, and if the number that is subtracted is larger than the number from which the difference is to be found, the numbers must be converted appropriately. This means that the years are based on 12 months and the months are based on 30 days. An example is shown in Figure 5.3.

Notice in Figure 5.3 that when subtracting the days, the number 30 is added to 2 to find the difference. When subtraction of days requires borrowing, a whole month, or 30 days, must be used. When borrowing to subtract months, the number 12 is added, because a whole year must be borrowed.

When determining the chronological age for testing, the days are rounded to the nearest month. Days are rounded up if there are 15 or more days by adding a month. The days are rounded down by dropping the days and using the month found through the subtraction process. Here are some examples:

	Years	Months	Days	
Chronological age:	7–	4–	17	rounded up to 7–5
Chronological age:	9–	10–	6	rounded down to 9–10
Chronological age:	11–	11–	15	rounded up to 12–0

Case Study for Determining Chronological Age

Mrs. Luke believed that Sandra was excelling in math ability and needed to be placed in a higher-level class. Mrs. Luke decided to administer a norm-referenced math test to find out how Sandra's math skills compared to a national sample. Once she had administered and scored the test, she discovered that the results were lower than she had expected. Mrs. Luke was confused because she knew that Sandra performed better than her grade peers. Mrs. Luke took another look at the test protocol and discovered these errors in her calculation. Can you identify the errors?

	Date of Test:	2005	6	15
	Date of Birth	1996	7	17
	Chronological Age	9	9	28

The correct chronological age should be

8 years   10 months   18 days

The incorrect calculation meant that Mrs. Luke compared Sandra with students who were nearly 10 years of age (9 years–10 months) when she should have compared Sandra with 8-year-old students. This error resulted in standard scores that placed Sandra in the low average range. When the error was corrected and Sandra was compared with the correct age group, her scores were within the high average range.

Check Your Understanding

Check your ability to calculate chronological age by completing Activity 5.2 below.

Activity 5.2

Calculate the chronological ages using the following birth dates and test dates.

			Year	**Month**	**Day**
1. Birth date:	3-2-1991	Date of test:	____	____	____
Test date:	5-4-2001	Date of birth:	____	____	____
		Chronological age:	____	____	____
2. Birth date:	7-5-1996	Date of test:	____	____	____
Test date:	11-22-2004	Date of birth:	____	____	____
		Chronological age:	____	____	____
3. Birth date:	10-31-1997	Date of test:	____	____	____
Test date:	06-20-2000	Date of birth:	____	____	____
		Chronological age:	____	____	____

Round the following chronological ages to years and months.

	Year	**Month**	**Day**	**Rounded to**
4.	7–	10–	23	____
5.	11–	7–	14	____
6.	14–	11–	29	____

Apply Your Knowledge

Why do you think it is so important to have the exact chronological age of a student before you administer and score a test? _____
_____
_____

Figure 5.4   Calculation for student who began with item 1 and correctly answered 8 of 15 attempted items.

1. __1__	11. __0__
2. __1__	12. __1__
3. __1__	13. __0__
4. __1__	14. __0__
5. __0__	15. __0__
6. __0__	16. _____
7. __1__	17. _____
8. __1__	18. _____
9. __0__	19. _____
10. __1__	20. _____

Raw Score: __8__

CALCULATING RAW SCORES

raw score The first score obtained in test administration; usually the number of items counted as correct.

The first score obtained in the administration of a test is the **raw score**. On most educational instruments, the raw score is simply the number of items the student answers correctly. Figure 5.4 shows the calculation of a raw score for one student. The student's correct responses are marked with a 1, incorrect responses with a 0. The number of items answered correctly on this test was 8, which is expressed as a raw score. The raw score will be entered into a table in the test manual to determine the derived scores, which are norm-referenced scores expressed in different ways. The administration of this test was stopped when the student missed three consecutive items because the test manual stated to stop testing when this occurred.

DETERMINING BASALS AND CEILINGS

The student whose scores are shown in Figure 5.4 began with item 1 and stopped after making three consecutive errors. The starting and stopping points of a test must be determined so that unnecessary items are not administered. Some tests contain hundreds of items, many of which may not be developmentally appropriate for all students.

Most educational tests contain starting rules in the manual, protocol, or actual test instrument. These rules are guides that can help the examiner begin testing with an item at the appropriate level. These guides may be given as age recommendations—for example, 6-year-olds begin with item 10—or as grade-level recommendations—for example, fourth-grade students begin with item 25. These starting points are meant to represent a level at which the student could answer all previous items correctly and are most accurate for students who are functioning close to age or grade expectancy.

Often, students referred for special education testing function below grade- and age-level expectancies. Therefore, the guides or starting points suggested by the test developers may be inappropriate. It is necessary to determine the **basal** level for the student, or the level at which the student could correctly answer all easier items, those items located at lower levels. Once the basal has been established, the examiner can proceed with testing the student. If the student fails to obtain a basal level, the test may be considered too difficult, and another instrument should be selected.

basal Thought to represent the level of skills below which the student would correctly answer all test items.

The rules for establishing a basal level are given in the test manuals, and many tests contain the information on the protocol. The basal rule may be the same as a ceiling rule, such as three consecutively correct responses and three consecutively incorrect responses. The basal rule may also be expressed as correctly completing an entire level. No matter what the rule, the objective is the same: to establish a level that is thought to represent a foundation and at which all easier items would be assumed correct.

The examples shown in Figure 5.5 illustrate a basal rule of three consecutive correct responses on Test I and a basal of all items answered correctly on an entire level of the test on Test II.

It may be difficult to select the correct item to begin with when testing a special education student. The student's social ability may seem to be age appropriate but academic ability may be significantly

Figure 5.5 Basal level established for test I for three consecutive correct responses; basal level for test II established when all items in one level (grade 1) are answered correctly.

TEST I		TEST II		
1.	_____	Level K	1.	_____
2.	_____		2.	_____
3.	_____		3.	_____
4.	_____		4.	_____
5.	_____	Grade 1	5.	___1___
6.	___1___		6.	___1___
7.	___1___		7.	___1___
8.	___1___		8.	___1___
9.	___0___			
10.	___1___	Grade 2	9.	___0___
			10.	___1___
			11.	___0___
			12.	___1___

below expectancy for the age and grade placement. The examiner may begin with an item that is too easy or too difficult. Although it is not desirable to administer too many items that are beneath the student's academic level, it is better to begin the testing session with the positive reinforcement of answering items correctly than with the negative reinforcement of answering several items incorrectly and experiencing a sense of failure or frustration. The examiner should obtain a basal by selecting an item believed to be a little below the student's academic level.

Even when the examiner chooses a starting item believed to be easy for a student, sometimes the student will miss items before the basal is established. In this case, most test manuals contain instructions for determining the basal. Some manuals instruct the examiner to test backward in the same sequence until a basal can be established. After the basal is determined, the examiner proceeds from the point where the backward sequence was begun. Other test manuals instruct the examiner to drop back an entire grade level or to drop back the number of items required to establish a basal. For example, if five consecutive correct responses are required for a basal, the examiner is instructed to drop back five items and begin administration. If the examiner is not familiar with the student's ability in a certain area, the basal may be even more difficult to establish. The examiner in this case may have to drop back several times. For this reason, the examiner should circle the number of the first item administered. This information can be used later in the test interpretation.

Students may establish two or more basals; that is, using the five-consecutive-correct rule, a student may answer five correct, miss an item, then answer five consecutive correct again. The test manual may address this specifically, or it may not be mentioned. Unless the test manual states that the examiner may use the second or highest basal, it is best to use the first basal established.

When calculating the raw score, all items that appear before the established basal are counted as correct. This is because the basal is thought to represent the level at which all easier items would be passed. Therefore, when counting correct responses, count items below the basal as correct even though they were not administered.

ceiling Thought to represent the level of skills above which all test items would be answered incorrectly; the examiner discontinues testing at this level.

Just as the basal is thought to represent the level at which all easier items would be passed, the **ceiling** is thought to represent the level at which more difficult items would not be passed. The ceiling rule may be three consecutive incorrect or even five items out of seven items answered incorrectly. Occasionally, an item is administered above the ceiling level by mistake, and the student may answer correctly. Because the ceiling level is thought to represent the level at which more difficult items would not be passed, these items usually are not counted. Unless the test manual states that the examiner is to count items above the ceiling, it is best not to do so.

USING INFORMATION ON PROTOCOLS

The protocol, or response form, for each test contains valuable information that can aid in test administration. Detailed instructions regarding the basal and ceiling rules for individual subtests of an educational test may be found on most protocols for educational tests.

Many tests have ceiling rules that are the same as the basal rules; for example, five consecutive incorrect responses are counted as the ceiling, and five consecutive correct responses establish the basal.

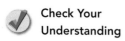

Check Your Understanding

Check your ability to calculate basals by completing Activity 5.3 below.

Activity 5.3

Using the following basal rules, identify basals for these students.

Test I (Basal: 5 consecutive correct)	**Test II** (Basal: 7 consecutive correct)	
1. _____	Grade 4	25. _____
2. _____		26. _____
3. _____		27. _____
4. _____		28. _____
5. _____		29. _____
6. __1__		30. _____
7. __1__	Grade 5	31. __1__
8. __1__		32. __1__
9. __1__		33. __1__
10. __1__		34. __1__
11. __0__		35. __1__
12. __1__	Grade 6	36. __1__
13. __0__		37. __1__
14. __1__		38. __0__
		39. __1__
		40. __0__

Basal items are:_____   Basal items are:_____

The instructions given in the test manual state that if a student fails to establish a basal with 5 consecutive correct items, the examiner must drop back 5 items from the first attempted item and begin testing. Which item would the examiner begin with in the following examples? _____

Example 1

22. _____
23. _____
24. _____
25. _____
26. _____
27. _____
28. _____
29. ___1___
30. ___0___
31. _____
32. _____

Drop to item: _____

Example 2

116. _____
117. _____
118. _____
119. _____
120. _____
121. ___1___
122. ___1___
123. ___0___
124. _____
125. _____
126. _____

Drop to item: _____

Apply Your Knowledge

What is the meaning of basal level, and how does it relate to a student's ability? _____

_____

_____

Since some tests have different basal and ceiling rules, it is necessary to read instructions carefully. If the protocol does not provide the basal and ceiling rules, the examiner is wise to note this at the top of the pages of the protocol for the sections to be administered.

The protocols for each test are arranged specifically for that test. Some forms contain several subtests that may be arranged in more than one order. On very lengthy tests, the manual may provide information about selecting only certain subtests rather than administering the entire test. Other tests have age- or grade-appropriate subtests, which must be selected according to the student's level. Some instruments use the raw score on the first subtest to determine the starting point on all other subtests. And finally, some subtests require the examiner to begin with item 1 regardless of the age or grade level of the student. Specific instructions for individual subtests may be provided on the protocol as well as in the test manual.

Educational tests often provide training exercises at the beginning of subtests. These training exercises help the examiner explain the task to the student and better ensure that the student understands the task before answering the first scored item. The student may be allowed to attempt the training tasks more than once, or the examiner may be instructed to correct wrong answers and explain the correct responses. These items are not scored, however, and a subtest may be skipped if the student does not understand the task. The use of training exercises varies.

ADMINISTERING TESTS: FOR BEST RESULTS

Students tend to respond more and perform better in testing situations with examiners who are familiar with them (Fuchs, Zern, & Fuchs, 1983). As suggested previously, the examiner should spend some time with the student before the actual evaluation. The student's regular classroom setting is a good place to begin. The examiner should talk with the student in a warm manner and repeat visits to the classroom before the evaluation. It may also be helpful for the student to visit the testing site to become familiar with the environment. The examiner may want to tell the student that they will work together later in the week or month. The testing session should not be the first time the examiner and student meet. Classroom observations and visits may aid the examiner in determining which tests to administer. Chances for successful testing sessions will increase if the student is not overtested. Although it is imperative that all areas of suspected disability be assessed, multiple tests that measure the same skill or ability are not necessary.

For **MORE PRACTICE** in the mechanics of determining chronological age, basals, ceilings, and raw scores, visit the Companion Website at *www.prenhall.com/overton.*

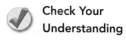

Check Your Understanding

Check your ability to calculate basal and ceiling scores by completing Activity 5.4 below.

Activity 5.4

Calculate the raw scores for the following protocol sections. Follow the given basal and ceiling rules.

Protocol 1	Protocol 2
(Basal: 5 consecutive correct; Ceiling: 5 consecutive incorrect)	**(Basal: 3 consecutive correct; Ceiling: 3 consecutive incorrect)**
223. _____	10. _____
224. _____	11. __1__
225. _____	12. __1__
226. _____	13. __1__
227. __1__	14. __1__
228. __1__	15. __1__
229. __1__	16. __1__
230. __1__	17. __1__
231. __1__	18. __1__
232. __0__	19. __0__
233. __1__	20. __1__
234. __1__	21. __1__

235. __0__
236. __0__
237. __0__
238. __0__
239. __0__

Raw score: ———

22. __1__
23. __0__
24. __0__
25. __0__
26. _____

Raw score: ———

1. Which protocol had more than one basal? _____
2. What were the basal items on protocol 1? _____
3. What were the ceiling items on protocol 1? _____
4. What were the basal items on protocol 2? _____
5. What were the ceiling items on protocol 2? _____

Apply Your Knowledge

What is the meaning of ceiling level, and how does it relate to the student's ability? _____

_____

_____

Check Your Understanding

Check your ability to calculate a raw score by completing Activity 5.5 below.

Activity 5.5

Using the protocol and the responses in Figure 5.6, determine the basal and ceiling items for this student.

1. How many trials are allowed for the training exercises on this subtest? _____
2. According to the responses shown, what items are included in the student's basal level? _____
3. What instructions are provided about establishing the basal?

   _____

4. According to the responses shown, what items are included in the student's ceiling level? _____

Apply Your Knowledge

What information are you able to learn from this page of the protocol?

_____

_____

_____

Figure 5.6 Basal and ceiling rules and response items for a subtest from the Peabody Individual Achievement Test—Revised.

SUBTEST 2
Reading Recognition

Training Exercises

	Trial 1	Trial 2	Trial 3
Exercise A.	(1) _____	(1) _____	(1) _____
Exercise B.	(3) _____	(3) _____	(3) _____
Exercise C.	(2) _____	(2) _____	(2) _____

Basal and Ceiling Rules
Basal: *highest* 5 consecutive correct responses
Ceiling: *lowest* 7 consecutive responses containing 5 errors

Starting Point
The item number that corresponds to the subject's raw score on General Information.

43.	ledge	1
44.	escape	1
45.	northern	1
46.	towel	1
47.	kneel	1
48.	height	0
49.	exercise	1
50.	observe	1
51.	ruin	0
52.	license	1
53.	uniforms	0
54.	pigeon	1
55.	moisture	0
56.	artificial	1
57.	issues	0
58.	quench	0
59.	hustle	0
60.	thigh	0

READING RECOGNITION
Ceiling Item _____
minus Errors _____
equals RAW SCORE _____

Source: From *Peabody Individual Achievement Test–Revised*, subtest 2, Reading Recognition, by F. C. Markwardt, 1989, Circle Pines, MN: American Guidance Service. Copyright 1989 by American Guidance Service. Reprinted by permission.

After the examiner and student are in the testing room, the examiner should attempt to make the student feel at ease. The examiner should convey the importance of the testing situation without making the student feel anxious. As suggested by McLoughlin and Lewis (2001), the examiner should encourage the student to work hard and should reinforce the student's attempts and efforts, not correct responses. Responses that reinforce the efforts of the student may include statements such as "You are working so hard today," or "You like math work," or "I will be sure to tell your teacher [or mother or father, etc.] how hard you worked." If the student asks about performance on specific items ("Did I get that one right?"), the examiner should again try to reinforce effort.

Young students may enjoy a tangible reinforcer upon the completion of the testing session. The examiner may tell the student near the end of the session to work just a few more items for a treat or surprise. Reinforcement with tangibles is not recommended during the assessment, because the student may lose interest in the test or no longer pay attention.

During the administration of the test, the examiner must be sure to follow all instructions in the manual. As stated in professional standards and IDEA, tests must be given in the manner set forth by the test developer, and adapting tests must be done by professionals with expertise in the specific area being assessed who are cognizant of the psychometric changes that will result.

Cole, D'Alonzo, Gallegos, Giordano, and Stile (1992) suggested that examiners consider several additional factors to decrease bias in the assessment process. The following considerations, adapted from Cole et al. (1992), can help the examiner determine whether the test can be administered in a fair way:

1. Do sensory or communicative impairments make portions of the test inaccessible?
2. Do sensory or communicative impairments limit students from responding to questions?
3. Do test materials or method of responding limit students from responding?
4. Do background experiences limit the student's ability to respond?
5. Does the content of classroom instruction limit students from responding?
6. Is the examiner familiar to the student?
7. Are instructions explained in a familiar fashion?
8. Is the recording technique required of the student on the test familiar? (p. 219)

OBTAINING DERIVED SCORES

The raw scores obtained during the test administration are used to locate other derived scores from norm tables included in the examiner's manuals for the specific test. The derived scores may include percentile ranks, grade equivalents, standard scores with a mean of 100 or 50, and other standardized scores, such as z scores.

There are advantages and disadvantages to using the different types of derived scores. Of particular concern is the correct use and interpretation of grade equivalents and percentile ranks. These two types of derived scores are used frequently because the basic theoretical concepts are thought to be understood; however, these two types of scores are misunderstood and misinterpreted by professionals (Huebner, 1988, 1989; Wilson, 1987). The reasons for this misinterpretation are the lack of understanding of the numerical scale used and the method used in establishing grade-level equivalents.

Percentile ranks are used often because they can be easily explained to parents. The concept, for example, of 75% of the peer group scoring at the same level or below a particular student is one that parents and professionals can understand. The difficulty in interpreting percentile ranks is that they do not represent a numerical scale with equal intervals. For example, the standard scores between the 50th and 60th percentiles are quite different from the standard scores between the 80th and 90th percentile ranks.

The development of grade equivalents needs to be considered when using these derived scores. Grade equivalents represent the average number of items answered correctly by the students in the standardization sample of a particular grade. These equivalents may not represent the actual skill level of particular items or of a particular student's performance on a test. Many of the skills tested on academic achievement tests are taught at various grade levels. The grade level of presentation of these skills depends on the curriculum used. The grade equivalents obtained therefore may not be representative of the skills necessary to pass that grade level in a specific curriculum.

TYPES OF SCORES

The concepts of standard scores, percentile ranks, and age and grade equivalents have been introduced. Standard scores and percentile ranks are scores used to compare an individual student with the larger norm group to determine relative standing in the areas assessed, such as mathematics skills or IQ. Standard scores include those scores with an average or mean of 100 as well as other scores such as T scores, which have an average of 50, or z scores, which convey the student's standing in terms of standard deviation units. Refer to Figure 3.9 to locate scores. For example, a z score of -1.0 indicates that the student is 1 standard deviation below average and if this score is converted to a standard score with a mean of 100, the standard score of this student is 85. If the student's z score is converted to T scores, the student's T score is 40 (T score average is 50; SD of 10).

Other scores that may be used to compare the student's standing to the norm group are stanine scores. Stanine scores, like percentile ranks, are not equidistant. Stanines are based on a system of dividing the distribution into 9 segments with an average or mean of 5 and a standard deviation of 2. This means that the previously presented student score of 85 and a z score of −1.0 would have a stanine score of 3. The data or student scores within the stanine sections represent large segments of ability and therefore do not convey very precise indications of a student's performance or ability.

GROUP TESTING: HIGH-STAKES ASSESSMENT

The protocol examples and basal and ceiling exercises presented thus far in the chapter are typical of individualized norm-referenced instruments. Other instruments commonly used in schools are norm-referenced standardized group achievement tests. These instruments are administered to classroom-size groups to assess achievement levels. Group achievement tests are increasingly used to assess accountability of individual students and school systems. These instruments are also known as high-stakes tests because the results of such tests often have serious implications of accountability, accreditation, and funding for school systems. States and districts use such instruments to be certain that students are meeting expected academic standards for their grade placement. In addition, at least 26 states use the results of statewide assessment to determine if students are allowed to graduate, and 6 states use such assessment for grade promotion (U.S. Department of Education, 2000).

Principles to guide the assessment of students for accountability have been proposed by Elliott, Braden, and White (2001), who suggest that school systems keep in mind that assessment should be logical and serve the purpose for which it is intended. They state that systems should set their standards or goals first before developing assessments. In addition, they remind school personnel that high-stakes testing should measure educational achievement rather than try to create achievement. As with individual assessment, these authors state, no single instrument has the capability to answer all achievement questions and multiple measures should be used. And finally, as with other educational instruments, high-stakes assessments should be reliable and valid for their specific purpose.

Brigham, Tochterman, and Brigham (2000) point out that in order for high-stakes assessment to be beneficial for students with special needs, such tests should provide useful information for planning. Such information would inform the teacher about what areas students have mastered, what areas are at the level of instruction, and the areas to which students have not been exposed. These authors further state that the information provided to teachers in high-stakes assessment is often not provided in a timely manner so that instructional interventions can occur. In addition, high-stakes

Barbara Schwartz/Merrill

assessment may not be completed annually but rather biannually, so that the results have little if any impact on the student's actual educational planning.

The 1997 IDEA Amendments require that students with disabilities be included in statewide and districtwide assessments. For some students, the assessments are completed with **accommodations** for their specific disabilities. The Amendments require that students who are unable to complete these assessments should be administered alternate assessments. When the 1997 Amendments required that students with disabilities be included in statewide accountability assessment, most states did not have such accountability systems in place for students eligible under IDEA (Thurlow, Elliott, & Ysseldyke, 1998). The Amendments required educators to decide and include in the IEP process which students would take statewide assessments, which students would require accommodations for the statewide assessments, and which students would require alternate assessment for accountability.

This decision-making process has proved to be complicated and should be reached by the IEP team. Educators must also address the issue of statewide assessment for students being served under Section 504, and the decisions should be included in the student's Section 504 plan (Office of Special Education and Rehabilitative Services, 2000). Thurlow et al. have proposed a decision-making form to assist educators in determining which students should be included in statewide assessment or require accommodations or alternate assessment.

According to Thurlow et al., the questions that should be considered when determining which students should be administered

accommodations
Necessary changes in format, response mode, setting, or scheduling that will enable a student with disabilities to complete the general curriculum or test.

statewide assessment, which students require accommodations, and which students should be provided alternate assessment, focus on the standards that the students are expected to master. If students are expected to master the standards expected of all general education students, the students should be administered the statewide assessment. For students who are given accommodations in the general education classroom in order to participate in the curriculum, accommodations should be included in the administration of statewide assessments. Finally, for students who are expected to meet general education standards, even with accommodations, these students should be administered an alternate assessment.

For students with disabilities who require accommodations for participation in statewide assessment, the accommodations must not alter what the test is measuring. Accommodations include possible changes in the format of the assessment, the manner in which the student responds, the setting of the assessment, or in scheduling (Office of Special Education and Rehabilitative Services, 2000). The team members determine the accommodations needed in order for the student to participate in the assessment and include such modifications in the student's IEP.

Students from culturally and linguistically diverse backgrounds who are considered to be English-language learners (limited English proficiency) may require accommodations to ensure that academic skills and knowledge are being assessed rather than English skills. As with assessment to determine eligibility, students must be assessed in specific areas of content or ability rather than for their English reading or communication skills. If required, accommodations may be included for the student's language differences (Office of Special Education and Rehabilitative Services, 2000).

The team determines to use an alternate assessment method when the student will not be able to participate, even with accommodations, in the statewide or districtwide assessments. Alternate assessments are to be designed that include the same areas or domains as the statewide assessments. The test content should reflect the appropriate knowledge and skills and should be considered a reliable and valid measure of the content.

ACCOMMODATIONS IN HIGH-STAKES TESTING

Students who participate in the general education curriculum with limited difficulty most likely will not require accommodations for high-stakes testing. Students who require accommodations in the general education or special education setting—such as extended time for task completion, or use of **assistive technology** (speech synthesizer, electronic reader, communication board)—to participate in the general curriculum will most likely require

assistive technology Necessary technology that enables the student to participate in a free, appropriate public education.

accommodations to participate in high-stakes testing. The purpose of accommodations during the assessment is to prevent measuring the student's disability and to allow a more accurate assessment of the student's progress in the general curriculum.

The determination of need for accommodations should be made during the IEP process. The types of accommodations needed must be documented on the IEP. Following the statewide or districtwide assessment, teachers should rate the accommodations that proved to be helpful for each specific student (Elliott, Kratochwill, & Schulte, 1998). The following adapted list of accommodations has been suggested by these authors:

1. Motivation—Some students may work best with extrinsic motivators such as verbal praise.

2. Providing assistance prior to administering the test—To familiarize the student with test format, test-related behavior or procedures that will be required.

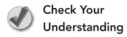

Check Your Understanding

Complete the questions of high-stakes assessment in Activity 5.6 below.

Activity 5.6

Match these terms to the statements that follow.

a. alternate assessment

b. statewide assessment

c. high-stakes assessment

d. accommodations

_____ 1. Juan is receiving special education support in the general classroom setting. Although he reads the same textbooks as other students, he must use a word processor to complete his writing assignments. His IEP team has determined that he will require _____ for his standardized statewide assessment.

_____ 2. When assessment determines promotion to the next grade in secondary school, the assessment is called _____.

_____ 3. Allowing students to complete assessment in a small group in a separate room is considered a type of _____.

_____ 4. The IEP team must include statements that address _____.

_____ 5. Lupitina has been receiving her education within a self-contained special education environment since she entered school. Her development is 5 years below the level of her peers. The IEP team must determine if Lupitina should have accommodations for her assessment, or if she will require _____.

3. Scheduling—Extra time or testing over several days.

4. Setting—Includes location, lighting, acoustics, specialized equipment.

5. Providing assistance during the assessment—To assist a student with turning pages, recording response, or allowing the child's special education teacher to administer the test.

6. Using aids—Any specialized equipment or technology the child requires.

7. Changes in test format—Braille edition or audiotaped questions.

Source: From "The Assessment Accommodations Checklist" by S. N. Elliott, T. R. Kratochwill, and A. G. Schulte, 1998, *Teaching Exceptional Children,* Nov./Dec. pp.10–14.

In the *Accommodations Manual* of the Council of Chief State School Officers (Thompson, Morse, Sharpe, & Hall, 2005), the following adapted list of accommodation categories are described for use in statewide assessment:

Presentation accommodations—An example might be a student with a significant reading disability may be provided the content through a means other than reading.

Response accommodations—An example of this type of accommodation would be a student who cannot respond in writing would be allowed to respond in another format such as use of a communication board or other technology.

Setting accommodations—This type of accommodation would be used when it is necessary to provide the assessment in a different location for reasons such as accessibility or when a student cannot process information in a distracting environment.

Timing and scheduling accommodations—students who require extended time or students who require frequent breaks to sustain attention would benefit from these accommodations.

ALTERNATE ASSESSMENT

Students who are not able to participate in the regular statewide assessment, or in the statewide assessment with accommodations, are required to complete an alternate assessment. The alternate assessment should be designed to reflect progress in the general education curriculum at the appropriate level. The intent of the alternate assessment is to measure the student's progress along the continuum of general education expectations.

States participating in statewide assessments determine individually how the state will provide alternate assessments for students who are not able to complete the assessments with accommodations. A state may use a statewide curriculum with set expectations for each grade level. These skills and expectations exist on a continuum, and this may be used as a basis for the alternate assessment. The skill level measured on the alternate assessment may actually be at a level below the expectations for students in school. For example, a young student with a significant cognitive disability may not be able to master the skills expected of a first- or second-grade student. The skills that may be measured for progress may be the preacademic skills necessary to progress toward the first- and second-grade skills.

The type and level of the assessment may be determined individually for each student requiring alternate assessments. Portfolio assessment, performance-based assessment, authentic assessment, and observations are methods used by states as alternate assessment for high-stakes testing. Many states are continuing to develop both acceptable accommodations and alternate tests (Elliott et al., 1998; Thurlow et al., 1998; Ysseldyke, Nelson, & House, 2000).

ISSUES IN HIGH-STAKES TESTING

Typically in the field of special education assessment new concepts and regulations in the assessment of students with special needs have been met with questions and issues that must be considered. The mandate in the 1997 Amendments to include all students in high-stakes assessment was added to the law as a measure of accountability. Student progress must be measured to determine if programs are effective. This mandate continues in IDEA 2004.

As this mandate has been implemented in schools, there have been problems and concerns. Ysseldyke, Thurlow, Kozleski, and Reschly (1998) identified 16 critical issues. Some of these issues include concerns about the inconsistency of definitions, federal law requirements, variability among states and districts, differences in standards of expectations for students with disabilities, lack of participation of students with disabilities in test development and standardization of instruments, and lack of consistency regarding decisions for accommodations and alternate assessment.

Other issues involve the conceptual understanding of the purpose and nature of the assessment. Gronna, Jenkins, and Chin-Chance (1998) state that students with disabilities have typically been excluded from national norming procedures, yet these students are now to be compared with these national samples to determine how much progress they have made. These authors raise the question of how to compare students with disabilities with the national norms when the students with disabilities, by definition, are expected to differ from the established norms. This is an area of continued research and debate in the field of special education. Nichols and Berliner (2007) argue that mandatory statewide assessments have resulted in damaging the American education system for all students and that alternate assessments may not be the best way to measure progress. Yeh (2006) found that some teachers reported that high-stakes assessment helped teachers target and individualize instruction, and that their students who disliked reading or had difficulties with academics felt more in control of their own learning. Yovanoff and Tindal (2007) suggest that performance task-based reading alternate tests can be scaled to statewide assessments, although determining the validity and reliability may be difficult. Perner (2007) states that the development of alternate assessments is difficult and that states require more time to develop appropriate measures.

In response to the difficulties often encountered by educators who must design alternative assessments or provide accommodations for assessments, there has been an interest in designing all assessments to be more fair and user friendly for all learners from the beginning rather than attempting to fit a test to a student's needs after it has been developed. This concept, known as Universal Design, has been gaining attention in both instructional methods and assessments. The Principles of Universal Design are presented in Table 5.4.

Table 5.4   Principles of Universal Design.

Principle One: Equitable Use: The design is useful and marketable to people with diverse abilities.

1a. Provide the same means of use for all users: identical whenever possible; equivalent when not.
1b. Avoid segregating or stigmatizing any users.
1c. Provisions for privacy, security, and safety should be equally available to all users.
1d. Make the design appealing to all users.

Principle Two: Flexibility in Use: The design accommodates a wide range of individual preferences and abilities.

2a. Provide choice in methods of use.
2b. Accommodate right- or left-handed access and use.
2c. Facilitate the user's accuracy and precision.
2d. Provide adaptability to the user's pace.

Principle Three: Simple and Intuitive Use: Use of the design is easy to understand, regardless of the user's experience, knowledge, language skills, or current concentration level.

3a. Eliminate unnecessary complexity.
3b. Be consistent with user expectations and intuition.
3c. Accommodate a wide range of literacy and language skills.
3d. Arrange information consistent with its importance.
3e. Provide effective prompting and feedback during and after task completion.

Table 5.4 continued.

Principle Four: Perceptible Information: The design communicates necessary information effectively to the user, regardless of ambient conditions or the user's sensory abilities.

4a. Use different modes (pictorial, verbal, tactile) for redundant presentation of essential information.
4b. Provide adequate contrast between essential information and its surroundings.
4c. Maximize "legibility" of essential information.
4d. Differentiate elements in ways that can be described (i.e., make it easy to give instructions or directions).
4e. Provide compatibility with a variety of techniques or devices used by people with sensory limitations.

Principle Five: Tolerance for Error: The design minimizes hazards and the adverse consequences of accidental or unintended actions.

5a. Arrange elements to minimize hazards and errors: most used elements, most accessible; hazardous elements eliminated, isolated, or shielded.
5b. Provide warnings of hazards and errors.
5c. Provide fail safe features.
5d. Discourage unconscious action in tasks that require vigilance.

Principle Six: Low Physical Effort: The design can be used efficiently and comfortably and with a minimum of fatigue.

6a. Allow user to maintain a neutral body position.
6b. Use reasonable operating forces.
6c. Minimize repetitive actions.
6d. Minimize sustained physical effort.

Principle Seven: Size and Space for Approach and Use: Appropriate size and space is provided for approach, reach, manipulation, and use regardless of user's body size, posture, or mobility.

7a. Provide a clear line of sight to important elements for any seated or standing user.
7b. Make reach to all components comfortable for any seated or standing user.
7c. Accommodate variations in hand and grip size.
7d. Provide adequate space for the use of assistive devices or personal assistance.

Source: The Center for Universal Design, North Carolina State University, 1997.

CHAPTER SUMMARY

This chapter provided information about norm-referenced instruments used in individual and group settings. Both types of instruments are used to measure academic achievement in schools. Group measures include statewide mandated achievement measures that may need to be adapted for students with disabilities.

THINK AHEAD

The most frequently used tests in education are achievement tests. In the next chapter, you will use portions of commonly used instruments to learn about achievement tests and how they are scored.

EXERCISES

Part I

Match the following terms with the correct definitions.

a. domain
b. norm-referenced tests
c. item pool
d. test manual
e. accommodations
f. ceiling
g. raw score
h. developmental version

i. grade equivalent
j. norm group
k. interpolated
l. chronological age
m. stanines
n. basal
o. field test
p. protocol

_____ 1. When a test is being developed, the test developer attempts to have this represent the population for whom the test is designed.

_____ 2. This step is completed using the developmental version to determine what changes are needed prior to the completion of the published test.

_____ 3. This represents the level of items that the student would most probably answer correctly, although they may not all be administered to the student.

_____ 4. When a teacher scores a classroom test including 10 items and determines that a student correctly answered 7, the number 7 represents a _____.

_____ 5. Information regarding how a test was developed is usually contained in the _____.

_____ 6. A student's standard score that compares the student with age peers is found by using the student's raw score and the student's _____ and the norm tables.

_____ 7. A teacher discovers that although only second, third, and fifth graders were included in the norm sample of a test, scores were presented for fourth grade. The fourth-grade scores were _____.

_____ 8. A student's actual skill level is not represented by the _____.

_____ 9. Both individual and group assessments may be _____ that compare students with age or grade expectations.

_____10. Students with disabilities who have IEPs and students who are served under Section 504 may need _____ for statewide assessments.

_____11. A student score that is reported to be exactly average with a score of 5 is reporting using _____ scores.

Part II

Select the type of accommodation and match with the following statements.

a. setting

b. scheduling

c. response mode

d. assessment format

_____ 1. Lorenzo, who participates in the general curriculum, requires Braille for all reading material. He will require changes in _____.

_____ 2. Lorenzo also requires the use of a stylus for writing or answers questions orally. He will also require changes in _____ .

_____ 3. When Susie is in the general classroom setting, she often is distracted and requires additional time to complete her assignments. On her Section 504 plan, the team members should include accommodations of _____.

_____ 4. George is a student with a specific reading disability. In his general education classroom, George's teacher and the classroom aide must read all instructions to him and often must read questions and multisyllabic words to him. On his IEP, the team has included a statement of accommodation of _____.

Part III

Discuss the issues and concerns of the statewide assessment of students with disabilities.

Part IV

Using the portions from the *KeyMath—Revised* (Connolly, 1988) protocol in Figure 5.7, determine the following:

1. Chronological age: _____

2. Domain scores: _____

3. Raw score: _____

4. Basal item: _____

5. Ceiling item: _____

Figure 5.7 Chronological age portion and Numeration subtest from the *KeyMath—Revised* protocol.

	YEAR	MONTH	DAY
Test date	91	10	5
Birth date	84	11	10
Chronological age	___	___	___

1 NUMERATION

General Directions:

Read Chapter 3 in the *Manual* carefully before administering and scoring the test. The correct procedures for establishing the subtest basal and ceiling are detailed in the chapter. Briefly, the criteria are as follows: *The basal is the 3 consecutive correct responses immediately preceding the easiest item missed; the ceiling is 3 consecutive errors.*

Begin administration at the Numeration item designated as the starting item for the student's grade level. Score items by penciling a 1 (correct) or 0 (incorrect) in the box. Continue administration until a basal and a ceiling have been extablished for the Numeration subtest. Use the Numeration basal item (the first item of the Numeration basal) to determine the starting points for the remaining subtests; for example, if the student's Numeration basal item is 18, begin the Rational Numbers subtest at item 2, begin the Geometry subtest at item 13, and so on.

The item-score boxes are positioned in columns indicating which domain each item belongs to. When totaling the scores in a domain column, count as *correct* the *un*administered items in that column that *precede* the easiest item administered. The resulting total for the column is the domain score. The sum of the domain scores is the subtest raw score.

GRADE	Item	Numbers 0-9	Numbers 0-99	Numbers 0-999	Multi-digit numbers
K,1 ▸	1. how many deer	1			
	2. as many fingers	1			
	3. read 5, 2, 7	1			
	4. read in order 5, 2, 7	1			
	5. how many people	0			
2,3 ▸	6. fourth person	1			
	7. ___ 20 ___		0		
	8. read in order 36 15 70 32		1		
	9. how many rods		0		
4 ▸	10. how many dots		0		
	11. order 643 618 305 648			1	
5-7 ▸	12. blue dot		0		
	13. 729 739 749 ___ ___			0	
	14. order 3,649 3,581 3,643				0
	15. how many small cubes				
8,9 ▸	16. round to nearest hundred				
	17. how many pencils				
	18. four-digit number				
	19. read 6,019,304				
	20. number in blue box				
	21. how many small cubes				
	22. three-digit number				
	23. less than positive four				
	24. what does 10^4 represent				

_____ CEILING ITEM   DOMAIN SCORES | | | | |

SUBTEST RAW SCORE (Sum of domain scores) | |

Source: From *KeyMath—Revised*, protocol B, individual test record (pp. 1, 2) by A. J. Connolly, 1988, Circle Pines, MN: American Guidance Service. Copyright 1988 by American Guidance Service. Reprinted by permission.

Companion
Website

Answers to these questions can be found in the Appendix of this text or you may also complete these questions and receive immediate feedback on your answers by going to the Think Ahead module in Chapter 5 of the Companion Website.

COURSE PROGRESS MONITORING ASSESSMENT

See how you are doing in the course after the conclusion of PART II by completing the following assessment. When you are finished, check your answers with your instructor or on the Companion Website *www.prenhall.com/overton.* Once you have your score, return to Figure 1.9, Student Progress Monitoring Graph in Chapter 1 and plot your progress.

Progress Monitoring Assessment

Select the best answer. Some of these terms may be used more than once.

A. Academic achievement tests
B. Curriculum-based measurement
C. Curriculum-based assessment
D. Behavior rating profile–2
E. Child behavior checklist
F. Estimated true score
G. Standard error of measurement

H. Content validity
I. Construct validity
J. Section 504
K. Age equivalent
L. High-stakes tests
M. FBA
N. Arena assessment
O. Reliability
P. Coefficient

_____ 1. The indicator of common variance of two variables.

_____ 2. This type of curriculum-based instrument does not have diagnostic capability unless an error analysis is completed on the student's work.

_____ 3. A developmental score that may not be very useful to interpret.

_____ 4. These measures are often used when assessing very young children.

_____ 5. This type of validity looks at difficult-to-measure concepts.

_____ 6. This behavior rating scale includes a classroom observation instrument.

_____ 7. This measure indicates how much error may be on a test based on the score's distance from the mean.

_____ 8. This curriculum-based measure assesses the student's performance to see if it is aligned with the goal or aim line.

_____ 9. This method of measuring error on a test uses the standard deviation in the computation.

_____10. This measurement of error is usually used to calculate confidence intervals.

Fill in the Blanks

11. Both _____ and _____ require that students be instructed using research-based interventions.

12. The _____ is a behavior rating system that includes forms for teachers, parents, and the student as well as a developmental interview for the parent.

13. The _____ includes a measure of the student's attitude toward math.

14. The _____ case resulted in more careful assessment for the determination of mental retardation.

15. The Stanford–Binet V categorizes scores within the 120–129 range as _____.

16. Regulatory disturbances might be assessed when the assessment involves _____.

17. The blending of isolated sounds into a whole word is called _____.

18. For each student served in special education, a _____ must be in place to plan the instruction.

19. Story starters might be useful in the informal assessment of _____.

20. As part of the process of the testing _____, previous educational experiences should be considered.

Assessing Students

Curriculum-Based Assessment and Other Informal Measures

curriculum-based assessment   direct measurement

curriculum-based measurement   subskill

formative assessment   task analysis

summative assessment   subtask

correct letter sequence   error analysis

probes   checklists

oral reading fluency   questionnaires

maze   work samples

baseline score   permanent products

aimline   authentic assessment

performance assessment   portfolio assessment

criterion-referenced tests

CHAPTER FOCUS

curriculum-based assessment Using content from the currently used curriculum to assess student progress.

Student academic performance in school is best measured using the actual curriculum materials that the student is expected to master. These assessment methods are collectively called **curriculum-based assessment**. This chapter introduces the various methods used in the classroom to assess student performance. These methods, also generally known as informal methods of assessment, provide valuable information to assist with planning and effective interventions.

CEC KNOWLEDGE AND SKILLS STANDARDS

The student completing this chapter will understand the knowledge and skills included in the following CEC Knowledge and Skills Standards from Standard 8: Assessment:

CC8K1—Basic terminology used in assessment

CC8K3—Screening, prereferral, referral, and classification procedures

GC8K4—Procedures for early identification of young children who may be at risk for disabilities

CC8S2—Administer nonbiased formal and informal assessments

UREMENT

ou learned that the Traditional Assessment Model the use of norm-referenced tests with the goal of udent's eligibility for special education support. n education and special education, the emphasis on strategies. Prevention and early intervention ocus of the Contemporary Assessment Model 7).

on methods prevent students from slipping ers in expected levels of academic achievement. One teachers can prevent students from falling behind their ers is to closely monitor their progress so that mistakes can be noticed early and interventions, such as a change in teaching strategies, can be implemented. **Curriculum-based measurement**, or CBM, is a method of monitoring instruction regularly. The student's CBM is based on the achievement goal for the school year (Fuchs, 2004). For example, if the goal is to comprehend fourth-grade-level reading material, the CBMs are based on fourth-grade-level reading passages even though at the beginning of the year the student reads at the third-grade level. The monitoring of progress lets the teacher know if the child is making adequate progress under the current educational conditions. This close monitoring, for the purpose of making instructional decisions in the classroom, has been found to result in better academic achievement (Fuchs & Fuchs, 1986; Fuchs, Butterworth, & Fuchs, 1989; Fuchs, Fuchs, Hamlett, & Stecker, 1991).

One reason that curriculum-based measurement is considered the optimal assessment technique for monitoring progress is that it is a **formative** type of evaluation. An evaluation is considered formative when the student is measured during the instructional period for acquisition of skills and goals. This formative evaluation allows the teacher to make observations and decisions about the student's academic performance in a timely manner. Curriculum-based measurement may also be called progress monitoring because it is a formative type of evaluation. An evaluation is considered **summative** if it is a measurement taken at the end of the instructional period. For example, end-of-chapter tests or end-of-year tests are summative.

To compare curriculum-based measurement, curriculum-based assessment, and commercially produced norm-referenced achievement tests, see Table 6.1.

-oased rement Fre-quent measurement comparing student's actual progress with expected rate of progress.

formative assessment Ongoing assessment that is completed during the acquisition of a skill.

summative assessment Assessment that is completed at the conclusion of an instructional period to determine level of acquisition or mastery.

HOW TO CONSTRUCT AND ADMINISTER CURRICULUM-BASED MEASUREMENTS

In the 1970s, research efforts by the University of Minnesota resulted in the initial development of curriculum-based measures

Table 6.1 Comparisons of curriculum-based measurement, curriculum-based assessment, and commercial academic achievement tests.

Curriculum-Based Measurements	Curriculum-Based Assessments	Commercial Academic Achievement Tests
1. Repeated measures of same academic skill level based on end-of-year goal (formative)	1. Usually given at end of instructional period (summative)	1. Given to students to determine possible eligibility for special education support
2. Administered one or two times per week during academic period (school year)	2. Each test represents new material	2. Many instruments do not have alternate forms and cannot be repeated frequently for valid results
3. Are standardized and have adequate reliability	3. May be teacher-made and not standardized	3. Have adequate reliability and construct validity but content may not be relevant for specific students
4. Have content validity	4. May not have adequate reliability and validity	4. Are summative measures
5. May be a more fair measure of academic progress for ethnically and linguistically diverse students	5. May or may not be considered more fair for ethnically and linguistically diverse students	5. May be more prone to bias
6. May be administered to group (spelling and math)	6. May be administered to groups	6. Individual administration (for purposes of determining eligibility)
7. Research supports use in early skills acquisition for elementary and middle grades; some support for use in secondary grades	7. Teacher-made instruments used for summative evaluation; have not been researched	7. Instruments designed to assess all grade levels from pre-academic through adulthood
8. Specific skills assessed for reading fluency, spelling letter sequences, and math skills	8. Assesses mastery of specific content or skill taught during academic period	8. Assesses the broad domain of academic skills and achievement
9. May be used diagnostically for specific skills assessed and rate of learning	9. No true diagnostic capability unless error analysis is completed	9. May have diagnostic capability for a variety of skills
10. Compares student with his or her own performance on skill measured; may be compared to peers in class, compared with local norms, or compared with norms of researched groups	10. Compares student against a standard of mastery (student must pass 80% of items at end of chapter)	10. Compares student with national norm group or with self for diagnostic analysis (strengths and weaknesses across domain)
11. May be part of data collected for eligibility consideration	11. May be part of data collected for eligibility consideration	11. May be part of data collected for eligibility consideration

(Deno, 1985; Deno, Marston, & Mirkin, 1982; Deno, Marston, Shinn, & Tindal, 1983). The result of the research and continuing work in the field of curriculum-based measurement was the identification of measures that have consistently been found to have reliability and validity for the measurement of progress in reading, spelling, writing, and mathematics. Deno stated that these measurements met specific design criteria in order to be considered CBMs. In brief, these criteria are

1. The measures must have sufficient reliability and validity so that they could be used confidently by classroom teachers to make educational decisions.

2. These measures must be easy to use and understand so that teachers could employ them easily and teach others how to use them.

3. The results found by using the CBMs would need to be easy to explain to others, such as parents and other school personnel.

4. Because these measures would be used frequently throughout the school year, they have to be inexpensive (Deno, 1985).

Significant research indicates that there are simple measures that can assist teachers with monitoring progress for the purpose of making data-based educational decisions. According to Shinn, Nolet, and Knutson (1990), most curriculum-based measures should include the following tasks:

1. In reading, students read aloud from basal readers for 1 minute. The number of words read correctly per minute constitutes the basic decision-making metric.

2. In spelling, students write words that are dictated at specific intervals (either 5, 7, or 10 seconds) for 2 minutes. The number of **correct letter sequences** and words spelled correctly are counted.

3. In written expression, students write a story for 3 minutes after being given a story starter (e.g., "Pretend you are playing on the playground and a spaceship lands. A little green person comes out and calls your name and. . ."). The number of words written, spelled correctly, and/or correct word sequences are counted.

4. In mathematics, students write answers to computational problems via 2-minute **probes**. The number of correctly written digits is counted. (p. 290)

correct letter sequence The sequence of letters in a specific word.

probes Tests used for in-depth assessment of the mastery of a specific skill or subskill.

oral reading fluency The number of words the student is able to read aloud in a specified period of time.

In the next sections you will learn how to construct CBMs for **oral reading fluency**, spelling, and mathematical operations.

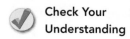

Check Your Understanding

Check your ability to recall the terms and concepts presented thus far in Chapter 6 by completing Activity 6.1 below.

Activity 6.1

Read each description below and determine if it illustrates **summative** or **formative evaluation**.

1. A classroom teacher administers a quiz following the introduction of each new concept in geometry. _____

2. The special education teacher requires her students to read oral passages twice a week to determine their rate of fluency and accuracy of reading. _____

3. In science, the teacher administers a unit test and uses the score as part of the end of term grade. _____

4. A third-grade language arts teacher uses curriculum based measurement twice each week to determine if students are correctly sequencing the letters in the spelling words. _____

5. Your assessment instructor administers a final exam to determine your mastery of assessment skills. _____

6. In this text, the pre-test and Part I, II, III, and IV tests are examples of _____ .

These methods are adapted from Fuchs and Fuchs (1992), Hosp and Hosp (2003), Marston (1989), and Scott and Weishaar (2003).

Constructing CBMs for Reading   In order to assess reading for a specific grade level, the teacher will need to have a sufficient number of passages to use for two types of activities at least two times per week. In addition to students reading the words orally so that the correct words can be counted for oral fluency, the **Maze** method has been found to provide valid results for comprehension. The Maze method requires that the student read a passage with missing words and select the correct word from three choices. Instructions for both of these types of assessment are presented next.

Maze A measure of reading comprehension that requires the student to supply a missing word in a passage.

Oral Reading Fluency Measure   For this measure, you will select three passages to be used to determine the baseline data for each student. For the repeated measures for the school year, you will need two passages per week. For example, if the instructional period is 25 weeks, you will need 50 passages plus the 3 passages for the baseline data. Select a total of 53 passages for oral reading fluency measures for each student reading at that grade level. It is important that the students not be exposed to these passages until the passages are used for the measurement. These passages can be taken from the basal reader or other books of the same readability level. If you are not certain of the readability level, the passage may be typed into a word processing program, such as Microsoft Word, that contains a readability calculator. Other methods for determining readability may also be used, such as the readability formulas found in reading textbooks. Research by Hintze and Christ (2004) supports closely controlling readability level for increased reliability of the reading measures. In their study, controlled readability was defined by carefully selecting passages that represented the middle 5 months of the grade-level readability level. This means that all passages for the third grade, for example, ranged from 3.3 to 3.7 in readability level.

For each passage used there will be one copy for the teacher and one for the student. The teacher's copy will have a cumlative sum of the number of words for each line. See Figure 6.1 for an example of a teacher passage. As the student reads each passage orally for the period of 1 minute, errors are scored on the teacher's copy and the number of words read correctly are totaled. The types of errors recorded are presented in Table 6.2.

baseline score The beginning score against which student progress is measured.

In order to determine the student's **baseline score**, the student reads three passages orally. The teacher notes the errors and sums the correct words. The scores for the three passages can be averaged for a baseline score or the median score can be selected as the baseline score. Because the data include only three scores, taking the median score may be more representative of the student's current oral reading ability.

The literature includes expected levels of progress for the tasks of oral reading fluency, spelling, written language, and mathematics operations (Deno, Fuchs, Marston, & Shin, 2001; Fuchs, Fuchs, & Hamlett, 1993). The expectations for reading are presented in Table 6.3.

aimline The goal line against which progress is measured in curriculum-based measurement.

Once the baseline number has been determined, the teacher can estimate the goal or number of words expected to be read by the end of the year and then plot an **aimline** to monitor progress. For example, a second-grade student who obtains a baseline of 55 correctly read words per minute can be expected to increase oral reading by approximately 38 words by the end of the year. This would result in a total of 93 correctly read words per minute. This is calculated in the following manner:

Baseline = 55

Weekly increase in number of words expected for 2nd grade = 1.5 per week

Figure 6.1   Example of teacher's passage of a CBM for oral reading fluency.

CBM #4/Grade 1

Student:	Teacher:
School:	Date:
Grade:	Examiner:

# attempted	# of errors	# read correctly

Instructions
You are going to read this story title <u>Taking Pictures</u> out loud. This story is about when Fox has his picture taken with different friends (place the reading passage in front of the student, face down). Try to read each word. You can use your finger to keep your place. If you come to a word you don't know, I'll tell it to you. You will read for one minute. Be sure to do your best reading. Do you have any questions? (Turn the passage right side up.) Put your finger on the first word. Begin.

Taking Pictures

On Monday Fox and Millie went to the fair.	7
"Let's have our picture taken," said Fox.	14
"Oh, yes, let's do," said Millie.	19
"Click," went the camera. And out came the pictures.	28
"Sweet," said Millie.	30
"One for you and one for me," said Fox.	39
On Tuesday Fox and Rose went to the fair.	46
"How about some pictures?" said Fox.	52
"Tee-hee," said Rose.	55
"Click," went the camera and out came the pictures.	64
"Tee-hee," said Rose.	67
"I'll keep mine always," said Fox.	73
On Wednesday Fox and Lola went to the fair.	80
"I don't have a picture of us," said Fox.	89
"Follow me," said Lola.	92
"Click," went the camera. And out came the pictures.	101
"What fun!" said Lola. "I'll carry mine everywhere."	108
"Me too," said Fox.	112

Source: Project AIM Staff, University of Maryland, 1999–2000 which was funded by the Department of Education, Office of Special Education. Deborah Speece, Lisa Pericola Case, and Dawn Eddy Molloy, Principle Investigators. Available from http://www.glue.umd.edu/%7Edlspeece/cbmreading/examinermat/grade1/pass4.pdf.

Number of weeks of instruction following baseline period = 25

$1.5 \times 25 = 38 + 55 = 93$

In order to plot the aimline, the teacher would begin at the baseline score (55 words) and draw a line to the goal (93 words), as shown in Figure 6.2. To monitor the instruction, the data are plotted two

Table 6.2   Oral reading errors for CBMs.

Type of Error	Example of Passage Text	Actual Student Response
Teacher-supplied word	The girl swam in the race.	The girl. . .in the race (teacher supplies "swam").
Student passes on word	The girl swam in the race.	The girl. . .pass, in the race.
Student mispronounces word	The girl swam in the race.	The girl swarm in the race.
Student omits word	The girl swam in the race.	The swam in the race.
Student reads words out of order	The girl swam in the race.	The girl swam the in race.
Student substitutes a word	The girl swam in the race.	The girl swam in the pool.

Source: Adapted from "Curriculum-based measurement for reading progress" by Scott, V. G., & Weishaar, M. K. (2003), *Intervention in School and Clinic, 38*(3), 153–159.

Table 6.3   Weekly growth rates for reading.

Grade	Realistic Growth Rate	Special Education Students	General Education Students	Ambitious Growth Rates
1	2 words	.83 word	1.8 words	3 words
2	1.5 words	.57 word	1.66 words	2 words
3	1 word	.58 word	1.18 words	1.5 words
4	.85 word	.58 word	1.01 words	1.1 words
5	.5 word	.58 word	.58 word	.8 word
6	.3 word	.62 word	.66 word	.65 word

Source: Copyright (as applicable) by the National Association of School Psychologists, Bethesda, MD. Reprinted with permission of the publisher. www.nasponline.org.

Figure 6.2   Oral reading fluency goal.

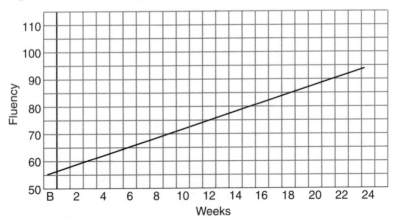

Figure 6.3   Curriculum-based measurement data for two interventions used with one student.

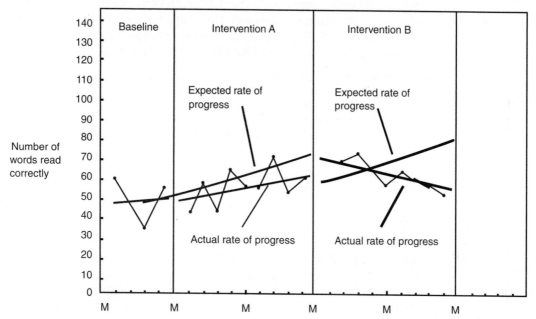

times per week. When a student falls below the aimline for three consecutive measures, the instruction should be adjusted. When the student excels above the aimline for three consecutive measures, the instruction should be made more challenging.

Figure 6.3 presents an example of how curriculum-based measurement is used to determine when an instructional change is indicated. The student in Figure 6.3 failed to make the projected progress and therefore needs an educational change to progress within the curriculum.

Maze Reading Method   One global measure of general reading ability is the Maze task. To construct CBMs to assess this aspect of reading ability, select passages in a manner similar to the oral reading passages. These passages must be passages new to the student, however, and they should represent the student's reading grade level. The first sentence in each passage is presented exactly as it is printed in the grade-level textbook. Following the first sentence, you delete one word from the next sentence and insert a blank. The student will have three word choices for each blank from which to select the correct word based on the meaning of the text. To complete the construction of these passage probes, you delete each *n*th word. For example, in the second sentence you delete the sixth word and every sixth word thereafter. In order to make certain that the task adequately assesses the comprehension aspect of reading, Fuchs and Fuchs (1992) used the following criteria to select distracters for the items. The distracters should not

> make contextual sense;
> rhyme with the correct choice;
> sound or look like the correct choice;
> be a nonsense word;
> require the student to read ahead to eliminate;
> be too high in vocabulary.

In addition, the distracters should be of approximately the same length as the correct word.

CAUTION ABOUT USING EXPECTED GROWTH RATES IN READING

In a study of more than 6,000 students, Silberglitt and Hintze (2007) found that not all student performance was consistent with expected growth rates when using averages of aggregated data. The results of this study suggest that teachers should employ other methods when establishing goals or aimlines that might be more representative of an individual student's ability to respond to interventions in reading. For example, these researchers suggested that the goal can be set using expected growth rates for the student's decile group (such as students who are ranked within the lowest decile group be compared with the expected growth rate of that decile group). Another alternative suggestion was for the teacher to establish a criterion-referenced goal rather than comparing students to the average of the aggregated data. These researchers state that adapting the expected goal for students based on where they are within the group (rather than comparing the students with the average of the group) may offer a method of monitoring progress effectively without the need for interventions to be provided through special education services. This method appears to be a more fair way to measure progress following interventions in reading for students who may be within the lower achievement group; however, they do not fall within the group of students who require special education services.

Constructing CBMs for Spelling   To assess spelling ability, both the number of correct letter sequences and the number of correctly spelled words can be plotted. The measures are constructed from grade-level spelling words and should include approximately 12 words for grades 1–3 and 18 words for grades 4–8 (Shinn, 1989). In order to score correct letter sequences, a point is given for each

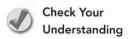

Check Your Understanding

Determine a baseline reading score and the aimline for a first-grade student by completing Activity 6.2 below.

Activity 6.2

Determine the baseline and the aimline for this first-grade student.

1. A first-grade teacher asked each student to read 3 passages aloud. Matt's scores were:

   10, 15, 13

   What is the baseline score? _____

2. Following the determination of the baseline score, the aimline should be determined. Refer to Table 6.3 in your text to determine the number of words a first-grade student is expected to increase each week. If there are 27 weeks remaining in the academic year, what is the goal? Draw the aimline.

3. What should teachers remember when establishing goals in reading using expected growth rates? _____

two letters that are in the correct sequence. For the correct beginning and ending letters, 1 point is given for each. For example, the number of correct letter sequences for the correctly spelled word *time* is 5. One point is scored for the *t*, one point for the correct sequence of *ti*, another point for *im*, another for *me*, and another for the correct ending letter of *e*.

For spelling, a baseline is taken in the same manner as for reading fluency and the aimline is plotted in the same manner, based on the weekly number of correct letter sequences expected. For the expected growth rate, see Table 6.4. An example of a CBM spelling measure is presented in Figure 6.4.

Constructing CBMs for Mathematics For a math CBM, the problems should be operational (addition, subtraction, multiplication, division). The two-minute math probes should be constructed of at least 25 math problems each (Fuchs & Fuchs, 1991). Select or generate 25 grade-level computational problems per probe and construct three math sheets or probes for the baseline score and two probes for each week during the academic period. Students

Table 6.4   Expected weekly growth rates for spelling: Correct letter sequences.

Grade	Realistic Growth Rate	Ambitious Growth Rate
2	1 letter sequence	1.5 letter sequences
3	.65 letter sequence	1 letter sequence
4	.45 letter sequence	.85 letter sequence
5	.3 letter sequence	.65 letter sequence
6	.3 letter sequence	.65 letter sequence

Source: Copyright (as applicable) by the National Association of School Psychologists, Bethesda, MD. Reprinted with permission of the publisher. www.nasponline.org.

Figure 6.4   Analysis of a spelling test.

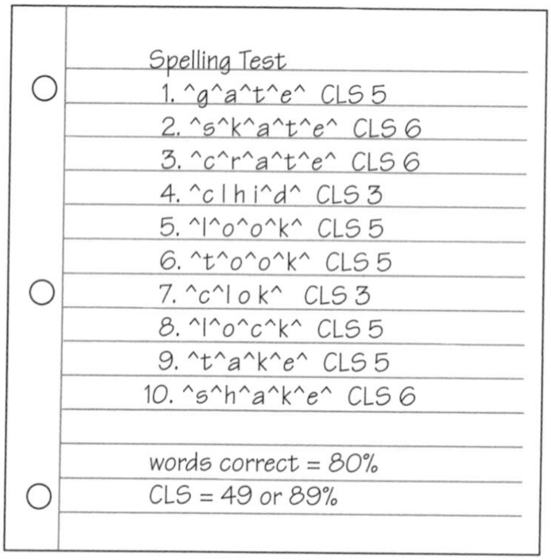

```
             Spelling Test
  O    1. ^g^a^t^e^  CLS 5
       2. ^s^k^a^t^e^  CLS 6
       3. ^c^r^a^t^e^  CLS 6
       4. ^c l h i^d^  CLS 3
       5. ^l^o^o^k^  CLS 5
       6. ^t^o^o^k^  CLS 5
  O    7. ^c^l o k^   CLS 3
       8. ^l^o^c^k^  CLS 5
       9. ^t^a^k^e^  CLS 5
      10. ^s^h^a^k^e^  CLS 6

      words correct = 80%
  O   CLS = 49 or 89%
```

complete as many problems as they can for the two-minute period. The teacher then counts the number of correct digits and plots the number on the student's graph. The weekly expected rate of growth for math is presented in Table 6.5.

REVIEW OF RESEARCH ON CURRICULUM-BASED MEASUREMENT

Curriculum-based measurement of progress has been found to noticeably affect academic achievement when the results are used to modify instructional planning. A brief review of many years of research studies supports the use of curriculum-based measurement, for several reasons.

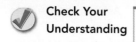

Determine a baseline spelling score and the aimline for a second-grade student by completing Activity 6.3 below.

Activity 6.3

1. Look at the student's performance on the following CBM in spelling. Determine the correct letter sequence score. If you convert this to the percentage of letter sequences correct, what is the percent? What is the spelling score on the test based simply on the number of words spelled correctly?

Word	Student's Spelling of Word
bat	bat
cat	cat
sat	sat
fat	fat
look	lok
book	book
took	took
cook	cook
seek	seek
meek	mek

2. The other two scores obtained to determine the baseline were 40 and 44. What is the baseline score? _____

3. Refer to Table 6.4 in your text. For a realistic growth rate, how many correct letter sequences is the student expected to increase each week in the 2nd grade? _____

4. There are 25 weeks remaining in the school year. What is the goal for this student? _____

5. Construct the aimline.

Table 6.5   Expected weekly growth rates for math: Number of correct digits.

Grade	Realistic Growth Rate	Ambitious Growth Rate
1	.3 correct digit	.5 correct digit
2	.3 correct digit	.5 correct digit
3	.3 correct digit	.5 correct digit
4	.70 correct digit	1.15 correct digits
5	.75 correct digit	1.20 correct digits
6	.45 correct digit	1 correct digit

When curriculum-based measurement was used for instructional programming, students were found to have somewhat greater gains than when it was used for testing purposes alone (Fuchs, Fuchs, & Hamlett, 1989). The more effective teachers were sensitive to the results of the assessment and used them to adapt or modify instruction rather than merely using curriculum-based measurement as a measurement device, such as grading or establishing a working level for IEP objectives.

The use of curriculum-based measurement has been linked to better understanding, by students, of the expectancies of their academic performance (Fuchs, Butterworth, & Fuchs, 1989). Students in this study indicated that they received more feedback than students not receiving curriculum-based measurement. Research has also indicated that teachers using curriculum-based measurement tended to set goals with higher expectations than did teachers who were not using these methods (Fuchs et al., 1989). Use of curriculum-based measurement along with providing instructional intervention strategies to general education teachers were promising in increasing the achievement of low-achieving students and students in general education classes with learning disabilities (Fuchs, Fuchs, Hamlett, Phillips, & Bentz, 1994). One study applied curriculum-based measurement in the general education classroom as part of a functional behavioral analysis (Roberts, Marshall, Nelson, & Albers, 2001). In this study, the use of curriculum-based measurement to determine appropriate instructional levels resulted in decreased off-task behaviors. When applied in this manner, curriculum-based measurement allowed instruction to be tailored; it may therefore be viewed as a prereferral strategy.

Curriculum-based measurement has been found effective for use in universal screening of students for early reading acquisition skills (Ardoin, Witt, Suldo, Connell, Koenig, Restar, Slider, & Williams, 2004; Marchand-Martella, Ruby, & Martella, 2007). In this study, the use of one reading probe was found to be sufficient for predicting overall reading achievement. Another study by Clarke and Shinn (2004) found that math CBMs for early math skills were reliable when used with first-grade students to identify students who may be at risk in mathematics. In a review of the use of CBMs in mathematics, Foegen, Jiban, and Deno (2007) found that there was adequate evidence for use of CBMs in the elementary grades for monitoring the acquisition of problem-solving and basic math facts. CBMs have also been found to predict future performance of students on high-stakes state achievement assessment (McGlinchey & Hixson, 2004).

In a study of curriculum-based measurement as one method of determining special education eligibility (Marston, Mirkin, & Deno, 1984), it was found to be an accurate screening measure for referral for special education and was less influenced by teacher variables.

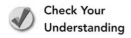

**Check Your
Understanding**

Determine a baseline math score and the aimline for a first-grade student by completing Activity 6.4 below.

Activity 6.4

1. A student was administered 3 math probes to determine the baseline score. Based on the scores below, what is the baseline score?

   _____

   17, 14, 16

2. Refer to Table 6.5 to determine the realistic expected growth rate for a first-grade student. There are 28 weeks remaining in the academic year. Determine the goal for this student. _____

3. Construct the aimline.

Its use appeared to result in less bias, as evidenced by more equity in the male–female ratio of referrals (Marston et al., 1984). Canter (1991) supported using curriculum-based measurement to determine eligibility for special education services by comparing the student's progress in the classroom curriculum to the expectations within the average range for the grade level. The student's actual progress may indicate the need for special education intervention.

Curriculum-based measurement has been found useful when the school employs a problem-solving model as the process for interventions (Deno, 1995; Marston, Muyskens, Lau, & Canter, 2003; Shinn, 2002). For this reason, CBM naturally fits within the Contemporary Assessment Model and is consistent with the movement for assessing learning difficulties by employing response-to-intervention strategies.

Curriculum-based measurement has been studied as a possible method of identifying students in special education placements who are ready to move back into the general education setting (Shinn, Habedank, Rodden-Nord, & Knutson, 1993). Using this method may help general education teachers smoothly integrate students from special education environments by providing data to assess progress and use in planning interventions. One study has also suggested that curriculum-based measures might be beneficial in measuring the effects of medication on students with attention disorders (Stoner, Carey, Ikeda, & Shinn, 1994). In this study, Stoner and colleagues (1994) replicated another study and found evidence suggesting that CBM may be one measure of determining the effect of methylphenidate on academic performance. Additional research in this area may add insight to the emerging field of effective treatment of students with attention deficit disorder.

One study found that when CBM was combined with peer tutoring, students in a general classroom setting made significantly greater achievement gains (Phillips, Hamlett, Fuchs, & Fuchs, 1993). Another study found substantial overall gains in reading fluency, although at-risk students did not progress at the same rate as their grade peers (Greenwood, Tapia, Abbott, & Walton, 2003). Meherns and Clarizio (1993) assert that CBM is helpful in determining when instruction should be adapted, but it does not necessarily provide information about what to change or how to provide the instruction. They advocate using CBM with other diagnostic assessment.

Baker and Good (1995) found that CBM used in assessing reading was as reliable and valid when used with bilingual students as when used with English-only students. They also found that CBM was a sensitive measurement of the reading progress made by bilingual students. Kamps et al. (2007) found that the use of progress monitoring of intensive interventions for students who are English-language learners offers effective tier two interventions. This study suggested that these methods were as effective with ELL students as they were with English-only students. Haager (2007) had inconsistent results when using RTI with ELL students and suggested that students receiving interventions in the first grade may require additional time for reading acquisition skills before they can be expected to meet the reading criteria set for the second grade.

performance assessment Assessment that requires the student to create an answer or product to demonstrate knowledge.

In their sample of fourth-grade students, Fuchs and Fuchs (1996) found that curriculum-based measurement combined with **performance assessment** provides teachers more in-depth assessment, which results in better instructional decisions. Another study found that general education teachers who employed CBM designed better instructional programs and had students who experienced greater gains in achievement than did teachers who did not use CBM (Fuchs et al., 1994). Allinder (1995) found that teachers who used CBM and had high teacher efficacy, set high student goals, and their students had significantly greater growth. In the Allinder study, special education teachers using CBM who had greater teaching efficacy set more goals for their students.

Teachers who were asked to compare CBM with norm-referenced assessments rated CBM as a more acceptable method of assessment (Eckert, Shapiro, & Lutz, 1995). Another study suggested that students enjoy participating in CBM and that their active participation in this process may increase their feelings of responsibility for learning (Davis, Fuchs, Fuchs, & Whinnery, 1995).

CAUTIONS

Several researchers have issued statements of caution about employing curriculum-based measurement. Like other types of assessment, curriculum-based measurement may be more useful in some situations and less useful in others. Heshusius (1991) cautions that curriculum-based assessment may not allow for measurement of some important constructs in education, such as creativity, areas of interest, and original ideas. Hintze, Shapiro, and Lutz (1994) found that CBM was more sensitive in measuring progress when used with traditional basal readers rather than literature samples, indicating that the materials contribute to difficulty in accurate measurement. Meherns and Clarizio (1993) suggest that CBM should be used as part of comprehensive assessment with other measures because of continuing concerns about the reliability and validity of CBM. Silberglitt and Hintze (2007) caution against using average aggregated growth rate expectations to establish reading goals.

When using data from CBMs to make educational decisions, teachers should keep in mind that time of day, presentation format of instruction, and other conditions should be considered (Parette, Peterson-Karlan, Wojcok, & Bardi, 2007). Stecker (2007) reminds educators that there are many variables of student performance and success that are not measured within CBMs, and that these variables, such as environment and family concerns, should be considered when using CBMs in the decision-making process.

Check Your Understanding

To review your understanding of the CBM literature, complete Activity 6.5 below.

Activity 6.5

Answer the following questions about curriculum-based assessment.

1. What did students report about using CBMs in classroom instruction according to Fuchs, Butterworth, and Fuchs? _____

2. One study reported the decrease in off-task behaviors when CBMs were employed. Why would this impact behavior? _____

3. One study by Marston, Mirkin, and Deno found that the use of CBMs was an effective measure to be used in the special education eligibility process. Why? _____

4. What did Baker and Good find in their research using CBMs with bilingual students? _____

CRITERION-REFERENCED ASSESSMENT

criterion-referenced tests Tests designed to accompany and measure a set of criteria or skill-mastery criteria.

Criterion-referenced tests compare the performance of a student to a given criterion. This criterion can be an established objective within the curriculum, an IEP criterion, or a criterion or standard of a published test instrument. The instrument designed to assess the student's ability to master the criterion is composed of many items across a very narrow band of skills. For example, a criterion-referenced test may be designed to assess a student's ability to read passages from the fifth-grade-level reading series and answer comprehension questions with 85% accuracy. For this student, the criterion is an IEP objective. The assessment is made up of several passages and subsequent comprehension questions for each passage, all at the fifth-grade reading level. No other curriculum materials or content items are included. The purpose is to determine if the student can answer the comprehension questions with 85% accuracy. Criterion-related assessment that uses curriculum materials is only one type of curriculum-based assessment.

Although many criterion-referenced instruments are non-standardized or perhaps designed by the teacher, a few criterion-referenced instruments are standardized. Some norm-referenced instruments yield criterion-related objectives or the possibility of adding criterion-related objectives with little difficulty. Examples of these instruments are the KeyMath–Revised (Connolly, 1988), K-TEA–II (Kaufman & Kaufman, 2004), and the WRMT–R (Woodcock, 1987). (See Chapter 5 for norm-referenced tests.)

Adapting standardized norm-referenced instruments to represent criterion-referenced testing is accomplished by writing educational objectives for the skills tested. To be certain that the skill or task has been adequately sampled, however, the educator may need to prepare additional academic *probes* to measure the student's skills. Objectives may represent long-term learning goals rather than short-term gains, determined by the amount of the material or the scope of the task tested by the norm-referenced test. Figure 6.5 illustrates how an item from the WRMT–R might be expanded to represent criterion-referenced testing.

In addition to adapting published norm-referenced instruments for criterion-related assessment, educators may use published criterion-referenced test batteries, such as the Brigance Inventories, that present specific criteria and objectives. Teachers may also create their own criterion-referenced tests.

THE BRIGANCE INVENTORIES

The Brigance Inventories (Brigance, 2004, 1999, 1977, 1981, 1991) are a standardized assessment system that provides criterion-referenced assessment at various skill levels. Norms are available

Figure 6.5   Examples of criterion-referenced testing.

Items missed	On the Word Attack subtest: the long a–e pattern in nonsense words—*gaked, straced;* the long i–e pattern in nonsense word—*quiles*
Deficit-skill	Decoding words with the long vowel-consonant-silent-*e* pattern
Probe	Decoding words orally to teacher: *cake, make, snake, rake, rate, lake, fake, like, bike, kite*
Criterion	Decode 10/10 words for mastery. Decode 8/10 words to 6/10 words for instructional level. Decode 5/10 words or fewer for failure level; assess pre - requisite skill level: discrimination of long/short vowels (vowels: *a, i*).

for some levels of the Brigance (Glascoe, 1999, 2004). Each battery contains numerous subtests, and each item is referenced by objectives that may be used in developing IEPs. The Brigance system includes three criterion-referenced instruments for the various age groups served in special education. These instruments include the Brigance Diagnostic Inventory of Early Development, the Brigance Diagnostic Comprehensive Inventory of Basic Skills–Revised, and the Brigance Diagnostic Inventory of Essential Skills. In each system, the educator should select only the areas and items of interest that identify specific strengths and weaknesses.

In addition to the three criterion-referenced instruments for the assessment of skills, a Brigance Diagnostic Life Skills Inventory and a Brigance Diagnostic Employability Skills Inventory are also available for secondary students in special education and vocational education programs. The Basic Skills Inventory is available in English and Spanish. The Brigance instruments should not be administered in their entirety.

Instruments   The Brigance Diagnostic Inventory of Early Development–Second Edition (Brigance, 2004) is an inventory within the system that was designed to assess the skills and development of children from birth to age 6 years and 11 months. Many of the subtests concern developmental areas of motor development. This test provides criterion-related measurement for self-help skills, prespeech and speech development, general knowledge, social and emotional development, reading readiness, manuscript writing, and beginning math. This instrument may be used along with additional data to support decisions regarding educational programming decisions as well as instructional decisions for the student's individual education program (IEP). This instrument has been norm-referenced, and raw scores can be

Patrick White/Merrill

converted to developmental scores (age equivalents), percentile ranks, and standard scores (Glascoe, 2004).

The Comprehensive Inventory of Basic-Skills–Revised is designed for use with elementary-aged students (Brigance, 1999). Table 6.6 presents the list of skills assessed on this inventory. A set of specific skills is listed within each of the skill areas assessed. The

Table 6.6   Skills assessed on the Brigance Diagnostic Comprehensive Inventory of Basic Skills–Revised.

Readiness	Math
Speech	Numbers
Listening	Number facts
Word recognition	Computation of whole numbers
Oral reading	Fractions and mixed numbers
Reading comprehension	Decimals
Word analysis	Percents
Functional word recognition	Time
Spelling	Money
Writing	U.S. customary measurement
Reference skills	Metrics
Graphs and maps	

Table 6.7 Functional word recognition.

Alphabetical Listing of Basic Sight Vocabulary	Assessments for Basic Skills
H-1 o	Basic Sight Vocabulary
H-2 o	Direction Words
H-3 o	Number words
❖H-4 o	Warning and Safety Signs
H-5 o	Informational Signs
H-6 o	Warning Labels
H-7 o	Food Labels
Supplemental and Related Lists/Skill Sequences	
H-1Sa	Contractions
H-1Sb	Abbreviations
H-2Sa	Direction Words for Writing Activities
H-2Sb	Direction Words for Speaking Activities
H-2Sc	Direction Words for Study Activities
H-2Sd	Direction Words for Physical Activities
H-4S	Warning and Safety Signs
H-5S	Informational Signs
H-6S	Warning Labels
H-7S	Labels on Packaged Foods

Source: Brigance Diagnostic Comprehensive Inventory of Basic Skills-Revised. (1999). A. H. Brigance. Curriculum Associates, North Billerica, MA. Reprinted with permission.

specific skills for the area of functional word recognition are presented in Table 6.7. A sample of one skill assessed, informational signs (H-5), is presented in Figure 6.6. Selected subtests have been norm-referenced, and developmental scores, percentiles, and standard scores exist for those specific subtests.

The Brigance system comprises large, multiple-ring notebook binders that contain both student and examiner pages. The pages may be turned to resemble an easel format, or the pages to be administered may be removed from the binder. A warning included in the test cautions the examiner to select the necessary subtests and avoid overtesting.

TEACHER-MADE CRITERION-REFERENCED TESTS

Instead of relying on published instruments, classroom teachers may develop their own criterion-referenced tests. This type of

Figure 6.6   Brigance Diagnostic Inventory of Basic Skills examiner page.

SKILL: Reads informational signs.

STUDENT RECORD BOOK: Page 23.

CLASS RECORD BOOK: Page 25.

ASSESSMENT METHOD: Individual oral response.

MATERIALS: S-240, S-241, and S-242.

DISCONTINUE: Your discretion, or after three consecutive errors.

TIME: Your discretion, or see **INDIVIDUALIZING THE TIME LIMIT**, on page 226.

ACCURACY: Give credit for each correct response.

NOTES: (See **NOTES** on pages 240–41.)

STUDENT-PAGE FORMAT FOR S-242

DIRECTIONS

This assessment is made by asking the student to read aloud the informational signs on S-240 through S-242.

Point to the informational signs on S-242, and

Say: **These are words we often see on signs. Look at each word carefully and read it aloud. Begin here.** Point to the word with which you want the student to begin.

If the student mispronounces a word,

Say: **Try it again.** Point to the word.

OBJECTIVE

By _____(date)_____, when shown a list of fifty-eight informational signs, _(student's name)_ will read _(quantity)_ of the signs.

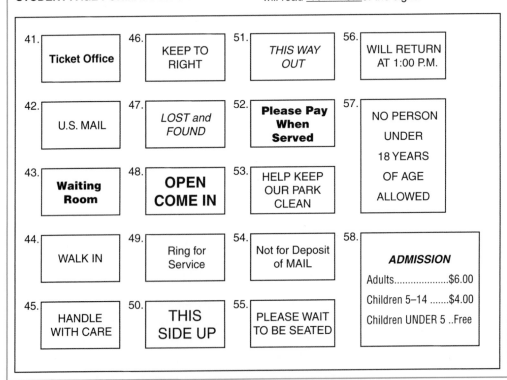

41. Ticket Office
42. U.S. MAIL
43. Waiting Room
44. WALK IN
45. HANDLE WITH CARE
46. KEEP TO RIGHT
47. LOST and FOUND
48. OPEN COME IN
49. Ring for Service
50. THIS SIDE UP
51. THIS WAY OUT
52. Please Pay When Served
53. HELP KEEP OUR PARK CLEAN
54. Not for Deposit of MAIL
55. PLEASE WAIT TO BE SEATED
56. WILL RETURN AT 1:00 P.M.
57. NO PERSON UNDER 18 YEARS OF AGE ALLOWED
58. ADMISSION
    Adults....................$6.00
    Children 5–14 ....$4.00
    Children UNDER 5 ..Free

---

assessment allows the teacher to directly link the assessment to the currently used curriculum. By writing the criterion to be used as the basis for determining when the student has reached or passed the objective, the teacher has created a criterion-referenced test. When the test is linked directly to the curriculum, it also becomes a curriculum-based assessment device and may be referred to as **direct measurement**. For example, the teacher may use the scope and sequence chart from the reading series or math text to write the objectives that will be used in the criterion-related assessment.

direct measurement
Measuring progress by using the same instructional materials or tasks that are used in the classroom.

Research supports the use of criterion-referenced assessment in the classroom and other settings (Glaser, 1963; Hart & Scuitto, 1996; McCauley, 1996). The first questions regarding the use of criterion-referenced assessment were raised in the literature in 1963 by Glaser. The issues Glaser raised seemed to be current issues in the debate about better measurement techniques to accurately determine student progress. Glaser stated that the knowledge educators attempt to provide to students exists on a continuum ranging from no acquisition to mastery. He stated that the criterion can be established at any level where the teacher wishes to assess the student's mastery or acquisition. This type of measurement is used to determine the student's position along the continuum of acquisition or mastery.

Hart and Scuitto (1996) concluded that using criterion-referenced assessment is practical, has social validity, and may assist with educational accountability. This type of assessment can be adapted to other areas, such as a child's speech and language development (McCauley, 1996). Criterion-referenced assessment has been shown to be useful in screening entering kindergarten and first-grade students for school readiness (Campbell, Schellinger, & Beer, 1991) and has also been used to determine appropriate adaptations for vocational assessments to assist in planning realistic job accommodations (Lusting & Saura, 1996). In a review of criterion-referenced assessment during the past 30 years, Millman (1994) concluded that to represent a true understanding of the student's ability, this type of assessment requires "item density." He suggests that to accurately assess whether a student has mastered a domain or area, the assessments need to have many items per domain. Teachers who construct their own criterion-referenced assessments should be certain that enough items are required of the student that they can determine accurately the level of mastery of the domain.

One difficulty that teachers may have in constructing criterion-referenced tests is establishing the exact criterion for whether the student has passed the objective or criterion. Shapiro (1989) suggested that one quantitative method of determining mastery would be to use a normative comparison of the performance, such as using a specific task that 80% of the peers in the class or grade have mastered. The teacher may wish to use a criterion that is associated with a standard set by the school grading policy. For example, answering 75% of the items correctly might indicate that the student needs improvement; 85% correct might be an average performance; and 95% correct might represent mastery. Or, the teacher might decide to use a criterion that the student can easily understand and chart. For example, getting 5 out of 7 items correct indicates the student could continue with the same objective or skill; getting 7 out of 7 items correct indicates the student is ready to move up to the next skill level. Often, the teacher sets the criterion using logical reasoning rather than a quantitative measurement (Shapiro, 1989).

Evans and Evans (1986) have suggested other considerations for establishing criteria for mastery:

> Does passing the test mean that the student is proficient and will maintain the skills?
>> Is the student ready to progress to the next level in the curriculum?
>> Will the student be able to generalize and apply the skills outside the classroom?
>> Would the student pass the mastery test if it were given at a later date? (p. 10)

The teacher may wish to use the following measures for criterion-referenced tests:

More than 95% = mastery of objective
90 to 95% = instructional level
76 to 89% = difficult level
Less than 76% = failure level

Similar standards may be set by the individual teacher, who may wish to adjust objectives when the student performs with 76 to 89% accuracy and when the student performs with more than 95% accuracy. It is important to remember that students with learning difficulties should experience a high ratio of success during instruction to increase the possibility of positive reinforcement during the learning process. Therefore, it may be better to design objectives that promote higher success rates. Figure 6.7 illustrates a criterion-referenced test written by a teacher for addition facts with sums of 10 or less. The objective, or criterion, is included at the top of the test.

Using criterion-referenced assessment may provide better information about student achievement levels and mastery of academic objectives; however, the criterion-referenced test may not always adequately represent growth within a given curriculum. To more effectively measure student progress within a curriculum, teachers should rely on measures that use that curriculum, such as curriculum-based assessment and direct measurement.

Figure 6.7   Teacher-made criterion-referenced test.

OBJECTIVE

John will correctly answer 9 out of 10 addition problems with sums of 10 or less.

5	3	8	9	4	6	7	2	4	1
+2	+2	+2	+1	+5	+2	+3	+4	+3	+6

Performance: _____

Objective passed: _____   Continue on current objective: _____

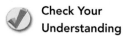

Check Your Understanding

subskill A small part of a skill, used in task analysis.

In Activity 6.6, you will determine whether the student responses illustrated indicate mastery of the **subskill** assessed by the *Basic Skills* test. Complete Activity 6.6 below.

Activity 6.6

1. Look at the student responses on the following teacher-made criterion-referenced test. Determine if the student met the criterion stated as the objective.

   Objective

   John will correctly answer 9 out of 10 addition problems with sums of 10 or less.

5	3	8	9	4	6	7	2	4	1
+2	+2	+2	+1	+5	+2	+3	+4	+3	+6
7	5	10	10	8	4	10	6	7	7

2. Can you describe the types of errors that John made?

   _____

Apply Your Knowledge

Using the suggested mastery level, instructional level, difficulty level, and failure level provided in your text, where does this student fall on this particular skill according to this criterion-referenced test?

_____
_____
_____

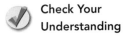

Check Your Understanding

The skills included in Activity 6.7 resemble those that would be included at the beginning level of a reading series. In this activity, you will select the information from one skill to write an objective and construct a short criterion-referenced test. The test should measure the student's mastery of the objective. Complete Activity 6.7 below.

Activity 6.7

Read the following list of skills necessary to complete level P1 of the Best in the Country Reading Series, adopted by all school systems in the country. Answer the questions that follow.

P1 Skills

- Associates pictures with story content.
- Follows sequence of story by turning pages at appropriate times.
- Associates the following letters with their sounds: b, d, c, g, h, j, k, l, m, n, p, q, r, s, t.
- Can match letters (from above) to pictures of objects that begin with the same sounds.
- Can correctly sequence the following stories:

  "A School Day": Mary gets on the bus, goes to school. George brings a rabbit to class; the rabbit gets out of the cage. Mary helps George catch the rabbit.

  "The Field Trip": Ralph invites the class to visit his farm. Sue, John, Mary, and George go on the trip. The animals are (a) a chicken, (b) a goat, (c) a cow, and (d) a horse. The goat follows the class; the goat tries to eat Ralph's shirt.

- Can name all characters in preceding stories.
- Can summarize stories and answer short comprehension questions.

Answer the Following

1. Select one P1 skill and write a behaviorally stated objective that includes the criterion acceptable for passing the objective. _____

2. Design a short criterion-referenced test to measure the skill objective written in number 1 of P1-level reading series. _____

Apply Your Knowledge

Write a behaviorally stated objective for students reading this chapter. _____
_____
_____

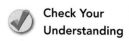

Check Your Understanding

Check your ability to complete a task analysis in Activity 6.8.

Activity 6.8

Answer the following questions.

1. Look at the following task analysis. Can you identify other smaller steps, or subskills, that should be included? Write the additional steps in the spaces provided.

   Skill: Adding numbers greater than 10

   Adds numbers 0–10 with sums greater than 10.

   Adds number facts 1–9 with sums greater than 10.

   Adds number facts 1–9 with sums less than 10.

   Adds number facts 1–8 with sums less than 10.

   Identifies numbers 1–10.

   Can count objects 1–10.

   Additional subskills: _____

2. Write a task analysis for the following skills.

   Skill: Recognizes initial consonant sounds and their association with the consonant letters of the alphabet.

   Necessary subskills: _____

Apply Your Knowledge

Select one of the subskills and write an idea or strategy for instruction.

_____

_____

_____

TASK ANALYSIS AND ERROR ANALYSIS

task analysis Breaking task down into parts to determine which part is causing difficulty for student.

subtask Small units of a task used to complete a task analysis.

Teachers often use task and error analyses without realizing that an analysis of student progress has been completed. **Task analysis** involves breaking down a task into the smallest steps necessary to complete the task. The steps actually reflect subskills, or **subtask**, which the student must complete before finishing a task. In academic work, many of these subskills and tasks form a hierarchy of skills that build throughout the school years. As students master skills and tasks, they face new, more advanced curricular tasks that depend on the earlier skills. In mathematics, for example, understanding of numerals and one-to-one correspondence must precede understanding of basic addition facts. A student must conquer addition and subtraction before tackling multiplication and division. Therefore, a thorough task analysis of skill deficits, followed by

error analysis Analyzing a student's learning problems by determining error patterns.

an informal assessment, may provide the teacher with information about what the student has or has not mastered.

Error analysis is an assessment method that a teacher can use with formal, informal, and direct measures, such as classwork. This is a method of discovering patterns of errors. A teacher may notice that a student who understands difficult multiplication facts, such as those of 11s, 12s, and 13s, continues to miss computation problems of those facts. With a careful error analysis of responses on a teacher-made test, the teacher determines that the student has incorrectly lined up the multiplicands. The student understands the math fact but has made a mistake in the mechanics of the operation.

One way that teachers can perform error analyses is to become familiar with the scope and sequence of the classroom curriculum materials. The teacher guides that accompany classroom materials are a good starting place to develop a thorough understanding of the materials and how to perform an error analysis of the students' responses. For example, a basal reading series may provide a sequence chart of the sounds presented in a given book at a specific level. Using this sequence chart, the teacher can first determine which

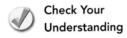 **Check Your Understanding**

Practice analyzing errors by completing Activity 6.9 below.

Activity 6.9

Look carefully at the student's responses in the following work sample from a language class. Analyze the errors the student made. Write your analysis in the space provided.

> *Items missed*—On a spelling test, the following words were missed by the student: break (spelled brak), dream (spelled dreem), and waist (spelled wast).

1. What is the deficit skill? _____

2. What words might be included in a probe written by the teacher to address this deficit skill? _____

> *Probe*—Decoding words orally to teacher:
> *Criterion*—Decode 10/10 words for mastery
>   Decode 9/10 words for instructional level
>   Decode 8/10 words or fewer indicates failure level

Apply Your Knowledge

Design a criterion-referenced probe for this skill and select the criterion necessary for mastery of the skill. _____
_____
_____

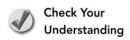
**Check Your
Understanding**

Check your ability to recall the terms introduced thus far in the chapter by completing Activity 6.10 below.

Activity 6.10

Use the terms discussed in the chapter to complete the following sentences.

1. Using material from the curriculum content in test items is called _____.

2. Using informal assessment composed of actual classwork curriculum materials is called _____.

3. A teacher who adds behavioral objectives following the analysis of test items on a standardized norm-referenced test has adapted the instrument to reflect _____ testing.

4. When a student has not mastered a specific skill, the teacher may wish to test the student more thoroughly on the one skill by developing a _____.

5. When a teacher assesses daily from the curriculum content, the assessment is called _____.

6. Assessing the subskills, or substeps, within a task is referred to as _____.

7. Analyzing the types of errors made on a test or on student work samples is called _____.

8. Teacher-made quizzes, curriculum-based assessment, criterion-referenced assessment, class assignments, and tests are all types of _____ assessment.

Apply Your Knowledge

Why would teachers prefer informal tests for measuring progress rather than commercial tests? _____
_____
_____

errors the student has made and then analyze the possible reason for the errors. Perhaps the student's errors are all errors in words with vowel combinations (such as ea, ie, ee, oa). The teacher can next perform a task analysis of the prerequisite skills the child needs to master those sounds and be able to decode words with those sounds.

Task analysis is a breaking down of the actual task or response expected to determine which prerequisite skills are lacking or have not been mastered. Error analysis often precedes task analysis because the teacher may need to look for a pattern of errors to determine exactly which task needs additional analysis.

TEACHER-MADE TESTS

Many of the types of informal assessment described in this chapter
are measures that can be designed by teachers. A study by Marso
and Pigge (1991) found that teachers made several types of errors
in test construction and tended to test items only at the knowledge
level. This study also found that the number of years of experience
teaching did not make a significant difference in the number and
type of errors made in test construction. The types of items developed by teachers in this study included short response, matching, completion, true-false, and multiple choice, with essay items
used infrequently. In constructing tests, these teachers made the
most errors in matching items, followed by completion, essay, and
true-false. Teachers may write test items using different levels of
learning, although many teachers use items at the knowledge level
because they are easier to write. Such items require the student to
merely recall, recognize, or match the material. Higher-order thinking skills are needed to assess a student's ability to sequence, apply
information, analyze, synthesize, infer, or deduct. These items may
be more difficult and time-consuming to construct.

Case Study for Teacher-Made Tests

Mr. Smithers was a first-year teacher of fourth-grade-level students.
One of the tasks he had difficulty with was constructing tests. He
had several commercially produced tests for many of the books he
was using with his students, but he often taught additional material and wanted to write his own items. He noticed that when he
constructed his own tests, students almost always made very high
grades. Although this was exciting for the students, he was not
certain that he was accurately measuring their ability.

Mr. Smithers decided to ask his mentor teacher, Mrs. Roberts,
to assist him. He showed Mrs. Roberts some examples of the items
he had written to assess the student's understanding of the concept of division.

1. $4 \div 2 =$
2. $8 \div 2 =$
3. $6 \div 2 =$

Mrs. Roberts pointed out that the items were assessing the
basic division facts that students in the fourth grade would be able
to learn by simple rote memory. In other words, this was at the simple skill level rather than at the conceptual level. Mrs. Roberts suggested that Mr. Smithers look over the scope-and-sequence chart
in the curriculum guide to determine the range of possible concepts
in the fourth-grade math curriculum. She noted that Mr. Smithers

might want to design some of his problems to assess more critical or higher-level thinking and problem solving. She also encouraged him to try to write some story or word problems to determine if his students knew when the process of division would be used rather than other operations such as addition or subtraction.

Mr. Smithers returned to his classroom and constructed the following problems to assess the conceptual understanding of division facts.

1. You and four of your friends decide to order two large 10-slice pizzas. You are all hungry and want to be sure everyone gets the same number of slices. How many pieces will each one get?

2. In your art class there are two long tables. Your art teacher tells you that you must all sit around the two tables. Since there are 16 students in the class, how many students will be at each table?

3. Your dog has been sick and your dad took him to the veterinarian. When he returns with your dog, he tells you that the veterinarian gave your dog a pill and said that he needs to take three more pills evenly spaced over the next 12 hours. How often will you need to give your dog a pill?

checklists Lists of academic or behavioral skills that must be mastered by the student.

For **MORE PRACTICE** constructing a teacher-made test, visit the Companion Website at *www.prenhall.com/overton*.

questionnaires Questions about a student's behavior or academic concerns that may be answered by the student or by the parent or teacher.

In addition to being aware of the level of difficulty of test items, teachers must be aware of types of errors made in constructing items, and how the items are associated on a test. Some of the most common types of errors made in Marso and Pigge's study are presented in Figure 6.8.

OTHER INFORMAL METHODS OF ACADEMIC ASSESSMENT

work samples Samples of a student's work; one type of permanent product.

Teachers employ many informal assessment methods to monitor the academic progress of students. Some of these methods combine the techniques of error analysis, task analysis, direct measurement, curriculum-based assessment, probes, and criterion-related assessment. These methods include making **checklists** and **questionnaires** and evaluating student **work samples** and **permanent products**.

permanent products Products made by the student that may be analyzed for academic or behavioral interventions.

Teacher-made checklists may be constructed by following an error analysis, identifying the problem area, and completing a task analysis. For each subskill that is problematic for the student, the teacher may construct a probe or a more in-depth assessment instrument. Probes may appear as short quizzes and may be timed to determine content mastery. For example, a teacher may give 10 subtraction facts for students to complete in 2 minutes. If the teacher

Figure 6.8 Most common test format construction errors.

Matching Items

Columns not titled

"Once, more than once, or not at all" not used in directions to prevent elimination

Response column not ordered

Directions do not specify basis for match

Answering procedures not specified

Elimination due to equal numbers

Columns exceed 10 items

Multiple-Choice Items

Alternatives not in columns or rows

Incomplete stems

Negative words not emphasized or avoided

"All or none of above" not appropriately used

Needless repetitions of alternatives

Presence of specific determiners in alternatives

Verbal associations between alternative and stem

Essay Exercises

Response expectations unclear

Scoring points not realistically limited

Optional questions provided

Restricted question not provided

Ambiguous words used

Opinion or feelings requested

Problem Exercises

Items not sampling understanding of content

No range of easy to difficult problems

Degree of accuracy not requested

Nonindependent items

Use of objective items when calculation preferable

Completion Items

Not complete interrogative sentence

Blanks in statement, "puzzle"

Textbook statements with words left out

More than a single idea or answer called for

Question allows more than a single answer

Requests trivia versus significant data

True-False Items

Required to write response, time waste

Statements contain more than a single idea

Negative statements used

Presence of a specific determiner

Statement is not question, give-away item

Needless phrases present, too lengthy

Interpretive Exercises

Objective response form not used

Can be answered without data present

Errors present in response items

Data presented unclear

Test Format

Absence of directions

Answering procedures unclear

Items not consecutively numbered

Inadequate margins

Answer space not provided

No space between items

Source: Adapted with permission from Ronald Marso and Fred Pigge, 1991, An analysis of teacher-made tests: Item types, cognitive demands, and item construction errors, *Contemporary Educational Psychology, 16*, pp. 284–285. Copyright 1991 by Academic Press.

uses items from the curriculum to develop the probe, the probe will be a curriculum-based assessment. The teacher may also establish a criterion for mastery of each probe or in-depth teacher-made test. This added dimension creates a criterion-referenced assessment device. The criterion may be 9 out of 10 problems added correctly. To effectively monitor the growth of the student, the teacher may set criteria for mastery each day as direct measurement techniques are employed. As the student meets the mastery criterion established for an objective, the teacher checks off the subskill on the checklist and progresses to the next most difficult item on the list of subskills.

Other informal methods that have been designed by teachers include interviews and checklists. These can be used to assess a variety of areas. Wiener (1986) suggested that teachers can construct interviews and questionnaires to assess report writing and test taking. For example, a teacher may wish to find out additional information about how students best can complete assignments such as reports or projects. A questionnaire may be designed to ask about student preferences for

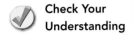

Check Your Understanding

Check your ability to correct errors in the items of a teacher-made test by completing Activity 6.11 below.

Activity 6.11

Use the information presented in Figure 6.8 to determine the errors made in the following examples of teacher-made test items. Write a corrected item for each of the following items.

True-False Items

T F 1. It is not true that curriculum-based assessment can be developed by the classroom teacher.

T F 2. Compared to norm-referenced assessment and other types of assessment used in general and special education to assess the classroom performance of students, curriculum-based assessment may be more sensitive to assessing the current classroom performance of students.

Multiple-Choice Items

1. In the assessment of students to determine the individual needs of learners, what types of assessment may be used?
    a. norm-referenced tests, curriculum-based assessment, teacher-made instruments
    b. norm-referenced instruments, curriculum-based assessment, teacher-made tests, classroom observations, probes
    c. any of the above
    d. only a and b
    e. only a and d
    f. none of the above

2. The results of assessment may assist the team in making an:
    a. goal
    b. IEP
    c. objectives
    d. decision

Apply Your Knowledge

Use the information in Figure 6.8 to write matching test items for the terms: curriculum-based assessment, direct assessment, and teacher-made tests. _____

_____

_____

teacher instructions, previous experiences with these types of tasks, and how assignments should be evaluated. A teacher may want to determine how students plan or think about their projects and what steps they have found useful in the past to complete these tasks.

Interviews and questionnaires can be written to determine students' study habits. These types of questions may include the type of environment the student prefers, what subjects are easier for the student to study independently, and which subjects are more problematic.

Teachers can also gather helpful information by informally reviewing students' work samples—actual samples of work completed by the student. Samples can include daily work, homework, tests, and quizzes. Work samples are one kind of permanent product. Other permanent products evaluated by the teacher include projects, posters, and art.

INFORMAL ASSESSMENT OF READING

Comprehension, decoding, and fluency are the broad areas of reading that teachers assess using informal methods. Comprehension is the ability to derive meaning from written language, whereas decoding is the ability to associate sounds and symbols. Fluency is the rate and ease with which a student reads orally.

Howell and Morehead (1987) presented several methods to informally assess comprehension. For example, students may be asked to answer comprehension questions about the sequence of the story and details of events in the story. Other techniques might include asking the students to paraphrase or tell the story or events in their own words, answering vocabulary items, or completing cloze or maze tasks.

A study by Fuchs and Fuchs (1992) found that the cloze and story retelling methods were not technically adequate and sensitive enough to measure the reading progress of students over time. The Maze method, however, was determined to be useful for monitoring student growth. This seems to suggest that the story retelling and the cloze methods may be best used for diagnostic information or as instructional strategies rather than as a means to monitor progress within a curriculum.

Barnes (1986) suggested using an error analysis approach when listening to students read passages aloud. With this approach, the teacher notes the errors made as the student reads and analyzes the errors to determine whether they change the meaning of the passage. The teacher then notes whether the substituted words look or sound like the original words.

Decoding skills used in reading can also be assessed informally. The teacher may design tests to measure the student's ability to

Orally read isolated letters, blends, syllables, and real words
Orally read nonsense words that contain various combinations of vowel sounds and patterns, consonant blends, and digraphs
Orally read sentences that contain new words. The teacher may sample the reader used by the student to develop a list of words to decode, if one has not been provided by the publisher. A sample may

be obtained by selecting every 10th word, selecting every 25th word, or, for higher-level readers, randomly selecting stories from which random words will be taken. Proper nouns and words already mastered by the student may be excluded (e.g., *a, the, me, I*).

Fluency is assessed to determine the reading rate and accuracy of a student using a particular reading selection. Reading fluency will be affected by the student's ability to decode new words and by the student's ability to read phrase by phrase rather than word by word. The teacher may assess oral reading fluency of new material and previously read material. Howell and Morehead (1987) suggested that the teacher listen to the student read a passage, mark the location reached at the end of 1 minute, and then ask the student to read again as quickly as possible. The teacher may note the difference between the two rates as well as errors.

Another assessment device used by teachers to measure reading skills is informal reading inventories, which assess a variety of reading skills. Inventories may be teacher-made instruments that use the actual curriculum used in instruction or commercially

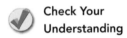

Check Your Understanding

Check your ability to write informal reading items by completing Activity 6.12 below.

Activity 6.12

Use the following passage to design brief informal assessment instruments in the spaces provided.

   Elaine sat on the balcony overlooking the mountains. The mountains were very high and appeared blue in color. The trees swayed in the breeze. The valley below was covered by a patch of fog. It was a cool, beautiful fall day.

1. Write an informal test using the cloze method. Remember to leave the first and last sentences intact. _____

2. Write an informal test using the Maze method. Remember to leave three word choices beneath each blank provided for the missing words. _____

3. Select a sentence from the passage and write an informal test using the sentence verification method. Write three sentences, one of which has the same meaning as the original sentence. _____

Apply Your Knowledge

Which of these methods was easiest for you to write? Why? _____
_____
_____

prepared devices. Commercially prepared instruments contain passages and word lists and diagnostic information that enable the teacher to analyze errors. One such instrument has been designed by Burns and Roe (1989).

Considerations When Using Informal Reading Inventories The cautions about grade levels and curriculum verification stated in the previous section should be considered when using any commercially prepared informal reading inventory. Gillis and Olson (1987) advised teachers and diagnosticians to consider the following guidelines when selecting commercially prepared informal reading inventories:

1. If possible, select inventories that have mostly narrative selections and mostly expository selections for placing elementary students in basal materials.

2. If possible, select inventories in which most of the selections are well organized.

3. When a passage on the form you are using is poorly organized or not of the appropriate text type for your purpose, use a passage at the same level from an alternate form. If an appropriate passage is not available, rewrite a passage from the inventory or write an appropriate passage.

4. When a student's comprehension scores are erratic from level to level, examine the passages to see whether the variability could be due to shifts between types of text or between well and poorly organized passages.

5. Finally, remember that the instructional level you find is just an estimate. Confirm it by observing the student's performance with classroom materials. Adjust placement if necessary. (pp. 36–44)

INFORMAL ASSESSMENT OF MATHEMATICS

The teacher may use curriculum-based assessment to measure all areas of mathematics. The assessment should be combined with both task analysis and error analysis to determine specific problem areas. These problem areas should be further assessed by using probes to determine the specific difficulty. In addition to using these methods, Liedtke (1988) suggested using an interview technique to locate deficits in accuracy and strategies. Liedtke included such techniques as asking the student to create a word problem to illustrate a computation, redirecting the original computation to obtain additional math concept information (e.g., asking the student to compare two of his answers to see which is greater), and asking the student to solve a problem and explain the steps used in the process.

Howell and Morehead (1987) suggested several methods for assessing specific math skills. Their techniques provide assessment of accuracy and fluency of basic facts, recall, basic concepts, operations, problem-solving concepts, content knowledge, tool and unit knowledge, and skill integration.

These authors suggest other techniques for checking recall and handwriting. For example, they suggest asking the student to orally respond to basic operations facts rather than responding in writing. The responses should be scored as correct or incorrect and can then be compared with the established criterion for mastery (such as 90% correct). When a student responds to written tasks such as copying numbers or writing digits, the student's ability to write the digits can be evaluated and compared with the student's oral mastery of math facts. In this way, the teacher may determine if the student's ability to write digits has an impact on responding to written math problems.

INFORMAL ASSESSMENT OF SPELLING

A common type of informal spelling assessment is a spelling test of standard format. The teacher states the word, uses the word in a sentence, and repeats the word. Most elementary spelling texts provide this type of direct curriculum-based assessment. The teacher may wish to assign different words or may be teaching at the secondary level, where typical spelling texts are not used. The teacher may also need to assess the spelling of content-related words in areas such as science or social studies. Or, the teacher may use written samples by the student to analyze spelling errors. One method of analyzing spelling errors, proposed by Guerin and Maier (1983), is shown in Table 6.8.

INFORMAL ASSESSMENT OF WRITTEN LANGUAGE

A student's written language ability may be assessed informally by collecting and analyzing written work samples. Written samples may be analyzed for spelling, punctuation, correct grammar and usage, vocabulary, creative ability, story theme, sequence, and plot. If the objective of instruction is to promote creativity, actual spelling, punctuation, and other mechanical errors should not be scored against the student on the written sample. These errors, however, should be noted by the teacher and used in educational planning for English and spelling lessons. One informal assessment technique for written language skills proposed by Shapiro (1996) includes the following steps:

1. A series of "story starters" should be constructed that can be used to give initial ideas for students to write about. These starters should contain items that most children will find of sufficient interest to generate a written story.

Table 6.8 Analysis of spelling errors used in informal assessment.

	Definitions	Example	
		Heard	Written
Phonetic Ability			
PS	Substitutions: placing another sound or syllable in place of the sound in the word	match nation	mach nashun
PO	Omissions: leaving out a sound or syllable from the word	grateful temperature	graful tempature
PA	Additions: adding a sound or syllable to the original	purchase importance	purchasing importantance
PSe	Sequencing: putting sounds or syllables in the wrong order	animal elephant	aminal elelant
Visualization			
VS	Substitutions: substitution of a vowel or consonant for those in the given word	him chapel	hin chaple
VO	Omissions: leaving out a vowel, or consonant, or syllable from those in the given word	allow beginning	alow begining
Phonetic Ability			
VA	Additions: adding a vowel, consonant, or syllable to those in the given word	welcome fragrant	wellcome fragerant
VSe	Sequencing: putting letters or syllables in the wrong order	guardian pilot	guardain pliot
Linguistic Performance			
LS	Substitution: substitution of a word for another having somewhat the same meaning	ring house	bell home
	Substitution: substituting another word because of different language structure (teacher judgment)	came ate	come et
	Substitution: substitution of a completely different word	pear polish	pair collage
LO	Omissions: omitting word endings, prefixes suffixes	pushed unhelpful	pusht helpful
LA	Additions: adding endings, prefixes, suffixes	cry forget	crys forgetting
LSe	Sequencing: reversing syllables	discussed disappoint	discuted dispapoint

Source: From *Informal Assessment in Education* (pp. 218–219) by G. R. Guerin and A. S. Maier, 1983, Palo Alto, CA: Mayfield Publishing. Copyright 1983 by Mayfield Publishing. Reprinted by permission.

2. The evaluator should give the child a copy of the story starter and read the starter to him or her. The evaluator then tells the student that he or she will be asked to write a story using the starter as the first sentence. The student should be given a minute to think about a story before he or she is asked to begin writing.

3. After 1 minute, the evaluator should tell the child to begin writing, start the stopwatch, and time for 3 minutes. If the child stops writing before the 3 minutes are up, he or she should be encouraged to keep writing until time is up.

4. The evaluator should count the number of words that are correctly written. "Correct" means that a word can be recognized (even if it is misspelled). Capitalization and punctuation are ignored. The rate of the correct and incorrect words per 3 minutes is calculated. If the child stops writing before the 3 minutes are up, the number of words correct should be multiplied by 180 for the number of words correct per 3 minutes. (p. 125)

Shapiro also suggested creating local norms to compare students. The number of words correct may be used as a basis for writing short-term objectives. This informal method may be linked directly to classroom curricula and may be repeated frequently as a direct measure of student writing ability. Writing samples may also be used to analyze handwriting. The teacher uses error analysis to evaluate the sample, write short-term objectives, and plan educational strategies. One such error analysis of handwriting skills is shown in Figure 6.9.

PERFORMANCE ASSESSMENT AND AUTHENTIC ASSESSMENT

Performance testing is designed so that the student creates a response from the student's existing knowledge base. The U.S. Office of Technology Assessment defines performance assessment as "testing methods that require students to create an answer product that demonstrates their knowledge or skills" (1992, p. 16). The teacher may use a variety of formats in performance assessment, including products that the student constructs. Harris and Graham (1994) state that performance assessment stresses the student's active construction in demonstrating knowledge.

The types of tasks that teachers may require a student to complete in performance assessment may include the student's explanation of process as well as the student's perception of the task and the material learned. This type of assessment may involve several levels of cognitive processing and reasoning and may allow educators to tap into areas not assessed by more traditional types of

Figure 6.9 One method of handwriting analysis.

Directions: Analysis of handwriting should be made on a sample of the student's written work, not from a carefully produced sample. Evaluate each task and mark in the appropriate column. Score each task "satisfactory" (1) or "unsatisfactory" (2).

I. Letter formation

A. Capitals (score each letter 1 or 2)

A _____	G _____	M _____	S _____	Y _____
B _____	H _____	N _____	T _____	Z _____
C _____	I _____	O _____	U _____	
D _____	J _____	P _____	V _____	
E _____	K _____	Q _____	W _____	
F _____	L _____	R _____	X _____	

Total _____

Score
(1 or 2)

B. Lowercase (score by groups)

1. Round letters
   a. Counterclockwise
     a, c, d, g, o, q _____
   b. Clockwise
     k, p _____
2. Looped letters
   a. Above line
     b, d, e, f, h, k, l _____
   b. Below line
     f, g, j, p, q, y _____
3. Retraced letters
   i, u, t, w, y _____
4. Humped letters
   h, m, n, v, x, z _____
5. Others
   r, s, b _____

C. Numerals (score each number 1 or 2)

1 _____	4 _____	7 _____	10–20 _____
2 _____	5 _____	8 _____	21–99 _____
3 _____	6 _____	9 _____	100–1,000 _____
			Total _____

continued.

Figure 6.9   continued.

II. Spatial relationships

                                                                                   Score
                                                                                   (1 or 2)

    A. Alignment (letters on line)   _____
    B. Uniform slant   _____
    C. Size of letters
       1. To each other   _____
       2. To available space   _____
    D. Space between letters   _____
    E. Space between words   _____
    F. Anticipation of end of line (hyphenates, moves to next line)   _____
                     Total   _____

III. Rate of writing (letters per minute)

                                                                                   Score
                                                                                   (1 or 2)

Grade 1:20
      2:30
      3:35
      4:45
      5:55
      6:65
      7 and above: 75   _____

Scoring	*Satisfactory*	*Questionable*	*Poor*
I. *Letter formation*			
A. Capitals	26	39	40
B. Lowercase	7	10	11
C. Numerals	12	18	19
II. *Spatial relationships*	7	10	11
III. *Rate of writing*	1	2	6

Source: From *Informal Assessment in Education* (p. 228) by G. R. Guerin and A. S. Maier, 1983, Palo Alto, CA: Mayfield Publishing. Copyright 1983 by Mayfield Publishing. Reprinted by permission.

authentic assessment
Assessment that requires the student to apply knowledge in the real world.

assessment. When considering performance assessment as an alternative for making educational placement decisions, Elliott and Fuchs (1997) caution that performance assessment should be used in conjunction with other types of assessment because of insufficient knowledge regarding psychometric evidence and the lack of professionals who are trained to use this type of assessment reliably. Glatthorn suggested criteria for educators to use in the evaluation of performance tasks (1998). These criteria are presented in Table 6.9.

    Authentic assessment differs from performance assessment in that students must apply knowledge in a manner consistent with

Table 6.9 Criteria for evaluating performance tasks.

Does the performance task

- Correspond closely and comprehensively with the standard and benchmarks it is designed to assess?
- Require the student to access prior knowledge in completing the task?
- Require the use of higher order thought processes including creative thinking?
- Seem real and purposeful, embedded in a meaningful context that seems authentic?
- Engage students' interest?
- Require the students to communicate to classmates and others the processes they used and the results they obtained, using multiple response modes?
- Require sustained effort over a significant period of time?
- Provide the student with options?
- Seem feasible in the context of schools and classrooms, not requiring inordinate resources or creating undue controversy?
- Convey a sense of fairness to all, being free of basis?
- Challenge the students without frustrating them?
- Include criteria and rubrics for evaluating student performance?
- Provide both group and individual work, with appropriate accountability?

Source: Performance Assessment and Standard-Based Curricula: The Achievement Cycle by A. A. Glatthorn (1998). Copyright by Eye on Education. Larchmont, NY.

generalizing into a real-world setting, or students may complete the task in the real world. Archbald (1991) states that authentic assessment requires a disciplined production of knowledge using techniques that are within the field in which the student is being assessed. The student's tasks are instrumental and may require a substantial amount of time to complete. The student may be required to use a variety of materials and resources that may include working in collaboration with other students.

PORTFOLIO ASSESSMENT

portfolio assessment
Evaluating student progress, strengths, and weaknesses using a collection of different measurements and work samples.

One method of assessing a student's current level of academic functioning is through **portfolio assessment**. A portfolio is a collection of student work that provides a holistic view of the student's strengths and weaknesses. The portfolio collection contains various work samples, permanent products, and test results from a variety of instruments and methods. For example, a portfolio of reading might include a student's test scores on teacher-made tests, including curriculum-based assessments, work samples from daily work and homework assignments, error analyses on work and test samples, and the results of an informal reading inventory with miscues noted and analyzed. The assessment of the student's progress would assess decoding skills, comprehension skills, fluency, and so on. These measures would be collected over a period of time. This type of assessment may be useful in describing the current progress of the student to his parents (Taylor, 1993).

The essential elements of effective portfolio assessment were listed by Shaklee, Barbour, Ambrose, and Hansford (1997), who included the following assessment elements:

> Assessment should:
> be authentic and valid.
> encompass the whole child.
> involve repeated observations of various patterns of behavior.
> be continuous over time.
> use a variety of methods for gathering evidence of student performance.
> provide a means for systematic feedback to be used in the improvement of instruction and student performance.
> provide an opportunity for joint conversations and explanations between students and teachers, teachers and parents, and students and parents. (p. 10)

Ruddell (1995) provides the following list of possible products that could be included in a portfolio for assessing literacy in the middle grades:

> samples of student writing
> story maps
> reading log or dated list of books student has read
> vocabulary journal
> artwork, project papers, photographs, and other products of work completed
> group work, papers, projects, and products
> daily journal
> writing ideas
> reading response log, learning log, or double-entry journal or writing from assigned reading during the year
> letters to pen pals, letters exchanged with teacher
> out-of-school writing and artwork
> unit and lesson tests collected over the grading period or academic year (p. 191)

Paratore (1995) reports that establishing common standards for assessing literacy through the use of portfolio assessment provides a useful alternative in the evaluation of students' reading and writing skills. Hobbs (1993) found portfolio assessment useful in providing supplemental information for eligibility consideration that included samples of the quality of work that was not evident in standardized assessment.

Portfolio data were also found to provide information to teachers that was more informative and led to different decisions for instructional planning (Rueda & Garcia, 1997). This study found that the recommendations were more specific and that student strengths were more easily identifiable using this form of assessment.

INFORMAL AND FORMAL ASSESSMENT METHODS

In Chapter 7 you will be introduced to norm-referenced testing. These tests are useful in assessing factors that cannot be reliably or validly assessed using informal measures. There are some difficulties with using norm-referenced tests, however, and this has led to the shift to the response-to-intervention method, problem-solving method, and the increased use of informal measures, such as CBMs, to collect data.

Some of the difficulties with the use of norm-referenced assessment are presented in the next section.

PROBLEMS OF NORM-REFERENCED ASSESSMENT

The weaknesses attributed to norm-referenced assessment include problems specific to the various instruments and problems with test administration and interpretation. Norm-referenced tests may not adequately represent material actually taught in a specific curriculum (Shapiro, 1996). In other words, items on norm-referenced tests may include content or skill areas not included in the student's curriculum. Salvia and Hughes (1990) wrote:

> The fundamental problem with using published tests is the test's content. If the content of the test—even content prepared by experts—does not match the content that is taught, the test is useless for evaluating what the student has learned from school instruction. (p. 8)

Good and Salvia (1988) studied the representation of reading curricula in norm-referenced tests and concluded that a deficient score on a norm-referenced reading test could actually represent the selection of a test with inadequate content validity for the current curriculum. Hultquist and Metzke (1993) determined that curriculum bias existed when using standardized achievement tests to measure the reading of survival words and reading and spelling skills in general.

In addition, the frequent use of norm-referenced instruments may result in bias because limited numbers of alternate forms exist, creating the possibility of test wiseness among students (Fuchs, Tindal, & Deno, 1984; Shapiro, 1996). Another study revealed that norm-referenced instruments are not as sensitive to academic growth as other instruments that are linked more directly to the actual classroom curriculum (Marston, Fuchs, & Deno, 1986). This means that norm-referenced tests may not measure small gains made in the classroom from week to week.

According to Reynolds (1982), the psychometric assessment of students using traditional norm-referenced methods is fraught with many problems of bias, including cultural bias, which may result in test scores that reflect intimidation or communication problems rather than ability level. These difficulties in using norm-referenced testing for special education planning have led to the emergence of alternative methods of assessment.

THINK AHEAD

When a student has academic difficulty and does not respond to the intensive interventions employed in a general education setting, a referral to special education may result. In order to make this determination, additional data, such as academic achievement and diagnostic data, may be required. Chapter 7 presents an overview of the assessment of academic achievement using norm-referenced methods.

EXERCISES

Part I

Match the terms with the correct definitions.

a. criterion-referenced assessment
b. curriculum-based measurement
c. task analysis
d. error analysis
e. informal assessment
f. questionnaire

g. formative
h. summative
i. probes
j. checklist
k. portfolio
l. aimline
m. authentic assessment
n. performance assessment

_____ 1. A teacher reviews the information provided in a student's norm-referenced achievement scores. She determines that the student has a weakness in the area of multiplication with regrouping, but she is not certain exactly how the student is completing the process. In order to determine this, the teacher decides to use _____.

_____ 2. A teacher who works with students in the range of mild mental retardation would like to assess the students' ability to return the correct amount of change when given a $10.00 bill to pay for an item that costs $2.85. How might the teacher decide to assess this skill? _____

_____ 3. To determine the specific skills applied in completing double-digit addition problems, the teacher can complete a _____.

_____ 4. In a daily living skills class, a teacher can assess the student's ability to make a complete meal by using _____.

_____ 5. A teacher assesses students' knowledge of the science unit by each student's book report, test grade, written classroom assignments, lab experiences, and journal. This group of science products demonstrates one example of _____.

_____ 6. Error analysis, checklists, direct measurement, authentic assessment, portfolio assessment, probes, and curriculum-based assessment are examples of _____.

_____ 7. A teacher sets a standard of reaching 90% mastery on the test assessing basic reading decoding skills of second-grade-level words. This test is an example of _____.

_____ 8. Asking the parent of a child to complete a survey about the specific behaviors observed during homework time is an example of using _____ as part of the assessment.

_____ 9. A teacher decides to evaluate the progress of her students following the conclusion of a science unit. This type of assessment is known as _____.

_____10. By adding the number of correct letter sequences found in the baseline to the number of weekly expected CLSs for the year, the teacher can then plot the _____.

Part II

Use the terms in Part I to select a method of informal assessment for the following situations. Write the reason for your selection.

1. Standardized test results you received on a new student indicate that she is performing two grade levels below expectancy. You want to determine which reading book to place her in.

   Method of assessment: _____

   Reason: _____

2. A student who understands division problems when presented in class failed a teacher-made test. You want to determine the reason for the failure.

   Method of assessment: _____

   Reason: _____

3. Following a screening test of fifth-grade level spelling, you determine that a student performs inconsistently when spelling words with short vowel sounds:

   Method of assessment: _____

   Reason: _____

4. A student seems to be performing at a different level than indicated by norm-referenced math test data. You think you

should meet with his parents and discuss actual progress in the classroom.

Method of assessment: _____

Reason: _____

5. A teacher wants to monitor the progress of students who are acquiring the basic addition computation skills. In order to determine if students are progressing toward the end-of-the-year goal, the teacher can employ:

Method of assessment: _____

Reason: _____

Answers to these questions can be found in the Appendix of this text or you may also complete these questions and receive immediate feedback on your answers by going to the Think Ahead module in Chapter 6 of the Companion Website.

CHAPTER

7

Academic Assessment

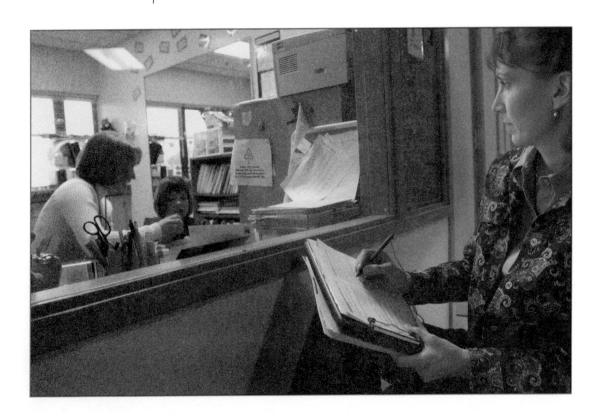

achievement tests

screening tests

aptitude tests

diagnostic tests

adaptive behavior scales

norm-referenced tests

curriculum-based assessment

diagnostic instruments

domain

language assessment

receptive language

expressive language

written language

CHAPTER FOCUS

This chapter includes several commonly used norm-referenced individual achievement tests. Information is presented that will enable you to understand how the basic methods of studying reliability and validity are applied to these instruments. You will learn some basic scoring methods that will allow you to generalize these skills to other instruments.

Professionals working with students who require special services are concerned with how students perform on educational measures. One way to measure educational performance is to use norm-referenced achievement tests. Of all standardized tests, individually administered achievement tests are the most numerous (Anastasi & Urbina, 1998).

CEC KNOWLEDGE AND SKILLS STANDARDS

The student completing this chapter will understand the knowledge and skills included in the following CEC Knowledge and Skills Standards from Standard 8: Assessment:

CC8K4—Use and limitations of assessment instruments

CC8S2—Administer nonbiased formal and informal assessments

CC8S5—Interpret information from formal and informal assessments

ACHIEVEMENT TESTS

achievement tests Tests used to measure academic progress, what the student has retained in curriculum.

Used in virtually every school, **achievement tests** are designed to measure what the student has learned. These tests may be developed to measure a specific area of the educational curriculum, such as written language, or to measure across several areas of the curriculum, such as math, reading, spelling, and science. Brief tests containing items that survey a range of skill levels, domains, or content areas are known as **screening tests.** Screening tests assess no one area in depth. Screening tests provide the educator with a method to determine weak areas that need additional assessment in order to determine specific skill mastery or weaknesses.

screening tests Brief tests that sample a few items across skills or domains.

aptitude tests Tests designed to measure strength, talent, or ability in a particular area or domain.

Aptitude tests contain items that measure what a student has retained but also are designed to indicate how much the student will learn in the future. Aptitude tests are thought to indicate current areas of strength as well as future potential. These tests are used in educational planning and include both group and individually administered tests. **Diagnostic tests** are those used to measure a specific ability, such as fine-motor ability. **Adaptive behavior scales** measure how well students adapt to different environments.

diagnostic tests Individually administered tests designed to determine specific academic problems or deficit areas.

adaptive behavior scales Instruments that assess a student's ability to adapt to the world in different situations.

STANDARDIZED NORM-REFERENCED TESTS VERSUS CURRICULUM-BASED ASSESSMENT

norm-referenced tests Tests designed to compare individual students with national averages, or norms of expectancy.

The use of **norm-referenced tests** to measure academic achievement helps educators make both placement and eligibility decisions. When selected and administered carefully, these tests yield fairly reliable and valid information. As discussed in the previous chapter, norm-referenced instruments are researched and constructed in a systematic way and provide educators with a method of comparing a student with a peer group evaluated during the standardization process of the test development. Comparing a student to a norm reference group allows the educator to determine whether the student is performing as expected for the age or grade. If the student appears to be significantly behind peers developmentally, special services may be recommended.

curriculum-based assessment Using content from the currently used curriculum to assess student progress.

Curriculum-based assessment tests students on the very curriculum used for instruction. In this method of determining mastery of skills or specific curriculum, the student may be compared with past performance on similar items or tasks. Curriculum-based testing, which is very useful and necessary in special education, is discussed further in Chapter 6.

REVIEW OF ACHIEVEMENT TESTS

This text is designed to involve the reader in the learning process and to help the reader develop skills in administering and interpreting tests. Rather than include numerous tests, many of which the future teacher may not use, this chapter presents achievement tests selected because of their frequent use in schools or because of their technical adequacy. The following are individually administered screening achievement tests used frequently by educators:

1. *Woodcock–Johnson III.* This revised edition of the Woodcock–Johnson–Revised Psychoeducational Battery includes two forms, A and B. It contains cognitive and achievement tests, each of which includes standard and extended batteries. The same sample was assessed using all components of the battery to establish the normative data. Using the same sample enhances the diagnostic capability for determining domain-specific skills and their associated cognitive abilities as well as discrepancies between ability and achievement (McGrew & Woodcock, 2001).

2. *Peabody Individual Achievement Test–4.* This test was listed as one of the most frequently used by professionals in Child Service Demonstration Centers (Thurlow & Ysseldyke, 1979), by school psychologists (LaGrow & Prochnow-LaGrow, 1982), by special education teachers who listed this as one of the most useful tests (Connelly, 1985), and by teachers who are in both self-contained and resource classrooms for students with learning disabilities (German, Johnson, & Schneider, 1985).

3. *Kaufman Test of Educational Achievement (K-TEA-II).* The K-TEA-II is a recent revision of the original K-TEA. It was conormed with the K-ABC.

4. *Wechsler Individual Achievement Test, Second Edition.* This revised instrument was designed to be used in conjunction with the Wechsler Intelligence Scales or other measures of cognitive ability and assesses the academic areas specified in special education regulations.

5. *Wide Range Achievement Test.* This test was listed as useful by teachers of students with emotional disabilities, learning disabilities, and mental retardation (Connelly, 1985); by teachers in self-contained and resource rooms for students with learning disabilities (German, Johnson, & Schneider, 1985); by school psychologists (LaGrow & Prochnow-LaGrow, 1982; Reschly, 1988); and by teachers in Child Service Demonstration Centers (Thurlow & Ysseldyke, 1979). This text describes the third edition of the Wide Range Achievement Test (Wilkinson, 1993).

6. *Mini-Battery of Achievement.* This is included as a fairly new screening achievement battery (Woodcock, McGrew, & Werder, 1994). This test has a format similar to the Woodcock-Johnson Tests of Achievement–Revised. It is presented as an alternative to the WRAT3.

These tests, which represent several academic areas, are discussed in the following sections. Their reliability and validity are presented in an effort to encourage future teachers to be wise consumers of assessment devices.

WOODCOCK-JOHNSON III TESTS OF ACHIEVEMENT (WJ III)

This new edition of the Woodcock-Johnson (Woodcock, McGrew, & Mather, 2001), presented in an easel type of format, comprises two parallel achievement batteries that allow the examiner to retest the same student within a short amount of time with less practice effect. The battery of subtests allows the examiner to select the specific clusters of subtests needed for a particular student. This achievement battery has standard tests and extended tests. An Examiner Training Workbook is included that will assist examiners in learning how to administer the subtests, understand basal and ceiling rules, and learn how to complete the scoring included on the protocol (Wendling & Mather, 2001). A checklist is provided in the manual for each subtest of the WJ III Achievement Tests. Each of the checklists states the specific skills and steps the examiner must follow in order to complete standardized administration of the instrument.

Some features of the WJ III Tests of Achievement include the following:

1. Basal and ceiling levels are specified by individual subtests. For many of the subtests, when the student answers six consecutive items correctly, the basal is established; and when the student answers six consecutive items incorrectly, the ceiling is established. Other subtests have basal levels of four consecutive correct and ceilings of four consecutive incorrect. Additional basal and ceiling rules include specific starting points and time limits for stopping the subtest administration. Examiners should study the basal and ceiling rules and refer to the protocol and the examiner's manual for specific rules.

2. Derived scores can be obtained for each individual subtest for estimations of age and grade equivalents only. Other standard scores are available using the computer scoring program.

3. The norm group ranged in age from 2 to 90 years and older and included students at the college/university level through graduate school.

4. The use of extended age scores provides a more comprehensive analysis of children and adults who are not functioning at a school grade level.

5. The WJ III Tests of Achievement include subtests that require the student to use paper and pencil as well as subtests that are administered using a tape player. The protocol contains icons to denote when the test response booklet or the tape player is needed as well as which subtests are timed.

6. The examiner's manual includes suggested guidelines for using the WJ III with individuals who are English language learners, individuals with reading and/or learning disabilities, individuals with attentional and behavioral difficulties, individuals with hearing or visual impairments, and individuals with physical impairments.

7. The computer scoring program includes an option for determining the individual's cognitive-academic language proficiency level.

8. A Test Session Observation Checklist is located on the front of the protocol for the examiner to note the individual student's behavior during the assessment sessions.

9. Transparent scoring templates are provided for reading and math fluency subtests.

The Woodcock-Johnson Tests of Achievement are organized into subtests and clusters. The subtests are grouped into broad clusters to aid in the interpretation of scores. The examiner may select the specific clusters needed to screen a student's achievement level and combine the administration of selected cognitive clusters to determine a pattern of strengths and weaknesses. For example, a student who is suspected of having difficulties with math reasoning would be administered the subtests of quantitative concepts and applied problems. A student who has had difficulty with beginning reading skills might be given the cluster to assess phoneme/grapheme knowledge which includes the subtests of word attack and spelling of sounds.

Standard Battery   The following paragraphs describe the subtests in the Standard Battery.

Letter-Word Identification. The student is presented with a picture, letter, or word and asked to identify it orally. The basal and ceiling levels are, respectively, six lowest consecutive items correct and the six highest items incorrect.

Reading Fluency. This timed subtest presents statements for the student to read and determine if the statements are true or not true. It assesses how quickly the student reads the sentences, makes decisions about the statement validity, and circles the correct response. The time limit is 3 minutes.

Story Recall. All items are presented using the audio recording provided. The student listens to the short stories and then tells the story to the examiner. Instructions for continuing and stopping the administration of the subtest are provided in the protocol and are based on the number of points the student earns.

Understanding Directions. This subtest requires the stimulus pictures on the easel and oral instructions by the examiner. As the student looks at the pictures, the examiner provides instructions such as "First point to the dog then the bird if the dog is brown." Specific instructions are provided in the protocol regarding when the student discontinues the subtest based on the number of points earned.

Calculation. Math problems are presented in a paper-and-pencil format. The problems include number writing on the early items and range from addition to calculus operations on the more advanced items. The basal and ceiling levels are, respectively, the six lowest consecutive items correct and the six highest consecutive items incorrect.

Math Fluency. This subtest is included in the student's response booklet. The student is required to complete problems of basic operations of addition, subtraction, multiplication, and division. This subtest is timed and the student solves as many problems as possible within 3 minutes.

Spelling. This subtest assesses the individual's ability to write words that are presented orally by the examiner. The early items include tracing lines and letters, and the more advanced items include multisyllabic words with unpredictable spellings. The basal and ceiling levels are, respectively, six consecutive correct and incorrect items.

Writing Fluency. This paper-and-pencil subtest consists of pictures paired with three words. The examiner instructs the student to write sentences about each picture using the words. The student is allowed to write for 7 minutes. Correct responses are complete sentences that include the three words presented.

Passage Comprehension. The examiner shows the student a passage with a missing word, and the student must orally supply the word. The basal and ceiling levels are, respectively, the six lowest consecutive items correct and the six highest incorrect items.

Applied Problems. The examiner reads a story math problem, and the student must answer orally. Picture cues are provided at the lower levels. The basal and ceiling levels are determined in the same manner as for the Calculation subtest.

Writing Samples. This subtest requires the student to construct age-appropriate sentences meeting specific criteria (for syntax, content, etc.). The items are scored as 2, 1, or 0 based on the quality of the responses. The examiner's manual provides a comprehensive scoring guide.

Story Recall—Delayed. On this subtest, the student is asked to recall the stories presented in a previous subtest, Story Recall. The delayed subtest can be presented from 30 minutes to 8 days following the initial administration of Story Recall.

Extended Battery   The subtests included in the Extended Battery are described in the following paragraphs.

Word Attack. The student is asked to read nonsense words aloud. This subtest measures the student's ability to decode and pronounce new words. The basal is established when a student answers six consecutive items correctly, and the ceiling is six consecutive incorrect responses.

Picture Vocabulary. The items in this subtest require the student to express the names of objects presented in pictures on the easel. The basal and ceiling levels are, respectively, the six lowest consecutive correct and six highest incorrect items.

Oral Comprehension. These items are presented on the audiotape and require that the student complete the missing word in the presented items. The items range from simple associations to more complex sentences. The basal and ceiling levels are, respectively, the six lowest consecutive correct and six highest incorrect items.

Editing. This subtest requires the student to proofread sentences and passages and determine the errors of punctuation, capitalization, usage, or spelling. The student is asked to correct errors in written passages shown on the easel page. The basal and ceiling levels are, respectively, the six lowest consecutive correct and six highest incorrect items.

Reading Vocabulary. This subtest contains three sections: Part A, Synonyms; Part B, Antonyms; and Part C, Analogies. All three sections must be completed in order to obtain a score for the subtest. The student is asked to say a word that means the same as a given word in Part A and to say a word that has the opposite meaning of a word in Part B. In Part C, the student must complete analogies. Only one-word responses are acceptable for the subtest items. The examiner obtains a raw score by adding the number of items correct in the two subtests. The basal and ceiling levels are, respectively, the four lowest consecutive items correct and four highest incorrect responses.

Quantitative Concepts. This subtest includes two parts: Part A, Concepts; and Part B, Number Series. Both sections must be completed in order to obtain a score for the subtest. Items cover math vocabulary, concepts, and the completion of missing numbers presented in various types of series. The examiner's manual states that no mathematical decisions are made in response to these test items. Picture cues are given for some items in the lower levels. The basal and ceiling instructions are different for each part and are contained in the protocol.

Academic Knowledge. This subtest contains three parts: Part A, Science; Part B, Social Studies; and Part C, Humanities. For the Science section, the examiner orally presents open-ended questions covering scientific content. The basal and ceiling levels are, respectively, the three lowest consecutive correct and three highest incorrect items. Picture cues are given at the lower and upper levels. The Social Studies section orally presents open-ended questions covering topics about society and government. The basal and ceiling levels are the same as for the Science section. Picture cues are given at the lower level. The questions in the Humanities section cover topics the student may have learned from the cultural environment. The basal and ceiling levels are the same as for the Science and Social Studies sections.

Spelling of Sounds. The examiner presents the first few items of this subtest orally and the remaining items are presented using the audiotape. The individual is asked to write the spellings of nonsense words. This requires that the student be able to associate the sounds heard with the written letter. The basal and ceiling levels are, respectively, the four lowest consecutive items correct and the highest four items incorrect.

Sound Awareness. This subtest contains four sections: Part A, Sound Awareness—Rhyming; Part B, Sound Awareness—Deletion; Part C, Sound Awareness—Substitution; and Part D, Sound Awareness—Reversal. The items for Part A require the student to determine and generate words that rhyme. Part B requires the student to say parts of the original stimulus provided on the audiotape. Part C requires that the individual change a specified part of the stimulus word. Part D requires the student to perform two tasks. First, the student is asked to reverse compound words. Then the student is required to reverse the sounds of letters to create new words. This subtest is arranged so that each part is more difficult than the previous part. Within each part, items are also sequenced from easier to more difficult items. The basal is one item correct for each of the sections, and the ceilings vary for each section.

Punctuation and Capitalization. This subtest includes items that require the student to write the correct punctuation for specific stimuli presented by the examiner and in the response booklet. For example, a sentence in the response booklet may

Check Your Understanding

Check your understanding of the Woodcock–Johnson III Tests of Achievement by completing Activity 7.1 below.

Activity 7.1

1. How many parallel forms are included in the third edition of the Woodcock–Johnson Tests of Achievement? What is the advantage of having different forms of the same instrument?_____

2. What is the age range of the WJ III?_____

3. What populations were included in the norming process of the third edition?_____

4. What new school level is included in the WJ III? Why?_____

Apply Your Knowledge

Refer to the WJ III subtest descriptions in your text. Which subtests would not be appropriate for a student to complete in the standard fashion if the student had a severe fine-motor disability and could not use a pencil or keyboard? What adaptations would be appropriate? Explain the ethical considerations that should be addressed by making such adaptations. _____

_____

_____

need quotation marks or a capital letter. The individual writes the needed punctuation or capitalization in the response booklet. The basal and ceiling levels are, respectively, the six lowest consecutive correct and the six highest incorrect items.

PEABODY INDIVIDUAL ACHIEVEMENT TEST–REVISED (PIAT–R)

The PIAT–R (Markwardt, 1989) is contained in four easels, called Volumes I, II, III, and IV. For this revision, the number of items has been increased on the existing subtests. The subtests are General Information, Reading Recognition, Reading Comprehension, Mathematics, Spelling, and Written Expression.

Subtests

General Information. Questions in this subtest are presented in an open-ended format. The student gives oral responses to questions that range in topic from science to sports. The examiner records all responses. A key for acceptable responses is given throughout the examiner's pages of the subtest and provides suggestions for further questioning.

Reading Recognition. The items at the beginning level of this subtest are visual recognition and discrimination items that require the student to match a picture, letter, or word. The student must select the response from a choice of four items. The more difficult items require the student to pronounce a list of words that range from single-syllable consonant-vowel-consonant words to multisyllable words with unpredictable pronunciations.

Reading Comprehension. This subtest is administered to students who earn a raw score of 19 or better on the Reading Recognition subtest. The items are presented in a two-page format. The examiner asks the student to read a passage silently on the first page of each item. On the second page, the student must select from four choices the one picture that best illustrates the passage. The more difficult-to-read items also have pictures that are more difficult to discriminate.

Mathematics. Math questions are presented in a forced-choice format. The student is orally asked a question and must select the correct response from four choices. Questions range from numeral recognition to trigonometry.

Spelling. This subtest begins with visual discrimination tasks of pictures, symbols, and letters. The spelling items are presented in a forced-choice format. The student is asked to select the correct spelling of the word from four choices.

Written Expression. This subtest allows for written responses by the student; level 1 is presented to students who are functioning at the kindergarten or first-grade level, level II to students functioning in the second- to twelfth-grade levels. The basal and ceiling levels do not apply.

Scoring The examiner uses the raw score on the first PIAT–R subtest, General Information, to determine a starting point on the following subtest, Reading Recognition. The raw score from the Reading Recognition subtest then provides a starting point for the Reading Comprehension subtest, and so on throughout the test. The basal and ceiling levels are consistent across subtests. A basal level is established when five consecutive items have been answered correctly. The ceiling level is determined when the student answers five of seven items incorrectly. Because the Written Expression subtest requires written responses by the student, the basal and ceiling levels do not apply.

The PIAT–R yields standard scores, grade equivalents, age equivalents, and percentile ranks for individual subtests and for a Total Reading and a Total Test score. The manual provides for standard error of measurement for obtained and derived scores. The raw score from the Written Expression subtest can be used with the raw score from the Spelling subtest to obtain a written language composite. Scoring procedures are detailed in Appendix I of the PIAT–R examiner's manual.

KAUFMAN TEST OF EDUCATIONAL ACHIEVEMENT, 2ND EDITION (K-TEA-II)

The K-TEA-II (Kaufman & Kaufman, 2004) is an individually administered achievement battery for children ages 4 years and 6 months to 25 years. This instrument provides subtests to assess children of preschool age through young adults in college. There are two forms of this comprehensive achievement measure, Form A and Form B. Having equivalent forms allows for repeated testing of constructs and items of equivalent difficulty and content while possibly decreasing the influence of the practice effect. The K-TEA-II was conormed with the Kaufman Assessment Battery for Children, Second Edition (K-ABC-II; Kaufman & Kaufman, 2004). Using both forms of this instrument permits a more valid comparison of cognitive and academic ability across instruments.

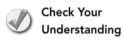

Check Your Understanding

Check your understanding of the PIAT–R protocol by completing Activity 7.2 below.

Activity 7.2

Refer to your text and Figure 7.1 to complete this exercise.

1. How is the starting point for the Reading Recognition subtest determined?_____

2. How is the Reading Comprehension start point determined? _____

3. What response mode is used on many of the items on this test?_____

4. How does this response mode impact scores?_____

5. Using the information provided on the portion of the PIAT–R protocol shown on page 262, determine the Total Reading Raw Score. Add the Reading Recognition and the Reading Comprehension raw scores. To determine the Total Test raw score, add all subtest raw scores. Write the sums in the appropriate spaces.

6. Using the raw score data, look up the standard scores on the following table and write the scores in the appropriate spaces on the protocol sheet._____

Apply Your Knowledge

Make a general statement regarding the student's academic functioning based on the standard scores you determined on the PIAT–R. Does the student have any academic strengths or weaknesses according to these scores?_____
_____
_____

The complete K-TEA-II, the Comprehensive Form and additional reading-related areas, includes the following composites, which are comprised of the respective subtests:

Reading—Letter & Word Identification; Reading Comprehension
Math—Math Concepts and Applications; Math Computation
Written Language—Written Expression; Spelling
Oral Language—Listening Comprehension; Oral Expression
Sound-Symbol—Phonological Awareness; Nonsense Word Decoding; Letter and Word Recognition
Decoding—Letter & Word Decoding; Nonsense Word Decoding

Figure 7.1   Basal and ceiling rules and response items for a subtest from the Peabody Individual Achievement Test–Revised.

SUBTEST 2
Reading Recognition

Training Exercises

	Trial 1	Trial 2	Trial 3
Exercise A.	(1) _____	(1) _____	(1) _____
Exercise B.	(3) _____	(3) _____	(3) _____
Exercise C.	(2) _____	(2) _____	(2) _____

Basal and Ceiling Rules
Basal: *highest* 5 consecutive correct responses
Ceiling: *lowest* 7 consecutive responses containing 5 errors

Starting Point
The item number that corresponds to the subject's raw score on General Information.

43. ledge _____ 1
44. escape _____ 1
45. northern _____ 1
46. towel _____ 1
47. kneel _____ 1
48. height _____ 0
49. exercise _____ 1
50. observe _____ 1
51. ruin _____ 0
52. license _____ 1
53. uniforms _____ 0
54. pigeon _____ 1
55. moisture _____ 0
56. artificial _____ 1
57. issues _____ 0
58. quench _____ 0
59. hustle _____ 0
60. thigh _____ 0

READING RECOGNITION
Ceiling Item _____
minus Errors _____
equals RAW SCORE _____

Oral Fluency—Associational Fluency; Naming Facility
Reading Fluency—Word Recognition Fluency; Decoding Fluency
(Kaufman & Kaufman, 2004, pp 2–3)

A description of each subtest, including the stimuli and the task demands, is presented in Table 7.1.

The K-TEA-II has increased the comprehensive and diagnostic capability of the original K-TEA. The teacher will be able to determine more specifically the strengths and weaknesses of the student's performance due to the increased coverage of error analyses by subtest and within-item performance. For example, the teacher can not only determine that the student has difficulty with fractions but also that

Table 7.1 Brief description of K-TEA-II Comprehensive Form subtests.

Subtest	Range	Description
Letter & Word Recognition	Ages 4:6–25:11	The student identifies letters and pronounces words of gradually increasing difficulty. Most words are irregular to ensure that the subject measures word recognition (reading vocabulary) more than decoding ability.
Reading Comprehension	Grade 1–Age 25:11	For the easiest items, the student reads a word and points to its corresponding picture. In following items, the student reads a simple instruction and responds by performing the action. In later items, the student reads passages of increasing difficulty and answers literal or inferential questions about them. Finally, the student rearranges five sentences into a coherent paragraph, and then answers questions about the paragraph.
Math Concepts & Applications	Ages 4:6–25:11	The student responds orally to test items that focus on the application of mathematical principles to real-life situations. Skill categories include number concepts, operation concepts, time and money, measurement, geometry, data investigation, and higher math concepts.
Math Computation	Grade K–Age 25:11	The student writes solutions to math problems printed in the Student Response Booklet. Skills assessed include addition, subtraction, multiplication, and division operations; fractions and decimals; square roots, exponents, signed number, and algebra.
Written Expression	Ages 4:6–25:11	Kindergarten and pre-kindergarten children trace and copy letters and write letters from dictation. At Grades 1 and higher, the student completes writing tasks in the context of an age-appropriate storybook format. Tasks at those levels include writing sentences from dictation, adding punctuation and capitalization filling in missing words, completing sentences, combining sentences, writing compound and complex sentences and, starting at Spring of Grade 1, writing an essay based on the story the student helped complete.

continued.

Table 7.1   continued.

Subtest	Range	Description
Spelling	Grade 1–Age 25:11	The student writes words dictated by the examiner from a steeply graded word list. Early items require students to write single letters that represent sounds. The remaining items require students to spell regular and irregular words of increasing complexity.
Listening Comprehension	Ages 4:6–25:11	The student listens to passages played on a CD and then responds orally to questions asked by the examiner. Questions measure literal and inferential comprehension.
Oral Expression	Ages 4:6–25:11	The student performs specific speaking tasks in the context of a real-life scenario. Tasks assess pragmatics, syntax, semantics, and grammar.
Phonological Awareness	Grades K–6	The student responds orally to items that require manipulation of sounds. Tasks include rhyming, matching sounds, blending sounds, segmenting sounds, and deleting sounds.
Nonsense Word Decoding	Grade 1–Age 25:11	The student applies phonics and structural analysis skills to decode invented words of increasing difficulty.
Word Recognition Fluency	Grade 3–Age 25:11	The student reads isolated words as quickly as possible for 1 minute.
Decoding Fluency	Grade 3–Age 25:11	The student pronounces as many nonsense words as possible in 1 minute.
Associational Fluency	Ages 4:6–25:11	The student says as many words as possible in 30 seconds that belong to a semantic category or have a specified beginning sound.
Naming Facility (RAN)	Ages 4:6–25:11	The student names objects, colors, and letters as quickly as possible.

Source: From *Kaufman Test of Educational Achievement, 2nd Edition: Comprehensive Form Manual.* (2004). Kaufman, A. S. and Kaufman, N. L., p. 4. Circle Pines, MN: AGS Publishing.

the student has not mastered the skills of adding or subtracting numerators or denominators or performing operations with equivalent fractions or determining common denominators. This information can then be used to write specific objectives, design teaching strategies, or create curriculum-based measures of mathematical operations.

The K-TEA-II includes four timed subtests that assess how quickly a student can retrieve or express specific information related to reading skills. When administering these subtests, particular care should be taken to the standardized requirements for administering and scoring because these are not all calculated in the same manner. For example, while some subtests are based on the student's actual performance within a specific time period, the

Naming Facility subtest score is based on the conversion of the student's performance to a point score (Kaufman & Kaufman, 2004).

The subtests on the K-TEA-II also have varying rules for the establishment of basal and ceiling levels. The examiner should carefully read and adhere to the specific administration procedures. Some of the subtests require that a student miss four consecutive items in order to establish a ceiling, another subtest may require four of five responses as incorrect in order to establish a ceiling, yet another may require five of six responses for the ceiling level. Some subtests follow different discontinue rules and others require that the examiner encourage the student to complete all of the items for a specific level. It is imperative that the examiner follow all of the standardized instructions during the administration in order to obtain a valid representation of the student's academic ability.

Scoring the Comprehensive Form of the K-TEA-II   Most items on the K-TEA-II are scored as 1 for correct response and 0 for incorrect. There are some exceptions to this scoring. The timed items are scored based on performance or a conversion score based on performance. The Written Expression subtest and the Oral Expression subtest include items that have multiple criteria for scoring. In addition to determining the raw scores and the error patterns, the K-TEA-II provides norm tables for converting the raw score data to standard scores for the subtests and composites. Norm tables for percentile ranks, confidence intervals, and developmental scores, such as age equivalents, are provided. An example of a scored protocol is presented in Figure 7.2.

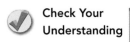

Check Your Understanding

Complete Activity 7.3 below to determine your general understanding of the K-TEA-II.

Activity 7.3

1. You are concerned about a student who is having difficulty answering questions about reading passages. In addition to assessing the student's ability with curriculum materials, you decide to assess the student's skills using a norm-referenced test. Which subtest of the K-TEA-II assesses a student's ability to answer literal and inferential questions?_____

2. Most of your kindergarten students have been making adequate progress in their ability to match sounds, blend sounds, segment sounds, and delete sounds. The data you collected using CBMs indicates that one student has not made adequate progress. You decided to assess this student using the K-TEA-II. Which subtests would you decide to use?_____

3. What is the difference between an item level error analysis and a within item error analysis?_____

Figure 7.2   Figure from page 18 of K-TEA-II manual.

KTEA·II

Comprehensive Form
Form A

Kaufman Test of Educational Achievement, Second Education
]Alan S. Kaufman & Nadeen L. Kaufman

	Year	Month	Day
Test Date	2004	5	26
Birth Date	1996	9	14
Age	7	6	12

Name: _Robyn Harris_   Sex: _F_ ID:_____

School: _____   Grade: _2_____

Teacher: _____ Examiner:_____

Medications: _____

Norms Used:
☐ Age
☐ Grade: Fall
☒ Grade: Spring

	Subtest Raw Score	Standard Score Subtest	Composite	CAC Subtests PreK–K	GR. 1–12⁺	Confidence Interval 90% Band	Interval	%ile Rank	Grade Equiv.	Age Other
2 Letter & Word Recognition	47	99			99	± 4	(95–103)	47	2.6	___
6 Reading Comprehension	25	98			98	± 5	(93–103)	45	2.6	___
Reading	Sum 197 →	98				± 3	(95–101)	45		___
3 Math Concepts & Applications	53	130			130	± 8	(122–138)	98	4.11	___
5 Math Computation	21	123			123	± 8	(115–131)	94	3.8	___
Math	Sum 253 →	129				± 6	(123–135)	97		
7 Written Expression	159	73			73	± 12	(61–85)	4	1.2	___
8 Spelling	18	85				± 6	(79–91)	16	1.6	___
Written Language	Sum 158 →	77				± 7	(70–84)	6		
9 Listening Comprehension	30	103			103	± 10	(93–113)	58	3.0	___
10 Oral Expression	65	105				± 10	(95–115)	63	3.4	___
Oral Language	Sum 208 →	104				± 8	(96–112)	61		

Comprehensive Achievement Composite (CAC)
Sum 626 ↓
Std. Score 105   ± 4 (101–109) 63   ___

Reading-Related Subtests	Raw Score	Standard Score						
1 Phonological Awareness	20	99	± 9	(90–108)	47	2.6	___
4 Nonsense Word Decoding	16	103	± 7	(96–110)	58	3.0	___
11 Word Recognition Fluency	___		± ___	(___–___)	___	___	___
12 Decoding Fluency	___		± ___	(___–___)	___	___	___
13 Associational Fluency	19	93	± 13	(80–106)	32	1.9	___
14 Naming Facility (RAN)	11	96	± 8	(88–104)	39	2.2	___

AGS PUBLISHING

© 2004 AGS Publishing
4201 Woodland Road,
Circle Pines, MN 55014-1796
800-328-2560 www.agsnet.com

Product Number: 32215-RF
A 0 9 8 7 6 5 4 3 2 1

Source: Kaufman Test of Educational Achievement (2nd ed.), (2004), page 18 of the Examiner's Manual. Circle Pines, MN: AGS publishers. Reprinted with permission.

Comparisons Within the K-TEA-II   Once the selected subtests or the entire K-TEA-II have been administered and scored, the examiner can compare subtests and composites of the student's scores in order to identify academic strengths and weaknesses. A completed portion of the protocol in which the subtest scores and the composite scores are compared is illustrated in Figure 7.3.

Remember that the level of significance selected indicates the amount of chance occurrence of the difference. In other words, if a level of significance of .05 is selected, this indicates that the difference between the two scores occurs by chance only 5 times out of 100. Also, if the .01 level of significance is selected, the amount of difference would occur only 1 time out of 100. In other words, there is a 99% chance that the difference is a truly significant difference.

Once it is determined that a difference is significant, the examiner also needs to find out how frequently the difference occurred in the norm sample. A difference can be significant statistically but that difference may also occur frequently within the general population. If it is a common occurrence, it may not require educational intervention. This is especially true if the difference is significant because one score is average and the other score is an even higher score. This may indicate a significant strength in a specific academic area. Tables are provided within the K-TEA-II manual to locate the frequency of occurrence and level of significance for comparisons between subtests, between composites, and between the K-ABC-II and the K-TEA-II.

Figure 7.3   K-TEA-II subset and composites comparisons.

Composite Comparisons   If difference is significant, circle composite with higher standard score.

	Standard Score	Diff.	Standard Score		Significance		Frequency of Occurrence		
Reading	98	31	129	(Math)	<.05	(<.01)	<15%	<10%	(<5%)
(Reading)	98	21	77	Written Language	<.05	(<.01)	<15%	<10%	(<5%)
Reading	98	6	104	Oral Language	<.05	<.01	<15%	<10%	<5%
(Math)	129	52	77	Written Language	<.05	(<.01)	<15%	<10%	(<5%)
(Math)	129	25	104	Oral Language	<.05	(<.01)	(<15%)	<10%	<5%
Written Language	77	27	104	(Oral Language)	<.05	(<.01)	<15%	(<10%)	<5%
Reading	98	4	102	Decoding	<.05	<.01	<15%	<10%	<5%
					<.05	<.01	<15%	<10%	<5%

Circle if significant or infrequent (refer to Appendix 1).

Subtest Comparisons   If difference is significant, circle subtest with higher standard score.

	Standard Score	Diff.	Standard Score		Significance		Frequency of Occurrence		
Reading Comprehension	98	5	103	Listening Comprehension	<.05	<.01	<15%	<10%	<5%
Written Expression	73	32	105	(Oral Expression)	<.05	(<.01)	<15%	(<10%)	<5%
Oral Expression	105	2	103	Listening Comprehension	<.05	<.01	<15%	<10%	<5%
					<.05	<.01	<15%	<10%	<5%
					<.05	<.01	<15%	<10%	<5%

Circle if significant or infrequent (refer to Appendix 1).

Source: Kaufman Test of Educational Achievement (2nd ed.), (2004), page 30 of the Examiner's Manual. Circle Pines, MN: AGS publishers. Reprinted by permission.

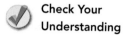

Check Your Understanding

To experience scoring a math achievement test, complete Activity 7.4 below.

Activity 7.4

A third-grade boy age 8-7 answered the items on a math calculation subtest in the following manner:

1.	11.	21. 1	31. 1
2.	12.	22. 1	32. 0
3.	13.	23. 1	33. 0
4.	14.	24. 0	34. 0
5.	15. 1	25. 1	35. 0
6.	16. 1	26. 1	36. 0
7.	17. 1	27. 0	37.
8.	18. 1	28. 0	38.
9.	19. 1	29. 0	39.
10.	20. 0	30. 0	40.

1. The basal for this subtest is 5 consecutive items correct and the ceiling is 5 consecutive items incorrect. What is the raw score?

   _____

2. The Daily Math Skills subtest has already been scored. The obtained raw score for the Daily Math Skills subtest was 38. Write the appropriate scores in the spaces provided on the sample protocol.

Math Composite

	Raw Score	Standard Score	Percentile Rank
Math Calculation			
Daily Math Skils			
Math Composite			

3. Add the raw scores and place the sum in the raw score box for the math composite score. Look at the norm table below. Locate the standard scores and percentile ranks for this student. Write the scores in the appropriate spaces.

Math Calculation

Raw Scores	Standard Score	Percentile Rank
23	83	13
24	82	12
25	80	10
26	79	9
27	78	8

Daily Math Skills

Raw Score	Standard Score	Percentile Rank
36	100	50
37	101	53
38	102	55
39	103	58
40	104	61

Math Composite Scores

Raw Score	Standard Score	Percentile Rank
62	89	24
61	90	26
62	91	28
63	92	30

Apply Your Knowledge

With the average standard score of 100 and the median percentile rank of 50, in what area(s) does this third-grade student appear to need intervention? _____

_____

_____

Determining Educational Needs Using the K-TEA-II The K-TEA-II provides several scores that can be used to determine educational needs of the individual student. The performance of the student can be analyzed for patterns of errors by comparing the types of items answered correctly and the types of items answered incorrectly. In addition, the within-items comparison for some subtests

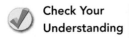

Check Your Understanding

Check your ability to calculate and determine significant differences in comparing composites of an achievement test by completing Activity 7.5 below.

Activity 7.5

On the test presented in Activity 7.4, an examiner can determine if there are any significant differences between composite scores. Look at the composite scores listed below. Subtract the scores to determine the amount of difference between the composite scores.

Math Composite	92
Written Language Composite	87
Reading Composite	72

On the following table, write the differences in the appropriate spaces. Look at the table and determine if any of the differences between composite scores are significant.

Composite Comparisons

Composites	Difference	Significant at the .05 Level	Significant at the .01 Level
Math-Written Language		17	20
Written Language-Reading		18	22
Math-Reading		16	19

Apply Your Knowledge

How would you explain the significant difference concept to the parents of this child? How might this significant difference impact educational interventions? _____

_____

_____

allows further analysis that can be used to determine educational needs. An example of a student's responses on the Nonsense Word Decoding subtest protocol is presented in Figure 7.4. The student's responses have been scored as pass or fail (a 0 or 1), and the specific pronunciations have been noted by the examiner. The raw score is determined and the errors are then analyzed on a separate form that allows the examiner to complete a within-item error analysis. The results of the error analysis within the items can be used to determine the educational needs of the student. These needs are the basis for writing educational objectives, designing teaching strategies, and identifying which specific skills will be

Figure 7.4 Portion of the Nonsense Word Decoding protocol, p.10, Form A.

#	Word	Score	Single/Double Consonant	Initial Blend	Medical Final Blend	Consonant Digraph	Wrong Vowel	Short Vowel	Long Vowel	Vowel Team/Diphthong	R-controlled Vowel	Silent Letter	Prefix/Word Beginning & Suffix/Inflection	Hard/Soft CGS	Initial/Final Sound	Insertion/Omission	Misordered Sounds	Whole Word Error
35	disenquoyment	0 ①				qu				oy			dis en ment					
36	bortioned	0 ① b	r								o		tion ed					
37	guarnal	0 ① g r n							ua				al					
38	cheigh	⓪ 1			ch				ei		gh							
39	gemnissent	0 ① g m n ss				e i						ent	✓				MPA
40	norpesious	⓪ 1 n r p s				e				o		ious					
41	dovign	⓪ 1 d v n					o ①			g							
42	quintabulent	0 ① b	i qu	nt		i a ⓤ					ent			✓		
43	slield	0 ①	sl	ld			le									
44	wredgiest	⓪ 1 r	g		e				w d	iest					
45	sydalogue	⓪ 1 s d l g			ⓨ a o				ue						
46	panpaudiatory	⓪ 1 p d			a i	au		pan tory					UN
47	cyctarious	⓪ 1 c c t t			y		ⓐ		ious				
48	shresplenescent	⓪ 1 ⓝ s shr	spl		e eⓔ			c	ent	✓			
49	pnoutiest	0 1 n t				ou		p	iest			
50	squertious	1 r	squ				e	tious			
	Total Errors by Category	2	2	0	0	1	3	2	1	1	1	1	1	2	4	1	4

CONSONANTS | **VOWELS** | **OTHER**

Source: Kaufman, A. S. and Kaufman, N. L., (2004). K-TEA-II Comprehensive Form A. Circle Pines, MN: AGS Publishing.

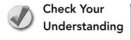

Check Your Understanding

Complete a within-item error analysis of the Nonsense Word Decoding subtest. Use the section of the protocol presented in Figure 7.4 to complete Activity 7.6.

Activity 7.6

Refer to Figure 7.4 of your text to answer the following questions.

1. The portion of this error analysis includes the student's performance on items 35–50. Based on this section of the error analysis, which short vowel sounds seem to be problematic?_____

2. In which categories did the student have no errors?_____

3. How many errors were made that were considered entire word mistakes?_____

4. How many types of vowel errors were made by this student? _____

5. What is meant by the term "misorderd sounds"?_____

Apply Your Knowledge

Give examples of words with insertion and omission errors._____
_____
_____

monitored through other classroom assessment methods, such as curriculum-based assessment.

Kaufman Test of Educational Achievement– II–Brief Form   The KTEA-II Brief Form is an instrument designed for screening students when an estimate of achievement is needed. For example, a student may be screened to determine if additional data are needed for a re-evaluation. This measure includes only three subtests: Reading, Math, and Written Expression. The Reading subtest includes reading recognition items and reading comprehension items. For example, a student is presented short paragraphs with comprehension questions and single words or letters for recognition. On the Math subtest, items include math computation as well as math application problems. The Written Expression items include both spelling and written language. This short assessment is presented in an easel format like the comprehensive battery, and the test publisher estimates administration time ranges from 10 to 40 minutes depending on the age of the child. This instrument was designed for children from 4 and ½ years of age to adults 90 years of age.

WECHSLER INDIVIDUAL ACHIEVEMENT TEST, SECOND EDITION (WIAT-II)

The WIAT-II (Psychological Corporation, 2001) is an individually administered achievement test made up of nine subtests. Students ages 4-0 to 19-11 or in grades PreK (age 5) through college may be administered this instrument. The administration of this instrument to college students and adults can be completed using the WIAT-II Supplement for College Students and Adults. This revised edition of the WIAT contains changes in individual items, subtests, and scoring. The revised edition expanded several subtests and added the new subtest, Pseudoword Decoding. The WIAT was designed to help educators in determining discrepancies between measured intellectual ability and academic achievement. The revised test format includes easels, paper-and-pencil tasks, and separate reading cards. Starting points and ceiling rules, which vary by subtests, are presented in the manual and on the protocol form. Some items are timed and cues are provided to the examiner in the test stimulus booklets and in the protocol. Examiners are also provided rules for reverse administration in the examiner's manual and on the protocol if the student does not establish a basal. A parent report form is included within the protocol.

The WIAT includes subtests in the areas of oral expression and listening comprehension. These areas are not typically included in other academic achievement tests and may offer the educator useful information for intervention. This test provides skill information on the protocol of the math subtests that can easily be adapted to write educational objectives. The protocol includes qualitative observation items that the examiner may simply check following the administration of each subtest. Additional information regarding each subtest follows.

Subtests

Word Reading. This subtest was called Basic Reading in the original version of the WIAT. This revised subtest has been expanded and includes items at the PreK level. The early items include visual memory and visual discrimination of letters. Items of letter recognition or letter naming are presented next, followed by items in which the student is asked to discriminate rhyming words. Students are then asked to generate rhyming words to specific stimuli. Then students are asked to determine two of three words that begin with the same sound followed by words with the same ending sounds. Students are then asked to discriminate the letters that make specific sounds; this includes isolated vowels, consonants, and consonant blends. On more difficult items, the student is presented with words on a card and asked to read the words aloud.

Numerical Operations. Items for PreK students include number recognition, number sequencing (1–10), dictation of specific numbers, and counting. Additional items require the student to respond in writing to solve calculation problems. More difficult items are problems that involve geometry, percent, decimals, and simple algebraic equations.

Reading Comprehension. In this subtest, the first-grade student is asked to point to the picture that matches the word. Simple sentence items follow with specific target words that are scored by the examiner. Beginning with second-grade items, the student reads written passages and then responds to questions asked by the examiner. In addition to passage items, sentences are also presented for oral reading accuracy. Beginning with the third-grade items, student reading speed is timed. Specific starting and stopping points are used rather than ceiling levels.

Spelling. The student responds in writing to letters, sounds, or words dictated by the examiner. Homonyms are presented in bold in the protocol.

Pseudoword Decoding. This subtest is presented on a reading card and is administered to students in grades 1 and above. The examiner should listen to the audiotape and become familiar with the correct pronunciation prior to the initial administration of the test. The student's responses are recorded exactly using correct pronunciation or phonetic symbols.

Math Reasoning. This subtest requires the student to solve math problems that require reasoning. The student is presented with items on the easel and may use pencil and paper if needed.

The PreK items include counting pictures and distinguishing pictures with more objects. Other early-level items include recognizing shapes and interpreting simple picture graphs. More difficult items include answering story-type problems and interpreting complex graphs.

Written Expression. This subtest contains the following five sections: alphabet writing, word fluency, sentences, paragraph, and essay. This subtest requires the student to respond in writing to various prompts. Written-expression paragraphs and essays are scored for mechanics, organization, and vocabulary.

Listening Comprehension. This subtest was revised to include receptive vocabulary items, sentence comprehension, and expressive vocabulary. Following orally presented items, the student responds to questions asked by the examiner. The items include picture cues, and the lower levels require the student to point to the answer.

Oral Expression. This subtest was revised to include the following four sections: sentence repetition (for the early grades only), word fluency, visual passage retell, and giving directions. Sentence repetition requires the student to repeat sentences. The word fluency subtest is timed. Other items assess the student's ability to use words to describe picture cues, give directions, or provide explanations. The student responds orally. The examiner must write the student's responses or use a tape recorder to tape the responses.

Scoring　　The scoring of the revised edition of the WIAT is more complex than the original version. Items on the Word Reading, Mathematics Reasoning, Spelling, Numerical Operations, Pseudoword Reading, and Listening Comprehension subtests receive a 1 when answered correctly and 0 when incorrect. Scoring for the Reading Comprehension and Written Expression subtests is slightly more complicated; the manual includes instructions and practice exercises. Raw scores are used to obtain derived scores that may be based on either grade- or age-normative data. Grade norm tables are presented for fall, winter, and spring. The correct table is determined by the date of testing according to the following guidelines: fall for August–November, winter for December–February, and spring for March–July. Standard scores—with a mean of 100, percentile ranks, age equivalents, and grade equivalents—are available for both subtests and composites. Supplemental scores, in quartiles and deciles, are available. Tables are provided to determine significant differences between individual subtest scores and composite scores. To assist in decisions regarding significant discrepancies between ability and achievement, tables are provided that display differences between scores on the WIAT-II and the Wechsler

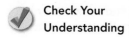

Check Your Understanding

Check your understanding of the WIAT-II by completing Activity 7.7 below.

Activity 7.7

Answer the following questions about the WIAT-II.

1. Which subtest includes items that assess phonemic awareness and early reading skills?_____

2. Which subtest includes expressive vocabulary and sentence comprehension?_____

3. A student who scored significantly below the levels expected on the subtests of word reading, reading comprehension, spelling, and pseudoword decoding but was within the range expected on other subtests might have been referred to determine if a _____exists.

4. A student in your class seems to take longer to respond in writing on tasks he is asked to do during class time. He also writes much shorter responses and often writes very short and simple words. His reading level is at the range expected, however, he may have difficulty with _____.

Apply Your Knowledge

Which subtests of the WIAT-II would you analyze closely for a student in your class who is struggling in math?_____
_____
_____

Intelligence Scale for Children, Third Edition, between the WIAT-II and the Wechsler Adult Intelligence Scale, Third Edition, and between the WIAT-II and the Wechsler Preschool and Primary Scale of Intelligence. Tables are provided with levels of statistical significance for differences between predicted and actual subtest scores and composite scores for using the predicted-achievement method.

WIDE RANGE ACHIEVEMENT TEST–REVISION 3 (WRAT3)

The WRAT3 is a screening achievement test that was designed to "measure the codes which are needed to learn the basic skills of reading, spelling, and arithmetic" (Wilkinson, 1993, p. 10). This test is composed of three subtests that may be administered in any order and may be given to persons ages 5 through 75. Because it is a screening instrument, the WRAT3 should be used not to diagnose learning problems but rather to determine whether additional testing is necessary. This third revision, unlike the WRAT–R, may be given to any person within the age range of 5–75 and is no longer divided by age levels. The test includes alternate forms, the Blue Test and Tan Test, which may be administered alone or together for a combined score. Students who are not administered the items for ages 5–7 are given credit for those items. The Spelling and Reading subtests use a 5/10 rule for the basal and ceiling. This means that individuals age 8 and above must be presented with the beginning items if they do not correctly answer the first 5 items presented, and that testing stops when students miss 10 consecutive items. The Arithmetic subtest uses a 5/15-minute criterion: Students age 8 and above must answer at least 5 items correctly or be given the beginning oral items, and testing stops at the 15-minute time limit.

Subtests

Reading. This subtest contains a plastic card with a small sample of letters and words that the student reads aloud to the examiner. The naming of letters is considered a prereading task. The student is allowed 10 seconds to recognize each word. The examiner scores the subtest by crossing out the first letter of incorrect words and by circling the item number for correct responses. Each correct item is worth 1 point. This subtest does not measure word attack or any form of reading comprehension.

Spelling. This subtest begins with name writing and letter writing for students ages 5 through 7. Students are asked to write their name and then to write letters spoken by the examiner. The student is then asked to spell words presented orally. The examiner pronounces a word, gives a sentence that includes the word, and then repeats the word; the student responds in writing on the protocol.

Arithmetic. This subtest contains a few counting items and oral response items, but the remainder of the subtest is a paper-and-pencil task of computation. Students may first solve a small sample of math problems presented on the protocol. Students ages 5 through 7 begin this subtest with the oral problems and progress to the calculation items. This subtest has a 15-minute time limit.

Scoring   The raw scores on the WRAT3 may be used to obtain standard scores, grade scores, and absolute scores. Absolute scores have a mean of 500 and were determined by using the Rasch analysis to determine item difficulty. The absolute scores allow for a person to be compared with the entire continuum of the domain or areas without using age or grade comparisons. Item analyses using the absolute scores are provided in the WRAT3 examiner's manual.

WOODCOCK–MCGREW–WERDER MINI-BATTERY OF ACHIEVEMENT

This instrument is an individually administered easel test designed to screen academic achievement across several areas.

Subtests   The test is structured to include the following subtests.

Reading. Reading is assessed using three subtests: reading identification, reading vocabulary, and reading comprehension. The reading identification subtest includes a list of letters and words that the student reads aloud. The reading vocabulary subtest assesses a student's ability to provide antonyms for given words. The reading comprehension subtest includes short passages with a word missing that the student must provide. The easier items present pictures and words. The student must find the picture that best represents the words.

Writing. A student's writing skills are screened by assessing writing mechanics such as spelling, punctuation, and grammar or usage. The subtests include dictation, which measures the student's ability to provide responses independently, and proofing, which requires the student to identify writing errors when presented with visual stimuli. This test does not include items that measure written expression but rather measures writing mechanics.

Mathematics. These skills are screened by assessing basic calculation using a pencil-and-paper format and by assessing math reasoning and concepts. The reasoning and concepts subtest includes visual stimuli in easel format as well as verbal cues.

Factual Knowledge. This is assessed through the use of questions presented orally. Information included on these items is information students learn through their environment and educational experiences.

Scoring   Items are scored as 1 or 0 for all subtests. Raw scores are entered into a computer scoring program that yields a one-page report of standard scores (mean of 100 and standard deviation of 15), percentile ranks, and age/grade equivalent for each subtest.

SELECTING ACADEMIC ACHIEVEMENT TESTS

The tests reviewed in this chapter represent the more commonly used instruments in public school assessment. One instrument may be particularly better to use in the situation than in another. The strengths and weaknesses are presented in Table 7.2 to provide some guidance in selecting instruments.

Table 7.2 Academic achievement tests.

Name of Instrument	Purpose of Test	Constructs Measured	Standardization Information	Reliability Information	Validity Information
Woodcock–Johnson Tests of Achievement, Third Edition	Comprehensive assessment of academic areas	Reading, oral language, math, written language, academic fluency, academic applications	More than 8,000 persons ages 2 to more than 90 years. Variables included race, sex, Hispanic/non-Hispanic, occupation, level of education, and community size.	Test-retest, interrater reliability, alternate forms reliability, and internal consistency. Most reliability coefficients for internal reliability in the .90s.	Concurrent validity research with other measures such as the K-TEA and the WIAT. Validity coefficients ranged from .79 to 65.
Kaufman Test of Educational Achievement, Second Edition	Comprehensive assessment of academic areas	Reading, reading-related composites, math, written language, oral language	Sample of 2,400 students in grades K–12. Variables included ethnicity, education level of parents, geographic region, sex.	Internal consistency reliability for subtests and composites; most in the .90s, alternate forms reliability, interrater reliability.	Construct validity, concurrent validity studies with the WJ–III, PIAT–R/NU, confirmatory factor analysis.
Wechsler Individual Achievement Test, Second Edition	Assessment of academic achievement	Reading, written expression, math, listening comprehension, oral expression	Included 3,600 students in grades PreK through 12 and ages 4–19. Variables included race/ethnicity, sex, geographic area, parents education level. Fall and spring testing periods.	Reliability research included internal consistency measures, test-retest, and interscorer reliability. Coefficients ranged from .81 to .99.	Construct validity, content validity, and criterion-related validity research included in manual.

278

Name of Instrument	Purpose of Test	Constructs Measured	Standardization Information	Reliability Information	Validity Information
Wide Range Achievement Test	Screening for three basic academic skills	Reading recognition, spelling, and math operations	More than 4,000 persons included in sample with consideration of age, sex, geographic region, race, and socioeconomic level.	Test-retest reliability, alternate forms reliability, and internal consistency research using coefficient alpha are included in manual.	Content and criterion-related validity studies included in the manual. Construct validity information included.
Mini-Battery of Achievement	Screening across several academic areas	Reading identification, comprehension, and vocabulary; writing mechanics and spelling; math calculation and reasoning; factual knowledge	The sample included more than 6,000 persons ranging in age from 4 to 95. Adequate demographic and geographic representation in norm sample.	Test-retest and split-half reliability research included, with coefficients ranging from .70 to .98. Greatest inconsistency noted in children younger than 6 years of age.	Concurrent validity research indicated coefficients ranging between .70s to upper .80s.

DIAGNOSTIC TESTING

diagnostic tests Tests used to obtain futher information about specific skills.

Teachers often need additional information to make the correct decisions for educational interventions. Instruments that can yield more detailed information for making such decisions are known as **diagnostic tests.**

REVIEW OF DIAGNOSTIC TESTS

The tests presented here represent those commonly used by teachers; they have also been selected because of existing research. The assessment of the basic skill areas of reading, mathematics, spelling, and written language is presented in this chapter. The uses of diagnostic tests are shown in Figure 7.5.

KEYMATH–3 DIAGNOSTIC ASSESSMENT (KEYMATH–3 DA)

The KeyMath–3 DA (Connolly, 2007) is presented in an easel format and consists of two equivalent forms, A and B. The KeyMath–3 is aligned with the Standards of the National Council of Teachers of Mathematics (NCTM, 2000) and the matrix reflecting this alignment is included in the appendix of the test manual. The alternate forms may be administered every three months to monitor progress of the student in mathematics. The third edition of this diagnostic mathematics battery includes computer scoring software and progress monitoring capability. The software program will provide a functional analysis of the student's responses on the instrument and will yield the specific items that require intervention. The functional analysis provides behavioral objectives that may be used to drive the math intervention process. The instrument may be administered to students who are 4 years and 6 months of age to students who are 21 years of age who are within the skill levels provided by the instrument. The estimated administration time ranges from 30–90 minutes.

On the KeyMath–3 DA, many of the items are presented orally by the examiner. The computation items for the basic math operations of addition, subtraction, multiplication, and division, are presented as paper-and-pencil tasks. This test includes subtests that are grouped into three areas: Basic Concepts, Operations, and Applications. Table 7.3 presents the areas, **domains**, and content of the revised KeyMath–3 DA.

domain Area of cognitive development or ability thought to be evidenced by certain behaviors or skills.

Subtests and Content Areas

Basic Concepts. In this content area, items are presented to assess the conceptual understanding of numeration, algebra, geometry, measurement, and data analysis and interpretation.

Table 7.3 Content specification of KeyMath–3 DA: Subtests and content of domains.

Areas	Basic Concepts	Operations	Applications
Strands and Domains	**Numeration** Early number awareness Place value and number sense Magnitude of numbers Fractions Decimals Percentages Exponents, integers, multiples, and factors **Algebra** Early algebraic awareness Algebraic uses of numbers and geometry Symbolic representation Ratio and proportion Coordinate graphing **Geometry** Early geometric awareness Two-dimensional shapes Three-dimensional shapes Lines and angles Formulas Grids and coordinate planes **Measurement** Early awareness of measurement Standard units Time Money Data analysis and probability Early awareness of data and probability Charts, tables, and graphs Graphical representation Statistics Probability	**Mental Computation and Estimation** Early awareness of mental computation Mental computation chains Mental computation with whole numbers Mental computation with rational numbers Estimation and whole numbers Estimation and rational numbers **Addition and Subtraction** Algorithms to add and subtract whole numbers Algorithms to add and subtract rational numbers Integers Algebra **Multiplication and Division** Algorithms to multiply and divide rational numbers Integers Algebra	**Foundations of Problem Solving** Analysis of problems Word problems **Applied Problem Solving** Numerations Algebra Geometry Measurement Data analysis and probability

Source: Adapted from *KeyMath–3 DA* (Appendix E pp.341–345) by A. J. Connolly, 2007, NCS Pearson, Inc. Minneapolis, MN: Pearson Assessments. Reprinted by permission.

Figure 7.5   Appropriate uses of diagnostic tests.

Initial assessment process	To assess areas in which questions remain regarding a student's ability in an academic skill—such as reading—or subskill—such as phonological awareness
Reevaluation	To assess specific areas that the team determines necessary in order to make a decision regarding continued eligibility for services or interventions
Assessment of progress	Classroom teacher uses to measure progress toward objectives in specific academic area
Additional data for classroom interventions	Classroom teacher needs additional information to adjust interventions or planning or to obtain in-depth information about student's mastery of a specific skill

Numeration. These items sample the student's ability to understand the number system and the functional application of that system. Items include tasks such as counting, identifying numbers, identifying missing numbers in a sequence, understanding concepts of more and less, and reading multidigit numbers.

Algebra. This subtest measures understanding of the concepts and skills used in pre-algebraic problems and includes items such as number sentences, functions, and equations.

Measurement. Items range from recognition and identification of units of measurement to problems that involve application and changing of the various units of measurement, and includes items of time and money.

Geometry. These items range from understanding spatial concepts and recognizing shapes to interpreting angles and three-dimensional figures.

Operations. This content area includes computation problems using paper and pencil and mental computation items that are presented in the easel format.

Mental Computation. This orally administered subtest includes math operations problems and more difficult problems that require several steps and operations to complete.

Addition and Subtraction. This subtest assesses the student's ability to perform addition and subtraction computation problems.

Multiplication and Division. This subtest is presented in the same format as the addition and subtraction subtests and includes simple grouping problems (sets) and more difficult multiplication of mixed numbers and fractions. The items cover a range of difficulty levels and contain some multistep, or "long" division, computations, addition and subtraction of fractions, and beginning algebraic computations.

Application. This content area includes problems that are representative of how mathematics is used in everyday life.

Foundations of Problem Solving. These items assess a student's early ability or "readiness" to complete application problems.

Applied Problem Solving. On these items, the student is presented with math problems of daily living such as calculating sales tax or categorization of objects.

Scoring   Grade level starting points are provided on the protocol. The basal is established when a student responds correctly to at least three items in the set before missing an item. If the student incorrectly responds to an item, the items are presented in reverse order until the student successfully answers three consecutive items correctly. The basal level is the three items prior to the first incorrect response. The ceiling is established when a student incorrectly answers four consecutive items. Once the raw scores for each subtest are calculated, they are used to locate the standard scores in the examiner manual.

The KeyMath–3 DA provides scale scores for the individual subtests. These scores have a mean of 10 and a standard deviation of 3. Each of the three areas and the total test score are presented as standard scores with a mean of 100 and a standard deviation of 15 for all age and grade groups. Norm tables are included for fall and spring for standard scores and percentile ranks. Age and grade equivalent developmental scores are also provided. Areas can be compared so that it may be determined if a student is significantly strong or weak in a specific math area.

Tables provide information regarding a student's functional range according to the subtest raw scores. There are tables that indicate which items are focus items that the student missed and yet the items fall below the student's functional range. These items may be in particular need of intervention. Information on a subsequent table indicates the items that the student answered correctly that were above the student's functional level.

Another score is provided to assist with measurement of ongoing progress. This is called the growth scale value or GSV. An example of the graphing of the GSV is presented in Figure 7.6.

Figure 7.6   Graphical display of the KeyMath–3 DA Progress Report.

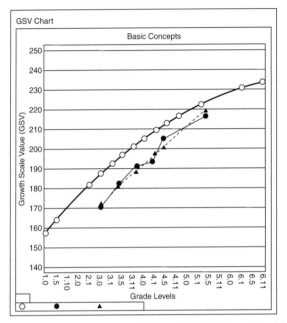

Source: KeyMath–DA, by J. A. Connolly, 2007. Page 32 of the Examiner's Manual, NCS Pearson, Inc. Minneapolis, MN. Reprinted with permission.

The examiner uses the raw scores to locate scaled scores for each subtest and then sums the raw scores of the subtests for the area raw score. The area raw scores are used to determine area standard scores, percentile ranks, and age or grade equivalents.

Comparing Area Standard Scores for Significance   The examiner compares the standard scores obtained on the three areas in the section of the protocol titled "Area Comparisons," shown in Figure 7.7. The examiner writes the standard scores in the appropriate spaces and writes or >, <, = on each of the lines between the boxes. The standard score differences are determined by subtracting the scores. To determine significance level, the examiner refers to a table in the manual that lists the differences that are considered significant. If the difference is listed as significant at the .05 level, this means that the chances are 95 out of 100 that a true difference exists and there are only 5 chances out of 100 that the difference is by error or chance. The level of .01 means that the difference exists with only 1 possibility of 100 that the difference is by error or chance.

In addition to an indication of the chance occurrence of such a difference, it is recommended that the frequency of such a difference be determined. For example, how often would a student have such a difference between areas happen? To determine this, the examiner refers to a table in the examiner's manual.

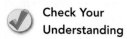

Check Your Understanding

Check your ability to score a portion of the KeyMath–3 DA by completing Activity 7.8 below.

Activity 7.8

Complete the following problems.

1. One student's responses for the Addition and Subtraction subtest are shown on the KeyMath–3 DA protocol in Figure A below. Calculate the raw score and then write your answer on the protocol.

Figure A

Addition and Subtraction

Note: Skip this subtest if the examinee's Numeration ceiling item is 6 or below.
See Chapter 2 in the KeyMath–3 DA manual for details.

OPERATIONS

Numeration Ceiling Item	Item	Score		Description	Correct Response
4–19 ▶	1.	①	0	1 + 2	3
	2.	①	0	0 + 5	5
	3.	①	0	6 − 0	6
20, 21 ▶	4.	①	0	7 + 2	9
	5.	①	0	4 − 2	2
	6.	1	⓪	8 − 8	0
22–25 ▶	7.	①	0	9 + 5	14
	8.	1	⓪	14 − 7	7
	9.	1	⓪	21 + 7	28
26–29 ▶	10.	1	⓪	14 + 6	20
	11.	1	⓪	56 − 5	51
	12.	1	0	13 + 47	60
30–34 ▶	13.	1	0	50 − 9	41
	14.	1	0	45 + 59	104
	15.	1	0	305 + 97	402

Ceiling Item — Errors = Raw Score*

[ ] − [ ] = [ ]

*Read the scoring instructions on page 10 of this record form before calculating the subtest raw score.

Source: p. 3 of KeyMath Protocol Copyright 1971, 1976, 1988, 1998, 2007 NCS Pearson, Inc. KeyMath is a trademark of NCS Pearson, Inc.

2. This student's other raw scores for the Operations subtests have been entered in Figure B. Write the raw score calculated in problem 1 in the appropriate space in Figure B below.

Figure B

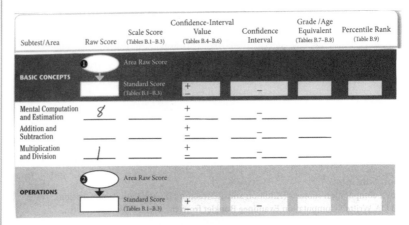

Source: KeyMath 3-Protocol Front Page KeyMath Protocol Copyright 1971, 1976, 1988, 1998, 2007. NCS Pearson, Inc. KeyMath is a trademark of NCS Pearson, Inc. Reprinted with permission.

Figure C

Mental Computation and Estimation	Addition and Subtraction	Multiplication and Division	Foundation of Problem Solving	Applied Problem Solving	Scale Score
37–40	30–35	22–31	26–27	32–35	19
35–36	29	21	25	30–31	18
33–34	—	20	—	29	17
31–32	28	18–19	24	27–28	16
29–30	27	17	23	26	15
27–28	26	15–16	21–22	24–25	14
24–26	25	14	20	23	13
22–23	24	13	19	21–22	12
21	23	11–12	17–18	20	11
19–20	22	—	15–16	18–19	10
17–18	20–21	9–10	14	16–17	9
15–16	18–19	8	12–13	14–15	8
12–14	16–17	7	11	12–13	7
10–11	14–15	5–6	9–10	10–11	6
7–9	12–13	4	7–8	8–9	5
5–6	9–11	2–3	5–6	6–7	4
3–4	6–8	1	4	5	3
2	4–5	0	3	3–4	2
0–1	0–3	—	0–2	0–2	1
1.0	1.4	0.9	1.2	1.2	68% CI

Source: From KeyMath-3 Examiner's Manual p. 237 Protocol Copyright 1971, 1976, 1988, 1998, 2007. NCS Pearson, Inc. KeyMath is a trademark of NCS Pearson, Inc. Reprinted with permission.

Figure D
From KeyMath–3 Examiner's Manual p. 237

Standard Score	Basic Concepts	Operations	Applications	Total Test
85	77	39	24	140–142
84	75–76	38	—	137–139
83	73–74	37	23	133–136
82	71–72	36	22	129–132
81	70	35	—	126–128
80	68–69	34	21	123–125
79	67	32–33	20	120–122
78	65–66	31	—	116–119
77	63–64	30	19	112–115
76	61–62	28–29	18	109–111
75	60	27	17	105–108
74	58–59	25–26	16	101–104
73	56–57	24	—	97–100
72	54–55	23	15	93–36
71	52–53	22	—	89–92
70	50–51	20–21	14	84–88
69	47–49	19	13	80–83
68	45–46	18	12	76–79
67	42–44	17	11	73–75
66	40–41	16	—	68–72
65	37–39	14–15	10	64–67
64	34–36	13	9	60–63
63	31–33	12	—	56–59
62	29–30	11	8	52–55
61	26–28	10	7	48–51
60	24–25	9	—	45–47
59	22–23	8	6	42–44
58	20–21	7	—	39–41
57	19	—	5	36–38
56	18	6	—	33–35
55	0–17	0–5	0–4	0–32
90% CI	5	7	8	4

Add the subtest raw scores to determine the area raw score and then write this score in the figure. Use the portions of the tables (Figures C and D) to locate scale scores and standard scores. Write these in the appropriate spaces.

Apply Your Knowledge
How would you interpret this student's standard scores for his parents? Write your explanation._____
_____
_____

The KeyMath–3 DA was normed on 3,630 people ages 4 years and 6 months through 21 years and 11 months of age. Persons who participated in the norming process were English proficient. The norm sample was representative of the population of the United

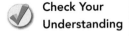

Check Your Understanding

Check your ability to determine if differences between scores are significant by completing Activity 7.9 below.

Activity 7.9

Complete the following problems.

1. A third-grade student obtained the KeyMath–3DA area standard scores shown at the bottom of Figure B. Write the standard scores in the appropriate spaces in Figure 7.7a. Indicate whether the comparisons are <, >, or = and determine the differences.

2. Using the information provided in Figures 7.7b and 7.7c, determine whether the differences found in problem 1 are significant. Write the significance level and write the frequency of occurrence in Figure 7.7a.

Apply Your Knowledge

Identify this student's strengths and weaknesses according to the information obtained regarding significant differences. How would you explain this to the student's parents? Write your explanation. _____

_____

_____

Figure 7.7a   KeyMath Protocol

Area	>, <, =	Area	Standard Score Difference	Significance Level	Frequency of Occurrence
75 **BASIC CONCEPTS**	___	**OPERATIONS**	___	___	___
75 **BASIC CONCEPTS**	___	*82* **APPLICATIONS**	___	___	___
OPERATIONS	___	*82* **APPLICATIONS**	___	___	___

Source: p. 9 KeyMath Protocol Copyright 1971, 1976, 1988, 2007 NCS Pearson, Inc. KeyMath is a trademark of NCS Pearson, Inc.

Figure 7.7b   KeyMath Examiners Manual p. 320.

Significance Levels Corresponding to Area Standard Score Differences

Grade	Signification Level	Basic Concepts vs. Operations	Basic Concepts vs. Applications	Operations vs. Applications
K	NS	0–12	0–13	0–13
	<.05	13–16	14–17	14–17
	<.01	17+	18+	18+
1	NS	0–9	0–9	0–7
	<.05	10–12	10–13	8–10
	<.01	13+	14+	11+
2	NS	0–10	0–10	0–10
	<.05	11–13	11–13	11–14
	<.01	14+	14+	15+
3	NS	0–8	0–9	0–10
	<.05	9–11	10–12	11–13
	<.01	12+	13+	14+
4	NS	0–7	0–8	0–9
	<.05	8–10	9–10	10–12
	<.01	11+	11+	13+

Figure 7.7c   KeyMath Examiner's Manual p. 320.

Frequencies of Occurrence Corresponding to Area Standard Score Differences

Grade	Frequency of Occurrence	Basic Concepts vs. Operations	Basic Concepts vs. Applications	Operations vs. Applications
K	>10%	0–20	0–12	0–21
	6–10%	21–28	13–17	22–29
	1–5%	29–34	18–24	30–44
	<1%	35+	25+	45+
1	>10%	0–16	0–14	0–16
	6–10%	17	15	17–19
	1–5%	18–24	16–26	20–26
	<1%	25+	27+	27+
2	>10%	0–14	0–13	0–15
	6–10%	15–18	14–15	16–18
	1–5%	19–21	16–17	19–25
	<1%	22+	18+	26+
3	>10%	0–13	0–13	0–18
	6–10%	14–15	14–15	19–21
	1–5%	16–19	16–19	22–24
	<1%	20+	20+	25+
4	>10%	0–12	0–11	0–14
	6–10%	13–14	12–14	15–16
	1–5%	15–19	15–17	17–20
	<1%	20+	18+	21+

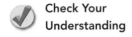

Check Your Understanding

Check your ability to determine a student's profile on the KeyMath–3 DA by completing Activity 7.10 below.

Activity 7.10

This student's scale scores and confidence intervals have been entered below on the score profile sheet. Complete the sheet by shading in the profile in Figure 7.8. Complete the profile of the area scores at the bottom of the profile. How would you interpret these scores for parents? _____
What would be the areas and skills of concern? _____

States in race/ethnicity, sex, parent's education level, and geographic location. The norm sample reflected the U.S. population based on the 2004 survey of the U.S. Bureau of Census.

The examiner's manual provides evidence of internal reliability including split-half reliability for subtests, area, and total test scores. Additional reliability information is provided for alternate forms and test-retest reliability. Validity information includes construct validity, content validity, and concurrent criterion related validity. Studies with clinical samples with the KeyMath included samples of children with attention-deficit hyperactivity disorder, learning disabilities in reading, in math, and in reading and math, and students with mild intellectual disabilities. A study with a sample of gifted students provided evidence of discrimnant validity with that sample of students who, on average, earned points that were consistently one-standard deviation above the mean of the instrument on both scale scores and standard scores.

Test of Mathematical Abilities–2 (TOMA–2) The TOMA (Brown, Cronin, & McEntire, 1994) was designed to assess some areas of math that may not be addressed by other instruments. This test, now in its second edition, was developed to be used with students who range in age from 8-0 to 18-11. The test authors present the following questions, not answered by other instruments, as their rationale for developing the TOMA:

1. What are the student's expressed attitudes toward mathematics?

2. What is the student's general vocabulary level when that vocabulary is used in a mathematical sense?

Figure 7.8 KeyMath–3 Protocol p.8 Form B.

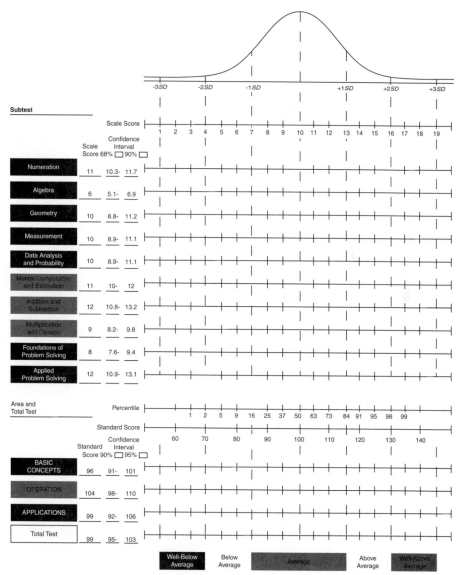

Source: page 8, KeyMath Protocol, Copyright 1971, 1976, 1988, 2007 NCS Pearson, Inc. KeyMath is a trademark of NCS Pearson, Inc.

3. How knowledgeable is the student (or group of students) regarding the functional use of mathematics facts and concepts in our general culture?

4. How do a student's attitudes, vocabulary, and general math information compare with the basic skills shown in the areas of computation and story problems?

5. Do the student's attitudes, vocabulary, and level of general math information differ markedly from those of a group of age peers? (Brown, Cronin, & McEntire, 1994, p. 1)

This instrument was developed to help the teacher find the answers to these questions. The TOMA–2 consists of five subtests, with the fifth subtest, Attitude Toward Math, considered supplemental. The remaining subtests are Vocabulary, Computation, General Information, and Story Problems. The subtests yield standard scores with a mean of 10, a math quotient with a mean of 100, age equivalents, and percentile ranks. The manual gives precautions against misinterpretation of test scores and encourages further diagnostic assessment if a math disability is suspected.

The test authors list three diagnostic questions that the TOMA–2 may help educators answer:

1. Where should the student be placed in a curriculum?
2. What specific skills or content has the student mastered?
3. How does this student's overall performance compare with that of age or grade peers? (Brown, Cronin, & McEntire, 1994, p. 1)

WOODCOCK READING MASTERY TESTS–REVISED (WRMT–R)

The WRMT–R (Woodcock, 1987) consists of two forms that are not exactly equivalent. One form, G, contains two additional reading-readiness subtests and a supplementary Letter Checklist. For this reason, Form G is the version that should be used with younger or lower-level readers. The other form, H, contains subtests equivalent to the four other subtests contained in Form G. A general screening of reading ability can be obtained by administering the Short Scale, which includes only the Word Identification and the Passage Comprehension subtests.

Subtests   For this revision of the WRMT, the subtests of Word Identification, Word Attack, and Passage Comprehension remained basically unchanged in presentation format. The Word Attack subtest contains an error analysis inventory, but the presentation format remains the same. Substantial changes have been made in some of the subtests, and these changes affect their presentation. A new subtest, Visual-Auditory Learning, has been added.

Visual-Auditory Learning. In this subtest, the examiner visually presents a picture or rebus type of symbol while orally presenting a word. After seeing four symbols and hearing their accompanying words, the student must use the newly learned symbols to "read" sentences presented on the subsequent easel page. The student then sees four new symbols and is asked to "read" sentences that include both the first symbols and the new symbols. This process continues throughout the subtest unless the student reaches a ceiling by making a specific number of errors. If the student reaches a ceiling, the cutoff score based on total errors is used to determine the raw score. If the student does not make the number of errors used to stop the testing but rather completes all of the stories on the subtest, the number of total errors is subtracted from the number 134 to determine the raw score. This subtest is found only on Form G of the WRMT–R.

Letter Identification and Supplementary Letter Checklist. These two subtests are contained only on Form G of the revised WRMT. The Letter Identification subtest does provide norm scores; however, the Supplementary Letter Checklist is used for error analysis only. The examiner has the option of presenting the task to measure the student's ability to name the letters or the sounds of the letters.

Word Identification. This subtest measures the student's ability to orally read the visually presented words. The words at the easiest level represent sight words and other words selected from several basal reading series. The more difficult words were selected from various sources. This subtest attempts to measure identification of the word. The student must say the word aloud; comprehension of the word is not measured.

Word Attack. This subtest visually presents nonsense words, which the student must decode orally. This test measures the student's ability to use phonetic attack and structural analysis in reading new words aloud. An error analysis page included in the protocol assists the examiner in identifying specific phonetic errors that need educational remediation.

Word Comprehension. This subtest samples the student's ability to provide missing words for analogies, synonyms, and antonyms. This subtest actually comprises three smaller subtests, which can be analyzed by categories for understanding vocabulary. The examiner calculates three raw scores and locates the *W* score on the protocol rather than from norm tables.

Passage Comprehension. This subtest presents a sentence or passage with a missing word. The student orally provides the missing word after silently reading the passage. The lower-level items contain picture cues, and most of the difficult items are fairly content specific. The most difficult items were taken from textbooks, newspaper articles, and the like.

Scoring On most of the WRMT–R subtests, the student establishes the basal after answering six consecutive items correctly and the ceiling after answering six consecutive responses incorrectly. The

Visual-Auditory Learning subtest, however, contains a cutoff score chart to determine when the student has reached a ceiling level.

Scoring the WRMT–R will result in comprehensive information about the student's individual reading ability. In addition to an error analysis for the Word Attack subtest and qualitative scoring of the Supplementary Letter Checklist, this battery can provide the examiner with the following information:

1. Standard error of measurement is provided for each *W* score, and confidence bands may be calculated for each subtest.

2. Space on the protocol for error responses helps the examiner complete an error analysis of reading ability.

3. Several diagnostic profiles may be plotted according to the student's performance based on percentile ranks, grade equivalents, and relative performance index scores.

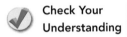

Check Your Understanding

Check your ability to obtain a raw score for a portion of the WRMT–R by completing Activity 7.11 below.

Activity 7.11

Complete the following problems.

1. A student taking the WRMT–R Visual-Auditory Learning subtest completed stories 1 through 4 and made 46 errors. In Figure H, find the row that contains stories 1–4, because the student completed four stories. Locate the number 46, and then locate the total error estimate beneath in the total errors row (stories 1–7). Write the total error estimate in the appropriate space in Figure H _____.

2. Subtract the total error estimate from 134 to obtain the raw score for this subtest. Write the score on Figure H _____.

Apply Your Knowledge

What is the purpose of using the cutoff score table?_____

_____

_____

Figure H

CUTOFF SCORE TO TOTAL ERRORS

Story 1:	- 9 -
Stories 1-2:	22 - 21 - - 20 - - 19 - - 18 - - 17 - - 16 - - 15 - - - - - - - -
Stories 1-4:	- 56 - 55 54 - 53 - 52 - 51 - 50 49 - 48 - 47 - 46 - 45 - 44 - 43 - 42 - 41 - 40 - 39 - 38 37
Stories 1-6:	105 104 103 102 - 101 100 99 98 97 96 95 94 - 93 92 91 90 89 88 - 87 86 85 84 83 82 - 81 80 79 78 77 - 76 75 74
TOTAL ERRORS (Stories 1-7)	133 132 131 130 129 128 127 126 125 124 123 122 121 120 119 118 117 116 115 114 113 112 111 110 109 108 107 106 105 104 103 102 101 100 99 98 97

Stories 1-4:	- 36 - 35 - 34 - 33 - 32 - 31 30 - 29 - 28 - 27 - 26 - - 25 - - - - - - - - - -
Stories 1-6:	73 72 71 70 69 68 67 - 66 65 64 63 62 61 60 59 - 58 57 56 - 55 54 53 52 51 50 49 48 47 46 45 44 43 42 41 40
TOTAL ERRORS (Stories 1-7)	96 94 93 92 91 90 89 88 87 86 85 84 82 81 80 79 78 77 76 75 74 73 72 71 70 69 67 66 65 63 62 61 60 59 57 56 55

134 − _____ = Test 1
Total   Raw
Errors   Score

Source: From *Woodcock Reading Mastery Tests–Revised Form G Protocol (p. 3).* By R. W. Woodcock 1987 Circle Pines, MN. American Guidance Service. Copyright 1976 by American Guidance Service.

Once having mastered the scoring, the examiner obtains a comprehensive evaluation of reading. The examiner uses raw scores to enter tables to obtain the derived scores of W scores, grade and age equivalents, and standard error of measurement for W scores. The examiner compares the student's obtained W scores with reference scores for age or grade-level comparisons.

The table that contains the reference scores also contains column numbers. The column numbers are used to find percentile ranks and standard scores on another table. Two column numbers are given for each reference score. After making the comparison by subtracting the reference score from the obtained W score, the examiner selects the correct column number and enters the relative performance index table, a portion of which is shown in Figure 7.9.

The examiner determines the correct column by the following criteria: If the difference between the W and the reference score is less than 100, the column number on the left is used to enter the table; if the difference is greater than 100, the column number on the right is used to enter the table. The column numbers may be different for the scores obtained in the standard error of measurement confidence bands. When the standard error of measurement is added to the difference score, the new score may be greater than 100 when the original difference score was less than 100. This means that the column number on the right would be used to determine the relative performance index and percentile rank for the confidence band scores. When the standard error of measurement is subtracted from the difference score, the new score may be less than 100 when the original score was not. Again, the new score found by using the standard error of measurement would require a different column number for the relative performance index table.

The WRMT–R presents cluster scores for reading as well as individual subtest scores. The clusters are Readiness (Form G only), Basic Skills, and Reading Comprehension. The Readiness cluster includes the Visual-Auditory and Letter Identification subtests. Word Identification and Word Attack subtests make up the Basic Skills cluster. The Reading Comprehension cluster is made up of the Word Comprehension and Passage Comprehension subtests. The cluster W scores are obtained by finding the average of the two subtest W scores in each cluster. A Total Reading cluster score is found by averaging the four subtests contained on both forms of the test: Word Identification, Word Attack, Word Comprehension, and Passage Comprehension.

PROCESS ASSESSMENT OF THE LEARNER: TEST BATTERY FOR READING AND WRITING (PAL–RW)

The PAL–RW is designed to assess the processes used in initial and emerging reading and writing skills as well as the skills expected

Figure 7.9 Table G all forms, columns 25 to 30, difference scores 115 to 144.

Table G. Relative Performance Indexes, Percentile Ranks, and Standard Scores (mean = 100, *SD* = 15)

			Column			
25	26	27	28	29	30	
PR/Std	PR/Std	PR/Std	PR/Std	PR/Std	PR/Std	DIFF
98 132	98 130	97 129	96 126	93 122	90 119	144
98 131	98 129	97 128	95 125	93 122	90 119	143
98 130	97 129	97 127	95 125	92 121	89 119	142
98 129	97 128	96 127	95 124	92 121	89 118	141
97 129	97 127	96 126	94 124	91 120	88 118	140
97 128	96 127	96 125	94 123	91 120	87 117	139
97 127	96 126	95 125	93 122	90 119	87 117	138
96 127	95 125	95 124	93 122	90 119	86 116	137
96 126	95 125	94 123	92 121	89 118	86 116	136
95 125	95 124	94 123	92 121	88 118	85 115	135
95 124	94 123	93 122	91 120	88 117	84 115	134
94 124	93 123	92 122	90 119	87 117	83 115	133
94 123	93 122	92 121	90 119	86 116	83 114	132
93 122	92 121	91 120	89 118	85 116	82 114	131
92 122	91 121	90 120	88 118	85 115	81 113	130
92 121	91 120	90 119	87 117	84 115	80 113	129
91 120	90 119	89 118	86 117	83 114	79 112	128
90 119	89 118	88 118	86 116	82 114	79 112	127
89 119	88 118	87 117	85 115	81 113	78 111	126
89 118	87 117	86 116	84 115	80 113	77 111	125
87 117	86 116	85 116	83 114	79 112	76 111	124
86 117	85 116	84 115	82 114	78 112	75 110	123
85 116	84 115	83 114	81 113	77 111	74 110	122
84 115	83 114	82 114	80 112	76 111	73 109	121
83 114	82 114	81 113	78 112	75 110	72 109	120
82 114	81 113	80 112	77 111	74 110	71 108	119
81 113	79 112	78 112	76 111	73 109	70 108	118
79 112	78 112	77 111	75 110	72 109	69 108	117
78 111	77 111	76 110	74 109	71 108	68 107	116
76 111	75 110	74 110	72 109	70 108	67 107	115

during the intermediate grades in school (through grade 6). This battery can be used for students ranging in age from 5 years to 13 years of age. It assesses the prerequisite and requisite skills needed to read, write, and take notes in school. Several skill areas are assessed. A brief description of each subtest is presented in the following section.

Alphabetic Writing. This subtest requires the student to write as many letters of the alphabet as possible under a timed format.

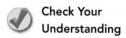

Check Your Understanding

Check your ability to score a portion of the WRMT–R by completing Activity 7.12 below.

Activity 7.12

Complete the problems and answer the questions that follow.

1. Use the information shown in Figure I to determine the difference between the obtained *W* score and the reference score for the Word Identification subtest. Choose from the figure the column number that will be used to find the relative performance index and the percentile rank for the obtained *W* score._____

2. Using the obtained difference score from problem 1, complete the confidence bands (Figure I) by adding and subtracting the standard error of measurement given in the figure. Write the answers in the appropriate spaces on the portion of the protocol in Figure I. Choose from the figure the column number that will be used to find the relative performance index and percentile ranks for the confidence band scores._____

3. The relative performance index for this student is 99/90. Write 99 in the appropriate spaces in Figure I. Use the previous table to find the standard score and percentile rank for the obtained difference score found in problem 1 for the Word Identification subtest. Write your answer in the appropriate spaces in Figure I.____

4. Use the table to obtain the standard scores and percentile ranks for the confidence bands. Write your answer in the appropriate spaces in Figure I._____

5. What do the confidence band scores represent?_____

Figure I   Protocol section for WRMT—R Word Identification subtest.

TEST 3: WORD IDENTIFICATION

Raw
Score _____ (106)   W $\frac{498}{\text{Table A}}$

OPTIONAL SCORES

SEM $\frac{4}{\text{Table A}}$ GE $\frac{4+7}{\text{Table A}}$ AE $\frac{9\text{-}10}{\text{Table A}}$

–R $\frac{374}{\text{Table E OR F}}$ COL $\frac{52/26}{\text{Table E OR F}}$ Other ☐ Std
☐ T ☐ NCE
☐ Starline

DIFF = _____   RPI $\frac{\quad}{\text{Table G}}$ /90   PR $\frac{\quad}{\text{Table G}}$ Table G or H

1:SEM CONFIDENCE BANDS

DIFF + *SEM* _____   RPI $\frac{\quad}{\text{Table G}}$ /90   PR $\frac{\quad}{\text{Table G}}$ _____ Table G or H

DIFF – *SEM* _____   RPI $\frac{\quad}{\text{Table G}}$ /90   PR $\frac{\quad}{\text{Table G}}$ _____ Table G or H

Source: From *Woodcock Reading Mastery Tests—Revised, Protocol* (p. 12) by R. W. Woodcock, 1987. Circle Pines, MN: American Guidance Service. Copyright 1987 by American Guidance Service. Reprinted by permission.

This assesses the child's memory of the alphabet as well as the child's ability to graphically represent the letters. Fluency or automaticity of this ability is considered due to the subtest time limit of 5 minutes. Qualitative analysis is included as part of the scoring, with omissions, reversals, inversions, sequencing errors, case confusions (upper and lower case), and cursive letters noted by the examiner. The test is administered to students in grades K–6.

Receptive Coding. The child is asked to match or discriminate letters within words. Letter sequencing is also assessed. These tasks tap into the child's visual memory of letters and sequences of letters. This subtest is administered to children in grades K–6.

Expressive Coding. Similar tasks as in receptive coding, however the student is required to write responses in a response booklet. The sequencing tasks require the child to understand concepts such as first or fifth to identify and correctly write the specific letter or letters. Children in grades 4–6 are administered this subtest.

Rapid Automatic Naming (RAN). Because automaticity or fluency is essential for mastery of reading and writing, there are several RAN subtests included on the PAL–RW. Qualitative analyses and quantitative analyses can be completed for each of the subtests of RAN–Letters (grades K–6), RAN–Words (grades 1–6), RAN–Digits (grades K–6), RAN–Digits and Words (grades 1–6).

Note Taking. There are two tasks for assessing the note-taking skills of students in grades 4–6. These tasks are scored both qualitatively and quantitatively. Students listen and take notes for a passage read by the examiner.

Rhyming. Two tasks assess the prereading skills of rhyming discrimination and rhyming fluency. This subtest is administered to students in kindergarten.

Syllables. Students in grades K–6 are administered this subtest. The task requires students to understand and manipulate the deletion of syllables they hear and say.

Phonemes. This subtest is administered to students in grades K–6, who must delete sounds of words and nonsense words. Tasks are differentiated by grade level.

Rimes. Students in grades 1–6 must hear, manipulate, and then say words in which they delete a sound.

Word Choice. This subtest assesses the student's ability to discriminate between words with correct written spellings and incorrect written spellings. The discriminations become more difficult according to the grade placement of the student, with students in grades 4–6 being required to discriminate more complex and unpredictable words. Visual memory and memory for visual sequencing of letters are required for this subtest.

Pseudoword Decoding. This subtest is for students in grades 1–6. Students are asked to read nonsense words.

Story Retell. This subtest is administered to students in kindergarten. Students are asked to listen to a story, answer specific questions about the story, and then retell the story. Scoring criteria for responses are provided.

Finger Sense. This subtest is administered to students in grades K–6. Students must physically respond to finger sequencing tasks and respond to tasks that require them to have adequate sensation within their fingers. Students are also required to determine specific letters that are "written" on their fingers by the examiner.

Sentence Sense. Students are required to read and discriminate which sentence, in sets of three sentences, make sense. Silent reading fluency and comprehension are necessary due to the timed format.

Copying. On these tasks, students are required to copy written sentences in a timed format. Both copying fluency and accuracy of writing is important, and scoring criteria are provided. Students in kindergarten complete Task A and students in grades 1–6 complete Task B.

This fairly new assessment instrument offers a variety of subtests that tap into the individual skills needed to read and write in school successfully. This test is not a comprehensive assessment of reading comprehension, but it offers a format in which to assess other skills needed, such as memory, sequencing, association, and fluency of the visual, aural, and motor abilities required for reading and written language skills. These skills are the skills that should be developmentally in place for students in kindergarten through grade 6 and therefore expand beyond the skills of phonemic awareness.

The scores available for this instrument are decile scores that are used to form a profile of the student's ability. Figure 7.10 illustrates a completed scored protocol with the decile profile.

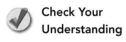

Check Your Understanding

Complete Activity 7.13 below.

Activity 7.13

Answer the following questions about the skills assessed on the PAL Test Battery for Reading and Writing.

1. One of the subtests of the PAL tests the student's ability to repeat sequences with their fingers. What is the name of this subtest? _____

2. Which subtest assesses a student's ability to select the correct spellings of words?_____

3. On which subtests are phonemic awareness and early prereading skills assessed?_____

4. Which complex subtest requires the student to be able to understand concepts such as position placement in a sequence of letters in order to respond to the task of the subtest?_____

Figure 7.10   Example of a completed score-profile page of the record form of the process assessment of the learner from the *PAL Test Battery for Reading and Writing Administration and Scoring Manual*, p. 24.

Subtest/Content	Raw Score	Decile Score	Profile									
Alphabet Writing Score	3	≤40	10	20	30	(40)	50	60	70	80	90	100
Receptive Coding Total Score	34	≤30	10	20	(30)	40	50	60	70	80	90	100
Expressive Coding Total Score			10	20	30	40	50	60	70	80	90	100
RAN												
Letters Total Time	89	≤20	10	(20)	30	40	50	60	70	80	90	100
Words Time	47	≤20	10	(20)	30	40	50	60	70	80	90	100
Digits Total Time	92	≤20	10	(20)	30	40	50	60	70	80	90	100
Words & Digits Time	93	≤10	(10)	20	30	40	50	60	70	80	90	100
Note-Taking Task A Score			10	20	30	40	50	60	70	80	90	100
Rhyming Total Score			10	20	30	40	50	60	70	80	90	100
Syllables Total Score	10	≤100	10	20	30	40	50	60	70	80	90	(100)
Phonemes Total Score	30	≤100	10	20	30	40	50	60	70	80	90	(100)
Rimes Total Score	6	≤70	10	20	30	40	50	60	(70)	80	90	100
Word Choice Total Score	1	≤10	(10)	20	30	40	50	60	70	80	90	100
Pseudoword Decoding Total Score	15	≤40	10	20	30	(40)	50	60	70	80	90	100
Story Retell Total Score			10	20	30	40	50	60	70	80	90	100
Finger Sense												
Repetition Item 1 Time	9	≤30	10	20	(30)	40	50	60	70	80	90	100
Repetition Item 2 Time	9	≤30	10	20	(30)	40	50	60	70	80	90	100
Succession Item 1 Time	14	≤50	10	20	30	40	(50)	60	70	80	90	100
Succession Item 2 Time	10	≤80	10	20	30	40	50	60	70	(80)	90	100
Localization Score	10	≤100	10	20	30	40	50	60	70	80	90	(100)
Recognition Score	10	≤100	10	20	30	40	50	60	70	80	90	(100)
Fingertip Writing Score	7	≤80	10	20	30	40	50	60	70	(80)	90	100
Sentence Sense Total Score	5	≤40	10	20	30	(40)	50	60	70	80	90	100
Copying												
Task A Score	27	≤100	10	20	30	40	50	60	70	80	90	(100)
Task B Score	60	≤100	10	20	30	40	50	60	70	80	90	(100)
Note-Taking Task B Score			10	20	30	40	50	60	70	80	90	100

Source: V. W. Beringer (2001). San Antonio, TX: The Psychological Corporation.

The PAL–RW manual contains a chapter on how the results of the assessment can be used for interventions. The appendices include criterion-referenced measures that may be reproduced for instructional purposes.

OTHER DIAGNOSTIC TESTS

The remainder of this chapter summarizes several other tests frequently used in the classroom. Some of these tests will not require the lengthy test administration time required by tests presented in the first section of the chapter. Some of these tests may be administered, in part or in their entirety, to groups of students. These tests are included here because they provide useful information to the educator for diagnosing deficits in specific academic areas and aid in educational planning.

GRAY ORAL READING TESTS–FOURTH EDITION (GORT–4)

The GORT–4 provides the teacher with a method of analyzing oral reading skills. This instrument is a norm-referenced test that may be administered to students ages 7-0 through 18-11. The GORT–4 has equivalent forms so that students may be reassessed using the same instrument. This newest version of the GORT has an additional story for the lowest level on both forms of the instrument to allow for better exploration of the emerging reading skills of young students. On this instrument, the student reads stories aloud to the teacher, who scores rate, accuracy, fluency, comprehension, and overall reading ability. The comprehension score is derived from answers to questions asked by the teacher following each story. The oral reading miscues may be analyzed in the following areas: meaning similarity, function similarity, graphic/phonemic similarity, multiple sources (of errors), and self-correction. The authors state that the purposes of the GORT–4 are to identify students with problems, determine strengths and weaknesses, document progress, and to conduct research using the GORT–4 (Wiederholt & Bryant, 2001, pp. 4–5).

TEST OF READING COMPREHENSION–THIRD EDITION (TORC–3)

The TORC–3 was designed to assess reading comprehension using eight subtests. The instrument includes four subtests in the reading comprehension core: general vocabulary, syntactic similarities, paragraph reading, and sentence sequencing. These skills are assessed using a variety of task formats, such as multiple-choice items for general vocabulary and discrimination of sentences for syntactic similarities. The diagnostic supplements include the following subtests: mathematics vocabulary, social skills vocabulary, science vocabulary, and reading the directions of schoolwork. The test manual includes suggestions for additional assessment methods.

TEST OF WRITTEN LANGUAGE–3 (TOWL–3)

The third edition of the TOWL includes two alternate forms test booklets (A and B) and is organized into three composites: Overall Written Language, Contrived Writing, and Spontaneous Writing (Hammill & Larsen, 1996). TOWL–3 contains eight subtests, of which three are calculated from the spontaneously written story. The student completes all test items in the student response booklet. This instrument may be administered in small groups, although for optimal monitoring of written responses, individual administration appears to be best. A description of each subtest follows:

1. Vocabulary—The student is provided a stimulus word and required to use the word in a sentence.
2. Spelling—The student is required to spell dictated words.
3. Style—The student writes dictated sentences and must punctuate sentences and capitalize properly.
4. Logical Sentences—The student is provided an illogical sentence and is required to edit it so that it is more logical.
5. Sentence Combining—The student is presented two or more sentences per item and must combine them into one meaningful and grammatically correct sentence.

   For subtests 6, 7, and 8, the student is asked to write a story when shown a stimulus picture. The requirements for each subtest are:

6. Contextual Conventions—The student's story response is scored for punctuation, capitalization, spelling, and other conventional rules of writing.
7. Contextual Language—The student's story response is scored for sentence construction, quality of vocabulary, and grammar.
8. The student's story response is scored for the following: plot, prose, development of characters, interest, and additional aspects of composition (Hammill & Larsen, 1996).

TEST OF WRITTEN SPELLING–4 (TWS–4)

A standardized spelling test, the TWS–4 (Larsen, Hammill, & Moats, 1999) consists of two alternate forms that can be administered to individual students or to groups of students ages 6-0 to 18-11. Instructions for starting points and basal and ceiling levels are presented in the examiner's manual. During administration of this test, the student begins at the appropriate entry level and continues until the ceiling has been reached. The ceiling is established when the student misses five words consecutively. Once the ceiling has been reached, the examiner checks to see that the basal of five consecutive items answered correctly was obtained. For students who did not establish a basal, the examiner administers items in reverse order until five consecutive items are spelled correctly, or until the student reaches item 1. All items below the established basal are scored as correct. Raw scores are used to enter tables for standard scores with a mean of 100, percentile ranks, age equivalents, and grade equivalents.

This revision of the TWS includes more elaboration for examiners regarding the theoretical bases of the test and a discussion of the skills of spelling in English. The authors also provide a useful chapter on additional assessment methods of spelling and other related skills, such as the assessment of phoneme awareness. These additional assessment methods offer the use of this instrument as part of a total evaluation effort in which teachers would use additional methods and may use an alternate form of the TWS for measuring gains following interventions.

ASSESSING OTHER LANGUAGE AREAS

language assessment Measuring verbal concepts and verbal understanding.

The ability to understand and express ideas using correct language is fundamental for school achievement. **Language assessment**, through tests that measure a student's understanding and use of language, is presented in this section. Tests administered by speech clinicians in an effort to diagnose and remediate speech disorders (articulation, voice, or fluency disorders) are beyond the scope of this text. Effective remediation of language disorders is considered a shared responsibility of the clinician, teacher, and parent, who each must be familiar with the tests to diagnose and monitor these skills. These tests assess a student's **receptive language** vocabulary, oral **expressive language**, and **written language** skills. In addition to actual test instruments, informal assessment of written language is conducted in the classroom as well and is presented in Chapter 6.

receptive language Inner language concepts applied to what is heard.

expressive language Language skills used in speaking or writing.

written language Understanding language concepts and using them in writing.

PEABODY PICTURE VOCABULARY TEST–4 (PPVT–4)

The PPVT–4 (Dunn & Dunn, 2007) measures the student's verbal comprehension skills by presenting a series of four visual stimuli and requesting the student to discriminate the stimulus that best represents the orally stated word. An example of this format is illustrated in Figure 7.11. Two equivalent forms of this individually

Figure 7.11 Example of visual stimuli presented to measure verbal comprehension skills in the PPVT–4.

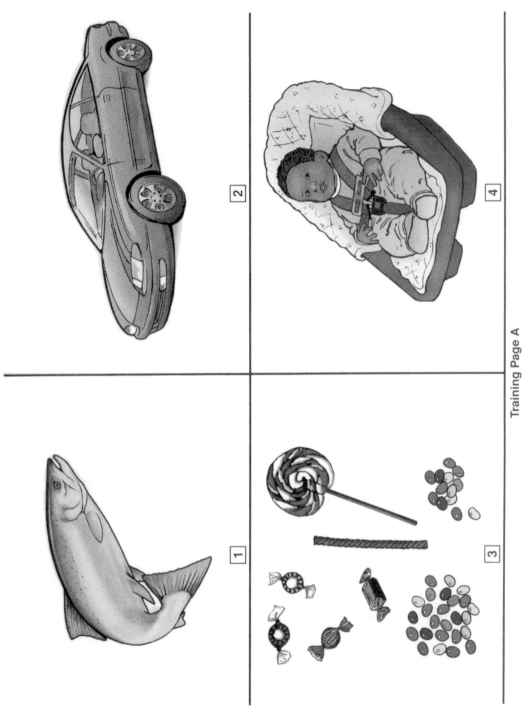

Source: From *Peabody Picture Vocabulary Test–4* (training plate D) by L. M. Dunn and L. M. Dunn, 2006. Reprinted by permission.

administered language test, form A and form B, allow retesting to monitor progress. This test includes an easel test, examiner's manual, norms booklet, and protocol. Derived scores include standard scores, percentile ranks, normal curve equivalents, stanines, age equivalents, and GSV or growth scale values. Scoring is fairly easy, and the basal level is determined when the student correctly answers all of the items in a set or misses only one item in the set. The ceiling is determined when the student incorrectly answers at least eight items in the set. The examiner's manual provides easy examples and cases to illustrate scoring and interpretation of raw scores. The examiner's manual also includes an analysis worksheet to determine if the student has more difficulty with the receptive vocabulary of nouns, verbs, or attributes. This may assist with planning interventions for promoting language development.

The examiner is cautioned to use this instrument with children who are English speakers because the PPVT–4 was normed on students who were proficient in English. The examiner's manual provides evidence of internal consistency, alternate forms reliability, test-retest reliability, content validity, concurrent criterion related validty, and discriminant validity comparing clinical groups with nonclinical groups. The PPVT–4 was conormed with the Expressive Vocabulary Test–2.

EXPRESSIVE VOCABULARY TEST–2

This instrument was conormed with the receptive language measure, the PPVT–4. This instrument was normed with persons ages 2 years and 6 months of age to those over 90 years of age. There are two forms of this measure, Forms A and B. The student's expressive vocabulary is assessed by asking the student to name a picture or to provide a synonym for a picture. Specific instructions with acceptable prompts are provided in the examiner's manual. Children are not penalized on this measure for mispronunciations or articulation errors if the work is recognizable. The examiner's manual includes worksheets that will assist the examiner in determining if the child has weaknesses in expressive vocabulary used at home or at school. An additional worksheet is provided for an analysis of parts of speech for each item of the instrument. Therefore, it can be determined that the student has a strength in nouns but has difficulty with verbs or attributes. These analyses may provide useful information to assist with language development interventions.

TEST OF LANGUAGE DEVELOPMENT–PRIMARY: THIRD EDITION (TOLD–P:3)

The Primary edition of the TOLD–P:3 (Newcomer & Hammill, 1997) was designed for use with students ranging in age from 4-0 to 8-11. The theoretical structure is based on a two-dimensional language model, described in the manual. TOLD–P:3 contains the following subtests: Picture Vocabulary, Relational Vocabulary, Oral Vocabulary, Grammatic Understanding, Sentence Imitation, Grammatic Completion, Word Discrimination, Phonemic Analysis, and Word Articulation. The standard scores on these subtests may be used to obtain quotients for the following composites: spoken language, listening, organizing, speaking, semantics, and syntax. Derived scores include standard scores (mean = 10), quotients (mean = 100), and percentile ranks. Age equivalents are available. The format of response includes both forced-choice and open-ended responses. The student is also asked to repeat sentences on the Sentence Imitation subtest and fill in missing words for the Grammatic Completion subtest. In the Word Discrimination subtest, the student must discriminate between same and different items, which the examiner states orally. The student must name pictured items and correctly pronounce the names in the Word Articulation subtest. Table 7.4 lists the skills measured by the subtests; understanding the skills enables the teacher to interpret results and use the interpretations to develop educational plans.

Table 7.4   Content within subtests of the TOLD–P:3.

I. *Picture Vocabulary* measures the ability to understand the meaning of individual words when spoken.

II. *Relational Vocabulary* measures the ability to organize incoming language into categories that permit the perception of relationships.

III. *Oral Vocabulary* measures the ability to define individual stimulus words precisely.

IV. *Grammatic Understanding* measures the ability to comprehend sentences having differing syntactic structures.

V. *Sentence Imitation* measures the ability to repeat complex sentences accurately.

VI. *Grammatic Completion* measures the ability to complete a partially formed sentence by supplying a final word that has a proper morphological form.

VII. *Word Discrimination* measures the ability to discern subtle phonological differences between two words spoken in isolation.

VIII. *Phonemic Analysis* measures the ability to segment spoken words into smaller phonemic units by remembering and uttering the component of a word that remains after a portion is removed from the original stimulus word.

IX. *Word Articulation* measures the ability to say (i.e., articulate) a series of single words properly.

Source: Examiner's Manual for Test of Language Development–Primary: Third Edition (p. 44). Austin, TX: Pro–Ed. 1997.

TEST OF LANGUAGE DEVELOPMENT–INTERMEDIATE: THIRD EDITION (TOLD–I:3)

The Intermediate edition of the TOLD–I:3 (Hammill & Newcomer, 1997) was constructed to aid in the diagnosis of students with language problems. The theoretical structure of the TOLD–I:3 is similar to the two-dimensional model of the TOLD–P:3. The following subtests are used to assess language skills for students aged 8-0 through 12-11: Sentence Combining, Picture Vocabulary, Word Ordering, Generals, Grammatic Comprehension, and Malapropisms. The examiner presents all subtests orally; items include forced-choice and open-ended questions. Derived scores of the TOLD–I:3 are standard scores (mean = 10), quotients (mean =100), and percentile ranks by age norms. Age equivalents are available.

SELECTING DIAGNOSTIC INSTRUMENTS

The instruments presented in this chapter are among those most used by educators to determine academic difficulties. Some instruments are recommended for specific academic areas or skills. Thus, an examiner may appropriately select one instrument because it contains subtests that will yield information necessary for academic planning and intervention. Table 7.5 presents a summary of the instruments in Chapter 7.

For **MORE PRACTICE** in deciding when to use achievement and diagnostic tests, visit the Companion Website at *www.prenhall. com/overton.*

RESEARCH AND ISSUES

Research is emerging on the newly revised versions of the tests presented in this chapter but is scant on the newly developed instruments, such as the KeyMath–3 DA. Selected research of the existing research and reviews of the instruments, and issues of academic assessment, are summarized here.

In a review of strengths and weaknesses of the WJ III Tests of Achievement, Mather, Wendling, and Woodcock (2001) noted that the inclusion of timed subtests may not be important in some settings and that students' performance on timed substests may be influenced by their culture. Moreover, these authors expressed concern that the complexity of some subtests, such as Understanding Directions and Story Recall, may result in responses that are difficult to interpret and score. They also stated that writing tasks on this instrument are limited to one-sentence responses.

Table 7.5 Diagnostic standardized academic tests.

Name of Test	Purpose of Test	Constructs Measured	Standardization Information	Reliability Information	Validity Information
KeyMath–3 DA	Comprehensive and diagnostic assessment of math skills	Basic math concepts, math operations, math applications	Sample included 3,630 persons ages 4 years 6 months–21 years 11 months Variables included geographic region, ethnicity, socioeconomic status, parental education level.	Alternate forms reliability coefficients .96–A .97–B for Total Test split-half reliability.	A variety of research supporting evidence for content validity, construct validity, concurrent criterion-related validity in manual.
Test of Mathematical Abilities–Second Edition	Assesses other aspects of math not found on other measures	Math vocabulary, attitude toward math, general math information	More than 2,000 students from 26 states. Variables included race, community, disability status.	Internal consistency coefficients and group coefficients ranged from .73 to .98; test-retest ranged from .66 to .93.	Concurrent criterion-related validity ranged from low to adequate; construct validity was supported.
Process Assessment of the Learner: Test Battery for Reading and Writing	Assessing the processes involved in reading and writing	Pre-reading and writing processes such as receptive and expressive coding, alphabetic writing, phonemic awareness skills, acquisition of written symbols, short-term memory of visual and oral symbols and sounds associated with reading, fluency of recall or rapid automatic naming	There were 868 students in the standardization sample ages 5–13 years. Variables considered include race/ethnicity, geographic region, and parent education level. Test developers sought to approximate the 1998 U.S. Census representation.	The manual includes reliability studies of internal consistency of alpha coefficients, test-retest reliability, and interscorer reliability. Coefficients ranged from adequate to high.	Evidence of content and construct validity provided. Concurrent criterion-related validity information provided with other diagnostic and reading/writing measures. Strong support for clinical discriminant validity provided.

Test	Purpose	Skills Assessed	Sample	Reliability	Validity
Woodcock Reading Mastery Tests–Revised	Assesses the skills of reading	Reading decoding skills, reading comprehension skills	More than 6,000 persons in sample from K to adult; variables include age, sex, race, geographic region.	Split-half reliability coefficients in the 90s.	Content and construct validity studies. Coefficients ranged from .48 to .91.
Gray Oral Reading Tests–Fourth Edition	Assesses oral reading skills	Accuracy, fluency, comprehension, and overall oral reading ability	More than 1,600 persons from four geographic regions. Variables included race, ethnicity, family income and educational status, age.	Alternative forms reliability, interscorer reliability, and test-retest reliability with coefficients ranging from .85 to .99	Content validity, differential item functioning, criterion-related validity research supports test validity.
Test of Reading Comprehension–Third Edition	Assesses reading comprehension skills	Reading comprehension, vocabulary from content-related areas	The sample included more that 1,900 students. Variables considered were age, sex, race, ethnicity, and geographic region.	Internal consistency, interscorer, content and time sampling were considered with reliability coefficients ranging from .79 to .98.	Information provided for content, construct, and criterion-related validity. Information provided for discriminant validity for specific groups.
Test of Written Language–Third Edition	Assessment of various written language skills	Written language, spelling skills, vocabulary	More than 2,000 students were included in the sample. Variables considered were sex, race and ethnicity, community type, disability, and geographic region.	Interscorer, coefficient alpha, split-half reliability, and test-retest reliability information ranged from adequate to high.	Concurrent criterion-related validity, factor analysis information provided and considered adequate.
Test of Language Development–Primary: Third Edition	Various aspects of language development of young children	Vocabulary, grammatical and syntactic understanding, articulation of words and phonemic analysis	The sample included 1,000 students ages 4-0 to 8-11. Variables considered were sex, race, community size, race, ethnicity, educational level of parents, family income and geographic region.	Reliability coefficients ranged from .77 to .99 for content sampling, internal consistency measures, time sampling, and interscorer reliability studies.	Content validity, construct validity, and criterion-related validity studies included in the manual, with coefficients ranging from .52 to .97.

Table 7.5 continued.

Name of Test	Purpose of Test	Constructs Measured	Standardization Information	Reliability Information	Validity Information
Test of Language Development–Intermediate: Third Edition	Assessment of general language skills of children ages 8-0 through 12-11	Vocabulary, grammatical comprehension	A portion of the sample was included from previous studies with a sample size of 779. Variables considered include sex, race, ethnicity, community size, parent occupation, and geographic area.	Internal consistency using coefficient alpha, content sampling, and interscorer reliability presented in the manual, with coefficients ranging from .83 to .97.	Criterion-related validity, construct validity, item validity, and factor analysis information included in the manual.
Test of Written Spelling–Fourth Edition	Assessment of spelling skills	Spelling skills	Over 4,000 students were included in the standardization of the TWS–2 and TWS–3 combined, with no new cases added for TWS–4. The sample considered the variables of race, sex, ethnicity, and geographic region.	Internal reliability coefficients were high, ranging from .93 to .99. Test-retest reliability studies were adequate although the sample sizes of the studies for reliability were small.	Content, criterion-related validity information, and construct validity research included and based on developmental gains.
Peabody Picture Vocabulary Test–Third Edition Expressive Vocabulary Text–2	Assessment of vocabulary skills through equivalent forms Assesses expressive vocabulary	Receptive vocabulary expressive vocabulary ability to name pictures and provide synonyms	Sample included 3,540 persons ranging in age from 2 years to 90+. Variables included sex, ethnicity, age, education level of person or parents, and geographic region. Representation based on 2004 U.S. Census survey data. Conormed with the PPVT–4, see above for standarization sample	Internal consistency studies included split-half and alternate forms. Test-retest information included. All coefficients ranged from the .83 to .90s for both forms Split-half reliability ranged from .88–.97	Examiner's manual provides various research studies providing evidence. of coustruct, Criterion related and content validity. Evidence provided for clinical discriminant validity. with clinical samples

Litchenberger and Smith (2005) pointed out some of the weaknesses of the WAIT–II. These authors report that the WIAT–II has a limited ceiling on some of the subtests and that this may cause difficulty in determining the functioning of students who are gifted. In addition, variability in standard errors of measurement across ages, indicates a weakness with reliability. For teachers who often interpret testing results and relate these results to instruction, it is also problematic that quartile and decile scores are unfamiliar. The WIAT–II also has limited items representing some skills that are found on the Skills Analysis.

The publishers of some achievement tests have renormed or updated the normative information available for the achievement batteries, for example, the PIAT–R–NU. When these tests undergo a normative update, there may be differences in between the groups of students who participate in one domain or on specific subtests. This may result in some variability between subtests on the same instrument (Johnson, 1999).

Berninger (2006) suggests that instruments such as the Process Assessment of the Learner and the WIAT–II should be used in combination with intensive interventions for reading and written language for students who are at risk for developing written language disabilities. This may offer an advantage over using CBM type progress monitoring alone since the student would be assessed and compared with age norms.

The K-TEA-II has weaknesses in the ceiling level and floor level when the test is administered to very young or old students on some subtests (Litchenberger & Smith, 2005). For example, on some subtests a young student with a raw score of 0 may earn a standard score between the low 60s and 80s. These authors also noted some weaknesses in the standard error of measurements for some specific age groups on specific subtests.

In a review by Cascella (2006), it was noted that some language assessments provide normative data on students with intellectual disabilities. This may be helpful when trying to determine if a student should receive additional speech and language therapy in the school setting. In this review, it was noted that the TOAL–3, the TOLD–I:3, the TOLD–P:3, the PPVT–3, and the EVT provided such norms.

In older reviews of the PIAT–R (Allinder & Fuchs, 1992), the authors cautioned that the format of the test instrument, including multiple choice on some subtests, may encourage guessing. These reviewers also cautioned that information obtained from multiple-choice items is diagnostically different from information obtained when a response must be produced independently by the student. They reminded consumers that this instrument was designed as a wide-range screening instrument and should therefore not be used in educational decision making involving placement, eligibility, or planning. Another study found that changing the visual stimuli associated with the PIAT–R Written Expression subtest resulted in significantly higher scores for structure (Cole, Muenz, Ouchi, Kaufman, & Kaufman, 1997).

Slate (1996) compared several measures frequently used in assessing students with learning disabilities. In this study, the WIAT, KeyMath–R, Woodcock–Reading Mastery–Revised, and the PIAT–R were compared. While many of the subtests were positively correlated, there remained significant variance and mean differences. In other words, although reading subtests may share common constructs and similar items, students may perform quite differently across such subtests of different achievement batteries. Therefore, what may be perceived as a true difference in abilities may really be the result of differences in the tests, not the student.

THINK AHEAD

How do you think student behaviors influence a student's ability to make successful progress in school? In the next chapter, you will learn a variety of methods used to study and assess behavior in a school setting.

EXERCISES

Part I

Match the following terms with the correct definitions.

a. individual achievement test
b. screening test
c. group achievement tests
d. diagnostic tests
e. composite scores
f. achievement tests
g. aptitude tests
h. receptive coding

i. expressive coding
j. norm-referenced tests
k. subtests
l. curriculum-based assessment
m. curriculum-based measurement
n. level of significance

_____ 1. This indicates the amount of chance occurrence of the difference between two scores _____.

_____ 2. Statewide assessment instruments are one form of _____.

_____ 3. The reading passages from the basal text are used to assess the students' levels at the end of each chapter. This is a form of _____.

_____ 4. When one student is compared with a national sample of students of the same age, it is called _____.

_____ 5. Reading decoding and reading comprehension of a test will yield an overall reading score for students. In this example, reading decoding and reading comprehension are _____.

_____ 6. The K-TEA-II and the PIAT–R are individually adminis-tered _____.

_____ 7. A broad-based instrument that samples a few items across the domains of a curriculum is called _____.

_____ 8. A student was administered a norm-referenced reading test and found to have inconsistent performance. The teacher was not certain that he had determined the difficulty using classroom informal methods. In order to obtain more in-depth information about reading, he decided to use differ-ent _____ for more specific skill assessment.

_____ 9. When informal methods and classroom interventions do not seem to have effective results, a teacher may need additional assessment information. One method is using _____ to compare the student to national average perfor-mance.

_____10. These instruments are designed to measure strength, tal-ent, or ability in a particular domain or area.

Part II

Match the following tests with the statements below.

a. Woodcock–Johnson Tests of Achievement–III
b. KeyMath–3
c. Kaufman Test of Educa-tional Achievement–II
d. Peabody Individual Achievement Test–R
e. Wide Range Achievement Test–3
f. Wechsler Individual Achievement Test–II

g. Woodcock–McGrew–Werder Mini-Battery of Achievement
h. Test of Mathematical Ability
i. Process Assessment of the Learner
j. Test of Written Spelling–4
k. PPVT–4
l. EVT–2

_____ 1. This diagnostic test is normed for students through the grade skill levels of 12th grade in mathematics.

_____ 2. This test, which includes a factual knowledge subtest, is a more comprehensive screening test than the WRAT3.

_____ 3. This test has standard and supplemental batteries.

_____ 4. This diagnostic test may be used in the very early grades to assess the cognitive abilities and functions required for reading.

_____ 5. This diagnostic test would not be used to assess complex calculus skills or other college level math.

_____ 6. This test provides cluster scores and individual subtest scores.

_____ 7. These academic achievement instruments were conormed with their cognitive assessment instruments.

_____ 8. This achievement test includes a Language Composite that measures both expressive language and receptive listening skills.

_____ 9. This academic achievement test includes many multiple-choice items that may encourage guessing.

_____10. This test includes measures for rapid naming.

_____11. This vocabulary assessment asks the student to name pictures or provide synonyms.

_____12. This vocabulary test was conormed with the PPVT–4.

Companion
Website

Answers to these questions can be found in the Appendix of this text or you may also complete these questions and receive immediate feedback on your answers by going to the Think Ahead module in Chapter 7 of the Companion Website.

Assessment of Behavior

academic engaged time
schoolwide positive behavioral
  support
manifestation determination
behavioral intervention plan
functional behavioral assessment
replacement behaviors
functional behavioral analysis
direct observation
event recording
interval recording
anecdotal recording
duration recording
latency recording
interresponse time
functional assessment interview

target behaviors
baseline
antecedent
setting events
establishing operation
frequency counting
time sampling
checklists
questionnaires
interviews
sociograms
ecological assessment
projective techniques
sentence completion tests
drawing tests
apperception tests

CHAPTER FOCUS

academic engaged time The time when the student is actively involved in the learning process.

This chapter addresses the assessment of behaviors that decrease **academic engaged time** and interfere with learning, such as externalizing (acting out) behaviors (including those attributed to attention deficit disorders), and the assessment of emotional and social difficulties of students. The 1997 IDEA Amendments included new mandates for the assessment of behaviors that may impede student academic success. These legal regulations for behavior remained in the 2004 IDEA. A discussion of tier one behavioral management is presented briefly at the beginning of this chapter. Methods used for functional behavioral assessment are discussed, followed by published instruments used to measure behavioral and emotional difficulties. Specific requirements for determining emotional disturbance are presented at the end of the chapter.

CEC KNOWLEDGE AND SKILLS STANDARDS

The student completing this chapter will understand the knowledge and skills included in the following CEC Knowledge and Skills Standards from Standard 8: Assessment:

CC8K1—Basic terminology used in assessment

CC8K2—Legal provisions and ethical principles regarding assessment of individuals

CCK83—Screening, prereferral, referral, and classification procedures

CG8K2—Laws and policies regarding referral and placement procedures for individuals with disabilities

CC8K5—Interpret information from formal and informal procedures

GC8S1—Implement procedures for assessing and reporting both appropriate and problematic social behaviors of individuals with disabilities

TIER ONE BEHAVIORAL INTERVENTIONS

schoolwide positive behavioral support Proactive strategies defined by school staff and based on behavioral principles.

Behavioral challenges, like educational challenges, are to be addressed within the three-tier structure in the school setting. This means that prior to a student receiving a referral for special education, teachers and staff should indicate the interventions that have been implemented and document that these interventions were not successful. As with educational interventions, these behavioral interventions are to be implemented consistently and with integrity. A well-known strategy to address the three-tier model is **schoolwide positive behavioral support systems**. These systems are structured by the local school and provide consistent schoolwide positive behavioral expectations. All adults consistently implement all school rewards, rules, and consequences. The implementation of such programs is most successful when all teachers and staff believe in and support the school's goals for improving behavior. This is considered a tier one intervention. The behavioral tiers are presented in Figure 8.1

Figure 8.1   Three tiers for behavioral interventions.

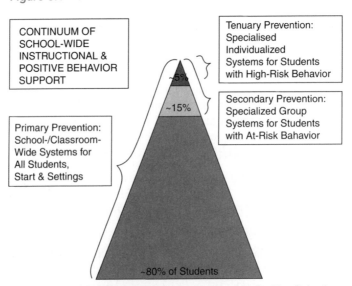

CONTINUUM OF SCHOOL-WIDE INSTRUCTIONAL & POSITIVE BEHAVIOR SUPPORT

Tenuary Prevention: Specialised Individualized Systems for Students with High-Risk Behavior

~5%

~15%

Secondary Prevention: Specialized Group Systems for Students with At-Risk Bahavior

Primary Prevention: School-/Classroom-Wide Systems for All Students, Start & Settings

~80% of Students

Source: From: *OSEP Technical Assistance Center on Positive Behavior Interventions and Supports.* www.pbis.org/schoolwide.htm. Reprinted with permission.

Tier two behavioral interventions include small group interventions and some specific intensive efforts for students at risk. Examples of these interventions include mentoring, classroom opportunities for the at risk student to be successful and be rewarded, and discussion with the student about expectations and rewards and consequences. When students fail to respond to these interventions, data may be collected through techniques such as functional behavioral assessments, behavioral analysis or frequency counts to determine baselines of behavior, attempt interventions, and observe increases in positive behavior or increases in negative behavior. These techniques are presented following the discussion of legal requirements.

REQUIREMENTS OF THE 1997 IDEA AMENDMENTS

The behavioral assessment and behavioral planning mandates of the 1997 IDEA Amendments were included as a method of ensuring procedural safeguards for students with behaviors that interfere with educational success. Prior to the Amendments, the application of discipline procedures for students with disabilities and students without disabilities was inconsistent (Yell, Drasgow, & Ford, 2000). Special education students who were repeatedly suspended from school for several days each time or who were expelled from school were no longer receiving a free appropriate education. In addition, these punitive types of disciplinary procedures often resulted in more harm to the student or caused the negative behaviors to escalate (Kubick, Bard, & Perry, 2000).

manifestation determination A hearing to determine if a student's behavior is the result of the student's disability.

Congress also sought to make schools safe for all learners and therefore provided educators with the means to discipline students fairly (Drasgow & Yell, 2001). To ensure that students requiring special education support were assisted with their behavioral needs rather than merely punished for behaviors, the 1997 IDEA Amendments and 2004 Amendments required schools to determine if the behaviors were the result of or manifested by the student's existing disability. This is referred to as a **manifestation determination**, which is a procedure required before a student receiving special education services can be suspended for more than 10 school days.

behavioral intervention plan A plan designed to increase positive behaviors and decrease negative behaviors before these become problematic.

The manifestation determination is required to be completed as quickly as possible and must meet federal regulations. Part of the requirements of manifestation determinations include confirming that the student's IEP was appropriately written and followed. The IEP must include the present levels of educational performance and behavioral functioning. In addition, the student exhibiting the behaviors should have a **behavioral intervention plan** in place that is based on a **functional behavioral assessment**.

functional behavioral assessment A multi-component assessment to determine the purpose of target behaviors.

The student's present levels of behavioral functioning are to be based on information obtained in the functional behavioral assessment and should be written in clear, understandable language (Drasgow, Yell, Bradley, & Shriner, 1999). The regulations required that the behavioral intervention plan include strategies for positive behavioral support and interventions that provide the student with acceptable **replacement behaviors** to be used by the student rather than the problematic behaviors.

replacement behaviors Appropriate behaviors that are incompatible with the negative behaviors they replace.

Functional behavioral assessments are measures to determine the function or purpose of a child's behavior. Functional behavioral assessment does not aim to label or name the type of behavior or disorder, such as hitting or depression, respectively, but rather seeks to answer the question of why. Why is the student using the behavior? Once this has been determined, interventions can be developed to promote positive acceptable replacement behaviors. A functional behavioral assessment should define the target behavior, determine when the behavior occurs and when it does not occur, and generate hypotheses about the possible function of the behavior. Once these have been determined, the hypotheses are tested or tried so that the exact function can be found (O'Neill, Horner, Albin, Sprague, Storey, & Newton, 1997). The testing out of hypotheses is also called **functional behavioral analysis**. Personnel who are responsible for this phase of the functional behavioral assessment should receive additional training in the procedures due to the possibility that manipulating the student's environment may result in more negative behaviors being exhibited (O'Neill et al., 1997). Drasgow and Yell summarized when functional behavioral assessments should be conducted and when they must be conducted. This information is presented in Figure 8.2.

functional behavioral analysis An analysis of the exploration of behaviors that occur when variables such as antecedents or consequences are manipulated.

Figure 8.2   IDEA '97 Requirements Regarding FBAs.

When an FBA *Should* Be Conducted	When an FBA *Must* Be Conducted
• When a student's problem behavior impedes his or her learning or the learning of others.	• When suspensions or placements in an alternative setting exceed 10 consecutive days or amount to a change in placement.
• When a student's behavior presents a danger to himself or herself or others.	• When a student is placed in an interim alternative educational setting for 45 days when his or her misconduct involves weapons or drugs.
• When a student's suspension or placement in an interim alternative educational setting approaches 10 cumulative days.	• When a due process hearing officer places a student in an interim alternative educational setting for behavior that is dangerous to himself or herself or others.

Source: Functional behavioral assessments: Legal requirements and challenges by Erik Drasgow and Mitchell Yell. In *School Psychology Review, 30*(2), 239–251, 243. Copyright 2001 by the National Association of School Psychologists. Reprinted by permission of the publisher.

direct observation
Observations of student behaviors in the environment in which the behaviors occur.

event recording
Recording the frequency of a target behavior; also called frequency counting.

interval recording
Sampling a behavior intermittently for very brief periods of time; used to observe frequently occurring behaviors.

Federal regulations require that both special education personnel and general education personnel participate in the functional behavioral assessment along with the student's parents (Conroy, Clark, Gable, & Fox, 1999). Initial efforts to apply functional behavioral assessments may have resulted in schools treating the requirements as merely a compliance issue (Gable, Hendrickson, & Smith, 1999). In other words, schools may not have completed extensive functional behavioral assessments but rather completed the minimal amount of paperwork needed to comply with the mandates. This resulted in numerous due process hearings brought by parents who believed that their children were not appropriately served or assessed prior to suspensions or other disciplinary actions (Drasgow & Yell, 2001). Most of these hearings found in favor of the parents due to inadequate or nonexistent functional behavioral assessments. It is necessary to fully understand the functional behavioral assessment process in order to fully comply with the law.

FUNCTIONAL BEHAVIORAL ASSESSMENTS

anecdotal recording
Observations of behavior in which the teacher notes all behaviors and interactions that occur during a given period of time.

duration recording
Observations that involve the length of time a behavior occurs.

latency recording
Observations involving the amount of time that elapses from the presentation of a stimulus until the response occurs.

interresponse time
The amount of time between target behaviors.

Information to determine why a student displays a specific behavior can be obtained through three broad methods of assessment (O'Neill et al., 1997; Witt, Daly, & Noell, 2000). The first method of assessment is the indirect method. It includes techniques such as interviewing the classroom teacher and parents, reviewing data in the school records, completing behavioral rating scales, checklists, and so on. These methods are presented later in the chapter. Another method used in functional behavioral assessment is called the **direct observation** or descriptive observational method. This requires that the student be observed in the environment in which the behaviors are occurring. During this part of the assessment, several techniques may be employed, such as **event recording**, **interval recording**, **anecdotal recording**, **duration recording**, **latency recording**, and **interresponse time**. These terms are presented in the following section of the chapter. Finally, the third broad method of assessment is the functional behavioral analysis method. During both the indirect assessment and the direct observation phases of the assessment, hypotheses are generated regarding the purpose or function of the behavior. In the functional behavioral analysis portion of the assessment, the variables believed to be triggering the behavior and the possible consequences following the behavior are manipulated. By this manipulation, it can be determined exactly why the student is using the behavior. For example, following the initial phases of the functional behavioral assessment, it is hypothesized that the reason a student is calling out in class is to receive peer attention. During the functional behavioral analysis, the hypothesis of peer attention is tested. Students in the class are instructed to ignore the calling-out behavior, and the calling out decreases. When students react to the calling-out behavior, such as by turning to look at the target student when calling out occurs, the calling out increases. Thus, the function of the calling out is to receive peer attention. Following the functional behavioral analysis and additional assessment, the students in the class are instructed to ignore all calling-out behavior and to reinforce appropriate hand raising by paying attention to the target student. This manipulation of the consequence (peer attention) resulted in decreasing the calling out and in an appropriate replacement behavior (raising hand).

functional assessment interviews The interview component of the functional behavioral assessment (FBA) that provides information about possible purposes of target behaviors.

Educational personnel may also need to use **functional assessment interviews** with teachers, parents, and the target student (Gresham, Watson, & Skinner, 2001). During these interviews, the goal is to obtain information that will assist in formulating a hypothesis about the function of the target behavior. These interviews will provide information concerning how the student functions in various environments. When interviewed, the student can share feelings and concerns about school and other areas of life.

DIRECT OBSERVATION TECHNIQUES

target behaviors Specific behaviors that require intervention by the teacher to promote optimal academic or social learning.

The first step in the intervention of behavioral problems is the identification of **target behaviors**. Once the exact behavior or behaviors have been identified, direct observations can begin. Direct observation enables the teacher to note how often a behavior occurs and to establish a **baseline**, which will be used to monitor the student's progress following intervention. Direct observation also enables the teacher to note the possible **antecedent** events that may trigger the target behavior or that may increase the likelihood that it will occur.

baseline The frequency, duration, or latency of a behavior determined before behavioral intervention.

Behavioral observations can be completed by the teacher or by another objective professional or trained paraprofessional. Behaviors may be observed for frequency, duration, intensity, or for the length of time between responses, or interresponse time (Gresham et al., 2001). The observer should remember two important guidelines for effective behavioral observation: Be objective and be specific. The observer should be fair and nonjudgmental and should precisely pinpoint or identify problem behaviors. The identified behaviors should be stated exactly so that two observers would be able to agree about whether the behavior is or is not occurring.

antecedent An event that occurs prior to the target behavior and increases or decreases the probability of the target behavior.

setting event A specific event that occurs before the target behavior but is removed from the actual environment in which the behavior occurs.

ANTECEDENTS

Antecedents may be actual events that increase the probability of target behaviors occurring. Antecedents may also be events that occur in another setting prior to the actual target behavior. These are called **setting events**. For example, a setting event may be that a student has an argument at home with an older sibling before coming to school. This antecedent may increase the probability that the student will exhibit externalizing target behaviors within the school environment. Other events that may increase the probability of a target behavior may be the events that make a consequence more attractive. For example, a student may be more anxious to receive an edible reward as a consequence when the student is hungry. This may increase the probability that a student will behave in a specific way, such as stealing another student's lunch. This type of an event is known as an **establishing operation**, or EO (Michael, 2000).

establishing operation Events occurring before the target behavior that alter the receptivity of the consequence and increase or decrease the probability of occurrence of the target behavior.

ANECDOTAL RECORDING

Behavioral intervention strategies are based on a clear understanding of why a behavior occurs. Behavioristic principle is founded in the theory that behaviors are maintained or increased by the reinforcing events that follow the event or behavior. Events that happen prior to the target behavior may increase the likelihood that the behavior will be exhibited. These conditions occurring prior to the exhibited behavior are known as antecedents. The teacher may recognize when a behavior occurs but not be able to identify the reinforcing event or the antecedent event. One behavioral observation technique that will enable the teacher to hypothesize about the exact antecedent event and reinforcing event, or consequence, is called anecdotal recording.

In the anecdotal recording method, the teacher observes the student and writes down everything that occurs in the situation. The teacher or other educational or behavioral professional observes the student for a specific time period, usually when the behavior seems to occur most frequently. The teacher may wish to observe during a particular academic subject time, such as math class, or during a nonacademic time when the behavior occurs, such as lunch or recess.

An anecdotal recording might look like this:

Name: Mary
Observation Time:

9:30 a.m.	Language Arts—Mary enters the classroom and walks around the room twice, then sits in her chair. Mary looks out of the window.
9:32 a.m.	Mary speaks out: Teacher, can I go to the office? Response: Mary, get your workbook out and turn to page 56.
9:33 a.m.	Mary gets workbook out and begins to look at the pictures on several of the pages. Continues for quite some time.
9:45 a.m.	Mary speaks out: What page, teacher? Teacher responds: Page 56.
9:47 a.m.	Mary speaks out: Teacher, can I use a pencil? Response: Here is a pencil, Mary.

Using the anecdotal format for observation provides a basis for analyzing the antecedent, behavior, and consequence. The antecedent is the event preceding the behavior, and the consequence is the event following the behavior. The antecedent may actually trigger the behavior, whereas the consequence is thought to maintain or reinforce the behavior. In the preceding example, the antecedent, behavior, and consequence analysis, or A-B-C, might look like this:

A	B	C
Mary enters room sits in chair and looks at the teacher	walks around talks out	allowed to walk freely teacher responds
looks at pages in workbook, then looks at teacher	talks out	teacher responds
looks at the teacher	talks out	teacher responds

This analysis provides information that will help the teacher plan a behavioral intervention strategy. It appears that the reinforcing event for Mary's talking out is the teacher responding to Mary. It also seems that the teacher has not provided an organizational intervention plan that will convey to Mary the behaviors expected of her when beginning academic work or instruction. Through this observation, two behaviors have been targeted for intervention: organizational behavior (ready for work) and talking out. The organizational behaviors expected can be broken down into specific behaviors for intervention: student in chair, pencils ready, books out, paper ready.

EVENT RECORDING

Event recording assesses the frequency with which behaviors occur. The teacher marks or tallies the number of times specific behaviors occur. This information, the initial recording of data, creates a baseline for the teacher to use as a comparison following intervention. This type of recording is useful for observing easily detectable behaviors for short periods of time. Examples of this type of behavior include time on task, talking out, and hitting. One illustration of **frequency counting**, another name for event recording, is shown in Figure 8.3.

Observations using event recording are typically completed for an entire class period or continuously for a specified time period. Other methods for observing behaviors intermittently or for short periods of time are **time sampling** and interval recording.

frequency counting Counting the occurrence of a specific behavior; same as event recording.

time sampling When the behavioral observation samples behavior through the day or class period.

Figure 8.3 An example of event recording (frequency counting).

Name	Joe

Target behavior: Out of seat

	Mon.	Tues.	Wed.
9:00 – 10:00	⊬⊬ ⊬⊬	⊬⊬ ⊬⊬ //	⊬⊬ ⊬⊬ /
10:00 – 11:00	//	/	///
11:00 – 12:00	/	///	//

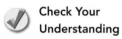

Check Your Understanding

Check your ability to analyze an anecdotal recording and a functional assessment interview by completing Activity 8.1 below.

Activity 8.1

Read the following anecdotal recording, which covers 2 days of class, and then answer the questions.

Name: John

Monday

John enters classroom.

Teacher (T): Let's get ready for math class.

   John (J): Can we go on the field trip Thursday?

      T: Yes, John. We will go on Thursday.

      J: I can't find my math book.

      T: Look in your desk, John. Now, let's work problems 1 to 10 on page 284.

      J: [Throws pencil on the floor. Picks pencil up.]

      T: John, let's get to work.

      J: [Crumbles paper up, throws on floor. Throws book on floor.]

      T: That's it, John! Go to the office.

      J: [Smiles. Leaves the room.]

Tuesday

John enters classroom.

T: Now class, let's get our math books out.

J: [Out of seat. Goes to pencil sharpener.]

T: John, when do we sharpen our pencils?

J: [No response.]

T: Pencil time is after lunch. Now, get your math book out. Turn to page 286. Let's check our homework.

J: [Slams book on desk. Groans.]

T: Today we will continue the division problems. John, get your book open.

J: [Throws book on floor.]

T: Okay! To the office!

J: [Smiles, leaves the room.]

Analyze the observations of John's behavior for antecedent, behavior, and consequence.

A	**B**	**C**
_____	_____	_____
_____	_____	_____
_____	_____	_____
_____	_____	_____
_____	_____	_____
_____	_____	_____

Functional Assessment Interview

During the functional assessment interview, John describes how he feels about his behavior. He reports that he is not happy in class and that the tasks have become too difficult. He states that he has not been able to keep up with the assignments the teacher gives each day for homework. Additional questioning about his homework routine reveals that John's parents work different shifts and that he often is responsible for younger siblings in the evenings until his father returns. He adds that due to child care difficulties, his mother wakes the children at 4:30 a.m. each day so that they may be at an aunt's house by 5:00, where he then sleeps for another hour before getting ready to come to school. He believes that he is too tired on some days to concentrate on his schoolwork. When asked if he has discussed these issues with his teachers, he states that it is too hard for him to talk about these concerns with other students in the classroom.

What additional important information was obtained in the functional interview? _____

Apply Your Knowledge

Based on your analysis of the antecedents, behaviors, and consequences, what purpose is the behavior serving for John? What would you recommend for an intervention plan? _____

_____

_____

Figure 8.4   Sample chart for time sampling of on-task and nontask behaviors.

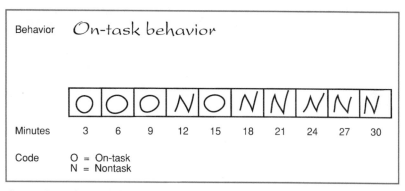

TIME SAMPLING

Time sampling uses frequency counting or event recording techniques for various times throughout the day or class period. The teacher identifies the target behaviors and records student activity for a time period, such as 2 or 5 minutes, throughout the period or day. The teacher is sampling the behavior to get an idea of how often the behavior occurs, without observing continuously. This enables the teacher to observe more than one student or more than one behavior throughout the day. An example of a time-sampling observation is shown in Figure 8.4.

INTERVAL RECORDING

Interval recording is used when the teacher wants to observe several students or behaviors at one time, record intermittently throughout the day or class period, and record behaviors that occur too frequently to record each event, such as stereotypical behaviors (Kerr & Nelson, 2002). During interval recording, the teacher notes whether the behavior is occurring or not occurring. The time intervals may be very short throughout the day. The observation might be for a very brief period of time, such as 2 minutes, during which the teacher notes every 30 seconds whether or not the behavior is occurring. An example of interval recording is shown in Figure 8.5.

DURATION RECORDING

The duration recording technique is used when the length of the behavior is the target variable of the behavior. For example, a student may need to increase the amount of time spent on task. The

Figure 8.5 Sample interval recording form.

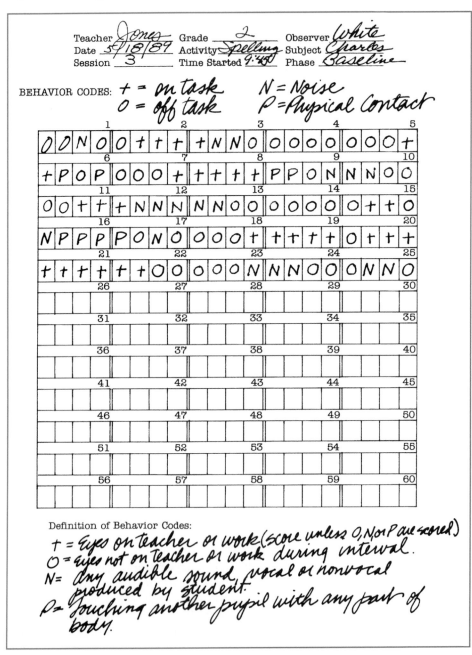

teacher will record how long the student remains on task following the directive to do so. The duration recording might look like this:

Name *Ralph*
Task *writing assignment*

On Task	Off Task
2 min	60 s
60 s	2 min
60 s	60 s

On-task/off-task ratio is 4:8 min = 50% on task

This brief duration recording revealed that Ralph is on task only 50% of the expected time. Following intervention by the teacher, such as a prompting signal or behavioral contract or other strategy, it is hoped that the student's on-task time would increase, while off-task time would decrease. Reinforcement for on-task time would increase the probability that Ralph would remain on task longer. A duration recording of on-task time during the intervention or treatment should be compared with the baseline data of 50% to note the effectiveness of the intervention strategies.

LATENCY RECORDING

The latency recording method of observation also involves the element of time. This is an observation in which the time is recorded from the moment a stimulus (such as a command) is given until the response occurs. The element of elapsed time is recorded. For example, the time is recorded from the moment the teacher gives spelling instructions until the student begins the assignment. If the student must be prompted several times during the completion of the task, the latency is recorded each time the student is prompted (Evans, Evans, & Schmid, 1989).

INTERRESPONSE TIME

Latency recording measures the amount of time elapsed between the specific stimulus and the actual response. Interresponse time assesses the length of time between the behaviors or responses (Gresham et al., 2001). For example, a student may be distracted or off task every 2 minutes between the observation period of 2:00 to 3:00 P.M., but become distracted only every 20 minutes during the observation period of 10:00 to 11:00 A.M. This assessment would then pose additional questions—such as, is the subject matter more interesting or easier in the morning observation, are there more hands-on activities, is the student tired in the afternoons, or has the student been prescribed a medication for distractibility that is administered only in the morning?

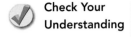

Check Your Understanding

Check your ability to complete a behavioral analysis for a fifth-grade student by completing Activity 8.2 below.

Activity 8.2

Use the following information to analyze the behavior of a fifth-grade student named Amber.

> Day 1
> Anecdotal recording:
> Amber was presented with her arithmetic worksheet following the direct instruction lesson with her group. After several minutes, she began to work on the first problem. During the time period of receiving the work and beginning the work, she was observed looking through her desk to find the necessary materials. When she located her pencil and paper, she dropped the assignment page on the floor. She picked the paper up and placed it on her desk. She sharpened her pencil and began to work. During the period that she was seated at her desk working, approximately 10 minutes, she was observed looking around the room and watching other students. When a sound occurred outside the room, she would look in the hallway or out the window. When papers were collected, she had completed the first 2 of 15 problems. One problem was correct, but the second problem was not calculated correctly because of a careless error.

> Day 2
> Latency recording: Time elapsed from assignment to working behavior: 5 minutes.

> Interval recording: Observations during work time:

+ = On task   **0 = Off task**

0	0	0	0	0	+	+	0	0	+

Minutes   1   2   3   4   5   6   7   8   9   10

1. Analyze the anecdotal recording. What are the antecedents, behaviors, and consequences? _____

        A   **B**   **C**

2. Analyze the latency recording information. _____
3. Analyze the interval recording data. How often is the student on task? _____

Apply Your Knowledge

Based on the information provided, why do you think Amber is having difficulty with this task? What recommendations would you suggest for Amber? _____

_____

_____

STRUCTURED CLASSROOM OBSERVATIONS

Observation methods discussed so far in this chapter may be teacher-made, informal instruments that can be used for prereferral, assessment, and intervention of behavioral problems. A structured classroom observation form called the Direct Observation Form (Achenbach, 1986) is one part of the Child Behavior Checklist (CBCL) system, a multiaxial system for assessment of behavioral and emotional problems. Other forms in this system are described throughout the chapter in the appropriate topical sections.

CHILD BEHAVIOR CHECKLIST: DIRECT OBSERVATION FORM, REVISED EDITION

The Direct Observation Form (Achenbach, 1986) is four pages in length, including general instructions and guidelines. The first page consists of the student's identifying information (name, date of birth, observation settings, and so on) and the general administration instructions. The inside pages of the form comprise three parts: an observation rating scale on which to mark observed behaviors and rate their intensity or severity, a space for anecdotal recording of all events during the observation period, and an interval recording form. The observer makes several observations of the target student across several different settings. The observer compares the target student with two grade and gender peers. When comparing the target student, the observer ascertains whether the student is significantly different from the two control students in on-task behavior. This method is often used to assess behavioral disorders such as attention deficit disorder. Often, the criterion for indicating possible attention problems is that the target student's off-task behavior score is 1.5 or 2 standard deviations above the control students' scores. The observer marks the items on the rating scale if the target child exhibits the behaviors during the observation. Figure 8.6 illustrates the types of items represented on the Direct Observation Form. These items are then scored, as are the other rating scales and interviews of the multiaxial CBCL system, for significant behavior problems. The behaviors are defined on two broad bands: (1) externalizing (acting out); and (2) internalizing (turning inward), which includes problems such as anxiety or withdrawal. In addition, the system notes the occurrence of several clinical behavioral syndromes, such as social problems, somatic complaints, aggressive behavior, and attention problems. The other components of the CBCL are scored along the same broad and narrow bands of behavior and emotional functioning.

Figure 8.6   Behavioral checklist.

	Yes	No
1. Student is prepared for work each period.	_____	_____
2. Student begins assignment on request.	_____	_____
3. Student stays on task with no distractions.	_____	_____
4. Student completes tasks.	_____	_____
5. Student stays on task but is sometimes distracted.	_____	_____
6. Student complies with teacher requests.	_____	_____
7. Student raises hand to speak.	_____	_____
8. Student talks out inappropriately.	_____	_____
9. Student completes homework.	_____	_____
10. Student is aggressive toward peers.	_____	_____
11. Student is disruptive during class.	_____	_____
12. Student talks out of turn.	_____	_____
13. Student is verbally aggressive.	_____	_____
14. Student has damaged property belonging to others.	_____	_____

OTHER TECHNIQUES FOR ASSESSING BEHAVIOR

checklists Lists of academic or behavioral skills that must be mastered by the student.

questionnaires Questions about a student's behavior or academic concerns that may be answered by the student or by the parent or teacher; also called interviews.

interviews Formal or informal questions asked orally by the examiner.

sociograms Graphic representation of the social dynamics within a group.

ecological assessment Analysis of the student's total learning environment.

Some techniques for assessing behavior do not involve direct observation of behavior. These techniques include **checklists**, **questionnaires**, **interviews**, **sociograms**, and **ecological assessment**. These methods rely on input from others, such as parents, teachers, or peers, rather than on direct observation of behavior. When these indirect methods are used with direct observation, the teacher can plan effective behavioral intervention strategies.

CHECKLISTS AND RATING SCALES

A checklist is a list of questions that the respondent completes by checking the appropriate responses. The respondent may answer yes or no or may check off the statements that apply to the student. The teacher, the parents, or both may complete the checklist. An example of a behavioral checklist was given earlier, in Figure 8.6.

A rating questionnaire may be similar in content to a checklist, although the respondent rates the answer. For example, the format of the checklist in Figure 8.6 would change so that the respondent would rate student behaviors as never, almost never, sometimes, somewhat often, frequently, or almost always. This format allows for interpretation of the extremes. The student behavior might be rated as almost never completing assignments, but frequently being verbally aggressive and sometimes damaging property. This information helps the teacher pinpoint areas that need observation and further evaluation.

Elliot, Busse, and Gresham (1993) suggested that the following issues be considered when using rating scales:

1. Ratings are summaries of observations of the relative frequency of specific behaviors.

2. Ratings of social behavior are judgments affected by one's environment and rater's standards for behavior.

3. The social validity of the behaviors one assesses and eventually treats should be understood.

4. Multiple assessors of the same child's behavior may agree only moderately.

5. Many characteristics of a student may influence social behavior; however, the student's sex is a particularly salient variable.

Several rating forms are commonly used in the assessment of behavior problems. Many of these include forms for teachers and parents. Common examples include the Teacher Report Form (Achenbach, 1991b) and the Child Behavior Checklist (Achenbach, 1991a), the Behavior Rating Profile-2 (Brown & Hammill, 1990), and the Conners Teacher Rating Scales and Conners Parent Rating Scales (1997). These forms and scoring systems ask a variety of questions about the student, and the parent or teacher rates the student on each item.

ASEBA—ACHENBACH SYSTEM OF EMPIRICALLY BASED BEHAVIOR ASSESSMENT (ASEBA) PARENT, TEACHER, AND YOUTH REPORT FORMS

The Achenbach System of Empirically Based Behavior Assessment (ASEBA), also known as the Child Behavior Checklist, (Achenbach, 1991a; Achenbach & Rescorla, 2001), includes a Parent Report Form, and companion forms such as the Teacher Report Form (Achenbach, 1991b, Achenbach & Rescorla, 2001) and the Youth Self-Report (Achenbach, 1991c). (The system's Direct Observation Form and interview form are discussed in other sections of this chapter.) This system also includes a preschool version with an informal language survey (Achenbach & Rescorla, 2000).

The Achenbach system allows for the student to be rated on both positive, or adaptive, behaviors and behavioral syndromes. In 1991, the author revised the system to allow the profiles to be scored consistently across the parent, teacher, and youth scales (McConaughy & Achenbach, 1993). The parent form includes, in addition to the rating scales, some open-ended questions, such as "What concerns you most about your child?"

The two ASEBA forms are available for parents: one for children aged $1\frac{1}{2}$–5 years and another for students aged 6–18 years. The

Teacher Report Form is for students aged 6–18. Items on these instruments are closely related so that both parents and teachers are rating the student on similar dimensions. An example of a Teacher Report Form profile is shown in Figure 8.7.

In addition to the teacher and parent forms, a self-rating form is available for students aged 11–18. The Youth Self-Report (Achenbach, 1991c, Achenbach & Rescorla, 2001) covers many of the same topics as the teacher and parent forms. This instrument can be evaluated qualitatively to determine the student's perceptions of himself. The student also answers items concerning current academic achievement and rates himself on social dimensions, such as getting along with family members.

Figure 8.7   CBCL. Teacher Report Form showing sample profile for female student.

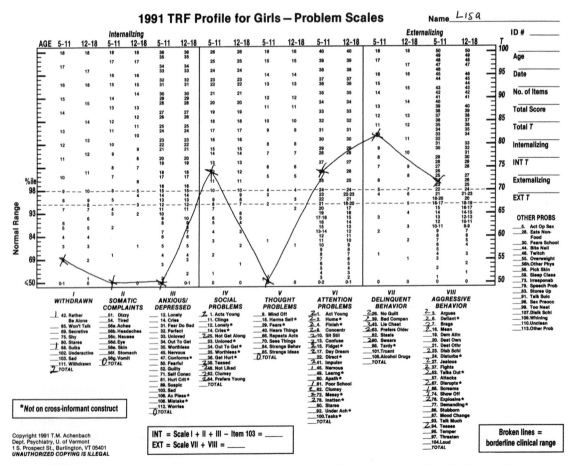

Examiner manuals address the issues of validity and reliability for each of the individual parts of the multiaxial ASEBA system by Achenbach (1991a, 1991b, 1991c, Achenbach & Recorla, 2000, 2001). The examiner is provided with detailed information about content and criterion-related validity and the discriminant validity of using cutoff scores to identify students with specific behavioral problems. Test-retest, testing across time, and reliability of raters are presented, and the technical quality of the systems appears to be adequate or above on all measures.

BEHAVIOR ASSESSMENT SYSTEM FOR CHILDREN, SECOND EDITION (BASC–2)

This assessment system includes rating scales for parents to complete, rating scales for teachers to complete, a developmental history form for parents, and self-reports for students ages 8–25 years. This system includes an observation form for recording observations within the classroom environment. The BASC–2 system was developed to be used with students ages 2 to 25 years of age. The system provides a method for distinguishing students with attention deficit disorder, depression, other behavioral concerns, and social maladjustments. Scores indicate students who are within a clinical range of significance; at risk for having difficulties; and average, low, and very low. The BASC–2 also indicates how well students are adapting in a positive manner. Scores on the adaptive scales are noted to be very high, high, average, at risk, and clinically significant. The BASC–2 includes an audiotape provided for students who have difficulty reading the self-report form in English but who understand spoken English. The student self-report form is presented in a true-false format. The instrument may be hand scored and computer scoring provides additional information such as the validity of the specific test administration. The BASC–2 provides a means of comparing the student with both the norm sample and clinical samples. This may be more helpful in determining the severity of behavioral difficulties.

The examiner's manual provides information regarding the standardization and norm samples for all components of the BASC–2. The total number of students and parents for the norm samples was 4,650 for the Teacher Rating Scale; 4,800 for the Parent Rating Scale; and 3,400 for the Self-Report of Personality. The samples were representative geographically, and gender and race/ethnicity were also considered and approximated U.S. population estimates.

The manual presents reliability and validity information for all scales. Ample technical data for internal consistency, test-retest reliability, interrater reliability, standard error of measurement, factor structure of scales, and concurrent validity data are presented.

Behavior Rating Profile–2 The Behavior Rating Profile–2 (Brown & Hammill, 1990) includes forms for the student, parent, and teacher. The student completes the rating by marking that items are true or false about herself. The teacher and parents rate the student by marking that the items are very much like the student, not like the student, like the student, or not at all like the student. This system allows the examiner to compare how the student, teacher, and parent perceive the student. It also categorizes the student's perceptions into the various environments of the student's life: school, home, and peer relationships. This enables the examiner to determine whether the student has more positive feelings about school, relationships with peers, or relationships with parents. The instrument is scored using a standard score with a mean of 10 and a standard deviation of 3. The examiner can plot a profile that presents a view of how the student, parent, and teacher perceive the student.

The manual provides reliability and validity information that includes studies conducted with relatively small samples. The internal consistency and test-retest coefficients seem to be adequate, with many reported to be in the .80s. Validity studies include criterion-related research, with reported coefficients ranging from below acceptable levels to adequate. The authors provide discussion of content and construct validity.

Conners Rating Scales–Revised The Conners system (Conners, 1997) includes the following scales:

Conners Parent Rating Scale–Revised: Long Version

Conners Parent Rating Scale–Revised: Short Version

Conners Teacher Rating Scale–Revised: Long Version

Conners Teacher Rating Scale–Revised: Short Version

Conners-Wells' Adolescent Self-Report Scale: Long Version

Conners-Wells' Adolescent Self-Report Scale: Short Version

Auxiliary Scales

Conners Global Index–Parent

Conners Global Index–Teacher

Conners ADHD/DSM-IV Scales–Parent

Conners ADHD/DSM-IV Scales–Adolescent

The revised version of this instrument includes several substantial changes. The author states that the revised version provides multidimensional scales that assess ADHD and other disorders that may exist with the attention disorders. The new version includes additional methods for assisting mental health professionals in making *DSM-IV* diagnoses (*Diagnostic and Statistical Manual*, 4th Edition, American Psychiatric Association, 1994). The former edition of the Conners included a Hyperactivity Index, which is now called the Conners' Global Index.

The Conners Rating Scales–Revised was developed with a large standardization sample (more than 8,000) with representative samples in the United States and Canada. In addition to representative norms, several studies are included in the manual that compare ethnic differences in samples of the following groups: African American/Black, Asian, Caucasian, Hispanic, Native American, and Other. These studies are presented in adequate detail in the manual, with main-effect differences by ethnic group provided for each scale. Consumers of this instrument are encouraged to read this section of the manual carefully when using the instrument for diagnostic purposes with the mentioned ethnic groups.

The dimensions of the Conners Rating Scales include oppositional, cognitive problems/inattention, hyperactivity, anxious-shy, perfectionism, social problems, and psychosomatic. The special "Quick Score" paper included with the rating scales enables the teacher or other member of the multidisciplinary team to score the short form in minutes. The long versions of the various rating scales involve much more effort to score, and hand scoring using the profile sheets is difficult because of the large number of columns included on the page. Computer scoring is available.

Reliability studies included internal reliability. Internal consistency for the various scales ranged from .72 to .95. Some variability exists on some scales with different age groups. For example, teacher ratings were more consistent for the younger and older age groups than for other age groups.

Validity studies in the Conners examiner's manual address factorial validity, convergent validity, divergent validity, discriminant validity, and concurrent validity. Information concerning this research is much more extensive than the previous edition and seems to range from below acceptable levels to adequate. Many of the studies included small samples. The author states that research in this area is continuing.

QUESTIONNAIRES AND INTERVIEWS

The questions found on questionnaires are similar to the items on checklists, but the respondent is encouraged to describe the behaviors or situations where the behavior occurs. The respondent answers with narrative statements. For example, the questions might appear as follows:

1. How is the student prepared for class each day?
2. Describe how the student begins assignments during class.
3. How does the student perform during distractions?
4. How often does the student complete homework assignments?
5. How does the student respond during class discussions?

Figure 8.8   Interview questions adapted for both parent and student.

Parent Interview	*Student Interview*
1. How do you think your child feels about school this year?	**1.** Tell me how you feel about school this year.
2. Tell me how your child completes homework assignments.	**2.** Describe how you go about finishing your homework.
3. Describe the responsibilities your child has at home.	**3.** What type of things are you expected to do at home? Do you think you complete those things most of the time?

The respondent should be encouraged to provide objective responses that describe as many variables of the behavior as possible. Interviews are completed using questions similar to those used on questionnaires. The evaluator verbally asks the respondent the questions and encourages objective, detailed information. The interview format may also be used with the student to obtain information about the student's feelings and perceptions about the target behaviors. Figure 8.8 illustrates how an interview could be adapted so that both parents and the student could provide answers.

Child Behavior Checklist: Semistructured Clinical Interview   Interviews may be conducted by different members of the multidisciplinary team. Often, these interviews are unstructured and informal. Achenbach and McConaughy (1989, 1990) developed a semistructured interview and observation form to be used with students aged 5–11. This interview assesses the student's feelings about school, family, and peers as well as affect or emotional functioning. The examiner is provided with, in addition to the interview, an observation form to rate behaviors of and comments by the student observed during the interview. The student is asked open-ended questions and guided through the interview process. This interview can be useful in determining the current social and emotional issues concerning the student.

SOCIOGRAMS

The sociogram method enables the teacher to obtain information about the group dynamics and structure within the classroom. This information can be interpreted to determine which students are well liked by their peers, which students are considered to be the leaders in the group, and which students are believed to be successful in school.

A sociogram is constructed by designing questions that all members of the class will be asked to answer. The questions might include, "Whom would you select to be in your group for the science project?" or "Whom would you invite to the movies?" The answers are then collected and interpreted by the teacher. The diagram in Figure 8.9a illustrates a sociogram; Figure 8.9b lists questions asked of a class of fourth-grade students.

The data are analyzed to determine who the class members perceive as being the class stars, the social isolates, and so on. The teacher also can determine where mutual choices exist (where two students share the same feelings about each other) and can identify cliques and persons who are neglected. The teacher can then use this information to intervene and structure social and academic situations that would promote fair social skills. Role plays, class projects, and school social activities could be used to increase the interpersonal interaction opportunities for social isolates and neglectees.

ECOLOGICAL ASSESSMENT

Ecological assessment analyzes the student's total learning environment. This analysis includes the student's interactions with others (peers, teachers, paraprofessionals, parents, and other persons who are directly involved with the student's learning process); the teacher's interactions with other students in the classroom; the methods of presentation of materials; materials used in the classroom; the physical environment; and the student's interactions with others in different settings, such as the playground or lunchroom. All of the informal behavioral assessment methods presented thus far may be used as a part of ecological assessment.

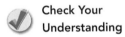

Check Your Understanding

Check your ability to analyze a sociogram of a classroom by completing Activity 8.3 below.

Activity 8.3

Use Figure 8.9a to analyze the social dynamics of this classroom.

1. Which students have made mutual choices? _____
2. Which students seem to be isolated from their peers? _____
3. Which students appear to be in cliques or groups? _____
4. Which students seem to be the most socially popular? _____
5. Who are the academic stars? _____

Apply Your Knowledge

List other questions that you may find useful in a sociogram: _____
_____
_____

Figure 8.9 Sociogram (a) and sociogram questions (b).

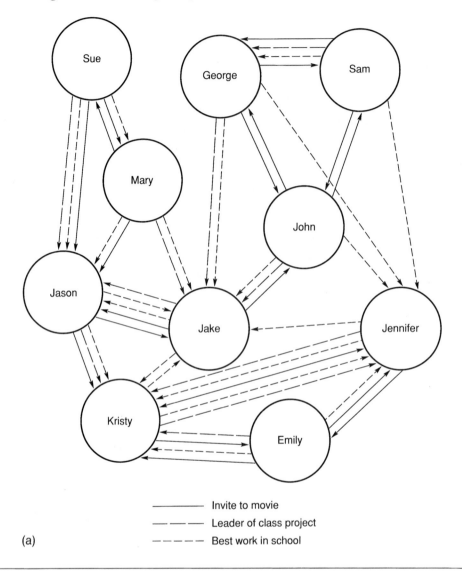

—————— Invite to movie

— — — Leader of class project

– – – – Best work in school

(a)

Sociogram questions.

1. Name two students in our class whom you would most like to invite to a movie (or other activity).

   a. _____

   b. _____

2. In our class, whom would you like to be the leader of our class project? _____

3. Name two students in our class who do the best work in school.

   a. _____

   b. _____

(b)

MORE PRACTICE-ANALYSIS OF BEHAVIORAL CASE

Mrs. Soto taught in a 7th grade resource setting. She was a new teacher and by November she began to feel that she was settling into her routine for lesson planning and instructional delivery. During the first week of December, she was notified that a new student would be transferring into her classroom from another city by the beginning of the second week of December. Following the appropriate meeting and review of the student's records by the IEP team, the new student, named Don, began attending her resource room each day for 1 hour. Don was receiving special education support services for mathematics. By Don's second week, Mrs. Soto noticed that Don had some organizational difficulties. She assisted him with strategies for organizing his books and papers. Don seemed to understand the expectations of the class and the school. Following the winter break in December, Don once again seemed to be disorganized. Mrs. Soto reviewed the organizational strategies and Don seemed to remember how the class was organized and what he was expected to do. Within a week, Mrs. Soto noticed that Don was coming to class without his materials. These were the observations she made:

Don—Preparation for work in resource room.

	Tardy	**Without Materials**
Monday	5 mins.	yes—another student brought materials to Don
Tuesday	7 mins.	yes—another student brought materials to Don
Wednesday	5 mins.	yes—another student brought materials to Don
Thursday	6 mins.	yes—Mrs. Soto sent Don for materials
Friday	7 mins.	yes—Don asked to go get materials

With this documentation, Mrs. Soto discussed the matter with Don. Don apologized and told Mrs. Soto he would be on time to class and try to improve.

The following week, Don was on time 3 of 5 days however, he continued to come to class without materials.

1. What questions would you ask Don?
2. What strategies would you use to change this behavior?
3. Write a behavioral objective for the strategies you would use and the behaviors you expect.

Once you have written the answers to these questions, read the next section.

Mrs. Soto investigated and determined that Don enjoyed talking with a student who worked in the office as a student assistant during the time period that he was in the resource room. Don would stop by and talk to this student and leave his books so that the friend could bring them to his class or he could return to visit with his friend again. How could you use this information in your behavior planning strategy?

The teacher variable is one area that can be assessed by direct observation and other techniques such as questionnaires. Guerin and Maier suggested surveying teachers to determine their level of teacher competency. This would include assessing areas such as level of instruction, teaching strategies, types of instruction, media used in the classroom, and general communication and interaction with students and parents. These types of questionnaires can be designed to be completed by the teacher or by an objective observer. The student's educational materials should be evaluated for their appropriateness for the individual student. The level of difficulty, format, and mode of presentation and response are important considerations. The following variables should be evaluated when assessing materials:

Analyzing Instructional Materials

1. Are the objectives of the materials appropriate for the student?
2. Do the ability/readability levels match the current instructional level of the student?
3. Is the interest level appropriate for the student?
4. Does the method of presentation match the student's strength for learning?
5. Are prerequisite steps needed before the student can attempt the task?
6. Does the format of the material contain extraneous stimuli that can confuse or distract the student?
7. Does the material contain information not necessary for task completion?
8. Are too many tasks contained on one page?
9. Is the student capable of completing the task in the amount of time allowed?
10. Does the task need to be broken down into smaller tasks?
11. Is the student capable of responding with relative ease in the manner required by the materials?
12. Can the criterion level for success be reduced?
13. Does the material allow the student to self-check or self-correct?
14. Does the material allow the student to observe progress? (Overton 1987, pp. 111–115)

Case Study for Behavior Analysis

Mr. Blackburn noticed that one of his students in his second-grade class, Gracelyn, was enthusiastic during the morning classes but had been having difficulty in the afternoon. She disturbed other students and generally seemed to be unhappy in class. Sometimes Gracelyn would say things to her peers that would result in an argument and she would be asked to leave the classroom. Mr. Blackburn collected the following data for afternoon classes:

	Off-Task Behaviors	Negative Remarks to Peers
Monday	5	2
Tuesday	6	3
Wednesday	1	0
Thursday	6	3
Friday	7	3

After he collected the data, he noticed that Wednesday Gracelyn's behavior was markedly better than the other days of the week. He began to analyze all the variables within the environment such as academic tasks, lunchroom behavior, seating arrangements, and other environmental factors. He concluded that the only variable that was different on Wednesday was that another student, Joyce, a student who came into the class in the afternoons, was absent on Wednesday. He decided the next step would be to discuss this with Gracelyn. When Mr. Blackburn talked to her, she reported that she and Joyce had been friends last year but now Joyce had a new best friend and she was afraid that she did not like her anymore. After the data analysis and the discussion with Gracelyn, Mr. Blackburn was able to intervene and assist Gracelyn with the social skills she needed to resolve this issue.

For **MORE PRACTICE** in the analysis of behavioral cases, visit the Companion Website at *www.prenhall.com/overton.*

PROJECTIVE ASSESSMENT TECHNIQUES

projective techniques
Techniques used to analyze a student's feelings by what the student projects into the story card or other stimulus.

The measures presented in this section are measures that are scored more subjectively; they are often referred to as **projective techniques**. These measures include sentence completion tests, drawing tests, and apperception tests, which require the student to tell a story about some stimulus, such as picture cards. These instruments are most likely administered by the school psychologist, school counselor, or other professional, such as a clinical psychologist, who has the training and experience required to administer such instruments. Teachers and other members of the multidisciplinary team may be required to make eligibility and planning decisions based on the results of these instruments. It is beneficial to teachers, therefore, to understand the nature of the instruments and how they might be used in the assessment process.

SENTENCE COMPLETION TESTS

sentence completion tests Stems of sentences that the student completes; analyzed for themes.

Sentence completion tests provide stems or beginnings of sentences that the student is required to finish. The stems have been selected to elicit comments from the student on such topics as relationships with parents and friends and feelings about oneself. The examiner analyzes the comments written by the student for themes rather than analyzing each sentence independently. The Rotter Incomplete Sentence Blank (Rotter & Rafferty, 1950) is an example of this type of instrument. Figure 8.10 presents stems similar to those on sentence completion tests.

DRAWING TESTS

drawing tests Tests in which student draws figures, houses, trees, or families; scored developmentally and projectively.

Drawing tests attempt to screen the student's feelings about self, home, and family. Each of these instruments follows a simple format. The student is presented with a form or a piece of plain paper and is asked to draw a picture of himself; of a house, a tree, and a person; or of his family doing something together. These tests are commonly known as the Draw-a-Person, Human-Figure Drawing, House-Tree-Person, and Kinetic Family Drawings. The drawings may be scored subjectively by an examiner who has had training and experience in this type of assessment. More empirically based scoring systems are also available: the Kinetic Family Drawing System for Family and School (Knoff & Prout, 1985), the Draw-a-Person: Screening Procedure for Emotional Disturbance (Naglieri, McNeish, & Bardos, 1991), and the Human-Figure Drawing Test (Koppitz, 1968). The Draw-a-Person can be scored developmentally using a system like that by Naglieri (1988) or Harris (1963).

The newer versions of scoring systems include standardization information and developmental information. The Kinetic Family Drawing System for Family and School includes questions that the examiner asks the student about the drawings. For example, one question is "What does this person need most?" (Knoff & Prout, 1985, p. 5). The scoring booklet provides various characteristics that the student may have included in the drawings. The examiner checks to see whether a characteristic, such as the omission of

Figure 8.10   Sample items from a sentence completion test.

1. Sometimes I wish _____ .
2. I wish my mother would _____ .
3. I feel sad when _____ .
4. My friends always _____ .
5. My father _____ .

body parts, is present in the student's drawing. Guidelines for interpreting these characteristics are provided in the manual through a listing of relevant research on drawing analysis. The examiner analyzes themes that exist within the drawing on such dimensions as figure characteristics and actions between figures. Several case studies are provided for the examiner to use as guidelines for learning how to interpret the drawings.

The scoring system of the Draw-a-Person: Screening Procedure for Emotional Disturbance uses scoring templates and a norm-referenced method of scoring the drawings. The instrument is to be used as a screening device to determine whether the student needs further emotional or behavioral assessment. The manual provides examples of using the templates and scoring exercises using case studies for learning the system. Derived scores include T scores with a mean of 50 and a standard deviation of 10 and percentile ranks. The scores are interpreted as follows (Naglieri et al., 1991):

Less than 55	Further evaluation is not indicated
55 to 64	Further evaluation is indicated
65 and above	Further evaluation is strongly indicated (p. 63)

An example of the template scoring system from the manual is presented in Figure 8.11.

Figure 8.11   Example of the Naglieri et al. template scoring system for the Draw-a-Person test.

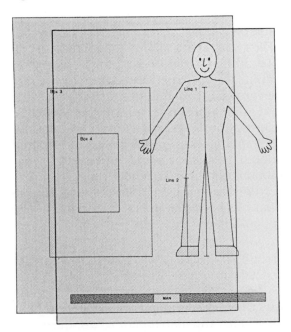
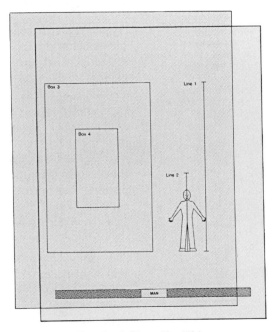

Source: From *Draw a Person: Screening Procedure for Emotional Disturbance, Examiner's Manual* (p. 23) by J. A. Naglieri, T. J. McNeish, and A. N. Bardos, 1991, Austin, TX: Pro-Ed. Copyright 1991 by Pro–Ed, Inc. Reprinted by permission.

The standardization information and technical data provided in the Naglieri et al. (1991) manual is fairly extensive and impressive for a projective drawing instrument. The sample included 2,260 students, ages 6 to 17 years. Approximately 200 students were represented in each age group. Consideration was given for age, sex, geographic region, population of community, ethnicity, race, parent occupation, and socioeconomic status. Internal consistency was researched using the coefficient alpha, and coefficients were adequate, ranging from .67 to .78. The standard error of measurement is approximately 5 for all ages. The test-retest information gives a coefficient of .67, although the sample for this study was fairly small (n = 67). Both intrarater and interrater agreement was studied and resulted in coefficients of .83 and .84, respectively. This study was also small, using 54 cases and 2 raters.

Descriptive statistics are included for validity studies that used the scoring system to compare students who had been clinically diagnosed with emotional or behavioral problems to students without such problems. The scoring system did discriminate between the groups, at least at the .05 significance level. Construct validity is supported by discriminant validity studies of intelligence testing and the Naglieri et al. Draw-a-Person scoring system. The research presented indicates that two separate areas are assessed by the Draw-a-Person and intelligence tests.

APPERCEPTION TESTS

apperception tests Student's feelings about what she perceives to be happening in a picture or other stimulus; influenced by personal experiences.

Apperception tests consist of a set of picture or story cards that have been designed to elicit responses about emotional issues. These instruments may be administered and interpreted only by professionals with the training and experience required by the test developers. Most of these projective techniques require that the examiner possess advanced graduate-level training in psychological assessment. Because apperception tests may contribute information used by the multidisciplinary team to determine educational and behavioral interventions, teachers should understand what these instruments attempt to measure and how they are interpreted. Two commonly used instruments are the Children's Apperception Test (Bellak & Bellak, 1949, 1952; Bellak & Hurvich, 1965) and the Roberts Apperception Test for Children (Roberts, 1982).

Children's Apperception Test (CAT) The CAT comprises two tests and a supplement for special situations (Bellak & Bellak, 1949, 1952; Bellak & Hurvich, 1965). The original test (animal figures) consists of 10 picture cards that depict animals engaged in human situations. The authors developed the instrument as an apperception method, which they define as "a method of investigating personality by studying the dynamic meaningfulness of the individual differences in perception of standard stimuli" (Bellak & Bellak, 1949, p. 1). The examiner evaluates a student's verbal responses to the picture cards in an effort to better understand how the student feels about herself and her relationships with family members.

The authors originally believed that younger children would identify more readily with animal figures and that these figures were more cultural and gender free. Figure 8.12 presents a picture-story card from the animal figures of the CAT. They later developed the CAT human figures as an answer to research studies that indicated the value of human-figure picture cards (Bellak & Hurvich, 1965). These picture-story cards maintain many of the same story themes and emotionally charged situations as in the animal figures; but the figures are now human, with some remaining fairly gender neutral.

The supplement to the CAT (Bellak & Bellak, 1952) contains various pictures depicting unusual situations using animal figures. Examples include a picture of a pregnant "mother" type of animal, an animal in a doctor's office, and an animal walking with crutches. Any of these specific cards may be selected by the examiner and used with the animal or human figures.

The CAT is scored subjectively along psychoanalytic themes such as regression, fear, anxiety, and denial; the manuals provide

Figure 8.12   Picture card 8 of the Children's Apperception Test.

Source: From *Children's Apperception Test (Animal Figures)* by L. Bellak and S.S. Bellak, 1999, Larchmont, NY: C.P.S. Copyright 1991 by C.P.S., Inc. Reprinted by permission of C.P.S., Inc., Box 83, Larchmont, NY 10538.

guidelines for scoring the instrument. Technical data provided in the manuals do not meet the standards set forth by many test developers in terms of reliability and validity.

Roberts–2   The second edition of the Roberts (Roberts & Gruber, 2005), like its original version, the Roberts Apperception Test for Children (McArthur & Roberts, 1982), presents story-picture cards of human figures engaged in situations with family members and peers. The second edition may be used with students ranging in age from 6 through 18 years. Of 27 stimulus cards, the student responds to 11 cards that are specific to the student's gender, as well as to 5 gender-neutral cards. This instrument has Hispanic cards and cards representing African American children as well as the set for Caucasian children. The cards were designed to elicit comments about the student's feelings about fear, parental relationships, dependency, peer and racial interaction, and so on. The examiner instructs the student to tell a story about what happened before, during, and after each scene pictured and to tell what the characters are doing, saying, and thinking. The examiner scores responses according to guidelines set forth in the manual, which gives information on adaptive indicators, clinical problems such as aggression or anxiety, and measures such as social cognitive functioning.

The manual includes information about the standardization of the instrument as well as studies comparing students within the normal range of emotional functioning with several different clinical samples. Reliability information includes interrater reliability and test-retest reliability studies. Median interrater reliability correlations ranged from .43 to 1.00. The validity information included in the manual presents several studies of the factors measured, as well as the instrument's ability to discriminate clinical from nonclinical groups. Generally, the information presented appears to be adequate for this type of behavior instrument.

COMPUTERIZED ASSESSMENT OF ATTENTION DISORDERS

Instruments have been developed for the assessment of sustained focused attention and impulsive responding patterns. Difficulty with these behaviors is believed to be characteristic of students with attention deficit disorders. This type of difficulty may be manifested as distractibility, impulsivity, and overactivity in classroom situations. These instruments should not be used as a single measure of attention problems, but rather should be used in combination with other measures, particularly classroom observations. Two such computerized systems currently used in clinical practice and research are the Continuous Performance Test (Gordon, 1983) and the Conners Continuous Performance Test (Conners, 1993). All tests of this general type are known as CPTs.

CONTINUOUS PERFORMANCE TEST

In Gordon's (1983) Continuous Performance Test, the student must discriminate between visual stimuli presented for a period of 9 minutes. The stimuli are numbers that appear at the rate of 1 per second. Scores are computed for the number of correct responses, omissions, and commissions. This instrument has been widely researched, and the author reports reliability coefficients ranging from .66 to .80.

CONNERS CONTINUOUS PERFORMANCE TEST

The Conners Continuous Performance Test is presented in much the same manner as Gordon's version (Conners, 1993; Conners, 1997). This CPT, however, lasts for 14 minutes, and the visual stimuli—letters—appear at varying rates throughout the administration. The student must maintain focused sustained attention, and the number of targets hit is calculated to determine impulsivity and loss of attention. Interpretive, computer-generated reports give derived scores for hit rate, reaction time, pattern for standard error or variability, omissions, commissions, attentiveness, and response tendencies such as risk taking. Data included in the manual and from computer reports compare the student with age and gender peers in a clinical group of students with attention deficit disorders.

DETERMINING EMOTIONAL DISTURBANCE

According to federal regulations, students may be found to be eligible for interventions under the category of emotional disturbance if they meet one the following criteria:

> An inability to learn that cannot be explained by other factors (such as a sensory or learning disorder)
> Difficulty in establishing and maintaining relationships with peers and adults
> Behaviors that are inappropriate for the circumstances
> A persistent mood of unhappiness or depression
> And
> Physical symptoms manifested as the result of fears or concerns about school or other problems.

It is important to note that a student may have some difficulties with emotion, such as a student who has depression, and not be eligible for services. For example, a student may be depressed; however; if there is no educational need for special education support, the student would not be found eligible for services. Students who manifest only mild behavioral problems without a coexisting emotional disorder, will also not likely be served under special education. For many students with such behavioral issues, it is simply a matter of poor learning or social maladjustment. It is also noteworthy that most students with attention deficit disorders or other physiologically based disorders such as Tourette's syndrome, will be served under the category of Other Health Impaired. The reasoning for this distinction is that although these disorders have behavioral manifestations, these disorders are not the result of an emotional disorder. This distinctions may be difficult for teachers to distinguish without additional assessment data from the school psychologist.

One instrument that may be used to assist in making such determinations, in combination with other behavioral and developmental data from parents and teachers, is the Scale for Assessing Emotional Disturbance (Epstein & Cullinan, 1998). The measures on this instrument are consistent with the five requirements of the federal regulations. The classroom teacher and other educators working with the student may be asked to complete a variety of questionnaires and checklists to assist in the determination. Students who are found to have emotional disturbance must manifest these behaviors across environments and in social interactions with a variety of peers and adults. The use of multiple checklists provides information about these multiple settings and social encounters.

RESEARCH AND ISSUES

The assessment of emotional and behavioral problems is by nature more ambiguous than other types of assessment, such as assessment of intellectual or academic achievement ability. The techniques range from systematic observations and computer assessment to projective techniques, such as telling stories about picture cards. The research on each of these methods has existed in volumes in the literature for many years. The research summarized in the following list represents some of the recent studies using the instruments often employed in settings that serve children and youth. Other measures, such as the Rorschach inkblot test (Rorschach, 1921, 1942), are more often used in clinical settings and therefore were not included in this text.

1. In a review of literature about functional behavioral assessment (FBA), it was found that FBA has largely studied high-rate behaviors in students with low-incidence disabilities, such as self-injurious behaviors in children with mental retardation (Ervin, Radford, Bertsch, Piper, Ehrhardt, & Poling, 2001). Additional research is needed on low-rate

behaviors (such as aggressive acts) in students with high-incidence disabilities, such as learning disabilities.

2. Northup and Gulley reviewed research that applied functional behavioral assessment in samples of students with attention deficit hyperactivity disorder and found that it is a useful technique to use in determining the interaction and effectiveness of medication with various environmental stimuli (2001).

3. Curriculum-based assessment used as part of a functional behavioral assessment was found to be an effective strategy in identifying escape-motivated behaviors of students within a general education classroom (Roberts, Marshall, Nelson, & Albers, 2001).

4. Information gained from functional behavioral assessments in preschool students at risk for attention deficit hyperactivity disorder was found to be an effective method of identifying specific strategies that decreased the problematic behaviors (Boyajian, DuPaul, Handler, Eckert, & McGoey, 2001).

5. In a review of the Behavior Rating Profile, Second Edition, the instrument's strengths include high criterion-related, concurrent, and construct validity, a sociogram, and the ability for assessment of behavioral, social, emotional, and interpersonal areas (Javorsky, 1998–1999). The weaknesses cited included the lack of students with behavioral/emotional difficulties in the norming group, lack of interrater reliability, lack of the ability to discriminate between different diagnostic categories of behavioral/emotional problems, limited use with younger students, and no information regarding intervention strategies.

6. In a study using school-referred males comparing the Teacher Report Form and the Child Behavior Checklist to the Youth Self-Report, it was found that the youth and the teacher and parent forms did not have high agreement, especially when the students rated themselves on externalizing behaviors (Lee, Elliott, & Barbour, 1994). The study found a somewhat higher agreement between parents and teachers in rating students. These findings seem to suggest that youth tend to underrate themselves on problem behaviors, which emphasizes the need for multimethod and multiinformant assessment.

7. An extensive review of the use of rating scales in different cultures resulted in noticeable differences related to culture (Reid, 1995). Because of the reliance of subjective interpretation by the rater, Reid suggests that use of rating scales in

other cultures may not be appropriate for use in diagnosing attention deficit disorder. He cautions that some symptoms may be influenced by variables related to culture, such as low socioeconomic status (SES) or other stressors.

8. In a study by Weine, Phillips, and Achenbach (1995) comparing results of the Child Behavior Checklist, differences were found in Chinese and American children. The Chinese children were found to be rated higher by their teachers for delinquent behavior, for being anxious/depressed, and on the internalizing scale. American children were rated higher on the Child Behavior Checklist on aggressive behavior. American children were rated higher by their teachers in attention problems.

9. A study comparing teacher responses on a teacher rating scale for Caucasian and African-American students found that teachers rated African-American students higher on all symptoms (Reid, DuPaul, Power, Anastopoulos, Rogers-Adkinson, Nell, & Ricco, 1998). Reid et al. caution that other measures should be used for diagnosis of attention deficit disorder for African Americans rather than relying on just teacher rating scales.

10. In a review by Walker of the Behavior Assessment System for Children, the BASC was stated to be fairly easy to administer and score, and it also had good evidence of interrater reliability (1998–1999). Walker stated that the weaknesses of the BASC were that no definitions were provided in the test manual, and students with disabilities were underrepresented in the normative sample, as well as students who are culturally, linguistically, and ethnically diverse. Walker noted that the instrument should be used only for screening purposes.

11. Oesterheld and Haber (1997) found that the items on the Conners test and the Child Behavior Checklist were difficult for Native-American parents to understand. The Native Americans often did not have similar words or concepts in their language or feared that their responses would be misinterpreted by the dominant culture.

12. Stanford and Hynd (1994) studied the difference between students with attention deficit disorder with and without hyperactivity and students with learning disabilities. Parents and teachers of students with hyperactivity endorsed more externalizing types of items on the Child Behavior Checklist. Parents and teachers of students who had attention deficit disorder without hyperactivity and students with learning disabilities endorsed fewer externalizing items.

13. The Child Behavior Checklist, Teacher Report Form, and Semistructured Clinical Interview for Children were found to have discriminant validity when comparing children with behavior disorders and nonreferred children (McConaughy & Achenbach, 1996). The discriminant validity was not as high when comparing children with behavior disorders and children with learning disabilities.

14. A study in a public school setting focused on interrater reliability among teachers using the Conners Teacher Rating Scale. Both certified teachers of students with emotional problems and their teacher aides were consistent in their ratings (Mattison, Bagnato, Mayes, & Felix, 1990). The strongest interrater correlations were on the scale's hyperactivity and conduct disorders factors. This seems to suggest that the Conners Teacher Rating Scale has adequate interrater reliability and may be an appropriate instrument in conjunction with other assessment techniques for screening for acting-out or externalizing behaviors.

15. Research of family drawings by students with divorced parents and those without divorced parents indicated differences around themes of interpersonal relationships (Spigelman, Spigelman, & Englesson, 1992). Students from homes with divorce seemed to have more omissions of family members and indications of conflict within relationships with siblings.

16. A study of human figure drawings with 5-year-old students found no significant differences between the drawings of aggressive and nonaggressive students (Norford & Barakat, 1990). It appears that this type of technique is not developmentally appropriate for use with students younger than 6.

17. Research using chronically ill children found that the Roberts Apperception Test for Children was able to differentiate children with adaptive coping styles from children with maladaptive coping styles (Palomares, Crowley, Worchel, Olson, & Rae, 1991).

18. Kroon, Goudena, and Rispens (1998) reviewed the Roberts Apperception Test for Children and stated that the psychometrics of the instrument appeared adequate, although the research presented in the manual is quite limited.

19. A study of students with and without attention deficit disorder identified both false positives and false negatives during use of a Continuous Performance Test (Trommer, Hoeppner, Lorber, & Armstrong, 1988). In addition, differences in these groups on other measures suggest that CPTs

may involve some higher-level cognitive tasks rather than pure attentive ability. Thus, CPTs should be interpreted with caution and always should be analyzed with data from multiple sources.

20. Research comparing CPT performance of students with learning disabilities and a matched control group indicated that students with learning disabilities made more omission errors but did not differ on the number of commission errors (Eliason & Richman, 1987). The authors suggest that the constructs of attention and memory are highly interrelated and may result in students with learning disabilities making more omission errors on this type of measure.

21. Research using a CPT determined favorable decreases in the number of errors made in a sample of students with attention deficit disorder following treatment with methylphenidate—Ritalin (Forness, Swanson, Cantwell, Guthrie, & Sena, 1992). This suggests that CPTs may be sensitive to measurement of the treatment of students with stimulant medication.

22. In a review of research, Loiser, McGrath, and Klein (1996) found that children with ADHD made a higher number of omission and commission errors than did non-ADHD children. They also found that children treated with methylphenidate made significantly fewer errors on the CPT than those who were not treated.

23. On a CPT, students with attention deficit disorder with hyperactivity made almost twice the number of errors of commission as did students with attention deficit disorder without hyperactivity (Barkley, DuPaul, & McMurray, 1990). This same study determined that students with attention deficit disorder and hyperactivity scored significantly worse on the ASEBA aggressive and delinquent scales than did students with attention deficit disorder without hyperactivity, students with learning disabilities, and the control sample of students.

24. Although the Children's Apperception Test has been revised, it continues to be criticized by professional reviewers due to the lack of adequate psychometric quality (Knoff, 1998; Reinehr, 1998).

25. Mueller, Brozovich, and Johnson reviewed the Conners Rating Scales–Revised (1998–1999). These reviewers noted the difficulty in scoring the Conners; they also noted that the readability level for the parent form was ninth grade. These reviewers questioned whether the readability level might be too high for some parents.

It is evident from the small sample of research reviewed in this chapter that many factors are to be considered in the assessment of students exhibiting behavioral and emotional problems. It is important that multiple measures and multiple informants be used and that the individual student's environment be assessed as well (Clarizio & Higgins, 1989). In a review of relevant research on assessment of attention and behavioral disorders, Schaughency and Rothlind (1991) stressed the need for a variety of methods, such as interviews, teacher ratings, observations, and peer nominations. These techniques may aid in determining whether the difficulties are reactions to the environment or reactions to current stress within the student's world. As with all assessment, a holistic view of the complete student and his environment is necessary.

THINK AHEAD

Cognitive abilities and the assessment of intelligence remain a part of the assessment process in determining the need for special education intervention. Chapter 9 presents the most commonly used measures of intelligence and adaptive behavior.

EXERCISES

Part I

Match the following terms with the statements.

a. checklist
b. direct observation
c. permanent product recording
d. setting event
e. anecdotal recording
f. interresponse time
g. functional behavior assessment
h. time sampling
i. projective techniques

j. target behavior
k. an apperception test
l. work samples
m. CPT
n. establishing operation
o. event recording
p. latency
q. interval recording
r. drawing tests
s. baseline

_____ 1. A teacher wants to determine the exact number of times a student inappropriately leaves his seat. The teacher needs this information before an intervention begins. This initial data collection technique about the student's behavior is referred to as the _____.

_____ 2. Although information can be obtained by questioning persons who work with a specific student, in order to determine what behavior occurs in a specific environment, the method of _____ will need to be used over multiple sessions.

_____ 3. By writing down information about a student's behavior that can later be analyzed for antecedent, behavior, and consequence, the teacher has used _____ as part of the functional behavioral assessment.

_____ 4. A teacher notices that one specific student has not been able to complete class work in the amount of time allotted. He notices that all other students in the class usually finish within the time frame expected. This specific student seems to take some time getting prepared to begin assignments. To establish a baseline about this specific behavior, the teacher will need to record the _____ time between the time the assignment is presented and the time the student begins to work.

_____ 5. A teacher and additional objective educational personnel have observed a student's off-task behavior in several settings. During the assessment process, the school psychologist may administer a _____ to measure distractibility and sustained focused attention on a computerized assessment.

_____ 6. A test that requires the psychologist to analyze story responses a student gives when shown specific picture cards is called _____.

_____ 7. Although much information can be obtained from norm-referenced standardized assessments, in order to analyze a student's progress and productivity in a curriculum, _____ should be collected and evaluated.

_____ 8. The evaluation of the information collected in question 7 is called _____.

_____ 9. An elementary teacher questions a third-grade student following a fight on the playground. The student is quite upset and relays to the teacher that his parents were fighting that morning before school and he witnessed his father shoving his mother. This incident may be referred to as the _____ of the child's behavior on the playground.

_____ 10. Assessment techniques such as completing sentence stems and drawing pictures of a house or person are called _____.

_____ 11. An assessment reveals that a child's continued calling out during class time is a method used by the child to gain the teacher's attention. This assessment, that identifies the reason for the student's calling out, is known as _____ .

_____ 12. Students display many varieties of behaviors during a school day. When specific behaviors are identified as problematic behaviors that require interventions, they are referred to as _____ .

Part II

Read the following scenario. Complete an analysis of the scenario and identify the **highlighted** phrases or words behaviorally.

A middle-school student has begun **arguing** and **getting into fights** during **unstructured times** during the school day. You observe that nobody seems to provoke the student, but rather the student becomes argumentative **whenever another student jokingly touches** or **comes near** the target student. The result of the student's problematic behaviors is that the student who was jokingly touching or coming near the target student **backs away** and **leaves the target student alone.** The target student seems to be happier during structured times during adult supervision. Upon questioning the target student, you learn that his older brother **has been hitting the target** student when **the parents are not at home.**

Provide your analysis below: _____

_____

_____

Anwers to these questions can be found in the Appendix of this text or you may also complete these questions and receive immediate feedback on your answers by going to the Think Ahead module in Chapter 8 of the Companion Website.

Measures of Intelligence and Adaptive Behavior

intelligence	acculturation
adaptive behavior	cross-battery assessment
IQ	simultaneous processing
innate potential	sequential processing
environmental influence	

CHAPTER FOCUS

Chapter 9 presents common assessment measures of cognitive ability and adaptive behavior. Teachers may be required to complete adaptive behavior measures and should also have an understanding of the use of intelligence tests.

CEC KNOWLEDGE AND SKILLS STANDARDS

The student completing this chapter will understand the knowledge and skills included in the following CEC Knowledge and Skills Standards from Standard 8: Assessment:

CC8K1—Basic terminology used in assessment.

CC8K2—Legal provisions and ethical principles regarding assessment of individuals.

CC8K4—Use and limitations of assessment instruments.

CC8K3—Screening, prereferral, referral, and classification procedures.

CC8S2—Administer nonbiased formal and informal assessments.

CC8S5—Interpret information from formal and informal assessments.

MEASURING INTELLIGENCE

intelligence A general concept of an individual's ability to function effectively within various settings; usually assessed by intelligence tests.

The measurement of **intelligence** has been a controversial issue in educational and psychological assessment for the past several years. Even though professionals in the field disagree to some extent about the definition of intelligence and about the fairness and importance of intelligence testing, the assessment of intellectual ability is mandated by IDEA for the diagnosis of many disabilities.

adaptive behavior One's ability to function in various environments.

This federal law also requires the assessment of **adaptive behavior**, or how a student functions within the environment, for the diagnosis of mental retardation.

This chapter presents a review of individual measures of intelligence and adaptive behavior that commonly are used in schools to diagnose students with learning or emotional disabilities. Group intelligence tests may be administered in school systems to students in the regular education curriculum; for special education diagnostic purposes, however, group IQ tests are not appropriate. Tests constructed to be administered in an individual setting are commonly used to measure cognitive abilities. Although teachers will not be responsible for administering intelligence tests, special education teachers should possess an understanding of the interpretation of intelligence test results and their possible implications for educational planning. A general discussion of intelligence testing and the court cases that have influenced current practice are presented before the review of intelligence tests.

THE MEANING OF INTELLIGENCE TESTING

IQ Intelligence quotient; expressed as a standard score, usually with a mean of 100.

The results of intelligence tests are usually reported in the form of a standardized **IQ** (intelligence quotient) score. The IQ score is a quotient that is derived in the following manner:

$$IQ = MA + CA \times 100$$

In this calculation, MA means the mental age of the student and CA is the chronological age of the student. Using this formula, a child with a mental age of 9 and a chronological age of 11 would have an IQ of around 82. A student with a mental age of 14 and a chronological age of 10 would have an IQ of 140. It is important for the special education professional to understand what an IQ score is and is not. To possess a basic understanding of IQ scores, the professional educator should consider what is measured by IQ tests, that is, the content and presentation of the items on an IQ test and what the items represent. It is a commonly held myth that IQ scores are measurements of potential that is innate in a person. The following statements illustrate some current views about intelligence and intelligence testing expressed in the literature:

> The IQ does not reflect a global summation of the brain's capabilities and is certainly not an index of genetic potential, but it does predict school achievement effectively. (Kaufman, 1979, p. 9)
>
> Ultimately, intelligence is not a kind of ability at all, certainly not in the same sense that reasoning, memory, verbal fluency, etc., are so regarded. Rather it is something that is inferred from the way these abilities are manifested under different conditions and circumstances. (Wechsler, 1974, p. 5)

Intelligence—unlike height and weight, but like all psychological constructs—must be measured indirectly; it must be inferred from intelligent behavior, past and present. (Hopkins, Stanley, & Hopkins, 1990, p. 374)

Measurement of current intellectual performance has become confused with measurement of innate potential. Intelligence tests do not assess potential; they sample behaviors already learned in an attempt to predict future learning. (McLoughlin & Lewis, 1990, p. 187)

Child-standardized intelligence performance provides a quantitative index of developmental status, but does not provide information on those functions that have not developed nor on the route by which the child arrived at his or her current developmental state. (Swanson & Watson, 1989, p. 93)

Historically, intelligence has been an enigmatic concept. It is a much valued construct or quality that is extremely difficult to define. Is intelligence the same as verbal ability? Analytical thinking? Academic aptitude? Strategic thinking? The ability to cope? Different theorists might argue for each, or a combination of these abilities. Similarly, they might ask whether intelligence is, or should be, defined in the same way for individuals of different cultural, ethnic, or social backgrounds. (Taylor, 1989, pp. 185–186).

Wasserman and Tulsky (2005) note that, "Over 100 years of debate have failed to lead to a consensus definition of this core psychological construct" (p. 14). The theories upon which these tests are based influence their use and interpretation. As the development of intelligence tests continue, and that development is based on researched theories, the measurement and interpretation of intelligence test results will continue to be more meaningful for interventions (Kamphaus, Winsor, Rowe, & Kim, 2005).

Even more controversial than the meaning of intelligence is the apparent bias that may occur by using individual IQ tests to classify and place students in special education (Reschly, 1981). Taylor (1989) questioned using the same definition of intelligence for individuals of all cultures, which reflects the concern that minority students are overrepresented in special education classrooms (Heller, Holtzman, & Messick, 1982). Specifically, African American students have been overrepresented in classrooms for students with mental retardation (Heller et al., 1982; Tucker, 1980), and Hispanic students have been increasingly found in classrooms for the learning disabled (Mick, 1985; Tucker, 1980). With the new regulations focused on decreasing disproportionality, it is even more important to make certain that formal assessment measures are free from ethnic, cultural, and linguistic bias.

Salvia and Ysseldyke (1988) underscored the importance that culture and background have on intellectual assessment:

Acculturation is the single most important characteristic in evaluating a child's performance on intelligence tests. . . . The culture in which a child lives and the length of time that the child has lived in that culture effectively determine the psychological demands a test item presents. (p. 149)

Taylor and Richards (1991) noted that persons obtaining similar scores on IQ tests manifest differences in their pattern of responding. These authors found that while white students scored higher on the Wechsler Scales than black and Hispanic students, different patterns were evident, with black students showing verbal strength and Hispanic students showing strength in perceptual ability.

innate potential Thought to be one's ability from birth.

environmental influence The impact of the environment on the student's learning ability.

acculturation The influence of one culture on another culture.

The issues of **innate potential**, learned behaviors, **environmental influence**, and **acculturation**, and their influence on intelligence testing, have fueled the fire of many professional debates (Herrnstein & Murray, 1994). Intelligence testing, however, like all testing in education, is simply the way that a student responds to a set of stimuli at a specific point in time. Reynolds (1982) reviewed and summarized the general problems with bias in assessment; these are presented, as adapted, in Figure 9.1. Some of the problems of intelligence testing stem from content validity, construct validity, predictive validity (Messick, 1980), and the mean differences obtained by groups of different cultural or ethnic backgrounds (Reschly, 1981), as well as problems that affect all types of standardized testing, such as examiner familiarity (Fuchs & Fuchs, 1989).

ALTERNATIVE VIEWS OF INTELLECTUAL ASSESSMENT

The use of traditional intelligence tests in schools has been criticized for producing different results for different groups (Canter, 1997). The movement toward change in special education assessment, accountability, and educational reform in schools has also had an influence on the use of traditional assessment methods. Due to these trends, it is likely that assessment personnel along with researchers will seek alternative types of assessment models and methods of determining intellectual ability. Canter stated that "intelligence testing as we practice it today seems increasingly out-of-step with the needs of tomorrow's schools" (1997, p. 256). Dissatisfaction with the traditional psychometric approach has stimulated research and theoretical exploration of additional definitions and techniques used to assess intellectual ability. For example, Gardner (1993) presents a model with seven intelligences:

> But there is an alternative vision that I would like to present—one based on a radically different view of the mind and one that yields a very different view of the school. It is a pluralistic view of mind, recognizing many different and discrete facets of cognition, acknowledging that people have different cognitive strengths and contrasting cognitive styles. . . . One such approach I have called my "theory of multiple intelligences." (1993, pp. 6–7)

Figure 9.1 Indicators of possible bias in assessment.

1. *Inappropriate content.* Black or other minority children have not been exposed to the material involved in the test questions or other stimulus materials. The tests are geared primarily toward white middle-class homes and values.

2. *Inappropriate standardization samples.* Ethnic minorities are underrepresented in the collection of normative reference group data.

3. *Examiner language bias.* Since most psychologists are white and speak primarily only standard English, they intimidate black and other ethnic minorities. They are also unable to accurately communicate with minority children. Lower test scores for minorities then are said to reflect only this intimidation and difficulty in the communication process and not lowered ability levels.

4. *Inequitable social consequences.* As a result of bias in educational and psychological tests, minority group members, who are already at a disadvantage in the educational and vocational markets because of past discrimination, are disproportionately relegated to dead-end educational tracts and are thought unable to learn. Labelling effects also fall under this category.

5. *Measurement of different constructs.* Related to (1) above, this position asserts that the tests are measuring significantly different attributes when used with children from other than the white middle-class culture.

6. *Differential predictive validity.* While tests may accurately predict a variety of outcomes for white middle-class children, they fail to predict at an acceptable level any relevant criteria for minority group members. Corollary to this objection is a variety of competing positions regarding the selection of an appropriate, common criterion against which to validate tests across cultural groupings. Scholastic or academic attainment levels are considered by a variety of black psychologists to be biased as criteria.

7. *Qualitatively distinct minority and majority aptitude and personality.* The idea here is that majority and minority cultures are so different that they result in substantial influences on personality and aptitude development. Due to these influences, different tests are required to accurately measure personality and aptitude.

Source: Adapted from "The Problem of Bias in Psychological Assessment" by C. R. Reynolds, P. A. Lowe, & A. L. Saenz; in C. R. Reynolds and T. B. Gutkin (Eds.), *The Handbook of School Psychology,* 3rd ed., 1999 (pp. 556–557), New York: John Wiley & Sons. Copyright 1999 by John Wiley & Sons. Adapted by permission.

The seven types of intellectual ability proposed by Gardner include linguistic intelligence, logical-mathematical intelligence, spatial intelligence, musical intelligence, bodily-kinesthetic intelligence, interpersonal intelligence, and intrapersonal intelligence. Gardner stresses the need for fair intellectual assessment that would assess all areas rather than only the linguistic and logical-mathematical assessment included in traditional intellectual assessment instruments.

Carroll had proposed a theory of intelligence that is based on three levels or stratums (Carroll, 2005). In this theory, a general or overarching intelligence influences the skills and abilities included within the other two levels or stratums. Level two includes more specific skills and abilities than the *g* or general factor of intelligence, and level three includes very specific abilities and skills.

The concept of dynamic assessment is another area of current research in the quest for alternate assessment models. This model uses the assessment experience to measure the precise task of learning. The tasks used in dynamic assessment are those in which the learner is presented with interventions to determine how the learner responds to those strategies or interventions. The learner begins a task and is assisted by the examiner rather than merely observed by the examiner. Lidz (1997) points out the differences between traditional and dynamic assessment:

> Most of our (traditional) procedures provide information only about the learner's independent level of performance and infer future from previous functioning.... Dynamic assessment begins where traditional psychometric assessment ends. Instead of terminating the procedure with the establishment of a ceiling, the dynamic assessor views the ceiling as an area of functioning that warrants assessment. (1997, pp. 281–282)

Others caution against the rapid adoption of alternative measures of intelligence without scientific basis for the changes (Lopez, 1997). While additional researchers call for the use of cross-battery assessment of cognitive abilities, noting that the use of multiple measures of cognitive skills and abilities can better account for the variety of abilities that must be measured (Flanagan & Ortiz, 2001). Brown, Reynolds, and Whitaker (1999) state that although many alternate assessment measures of IQ have been proposed, professionals should rely on research-based methods, including traditional standardized assessment instruments. Therefore, in most states, traditional IQ tests continue to be used as a part of the assessment process. Based on the individual student's measured performance on tasks on the IQ tests, the team members infer the student's intellectual ability (Turnbull, Turnbull, Shank, Smith, & Leal, 2002).

Even though IQ testing has received much criticism, MacMillan and Forness remind assessment personnel that traditional IQ scores derived from traditional methods serve a function in schools today (1998). As these authors point out,

> What IQ tells us is that if nothing is done and the child remains in general education with no adjustment to instructional strategies, the child with a low score is likely to experience failure—the lower the score, the greater the probability and the greater the degree of failure that the child will encounter. (1998, p. 251)

The most important consideration for school personnel using or interpreting IQ assessment data is that the data obtained from these assessments are only a small part of the information employed in the decision-making process (Prifitera, Saklofske, Weiss, & Rolfhus, 2005). Therefore, it is most important to select measures that will provide useful information and assist in making educational and behavioral interventions.

LITIGATION AND INTELLIGENCE TESTING

The issues of intelligence testing and the overrepresentation of minorities in special education classrooms led to litigation that has affected current practice in the field, including the decreased use of intelligence tests by some state and local education agencies for the diagnosis of disabling conditions (Bersoff, 1981). Major court cases that have involved the assessment of intellectual ability are *Larry P. v. Riles* (1984) and *PASE v. Hannon* (1980). Other cases have involved assessment and placement procedures: *Diana v. State Board of Education* and *Lora v. New York City Board of Education*. These cases are summarized in Figure 9.2.

Figure 9.2   Summary of court cases involving IQ assessment.

Larry P. v. Riles (1984). This case resulted in the court's finding that schools could no longer use standardized but unvalidated IQ tests for the purpose of identifying and placing black children into segregated special education classes for children designated as educable mentally retarded (EMR) (Turnbull, 1990, p. 92).

PASE v. Hannon (1980). Although PASE (Parents in Action on Special Education) found that some of the items in the tests were discriminatory, the court upheld that the tests were generally nondiscriminatory. More important, it found that the tests were not the sole basis for classification and that the school district therefore was complying with the Education of the Handicapped Act, EHA, which requires multifaceted testing (Turnbull, 1990, p. 95).

Diana v. State Board of Education (1970). In this case, the state board of education of California agreed to test students in their native language, to omit unfair test items of a verbal nature, to construct tests that would reflect the culture of Mexican American students, and to provide tests that would be standardized for Mexican Americans (Ysseldyke & Algozzine, 1982).

Lora v. New York City Board of Education (1984). This case required that the school system use objective and improved referral and assessment methods and multidisciplinary evaluations to reach decisions for diagnosis of students with emotional disturbance. The court found that the method previously in use was racially discriminatory and ruled that the school system could no longer consider school monetary problems or availability of services as reasons to place or not to place students in special education (Wood, Johnson, & Jenkins, 1990).

Due to the recent litigation involving the testing of intelligence as well as the information included in the assessment sections of IDEA, a movement toward more objective testing practices is currently under way in the assessment field. In addition, professionals are reminded to follow the *Code of Fair Testing Practices in Education* (see Chapter 2) by the Joint Committee on Testing Practices and the standards set forth by the AERA (1999).

For **MORE PRACTICE** on understanding what IQ tests measure, visit the Companion Website at *www.prenhall.com/overton.*

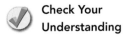 **Check Your Understanding**

Complete Activity 9.1 below to assess your knowledge of content on legal considerations and concepts of intelligence.

Activity 9.1

Match the following terms to the descriptions.

A. *PASE v. Hannon*

B. *Diana v. State Board of Education*

C. inappropriate content

D. inequitable social consequences

E. inappropriate standardization sample

F. differential predictive validity

G. *Lora v. New York City Board of Education*

H. *Larry P. v. Riles*

I. examiner language bias

J. measurement of different constructs

K. IQ score

L. intelligence testing

_____ 1. Case involving administering tests in a language other than the child's native language.

_____ 2. Case concerning students who were placed in a school for students with emotional disturbance without the benefit of nondiscriminatory assessment.

_____ 3. Standardized norm-referenced assessment of cognitive abilities; the indirect measurement of the construct of intelligence.

_____ 4. When, as the result of discriminatory assessment, minority students are placed in dead-end educational or vocational tracts.

_____ 5. When a test measures different constructs for people of different groups.

_____ 6. A test may accurately predict for one group of students but not as accurately for another group, which results in this.

_____ 7. A numerical representation of intellectual ability.

_____ 8. When the examiner does not possess skill in communicating in the student's native language, it may result in this.

_____ 9. Case finding that the use of IQ tests to place black students in classes for persons with mental retardation was a discriminatory practice.

_____ 10. Case finding the same IQ tests to be nondiscriminatory even though a few items were found to be biased.

Apply Your Knowledge

Summarize how court cases have influenced the use of intelligence tests. _____

_____

_____

USE OF INTELLIGENCE TESTS

The use of intelligence tests remains controversial in part because of inappropriate use in the past. Revised instruments, alternative testing practices, and understanding of the ethnic or cultural differences that may occur are promising improvements in the assessment of intelligence. Intelligence testing is likely to remain a substantial part of the assessment process because of the known correlation between performance on IQ tests and school achievement (Reschly & Grimes, 1995). Kaufman (1994) states that intelligence tests should be used "as a helping agent rather than an instrument for placement, labeling, or other types of academic oppression" (p. 1). Kaufman has long advocated for the intelligent use of intelligence tests. McGrew and Flanagan (1998) state that to have a complete picture of a person's true intellectual ability, a cross battery or multiple measures of intelligence tests should be used. Given that IQ tests will continue to be used, educators must promote fair and appropriate use of intelligence measures. Reschly and Grimes (1995) set forth the following guidelines for appropriate use of IQ tests:

1. Appropriate use requires a context that emphasizes prevention and early intervention rather than eligibility determination as the initial phase in services to students with learning and behavior problems.

2. Intellectual assessment should be used when the results are directly relevant to well-defined referral questions and other available information does not address those questions.

3. Mandatory use of intellectual measures for all referrals, multifactored evaluations, or reevaluations is not consistent with best practices.

4. Intellectual assessment must be part of a multifactored approach, individualized to a child's characteristics and the referral problems.

5. Intellectual assessment procedures must be carefully matched to characteristics of children and youth.

6. Score reporting and interpretation must reflect known limitations of tests, including technical adequacy, inherent error in measurement, and general categories of performance.

7. Interpretation of performance and decisions concerning classification must reflect consideration of overall strengths and weaknesses in intellectual performance, performance on other relevant dimensions of behavior, age, family characteristics, and cultural background.

8. Users should implement assertive procedures to protect students from misconceptions and misuses of intellectual test results. (pp. 436–437)

Special education professionals can obtain meaningful information from IQ test results if they understand the types of behavior that are assessed by individual subtests and items. Readers should take notice of the possible areas of testing bias as well as previous court decisions as they study the tests reviewed in this chapter.

REVIEW OF INTELLIGENCE TESTS

This chapter reviews some of the tests most commonly used by schools to measure cognitive ability or intelligence. Perhaps the best-known intelligence measures are the Wechsler Scales, three separate tests designed to assess intellectual functioning at different age levels. The Wechsler Preschool and Primary Scale of Intelligence–Revised (WPPSI–III) was developed for use with children aged 2–6 to 7–3; it is reviewed in Chapter 10, "Special Considerations of Assessment in Early Childhood and Transition." The Wechsler Adult Intelligence Scale–Third Edition (WAIS–III) (discussed later) is used with youth 16 years of age through adulthood. The Wechsler Intelligence Scale for Children–Fourth Edition assesses school-aged children ranging in age from 6 through 16–11.

A newly revised Kaufman Assessment Battery for Children, Second Edition (K-ABC-II) has an even stronger theoretical base than the original version (Kufman & Kaufman, 2004). It allows the examiner to score the test based on one of two theoretical viewpoints, with one theoretical framework yielding a composite score that is not as heavily influenced by language or linguistic differences. This instrument will no doubt receive attention in those schools where an increasingly larger percentage of students whose primary language is not English are currently enrolled.

Other measures of intelligence are commonly used with school-aged children. The following are reviewed briefly in this chapter: the Woodcock-Johnson–Tests of Cognitive Ability, Third Edition, Stanford–Binet Intelligence Scale–Fifth Edition, Detroit Tests of Learning Aptitude–4, and the Kaufman Adolescent and Adult Intelligence Test. As with the Wechsler Scales and the K-ABC-II, these tests may not be administered by the teacher; however, test results provided by the psychologist or diagnostician may be useful to the teacher.

WECHSLER INTELLIGENCE SCALE FOR CHILDREN–FOURTH EDITION

The WISC–IV (Wechsler, 2003a) is designed to assess the global intellectual ability and processing ability of children ages 6–0 through 16–11. Unlike the earlier editions, this test does not provide verbal and performance IQ scores. The structure of the scoring system is based on the supported factor structure of the test. Therefore, the test results are presented with a Full Scale IQ score as well as index or processing scores. The test developers report that the basal and ceiling levels of the instrument have been expanded so that a more accurate assessment of intellectual ability can be obtained for very young students (6 years of age) as well as students in the older age group (aged 16 years). This provides more accuracy in measurement of ability for children who have cognitive limitations at the younger end and who have superior cognitive functioning at the upper end.

The constructs that are assessed on this instrument are presented in Figure 9.3. The subtests are included within each index cluster. The subtests presented in italics are the supplemental subtests or the subtests that can be used if a particular subtest is spoiled during the administration. A discussion of each subtest is presented in the following section.

Subtests of the WISC–IV   The following subtests are grouped by index scores. For example, the Similarities, Vocabulary, Comprehension, Information, and Word Reasoning subtests all support the factor structure of the Verbal Comprehension Index score. This means that research using the scores obtained during the standardization process indicates that these subtests all contribute to the Verbal Comprehension Index. In other words, a student who scores high on these subtests is likely to have strength in the area of verbal comprehension. We would anticipate that students with strength in this area would be able to score consistently across the subtests. When a student scores very low on one or two subtests,

Figure 9.3   From the *WISC–IV Technical and Interpretive Manual*, p. 6.

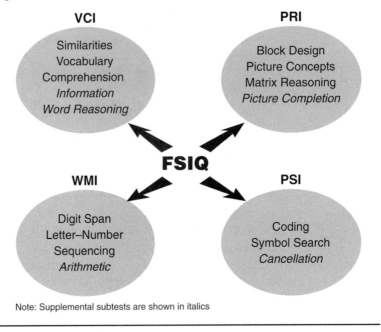

VCI—Verbal Comprehension Index
PRI—Perceptual Reasoning Index
WMI—Working Memory Index
PSI—Processing Speed Index

Source: David Wechsler, 2003, *Wechsler Intelligence Scale for Children,* 4th ed.
San Antonio, TX: The Psychological Corporation.

cross-battery assessment Administering subtests from two or more tests to determine if a weakness exists in a particular skill or ability.

the psychologist may give additional instruments to determine if this is a true weakness. The psychologist may also complete additional assessment or collect additional data when a student scores lower on one index than other indicates. This type of assessment is called **cross-battery assessment**.

Verbal Comprehension Subtests   The following subtests support the construct of verbal comprehension. These subtests have been found to be heavily weighted in the understanding of language concepts.

Similarities. On this subtest students are required to compare two words read by the examiner to determine how the two words are alike. The responses may be scored as a 0, 1, or 2.

Vocabulary. The student is asked to define common words. For the younger child, pictures serve as the stimulus for the item. For children aged 9 to 16 years, the written form of the words are presented as the item stimulus.

Comprehension. The items on this subtest assess the child's knowledge of common concepts learned incidentally or from experiences or the environment. For example, some questions tap into understanding of social issues, such as keeping your word to a friend; other items assess information for everyday functioning such as paying bills or maintaining good health. These items may therefore be influenced by the child's experiences or environment, whether that environment is limited or enriched.

Information. These items assess information that may also be obtained from experiences or education. Items may include questions similar to the number of legs a cat has or the number of weeks in a month. In other words, this information is likely to have been learned prior to test administration and the child is simply using recall to respond to the question. This is a supplemental subtest of the Verbal Comprehension Index.

Word Reasoning. This subtest presents clues that the child must use to respond with a specific word for a common object. A series of clues are presented and the student is given a chance with each clue to respond with the correct answer. This is a supplemental subtest of the Verbal Comprehension Index.

Perceptual Reasoning Subtests. Perceptual reasoning means that a person is able to look at visual stimuli and tap into reasoning skills to solve novel problems. In other words, these types of items may not be as heavily influenced by previous education experiences, but rather require the student to see a stimulus, process that visual concept mentally, and respond with a solution.

Block Design. On this subtest, students are required to manipulate and copy a pattern of red and white blocks. This is a timed subtest and students are awarded additional points when the pattern is copied quickly and accurately. The task requires that students use visual-motor responses and that they have the visual-perceptual ability to understand and reproduce the stimulus.

Picture concepts. The student is presented with one picture and several rows of pictures. The student must select pictures from the rows of pictures to form a common concept. This task requires the child to use abstract verbal reasoning skills.

Matrix Reasoning. This subtest presents visual stimuli that represent incomplete matrices. The child is asked to select the representation that would complete the matrix. There are four types of matrices on this subtest, including pattern completions, classifications, and analogical and serial reasoning (Wechsler, 2003b).

Picture Completion. The child is required to scan pictures and either name or point to a missing part. This task may be influenced by previous experiences because many of the pictures are common objects in the environment. This is a supplemental subtest of the Perceptual Reasoning Index.

Working Memory Subtests When an item is presented that requires the student to hold on to the stimuli for a period of time in order to solve the task, it is referred to as a working memory item. These items may require visual or auditory working memory.

Digit Span. On this subtest, the examiner says a series of numbers to the child that the child must repeat as a series. The series become increasingly longer. The series of numbers are presented forward and backward.

Letter-Number Sequencing. On this subtest, the student hears a series of letters with numbers and is required to recall the numbers in ascending order and also the letters in alphabetical order. Children 6 and 7 years old perform the simpler tasks of counting and reciting part of the alphabet.

Arithmetic. This is a supplemental subtest of the Working Memory Index. On this subtest, the child is presented with math problems that must be solved mentally. This subtest requires working memory and some knowledge of math operations and reasoning.

Processing Speed Subtests   The subtests included in this index score assess how quickly a person can complete a task. The subtests included in the index require visual-motor processing and fine-motor skills required to respond to the items. All subtests in this index are timed.

Coding. On this subtest, the student is required to copy visual symbols that correspond to visually presented numbers.

Symbol Search. The student is presented with an initial symbol or with two symbols at the beginning of each row of symbols. The child must scan the row of symbols and determine if one or the initial symbols is present in that row. The task requires visual discrimination and memory.

Cancellation. On this subtest the student is presented with a page of small pictures and asked to mark all animals on the page of pictures. The subtest has two formats of presentation, random and organized. This is a supplemental subtest on the Processing Speed Index.

Scores Obtained on the WISC–IV   Subtests are scored by using the raw scores to obtain the derived scaled scores. The scaled scores have a mean of 10. A score is obtained for each of the indices along with the Full Scale Intelligence Quotient. The index scores and the FSIQ score are based on the standard score with a mean of 100 and a standard deviation of 15. Additional process scores may be obtained; however, these are obtained from data collected by the administration of the existing subtests and are used primarily for diagnostic purposes. For example, data collected during the administration of the Digit Span subtest can be used to obtain the Digit Span Forward and Digit Span Backward scaled scores.

Figure 9.4 illustrates a portion of the completed protocol of the WISC–IV. This illustration shows the student's scaled scores, composite scores, percentile ranks, confidence intervals, FSIQ, and the score profiles. The composite scores, which are based on the mean

Figure 9.4 Example of completed summary page.

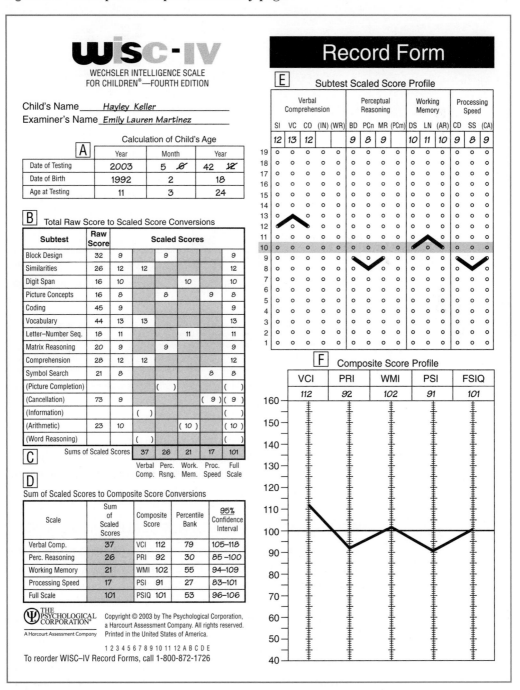

373

Figure 9.5   Portion of WISC–IV Protocol.

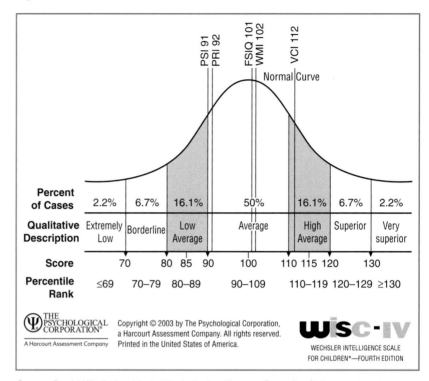

Source: David Wechsler, 2003, *Wechsler Intelligence Scale for Children,* 4th ed. San Antonio, TX: The Psychological Corporation.

of 100, can be related to the normal distribution. On one page of the protocol, the scores may be plotted on a bell curve. This curve also includes the descriptive terms or categories often used when the WISC–IV is interpreted. This portion of the protocol is represented in Figure 9.5.

WECHSLER ADULT INTELLIGENCE SCALE–THIRD EDITION

The Wechsler Adult Intelligence Scale–Third Edition (WAIS–III) was published in 1997. Many of the same subtests of the children's version are included on the scales for adults.

Subtests   Examples of the subtests included on the WAIS–III are:

> *Letter-Number Sequencing.* This additional verbal subtest presents a mixed series of numbers and letters that the examinee must repeat back to the examiner, with the numbers in ascending order and the letters in alphabetical order. This subtest assesses short-term auditory memory as well as the ability to mentally manipulate stimuli according to specific parameters and to respond orally. This subtest is optional and is not required to determine IQ scores.

Matrix Reasoning. This additional performance subtest presents visual stimuli that the examinee must evaluate to determine which of the stimuli will complete the visual pattern. This subtest assesses visual analytical and abstract reasoning.

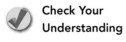

Check Your Understanding

Check your knowledge of the terms presented in association with the Wechsler Scales by completing Activity 9.2 below.

Activity 9.2

Match the following terms with the correct descriptions.

A. WAIS–III

B. WPPSI–R

C. WISC–IV

D. Verbal Comprehension Index

E. Perceptual Reasoning Index

F. Full-scale IQ

G. Digit span

H. Coding

I. K-ABC-II

J. Similarities

K. Block design

L. Information

M. Picture completion

N. Working Memory Index

O. Vocabulary

P. Processing Speed Index

Q. Word reasoning

R. Processing Speed Index

S. Comprehension

T. Arithmetic

U. Matrix reasoning

_____ 1. This edition has four index scores: perceptual reasoning, verbal comprehension, working memory, and processing speed.

_____ 2. This Wechsler test is designed to be used through adulthood.

_____ 3. This subtest presents math story problems, and performance can be influenced by attention span and concentration or working memory.

_____ 4. On this subtest, the examiner asks the student how two things are alike.

_____ 5. This index score represents the student's ability to attend and process infomation and complete tasks with this information.

_____ 6. On this subtest, the examiner provides clues and the student uses the clues to provide a specific word.

_____ 7. The subtests on this index represent the student's ability to quickly respond on fine motor tasks.

_____ 8. This instrument includes subtests that assess tasks believed to measure one's simultaneous and successive processing ability on cognitive tasks.

_____ 9. This subtest contains red and white cubes and measures perceptual organization, spatial ability, synthesis, and reproduction of models.

_____10. Performance on this Verbal Comprehension subtest can be influenced by the student's conscience or moral sense.

_____11. This subtest is divided into two parts, forward and backward, and measures auditory short-term memory and freedom from distractibility.

_____12. This IQ score reflects the performance of the student on all four indexes.

_____13. This Wechsler test was designed to be used with children from the ages of 2 years and 6 months to 7 years and 3 months.

_____14. Which of the cognitive assessment instruments can be administered to school age students ages 6–16 ?

Apply Your Knowledge

Which of the subtests described for the Wechsler Scales can be influenced by weakness in the visual-motor areas? _____

_____

_____

The third edition provides additional items on the lower end and additional practice items on some of the subtests. This instrument is clinically more user friendly for examinees who are functioning significantly below the average. These additional items may allow examinees at the lower end to respond to more items before reaching a ceiling, providing the clinician with a better picture of an examinee's ability.

This edition eliminated several items of the WAIS–R that proved to be biased or outdated (Wechsler, 1997). The third edition moved Object Assembly to optional status rather than keep it as a mandatory subtest. In general, the materials are more attractive, sturdier, and easier to handle. The sequence of administration is also improved and is easier to administer.

KAUFMAN ASSESSMENT BATTERY FOR CHILDREN, SECOND EDITION

The Kaufman Assessment Battery for Children, Second Edition (K-ABC-II) assesses the cognitive ability of children aged 3-0 to 18-11. This newly revised instrument includes a revised method of scoring and interpretation. Although this instrument will not be administered by teachers, an understanding of the theoretical bases of the scoring will assist the teacher in interpreting the results and considering the results for interventions.

Before the test is administered, the psychologist must decide which theoretical base will be used to administer and score the instrument. A brief explanation of each theoretical base follows.

One theoretical base, Luria's neurological processing theory, is quite extensive; however, one of the major premises of the theory is that the brain functions using two modes of processing: **simultaneous** and **sequential processing**. The K-ABC-II includes subtests that assess a student's ability to perceive and process information that is presented sequentially. This means that each stimulus that the child processes is linked to the previous stimulus and must be processed sequentially in order to perform the task or solve the problem. Other subtests include items that must be processed simultaneously, that is, the stimuli must be processed and integrated at the same time in order to perform the task.

The scoring of the K-ABC-II using the Luria model will yield Scale Index scores for Sequential processing, Simultaneous processing, Learning, Planning, and the Mental Processing Index for the general measure of cognitive ability.

The other theoretical base for scoring is based on the Cattell-Horn-Carol theory of intelligence. This theory is founded on three levels or stratums of intellectual ability. The first level is general intellectual functioning, commonly called the *g* factor. The next level is comprised of broad cognitive abilities, and the final level is made up of narrow abilities of cognitive functioning. The CHC theory is sometimes described as broad fluid and crystallized abilities. On the K-ABC-II, scoring according to the CHC theory will provide a Fluid Crystallized Index score for the global cognitive score.

Additional Scale Indexes include Gsm for short-term memory, Gv for visual processing, Glr for learning, Gf for fluid reasoning, and Gc for crystallized ability. Tasks that assess the Gsm processing include those that require short-term and working memory. Tasks that assess Gv are those that require for example, visual memory, spatial relations, spatial screening, and visualization. Tasks that measure Glr require long-term memory and recall. The assessment of the Gf scale requires fluid reasoning or adapting and solving novel problems or figuring out how to do something one has not been exposed to in the past. The Gc scale assesses general information learned from the environment or previous experiences.

Another index that is available for scoring on the K-ABC-II is the Nonverbal Index. This index includes subtests that do not rely heavily on language skills or learned verbal concepts. For example, students may be asked to solve problems that require copying visual patterns using manipulatives or to imitate hand movements. This scale is

---

simultaneous processing
Presenting one stimulus at a time that is processed in sequence and linked to previous stimulus.

sequential processing
Presenting stimuli at the same time to be processed and integrated.

especially appropriate for students who may not have mastery of the English language or may have other language difficulties. It can be used to provide an estimate of cognitive functioning without using subtests that are heavily weighted in language or verbal concepts.

For very young children, only a general cognitive score is available. Either the Fluid Crystallized Index or the Mental Processing Index scores may be obtained.

STANFORD–BINET, FIFTH EDITION

The fifth edition of the Stanford-Binet may be administered to persons ages 2–85+ years (Roid, 2003b). This instrument consists of 10 subtests and can yield a Full Scale IQ score, a Nonverbal IQ score, and a Verbal IQ score. The factors assessed on this instrument include Fluid Reasoning, Knowledge, Quantitative Reasoning, Visual-Spatial Reasoning, and Working Memory. Within each factor or area, a variety of activities are administered to obtain the score for the factors. The activities included within the factors are presented in Figure 9.6, which provides a brief description of the tasks and the performance requirements for them. For example, you will note that the Visual-Spatial Processing factor is assessed verbally and non-verbally. For the nonverbal task requirement, the student works puzzles that are solved using visual-perceptual motor skills. For the verbal task requirement, of the Visual-Spatial Processing factor, the student must respond to questions and problems verbally. The

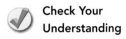

Check Your Understanding

Complete Activity 9.3 below.

Activity 9.3

Answer the following questions about the K-ABC-II.

1. What is the term that means a student processes each bit of information, one bit at a time, and that each new piece of information is linked to the previous bit of information? _____

2. What two broad cognitive abilities are included in the CHC theory of intelligence? _____

3. Which index may be particularly useful when assessing a student who has Spanish as a primary language? _____

4. For very young students, what type of scores are available?
_____

Apply Your Knowledge

What type of information is represented on a test that assesses crystallized intelligence? _____
_____
_____

Figure 9.6   Organization of the Stanford-Binet V.

Factors		Domains	
		Nonverbal (NV)	**Verbal (V)**
	Fluid Reasoning (FR)	**Nonverbal Fluid Reasoning*** Activities: Object Series/ Matrices (Routing)	**Verbal Fluid Reasoning** Activities: Early Reasoning (2–3), Verbal Absurdities (4), Verbal Analogies (5–6)
	Knowledge (KN)	**Nonverbal Knowledge** Activities: Procedural Knowledge (2–3), Picture Absurdities (4–6)	**Verbal Knowledge*** Activities: Vocabulary (Routing)
	Quantitative Reasoning (OR)	**Nonverbal Quantitative Reasoning** Activities: Quantitative Reasoning (2–6)	**Verbal Quantitative Reasoning** Activities: Quantitative Reasoning (2–6)
	Visual-Spatial Processing (VS)	**Nonverbal Visual-Spatial Processing** Activities: Form Board (1–2), Form Patterns (3–6)	**Verbal Visual-Spatial Processing** Activities: Position and Direction (2–6)
	Working Memory (WM)	**Nonverbal Working Memory** Activities: Delayed Response (1), Block Span (2–6)	**Verbal Working Memory** Activities: Memory for Sentences (2–3), Last Word (4–6)

Note: Names of the 10 subtests are in ***bold italic***. Activities include the levels at which they appear.

* = Routing subtests

Organization of the SB5.

Source: Roid, G. H. (2003) Stanford Binet Intelligence Scales, Fifth Edition, Examiner's Manual, p.24. Itasca, IL. Riverside Publishing. Reprinted with permission.

problems for this task involve directional terms or prepositional words for correct responses. Yet both the verbal and nonverbal tasks are concerned with Visual-Spatial Processing.

The categories of IQ scores on the Binet–V are the following:

145–160	Very gifted or highly advanced
130–144	Gifted or highly advanced
120–129	Superior
110–119	High Average
90–109	Average
80–89	Low Average
70–79	Borderline impaired or delayed
55–69	Mildly impaired or delayed
40–54	Moderately impaired or delayed

(Roid, 2003c, p.150)

WOODCOCK–JOHNSON III TESTS OF COGNITIVE ABILITIES

The Woodcock-Johnson III Tests of Achievement are interpreted for general academic areas such as reading, math, and written language. Students may also be assessed in areas such as oral language, academic skills, academic fluency, and phoneme/ grapheme knowledge. The Woodcock-Johnson III Tests of Cognitive Abilities include assessment of areas such as general intellectual ability, cognitive factors like visual-spatial thinking and auditory processing, and clinical clusters such as working memory and phonemic awareness. These two batteries together can provide a comprehensive assessment of cognitive abilities and academic skills.

The cognitive tests, like the achievement measures, are divided into the standard battery and the extended battery. The subtests

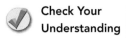

Check Your Understanding

Use the information provided in Figure 9.6 to apply the test results of the Stanford–Binet-V to a case with classroom implications in Activity 9.4 below.

Activity 9.4

Case study using SB–V

The following scores were obtained by a 4th grade student who was referred for learning difficulties following several interventions. After reading the scores below, answer the questions about the student's performance. Refer to your text as needed for information about the SB–V.

	Domains	
	Nonverbal	**Verbal**
Fluid Reasoning	11	9
Knowledge	9	9
Quantitative Reasoning	12	8
Visual-Spatial Processing	14	10
Working Memory	7	7

Composite Profile

Nonverbal	IQ	108
Verbal	IQ	93
Full Scale	IQ	101
Fluid Reasoning		100
Knowledge		92
Quantitative Reasoning		99
Visual-Spatial Reasoning		109
Working Memory		80

1. What areas appear to represent strengths in cognitive processing? _____

2. What areas represent the areas of concern? _____

3. As a teacher, what areas would be of concern to you when thinking about instruction? _____

4. As you look at the domain scores, in what way was the student able to process math best? _____

Apply Your Knowledge

What recommendations would you make to parents about homework assignments that need to be completed at home? _____

_____

_____

included on the standard battery are verbal comprehension, visual-auditory learning, spatial relations, sound blending, concept formation, visual matching, numbers reversed, incomplete words, auditory working memory, and visual-auditory learning-delayed.

The WJ III Tests of Cognitive Abilities, like the achievement tests, are computer scored. The scoring program is easy to use, and comparative data for age and grade norms, confidence intervals, standard scores, and percentile ranks are available.

DETROIT TESTS OF LEARNING APTITUDE–4 (DTLA–4)

The DTLA–4 contains 10 subtests, which are grouped into a variety of composites. These composites include the General Mental Ability Composite, the Optimal Composite, the Domain Composites, and the Theoretical Composites. The General Mental Ability Composite is made up of the scores of all 10 of the subtests. The Optimal Composite is found by using the four highest scores obtained on the individual subtests in an effort to find the "best estimate of a person's overall 'potential'" (Hammill, 1998, p. 20). The Domain Composites include the following four domains: Linguistic Domain, Cognitive Domain, Attentional Domain, and Motoric Domain. The Theoretical Composites comprise a variety of combinations of subtests that the author believes represent assessment of abilities according to theoretical models such as those set forth by Cattell and Horn, Das, Jensen, and Wechsler.

The author presents additional research in this fourth edition of the DTLA in an effort to support the validity of test constructs and theoretical foundation. The research presented is an improvement over previous editions, although the studies do not appear to have been carried out with the same rigor expected of other well-known tests that measure intelligence and abilities.

As suggested by the subtest and composite titles, some of the subtests are verbal, some are presented visually and require fine-motor responses such as reproducing line drawings, and still others require short-term auditory memory and the ability to follow oral directions. This instrument may be used, along with other measures, to document the possibility of distractibility or visual-motor difficulties. This instrument may provide insight into a student's abilities in some areas, although it seems to lack adequate research to stand alone as a measure of intelligence for the purposes of placement and intervention decisions.

KAUFMAN BRIEF INTELLIGENCE TEST (KBIT)

Designed as a screening instrument, the KBIT (Kaufman & Kaufman, 1990) should not be used as part of a comprehensive evaluation to determine eligibility or placement. According to the manual, the test serves to screen students who may be at risk for developing educational problems and who then should receive a comprehensive evaluation. The test takes about 15–30 minutes to administer and consists of two subtests: Vocabulary and Matrices. The Vocabulary subtest has two parts: Expressive and Definitions. These two subtests are designed to measure crystallized intelligence (Vocabulary) and fluid intelligence (Matrices).

NONVERBAL INTELLIGENCE TESTS

Three commonly used measures—the Universal Test of Nonverbal Intelligence, the Comprehensive Test of Nonverbal Intelligence, and

Check Your Understanding

Check your ability to answer questions about measures of cognitive ability by completing Activity 9.5 below.

Activity 9.5

Answer the following questions about the measures of cognitive ability.

1. _____ has a strong theoretical base that includes different ways to interpret the test based on those theories.

2. _____ is the Wechsler Scale that assesses adults.

3. The _____ includes both verbal and nonverbal domains.

4. Which test includes an attentional domain? _____

Apply Your Knowledge

When would a school psychologist give more than one measure of cognitive evaluation for an inital evaluation? _____

_____

_____

the Nonverbal Test of Intelligence, Third Edition, are reviewed here to provide examples of this type of assessment.

UNIVERSAL NONVERBAL INTELLIGENCE TEST

The Universal Nonverbal Intelligence Test (UNIT) is an intellectual assessment measure for children ages 5 years through 17 years 11 months. It includes six subtests and may be given as a standard battery, abbreviated battery, or extended battery (Bracken & McCallum, 1998). The most typical administrations are the standard battery, which includes four subtests, and the extended battery, which includes all subtests. The abbreviated battery of two subtests is given for screening rather than diagnostic purposes. The test measures reasoning and memory skills through the nonverbal presentation of the subtests. The subtest descriptions are presented in Figure 9.7.

The test developers designed this instrument to be a fair measure of intellectual ability for children and adolescents for whom it may be difficult to obtain an accurate estimate of ability on tests that are heavily weighted with verbal items and content. For example, children and adolescents who have hearing impairments, who are from culturally or linguistically diverse environments, or who have not mastered the English language. This assessment instrument may also be a more fair estimate of intellectual ability for students with mental retardation and for students with other disorders that impact verbal communication, such as autism.

In order to present a nonverbal assessment in a manner that does not require spoken language, several gestures for communication during the administration are provided in the manual. For example, palm rolling conveys a message to the student to continue, keep going, or take your turn now. These gestures are illustrated in the manual; the gesture called palm rolling is presented in Figure 9.8.

The possible test scores that can be obtained on the UNIT include scores for the various subtests, scale scores, and a full scale IQ score. The scale scores are for the four scales of memory, reasoning, and symbolic and nonsymbolic concepts. The memory scale assesses not only the storing of information but also the skills and abilities needed for memory, such as attending, encoding, and organization. The reasoning subtest taps into problem-solving ability. The symbolic scale assesses abilities that are believed to be precursors to understanding and using language, and the nonsymbolic scale assesses processing, perception, and integration of information. The symbolic and nonsymbolic scales both assess mediation, or what one does cognitively with the material as it is processed, associated, and retained or used to solve problems.

Figure 9.7   Descriptions of the UNIT subtests.

Overview of the UNIT

Table 1.1	Descriptions of the UNIT Subtests

Symbolic Memory

The examinee views a sequence of universal symbols for a period of 5 seconds. After the stimulus is removed, the examinee re-creates the sequence using the Symbolic Memory Response Cards. Each item is a series of universal symbols for *baby, girl, boy, woman,* and *man,* depicted in green or black. Symbolic Memory is primarily a measure of short-term visual memory and complex sequential memory for meaningful material.

Spatial Memory

The examinee views a random pattern of green, black, or green and black dots on a 3 × 3 or 4 × 4 grid for a period of 5 seconds. After the stimulus is removed, the examinee re-creates the spatial pattern with green and black circular chips on the blank response grid. Spatial Memory is primarily a measure of short-term visual memory for abstract material.

Object Memory

The examinee is presented a random pictorial array of common objects for 5 seconds. After the stimulus is removed, a second pictorial array is presented, containing all of the previously presented objects and additional objects to serve as foils. The examinee recognizes and identifies the objects presented in the first pictorial array by placing response chips on the appropriate pictures. Object Memory is primarily a measure of short-term recognition and recall of meaningful symbolic material.

Cube Design

Cube Design involves the presentation and direct reproduction of two-color, abstract, geometric designs. While viewing the stimulus design, the examinee reconstructs the design directly on the stimulus book or response mat, using green-and-white one-inch cubes. Cube Design is primarily a measure of visual–spatial reasoning.

Analogic Reasoning

Analogic Reasoning presents incomplete conceptual or geometric analogies in a matrix format and requires only a pointing response. The items feature either common objects or novel geometric figures. The examinee completes the matrix analogies by selecting from four response options. Analogic Reasoning is primarily a measure of symbolic reasoning.

Mazes

The examinee uses paper and pencil to navigate and exit mazes by tracing a path from the center starting point of each maze to the correct exit, without making incorrect decisions en route. Increasingly complex mazes are presented. Mazes is primarily a measure of reasoning and planful behavior.

Source: From *The Universal Nonverbal Intelligence Test: Examiner's Manual,* p. 3, by B. A. Bracken and R. S. McCallum, 1998. Itasca, IL: Riverside Publishing Company.

Figure 9.8

Palm Rolling

Source: From *The Universal Nonverbal Intelligence Te*
B. A. Bracken and R. S. McCallum, 1998. Itasca, IL: Riv̷   ̶any.

The subtest scores have a mean of 10̷   ̷ne scales have
quotients with a mean of 100. The standard s̷ ̸res are interpreted
using the following guidelines:

Very superior	>130
Superior	120–130
High average	110–120
Average	90–110
Low average	80–90
Delayed	70–80
Very delayed	>70

Case Study for Intellectual Assessment

Read the following background information about a second-grade
student named Lupita.

Name: Lupita Garcia
Date of Birth: 2-1-1996
Date of Evaluation: 4-6-2004
Age: 8-2
Grade Placement: 2.8

BACKGROUND AND REFERRAL INFORMATION

Lupita is currently enrolled in the second grade at Wonderful
Elementary School. She has been attending this school since
October of the current school year. There was a delay in receiving

om another state and, therefore, it was not
al months that Lupita had been in the referral
er previous school. School records from her previous
ndicate that she has attended three schools since she
ered kindergarten about 3 years ago.

Lupita lives with her mother and father, who until recently were migrant farm workers. Her parents now have full-time employment in the city and plan to make this community their home. Lupita has two older sisters.

Information provided through a home study reveals that all family members speak both English and Spanish. Lupita's mother, who was born in the United States, reported that she learned English while growing up because in school she was not allowed to speak Spanish as her parents did at home. Lupita's father was raised in Mexico, where he attended school until he was 12 years of age. At that time, he stopped going to school in order to work the field with his parents. Mr. Garcia reported that his English is not as good as his wife's, and therefore she helps Lupita with all of her homework assignments.

Mrs. Garcia said that she has taught her children to speak English first because she knew that would be important for school. Although she has emphasized English in the home, Mr. Garcia usually speaks to the children in Spanish. Mr. Garcia is very proud of his daughter's ability to use English so well because he often must rely on his daughters to translate for him when they are in the community.

Lupita's reason for referral is due to academic difficulties in learning to read. The child study team met four times to plan and implement strategies for intervention in an attempt to assist Lupita. Lupita has been receiving additional assistance from the school system's bilingual program. As part of the referral process, Mrs. Garcia completed a home language assessment. The results of that assessment indicate that while both languages are spoken in the home, English is the primary language and is used in approximately 75% of communication within the home. Despite these findings, the team members were not certain about Lupita's mastery of English, particularly at the level required for academic learning and especially in the area of reading.

Following the last meeting of the team, the members agreed, at the urging of Mrs. Garcia, to complete a comprehensive evaluation.

Given the background information about Lupita, the team members decided that the K-ABC-II nonverbal index and the UNIT would yield the most fair estimate of Lupita's intellectual ability.

COMPREHENSIVE TEST OF NONVERBAL INTELLIGENCE (CTONI)

This instrument includes six subtests that may be used with persons ages 6-0 to 89-11 years of age (Hammill, Pearson, & Wiederholt, 1996).

Figure 9.9   Examples of pictorial categories and geometric categories.

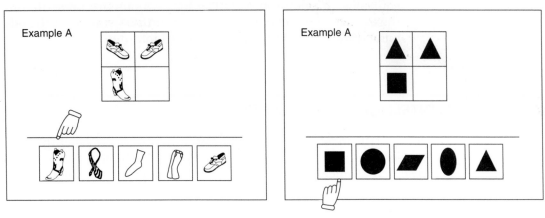

Source: From *Comprehensive Test of Nonverbal Intelligence, Examiner's Manual,* p. 11. *Examiner's Manual for the Comprehensive Test of Nonverbal Intelligence,* by D. D. Hammill, N. A. Pearson, & J. L. Wiederholt, 1997. Austin, Tx: Pro–ED. Reprinted by permission.

The six subtests include: pictorial analogies, geometric analogies, pictorial categories, geometric categories, pictorial sequences, and geometric sequences. Examples of the pictorial and geometric categories are shown in Figure 9.9. The administration of all subtests will yield a nonverbal intelligence composite, the administration of the pictorial subtests will provide a pictorial nonverbal composite, and administration of the geometric subtests will provide a geometric nonverbal intelligence component.

The CTONI has three principal uses according to the authors. It can be used with persons for whom other instruments assessing intelligence would be inappropriate or biased; to make comparisons between verbal measures and nonverbal intelligence; and for research. The authors report that the instrument was developed using multiple theoretical bases rather than a single theory.

This test may be administered by using oral instructions or by presenting the instructions through pantomime. The instrument should be administered through pantomime for all persons who are hearing impaired and for persons who speak a language other than English.

TEST OF NONVERBAL INTELLIGENCE–THIRD EDITION (TONI–3)

This instrument was designed to assess a single cognitive process of solving novel abstract problems (Brown, Sherbenou, & Johnsen, 1997). The authors state that the TONI–3 is a language- and motor-reduced instrument that also reduces cultural influence. It may be used with students ages 6-0 to 89-11. This test includes two equivalent forms, A and B. The instructions are presented to the examinee using pantomime. The authors state that the administration time is approximately 45 minutes.

RESEARCH ON INTELLIGENCE MEASURES

Many of the most popular intelligence measures have recently been revised, and research continues to emerge in the literature. Some research studies on earlier editions and test reviews are summarized here.

1. After an extensive review of evidence in the literature and other sources, Schrank and Flanagan conclude that the WJ–III Tests of Cognitive Ability are well grounded in the CHC theory, or Three Stratum Theory, proposed by Carroll (2003).

2. Miller (2007) reports that the theoretical structure of the WJ–III Tests of Cognitive Ability make this instrument useful in assessing persons referred for school neuropsychological assessment. The abilities assessed on this instrument fall within an assessment model employed in the field of school neuropsychology.

3. Schrank, et al. (2002) noted that the WJ–III Tests of Cognitive Achievement needed additional research to support the use with various clinical groups.

4. Prewett (1992) found that the KBIT's correlation with the WISC–III supports its use as a screening instrument. Prewett and McCaffery (1993) found that the KBIT should be interpreted as only a rough estimate of the IQ that can be obtained on the Stanford–Binet. Kaufman and Wang (1992) found that the differences in means obtained by blacks, Hispanics, and whites on the KBIT are in agreement with mean differences found on the WISC–R. Canivez (1996) found high levels of agreement between the KBIT and the WISC—III in the identification of students with learning disabilities using discrepancies between these measures and the WJ–R.

5. Differences in scores were found between Asian and white children on the K-ABC (Mardell-Czudnowski, 1995). In this study, the Asian children scored higher on the sequential processing scale but showed no differences on the mental processing scales. The achievement scale scores were

higher for children who had previously lived in the United States for at least 4 years.

6. Valencia, Rankin, and Livingston (1995) found evidence of content bias in the items of the K-ABC. In this study, 14% of the items on the Mental Processing scale and 63% of the items on the Achievement scale were determined to be biased against the Mexican American children who participated in the research. These authors suggest that the opportunity to learn specific test content may be the contributing reason for the bias of these items.

7. On the K-ABC, an analysis of data from the standardization sample indicated that the construct validity was similar for both African American and white children (Fan, Wilson, & Reynolds, 1995). This research included four statistical analyses of existing data. An analysis of the data by Keith et al. (1995) determined a similar conclusion.

8. Kaufman, Litchenberger, Fletcher-Janzen, and Kaufman (2005) note that the KABC–II provides limited assessment of expressive language skills and that some clinical comparisons are not possible due to age limitations on specific subtests such as Story Completion and Rover.

9. Several researchers have questioned the factor structure of the WISC–III indicating that there is evidence for the first two factors of verbal comprehension and performance; however, the freedom from distractibility and processing speed factors appear to be weak and perhaps misnamed (Carroll, 1997; Keith & Witta, 1997; Kranzler, 1997; Kush, 1996; Ricco, Cohen, Hall, & Ross, 1997).

10. In one study using the Stanford–Binet IV, students in a general education classroom were found to have more variability in their scores than students already receiving special education services. This may be due in part to the greater degree of homogeneity of the group of students receiving services. Gridley and McIntosh (1991) found that the scores of children aged 2 to 6 years and 7 to 11 years did not support the factor theory purported by the test authors.

11. In a study by Roid and Pomplin (2005), it was found that using the scores for assistance in differential diagnosis between clinical groups, such as distinguishing between students with mental retardation and students with low-functioning autism, could not be done without additional assessment measures. The use of the scores from the Binet IV alone did not differentiate between some clinical groups.

12. In a concurrent validity study, Canivez (1995) found similarities in the WISC–III and KBIT scores. However, he suggested that the KBIT be used only for screening and more comprehensive measures should be used for detailed interpretations of ability. Other researchers have found that the KBIT may be suitable for screening but it is not suitable for determining other comprehensive information (Parker, 1993; Prewett & McCaffery, 1993).

13. Vig and Jedrysek (1996) researched the performance of children with language impairments on the Stanford-Binet and found that the Stanford–Binet IV may be inappropriate for use with 4- and 5-year-olds because of the minimal expectations of this age group on the Binet.

14. In a review of the CTONI, Nicholson warned examiners to use additional assessment instruments when using the CTONI (1998–1999). Nicholson noted that the CTONI does not provide a comprehensive measure of intelligence or nonverbal intelligence.

15. Smith reviewed the KBIT and noted that use of the instrument with persons of different cultural backgrounds may be measuring acculturation rather than ability, especially on the vocabulary subtest (1998–1999). The review also pointed out the strong psychometric characteristics of this screening instrument.

ASSESSING ADAPTIVE BEHAVIOR

Adaptive behavior is a term used to describe how well a student adapts to the environment. The importance of this concept was underscored by the passage of PL 94-142, which contained the requirement of nondiscriminatory assessment-specifically, the mandate to use more than one instrument yielding a single IQ score for diagnosis (*Federal Register*, 1977). The measurement of adaptive behavior must be considered before a person meets the criteria for mental retardation. A student who functions within the subaverage range of intelligence as measured on an IQ test but who exhibits age-appropriate behaviors outside the classroom should not be placed in a setting designed for students with mental retardation.

Adaptive behavior measurement is also emphasized as one possible method of promoting nonbiased assessment of culturally different students (Mercer, 1979; Reschly, 1982). Use of adaptive behavior scales in the assessment of students with learning problems can add another perspective that may be useful in planning educational interventions (Bruininks, Thurlow, & Gilman, 1987; Horn & Fuchs, 1987). Other researchers have found the assessment of adaptive behavior useful in educational interventions for learning-disabled students (Bender & Golden, 1988; Weller, Strawser, & Buchanan, 1985). Adaptive behavior scales are instruments that usually are designed to be answered by a parent or teacher or some other person familiar with the student's functioning in the everyday world. The questions are constructed to obtain information about the student's independent functioning level in and out of school. Many of the items measure self-reliance and daily living skills at home and in the community.

Reschly (1982) reviewed the literature on adaptive behavior and determined that several common features were presented. The measuring of adaptive behavior had the common concepts of (a) developmental appropriateness, (b) cultural context, (c) situational or generalized behaviors, and (d) domains. Reschly found that definitions of adaptive behavior and the measurement of that behavior were based on expectations of a particular age, within the person's culture, and in given or general situations and that the behaviors measured were classified into domains.

Harrison (1987) reviewed research on adaptive behavior and drew the following conclusions:*

1. There is a moderate relationship between adaptive behavior and intelligence.

2. Correlational studies indicate that adaptive behavior has a low relationship with school achievement, but the effect of adaptive behavior on achievement may be greater than the correlations indicate and adaptive behavior in school may have a greater relationship with achievement than adaptive behavior outside school.

3. There is typically a moderate to a moderately high relationship between different measures of adaptive behavior.

4. Adaptive behavior is predictive of certain aspects of future vocational performance.

5. There is a possibility that the use of adaptive behavior scales could result in the declassification of mentally retarded individuals, but no evidence was located to indicate that this is actually happening.

6. There are few race and ethnic group differences on adaptive behavior scales.

7. There are differences between parents' and teachers' ratings on adaptive behavior scales.

*From "Research with Adaptive Behavior Scales" by P. Harrison, 1987, *The Journal of Special Education, 21*, pp. 60–61. Copyright 1987 by PRO–ED, Inc. Reprinted by permission.

8. Adaptive behavior scales differentiate among different classification groups such as normal, mentally retarded, slow learner, learning disabled, and emotionally disturbed.

9. Adaptive behavior scales differentiate among mentally retarded people in different residential and vocational settings.

10. Adaptive behavior is multidimensional.

11. Adaptive behavior can be increased through placement in settings which focus on training adaptive behavior skills.

12. Adaptive behavior scales exhibit adequate stability and interrater reliability.

Although earlier research found that there were differences between parent and teacher ratings on adaptive behavior, Foster-Gaitskell and Pratt (1989) found that when the method of administration and familiarity with the adaptive behavior instrument were controlled, differences between parent and teacher ratings were not significant.

The formal measurement of adaptive behavior began with the development of the Vineland Social Maturity Scale (Doll, 1935). The assessment of adaptive behavior as a common practice in the diagnosis of students, however, did not occur until litigation found fault with school systems for the placement of minority students based only on IQ results (Witt & Martens, 1984). Some researchers feel that the assessment of adaptive behavior in students being evaluated for special education eligibility should not be mandated until further research on adaptive behavior instruments has occurred (Kamphaus, 1987; Witt & Martens, 1984). After reviewing several of the newer adaptive behavior scales, Evans and Bradley-Johnson (1988) cautioned examiners to select instruments carefully because of the low reliability and validity of the instruments. These authors issued the following considerations for professionals using adaptive behavior instruments:[*]

a. Scales must be selected that were standardized using the type of informant to be employed in the assessment (e.g., ABI [Adaptive Behavior Inventory] with teachers and Vineland Survey Form or SIB [Scales of Independent Behavior] with caregivers).

b. If valid information is to be obtained, the response format of the scale must be readily understood by the informant, i.e., not be confusing.

---

[*]From "A Review of Recently Developed Measures of Adaptive Behavior" by L. Evans and S. Bradley-Johnson, 1988, *Psychology in the Schools, 25,* p. 286. Copyright 1988 by Psychology in the Schools. Reprinted by permission.

c. In some cases it will be helpful to select a scale with both normative data on both a nonretarded and a retarded group.

d. If information on maladaptive behavior is desired, only ABS:SE [Adaptive Behavior Scale, School Edition], the SIB, and the Vineland Survey Form address this area.

e. The number of items on subtests of interest should be considered in interpretation to insure that an adequate sample of behavior has been obtained.

f. For eligibility decisions, total test results, rather than subtest scores, should be used. Total test results are based upon a larger sample of behavior and are much more reliable and valid.

g. If different scales are used for the same student, quite different results may be obtained due to many factors, including different response formats, content, and technical adequacy.

h. Different informants (teacher vs. parent) may perceive a student's performance differently due to personal biases and the different demands of the settings.

i. Validity of results must be evaluated in each case based upon problems inherent to rating scales (e.g., informant bias, avoidance of extreme choices).

The examiner should remember these considerations when selecting an adaptive behavior scale and choose the instrument that best suits the needs of the student.

Check Your Understanding

Check your ability to answer questions about adaptive behavior by completing Activity 9.6 below.

Activity 9.6

1. Adaptive behavior is the ability one has to _____.
2. Assessments of adaptive behavior may be used to _____.
3. According to Reschly (1982), what are the four concepts of the assessment of adaptive behavior? _____

Apply Your Knowledge

What are some of the findings summarized by Harrison (1987) about the research of adaptive behavior? _____
_____
_____

REVIEW OF ADAPTIVE BEHAVIOR SCALES

The adaptive behavior scales reviewed in this chapter are the Vineland Adaptive Behavior Scales (Survey Form, Expanded Form, and Classroom Edition), the AAMR Adaptive Behavior Scale— School, Second Edition, the Adaptive Behavior Inventory (ABI and ABI Short Form), and the Adaptive Behavior Inventory for Children. As stated previously, examiners should be cautious in selecting the scale appropriate for the student's needs. Some scales have been normed using special populations only, some scales have been normed using both special and normal populations, and some scales contain items for assessing maladaptive behavior as well as adaptive behavior. The size of the samples used during standardization and the reliability and validity information should be considered.

VINELAND–II: VINELAND ADAPTIVE BEHAVIOR SCALES, SECOND EDITION

A revision of the original Vineland Social Maturity Scale (Doll, 1935), and the Vineland Adaptive Behavior Scales (Sparrow, Balla, & Cicchetti, 1984), this edition of these adaptive behavior scales contain additional items at the lower levels and is consistent with the recommendations of the American Association on Mental Deficiency (Sparrow, Cicchetti, & Balla, 2005). The scales include the Survey Interview Form, the Parent/Caregiver Form, and the Teacher Rating Form. The Parent Form is available in Spanish. The Interview Form and the Parent Rating Form assess the same skills; however, the Parent Form is in a rating scale format.

The Survey and Parent Forms may be used to obtain information about individuals who range in age from 0 to 90 years. The Teacher Form was designed for students ages 3 to 21 years and 11 months. The areas assessed include communication, daily living skills, socialization, motor skills, and an optional maladaptive behavior scale. Computer scoring is available. Scores that are provided using the Vineland–II include scale scores, percentile ranks, standard scores, age equivalents, and domain and adaptive behavior composite scores.

AAMR ADAPTIVE BEHAVIOR SCALE–SCHOOL, SECOND EDITION (ABS–S2)

Test developers constructed the ABS–S2 (Lambert, Nihira, & Leland, 1993) as one method to determine whether persons meet the criteria for the diagnosis of mental retardation. The ABS–S2 is divided into two parts based on (a) independent living skills and (b) social behavior. The domains assessed in each are listed in Figure 9.10.

Figure 9.10   Areas assessed by the AAMR Adaptive Behavior Scale–School, Second Edition.

Part I: Independent Living Domains	Part II: Social Behavior Domains
Independent Functioning	Social Behavior
Physical Development	Conformity
Economic Activity	Trustworthiness
Language Development	Stereotyped and Hyperactive Behavior
Numbers and Time	Self-Abusive Behavior
Prevocational/Vocational Activity	Social Engagement
Self-Direction	Disturbing Interpersonal Behavior
Responsibility	
Socialization	

The person most familiar with the student may administer the scale by completing the items, or a professional who is familiar with the child may complete the items. The information is plotted on a profile sheet to represent the student's adaptive behavior functioning. Standard scores, percentile ranks, and age equivalents are provided in the manual.

INTELLIGENCE AND ADAPTIVE BEHAVIOR: CONCLUDING REMARKS

Intelligence tests for diagnosis of learning problems should be applied with caution. Refer to Tables 9.1 and 9.2 for a summary of the instruments presented in Chapter 9. In addition to the many problems and issues surrounding the use of intelligence tests, the interpretation of test results is largely dependent on the training of the individual examiner. Some professionals believe that appropriate classification can occur only after numerous formal and informal assessments and observations. Others rely on only quantitative test data. Some professionals may use a factor analysis approach to determine learning disabilities, whereas others use informal and curriculum-based achievement measures.

The determination of the classification of mild mental retardation or educational disability is complicated by many social and legal issues. In a review of the problems and practices in the field for the past 20 years, Reschly (1988) advocated the need for a change of focus in the diagnosis and classification of students with mental retardation.

Table 9.1   Instruments for assessment of IQ.

Name of Instrument	Purpose of Test	Constructs Measured	Standardization Information	Reliability Information	Validity Information
Wechsler Intelligence Scale for Children–IV	Assess overall intellectual ability for children ages 6-0 to 16-11	Verbal Comprehension, Perceptual Reasoning, Working Memory, Processing Speed, Full Scale IQ	Sample based on U.S. Census of 2000. Variables include geographic region, ethnicity, gender, age, parental education level.	Adequate to high evidence of split-half reliability, test-retest reliability SEMs, inter-scorer reliability.	Evidence supports validity based on content validity, construct validity, confirmatory factor analysis.
Kaufman Assessment Battery for Children–II	Assess processing and cognitive abilities of children ages 3–18	Fluid/ Crystalized intelligence factors and Mental Processing factors	Total sample of 3,025 children ages 3–18. Variables include sex, age, ethnicity, parental education level, and geographic region.	Evidence of test-retest reliability, internal consistency, SEMs, reliability of nonstandard administration, differences by ethnicity, sex, and parental education level.	Evidence of construct validity, factor analytic data, concurrent criterion-related validity data
Stanford–Binet V	General and specific cognitive and processing abilities	Fluid reasoning, knowledge quantitative reasoning, visual-spatial processing, working memory	Total sample of 4,800 persons in norming and standardization process. Variables considered include sex, age, community size, ethnicity, socioeconomic status, and geographic region.	Internal consistency SEM, test-retest reliability, and interscorer reliability research supports consistency of instrument.	Validity research includes content and construct validity and concurrent criterion-related validity. Factor analytic studies also support validity.

Test	Purpose/Construct	Standardization Sample	Reliability	Validity
Woodcock–Johnson III Tests of Cognitive Ability	Measures cognitive factors, clinical clusters, intracognitive discrepancies. Instrument designed to be used with the WJ III tests of Achievement	Global cognitive ability, specific processing clusters, predicted academic achievement	More than 8,000 persons included in the sample. Variables included ethnicity, community size, geographic region. Adult sample includes educational and occupational variables.	Information regarding test-retest reliability, interrater reliability, alternate forms reliability, and internal consistency reliability included. Most reliability coefficients for internal consistency are reported to be in the .90s.	Concurrent criterion-related validity research included. Evidence of construct and content validity included.
Detroit Tests of Learning Aptitude	General mental processing composites of cognitive skills	General mental composite, linguistic, attention, and motor domains	1,350 students in 37 states were included. Demographic variables considered were gender, rural or urban community, race (white, black, other), ethnicity (African American, Hispanic, Native American, or other), and geographic region. Family income, educational attainment of parents, disability status, and age (6 years to 17 years of age) were also considered.	Internal consistency coefficients were calculated using coefficient alpha and ranged from .71 to .97. Test-retest reliability yielded coefficients ranging from .71 to .99 when compared across the various age groups.	Content validity, criterion-related validity, and construct validity information are presented in the manual.

continued.

Table 9.1 continued.

Name of Instrument	Purpose of Test	Constructs Measured	Standardization Information	Reliability Information	Validity Information
Universal Nonverbal Intelligence Test	Assesses nonverbal reasoning and cognitive abilities	Memory, reasoning, symbolic mediation, nonsymbolic mediation	The standardization sample included more than 2,000 students, with the variables of sex, age, race, Hispanic origin, region, parental educational level, and general or special education placement.	A sample of 1,765 children participated in the reliability and validity studies. Evidence of internal consistency in general, clinical, and special samples, test-retest reliability.	A sample of 1,765 children participated in the reliability and validity studies. Evidence of content validity, confirmatory factor analysis, concurrent criterion-related validity.
Comprehensive Test of Nonverbal Intelligence	Assesses various nonverbal cognitive abilities	Nonverbal analogies, categories, and sequences	The norm sample of the CTONI included 2,901 persons in 30 states. The characteristics of geographic area, gender, race (white, black, other) urban/rural residence, ethnicity (Native American, Hispanic, Asian, African American, other), family income, and parents' educational level were considered in the norm sample.	Reliability information was provided for internal consistency, standard error of measurement, test-retest reliability, and interrater reliability. All coefficients were within the adequate to high range.	Validity information for content validity, including analyses of the content validity of other measures of nonverbal intelligence, relationship to theories of intelligence, item analysis, and differential item functioning analysis.

| Test of Nonverbal Intelligence—Third Edition | Brief measure of nonverbal cognitive ability | Abstract problem-solving skills of nonverbal items | A total of 3,451 persons representing 28 states were included in the norming sample. The demographic considerations in the norming process were based on the 1997 *Statistical Abstracts of the United States* (U.S. Bureau of the Census, 1997). These factors included geographic region, gender, race (white, black, other), residence (urban/rural), ethnicity (Native American, Hispanic, Asian, African American, and other), disability status (no disability, learning disability, speech-language disorder, mental retardation, other disability). In addition, the family income of parents, educational level of parents, and educational level of adult subjects were considered. | Evidence of reliability includes internal consistency measures using coefficient alpha and standard error of measurement, alternate forms reliability, test-retest reliability, and interrater reliability. All reliability coefficients presented in the manual were within the .90s. | Adequate evidence of content validity, criterion-related validity, and some evidence of construct validity. |

Table 9.2 Adaptive behavior instruments.

Name of Instrument	Purpose of Test	Constructs Measured	Standardization Information	Reliability Information	Validity Information
Vineland–II	Assesses adaptive behavior for persons ranging in age from 0 to 90	Communication, daily living skills, socialization, motor skills, and maladaptive behavior	The standardization sample for the Vineland included 3,695 persons ranging in age from birth to 18-11 years. Variables considered in the sample were sex, geographic region, parental educational level, race or ethnic group, community size, educational placement and age. Additional clinical groups who were also in norm group included students with ADHD, emotional disturbance, learning disabilities, mental retardation, noncategorical developmentally delayed, speech and/or language impaired, and other (such as OHI, multiple disabilities)	Evidence of split-half, test-retest, and interrater reliability. Reliability coefficients range from adequate to high.	Information included construct validity, content validity, and criterion-related validity studies. Construct validity was based on developmental progression and factor analysis of domains and subdomains. Content validity information also provided.

Vineland Adaptive Behavior–Expanded Form	Expanded form of adaptive behavior assessment	More detailed assessment of communication, daily living skills, socialization, motor skills, and maladaptive behavior.	The same norming sample used for the expanded form	The manual reports on reliability studies using split-half, test-retest, and interrater reliability measures. Split-half reliability coefficients were in the .80s for the standardization sample, and in the .80s and .90s for supplementary norms. Information for the test-retest and interrater reliability is based on the Survey Form information.	Information given includes construct validity, content validity, and criterion-related validity. Studies were based on the Survey Form, and discussion of estimating coefficients for the Expanded Form is included.
AAMR–Adaptive Behavior Scale–2	Assessment of adaptive behavior	Independent living skills and social skills	The ABS–S2 was normed on a sample of 2,074 persons with mental retardation and 1,254 persons who were nondisabled. The variables of race, gender, ethnicity, urban and rural residence, geographic region, and age (3–18) were considered in the sample.	Information on interrater reliability, internal consistency, and test-retest reliability is presented in the manual. All coefficients presented range from adequate to high.	The examiner's manual addresses construct and item validity for students with and without mental retardation.

The classification system reforms advocated would place more emphasis on three dimensions: (1) severe, chronic achievement deficits; (2) significantly deficient achievement across most if not all achievement areas; and (3) learning problems largely resistant to regular interventions. The students meeting these criteria will be virtually the same as the current population with MMR; however, their classification will not carry the stigma of comprehensive incompetence based on biological anomaly that is permanent. (p. 298)

For **MORE PRACTICE** in understanding intellectual and adaptive behavior assessment, visit the Companion Website at *www. prenhall.com/overton.*

THINK AHEAD

This text has been concerned primarily with the assessment of students within school age, typically from about age 6 to 18. Students who require the assistance of special education services as part of their educational intervention often require services during preschool years and have additional needs for postsecondary years. The assessment of students in the years of early childhood and in the years requiring special considerations for transition to adulthood are presented in Chapter 10.

EXERCISES

Part I

Select the terms to complete the statements that follow.

a. intelligence
b. adaptive behavior
c. IQ
d. achievement
e. bidialectal
f. traditional measures of IQ

g. nonverbal
h. acculturation
i. multiple intelligences
j. environmental influence
k. dynamic assessment

_____ 1. Because many of the instruments used to assess intelligence and achievement include numerous items of a verbal nature, the assessment of students whose primary language is not English should be given a _____ measure _____ in addition to other measures.

_____ 2. IDEA includes statements of determining eligibility that require the team to exclude _____ as the primary reason for a disability before determining a student as eligible for special education services.

_____ 3. Minority students who may appear to be within the range of mental retardation on measures developed for use with students from the majority culture may not be within the range of mental retardation on _____ measures.

_____ 4. Students who have a dominant language other than English are often referred to as being bilingual, and students whose primary language is English and nonstandard English are referred to as _____.

_____ 5. Bilingual students may have difficulty with both the language items on standardized assessments and the level of _____ required to perform well on the items.

_____ 6. Once the standardized assessment has been completed, an examiner may use the method of _____, incorporating teaching, to determine the student's potential to learn the failed items.

_____ 7. The measure of this is actually a ratio comparing a student's mental age and chronological age.

Companion
Website

Answers to these questions can be found in the Appendix of this text or you may also complete these questions and receive immediate feedback on your answers by going to the Think Ahead module in Chapter 9 of the Companion Website.

Special Considerations of Assessment in Early Childhood and Transition

Public Law 99-457
developmental delay
at risk for developmental delay
biological risk factors
environmental risk factors
Individual Family Service Plan
family-centered program
family-focused program
expressive language disorders
receptive language disorders
play evaluations
arena assessment

interactive strategies
observations
situational questionnaires
ecobehavioral interviews
phonemic awareness
phonemic synthesis
phonemic analysis
autism spectrum disorders
assistive technology
assistive technology evaluation
transition planning
supported employment

CHAPTER FOCUS

The assessment process included thus far in the text concerns primarily the assessment of students of school age. This chapter includes the issues and procedures needed to assess very young children and older students with transition needs. The assessment of infants and young children involves different procedures and methods from assessment of school-aged children. Federal regulations require that much of the assessment process include extensive interviews with parents and that the family needs be considered. Federal regulations also require additional procedures to assist students and parents with the transition from school to adulthood. These methods and issues are presented in this chapter.

CEC KNOWLEDGE AND SKILLS STANDARDS

The student completing this chapter will understand the knowledge and skills included in the following CEC Knowledge and Skills Standards from Standard 8: Assessment:

GCK8K2—Laws and policies regarding referral and placement procedures for individuals with disabilities

GCK8K3—Types and importance of information concerning individuals with disabilities available from families and public agencies

GCK84—Procedures for early identification of young children who may be at risk for disabilities

CC8S1—Gather relevant background information

GC8S2—Use exceptionality specific assessment instruments with individuals with disabilities

LEGAL GUIDELINES OF EARLY CHILDHOOD EDUCATION

Public Law 99-457
IDEA amendments
that extend services
for special-needs
children through
infancy and
preschool years;
mandates services
for children ages 3–5
with disabilities.

Public Law 99-457 is the law that set forth many of the guidelines and provisions of serving infants and toddlers. Many of the guidelines were incorporated into the 1997 amendments. The assessment of infants and young children presents several issues and concerns not found in the assessment of school-age children. Many of these issues are related to the young age of the child. For example, these young children present unique challenges in assessment because they must be evaluated in domains and areas that are not based on school-related competencies such as academic achievement. These children are evaluated in other areas such as physical challenges, developmental motor skills, functional communication skills, behaviors in specific situations, and developmental competence. The assessment of young children and infants also includes the unique component of family needs and a family plan for appropriate intervention.

IDEA provides for educational intervention for children beginning at age 3. Part C of the IDEA Amendments of 1997 authorizes funding to states for intervention for special-needs infants and toddlers. The aspects of IDEA that pertain to the assessment of infants, toddlers, and preschool children are presented in the following section.

INFANTS, TODDLERS, AND YOUNG CHILDREN

Federal regulations define the population of children eligible to be served, define the methods of assessment, provide procedural safeguards, and outline procedures to be used for intervention based on the family's needs.

developmental delay When an infant or child experiences delay in physical, cognitive, communicative, social, emotional, or adaptive development.

at risk for developmental delay When a child is believed to be at risk for delay in one or more areas if interventions are not provided.

ELIGIBILITY

Infants and toddlers from birth to age 2 who are experiencing **developmental delays** in one or more of the following areas are eligible for services: cognitive development, physical development (includes vision and hearing), communication development, social or emotional development, and adaptive development. Infants and toddlers may also be eligible for services if they have a diagnosed physical or mental condition that is likely to result in developmental delay. The law gives the individual states discretion to determine the lead agency to provide services for infants and toddlers with special needs. The states also have the option to provide services for children 3 years of age and younger considered to be **at risk for developmental delay** unless the child has appropriate interventions.

Children eligible for early childhood services are those with the same disabilities defined for school-aged children: autism, deaf-blindness, deafness, hearing impairment, mental retardation, multiple disabilities, orthopedic impairment, other health impairment, serious emotional disturbance, specific learning disability, speech or language impairment, traumatic brain injury, and visual impairment. Infants and toddlers who have a diagnosed physical or mental condition that is known to have a high probability of resulting in developmental delay are also eligible (IDEA Amendments, 1997).

Although not all states choose to serve infants and toddlers who are at risk for developmental delays, many states have responded to this category of infants and toddlers and provide intervention services. Katz (1989) lists as **biological risk factors** "prematurity associated with low birth weight, evidence of central nervous system involvement (intraventricular hemorrhage, neonatal seizures), prolonged respiratory difficulties, prenatal maternal substance use or abuse" (p. 100). These risk factors may not always result in an early diagnosed physical condition but may prove problematic as the child develops.

biological risk factors Health factors, such as birth trauma, that place a child at risk for developmental disabilities.

In addition to biological risk factors, **environmental risk factors** often exist. The most often cited environmental risk factors found by Graham and Scott (1988) are poor infant/child interaction patterns, low maternal educational level, young maternal age, disorganization or dysfunction of the family, and few family support networks. Suggestions for assessing infants at risk are given later in this chapter.

environmental risk factors Environmental influences, such as the mother's young age, that place a child at risk for developmental disabilities.

EVALUATION AND ASSESSMENT PROCEDURES

The 1997 IDEA Amendments define evaluation as the ongoing procedures used by qualified personnel to determine the child's eligibility and continued eligibility while the child is served under this law. The amendments state that

§ 636
a. ...the state shall provide, at a minimum for each infant or toddler with a disability, and the infant's or toddler's family, to receive—
   1. a multidisciplinary assessment of the unique strengths and needs of the infant or toddler and the identification of services appropriate to meet such needs;
   2. a family-directed assessment of the resources, priorities, and concerns of the family and the identification of the supports and services necessary to enhance the family's capacity to meet the developmental needs of the infant or toddler. (IDEA Amendments of 1997, p. 62)

Individual Family Service Plan (IFSP) Plan required by PL 99-457 that includes the related needs of the family of the child with disabilities.

The regulations require that an IFSP, or **Individual Family Service Plan**, be developed for each infant or toddler and its family. This family service plan shall include

1. a statement of the infant's or toddler's present levels of physical development, cognitive development, communication development, social or emotional development, and adaptive development, based on objective criteria;
2. a statement of the family's resources, priorities, and concerns relating to enhancing the development of the family's infant or toddler with a disability;
3. a statement of the major outcomes expected to be achieved for the infant or toddler and the family, and the criteria, procedures, and timelines used to determine the degree to which progress toward achieving the outcomes is being made and whether modifications or revisions of the outcomes or services are necessary;

 **Check Your Understanding**

Check your ability to define terms used in the discussion of serving infants and toddlers by completing Activity 10.1.

Activity 10.1

Complete the sentences using the following terms.

> developmental delay
> at risk for developmental delay
> family's
> 6 months
> IFSP

1. Family assessment includes determining the _____ priorities and concerns related to enhancing the development of the child.
2. A child with _____ may be measured by the appropriate instruments and found in one or more of the following areas: cognitive development, physical development, communication development, social or emotional development, adaptive development.
3. _____ must incorporate the family's description of its resources, priorities, and concerns related to the development of the child.
4. The time set for a review of the IFSP of infants and young children is _____.

Apply Your Knowledge

Explain why the family involvement is emphasized in both the assessment stage and the development and implementation of the IFSP.

_____

_____

_____

4. a statement of specific early intervention services necessary to meet the unique needs of the infant or toddler and the family, including the frequency, intensity, and method of delivering services. (IDEA Amendments of 1997, pp. 62–63)

In addition, this plan must include a statement detailing how the services will be provided within the child's natural environment and to what extent any services will not be provided in the child's natural environment. The plan must also include the anticipated dates for the services to begin and a statement about the expected duration of the services. The coordinator of the services must be named, and the steps that will be taken to transition the child to preschool or other services must be outlined (IDEA Amendments, 1997).

The amendments require that the IFSP be reviewed every 6 months (or more frequently as appropriate) and the family given the review of the plan. The IFSP must be evaluated at least once a year.

The assessment of infants and young children must also follow IDEA's regulations concerning nondiscriminatory assessment, parental consent, confidentiality, and due process procedural safeguards. The law requires annual evaluation of progress but notes that because of the rapid development during this period of a child's life, some evaluation procedures may need to be repeated before the annual review.

ISSUES AND QUESTIONS ABOUT SERVING INFANTS AND TODDLERS

A goal of PL 99-457 was to incorporate family members as partners in the assessment of and planning for the infant or child with developmental disabilities. Since the law's passage in 1986, many concerns have been raised by clinical practitioners working with these regulations. Of chief concern is the role of the parents in the assessment and planning process (Dunst, Johanson, Trivette, & Hamby, 1991; Goodman & Hover, 1992; Katz, 1989; Minke & Scott, 1993).

The issues raised by Goodman and Hover include confusion with the interpretation and implementation of the family assessment component. The regulations may be misunderstood as requiring mandatory assessment of family members rather than voluntary participation by the parents. The family's strengths and needs as they relate to the child, not the parents themselves, are the objects of the assessment. Furthermore, these authors contended that a relationship based on equal standing between parents and professionals may not result in a greater degree of cooperation and respect than the traditional client-professional relationship. When the parents and professionals are viewed as equal partners, the professional surrenders the role of expert. Goodman and Hover suggested that the relationship be viewed as reciprocal rather than egalitarian. An assessment process directed by the parents may not be in the child's best interest, because the parents retain the right to restrict professional inquiry.

Katz (1989) observed that the family's view of the child's most important needs takes precedence over the priorities perceived by the professional team members. In some instances, parents and professionals must negotiate to agree on the goals for the child. The family will be more motivated to achieve the goals that they believe are important.

The law clearly states that the IFSP be developed with parent participation. This is true whether or not the family participates in the assessment process. In practice, parent participation varies, according to a study of the development of IFSPs in three early-childhood intervention programs (Minke & Scott, 1993). This study found that parents do not always participate in goal setting for their children, play a listening role without soliciting input from professionals, appear to need better explanations by professionals, and may become better child advocates with early participation. These issues are similar to issues associated with parent participation during eligibility meetings for school-aged children (refer to Chapter 2).

Differences in the implementation of PL 99-457 may be the result of state-determined policies and procedures. One area of difference seems to be in the interpretation of how families should be involved in the early intervention process. Dunst et al. (1991) described the

family-centered program Program in which the assessment and goals are driven by the family's needs and priorities.

family-focused program Program in which the family's needs are considered but goals and plans are reached through mutual agreement between the family and education professionals.

family-centered program and the **family-focused program** as paradigms representing two such interpretations. In the family-centered program paradigm, family concerns and needs drive the assessment, anything written on the IFSP must have the family's permission, and the family's needs determine the actual roles played by case managers. The family-focused program paradigm restricts assessment to the family's needs only as they relate to the child's development, the goals are agreed on mutually by professionals and parents, and the case manager's role is to encourage and promote the family's use of professional services. It seems clear that the interpretation and implementation of PL 99-457 differ from state to state and may yet be problematic.

Another type of assessment of young children and their families, called Intervention-Based Multifactored Evaluation, has been proposed (Barnett, Bell, Gilkey, Lentz, Graden, Stone, Smith, & Macmann, 1999). These authors suggest that the assessment and eligibility process should be directly linked to the level of interventions required for instruction. Further, these authors believe that a child should be found eligible for services only when there are notable discrepancies between the child's ability and the peers within the environment. For example, the target child may have discrepancies between the level of assistance required and the rate of learning, the level of caregiver monitoring, or the adaptations of the curriculum, when compared to age peers. When these differences require more time or adaptation than can be accomplished within the general educational environment, special education support services are required. These authors propose a data collection method across tasks and behaviors, similar to the assessment methods used in curriculum-based measurement and in functional behavioral assessments. This method of assessment would be within the spirit of the federal regulations, which require that assessment results be linked directly to interventions.

In addition to involvement of the family in the assessment process, the Division of Early Childhood, or DEC, of the Council for Exceptional Children (CEC) recommends that all assessment be developmentally appropriate, include familiar environments and people, and be functional (Sandall, Hemmeter, Smith, & McLean, 2005). An assessment is considered functional when data is collected

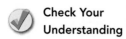

Check Your Understanding

Check your ability to answer questions about IFSPs and serving infants and toddlers by completing Activity 10.2 below.

Activity 10.2

Answer the questions and complete the sentences.

1. What five areas of child development must the IFSP address? _____

2. The IFSP must include the expected _____ of the interventions and the degree to which _____ toward achieving them is being made.

3. In which of the program paradigms does the parent play a more active role in the assessment and planning process? _____

4. According to Minke and Scott (1993), parents may need better _____ from professionals.

5. Katz (1989) stated that in some instances, parents and professionals must _____ on goals for the child.

6. According to Goodman and Hover (1992), when assessment is directed by the parents, what problems may occur? _____

7. What are the assessment recommendations of the Division of Early Childhood? _____

Apply Your Knowledge

Discuss how the IFSP must balance the parents' and child's needs.
_____
_____
_____

in situations that are common in the child's daily routine. This type of assessment will result in more reliable and valid information.

An issue in the implementation of services for infants and toddlers is the identification of young children. A study by Snyder, Bailey, and Auer (1994) found that when children were identified, they may be identified differently than school-aged children. Snyder et al. found that 72% of the states used determination systems that included combinations or noncategorical systems.

METHODS OF EARLY-CHILDHOOD ASSESSMENT

As previously noted, many states serve children who are considered at risk for developmental disabilities. The discussion of assessment methods presented in this text applies to children with existing developmental disabilities as well as to those who may be at risk for developmental disabilities if they do not receive early childhood intervention.

Regulations require that qualified personnel assess children in many developmental areas; for example, assessments of vision, hearing, speech, and medical status are part of a multifactored evaluation. Detailed assessment in these areas is beyond the scope of this text. Measures presented include behavior questionnaires, observations, interviews, checklists, and measures of cognitive and language functioning. Techniques used in the assessment process are also presented.

ASSESSMENT OF INFANTS

Documenting developmental milestones and health history is primarily the responsibility of health professionals. Infants may be suspected of having developmental delays or of being at risk for developmental delays if there are clinical indications of concern. Mayes (1991) cited the following indications of need for an infant assessment:

1. Regulatory disturbances—Sleep disturbances, excessive crying or irritability, eating difficulties, low frustration tolerance, self-stimulatory or unusual movements.

2. Social/environmental disturbances—Failure to discriminate mother, apathetic, withdrawn, no expression of affect or interest in social interaction, excessive negativism, no interest in objects or play, abuse, neglect, or multiple placements, repeated or prolonged separations.

3. Psychophysiological disturbances—Nonorganic failure to thrive, recurrent vomiting or chronic diarrhea, recurrent dermatitis, recurrent wheezing.

4. Developmental delays—Specific delays (gross motor, speech delays). General delays or arrested development. (p. 445)

The prenatal, birth, and early neonatal health history is an important component of the evaluation of infants and is required by PL 99-457. Following the careful history taking of the infant's health factors, Greenspan (1992) organizes the infant/toddler/young child assessment using the following factors:

1. Prenatal and perinatal variables.

2. Parent, family, and environmental variables.

3. Primary caregiver and caregiver/infant-child relationship.

4. Infant variables: Physical, neurologic, physiologic, and cognitive.

5. Infant variables: Formation and elaboration of emotional patterns and human relationships. (pp. 316–317)

Of particular concern in assessing the infant are regulatory patterns, or how the infant reacts to stimuli in the environment and processes sensory information (Greenspan, 1992; Mayes, 1991). This includes how the infant interacts with and reacts to caregivers, the infant's sleeping habits, level of irritability, and so on. This type of assessment relies on observations using checklists and parent interviews or questionnaires. One commonly used observation assessment instrument for newborn infants is the Neonatal Behavioral Assessment Scale (Brazelton, 1984), which includes both reflex items and behavioral observation items. Use of this scale to determine control states (such as sleeping, alert) underscores the importance of this aspect of infant behavior to more complex functions, such as attention (Mayes, 1991). This scale can be used with infants up to 1 month of age.

The Uzgiris-Hunt Ordinal Scales of Psychological Development (Uzgiris & Hunt, 1975) present a Piagetian developmental perspective for assessment during the first 2 years of the infant's life. These six scales include assessment for such skills as visual pursuit, object permanence, manipulation of and interaction with factors in the environment, development of vocal and gestural imitation, and development of schemes for relating to the environment. This instrument requires the use of several objects and solicitation of reactions and responses of the infant. This system, a comprehensive assessment based on the Piagetian model, has been criticized for being developed using primarily infants from middle-class families (Mayes, 1991).

Another instrument used to assess young children and toddlers (ages 1–42 months) is the Bayley Scales of Infant Development-II

(Bayley, 1993). This revised formal instrument now includes in the manual improved statistical research regarding reliability and validity. Like most infant/toddler instruments, the Bayley requires the examiner to manipulate objects and observe the reactions and behavior of the infant. The scale assesses mental functions such as memory, problem solving, verbal ability, and motor functions such as coordination and control; it also includes a behavioral rating scale. In addition to the standardization sample, clinical samples were included in the development of this revision. The clinical samples included infants and young children who were premature, HIV positive, exposed prenatally to drugs, or asphyxiated at birth, and those who had Down syndrome, autism, developmental delays, or otitis media.

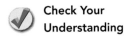

Check Your Understanding

Check your knowledge of assessment instruments used in serving infants and toddlers by completing Activity 10.3 below.

Activity 10.3

Match the following terms with the correct descriptions.

A. Uzgiris-Hunt Ordinal Scales of Psychological Development

B. Bayley Scales of Infant Development–II

C. Neonatal Behavioral Assessment Scale

D. regulatory disturbances

E. infant variables

F. developmental delays

1. This measure of infant assessment is used to determine the possible risk of developmental disabilities of infants from birth to 1 month of age _____.

2. These include physical, neurological, and emotional factors that influence the child's development _____.

3. This instrument is based on Piagetian developmental theory and is used for infants through 2 years of age _____.

4. These include sleep disturbances, irritability, and unusual movements _____.

5. This revised instrument includes research on several clinical samples and is used for children aged 1 to 42 months _____.

Apply Your Knowledge

How do you think regulatory disturbances might influence a child's ability to learn? _____

_____

_____

ASSESSMENT OF TODDLERS AND YOUNG CHILDREN

Many of the instruments discussed in earlier chapters contain basal-level items for toddlers and young children, including the K-ABC-II, WJ III Tests of Achievement, Vineland Adaptive Behavior Scales, Achenbach's Child Behavior Checklist, and Stanford-Binet V. Following is a brief survey of some of the most commonly used and newest instruments that are specifically designed to assess the development and behavior of young children. Instruments that assess general developmental ability of toddlers and young children can also be used to collect additional data to determine the likelihood of disorders in language. For example, young children may appear to have global developmental delays; however, assessment of general development may indicate development is progressing as expected with the exception of language disorders, such as **expressive** or **receptive language disorders**.

expressive language disorders Significant difficulty with oral expression.

receptive language disorders Significant difficulty understanding spoken language.

MULLEN SCALES OF EARLY LEARNING: AGS EDITION

This instrument assesses the cognitive functioning of children ages birth through 68 months (Mullen, 1995) and is to be used by assessment personnel with experience in the evaluation of infants and young children. The test author estimates the test administration time to range from 15 minutes to 60 minutes depending on the age of the child. The instrument uses many common manipulative objects to assess the child's gross motor, visual, fine-motor, and receptive and expressive language abilities.

The theoretical basis of the test design is included in the manual and is presented in developmental stages. The expectations of a given developmental stage are listed, followed by the tasks used to assess each of the expected developmental indicators. For example, at stage 2–4 months 0 days to 6 months 30 days—a child's vision is refined and visual reception is assessed using the following items: stares at hand, localizes on objects and people, looks for an object in response to a visual stimulus followed by an auditory stimulus.

Technical Data

Norming Process The manual provides information regarding the standardization process, which included 1,849 children. The standardization process was completed over an 8–year time span and was conducted within the south, northeast, west, north, and south-central regions. The variables of gender, ethnicity, race, age, and community size were considered in construction of the sample.

Reliability   The reliability studies contained in the manual were split-half reliability for internal consistency, test-retest reliability, and interscorer reliability. The reliability coefficients ranged from adequate and low/adequate to high. This may in part reflect the instability of developmental scores at the very early ages. Several of the sample sizes used in the reliability studies for some ages were small (38 for test-retest of the gross motor scale for ages 1 to 24 months).

Validity   Evidence of construct validity, concurrent validity, and exploratory factor analyses is presented in the examiner's manual. The research regarding developmental progression to support the constructs being measured suggests validity of the scales as developmental indicators.

THE WECHSLER PRESCHOOL AND PRIMARY SCALE OF INTELLIGENCE, 3RD EDITION

The Wechsler Preschool and Primary Scale of Intelligence, 3rd Edition (WPPSI-III) was developed for use with children ages 2 years and 6 months of age to age 7 years and 3 months. This test provides three composite scores of intellectual ability: Verbal Intelligence Quotient, Performance Intelligence Quotient, and Full Scale Intelligence Quotient.

Test developers note that the recent revision of this instrument focused on five major goals. These goals were to:

- update theoretical foundations
- increase developmental appropriateness
- enhance clinical utility
- improve psychometric properties, and
- increase user-friendliness (Wechsler, 2002, p. 10).

In an effort to meet these goals, the revised instrument has items for younger children and increased the number of items for the younger and older age groups. This instrument now has more comprehensive measures of fluid reasoning than the previous edition. The instructions for both the child and the examiner have been improved by including easier to understand instructions for the child and more clear instructions for the examiner. Moreover, this revised edition includes additional items for teaching and expanded and additional queries.

The WPPSI-III has separate subtests for the major age divisions. The age divisions include children ages 2 years 6 months to 3 years 11 months and children ages 4 years to 7 years and 3 months. The third edition of the WPPSI is organized in the following manner:

For ages 2 years and 6 months to 3 years and 11 months—Children are administered the following Core Subtests and may be administered the following Supplemental subtest:

Core Subtests   For the Verbal IQ:

Receptive Vocabulary   On this subtest the child is presented 4 pictures and asked to identify 1 of those pictures. This subtest may be influenced by auditory and visual memory.

Information   This subtest assesses the child's previously learned factual information. The child's responses may be influenced by experiences and environment.
For the Performance IQ:

Block Design   This subtest requires the child to copy a visual pattern and assesses the child's ability to use visual motor skills and visual organizational skills. This subtest is a core subtest for all age groups.

Object Assembly   This is a timed subtest that is a core subtest for the younger age group and a supplemental subtest for the older age group. Children are required to complete a series of puzzles. This task may be influenced by visual perceptual, visual spatial, and visual motor organizational skills. This taps into the child's ability to analyze pieces of a whole and to construct the whole object.

Supplemental Subtest

Picture Naming   This is a supplemental subtest for the younger age group and an optional subtest for the older age group. On this subtest, the child is presented with pictures and is asked to name the picture. This subtest may be influenced by visual and auditory long term memory, word knowledge, and expressive language skills.
For ages 4 years to 7 years and 3 months—Children are administered the following Core Subtests and may be administered the following Supplemental subtests and optional subtests:

Core Subtests   For the Verbal IQ:

Information   This subtest assesses the child's previously learned factual information. The child's responses may be influenced by experiences and environment. This is a required core subtest for all age divisions.

Vocabulary   This subtest requires the student to respond to items assessing basic word knowledge and may be influenced by the child's previous experience and environment. These items are a measure of long term memory for verbal information.

Word Reasoning   This subtest assesses verbal knowledge and reasoning skills.

For the Performance IQ:

Block Design   This subtest requires the child to copy a visual pattern and assesses the child's ability to use visual motor skills and visual organization skills. This subtest is a core subtest for all age groups.

Matrix Reasoning   The skills visual processing and abstract reasoning may influence the child's ability to successfully complete these tasks. This subtest presents visual stimuli consisting of an incomplete matrix. The child is asked to scan several choices and select the missing piece from those choices.

Picture Concepts   The child is shown rows of pictures and then asked to select another picture with the same characteristics. The child's performance on this subtest may be influenced by visual reasoning and visual conceptual memory.

Coding   The Coding Subtest contributes to a Full Scale IQ but not to the Verbal or Performance IQ.

Supplemental Subtests

Comprehension   This subtest is largely influenced by verbal concepts learned from previous experiences and also requires practical knowledge and the ability to reason or analyze specific situations.

Picture Completion   This subtest assesses the child's ability to scan pictures and determine what essential detail is missing.

Similarities   This subtest uses a sentence completion format to assess the child's ability to analyze how 2 things are alike.

Object Assembly   Children are required to complete a series of puzzles. This task may be influenced by visual perceptual, visual spatial, and visual motor organizational skills. This taps into the child's ability to analyze pieces of a whole and construct the whole object.

Additional optional subtests are included for the older age division. These subtests are:

Receptive Vocabulary   This is a core subtest for the younger age division and presents the same task demands for the older age group as the younger age group.

Picture Naming On this subtest, the child is presented with pictures and is asked to name the picture. This subtest may be influenced by visual and auditory long-term memory, word knowledge, and expressive language skills.

Technical Data Norming Process—During the development of this revision, children from the general population and special clinical groups were assessed. The standardization sample included 1,700 children in stratified age groups from age 2 years 6 months to 7 years and 3 months. The variables considered in the norm group included age, sex, race/ethnicity (white, African American, Hispanic, Asian, other), parental education level, and geographic region. The standardization sample was selected to correspond with the 2000 U.S. Census.

The special groups studied during the development of the test include the following groups: intellectually gifted, mental retardation, developmental delay, at risk, developmental risk factors, autistic disorder, expressive language delay, mixed expressive-receptive language delay, limited English proficiency, attention deficit/hyperactivity disorder, and motor impairment.

Reliability The manual provides evidence of adequate internal consistency as measured by split-half reliability for both age divisions and the overall standardization sample. The manual includes evidence of small standard errors of measurement across age groups. Test-retest stability and interrater reliability are adequate.

Validity Evidence of validity is presented in the manual and includes measures of criterion-related validity, confirmatory factor analysis, and validity of use with special groups. The evidence presented indicates that the WPPSI-III successfully discriminates between the special groups and the norm sample. The manual presents a discussion of the study of content validity.

AGS EARLY SCREENING PROFILES

The AGS Early Screening Profiles (Harrison et al., 1990) present a comprehensive screening for children aged 2 to 6-11 years. The battery contains items that are administered directly to the child and surveys that are completed by parents, teachers, or both. The components, shown in Figure 10.1, are described in the following paragraphs.

Components

Cognitive/Language Profile The child demonstrates verbal abilities by pointing to objects named or described by the examiner,

Figure 10.1 Components of the AGS Early Screening Profiles.

PROFILES

Cognitive/Language Profile

Source: direct testing of child
Time: 5 to 15 minutes

Cognitive Subscale
Visual Discrimination Subtest (14 items)

Logical Relations Subtest (14 items)
Language Subscale
Verbal Concepts Subtest (25 items)
Basic School Skills Subtest (25 items)

Motor Profile

Source: direct testing of child
Time: 5 to 15 minutes

Gross-Motor Subtest (5 items)
Fine-Motor Subtest (3 items)

Self-Help/Social Profile

Source: parent, teacher questionnaires
Time: 5 to 10 minutes

Communication Domain (15 items)
Daily Living Skills Domain
    (15 items)
Socialization Domain (15 items)
Motor Skills Domain (15 items)

SURVEYS

Articulation Survey

Source: direct testing of child
Time: 2 to 3 minutes

Articulation of Single Words
    (20 items)
Intelligibility During
    Continuous Speech (1 rating)

Home Survey

Source: parent questionnaire
Time: 5 minutes

    (12 items)

Health History Survey

Source: parent questionnaire
Time: 5 minutes

    (12 items)

Behavior Survey

Source: examiner questionnaire
Time: 2 to 3 minutes

Cognitive/Language
    Observations (9 items)
Motor Observations
    (13 items)

Source: From *Screening Profiles* by Patti Harrison, Alan Kaufman, Nadeen Kaufman, Robert Bruininks, John Rynders, Steven Ilmer, Sara Sparrow & Domenic Cicchetti. © 1990 American Guidance Service, Inc., 4201 Woodland Road, Circle Pines, MN 55014-1796. Reproduced with permission of the Publisher. All rights reserved.

discriminates pictures and selects those that are the same as the stimulus, solves visual analogies by pointing to the correct picture, and demonstrates basic school skills such as number and quantity concepts and the recognition of numbers, letters, and words. Items are presented in an easel format, and sample items are included to teach the tasks.

Motor Profile These items assess both gross-motor and fine-motor developmental skills. Gross-motor skills measured include imitating movements, walking on a line, standing on one foot, walking heel-to-toe, and performing a standing broad jump. Fine-motor tasks include stringing beads, drawing lines and shapes, and completing mazes.

Self-Help/Social Profile Questionnaires completed by teachers and parents measure the child's understanding of oral and written language, daily self-care skills such as dressing and eating, ability to do chores, and community skills such as telephone manners. Social skills that assess how well the child gets along with others and questions measuring the child's fine- and gross-motor skills are included in this section of the instrument.

Articulation Survey In this easel-format task, the examiner asks the child to say words that sample the child's ability to articulate sounds in the initial, medial, and final position.

Home Survey and Health History Survey These questionnaires completed by the parents assess parent-child interactions; types of play; frequency of parent reading to the child; health problems of the mother's pregnancy, labor, and delivery; and health history of the child, such as immunization schedule.

Behavior Survey An observation form is used to rate the child's behavior in several categories such as attention, independence, activity level, and cooperativeness.

Technical Data

Norming Process The test manual provides detailed descriptions of the development of test items and questions included on parent and teacher questionnaires. The following variables, representative of the 1986 U.S. Census data, were considered in the national standardization sample: age, gender, geographic region, parental educational level, and race or ethnic group.

Reliability Reliability research presented in the manual includes coefficient alpha for internal consistency and immediate test-retest and delayed test-retest research. Coefficients are adequate to moderately high for all measures.

Validity Validity studies presented in the manual include content validity, construct validity, part-total correlations, and concurrent validity research with cognitive measures used with early childhood students. Many of the validity coefficients are low to adequate.

KAUFMAN SURVEY OF EARLY ACADEMIC AND LANGUAGE SKILLS (K-SEALS)

The K-SEALS (Kaufman & Kaufman, 1993) was developed as an expanded version of the language measure of the AGS Early Screening Profiles. Normed for children aged 3-0 to 6-11, the instrument includes three subtests: Vocabulary; Numbers, Letters, and Words; and Articulation Survey. Scores for expressive and receptive language skills may be obtained from the administration of the Vocabulary and Numbers, Letters, and Words subtests. Scores for early academic skills, such as number skills and letter and word skills, may be computed for children aged 5-0 to 6-11. Items are presented in an easel format with visual and verbal stimuli and are similar to the items on the AGS Early Screening Profiles. Half of the items from the Vocabulary and Numbers, Letters, and Words subtests are identical to those on the AGS Early Screening Profiles. The Articulation Survey from the AGS test is repeated in its entirety on the K-SEALS, but the error analysis is expanded on the K-SEALS.

Scoring The manual includes norm tables for converting raw scores into percentile ranks and cutoff scores for the categories of "potential delay" or "OK."

Technical Data The K-SEALS was standardized as part of the standardization of the AGS Early Screening Profiles. The same variables were considered to promote representativeness in the sample. Reliability and validity information for the K-SEALS includes split-half reliability, test-retest reliability, intercorrelations, construct validity, content validity, concurrent validity, and predictive validity. Individual subtest coefficients for reliability and validity studies ranged from low to adequate, but total test coefficients appear adequate for most studies cited.

BRIGANCE SCREENS

The Brigance Screens (Brigance, 1997, 1998a, 1998b; Glascoe, 1998) are a system of assessment instruments designed to screen for both development risk and potential advanced development. The screens are designed for the ages of 1-9 to 7-6 and are arranged in easel format for administration. Parent and teacher ratings are included.

The domains assessed in the Brigance Screens include visual/fine/and graphmotor, gross motor, quantitative concepts, personal information, receptive vocabulary, prereading/reading skills, expressive vocabulary, and articulation/verbal fluency/syntax. These domains are assessed using the criterion-referenced approach. The instrument was designed to be administered in approximately 15 minutes.

Scoring   Norm tables are provided for age-equivalent scores for motor development, communication development, and cognitive development. Percentile ranks are presented for total scores.

Technical Data   The standardization sample for the 1995 re-standardization included a total of 408 students. Demographic information is provided in the technical manual, which includes tables for the following characteristics: geographic sites, educational level of child, gender, racial and ethnic background, educational level of parents, family income (participation in free lunch program), parents' marital status, and ages. The technical manual also presents information regarding the performance of the sample by demographic characteristics (such as participation in free lunch program).

Reliability   The technical manual presents information for internal consistency, test-retest reliability, and interrater reliability. Total internal reliability coefficients are in the .90s for 2-year-olds to first graders. The end-of-first-grade reliability coefficient was .52. Test-retest reliability coefficients ranged from the mid-.50s to the upper-.90s. Interrater reliability coefficients were reported to be in the mid- to upper-.90s.

Validity   The technical manual reports information on content validity, construct validity, concurrent validity, predictive validity, and discriminant validity. Coefficients ranged widely from low to adequate.

DEVELOPMENTAL INDICATORS FOR THE ASSESSMENT OF LEARNING–THIRD EDITION (DIAL–3)

This instrument was developed in an effort to screen young children who may be at risk for future learning difficulties (Mardell-Czudnowski & Goldenberg, 1998). The test authors state that the purpose of this instrument is to "identify young children in need of further diagnostic assessment" (Mardell-Czudnowski & Goldenberg, 1998, p. 1). The test may be used to assess children ages 3 years through 6-11. The test assesses the areas mandated by IDEA 1997, including motor skills, concepts, language, self-help, and social skills. The motor, concepts, and language skills are assessed through performance items presented to the child. The self-help or adaptive skills and social skills areas are assessed through parent questionnaires. Instructions are also presented for the examiner to assess social adjustment through observations obtained during the assessment session. A fairly detailed theoretical basis for the development of the test and research pertaining to specific areas assessed are presented in the manual.

The DIAL–3 has been developed in both English and Spanish, although there are no separate Spanish norms. Using item response theory (Rasch one-parameter model), the Spanish and English versions were equated so that the performance of the Spanish-speaking children could be compared with the performance of the English-speaking children (Mardell-Czudnowski & Goldenberg, 1998, p. 75). The test includes several concrete manipulative items, including three dials to be used as stimuli for items in the concepts, motor, and language areas. Pictures, blocks, and a color chart are among the other items included.

Components

Motor   This component of the DIAL–3 includes both fine- and gross-motor tasks. The child is requested to complete such items as jumping, cutting, and writing his name (as appropriate).

Concepts   This component assesses the child's ability to identify colors and parts of the body as well as concepts such as biggest, cold, and longest. The child is also assessed in counting skills and ability to sort by shape and name shapes.

Language   This component assesses the child's ability to provide some personal information, such as name and age, identify pictures of objects, and name letters. In addition, the child's articulation is assessed for developmental risk.

Parent Questionnaire   Composed of several parts, this questionnaire is used to assess developmental history and self-help skills on a 15-item rating scale. It includes a social skills rating scale, a rating scale for areas of parental concern, and a section for rating the screening program using the DIAL–3.

Technical Data   The standardization sample included 1,560 children who ranged in age from 3 to 6-11. The sample matched the 1994 Census data. The following variables were considered in selecting the sample: age, gender, geographic region, race/ethnicity, and parent educational level. Information is also provided in the manual regarding the children in the sample who were receiving special services.

Reliability   Internal reliability was researched using coefficient alpha. The coefficients ranged from .66 to .87 (for median coefficients). The total DIAL–3 test-retest reliability coefficients for two age groups were .88 and .84.

Validity   Extensive information is provided in the manual about the development of the items in both the English and the Spanish versions. Information is presented concerning the reviews of items for content and potential bias as well as the rationale for selection of specific items. Concurrent validity studies were conducted with the DIAL–R, the Early Screening Profiles, the Battell, the Bracken Screening Test, the Brigance Preschool Screen, the PPVT–III, and the Social Skills Rating System. Corrected coefficients were scattered considerably, from extremely low to adequate.

TECHNIQUES AND TRENDS IN INFANT AND EARLY-CHILDHOOD ASSESSMENT

The assessment methods presented in this chapter are formal methods of assessment. Current literature suggests that alternative methods of assessment be used with or in place of traditional assessment of infants and young children (Cohen & Spenciner, 1994; Fewell, 1991; Paget, 1990; Sinclair, Del'Homme, & Gonzalez, 1993). Among the alternative methods suggested by various studies are play evaluations, arena assessment, interactive strategies, observations, situational questionnaires, and ecobehavioral interviews.

play evaluations
Observational informal assessment in a natural play environment.

Play evaluations can yield useful information about how the child interacts with people and objects and can be completed in a naturalistic environment. They can be useful in determining the child's activity level, reaction to novel stimuli, and affect. The characteristics of play listed by Bailey and Wolery (1989) are presented in Table 10.1. Using these characteristics as guidelines, the examiner can assess many behaviors of the child in a naturalistic environment for developmental progress in social skills, activity level, motor skills, frustration tolerance, communication skills with the examiner or caretaker while playing, and so on.

arena assessment
Technique that places the child and facilitator in the center of the multidisciplinary team members during the evaluation.

Arena assessment can be arranged for any method of assessment defined in this chapter, except perhaps for formal cognitive assessment on standardized instruments. Arena assessment is a technique in which all members of the multidisciplinary team surround the child and examiner or facilitator and observe as they interact in multiple situations. Play evaluations, formal play or preacademic tasks,

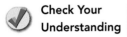

Check your ability to answer questions about assessment instruments used with young children by completing Activity 10.4 below.

Activity 10.4

Answer the following questions about the assessment instruments used with young children.

1. Which instrument for younger ages includes many of the same subtests as the WISC–IV? _____

2. Which instrument was standardized at the same time as the AGS Early Screening Profiles? _____

3. What instrument provides scores for expressive and receptive language skills as well as early academic skills for children aged 5 and 6 years? _____

4. Which instrument includes an articulation survey but does not have the expanded error analysis included in the K-SEALS? _____

5. Which instrument includes both direct assessment and questionnaires/ratings to be completed by caretakers? _____

Apply Your Knowledge

Language development is consistently evaluated in preschool evaluations. What other areas of development does language development influence? _____

_____

_____

Table 10.1   Characteristics of play.

Characteristic	Description
Intrinsic motivation	Play is not motivated by biological drives (e.g., hunger) but comes from within the child and not from the stimulus properties of the play objects.
Spontaneous and voluntary	Play involves free choice; children engage in play because they want to, not because someone assigns it to them.
Self-generated	Play involves the child actively generating the activities.
Active engagement	Play involves active attention to the activities of play.
Positive affect	Play involves pleasurable or enjoyable activities or results in pleasurable or enjoyable consequences.
Nonliterality	Play involves activities that are carried out in a pretend or "as-if" nature—less serious or real.
Flexibility	Play involves variability in form or context and can be done in a variety of ways or situations.
Means more than ends	Play involves emphasis on the activity itself rather than on the goal of the activity.

Source: From *Assessing Infants and Preschoolers with Handicaps* (p. 432) by D. B. Bailey and M. Wolery, 1989, Upper Saddle River, NJ: Merrill/Prentice Hall. Reprinted by permission.

Figure 10.2   Team members conducting an arena assessment.

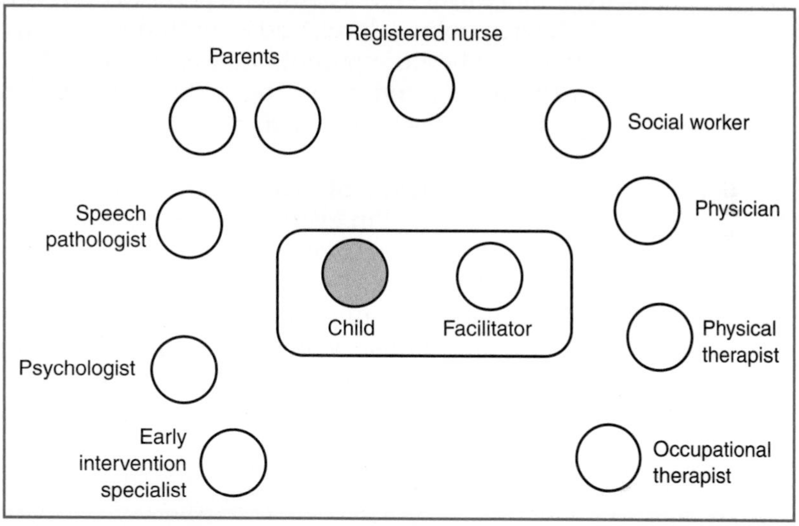

Source: From *Assessment of Young Children* by Libby G. Cohen and Loraine Spenciner. Copyright © 1992 by Longman Publishers. Reprinted with permission.

communication items, and so on may all be presented in this format. All members of the team record the child's responses throughout the evaluation session. This might be a more effective method of assessment of infants and young children because it may reduce the number of assessment sessions (Cohen & Spenciner, 1994). Figure 10.2 illustrates the arena assessment model.

interactive strategies Strategies used by the examiner that encourage the child to use communication to solve problems.

Interactive strategies can be useful in the assessment of young children. These strategies assess the child's abilities to solve problems through interpersonal interactions with the examiner (Paget, 1990). The examiner may alter the problems presented to observe the child's responses to frustration, humor, or different types or objects of play. The strategies are aimed at encouraging the child to communicate with the examiner to solve the problem.

observations An informal assessment method of activities, language, and interactions in various settings.

Observations can be used in a variety of settings and across a variety of tasks. The child may be observed in the home or preschool classroom environment with peers, siblings, and caretakers. All areas of assessment in early childhood can be enhanced through observations. The child's behavior, social skills, communication skills, cognitive level, speech, motor skills, motor planning, adaptive behaviors, activity level, frustration tolerance level, attention span, and self-help skills can be assessed through multiple observations. When observations are combined with information from parent questionnaires and more formal assessment measures, the examiner can gain a holistic view of the child's developmental progress.

situational questionnaires Questionnaires that assess the child's behavior in various situations.

Situational questionnaires are useful when comparing the child's behavior in specific situations. Examples of these are the

Home Situations Questionnaire and the School Situations Questionnaire (Barkley, 1990). The parents and teachers rate the child's behavior, activity level, and attention span in a variety of situations, such as when the parents talk on the telephone, when visitors are in the home, and when the child is interacting with peers. These questionnaires allow for more direct analysis and intervention for problematic behaviors.

ecobehavioral interviews
Interviews of parents and teachers that assess behavior in different settings and routines.

In **ecobehavioral interviews**, parents and teachers describe a child's behaviors in everyday situations, such as during daily routines, bedtimes, class activities, and transitions from one activity to the next (Barnett, Macmann, & Carey, 1992). These responses are analyzed to determine problem behaviors that occur across settings or situations. Behavioral interventions are then targeted to remediate the behaviors in the situations described by the parents and teachers.

OTHER CONSIDERATIONS IN ASSESSING VERY YOUNG CHILDREN

The best practice of assessment across all ages of children involves multiple measures, multiple examiners, and multiple situations or environments. This is especially important for infants, toddlers, and young children because of the influence that temperament, physical health, and current physical state (alertness or sleepiness) may have during an evaluation period. A holistic view of the child's developmental level can be gained by observing the child in many different settings, using both formal and informal assessment, and analyzing the observed behaviors.

Because of the very rapid pace of development of young children, assessment and monitoring of progress should be ongoing, as stated in PL 99-457 (*Federal Register*, 1993). This rapid progress contributes to the instability of scores obtained at very young ages. The variability of the educational and home environments can also contribute to the instability of scores.

Analysis of formal early-childhood assessment instruments indicates that the reliability and validity of the subtests are moderately adequate to below acceptable levels. The coefficients tend to be more acceptable for total test or total instrument scores. Barnett et al. (1992) cautioned against using profile analysis of individual subtests at young ages and suggested that only global scores be used. Katz (1989) warned of the dangers that could occur when very young children are falsely identified through assessment. That is, the child's scores might indicate developmental difficulties, but in reality, the child is not disabled. This false identification may result in changes in parent-child interactions and diminished expectations held for the child.

At the other end of the identification process are the children who need services but remain unidentified. In a study by Sinclair et al. (1993), students who were previously undiagnosed were referred for assessment of behavioral disorders. This study involved a three-stage, multiple-gating system that was used to screen preschool children for behavioral disorders. In this study, 5% of the sample who had not previously been identified as having behavioral difficulties were referred for a comprehensive evaluation.

Review of the literature on the assessment of infants and young children indicates that new trends are emerging. It is hoped that these trends will remedy some of the difficulties of assessing children at very young ages.

Table 10.2 summarizes the strengths and weaknesses of the instruments presented in this chapter.

Table 10.2   Summary of instruments of early childhood assessment.

Instrument	Strengths	Weaknesses
Neonatal Behavioral Assessment Scale	Useful for infants through 1 month of age Assesses behavior and reflex actions	Not typically used in educational setting Requires specific training for use
Uzgiris-Hunt Ordinal Scales of Psychological Development	For children up to 2 years of age Good theoretical basis	Lengthy administration time Norm sample not representative
Bayley Scales of Infant Development-II	Manual has improved statistical data Standardization included clinical samples Assess many areas of development	Lengthy administration time Specific training necessary
Mullen Scales of Early Learning: AGS Edition	Integration of developmental concepts and theoretical foundations included in manual Includes ages birth–68 months	Small sample sizes for reliability, validity data
Wechsler Preschool and Primary Scales of Intelligence, 3rd Edition	Subtests are like those in other Wechsler Scales Appropriate for ages 2-6 to 7-3	Reliability and validity improved in 3rd edition, motor-performance subtests continue to have lower ability
AGS Early Screening Profiles	Include both direct and indirect assessment across multiple situations and skills	Low to adequate reliability and validity coefficients
Kaufman Survey of Early Academic and Language Skills	Expands the language sections of the AGS Early Screening Profiles Offers expanded analysis of articulation errors	Subtest coefficients low to adequate

continued.

Table 10.2 continued.

Instrument	Strengths	Weaknesses
Brigance Screens	Assesses across various ages; criterion-referenced; provides parent and teacher rating system	Norms could be expanded
Developmental Indicators for the Assessment of Learning	Spanish and English versions; parent questionnaire included; fairly comprehensive	Does not provide age-equivalent scores

PHONEMIC AWARENESS

phonemic awareness
Comprehension of individual sounds that make up words.

Legal regulations require that the child's level of functioning in the areas of physical development, cognitive development, communication development, social or emotional development, and adaptive development be addressed during the assessment process. Assessment in these areas provides information for educational personnel about how to implement interventions necessary for childhood development and future educational success. One skill area that may assist assessment personnel in understanding the preschool child's readiness for academic tasks is the area of **phonemic awareness**. A child with this skill is able to determine the separate sounds in spoken words. This awareness is a conscious awareness that words are made up of phonemes or sounds (Snider, 1995).

The skills involved in being able to distinguish the sounds of words are important in learning to read (Turnbull, Turnbull, Shank, Smith, & Leal, 2002). A comprehensive review of the literature regarding the effects of instruction in phonemic awareness on reading skills indicated that both word reading skills and reading comprehension improved with phonemic awareness (Ehri, Nunes, Willows, Schuster, Yaghoub-Zadeh, & Shanahan, 2001). Research also suggests that early interventions that promote phonemic awareness may reduce the number of young students referred for special education services (Lennon & Slesinski, 1999).

phonemic synthesis
The blending of isolated sounds into a whole word.

phonemic analysis
The breaking up of a word into isolated sounds.

Phonemic awareness is composed of subskills and tasks that can be assessed by informal methods. For example, the skills of **phonemic synthesis** or blending of sounds, **phonemic analysis** or breaking the words into sounds, rhyming, and substitution, are some of the phonemic awareness skills that may be evaluated by educators (Snider, 1995). Assessment of subskills in preschool, such as rhyming, have been found to be significant predictors of later reading skills in first grade readers (Missall, Reschly, Betts,

McConnell, Heistad, et al 2007). Specific tasks used to assess phonemic awareness listed by Ehri et al. (2001) include

1. Phonemic isolation, which requires recognizing individual sounds in words; for example, "Tell me the first sound in paste." (/p/)

2. Phoneme identity, which requires recognizing the common sound in different words; for example; "Tell me the sound that is the same in bike, boy, and bell." (/b/)

3. Phoneme categorization, which requires recognizing the word with the odd sound in a sequence of three or four words, for example, "Which word does not belong? bus, bun, rug." (rug)

4. Phoneme blending, which requires listening to a sequence of separately spoken sounds and combining them to form a recognizable word; for example, "What word is /s//k//u//l/?" (school)

5. Phoneme segmentation, which requires breaking the word into its sounds by tapping out or counting the sounds or by pronouncing and positioning a marker for each sound; for example, "How many phonemes in sip?" (3:/s//i//p/)

6. Phoneme deletion, which requires recognizing what word remains when a specified phoneme is removed; for example, "What is smile without /s/?" (mile) (Ehri et al., 2001, p. 252)

An informal assessment instrument for assessing phonemic awareness was constructed by Snider (1997). This instrument, along with other published instruments to assess emerging reading skills, may be used to assess phonemic awareness in kindergarten students. Figure 10.3 presents sample items for the Test of Phonemic Awareness.

In addition to using informal assessment instruments designed by teachers, preacademic reading skills, such as identifying the sounds of letters or rhyming, may be assessed using many of the instruments previously presented in this text, such as the Woodcock Reading Mastery Test–Revised and instruments designed for use with preschool children, such as the Developmental Indicators for the Assessment of Learning, 3rd ed. (DIAL–3), and the Kaufman Brief Survey of Early Academic and Language Skills. The Woodcock–Johnson III Tests of Achievement include the subtest called Sound Awareness that contains rhyming, deletion, and substitution sections. The Wechsler Individual Achievement Test II includes items that assess rhyming and ability to determine words with the same initial and ending sounds. These instruments may assist with determining how a student compares to a norm sample population as well as determining the specific skills mastered.

In the following activity, you will construct a teacher-made instrument to measure phonemic awareness. Use the information presented in Figure 10.4 to develop your items.

Figure 10.3   Sample items from Test of Phonemic Awareness.

Phoneme Segmentation

Model: Today we're going to play a word game. I'm going to say a word and I want you to break the word apart. You are going to tell me each sound in order. For example, if I say cat, you say /c/ /a/ /t/. Let's try a few more words.

Directions: Say the sounds in _____.

Practice Items: to, dog

Test Items:

1. she

2. red

3. lay

Strip Initial Consonant

Model: Listen to the word task. If I take away the sound /t/, ask is left. What word is left? Let's try some more.

Directions: Listen to the word _____. If you take away the // sound, what word is left?

Practice items: ball, pink

Test Items:

1. told

2. hill

3. nice

Source: From "The relationship between phonemic awareness and later reading achievement, Test of Phonemic Awareness," by Vicki Snider. In *Journal of Educational Research* (Mar/Apr/97) *90*(4), pp. 203–212. Reprinted with permission of the Helen Dwight Reid Educational Foundation. Published by Heldref Publications, 1319 Eighteenth St., NW, Washington, DC 20036-1802. Copyright 1997.

ASSESSMENT OF CHILDREN REFERRED FOR AUTISM SPECTRUM DISORDERS

autism spectrum disorders A group of pervasive disorders that are characterized by significant difficulties in capacity for social reciprocity, communication delays, and repetitive behavior patterns.

The number of children with autism and **autism spectrum disorders** has been increasing in recent years. The Center for Disease Control and Prevention(CDC) estimates that approximately 1 in every 150 children who have an autism spectrum disorder (CDC, 2007). These disorders are under the category of Pervasive Developmental Disorders that include three primary areas of potential impairment (American Psychiatric Association, 2000). The areas of impairment include communication delays or abnormalities,

Figure 10.4 Sample Words for teaching letter sounds and phonemic awareness.

Lesson	New Letter Sound	Review	Rhyming [onset][rime]	Blending/ Segmenting
1	/a/		[s,f,m,r] {at} [z,l,r,sh] {ip}	am, an, if, at
2	/m/	a,m	[f,m,r,v] {an} [f,m,n,s] {eat}	am, me, up, mat
3	/t/	a,m,t	[s,v,m,n] {et} [l,r,s] {ock}	mat, miss, at, Sam, mit
4	/s/	a,m,t	[s,l,th,k] {ick} [l,r,s,p] {ay}	sat, fat, fit, sit, am, mad
5		a,m,t,s	[m,s,b,t] {ee} [f,n,g,s] {ame}	it, am, mat, fit, Sam, Sid
6	/i/	a,m,t,s	[f,c,v,p] {an} [b,f,r,h] {ed}	at, sit, if, fit, sad, mat
7		a,m,t s,i	[b,n,s,r] {ag} [k,l,p,th] {ick}	sat, it, am, fat, fit, miss
8	/f/	a,m,t s,i	[b,c,f,t] {all} [b,s,f,sh] {ell}	mad, Sid, fit, rat, dad, at
9		a,m,t s,i,f	[d,f,m,sh] {ine} [b,j,qu,t] {ack}	rad, fit, sad, add, rat, mit
10		a,m,t s,i,f	[b,h,l,s] {and} [b,d,j,l] {ump}	rag, sad, did, fit, at, mad

Source: Copyright (as applicable) by the National Association of School Psychologists, Bethesda, MD. Reprinted with permission of the publisher. www.nasponline.org.

difficulties with social reciprocity or interactions with people, and patterns of unusual or repetitive behaviors. This disorder is typically manifested by the age of three but may not be recognized or diagnosed until later ages due to a variety of complicating issues (Overton, Fielding, Garcia de Alba, 2007).

Early indications that a child may have an autism spectrum disorder are that the child fails to have the social communication skills expected of a youngster (Filipek, 1999). These skills are expected to develop during the early toddler years and therefore children who do not begin to develop these skills may be referred for assessments during this developmental period. Although children may be assessed prior to their third birthday, generally, the

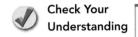

Check your ability to construct a teacher-made test of phonemic awareness by completing Activity 10.5 below.

Activity 10.5

Construction of a Teacher-Made Test of Phonemic Awareness

Look at the letter sounds and tasks presented in Figure 10.3 and Figure 10.4. Use these to construct a teacher-made test on phonemic awareness. For example, the first sound to assess is /a/. In order to make a rhyming item, provide an example of a rhyming word that uses the sounds /a//t/ or at. The words that may be formed using at and the other consonants provided are: sat, fat, mat, and rat.

Model: Listen to this word "at." I know some words that rhyme with "at": "mat and fat."

Next sound to be assessed is /i/.

Directions: Now listen to this word: zip. Tell me a word that rhymes with zip. (Acceptable responses might be lip, rip, ship).

Continue with the construction of the test for the following items:

Blending/segmenting of am, an, if, at. To blend, you ask the student to say sounds together that you first say in isolation. When the sounds are said together, they form a word (/a//m/ together is am). To make segmenting items, you provide an example of how a word sounds, then how it sounds when each sound is pronounced (am then /a//m/).

1. Model (blending):

2. Directions:

3. Model (segmenting):

4. Directions:

Substitution Items. These items make new words when one sound is replaced with another sound. (fat/rat). Use any of the words presented in Figure 10.4 for the items.

5. Model (substitution):

6. Directions:

Apply Your Knowledge

Use the information provided in Figure 10.3 and Figure 10.4 to complete an additional phonemic awareness item. This time, construct an item (model and directions) for the task of phoneme categorization. For this task, the student must tell you which word does not belong to a list of words.

Model:

Directions:

younger the child, the less reliable the assessment results. This lack of reliability at younger ages reflects the differences in development that occur during the early years.

The assessment of autism spectrum disorders, like other types of assessment for potential disabilities, involves observations and data collection from a variety of sources and environments. Moreover, the assessment of children referred for autism spectrum disorders should be developmentally appropriate as suggested by DEC (Sandall et al, 2005). Data should be collected from parents, early childhood caregivers, teachers, and most importantly, from direct assessment of the child. These methods should include rating scales, interviews, observations in the natural environment (home or early childhood classroom or daycare setting), and age appropriate assessment with specific diagnostic instruments for children referred for autism spectrum disorders. Selected screening and diagnostic instruments are presented below.

GILLIAM AUTISM RATING SCALE-2 (GARS-2)

The GARS-2 is a rating scale that can be used as a first step screening assessment for children who are suspected of having characteristics of an autism spectrum disorder. Children between the ages of 3 years to 22 years can be screened with this instrument. The GARS-2 may be completed by parents, teachers, or other educators or professionals who know the child. This brief screener requires approximately 10 minutes to complete. The three core areas of autism spectrum disorders, communication, social interactions, and stereotyped behaviors, are included within the items of this assessment. More than 1,100 children were included in the norming of this instrument and the sample was modeled on the U.S. 2000 Census data. This rating scale should be used for screening purposes only and children who appear to have characteristics within the three areas assessed should be referred for additional assessments.

CHILDHOOD AUTISM RATING SCALE (CARS)

The CARS is a rating scale that should be used as part of the screening for possible autism spectrum disorders. This is a very brief, fifteen item, rating scale that the examiner completes after observing the child. The items provide a means of rating the child on indicators such as adaptation to change, relating to people, and imitation. On each item, the child is rated as apropriate for the specific behavior, mildly abnormal, moderately abnormal, and severely abnormal. The child's total score falls within three diagnostic categories: Nonautistic, Autistic (mild to moderate autism), and Autistic (severe autism).

The examiner's manual includes data on the clinical sample of children upon which the instrument was developed. The results of assessment of more than 1,600 children were used to develop the instrument over a period of fourteen years. The ages of the children included in the initial development of the instrument range from 0 to 11 + years. The sample included 75% males and 25% females. Ethinic groups included in the manual were described as Black, White, and Other. IQ ranges presented for the sample were 0-69, 70-84, and 85 and older. Reliability information included internal consistency reliability research, interrater reliability information and test-retest reliability information. Validity information included criterion-related validity information. The manual is very short and contains guidance on the scoring criteria. This instrument, due to the limited number of items, is best used for screening purposes. Children who were initially assessed with this instrument and who appear to have the characteristics of an autism spectrum disorder, should be evaluated with additional direct assessment instruments and multiple observations in natural settings.

THE AUTISM DIAGNOSTIC OBSERVATION SCHEDULE (ADOS)

The ADOS has been referred to as the "gold standard" in the assessment of autism spectrum disorders. This instrument provides a method for direct assessment of children and adults who manifest the characteristics of autism. The ADOS assesses all behavioral areas of autism; however, cut-off scores are provided only for abnormalities in communication and abnormalities in reciprocal social interactions (Lord, Rutter, DiLavore, Risi, 2002). In order to assess repetitive stereotyped behaviors, additional assessments, such as the Autism Diagnostic Interview—Revised (Rutter, LeCourteur, & Lord, 2002), should be administered. The ADOS has four levels or modules of administration. The appropriate level for administration for a specific child is determined by their level of language development. For example, children who are nonverbal are administered Module 1 and adults who are verbal are administered Module 4.

The ADOS is difficult to learn and complex to score and it is recommended that a team of professionals administer the instrument and discuss the behavioral score for each item following the administration. It is also recommended that the administration of the instrument be video recorded so that the behaviors in question can be reviewed during the scoring process.

The instrument was developed using the results obtained employing earlier versions of the instrument, the PL-ADOS (pre-linguistice Autism Diagnostic Obsevation Schedule, DiLavore, Lord, & Rutter, 1995), and the 1989 version of the ADOS (Lord et al, 1989). The current ADOS includes items from these earlier versions and additional items developed to assess older and more verbal individuals (Lord et al, 2002).

The ADOS was developed primarily by using results of samples of children who were referred for evaluations for potential developmental disorders (Lord et al, 2002). Results from clinical centers were combined and the final sample upon which the ADOS was validated included all English speaking children and adults. The ethnicity was 80% Caucasion, 11% African American, 4% Hispanic, 2% Asian American, and 2% other or mixed ethnic groups. Information provided in the manual includes summary statistics for all four modules for autistic, PDD-NOS, and Non-Spectrum children and adults. Consistency was researched on the instrument by analysis of test-retest, interrater reliability, and internal consistency across all groups for the four modules. Even though this instrument is considered to be the highest standard for assessment of autism spectrum disorders, it is nonetheless a fairly new technique and research continues in the investigation of sensitivity and specificity (Gotham, Risi, Pickles, & Lord, 2007; Overton, Fielding, Garcia de Alba, 2007; Overton, Fielding, Garcia de Alba, in press).

THE AUTISM DIAGNOSTIC INTERVIEW-REVISED (ADI-R)

The ADI-R (Rutter et al, 2002), is an extensive clinical interview that should be completed by a professional trained in conducting interviews. In the school setting, the person most likely to conduct this type of interview would be the school psychologist, counselor, or clinical social worker. The interview may take up to 2 and 1/2 hours. The results of the interview can assist the clinical team in determining if the referred child has an autistic spectrum disorder and can assist the team in knowing what additional data may need to be collected. The ADI-R includes questions about early behaviors that may be characteristic of an autistic spectrum disorder. For example, there are several questions about regression of language skills and questions about repetitive behavior patterns. These items are not accounted for in the scoring of the ADOS and, therefore, it is recommended that both the ADOS and the ADI-R be used in the evaluation. These instruments, when used together along with other assessment techniques, are helpful in determining the specific disorder that may be manifest if it is not an autism spectrum disorder and can provide data to determine if more than one disorder is present (Overton, Fielding, Garcia de Alba, 2007). For example, children with autism may also exhibit symptoms of anxiety or depression. The team should employ a variety of methods to determine if the child has more than one area of concern.

ASSISTIVE TECHNOLOGY AND ASSESSMENT

assistive technology Any assistive device that enables persons with disabilities to function better in their environments.

Assistive technology is a term that is used to designate any device that a student requires to function within the academic environment. Such devices range from a specially designed spoon for eating to computer software that can transfer spoken language to written language. Assistive technology may also include computer

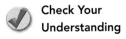

**Check Your
Understanding**

Check your understanding of assessment for children who are referred for possible autism spectrum disorders by completing Activity
10.6 below.

Activity 10.6

Select the correct term for each statement below.

A. autism spectrum disorders   F.   CARS

B. expressive language disor-
    ders   G.   GARS-2

       H.   communication

C. receptive language disorders   I.   repetitive patterns of behavior

D. ADOS   J.   reciprocal social Interaction

E. ADI-R

_____ 1. The _____ is an instrument that a parent, teacher, or other
professional uses to rate observations for children referred
for autism spectrum disorders.

_____ 2. The _____ should be administered by a professional with
training in clinical interviewing techniques.

_____ 3. A child who does not have oral language but may be average in other skills may have a(n) _____.

_____ 4. This instrument is considered the standard for direct assessment of autism spectrum disorders.

Apply Your Knowledge

What is the difference between the direct assessment methods and
indirect assessment methods for assessing children referred for
autism spectrum disorders? _____
_____
_____

software programs that are necessary for instructional purposes
due to the specific type of disability manifested by the child.

     In order to determine if any assistive technology devices may be
required for a student with special needs, an **assistive technology
evaluation** is conducted. This evaluation should be conducted by
professionals who are knowledgeable about such techniques and
equipment, and how to implement their use. The evaluation should
include assessing the student's method of mobility, fine and gross
motor needs, visual and auditory perceptual needs, accessibility
needs to function within the environment, computer technology
needs, communication needs, and any other area in which the
child may require assistive devices.

     Before the actual devices are selected, the student's general
cognitive ability should be considered so that developmentally

**assistive
technology
evaluation** An
assessment to
determine what
devices are needed to
promote successful
functioning within
the school
educational
environment.

appropriate techniques and devices are employed. Once the student's assistive technology needs are determined, the evaluation must consider how the actual devices will be used within the environment. In addition to acquiring such devices, the student may need accommodations in order to use the devices. It is important that all devices be tested with the student so that it can be determined that selected devices fit the student's needs. All of these considerations will promote the student's ability to have access to the general educational curriculum as much as possible. The techniques and equipment that are required for a successful education should be documented in the student's IEP. It is imperative that the team monitor the student's use and success with any assistive technology deemed necessary for the student's education. As pointed out by Bryant (1998), part of the follow-up should include assessing the teacher's understanding and skill in using the assistive technology in the school setting.

TRANSITION AND POSTSECONDARY CONSIDERATIONS

The legal requirements stated in the IDEA 2004 Amendments were presented in Chapter 2. The important components for educators include the inclusion within the IEP of the transitional needs of students from the beginning age of 16. The statement addressing these needs in the IEP must be updated each year and include the specific **transition planning** needed, as well as the areas of study required to meet those needs. By the time the student reaches 16, or sooner if determined necessary for the transition goals set out by the IEP team, the IEP must include information regarding other agencies and the responsibilities of stated agencies.

transition planning
Planning for meeting students' needs following high school.

The other component that educators must remember is that one year before the student reaches the age of majority expressed in state law, the student must be informed of his or her rights that will be transferred to the student as the student reaches the age of majority. This is to be acknowledged in a statement of the IEP.

The emphasis on transitional services that assist students in their movement from school to adult life is a reflection of the data indicating negative outcomes for students with disabilities (Levinson, 1995; U.S. Department of Education, 1999; U.S. Department of Education, 2000). The number of students graduating from high school with a standard diploma has increased to 47.6% (U.S. Department of Education, 2004). The remaining 52.4% of students with disabilities who leave high school receive a certificate of completion, reach the maximum age for services, or simply drop out of school. Students with disabilities who are least likely to receive a high school diploma are students with emotional disturbance, mental retardation, multiple disabilities, and autism. Some of the disability groups for low incidence disorders had very few students included in the analysis (deafblindness). The graduate rates by disability are presented in Table 10.3.

One factor that may influence the number of students with disabilities who graduate from high school is the requirement by some states of exit examinations as criteria for graduation. Research indicates that students with disabilities are less likely to graduate if they are required to pass a high school exit examination. This finding was consistent regardless of the disability category; however, it

Table 10.3 Students ages 14 and older with disabilities who graduated with a standard diploma[a]: 1993–94[b] through 2001–02[b].

Disability	1993–94	1994–95	1995–96	1996–97	1997–98	1998–99[c]	1999–2000	2000–01	2001–02
					Percent				
Specific learning disabilities	49.1	47.7	48.2	48.8	51.0	51.9	51.6	53.6	56.9
Speech/language impairments	42.9	41.7	42.2	44.8	48.1	51.2	53.2	52.3	55.7
Mental retardation	35.0	33.8	34.0	33.0	34.3	36.0	34.4	35.0	37.8
Serious emotional disturbance	27.0	26.0	25.1	25.9	27.4	29.2	28.6	28.9	32.1
Multiple disabilities	36.1	31.4	35.3	35.4	39.0	41.0	42.3	41.6	45.2
Hearing impairments	61.9	58.2	58.8	61.8	62.3	60.9	61.4	60.3	66.9
Orthopedic impairments	56.7	54.1	53.6	54.9	57.9	53.9	51.5	57.4	56.4
Other health impairments	54.6	52.6	53.0	53.1	56.8	55.0	56.5	56.1	59.2
Visual impairments	63.5	63.7	65.0	64.3	65.1	67.6	66.4	65.9	70.8
Autism	33.7	35.5	36.4	35.9	38.7	40.5	40.8	42.1	51.1
Deaf-blindness[d]	34.7	30.0	39.5	39.4	67.7	48.3	37.4	41.2	49.1
Traumatic brain injury	54.6	51.7	54.0	57.3	58.2	60.6	56.8	57.5	64.4
All disabilities	43.5	42.1	42.4	43.0	45.3	46.5	46.1	47.6	51.1

Source: U.S. Department of Education, Office of Special Education Programs, Data Analysis System (DANS). Table 4-1 in vol 2. These data are for the 50 States, DC, Puerto Rico, and the four outlying areas.

[a]The percentage of students with disabilities who exited school with a regular high school diploma and the percentage who exit school by dropping out are performance indicators used by OSEP to measure progress in improving results for students with disabilities. The appropriate method for calculating graduation and dropout rates depends on the question to be answered and is limited by the data available. For reporting under the *Government Performance and Results Act* (GPRA), OSEP calculates the graduation rate by dividing the number of students age 14 and older who graduated with a regular high school diploma by the number of students in the same age group who are known to have left school (i.e., graduated with a regular high school diploma, received a certificate-of-completion, reached the maximum age for services, died, moved and are not known to be continuing in an education program or dropped out). These calculations are presented here.

[b]Data are based on a cumulative 12-month count.

[c]Two large states appear to have underreported dropouts in 1988–99. As a result, the graduation rate is somewhat inflated that year.

[d]Percentage is based on fewer than 200 students exiting school.

proved to be most significant for students with mental retardation and speech and language impairments (Thurlow, Ysseldyke, & Anderson, 1995). This may continue to have an impact on the numbers of students with disabilities who are able to graduate due to the assessment requirements of the IDEA 1997 Amendments. Recall that the 1997 Amendments mandate that the assessments for students with disabilities be consistent with the assessment of students without disabilities.

Individuals with disabilities who leave the school environment are less likely to be employed than persons without disabilities, and those who are employed are more likely to earn less than persons without disabilities (Kaye, 1998; Levinson, 1995). Persons with disabilities are likely to live at home with their parents or have other nonindependent arrangements (Levinson, 1995; U.S. Department of Education, 1995). Persons with disabilities who are able to live in the community are more likely to live alone with little social participation (Kaye, 1998). As Levinson states,

> There is little doubt that, given the high unemployment and underemployment rates among persons with disabilities, the high percentage who continue to live at home following the completion of high school, and the elevated dropout rate among students with disabilities, efforts in the area of special education have not resulted in their successful integration into society. (Levinson, 1995, p. 910)

The research findings and requirements of the federal regulations result in additional assessment responsibilities of educational personnel to meet students' needs as they exit the educational system. The assessment process should begin before the student reaches age 14 and needs to continue until the student has exited from the educational system.

ASSESSMENT OF TRANSITION NEEDS

The focus of the assessment process of students nearing their teen years should change to reflect postsecondary school needs. The student's functioning and needs should be determined in the areas of educational or instructional needs, vocational training or employment needs such as **supported employment**, community experiences, and adult daily living skills. The goals and objectives must include consideration of future plans to enter the adult world as independently as possible.

supported employment
Employing a person with a disability with persons without disabilities. Arrangement is for at least minimum wage and may include a job coach or other supports.

Research regarding best practice for transition assessment and planning has shown that the most successful transition plans with more successful outcomes result from involvement of both students and parents in the assessment and planning process (Brotherson & Berdine, 1993; Thoma, Rogan, & Baker, 2001). Student participation includes teaching students how to advocate for their needs or use the skills of self-determination (Lindsey, Whemeyer, Guy, & Martin,

2001). Self-determination has been defined as "a combination of skills, knowledge, and beliefs that enable a person to engage in goal directed, self-regulated, autonomous behavior" (Field, Martin, Miller, Ward, & Wehmeyer, 1998, p. 2). In order to assist students with their transition needs, educators must assess the student's ability to advocate for their own needs.

Assessment for transition planning incorporates both standardized assessment methods to determine educational achievement, cognitive functioning, behavioral functioning, and other areas as needed. For example, assessment measures such as the Wechsler Intelligence Scales for Children, Fourth Edition; the Wechsler Intelligence Scales for Adults, Third Edition, the Stanford-Binet V, the Woodcock-Johnson III Tests of Achievement and Tests of Cognitive Abilities, and the Wechsler Individual Achievement Tests II may be used throughout the school and transitional periods to assess intelligence and achievement.

Assessment for transition also includes assessing the career and vocational interests, skills, life skills, and social and leisure skills. Clark offered several suggestions for assessment to plan for transition (Clark, 1996, pp. 89–90). The following list is adapted from Clark:

1. Select assessment instruments and procedures on the basis of how to answer key questions in a student's individual transition planning: Who am I? What do I want in life, now and in the future? What are some of life's demands that I can meet now?

Anne Vega/Merrill

2. Make assessment ongoing starting as early as possible, but no later than age 14, and continuing through life.

3. Use multiple types and levels of assessment.

4. Make 3-year reevaluations for all secondary students--useful for their next placement or environment.

5. Assessment procedures should be efficient and effective.

6. Organize assessment data for easy access for IEP planning and instructional planning.

7. Arrange for one person to be responsible for coordinating the assessment process.

8. Develop a transition assessment approach that is not only cultural/language fair, but also culture/language enhanced–questions should be posed in culturally appropriate ways rather than reflecting only majority culture/language values.

Methods of determining the transitional needs of students include conducting a needs interview or using a commercially published instrument to determine such transition needs. One such instrument is the Transition Planning Inventory (Clark & Patton, 1997).

TRANSITION PLANNING INVENTORY: UPDATED VERSION (TPI-UV)

This inventory contains four inventory forms: Student Form, Home Form, School Form, and Further Assessment Recommendations Form (Clark & Patton, 2006). The forms contain items on which the student, parent, and educational personnel rate the student's current functioning. The Home Form is available in the following languages: Spanish, Chinese, Japenese, and Korean. The items survey the domains of employment, further education and training, daily living, leisure activities, community participation, health, self-determination, communication, and interpersonal relationships. The student form also includes questions of career awareness, future plans for living and working, community participation, and leisure and hobby interests. The forms are easy to administer. This instrument allows for multiple informants to participate in assessing transition needs for the student. The authors state that this instrument may be used to determine the future transition needs of any student. The updated edition of the TPI includes the additional resource publication, Informal Assessments for Transition Planning (Clark, Patton, and Moulton, 2000). Another publication is available that incorporated the TPI, Case Studies in Assessment for Transition Planning (Trainor, Patton, & Clark, 2005).

Technical Data

Instrument Construction Because the TPI is not a norm-referenced instrument, the information included in the test manual focuses on test development and on the reliability and validity of the inventory. The authors indicate that the 46 transition planning statements reflect the domains used across various states. The instrument may be administered in alternative ways for students with special needs. An explanation of the expected student behaviors for each item is included in the manual. For example, for an education/training item of "Knows how to gain entry to an appropriate post-school community employment training program," the explanation provided is: "Student knows how to find and get into an on-the-job training program of interest to the student" (Clark & Patton, 2006).

Reliability The internal reliability was studied using coefficient alpha, and the reliability coefficients ranged between .70 and .95. Test-retest reliability coefficients ranged from .70 to .98.

Validity Information for evidence of content and criterion-related validity is included in the manual. Evidence suggests that the TPI was viewed as including necessary content for transition planning.

ASSESSING FUNCTIONAL ACADEMICS

As previously stated, the standardized assessment instruments as well as informal methods may be used to assess the current level of academic functioning of students with transition needs. The informal methods presented in Chapter 8 are very appropriate for determining the level of academic functioning as it applies to everyday living situations.

In addition to previously mentioned methods and tests, the Kaufman Functional Academic Skills Test (K-FAST) may be used (Kaufman & Kaufman, 1994). It is presented in the following section.

KAUFMAN FUNCTIONAL ASSESSMENT SKILLS TEST (K-FAST)

The K-FAST was designed to be administered individually to adolescent and adult students (Kaufman & Kaufman, 1994). This instrument assesses the skills needed for the math and reading skills required in everyday life situations. The authors state that this test was not designed to replace other existing achievement batteries, but rather to add information regarding a student's competency for functioning outside the school environment. The instrument

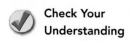

Check Your Understanding

Check your ability to determine the transition needs of a student by completing Activity 10.7 below.

Activity 10.7

Use the student profile from the Transition Planning Inventory to determine the transition needs for Jimmy.

List possible needs below:

1. Employment needs:

2. Further education/training:

3. Daily living:

4. Leisure activities:

5. Community participation:

6. Health:

7. Self-determination:

8. Communication:

9. Interpersonal relationships:

Apply Your Knowledge

Use the information obtained from the TPI to write a behavioral objective for Jimmy's self-determination needs. _____

_____

_____

presents the items in an easel format with oral instructions by the examiner. The math items include such content as the value of money, telling time, reading graphs, and more difficult items covering percentages and calculating the area of a room. The reading items include reading signs, symbols, recipes, and want ads. The test may be administered to persons ranging from age 15 to age 75 and older. The scores provided include standard scores, percentile ranks, and descriptive categories.

Technical Data

Norming Process The development of the K-FAST included developmental versions and tryout exams. The total representative standardization sample included 1,424 people from 27 states. The variables were age, gender, geographic region, socioeconomic status of parents or of examinees, and race/ethnic groups. The sample reflected the U.S. population in terms of characteristics and distribution of abilities when compared with the theoretical normal distribution.

Reliability Two measures of reliability were obtained for the K-FAST, including split-half reliability for internal consistency and test-retest reliability for consistency across time. Internal reliability coefficients ranged from .83 to .97. The test-retest coefficients ranged from .84 to .91.

Validity The validity was studied using factor analytic studies for construct validity, developmental changes as support for construct validity, and concurrent criterion-related validity with general intellectual measures. The validity coefficients varied on the comparisons with tests of general intelligence; however, validity appears to range from adequate to high.

Case Study on Transition Planning

Eric's parents met with his teacher and the school counselor for a conference about Eric's future plans. His parents reported that Eric gets along very well with all family members and with the other children in the neighborhood. They stated that they are allowing Eric to participate in the driver's education course at school. They have not decided if Eric will be able to take his driver's test and stated they are waiting to hear from the instructor regarding Eric's ability to drive. Eric's father said that he has taken Eric out for some practice runs in a neighborhood parking lot on Sundays when there is no traffic in the area.

Eric's parents expressed concern about Eric's independence and were especially eager to learn ways to assist Eric in learning independent living skills. His mother reported that she has made attempts to engage Eric in learning how to cook but that he is not really interested. She said that he would live on pizza if the choice were left to him. Eric's parents said that they envision Eric living in his own apartment someday and marrying. They hope that he will be able to have a steady job and be able to support a family. They also stated that Eric currently has a crush on a neighborhood girl who lives on their block, but that she is not very interested in Eric.

This has been a little difficult for Eric to understand, but his father reported that Eric seems to be feeling better about this issue. Mr. and Mrs. Parks are interested in Eric continuing with a vocational training program as long as possible. They also reported that they will assist Eric financially, if needed, to complete enough training so that he can maintain a job. They were interested in learning of outside community agencies where they could go for assistance after Eric leaves the public school setting.

Transitional Planning Inventory

Areas of Need Indicated by Student (Completed with assistance of teacher)

Employment

How to get a job

General job skills and work attitude

Further Education and Training

How to gain entry into a community employment training program

Daily Living

How to locate a place to live

How to set up living arrangements

How to manage money

Community Participation

Understanding basic legal rights

How to make legal decisions

How to locate community resources

How to use community resources

How to obtain financial assistance

PARENT INTERVIEW

Eric's parents agreed with the areas of need identified by Eric and added the following concerns:

Self-Determination

How to recognize and accept his own strengths and limitations

How to express his ideas and feelings appropriately

How to set personal goals

Interpersonal Relationships

How to get along with supervisor

INTERVIEW WITH ERIC

Eric was excited to come into the office for his interview. He said that his parents had told him about their interview the day before and now it was his turn to talk about getting a job and an apartment someday. Eric said that his favorite part of school is when he goes to the vocational training center in the afternoons. He likes learning about the mechanical aspects of cars. He also reported that the last activity of the day is his driver's education class. He hopes to be able to pass his driving test by the end of the school year but remarked that he may not be able to do that until next year.

Eric stated that he wants to get an apartment someday when he is older, "like when I am about 40." He said that he enjoys living with his parents and he enjoys living in his neighborhood. He stated that even if he moved into an apartment, he wanted to remain in the area where he currently lives. He said that he knows his way around and wants to live close to his friends.

Eric reported that he wants to learn more about how to get a job so that when his training is completed, he can start to work right away. He said he would like to save his money to buy a car. He said that he is not really anxious to live by himself and that he doesn't know much about buying groceries or doing laundry. He said his mother usually helps him with these chores.

With this information, Eric's teacher was able to complete task analyses on the target skills. Following this analysis, Eric's teacher and parents designed specific objectives and interventions to assist Eric with his transition needs. To monitor the progress of Eric as this instruction was implemented, his teacher used curriculum-based measurement to determine if Eric was making adequate progress.

RESEARCH AND ISSUES RELATED TO TRANSITION PLANNING AND ASSESSMENT

The outcomes for students with disabilities continue to be problematic. Research indicates, for example, that young women with learning disabilities tend to be at risk for early-age pregnancy and for single motherhood (Levine & Nourse, 1998).

Although self-determination has been cited as best practice for the development of effective transition planning, research indicates that students are not participating in a manner reflecting self-determination in the transition/IEP process (Thoma et al., 2001). These researchers found that students with cognitive disabilities attended meetings but were not active during the meetings. Moreover, teachers and parents tended to discuss issues about the students rather than engaging the students in the discussion.

Postsecondary research assessing the admission process and accommodations for students continuing their education in 2- and 4-year schools indicates that accommodations are applied inconsistently (Vogel, Leonard, Scales, Hayeslip, Hermansen, & Donnells, 1998). Differences were found in where and how services were delivered to students with disabilities.

Even though students are to be told their rights in the education process that will transfer to them upon reaching the age of majority, individuals with cognitive disabilities are often assumed to lack the competence to assert their opinions about their own education (Lindsey et al., 2001). This appears to be the case even though most students have not legally been declared as incompetent under state law.

Even when students are included in the formal planning process, there are a number of areas that should be evaluated to assist in determining the student's ability to transition well after the secondary school years. For example, students should be evaluated to determine their strengths and weakness in problem-solving, self-evaluation, self-monitoring, and communication skills (Hong, Ivy, Gonzalez, & Ehrensberger, 2007). These skills, along with self-determination, may increase the likelihood of post-secondary success.

In a study analyzing how parenting and family patterns influence post-secondary outcomes for students with disabilities, it was determined that students from families in which the parents exposed their children to employment and career activities fared better after high school (Lindstrom, Doren, Metheny, Johnson, & Zane, 2007). It was also noted that students whose parents acted as advocates tended to have better employment adjustments than students whose parents were protective and better than students whose parents were disengaged from the post-secondary process. This may suggest that these parents modeled more deterministic behavior and that their children were more engaged themselves in the post-secondary planning and outcomes.

THINK AHEAD

Once the student has been administered a battery of tests, the teacher must be able to interpret the results and make educational recommendations. The next chapter includes the steps for test interpretation.

EXERCISES

Part I

Match the correct terms with the statements that follow.

a. PL 99-457
b. developmental delays
c. phonemic synthesis
d. biological risk factors
e. environmental risk factors
f. IFSP
g. family-centered program
h. family-focused program
i. arena assessment
j. phoneme awareness
k. situational questionnaire
l. ecobehavioral interview
m. play evaluations
n. phonemic analysis

_____ 1. This technique used in the assessment of infants and tod-dlers may decrease the time spent in assessment.

_____ 2. Once the family's needs and the young child's needs are de-termined, the information is used to complete _____ .

_____ 3. When a child is asked to sound out each isolated sound in a whole word, the teacher is requiring the child to use _____ .

_____ 4. Among the possible reasons for _____ are physical development behind that of age peers and cognitive func-tioning below the levels expected.

_____ 5. The transition needs of students age 16 years and older are required to be included in a student's IEP by the 1997 Amendments of IDEA; _____ mandate services for children aged 3 to 5 with disabilities.

_____ 6. When a child appears to behave and function differently in specific situations, a _____ may be used to assess these behaviors or abilities.

_____ 7. When a child is able to hear and say isolated sounds, rec-ognize that sounds make up words, discriminate between sounds, provide rhyming words to target words, substi-tute sounds upon request, and identify words with specific sounds, the child is demonstrating evidence of _____ .

Part II

Answer the following questions.

1. What are some criticisms and issues of family involvement as specified in early-childhood assessment?

_____

_____

2. What are the clinical indications that an infant may need a full evaluation according to Mayes (1991)?

_____

_____

3. What areas are assessed when infants are evaluated? Describe these areas in your answer.

_____

_____

4. What are some general considerations and problems of assess-ing infants, toddlers, and young children?

_____

_____

Part III

List and discuss some of the issues related to transition assessment and planning.

1. _____

_____

2. _____

_____

3. _____

_____

4. _____

_____

Answers to these questions can be found in the Appendix of this text or you may also complete these questions and receive immediate feedback on your answers by going to the Think Ahead module in Chapter 10 of the Companion Website.

COURSE PROGRESS MONITORING ASSESSMENT

See how you are doing in the course after the conclusion of PART I chapters by completing the following assessment. When you are finished, check your answers with your instructor or on the Companion Website *www.prenhall.com/overton*. Once you know your score, return to Figure 1.8, Student Progress Monitoring Graph in Chapter 1 and plot your progress.

Progress Monitoring Assessment

Select the best answer. Some of these terms may be used more than once.

a. Standardized tests
b. Age Equivalent
c. Reliability coefficient
d. Negatively skewed
e. RTI
f. WISC-IV
g. FBA

h. ADI-R
i. IDEA 2004
j. Estimated true score
k. Disproportionality
l. Progress Monitoring
m. TPI-UV
n. NCLB

_____ 1. The indicator of common variance of two variables.

_____ 2. A developmental score that may not be very useful to interpret.

_____ 3. The visual representation when more scores are located above the mean.

_____ 4. This is an extensive clinical developmental interview that is used to make a determination of an autism spectrum disorder.

_____ 5. One component of this legislation was to improve teacher quality.

_____ 6. This test includes a working memory index, perceptual reasoning index, and a processing speed index as well as verbal measures.

_____ 7. This measure indicates how much error may be on a test based on the score's distance from the mean.

_____ 8. When students from a specific group are over/under represented in specific eligibility categories.

_____ 9. These instruments are structured to ensure that all students are administered the items in the same manner so that comparisons can be made more reliably.

_____10. This will assist teachers in determining the function of problematic behaviors.

Fill in the Blanks

_____11. Both _____ and _____ require that students be instructed using research-based interventions.

_____12. The _____ includes a measure of the student's attitude toward math.

_____13. The square root of $1 - .r$ is one variable used to determine the _____.

_____14. On the UNIT, the _____ subtest uses a pencil and paper to measure reasoning and planful behavior.

_____15. _____ is noted by a vertical line on the student data graph.

_____16. The blending of isolated sounds into a whole word is called _____.

_____17. The _____ is a measure of preschool students' language development that is based on a two-dimensional language model.

_____18. In order to determine if a student is within the range of mental retardation, cognitive ability and _____ are assessed.

_____19. IDEA requires that _____ is obtained prior to assessment.

_____20. _____ are a group of disorders that are characterized by abnormalities in communication, social interactions, and repetitive patterns of behavior.

PART

4

Interpretation of Assessment Results

CHAPTER 11
Interpreting Assessment for Educational Intervention

Interpreting Assessment for Educational Intervention

CHAPTER FOCUS

When students have not responded to interventions made by teachers and other professionals, the student may then be referred for a more comprehensive assessment as part of the problem-solving process. Following the assessment, the meeting with the team is conducted to determine if a student requires special education support in order to make educational progress. In some cases, these students will be determined eligible for services through special education. The team must then use the test data to design educational goals and objectives.

This chapter provides suggestions for interpreting test results and designing educational goals for appropriate interventions. You will be presented with a complete case that includes test scores, interpretations, goals, and objectives. Test results help educators make decisions about educational interventions, planning, and possible eligibility for special education services. After the professional interprets a student's test results from norm-referenced tests, classroom observations, informal assessment, and parental input, the team members use the results as part of the data to make a decision concerning eligibility, interventions, and if age appropriate, long-term transition plans. The teacher then uses curriculum-based assessment, teacher-made tests, and direct measurement techniques to monitor progress and adapt instruction.

CEC KNOWLEDGE AND SKILLS STANDARDS

The student completing this chapter will understand the knowledge and skills included in the following CEC Knowledge and Skills Standards from Standard 8: Assessment:

CC8S5—Interpret information from formal and informal assessments.

CC8S6—Use assessment information in making eligibility, program, and placement decisions for individuals with exceptional learning needs, including those from culturally and/or linguistically diverse backgrounds.

CC8S7—Report assessment results to all stakeholders using effective communication skills.

Test results are most useful when interpreted and presented in a clear format with specific information relating to educational and behavioral strategies. The regulations of the 1997 Amendments to IDEA require that assessment data be interpreted and used to develop educational and behavioral interventions that will be of benefit to the student. Hoy and Retish (1984) determined that test reports generally lacked the characteristics necessary for ease of **educational planning**. In this chapter, a model of interpreting test results to assist with **eligibility decisions** and plan program interventions is presented. The second part of the chapter illustrates how to use test results to write effective **behaviorally stated short-term objectives**, **benchmarks**, and **long-term goals** and how to continue to monitor student progress through direct assessment.

When interpreting the results of standardized tests, classroom observations, student interviews, parent interviews, questionnaires, surveys, and other methods of assessment, it is important to remember the holistic view of the child or adolescent as well as the environment from which the child comes. Tharinger and Lambert (1990) offered the following guidelines for the assessment and interpretive process*:

1. A child is dependent on the environment to fulfill basic physiological and psychological needs.
2. A child's family is the most active shaper of her or his environment.
3. A child is also an active participant in shaping her or his environment.
4. A child's functioning is multiply and transactionally determined.
5. A child strives to adapt to her or his environment regardless of the health of the environment.
6. A child's motivations for her or his behavior may not be conscious.
7. A child's attachment, separations, and losses are very significant factors in her or his psychological development.
8. A child's current functioning must be evaluated in light of her or his past functioning.
9. A child's behavior can only be understood in relation to current context and the influence of past contexts.
10. As a child develops, conflicts, tensions, and problems are inevitable and necessary. The important factor for assessment is how the child and significant others respond to these conflicts.

educational planning Interventions and strategies used to promote educational success.

eligibility decisions The determination of whether a student will receive special education services.

behaviorally stated short-term objectives Observable and measurable objectives that provide evidence of a student's progress toward annual goals.

benchmarks The major markers that provide evidence of a student's progress toward annual goals.

long-term goals Statements of anticipated progress that a student will make in one year upon which the short-term objectives and benchmarks are based.

11. If the child's thoughts, behaviors, or feelings appear atypical, it is important to consider where, under what circumstances, and at what developmental level this thought pattern, behavior, or emotional expression would make sense.

12. Both the child and her significant environments (i.e., school and home) need to be assessed. (p. 95)

INTERPRETING TEST RESULTS FOR EDUCATIONAL DECISIONS

One purpose of the assessment process is to consider test results to determine if a student requires interventions provided through special education services. Eligibility is determined by using set criteria stated in IDEA. These criteria may vary from state to state for the different types of disabilities but must remain within the IDEA guidelines. This means that the definitions and criteria may be written by the state; however, students who would be found eligible according to the federal law must not be excluded by the state criteria. The scope of this text focuses primarily on mild to moderate disabilities. The most common types of mild to moderate disabilities are learning disabilities, mental retardation, speech/language impairment, and emotional or behavioral disturbances. Students with attention disorders are also often served by educators who teach students with mild to moderate disabilities. These students may be served in the general education environment under the provisions of Section 504 of the Rehabilitation Act of 1973 (refer to Chapter 2) or under the IDEA category of "other health impaired" if the attention problem does not coexist with another disability, such as a learning disability.

The criteria for the qualification of a specific category and eligibility for special education services as stated in IDEA are used as a basis for interpreting test results. Table 11.1 lists the criteria for mild to moderate disabilities as well as the common characteristics of students with attention deficit disorders.

THE ART OF INTERPRETING TEST RESULTS

Most of this text has focused on quantitative measurement, informal data collection, and information from multiple informants about student abilities. A teacher or diagnostician may know how to effectively administer test items, score tests, and collect data; however, the art of interpreting meaning from all of the data and information must also be mastered. Accurate interpretation involves

Table 11.1   Key diagnostic criteria of IDEA for attention disorders and mild/moderate disabilities.

Disability	Key Criteria	Assessment Devices
Mental retardation	Subaverage intellectual, academic, and adaptive behavior (2 or more standard deviations below expectancy for age and according to generally accepted guidelines)	Standardized IQ tests, academic achievement and diagnostic tests, adaptive behavior scales, parent interviews, classroom observations
Learning disability	Average or above in intelligence; specific deficits in academics, cognitive language, or perceptual processing weaknesses may be used. Discrepancy between cognitive ability and achievement NOT required. Response to evidence-based or research-based interventions and performance on academic work should be considered in the decision-making process.	Standardized IQ test, academic achievement and diagnostic tests, classroom observations, permanent products, informal measures, parent interviews, perceptual-motor tests, curriculum-based measurement
Emotional disturbance	Behavioral or emotional difficulties that interfere with academic or developmental progress: unexplained physical problems, pervasive unhappiness, withdrawal, and so on	Standardized IQ tests, academic achievement and diagnostic tests, clinical interviews, parent interviews, classroom observations, projective tests, personality or behavioral inventories, DSM-IV criteria
Speech/language impairment	Communication difficulty that interferes with academic progress, ability to speak, or normal developmental progress	Speech or language diagnostic tests, classroom observations, parent interviews, academic achievement tests
Attention deficit disorders		
1. With hyperactivity	Externalizing behaviors, talking out, talking too much, impulsive actions, activity level beyond developmental expectations, poor schoolwork, incomplete or missing assignments	DSM–IV evaluation, behavioral ratings by different persons and in different environments, Continuous Performance Tests, cognitive and achievement tests, multiple direct classroom observations
2. Inattentive type	Poor schoolwork, incomplete or missing assignments, confusion, excessive daydreaming, self-distracting behavior, difficulty following directions and following through	Same as for hyperactive type

Disability	Key Criteria	Assessment Devices
3. Combined (hyperactivity and inattention)	Combination of characteristics found in hyperactive and inattentive ADD	Same as for hyperactive type
4. Autism spectrum disorders	Significant deficits in the capacity for social reciprocity, abnormalities in communication, repetitive, restrictive, stereotyped patterns of behavior	Indirect assessment using rating scales, observations in natural environment, direct assessment of child (ADOS for example) developmental clinical interview with caregivers

interindividual interpretation Comparing a student to a peer norm group.

intra-individual interpretation Comparing a student with his or her own performance.

both **interindividual** and **intra-individual interpretation** of test results. Interindividual interpretation involves comparing the student with other students in the norm group to determine how different the student is from that group. Intra-individual interpretation may be even more important than interindividual interpretation. For intra-individual interpretation, the teacher uses the test results and other data collected to compare the student's own performances in determining strengths and weaknesses. These strengths and weaknesses are then used in effective educational and behavioral planning.

Generally, all possible areas of suspected disability are assessed according to the recommended tests and evaluation measures given in Table 11.1. The following procedures are suggested for evaluating the student and interpreting test results.

1. *Parental permission.* The professional must secure parental permission before conducting an individual assessment or making a referral.

2. *Screening for sensory impairments or physical problems.* Before a psychoeducational evaluation is recommended, the student's vision, hearing, and general physical health should be screened. When these areas are found to be normal or corrections for vision/hearing impairments are made, the evaluation procedure can continue.

3. *Parent interview.* The professional should question the parent regarding the student's progress, development, developmental history, family structure, relationships with family and peers, and independent adaptive behavior functioning.

4. *Intellectual and academic assessment.* The team members should administer an intelligence measure and academic

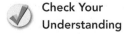

Check Your Understanding

To check your understanding of the mild/moderate criteria, complete Activity 11.1 below.

Activity 11.1

Answer the following questions.

1. What are the general criteria used to determine if a student is functioning within the range of mental retardation? _____

2. Which term listed in Table 11.1 is used when the student has communication problems affecting developmental progress? _____

3. Which term listed in Table 11.1 indicates that a student has discrepancies between ability and academic performance? _____

4. In determining _____, behavioral observations, clinical interviews, information from multiple informants, and projective tests may be used. _____

5. Which tests are typically administered to assess for the possibility of learning disabilities? _____

6. For what categories of disabilities are classroom observations recommended as part of the assessment process? _____

7. What are the key components for the assessment of autism spectrum disorders? _____

Apply Your Knowledge

How are the characteristics of students with attention disorders with hyperactivity and the characteristics of students with attention disorders, inattentive type, similar? How are they different?

_____

_____

_____

achievement or diagnostic instrument, conduct classroom observations, and complete an informal evaluation.

5. *Behavioral assessment.* If the assessment and the information from the parents and teacher indicate behavioral, emotional, or attention problems, the student should also be assessed by a school or clinical psychologist to obtain behavioral, emotional, and personality information.

6. *Test interpretation.* Several members of the evaluation team may interpret test results. The team members may write separate or combined reports. In interpreting results, the assessment team should accomplish the following:

a.

b.

c.

PART 4

To check your unders
plete Activity 11.2

Activity 11.2

Complete

1. Be

h.
per.
quent

d. If appro
sessment **461**
(assessment
completed dur to or
terviews to determ are
for bilingual student
in both languages).

e. Determine whether lea
exhibited in a particular sc
tured play or lunchroom) or
subject area or a particular teacher, peer, or adult.

f. Compare ability on intellectual, academic, or adaptive behavior measures. Are there apparent discrepancies in functioning? Do perceptual or motor deficits appear to influence ability in specific academic areas? Is the student functioning higher in one area than in others? Is the student functioning significantly below expectancy in one or more areas? How do the formal test results compare with classroom assessments?

g. Determine whether emotional/behavioral problems exist. Does the student appear to be progressing slowly because of behavioral or emotional difficulties? Does the student adapt well in various situations? Does the student have good relationships with peers and adults? Is attention or activity level interfering with academic and social progress? Does a functional behavioral assessment need to be completed?

h. Determine whether speech/language problems are present. Is the student having difficulty understanding language or following oral lectures or directions? Does the student make articulation errors that are not age appropriate?

standing of the procedures for evaluation, com-
below.

the following sentences.

ore a decision is made that involves educational or intellectual
ability, screening for _____ should be completed.

2. If there appears to be a conflict in the home or emotional or
behavioral problems are suspected, the student should be
referred for _____.

3. If a student has average or above intellectual functioning, average emotional/behavioral functioning, and average adaptive
behavior skills but has significant difficulty in academic areas
and specific fine-motor ability, he may be determined to have
_____.

4. A student who is below expectancy in all academic areas, is subaverage in intellectual functioning, and has below-average adaptive behavior may be found to be functioning within the range of
_____.

5. A student who has a communication problem that is affecting her
relationships with peers and her ability to progress in school may
have a _____.

6. A student who has impulsive behavior, acts out, has difficulty
completing schoolwork, exhibits too much activity when observed,
and whose parents and teachers rate as having these types of
behavioral problems may be found to have _____.

Apply Your Knowledge

The initial stage of the assessment process should be concerned
with _____
_____
_____

As these questions are answered, the diagnostician or special
education teacher begins to form a picture of how the student
processes information and how the strengths and weaknesses
noted during test performance and observations may affect learning and behavior. From these interpretations, the teacher can make
recommendations that will provide educational intervention and
support to benefit the student and promote academic progress. The
psychoeducational report or reports are then written to facilitate
appropriate intervention strategies.

INTELLIGENCE AND ADAPTIVE BEHAVIOR TEST RESULTS

Cognitive or intellectual measures are generally administered by school psychologists, clinical psychologists, or educational diagnosticians. The results from these tests should be interpreted and used to plan educational interventions. Interindividual interpretations may indicate that the student is within the range of mental retardation or, has a specific learning disability, emotional disturbance, developmental immaturity, or average or above-average intellectual functioning. Intra-individual interpretations should be provided by the person who administered the tests. These interpretations may pinpoint specific demonstrated strengths as well as problems with distractibility, attention deficits, auditory short-term memory, visual retention, verbal comprehension, abstract visual reasoning, visual memory difficulties, and so on. Interpretation of the cognitive measures may refer to patterns of functioning noticed. Patterns of functioning may be explained as significant differences between verbal areas of functioning and visual-motor abilities, spatial reasoning or functioning, or perceptual-organization abilities. These patterns may be indicated by significant weaknesses in particular areas or by more global scores, such as significant differences between verbal and performance IQ scores (e.g., a verbal IQ of 108 and a performance IQ of 71). These weaknesses or discrepancies may be linked to particular learning difficulties. The examiner's descriptions of the student's performance may help the team plan effective educational strategies.

A more in depth analysis of cognitive processing scores across several instruments may be included in the interpretation of results by the school psychologist, school neuropsychologist, or a clinical psychologist. This type of analysis, in which a student's skills and abilities are analyzed across several instruments is known as **cross-battery assessment** (Flanagan & Harrison, 2005; Flanagan & Ortiz, 2001). Specifically, this type of interpretation has a theoretical basis in the CHC theory of cognitive ability. This type of analysis is often used to evaluate the abilities of students who are referred for learning disabilities, traumatic brain injury, neurodevelopmental disorders, or other types of disabilities that originate from frank organic brain abnormalities (Miller, 2007).

cross-battery assessment
Comparing a student's performance in specific areas of processing or skills across more than one instrument.

EDUCATIONAL ACHIEVEMENT AND DIAGNOSTIC TEST RESULTS

The educator may be responsible for administering norm-referenced educational achievement and other diagnostic tests. Scoring these instruments may be somewhat mechanical, although great care should be taken when scoring tests and interpreting the results. The first method of interpretation involves interindividual interpretation: Compare the student with age/grade expectations.

Data provided on norm tables will enable the examiner to determine how a student compares with age/grade peers. Is the student significantly above expectations (in the 90th percentile, for example)? Is the student average (in the 50th percentile range) on some measures but significantly below peers (below the 10th percentile) on other measures? The examiner must plot a profile of how the student performs when compared to these expectations.

Intra-individual interpretation means that the examiner will identify specific strengths and weaknesses in academic achievement, other abilities, and behavioral areas. Because the areas of strength and weakness should be defined as specifically as possible, tests that provide error analysis are most helpful. This analysis can be broken down further by task and used to develop teacher-made tests or informal probes if more information is needed.

WRITING TEST RESULTS

Interpreting and writing test results so that meaningful information is available for the persons responsible for the delivery of educational service is the most important concern when preparing reports. Bagnato (1980) suggested the following guidelines for making psychoeducational reports easy to use in the development of IEPs:

1. Be organized by multiple developmental or functional domains rather than only by tests given.
2. Describe specific areas of strength and skill deficits in clear behavioral terms.
3. Emphasize process variables and qualitative features regarding the child's learning strategies.
4. Highlight lists of developmental ceilings, functional levels, skill sequences, and instructional needs upon which assessment/curriculum linkages can be constructed to form the IEP.
5. Detail efficient suggestions regarding behavioral and instructional management strategies. (p. 555)

Although psychoeducational reports may differ in format, they include the same general content. Typically, the identifying information is presented first: student name, date of birth, parents' names, address, grade placement, date(s) of evaluation, methods of evaluation, and the name of the examiner. Presented next is the background and referral information, which may include sociological information such as the size of family, student's relationship with family members, other schools attended, and any previous academic, behavioral, developmental, or health problems.

Following the preliminary information are the test results. An interpretation is presented, and recommendations for interventions, further evaluations, or changes in placement are then suggested. The following is an outline of a psychoeducational report.

I. Identifying Data
II. Background and Referral Information
    A. Background
    B. Referral
    C. Classroom Observation
    D. Parent Information
III. Test Results
IV. Test Interpretations
V. Summary and Conclusions
    A. Summary
    B. Recommendations for Educational Interventions
    C. Recommendations for Further Assessment

Writing style is also important in writing test results. Words should be selected carefully to convey an objective assessment. Goff (2002) suggested specific guidelines for educators to follow in report preparation when normative tests are used. These guidelines, presented in Table 11.2, include samples of educators' reports and suggested improvements.

Table 11.2 Guidelines for writing objective reports.

Background Information

- Make sure that all statements are attributed. The statement *Jack's mother is very supportive, which contributes to his academic success* is not attributed. Jack's father may strongly disagree if there is a custody battle. This statement could easily be rewritten to attribute the comment to its source: *Ms. Jones, Jack's teacher, reported that Jack's mother has been very supportive and that this support has contributed to Jack's academic success.*

- Do not ask the reader to make assumptions. The statement *Her teacher reports a noticeable difference in Jill's attention span when she does not take her medication* requires the reader to make an assumption. Some students will perform better when not on medication because they become more diligent in monitoring their own behavior to prove they do not need it.

Classroom Observations and Test Observations

- Make sure that you provide observations, not interpretations of behavior. The statement *James really liked the lesson* is an interpretation. This could be rewritten as *James stated, "I really like this work."* NOTE: This is not an interpretation because you are directly quoting Jack. The statement *The work he was given was too hard for James* is also an interpretation and could be rewritten as *James did not complete the more difficult items successfully.*

Test Results

- Make a standard comment about the mean and standard deviation of the test used. For example: *The standard scores for the WJ—III have a mean of 100 and a standard deviation of 15.*

- Report standard scores, percentile ranks, and standard errors of measure. Report both subtest scores and composite or broad area scores. A table in the body of the report or at the end is usually the clearest way to communicate this information.

continued.

Table 11.2   continued.

Test Interpretation

- Discuss clear strengths and weaknesses in performance only if variation in scores reaches statistical significance (usually to the .05 level). Otherwise, the variation should be considered to be normal variability.

Summary and Conclusions

- Tie a review of the Background Information, Observations, Test Results, and Test Interpretation together in summary form. Your summary should pull everything together.
- Your strongest conclusions will be based on concerns supported by Background Information, Observations, and Test Interpretation.
  Observations and evaluation data support the parents' and teacher's concern that Billy has a reading deficit. In addition, he scored well below average on assessments of written language. This supports a recommendation of remediation services in language arts.
- If a student does better in one part of a domain than another, note this difference. *Tonya performed at an average level on a subtest that assesses reading comprehension, but scored well below average on a subtest that assesses word identification skills.* This supports a recommendation that, while remediating word attack skills, the student could continue to be presented with age-appropriate content.
- If the testing data do not support a claim of weakness, look first to differences in task demands of the testing situation and the classroom when hypothesizing a reason for the difference.
- *Although weaknesses in mathematics were noted as a concern by his teacher, Billy scored in the average range on assessments of mathematics skills. These tests required Billy to perform calculations and to solve word problems that were read aloud to him. It was noted that he often paused for 10 seconds or more before starting pencil-and-paper tasks in mathematics.*
- This supports a recommendation that the teacher attempt to redirect him to task frequently and to avoid the assumption that a long pause means that Billy is unable to solve a problem.
- If the testing data indicate a weakness that was not identified as a concern, give first priority to explaining the discrepancy to the limitations with the testing.
- *Billy's teacher stated that he does well in spelling. However, he scored well below average on a subtest of spelling skills. Billy appeared to be bored while taking the spelling test so a lack of vigilance in his effort may have depressed his score. Also, the spelling tests he takes in school use words he has been practicing for a week. The lower score on the Spelling subtest of this assessment may indicate that he is maintaining the correct spelling of words in long-term memory.*
- Do not use definitive statements of the "real" child when reporting assessment results. A 45-minute test does not give you definitive knowledge of the student. The statement *The results of this screening show that Jack has strength in language arts and is weak in mathematics* could be rewritten as *Based on the results of this screening, Jack's language arts skills were assessed to be an area of strength while his mathematics skills were assessed to be an area of weakness.*

Recommendations

- Be careful of using "should" in your recommendations. It means that you are directing another professional on how to do his or her job even though that other professional may have a much more comprehensive knowledge of the child than you.
- Do not make placement recommendations based solely on the results of an achievement test. Make academic recommendations only if your full assessment provides adequate information to make these recommendations with confidence. Remember, specific recommendations can only be made by someone with thorough knowledge of the curriculum and the domain being assessed.

Source: Guideline for Writing Reports. Reprinted with permission of author: W. H. Goff (2002).

The following case study presents test results and interpretations. Read the results and notice interpretations and how they are implemented in the educational recommendations. For instructional purposes, the reasons for the recommendations are given with each recommendation. The reasons for recommendations are not typically included in reports.

Case Study 1: Sue

Name: Sue Smith

Date of Birth: 6-8-94

Dates of Evaluation: 11-20-04, 11-28-04

Age: 10-6

Current Grade Placement: 3.3

Examiner: Hazel Competent

Instruments: Wechsler Intelligence Scale for Children–Fourth Edition

Woodcock-Johnson III Tests of Achievement: Standard and Extended Battery

Test of Auditory Perceptual Skills

Teacher Report Form (Achenbach)

Work sample analysis

Classroom observations

Conference with parents

BACKGROUND INFORMATION AND REFERRAL

Sue was referred for testing by her parents for the possible consideration of special education services. Sociological information reported normal developmental progress and a warm, caring home environment. Sue's parents reported that they felt education was important and wanted Sue's progress to improve. Sue appears to have good relationships with both parents and her two older brothers.

Sue repeated kindergarten and received low grades during her first- and second-grade years. Sue is currently enrolled in third grade, and the teacher reported that Sue has difficulty with phonics and reading words that "she should know." Sue attended a special summer program in an attempt to improve her reading skills.

Sue has normal vision and hearing and no apparent physical problems. Peer relationships are as expected for her age.

PARENT CONFERENCE

Sue's parents reported that Sue is a well-adjusted child who enjoys playing outside, listening to music, and playing on the computer. Her parents believe that Sue's academic difficulties began to surface over a year ago. They stated that they thought Sue would be able to catch up with her peers in reading; however, she still doesn't seem to "get it." Her parents have hired a tutor in the neighborhood to help Sue with her homework. They said that Sue seems to enjoy working with this high school student because she enjoys having another girl to talk to rather than her brothers. Her parents said Sue doesn't appear to get as frustrated as when she works with her parents.

CLASSROOM OBSERVATIONS

Sue was observed on three separate occasions before the testing sessions. She seemed to stay on task and attempted all assigned work. Her teacher reported that more than half of Sue's assignments were incomplete. It appeared that the pace of the class might be too rapid, especially in reading and language arts. Sue did not exhibit many inappropriate behaviors for her age and seemed to have friends within the classroom. Sue's teacher used peer tutors for some of the reading and language arts assignments, which she reports helped Sue to finish some of her work.

TEST RESULTS

Wechsler Intelligence Scale for Children—IV

Block Design	7
Similarities	7
Digit Span	4
Picture Concepts	10
Coding	5
Vocabulary	7
Letter-Number Sequencing	5
Matrix Reasoning	7
Comprehension	7
Symbol Search	5

	Standard Score	95 % Confidence Interval	Percentile Rank
Verbal Comprehension	83	(77–91)	13
Receptual Reasoning	88	(81–97)	21
Working Memory	68	(63–78)	2
Processing Speed	73	(67–85)	4
Full Scale	73	(69–79)	4

Woodcock–Johnson III Tests of Achievement: Standard and Extended Batteries

Cluster/Test	PR	SS	(90% BAND)	GE
Oral Language (Ext)	5	76	(69–82)	2.0
Oral Expression	12	83	(74–92)	2.1
Listening Comprehension	9	80	(73–86)	1.9
Total Achievement	.3	59	(56–62)	1.9
Broad Reading	.2	57	(54–60)	1.5
Broad Math	23	89	(85–93)	3.5
Broad Written Language	0.4	60	(54–66)	1.6
Basic Reading Skills	0.3	59	(55–63)	1.3
Reading Comprehension	1	67	(62–72)	1.7
Math Calculation Skills	39	96	(90–101)	4.4
Math Reasoning	30	92	(87–97)	3.8
Basic Writing Skills	2	68	(63–73)	1.7
Written Expression	4	74	(66–81)	2.3
Academic Skills	1	66	(63–69)	1.7
Academic Fluency	3	72	(69–76)	2.2
Academic Applications	4	75	(70–79)	1.9
Academic Knowledge	35	94	(87–101)	4.3
Phoneme/Grapheme Knowledge	0.2	56	(49–63)	1.0

The following achievement tests of Form A were administered:

	PR	SS	(90% BAND)	GE
Letter-Word Identification	<0.1	48	(43–52)	1.1
Reading Fluency	5	76	(72–79)	2.2
Story Recall	2	68	(50–86)	K.3
Understanding Directions	<0.1	50	(43–57)	K.0
Calculation	76	110	(101–120)	6.2
Math Fluency	1	62	(56–67)	1.5
Spelling	<0.1	52	(45–60)	K.9
Writing Fluency	5	75	(66–83)	2.5
Passage Comprehension	2	68	(61–74)	1.5
Applied Problems	12	82	(76–89)	2.6
Writing Samples	8	79	(68–90)	1.9
Word Attack	5	75	(68–82)	1.6
Picture Vocabulary	29	92	(84–100)	3.1
Oral Comprehension	47	99	(91–107)	4.5
Editing	14	84	(77–91)	2.9
Reading Vocabulary	7	78	(73–83)	1.9
Quantitative Concepts	70	108	(98–117)	5.9
Academic Knowledge	35	94	(87–101)	4.3
Spelling of Sounds	<0.1	26	(11–41)	<K.0
Sound Awareness	11	82	(76–88)	1.9
Punctuation & Capitals	<0.1	49	(35–62)	K.9
Handwriting	38	96	(85–106)	3.9

Test of Auditory-Perceptual Skills

	Scaled Score	Percentile Rank
Auditory Number Memory		
Forward	6	9
Reversed	5	5
Auditory Sentence Memory	8	25
Auditory Word Memory	5	5
Auditory Interpretation of Directions		
Total Correct Sentences	7	16
Auditory Word Discrimination	3	1
Auditory Processing (thinking and reasoning)	7	16
Auditory Quotient	70	

TEST INTERPRETATIONS

On measures of intellectual ability, Sue performed within the low-average/borderline range. This indicates that on this assessment, Sue is considered to have a range of abilities that are consistent with the low end of average and bordering in the below-average range. Discrepancies exist between her higher-end scores of verbal comprehension and perceptual reasoning skills and her lower scores of working memory and processing speed. Sue performed with relative strength on tasks requiring verbal skills and concepts and on tasks requiring abstract visual-perceptual reasoning skills. Sue seems to have more difficulty with tasks requiring her to sustain attention to encode and sequence information using auditory memory skills. She worked at a somewhat slow and deliberate pace on some tasks, which may have influenced her processing speed score.

On overall achievement measures of the Woodcock–Johnson III Tests of Achievement, Sue performed as expected for her age on items of math calculation and math reasoning. Sue's general academic knowledge was in the range expected for her age when she completed tasks of science, social studies, and humanities. Sue also demonstrated age-appropriate skills in the ability to comprehend orally and in handwriting ability. She performed within the low-average to slightly below the average range in areas of oral expression, oral language, and listening comprehension.

Sue's difficulties in academics were demonstrated through formal assessment in the areas of written language, including reading, spelling, sound awareness, and phoneme/grapheme knowledge. The weaknesses result in the inability to decode new words, spell sounds, and comprehend content that is read. An error analysis of word attack skills revealed weaknesses in decoding single consonants, digraphs, consonant blends, vowels, and multisyllabic words.

Sue demonstrated weakness in most areas assessed by the Test of Auditory-Perceptual Skills. She seems to have relative weaknesses on subtests that measure memory for isolated words and numbers. She appears to have slightly higher ability to remember meaningful auditory stimuli, such as sentences or directions. However, she had difficulty on similar items of the WJ III, indicating inconsistent skill mastery or inconsistent abilities.

On items requiring oral language responses, Sue was somewhat shy and tended to limit her responses to one-word answers. This may have affected some of her scores on tests assessing the language areas. These scores may underestimate her true ability.

Responses provided by Sue's teacher on the Teacher Report Form of the Child Behavior Checklist indicated that Sue is unable to complete most of her schoolwork as expected of students her age. The teacher endorsed items that indicate Sue may be having some emerging problems with anxiety. Items were also endorsed that are consistent with difficulties with concentration and attention. These may be related to her current performance in school. None of the scores were within a clinical range for behavior problems.

Work sample analysis indicated that Sue has a relative strength in the ability to compute simple math operations and to understand math concepts and math reasoning. Her samples for spelling, writing, and reading comprehension were within the failure range. The work samples indicated difficulty with her ability to associate written letters with sounds consistently, which is consistent with her performance on standardized achievement measures.

Three separate classroom observations indicated that Sue was cooperative and remained quiet during all of the observation periods. She attempted to begin her work when instructed to do so but was unable to complete language arts assignments as instructed. She also appeared to increase the amount of time that she was off task during language arts classes compared with her ability to concentrate during math class.

SUMMARY AND CONCLUSIONS

Sue is currently functioning in the low-average range of intellectual ability, with significant weaknesses in phoneme/grapheme awareness and short-term auditory memory. These weaknesses influence Sue's ability to decode words, spell, and comprehend new material. The weakness may also decrease the efficiency with which Sue can obtain new information through a standard teaching (lecture) format. Sue's performance on standardized and informal

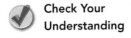

To check your understanding of this case, complete Activity 11.3 below.

Activity 11.3

Answer the following questions about the case study.

1. Why was Sue referred for testing? _____
2. How is Sue functioning intellectually? _____
3. What are the discrepancies in Sue's functioning according to the test results? _____
4. What are Sue's strengths as indicated through the assessment process? _____
5. What are Sue's weaknesses, and how do these weaknesses appear to influence Sue's academic functioning? _____
6. What additional assessment was recommended for Sue? _____
7. According to these results, what are Sue's specific academic skill deficits? _____
8. What types of educational interventions and strategies were recommended? _____

Apply Your Knowledge

Write any additional concerns you may have about Sue after reading this report. _____
_____
_____

assessment instruments resulted in a profile consistent with that of a student with specific learning disabilities in the areas of reading and written language skills. This may be the result of her difficulties with processing information presented auditorily and an inability to form sound-symbol relationships.

RECOMMENDATIONS

1. Sue may benefit from additional educational support in the areas of reading and language arts. (Reasons: Student has difficulty with sound awareness, phoneme/grapheme awareness, auditory memory, verbal skills, and attention; this would support the decision that she may benefit from additional educational interventions.)

2. New material should be presented through both visual and auditory formats. (Reasons: Weakness appears to be auditory memory; pairing all auditory material with visual cues may help student to focus attention.)

3. Sue will benefit from direct instruction techniques that require her to actively respond to new material. (Reasons: Student may increase academic engaged time; active responding may help student to focus attention and receive positive feedback from teacher.)

4. Sue may benefit from phonemic awareness training activities. (Assessment results are consistently low in these areas; additional instruction may decrease her difficulties with reading).

5. Sue may benefit from advanced organizers in content areas, introduction of new vocabulary terms before reading them in new chapters, outlines of class lectures or presentations, and note-taking training. (Reasons: Student may increase ability to focus on relevant material, increase attention to task.)

Hazel Competent, M. Ed.

Educational Diagnostician

WRITING EDUCATIONAL OBJECTIVES

At the eligibility meeting, team members discuss the results and recommendations of the psychoeducational reports with the parents. If the student is eligible for special education services, the team writes the specific educational objectives that the student's IEP will comprise. If the student does not meet eligibility criteria, the student may be considered to need accommodations under Section 504. The team may also decide that the student does not need additional services under 504 or IDEA, but additional referrals, programs, or interventions may be suggested within the general curriculum. Let's continue with the example of Sue Smith to see how the team would use its results to write Sue's educational objectives.

IEP TEAM MEETING RESULTS

The following results were presented in the IEP team meeting along with additional information from Sue's parents, school psychologist, and classroom teachers. At that time, the team agreed that Sue would receive reading and language arts instruction in a resource room setting. This decision was made so that Sue could receive intensive training in phonemic awareness, reading decoding, reading comprehension, reading fluency, and spelling in a one-on-one and small-group environment. Additional assessments would be completed to further pinpoint the specific weaknesses in phoneme/grapheme awareness and other areas of language arts.

The resource room teacher plans to use curriculum-based measurement to monitor progress.

SUE'S IEP

During the IEP meeting, the IEP was developed. Portions of the IEP are presented here.

Student's Present Level of Educational Performance

Cognitive Abilities. Current assessment data indicate that Sue is functioning in the low-average range of intelligence. Sue's strengths are in the areas of performance or nonverbal skills.

Reading

- *Basic Reading Skills.* Formal assessment, curriculum-based assessments, and informal measures indicate that Sue is performing below the range expected for her age on tasks of reading decoding—specifically, word attack and phoneme/grapheme awareness. Her performance in curriculum-based measures are at the first- to second-grade level.
- *Comprehension.* Comprehension skills were at the first- to second-grade level on all measures.
- *Fluency.* Reading fluency was assessed to be at the first- to second-grade level.

Spelling. Sue's spelling skills were measured to be at the first-grade level. Sue has difficulty with the spelling of basic cvc (consonant-vowel-consonant) words.

Written Language. Sue's written language skills were measured to be at the first- to second-grade level on both formal and informal classroom measures.

Mathematics. Sue is performing at the level expected for her age in areas of math calculation and math reasoning.

Science. Sue's standardized achievement scores and classroom measures indicate that Sue is comprehending science at the level expected for her age.

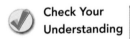

Check Your Understanding

To check your understanding of writing objectives, complete Activity 11.4 below.

Activity 11.4

Additional classroom assessment indicated that Sue has difficulty with the following sound/letter associations when asked to decode words. She also had difficulty with spelling of first-grade-level words. Using the following information, write behaviorally stated short-term objectives for these skills.

> Reading Decoding Errors; Letter/Sound Association Errors: /cr/, /pl/, /dr/, /st/, /sh/, /ch/
>
> Spelling Errors: tree, church, play, drop, drip, drank, drink, meat, meet, hand, sand, band, milk, silk, some, come, home
>
> 1. When presented with _____, Sue will be able to _____ with % accuracy by _____.
>
> 2. _____
>
> 3. _____
>
> 4. _____
>
> *Apply Your Knowledge*
>
> Using the information provided for this case, write a long-term annual goal for written expression. _____
> _____
> _____

Social Studies. Sue's standardized achievement scores and classroom measures indicate that Sue is performing at the level expected for her age.

Listening. Assessment results of Sue's listening comprehension were inconsistent with comprehension measured to be within the low-average range, consistent with her measured cognitive abilities. Other areas were assessed to be below the level expected for her age. Auditory discrimination and memory were below the level expected for her age.

Sample IEP Annual Goal for Basic Reading Skills Sue will master the decoding skills required in the reading series, Spinners, at the mid-second-grade level by the end of the school year.

Sample IEP Short-term Objective When given a list of 20 random words from the highest-level first-grade reader (1.E Level) from the series Spinners, Sue will be able to decode the list with 85% accuracy at the end of the 6-week reporting period.

Methods and Evaluation

Methods/Material Used	Method of Monitoring/Assessment
Spinners Reader Level 1.E	Curriculum-based measurement

Following is the general format for writing an educational behaviorally stated short-term objective:

When presented with _____, Sue will be able to _____ with _____% accuracy by _____.

REEVALUATIONS

The 1997 IDEA Amendments changed the focus of the reevaluation process. In the past, students were assessed in the same areas they were assessed for their initial evaluations (cognitive, academic, speech/language, adaptive functioning, and so on). The regulations now state that data is collected only in the areas that the team members feel they need additional information in order to make a decision regarding continued eligibility and interventions. For example, a student with a specific learning disability in math may need only additional data and/or assessment in the area of math. Rather than requiring total comprehensive evaluations every 3 years, reevaluations now consist of only the additional assessment determined to be needed in order to thoroughly review the case.

Case Study 2: Travis

Name: Travis Shores

Date of Birth: 8-9-84

Date of Evaluation: 10-28-02

Age: 18-2

Examiner: Mark House

Instruments: Wechsler Adult Intelligence Scale–Third Edition

Conners' Continuous Performance Test

Woodcock Language Proficiency Battery–Revised

Clinical interview

BACKGROUND AND REFERRAL INFORMATION

Travis is currently enrolled as a freshman in Anywhere Community College and reported having difficulty with study habits, time management, spelling skills, writing skills, reading comprehension, and grammar. He also expressed concern about his ability to master a foreign language at the college level. Travis said that he has difficulty with attention span, finishing tasks, test taking, and listening in class. He reported that he gets distracted easily in lecture classes.

Travis reported that he has no history of testing for learning or attention difficulties. He stated that he had a difficult time in high school during his sophomore year but then felt that things were better for him during his junior and senior years. Travis attempted to take Spanish this semester and decided to drop the course because of his inability to make the progress he expected. He is taking economics and believes he is doing well in that class.

TEST RESULTS

Wechsler Adult Intelligence Scale–Third Edition

Verbal Tests		Performance Tests	
Vocabulary	9	Picture Completion	12
Similarities	11	Digit Symbol-Coding	10
Arithmetic	8	Block Design	14
Digit Span	8	Matrix Reasoning	13
Information	8	Picture Arrangement	9
Comprehension	12		

Verbal IQ	95
Performance IQ	110
Full-Scale IQ	96

Conners' Continuous Performance Test

Measure	Percentile	Range of Performance
Number of Hits	99.59	Markedly atypical
Number of Omissions	94.86	Markedly atypical
Number of Commissions	50.90	Within average range
Hit Rate	21.46	Within average range
Hit Rate Standard Error	93.44	Markedly atypical
Variability of SES	77.87	Within average range
Attentiveness	84.42	Mildly atypical
Risk Taking	99.00	Markedly atypical
Hit RT Block Change	95.96	Markedly atypical
Hit SE Block Change	82.60	Within average range
Hit RT ISI Change	80.90	Within average range
Hit SE ISI Change	76.78	Within average range

Travis performed with some inconsistency on the Conners Continuous Performance Test. He performed like students his age with attention problems on several indices. He was within the average range on other indices. His performance indicates that he may have difficulty sustaining attention on some tasks but not others. His performance showed some evidence of an impulsive responding pattern.

Woodcock Language Proficiency Battery—Revised

Subtest	Standard Score	Percentile Rank	Grade Equivalent
Memory for Sentences	95	38	10.2
Picture Vocabulary	85	15	9.3
Oral Vocabulary	86	17	9.6
Listening Comprehension	103	57	14.2
Verbal Analogies	81	10	6.2

	Standard Score	Percentile Rank	Grade Equivalent
Letter-Word Identification	96	39	11.9
Passage Comprehension	90	25	10.0
Word Attack	103	57	14.4
Dictation	90	25	9.8
Writing Samples	136	99	16.9
Proofing	70	2	5.0
Writing Fluency	88	22	9.5
Punctuation	71	3	5.7
Spelling	92	29	10.5
Usage	86	18	8.8
Cluster Scores			
Oral Language	88	22	9.6
Broad Reading	93	31	10.9
Basic Reading Skills	99	47	12.5
Broad Written Language	107	67	16.0
Basic Writing Skills	77	6	7.2
Written Expression	110	74	16.1

Travis is currently functioning within the average range of intellectual ability. A significant discrepancy exists between his verbal IQ score of 95 and his performance IQ score of 110. This indicates that Travis is able to use nonverbal strategies rather than verbal strategies for most problem solving. This discrepancy also indicates that Travis's full scale IQ score may not be representative of his true ability. Travis's performance IQ score may better represent his true cognitive potential. Analysis of individual subtests and factors also indicates strengths and weaknesses in processing. Travis demonstrated significant strength in the ability to comprehend common verbal concepts. He also demonstrated significant strength in visual perceptual organization of nonverbal stimuli. His performance on this instrument indicates relative weakness in short-term auditory memory and in the ability to remain free from distraction. Travis appears to have relative weakness in long-term retention of factual information.

Travis was administered the Conners Continuous Performance Test to determine whether he has significant difficulty maintaining sustained, focused attention. On this instrument, the more measures found to be within the atypical range, the greater the likelihood that attention problems exist. On this test, Travis gave slower responses at the end than at the beginning of the test, indicating an ability to sustain attention. He made a larger number of omission errors, indicating poor attention to the task. He was highly inconsistent in responding, indicating inattentiveness as measured by standard error. Numerous indices strongly suggest that Travis has attention problems according to his performance on this test.

SUMMARY

Write your summary for the assessment data in the space provided.

_____
_____
_____
_____
_____

RECOMMENDATIONS

Write recommendations: discuss appropriate interventions in class and for studying outside of class. Include accommodations for the college environment based on data provided. Should Travis be referred for additional services in any other agencies or with other professionals? What considerations should be discussed with Travis regarding his future plans and course of study at the college level? What issues regarding his functioning as an adult should be considered?

Recommendations:

1. _____
   _____

2. _____
   _____

3. _____
   _____

4. _____
   _____

Case Study 3: Burt

Name: Burt Down
Date of Birth: 5-10-1989
Date of Evaluation: 11-27-2003
Age: 14-7
Current Grade Placement: 9.3
Examiner: Phil Mood
Instruments: Selected subtests of the Woodcock–Johnson III
Math Work Samples
Behavior Assessment System for Children: Self-Report (ages 12–18)
Behavioral Observation Data
Functional Behavioral Assessment

BACKGROUND AND REFERRAL INFORMATION

Burt was referred for a reevaluation due to recent behavioral difficulties. Burt has been receiving special education support for specific learning disabilities since he was in the fourth grade. He receives his English instruction in the resource room setting. He has previously been found to have attention deficit hyperactivity disorder and has been prescribed medication as part of his treatment for this disorder. His parents and teachers agree that his behavior improves when he complies with his medication treatment. His parents also acknowledge that things have been rough at home lately. They told the team that they have not been able to manage Burt's behavior within the home and attribute this to "just his age." They report that Burt has been staying out later than he is supposed to and that he argues with them about school and homework. They said that Burt tells them he is old enough to make up his own mind about curfews and selecting his friends. Mr. and Mrs. Down said they do not approve of Burt's friends.

Burt was assessed last year for his regular triennial evaluation. His cognitive ability has been assessed to be within the average range (full scale IQ 108). Due to recent difficulties in mathematics and his behavioral difficulties, another reevaluation was requested. The team members, including Burt's parents, met to discuss possible data needed to analyze the current areas of difficulty. All members agreed that a behavioral analysis and other measures of behavior would be collected. In addition, selected subtests of the WJ III and math work samples would be analyzed.

TEST RESULTS

Woodcock–Johnson III Tests of Achievement

Clusters	PR	SS (90% BAND)	GE
Broad Math	6	77 (73–81)	4.7
Math Calculation Skills	7	78 (72–84)	5.2
Math Reasoning	16	85 (80–90)	5.3
Subtest			
Calculation	15	84 (76–93)	5.7
Math Fluency	3	71 (67–75)	4.2
Applied Problems	8	79 (74–84)	4.1
Quantitative Concepts	40	96 (89–104)	7.5

Math Work Samples

An analysis of Burt's math class work indicates that he attempted to answer 80% of the problems he was assigned in class; however, he successfully completed 35% of the problems he was given to complete in class. His errors included miscalculations, errors of alignment, errors of wrong applications in story problems (adding when he should subtract), and skipping steps needed in multiple-step problems. Burt was not able to complete an entire math assignment, working only about 75% to 85% of the problems before he either quit or ran out of time.

Burt's homework assignments did not show much evidence of his understanding the tasks presented. He turned in only 6 of 15 assignments since the beginning of the school year, and he successfully completed 38% of the problems assigned. His errors on homework assignments were consistent with the errors made on his classwork assignments.

Behavioral Assessments
Behavioral Assessment System for Children: Self-Report (ages 12–18)

Rank*	T-Score*	Percentile
Clinical Profile		
Attitude to School	68	95
Attitude to Teachers	68	94
Sensation Seeking	67	95
School Maladjustment Composite	72	99
Atypicality	52	65
Locus of Control	74	98
Somatization	50	62
Social Stress	64	94
Anxiety	49	51
Clinical Maladjustment Composite	60	81
Depression	85	99
Sense of Inadequacy	83	99

*On the clinical scales, a *T*-score greater than 70 is considered to be the area of caution for the student's current behaviors. For percentile ranks on clinical scales, the higher the score, the more significant. A percentile rank of 50 is average.

Rank*	T-Score*	Percentile
Adaptive Profile		
Relations with Parents	12	1
Interpersonal Relations	43	18
Self-Esteem	26	4
Self-Reliance	39	15
Personal Adjustment Composite	23	2

*High scores on the adaptive scales indicate high levels of adaptive skills.

On the BASC, Burt endorsed critical items indicating that he feels he has trouble controlling his behavior, he feels he does not do anything right, he thinks no one understands him, he doesn't care anymore, he feels that nothing goes his way and that no one listens to him.

Figure 11.1 illustrates the behavioral observations for Burt during math class for "off-task" behavior across three observation periods.

Figure 11.1   Frequency of off-task behavior in Math class (Burt).

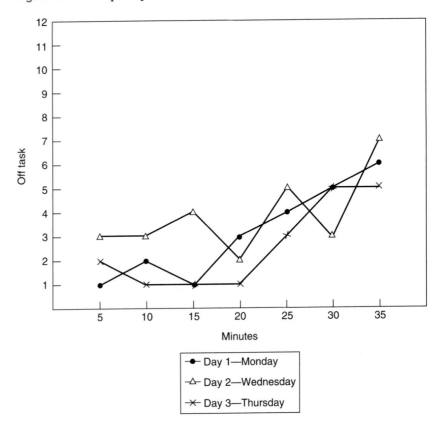

To compare Burt's behavior in additional settings, he was observed in his resource room, where he receives English instruction (Figure 11.2), and in his art class (Figure 11.3).

Functional Behavioral Interview

Following the observations sessions, Burt was interviewed by the school psychologist to determine Burt's perspective on his recent behavioral difficulties and to determine the function of these behaviors. Burt told the psychologist he knows that he is not doing well in math and that he just can't seem to keep up. He stated that he was able to do math last year and felt his teacher was "nicer to me." He stated that his teacher last year offered to stay after school and help him so he could complete his homework assignments. Burt reported that he feels lost in math so he gets bored and wants to do something else. He figures there is no use in trying to do the work, because "I just get Fs anyway."

When Burt is in his other classes, he says he can get along just fine. He says he has lots of friends in his other classes who help him with things he doesn't understand.

Figure 11.2 Frequency of off-task behavior in English class (Burt).

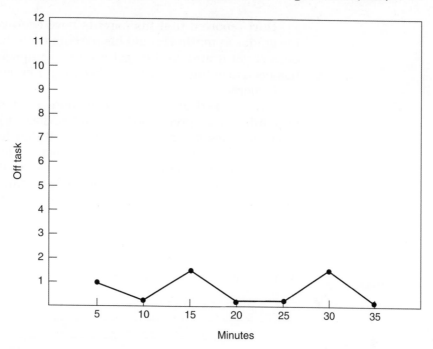

Figure 11.3 Frequency of off-task behavior in art class (Burt).

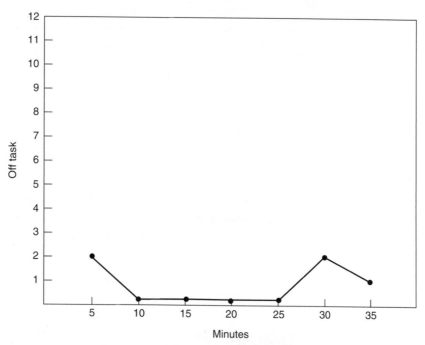

Source: From D. J. Tharinger and N. M. Lambert (1990). "The Contributions of Developmental Psychology to School Psychology," in T. Gutkin and C. R. Reynolds (Eds.), *The Handbook of School Psychology* (2nd ed.). New York: Wiley, pp. 74–103. (© John Wiley & Sons, Inc. Reprinted by permission of the publisher.)

Burt reported that his parents have been yelling at him about his grades in math. He said his parents try to help him, but he still doesn't get it and so they get even more upset. He stated that he has been avoiding going home, because "I know they will yell at me some more."

When asked about his medication, Burt said that he hasn't been taking it as prescribed. He said he doesn't like the way he feels when he takes it even though he agreed that he can pay attention better in school when he takes his medicine. He reported that some of his friends found out that he has to take medicine and that they began calling him names like "hyper" and "dummy." He said that he doesn't feel as good about himself or his relationships with his peers as he did last year.

SUMMARY

Write your summary in the space provided.

_____
_____
_____
_____
_____
_____
_____

RECOMMENDATIONS

Write recommendations, discussing appropriate interventions in class, including determining any changes in setting or any needed additional assessment information based on data provided.

Recommendations:

1. _____
   _____
2. _____
   _____
3. _____
   _____
4. _____
   _____

TEAM MEETING

Write the team's discussion and deliberations in the space provided. What are the decisions for Burt? What types of services are needed? Where will these services take place? Who will provide services?

_____
_____
_____
_____
_____

Write the present levels of performance for Burt:

_____
_____
_____

Write behavioral objectives for Burt that will be the basis of the behavioral intervention plan for him:

_____
_____
_____
_____
_____

Write the short-term objectives for Burt relating to the areas assessed in the reevaluation:

_____
_____
_____
_____
_____
_____
_____
_____

Case Study 4: Alicia

Name: Alicia Young
Date of Birth: 2-7-98
Date of Evaluation: 4-7-01
Age: 3-2
Current Grade Placement: None
Examiner: Beth Child
Stanford–Binet V
Vineland Adaptive Behavior Scales
Evaluation Methods: AGS Early Screening Profiles

Play evaluation

Home visit

Parent interview

BACKGROUND AND REFERRAL INFORMATION

Alicia was referred by her maternal grandmother, who is her legal guardian. Sociological information indicates that Alicia's grandmother does not know her daughter's residence at this time. Health information provided by the grandmother on the Health History Survey indicates that Alicia was born prematurely and that Alicia's mother has a long history of substance abuse. At the time of Alicia's birth, Alicia's mother was 17 years of age. Alicia has one older sibling, a 6-year-old brother who is currently receiving special education support services. Alicia's grandmother believes that Alicia is not developing at the expected pace and requested a screening evaluation to determine whether Alicia might be considered for the early childhood at-risk program.

TEST RESULTS

K-ABC-II

Age 3: Global Scale Index

Mental Processing Composite

	Scaled Scores
Atlantis	6
Conceptual Thinking	7
Face Recognition	6
Triangles	6
Word Order	6
Mental Processing Composite Standard Score	66
95% Confidence Interval	59–77

Vineland Adaptive Behavior Scales: Interview Edition (Expanded Form)

Communication	
Receptive	Moderately low
Expressive	Low
Written	Low

Daily Living Skills	
Personal	Moderately low
Domestic	Low
Community	Low

Socialization	
Interpersonal Relationships	Low
Play and Leisure Time	Moderately low
Coping Skills	Low

AGS Early Screening Profile

	Standard Score	Percentile Rank	Age Equivalent
Cognitive/Language	60	1	2-0
Motor	75	5	2-1
Self-Help/Parent	68	2	2-0

Survey Scores

Articulation	Below average/poor
Home Behavior	Average
Cognitive/Language	Below average
Motor	Below average

Play Evaluation and Home Visit

Alicia sat quietly on the carpet during the play evaluation. Alicia's grandmother was present during the first part of the evaluation. When her grandmother left the room to complete a survey, Alicia sat motionless and did not exhibit any change in her behavior following the separation. Alicia did not initiate any spontaneous use of language or communication, such as gesturing. She did not interact with the examiner when encouraged to do so and played with only one object, a stuffed toy. Her play can be best described as mechanistic and without any noticeable motive or affect exhibited. Alicia did not react to her grandmother when she returned, but joined her grandmother on the sofa when requested.

A home visit was made 2 days following the evaluation. The home environment was clean, and several educational toys and materials were available. All interactions between the grandmother and Alicia were initiated by the grandmother. Alicia displayed very flat affect during both the home visit and the evaluation. Alicia's grandmother stated that the only reaction she sees from Alicia is when it is time to eat. She described Alicia's appetite as fair because Alicia likes only a few types of food. When she is given something new to taste, she usually spits it out after she tries it.

Parent Interview

When Alicia's grandmother was asked to list her priorities and concerns for Alicia, she expressed the need for some support to help her toilet train Alicia, improve Alicia's speech development, and improve Alicia's self-help skills, such as dressing and washing her face. Alicia's grandmother believes that Alicia's motor skills are different from her grandson's. She believes that Alicia is somewhat clumsy and too dependent on her for routine activities that other 3-year-olds are learning to do, such as self-feed with a spoon.

Alicia's grandmother reported that she has been able to access monetary assistance using public resources including Medicaid for

Alicia's medical needs and transportation to and from the community agencies for Alicia's care. She reported that Alicia's needs are primarily being met within the home environment but expressed desire for additional assistance in training Alicia within the home environment and in managing her behavior.

SUMMARY

Write your summary for Alicia's assessment data in the space provided.

_____

_____

_____

_____

_____

_____

_____

RECOMMENDATIONS

Write recommendations, discussing appropriate interventions including interventions within the home and between the home and school environment. For this case, you must first determine how children of Alicia's age are served in your state and local community. Following the discussion, complete the "Team Meeting" section with members in your class.

Recommendations:

1. _____

   _____

2. _____

   _____

3. _____

   _____

4. _____

   _____

TEAM MEETING

Write the team's discussion and deliberations in the space provided. What are the decisions for Alicia? What types of services are needed? Where will these services take place? Who will provide services? Include statements about Alicia's inclusion activities with children who do not have disabilities. After discussing the results with members in your class, complete the IEP.

_____

_____

_____

_____

_____

_____

_____

IEP

Write the present levels of development for Alicia in the following areas: physical development, cognitive development, social/emotional development, and adaptive development.

_____

_____

_____

_____

Write annual goals for Alicia:

_____

_____

_____

_____

_____

_____

Write the short-term objectives or benchmarks for Alicia:

_____

_____

_____

_____

_____

_____

_____

_____

_____

THINK AHEAD

EXERCISES

Part I

Match the following terms with the correct definitions.

a. educational planning
b. eligibility decision
c. behaviorally stated objective
d. Section 504
e. benchmarks
f. interindividual interpretation
g. intra-individual interpretation
h. projective tests
i. reevaluations

_____ 1. This level of test interpretation compares the student with the age or grade expectations according to the norm-group statistics.

_____ 2. These are based on specific criteria included in state and federal regulations.

_____ 3. Interventions and strategies used to promote educational success.

_____ 4. This is a method of comparing a student's own strengths and weaknesses to determine a pattern of functioning that may be influencing a student's educational performance.

_____ 5. The 1997 and 2004 IDEA Amendments changed this process so that less testing may be necessary for some students.

Answers to these questions can be found in the Appendix of this text or you may also complete these questions and receive immediate feedback on your answers by going to the Think Ahead module in Chapter 11 of the Companion Website.

COURSE PROGRESS MONITORING ASSESSMENT

See how you are doing in the course after the conclusion of Part IV chapters by completing the following assessment. When you are finished, check your answers with your instructor or on the Companion Website at *www.prenhall.com/overton*. Once you know your score, return to Figure 1.9, Student Progress Monitoring Graph in Chapter 1 and plot your progress.

Progress Monitoring Assessment

Select the best answer. Some of these terms may be used more than once.

A. diagnostic tests
B. abnormalities in social reciprocity
C. school neuropsychologist
D. mental retardation
E. FBA

F. CBMs
G. norm-referenced tests
H. standard error of
   measurement
 I. interresponse time
J. duration recording

K. criterion referenced tests
L. TBI
M. Ecological Assessment
N. developmental version
O. standardized tests

_____ 1. The core features of an autism spectrum disorder are abnormalities in communication, repetitive patterns of behavior, and ?

_____ 2. The use of a cognitive processing cross battery analysis may be part of an evaluation for ?

_____ 3. This person may conduct cross-battery assessments.

_____ 4. The initial administration of an instrument to a sample population.

_____ 5. These instruments may provide additional information used for specific academic or other weaknesses.

_____ 6. Tests designed to accompany a set of skills.

_____ 7. Assessing the learning environment.

_____ 8. These instruments provide comparisons with students the same age across the United States.

_____ 9. This measurement of error is usually used to calculate confidence intervals.

_____ 10. Measure of time between the presentation of a stimulus and a response.

Fill in the Blanks

11. When writing test reports the analysis of the comprehensive results are included in the _____ section.

12. The purpose of assessment is to _____ .

13. _____ is the type of validity that indicates a measure has items that are representative across the possible items in the domain.

14. _____ validity and _____ validity are differentiated by time.

15. _____ is a behavioral measure that indicates how students in a class view each other.

16. _____ is a computerized assessment of a student's ability to sustain attention across time.

17. Regulatory disturbances might be assessed when the assessment involves _____ .

18. Story starters might be useful in the informal assessment of _____ .

19. Any device that is necessary for a student to function within the educational environment is known as _____.

20. The final result of a comprehensive evaluation is to provide _____.

Appendix

KEY TO END-OF-CHAPTER EXERCISES

CHAPTER 1

Part I
1. overidentification
2. assessment
3. error analysis
4. dynamic assessment
5. eligibility meeting
6. standardized tests
7. prereferral intervention strategies
8. norm-referenced test
9. IFSP (Individual Family Service Plan)
10. CBA (curriculum-based assessment)

Part II
1. Prereferral checklist.
2. High-stakes assessment may be used to make high-stakes decisions, such as funding for school systems.
3. High-stakes assessment provides an accountability measure for all students in schools. This means that all students, including students who are receiving special education support services, should receive the appropriate education that will allow them to achieve as expected.
4. Whole-school approaches and prereferral interventions.
5. Frequent measurement of progress in the general education classroom, early prereferral interventions monitored for integrity, data collected and analyzed by intervention team, additional interventions tried, assessment plan designed, comprehensive assessment completed, team meeting held to determine eligibility, IEP or alternative plan designed and implemented.

CHAPTER 2

Part I

1. o	5. b, e	9. b
2. h	6. bb	10. m
3. w	7. x	11. s
4. d	8. i	

Part II
1. Parents, professionals, litigation.
2. If the student will need accommodations or an alternate test.
3. (a) Upon initial referral for evaluation,
   (b) Upon each notification of an individual education program meeting,

      (c) Upon reevaluation of the child,

      (d) Upon registration of a complaint.

4. (a) Are selected and administered so as not to be discriminatory on a racial or cultural basis,

    (b) Are provided and administered in the child's native language or other mode of communication, unless it is clearly not feasible to do so,

    (c) Measure the extent to which the child has a disability and needs special education, rather than measuring the child's English language skills,

    (d) Have been validated for the specific purpose for which they are used,

    (e) Are administered by trained and knowledgeable personnel in accordance with any instructions provided by the producer of such tests,

    (f) Include those tailored to assess specific areas of educational need and not merely those that are designed to provide a single, general intelligence quotient,

    (g) Are selected and administered so as best to ensure that if a test is administered to a child with impaired sensory, manual, or speaking skills, the test results accurately reflect the child's aptitude or achievement level or whatever other factors the test purports to measure, rather than reflecting the child's impaired sensory, manual, or speaking skills (unless those skills are the factors that the test purports to measure),

    (h) Are technically sound instruments that may assess the relative contribution of cognitive and behavioral factors, in addition to physical or developmental factors.

Part III

1. In the past traditional IEP conference, parents were found to be passive and to attend merely to receive information. Parents are now considered to be equal team members in the IEP process. Additionally, when working with parents from culturally diverse backgrounds, their level of acculturation should be considered.

2. Due process may be discriminatory because its cost may prohibit some families from following this procedure: actual financial costs, emotional and psychic costs, and time spent costs. Therefore, mediation is a free alternative for parents.

3. Evaluation procedures should not be racially or culturally discriminatory. Test bias may have greater implications for students who have linguistic differences and those who may come from culturally different backgrounds or deprived environments. Problems with bias in assessment include inappropriate test content; inappropriate standardization

samples, examiner and language issues, inequitable social consequences, measurement of different constructs, different predictive validity, and qualitatively distinct minority and majority aptitude and achievement. Additionally, there may be problems in biased assessment that also include overinterpretation of test results and problems that may arise in testing students whose dominant language is not English. It has even been recommended that norm-referenced instruments should not be used with bilingual students because norms are usually limited to small samples of minority children, norming procedures routinely exclude students with limited English proficiency, test items tap information that minority children may not be familiar with due to their linguistically and culturally different backgrounds, testing formats do not allow examiners the opportunity to provide feedback or to probe into the children's quality of responses, test scoring systems arbitrarily decide what are the correct responses based on majority culture paradigms, standardized testing procedures assume that the child has appropriate test-taking skills.

CHAPTER 3

Part I

1. s and q
2. t
3. g
4. a

5. p
6. c
7. o

8. e
9. t
10. j

Part II

mean = <u>81.16</u>   median = <u>83</u>   mode = <u>74, 78, 84, 85</u>

range = <u>41</u>   variance = <u>103.086</u>   standard deviation = <u>10.153</u>

Scores that are a significant distance from the mean are <u>58, 60, 63, 70, 72, 95, 96, 97, 99</u>

1. 95.44
2. 50
3. >99

4. between 3 and 4
5. .13% or less than 1%

CHAPTER 4

Part I

1. j
2. i
3. d
4. o

5. g or u
6. r
7. b

8. c
9. m
10. l

Part II

1. error	4. reliable
2. estimated true score	5. age
3. standard error of measurement	6. reliable

7. mean = <u>72.92</u> median = <u>76</u> mode = <u>76</u>

range = <u>61</u> variance = <u>277.91</u> standard dev. = <u>16.67</u>

SEM = <u>6.5</u>

(a) from 43.5 to 56.5
(b) from 68.5 to 81.5
(c) from 24.5 to 37.5
(d) from 70.5 to 83.5
(e) from 58.5 to 71.5
(f) from 74.5 to 87.5
(g) from 83.5 to 96.5
(h) from 85.5 to 98.5
(i) from 69.5 to 82.5
(j) from 67.5 to 80.5
(k) from 81.2 to 94.5
(l) from 81.5 to 94.5

CHAPTER 5

Part I

1. j	5. d	9. b
2. o	6. l	10. e
3. n	7. k	11. m
4. g	8. i	

Part II

1. d
2. c
3. a and b
4. d

Part III

Answers will vary but should include the concepts presented in the chapter, such as when students are not able to participate in the assessments, variability across states, purpose of assessment, and what is meant by high stakes.

Part IV

1. Chronological age: 7-10-25
2. Domain scores: 5 1 1 0
3. Raw score: 7

4. Basal item: 4
5. Ceiling item: 8

CHAPTER 6

Part I

1. d	5. k	8. f
2. m	6. e	9. h
3. c	7. a	10. l
4. n		

Part II
1. Curriculum-based assessment, to determine where to place the student in classroom reading texts.
2. Error analysis, to learn where the student seems to have difficulty working with the problems.
3. Error analysis, probes, direct measurement, to assist in determining a pattern of errors.
4. Curriculum-based, direct measurement—these methods are more sensitive and specific than norm-referenced tests.
5. Curriculum-based assessment and the aim line—to monitor progress.

CHAPTER 7

Part I

1. n	5. k	8. d
2. c	6. f	9. j
3. l	7. b	10. g
4. j		

Part II

1. b	5. h	8. f
2. g	6. a	9. d
3. a	7. a, c, f	10. i
4. i		

CHAPTER 8

Part I

1. s	5. m	9. d
2. b	6. k	10. i
3. e	7. l	11. g
4. p	8. c	12. j

Part II
The older brother's aggression is the setting event. The purpose of the student's aggression is to keep others from being aggressive toward him.

CHAPTER 9

Part I

1. g
2. j
3. b
4. e

5. d
6. k
7. c

CHAPTER 10

Part I

1. i
2. f
3. n
4. b

5. a
6. k
7. j

Part II

1. Confusion with the interpretation and implementation of the family assessment component, family's strengths and needs as they relate to the child rather than the parents, equal standing between parents and professionals may not result in a greater degree of cooperation and respect, etc. Answers may vary.
2. Regulatory disturbances, social/environmental disturbances, physiological disturbances, developmental delays.
3. Strengths and needs of the infant or toddler in the areas of physical and cognitive development, communication development, and adaptive development, and the identification of services appropriate to meet such needs, resources, priorities, and concerns of the family, identification of supports and services necessary, etc. Answers may vary.
4. Family involvement component, level of disability necessary for eligibility, assessment instruments, etc. Answers may vary, but should include the considerations presented in this chapter.

Part III

Answers may vary, but should include the concepts presented in this chapter, such as difficulties with implementing self-determination and transferring the rights of majority age.

CHAPTER 11

Part I

1. f
2. b
3. a

4. g
5. i

REFERENCES

Achenbach, T. M. (1986). *Child Behavior Checklist: Direct Observation Form, Revised Edition.* Burlington: University of Vermont Center for Children, Youth, and Families.

Achenbach, T. M. (1991a). *Manual for the Child Behavior Checklist/4–18 and 1991 profile.* Burlington: University of Vermont Department of Psychiatry.

Achenbach, T. M. (1991b). *Manual for the Teacher Report Form and 1991 profile.* Burlington: University of Vermont Department of Psychiatry.

Achenbach, T. M. (1991c). *Manual for the Youth Self-Report and 1991 Profile.* Burlington: University of Vermont Department of Psychiatry.

Achenbach, T. M. (1992). *Manual for the Child Behavior Checklist/2–3 and the 1992 Profile.* Burlington: University of Vermont Department of Psychiatry.

Achenbach, T. M., & McConaughy, S. H. (1989, 1990). *Semistructured Clinical Interview: Observation Form.* Burlington: University of Vermont Center for Children, Youth, and Families.

Achenbach, T. M., & Rescorla, L. A. (2000). *Manual for the ASEBA preschool forms & profiles: An integrated system of multi-informant assessment.* Burlington, VT: Authors.

Achenbach, T. M., & Rescorla, L. A. (2001). *Manual for the ASEBA school-age forms & profiles.* Burlington, VT: University of Vermont, Research Center for Children, Youth, & Families.

Algozzine, B., Christenson, S., & Ysseldyke, J. (1982). Probabilities associated with the referral-to-placement process. *Teacher Education and Special Education, 5,* 19–23.

Algozzine, B., Ysseldyke, J. E., & Christenson, S. (1983). An analysis of the incidence of special class placement: The masses are burgeoning. *The Journal of Special Education, 17,* 141–147.

Allinder, R. N. (1995). An examination of the relationship between teacher efficacy and curriculum-based measurement and student achievement. *Remedial and Special Education, 16,* 247–254.

Allinder, R. N., & Fuchs, L. S. (1992). Screening academic achievement: Review of the Peabody Individual Achievement Test–Revised. *Learning Disabilities Research & Practice, 7*(1), 45–47.

American Educational Research Association (AERA), American Psychological Association (APA) & National Council on Measurement in Education (NCME). (1999). *Standards for educational and psychological testing.* Washington, DC: AERA.

American Psychiatric Association. (1994). *Diagnostic and statistical manual of mental disorders* (4th ed.). Washington, DC: Author.

American Psychiatric Association. (2000). *Diagnostic and statistical manual of mental disorders,* (4th ed. Revised). Arlington, VA: Author.

American Psychological Association. (1985). *Standards for educational and psychological testing.* Washington, DC: Author.

Anastasi, A. (1988). *Psychological testing* (6th ed.). New York: Macmillan.

Anastasi, A., & Urbina, S. (1998). *Psychological testing* (7th ed.). Upper Saddle River, NJ: Prentice Hall.

Andrews, T. J., Wisnieswski, J. J., & Mulick, J. A. (1997). Variables influencing teachers' decisions to refer children for psychological assessment services. *Psychology in the Schools, 34,* 239–244.

Archbald, D. A. (1991). Authentic assessment: Principles, practices, and issues. *School Psychology Quarterly, 6,* 279–293.

Ardoin, S. P., Witt, J. C., Suldo, S. M., Connell, J. M., Koenig, J. L., Resetar, J. L., Slider, N. J., & Williams, K. L. (2004). Examining the incremental benefits of administering maze and three versus one curriculum-based measurement reading probes when conducting universal screening. *School Psychology Review, 33*(2), 218–233.

Bagnato, S. (1980). The efficacy of diagnostic reports as individualized guides to prescriptive goal planning. *Exceptional Children, 46,* 554–557.

Bailey, D. B., & Wolery, M. (1989). *Assessing infants and preschoolers with handicaps.* Upper Saddle River, NJ: Merrill/Prentice Hall.

Baker, S. K., & Good, R. (1995). Curriculum-based measurement of English reading with bilingual Hispanic students: A validation study with second grade students. *School Psychology Review, 24*(4), 561–578.

Barkley, R. A. (1990). *Attention deficit hyperactivity disorder: A handbook for diagnosis and treatment.* New York: Guilford.

Barkley, R. A., DuPaul, G. J., & McMurray, M. B. (1990). Comprehensive evaluation of attention deficit disorder with and without hyperactivity as defined by research criteria. *Journal of Consulting and Clinical Psychology, 58,* 775–789.

Barnes, W. (1986). Informal assessment of reading. *Pointer, 30,* 42–46.

Barnett, D., Zins, J., & Wise, L. (1984). An analysis of parental participation as a means of reducing bias in the education of handicapped children. *Special Services in the Schools, 1,* 71–84.

Barnett, D. W., Bell, S. H., Gilkey, C. M., Lentz, F. E., Graden, J. L., Stone, C. M., Smith, J. J., & Macmann, G. M. (1999). The promise of meaningful eligibility determination: Functional intervention-based multifactored preschool evaluation. *Journal of Special Education, 33*(2), 112–124.

Barnett, D. W., Macmann, G. M., & Carey, K. T. (1992). Early intervention and the assessment of developmental skills: Challenges and directions. *Topics in Early Childhood Special Education, 12*(1), 21–43.

Bayley, N. (1993). *Bayley scales of infant development-II.* San Antonio: Psychological Corporation.

Bellak, L., & Bellak, S. S. (1949). *Children's Apperception Test (animal figures).* Larchmont, NY: C.P.S.

Bellak, L., & Bellak, S. S. (1952). *Manual for the Supplement for the Children's Apperception Test.* Larchmont, NY: C.P.S.

Bellak, L., & Hurvich, M. S. (1965). *Children's Apperception Test (human figures) Manual.* Larchmont, NY: C.P.S.

Bender, W., & Golden, L. (1988). Adaptive behavior of learning disabled and non-learning disabled children. *Learning Disability Quarterly, 11,* 55–61.

Bennett, R. (1981). Professional competence and the assessment of exceptional children. *Journal of Special Education, 15,* 437–446.

Bennett, R. (1982). Cautions for the use of informal measures in the educational assessment of exceptional children. *Journal of Learning Disabilities, 15,* 337–339.

Bennett, R., & Shepherd, M. (1982). Basic measurement proficiency of learning disability specialists. *Learning Disabilities Quarterly, 5,* 177–183.

Bennett, T., Lee, H., & Lueke, B. (1998). Expectations and concerns: What mothers and fathers say about inclusion. *Education and Training in Mental Retardation and Developmental Disabilities, 33*(2), 108–122.

Berninger, V. L. (2006). Research-supported ideas for implementing reauthorized IDEA with intelligent professional psychological services. *Psychology in the Schools, 43*(7), 781–796.

Berninger, V. W. (2001). *Process assessment of the learner: Test battery for reading and writing.* San Antonio, TX: The Psychological Corporation.

Bersoff, D. N. (1981). Testing and the law. *American Psychologist, 36,* 1047–1056.

Bocian, K. M., Beebe, M. E., MacMillan, D., & Gresham, F. M. (1999). Competing paradigms in learning disabilities classification by schools and the variations in the meaning of discrepant achievement. *Learning Disabilities Research, 14*(1), 1–14.

Borg, W., Worthen, B., & Valcarce, R. (1986). Teachers' perceptions of the importance of educational measurement. *Journal of Experimental Education, 5,* 9–14.

Bracken, B. A. & McCallum, R. S. (1998). *Universal Test of Non-verbal Intelligence: Examiner's manual.* Itasca, IL: Riverside Publishing Company.

Brantlinger, E. (1987). Making decisions about special education placement: Do low-income parents have the information they need? *Journal of Learning Disabilities, 20*, 94–101.

Brazelton, T. (1984). *Neonatal Behavioral Assessment Scale-Second Edition*. Philadelphia: Lippincott.

Brigance, A. H. (1981). *Brigance diagnostic inventory of essential skills*. N. Billerica, MA: Curriculum Associates.

Brigance, A. H. (1997). *K & 1 screen*. North Billerica, MA: Curriculum Associates.

Brigance, A. H. (1998a). *Early preschool screen*. North Billerica, MA: Curriculum Associates.

Brigance, A. H. (1998b). *Preschool screen*. North Billerica, MA: Curriculum Associates.

Brigance, A. H. (1999). *Brigance Diagnostic Comprehensive Inventory of Basic Skills*. N. Billerica, MA: Curriculum Associates.

Brigance, A. H. (2004). *Brigance Diagnostic Inventory of Early Development-Second Edition*. N. Billerica, MA: Curriculum Associates.

Brigham, F. J., Tochterman, S., & Brigham, M. S. P. (2000). Students with emotional and behavioral disorders and their teachers in test-linked systems of accountability. *Assessment for Effective Intervention, 26*(1), 19–27.

Brotherson, M. J., & Berdine, W. H. (1993). Transition to adult services: Support for ongoing parent participation. *Remedial & Special Education, 14*(4), 44–52.

Brown, L., & Hammill, D. (1990). *Behavior Rating Profile* (2nd ed.). Austin, TX: Pro-Ed.

Brown, L., & Leigh, J. E. (1986). *Adaptive Behavior Inventory*. Austin, TX: Pro-Ed.

Brown, L., Sherbenou, R. J., & Johnsen, S. K. (1997). *Test of Nonverbal Intelligence, 3rd Edition*. Austin, TX: Pro-Ed.

Brown, T., Reynolds, C. R., & Whitaker, J. S. (1999). Bias in mental testing since Bias in Mental Testing. *School Psychology Quarterly, 14*(3), 208–238.

Brown, V. L., Cronin, M. E., & McEntire, E. (1994). *Test of mathematical abilities* (2nd ed.). Austin, TX: Pro-Ed.

Brown, V. L., Hammill, D. D., & Wiederholt, J. L. (1995). *The test of reading comprehension* (3rd ed.). Austin, TX: Pro-Ed.

Bruininks, R., Thurlow, M., & Gilman, C. (1987). Adaptive behavior and mental retardation. *Journal of Special Education, 21*, 69–88.

Bryant, B. R. (1998). Assistive technology: An introduction. *Journal of Learning Disabilities, 31*(1), 2–3.

Budoff, M., & Orenstein, A. (1981). Special education appeals hearings: Are they fair and are they helping? *Exceptional Education Quarterly, 2*, 37–48.

Burger, S. E., & Burger, D. L. (1994). Determining the validity of performance-based assessment. *Educational Measurement: Issues and Practices, 13*, 9–15.

Burnette, J. (1998, March). Reducing the disproportionate representation of minority students in special education. ERIC/OSEP Digest E566.

Burns, P. C., & Roe, B. D. (1989). *Informal Reading Inventory* (3rd ed.). Boston: Houghton Mifflin.

Cahan, S. (1989). Don't throw the baby out with the bath water: The case for using estimated true scores in normative comparisons. *Journal of Special Education, 22*, 503–506.

Campbell, E., Schellinger, T., & Beer, J. (1991). Relationship among the ready or not parental checklist for school readiness, the Brigance kindergarten and first grade screen, and SRA scores. *Perceptual and Motor Skills, 73*, 859–862.

Canivez, G. L. (1995). Validity of the Kaufman Brief Intelligence Test: Comparisons with the Wechsler Intelligence Scale for Children-Third Edition. *Psychological Assessment Resources, Inc. 2*(2), 101–111.

Canivez, G. L. (1996). Validity and diagnostic efficiency of the Kaufman Brief Intelligence Test in reevaluating students with learning disability. *Journal of Psychoeducational Assessment, 14*, 4–19.

Canter, A. (1991). Effective psychological services for all students: A data-based model of service delivery. In G. Stoner, M. R. Shinn, & H. M. Walker (Eds.), *Interventions for achievement and behavioral problems* (pp. 49–78). Silver Spring, MD: National Association of School Psychologists.

Canter, A. S. (1997). The future of intelligence testing in the schools. *School Psychology Review, 26*(2), 255–261.

Carroll, J. B. (1997). Commentary on Keith and Witta's hierarchical and cross-age confirmatory factor analysis of the WISC-III. *School Psychology Quarterly, 12*(2), 108–109.

Carroll, J. B. (2005). The three stratum theory of cognitive abilities. In D. P. Flanagan & P.L. Harrison (Eds.), *Contemporary intellectual assessment: Theories, tests, and issues* (pp. 69–76). New York: The Guilford Press.

Carter, J., & Sugai, G. (1989). Survey on pre-referral practices: Responses from state departments of education. *Exceptional Children, 55*, 298–308.

Cascella, P. W. (2006). Standardised speech-language tests and students with intellectual disability: A review of normative data. *Journal of Intellectual & Developmental Disability, 3*(2), 120–124.

Centers for Disease Control and Prevention (2007). Autism Information Center, ADDM, 2007. Available from the Centers for Disease Control and Prevention Web site, *http://www.cdc.gov/ncbddd/autism/overview.htm*

Chalfant, J. C., & Psyh, M. (1989). Teachers assistance teams: Five descriptive studies on 96 teams. *Remedial and Special Education, 10*(6), 49–58.

Clarizio, H. F., & Higgins, M. M. (1989). Assessment of severe emotional impairment: Practices and problems. *Psychology in the Schools, 26*, 154–162.

Clark, G. M. (1996). Transition planning assessment for secondary-level students with learning disabilities. *Journal of Learning Disabilities, 29*(1), 79–93.

Clark, G., & Patton, J. (1997). *Transition Planning Inventory.* Austin, TX: Pro-Ed.

Clark, G. M., & Patton, J. R. (2006). *Transition planning inventory: Update version.* Austin, TX: Pro-Ed.

Clark, G. M., Patton, J. R., & Moulton, L. R. (2000). *Informal assessments for transition planning.* Austin, TX: Pro-Ed.

Clarke, B., & Shinn, M. R. (2004). A preliminary investigation into the identification and development of early mathematics curriculum-based measurement. *School Psychology Review, 33*(2), 234–248.

Cohen, L. G., & Spenciner, L. J. (1994). *Assessment of young children.* New York: Longman.

Cole, J., D'Alonzo, B., Gallegos, A., Giordano, G., & Stile, S. (1992). Test biases that hamper learners with disabilities. *Diagnostique, 17*, 209–225.

Cole, J. C., Muenz, T. A., Ouchi, B. Y., Kaufman, N. L., & Kaufman, A. S. (1997). The impact of pictorial stimulis on written expression output of adolescents and adults. *Pyschology in the Schools, 34*, 1–9.

Cole, N. (1981). Bias in testing. *American Psychologist, 36*, 1067–1075.

Connelly, J. (1985). Published tests: Which ones do special education teachers perceive as useful? *Journal of Special Education, 19*, 149–155.

Conners, C. K. (1993). *Conners' Continuous Performance Test.* North Tonawanda, NY: Multi-Health Systems.

Conners, C. K. (1997). *Conners' Rating Scales–Revised: Technical Manual.* North Tonawanda, NY: Multi-Health Systems.

Connolly, A. J. (1988). *KeyMath-Revised: A Diagnostic Inventory of Essential Mathematics, manual. Forms A and B.* Circle Pines, MN: American Guidance Service.

Connolly, A. J. (2007). *KeyMath 3: Diagnostic battery.* Minneapolis, MN: NCS Pearson, Inc.

Conroy, M. A., Clark, D., Gable, R. A., & Fox, J. (1999). Building competence in the use of functional behavioral assessment. *Preventing School Failure, 43*(4), 140–144.

Council for Exceptional Children (1993). CEC policies for delivery of services: Ethnic and multicultural groups. *CEC Policy Manual*, section 3, part 1 (pp. 6, 20–21). Reston, VA: Author.

Council for Exceptional Children (1997–1999). *Standards for professional practice.* Reston, VA: Author.

Cronis, T. G., & Ellis, D. N. (2000, Summer). Issues facing special educators in the new millennium. *Education, 120*(4), 639–648.

Daly, E. J., Witt, J. C., Martens, B. K., & Dool, E. J. (1997). A model for conducting a functional analysis of academic performance problems. *School Psychology Review, 26*, 554–574.

Davis, L. B., Fuchs, L. S., Fuchs, D., & Whinnery, K. (1995). "Will CBM help me learn?" Students' perception of the benefits of curriculum-based measurement. *Education and Treatment of Children, 18,* 19–32.

Davis, W., & Shepard, L. (1983). Specialists' use of tests and clinical judgments in the diagnosis of learning disabilities. *Learning Disabilities Quarterly, 6,* 128–137.

deGruijter, D. N. M. (1997). On information of percentile ranks. *Journal of Educational Measurement, 34,* 177–178.

Del'Homme, M., Kasari, C., Forness, S. R., & Bagley, R. (1996). Prereferral intervention and students at risk for emotional or behavioral disorders. *Education and Treatment of Children, 19,* 272–285.

Demaray, M. K., & Elliott, S. N. (1998). Teachers' judgment of students' academic functioning: A comparison of actual and predicted performances. *School Psychology Quarterly, 13*(1), 8–24.

Deno, S. L. (1985). Curriculum-based measurement: The emerging alternative. *Exceptional Children, 52*(3), 219–232.

Deno, S. L. (1989). Curriculum-based measurement and alternative special education services: A fundamental and direct relationship. In M. R. Shinn (Ed.), *Curriculum-based measurement: Assessing special children* (pp. 1–17). New York: Gilford Press.

Deno, S. L. (2003). Developments in curriculum-based measurement. *The Journal of Special Education, 37*(3), 184–192.

Deno, S. L., Fuchs, L. S., Marston, D., & Shin, J. (2001). Using curriculum-based measurement to establish growth standards for students with learning disabilities. *School Psychology Review, 30*(4), 507–524.

Deno, S. L., Marston, D., & Mirkin, P. (1982). Valid measurement procedures for continuous evaluation of written expression. *Exceptional Children, 48*(4), 368–371.

Deno, S. L., Marston, D., Shinn, M., & Tindal, G. (1983). Oral reading fluency: A simple datum for scaling reading disability. *Topics in Learning and Learning Disabilities, 2*(4), 53–59.

Detterman, D. K., & Thompson, L. A. (1997). What is so special about special education? *American Psychologist, 52*(10), 1082–1090.

Detterman, D. K., & Thompson, L. A. (1998). They doth protest too much. *American Psychologist, 53*(10), 1162–1163.

Diana v. State Board of Education, Civil Act. No. C-70–37 (N.D. Cal, 1970, further order, 1973).

DiLavore, P., Loard, C., & Rutter, M. (1995). Pre-Linguistic Autism Diagnostic Observation Schedule (PL-ADOS). *Journal of Autism and Pervasive Developmental Disorders, 25,* 355–379.

Doll, E. A. (1935). A genetic scale of social maturity. *American Journal of Orthopsychiatry, 5,* 180–188.

Drasgow, E. & Yell, M. (2001). Functional behavioral assessments: Legal requirements and challenges. *School Psychology Review, 30*(2), 239–251.

Drasgow, E., Yell, M. L., Bradley, R., Shriner, J. G. (1999). The IDEA Amendments of 1997: A school-wide model for conducting functional behavioral assessments and developing behavioral intervention plans. *Education and Treatment of Children, 22*(3), 244–266.

Dunn, L. M., & Dunn, D. M. (1997). *Peabody picture vocabulary yest-III.* Circle Pines, MN: American Guidance Service.

Dunn, L.M., & Dunn, D.M. (2007). *Peabody Picture Vocabulary Test-4.* Wascana Limited Partnership. Minneapolis, MN. NCS Pearson, Inc.

Dunst, C. J., Johanson, C., Trivette, C. M., & Hamby, D. (1991). Family-oriented early intervention policies and practices: Family-centered or not? *Exceptional Children, 58,* 115–126.

Eaves, R. (1985). Educational assessment in the United States [Monograph]. *Diagnostique, 10,* 5–39.

Eckert, T. L., Shapiro, E. S., & Lutz, J. G. (1995). Teachers' ratings of the acceptability of curriculum-based assessment methods. *School Psychology Review, 24,* 497–511.

Education of the Handicapped Act (1975, 1977). PL 94–142, 20 U.S.C. §§ 1400–1485, 34 CFR-300.

Ehri, L. C., Nunes, S. R., Willows, D. M., Schuster, B. V., Yaghoub-Zadeh, Z., & Shanahan, T. (2001). Phonemic awareness instruction helps children learn to read: Evidence from the national reading panel's meta-analysis. *Reading Research Quarterly, 36*(3), 250–287.

Eliason, M. J., & Richman, L. C. (1987). The Continuous Performance Test in learning disabled and nondisabled children. *Journal of Learning Disabilities, 20,* 614–619.

Elliott, S. N., Braden, J. P., & White, J. L. (2001). *Assessing one and all: Educational accountability for students with disabilities.* Arlington, VA: Council for Exceptional Children.

Elliot, S. N., Busse, R. T., & Gresham, F. M. (1993). Behavior rating scales: Issues of use and development. *School Psychology Review, 22,* 313–321.

Elliott, S. N., & Fuchs, L. S. (1997). The utility of curriculum-based measurement and performance assessment as alternatives to traditional intelligence and achievement tests. *School Psychology Review, 26*(3) 224–233.

Elliott, S. N., Kratochwill, T. R., & Schulte, A. G. (1998). The assessment accommodation checklist. *Teaching Exceptional Children,* Nov./Dec., 10–14.

Engiles, A., Fromme, C., LeResche, D., & Moses, P. (1999). *Keys to access: Encouraging the use of mediation by families from diverse backgrounds.* (Document No. EC 307 554). Consortium for Appropriate Dispute Resolution in Special Education. (ERIC Document Reproduction Service No. ED 436 881)

Epstein, M.H., & Cullinan, D. (1998). *Scale for assessing emotional disturbance.* Austin, TX: Pro-Ed.

Ervin, R. A., Radford, P. M., Bertsch, K., Piper, A. L., Ehrhardt, K. E., & Poling, A. (2001). A descriptive analysis and critique of the empirical literature on school-based functional assessment. 193–210.

Etscheidt, S., & Knesting, K. (2007). A qualitative analysis of factors influencing the interpersonal dynamics of a prereferral team. *School Psychology Quarterly, 22*(2), 264–288.

Evans, L., & Bradley-Johnson, S. (1988). A review of recently developed measures of adaptive behavior. *Psychology in the Schools, 25,* 276–287.

Evans, S., & Evans, W. (1986). A perspective on assessment for instruction. *Pointer, 30,* 9–12.

Evans, W. H., Evans, S. S., & Schmid, R. E. (1989). *Behavioral and instructional management: An ecological approach.* Boston: Allyn & Bacon.

Fan, X., Wilson, V. L., & Reynolds, C. R. (1995). Assessing the similarity of the factor structure of the K-ABC for African American and white children. *Journal of Psychoeducational Assessment, 13,* 120–131.

Federal Register (1977, August 23). Washington, DC: U.S. Government Printing Office.

Federal Register. (1992, September 29). Washington, DC: U.S. Government Printing Office.

Federal Register (1993, July 30). Washington, DC: U.S. Government Printing Office.

Federal Register. (1999, March 12). Washington, DC: U.S. Government Printing Office.

Federal Register (2006, August 14). Washington, DC: U.S. Government Printing Office.

Feldt, L., Sabers, D., & Reschly, D. (1988). Comments on the reply by Salvia and Ysseldyke. *Journal of Special Education, 22,* 374–377.

Felton, R. H., & Pepper, P. P. (1995). Early identification and intervention of phonological deficits in kindergarten and early elementary children at risk for reading disability. *School Psychology Review, 24*(3), 405–414.

Fewell, R. R. (1991). Trends in the assessment of infants and toddlers with disabilities. *Exceptional Children, 58,* 166–173.

Field, S. Martin, J., Miller, R., Ward, M., & Wehmeyer, M. (1998). *A practical guide to teaching self-determination.* Reston, VA: Council for Exceptional Children.

Filipek, P. A., Accardo, P. J., Baranek, G. T., Cook, E. H., Jr., Dawson, G., Gordon, B., et al. (1999). The screening and diagnosis of autism spectrum disorders. *Journal of Autism and Developmental Disabilities, 29*(6), 439–484.

Flanagan, D. P., & Harrison, P. L. (Eds.) (2005). *Contemporary intellectual assessment: Theories, tests, and issues.* New York: The Guilford Press.

Flanagan, D. P., & Ortiz, S. (2001). *Essentials of cross-battery assessment.* New York: John Wiley & Sons, Inc.

Flaugher, R. (1978). The many definitions of test bias. *American Psychologist, 33,* 671–679.

Foegen, A., Jiban, C., Deno, S. (2007). Progress monitoring measures in mathematics: A review of the literature. *The Journal of Special Education, 4*(2), 121–139.

Forness, S. R., Swanson, J. M., Cantwell, D. P., Guthrie, D., & Sena, R. (1992). Responses to stimulant medication across six measures of school related performance in children with ADHD and disruptive behavior. *Behavioral Disorders,* 18, 42–53.

Foster-Gaitskell, D., & Pratt, C. (1989). Comparison of parent and teacher ratings of adaptive behavior of children with mental retardation. *American Journal of Mental Retardation, 94,* 177–181.

Fradd, S., & Hallman, C. (1983). Implications of psychological and educational research for assessment and instruction of culturally and linguistically different students. *Learning Disabilities Quarterly, 6,* 468–477.

Fuchs, D. (1991). Mainstream assistance teams: A prereferral intervention system for difficult to teach students. In Stoner, G., Shinn, M. R., & Walker, H. M. (Eds.), *Interventions for achievement and behavior problems* (pp. 241–267). Silver Spring, MD: National Association of School Psychologists.

Fuchs, D., & Fuchs, L. (1989). Effects of examiner familiarity on Black, Caucasian, and Hispanic children: A meta-analysis. *Exceptional Children, 55,* 303–308.

Fuchs, D., Fuchs, L., Benowitz, S., & Barringer, K. (1987). Norm-referenced tests: Are they valid for uses with handicapped students? *Exceptional Children, 54,* 263–271.

Fuchs, D., Zern, D., & Fuchs, L. (1983). A microanalysis of participant behavior in familiar and unfamiliar test conditions. *Exceptional Children, 50,* 75–77.

Fuchs, L. S. (2004). The past, present, and future of curriculum-based measurement research. *School Psychology Review, 33*(2), 188–192.

Fuchs, L., Butterworth, J., & Fuchs, D. (1989). Effects of ongoing curriculum-based measurement on student awareness of goals and progress. *Education and Treatment of Children, 12,* 41–47.

Fuchs, L. S., Deno, S. L., & Mirkin, P. (1984). Effects of frequent curriculum-based measurement and evaluation on pedagogy, student achievement, and student awareness of learning. *American Educational Research Journal, 21,* 449–460.

Fuchs, L. S., & Fuchs, D. (1986). Effects of a systematic formative evaluation: A meta-analysis. *Exceptional Children, 53,* 199–208.

Fuchs, L., & Fuchs, D. (1992). Identifying a measure for monitoring student reading progress. *School Psychology Review, 21,* 45–58.

Fuchs, L. S., & Fuchs, D. (1996). Combining performance assessment and curriculum-based measurement to strengthen instructional planning. *Learning Disabilities Research & Practice, 11,* 183–192.

Fuchs, L. Fuchs, D., & Hamlett, C. (1989). Effects of instrumental use of curriculum-based measurement to enhance instructional programs. *Remedial and Special Education, 10,* 43–52.

Fuchs, L. Fuchs, D., Hamlett, C. L., Phillips, N. B., & Bentz, J. (1994). Classwide curriculum-based measurement: Helping general educators meet the challenge of student diversity. *Exceptional Children, 60,* 518–537.

Fuchs, L. S., Fuchs, D., Hamlett, C. L., Walz, C. L., & Germann, G. (1993). Formative evaluation of academic progress: How much growth can we expect? *School Psychology Review, 22*(1), 27–48.

Fuchs, L. S., Fuchs, D., Hamlett, C. L., & Stecker, P. M. (1991). Effects of curriculum-based measurement and consultation on teacher planning and student achievement in mathematics operations. *American Educational Research Journal, 28,* 617–641.

Fuchs, L., Tindal, G., & Deno, S. (1984). Methodological issues in curriculum-based assessment. *Diagnostique, 9,* 191–207.

Fugate, D. J., Clarizio, H. F., & Phillips, S. E. (1993). Referral-to-placement ratio:

A finding in need of reassessment? *Journal of Learning Disabilities, 26*(6), 413–416.

Fujiura, G. T., & Yamaki, K. (2000). Trends in demography of childhood poverty and disability. *Exceptional Children, 66*(2), 187–199.

Gable, R. A., Hendrickson, J. M., & Smith, C. (1999). Changing discipline policies and practices: Finding a place for functional behavioral assessments in schools. *Preventing School Failure, 43*(4), 167–170.

Gardner, H. (1993). *Multiple intelligences: The theory in practice.* New York: Basic Books.

German, D., Johnson, B., & Schneider, M. (1985). Learning disability vs. reading disability: A survey of practitioners' diagnostic populations and test instruments. *Learning Disability Quarterly, 8,* 141–156.

Gilliam, J.E. (2006). *Gilliam autism rating scale: Examiner's manual.* Austin, TX: Pro-Ed.

Gillis, M., & Olson, M. (1987). Elementary IRIs: Do they reflect what we know about text/type structure and comprehension? *Reading Research and Instruction, 27,* 36–44.

Gindis, B. (1999). Vygotsky's vision: Reshaping the practice of special education for the 21st century. *Remedial and Special Education, 20,* 333–340.

Glascoe, F. P. (1998). *Technical report for the Brigance screens.* North Billerica, MA: Curriculum Associates.

Glascoe, F. P. (1999). *CIBS-R standardization and validation manual.* N. Billerica, MA: Curriculum Associates.

Glascoe, F. P. (2004). *IED-II standardization and validation manual.* N. Billerica, MA: Curriculum Associates.

Glaser, R. (1963). Instructional technology and the measurement of learning outcomes: Some questions. *American Psychologist, 18*(2), 519–521.

Glatthorn, A. A. (1998). *Performance assessment and standards-based curricula: The achievement cycle.* Larchmont, NY: Eye on Education.

Goff, W. H. (2002). *Guidelines for writing objective reports.* Unpublished manuscript.

Goldstein, S., Strickland, B., Turnbull, A., & Curry, L. (1980). An observational analysis of the IEP conference. *Exceptional Children, 46,* 278–286.

Goldstein, S., & Turnbull, A. (1982). Strategies to increase parent participation in IEP conferences. *Exceptional Children, 48,* 360–361.

Good, R., & Salvia, J. (1988). Curriculum bias in published, norm-referenced reading tests: Demonstrable effects. *School Psychology Review, 17,* 51–60.

Goodman, J. F., & Hover, S. A. (1992). The Individual Family Service Plan: Unresolved problems. *Psychology in the Schools, 29,* 140–151.

Gopaul-McNicol, S., & Thomas-Presswood, T. (1998). *Working with linguistically and culturally different children: Innovative clinical and educational approaches.* Boston: Allyn & Bacon.

Gordon, M. (1983). *Gordon Diagnostic System.* DeWitt, NY: Gordon Diagnostic Systems.

Gotham, K., Risi, S., Pickles, A., Lord, C. (2007). The Autism Diagnostic observation schedule: Revised algorithms for improved diagnostic validity. *Journal of Autism and Developmental Disorders, 37*(4), 613–627.

Graden, J., Casey, A., & Bonstrom, O. (1985). Implementing a prereferral intervention system: Part II. The data. *Exceptional Children, 51,* 487–496.

Graden, J., Casey, A., & Christenson, S. (1985). Implementing a prereferral intervention system: Part I. The model. *Exceptional Children, 51,* 377–384.

Graham, M., & Scott, K. (1988). The impact of definitions of high risk on services of infants and toddlers. *Topics in Early Childhood Special Education, 8*(3), 23–28.

Granville, R., Shaver, R. B., & McGrew, K. S. (2003). Interpretation of the Woodcock-Johnson III Tests of Cognitive Abilities: Acting on evidence. In F. A. Schrank & D. P. Flanagan (Eds.), WJ III clinical use and interpretation (pp. 3–39). San Diego, CA: Academic Press.

Greenspan, S. I. (1992). *Infancy and early childhood: The practice of clinical assessment and intervention with emotional and developmental challenges.* Madison, CT: International University Press.

Greenwood, C. R., Tapia, Y., Abott, M., & Walton, C. (2003). A building-based case study of evidence-based literacy practices: Implementation, reading behavior, and growth in reading fluency, K-4. *Journal of Special Education, 37*(2), 95–111.

Gresham, F. M., MacMillan, D. L., & Bocian, K. M. (1998). Agreement between school study team decisions and authoritative definitions in classifications of students at-risk for mild disabilities. *School Psychology Quarterly, 13*(3), 181–191.

Gresham, F. M., Watson, T. S., & Skinner, C. H. (2001). Functional behavioral assessment: Principles, procedures, and future directions. *School Psychology Review, 30*(2), 156–172.

Gridley, B. E., & McIntosh, D. E. (1991). Confirmatory factor analysis of the Stanford–Binet: Fourth Edition for a normal sample. *Journal of School Psychology, 29*, 237–248.

Gronna, S., Jenkins, A., & Chin-Chance, S. (1998). The performance of students with disabilities in a norm-referenced, statewide standardized testing program. *Journal of Learning Disabilities, 31*(5), 482–493.

Guerin, G. R., & Maier, A. S. (1983). *Informal assessment in education.* Palo Alto, CA: Mayfield.

Haager, D, (2007). Promises and cautions regarding using response to intervention with English Language Learners. Learning Disabilities Quarterly, *30*(3), 213–218.

Halgren, D. W., & Clarizio, H. F. (1993). Categorical and programming changes in special education services. *Exceptional Children, 59*, 547–555.

Hammill, D. D. (1998). *Detroit Tests of Learning Aptitude-4.* Austin, TX: Pro-Ed.

Hammill, D. D., & Hresko, W. P. (1994). *Comprehensive Scales of Student Abilities.* Austin, TX: Pro-Ed.

Hammill, D. D., & Larsen, S. C. (1996). *Test of Written Language.* Austin, TX: Pro-Ed.

Hammill, D. D., & Newcomer, P. L. (1997). *Test of Language Development-Intermediate: Third edition.* Austin, TX: Pro-Ed.

Hammill, D. D., Pearson, N. A., & Wiederholt, J. L. (1996). *Comprehensive Test of Nonverbal Intelligence.* Austin, TX: Pro-Ed.

Hammill, D. D., & Larsen, S. C. (1999). *Test of Written Language, Third Edition.* Austin, TX: Pro-Ed.

Harris, D. B. (1963). *Goodenough–Harris drawing test.* New York: Harcourt Brace.

Harris, K., & Graham, S. (1994). Constructivism: Principles, paradigms, and integration. *Journal of Special Education, 28*, 233–247.

Harrison, P. (1987). Research with adaptive behavior scales. *Journal of Special Education, 21*, 37–61.

Harrison, P. L., Kaufman, A. S., Kaufman, N. L., Bruininks, R. H., Rynders, J., Ilmer, S., Sparrow, S. S., & Cicchetti, D. V. (1990). *AGS early screening profiles.* Circle Pines, MN: American Guidance Service.

Harrison, P. L., & Robinson, B. (1995). Best practices in the assessment of adaptive behavior. In A. Thomas & J. Grimes (Eds.), *Best practices in school psychology* (3rd ed.). Washington, DC: National Association of School Psychologists.

Harry, B., & Anderson, M. G. (1995). The disproportionate placement of African American males in special education programs: A critique of the process. *Journal of Negro Education, 63*(4), 602–619.

Hart, K. E., & Scuitto, M. J. (1996). Criterion-referenced measurement of instructional impact on cognitive outcomes. *Journal of Instructional Psychology, 23*, 26–34.

Harvey, V. (1991). Characteristics of children referred to school psychologists: A discriminant analysis. *Psychology in the Schools, 28*, 209–218.

Hasazi, S. B., Johnston, A. P., Liggett, A. M., & Schattman, R. A. (1994). A qualitative policy study of the least restrictive environment provision of the Individuals with Disabilities Education Act. *Exceptional Children, 60*, 491–507.

Heller, K., Holtzman, W., & Messick, S. (Eds.). (1982). *Placing children in special education: A strategy for equity.* Washington, DC: National Academy Press.

Herrnstein, R. J., & Murray, C. (1994). *The bell curve: Intelligence and class structure in American life.* New York: The Free Press.

Heshusius, L. (1991). Curriculum-based assessment and direct instruction: Critical reflections on fundamental assumptions. *Exceptional Children, 57*, 315–328.

Hintze, J. M., & Christ, T. J. (2004). An examination of variability as a function of passage variance in CBM monitoring. *School Psychology Review, 33*(2), 204–217.

Hintze, J. M., Shapiro, E. S., & Lutz, J. G. (1994). The effects of curriculum on the sensitivity of curriculum-based measurement in reading. *Journal of Special Education, 28*, 188–202.

Hobbs, R. (1993). Portfolio use in a learning disabilities resource room. *Reading & Writing Quarterly: Overcoming Learning Difficulties, 9*, 249–261.

Hong, B. S. S., Ivy, W. F., Gonzalez, H. R., & Ehrensberger, W.(2007). Preparing students for post-secondary education. *Teaching Exceptional Children, 40*(1), 32–38.

Hopkins, K. D., Stanley, J. C., & Hopkins, B. R. (1990). *Educational and psychological measurement and evaluation* (7th ed.). Upper Saddle River, NJ: Prentice Hall.

Horn, E., & Fuchs, D. (1987). Using adaptive behavior in assessment and intervention. *Journal of Special Education, 21*, 11–26.

Hosp, M. K., & Hosp, J. L. (2003). Curriculum-based measurement for reading, spelling, and math: How to do it and why. *Preventing School Failure, 48*(1), 10–18.

Howell, K. W., & Morehead, M. K. (1987). *Curriculum-based evaluation for special and remedial education.* Columbus, OH: Merrill.

Hoy, M., & Retish, P. (1984). A comparison of two types of assessment reports. *Exceptional Children, 51*, 225–229.

Huebner, E. (1988). Bias in teachers' special education decisions as a further function of test score reporting format. *Journal of Educational Researcher, 21*, 217–220.

Huebner, E. (1989). Errors in decision making: A comparison of school psychologists' interpretations of grade equivalents, percentiles, and deviation IQs. *School Psychology Review, 18*, 51–55.

Huebner, E. S. (1991). Bias in special education decisions: The contribution of analogue research. *School Psychology Quarterly, 6*(1), 50–65.

Huefner, D. S. (2000). The risks and opportunities of the IEP requirements under the IDEA 1997. *Journal of Special Education, 33*(4), 195–204.

Hultquist, A. M., & Metzke, L. K. (1993). Potential effects of curriculum bias in individual norm-referenced reading and spelling achievement tests. *Journal of Psychoeducational Assessment, 11*, 337–344.

Individuals with Disabilities Education Act Amendments of 1997, PL. 105–17, 105th Congress.

Individuals with Disabilities Education Act (IDEA, 20 U.S.C. § 1400 et seq. (1997).

Individuals with Disabilities Education Improvement Act of 2004, P. L. 108–446, 20 U.S.C. § 1400 et seq.

Individuals with Disabilities Education Act Regulations, 34, CFR. §§ 300 and 303 (1999).

Jackson, G. D. (1975). Another psychological view from the Association of Black Psychologists. *American Psychologist, 30*, 88–93.

Javorsky, J. (1998–1999). Behavior-Rating Profile, Second Edition. *Monograph: Assessment for the New Decade, Diagnostic, 24*(1–4), 33–40.

Jensen, A. R. (1998). *The g factor: The science of mental ability.* Westport, CT: Praeger.

Johnson, S. B. (1999). Test reviews: Normative update for Kaufman Educational Achievement, Peabody Individual Achievement Test–Revised, KeyMath–Revised, and Woodcock Reading Mastery Test–Revised. *Psychology in the Schools, 36*(2),175–176.

Kamphaus, R. (1987). Conceptual and psychometric issues in the assessment of adaptive behavior. *Journal of Special Education, 21*, 27–35.

Kamphaus, R. W., Winsor, A. P., Rowe, E. W., & Kim, S. (2005). A history of intelligence test interpretation. In D. P. Flanagan & P. L. Harrison (Eds.), *Contemporary intellectual assessment: Theories, tests, and issues* (pp. 23–37). New York: The Guilford Press.

Kamps, D., Abbott, M., Greenwood, C., Arregaga-Mayer, C., Wills, H., et al. (2007). Use of evidence-based, small group reading instruction for English language learners in elementary grades: Secondary-tier intervention. *Learning Disability Quarterly, 30*(3), 153–168.

Katsiyannis, A. (1994). Prereferral practices: Under Office of Civil Rights scrutiny.

Journal of Developmental and Physical Disabilities, 6, 73–76.

Katz, K. S. (1989). Strategies for infant assessment: Implications of P.L. 99-457. *Topics in Early Childhood Special Education, 9*(3), 99–109.

Kaufman, A. S. (1979). *Intelligent testing with the WISC–R.* New York: Wiley.

Kaufman, A. S. (1994). *Intelligent Testing With the WISC–III.* New York: Wiley.

Kaufman, A. S., & Horn, J. L. (1996). Age changes on tests of fluid and crystallized ability for women and men on the Kaufman Adolescent and Adult Intelligence Test (KAIT) at ages 17–94 years. *Archives of Clinical Neuropsychology, 11,* 97–121.

Kaufman, A. S., & Kaufman, N. L. (1990). *Kaufman Brief Intelligence Test.* Circle Pines, MN: American Guidance Service.

Kaufman, A. S., & Kaufman, N. L. (1993). *Kaufman Adolescent and Adult Intelligence Test.* Circle Pines, MN: American Guidance Service.

Kaufman, A. S., & Kaufman, N. L. (1993). *K-SEALS: Kaufman survey of early academic and language skills.* Circle Pines, MN: American Guidance Service.

Kaufman, A. S., & Kaufman, N. L. (1994). *Kaufman functional academic skills test.* Circle Pines, MN: American Guidance Service, Inc.

Kaufman, A. S., & Kaufman, N. L. (2004). *Kaufman Test of Educational Achievement* (2nd ed.) Circle Pines, MN: AGS Publishing.

Kaufman, A. S., Litchenberger, E. O., Fletcher-Janzen, E., & Kaufman, N. L. (2005). *Essentials of KABC-II assessment.* New York: John Wiley & Sons, Inc.

Kaufman, A. S., McLean, J. E., & Kaufman, J. C. (1995). The fluid and crystallized abilities of White, Black, and Hispanic adolescents and adults, both with and without an education covariate. *Journal of Clinical Psychology, 51,* 636–647.

Kaufman, A. S., & Wang, J. (1992). Gender, race, and education differences on the K-BIT at ages 4 to 90 years. *Journal of Psychoeducational Assessment, 10,* 219–229.

Kaye, H. S. (1998). Is the status of people with disabilities improving? *Abstract 21: Disability Statistics Center.* San Francisco: University of California.

Keith, T. Z., Fugate, M. H., DeGraff, M., Diamond, C. M., Shadrach, E. A., & Stevens, M. L. (1995). Using multi-sample confirmatory factor analysis to test for construct bias: An example using the K-ABC. *Journal of Psychoeducational Assessment, 13,* 347–364.

Keith, T. Z., & Witta, E. L. (1997). Hierarchical and cross-age confirmatory factor analysis of the WISC-III: What does it measure? *School Psychology Quarterly, 12*(2), 89–107.

Keogh, B. K., Forness, S. R., & MacMillan, D. L. (1998). The real world of special education. *American Psychologist, 53*(10), 1161–1162.

Kerr, M. M., & Nelson, C. M. (2002). *Strategies for addressing behavioral problems in the classroom* (4th ed.). Upper Saddle River, NJ: Merrill/Prentice Hall.

Klinger, J. K., Vaughn, S., Schumm, J. S., Cohen, P., & Forgan, J. W. (1998). Inclusion or pull-out: Which do students prefer? *Journal of Learning Disabilities, 31,* 148–158.

Knoff, H. M. (1998). Review of the Children's Apperception Test (1991 Revision). In J. C. Impara and B. S. Plake (Eds.), *The thirteenth mental measurements yearbook* (pp. 231–233). Lincoln: University of Nebraska Press.

Knoff, H. M., & Prout, H. T. (1985). *Kinetic Family Drawing System for Family and School: A handbook.* Los Angeles: Western Psychological Services.

Koppitz, E. (1968). *Human Figure Drawing Test.* New York: Grune & Stratton.

Kranzler, J. H. (1997). What does the WISC–III measure? Comments on the relationship between intelligence, working memory capacity, and information processing speed and efficiency. *School Psychology Quarterly, 12*(2), 110–116.

Kroon, N., Goudena, P. P., & Rispens, J. (1998). Thematic apperception tests for child and adolescent assessment: A practitioner's consumer guide. *Journal of Psychoeducational Assessment, 16,* 99–117.

Kubicek, F. C. (1994). Special education reform in light of select state and federal court decisions. *Journal of Special Education, 28,* 27–42.

Kubick, R. J., Bard, E. M., & Perry, J. D. (2000). Manifestation determinations: Discipline guidelines for children with disabilities. In Telzrow, C. F., & Tankersley, M. (Eds.), *IDEA: Amendments of 1997: Practice guidelines for school-based teams* (pp. 1–28). Bethesda, MD: National Association of School Psychologists.

Kush, J. C. (1996). Factor structure of the WISC–III for students with learning disabilities. *Journal of Psychoeducational Assessment, 14,* 32–40.

LaGrow, S., & Prochnow-LaGrow, J. (1982). Technical adequacy of the most popular tests selected by responding school psychologists in Illinois. *Psychology in the Schools, 19,* 186–189.

Lambert, N., Nihira, K., & Leland, H. (1993). *AAMR adaptive behavior scale-school, second edition.* Austin, TX: Pro-Ed.

Larry P. v. Riles, 343 F. Supp. 1306, aff'd., 502 F.2d 963, further proceedings, 495 F. Supp. 926, aff'd., 502 F.2d 693 (9th Cir. 1984).

Larsen, S. C., Hammill, D. D., & Moats, L. C. (1999). *Test of Written Spelling–4.* Austin, TX: Pro-Ed.

Lavin, C. (1996). The Wechsler Intelligence Scale for Children–Third Edition and the Stanford–Binet Intelligence Scale, Fourth Edition: A preliminary study of validity. *Psychological Reports, 78,* 491–496.

Lee, S. W., Elliott, J., & Barbour, J. D. (1994). A comparison of cross-informant behavior ratings in school-based diagnosis. *Behavioral Disorders, 192,* 87–97.

Lennon, J. E., & Slesinski, C. (1999). Early intervention in reading: Results of a screening and intervention program for kindergarten students. *School Psychology Review, 28,* 353–365.

Levine, P., & Nourse, S. W. (1998). What follow-up studies say about postschool life for young men and women with learning disabilities: A critical look at the literature. *Journal of Learning Disabilities, 31*(3), 212–233.

Levinson, E. M. (1995). Best practices in transition services. In A. Thomas & J. Grimes (Eds.), *Best practices in school psychology-III*

(pp. 909–915). Washington, DC: The National Association of School Psychologists.

Lidz, C. S. (1997). Dynamic assessment approaches. In D. P. Flanagan, J. L. Genshaft, & P. L. Harrison (Eds.), *Contemporary intellectual assessment: Theories, tests, and issues* (pp. 281–296). New York: Guilford Press.

Linan-Thompson, S., Vaughn, S., Prater, K., & Cirino, P. T. (2006). The response to intervention of English language learners at risk for reading problems. *Journal of Learning Disabilities, 39*(5), 390–398.

Lindsey, P., Wehmeyer, M. L., Guy, B., & Martin, J. (2001). Age of majority and mental retardation: A position statement of the division on mental retardation and developmental disabilities. *Education and Training in Mental Retardation and Developmental Disabilities, 36*(1), 3–15.

Lindstrom, L., Doren, B., Metheny, J., Johnson, P., & Zane, C. (2007). Transition to employment: Role of the family in career development. *Exceptional Children, 73*(3), 348–366.

Lipsky, D. K., & Gartner, A. (1997). *Inclusion and school reform: Transforming America's classrooms.* Baltimore, MD: Brookes Publishing.

Litchenberger, E. O., & Smith, D. R. (2005). *Essentials of WIAT-II and KTEA-II assessment.* Hoboken, NJ: John Wiley & Sons, Inc.

Loiser, B. J., McGrath, P. J., & Klein, R. M. (1996). Error patterns on the continuous performance test in nonmedicated and medicated samples of children with and without ADHD: A meta-analytic review. *Journal of Child Psychology and Psychiatry, 37,* 971–987.

Lopez, E. C. (1995). Best practices in working with bilingual children. In Alex Thomas and Jeff Grimes (Eds.), *Best practices in school psychology* (3rd ed., p. 1113). Bethesda, MD: National Association of School Psychologists.

Lopez, R. (1997). The practical impact of current research and issues in intelligence test interpretation and use for multicultural populations. *School Psychology Review, 26*(2), 249–254.

Lora v. New York City Board of Education, 1984: Final order, August 2, 1984, 587F. Supp. 1572 (E.D.N.Y. 1984).

Lord, C., Rutter, M., DiLavore, P. C., & Risi, S. (2002). Autism diagnostic observation schedule. Los Angeles, CA: Western Psychological Services.

Lord, C., Rutter, M., Goode, S., Heemsbergen, J., Jordan, H., Mawhood, L., & Schopler, E. (1989). Autism Diagnostic Observation Schedule: A standardized observation of communicative and social behavior. Journal of Autism Spectrum Disorders, 19, 185–212.

Lusting, D. D., & Saura, K. M. (1996, Spring). Use of criterion-based comparisons in determining the appropriateness of vocational evaluation test modifications for criterion-referenced tests. Vocational Evaluation and Work Adjustment Bulletin.

MacMillan, D. L., & Forness, S. R. (1998). The role of IQ in special education placement decisions: Primary and determinative or peripheral and inconsequential. Remedial and Special Education, 19, 239–253.

MacMillan, D. L., Gresham, F. M., & Bocian, K. (1998). Discrepancy between definitions of learning disabilities and school practices: An empirical investigation. Journal of Learning Disabilities, 32(4), 314–326.

Macready, T. (1991). Special education: Some thoughts for policy makers. Educational Psychology in Practice, 7(3), 148–152.

Marchand-Martella, N. E., Ruby, S. F., & Martella, R. C. (2007). Intensifying reading instruction for students within a three-tier model: Standard protocol and problem solving approaches within a response-to-intervention (RTI) system. Teaching Exceptional Children Plus: 3, 5, Article 2. Retrieved October 1, 2007 from: http://escholarship.bc.edu/education/tecplus/vol13/iss5/art2

Mardell-Czudnowski, C. (1995). Performance of Asian and White children on the K-ABC: Understanding information processing differences. Psychological Assessment Resources, Inc., 2(1), 19–29.

Mardell-Czudnowski, C., & Goldenberg, D. (1998). Developmental indicators for the assessment of learning (3rd ed.). Circle Pines, MN: American Guidance Service.

Markwardt, F. C. (1989). Peabody Individual Achievement Test-Revised. Circle Pines, MN: American Guidance Service.

Marsh, T. Y., & Cornell, D. G. (2001). The contributions of student experiences to understanding ethnic differences in high risk behaviors at school. Behavior Disorders, 26(2), 152–163.

Marso, R. N., & Pigge, F. L. (1991). An analysis of teacher-made tests: Item types, cognitive demands, and item construction errors. Contemporary Educational Psychology, 16, 279–286.

Marston, D., Fuchs, L., & Deno, S. (1986). Measuring pupil progress: A comparison of standardized achievement tests and curriculum related measures. Diagnostique, 11, 77–90.

Marston, D., Mirkin, P. K., & Deno, S. L. (1984). Curriculum-based measurement: An alternative to traditional screening, referral, and identification. Journal of Special Education, 18, 109–118.

Marston, D., Muyskens, P., Lau, M., & Canter, A. (2003). Problem-solving model for decision making with high incidence disabilities: The Minneapolis experience. Learning Disabilities Research & Practice, 18(3), 187–201.

Marston, D. B. (1989). A curriculum-based measurement approach to assessing academic performance: What it is and why we do it. In M. R. Shinn (Eds.), Curriculum-based measurement: Assessing special children (pp.18–78). New York: Guilford.

Mather, N., Wendling, B. J., & Woodcock, R. W. (2001). Essentials of WJ III Tests of Achievement assessment. Hoboken, NJ: John Wiley & Sons, Inc.

Mather, N., & Woodcock, R. W. (2001). Examiner's manual. Woodcock–Johnson III Tests of Achievement. Itasca, IL: Riverside Publishing.

Mattison, R. E., Bagnato, S. J., Mayes, S. D., & Felix, B. C. (1990). Reliability and validity of teacher diagnostic ratings for children with behavioral and emotional disorders. Journal of Psychoeducational Assessment, 8, 509–517.

Maxam, S., Boyer-Stephens, A., & Alff, M. (1986). *Assessment: A key to appropriate program placement.* (Report No. CE 045 407, pp. 11–13). Columbia: University of Missouri Columbia, Department of Special Education and Department of Practical Arts and Vocational-Technical Education. (ERIC Document Reproduction Service No. ED 275 835)

May, K., & Nicewander, W. A. (1994). Reliability and information functions for percentile ranks. *Journal of Educational Measurement, 31,* 313–325.

May, K. O., & Nicewander, W. A. (1997). Information and reliability for percentile ranks and other monotonic transformations of the number-correct score: Reply to De Gruijter. *Journal of Educational Measurement, 34,* 179–183.

Mayes, L. C. (1991). Infant assessment. In M. Lewis (Ed.), *Child and adolescent psychiatry: A comprehensive textbook* (pp. 437–447). Baltimore: Williams & Wilkins.

McArthur, D. S., & Roberts, G. E. (1982). *Roberts Apperception Test for Children: Manual.* Los Angeles: Western Psychological Services.

McConaughy, S. H., & Achenbach, T. M. (1993). Advances in empirically based assessment of children's behavioral and emotional problems. *School Psychology Review, 22,* 285–307.

McConaughy, S. H., & Achenbach, T. M. (1996). Contributions of a child interview to multimethod assessment of children with EBD and LD. *School Psychology Review, 25,* 24–39.

McGlinchey, M. T., & Hixson, M. D. (2004). Using curriculum-based measurement to predict performance on state assessments in reading. *School Psychology Review, 33*(2), 193–203.

McGrew, K. S., & Flanagan, D. P. (1998). *The intelligence test desk reference (ITDR): Gf-Gc cross-battery assessment.* Boston: Allyn & Bacon.

McGrew, K. S., & Woodcock, R. W. (2001). *Technical manual. Woodcock–Johnson III.* Itasca, IL: Riverside Publishing.

McIntyre, L. (1988). Teacher gender: A predictor of special education referral? *Journal of Learning Disabilities, 21,* 382–384.

McLaughlin, M. J., & Owings, M. F. (1992). Relationship among states' fiscal and demographic data and the implementation of P. L. 94–142. *Exceptional Children, 59,* 247–261.

McLoughlin, J. (1985). Training educational diagnosticians [Monograph]. *Diagnostique, 10,* 176–196.

McLoughlin, J. A., & Lewis, R. B. (1994). *Assessing special students* (4th ed.). Upper Saddle River, NJ: Merrill/Prentice Hall.

McLoughlin, J., & Lewis, R. (2001). *Assessing special students* (5th ed.). Upper Saddle River, NJ: Merrill/Prentice Hall.

McNamara, K., & Hollinger, C. (2003). Intervention-based assessment: Evaluation rates and eligibility findings. *Exceptional Children, 69*(2), 181–193.

McNutt, G., & Mandelbaum, L. (1980). General assessment competencies for special education teachers. *Exceptional Education Quarterly, 1,* 21–29.

Mehrens, W., & Lehmann, I. (1978). *Standardized tests in education.* New York: Holt, Rinehart & Winston.

Meherns, W. A., & Clarizio, H. F. (1993). Curriculum-based measurement: Conceptual and psychometric considerations. *Psychology in the Schools, 30,* 241–254.

Mercer, J. *System of Multicultural Assessment,* NY: The psychological corporation.

Messick, S. (1980). Test validity and the ethics of assessment. *American Psychologist, 35,* 1012–1027.

Messick, S. (1984). Assessment in context: Appraising student performance in relation to instructional quality. *Educational Researcher, 13,* 3–8.

Michael, J. (2000). Implications and refinements of the establishing operation concept. *Journal of Applied Behavior Analysis, 33,* 401–410.

Mick, L. (1985). Assessment procedures as related to enrollment patterns of Hispanic students in special education. *Educational Research Quarterly, 9,* 27–35.

Miller, D. C. (2007). *Essentials of school neuropsychological assessment.* New York: John Wiley & Sons, Inc.

Millman, J. (1994). Criterion-referenced testing 30 years later: Promise broken, promise kept. *Educational Measurement: Issues and Practices, 13*, 19–20, 39.

Minke, K. M., & Scott, M. M. (1993). The development of Individualized Family Service Plans: Roles for parents and staff. *Journal of Special Education, 27*, 82–106.

Missall, K., Reschly, A., Betts, J., McConnell, Heistad, et al. (2007). Examination of the predictive validity of preschool early literacy skills. *School Psychology Review, 36*(3), 433–452.

Morsink, C. V., & Lenk, L. L. (1992). The delivery of special education programs and services. *Remedial and Special Education, 13*(6), 33–43.

Mueller, F., Brozovich, R., & Johnson, C. B. (1998–1999). Conners' Rating Scales—Revised (CRS—R). *Monograph: Assessment for the New Decade, Diagnostic, 24*(1–4), 83–97.

Mullen, E. M. (1995). *Mullen scales of early learning: AGS edition*. Circle Pines, MN: American Guidance Service, Inc.

Naglieri, J. A. (1988). *Draw-a-person: A quantitative scoring system*. New York: Psychological Corporation.

Naglieri, J. A., McNeish, T. J., & Bardos, A. N. (1991). *Draw-a-person: Screening procedure for emotional disturbance*. Austin, TX: Pro-Ed.

National Association of School Psychologists (2000). *National Association of School Psychologists professional conduct manual: Principles for professional ethics; guidelines for the provision of school psychologists*. Bethesda, MD: Author.

NCTM (2000). *Principles and standards for mathematics*. Available from http://standards.nctm.org.

Nelson, J. R., Smith, D. J., Taylor, L., Dodd, J. M., & Reavis, K. (1992). A statewide survey of special education administrators regarding mandated prereferral interventions. *Remedial and Special Education, 13*(4), 34–39.

Newcomer, P. L., & Hammill, D. D. (1997). *Test of Language Development—Primary: Third Edition*. Austin, TX: Pro-Ed.

Nichols, S. L., & Berliner, D. C. (2007) *Collateral damage: How high stakes testing corrupts America's schools*. Cambridge, MA. Harvard Educational Press.

Nicholson, C. L. (1998–1999). Comprehensive test of nonverbal intelligence (CTONI). *Monograph: Assessment for the New Decade, Diagnostic, 24*(1–4), 57–68.

Nihira, K., Foster, R., Shellhaas, M., & Leland, H. (1974). *AAMD adaptive behavior scale*. Washington, DC: American Association on Mental Deficiency.

No Child Left Behind Act of 2001, PL 107-110, 115 Stat. 1425 (2002).

Norford, B. C., & Barakat, L. P. (1990). The relationship of human figure drawings to aggressive behavior in preschool children. *Psychology in the Schools, 27*, 318–325.

Northup, J., & Gulley, V. (2001). Some contributions of functional analysis to the assessment of behaviors associated with attention deficit hyperactivity disorder and the effects of stimulant medication. *School Psychology Review, 30*(2), 227–238.

Nunnally, J. (1967). *Psychometric theory*. New York: McGraw-Hill.

Oesterheld, J. R., & Haber, J. (1997). Acceptability of the Conners parent rating scale and child behavior checklist to Dakotan/Lakotan parents. *Journal of the American Academy of Child and Adolescent Psychiatry, 36*, 55–64.

Office of Special Education and Rehabilitative Services (2000). *Questions and answers about provisions in the Individuals with Disabilities Education Act Amendments of 1997 related to students with disabilities and state and district wide assessments*. Washington, DC: Author.

O'Neill, R. E., Horner, R. H., Albin, R. W., Sprague, J. R., Storey, K., & Newton, J. S. (1997). *Functional assessment and program development for problem behavior*. Pacific Grove, CA: Brooks/Cole Publishing Company.

Overton, T. (1987). Analyzing instructional material as a prerequisite for teacher effectiveness. *Techniques: A Journal for Remedial Education and Counseling, 3*, 111–115.

Overton, T. (2003). Promoting academic success through assessment of the academic environment. *Intervention in School and Clinic, 39*(3), 147–153.

Overton, T., Fielding, C., & Garcia de Alba, R. (2007). Differential diagnosis of Hispanic children referred for autism spectrum disorders. *Journal of Autism and Developmental Disorders, 37*(2), 1996–2007.

Overton, T., Fielding, C., & Garcia de Alba, R. (In Press). Application of the ADOS revised algorithm: Exploratory analysis of specificity and predictive value with Hispanic children referred for autism spectrum disorders. *Journal of Autism and Developmental Disabilities.*

Paget, K. D. (1990). Best practices in the assessment of competence in preschool-age children. In A. Thomas & J. Grimes (Eds.), *Best practices in school psychology-II* (pp. 107–119). Washington, DC: National Association of School Psychologists.

Palomares, R. S., Crowley, S. L., Worchel, F. F., Olson, T. K., & Rae, W. A. (1991). The factor analytic structure of the Roberts Apperception Test for Children: A comparison of the standardization sample with a sample of chronically ill children. *Journal of Personality Assessment, 53,* 414–425.

Paratore, J. R. (1995). Assessing literacy: Establishing common standards in portfolio assessment. *Topics in Language Disorders, 16,* 67–82.

Parette, H. P., Peterson-Karlan, G. R., Wojcok, B. W., & Bardi, N. (2007). Monitor that progress: Interpreting data trends for assistive technology decision making. *Teaching Exceptional Children, 40*(1), 22–29.

Parker, L. D. (1993). The Kaufman Brief Intelligence Test: An introduction and review. *Measurement and Evaluation in Counseling and Development, 26,* 152–156.

PASE (Parents in Action in Special Education) *v. Hannon,* 506 F. Supp. 831 (N.D. Ill. 1980).

Patton, J. M. (1998). The disproportionate representation of African Americans in special education: Looking behind the curtains for understanding and solutions. *Journal of Special Education, 32*(1), 25–31.

Perner, D. E. (2007). No Child Left Behind: Issues of assessing students with the most significant cognitive disabilities. *Education and Training in Developmental Disabilities, 42*(3), 243–251.

Phillips, N. B., Hamlett, C. L., Fuchs, L. S., & Fuchs, D. (1993). Combining classwide curriculum-based measurement and peer tutoring to help general educators provide adaptive education. *Learning Disabilities Research & Practice, 8,* 148–156.

Poon-McBrayer, F., & Garcia, S. B. (2000). Profiles of Asian American students with learning disabilities at initial referral, assessment, and placement in special education. *Journal of Learning Disabilities, 33*(1), 61–71.

Portes, P. R. (1996). Ethnicity and culture in educational psychology. In D. C. Berliner & R. C. Calfee (Eds.), *Handbook of Educational Psychology* (pp. 331–357). New York: Simon Schuster McMillan.

Prewett, P. N. (1992). The relationship between the Kaufman Brief Intelligence Test (K-BIT) and the WISC–R with referred students. *Psychology in the Schools, 29,* 25–27.

Prewett, P. N., & McCaffery, L. K. (1993). A comparison of the Kaufman Brief Intelligence Test (K-BIT) with the Stanford–Binet, a two-subtest short form, and the Kaufman Test of Educational Achievement (K-TEA) Brief Form. *Psychology in the Schools, 30,* 299–304.

Prifitera, A., Saklofske, D. H., & Weiss, L. G. (2005). *WISC-IV: Clinical use and interpretation.* Burlington, MA: Elsevier Academic Press.

Psychological Corporation. (1997). *WAIS-III WMS-III Technical Manual.* San Antonio: Author.

Psychological Corporation. (2001). *Wechsler Individual Achievement Test, Second Edition.* San Antonio, TX: Author.

Reid, R. (1995). Assessment of ADHD with culturally different groups: The use of behavioral rating scales. *School Psychology Review, 24,* 537–560.

Reid, R., DuPaul, G. J., Power, T. J., Anastopoulos, A. D., Rogers–Adkinson, D., Nell, M., & Ricco, C. (1998). Assessing culturally different students for attention deficit hyperactivity disorder using behavior rating scales. *Journal of Abnormal Child Psychology, 26,* 187–198.

Reinehr, R. C. (1998). Review of the Children's Apperception Test (1991 Revision). In J. C.

Impara and B. S. Plake (Eds.), *The thirteenth mental measurements yearbook* (pp. 233–234). Lincoln: University of Nebraska Press.

Reschly, D. (1981). Psychological testing in educational classification and placement. *American Psychologist, 36,* 1094–1102.

Reschly, D. (1982). Assessing mild mental retardation: The influence of adaptive behavior, sociocultural status, and prospects for nonbiased assessment. In C. R. Reynolds & T. B. Gutkin (Eds.), *The handbook of school psychology* (pp. 209–242). New York: Wiley.

Reschly, D. (1986). Functional psychoeducational assessment: Trends and issues. *Special Services in the Schools, 2,* 57–69.

Reschly, D. (1988). Assessment issues, placement litigation, and the future of mild mental retardation classification and programming. *Education and Training in Mental Retardation, 23,* 285–301.

Reschly, D. (1988). Special education reform. *School Psychology Review, 17,* 459–475.

Reschly, D. J., & Grimes, J. P. (1995). Best practices in intellectual assessment. In A. Thomas & J. Grimes (Eds.), *Best practices in school psychology-II.* Washington, DC: National Association of School Psychologists.

Reynolds, C. R. (1982). The problem of bias in psychological assessment. In C. R. Reynolds & T. B. Gutkin (Eds.), *The handbook of school psychology,* (pp. 178–208). New York: Wiley.

Reynolds, C. R., & Kamphaus, R. W. (1998). *Behavior assessment system for children.* Circle Pines, MN: American Guidance Service.

Reynolds, C. R., & Kamphaus, R.W. (2004). *Behavior assessment system for children, second edition.* Circle Pines, MN: American Guidance Service.

Reynolds, C. R., Lowe, P. A., & Saenz, A. L. (1999). The problems of bias in psychological assessment. In C. R. Reynolds & T. Gutkin (Eds.), *The handbook of school psychology* (3rd ed., pp. 556–557). New York: Wiley.

Ricco, C. A., Cohen, M. J., Hall, J., & Ross, C. M. (1997). The third and fourth factors of the WISC-III: What they don't measure. *Journal of Psychoeducational Assessment, 15,* 27–39.

Roberts, G. E. (1982). *Roberts apperception test for children: Test pictures.* Los Angeles: Western Psychological Services.

Roberts, G. E., & Gruber, C. (2005). *Roberts-2.* Los Angeles: Western Psychological Services.

Roberts, M. L., Marshall, J., Nelson, J. R., & Albers, C. A. (2001). Curriculum-based assessment procedures embedded within functional behavioral assessments: Identifying escape-motivated behaviors in a general education classroom. *School Psychology Review, 30*(2), 264–277.

Roid, G. H. (2003a). *Stanford–Binet intelligence scales* (5th ed.) Itasca, IL: Riverside Publishing.

Roid, G. H. (2003b). *Stanford–Binet intelligence scales* (5th ed.). *Examiner's manual.* Itasca, IL: Riverside Publishing.

Roid, G. H. (2003c). *Stanford–Binet intelligence scales* (5th ed.). *Technical manual.* Itasca, IL: Riverside Publishing.

Roid, G. H., & Pomplin, M. (2005). Interpreting the Stanford-Binet Intelligence Scales, Fifth Edition. In D. P. Flanagan & P. L. Harrison (Eds.), *Contemporary intellectual assessment: Theories, tests, and issues* (pp. 325–343). New York: The Guilford Press.

Rorschach, H. (1921, 1942). *Psycho-Diagnostics: A diagnostic test based on perception* (P. Lemkau & B. Kroenburg, Trans.). Berne: Heber. (First German Edition, 1921. Distributed in the United States by Grune & Stratton.)

Rosenfield, S., & Kurait, S. K. (1990). Best practices in curriculum-based assessment. In A. Thomas & J. Grimes (Eds.), *Best practices in school psychology-II* (pp. 275–286). Washington, DC: National Association of School Psychology.

Rotter, J., & Rafferty, J. (1950). *The Rotter incomplete sentence test.* New York: Psychological Corporation.

Ruddell, M. R. (1995). Literacy assessment in middle level grades: Alternatives to traditional practices. *Reading & Writing Quarterly: Overcoming Learning Difficulties, 11,* 187–200.

Rueda, R., & Garcia, E. (1997). Do portfolios make a difference for diverse students?

The influence of type of data on making instructional decisions. *Learning Disabilities Research & Practice*, *12*(2), 114–122.

Ruehl, M. E. (1998). Educating the child with severe behavioral problems: Entitlement, empiricism, and ethics. *Behavioral Disorders, 23*, 184–192.

Rutter, M., LeCouteur, A., & Lord, C. (2002). *Autism diagnostic interview, revised.* Los Angeles, CA: Western Psychological Services.

Rutter, M., LeCouteur, A., & Lord, C. (2003). *Autism Diagnostic Interview–Revised.* Los Angeles, CA: Western Psychological Services.

Sabers, D., Feldt, L., & Reschly, D. (1988). Appropriate and inappropriate use of estimated true scores for normative comparisons. *Journal of Special Education, 22*, 358–366.

Salend, S. J., & Taylor, L. (1993). Working with families: A cross-cultural perspective. *Remedial and Special Education, 14*(5), 25–32, 39.

Salvia, J., & Hughes, C. (1990). *Curriculum-based assessment: Testing what is taught.* New York: Macmillan.

Salvia, J., & Ysseldyke, J. (1988a). *Assessment in remedial and special education* (4th ed.). Dallas: Houghton Mifflin.

Salvia, J., & Ysseldyke, J. (1988b). Using estimated true scores for normative comparisons. *Journal of Special Education, 22*, 367–373.

Salvia, J., & Ysseldyke, J. E. (1988). *Assessment in special and remedial education* (4th ed.). Boston: Houghton Mifflin.

Sandall, S., Hemmeter, M. L., Smith, B. J., McLean, M. E. (2005). DEC recommended practices: A comprehensive guide for practical approaches in early intervention/early childhood. Copyright 2005 by the Division of Early Childhood (DEC) of the Council for Exceptional Children (CEC). Longmont, CO: Sopris West.

Sapp, G., Chissom, B., & Horton, W. (1984). An investigation of the ability of selected instruments to discriminate areas of exceptional class designation. *Psychology in the Schools, 5*, 258–262.

Schaughency, E. A., & Rothlind, J. (1991). Assessment and classification of attention deficit hyperactive disorders. *School Psychology Review, 20*, 187–202.

Schopler, E., Reichler, R. J., Renner, B. R. (1998). Childhood autism rating scale. Los Angeles, CA: Western Psychological Services.

Schrank, F. A., & Flanagan, D. P. (Eds.) (2003). *WJ III clinical use and interpretation.* San Diego, CA: Academic Press.

Schrank, F. A., Flanagan, D. P., Woodcock, R. W., & Mascolo, J. T. (2002). *Essentials of WJ III cognitive abilities assessment.* New York: John Wiley & Sons.

Scott, V. G., & Weishaar, M. K. (2003). Curriculum-based measurement for reading progress. *Intervention in School and Clinic, 38*(3), 153–159.

Scruggs, T. E., & Mastropieri, M. A. (1996). Teacher perceptions of mainstreaming/inclusion, 1958–1995: A research synthesis. *Exceptional Children, 63*, 59–74.

Section 504 of the Rehabilitation Act of 1973, 29 U.S.C. § 794 et seq.

Serna, L. A., Forness, S. R., & Nielsen, M. E. (1998). Intervention versus affirmation: Proposed solutions to the problem of disproportionate minority representation in special education. *Journal of Special Education, 32*(1), 48–51.

Shaklee, B. D., Barbour, N. E., Ambrose, R., & Hansford, S. J. (1997). *Designing and using portfolios.* Boston: Allyn & Bacon.

Shapiro, E. S. (1989). *Academic skills problems: Direct assessment and intervention.* New York: Guilford.

Shapiro, E. S. (1996). *Academic skills problems: Direct assessment and intervention* (2nd ed.). New York: Guilford.

Sheridan, S. M., Cowan, P. J., & Eagle, J. W. (2000). Partnering with parents in educational programming for students with special needs. In C. F. Telzrow & M. Tankersley (Eds.), *IDEA Amendments of 1997: Practice guidelines for school-based teams.* Bethesda, MD: National Association of School Psychologists.

Sherman, A. (1994). *Wasting America's future: The Children's Defense Fund report on the cost of child poverty.* Boston: Beacon Press.

Shinn, M. R. (1989). *Curriculum-based measurement: Assessing special children.* New York: Guilford.

Shinn, M. R. (2002). Best practices in using curriculum-based measurement in a problem-solving model. In A. Thomas & J. Grimes (Eds.), *Best practices in school psychology* (Vol. 4, pp. 671–697). Silver Springs, MD: National Association of School Psychologists.

Shinn, M. R., Habedank, L., Rodden-Nord, K., & Knutson, N. (1993). Using curriculum-based measurement to identify potential candidates for reintegration into general education. *Journal of Special Education, 27*, 202–221.

Shinn, M. R., Nolet, V., & Knutson, N. (1990). Best practices in curriculum-based measurement. In A. Thomas & J. Grimes (Eds.), *Best practices in school psychology*. Washington, DC: National Association of School Psychologists.

Silberglitt, B., & Hintze, J. M. (2007). How much growth can we expect? A conditional analysis of R-CBM growth rates by level of performance. *Exceptional Children, 74*(1), 71–99.

Silver, S. (1987). *Compliance with PL 94-142 mandates: Policy implications.* (ERIC Document Reproduction Service No. ED 284 705)

Sinclair, E., Del'Homme, & M. Gonzalez. (1993). Systematic screening for preschool assessment of behavioral disorders. *Behavioral Disorders, 18*, 177–188.

Slate, J. R. (1996). Interrelations of frequently administered achievement measures in the determination of specific learning disabilities. *Learning Disabilities Research & Practice, 11*(2), 86–89.

Smith, C. R. (1997). Advocacy for students with emotional and behavioral disorders: One call for redirected efforts. *Behavioral Disorders, 22*(2), 96–105.

Smith, D. K. (1998–1999). Kaufman Brief Intelligence Test (K-BIT). *Monograph: Assessment for the New Decade, Diagnostic, 24*(1–4), 125–134.

Snider, V. E. (1995). A primer on phonemic awareness: What it is, why it is important, and how to teach it. *School Psychology Review, 24*(3), 443–455.

Snider, V. E. (1997). The relationship between phonemic awareness and later reading achievement. *Journal of Educational Research, 90*(4), 203–212.

Snyder, P., Bailey, D., & Auer, C. (1994). Preschool eligibility determination for children with known or suspected learning disabilities under IDEA. *Journal of Early Intervention, 18*, 380–390.

Soodak, L. C., & Podell, D. M. (1993). Teacher efficacy and student problem as factors in special education referral. *Journal of Special Education, 27*(1), 66–81.

Sparrow, S. S., Balla, D. A., & Cicchetti, D. V. (1984). *Vineland adaptive behavior scales.* Circle Pines, MN: American Guidance Service.

Sparrow, S.S., Cicchetti, D.V., & Balla, D.A. (2005). *Vineland-II: Vineland Adaptive Behavior Scales, Second Edition.* Circle Pines, MN: AGS Publishing Company.

Spigelman, G., Spigelman, A., & Englesson, I. L. (1992). Analysis of family drawings: A comparison between children from divorce and nondivorce families. *Journal of Divorce & Remarriage, 18*, 31–51.

Stanford, L. D., & Hynd, G. W. (1994). Congruence of behavioral symptomology in children with ADD/H, ADD/WO, and learning disabilities. *Journal of Learning Disabilities, 27*, 243–253.

Stecker, P. M. (2007). Tertiary intervention: Using progress monitoring with intensive services. *Teaching Exceptional Children,* May/June 2007, 50–57.

Stoner, G., Carey, S. P., Ikeda, M. J., & Shinn, M. R. (1994). The utility of curriculum-based measurement for evaluating the effects of methylphenidate on academic performance. *Journal of Applied Behavior Analysis, 27*, 101–113.

Swanson, H. L., & Watson, B. L. (1989). *Educational and psychological assessment of exceptional children* (2nd ed.). Upper Saddle River, NJ: Merrill/Prentice Hall.

Symons, F. J., & Warren, S. F. (1998). Straw men and strange logic issues and pseudo-issues in special education. *American Psychologist, 53*(10), 1160–1161.

Taylor, R. L. (1993). *Assessment of exceptional students: Educational and psychological procedures* (3rd ed.). Boston: Allyn & Bacon.

Taylor, R. L., & Richards, S. B. (1991). Patterns of intellectual differences of black, Hispanic, and white children. *Psychology in the Schools, 28*, 5–9.

Telzrow, C. F., & Tankersley, M. (2000). *IDEA: Amendments of 1997: Practice Guidelines for School-Based Teams.* Bethesda, MD: National Association of School Psychologists.

Tharinger, D. J., & Lambert, N. M. (1990). The contributions of developmental psychology to school psychology. In T. Gutkin & C. R. Reynolds (Eds.), *The handbook of school psychology* (2nd ed.), pp. 74–103. New York: Wiley.

Thoma, C. A., Rogan, P., & Baker, S. R. (2001). Student involvement in transition planning: Unheard voices. *Education and Training in Mental Retardation and Developmental Disabilities, 36*(1), 16–29.

Thomas, A., & Grimes, J. (1990). *Best practices in school psychology-II.* Silver Spring, MD: National Association of School Psychologists.

Thompson, S. J., Morse, A. B., Sharpe, M., & Hall, S. (2005). *Accommodations manual: How to select, administer, and evaluate use of accommodations for instruction and assessment of students with disabilities, 2nd edition.* Washington, DC: Council of Chief State School Officers.

Thompson, S. J., Johnstone, C. J., & Thurlow, M. L. (2002). *Universal design applied to large scale assessments* (Synthesis Report 44). Minneapolis, MN: University of Minnnesota, National Center on Educational Outcomes Retrieved July 7, 2007, from: *http://education.umn.edu? NCeO/ OnlinePubs/Synthesis44. html*

Thurlow, M., Christenson, S., & Ysseldyke, J. (1983). *Referral research: An integrative summary of findings* (Research Report No. 141). Minneapolis: University of Minnesota, Institute for Research on Learning Disabilities.

Thurlow, M. L., Elliott, J. L., & Ysseldyke, J. E. (1998). *Testing students with disabilities: Practical strategies for complying with district and state requirements.* Thousand Oaks, CA: Corwin Press, Inc.

Thurlow, M., & Ysseldyke, J. (1979). Current assessment and decision-making practices in model programs. *Learning Disabilities Quarterly, 2,* 14–24.

Thurlow, M. L., Ysseldyke, J. E., & Anderson, C. L. (1995). *High school graduation requirements: What's happening for students with disabilities?* Minneapolis: National Center on Educational Outcomes.

Tindal, G. (1991). Operationalizing learning portfolios: A good idea in search of a method. *Diagnostique, 2,* 127–133.

Trainor, A. A., Patton, J. R., & Clark, G. M. (2005). Case studies in assessment for transition planning. Austin, TX: Pro-Ed.

Trommer, B. L., Hoeppner, J. B., Lorber, R., & Armstrong, K. (1988). Pitfalls in the use of a Continuous Performance Test as a diagnostic tool deficit disorder. *Developmental and Behavioral Pediatrics, 9,* 339–345.

Truscott, S. D., Cohen, C. E., Sams, D. P., Sanborn, K. J., & Frank, A. J. (2005). The current state(s) of prereferral teams: A report from two national surveys. *Remedial and Special Education, 26*(3), 130–140.

Tucker, J. (1980). Ethnic proportions in classes for the learning disabled: Issues in nonbiased assessment. *Journal of Special Education, 14,* 93–105.

Turnbull, H. R. (1986). *Free and appropriate public education: The law and children with disabilities.* Denver: Love Publishing.

Turnbull, H. R. (1990). *Free and appropriate public education: The law and children with disabilities* (3rd ed.). Denver: Love Publishing.

Turnbull, H. R., Turnbull, A. P., & Strickland, B. (1979). Procedural due process: The two-edged sword that the untrained should not unsheath. *Journal of Education, 161,* 40–59.

Turnbull, R., Turnbull, A., Shank, A., Smith, S., & Leal, D. (2002). *Exceptional lives: Special education in today's schools (3rd ed.).* Upper Saddle River, NJ: Merrill/Prentice Hall.

U.S. Bureau of the Census. (1997). *Statistical abstract of the United States: 1997* (117th ed.). Washington, DC: Author.

U.S. Congress. (1993, March). *Goals 2000: Educate America Act.* PL 103-227, 103rd Congress.

U.S. Department of Education. (1991). *Memorandum to chief state school officers.* Washington, DC: Author.

U.S. Department of Education. (1995). *The Seventeenth annual report to Congress on* the implementation of the Individuals with Disabilities Education Act. Washington, DC: Author.

U.S. Department of Education. (1997). Nineteenth annual report to Congress on the implementation of the Individuals with Disabilities Education Act. Washington, DC: Author.

U.S. Department of Education. (1999). Assistance to states for the education of childern with disabilities and the early intervention Program for infants and toddlers with disabilities: final regulation. Washington, DC: Author.

U.S. Department of Education. (2000). The use of tests when making high-stakes decisions for students: A resource guide for educators and policymakers. Washington, DC: Author.

U.S. Department of Education. (2000). Twenty-second annual report to Congress on the implementation of the Individuals with Disabilities Education Act. Washington, DC: Author.

U.S. Department of Education. (2001). Twenty-third annual report to Congress on the implementation of the Individuals with Disabilities Education Act. Washington, DC: Author.

U.S. Department of Education. (2002). Twenty-fourth annual report to Congress on the implementation of the Individuals with Disabilities Education Act. Washington, DC: Author.

U.S. Department of Education. (2003). Twenty-fifth annual report to Congress on the implementation of the Individuals with Disabilities Education Act. Washington, DC: Author.

U.S. Department of Education. (2004). Twenty-sixth annual report to Congress on the implementation of the Individuals with Disabilities Education Act. Washington, DC: Author.

U.S. Department of Education. (2006). IDEA regulations: Disproportionality and over identification. Washington, DC: Office of Special Education and Rehabilitative Services. Retrieved from http://www.nichcy.org/reauth/tboverident.pdf

U.S. Office of Technology Assessment. (1992, February). Testing in American schools: Asking the right questions (OTA-SET-519). Washington, DC: U.S. Government Printing Office.

Uzgiris, I. C., & Hunt, J. McV. (1975). Assessment in infancy: Ordinal Scales of Psychological Development. Urbana: University of Illinois Press.

Valencia, R. R., Rankin, R. J., & Livingston, R. (1995). K-ABC content bias: Comparisons between Mexican American and White children. Psychology in the Schools, 32, 153–169.

Valles, E. C. (1998). The disproportionate representation of minority students in special education: Responding to the problem. Journal of Special Education, 32(1), 52–54.

VanDerHeyden, A. M., Witt, J. C., Naquin, G. (2003). Development and validation of a process for screening referrals to special education. School Psychology Review, 32(2), 204–227.

Vaughn, S., Bos, C., Harrell, J., & Lasky, B. (1988). Parent participation in the initial placement/IEP conference ten years after mandated involvement. Journal of Learning Disabilities, 21, 82–89.

Vig, S., & Jedrysek, E. (1996). Stanford–Binet Fourth Edition: Useful for young children with language impairment? Psychology in the Schools, 33, 124–131.

Vogel, S. A., Leonard, F., Scales, W., Hayeslip, P., Hermansen, J., & Donnells, L. (1998). The national learning disabilities postsecondary data bank: An overview. Journal of Learning Disabilities, 31(3), 234–247.

Vygotsky, L. S. (1993). The collected works of L. S. Vygotsky: Vol. 2, The fundamentals of defectology (abnormal psychology and learning disabilities (J. E. Knox & C. B. Stevens, Trans.). New York: Plenum.

Walsh, B., & Betz, N. (1985). Tests and assessment. Upper Saddle River, NJ: Prentice Hall.

Ward, S. B., Ward, T. J., & Clark, H. T. (1991). Classification congruence among school psychologists and its relationship to type of referral question and professional experience. Journal of School Psychology, 29, 89–108.

Wasserman, J. D., & Tulsky, D. S. (2005). A history of intelligence assessment. In D. P. Flanagan & P.L. Harrison (Eds.), Contemporary intellectual assessment: Theories, tests, and issues (pp. 3–22). New York: The Guilford Press.

Weber, J., & Stoneman, Z. (1986). Parental nonparticipation as a means of reducing bias in the education of handicapped children. *Special Services in the Schools, 1,* 71–84.

Wechsler, D. (1974). *Manual for the Wechsler intelligence scale for children–revised.* San Antonio: Psychological Corporation.

Wechsler, D. (1997). *Wechsler adult intelligence scale, 3rd edition: Administration and scoring manual.* San Antonio: Psychological Corporation.

Wechsler, D. (2002). *Wechsler preschool and primary scales of intelligence, third edition.* San Antonio, TX: The Psychological Corporation.

Wechsler, D. (2003). *Wechsler intelligence scale for children* (4th ed.). *Administration and scoring manual.* San Antonio, TX: The Psychological Corporation.

Wechsler, D. (2003). *Wechlser intelligence scale for children* (4th ed.). *Technical and interpretive manual.* San Antonio, TX: The Psychological Corporation.

Weine, A. M., Phillips, J. S., & Achenbach, T. M. (1995). Behavioral and emotional problems among Chinese and American Children: Parent and teacher reports for ages 6 to 13. *Journal of Abnormal Child Psychology, 23,* 619–639.

Weller, C., Strawser, S., & Buchanan, M. (1985). Adaptive behavior: Designator of a continuum of severity of learning disabled individuals. *Journal of Learning Disabilities, 18,* 200–203.

Wendling, B. J., & Mather, N. (2001). *Examiner training workbook Woodcock–Johnson III Tests of Achievement.* Itasca, IL: Riverside Publishing.

Wiederholt, J. L., & Bryant, B. R. (2001). *Gray Oral Reading Tests* (4th ed). Austin, TX: Pro-Ed.

Wiener, J. (1986). Alternatives in the assessment of the learning disabled adolescent: A learning strategies approach. *Learning Disabilities Focus, 1,* 97–107.

Wilkinson, G. S. (1993). *The wide range achievement test: Administration manual.* Wilmington, DE: Jastak, Wide Range.

Williams, R., & Zimmerman, D. (1984). On the virtues and vices of standard error of measurement. *Journal of Experimental Education, 52,* 231–233.

Wilson, C. P., Gutkin, T. B., Hagen, K. M., & Oats, R. G. (1998). General education teachers' knowledge and self-reported use of classroom interventions for working with difficult-to-teach students: Implications for consultation, prereferral intervention and inclusive services. *School Psychology Quarterly, 13*(1), 45–62.

Wilson, V. (1987). Percentile scores. In C. R. Reynolds & L. Mann (Eds.), *Encyclopedia of special education: A reference for the education of the handicapped and other exceptional children and adults* (p. 1656). New York: Wiley.

Witt, J., & Martens, B. (1984). Adaptive behavior: Tests and assessment issues. *School Psychology Review, 13,* 478–484.

Witt, J. C., Daly, E., & Noell, G. H. (2000). *Functional assessments: A step-by-step guide to solving academic and behavior problems.* Longmont, CO: Sopris West.

Wood, F., Johnson, J., & Jenkins, J. (1990). The Lora case: Nonbiased referral, assessment, and placement procedures. *Exceptional Children, 52,* 323–331.

Woodcock, R. W. (1987). *Woodcock Reading Mastery Tests-Revised.* Circle Pines, MN: American Guidance Service.

Woodcock, R. W., McGrew, K. S., & Mather, N. (2001). *Woodcock–Johnson III tests of cognitive abilities.* Itasca, IL: Riverside Publishing.

Woodcock, R. W., McGrew, K. S., & Werder, J. K. (1994). *Woodcock–McGrew–Werder Mini-Battery of Achievement.* Itasca, IL: Riverside Publishing.

Yeh, S. S. (2006). High stakes testing: Can rapid assessment reduce the pressure? *Teachers College Record, 108*(4), 621–661.

Yell, M. L. (1995). Least restrictive environment, inclusion and students with disabilities: A legal analysis. *Journal of Special Education, 28,* 389–404.

Yell, M. L. (1997). *The law and special education.* Upper Saddle River, NJ: Merrill/ Prentice Hall.

Yell, M. L., Drasgow, E., & Ford, L. (2000). The individuals with disabilities education act amendments of 1997: Implications for school-based teams. In Telzrow, C. F., & Tankersley, M. (Eds.), *IDEA: Amendments of 1997: Practice guidelines for school-based teams* (pp. 1–28). Bethesda, MD: National Association of School Psychologists.

Yovanoff, P., & Tindal, G. (2007). Scaling early reading alternate assessments with statewide measures. *Exceptional Children, 73*(2), 184–201.

Ysseldyke, J., & Algozzine, B. (1982). *Critical issues in special and remedial education.* Boston: Houghton Mifflin.

Ysseldyke, J., Algozzine, B., Regan, R., & Potter, M. (1980). Technical adequacy of tests used by professionals in simulated decision making. *Psychology in the Schools, 17*, 202–209.

Ysseldyke, J., Algozzine, B., Richey, L., & Graden, J. (1982). Declaring students eligible for learning disability services: Why bother with the data? *Learning Disabilities Quarterly, 5*, 37–44.

Ysseldyke, J., Christenson, S., Pianta, B., & Algozzine, B. (1983). An analysis of teachers' reasons and desired outcomes for students referred for psychoeducational assessment. *Journal of Psychoeducational Assessment, 1*, 73–83.

Ysseldyke, J. E., Nelson, J. R., & House, A. L. (2000). Statewide and district wide assessments: Current status and guidelines for student accommodations and alternate assessments. In C. F. Telzrow and M. Tankersley (Eds.), *IDEA Amendments of 1997: Practice guidelines for school-based teams.* Bethesda, MD: National Association of School Psychologists.

Ysseldyke, J. E., Thurlow, M. L., Kozleski, E., & Reschly, D. (1998). *Accountability for the results of educating students with disabilities: Assessment conference report on the new assessment provisions of the 1997 Amendments to the Individuals with Disabilities Education Act.* (EC 306929) National Center on Educational Outcomes. (ERIC Document Reproduction Service No. ED 425 588)

Ysseldyke, J. E., Nelson, J. R., & House, A. L. (2000). Statewide and district wide assessments: Current status and guidelines for student accommodations and alternate assessments. In C. F. Telzrow & M. Tankersley (Eds.), *IDEA Amendments of 1997: Practice guidelines for school-based teams.* Bethesda, MD: National Association of School Psychologists.

Ysseldyke, J., & Thurlow, M. (1983). *Identification/classification research: An integrative summary of findings* (Research Report No. 142). Minneapolis: University of Minnesota, Institute for Research on Learning Disabilities.

Zins, J., Graden, J., & Ponti, C. (1989). Prereferral intervention to improve special services delivery. *Special Services in the Schools, 4*, 109–130.

NAME INDEX

Note: *Italicized* page numbers indicate illustrations.

Note: *Italicized* page numbers indicate illustrations.

Arctic Ocean

80N

NORWAY
SWEDEN
FINLAND
RUSSIA
ARCTIC CIRCLE
60N

Sungir

Spy
Neander Valley
Heidelberg (Mauer)
Mladeč, Předmostí, Dolní Věstonice
KAZAKHSTAN
Krapina
Oase
MONGOLIA
Arago
Dmanisi
UZBEKISTAN
Teshik Tash
Jinniushan
40N
Ceprano
Petralona
KYRGYZSTAN
Zhoukoudian/Tianyuan
NORTH
KOREA
JAPAN
Tighenif
TURKEY
TAJIKISTAN
Ordos
SOUTH
KOREA
Amud
IRAN
Lantian
Dali
CHINA
Skhūl/Tabun
Jebel
Qafzeh
Shanidar
AFGHANISTAN
PAKISTAN
Hexian

ALGERIA
LIBYA
EGYPT
SAUDI
ARABIA
Liujiang
Maba
TAIWAN
TROPIC OF CANCER
20N

NIGER
CHAD
SUDAN
YEMEN
INDIA
MYANMAR
(BURMA)
LAOS
HONG KONG
MACAU
Pacific
Ocean
NORTHERN
MARIANA
ISLANDS
(U.S.)
REPUBLIC OF THE
MARSHALL ISLANDS

Toros-Menalla

Hadar/Gona
Middle Awash (Aramis, Daka,
Herto, Dikika)
ETHIOPIA
THAILAND
CAMBODIA
VIETNAM
PHILIPPINES
Bodo
Omo
East and West Turkana
UGANDA
KENYA
SRI LANKA
MALDIVES
BRUNEI
MALAYSIA
Niah Cave
FEDERATED STATES
OF MICRONESIA
EQUATOR
0
Kanapoi
Tugen Hills
RWANDA
SINGAPORE
Sumatra
Olduvai/Laetoli
BURUNDI
TANZANIA
SEYCHELLES
INDONESIA
Ngandong
PAPUA
NEW GUINEA
SOLOMON
ISLANDS
TUVALU

COMOROS IS.
Indian Ocean
Sangiran
Trinil
Flores
Kabwe
ZAMBIA
MALAWI
20S
VANUATU
FIJI
NAMIBIA
ANGOLA
ZIMBABWE
MADAGASCAR
MAURITIUS
NEW
CALEDONIA
(Fr.)
TROPIC OF CAPRICORN

AUSTRALIA

WALVIS BAY
(Status to be
determined)
Taung
Sterkfontein/Swartkrans/Drimolen
BOTSWANA
Florisbad
SWAZILAND
LESOTHO
Border Cave
SOUTH
AFRICA
Lake Mungo
Klasies River Mouth
Kow Swamp
NEW
ZEALAND
40S

1. SLOVENIA
2. CROATIA
3. BOSNIA AND HERZEGOVINA
4. ALBANIA
5. MACEDONIA
6. SERBIA AND MONTENEGRO

60S

ANTARCTIC CIRCLE

ANTARCTICA
80S

0   20E   40E   60E   80E   100E   120E   140E   160E   180

Brief Contents

Contents

Lynn Kilgore

Heredity and Evolution

Chapter 4
Heredity and Evolution

Chapter 5
Macroevolution: Processes of Vertebrate and Mammalian Evolution

Drawing by Robert Greisen

Primates

Nelson Ting

San Francisco Zoo

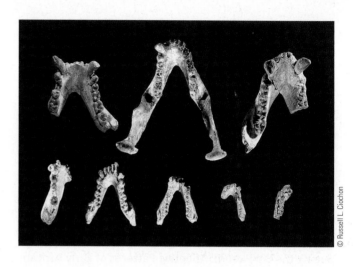

Hominin Evolution

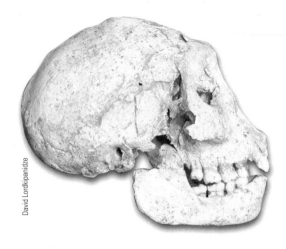

David Lordkipanidze

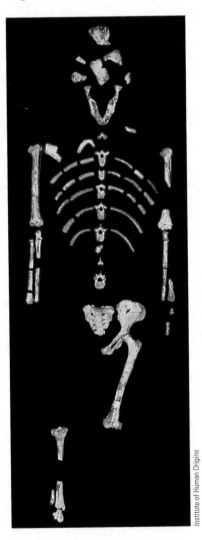

Institute of Human Origins

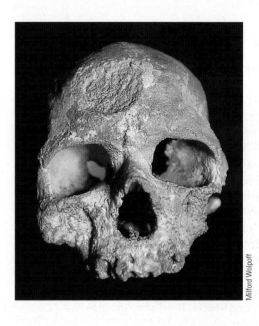

Milford Wolpoff

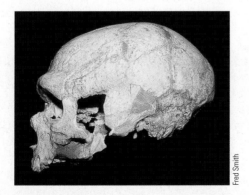

Fred Smith

Contemporary Human Evolution

List of Features

A Closer Look

At a Glance

What's Important

New Frontiers in Research

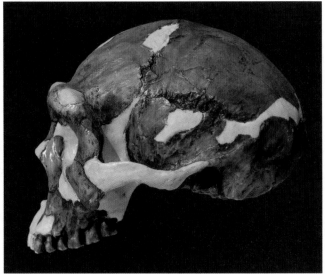

© Russell L. Ciochon

Preface

Welcome, students and instructors, to our latest edition of *Introduction to Physical Anthropology*. In this edition, we're pleased to bring you news of exciting discoveries and fresh insights regarding newly found genetic mechanisms and ancient fossils. With the benefit of this new material, this book is both more up-to-date and much improved from the last edition.

Of the four fields of anthropology, physical anthropology relies most heavily on the biological sciences as a foundation. Because our discipline is a scientific one, many of the topics covered in this book will seem complex to introductory students. What's more, new and extraordinarily powerful genetic techniques of analysis continue to revolutionize our field, further complicating some of the material we will cover. These exciting developments pose a challenge for students, instructors, and textbook authors alike, but they also provide the opportunity for a deeper understanding of our subject.

Each of the authors has taught the introductory physical anthropology course over many, many years. From this long experience, we realize that due to generally superficial biological training as well as a lack of anthropological instruction at the high school level, much of the material in this textbook may be entirely new to our readers. To ease the transition into this new subject area, we aim for maximum clarity in writing style and provide many visual aids to further assist readers. Within these pages, there are many places where students can seek help in learning about topics, ideas, and developments encountered for the first time. To provide even more assistance than in previous editions, much of the artwork has been completely redrawn, and we have also added many new photos. All these changes reflect our long-term commitment to make our textbook an effective teaching and learning instrument. There are also several printed and online learning aids, many of which are specifically designed to accompany this text (see Supplements for Students on pp. xix–xx). Nevertheless, we believe that the first (and best) place for students to find help in mastering new material is the textbook (although we encourage you, of course, to ask your instructor or teaching assistant a variety of questions).

This physical anthropology textbook is about human biology, especially from an evolutionary perspective. New techniques and rapid advances, such as in DNA research (genomics), have fueled a massive revolution in all the biological sciences, including physical anthropology. Knowledge is proliferating so fast that researchers race to stay up-to-date. Sometimes, what was adequate knowledge last month is now deemed incomplete.

Significant, and increasingly indispensable, medical applications taken directly from the biological sciences will impact all of us in coming years. Many of you who are taking a course in physical/biological anthropology are doing so to fulfill a general education life science requirement. As engaged citizens in a twenty-first-century democracy, it's crucial that you be well informed. Consequently, another major goal of this text is to provide students with essential tools for understanding scientific information; in this way, you'll be better prepared to deal with the rapidly changing world you'll face in the years ahead.

Because genetic mechanisms lie at the heart of understanding evolution, we'll address basic aspects of life, cells, DNA, and the ways species change in the early chapters of this text (Chapter 2 through 5). We'll next turn (in Chapters 6 through 8) to an exploration of our evolutionary cousins, the nonhuman primates, and how they relate to us both physically and behaviorally. In Chapter 9, we'll discuss the evolutionary history of early primates to better understand the many ways in which primates have adapted to their environments.

More details of our specific human evolutionary history over the past 7 million years are covered over the next five chapters. We'll begin with our small-brained ancestors in Africa and follow the development of their descendants through time and over their expanding ranges into Asia and Europe—and much later into Australia and the Americas.

In the last section of this book (Chapters 15 through 17), we'll conclude our journey of human evolution with a discussion of modern human biology and trace the ongoing evolution of our species. Our major topics will include the nature of human variation (including the meaning of "race") and patterns of adaptation in recent human populations.

What's New in the 2009–2010 Edition

First of all, we have added many updates throughout the book, reflecting recent advances in virtually every field of physical anthropology. In our genetics section (Chapters 3 and 4) we show how DNA is organized and how it works, with new material on the crucial function of regulatory genes (Chapter 3) and how these genes interact to affect physical features like eye color (Chapter 4). For those of you who perhaps learned in high school about how eye color is inherited, you're in for a surprise. In the section on nonhuman primates (Chapters 6–8) we report on fascinating new discoveries about chimpanzee behavior. For example, they use sharpened sticks as spears while preying on smaller animals and capuchin monkeys use stones to crack nuts (as shown on the book's cover). The primate classification in Chapter 9 has been updated to support the most current views, and a new molecularly based evolutionary tree shows divergence dates of major primate groups discussed in the text. We've also added a new section on the earliest known primate, and enhanced visuals have been developed to better show evolutionary relationships among our primate relatives.

There are also many intriguing new discoveries of fossil hominins, which we cover in Chapters 10 through 14. Among these are late-surviving early members of genus *Homo* in East Africa (Chapter 11) and discoveries of limb bones of the first hominin migrants out of Africa (found in the Republic of Georgia in southeastern Europe; Chapter 12). From sites a little later in time from Spain, new fossils have provided the earliest evidence of hominins in western Europe (Chapter 13). Further evidence has also emerged from analysis of Neandertal DNA, providing new clues regarding their language capabilities and even their skin color (Chapter 13). And recent discoveries have also added to our knowledge about the earliest modern humans found in Asia (Chapter 14). Then, too, there are the "little people" from an island in Indonesia, whom the press have dubbed "hobbits." These unusual hominins were discussed in our previous edition, but since then, anthropologists have intensely debated what sort of hominins these fossils represent. The debate continues and is discussed in some detail in Chapter 14; as you'll see, the latest and most detailed studies provide more conclusive evidence than was previously available.

In Chapters 15 through 17, our focus turns to modern human biology. There we provide new information on the biocultural evolution of the gene influencing milk digestion in human populations (Chapter 15) as well as

significant new findings helping explain the evolutionary adaptations relating to human skin color (Chapter 16). Chapter 17 includes a new section on global warming, another phenomenon with far-reaching consequences that we will have to deal with in the near future.

For previous users of the book, you will notice some important changes in how we classify primates (discussed in Chapters 6 and 9 and complemented by our new Appendix B, "Taxonomy of Living and Selected Extinct Primates"). Throughout the text, we have introduced what may seem like a small change in terminology regarding the way the human lineage is classified. In place of the former term *hominid*, we now use the term *hominin*. This new terminology, in fact, reflects a major change in how the human lineage is now classified relative to the great apes, especially our *very* close cousins, the chimpanzee and gorilla.

Features

New Frontiers in Research features highlight some of the newest and most innovative research in physical anthropology. Five areas of research are covered:

- Molecular Applications in Forensic Anthropology (following Chapter 3)
- Evo-Devo: The Evolution Revolution (following Chapter 5)
- Molecular Applications in Primatology (following Chapter 7)
- Ancient DNA (following Chapter 13)
- Molecular Applications in Modern Human Biology (following Chapter 15)

Boxed highlights titled A Closer Look are high-interest features found throughout the book. They expand on the topic under discussion in the chapter by providing a more in-depth perspective.

In-Chapter Learning Aids

- Chapter outlines at the beginning of each chapter list all major topics covered.
- Key Questions appear at the beginning of each chapter and highlight the central topic of that chapter.
- A running glossary in the margins provides definitions of terms immediately adjacent to the text when the term is first introduced. A full glossary is provided at the back of the book.

- At a Glance boxes found throughout the book briefly summarize complex or controversial material in a visually simple fashion.

- Figures, including numerous photographs, line drawings, and maps, most in full color, are carefully selected to clarify text materials and directly support the discussion in the text. Much of the art, especially anatomical drawings, have been redrawn for this edition.

- Critical Thinking Questions at the end of each chapter reinforce key concepts and encourage students to think critically about what they have read.

- Full bibliographical citations throughout the book provide sources from which the materials are drawn. This type of documentation guides students to published source materials and illustrates for students the proper use of references. All cited sources are listed in the comprehensive bibliography at the back of the book.

- A "Click!" guide at the beginning of each chapter directs students to the appropriate media covering materials pertinent to that chapter. One or more of the three supplemental multimedia products will be listed: Virtual Laboratories for Physical Anthropology, Version 4.0; Basic Genetics for Anthropology CD-ROM: Principles and Applications, Version 2.0; and Hominid Fossils CD-ROM: An Interactive Atlas.

Acknowledgments

Over the years, many friends and colleagues have assisted us with our books. For this edition we are especially grateful to the reviewers who so carefully commented on the manuscript and made such helpful suggestions: Susan Cachel, Rutgers University; Arthur Durband, Texas Tech University; John G. Fleagle, Stony Brook University; Sandra Gray, University of Kansas; Gregg F. Gunnell, University of Michigan; Terry Harrison, New York University; Li Jian, University of Northern Iowa; John Krigbaum, University of Florida; Monte L. McCrossin, New Mexico State University; Robert R. Paine, Texas Tech University; and Melissa Remis, Purdue University.

We wish to thank the team at Cengage Learning: Marcus Boggs, Lin Marshall Gaylord, Andrew Keay, Arwen Petty, Liana Monari, Erin Abney, Caryl Gorska, and Jerilyn Emori. Moreover, for their unflagging expertise and patience, we are grateful to our copy editor, Janet Greenblatt, our production coordinator, Gary Hespenheide, and his skilled staff at Hespenheide Design: Patti Zeman, Bridget Neumayr, and Randy Miyake.

To the many friends and colleagues who have generously provided photographs, we are greatly appreciative: Zeresenay Alemsegel, Berhane Asfaw, Chris Beard, David Begun, Brenda Benefit, Jonathan Bloch, C. K. Brain, Günter Bräuer, Michel Brunet, Peter Brown, Chip Clark, Desmond Clark, Ron Clarke, Bill Clemens, Raymond Dart, Henri de Lumley, Louis de Bonis, Jean deRousseau, Tiago Falótico, John Fleagle, Dorothy Fragaszy, Diane France, Robert Franciscus, David Frayer, Kathleen Galvin, Philip Gingerich, Laurie Godfrey, Gregg Gunnell, David Haring, Terry Harrison, John Hodgkiss, Almut Hoffman, Pat Holroyd, Ellen Ingmanson, Fred Jacobs, Peter Jones, John Kappelman, Richard Kay, William Kimbel, Leslie Knapp, Arlene Kruse, Richard Leakey, Carol Lofton, David Lordkipanidze, Giorgio Manzi, Margaret Maples, Monte McCrossin, Lorna Moore, Stephen Nash, Gerald Newlands, Xijum Ni, John Oates, Bonnie Pedersen, Lorna Pierce, David Pilbeam, William Pratt, Judith Regensteiner, Sastrohamijoyo Sartono, Jeffrey Schwartz, Eugenie Scott, Rose Sevick, Elwyn Simons, Meredith Small, Fred Smith, Thierry Smith, Noemi Spagnoletti, Kiristin Sterner, Judy Suchey, Gen Suwa, Masanaru Takai, Heather Thew, Nelson Ting, Phillip Tobias, Erik Trinkaus, Alan Walker, Carol Ward, Dietrich Wegner, James Westgate, Randy White, Milford Wolpoff, Barth Wright, and Xinzhi Wu.

To the many students who have pledged their time and expertise, we would like to thank Audrey Dunn, Lindsay Eaves-Johnson, Scott Maddux, Hannah Marsh, Nathan Holton, and Anna Waterman for their help editing and researching the manuscript; James Rogers, Nathan Totten, and Joshua Gruber for their help with computer graphics; and Audrey Dunn, Lindsay Eaves-Johnson, Anna Waterman, and Kara Bantz for their meticulous work on the index and bibliography. Special mention goes to Lindsay Eaves-Johnson and James Rogers for their valued assistance in facilitating coordination of the text and art within the context of the Ciochon Lab. These students have worked to ensure that the text is as accessible as possible for their peers. Also at the University of Iowa, Linda Maxson, Dean of the College of Liberal Arts and Sciences, provided invaluable support. Others who have assisted in forming the concepts that we have put into written form include John Fleagle, Eric Delson, Terry Harrison, Gregg Gunnell, Philip Rightmire, Kirstin Sterner, Nelson Ting, and Tim White.

Robert Jurmain
Lynn Kilgore
Wenda Trevathan
Russell Ciochon
January 2009

Dedicated to the memory of
Wenoma Fosdick Copple
1915–2008

Supplements

Introduction to Physical Anthropology 2009–2010 comes with an outstanding supplements program to help instructors create an effective learning environment so that students can more easily master the latest discoveries and interpretations in the field of physical anthropology.

Supplements for Instructors

Instructor's Edition for Jurmain/Kilgore/Trevathan/ Ciochon's *Introduction to Physical Anthropology 2009– 2010 Edition* The Instructor's Edition contains the student version of the book as well as an informative visual preface. (ISBN: 0-495-59980-8)

Online Instructor's Manual with Test Bank for Jurmain/ Kilgore/Trevathan/Ciochon's *Introduction to Physical Anthropology 2009–2010 Edition* This online resource includes a sample syllabus showing how to integrate the Anthropology Resource Center with the text, as well as chapter outlines, learning objectives, key terms and concepts, lecture suggestions, enrichment topics, and 40 to 60 test questions per chapter. (ISBN: 0-495-60334-1)

PowerLecture with Exam View® (Windows/Macintosh) and JoinIn™ for Jurmain/Kilgore/Trevathan/Ciochon's *Introduction to Physical Anthropology 2009–2010 Edition* This easy-to-use tool includes the following: Preassembled Microsoft® PowerPoint® presentations using charts, graphs, line art, and photographs with a zoom feature; ExamView® testing software that lets you create, deliver, and customize tests and study guides (both print and online) in minutes with an easy-to-use assessment and tutorial system. ExamView® offers both a Quick Test Wizard and an Online Test Wizard that guide you step by step throughout the process of creating tests, while its unique WYSIWYG capability allows you to see the test you are creating on screen exactly as it will print or display online. You can build tests of up to 250 questions, using up to 12 question types. Using ExamView's® complete word processing capabilities, you can enter an unlimited number of new questions or edit existing questions. This instructor CD-ROM also includes JoinIn™ on Turning Point® (clicker) content for Audience Response Systems tailored to this text. Use the program to take roll, give opinion polls on issues important to each chapter in the text (5 questions per chapter), give a paperless quiz for each chapter, or pose your own questions and display students' answers instantly within the Microsoft PowerPoint slides of your existing lecture. Enhance how your students interact with you, your lecture, and each other. For college and university adopters only. Contact your local Cengage sales representative to learn more. (ISBN: 0-495-60336-8)

Wadsworth Anthropology Video Library Qualified adopters may select full-length videos from an extensive library of offerings drawn from such excellent educational video sources as Films for the Humanities and Sciences.

ABC Anthropology Video Series This exclusive video series was created jointly by Wadsworth and ABC for the anthropology course. Each video contains approximately 60 minutes of footage originally broadcast on ABC within the past several years. The videos are broken into short 2- to 7-minute segments, perfect for classroom use as lecture launchers. An annotated table of contents accompanies each video, providing descriptions of the segments and suggestions for their possible use within the course.

Online Resources for Instructors and Students

WebTutor™ Toolbox on WebCT® or Blackboard® WebTutor Toolbox provides access to all the content of this text's rich Book Companion Website from within your course management system. Robust communication tools—such as course calendar, asynchronous discussion, real-time chat, a whiteboard, and an integrated e-mail system— make it easy for your students to stay connected to the course. (On WebCT, ISBN 0-534-27488-9; on Blackboard, ISBN 0-534-27489-7)

Anthropology Resource Center This hands-on online center offers a wealth of information and useful tools for both instructors and students in all four fields of anthropology: cultural anthropology, physical anthropology, archaeology, and linguistics. For students, it provides interactive maps, learning modules, video clip exercises, breaking news in anthropology, and more. For instructo the Resource Center is a gateway to time-saving teaching tools, such as image banks and sample syllabi. Access to the website is available free when bundled with the text or for purchase for a fee. To purchase online, students are directed to iChapters.com. (ISBN: 0-495-39454-8)

Website for Jurmain/Kilgore/Trevathan/Ciochon's *Introduction to Physical Anthropology 2009–2010* This text-specific website provides students with a variety of basic learning resources, including tutorial quizzes, a final practice exam, learning objectives, Web links, flash cards, crossword puzzles, and more! (ISBN: 0-495-60338-4)

Online Virtual Laboratories for Physical Anthropology, Version 4.0, by John Kappelman Virtual Laboratories provides students with an interactive learning environment to complete lab assignments at school, at home, or in the library. Each laboratory is a self-contained instructional module that combines a wide range of digital images, 3-D animation, video, and sound to help students master the many techniques and concepts taught in the normal laboratory class. Students actively participate in the physical anthropology labs and develop critical-thinking and problem-solving skills by taking measurements and plotting data, assessing primates in the wild, evaluating data, and much more. When you order Virtual Laboratories on the web-based CengageNOW platform, a powerful course management component allows you to change the order of the labs, move content within the labs, utilize the pre- and post-lab tests for each lab, and track how much time students spend on each lab. Virtual Laboratories includes Web links, outstanding fossil images, exercises, a notebook feature, and a post-lab self-quiz. (Virtual Laboratories is also available on CD with a portion of the features and functionality of the online version.) (ISBN: 0-495-00992-X)

Basic Genetics in Anthropology CD-ROM: Principles and Applications, Version 2.0, by Jurmain/Kilgore/Trevathan Available free bundled with the text, this student CD-ROM reviews and expands on basic biological concepts covered in the book, focusing on biological inheritance (for example, genes and DNA sequencing) and its applications to modern human populations at the molecular level (including disease, diet, and growth and development). Interactive animations and simulations bring these important concepts to life for students so they can fully understand the essential biological principles underlying human evolution. Also available are quizzes and interactive flash cards for further study. (ISBN: 0-495-64849-3)

ominid Fossils CD-ROM: An Interactive Atlas, by James rn This CD-based interactive atlas explores more than 75 key fossils that are important for a clear understanding of human evolution. The QuickTime® Virtual Reality (QTVR) format enables each fossil to be rotated 360 degrees. Compelling and highly visual Tutorials help students learn fossil and species identification, while a compare/contrast feature aids in student mastery of key fossils. "Hot Spot" labeling, an audio glossary, and a dynamic quizzing section geared to users with varying levels of prior knowledge further enhance student learning. An online instructor's manual is available. (ISBN: 0-534-63841-4)

Cengage InSite™ for Writing and Research with Turnitin™ Originality Checker InSite features a full suite of writing, peer review, online grading, and e-portfolio applications. It is an all-in-one tool that helps instructors manage the flow of papers electronically and allows students to submit papers and peer reviews online. Also included in the suite is Turnitin, an originality check that offers a simple solution for instructors who want a strong deterrent against plagiarism, as well as encouragement for students to employ proper research techniques. Access is available for packaging with each copy of this book. For more information, visit www.insite.cengage.com.

Supplements for Students

Study Guide This useful guide enables students to fully comprehend and appreciate what the text has to offer. Each chapter of the study guide features learning objectives, chapter outlines, key terms, concept applications, and practice tests consisting of 30 to 40 multiple-choice questions and 5 to 10 true/false questions with answers and page references, in addition to several short-answer and essay questions. (ISBN: 0-495-60335-X)

Distance Learning Course A new distance learning course entitled Physical Anthropology: The Evolving Human provides online and print companion study guide options that include quizzing, study aids, interactive exercises, video, and more, for the distance learning class. (ISBN: 0-495-80785-0)

Classic and Contemporary Readings in Physical Anthropology, by Mary K. Sandford with Eileen Jackson This accessible reader includes 23 selections that help students examine the question, What does it mean to be human? Mirroring the organization of most introductory courses in biological anthropology, the book covers five main areas of interest: the nature of science, evolution and heredity, primate behavior, human evolution, and modern human variation. The book's collection of classic and contemporary readings reflects Sandford and Jackson's careful consideration of the available literature, stressing the importance of scientific principles and methods as well as the historical development of physical anthropology and the applications of new technology to the discipline. Available for packaging at a price advantage with the text. (ISBN: 0-495-51014-9)

Lab Manual and Workbook for Physical Anthropology, Sixth Edition, by Diane L. France Now in full color, France's Lab Manual balances the study of genetics, biological classification, human osteology, primates, human evolution, and anthropometry. It contains material on forensic anthropology and a new chapter on growth and development that includes more material on disease and new information on the anomalies of the human skeleton caused by disease and mechanical stress. This edition's art program has been greatly enhanced with color images that include scales and orientation information, as well as reprinted images for chapter exercises where needed. With hands-on lab assignments that help students apply physical anthropology perspectives and techniques to real situations, the Lab Manual provides a wealth of solid information and photographs that help make the concepts of physical anthropology easier to understand. Contact your Cengage sales representative to package with the text. (ISBN: 0-495-09399-8)

Modules in Physical Anthropology

Cengage Modules in Physical Anthropology series Each free-standing module is actually a complete text chapter, featuring the same quality of pedagogy and illustration contained in Cengage's physical anthropology texts. Available free bundled with the text.

Evolution of the Brain, by Daniel D. White The human species is the only species that has ever created a symphony, written a poem, developed a mathematical equation, or studied its own origins. The biological structure that has enabled humans to perform these feats of intelligence is the human brain. This module explores the basics of neuroanatomy, brain development, lateralization, sexual dimorphism, and the fossil evidence for hominin brain evolution.

Human Environment Interactions, by Cathy Galvin This module begins with a brief discussion of the history and core concepts of the field of human ecology before looking in depth at how the environment influences cultural practices (environmental determinism) and how aspects of culture, in turn, affect the environment. Human behavioral ecology is presented within the context of natural selection and how ecological factors influence the development of cultural and behavioral traits and how people subsist in different environments. The module concludes with a discussion of resilience and global change as a result of human-environment interactions.

Molecular Anthropology Module, by Leslie Knapp This module explores how molecular genetic methods are used to understand the organization and expression of genetic information in humans and nonhuman primates. Students will learn about the common laboratory methods used to study variation and evolution in molecular anthropology. Examples are drawn from up-to-date research on human evolutionary origins and comparative primate genomics to demonstrate that scientific research is an ongoing process with theories frequently being questioned and reevaluated.

Forensic Anthropology Module, by Diane France This module introduces students to the essentials of forensic anthropology as it is practiced in the United States and Canada. It explores the field's myths and realities of the search for human remains at crime scenes, the expectations of a forensic anthropology expert in the courtroom, some of the challenges of mass fatality incident responses, and the issues a student should consider if pursuing a career in forensic anthropology.

These resources are available to qualified adopters, and ordering options for student supplements are flexible. Please consult your local Cengage sales consultant for more information or to evaluate examination copies of any of these resources or to receive product demonstrations. You may also contact the Wadsworth Academic Resource Center at 800-423-0563 or visit us at academic.cengage.com. Additional information is also available at www.academic.cengage.com/anthropology/Jurmain.

1

Introduction to Physical Anthropology

Key Questions

What do physical anthropologists do?

Why is physical anthropology a scientific discipline, and what is its importance to the general public?

Click!

Go to the following media for interactive activities and exercises on topics covered in this chapter:

- Online Virtual Laboratories for Physical Anthropology, Version 4.0

- Genetics in Anthropology: Principles and Applications CD-ROM, Version 2.0

- Hominid Fossils: An Interactive Atlas CD-ROM

Introduction

One day, perhaps during the rainy season some 3.7 million years ago, two or three animals walked across a grassland savanna in what is now northern Tanzania, in East Africa. These individuals were early **hominins**, members of the evolutionary lineage that also includes our own species, *Homo sapiens*. Fortunately for us, a record of their passage on that long-forgotten day remains in the form of fossilized footprints, preserved in hardened volcanic deposits.

As chance would have it, shortly after heels and toes were pressed into the dampened soil, a nearby volcano erupted. The ensuing ashfall blanketed everything on the ground. In time, the ash layer hardened into a deposit that remarkably preserved the tracks of numerous animals, including those early hominins (Fig. 1-1).

These now famous prints indicate that two individuals, one smaller than the other and perhaps walking side by side, left parallel sets of tracks. But because the

Figure 1-1

Early hominin footprints at Laetoli, Tanzania. The tracks to the left were made by one individual, while those to the right appear to have been formed by two individuals, the second stepping in the tracks of the first.

Peter Jones

hominins Colloquial term for members of the evolutionary group that includes modern humans and now extinct bipedal relatives.

larger individual's prints are obscured, possibly by those of a third, it's unclear how many actually made that journey so long ago. But it is clear that the prints were made by an animal that habitually walked **bipedally** (on two feet), and that fact tells us that those ancient travelers were hominins.

Besides the footprints, scientists working at this site (called Laetoli) and at other locations have discovered many fossilized parts of skeletons of an animal we call *Australopithecus afarensis*. After analyzing these remains, we know that these hominins were anatomically similar to ourselves, although their brains were only about one-third the size of ours. And even though they may have used stones and sticks as simple tools, there's no evidence that they actually made stone tools. In fact, they were very much at the mercy of nature's whims. They certainly couldn't outrun most predators, and since their canine teeth were fairly small, they were pretty much defenseless.

We've asked hundreds of questions about the Laetoli hominins, but we'll never be able to answer them all. Those individuals walked down a path into what became their future, and their immediate journey has long since ended. So it remains for us to learn as much as we can about them and their **species**; and as we continue to do this, their greater journey continues.

On July 20, 1969, a television audience numbering in the hundreds of millions watched as two human beings stepped out of a spacecraft onto the surface of the moon. To anyone born after that date, this event may be taken more or less for granted. But the significance of that first moonwalk can't be overstated, because it represents humankind's presumed mastery over the natural forces that govern our presence on earth. For the first time ever, people actually walked upon the surface of a celestial body that has never given birth to biological life (as far as we know).

As the astronauts gathered geological specimens and frolicked in near weightlessness, they left traces of their fleeting presence in the form of footprints in the lunar dust (Fig. 1-2). On the surface of the moon, where no rain falls and no wind blows, the footprints remain undisturbed to this day. They survive as mute testimony to a brief visit by a medium-sized, big-brained creature who presumed to challenge the very forces that created it.

You may be wondering why anyone would care about early hominin footprints and how they can possibly be relevant to your life. And even though you know that there was a moon landing in the late 1960s, you may not have spent much time actually thinking about it. You may also wonder why a physical **anthropology** textbook would begin by discussing two such seemingly unrelated events as hominins walking across an African savanna and a moonwalk. The fact is, these two events are very closely related.

Physical, or biological, anthropology is a scientific discipline concerned with the biological and behavioral characteristics of human beings; our closest relatives, the nonhuman **primates** (apes, monkeys, lemurs, lorises, and tarsiers); and their ancestors. This kind of research helps us explain what it means to be human. This is a pretty ambitious goal, and it's probably not completely attainable. But it's certainly worth pursuing. We're the only species to ponder our own existence and wonder how we fit into the spectrum of life on earth. Most people view humanity as separate from the rest of the animal kingdom. But at the same time, many are curious about the similarities we share with other species. Maybe you've looked at your dog and tried to figure out how her front legs might correspond to your arms. During a visit to the zoo, you may have recognized the similarities between a chimpanzee's hands or facial expressions and your own. Perhaps you wondered if they also shared your thoughts and feelings. If you've ever had thoughts and questions like these, then you've indeed been curious about humankind's place in nature.

© Bettmann/Corbis

Figure **1-2**

Human footprints left on the lunar surface during the *Apollo* mission.

bipedally On two feet. Walking habitually on two legs.

species A group of organisms that can interbreed to produce fertile offspring. Members of one species are reproductively isolated from members of all other species (i.e., they cannot mate with them to produce fertile offspring).

anthropology The field of inquiry that studies human culture and evolutionary aspects of human biology; includes cultural anthropology, archaeology, linguistics, and physical, or biological, anthropology.

primates Members of the order of mammals Primates (pronounced "pry-may´-tees"), which includes lemurs, lorises, tarsiers, monkeys, apes, and humans.

We humans, who can barely comprehend a century, can't begin to grasp the enormity of nearly 4 million years. But we still want to know more about those creatures who walked across the savanna that day. We want to know how an insignificant but clever bipedal primate such as *Australopithecus afarensis*, or perhaps a close relative, gave rise to a species that would eventually walk on the surface of a moon some 230,000 miles from earth.

How did *Homo sapiens*, a result of the same evolutionary forces that produced all other forms of life on this planet, gain the power to control the flow of rivers and perhaps even change the very climate in which we live? As tropical animals, how were we able to leave the tropics and eventually occupy most of the earth's land surfaces? How did we adjust to different environmental conditions as we moved into new areas? How could our species, which numbered fewer than 1 billion until the mid-nineteenth century, come to number almost 7 billion worldwide today and, as we now do, add another billion people every 11 years?

These are some of the many questions that physical anthropologists try to answer, and they're largely the focus of the study of human **evolution**, variation, and **adaptation**. These issues, and many others, are the topics covered directly or indirectly in this textbook, because physical anthropology is, in part, human biology seen from an evolutionary perspective.

As biological organisms, humans are subjected to the same evolutionary forces as all other species. On hearing the term *evolution*, most people think of the appearance of new species. Certainly, new species are one important consequence of evolution; but it isn't the only one, because evolution is an ongoing biological process with more than one outcome. Simply stated, evolution is a change in the **genetic** makeup of a population over time, and it can be defined and studied at two levels. Sometimes genetic changes in populations over time do result in the appearance of a new species (or *speciation*), especially when those populations are isolated from one another. Change at this level is called *macroevolution*. At the other level, there are genetic alterations *within* populations; and while this type of change may not lead to speciation, it does cause populations of a species to differ from one another in the frequency of certain traits. Evolution at this level is referred to as *microevolution*. Evolution as it occurs at both these levels will be discussed in this book.

But physical anthropologists don't just study physiological and biological systems. When these topics are considered within the broader context of human evolution, another factor must be considered, and that factor is **culture**. Culture is an extremely important concept, not only as it relates to modern humans but also because of its critical role in human evolution. Quite simply, and in a very broad sense, culture can be defined as the strategy by which humans adapt to the natural environment. In fact, culture is the environment we live in. Culture includes technologies ranging from stone tools to computers; subsistence patterns, from hunting and gathering to global agribusiness; housing types, from thatched huts to skyscrapers; and clothing, from animal skins to high-tech synthetic fibers (Fig. 1-3). Technology, religion, values, social organization, language, kinship, marriage rules, gender roles, inheritance of property—these are all aspects of culture. And each culture shapes people's perceptions of the external environment, or **worldview**, in particular ways that distinguish that culture from all others.

One important point to remember is that culture isn't genetically passed from one generation to the next. We aren't born with innate knowledge that leads us to behave in ways appropriate to our own culture. Culture is *learned*, and the process of learning one's culture begins, quite literally, at birth. As we just discussed, all humans are products of the culture they're raised in, and since most of human

---

evolution A change in the genetic structure of a population. The term is also frequently used to refer to the appearance of a new species.

adaptation An anatomical, physiological, or behavioral response of organisms or populations to the environment. Adaptations result from evolutionary change (specifically, as a result of natural selection).

genetic Having to do with the study of gene structure and action and the patterns of inheritance of traits from parent to offspring. Genetic mechanisms are the foundation for evolutionary change.

culture Behavioral aspects of human adaptation, including technology, traditions, language, religion, marriage patterns, and social roles. Culture is a set of learned behaviors transmitted from one generation to the next by nonbiological (i.e., nongenetic) means.

worldview General cultural orientation
perspective shared by members of a
ty.

(a)

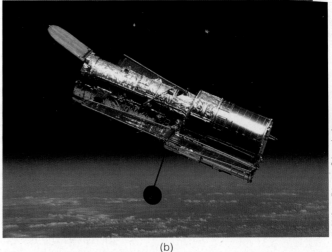

(b)

Lynn Kilgore

NASA/Space Telescope Science Institute

(c)

(d)

Lynn Kilgore

Justin Horocks/iStockphoto

behavior is learned, it follows that most behaviors, perceptions, values, and reactions are shaped by culture.

At the same time, however, it's important to emphasize that even though culture isn't genetically determined, the human predisposition to assimilate culture and function within it is very much influenced by biological factors. Most nonhuman animals, including birds and especially primates, rely to varying degrees on learned behavior; and this is especially true of the great apes, which exhibit several aspects of culture (see Chapter 7).

The predisposition for culture is perhaps the most critical component of human evolutionary history, and it was inherited from our early hominin or even pre-hominin ancestors. In fact, the common ancestor we share with chimpanzees may have had this predisposition. But during the course of human evolution, the role of culture became exceptionally important. Over time, culture influenced many aspects of our biological makeup; and in turn, aspects of biology influenced cultural practices. For this reason, humans are the result of long-term interactions

Figure **1-3**

(a) An early stone tool from East Africa. This artifact represents one of the oldest types of stone tools found anywhere. (b) The Hubble Space telescope orbits the earth every 96 minutes at an altitude of 360 miles. Because it is above the earth's atmosphere, it provides distortion-free images of objects in deep space. (c) A Samburu woman in East Africa building a traditional dwelling of stems, small branches, and mud. (d) These Hong Kong skyscrapers are typical of cities in industrialized countries today.

between biology and culture, and we call this interaction **biocultural evolution**; in this respect, humans are unique.

In humans, biocultural interactions have resulted in many anatomical, biological, and behavioral changes: the shape of the pelvis, increased brain size, reorganization of neurological structures, smaller teeth, and the development of language, to list a few. Today, biocultural interactions are as important as they've ever been. For example, air pollution and exposure to dangerous chemicals have increased the prevalence of respiratory diseases and cancer. Air travel makes it possible for infectious diseases to spread, literally within hours, across the globe. Many human activities have changed the patterns of such infectious diseases as tuberculosis and malaria. Because we've overused antibiotics, we've made some strains of tuberculosis resistant to treatment, and even deadly. Likewise, although we're making progress in treating malaria, the microorganism that causes it has developed resistance to some treatments and preventive medications. We've also increased the geographical distribution of malaria-carrying mosquitoes through agricultural practices and global climate change. So it's clear that we humans have influenced the development and spread of infectious disease; but what isn't so clear, at least to most people, is that the changes in infectious disease patterns have also affected human biology and behavior. Anthropological research in this one topic alone is extremely relevant, and there are many other critical topics that anthropologists explore.

What Is Anthropology?

Many anthropology students are forced to contemplate this question when they are inevitably asked by friends or parents, "What are you studying?" The answer is often followed by blank stares or a comment relating to Indiana Jones or dinosaurs. Well, what *is* anthropology, and how is it different from several related disciplines?

Human biologists and anatomists also investigate human adaptation and evolution; and historians and sociologists also study aspects of human societies, past and present. But when biological or social research also considers the interactions between evolutionary and cultural factors, such research is placed within the discipline of anthropology.

In the United States, anthropology is divided into four main subfields: cultural, or social, anthropology; linguistic anthropology; archaeology; and physical, or biological, anthropology. Each of these, in turn, is divided into several specialized areas of interest. This four-field approach concerns all aspects of humanity across space and time. Each approach emphasizes different facets of humanity, but together, these four fields offer a powerful means of explaining variation in human adaptations. In addition, each of these subfields has practical applications, and many anthropologists pursue careers outside the academic environment. This kind of anthropology is called **applied anthropology**, and it's extremely important today.

Cultural Anthropology

Cultural, or social, anthropology is the study of the global patterns of belief and behavior found in human cultures both past and present. The origins of cultural anthropology can be traced to the nineteenth century, when travel increasingly

biocultural evolution The mutual, interactive evolution of human biology and culture; the concept that biology makes culture possible and that developing culture further influences the direction of biological evolution; a basic concept in understanding the unique components of human evolution.

applied anthropology The practical application of anthropological and archaeological theories and techniques. For example, many biological anthropologists work in the public health sector.

brought Europeans in contact (and sometimes in conflict) with various cultures in Africa, Asia, and the New World.

With this contact grew an interest in so-called "traditional" societies, leading numerous early anthropologists to study and record lifeways that are now all but extinct. These studies produced many descriptive **ethnographies** that emphasized various phenomena, such as religion, ritual, myth, use of symbols, diet, **subsistence strategies**, technology, gender roles, and child-rearing practices. Ethnographic accounts, in turn, formed the basis for comparative studies of numerous cultures. Such *cross-cultural* studies, called *ethnologies*, broadened the context within which cultural anthropologists studied human behavior.

The focus of cultural anthropology shifted over the course of the twentieth century. Cultural anthropologists still work in remote areas, but increasingly they've turned their gaze inward, toward their own cultures and the people around them. Increasingly, ethnographic techniques have been applied to the study of diverse subcultures and their interactions with one another in contemporary metropolitan areas (urban anthropology). The population of any city is composed of many subgroups defined by economic status, religion, ethnic background, profession, age, level of education, and so on. Even the student body of your own college or university is made up of many subcultures, and as you walk across campus, you'll see students of many nationalities and diverse religious and ethnic backgrounds. You may also be aware of more recent cultural identities such as LGBT, goths, and emos, to name a few.

Linguistic Anthropology

Linguistic anthropology is the study of human speech and language, including the origins of language in general as well as specific languages. By examining similarities between contemporary languages, linguists have been able to trace historical ties between languages and groups of languages, thus facilitating the identification of language families and perhaps past relationships between human populations.

Because the spontaneous acquisition and use of language is a uniquely human characteristic, it's an important topic for linguistic anthropologists, who, along with specialists in other fields, study the process of language acquisition in infants. Since insights into the process may well have implications for the development of language in human evolution, as well as in growing children, it's also an important subject to physical anthropologists.

Archaeology

Archaeology is the study of earlier cultures and lifeways by anthropologists who specialize in the scientific recovery, analysis, and interpretation of the material remains of past societies. Archaeologists are concerned with culture, but instead of interviewing living people, they collect information from artifacts and structures left behind by earlier societies. Obviously, no one has ever excavated such aspects of culture as religious belief, spoken language, or a political system. But archaeologists assume that the surviving evidence of human occupation reflects some of those important but less-tangible features of the culture that created them.

ethnographies Detailed descriptive studies of human societies. In cultural anthropology, an ethnography is traditionally the study of a non-Western society.

subsistence strategies Activities and behavioral patterns aimed at obtaining food. These can include hunting, gathering wild plant foods, agriculture, and raising domesticated animals for meat and other products.

Unlike in the past (or in movies like *Tomb Raider* or *Indiana Jones*), sites aren't excavated just because they exist or for the artifacts or "treasures" they may contain. Rather, they're excavated to gain information about human behavior. For example, patterns of behavior are reflected in the dispersal of human settlements across a landscape and in the distribution of cultural remains within them. Archaeological research questions may focus on specific localities or peoples and attempt to identify, for example, various aspects of social organization, subsistence techniques, or factors that led to the collapse of a civilization. Alternatively, inquiry may reflect an interest in broader issues relating to human culture in general, such as the development of agriculture or the rise of cities.

Archaeological techniques are used to identify and excavate not only remains of human cities and settlements but also sites that contain remains of extinct species, including everything from dinosaurs to early hominins. Together, prehistoric archaeology and physical anthropology form the core of a joint science called *paleoanthropology*, described later in this book.

Physical Anthropology

As we've already said, physical anthropology is the study of human biology within the framework of evolution and with an emphasis on the interaction between biology and culture. This subdiscipline is also referred to as *biological anthropology*, and you'll find the terms used interchangeably. *Physical anthropology* is the original term, and it reflects the initial interests anthropologists had in describing human physical variation. The American Association of Physical Anthropologists, its journal, many college courses, and numerous publications retain this term. The designation *biological anthropology* reflects the shift in emphasis to more biologically oriented topics, such as genetics, evolutionary biology, nutrition, physiological adaptation, and growth and development. This shift occurred largely because of advances in the field of genetics and molecular biology since the late 1950s. Although we've continued to use the traditional term in the title of this textbook, you'll find that all our major topics pertain to biological issues.

The origins of physical anthropology can be traced to two principal areas of interest among eighteenth- and nineteenth-century European and American scientists (at that time called naturalists or natural historians): the origins of modern species and human variation. Although most of these naturalists held strong religious convictions, they were beginning to doubt the literal interpretation of the biblical account of creation and to support explanations that emphasized natural processes rather than supernatural phenomena. Eventually, the sparks of interest in biological change over time were fueled into flames by the publication of Charles Darwin's *On the Origin of Species* in 1859.

Today, **paleoanthropology**, the study of anatomical and behavioral human evolution as shown in the fossil record, is a major subfield of physical anthropology (Fig. 1-4). Thousands of fossilized remains of human ancestors are now kept in research collections. Taken together, these fossils span at least 46 million years (and maybe more!) of human prehistory. Although most of these fossils are fragmentary, they provide us with a significant wealth of knowledge that increases every year. It's the ultimate goal of paleoanthropological research to identify the various early human and humanlike species, establish a chronological sequence of relationships among them, and gain insights into their adaptation and behavior. Only then will we have a clear picture of how and when humankind came into being.

paleoanthropology The interdisciplinary approach to the study of earlier hominins—their chronology, physical structure, archaeological remains, habitats, and so on.

(a)

To some extent, **primate paleontology** can be viewed as a subset of paleoanthropology. Primate paleontology is the study of the primate fossil record, which extends back to the beginning of primate evolution some 65 million years ago (mya). Virtually every year, fossil-bearing beds in North America, Africa, Asia, and Europe yield important new discoveries. By studying fossil primates and comparing them with anatomically similar living species, primate paleontologists are learning a great deal about factors such as diet or locomotion in earlier forms. They can also try to identify aspects of behavior in some extinct primates and attempt to clarify what we know about evolutionary relationships between extinct and modern species, including ourselves.

Visible physical variation was the other major area of interest for early

(b)

Figure 1-4

(a) Paleoanthropologists excavating at the Drimolen site, South Africa. (b) Russ Ciochon and Vietnamese colleague examine fossils from a 450,000-year-old site that contains fossil remains of *Gigantopithecus* site in Vietnam. *Gigantopithecus* is the name given to the largest apes that ever lived. In the background is a reconstruction of this enormous animal.

primate paleontology The study of fossil primates, especially those that lived before the appearance of hominins.

9

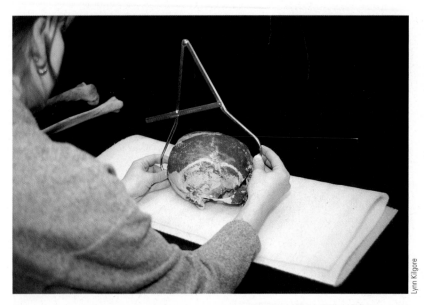

Figure 1-5

Anthropology student using spreading calipers to measure cranial length.

anthropometry Measurement of human body parts. When osteologists measure skeletal elements, the term *osteometry* is often used.

DNA (deoxyribonucleic acid) The double-stranded molecule that contains the genetic code. DNA is a main component of chromosomes.

physical anthropologists. Enormous effort was spent in measuring, describing, and explaining the obvious differences among various human populations, with particular attention being focused on skin color, body proportions, and shape of the head and face. Although some approaches were misguided, they gave rise to hundreds of body measurements. The techniques of **anthropometry** are still used today, although with very different goals. In fact, they've been applied to the design of everything from wheelchairs to body armor for soldiers. (Undoubtedly, they've also been used to determine the absolute minimum amount of leg room a person must have to complete a 3-hour flight on a commercial airliner and remain sane.) They're also very important to the study of skeletal remains from archaeological sites (Fig. 1-5).

Today, anthropologists are concerned with human variation because of its possible *adaptive significance*. In other words, many traits that typify certain populations can be seen as having evolved as biological adaptations, or adjustments, to local environmental conditions, including infectious disease. Other characteristics may be the results of geographical isolation or the descent of populations from small founding groups.

Since the early 1990s, the focus of human variation studies has shifted completely away from the visible differences we see in people to the underlying genetic factors that influence these and many other traits. This shift occurred partly because examining genetic variation between populations and individuals of any species helps explain biological change over time; and that is really what the evolutionary process is all about.

Modern population studies also examine other important aspects of human variation, including how various groups respond physiologically to different kinds of environmentally induced stress (Fig. 1-6). Such stresses may include high altitude, cold, or heat. *Nutritional anthropologists* study the relationships between various dietary components, cultural practices, physiology, and certain aspects of health and disease (Fig. 1-7). Investigations of human fertility, growth, and development also are closely related to the topic of nutrition. These fields of inquiry, which are fundamental to studies of adaptation in modern human populations, can provide insights into hominin evolution too.

As you've just seen, genetics is a crucial field for physical anthropologists. As Charles Darwin discovered (see p. 42), it's extremely difficult (actually impossible) to effectively study evolutionary processes without knowing how traits are inherited. Therefore, modern physical anthropology wouldn't exist as an evolutionary science if it weren't for advances in the understanding of genetic mechanisms. In fact, many biological anthropologists (called molecular anthropologists) specialize in genetics.

Molecular anthropologists use cutting-edge technologies to investigate evolutionary relationships between human populations as well as between humans and nonhuman primates. To do this, they examine similarities and differences in **DNA** among individuals, populations, and species. What's more, by extracting

DNA from certain fossils, these researchers have contributed to our understanding of relationships between extinct and living species. As genetic technologies continue to be developed, molecular anthropologists will play a key role in explaining human evolution, adaptation, and our biological relationships with other species (Fig. 1-8).

However, before genetic and molecular techniques became widespread, **osteology**, the study of the skeleton, was the only way that anthropologists could study our immediate ancestors. In fact, a thorough knowledge of skeletal structure and function is still critical to the interpretation of fossil material today. For this reason, osteology has long been viewed as central to physical anthropology. In fact, it's so important that when many people think of biological anthropology, the first thing they think of is bones!

In addition to paleontology, bone biology and physiology are of major importance to many other aspects of physical anthropology. One subdiscipline of osteology, called **paleopathology**, is the study of disease and trauma in ancient skeletal populations. Paleopathologists investigate the prevalence of trauma, certain

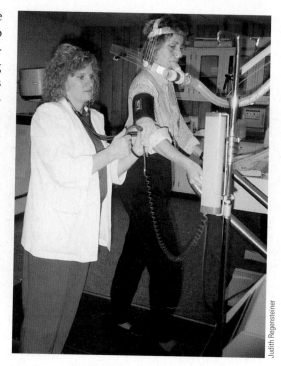

Figure **1-6**

This researcher is using a treadmill test to assess a subject's heart rate, blood pressure, and oxygen consumption.

Judith Regensteiner

Kathleen Galvin

Figure **1-7**

Dr. Kathleen Galvin measures upper arm circumference in a young Maasai boy in Tanzania. Data derived from various body measurements, including height and weight, were used in a health and nutrition study of groups of Maasai cattle herders.

osteology The study of skeletal material. Human osteology focuses on the interpretation of the skeletal remains from archaeological sites, skeletal anatomy, bone physiology, and growth and development. Some of the same techniques are used in paleoanthropology to study early hominins.

paleopathology The branch of osteology that studies the evidence of disease and injury in human skeletal (or, occasionally, mummified) remains from archaeological sites.

(a) *Robert Jurmain*

(b) *Nelson Ting*

Figure 1-8

(a) Cloning and sequencing methods are frequently used to identify genes in humans and nonhuman primates. This graduate student identifies a genetically modified bacterial clone. (b) Molecular anthropologist Nelson Ting collecting red colobus fecal samples for a study of genetic variation in small groups of monkeys isolated from one another by agricultural clearing.

Figure 1-9

Two examples of pathological conditions in human skeletal remains from the Nubian site of Kulubnarti in Sudan. These remains are approximately 1,000 years old. (a) A partially healed fracture of a child's left femur (thigh bone). The estimated age at death is 6 years, and the cause of death was probably an infection resulting from this injury. (b) Very severe congenital scoliosis in an adult male from Nubia. The curves are due to developmental defects in individual vertebrae. (This is not the most common form of scoliosis.)

forensic anthropology An applied anthropological approach dealing with legal matters. Forensic anthropologists work with coroners and others in identifying and analyzing human remains.

infectious diseases (such as syphilis and tuberculosis), nutritional deficiencies, and numerous other conditions that may leave evidence in bone (Fig. 1-9). This research tells us a great deal about the lives of individuals and populations from the past. Paleopathology also yields information regarding the history of certain disease processes, and for this reason it's of interest to scientists in biomedical fields.

Forensic anthropology, an area directly related to osteology and paleopathology, has become of increasing interest to the public because of forensic TV shows like *Bones* (based on a character created by a practicing forensic anthropologist) and *Crime Scene Investigation: CSI*. Technically, this approach is the application of

(a) *Lynn Kilgore*

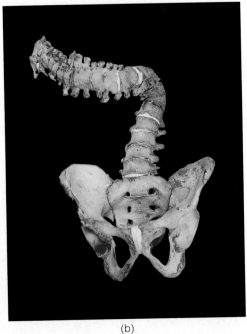

(b) *Lynn Kilgore*

anthropological (usually osteological and sometimes archaeological) techniques to legal issues (Fig. 1-10a). Forensic anthropologists help identify skeletal remains in mass disasters or other situations where a human body has been found. They've been involved in numerous cases having important legal, historical, and human consequences. They were instrumental in identifying the skeletons of most of the Russian imperial family, executed in 1918; and many participated in the overwhelming task of trying to identify the remains of victims of the September 11, 2001, terrorist attacks in the United States (Fig.1-10b).

Anatomy is yet another important area of interest for physical anthropologists. In living organisms, bones and teeth are intimately linked to the soft tissues that surround and act on them. Consequently, a thorough knowledge of soft tissue anatomy is essential to understanding the biomechanical relationships involved in movement. Such relationships are important in assessing the structure and function of limbs and other components of fossilized remains. For these reasons and others, many physical anthropologists specialize in anatomical studies. In fact, several physical anthropologists hold professorships in anatomy departments at universities and medical schools (Fig. 1-11).

But humans aren't the only species studied by biological anthropologists. Given our evolutionary focus and the fact that we ourselves are primates, it's natural that **primatology**, the study of the living nonhuman primates, has become increasingly important since the 1960s (Fig. 1-12). A few scientists had begun systematically studying nonhuman primates in the 1950s, but in 1960 a young English woman named Jane Goodall went to Africa to study chimpanzees. As news of her work became popularized in *National Geographic* films and magazines, she and her research became world famous, and for the first time, people began to understand how similar we are to our closest relatives. Today, dozens of nonhuman primate species have been, and are being, studied, and because this research focuses primarily on behavior, it has implications for many scientific disciplines. Moreover, because nonhuman primates are our closest living relatives, identifying the underlying factors related to social behavior, communication, infant care, reproductive

primatology The study of the biology and behavior of nonhuman primates (lemurs, lorises, tarsiers, monkeys, and apes).

Figure **1-10**

(a) Forensic anthropologists at the location on Staten Island where all materials from the World Trade Center were taken for investigation after September 11, 2001. The scientists are wearing HAZMAT (hazardous materials) suits for protection (b) Forensic anthropologists assisting in a dog training session. The dog has just found a concealed human cranium.

(a)

D. France

(b)

Lorna Pierce/Judy Suchey

Figure **1-11**
Dr. Linda Levitch teaching a human anatomy class at the University of North Carolina School of Medicine.

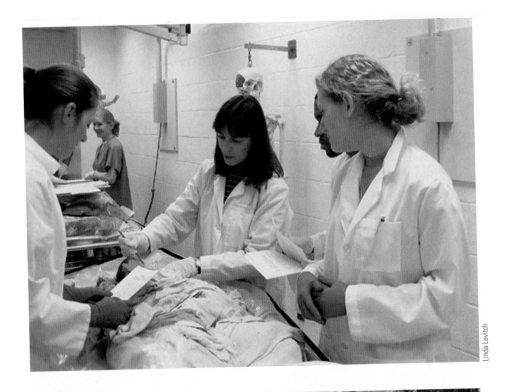

Linda Levitch

Figure **1-12**
Primatologist Jill Pruetz follows a chimpanzee in Senegal, in west Africa.

Julie Lesnik

behavior, and so on, helps us to develop a better understanding of the natural forces that have shaped so many aspects of modern human behavior.

Nonhuman primates are also important to study in their own right. This is particularly true today because the majority of primate species are threatened or seriously endangered. Only through study will scientists be able to recommend policies that can better ensure the survival of many nonhuman primates and thousands of other species as well.

Interdisciplinary Approaches

Today, there are many areas where the four main subfields of anthropology overlap, so that the different areas of expertise are combined in both academic and nonacademic settings. *Biocultural anthropology* and applied anthropology are two such areas.

Biocultural Anthropology

Because medical and nutritional anthropology sit at the intersection of cultural and biological anthropology, they can best be described as examples of *biocultural anthropology*. On the cultural side are explorations of the relationship between a cultural attribute (such as gender, religion, or ideology) and diet or health. For example, ideas about what is considered food may vary from one culture to another. (Consider dogs and horses, both of which are perfectly adequate protein sources for humans, but show great variation across cultures as to whether or not they are considered food.)

Food as a way of expressing identity is another topic in the realm of cultural anthropology. But population variation in the genetically controlled ability to digest milk products is more typically studied by physical anthropologists and geneticists.

In general, anthropologists see health as a product of both our biological and cultural environments and heritage. But whether or not a particular attribute is perceived as healthful often varies from one culture to another, despite somewhat objective biomedical measures. So while obesity, for example, is seen as a major health problem in industrialized nations, in some cultures it's viewed as evidence of good health and prosperity.

Applied Anthropology

Applied approaches in anthropology are numerous. While *applied anthropology* is the practical application of anthropological theories and methods outside the academic setting, applied and academic anthropology aren't mutually exclusive approaches. In fact, applied anthropology relies on the research and theories of academic anthropologists and at the same time has much to contribute to theory and techniques. While most applied anthropologists were trained as cultural anthropologists, the term *applied* is also increasingly used to describe the work of archaeologists and physical anthropologists.

One area of applied anthropology of interest to cultural anthropologists is the welfare of refugees and their resettlement and cultural integration (or lack thereof) in countries such as the United States or Canada. But perhaps *medical anthropology* is an even more common approach that explores the relationship between various cultural attributes and health and disease (Fig. 1-13). For instance, one area of interest is how different groups view disease processes and how these views affect treatment or the willingness to accept treatment. Today, most innovative hospitals that are interested in transforming health care have cultural anthropologists on staff (Chin, pers. comm.).

While for cultural medical anthropologists the focus is primarily the social dimensions of disease, many physical anthropologists describe what they do as *biomedical anthropology*. Research topics in biomedical anthropology include population variation in susceptibility to disease; the relationship between genes, environment, diet, and health; and the evolutionary history of disease.

In the United States, the greatest expansion in archaeology since the 1970s has been in an applied subfield called *cultural resource management (CRM)*. CRM arose from environmental legislation requiring archaeological evaluation and sometimes excavation of sites that may be threatened by development. (Canada and many European countries have similar legislation.) Many contract archaeologists (so called because their services are contracted out to builders and developers) are affiliated with private consulting firms, state or federal agencies, or educational institutions.

Within physical anthropology, forensic anthropology is a good example of the applied approach, and quite often forensic anthropologists work with archaeologists to search for human remains or for various kinds of evidence at crime scenes (see p. 12). But the practical application of the techniques of physical anthropology came about before the development of forensic anthropology. During World War II, for example, physical anthropologists, using anthropometric techniques, were extensively involved in designing gun turrets and airplane cockpits. Today, physical anthropologists pursue careers in genetic and biomedical research, public health, evolutionary medicine, medical anthropology, and conservation of nonhuman primates. Moreover, many physical anthropologists hold positions in museums and zoos. In fact, a background in physical anthropology is excellent preparation for almost any career in the medical and biological fields.

Physical Anthropology and the Scientific Method

science A body of knowledge gained through observation and experimentation; from the Latin *scientia*, meaning "knowledge."

hypotheses (*sing.*, hypothesis) A provisional explanation of a phenomenon. Hypotheses require verification or falsification through testing.

empirical Relying on experiment or observation; from the Latin *empiricus*, meaning "experienced."

scientific method An approach to research whereby a problem is identified, a hypothesis (provisional explanation) is stated, and that hypothesis is tested by collecting and analyzing data.

data (*sing.*, datum) Facts from which conclusions can be drawn; scientific information.

Science is a process of explaining natural phenomena through observation, developing explanations or **hypotheses**, and then devising a research design or series of experiments to test those hypotheses. This is an **empirical** approach to gaining information. Because biological anthropologists are engaged in scientific pursuits, they adhere to the principles of the **scientific method**, whereby they identify a research problem and then gather information to solve it.

Once a question has been asked, the first step usually is to explore the existing literature (books and journals) to determine what other people have done to resolve the issue. Based on this preliminary research and other observations, one or even several tentative explanations (hypotheses) are then proposed. The next step is to develop a research design or methodology aimed at testing the hypothesis. These methods involve collecting information, or **data**, that can then be studied and analyzed. Data can be analyzed in many ways, most of them involving various statistical tests. During the data collection and analysis phase, it's important for scientists to use a rigorously controlled approach so they can precisely describe

(a)

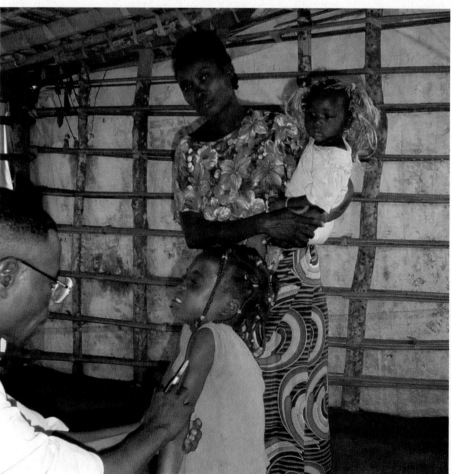

(b)

Nanette Barkey

Figure 1-13

(a) Dr. Soo Young Chin, Lead Partner of Practical Ethnographics at Ascension Health, pointing to pilot locations for a study of a new health care plan.
(b) Nanette Barkey, a medical anthropologist involved in a repatriation project in Angola, photographed this little girl being vaccinated at a refugee transit camp. Vaccinations were being administered to Angolan refugees returning home in 2004 from the Democratic Republic of Congo, where they had fled to escape warfare in their own country.

A Closer Look

Evaluation in Science: Lessons in Critical Thinking

Every day, we're bombarded through the media with innumerable claims relating to health, financial success, self-improvement, and just about anything else that someone wants us to believe. But we must always be careful how we evaluate such information while not being overly swayed by our personal opinions, and we should be reluctant to accept a view based solely on its personal appeal. Accepting or rejecting an idea based on personal feelings is as good a definition of bias as one could devise. Science is an approach—indeed, a tool—used to eliminate (or at least minimize) bias.

Scientific evaluation is, in fact, part of a broader framework of intellectual rigor called critical thinking. The development of critical thinking skills should be an important and lasting benefit of a college education. These skills are valuable in everyday life because they enable people to evaluate, compare, analyze, critique, and synthesize information so they won't accept everything they hear and read at face value.

The advertising industry provides an excellent illustration of the need for critical thinking. Cosmetics companies tell us, among other things, that collagen creams will reduce wrinkles because collagen is a principal protein component of connective tissue, including skin. It's true that collagen is a major protein constituent of skin tissue. Moreover, collagen fibers do break down over time, and this damage is one factor that contributes to the development of wrinkles. But the most beneficial properties of the creams are probably the UV filters and moisturizers they contain, although they won't eliminate wrinkles. What's more, the collagen isn't absorbed into skin cells, and even if it were, it still wouldn't be incorporated in a way that would replenish what's been destroyed. But most people don't know what collagen is. Thus, when they hear that it's an important component of skin tissue and therefore can help reduce wrinkles, the argument sounds reasonable; so they buy the cream, which won't reduce wrinkles and is usually expensive.

Critical thinking skills may be most important in the area of politics. Politicians routinely make claims, frequently in 30-second sound bites that use catchphrases and misleading statistics. (Remember, their speechwriters are well informed and skillful at manipulating language, and they know they're targeting a generally uninformed public.)

An informed public can—and should—call its political leaders to task when necessary. For example, global climate change has become a political issue, especially in the United States. The vast majority of scientists worldwide now agree that global warming is happening and that it's largely caused by human activity. Fortunately, many governments, especially in Europe, are beginning to formulate policies aimed at slowing the warming trend. However, many politicians in the United States and a few other countries continue to say that we still don't have enough scientific data to justify spending billions of dollars on preventive measures that may not even work. Given the stakes involved, if the concerns expressed by so many scientists today are real, an informed populace should take it upon itself to investigate these issues and ask why some governments are concerned while others aren't.

When politicians say, "Scientists aren't in complete agreement on the issue of global warming," what they imply—and what most people hear—is that scientists aren't in agreement that the climate is changing. Certainly, some climate scientists still aren't convinced, but most of them are. If you understand the nature of science and the scientific method, then you realize that much of the disagreement among scientists isn't whether warming is happening, or if human activities are a factor, but rather how fast it's happening, how warm it will get, and how disastrous the consequences will be (Gregory et al., 2004).

Most people tend to be ambivalent toward science and maybe even intimidated by it. In general, people accept scientific results when they support their personal views and reject them when they don't. They're also sometimes confused because science changes so rapidly. A study in 2004, before the presidential election, revealed that one-third of Americans had never heard of stem cells, even though stem cell research was a major political issue and had been prominent in the news. Since most respondents in the survey were older (or not young), they hadn't learned about stem cells in school, and once out of school, most people avoid scientific issues. Moreover, science and math education in the United States has suffered a deplorable decline in recent years and now ranks behind that of all European countries (Gross, 2006). And over half of high school graduates don't complete a college degree. Fortunately, most colleges and universities require at least one year of science for a degree—in fact, that may be why you're taking this course.

Education is crucial for developing the critical thinking skills that will help us make important decisions and understand the many profound issues that confront us. Moreover, critical thinkers are able to assess the evidence supporting their own beliefs (in a sense, to step outside themselves) and to identify the weaknesses in their own positions. They recognize that knowledge is not merely a collection of facts, but an ongoing process of examining information to expand our understanding of the world. Critical thinkers look beyond the often superficial or ill-informed statements made by political leaders and advertisements and ask questions aimed at assessing the claims: "What is the evidence for that?" "Who made that statement?" "What research supports that claim?" "Was the research published in a peer-reviewed journal or quoted out of context or in a biased publication?" They also may take the time to research issues before making up their minds about them.

Throughout this book, you'll be presented with the results of numerous studies using numerical data. For example, we might tell you that the gene for cystic fibrosis is more common in European populations than in other groups. Always be cautious of generalizations. What is the specific nature of the argument? What data support it? Can these data be quantified? If so, how is this information presented? (*Note*: Always carefully read the tables that appear in textbooks or articles.)

Regardless of the discipline you ultimately study, at some point in your college career you should take a course in statistics. Many universities now make statistics a general education requirement (sometimes under the category "quantitative reasoning"). Statistics often seems like a difficult and boring subject, and many students are intimidated by the math it requires. Nevertheless, perhaps more than any other skill you'll acquire in your college years, quantitative critical reasoning is a tool you'll be able to use every day of your life.

One responsibility of an educated society is to be both informed and vigilant. The knowledge we possess and attempt to build on is neither good nor bad; however, the ways that knowledge may be used can have highly charged moral and ethical implications. Here are some useful questions to ask in making critical evaluations about any controversial scientific topic:

1. What data are presented?
2. What conclusions are presented, and how are they organized (as tentative hypotheses or as more dogmatic assertions)?
3. Are these views simply the authors' opinions, or are they supported by a larger body of research?
4. What are the research findings? Are they adequately documented?
5. Is the information consistent with information that you already possess? If not, can the inconsistencies be explained?
6. Are the conclusions (hypotheses) testable? How might one go about testing the various hypotheses that are presented?
7. If new research findings are at odds with previous hypotheses (or theories), must these hypotheses now be modified (or completely rejected)?
8. How do your own personal views bias you in interpreting the results?
9. Once you've identified your own biases, are you able to set them aside in order to evaluate the information objectively?
10. Can you discuss both the pros and cons of a scientific topic in an evenhanded manner?

their techniques and results. This precision is critical because it enables others to repeat the experiments and allows scientists to make comparisons between their study and the work of others.

For example, when scientists collect data on tooth size in hominin fossils, they must specify which teeth are being measured, how they're measured, and the results of the measurements (expressed numerically, or **quantitatively**). Then, by analyzing the data, the investigators try to draw conclusions about the meaning and significance of their measurements. This body of information then becomes the basis of future studies, perhaps by other researchers, who can compare their own results with those already obtained.

Hypothesis testing is the very core of the scientific method, and although it may seem contradictory at first, it's based on the potential to *falsify* the hypothesis. Falsification doesn't mean that the entire hypothesis is untrue, but it does indicate that the hypothesis may need to be refined and subjected to further testing.

Eventually, if a hypothesis stands up to repeated testing, it may become part of a **theory** or perhaps a theory itself. There's a popular misconception that a theory is mere conjecture, or a "hunch." But in science, theories are proposed explanations of relationships between natural phenomena. Theories usually concern a broader, more universal view than hypotheses, which have a narrower focus and deal with more specific relationships between phenomena. But like hypotheses, theories aren't facts. *They're tested explanations of facts.* For example, it's a fact that when you drop an object, it falls to the ground. The explanation for this fact is the theory of gravity. But, like hypotheses, theories can be altered over time with further experimentation and by using newly developed technologies in testing.

There's one more important fact about hypotheses and theories: *Any proposition that's stated as absolute or does not allow the possibility of falsification is not a scientific hypothesis, and it should never be considered as such.* We've emphasized that a crucial aspect of scientific statements is that there must be way to evaluate their validity. Statements such as "Heaven exists" may well be true (that is, they describe some actual state), but there's no rational, empirical means (based on experience or experiment) of testing them. Therefore, acceptance of such a view is based on faith rather than on scientific verification. The purpose of scientific research isn't to establish absolute truths; rather, it's to generate ever more accurate and consistent explanations of phenomena in our universe, based on observation and testing. At its very heart, scientific methodology is an exercise in rational thought and critical thinking (see "A Closer Look," pp. 18–19).

Scientific testing of hypotheses may take several years (or longer) and may involve researchers who weren't involved with the original work. What's more, new methods may permit different kinds of testing that weren't previously possible, and this is a strength of scientific research. For example, since the 1970s, primatologists have reported that male nonhuman primates (as well as males of many other species) sometimes kill infants. One hypothesis has been that since the males were usually new to a group, they were killing infants fathered by other males. But many scientists have objected to this hypothesis, and they've proposed several alternatives. For one thing, there was no way to know for certain that the males weren't killing their own offspring; but if they were, this would argue against the hypothesis. However, in a fairly recent study, scientists collected DNA samples from dead infants and the males who killed them and showed that most of the time, the males weren't related to their victims. This result doesn't prove that the original hypothesis is accurate. But it does strengthen it. This study is described in more detail in Chapter 7, but we mention it here to emphasize that science is an ongoing process

quantitatively Pertaining to measurements of quantity and including such properties as size, number, and capacity. When data are quantified, they're expressed numerically and can be tested statistically.

theory A broad statement of scientific relationships or underlying principles that has been substantially verified through the testing of hypotheses.

scientific testing The precise repetition of an experiment or expansion of observed data to provide verification; the procedure by which hypotheses and theories are verified, modified, or discarded.

that builds on previous work and benefits from newly developed techniques (in this case, DNA testing) in ways that constantly expand our knowledge.

Using the scientific method allows for the development and testing of hypotheses, and it allows scientists to try to eliminate various types of *bias*. It's important to realize that bias occurs in all studies. Sources of bias include how the investigator was trained and by whom; what particular questions the researcher is asking; what specific skills and talents he or she possesses; what earlier results (if any) have been established in this realm of study and by whom (for example, the researcher, close colleagues, or those with rival approaches or even rival personalities); and what sources of data are available (such as in accessible countries or museums) and thus what samples can be collected.

The Anthropological Perspective

Perhaps the most important benefit you'll receive from this textbook, and this course, is a wider appreciation of the human experience. To understand human beings and how our species came to be, we must broaden our viewpoint through both time and space. All branches of anthropology fundamentally seek to do this in what we call the *anthropological perspective*.

Physical anthropologists, for example, are interested in how humans differ from—and are similar to—other animals, especially nonhuman primates. For example, we've defined *hominins* as bipedal primates, but what are the major anatomical components of bipedal locomotion, and how do they differ from, say, those in a quadrupedal ape? To answer these questions, we would need to study the anatomical structures involved in human locomotion (muscles, hips, legs, and feet) and compare them with the same structures in various nonhuman primates.

In addition to broadening perspectives over space (that is, encompassing many cultures and ecological circumstances as well as nonhuman species), an anthropological perspective also extends our horizons *through time*. For example, in Chapter 17, we'll discuss human nutrition. The vast majority of the foods people eat today (coming from domesticated plants and animals) were unavailable prior to the development of agriculture, approximately 10,000 years ago. Human physiological mechanisms for chewing and digesting foods nevertheless were already well established long before that date; these adaptive complexes go back millions of years. Moreover, earlier hominins might well have differed from humans today in average body size, metabolism, and activity patterns. How, then, does the basic evolutionary "equipment" (that is, physiology) inherited from our hominin forebears accommodate our modern diets? Clearly, the way to understand such processes is not just by looking at contemporary human responses, but by placing them in the perspective of evolutionary development through time.

Through a perspective that is broad in space and time, we can begin to grasp the diversity of the human experience within the context of biological and behavioral continuity with other species. In this way, we may better understand the limits and potentials of humankind. And by extending our knowledge to include cultures other than our own, we may hope to avoid the **ethnocentric** pitfalls inherent in a more limited view of humanity.

We hope that after reading this text, you'll have an increased understanding not only of the similarities we share with other biological organisms, but also of the processes that have shaped the traits that make us unique. We live in what may well be our planet's most crucial period in the past 65 million years.

ethnocentric Viewing other cultures from the inherently biased perspective of one's own culture. Ethnocentrism often results in other cultures being seen as inferior to one's own.

We are members of the one species that, through the very agency of culture, has wrought such devastating changes in ecological systems that we must now alter our technologies or face potentially unspeakable consequences. In such a time, it's vital that we attempt to gain the best possible understanding of what it means to be human. We believe that the study of physical anthropology is one endeavor that aids in this attempt, and that is indeed the goal of this text.

Summary

In this chapter, we've introduced you to the field of physical, or biological, anthropology, placing it within the overall context of anthropological studies. As a major academic discipline within the social sciences, anthropology also includes cultural anthropology, archaeology, and linguistic anthropology as major subfields.

Physical anthropology is the study of many aspects of human biology, including genetics, genetic variation, adaptations to environmental factors, nutrition, and anatomy. These topics are discussed within an evolutionary framework because all human characteristics are either directly or indirectly the results of biological evolution, which in turn is driven by genetic change. Humans are a product of the same forces that produced all life on earth. As such, we're just one contemporary component of a vast biological **continuum** at one point in time. Hence, biological anthropologists also study our closest relatives, the nonhuman primates, primate evolution, and the genetic and fossil evidence for human evolution.

Because biological anthropology is a scientific discipline, we also discussed the role of the scientific method in research. We presented the importance of objectivity, observation, data collection, and analysis; and we described the formation and testing of hypotheses to explain natural phenomena. We emphasized that this approach is an empirical one that doesn't rely on supernatural explanations.

Because evolution is the core of physical anthropology, in the next chapter we present a brief historical overview of changes in Western scientific thought that led to the discovery of the basic principles of biological evolution. As you're probably aware, evolution is a highly controversial subject in the United States; however, it's not so controversial in other countries. In the next chapter, we'll address some of the reasons for this controversy and explain the evidence for evolution as the single thread uniting all the biological sciences.

Critical Thinking Questions

1. Given that you've only just been introduced to the field of physical anthropology, why do you think subjects such as anatomy, genetics, nonhuman primate behavior, and human evolution are integrated into a discussion of what it means to be human?

2. Is it important to you, personally, to know about human evolution? Why or why not?

3. Do you see a connection between hominin footprints that are almost 4 million years old and human footprints left on the moon in 1969? If so, do you think this relationship is important? What does the fact that there are human footprints on the moon say about human adaptation? (Consider both biological and cultural adaptation.)

continuum A set of relationships in which all components fall along a single integrated spectrum. All life reflects a single biological continuum.

CHAPTER

2

The Development of Evolutionary Theory

Key Questions

What are the basic premises of natural selection?

What were the technological and philosophical changes that led people to accept notions of evolutionary change?

Introduction

Has anyone ever asked you, "If humans evolved from monkeys, then why do we still have monkeys?" Or maybe, "If evolution happens, then why don't we ever see new species?" These are the kinds of questions people sometimes ask if they don't understand evolutionary processes or if they don't believe evolution occurs. Evolution is one of the most fundamental biological processes, and yet it's one of the most misunderstood. The explanation for the misunderstanding is simple: Evolution isn't taught in most primary and secondary schools; in fact, it's frequently avoided. And in colleges and universities, evolution is covered only in classes that directly relate to it. If you're not an anthropology or biology major and you're taking a class in biological anthropology mainly to fill a science requirement, you'll probably never study evolution again.

By the end of this course, you'll know the answers to the questions in the preceding paragraph. Briefly, no one who studies evolution would ever say that humans evolved from monkeys, because we didn't. We didn't evolve from chimpanzees either. The earliest human ancestors evolved from a species that lived some 6 to 8 million years ago (mya). That ancestral species was the *last common ancestor* we share with chimpanzees. In turn, the lineage that eventually gave rise to the apes and humans separated from a monkey-like ancestor some 20 mya, and monkeys are still around because as lineages diverged from a common ancestor, each group went its separate way. Over millions of years, some of these groups became extinct while others evolved into the species we see today. So each living species is the current product of processes that go back millions of years. Because evolution takes time, and lots of it, we rarely witness the appearance of new species except in microorganisms. But we do see *microevolutionary* changes (briefly referred to in Chapter 1) in many species, including our own.

The subject of evolution is controversial, especially in the United States, because some religious views hold that evolutionary statements run counter to biblical teachings. In fact, as you're probably aware, there is strong opposition to the teaching of evolution in public schools.

Opponents of evolution often say, "It's just a theory," implying that evolution is just an idea. As we pointed out in Chapter 1, scientific theories aren't just ideas or suppositions, although that's how the word *theory* is commonly used in everyday conversation. Actually, when dealing with scientific issues, referring to a concept as "theory" supports it. As we discussed in Chapter 1, theories have been tested and subjected to verification through accumulated evidence—and they haven't been disproved, sometimes even after decades of experimentation. It's true; evolution is a theory, one that's being supported by a mounting body of genetic evidence that, quite literally, grows daily. It's a theory that explains how biological change occurs in species over time, and it's stood the test of time. Today, evolutionary theory stands as the most fundamental unifying force in biological science, and evolutionary biologists are now able to explain many evolutionary processes.

Because physical anthropology is concerned with all aspects of how humans came to be and how we adapt physiologically to the external environment, the details of the evolutionary process are crucial to the field. And given the central importance of evolution to biological anthropology, it's helpful to know how the mechanics of the process came to be discovered. Also, if we want to understand and make critical assessments of the controversy that surrounds the issue today, we need to explore the social and political events that influenced the discovery of evolutionary principles.

A Brief History of Evolutionary Thought

The discovery of evolutionary principles first took place in western Europe and was made possible by advances in scientific thinking that date back to the sixteenth century. Having said this, we must recognize that Western science borrowed many of its ideas from other cultures, especially the Arabs, Indians, and Chinese. In fact, intellectuals in these cultures and in ancient Greece had developed notions of biological evolution centuries before Charles Darwin (Teresi, 2002), but they never formulated them into a cohesive theory.

Charles Darwin was the first person to explain the basic mechanics of the evolutionary process. But while he was developing his theory of **natural selection**, a Scottish naturalist named Alfred Russel Wallace independently reached the same conclusion. That natural selection, the single most important force of evolutionary change, was proposed at more or less the same time by two British men in the mid-nineteenth century may seem like a strange coincidence. But actually, if Darwin and Wallace hadn't made their simultaneous discoveries, someone else soon would have, and that someone would probably have been British or French. That's because the groundwork had already been laid in Britain and France, and many scientists there were prepared to accept explanations of biological change that would have been unacceptable even 25 years before.

Like other human endeavors, scientific knowledge is usually gained through a series of small steps rather than giant leaps. And just as technological change is based on past achievements, scientific knowledge builds on previously developed theories. For this reason, it's informative to examine the development of ideas that led Darwin and Wallace to independently develop the theory of evolution by natural selection.

Throughout the Middle Ages, one predominant feature of the European worldview was that all aspects of nature, including all forms of life and their relationships to one another, never changed. This view was partly shaped by a feudal society that was itself a rigid class system that hadn't changed much for centuries. But the most important influence was an extremely powerful religious system wherein the teachings of Christianity were taken literally. Consequently, it was generally accepted that all life on earth had been created by God exactly as it existed in the present, and the belief that life-forms couldn't and didn't change came to be known as **fixity of species**. Anyone who questioned the assumptions of fixity, especially in the fifteenth and sixteenth centuries, could be accused of challenging God's perfection, and that was heresy. Generally, it was a good idea to avoid being accused of heresy because it was a crime that could punished by a nasty and potentially fiery death (Fig. 2-1).

natural selection The most critical mechanism of evolutionary change, first described by Charles Darwin; refers to genetic change or changes in the frequencies of certain traits in populations due to differential reproductive success between individuals.

fixity of species The notion that species, once created, can never change; an idea diametrically opposed to theories of biological evolution.

The plan of the entire universe was viewed as God's design. In what's called the "argument from design," anatomical structures were engineered to meet the purpose for which they were required. Limbs, internal organs, and eyes all fit the functions they performed; and they, along with the rest of nature, were a deliberate plan of the Grand Designer. Also, pretty much everybody believed that the Grand Designer had completed his works fairly recently. An Irish archbishop named James Ussher (1581–1656) analyzed the "begat" chapter of Genesis and determined that the earth was created the morning of October 23 in 4004 B.C. While Ussher wasn't the first person to suggest a recent origin of the earth, he was the first to propose a precise date for it.

Figure **2-1**

Portion of a Renaissance painting depicting the execution of Father Girolamo Savonarola, in 1498 in Florence, Italy. (Artist unknown.) Although Savonarola wasn't promoting scientific arguments, as virtual ruler of Florence, he was openly critical of the Renaissance, and opposed the Church for being overly materialistic. Many scientists and philosophers of the day met a similar fate.

The prevailing notion of the earth's brief existence, together with fixity of species, was a huge obstacle to the development of evolutionary theory. Evolution takes time; and the idea of immense geological time, which today we take for granted, simply didn't exist. In fact, until the concepts of fixity and time were fundamentally altered, it was impossible to conceive of evolution by means of natural selection.

The Scientific Revolution

So, what transformed centuries-old beliefs in a rigid, static universe to a view of worlds in continuous motion? How did the earth's brief history become an immense expanse of incomprehensible time? How did the scientific method as we know it today develop? These are important questions, but it would also be appropriate to ask why it took so long for Europe to break away from traditional beliefs. After all, Arab and Indian scholars had developed concepts of planetary motion, for example, centuries earlier.

For Europeans, the discovery of the New World and circumnavigation of the globe in the fifteenth century overturned some very basic ideas about the planet. For one thing, the earth could no longer be thought of as flat. Also, as Europeans began to explore the New World, their awareness of biological diversity was greatly expanded as they became aware of plants and animals they'd never seen before.

There were other attacks on traditional beliefs. In 1514, a Polish mathematician named Copernicus challenged a notion proposed more than 1,500 years earlier by the fourth-century B.C. Greek philosopher Aristotle. Aristotle had taught that the sun and planets existed in a series of concentric spheres that revolved around the earth (Fig. 2-2). This system of planetary spheres was, in turn, surrounded by the stars; and this meant that the earth was the center of the universe. In fact, in India, scholars had figured out that the earth orbited the sun long before

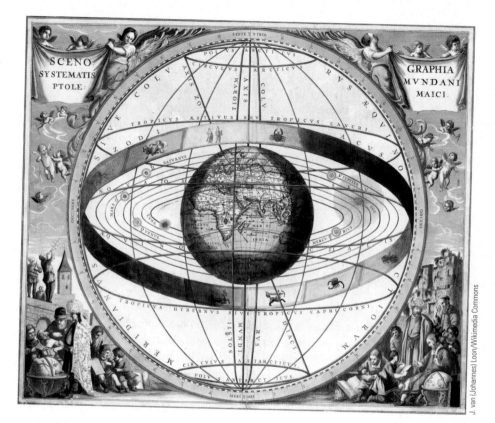

Figure 2-2

This beautifully illustrated seventeenth-century map shows the earth at the center of the solar system. Around it are seven concentric circles depicting the orbits of the moon, sun, and the five planets that were known at the time. (Note also the signs of the zodiac.)

Copernicus did; but Copernicus is generally credited with removing the earth as the center of all things.

Copernicus' theory was discussed in intellectual circles, but it didn't attract much attention from the Catholic Church. (Catholicism was the only form of Christianity until the 1520s.) Nevertheless, the theory did contradict a major premise of church doctrine, which at that time wholeheartedly embraced the teachings of Aristotle. By the 1300s, the church had accepted this view as dogma because it reinforced the notion that the earth, and the humans on it, were the central focus of God's creation and must therefore have a central position in the universe.

However, in the early 1600s, an Italian mathematician named Galileo Galilei restated Copernicus' views in print, and he used logic and mathematics to support his claim. (In fact, Galileo is credited with having introduced the empirical approach to Western science.) To his misfortune, Galileo was eventually confronted by the highest-ranking officials of the Catholic Church (including the pope), and he spent the last nine years of his life under house arrest. Nevertheless, in intellectual circles, the solar system had changed from being earth centered to being sun centered and from being fixed to being in motion.

Throughout the sixteenth and seventeenth centuries, European scholars developed methods and theories that revolutionized scientific thought. The seventeenth century, in particular, saw the discovery of the principles of physics, motion, and gravity. Other achievements included the discovery of the function of the heart and circulatory system and the invention of numerous scientific instruments, such as the telescope (perfected by Galileo), barometer, and microscope. These advances permitted the investigation of many previously misunderstood natural phenomena and opened up entire new worlds for previously unimagined discoveries. But even with these advances, the idea that living forms could change over time simply didn't occur to people.

Precursors to the Theory of Evolution

Before early naturalists could begin to understand the many forms of organic life, they needed to list and describe them. And as research progressed, scholars were increasingly impressed with the amount of biological diversity they saw.

The concept of species, as we think of it today, wasn't proposed until the seventeenth century, when John Ray, a minister educated at Cambridge University, developed the concept. He recognized that groups of plants and animals could be differentiated from other groups by their ability to mate with one another and produce offspring. He placed such groups of **reproductively isolated** organisms into single categories, which he called species (*sing.*, species). Thus, by the late 1600s, the biological criterion of reproduction was used to define species, much as it is today (Young, 1992).

Ray also recognized that species frequently share similarities with other species, and he grouped these together in a second level of classification he called the genus (*pl.*, genera). He was the first to use the labels *genus* and *species* in this way, and they're the terms we still use today.

Carolus Linnaeus (1707–1778) was a Swedish naturalist who developed a method of classifying plants and animals. In his famous work, *Systema Naturae* (Systems of Nature), first published in 1735, he standardized Ray's use of genus and species terminology and established the system of **binomial nomenclature**. He also added two more categories: class and order. Linnaeus' four-level system became the basis for **taxonomy**, the system of classification we continue to use.

Linnaeus also included humans in his classification of animals, placing them in the genus *Homo* and species *sapiens*. (Genus and species names are always italicized.) Placing humans in this scheme was controversial because it defied contemporary thought that humans, made in God's image, should be considered unique and separate from the rest of the animal kingdom.

For all his progressive tendencies, Linnaeus still believed in fixity of species, although in later years, faced with mounting evidence to the contrary, he came to question it. Indeed, fixity was being challenged on many fronts, especially in France, where voices were being raised in favor of a universe based on change and, more to the point, in favor of a biological relationship between similar species based on descent from a common ancestor.

A French naturalist, Georges-Louis Leclerc de Buffon (1707–1788), recognized the dynamic relationship between the external environment and living forms. In his *Natural History*, first published in 1749, he stressed the importance of change in the universe and in the changing nature of species. Buffon believed that when groups of organisms migrate to new areas, they gradually become altered as a result of adapting to a different environment. Although Buffon rejected the idea that one species could give rise to another, his recognition of the external environment as an agent of change in species was extremely important.

Today, Erasmus Darwin (1731–1802) is best known as Charles Darwin's grandfather. But he was also a physician, a poet, and a leading member of an important intellectual community in Lichfield, England. In fact, Darwin counted among his friends some of the leading figures of industrial revolution, a time of rapid technological and social change.

In his most famous poem, Darwin expressed the view that life had originated in the seas and that all species had descended from a common ancestor. Thus, he introduced many of the ideas that his grandson would propose 56 years later. These concepts include vast expanses of time for life to evolve, competition for resources, and the importance of the environment in evolutionary processes. From letters

reproductively isolated pertaining to groups of organisms that, mainly because of genetic differences, are prevented from mating and producing offspring with members of other groups.

binomial nomenclature (*binomial*, meaning "two names") In taxonomy, the convention established by Carolus Linnaeus whereby genus and species names are used to refer to species. For example, *Homo sapiens* refers to human beings.

taxonomy The branch of science concerned with the rules of classifying organisms on the basis of evolutionary relationships.

and other sources, we know that Charles Darwin read his grandfather's writings; but the degree to which his theories were influenced by Erasmus isn't known.

Neither Buffon nor Erasmus Darwin attempted to *explain* the evolutionary process. The first person to attempt this was a French naturalist named Jean-Baptiste Lamarck (1744–1829). Lamarck (Fig. 2-3) suggested a dynamic relationship between species and the environment such that if the external environment changed, an animal's activity patterns would also change to accommodate the new circumstances. This would result in the increased or decreased use of certain body parts; consequently, those body parts would be modified. According to Lamarck, the parts that weren't used would disappear over time. However, the parts that continued to be used, perhaps in different ways, would change over time. Such physical changes would occur in response to bodily "needs," so that if a particular part of the body felt a certain need, "fluids and forces" would be directed to that point, and the structure would be modified. Since the alteration would make the animal better suited to its habitat, the new trait would be passed on to offspring. This theory is known as the *inheritance of acquired characteristics*, or the *use-disuse* theory.

American Museum of Natural History

Figure **2-3**

Lamarck believed that species change was influenced by environmental change. He is best known for his theory of the inheritance of acquired characteristics.

One of the most frequently given hypothetical examples of Lamarck's theory is that of the giraffe, which, having stripped all the leaves from the lower branches of a tree (environmental change), tries to reach leaves on upper branches. As "vital forces" move to tissues of the neck, it becomes slightly longer, and the giraffe can reach higher. The longer neck is then transmitted to offspring, with the eventual result that all giraffes have longer necks than their predecessors had (Fig. 2-4). So, according to this theory, *a trait acquired by an animal during its lifetime can be passed on to offspring.* Today we know that this explanation is wrong because only those traits that are influenced by genetic information contained within sex cells (eggs and sperm) can be inherited (see Chapter 3).

Because Lamarck's explanation of species change isn't genetically correct, it's frequently dismissed. But in fact, Lamarck deserves a lot of credit because he emphasized the importance of interactions between organisms and the external environment in the evolutionary process. He also coined the term *biology* to refer to the study of living organisms, and a central feature of this new discipline was the idea of species change.

Lamarck's most vehement opponent was a French vertebrate paleontologist named Georges Cuvier (1769–1832). Cuvier (Fig. 2-5) introduced the concept of extinction to explain the disappearance of animals represented by fossils. Although he was a brilliant anatomist, Cuvier never grasped the dynamic concept of nature and continued to insist on the fixity of species. So, rather than assuming that similarities between fossil forms and living species indicate evolutionary relationships, Cuvier proposed a variation of a doctrine known as **catastrophism**.

Catastrophism was the belief that the earth's geological features are the results of sudden, worldwide cataclysmic events. Cuvier's version of catastrophism suggested that a series of regional disasters had destroyed most or all of the local plant and animal life in many places. These areas were then restocked with new, similar forms that migrated in from unaffected regions. Since he needed to

catastrophism The view that the earth's geological landscape is the result of violent cataclysmic events. Cuvier promoted this view, especially in opposition to Lamarck.

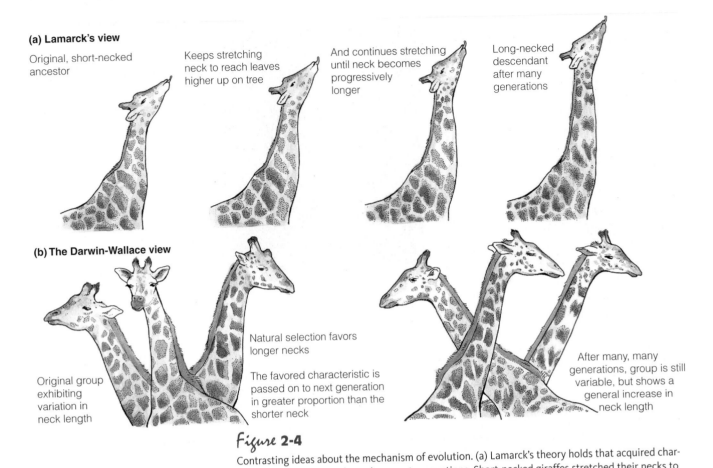

(a) Lamarck's view

Original, short-necked ancestor

Keeps stretching neck to reach leaves higher up on tree

And continues stretching until neck becomes progressively longer

Long-necked descendant after many generations

(b) The Darwin-Wallace view

Original group exhibiting variation in neck length

Natural selection favors longer necks

The favored characteristic is passed on to next generation in greater proportion than the shorter neck

After many, many generations, group is still variable, but shows a general increase in neck length

Figure 2-4

Contrasting ideas about the mechanism of evolution. (a) Lamarck's theory holds that acquired characteristics can be passed to subsequent generations. Short-necked giraffes stretched their necks to reach higher into trees for food, and, according to Lamarck, this acquired trait was passed on to offspring, who were born with longer necks. (b) The Darwin-Wallace theory of natural selection states that among giraffes there is variation in neck length. If having a longer neck provides an advantage for feeding, the trait will be passed on to a greater number of offspring, leading to an overall increase in the length of giraffe necks over many generations.

Figure 2-5

Cuvier explained the fossil record as the result of a succession of catastrophes followed by new creation events.

Wikipedia

be consistent with emerging fossil evidence, which indicated that organisms had become more complex over time, Cuvier proposed that after each disaster, the incoming migrants had a more modern appearance because they were the results of more recent creation events. (The last of these creations was the Noah flood, described in Genesis.) In this way, Cuvier's explanation of increased complexity over time avoided any notion of evolution while still accounting for the evidence of change so well preserved in the fossil record.

In 1798, an English economist named Thomas Malthus (1766–1834) wrote *An Essay on the Principle of Population* (Fig. 2-6). This important essay inspired both Charles Darwin and Alfred Russel Wallace in their separate discoveries of natural selection. Considering the enormous influence that Malthus had on these two men, it's noteworthy that he wasn't interested in species change at all. Instead, he was arguing for limits to human population growth because, as he pointed out, in nature the tendency for populations to increase is constantly being held in check by the availability of resources.

With permission from the Master of Haileybury

Figure 2-6

Thomas Malthus' *Essay on the Principle of Population* led both Darwin and Wallace to the principle of natural selection.

© National Portrait Gallery, London

Figure 2-7

Portrait of Charles Lyell.

That is, population size increases exponentially while food supplies remain relatively stable. Even though humans can reduce constraints on population size by producing more food, Malthus argued that the lack of resources would always be a constant source of "misery" and famine for humankind if our numbers continued to increase.

Both Darwin and Wallace extended Malthus' principles to all organisms, not just humans. Moreover, they recognized the important fact that when population size is limited by resource availability, there must be constant competition for food and water. And competition between individuals is the ultimate key to understanding natural selection.

Charles Lyell (1797–1875) is considered the founder of modern geology (Fig. 2-7). He was a lawyer, a geologist, and, for many years, Charles Darwin's friend and mentor. Before meeting Darwin in 1836, Lyell had earned acceptance in Europe's most prestigious scientific circles, thanks to his highly praised *Principles of Geology*, first published during the years 1830–1833.

In this extremely important work, Lyell argued that the geological processes we see today are the same as those that occurred in the past. This theory, called geological **uniformitarianism**, didn't originate entirely with Lyell, having been proposed by James Hutton in the late 1700s. Even so, it was Lyell who demonstrated that forces such as wind, water erosion, local flooding, frost, decomposition of vegetable matter, volcanoes, earthquakes, and glacial movements had all contributed in the past to produce the geological landscape that we see today. What's more, these processes were ongoing, indicating that geological change was still happening and that the forces driving such change were consistent, or *uniform*, over time. In other words, various aspects of the earth's surface (for example, climate, plants, animals, and land surfaces) vary through time, but the *underlying processes* that influence them are constant.

Lyell also emphasized the obvious: namely, that for such slow-acting forces to produce momentous change, the earth must be far older than anyone had

uniformitarianism The theory that the earth's features are the result of long-term processes that continue to operate in the present as they did in the past. Elaborated on by Lyell, this theory opposed catastrophism and contributed strongly to the concept of immense geological time.

(a)

(b)

Lynn Kilgore

Figure 2-8

(a) These limestone cliffs in southern France were formed around 300 million years ago from shells and the skeletal remains of countless sea creatures. (b) Part of a block of stone cut from the same limestone containing fossilized shells.

previously suspected. By providing an immense time scale and thereby changing perceptions of the earth's history from a few thousand to many millions of years, Lyell changed the framework within which scientists viewed the geological past. So the concept of "deep time" (Gould, 1987) remains one of Lyell's most significant contributions to the discovery of evolutionary principles. The immensity of geological time permitted the necessary time depth for the inherently slow process of evolutionary change (Fig. 2-8).

As you can see, the roots of evolutionary theory are deeply imbedded in the late eighteenth and early nineteenth centuries. During that time, many lesser-known people also contributed to this intellectual movement. One such person was Mary Anning (1799–1847), who lived in the town of Lyme Regis, on the south coast of England (Fig. 2-9).

Anning's father died when she was 11 years old, leaving his wife and two children destitute. Fortunately, he had taught Mary to recognize marine fossils embedded in the cliffs near the town. Thus, she began to earn a living by collecting and selling fossils to collectors who were becoming increasingly interested in the remains of creatures that many people believed had been killed in the Noah flood.

After Anning's discovery of the first *complete* fossil of *Ichthyosaurus*, a large fishlike marine reptile, and the first *Pleiosaurus* fossil (another ocean-dwelling reptile), some of the most famous scientists in England repeatedly visited her home. Eventually, she became known as one of the world's leading "fossilists," and by sharing her extensive knowledge of fossil species with many of the leading scientists of the day, she contributed to the understanding of the evolution of marine life that spanned over 200 million years. But because she was a woman, and of lowly social position, Anning wasn't acknowledged in the numerous scientific publications she facilitated. In recent years, however, she has achieved the recognition she deserves; her portrait hangs prominently in the British Museum (Natural History) in London, near one of her famous *Pleiosaurus* fossils.

The Discovery of Natural Selection

Having already been introduced to Erasmus Darwin, you shouldn't be surprised that his grandson Charles grew up in an educated family with ties to intellectual circles. Charles Darwin (1809–1882) was one of six children of Dr. Robert and Susanna Darwin (Fig. 2-10). Being the grandson not only of Erasmus Darwin but also of the wealthy Josiah Wedgwood (of Wedgwood china fame), Charles grew up enjoying the comfortable lifestyle of the landed gentry in rural England.

As a boy, Darwin had a keen interest in nature and spent his days fishing and collecting shells, birds' eggs, and rocks. However, this interest in natural history didn't dispel the generally held view of family and friends that he was in no way remarkable. In fact, his performance at school was no more than ordinary. (Perhaps this can be a source of inspiration to us all!)

After his mother's death when he was eight years old, Darwin was raised by his father and older sisters. Because he showed little interest in anything except hunting, shooting, and perhaps science, his father sent him to Edinburgh University to study medicine. It was there that Darwin first became acquainted with the evolutionary theories of Lamarck and others.

During that time (the 1820s), notions of evolution were becoming feared in England and elsewhere. Anything identified with postrevolutionary France was viewed with suspicion by the established order in England, and Lamarck, partly because he was French, was especially vilified by British scientists.

It was also a time of growing political unrest in Britain. The Reform Movement, seeking to undo many inequalities of the traditional class system, was under way, and like most social movements, it had a radical faction. Because many of the radicals were atheists and socialists who also supported Lamarck's ideas, many people came to associate evolution with atheism and political subversion. The growing fear of evolutionary ideas led many to believe that if these ideas were generally accepted, "the Church would crash, the moral fabric of society would be torn apart, and civilized man would return to savagery" (Desmond and Moore, 1991, p. 34). It's unfortunate that some of the most outspoken early proponents of species change were so vehemently anti-Christian, because their rhetoric helped establish the entrenched suspicion and misunderstanding of evolutionary theory that persists today.

While at Edinburgh, Darwin studied with professors who were outspoken supporters of Lamarck. So, even though he hated medicine and left Edinburgh after two years, his experience there was a formative period in his intellectual development.

Although Darwin was fairly indifferent to religion, he next went to Christ's College, Cambridge, to study theology. It was during his Cambridge years that he cultivated his interests in natural science, immersing himself in botany and geology. It's no wonder that following his graduation in 1831, he was invited to join a scientific expedition that would circle the globe (Fig. 2-11). And so it was that Darwin set sail aboard HMS

The Natural History Museum, London

Figure **2-9**

Portrait of Mary Anning

© Bettmann/Corbis

Figure **2-10**

Charles Darwin, photographed five years before the publication of *Origin of Species*.

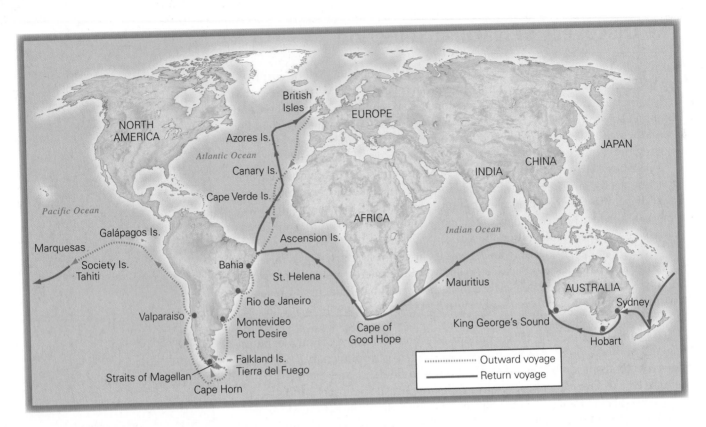

Figure 2-11

The route of HMS *Beagle*.

Beagle on December 17, 1831. The famous voyage of the *Beagle* would take almost five years and would forever change not only the course of Darwin's life but also the history of biological science.

Darwin went aboard the *Beagle* believing in fixity of species. But during the voyage, he privately began to have doubts. For example, he came across fossils of ancient giant animals that, except for size, looked very much like species that still lived in the same vicinity, and wondered if the fossils represented ancestors of those living forms.

During the famous stopover at the Galápagos Islands, off the coast of Ecuador, Darwin noticed that the vegetation and animals (especially birds) shared many similarities with those on the mainland of South America. But they weren't identical to them. What's more, the birds varied from island to island. Darwin collected 13 varieties of Galápagos finches, and it was clear that they represented a closely affiliated group; but some of their physical traits were different, particularly the shape and size of their beaks (Fig. 2-12). Darwin also collected finches from the mainland, and these appeared to represent only one group, or species.

The insight that Darwin gained from the finches is legendary. He realized that the various Galápagos finches had all descended from a common, mainland ancestor and had been modified over time in response to different island habitats and dietary preferences. But actually, it wasn't until *after* he returned to England that he recognized the significance of the variation in beak structure. In fact, during the voyage, he had paid little attention to the finches. It was only later that he considered the factors that could lead to the modification of one species into many (Gould, 1985; Desmond and Moore, 1991).

Darwin arrived back in England in October of 1836 and was immediately accepted into the most prestigious scientific circles. He married his cousin, Emma Wedgwood, and moved to the village of Down, near London, where he spent the

(a) Ground finch
Main food: seeds
Beak: heavy

(b) Tree finch
Main food: leaves, buds,
blossoms, fruits
Beak: thick, short

(c) Tree finch (called
woodpecker finch)
Main food: insects
Beak: stout, straight

(d) Ground finch (known
as warbler finch)
Main food: insects
Beak: slender

rest of his life writing on topics ranging from fossils to orchids. But the question of species change was his overriding passion.

At Down, Darwin began to develop his views on what he called *natural selection*. This concept was borrowed from animal breeders, who choose, or "select," as breeding stock those animals that possess certain traits they want to emphasize in offspring. Animals with undesirable traits are "selected against," or prevented from breeding. A dramatic example of the effects of selective breeding can be seen in the various domestic dog breeds shown in Figure 2-13. Darwin applied his knowledge of domesticated species to naturally occurring ones, and he recognized that in undomesticated organisms, the selective agent was nature, not humans.

Figure **2-12**

Beak variation in Darwin's Galápagos finches.

Figure **2-13**

All domestic dog breeds share a common ancestor, the wolf. The extreme variation exhibited by dog breeds today has been achieved in a relatively short time through artificial selection. In this situation, humans allow only certain dogs to breed to emphasize specific characteristics. (We should note that not all traits desired by human breeders are advantageous to the dogs themselves.)

By the late 1830s, Darwin had realized that biological variation within a species (that is, differences among individuals) was crucial. Furthermore, he realized that sexual reproduction increased variation, although he didn't know why. Then, in 1838, he read Malthus' essay; and there he found the answer to the question of how new species came to be. He accepted Malthus' idea that populations increase at a faster rate than resources do, and he recognized that in nonhuman animals, population size is always limited by the amount of food and water available. He also recognized that these two facts lead to a constant "struggle for existence." The idea that in each generation more offspring are born than survive to adulthood, coupled with the notions of competition for resources and biological diversity, was all Darwin needed to develop his theory of natural selection. He wrote: "It at once struck me that under these circumstances favourable variations would tend to be preserved, and unfavourable ones to be destroyed. The result of this would be the formation of a new species" (F. Darwin, 1950, pp. 53–54). Basically, this quotation summarizes the entire theory of natural selection.

By 1844, Darwin had written a short summary of his views on natural selection, but he didn't think he had enough data to support his hypothesis, so he continued his research without publishing. He also had other reasons for not publishing what he knew would be, to say the least, a highly controversial work. He was deeply troubled that his wife, Emma, saw his ideas as running counter to her strong religious convictions (Keynes, 2002). Also, as a member of the established order, he knew that many of his friends and associates were concerned with threats to the status quo, and evolutionary theory was viewed as a very serious threat.

In Darwin's Shadow

Unlike Darwin, Alfred Russel Wallace (1823–1913) was born into a family of modest means (Fig. 2-14). He went to work at the age of 14, and with little formal education, he moved from one job to the next. He became interested in collecting plants and animals, and in 1848 he joined an expedition to the Amazon, where he acquired firsthand knowledge of many natural phenomena.

Figure **2-14**
Alfred Russel Wallace independently discovered the key to the evolutionary process.

© National Portrait Gallery, London

In 1855, Wallace published an article suggesting that current species were descended from other species and that the appearance of new ones was influenced by environmental factors (Trinkaus and Shipman, 1992). This article caused Lyell and others to urge Darwin to publish, but he still hesitated.

Then, in 1858, Wallace sent Darwin another paper, "On the Tendency of Varieties to Depart Indefinitely from the Original Type." In this paper, Wallace described evolution as a process driven by competition and natural selection. When he received Wallace's paper, Darwin was afraid that Wallace might get credit for a theory (natural selection) that he himself had developed. He quickly wrote a paper presenting his ideas, and both men's papers were read before the Linnean Society of London. Neither author was present. Wallace was out of the country, and Darwin was mourning the recent death of his young son.

The papers received little notice at the time. But in December 1859, when Darwin completed and published his greatest work, *On the Origin of Species,** the storm broke; and it still hasn't abated (Fig. 2-15). Although public opinion was negative, there was much scholarly praise for the book, and scientific opinion gradually came to Darwin's support. The riddle of species was now explained: Species could change, they weren't fixed, and they evolved from other species through the mechanism of natural selection.

Natural Selection

Early in his research, Darwin had realized that natural selection was the key to evolution. With the help of Malthus' ideas, he saw *how* selection in nature could be explained. In the struggle for existence, those *individuals* with favorable variations would survive and reproduce, but those with unfavorable variations wouldn't. For Darwin, the explanation of evolution was simple. The basic processes, as he understood them, are as follows:

1. All species are capable of producing offspring at a faster rate than food supplies increase.
2. There is biological variation within all species. (Today we know that, except for identical twins, no two individuals are genetically the same.)
3. Since in each generation more offspring are produced than can survive, and because of limited resources, there is competition among individuals. (*Note:* This statement doesn't mean that there is constant fierce fighting.)
4. Individuals who possess favorable variations or traits (for example, speed, resistance to disease, protective coloration) have an advantage over those who don't have them. In other words, they have greater **fitness** because favorable traits increase the likelihood of survival and reproduction.
5. The environmental context determines whether or not a trait is beneficial. What is favorable in one setting may be a liability in another. Consequently, the traits that become most advantageous are the results of a natural process.
6. Traits are inherited and passed on to the next generation. Because individuals who possess favorable traits contribute more offspring to the next generation than others do, over time, those favorable traits become more common in the population. Less favorable characteristics aren't passed as frequently, so they become less common over time and are "weeded out." Individuals who produce more offspring in comparison to others are said to have greater **reproductive success** or fitness.
7. Over long periods of geological time, successful variations accumulate in a population, so that later generations may be distinct from ancestral ones. Thus, in time, a new species may appear.

*The full title is *On the Origin of Species by Means of Natural Selection, or the Preservation of Favoured Races in the Struggle for Life.*

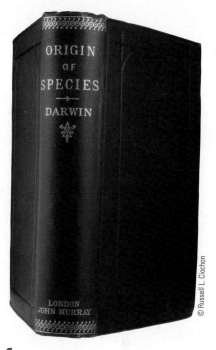

Figure **2-15**

Charles Darwin's, *Origin of Species,* the book that revolutionized biological science.

fitness Pertaining to natural selection, a measure of the relative reproductive success of individuals. Fitness can be measured by an individual's genetic contribution to the next generation compared to that of other individuals. The terms *genetic fitness, reproductive fitness,* and *differential reproductive success* are also used.

reproductive success The number of offspring an individual produces and rears to reproductive age; an individual's genetic contribution to the next generation.

8. Geographical isolation also contributes to the formation of new species. As populations of a species become geographically isolated from one another, for whatever reasons (for example, distance or natural barriers such as oceans), they begin to adapt to different environments. Over time, as populations continue to respond to different **selective pressures** (that is, different ecological circumstances), they may become distinct species. The 13 species of Galápagos finches are presumably all descended from a common ancestor on the South American mainland, and they provide an example of the role of geographical isolation.

Before Darwin, individual members of species weren't considered important, so they weren't studied. But as we've seen, Darwin recognized the uniqueness of individuals and realized that variation among them could explain how selection occurs. Favorable variations are selected, or chosen, for survival by nature; unfavorable ones are eliminated. *Natural selection operates on individuals*, either favorably or unfavorably, but *it's the population that evolves*. It's important to emphasize that the unit of natural selection is the individual; the unit of evolution is the population. This is because individuals don't change genetically, but over time, populations do.

Natural Selection in Action

The most frequently cited example of natural selection relates to changes in the coloration of a species of moth. In recent years, the moth story has come under some criticism; but the premise remains valid, so we use it to illustrate how natural selection works.

Before the nineteenth century, the most common variety of the peppered moth in England was a mottled gray color. During the day, as the moths rested on lichen-covered tree trunks, their coloration provided camouflage (Fig. 2-16). There was also a dark gray variety of the same species, but since the dark moths weren't as well camouflaged, they were more frequently eaten by birds and so they were less common. (In this example, the birds are the *selective agent*, and they apply *selective pressures* on the moths.) Yet, by the end of the nineteenth century, the darker form had almost completely replaced the common gray one.

The cause of this change was the changing environment of industrialized nineteenth-century England. Coal dust from factories and fireplaces settled on trees, turning them dark gray and killing the lichen. The moths continued to rest on the trees, but the light gray ones became more conspicuous as the trees became darker, and they were increasingly targeted by birds. Since fewer of the light gray moths were living long enough to reproduce, they contributed fewer genes to the next generation than the darker moths did, and the proportion of lighter moths decreased while the dark moths became more common. A similar color shift also occurred in North America. But with the advent of clean air acts in both Britain and the United States reducing the amount of air pollution (at least from coal), the predominant color of the peppered moth once again became the light mottled gray. This kind of evolutionary shift in response to environmental change is called *adaptation*.

In the 1950s, a series of experiments, conducted under somewhat artificial conditions, seemed to confirm that the color shift was due to the absence of lichen (Kettlewell, 1956). But some aspects of the study were questionable. For instance, the same shift in coloration had occurred in North America, where lichen wasn't

selective pressures Forces in the environment that influence reproductive success in individuals.

(a)

Figure **2-16**

Variation in the peppered moth. (a) The dark form is more visible on the light, lichen-covered tree. (b) On trees darkened by pollution, the lighter form is more visible.

(b)

generally present on trees. Besides, there is evidence that birds can see ultraviolet (UV) light, and in the UV spectrum, moths and lichen wouldn't look like each other. For these reasons, a resemblance to lichen may not have played a significant part in protecting the moths (Weiss, 2003). Yet, the color shift occurred in both regions during periods of increased air pollution. So, even though the explanation for the observed changes in moth color is probably more complex than originally believed and may involve factors in addition to bird predation, this phenomenon is still a very good example of microevolution in a contemporary population.

The medium ground finch of the Galápagos Islands gives us another example of natural selection. In 1977, drought killed many of the plants that produced the smaller, softer seeds favored by these birds. This forced a population of finches on one of the islands to feed on larger, harder seeds. Even before 1977, some birds had smaller, less robust beaks than others (that is, there was variation); and during the drought, because they were less able to process the larger seeds, more smaller-beaked birds died than larger-beaked birds. So, although overall population size declined, average beak thickness in the survivors and their offspring increased, simply because thicker-beaked individuals were surviving in greater numbers and producing more offspring. In other words, they had greater reproductive success. But during heavy rains in 1982–1983, smaller seeds became more plentiful again and the pattern in beak size reversed itself, demonstrating again how reproductive success is related to environmental conditions (Grant, 1986; Ridley, 1993).

The best illustration of natural selection, however—and certainly one with potentially grave consequences for humans—is the recent increase in resistant strains of disease-causing microorganisms. When antibiotics were first introduced in the 1940s, they were seen as the cure for bacterial disease. But that optimistic view didn't take into account that bacteria, like other organisms, possess genetic variability. Consequently, while an antibiotic will kill most bacteria in an infected person, any bacterium with an inherited resistance to that particular therapy will survive. In turn, the survivors reproduce and pass their drug resistance to future generations so that eventually, the population is mostly made up of bacteria that don't respond to treatment. What's more, because bacteria produce new generations every few hours, antibiotic-resistant strains are continuously appearing. As a result, many types of infection no longer respond to treatment. For example, tuberculosis was once thought to be well controlled, but there's been a resurgence of TB in recent years because some strains of the bacterium that causes it are resistant to most of the antibiotics used to treat TB.

These three examples (moths, finches, and bacteria) provide the following insights into the fundamentals of evolutionary change produced by natural selection:

1. *A trait must be inherited if natural selection is to act on it.* A characteristic that isn't hereditary (such as a temporary change in hair color produced by the hairdresser) won't be passed on to offspring. In finches, for example, beak size is a hereditary trait.
2. *Natural selection can't occur without population variation in inherited characteristics.* If, for example, all the peppered moths had initially been gray and the trees had become darker, the survival and reproduction of the moths could have been so low that the population might have become extinct. *Selection can work only with variation that already exists.*
3. *Fitness is a relative measure that changes as the environment changes.* Fitness is simply differential reproductive success. In the initial stage, the lighter moths were more fit because they produced more offspring. But as the environment changed, the dark gray moths became more fit. Later, a further change reversed the pattern again. Likewise, the majority of Galápagos finches will have larger or smaller beaks, depending on external conditions. So it should be obvious that statements regarding the "most fit" don't mean anything without reference to specific environments.
4. *Natural selection can act only on traits that affect reproduction.* If a characteristic isn't expressed until later in life, after organisms have reproduced, then natural selection can't influence it. This is because the trait's inherited components have already been passed on to offspring. Many forms of cancer and cardiovascular disease are influenced by hereditary factors, but because these diseases usually affect people after they've had children, natural selection can't act against them. By the same token, if a condition usually kills or compromises the individual before he or she reproduces, natural selection can act against it because the trait won't be passed on.

So far, our examples have shown how different death rates influence natural selection (for example, moths or finches that die early leave fewer offspring). But mortality isn't the complete picture. Another important aspect of natural selection is **fertility**, because an animal that gives birth to more young passes its genes on at a faster rate than one that bears fewer offspring. But fertility isn't the entire story either, because the crucial element is the number of young raised successfully to

fertility The ability to conceive and produce healthy offspring.

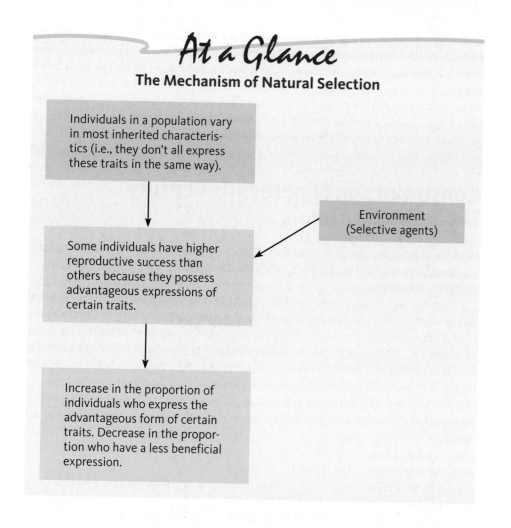

At a Glance

The Mechanism of Natural Selection

Individuals in a population vary in most inherited characteristics (i.e., they don't all express these traits in the same way).

↓

Environment (Selective agents)

Some individuals have higher reproductive success than others because they possess advantageous expressions of certain traits.

↓

Increase in the proportion of individuals who express the advantageous form of certain traits. Decrease in the proportion who have a less beneficial expression.

the point where they themselves reproduce. We call this *differential net reproductive success*. The way this mechanism works can be demonstrated through another example.

In swifts (small birds that resemble swallows), data show that producing more offspring doesn't necessarily guarantee that more young will be successfully raised. The number of eggs hatched in a breeding season is a measure of fertility. The number of birds that mature and are eventually able to leave the nest is a measure of net reproductive success, or successfully raised offspring. The following table shows the correlation between the number of eggs hatched (fertility) and the number of young that leave the nest (reproductive success), averaged over four breeding seasons (Lack, 1966):

Number of eggs hatched (fertility)	2 eggs	3 eggs	4 eggs
Average number of young raised (reproductive success)	1.92	2.54	1.76
Sample size (number of nests)	72	20	16

As you can see, the most efficient number of eggs is three, because that number yields the highest reproductive success. Raising two offspring is less beneficial to the parents since the end result isn't as successful as with three eggs. Trying to raise more than three is actually detrimental, since the parents may not be able to provide enough nourishment for any of the offspring. Offspring that die before reaching reproductive age are, in evolutionary terms, equivalent to never being born. Actually, death of an offspring can be a minus to the parents, because before it dies, it drains parental resources. It may even inhibit their ability to raise other offspring, thus reducing their reproductive success even further. Selection favors those genetic traits that yield the maximum net reproductive success. If the number of eggs laid is a genetic trait in birds (and it seems to be), natural selection in swifts should act to favor the laying of three eggs as opposed to two or four.

Constraints on Nineteenth-Century Evolutionary Theory

Darwin argued for the concept of evolution in general and the role of natural selection in particular. But he didn't entirely comprehend the exact mechanisms of evolutionary change.

As we've already seen, natural selection acts on *variation* within species, though neither Darwin nor anyone else in the nineteenth century understood the actual source of this variation. Also, no one understood how parents pass traits to offspring. Almost without exception, nineteenth-century scientists believed that inheritance is a *blending* process in which parental characteristics are mixed together to produce intermediate expressions in offspring. Given this notion, we can see why the true nature of genes was unimaginable; and with no alternative explanations, Darwin accepted it. As it turns out, a contemporary of Darwin's had actually worked out the rules of heredity. However, the work of this Augustinian monk named Gregor Mendel (whom you'll meet in Chapter 4) wasn't recognized until the beginning of the twentieth century.

The first three decades of the twentieth century saw the merger of natural selection theory and Mendel's discoveries. This was a crucial development because until then, scientists thought these concepts were unrelated. Then, in 1953, the structure of DNA was discovered. This landmark achievement has been followed by even more amazing advances in the field of genetics. The human and chimpanzee **genomes** were sequenced in 2003 and 2005 respectively. The genomes of many other species (including dogs, mice, and rhesus macaques, to name a few) have also now been sequenced. By comparing different species' genomes, scientists can examine how genetically similar (or different) the species are, and this will explain many aspects of how these species evolved. Also, since the early 1990s, several scientists have merged the fields of evolutionary and developmental biology into a new field called "evo-devo" (see p. 138). This approach, which compares the actions of different developmental genes and the factors that regulate them, are making it possible to explain evolution in ways that were impossible even 15 years ago. Scientists are truly on the threshold of revealing the remaining secrets of the evolutionary process. The year 2009 marks the 200th anniversary of Charles Darwin's birth and the 150th anniversary of the publication of *Origin of Species*. At Cambridge University and elsewhere in England, events are being planned that will include presentations from evolutionary biologists from around the world. Moreover, an exact replica of the HMS *Beagle* is now under construction (Fig. 2-17). In 2009, this ship will begin a scientific voyage during which it will circumnavigate the globe, following the route of the original voyage. How wonderful it would be if, for Darwin's 200th birthday, we could show him how far the field of evolutionary biology has come!

genomes The term "genome" refers to the entire genetic makeup of an individual or species.

Figure **2-17**

A painting by John Chancellor of the HMS *Beagle* sailing through the Galápagos Islands in 1835.

© Gordon Chancellor

Opposition to Evolution Today

One hundred and fifty years after the publication of *Origin of Species*, the debate over evolution is far from over, especially in the United States and, increasingly, in several Muslim countries. For the majority of biological scientists today, evolution is indisputable. The genetic evidence for it is solid and accumulating daily. Anyone who appreciates and understands genetic mechanisms can't avoid the conclusion that populations and species evolve. What's more, the majority of Christians don't believe that biblical depictions should be taken literally. But at the same time, some surveys show that about half of all Americans don't believe that evolution occurs. There are a number of reasons for this.

The mechanisms of evolution are complex and don't lend themselves to simple explanations. Understanding them requires some familiarity with genetics and biology, a familiarity that most people don't have unless they took related courses in school. What's more, many people want definitive, clear-cut answers to complex questions. But as you learned in Chapter 1, science doesn't always provide definitive answers to questions; it doesn't establish absolute truths; and it doesn't *prove* facts. Another thing to consider is that regardless of their culture, most people are raised in belief systems that don't emphasize **biological continuity** between species or offer scientific explanations for natural phenomena.

The relationship between science and religion has never been easy (remember Galileo), even though both systems serve, in their own ways, to explain natural phenomena. Scientific explanations are based in data analysis, hypothesis testing, and interpretation. Religion, meanwhile, is a system of faith-based beliefs that, like science, often attempts to explain natural phenomena. One difference between science and religion is that religious beliefs and explanations aren't amenable to scientific testing. Religion and science concern different aspects of the human experience, and they aren't inherently mutually exclusive approaches. That is, belief in God doesn't exclude the possibility of biological evolution; and

biological continuity Refers to a biological continuum. When expressions of a phenomenon continuously grade into one another so that there are no discrete categories, they exist on a continuum. Color is one such phenomenon, and life-forms are another.

acknowledgment of evolutionary processes doesn't preclude the existence of God. What's more, evolutionary theories aren't rejected by all religions or by most forms of Christianity.

Some years ago, the Vatican hosted an international conference on human evolution; and in 1996, Pope John Paul II issued a statement that "fresh knowledge leads to recognition of the theory of evolution as more than just a hypothesis." Today, the official position of the Catholic Church is that evolutionary processes do occur, but that the human soul is of divine creation and not subject to evolutionary processes. Likewise, mainstream Protestants don't generally see a conflict. Unfortunately, those who believe in an absolutely literal interpretation of the Bible (called *fundamentalists*) accept no compromise.

A Brief History of Opposition to Evolution in the United States

Although there are small movements that argue against evolution in other parts of the world, opposition to evolution is far more prevalent in the United States, and there are historical reasons for this. Reacting to rapid cultural change after World War I, conservative Christians in the United States sought a revival of what they considered "traditional values." In their view, one way to do this was to prevent any mention of Darwinism in public schools. One result of this effort was a state law passed in 1925 that banned the teaching of any theory (particularly evolution) that doesn't support the biblical version of the creation of humankind. To test the validity of the law, the American Civil Liberties Union persuaded a high school teacher named John Scopes to submit to being arrested and tried for teaching evolution (Fig. 2-18). The subsequent trial, called the Scopes Monkey Trial, was a 1920s equivalent of current celebrity trials. In the end, Scopes was convicted and fined $100, though the conviction was later overturned. Although most states didn't actually forbid the teaching of evolution, Arkansas, Tennessee, and a few others continued to prohibit any mention of it until 1968, when the U.S. Supreme Court struck down the ban against teaching evolution in public schools. (One coauthor of this textbook remembers when her junior high school science teacher was fired for mentioning evolution in Little Rock, Arkansas.)

As coverage of evolution in textbooks increased by the mid-1960s, **Christian fundamentalists** renewed their campaign to eliminate evolution from public school curricula or to introduce antievolutionary material into public school classes. Out of this effort, the *creation science* movement was born.

Proponents of creation science are called "creationists" because they explain the existence of the universe as the result of a sudden creation event that occurred over the course of six 24-hour days as described in the book of Genesis. The premise of creation science is that the biblical account of the earth's origins and the Noah flood can be supported by scientific evidence.

Creationists have insisted that what they used to call "creation science" and now call "intelligent design" (ID) is as much a scientific endeavor as is evolution and that there's scientific evidence to support creationist views. They've argued that in the interest of fairness, a balanced view should be offered: If evolution is taught as science, then creationism should also be taught as science. Sounds fair, doesn't it? But ID isn't science at all, for the simple reason that creationists insist that their view is absolute and infallible. Therefore, creationism isn't a hypothesis that can be tested, nor is it amenable to falsification. And because hypothesis testing is the basis of all science, creationism, by its very nature, cannot be considered science.

Christian fundamentalists Adherents to a movement in American Protestantism that began in the early twentieth century. This group holds that the teachings of the Bible are infallible and the scriptures are to be taken literally.

Figure **2-18**

Photo taken at the "Scopes Monkey Trial". The well-known defense attorney Clarence Darrow is sitting on the edge of the table. John Scopes, the defendant, is sitting with his arms folded behind Darrow.

Since the 1970s, creationists have become increasingly active in local school boards and state legislatures, promoting laws that mandate the teaching of creationism in public schools. In Dover, Pennsylvania, ID proponents suffered a setback in 2004 when voters ousted all eight of the nine-member Dover Area School Board who were up for reelection. This school board, composed entirely of ID supporters, had established a policy requiring high school teachers to discuss ID as an alternative to evolution. Then, in late 2005, U.S. District Judge John Jones struck down the policy because it violated the First Amendment to the Constitution.

In fact, state and federal courts consistently overrule these and similar laws because they violate the "establishment clause" of the First Amendment of the U.S. Constitution, which states that "Congress shall make no law respecting an establishment of religion, or prohibiting the free exercise thereof." This statement guarantees the separation of church and state, and it means that the government can neither promote nor inhibit the practice of any religion. Therefore, the use of public institutions (including schools) paid for by taxpayers' dollars to promote any particular religion is unconstitutional. Of course, this doesn't mean that individuals can't have private religious discussions or pray in public places; but it does mean that such places can't be used for organized religious events.

The establishment clause was initially proposed to ensure that the government could neither promote nor restrict any particular religious view, as it did in England at the time the U.S. Constitution was written. But this hasn't stopped creationists, who encourage teachers to claim "academic freedom" to teach creationism. To avoid objections based on the guarantee of separation of church and state, proponents of ID claim that they don't emphasize any particular religion. But this argument doesn't address the essential point that teaching *any* religious views in a way that promotes them in publicly funded schools is a violation of the U.S. Constitution.

CHAPTER 2

Summary

Our current understanding of evolutionary processes is directly traceable to developments in intellectual thought in western Europe, with significant influences from the East, over the past 400 years. Many people contributed to this shift in perspective, and we've named only a few. Linnaeus placed humans in the same taxonomic scheme as all other animals. With remarkable insight, Lamarck and Buffon both recognized that species could change in response to environmental circumstances; Lamarck also attempted to explain how the changes occur. He proposed the idea of the inheritance of acquired characteristics, which was later discredited. Lyell, in his theory of geological uniformitarianism, provided the necessary expanse of time for evolution to occur, and Malthus discussed how population size is kept in check by the availability of resources.

Darwin and Wallace, influenced by their predecessors, independently recognized that because of competition for resources, individuals with favorable characteristics would tend to survive and pass those traits on to offspring. Those lacking beneficial traits would produce fewer offspring if they survived to reproductive age at all. That is, they would have lower reproductive success and reduced fitness. Thus, over time, advantageous characteristics accumulate in a population (because they have been selected for) while disadvantageous ones are eliminated (selected against). This, in a nutshell, is the theory of evolution by means of natural selection.

Despite mounting evidence in support of evolutionary theory for almost 150 years, there is still very strong public sentiment against it, especially in the United States. The opposition has been fueled mostly by fundamentalist Christian groups attempting to either ban the teaching of evolution in public schools or introduce religiously based views into public school curricula in the name of "fair and balanced treatment." These attempts have repeatedly been struck down in state and federal courts because they violate the First Amendment to the U.S. Constitution.

Critical Thinking Questions

1. After having read this chapter, how would you respond to the question, "If humans evolved from monkeys, why do we still have monkeys?"
2. Given what you've read about the scientific method in Chapter 1, how would you explain the differences between science and religion as methods of explaining natural phenomena? Do you personally see a conflict between evolutionary and religious explanations of how species came to be?
3. Can you think of some examples of artificial and natural selection that weren't discussed in this chapter? For your examples, what traits have been selected for? In the case of natural selection, what was the selective agent?

CHAPTER

3

The Biological Basis of Life

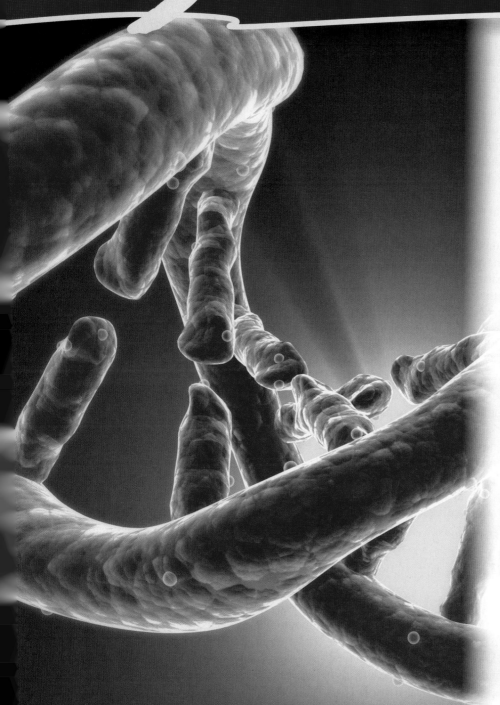

MedicalRF.com/Corbis

Key Questions

What is the molecular basis for life? Does it vary from species to species?

How do human beings fit into a biological continuum?

 Click!

Go to the following media for interactive activities and exercises on topics covered in this chapter:

• Genetics in Anthropology: Principles and Applications CD-ROM, Version 2.0

Introduction

After a rotten day, you've turned on the TV to watch the news. The first story, after about 20 minutes of commercials, is about genetically modified foods, a newly cloned species, or the controversy over stem cell research. What do you do? Change the channel? Press the mute button? Go to sleep? Or do you listen to the story? If you do listen to it, do you understand it? Do you think it's important or relevant to you personally? Actually, it's very relevant to you personally because you live in an age when genetic discoveries and genetically based technologies are advancing daily, and they're going to profoundly affect your life.

At some point, you or someone you love will probably need lifesaving medical treatment, perhaps for cancer, and this treatment may be based on genetic research. Like it or not, you already eat genetically modified foods. You might at some point take advantage of developing reproductive technologies, and sadly, you may soon see the development of biological weapons based on genetically altered bacteria and viruses. But you'll also probably live to see many of the secrets of evolution revealed through genetic research. So even if you haven't been interested in genetic issues, you should be aware that they affect your life every day.

As you already know, this book is about human evolution and adaptation, both of which are intimately linked to life processes that involve cells, the duplication of genetic information, and the transmission of this information from one generation to the next. So, to discuss human evolution and adaptation in the broad sense, we need to examine how life is organized at the cellular and molecular levels. This, in turn, requires a discussion of the fundamental principles of genetics.

Genetics is the study of how **genes** work and how traits are transmitted from one generation to the next. Because physical anthropologists are concerned with human evolution, adaptation, and variation, they need to understand the factors that lie at the root of these phenomena. In fact, although many physical anthropologists don't actually specialize in genetics, it's genetics that ultimately links the various subdisciplines of biological anthropology.

Cells

genes Sequences of DNA bases that specify the order of amino acids in an entire protein, a portion of a protein, or any functional product. A gene may be made up of hundreds or thousands of DNA bases organized into coding and noncoding segments.

To discuss genetic and evolutionary principles, it's first necessary to understand basic cell functions. Cells are the fundamental units of life in all living organisms. In some forms, such as bacteria, the entire organism consists of only a single cell. However, more complex *multicellular* forms, such as plants, insects, birds, and mammals, are composed of billions of cells. As a matter of fact, an adult human is made up of perhaps as many as 1,000 billion (1,000,000,000,000) cells, all functioning in complex ways that ultimately promote the survival of the individual.

Life on earth began at least 3.7 billion years ago in the form of single-celled organisms, represented today by bacteria (Fig. 3-1) and blue-green algae. Structurally more complex cells, called eukaryotic cells, appeared approximately 1.2 billion years ago, and since they're the kind of cell that multicellular organisms are made of, they're the focus of this discussion. In spite of the many differences among life-forms, the cells of all living organisms share many similarities as a result of their common evolutionary past.

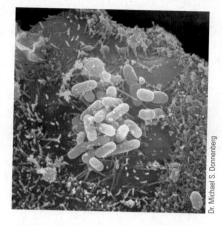

<figure>

Figure **3-1**

Each one of these sausage-shaped structures is a single-celled bacterium.

Dr. Michael S. Donnenberg

In general, a eukaryotic cell is a three-dimensional structure composed of *carbohydrates, lipids (fats), nucleic acids,* and *proteins*. It also contains several kinds of substructures, one of which is the **nucleus** (*pl.,* nuclei), a discrete unit surrounded by a thin membrane called the *nuclear membrane* (Fig. 3-2). Inside the nucleus are two kinds of **molecules** that contain the genetic information that controls the cell's functions: These two molecules are **DNA (deoxyribonucleic acid)** and **RNA (ribonucleic acid)**. The nucleus is surrounded by a gel-like substance called the **cytoplasm**. In addition to the nucleus, the cytoplasm contains many other types of organelles, or subunits within cells that are involved in various activities. These activities include breaking down nutrients and converting them to other substances, storing and releasing energy, eliminating waste, and manufacturing **proteins** through a process called **protein synthesis**.

We need to say a bit more about two kinds of organelles: **mitochondria** (*sing.,* mitochondrion) and **ribosomes**. Mitochondria (see Fig. 3-3) are responsible for

nucleus   A structure (organelle) found in all eukaryotic cells. The nucleus contains chromosomes (nuclear DNA).

molecules   Structures made up of two or more atoms. Molecules can combine with other molecules to form more complex structures.

DNA (deoxyribonucleic acid)   The double-stranded molecule that contains the genetic code. DNA is a main component of chromosomes.

RNA (ribonucleic acid)   A single-stranded molecule, similar in structure to DNA. Three forms of RNA are essential to protein synthesis: messenger RNA (mRNA), transfer RNA (tRNA), and ribosomal RNA (rRNA).

cytoplasm   The portion of the cell contained within the cell membrane, excluding the nucleus. The cytoplasm consists of a semifluid material and contains numerous structures involved with cell function.

proteins   Three-dimensional molecules that serve a wide variety of functions through their ability to bind to other molecules.

protein synthesis   The assembly of chains of amino acids into functional protein molecules. The process is directed by DNA.

mitochondria   (*sing.,* mitochondrion) Structures contained within the cytoplasm of eukaryotic cells that convert energy, derived from nutrients, to a form that can be used by the cell.

ribosomes   Structures composed of a form of RNA called ribosomal RNA (rRNA) and protein. Ribosomes are found in a cell's cytoplasm and are essential to the manufacture of proteins.

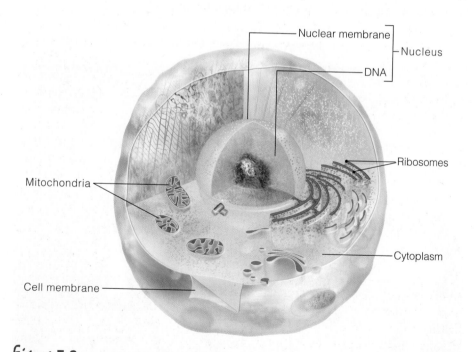

Nuclear membrane
Nucleus
DNA
Ribosomes
Mitochondria
Cytoplasm
Cell membrane

Figure **3-2**

Structure of a generalized eukaryotic cell, illustrating the cell's three-dimensional nature. Various organelles are shown, but for simplicity only those we discuss are labeled.

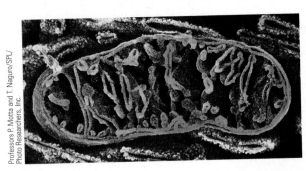

Figure 3-3

Scanning electron micrograph of a mitochondrion.

producing energy within the cell, and they can be loosely thought of as the cell's engines. Mitochondria are oval structures enclosed within a folded membrane, and they contain their own distinct DNA, called **mitochondrial DNA (mtDNA)**, which directs mitochondrial activities. Mitochondrial DNA has the same molecular structure and function as nuclear DNA (that is, DNA found in the nucleus), but it's organized somewhat differently. In recent years, mtDNA has attracted a lot of attention because it has several forensic applications and is also important in the study of certain evolutionary processes. For these reasons, we'll discuss mitochondrial inheritance in more detail in Chapters 4 and 14. We'll also discuss ribosomes because they're partly composed of RNA and are essential to protein synthesis (see p. 57).

There are basically two types of cells: **somatic cells** and **gametes**. Somatic cells are the cellular components of body tissues, such as muscle, bone, skin, nerve, heart, and brain. Gametes, or *sex cells*, are specifically involved in reproduction and aren't important as structural components of the body. There are two types of gametes: egg cells, produced in female ovaries, and sperm cells, which develop in male testes. The sole function of a sex cell is to unite with a gamete from another individual to form a **zygote**, which has the potential of developing into a new individual. In this way, gametes transmit genetic information from parent to offspring.

The Structure of DNA

DNA is the very basis of life because it directs all cellular functions. So if we want to understand these functions and how characteristics are inherited, we need to know something about the structure and function of DNA.

Figure 3-4

James Watson (left) and Francis Crick in 1953 with their model of the structure of the DNA molecule.

mitochondrial DNA (mtDNA) DNA found in the mitochondria; mtDNA is inherited only from the mother.

somatic cells Basically, all the cells in the body except those involved with reproduction.

gametes Reproductive cells (eggs and sperm in animals) developed from precursor cells in ovaries and testes.

zygote A cell formed by the union of an egg cell and a sperm cell. It contains the full complement of chromosomes (in humans, 46) and has the potential of developing into an entire organism.

A Closer Look

Rosalind Franklin: The Fourth (But Invisible) Member of the Double Helix Team

In 1962, three men, James Watson, Francis Crick, and Maurice Wilkins, won the Nobel Prize for medicine and physiology. They earned this most prestigious of all scientific honors for their discovery of the structure of the DNA molecule, which they had published in 1953. But due credit was not given to a fourth, equally deserving but unacknowledged person named Rosalind Franklin, who had died of ovarian cancer in 1958. But even if she had been acknowledged in 1962, Franklin still wouldn't have been a Nobel recipient because the Nobel Prize isn't awarded posthumously.

Franklin was a chemist who went to the University of Cambridge in 1951, after being invited there to study the structure of DNA. Before that, she'd been in Paris using a technique called X-ray diffraction, a process that reveals the positions of atoms in crystalline structures. What Franklin didn't know was that a colleague in her Cambridge lab, Maurice Wilkins, was working on the same DNA project. To make matters worse, Wilkins hadn't been told what her position was, so he thought she'd been hired as his assistant. Needless to say, this was hardly a good way to begin a working relationship, and as you might expect, there were a few tense moments between them.

Franklin soon produced some excellent X-ray diffraction images of some DNA fibers that Wilkins had provided,

Figure 1
Rosalind Franklin

The Novartis Foundation

and the images clearly showed that the structure was helical. Furthermore, she worked out that there were two strands, not one. Wilkins innocently (but without Franklin's knowledge) showed the images to Watson and Crick, who were working in another laboratory, also at Cambridge. Within two weeks, Watson and Crick had developed their now-famous model of a double-stranded helix without Franklin's knowledge.

Desperately unhappy at Cambridge, Franklin took a position at King's College, London, in 1953. In April of that year, she and a student published an article in the journal *Nature* that dealt indirectly with the helical structure of DNA. The article by Watson and Crick was published in the same issue.

During her lifetime, Franklin gained recognition for her work in carbons, coal, and viruses, topics on which she published many articles; and she was happy with the reputation she achieved. After her death, Watson made many derogative comments about Rosalind Franklin, including several in print. Even so, it appears they remained on friendly terms until she died at the age of 37. She also remained friendly with Crick, but she never knew that their revolutionary discovery was partly made possible by her photographic images.

The exact physical and chemical properties of DNA were unknown until 1953, when, at the University of Cambridge in England, an American researcher named James Watson and three British scientists, Francis Crick, Maurice Wilkins, and Rosalind Franklin, developed a structural and functional model (Fig. 3-4) of DNA (Watson and Crick, 1953a, 1953b). It's impossible to overstate the importance of this achievement because it completely revolutionized the fields of biology and medicine and forever altered our understanding of biological and evolutionary mechanisms (see "A Closer Look").

The DNA molecule is composed of two chains of even smaller molecules called **nucleotides**. A nucleotide, in turn, is made up of three components: a sugar molecule (deoxyribose), a phosphate unit, and one of four nitrogenous bases (Fig. 3-5). In DNA, nucleotides are stacked on top of one another to form a chain that is bonded along its bases to another nucleotide chain. Together these two chains twist to form a spiral, or helical, shape. Therefore, the DNA molecule is double-stranded and is described as forming a *double helix* that resembles a twisted ladder. If we

nucleotides Basic units of the DNA molecule, composed of a sugar, a phosphate, and one of four DNA bases.

Figure 3-5

Part of a DNA molecule. The illustration shows the two DNA strands with the sugar and phosphate backbone (blue/green) and the bases (labelled T, A, G, and C) extending toward the center.

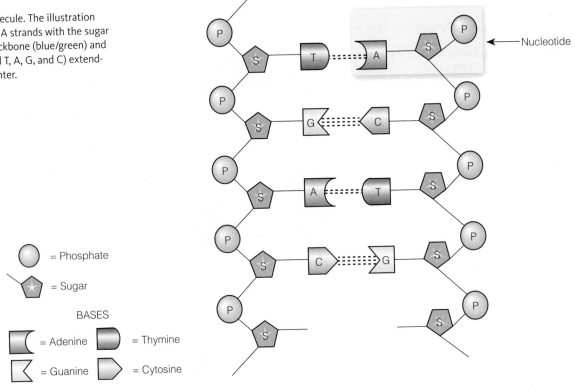

follow the twisted ladder analogy, the sugars and phosphates represent the two sides, while the bases and the bonds that join them form the rungs (Fig. 3-5).

The four bases are the key to how DNA works. These bases are *adenine, guanine, thymine,* and *cytosine,* and they're usually referred to by their initial letters: A, G, T, and C. When the double helix is formed, one type of base can pair, or bond, with only one other type. Therefore, base pairs (two DNA bases joined together) can form *only* between adenine and thymine, or between guanine and cytosine (see Fig. 3-5). This specificity is absolutely essential to the DNA molecule's ability to *replicate,* or make an exact copy of itself.

DNA Replication

For organisms to develop and grow, and for injured tissues to heal, somatic (body) cells have to multiply; and they do this by dividing to make exact copies of themselves. A cell divides one time to produce two "daughter" cells, each of which receives a full set of genetic material. This process is important because a cell can't function properly without the appropriate amount of DNA. But before a cell can divide, its DNA must first replicate or make an identical copy of itself.

Replication begins when **enzymes** break the bonds between bases throughout the DNA molecule, leaving the two previously joined strands of nucleotides with their bases exposed (Fig. 3-6). These exposed bases then attract unattached DNA nucleotides that are free-floating in the cell nucleus. (These free-floating nucleotides have been made by genes located elsewhere in the cell's DNA.) Since each base can pair with only one other type of base, the attraction between bases

enzymes Specialized proteins that initiate and direct chemical reactions in the body.

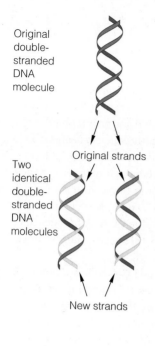

Original double-stranded DNA molecule

Original strands

Two identical double-stranded DNA molecules

New strands

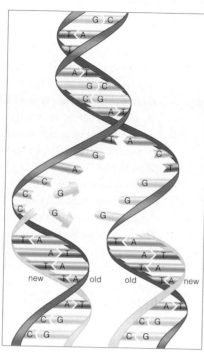

DNA double helix

Replication under way

Unattached nucleotides are attracted to their complementary nucleotides and thereby form a new strand

Replication complete

Figure 3-6

DNA replication. During DNA replication, the two strands of the DNA molecule (blue) are separated, and each strand serves as a template for the formation of a new strand (yellow). When replication is complete, there are two DNA molecules. Each molecule consists of one new and one original DNA strand.

occurs in a **complementary** way. What this means is that the two previously joined parental nucleotide chains serve as models, or templates, for forming new strands of nucleotides. As each new strand is formed, its bases are joined to the bases of an original strand. When the process is complete, there are two double-stranded DNA molecules exactly like the original one. Also, each newly formed molecule consists of one original nucleotide chain joined to a newly formed chain (see Fig. 3-6).

Protein Synthesis

The most important thing about DNA is that it directs cells to make proteins in a process called *protein synthesis*. Proteins are complex, three-dimensional molecules that function through their ability to bind to other molecules (Fig. 3-7). For example, the protein **hemoglobin**, found in red blood cells, is able to bind to oxygen, which it carries to cells throughout the body.

Proteins function in thousands of ways. Some are structural components of tissues. Collagen, which we mentioned in Chapter 1, is the most common protein in the body and is a major component of all connective tissues. Enzymes are also proteins, and they initiate and enhance chemical reactions. For instance, a digestive enzyme called *lactase* breaks down *lactose*, or milk sugar, into two simpler sugars. Another class of proteins includes many types of **hormones**. Hormones are produced by specialized

complementary In genetics, referring to the fact that DNA bases form pairs (called base pairs) in a precise manner. For example, adenine can bond only to thymine. These two bases are said to be complementary because one requires the other to form a complete DNA base pair.

hemoglobin A protein molecule that occurs in red blood cells and binds to oxygen molecules.

hormones Substances (usually proteins) that are produced by specialized cells and that travel to other parts of the body, where they influence chemical reactions and regulate various cellular functions.

Alpha chain   Alpha chain

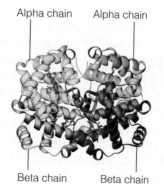

Beta chain   Beta chain

Figure 3-7

Diagrammatic representation of a hemoglobin molecule. Hemoglobin molecules are composed of four chains of amino acids (two alpha chains and two beta chains).

A Closer Look

Characteristics of the DNA Code

1. **The code is triplet.** Each amino acid is specified by a sequence of three bases in the mRNA (the codon), which in turn is coded for by three bases in the DNA (the triplet).

2. **The code is continuous, without pauses.** There are no pauses separating one triplet or codon from another. Thus, if a base should be deleted, the entire frame would be moved, drastically altering the message downstream for successive triplets or codons. Such a gross alteration is called a frameshift mutation. Note that although the code lacks "commas," it does contain "periods" in the form of three specific codons that act to stop translation.

3. **The code is redundant.** While there are 20 amino acids, there are 4 DNA bases and 64 possible DNA triplets or mRNA codons. Even considering the three "stop" messages, that still leaves 61 codons specifying the 20 amino acids. Thus, many amino acids are specified by more

than one codon (see Table 3-1). For example, leucine and serine are each coded for by six different codons. In fact, only two amino acids (methionine and tryptophan) are coded for by a single codon. Redundancy is useful. For one thing, it serves as a safety net by helping to reduce the likelihood of severe consequences if there is a change, or mutation, in a DNA base. For example, four different DNA triplets—CGA, CGG, CGT, and CGC—code for the amino acid alanine. If, in the codon CGA, A mutates to G, the resulting triplet, CGG, will still specify alanine; thus, there will be no functional change.

4. **The code is universal.** The same DNA code applies to all life on earth, from bacteria to oak trees to humans. That is, the same DNA triplets specify the same amino acids in all forms of life. This commonality is the basis for the methods used in recombinant DNA technology, and it implies biological continuity between species.

cells and then released into the bloodstream to circulate to other areas of the body, where they produce specific effects in tissues and organs. Insulin, for example, is a hormone produced by cells in the pancreas, and it causes cells in the liver and certain types of muscle tissue to absorb energy-producing glucose (sugar) from the blood. (Enzymes and hormones are discussed in more detail in Chapter 17.) Lastly, there are many kinds of proteins called **regulatory proteins** or *regulatory molecules*, which can attach directly to DNA segments to regulate the activities of genes (see p. 58). From this brief description, you can see that proteins make us what we are. For this reason, protein synthesis has to occur accurately, because if it doesn't, physiological development and cellular activities can be disrupted or even prevented.

Proteins are made up of chains of smaller molecules called **amino acids**. In all, there are 20 amino acids, 8 of which must be obtained from foods (see Chapter 17). The remaining 12 are produced by cells. These 20 amino acids are combined in different amounts and sequences to produce at least 90,000 different proteins. What makes proteins different from one another is the number and sequence of their amino acids; and for a protein to function accurately, its amino acids must be arranged in the correct order.

In part, DNA is a recipe for making a protein, since it's the sequence of DNA bases that ultimately determines the order of amino acids in a protein molecule. In the DNA instructions, a triplet, or group of three bases, specifies a particular amino acid (see "A Closer Look). For example, if a triplet consists of the base sequence cytosine, guanine, and adenine (CGA), it specifies the amino acid alanine (Table 3-1). If the next triplet in the chain consists of the sequence guanine, thymine, and cytosine (GTC), it refers to another amino acid—glutamine. So a DNA recipe might look like this: AGA CGA ACA ACC TAC TTT TTC CTT AAG GTC (but without the spaces).

regulatory proteins Proteins that can bind to certain DNA segments and modify the action of genes. Many are active only during certain stages of development.

amino acids Small molecules that are the components of proteins.

Table 3-1 The Genetic Code

Amino Acid Symbol	Amino Acid	mRNA Codon	DNA Triplet
Ala	Alanine	GCU, GCC, GCA, GCG	CGA, CGG, CGT, CGC
Arg	Arginine	CGU, CGC, CGA, CGG, AGA, AGG	GCA, GCG, GCT, GCC, TCT, TCC
Asn	Asparagine	AAU, AAC	TTA, TTG
Asp	Aspartic acid	GAU, GAC	CTA, CTG
Cys	Cysteine	UGU, UGC	ACA, ACG
Gln	Glutamine	CAA, CAG	GTT, GTC
Glu	Glutamic acid	GAA, GAG	CTT, CTC
Gly	Glycine	GGU, GGC, GGA, GGG	CCA, CCG, CCT, CCC
His	Histidine	CAU, CAC	GTA, GTG
Ile	Isoleucine	AUU, AUC, AUA	TAA, TAG, TAT
Leu	Leucine	UUA, UUG, CUU, CUC, CUA, CUG	AAT, AAC, GAA, GAG, GAT, GAC
Lys	Lysine	AAA, AAG	TTT, TTC
Met	Methionine	AUG	TAC
Phe	Phenylalanine	UUU, UUC	AAA, AAG
Pro	Proline	CCU, CCC, CCA, CCG	GGA, GGG, GGT, GGC
Ser	Serine	UCU, UCC, UCA, UCG, AGU, AGC	AGA, AGG, AGT, AGC, TCA, TCG
Thr	Threonine	ACU, ACC, ACA, ACG	TGA, TGG, TGT, TGC
Trp	Tryptophan	UGG	ACC
Tyr	Tyrosine	UAU, UAC	ATA, ATG
Val	Valine	GUU, GUC, GUA, GUG	CAA, CAG, CAT, CAC
Terminating triplets		UAA, UAG, UGA	ATT, ATC, ACT

Protein synthesis actually takes place outside the cell nucleus, in the cytoplasm, at one of the types of organelles we mentioned earlier, the ribosomes. But the DNA molecule can't leave the cell's nucleus. So the first step in protein synthesis is to copy the DNA message into a form of RNA called **messenger RNA (mRNA)**, which can pass through the nuclear membrane into the cytoplasm. RNA is similar to DNA, but it differs in some important ways:

1. It's single-stranded. (This is true for the forms we discuss here, but it's not true for all forms of RNA.)
2. It contains a different type of sugar.
3. It contains the base uracil as a substitute for the DNA base thymine. (Uracil binds to adenine, just as thymine does.)

The mRNA molecule forms on the DNA template in much the same way that new DNA molecules are assembled. As in DNA replication, the two DNA strands separate, but only partially, and one of these strands attracts free-floating RNA nucleotides (also produced in the cell), which are joined together on the DNA template. The formation of mRNA is called *transcription* because, in fact, the DNA code is being copied, or transcribed (Fig. 3-8). Transcription continues until a section of DNA called a terminator region (composed of one of three DNA triplets) is reached and the process stops (see Table 3-1). At this point, the mRNA strand, comprising anywhere from 5,000 to perhaps as many as 200,000 nucleotides, peels away from the DNA model, and a portion of it travels through the nuclear membrane to the

messenger RNA (mRNA) A form of RNA that's assembled on a sequence of DNA bases. It carries the DNA code to the ribosome during protein synthesis.

ribosome. Meanwhile, the bonds between the DNA bases are reestablished, and the DNA molecule is once more intact.

As the mRNA strand arrives at the ribosome, its message is translated in groups of three mRNA bases called "codons." (This stage of the process is called *translation* because at this point, the genetic instructions are decoded and implemented.) Therefore, mRNA codons specify one amino acid, just as DNA triplets do.

Another form of RNA, **transfer RNA (tRNA)**, is also essential to the assembly of a protein. Each tRNA molecule can bind to one specific amino acid, and during protein synthesis, a tRNA molecule takes the amino acid that matches the codon that is being translated to the ribosome (Fig. 3-9). The ribosome then joins that amino acid to another one in the order dictated by the sequence of mRNA codons. In this way, amino acids are linked together to form a structure that eventually functions as a protein or part of a protein.

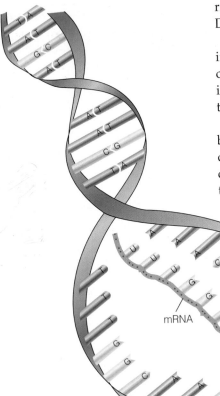

mRNA

DNA template strand

Figure 3-8

Transcription. In this illustration, the two DNA strands have partly separated. Messenger RNA (mRNA) nucleotides have been drawn to the template strand, and a strand of mRNA is being made. Note that the mRNA strand will exactly complement the DNA template strand, except that uracil (U) replaces thymine (T).

transfer RNA (tRNA) The type of RNA that binds to specific amino acids and transports them to the ribosome during protein synthesis.

mutation A change in DNA. The term can refer to changes in DNA bases (specifically called point mutations) as well as to changes in chromosome number and/or structure.

What Is a Gene?

The answer to this question is complicated, and the definition of the term "gene" is now a subject of debate. Textbooks used to compare genes to a string of beads, with each bead representing one gene on a chromosome. This analogy was used for more than 50 years because genes mostly occur in linear sequence along a chromosome. But now we know that DNA sequences that code for proteins may overlap. Also, it was previously thought that each gene codes for the production of only one particular protein. However, if this were true, we would need as many as 100,000 genes to produce the thousands of different kinds of proteins that we have. But when the human genome was sequenced in 2001 (International Human Genome Sequencing Consortium, 2001; Venter et al., 2001), scientists learned that humans have only between 25,000 and 30,000 genes, pretty much the same number as in most other mammals. Furthermore, protein coding genes (also called *coding sequences*), the DNA segments that actually are transcribed into proteins, make up only about 2 percent of the entire human genome! The other 98 percent is composed of various things, including so-called "noncoding DNA" (see p. 59). Clearly, these discoveries show that gene action was much more complicated than previously believed.

In this book, most of our discussion is confined to coding DNA segments, and we can loosely define a gene as *a segment of DNA that specifies the sequence of amino acids in a particular protein.* Those proteins composed of only a single such chain are produced through the action of a single gene. However, some proteins (such as collagen and hemoglobin) are composed of two or more amino acid chains, each resulting from the action of a different gene. So while some proteins result from the action of only one gene, others are produced by two or more. A gene may be composed of only a few hundred bases, or it may comprise thousands. If the sequence of bases is altered by **mutation** (a change in the DNA), then the manufacture of proteins may not happen, and the cell (or indeed the organism) may not function properly, if it functions at all.

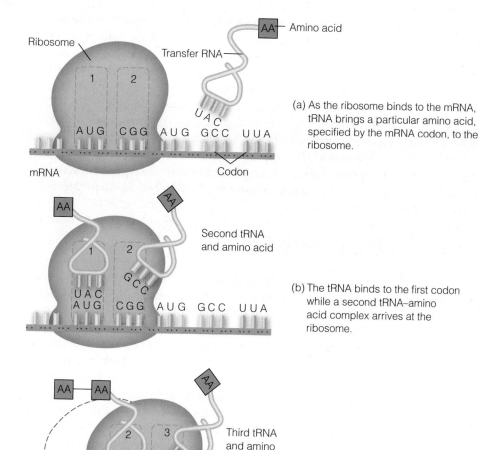

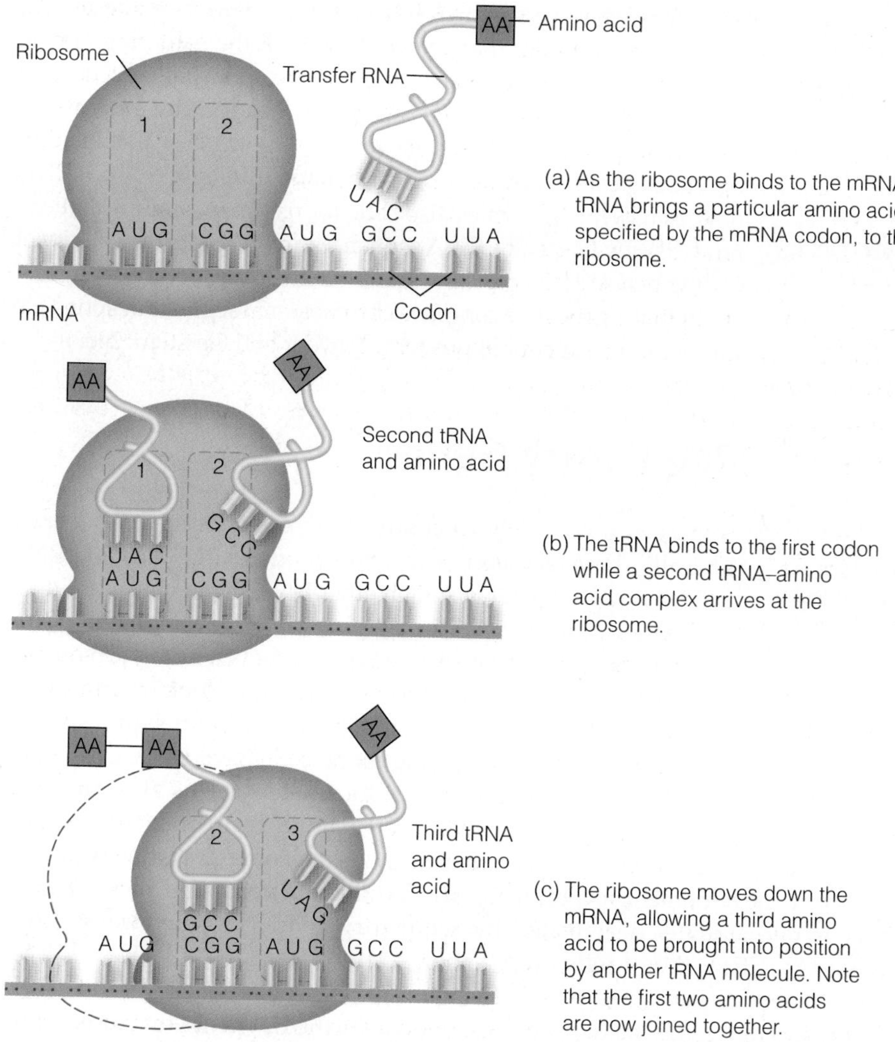

<figure>

Ribosome

Transfer RNA

AA — Amino acid

1   2

U A C

AUG CGG AUG GCC UUA

mRNA

Codon

(a) As the ribosome binds to the mRNA, tRNA brings a particular amino acid, specified by the mRNA codon, to the ribosome.

AA   AA

1   2

G C C

U A C

AUG CGG AUG GCC UUA

Second tRNA and amino acid

(b) The tRNA binds to the first codon while a second tRNA–amino acid complex arrives at the ribosome.

AA — AA   AA

2   3

G C C

U A G

AUG CGG AUG GCC UUA

Third tRNA and amino acid

(c) The ribosome moves down the mRNA, allowing a third amino acid to be brought into position by another tRNA molecule. Note that the first two amino acids are now joined together.

</figure>

Figure 3-9

Assembly of an amino acid chain in protein synthesis.

In recent years, geneticists have learned that only some parts of a gene, called **exons**, are actually transcribed into mRNA and thus code for specific amino acids, while most of the nucleotide sequences in a gene aren't expressed during protein synthesis. (By *expressed*, we mean that the DNA sequence is actually making a product.) In fact, some noncoding sequences, called **introns**, are initially transcribed into mRNA and then clipped out (Fig. 3-10; also see "A Closer Look," p. 59). This means that introns aren't represented in the newly formed mature mRNA segment, so they aren't translated into amino acid sequences. But they're still a part of the DNA molecule, and it's the combination of introns and exons, interspersed along a strand of DNA, that makes up the unit we call a gene.

But it gets even more complicated. The introns that are snipped out of a gene aren't always the same ones. This means that the exons can be combined in different ways to make segments that code for more than one protein. Therefore, genes can overlap one another, and there can also be genes within genes (Fig. 3-11)! So much for beads on a string.

Our earlier definition of a gene is a traditional one, but as we mentioned, the definition has changed in response to new information. (Incidentally, this

exons Segments of genes that are transcribed and are involved in protein synthesis. (The prefix "ex" denotes that these segments are expressed.)

introns Segments of genes that are initially transcribed and then deleted. Because they aren't expressed, they aren't involved in protein synthesis.

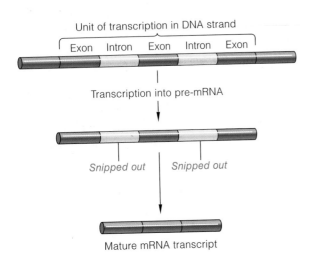

Unit of transcription in DNA strand

Exon | Intron | Exon | Intron | Exon

Transcription into pre-mRNA

Snipped out   Snipped out

Mature mRNA transcript

Figure **3-10**

Diagram of a DNA sequence being transcribed. The introns are deleted from the pre-mRNA before it leaves the cell's nucleus. The remaining mature RNA contains only exons, which will code for a protein or part of a protein.

homeobox genes An evolutionarily ancient family of regulatory genes that directs the development of the overall body plan and the segmentation of body tissues.

Figure **3-11**

Diagrammatic representation of how our views of gene function have changed. (a) According to the traditional view, genes are discrete segments of DNA, each coding for a specific protein, and only one of the two DNA strands are involved in protein synthesis. (b)We now know that as different introns are deleted during translation, the remaining exons can form several overlapping coding sequences, each of which can be considered a gene. That is, a portion of one gene can also be part of another gene. Also, both DNA strands are functional.

illustrates what we said in Chapter 1 about how hypotheses and theories can, and do, change over time with the gathering of new data.) The notion of a *one gene–one protein* relationship, which was a core concept of biology for a few decades, has gone by the wayside for a number of reasons. For one thing, we now know that in addition to proteins, DNA also codes for many different kinds of RNA not discussed here. Genes also code for *regulatory proteins* that can bind directly to specific DNA sequences and regulate the activity of coding genes. Thus, one new and more inclusive definition simply states that a gene is "a complete chromosomal segment responsible for making a functional product" (Snyder and Gerstein, 2003).

Regulatory Genes

Some genes act solely to control the expression of other genes. Basically, these *regulatory genes* make products (proteins and RNA and DNA segments) that switch other DNA segments on or off.

DNA deactivation during embryonic development is one example of how regulatory genes work. As you know, all somatic cells contain the same genetic information; but in any given cell, only a fraction of the DNA is actually involved in protein synthesis. For example, like the cells of the stomach lining, bone cells have DNA that codes for the production of digestive enzymes. But fortunately for us all, bone cells don't produce digestive enzymes. Instead, they manufacture collagen, the main organic component of bone. This is because cells become specialized during embryonic development to perform only certain functions, and most of their DNA is permanently deactivated by regulatory genes. In other words, they become specific types of cells, such as bone cells.

Homeobox genes are extremely important regulatory genes, and there are several different kinds. Perhaps the best known are the *Hox* genes that direct early segmentation of embryonic tissues, including those that give rise to the spine and

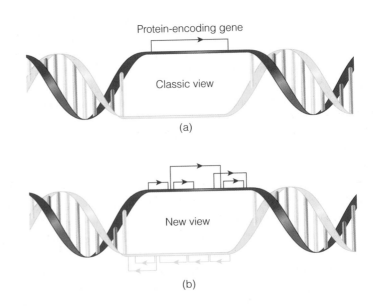

Protein-encoding gene

Classic view

(a)

New view

(b)

A Closer Look

What's All This Junk? Or Is It Junk?

In all fields of inquiry, important discoveries always raise new questions that eventually lead to further revelations. There's probably no statement that could be more appropriately applied to the field of genetics. For example, in 1977, geneticists recognized that during protein synthesis, the initially formed mRNA molecule contains many more nucleotides than are represented in the subsequently produced protein. This finding led to the discovery of *introns*, portions of genes that don't code for, or specify, proteins. What happens is that once the mRNA molecule peels away from the DNA template, but before it leaves the cell's nucleus, enzymes snip out the introns. The original mRNA molecule is sometimes called pre-mRNA, but once the introns have been deleted, the remainder is mature mRNA. It's the mature mRNA that leaves the nucleus carrying its code for protein production.

In the 1980s, geneticists learned that only about 2 percent of the roughly 3 billion DNA bases in the human genome is contained within *exons*, the segments that actually provide the code for protein synthesis. This means that while an estimated 28 percent of human DNA is composed of genes (including introns and exons), only 5 percent of the DNA within these genes is actually composed of coding sequences (Baltimore, 2001). And we also know that a human gene can specify the production of as many as three different proteins by using different combinations of the exons interspersed within it (Pennisi, 2001).

With only 2 percent of the human genome directing protein synthesis, humans have more noncoding DNA than any other species so far studied (Vogel, 2001). Invertebrates and some vertebrates have only small amounts of noncoding sequences, and yet they're fully functional organisms. So just what does all this noncoding DNA (originally called "junk DNA") do in humans?

Almost half of all human DNA consists of noncoding segments that are repeated over and over and over. Depending on their length, these segments have been referred to as *tandem repeats*, *satellites*, or *microsatellites*, but now they're frequently lumped together and called *copy number variants (CNVs)*. Microsatellites have an extremely high mutation rate and can gain or lose repeated segments and then return to their former length. But this tendency to mutate means that the number of repeats in a given microsatellite varies between individuals. And this tremendous variation has been the basis for DNA fingerprinting, a technique commonly used to provide evidence in criminal cases (see p. 73). Actually, anthropologists are now using microsatellite variation for all kinds of research, from tracing movements of peoples to paternity testing in nonhuman primates (see p. 182).

Some of the variations in microsatellite composition are associated with various disorders, so we can't help wondering why humans have them. One possible answer is that some noncoding regions may switch functioning genes on and off. Or they may modulate the activities of genes in other ways. Also, by losing or adding material, they can alter the sequences of bases in genes, thus becoming a source of mutation in functional genes. And these mutations are a source of genetic variation..

Lastly, there are transposable elements (TEs), the so-called *jumping genes*. These are DNA sequences that can make thousands of copies of themselves, and these copies are then scattered throughout the genome. One family of TEs, called *Alu*, is found only in primates. About 5 percent of the human genome is made up of *Alu* sequences, and although most of these are shared with other primates, about 7,000 are unique to humans (Chimpanzee Sequencing and Analysis Consortium, 2005).

TEs mainly code for proteins that enable them to move about, and because they can land right in the middle of coding sequences (exons), TEs cause mutations. Some of these mutations are harmful, and TEs have been associated with numerous disease conditions, including some forms of cancer (Deragon and Capy, 2000). But at the same time, TEs essentially create new exons, and by doing this they actually generate variations for natural selection to act on. Moreover, they also regulate the activities of many genes, including those involved in development. So, rather than being junk, TEs are increasingly being recognized as serving extremely important functions in the evolutionary process, including the introduction of genetic change that has led to the origins of new lineages.

thoracic muscles. They also interact with other genes to determine the identity and characteristics of developing body segments and structures, but not their actual development. For example, *Hox* genes determine where, in a developing embryo, limb buds will appear. They also establish the number and overall pattern of the different types of vertebrae, the bones that make up the spine (Fig. 3-12).

All homeobox genes are highly conserved, meaning they've been maintained pretty much throughout evolutionary history. They're present in worms, insects, and vertebrates, and they don't vary greatly from species to species. Counterparts of human homeobox genes are present in fruit flies, for example, where they perform similar functions. This type of conservation means that not only are these genes vitally important, but they also evolved from genes that were present in some of the earliest forms of life. Also, changes in the behavior of homeobox genes are probably responsible for various physical differences between closely related species. For example, some of the anatomical differences between humans and chimpanzees are almost certainly the results of evolutionary changes in homeobox and other regulatory genes in both lineages. For these reasons, homeobox genes are now a critical area of research in evolutionary and developmental biology (see p. 136).

In spite of all the recently obtained information that has changed some of our views about DNA, there is one fact that doesn't change. The genetic code is universal, and, at least on earth, DNA is the genetic material in all forms of life. The DNA of all organisms, from bacteria to fruit flies to human beings, is composed of

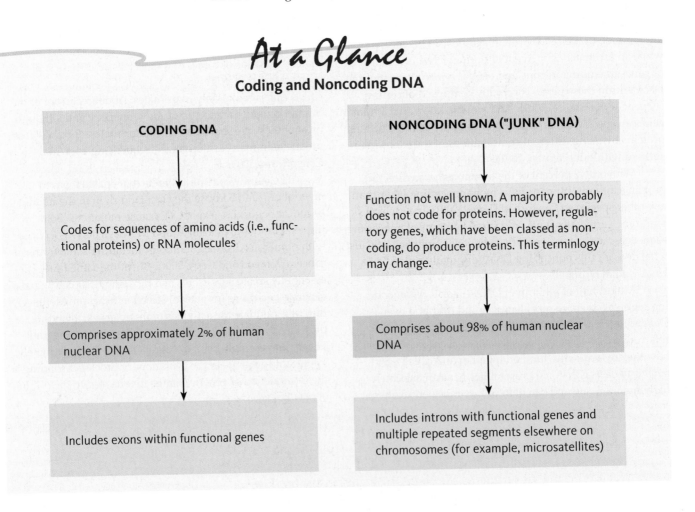

At a Glance
Coding and Noncoding DNA

CODING DNA	NONCODING DNA ("JUNK" DNA)
Codes for sequences of amino acids (i.e., functional proteins) or RNA molecules	Function not well known. A majority probably does not code for proteins. However, regulatory genes, which have been classed as noncoding, do produce proteins. This terminlogy may change.
Comprises approximately 2% of human nuclear DNA	Comprises about 98% of human nuclear DNA
Includes exons within functional genes	Includes introns with functional genes and multiple repeated segments elsewhere on chromosomes (for example, microsatellites)

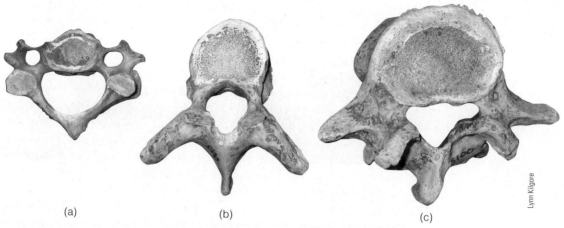

(a) (b) (c)

Lynn Kilgore

Figure 3-12

The differences in these three vertebrae, from different regions of the spine, are caused by the action of *Hox* genes during embryonic development. The cervical (neck) vertebrae (a) have characteristics that differentiate them from the thoracic vertebrae (b), attached to the ribs, and also from the lumbar vertebrae (c) of the lower back. *Hox* genes determine the overall pattern not only of each type of vertebra but also of each individual vertebra.

the same molecules using the same kinds of instructions. Consequently, the DNA triplet CGA, for example, specifies the amino acid alanine, regardless of species. These similarities imply biological relationships among, and an ultimate common ancestry for, all forms of life. What makes fruit flies distinct from humans isn't differences in the DNA material itself, but differences in how that material is arranged and how it's regulated.

Mutation: When Genes Change

The best way to understand how genetic material functions is to see what happens when it changes, or mutates. Normal adult hemoglobin is made up of four amino acid chains (two *alpha* chains and two *beta* chains) that are the direct products of gene action. Each beta chain is in turn composed of 146 amino acids. There are several hemoglobin disorders with genetic origins, and perhaps the best known of these is **sickle-cell anemia**, which results from a defect in the beta chain. People with sickle-cell anemia inherit, from *both* parents, a mutated form of the gene that directs the formation of the beta chain. This mutation is caused by the substitution of one amino acid (*valine*) for the amino acid that's normally present (*glutamic acid*). This single amino acid substitution on the beta chain results in the production of a less-efficient form of hemoglobin called hemoglobin S (Hb^S) instead of the normal form, which is called hemoglobin A (Hb^A). In situations where the availability of oxygen is reduced, such as at high altitude, or when oxygen requirements are increased through exercise, red blood cells with Hb^S collapse and become sickle-shaped (Fig. 3-13). What follows is a cascade of events, all of which result in severe anemia and its consequences (Fig. 3-14). Briefly, these consequences include impaired circulation from blocked capillaries, red blood cell destruction, oxygen deprivation to vital organs (including the brain), and, without treatment, death.

sickle-cell anemia A severe inherited hemoglobin disorder in which red blood cells collapse when deprived of oxygen. It results from inheriting two copies of a mutant allele. This allele is caused by a single base substitution in the DNA.

Figure 3-13

(a) Scanning electron micrograph of a normal, fully oxygenated red blood cell.
(b) Scanning electron micrograph of a collapsed, sickle-shaped red blood cell that contains HB^S.

(a)

(b)

© Dr. Stanley Flegler / Visuals Unlimited

Figure 3-14

Diagram showing the cascade of symptoms that can occur in people with sickle-cell anemia.

People who inherit the altered form of the gene from only one parent don't have sickle-cell anemia, but they do have what's called *sickle-cell trait*. But fortunately for them, they're much less severely affected because only about 40 percent of their hemoglobin is abnormal.

The cause of all the serious problems associated with sickle-cell anemia is a change in the *Hb* gene. Remember that the beta chains of normal hemoglobin and the sickle-cell variety each have 146 amino acids, and 145 of the amino acids in both forms are identical. What's more, to emphasize the importance of a seemingly minor alteration, consider that triplets of DNA bases are required to specify amino acids. Therefore, it takes 438 bases (146 × 3) to produce the chain of 146 amino acids that forms the adult hemoglobin beta chain. But a change in only one of these 438 bases produces the life-threatening complications seen in sickle-cell anemia. Figure 3-15 shows a DNA base sequence and the resulting

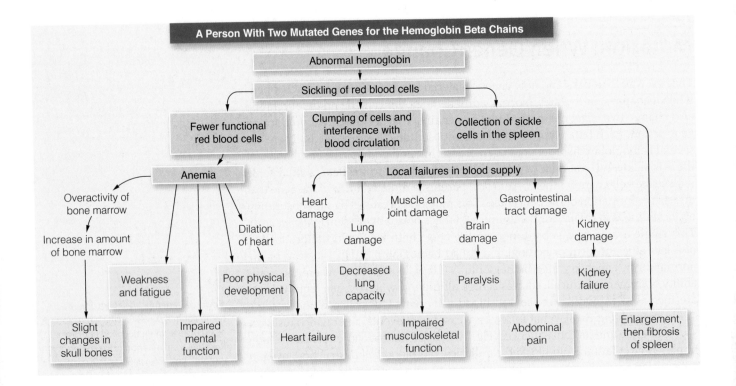

amino acid products for both normal and sickling hemoglobin. As you can see, a single base substitution (from CTC to CAC) can result in an altered amino acid sequence, from

. . . proline—*glutamic acid*—glutamic acid . . .

to

. . . proline—*valine*—glutamic acid . . .

This kind of change in the genetic code is referred to as a **point mutation**, and in evolution, it's a common and important source of new genetic variation in populations. Point mutations, like the one that causes sickle-cell anemia, probably occur fairly frequently. But for a new mutation to be evolutionarily significant, it must be passed on to offspring and eventually become more common in a population. Once point mutations occur, their fate in populations depends on the other evolutionary forces, especially natural selection. Depending on how beneficial a mutation is, it may become more common over time; if it's disadvantageous, it probably won't. Sickle-cell anemia is the best-demonstrated example of natural selection acting on humans; it shows us how, under certain circumstances, a disadvantageous mutation can become more frequent in some environments. This is a point that we'll consider in more detail in Chapter 4.

POINT MUTATION				
Normal Hemoglobin			**Sickling Hemoglobin**	
DNA sequence	Amino acid		Amino acid	DNA sequence
• • • • •	#1		#1	• • • • •
T G A	#4 Threonine		#4 Threonine	T G A
G G A	#5 Proline		#5 Proline	G G A
C T C	#6 Glutamic acid		#6 Valine	C A C
C T C	#7 Glutamic acid		#7 Glutamic acid	C T C
T T T	#8 Lysine		#8 Lysine	T T T
• • • • •	#146		#146	• • • • •
#1652 (including intron sequences)			#146	#1652

Figure **3-15**

Substitution of one base at position 6 produces sickling hemoglobin.

point mutation   A chemical change in a single base of a DNA sequence.

Chromosomes

Throughout much of a cell's life, its DNA (all six feet of it!) is involved in directing cellular functions and exists as an uncoiled, granular substance called **chromatin**. However, at various times in the life of most types of cells, normal functions are interrupted and the cell divides. Cell division produces new cells, and it's during this process that the chromatin becomes tightly coiled and is visible under a microscope as a set of discrete structures called **chromosomes** (Fig. 3-16).

A chromosome is composed of a DNA molecule and proteins (Fig. 3-17). During normal cell function, if chromosomes were visible, they would look like single-stranded structures. But during the early stages of cell division, they're made up of two strands, or two DNA molecules, joined together at a constricted area called the **centromere**. The reason there are two strands is simple: The DNA molecules have *replicated*, and one strand of a chromosome is an exact copy of the other.

Every species has a specific number of chromosomes in somatic cells (Table 3-2). Humans have 46, while chimpanzees and gorillas have 48. This difference doesn't mean that humans have less DNA than chimpanzees and gorillas do. It just means that the DNA is packaged differently.

There are two basic types of chromosomes: **autosomes** and **sex chromosomes**. Autosomes carry genetic information that governs all physical characteristics except primary sex determination. The two sex chromosomes are the X and Y chromosomes; in mammals, the Y chromosome is directly involved in determining maleness. Although the X chromosome is called a sex chromosome, it actually functions more like an autosome because it's not involved in primary sex determination, and it influences several other traits.

Among mammals, all genetically normal females have two X chromosomes (XX), and they're female only because they don't have a Y chromosome. (In other words, female is the default setting.) All genetically normal males have one X and one Y chromosome (XY). In other classes of animals, such as birds or insects, primary sex determination is governed by various other chromosomal mechanisms.

chromatin The loose, diffuse form of DNA seen when a cell isn't dividing. When it condenses, chromatin forms into chromosomes.

chromosomes Discrete structures composed of DNA and protein found only in the nuclei of cells. Chromosomes are visible under magnification only during certain phases of cell division.

centromere The constricted portion of a chromosome. After replication, the two strands of a double-stranded chromosome are joined at the centromere.

autosomes All chromosomes except the sex chromosomes.

sex chromosomes In mammals, the X and Y chromosomes.

Figure 3-16

Scanning electron micrograph of human chromosomes during cell division. Note that these chromosomes are composed of two strands, or two DNA molecules.

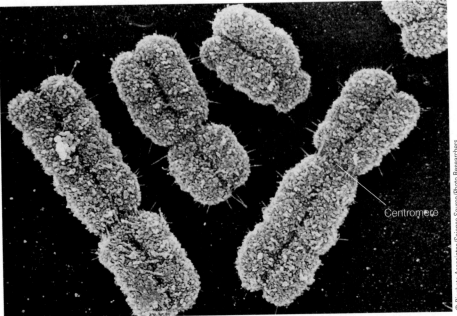

Centromere

© Biophoto Associates/Science Source/Photo Researchers

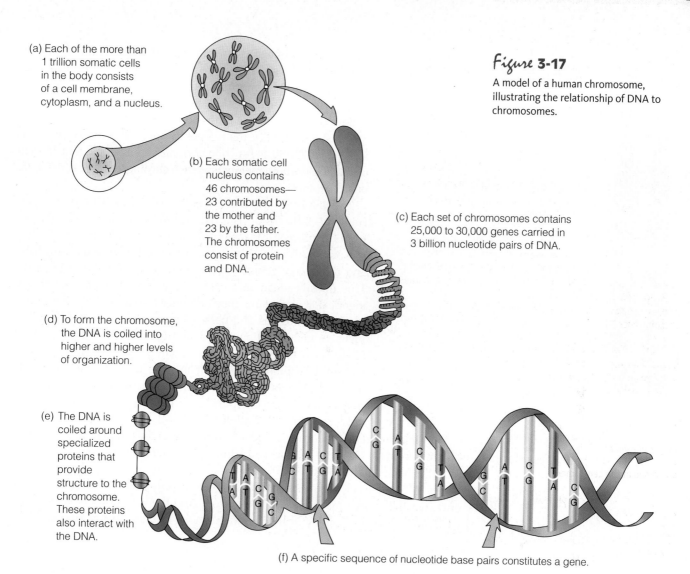

(a) Each of the more than 1 trillion somatic cells in the body consists of a cell membrane, cytoplasm, and a nucleus.

Figure 3-17

A model of a human chromosome, illustrating the relationship of DNA to chromosomes.

(b) Each somatic cell nucleus contains 46 chromosomes— 23 contributed by the mother and 23 by the father. The chromosomes consist of protein and DNA.

(c) Each set of chromosomes contains 25,000 to 30,000 genes carried in 3 billion nucleotide pairs of DNA.

(d) To form the chromosome, the DNA is coiled into higher and higher levels of organization.

(e) The DNA is coiled around specialized proteins that provide structure to the chromosome. These proteins also interact with the DNA.

(f) A specific sequence of nucleotide base pairs constitutes a gene.

Table 3-2 Standard Chromosomal Complement in Various Organisms

Organism	Chromosome Number in Somatic Cells	Chromosome Number in Gametes
Human (*Homo sapiens*)	46	23
Chimpanzee (*Pan troglodytes*)	48	24
Gorilla (*Gorilla gorilla*)	48	24
Dog (*Canis familiaris*)	78	39
Chicken (*Gallus domesticus*)	78	39
Frog (*Rana pipiens*)	26	13
Housefly (*Musca domestica*)	12	6
Onion (*Allium cepa*)	16	8
Corn (*Zea mays*)	20	10
Tobacco (*Nicotiana tabacum*)	48	24

Source: Cummings, 2000, p. 16.

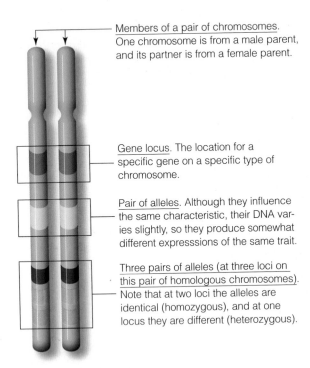

Members of a pair of chromosomes. One chromosome is from a male parent, and its partner is from a female parent.

Gene locus. The location for a specific gene on a specific type of chromosome.

Pair of alleles. Although they influence the same characteristic, their DNA varies slightly, so they produce somewhat different expresssions of the same trait.

Three pairs of alleles (at three loci on this pair of homologous chromosomes). Note that at two loci the alleles are identical (homozygous), and at one locus they are different (heterozygous).

Figure 3-18

As this diagram illustrates, alleles are located at the same locus on paired chromosomes, but they aren't always identical. For the sake of simplicity, they are shown here on single-stranded chromosomes.

locus   (pl., loci) (lo´-kus, lo-sigh´) The position on a chromosome where a given gene occurs. The term is sometimes used interchangeably with *gene*.

alleles   Alternate forms of a gene. Alleles occur at the same locus on paired chromosomes and thus govern the same trait. But because they're different, their action may result in different expressions of that trait. The term *allele* is sometimes used synonymously with *gene*.

karyotype   The chromosomal complement of an individual, or what is typical for a species. Usually displayed in a photo micrograph, the chromosomes are arranged in pairs and according to size and position of the centromere.

Chromosomes occur in pairs, so all normal human somatic cells have 22 pairs of autosomes and one pair of sex chromosomes (23 pairs in all). Abnormal numbers of autosomes, with few exceptions, are fatal—usually soon after conception. Although abnormal numbers of sex chromosomes aren't usually fatal, they may result in sterility and frequently have other consequences as well (see p. 72). So, to function normally, it's essential for a human cell to possess both members of each chromosomal pair, or a total of 46 chromosomes.

Offspring inherit one member of each chromosomal pair from the father (the paternal chromosome) and one member from the mother (the maternal chromosome). Members of chromosomal pairs are alike in size and position of the centromere, and they carry genetic information governing the same traits. This doesn't mean that partner chromosomes are genetically identical; it just means they influence the same traits. For example, on both copies of a person's ninth chromosomes, there's a **locus**, or gene position, that determines which of the four ABO blood types (A, B, AB, or O) he or she will have. However, these two ninth chromosomes might not have identical DNA segments at the ABO locus. In other words, at numerous genetic loci, there may be more than one possible form of a gene, and these different forms are called **alleles** (Fig 3-18).

Alleles are alternate forms of a gene that can direct the cell to produce slightly different forms of the same product and, ultimately, different expressions of traits—as in the hemoglobin S (Hb^S) example. At the ABO locus, there are three possible alleles: *A*, *B*, and *O*. However, since individuals have only two ninth chromosomes, only two alleles are present in any one person. And the variation in alleles at the ABO locus is what accounts for the variation among humans in ABO blood type.

Karyotyping Chromosomes

One method frequently used to examine chromosomes in an individual is to produce a **karyotype**. (An example of a human karyotype is shown in Fig. 3-19.) Chromosomes used in karyotypes are obtained from dividing cells. (You'll remember that chromosomes are visible only during cell division.) For example, white blood cells, because they're easily obtained, can be cultured, chemically treated, and microscopically examined to identify the ones that are dividing. These cells are then photographed through a microscope to produce *photomicrographs* of intact, double-stranded chromosomes. Partner chromosomes are then matched up, and the entire set is arranged in descending order by size so that the largest (chromosome 1) appears first.

Karyotyping has numerous practical applications. Physicians and genetic counselors routinely use karyotypes to help diagnose chromosomal disorders in patients, and they're used in prenatal testing to identify chromosomal abnormalities in developing fetuses. Karyotype analysis has also revealed many chromosomal similarities shared by different species, including humans and nonhuman primates. However, now that scientists can compare the genomes of species directly, karyotyping probably won't continue being used for this purpose.

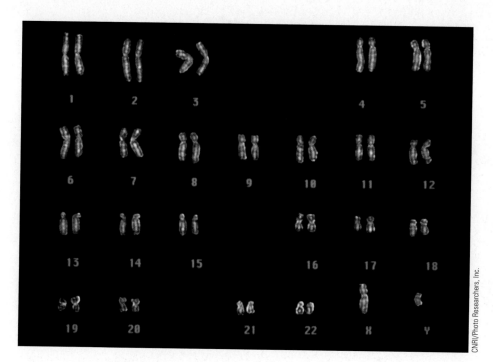

CNRI/Photo Researchers, Inc.

Figure **3-19**

A karyotype of a human male with the chromosomes arranged by size, position of the centromere, and banding pattern.

Cell Division

As we mentioned earlier, normal cellular function is periodically interrupted so the cell can divide. Cell division in somatic cells is called **mitosis**, and it's the way these cells reproduce. Mitosis occurs during growth and development; it also repairs injured tissues and replaces older cells with newer ones. But while mitosis produces new somatic cells, another type of cell division, called **meiosis**, may lead to the development of new individuals, since it produces reproductive cells, or gametes.

Mitosis

In the early stages of mitosis, a human somatic cell has 46 double-stranded chromosomes, and as the cell begins to divide, these chromosomes line up in random order along the center of the cell (Fig. 3-20). As the cell wall starts to constrict at the center, the chromosomes split apart at the centromere, so that the two strands are separated. Once the two strands are apart, they pull away from each other and move to opposite ends of the dividing cell. Each strand is now a distinct chromosome, composed of one DNA molecule. Following the separation of chromosome strands, the cell membrane pinches in and becomes sealed, so that two new cells are formed, each with a full complement of DNA, or 46 chromosomes.

Mitosis is referred to as *simple cell division* because a somatic cell divides one time to produce two daughter cells that are genetically identical to each other and to the original cell. In mitosis, the original cell possesses 46 chromosomes, and each new daughter cell inherits an exact copy of all 46. This precision is made possible by the DNA molecule's ability to replicate. Therefore, DNA replication is what ensures that the quantity and quality of the genetic material remain constant from one generation of cells to the next.

We should mention here that certain types of somatic cells don't divide. Red blood cells are produced continuously by specialized cells in bone marrow, but

mitosis Simple cell division; the process by which somatic cells divide to produce two identical daughter cells.

meiosis Cell division in specialized cells in ovaries and testes. Meiosis involves two divisions and results in four daughter cells, each containing only half the original number of chromosomes. These cells can develop into gametes.

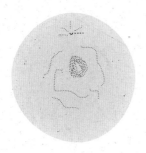
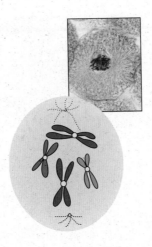
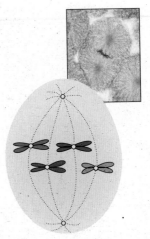

(a) The cell is involved in metabolic activities. DNA replication occurs, but chromosomes are not visible.

(b) The nuclear membrane disappears, and double-stranded chromosomes are visible.

(c) The chromosomes align themselves at the center of the cell.

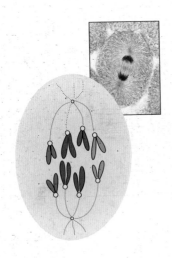
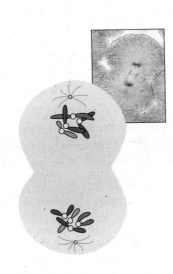

(d) The chromosomes split at the centromere, and the strands separate and move to opposite ends of the dividing cell.

(e) The cell membrane pinches in as the cell continues to divide. The chromosomes begin to uncoil (not shown here).

(f) After mitosis is complete, there are two identical daughter cells. The nuclear membrane is present, and chromosomes are no longer visible.

Figure **3-20**
Mitosis. The blue images next to some of these illustrations are photomicrographs of actual chromosomes in a dividing cell.

they can't divide because they have no nucleus and no nuclear DNA. Once the brain and nervous system are fully developed, brain and nerve cells (neurons) don't divide either, although there's currently some debate about this. Liver cells also don't divide after growth has stopped unless this vital organ is damaged through injury or disease. With these three exceptions (red blood cells, mature neurons, and liver cells), somatic cells are regularly duplicated through the process of mitosis.

Meiosis

In some ways, meiosis is similar to mitosis, but it's a more complicated process. In meiosis there are two divisions instead of one. Also, meiosis produces four daughter cells, not two, and each of the four cells contains only half the original number of chromosomes.

During meiosis, specialized cells in male testes and female ovaries divide and eventually develop into sperm and egg cells. Initially, these cells contain the full complement of chromosomes (46 in humans), but after the first division (called *reduction division*), the number of chromosomes in the two resulting daughter cells is 23, or half the original amount (see Fig. 3-21). This reduction of chromosome number is a critical feature of meiosis because the resulting gamete, with its 23 chromosomes, may eventually unite with another gamete that also has 23 chromosomes. The product of this union is a *zygote*, or fertilized egg, in which the original number of chromosomes (46) has been restored. In other words, a zygote inherits the exact amount of DNA it needs (half from each parent) to develop and function normally. If it weren't for reduction division in meiosis, it wouldn't be possible to maintain the correct number of chromosomes from one generation to the next.

During the first meiotic division, partner chromosomes come together to form *pairs* of double-stranded chromosomes. Then these pairs line up along the cell's center. Pairing of partner chromosomes is essential, because while they're together, members of pairs exchange genetic information in a process called **recombination**. Pairing is also important because it ensures that each new daughter cell receives only one member of each pair.

As the cell begins to divide, the chromosomes themselves remain intact (that is, double-stranded), but *members of pairs* separate and migrate to opposite ends of the cell. After the first division, there are two new daughter cells, but they aren't identical to each other or to the parental cell. They're different because each cell contains only one member of each chromosome pair (that is, only 23 chromosomes), each of which still has two strands. Also, because of recombination, each chromosome is somewhat different from its predecessor because it now contains some alleles it didn't have before.

The second meiotic division happens pretty much the same way as in mitosis. In the two newly formed cells, the 23 double-stranded chromosomes line up at the cell's center, and the strands of each chromosome separate and move apart. Once this second division is completed, there are four daughter cells, each with 23 single-stranded chromosomes, or 23 DNA molecules. (For a simplified comparison of mitosis and meiosis, see Fig. 3-22.)

The Evolutionary Significance of Meiosis

Meiosis occurs in all sexually reproducing organisms, and it's an extremely important evolutionary innovation because it increases genetic variation in populations. Members of sexually reproducing species aren't genetically identical **clones** of other individuals because they receive genetic contributions from two parents. In human matings, a staggering number of genetic combinations can result in the possible offspring of two parents. From just the **random assortment** of chromosome pairs lining up along the center of the cell during the first division of meiosis, each parent can produce around 8 million genetically different gametes. And given the combined probability accounting for both parents, the total number of possible genetic combinations for any human mating is about 70 trillion! Each individual thus

recombination The exchange of genetic material between homologous chromosomes during meiosis; also sometimes called *crossing over*.

clones Organisms that are genetically identical to another organism. The term may also be used to refer to genetically identical DNA segments, molecules, or cells.

random assortment The chance distribution of chromosomes to daughter cells during meiosis; along with recombination, the source of variation resulting from meiosis.

Figure **3-21**

Diagrammatic representation of meiosis. The gray circles are photomicrographs of actual chromosomes in a dividing cell.

Chromosomes are not visible as DNA replication occurs in a cell preparing to divide.

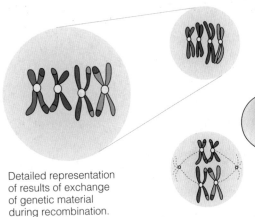

Double-stranded chromosomes become visible, and partner chromosomes exchange genetic material in a process called recombination or crossing over.

Detailed representation of results of exchange of genetic material during recombination.

Chromosome pairs migrate to the center of the cell.

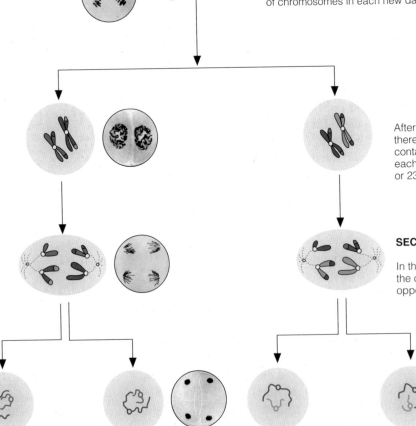

FIRST DIVISION (reduction division)

Partner chromosomes separate, and members of each pair move to opposite ends of the dividing cell. This results in only half the original number of chromosomes in each new daughter cell.

After the first meiotic division, there are two daughter cells, each containing only one member of each original chromosomal pair, or 23 nonpartner chromosomes.

SECOND DIVISION

In this division, the chromosomes split a the centromere, and the strands move to opposite sides of the cell.

After the second division, meiosis results in four daughte cells. These may mature to become functional gametes, containing only half the DNA in the original cell.

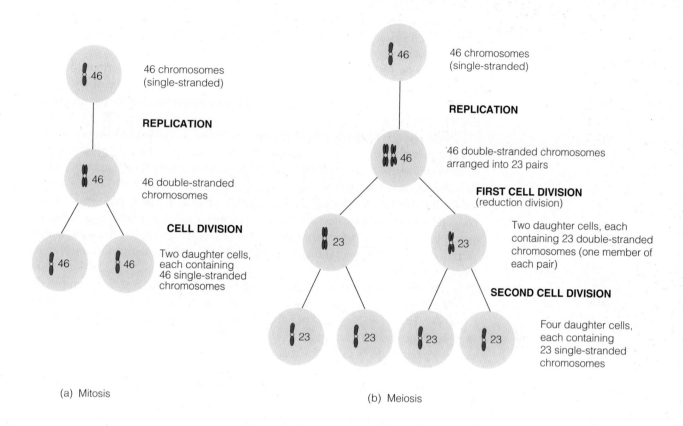

(a) Mitosis

(b) Meiosis

represents a unique combination of genes that in all likelihood has never occurred before and will never occur again.

As you can see, genetic diversity is considerably enhanced by meiosis, and this diversity is essential if species are to adapt to changing selective pressures. As we mentioned in Chapter 2, natural selection acts on genetic variation in populations; so if all individuals were genetically identical, natural selection would have nothing to act on and evolution couldn't occur. In all species, *mutation* is the only source of new genetic variation because it produces new alleles. But sexually reproducing species have an additional advantage because recombination produces new *arrangements* of genetic information, potentially providing additional material for selection to act on. In fact, the influence of meiosis on genetic variation is the main advantage of sexual reproduction. Thus, sexual reproduction and meiosis are of major evolutionary importance because they contribute to the role of natural selection in populations.

Problems with Meiosis

If the process of meiosis doesn't go exactly right, normal fetal development can't occur. If chromosomes or chromosome strands don't completely separate during either of the two meiotic divisions, serious problems can develop. This failure to separate is called **nondisjunction**. The result of nondisjunction is that one of the daughter cells receives two copies of the affected chromosome, while the other daughter cell receives none. If such an affected gamete unites with a normal gamete containing 23 chromosomes, the resulting zygote will have either 45 or 47 chromosomes. Having only one member of a chromosome pair is referred to as *monosomy*. The term *trisomy* refers to the presence of three copies of a particular chromosome.

Figure **3-22**

Mitosis and meiosis compared. In mitosis, one division produces two daughter cells, each of which contains 46 chromosomes. Meiosis is characterized by two divisions. After the first, there are two cells, each containing only 23 chromosomes (one member of each original chromosome pair). Each daughter cell divides again, so that the final result is four cells, each with only half the original number of chromosomes.

nondisjunction   The failure of partner chromosomes or chromosome strands to separate during cell division.

You can appreciate the potential effects of an abnormal number of chromosomes if you think about the fact that a zygote reproduces itself through mitosis. Every cell of the developing body is a descendant of that one-celled zygote and will therefore have the abnormal number of chromosomes. This is so serious that most abnormal numbers of autosomes are lethal, and embryos with more or fewer than 44 autosomes are usually spontaneously aborted, frequently before the pregnancy is even recognized.

Trisomy 21, formerly called Down syndrome, is caused by the presence of three copies of chromosome 21, and it's the only example of an abnormal number of autosomes that's compatible with life beyond the first few years after birth. Trisomy 21 occurs in approximately 1 out of every 1,000 live births and is associated with various developmental and health problems. These problems include congenital heart defects (seen in about 40 percent of affected newborns), increased susceptibility to respiratory infections, and leukemia. However, the most widely recognized effect is mental impairment, which is variably expressed and ranges from mild to severe.

Trisomy 21 is partly associated with advanced maternal age. For example, the risk of a 20-year-old woman giving birth to an affected infant is just 0.05 percent (5 in 10,000). However, 3 percent of babies born to mothers 45 and older are affected (a 60-fold increase). Actually, most affected infants are born to women under the age of 35, but that's because the majority of women who have babies are less than 35 years old. The increased prevalence of trisomy 21 with maternal age is thought to be related to the fact that meiosis actually begins in females during their own fetal development and then stops, only to be resumed and completed at ovulation. This means that a woman's gametes are as old as she is, and age-related changes in the chromosomes themselves appear to increase the risk of nondisjunction at least for some chromosomes.

Nondisjunction also occurs in sex chromosomes, producing individuals who, for example, are XXY (47 chromosomes), XO (45 chromosomes), XXX (47 chromosomes), or XYY (47 chromosomes). While these conditions don't result in death, some are associated with impaired mental function and/or sterility (Table 3-3). What's more, still greater numbers of X chromosomes, such as XXXX or XXXY, result in

Table 3-3 Examples of Nondisjunction in Sex Chromosomes

Chromosomal Complement	Condition	Estimated Incidence	Manifestations
XXX	Trisomy X	1 per 1,000 female births	Affected women are usually clinically normal, but there is a slight increase in sterility and mental impairment compared to the general population. In cases with more than three X chromosomes, mental retardation can be severe
XYY	XYY syndrome	1 per 1,000 male births	Affected males are fertile and tend to be taller than average.
XO	Turner syndrome	1 per 10,000 female births	Affected females are short-statured, have broad chests and webbed necks, and are sterile. There is usually no mental impairment, but concepts relating to spatial relationships, including mathematics, can pose difficulties. Between 95 and 99 percent of affected fetuses die before birth.
XXY	Klinefelter syndrome	1 per 1,000 male births	Symptoms are noticeable by puberty: reduced testicular development, reduced facial and body hair, some breast development in about half of all cases, and reduced fertility or sterility. Some individuals exhibit lowered intelligence. Additional X chromosomes (XXXY) are associated with mental impairment.

marked mental deficiency, and some nondisjunctions of sex chromosomes are lethal. It's possible to survive without a Y chromosome (roughly half of all humans do), but it's impossible for an embryo to survive without an X chromosome. Clearly, normal development depends on having the correct number of chromosomes.

New Frontiers

Since the discovery of DNA structure and function in the 1950s, the field of genetics has revolutionized biological science and reshaped our understanding of inheritance, genetic disease, and evolutionary processes. For example, a technique developed in 1986, called **polymerase chain reaction (PCR)**, enables scientists to make thousands of copies of small samples of DNA that can then be analyzed. In the past, DNA samples from crime scenes or fossils were usually too small to be studied. But PCR has made it possible to examine nucleotide sequences in, for example, Neandertal fossils and Egyptian mummies. As you can imagine, PCR has limitless potential for many disciplines, including forensic science, medicine, and paleoanthropology.

Another application of PCR allows scientists to identify *DNA fingerprints*, so called because they appear as patterns of repeated DNA sequences that are unique to each individual (Fig. 3-23). For example, one person might have a segment of six bases such as ATTCTA repeated 3 times, while another person might have 20 copies of the same sequence.

DNA fingerprinting is perhaps the most powerful tool available for human identification. Scientists have used it to identify scores of unidentified remains, including members of the Russian royal family murdered in 1918 and victims of the September 11, 2001, terrorist attacks. It also provided the DNA evidence in the O. J. Simpson murder trial. Moreover, the technique has been used to exonerate many innocent people wrongly convicted of crimes, in some cases decades after they were imprisoned.

Over the last two decades, scientists have used the techniques of **recombinant DNA technology** to transfer genes from the cells of one species into those of another. One common method has been to insert human genes that direct the production of various proteins into bacterial cells in laboratories. The altered bacteria can then produce human gene products such as insulin. Until the early 1980s, diabetic patients relied on insulin derived from nonhuman animals. However, this insulin wasn't plentiful, and some patients developed allergies to it. But since 1982, abundant supplies of human insulin, produced by bacteria, have been available; and bacteria-derived insulin doesn't cause allergic reactions.

In recent years, genetic manipulation has become increasingly controversial owing to questions related to product safety, environmental concerns, animal welfare, and concern over the experimental use of human embryos. For example, the insertion of bacterial DNA into certain crops has made them toxic to leaf-eating insects, thus reducing the need for pesticides. Cattle and pigs are commonly treated with antibiotics and genetically engineered growth hormone to increase growth rates. (There's no concrete evidence that humans are susceptible to the insect-repelling bacterial DNA or harmed by consuming meat and dairy products from animals treated with growth hormone. But there are concerns over the unknown effects of long-term exposure.)

No matter how contentious these new techniques may be, nothing has generated as much controversy as cloning. The controversy escalated in 1997 with the

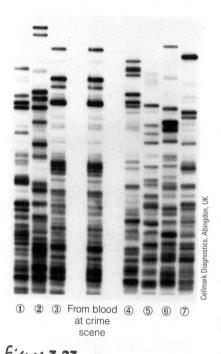

① ② ③ From blood at crime scene ④ ⑤ ⑥ ⑦

Cellmark Diagnostics, Abingdon, UK

Figure **3-23**

Eight DNA fingerprints, one of which is from a blood sample left at an actual crime scene. The other seven are from suspects. By comparing the banding patterns, it is easy to identify the guilty party.

polymerase chain reaction (PCR)
A method of producing thousands of copies of a DNA sample.

recombinant DNA technology A process in which genes from the cell of one species are transferred to somatic cells or gametes of another species.

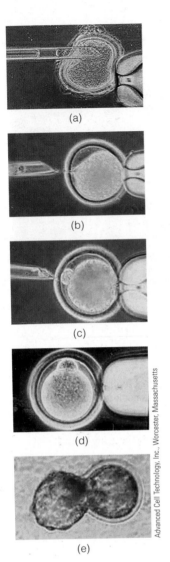

Advanced Cell Technology, Inc., Worcester, Massachusetts

Figure 3-24

A series of photomicrographs showing a nuclear transfer process. (a) The nucleus of an egg cell (from a donor) is drawn into a hollow needle. (b) Only the cytoplasm remains in the donor egg. (c) The nucleus of a skin cell from the individual being cloned is injected into the egg. (d) Electric shock causes the nucleus of the skin cell to fuse with the egg's cytoplasm. (e) The egg begins to divide, and a few days later the cloned embryo will be transferred into the uterus of a host animal.

Human Genome Project An international effort aimed at sequencing and mapping the entire human genome, completed in 2003.

genome The entire genetic makeup of an individual or species. In humans, it's estimated that each individual possesses approximately 3 billion DNA nucleotides.

birth of Dolly, a clone of a female sheep (Wilmut et al., 1997). Actually, cloning isn't as new as you might think. Anyone who has ever taken a cutting from a plant and rooted it to grow a new one has produced a clone. Many species have now been cloned. Cloned mammals include mice, rats, rabbits, cats, sheep, cattle, horses, a mule, and dogs. Moreover, researchers recently produced clones of dead mice that were frozen for as long as 16 years. This gives rise to hopes that eventually it may be possible to clone extinct animals, such as mammoths, from the frozen bodies of animals that died several thousand years ago (Wakayama et al., 2008), but this is extremely unlikely.

Cloning involves a technique called nuclear transfer, a process that has several stages (Fig. 3-24). First, an egg cell is taken from a donor animal, and the nucleus is removed. Then a DNA-containing nucleus is taken from a tissue cell of another animal (the animal actually being cloned). This nucleus is then inserted into the donor egg cell. The fused egg is placed in the uterus of a host mother. If all goes well, that mother eventually gives birth to an infant that's genetically identical to the animal that provided the tissue cells containing the DNA.

How successful cloning will be hasn't been determined yet. Dolly, who had developed health problems, was euthanized in February 2003 at the age of 6 years (Giles and Knight, 2003). Long-term studies have yet to show whether cloned animals live out their normal life span, but some evidence from mice suggests that they don't.

As exciting as these innovations are, probably the single most important advance in genetics has been the progress made by the **Human Genome Project** (Human Genome Sequencing Consortium, 2001; Venter et al., 2001). The goal of this international effort, begun in 1990, was to sequence the entire human **genome**, which consists of some 3 billion bases making up approximately 25,000 protein-coding genes. In 2003, the project was completed.

The potential for anthropological applications is enormous. While scientists were sequencing human genes, the genomes of other organisms were also being studied. As of now, the genomes of hundreds of species have been sequenced. In December 2002, the mouse genome had been completely sequenced (Waterston et al., 2002). The sequence of the chimpanzee genome was announced in 2005 (The Chimpanzee Sequencing and Anaysis Consortium, 2005). And in 2007, the genome of the rhesus macaque was published (The Rhesus Macaque Genome Sequencing and Analysis Consortium, 2007). Two different groups are also currently working to reveal the Neandertal genome (Green et al., 2006; Noonan et al., 2006). The availability of these genomes will allow DNA comparisons between modern humans, Neandertals, and nonhuman primates. This research, called *comparative genomics*, has enormous implications not only for biomedical research but also for studies of evolutionary relationships among species, including ourselves.

Eventually, comparative genome analysis should provide a thorough assessment of genetic similarities and differences, and thus the evolutionary relationships, between humans and other primates. What's more, we can already look at human variation in an entirely different light than we could even 10 years ago (see Chapter 15). Among other things, genetic comparisons between human groups can inform us about population movements in the past and what selective pressures may have been exerted on different populations to produce some of the variability we see. We may even be able to speculate to some extent on patterns of infectious disease in the past. The possibilities are extraordinary, and it wouldn't be exaggerating to say that this is the most exciting time in the history of evolutionary biology since Darwin published *On the Origin of Species*.

Summary

The topics covered in this chapter relate to discoveries made after Darwin and Wallace described the fundamentals of natural selection. But all the issues presented here are basic to an understanding of biological evolution, adaptation, and human variation.

Cells are the fundamental units of life, and in multicellular organisms, there are basically two types. Somatic cells make up body tissues, while gametes (eggs and sperm) are reproductive cells that transmit genetic information from parents to offspring.

Genetic information is contained in the DNA molecule, found in the nuclei of cells. The DNA molecule is capable of replication, or making copies of itself. Replication makes it possible for daughter cells to receive a full complement of DNA (contained in chromosomes).

DNA also controls protein synthesis by directing the cell to arrange amino acids in the proper sequence for each particular type of protein. Also involved in the process of protein synthesis is another, similar molecule called RNA.

There are many genes that regulate the function of other genes. Some homeobox genes are expressed only in embryonic development, and they direct the development of the body plan. Other regulatory genes turn genes on and off. In some cases, this results in the production of different forms of a protein during different stages of life. Also, most of our DNA doesn't actually code for protein production, and much of its function is unknown. Some of these noncoding sequences, called introns, are contained within genes, and these are initially transcribed into mRNA but are then deleted before the mRNA leaves the cell nucleus.

Cells multiply by dividing, and during cell division, DNA is visible under a microscope in the form of chromosomes. In humans, there are 46 chromosomes (23 pairs). If the full complement isn't precisely distributed to succeeding generations of cells, there may be serious consequences.

Somatic cells divide during growth or tissue repair or to replace old, worn-out cells. Somatic cell division is called mitosis. A cell divides one time to produce two daughter cells, each possessing a full and identical set of chromosomes. Sex cells are produced when specialized cells in the ovaries and testes divide during meiosis. Unlike mitosis, meiosis is characterized by two divisions that produce four nonidentical daughter cells, each containing only half the amount of DNA (23 chromosomes) that's carried by the original cell.

Critical Thinking Questions

1. We only briefly touched on the topic of recombinant DNA technologies. From what we said and from things you've heard elsewhere, what is your view on this important topic? Are you generally in favor of most of the goals of recombinant DNA research? What are your objections?
2. Before reading this chapter, were you aware that the DNA in your body is structurally the same as in all other organisms? Do you see this fact as having potential to clarify some of the many questions we still have regarding biological evolution? Why?
3. Do you think proteins are exactly the same in all species? If not, how do you think they would differ in terms of their composition, and why might these differences be important to physical anthropologists?

Molecular Applications in Forensics

No doubt you know of instances in which DNA analysis has been used for forensic purposes to identify a criminal. Likewise, you've probably heard of cases in which mistakenly imprisoned individuals have been released when DNA evidence cleared them of criminal involvement—sometimes several years following conviction.

Since the 1980s, molecular applications have greatly assisted law enforcement agencies. In fact, immediately following development of the polymerase chain reaction (PCR) technique in the mid-1980s, the first widely applied examples of precise DNA genotyping were for forensic purposes.

Forensic anthropologists, from the outset, have been central contributors in these molecular applications. It must be emphasized that forensic science is a coordinated *team effort*. Thus, forensic anthropologists work in close collaboration with law enforcement agencies, medical examiners, forensic odontologists (dental experts), entomologists (experts who identify insects, which provide keys to how long it's been since an individual died), and DNA identification laboratories.

The standard methods used in these laboratories include PCR and DNA fingerprinting (see p. 73). Both mitochondrial and nuclear DNA are used to identify individuals. PCR makes it possible to make a reliable identification of individuals from extremely small samples of tissue (for example, blood, semen, teeth, and bone). Thus, even in cases where the remains have deteriorated badly over time or were crushed or burned in a mass disaster, proper collection and precise laboratory controls can often yield useful results. For example, a person missing for several years can be identified from just a small scrap of bone if the DNA fingerprint can be matched with that of a close relative. Because initial analysis of physical attributes of the skeleton (for example, age, sex, stature) can greatly narrow the range of possible matches (so that fewer potential relatives need to be tested), anthropologists provide crucial assistance in the identification process. At present, existing data banks are insufficient to accomplish the task without such initial corroborating clues.

To successfully make a positive genetic ID, the DNA must be (1) extracted (from bone, by cutting a small section with a saw); (2) purified to remove chemicals that interfere with PCR; (3) amplified (that is, replicated millions of times by PCR); and (4) sequenced (usually by use of "fingerprinting"—that is, characterizing for particular chromosomal regions (unique repeated arrays of small DNA segments).

One renowned case of DNA identification from skeletal remains is that of the last tsar of Russia, Nicholas II.

As is well known, Nicholas and all his immediate family were executed in July 1918. The bodies were long thought to have been completely destroyed, but the true location of the graves of the Russian royal family was discovered several years ago. Only after the fall of communism, however, were skeletal remains finally exhumed in 1991.

A team led by the late William Maples was permitted to examine the remains and attempt to establish the exact identities of all the individuals (more than 1,000 bone fragments were mixed together; Fig. 1). Anthropological analysis of the skeletons suggested that five members of the royal family were represented (Tsar Nicholas, Empress Alexandra, and three of their daughters).

Molecular results agreed with the anthropological findings (Gill et al., 1994), except that some lingering questions remained concerning the identification of the tsar's mtDNA. Further tests comparing the presumed tsar's DNA with that of living relatives (including members of the British royal family) as well as DNA from the skeleton of Nicholas's brother (who died in 1899) showed beyond any

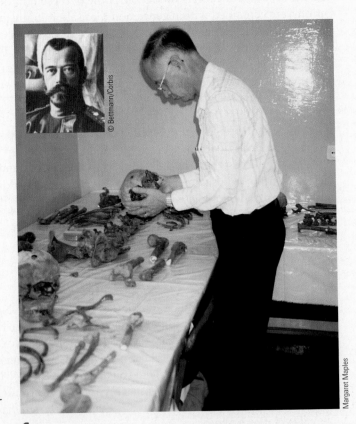

© Bettmann/Corbis

Margaret Maples

Figure 1

Forensic anthropologist Bill Maples examines the cranium of Tsar Nicholas II (inset).

doubt that the skeleton was indeed that of Tsar Nicholas II (Ivanov et al., 1996).

Further excavations in 2007 discovered the remains of the last two members of the Russian royal family who were executed in 1917. A positive DNA identification confirmed the two individuals were Romanov children, one of whom was the 13-year-old tsarevich (and heir) Alexei. The other individual was either the 17-year-old princess Anastasia or perhaps her 19-year-old sister, Maria. (DNA analysis can't distinguish the two sisters, nor can the standard bone indicators of age match the skeletal remains of one sister versus the other with certainty.)

Popular television programs like CSI have greatly widened people's knowledge of these DNA techniques as they apply to crime scenes and criminal prosecutions. Over the last couple of decades, a growing number of convicted individuals, some who'd been in prison for more than 20 years, have been cleared of their crimes and released from prison. As of August 2008, 218 such miscarriages of justice had been corrected and the victims released from prison —all with the help of DNA analysis (www.innocence project.org).

A recent further innovation is now allowing accurate identifications from crime scenes using samples that are microscopic. Known as "touch DNA," this procedure identifies individuals from just a few skin cells that were shed while touching a person's body, their clothes, a weapon, or any object present at a crime scene. The technique has been used in the United Kingdom for a couple of years and has recently been put to use in the United States, providing new evidence relating to the infamous murder in 1996 of 6-year-old JonBenet Ramsey in Boulder, Colorado (*Scientific American*, 2008).

Police and others interested in wider use of DNA technology to identify criminals have advocated national data bases containing DNA information on large numbers of individuals. Such data banks have been initiated in both the United States and United Kingdom, although the total amount of information is still not extremely large. In the United States, approximately 6 million individuals have been added to the National Data Index System; in the United Kingdom, the National DNA Database has information for approximately 4 million people (although in the latter, a much higher proportion of the population is represented: 2 percent in the United States versus 7 percent in the United Kingdom). Many in law enforcement would like to see the DNA data bases greatly expanded, some even arguing that everyone should be required to be tested and have their DNA profile on permanent record.

There are obviously significant ethical and human rights issues involved, and at present, no serious efforts are contemplated to make testing compulsory in either the United States or the United Kingdom.

Scenes of mass disaster (such as fires, earthquakes, tsunamis, or plane crashes) are another context in which both forensic anthropology and DNA analysis play crucial roles. To respond quickly and effectively to such disasters, the federal government has organized regional disaster reaction work groups called DMORT (Disaster Mortuary Operational Response Team). A forensic anthropologist is included in all these teams, and sometimes the anthropologist is the team leader. In fact, following the tragic events of September 11, 2001, Paul Sledzik (a forensic anthropologist then at the Armed Forces Institute of Pathology) was the DMORT leader at the Pennsylvania crash site of United Flight 93.

During the recovery, the team followed strict procedures in the collection and analysis of the human remains and other evidence. It must be remembered that in addition to a site of immense personal tragedy, this was also a crime scene. Accordingly, as in all such circumstances, close interaction with law enforcement agencies was essential; in this case, the FBI led the criminal investigation.

Forensic anthropologists also assisted in the recovery of human remains at the World Trade Center. Here procedures differed, as millions of tons of debris had to be sifted through, and the few human remains that were present were extremely fragmentary and severely burned.

In Pennsylvania, although burned, the remains of victims were much more complete. Thus, the DMORT staff could select the material most likely to provide the best DNA results. Moreover, clothing and other personal items found with the remains could provide an exact identification (which could be further corroborated through basic anthropological observations of age, sex, and so on). Where identification was unambiguous, DNA analysis was not required (see DMORT website for Flight 93 Morgue Protocols).

From the World Trade Center, few remnants of associated clothing or personal effects were found. Moreover, since the bone and tooth fragments were so small and were often altered by intense heat, few of the standard anthropological skeletal observations were possible. As a result, basically all the presumed bone and dental remains have been analyzed for DNA. Most of the work identifying the 2,749 victims was completed in 2005, but only about 58 percent of those killed were able to be identified. However, the work continues.

Molecular Applications in Forensics (continued)

Large numbers of civilian deaths also occur during wars and ethnic conflicts. Forensic anthropologists are often asked to assist in these circumstances as well, since victims of atrocities sometimes are left in mass graves. When possible, these graves are intensively investigated, often revealing decomposed bodies as well as partial skeletons. Such work has sadly become more commonplace, keeping pace with the increase in brutality seen throughout the world. (Consider, for example, the tragedies of Argentina, Guatemala, Rwanda, the Balkans, and Iraq.)

Recovery efforts are concerned first with identifying the victims. Successful personal identification allows family members to learn the fate of missing loved ones. Then the evidence obtained can be used in legal proceedings in which perpetrators are tried for genocide or other crimes against humanity. (Such trials are now being conducted in Africa, in Iraq, and at the World Court.)

As with the circumstances at the 9/11 disaster sites, DNA analyses are sometimes required; but in other cases, accurate personal identification can be done more quickly and more economically by using standard anthropological criteria and associated personal items (the latter corroborated by relatives of the deceased). Such methods are especially important in very poor, war-torn regions (where large-scale DNA testing is not affordable).

In addition to the field collection and analysis contexts discussed above, forensic anthropologists are also becoming directly involved in molecular research in the laboratory. Several anthropologists working in cooperation with molecular biologists are investigating how to refine procedures to make DNA sequencing more accurate (Kontanis, 2004; Latham et al., 2004). For example, at the Armed Forces DNA Identification Laboratory (AFDIL), anthropologist Heather Thew is a DNA analyst directly involved in all steps of sample preparation and molecular analysis. Much of her work concerns the mtDNA testing of the remains of military personnel—some of whom have been missing since World War II; thus, the physical remains consist only of very fragmented bone pieces. Thew credits her anthropology training in human skeletal analysis and modern population biology for providing her with both a solid background and specialized skills that allow her to better perform many of the laboratory duties at AFDIL (Fig. 2).

SOURCES

Flight 93 Morgue Protocols.
2009 www.dmort.org/FilesforDownload/Protocol_Flight_93.pdf

Gill, P., P. L. Ivanov, C. Kimpton, et al.
1994 Identification of the remains of the Romanov family by DNA analysis. *Nature Genetics* 6:130–135.

Ivanov, Pavel L., Mark J. Wadhams, Rhonda K. Roby, et al.
1996 Mitochondrial DNA sequence heteroplasmy in the Grand Duke of Russia Georgij Romanov establishes the authenticity of the remains of Tsar Nicholas II. *Nature Genetics* 12:417–420.

Kotanis, Elias J.
2004 Using real-time PCR quantifications of nuclear and mitochondrial DNA to develop degradation profiles for various tissues. Paper presented at Annual Meetings of the American Academy of Forensic Sciences, Dallas, February 2004.

Latham, Krista E.
2004 The ability to amplify skeletal DNA after heat exposure due to maceration. Paper presented at Annual Meetings of the American Academy of Forensic Sciences, Dallas, February 2004.

Scientific American
2008 www.sciam.com, August 8, 2008.

Figure 2

DNA analyst Heather Thew prepares a bone sample at the Armed Forces DNA Identification Laboratory.

CHAPTER

4

Heredity and Evolution

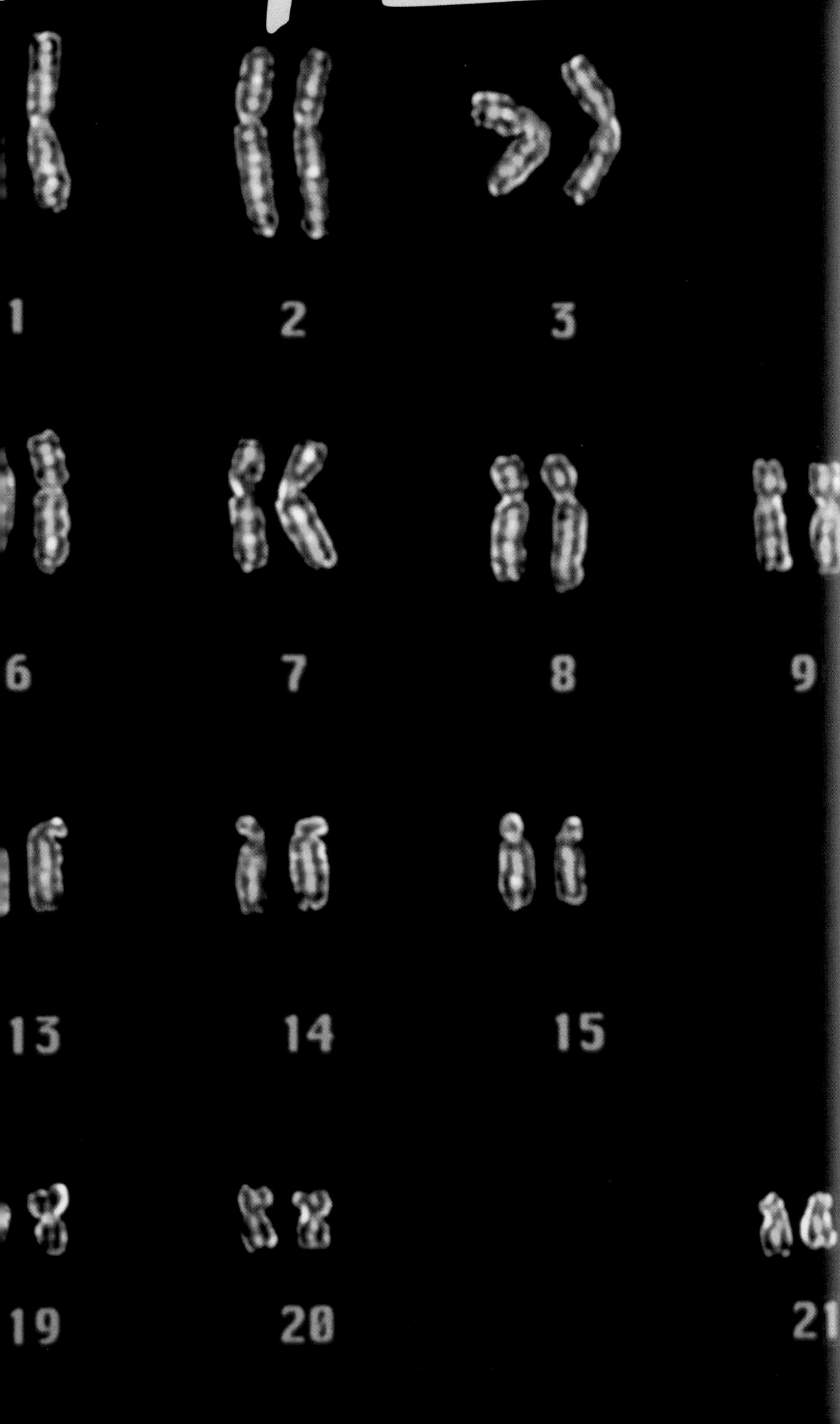

1   2   3   4

6   7   8   9   11

13   14   15

19   20   21

CNRI/Photo Researchers

Key Questions

Why is it important to know the basic mechanisms of inheritance to understand the processes of evolution?

How do the patterns of human inheritance compare with those of other organisms?

Click!

Go to the following media for interactive activities and exercises on topics covered in this chapter:

- Genetics in Anthropology: Principles and Applications CD-ROM, Version 2.0

Introduction

Have you ever had a cat with five, six, or even seven toes? Even if you haven't, you may have seen one, because it's fairly common in cats. Or maybe you've known someone with an extra finger or toe. Anne Boleyn, mother of England's Queen Elizabeth I and the first of Henry VIII's wives to lose her head, apparently had at least part of an extra little finger. (Of course, this had nothing to do with her early demise; that's another story.)

Having extra digits (fingers or toes) is called polydactyly, and it's likely that one of Anne Boleyn's parents was also polydactylous (Fig. 4-1). It's also likely that any polydactylous cat has a parent with extra toes. But how can we know this? Actually, it's fairly simple. We know this because polydactyly is a Mendelian characteristic, meaning that its pattern of inheritance is one of those discovered almost 150 years ago by a monk named Gregor Mendel. And by the time you finish reading this chapter, you'll understand these principles and be able to explain how we know that polydactylous cats and people probably have a polydactylous parent, even if we've never seen their parents.

For at least 10,000 years, beginning with the domestication of plants and animals, people have tried to explain how offspring inherit characteristics from their parents. Farmers knew that they could increase the frequency and expression of desirable attributes through **selective breeding**, but they didn't know why.

From the time the ancient Greek philosophers considered the problem of inheritance until well into the nineteenth century, the prevailing belief was that the traits seen in offspring resulted from the *blending* of parental traits. Blending supposedly happened because of certain particles that existed in every part of the body. These particles contained miniature versions of the body part (limbs, organs, bones, and so on) they came from, and they traveled through the blood to the

Figure 4-1

(a) Hand of a polydactylous child.
(b) Front foot of a polydactylous cat.

selective breeding A practice whereby animal or plant breeders choose which individual animals or plants will be allowed to mate based on the traits (such as coat color or body size) they hope to produce in offspring. Animals or plants that don't have the desirable traits aren't allowed to breed.

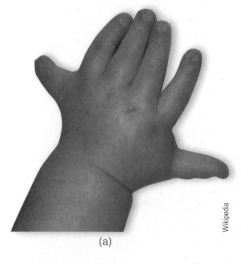

(a) (b)

reproductive organs and ultimately blended with particles of another individual during reproduction. There were variations on this theme, and numerous scholars, including Charles Darwin, adhered to some aspects of the theory.

The Genetic Principles Discovered by Mendel

It may seem odd that after discussing recent discoveries about DNA we now turn our attention back to the middle of the nineteenth century, but that's when the science of genetics was born. By examining how the basic principles of inheritance were discovered, we can more easily understand them. It wasn't until Gregor Mendel (1822–1884) addressed the question of heredity that it began to be resolved (Fig. 4-2). Mendel was living in an abbey in what is now the Czech Republic, and by the time he began his research, he'd already studied botany, physics, and mathematics at the University of Vienna. Moreover, he'd also done various experiments in the monastery gardens. These experiments led him to explore how physical traits, such as color or height, could be expressed in plant **hybrids.**

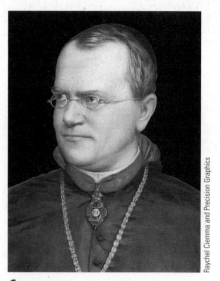

Raychel Ciemma and Precision Graphics

Figure **4-2**
Portrait of Gregor Mendel.

Figure **4-3**
The traits Mendel studied in peas.

Trait Studied	Dominant Form	Recessive Form
Seed shape	round	wrinkled
Seed color	yellow	green
Pod shape	inflated	wrinkled
Pod color	green	yellow
Flower color	purple	white
Flower position	along stem	at tip
Stem length	tall	short

hybrids Offspring of parents that differ from each other with regard to certain traits or certain aspects of genetic makeup; heterozygotes.

Mendel worked with garden peas, concentrating on seven different traits, each of which could be expressed in two different ways (Fig. 4-3). You may think it strange to discuss garden peas in an anthropology book, but they provide a simple example of the basic rules of inheritance. The principles Mendel discovered apply not just to peas, but to all biological organisms, including humans.

Segregation

First Mendel produced groups of pea plants that were the same with regard to the expression of at least one trait. For example, in one group all the plants were tall; in another, they were all short. In other words, there was no variation in height in each group.

To see how the expression of height would change from one generation to the next, Mendel began by crossing parent (P) plants that produced only tall plants with other plants that produced only short ones. According to blending theories of inheritance, all the hybrid offspring, which he called the F_1 *generation*, should have been intermediate in height. But they weren't. Instead, they were all tall (Fig. 4-4).

Figure **4-4**

Results of crosses when only one trait (height) at a time is considered.

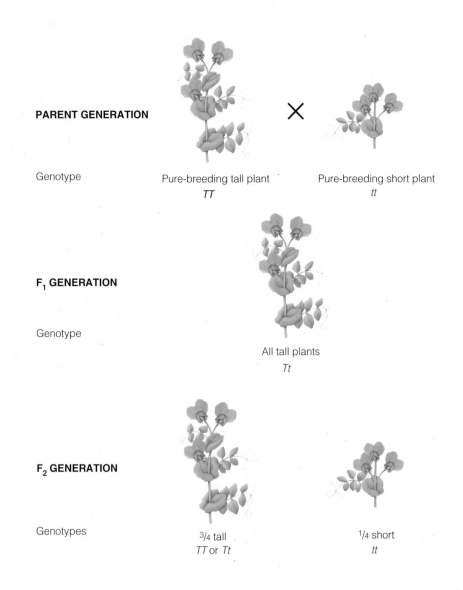

PARENT GENERATION

Genotype

Pure-breeding tall plant
TT

Pure-breeding short plant
tt

F₁ GENERATION

Genotype

All tall plants
Tt

F₂ GENERATION

Genotypes

3/4 tall
TT or *Tt*

1/4 short
tt

Next, he allowed the F_1 plants to self-fertilize to produce a second generation (the F_2 *generation*). But this time, only about ¾ of the offspring were tall, and the remaining ¼ were short. One expression (short) of the trait (height) had completely disappeared in the F_1 generation and then reappeared in the F_2 generation. What's more, the expression he saw in all the F_1 plants was more common in the F_2 plants, occurring in a ratio of approximately 3:1 (three tall plants for every short one).

These results suggested that different expressions of traits were controlled by discrete units (what Mendel called "particles" and we would call genes) occurring in pairs and that offspring inherited one unit from each parent. Mendel realized that the members of a pair of units somehow separated into different sex cells and were again united with another member during fertilization of the egg. This is Mendel's *first principle of inheritance*, known as the **principle of segregation.**

Today we know that meiosis explains Mendel's principle of segregation. During meiosis, paired chromosomes and the genes they carry separate from each other and end up in different gametes. But in the zygote, the original number of chromosomes is restored, and both members of each chromosome pair are present in the offspring.

Dominance and Recessiveness

Mendel also realized that the expression that was absent in the F_1 plants hadn't actually disappeared at all. It was still there, but somehow it was masked and couldn't be expressed. Mendel described the trait that seemed to be lost as **recessive**, and he called the expressed trait **dominant**. Thus he formulated the important principles of *dominance* and *recessiveness*, and today they're still extremely important concepts in the field of genetics.

As it turns out, height in pea plants is controlled by two different alleles at the same genetic locus.(We'll call it the height locus.) The allele that determines that a plant will be tall is dominant to the allele for short. (It's worth mentioning that height isn't controlled this way in all plants.) In Mendel's experiments, all the parent (P) plants had two copies of the same allele, either dominant or recessive, depending on whether they were tall or short. When two copies of the same allele are present, the individual is said to be **homozygous**. So, all the tall parent plants were homozygous for the dominant allele, and all the short parent plants were homozygous for the recessive allele. (This homozygosity explains why tall plants crossed with tall plants produced only tall offspring, and short plants crossed with short plants produced only short offspring. Because the parent plants were homozygous, they had no genetic variation at the height locus and therefore they only had one type of allele to pass on. However, all the hybrid F_1 plants had inherited one allele from each parent plant (one tall and one short). And since *heterozygotes* have two different alleles at a particular locus, they can pass on two variants of the gene.

Figure 4-4 illustrates the crosses that Mendel initially performed. Letters that represent alleles or genes are conventionally italicized. Uppercase letters refer to dominant alleles (or dominant traits), and lowercase letters refer to recessive alleles (or recessive traits). Therefore,

$$T = \text{the allele for tall}$$
$$t = \text{the allele for short}$$

The same symbols are combined to describe an individual's actual genetic makeup, or **genotype**. The term *genotype* can be used to refer to an organism's entire

principle of segregation Genes (alleles) occur in pairs because chromosomes occur in pairs. During gamete formation, the members of each pair of alleles separate, so that each gamete contains one member of each pair. During fertilization, the full number of chromosomes is restored, and members of gene or allele pairs are reunited.

recessive Describing a trait that isn't expressed in heterozygotes; also refers to the allele that governs the trait. For a recessive allele to be expressed, an individual must have two copies of it (i.e., the individual must be homozygous).

dominant Describing a trait governed by an allele that's expressed in the presence of another allele (i.e., in heterozygotes). Dominant alleles prevent the expression of recessive alleles in heterozygotes. (This is the definition of *complete* dominance.)

homozygous Having the same allele at the same locus on both members of a pair of chromosomes.

genotype The genetic makeup of an individual. Genotype can refer to an organism's entire genetic makeup or to the alleles at a particular locus.

Figure 4-5

Punnett square representing possible genotypes and phenotypes and their proportions in the F$_2$ generation. The circles across the top and at the left of the Punnett square represent the gametes of the F$_1$ parents. Each square receives one allele from the gamete above it and another from the gamete to the left. Thus the square at the upper left has two dominant (T) alleles. Likewise, the upper right square receives a recessive (t) from the orange gamete above it and a dominant (T) from the green gamete to its left. In this way, the four squares illustrate that ¼ of the F$_2$ plants can be expected to be homozygous tall (*TT*); another ½ of the plants can also be expected to be tall but will be heterozygous (*Tt*); and the remaining ¼ can be expected to be short because they are homozygous for the recessive "short" allele (*tt*). Thus, ¾ can be expected to be tall and ¼ to be short.

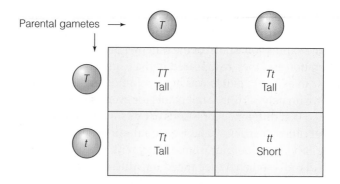

phenotypes The observable or detectable physical characteristics of an organism; the detectable expressions of genotypes, frequently influenced by environmental factors.

heterozygous Having different alleles at the same locus on members of a pair of chromosomes.

principle of independent assortment The distribution of one pair of alleles into gametes does not influence the distribution of another pair. The genes controlling different traits are inherited independently of one another.

assort To sort out or separate.

random assortment The chance distribution of chromosomes to daughter cells during meiosis; along with recombination, a source of genetic variation (but not new alleles) from meiosis.

genetic makeup or to the alleles at a specific genetic locus. Thus, the genotypes of the plants in Mendel's experiments were

$$TT = \text{homozygous tall plants}$$
$$Tt = \text{heterozygous tall plants}$$
$$tt = \text{homozygous short plants}$$

Figure 4-5 is a *Punnett square*. It shows the different ways alleles can be combined when the F$_1$ plants are self-fertilized to produce an F$_2$ generation. Therefore, the figure shows all the *genotypes* that are possible in the F$_2$ generation, and statistically speaking, it demonstrates that we would expect ¼ of the F$_2$ plants to be homozygous dominant (*TT*), ½ to be heterozygous (*Tt*), and the remaining ¼ to be homozygous recessive (*tt*).

The Punnett square also shows the proportions of F$_2$ **phenotypes** (the observed physical manifestations of genes), illustrating why Mendel saw approximately three tall plants for every short plant in the F$_2$ generation. You can see that ¼ of the F$_2$ plants are tall because they have the *TT* genotype. Furthermore, an additional ½, which are **heterozygous** (*Tt*), are also tall because *T* is dominant to *t* and so it's expressed in the phenotype. The remaining ¼ are homozygous recessive (*tt*), and they're short because no dominant allele is present. It's important to note that the *only* way a recessive allele can be expressed is if it occurs with another recessive allele, that is, if the individual is homozygous recessive at the particular locus in question.

Independent Assortment

Mendel also demonstrated that different characteristics aren't necessarily inherited together by showing that plant height and seed color are independent of each other (Fig. 4-6). That is, he saw that any tall pea plant had a 50-50 chance of producing either yellow or green peas. Because of this fact, he developed what is called the **principle of independent assortment**. According to this principle, the units (genes) that code for different traits (in this example, plant height and seed color) **assort** independently of each other during gamete formation. Today we know that this happens because the genes that control plant height and seed color are located on different, nonpartner chromosomes, and during meiosis, these chromosomes travel to newly forming cells independently of one another in a process called **random assortment**.

But if Mendel had used just *any* two traits, his results would have been different at least some of the time. This is because genes on the same chromosome aren't

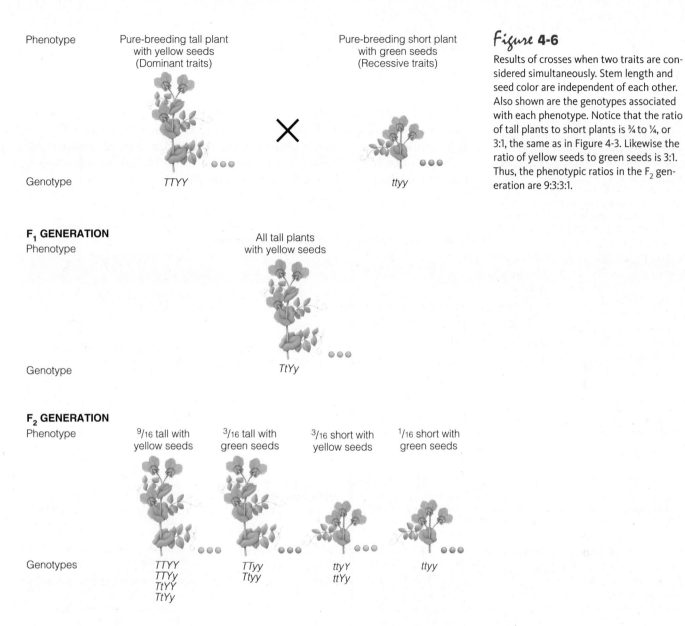

Figure 4-6
Results of crosses when two traits are considered simultaneously. Stem length and seed color are independent of each other. Also shown are the genotypes associated with each phenotype. Notice that the ratio of tall plants to short plants is ¾ to ¼, or 3:1, the same as in Figure 4-3. Likewise the ratio of yellow seeds to green seeds is 3:1. Thus, the phenotypic ratios in the F_2 generation are 9:3:3:1.

independent of each other and, unless they're separated during recombination, they stay together during meiosis. Therefore, the traits they influence don't conform to Mendel's rule of independent assortment. Even though Mendel didn't know about chromosomes, he certainly knew that all characteristics weren't independent of one another. But because independence was what he wanted to emphasize, he reported only on those traits that did in fact illustrate independent assortment.

In 1866, Mendel's results were published, but the methodology and statistical nature of the research were beyond the thinking of the time, and their significance was overlooked and unappreciated. However, by the end of the nineteenth century, several investigators had made important contributions to the understanding of chromosomes and cell division. These discoveries paved the way for the acceptance of Mendel's work in 1900, when three different groups of scientists came across his paper. Regrettably, Mendel had died 16 years earlier and never saw his work vindicated.

Mendelian Inheritance in Humans

Mendelian traits Characteristics that are influenced by alleles at only one genetic locus. Examples include many blood types, such as ABO. Many genetic disorders, including sickle-cell anemia and Tay-Sachs disease, are also Mendelian traits.

Mendelian traits, also called *discrete traits* or *traits of simple inheritance,* are characteristics controlled by alleles at only one genetic locus. The most comprehensive listing of Mendelian traits in humans is V. A. McKusick's (1998) *Mendelian Inheritance in Man,* first published in 1965 and now in its twelfth edition. This volume, as well as its continuously updated Internet version, *Online Mendelian Inheritance in Man* (www.ncbi.nlm.nih.gov/omim/), currently lists over 18,000 human characteristics that are inherited according to Mendelian principles.

Table 4-1 Some Mendelian Traits in Humans

Dominant Traits Condition	Manifestations	Recessive Traits Condition	Manifestations
Achondroplasia	Dwarfism due to growth defects involving the long bones of the arms and legs; trunk and head size usually normal.	Cystic fibrosis	Among the most common genetic (Mendelian) disorders among European Americans; abnormal secretions of the exocrine glands, with pronounced involvement of the pancreas; most patients develop obstructive lung disease. Until the recent development of new treatments, only about half of all patients survived to early adulthood.
Brachydactyly	Shortened fingers and toes.		
Familial hyper-cholesterolemia	Elevated cholesterol levels and cholesterol plaque deposition; a leading cause of heart disease, with death frequently occurring by middle age.		
Neurofibromatosis	Symptoms range from the appearance of abnormal skin pigmentation to large tumors resulting in severe deformities; can, in extreme cases, lead to paralysis, blindness, and death.	Tay-Sachs disease	Most common among Ashkenazi Jews; degeneration of the nervous system beginning at about 6 months of age; lethal by age 2 or 3 years.
Marfan syndrome	The eyes and cardiovascular and skeletal systems are affected; symptoms include greater than average height, long arms and legs, eye problems, and enlargement of the aorta; death due to rupture of the aorta is common. Abraham Lincoln may have had Marfan syndrome.	Phenylketonuria (PKU)	Inability to metabolize the amino acid phenylalanine; results in mental retardation if left untreated during childhood; treatment involves strict dietary management and some supplementation.
Huntington disease	Progressive degeneration of the nervous system accompanied by dementia and seizures; age of onset variable but commonly between 30 and 40 years.	Albinism	Inability to produce normal amounts of the pigment melanin; results in very fair, untannable skin, light blond hair, and light eyes; may also be associated with vision problems. (There is more than one form of albinism.)
Camptodactyly	Malformation of the hands whereby the fingers, usually the little finger, is permanently contracted.	Sickle-cell anemia	Abnormal form of hemoglobin (Hb^S) that results in collapsed red blood cells, blockage of capillaries, reduced blood flow to organs, and, without treatment, death.
Hypodontia of upper lateral incisors	Upper lateral incisors are absent or only partially formed (peg-shaped). Pegged incisors are a partial expression of the allele.	Thalassemia	A group of disorders characterized by reduced or absent alpha or beta chains in the hemoglobin molecule; results in severe anemia and, in some forms, death.
Cleft chin	Dimple or depression in the middle of the chin; less prominent in females than in males.	Absence of permanent dentition	Failure of the permanent dentition to erupt. The primary dentition is not affected.
PTC tasting	The ability to taste the bitter substance phenylthiocarbamide (PTC). Tasting thresholds vary, suggesting that alleles at another locus may also exert an influence.		

Table 4-2 ABO Genotypes and Associated Phenotypes

Genotypes	Antigens on Red Blood Cells	ABO Blood Type (Phenotype)
AA, AO	A	A
BB, BO	B	B
AB	A and B	AB
OO	None	O

Although some Mendelian characteristics have readily visible phenotypic expressions (for example, polydactyly), most don't. Most Mendelian traits are biochemical in nature, and many genetic disorders result from harmful alleles inherited in Mendelian fashion. So if it seems like textbooks overly emphasize genetic disease when they discuss Mendelian traits, it's because many of the known Mendelian characteristics are the results of harmful alleles.

Some genetic disorders are inherited as dominant traits (Table 4-1). This means that if a person inherits only one copy of a harmful, dominant allele, the condition it causes will be present, regardless of the existence of a different, recessive allele on the partner chromosome.

Recessive conditions are commonly associated with the lack of a substance, usually an enzyme (see Table 4-1). For a person actually to have a recessive disorder, he or she must have two copies of the recessive allele that causes it. Heterozygotes who have only one copy of a harmful recessive allele are unaffected, but they're frequently called *carriers* because they can pass the allele to their children. (Remember, half their gametes will carry the recessive allele.) If their mate is also a carrier, it's possible for them to have a child who will be homozygous for the allele, and that child will be affected. In fact, in a mating between two carriers, the risk of having an affected child is 25 percent (look back to Fig. 4-5).

The blood groups, like the ABO system, provide some of the best examples of Mendelian traits in humans. The ABO system is governed by three alleles, *A*, *B*, and *O*, found at the *ABO* locus on the ninth chromosome. These alleles determine which ABO blood type an individual has by coding for the production of molecules called **antigens** on the surface of red blood cells. If only antigen A is present, the blood type (phenotype) is A; if only B is present, the blood type is B; if both are present, the blood type is AB; and when neither is present, the blood type is O (Table 4-2).

Dominance and recessiveness are clearly illustrated by the ABO system. The *O* allele is recessive to both *A* and *B*, so if a person has type O blood, he or she must be homozygous for (have two copies of) the *O* allele. But since both *A* and *B* are dominant to *O*, an individual with blood type A can actually have one of two genotypes: *AA* or *AO*. The same is true of type B, which results from the genotypes *BB* and *BO*. Type AB presents a slightly different situation and is an example of **codominance.**

Codominance is seen when a person has two different alleles, but neither allele can mask the other; therefore, the products of *both* alleles are expressed in the phenotype. So when both *A* and *B* alleles are present, both A and B antigens can be detected on the surface of red blood cells.

Misconceptions about Dominance and Recessiveness

Traditional methods of teaching genetics have led to some misunderstanding of dominance and recessiveness. Probably the most famous example is something

antigens Large molecules found on the surface of cells. Several different loci govern various antigens on red and white blood cells. (Foreign antigens provoke an immune response.)

codominance The expression of two alleles in heterozygotes. In this situation, neither allele is dominant or recessive so they both influence the phenotype.

many of us learned in high school—namely, that eye color is a Mendelian characteristic and that brown eyes are dominant to blue eyes. This would mean that eye color is controlled by alleles at one genetic locus and that the brown allele is dominant to the blue allele. But eye color isn't a Mendelian trait. Rather, it's influenced by alleles at several genetic loci (see p. 93).

Most people have the impression that the inheritance of Mendelian characteristics is an all-or-nothing situation. This misconception especially pertains to recessive alleles, and the general view is that when recessive alleles occur in heterozygotes (that is, carriers), they have absolutely no effect on the phenotype. That is, they are completely inactivated by the other allele. Certainly, this is how it appeared to Gregor Mendel and, until the last two or three decades, to most geneticists.

However, modern biochemical techniques have shown that recessive alleles actually do have some effect on the phenotype, although these effects aren't always apparent through simple observation. It turns out that in heterozygotes, many recessive alleles act to reduce, but not eliminate, the gene products they influence. In fact, it's now clear that our *perception* of recessive alleles greatly depends on whether we examine them at the directly observable phenotypic level or the biochemical level.

Consider Tay-Sachs disease, a lethal condition resulting from the inability to produce an enzyme called hexosaminidase A (see Table 4-1). This inability, seen in people who are homozygous for a recessive allele (*ts*) on chromosome 15, invariably results in death by early childhood. Carriers don't have the disease; and practically speaking, they're unaffected. But carriers, although functionally normal, actually have only about 40 to 60 percent of the amount of the enzyme seen in people with normal amounts of the enzyme. This fact has led to the development of voluntary tests to screen carriers in populations at risk for Tay-Sachs disease.

There are also several misconceptions about dominant alleles. Most people think of dominant alleles as somehow stronger or even better. There's also the notion that dominant alleles are more common in populations because natural selection favors them. These misconceptions undoubtedly stem partly from the label "dominant" and its connotations of power or control. But in genetic usage, those connotations are misleading. Just think about it. If dominant alleles were always more common, then most people would have conditions such as achondroplasia and Marfan syndrome (see Table 4-1). But clearly, this isn't the case.

The relationships between recessive and dominant alleles and their functions are more complicated than they first appeared to be. Previously held views of dominance and recessiveness were guided by available technologies. But as genetic technologies continue to change, new theories will emerge, and our perceptions will be further altered. (This is another example of how new techniques and continued hypothesis testing can lead to a revision of hypotheses and theories.) In fact, although dominance and recessiveness will remain important factors in genetics, it's clear that the ways in which these concepts are taught will be adapted to accommodate new discoveries.

Patterns of Inheritance

It's important to be able to establish the pattern of inheritance of genetic traits, especially those that cause serious disease. Also, in families with a history of inherited disorders, it's important to determine an individual's risk of inheriting harmful alleles or expressing symptoms. The principal technique traditionally used to assess risk of genetic disease has been the construction of a **pedigree chart,** or a diagram of matings and offspring in a family over the span of a few generations.

Pedigree analysis helps researchers determine if a trait is Mendelian. It also helps establish the mode of inheritance. By determining whether the locus that influences a particular trait is located on an autosome or sex chromosome and whether a particular allele is dominant or recessive, researchers have identified six different modes of Mendelian inheritance in humans: *autosomal dominant, autosomal recessive, X-linked recessive, X-linked dominant, Y-linked,* and *mitochondrial.* We'll discuss the first three in some detail.

Standardized symbols are used in pedigree charts. Squares and circles represent males and females, respectively. Horizontal lines connecting individuals indicate matings, and offspring are connected to horizontal mating lines by vertical lines. Siblings are joined by a horizontal line connected to a vertical line that descends from the parents (Fig. 4-7).

Autosomal Dominant Traits As the term implies, autosomal dominant traits are governed by dominant alleles located on autosomes (that is, any chromosome except X or Y). One example of an autosomal dominant trait is brachydactyly, a condition characterized by malformed hands and shortened fingers (see Table 4-1).

Because brachydactyly is caused by a dominant allele, anyone who inherits just one copy of it will have the trait. (In this discussion, we'll use the symbol *B* to refer to the dominant allele that causes the condition and *b* for the recessive, normal allele.) Since the allele is rare, virtually everyone who has brachydactyly is a heterozygote (*Bb*). Unaffected individuals (that is, almost everybody) are homozygous recessive (*bb*).

Figure 4-8 is a partial pedigree for brachydactyly. It's apparent from this pedigree that all affected members have at least one affected parent, so the abnormality doesn't skip generations. This pattern is true of all autosomal dominant traits. Another characteristic of autosomal dominant traits is that there is no sex bias, so males and females are more or less equally affected.

One other fact illustrated by Figure 4-9 is that approximately half the offspring of affected parents are also affected. This proportion is what we would predict for an autosomal dominant trait where only one parent is affected, because half of that parent's gametes will have the dominant but harmful allele (refer back to Fig. 4-5).

Autosomal Recessive Traits Autosomal recessive traits are also influenced by loci on autosomes but show a different pattern of inheritance. A good example is shown in Figure 4-10, a pedigree for albinism. Albinism is a metabolic disorder caused by an autosomal recessive allele that prevents the production of a pigment

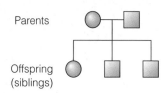

Figure 4-7

Typical symbols used in pedigree charts. Circles and squares represent females and males respectively. Horizontal lines connecting two individuals indicate mating. Vertical lines connect generations.

pedigree chart A diagram showing family relationships. It's used to trace the hereditary pattern of particular genetic (usually Mendelian) traits.

Figure 4-8

Inheritance of an autosomal dominant trait: a human pedigree for brachydactyly. How can individuals 5, 11, 14, 15, and 17 be unaffected? What is the genotype of all affected individuals?

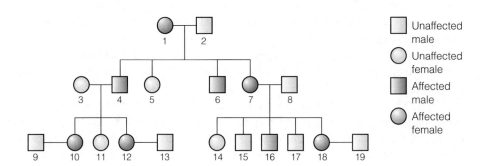

	Unaffected male
	Unaffected female
	Affected male
	Affected female

(a)   (b)

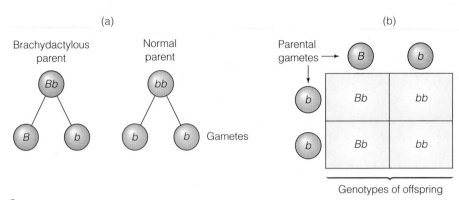

Figure **4-9**

The pattern of inheritance of autosomal dominant traits is the direct result of the distribution of chromosomes, and the alleles they carry, into gametes during meiosis. (a) A diagram of possible gametes produced by two parents, one with brachydactyly and another with normal hands and fingers. The brachydactylous individual can produce two types of gametes: half with the dominant allele (*B*) and half with the recessive allele (*b*). All gametes produced by the normal parent will carry the recessive allele. (b) A Punnett square depicting the possible genotypes in the offspring of one parent with brachydactyly (*Bb*) and one with normal hands and fingers (*bb*). Statistically, we would expect half the offspring to have the *Bb* genotype and thus brachydactyly. The other half would be homozygous recessive (*bb*) and would be normal.

Figure **4-10**

Partial pedigree for albinism, an autosomal recessive trait. Why are some of the offspring of affected individuals unaffected? Individuals 6 and 7, children of unaffected parents, are affected. Why? Four individuals are definitely unaffected carriers. Which ones are they?

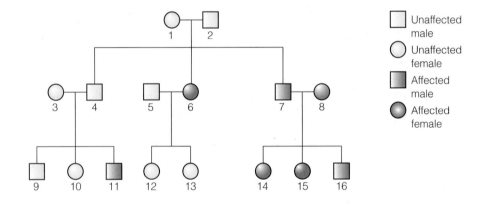

Figure **4-11**

An African albino. This young man has a greatly increased likelihood of developing skin cancer.

called melanin (see Chapter 16). People who inherit the most common variety of albinism have unusually light hair, skin, and eyes (Fig. 4-11). The frequency of this particular form of albinism varies widely among populations, with a prevalence of about 1 in 37,000 people of European ancestry. But approximately 1 in 200 Hopi Indians are affected.

Pedigrees for autosomal recessive traits show obvious differences from those for autosomal dominant characteristics. For one thing, an affected offspring can be produced by two phenotypically normal parents. In fact, most people who express recessive conditions have unaffected parents. In addition, the proportion of affected offspring from most matings is less than half. But when both parents have the trait, all the offspring will be affected. As in the pattern for autosomal dominant traits, males and females are equally affected.

The Mendelian principle of segregation explains the pattern of inheritance of autosomal recessive traits. In fact, this pattern is the very one Mendel first described in his pea experiments (look back at Fig. 4-3). Unaffected parents who produce an albino child *must both be carriers*, and their child is homozygous for the recessive allele that causes the abnormality. The Punnett square in Figure 4-12 shows how such a mating produces both unaffected and affected off-spring in predictable proportions—the typical *phenotypic ratio* of 3:1.

Sex-Linked Traits Sex-linked traits are controlled by genes located on the X and Y chromosomes. Almost all of the more than 450 sex-linked traits listed in OMIM (see p. 86) are influenced by genes on the X chromosome (Table 4-3). Most of the coding sequences (that is, those segments that actually specify a protein) on the Y chromosome are involved in determining maleness and testis function. Although some Y-linked genes are expressed in areas other than the testes (Skaletsky et al., 2003), their functions aren't well known. For this reason, our discussion concerns only the X chromosome.

Hemophilia, one of the best known of the X-linked traits, is caused by a recessive allele on the X chromosome. This allele prevents the formation of a clotting factor in the blood, and affected individuals suffer bleeding episodes and may actually bleed to death from injuries that most of us would consider trivial.

The most famous pedigree illustrating this condition is that of Queen Victoria (1820–1901) of England and her descendants (Fig. 4-13). The most striking feature shown by this pattern of inheritance is that almost all affected people are males, because males have only one X chromosome and therefore only one copy of X-linked genes. This means that *any allele*, even a recessive one, located on their X chromosome will be expressed, because there's no possibility of a dominant allele on a partner chromosome to block it.

Females, on the other hand, show the same pattern of expression of X-linked traits as for autosomal traits, because they have two X chromosomes. That is, just as with any other pair of chromosomes, the only way an X-linked recessive allele can be expressed in a female is if she has two copies of it. However, females who have one copy of the hemophilia allele are carriers, and they may have some tendency toward bleeding, even though they aren't severely affected.

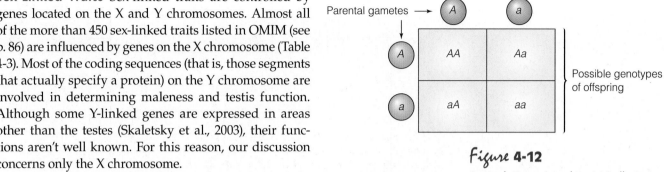

Figure 4-12

A cross between two phenotypically normal parents, both of them carriers of the albinism allele. From a mating such as this between two carriers, we would expect the following possible proportions of genotypes and phenotypes in the offspring: homozygous dominants (*AA*) with normal phenotype, 25 percent; heterozygotes, or carriers (*Aa*) with normal phenotype, 50 percent; and homozygous recessives (*aa*) with albinism, 25 percent. This yields the phenotypic ratio of 3 normal to 1 albino.

Table 4-3 Some Mendelian Disorders Inherited as X-Linked Recessive Traits in Humans

Condition	Manifestations
G-6-PD (glucose-6-phosphate dehydrogenase) deficiency	Lack of an enzyme (G-6-PD) in red blood cells; produces severe, sometimes fatal anemia in the presence of certain foods (e.g., fava beans) and/or drugs (e.g., the antimalarial drug primaquin).
Muscular dystrophy	One form; other forms can be inherited as autosomal recessives; progressive weakness and atrophy of muscles beginning in early childhood; continues to progress throughout life; some female carriers may develop heart problems.
Red-green color blindness	Actually, there are two separate forms, one involving the perception of red and the other affecting only the perception of green. About 8 percent of European males have an impaired ability to distinguish green.
Lesch-Nyhan disease	Impaired motor development noticeable by 5 months; progressive motor impairment, diminished kidney function, self-mutilation, and early death.
Hemophilia	There are three forms; two (hemophilia A and B) are X-linked. In hemophilia A, a clotting factor is missing; hemophilia B is caused by a defective clotting factor. Both produce abnormal internal and external bleeding from minor injuries; severe pain is a frequent accompaniment; without treatment, death usually occurs before adulthood.
Ichthyosis	There are several forms; one is X-linked. A skin condition due to lack of an enzyme; characterized by scaly, brown lesions on the extremities and trunk. In the past, people with this condition were sometimes exhibited in circuses and sideshows as "the alligator man."

Figure **4-13**

Pedigree for Queen Victoria and some of her descendants, showing inheritance of hemophilia, an X-linked recessive trait in humans.

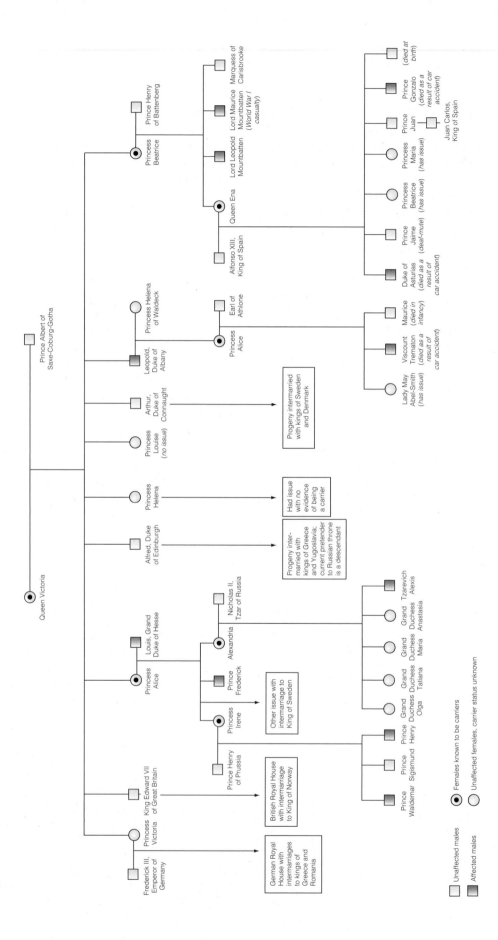

Non-Mendelian Inheritance

Polygenic Inheritance

Mendelian traits are described as *discrete*, or *discontinuous*, because their phenotypic expressions don't overlap; instead, they fall into clearly defined categories. For example, Mendel's pea plants were either short or tall, but none was intermediate in height. In the ABO system, the four phenotypes are completely distinct from one another; that is, there's no intermediate form between type A and type B. In other words, Mendelian traits don't show *continuous* variation.

However, many traits do have a wide range of phenotypic expressions that form a graded series. These are called **polygenic**, or *continuous*, traits (Fig. 4-14).

polygenic Referring to traits that are influenced by genes at two or more loci. Examples include stature, skin color, eye color, and hair color. Many, but not all (eye color, for example), polygenic traits are influenced by environmental factors such as nutrition.

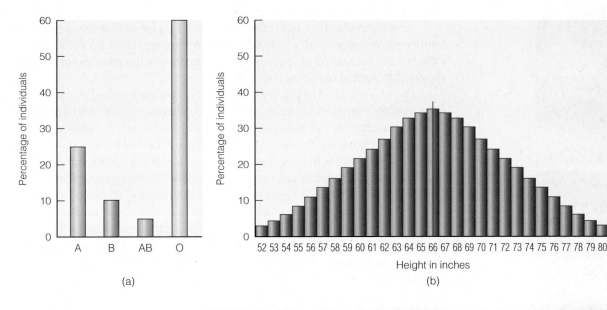

(a) (b)

(c)

Figure 4-14

(a) This bar graph shows the discontinuous distribution of a Mendelian trait (ABO blood type) in a hypothetical population. Expression of the trait is described in terms of frequencies. (b) This histogram represents the continuous expression of a polygenic trait (height) in a large group of people. Notice that the percentage of extremely short or tall individuals is low; most people are closer to the mean, or average, height, represented by the vertical line at the center of the distribution. (c) A group of male students arranged according to height. The most common height is 70 inches, which is the mean, or average, for this group.

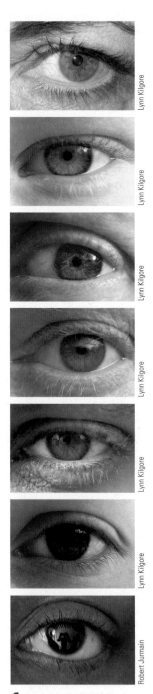

Figure 4-15

Examples of the continuous variation seen in human eye color. The person whose blue eye is shown at top is probably homozygous for the allele that regulates the *OCA2* gene. However, the variable expression of blue combined with brown and different shades of brown and even green are due to the interactions between *OCA2* and other genes.

While Mendelian traits are governed by only one genetic locus, polygenic characteristics are influenced by alleles at two or more loci, and each locus contributes in some way to the phenotype. For example, one of the most frequently cited examples of polygenic inheritance in humans is skin color, and the single most important factor influencing it is the amount of the pigment melanin that skin cells produce.

Melanin production is influenced by the interactions between several different loci; and some of these loci have now been identified. A recent study by Lamason and colleagues (2005) showed that one single highly conserved gene (called *MC1R*) with two alleles makes a significant (and probably disproportionate) contribution to the amount of melanin that cells produce (see p. 451 for further discussion). In addition, at least four other pigmentation genes have been identified, and this is very important, because until recently, none had been. Thus, it appears that many long-standing questions about variation in human skin color may be answered in the foreseeable future.

As we stated earlier, eye color is influenced by more than one gene, and certainly some of the genes that influence skin color are also involved. However, a gene called *OCA2*, located on chromosome 15, is apparently the most important gene in the development of blue eyes (Fig. 4-15).

OCA2 is involved in pigmentation of the iris of the eye, and mutations in this gene lead to a form of albinism. Sturm and colleagues (2008) demonstrated that this gene accounts for 74 percent of the variation in human eye color in European populations. (Northern European populations and their descendants exhibit more variability in eye color than is seen in all other human populations; and they're the only ones in which significant numbers of people have blue eyes.) Moreover, specific variations of the *OCA2* gene were found in virtually 100 percent of blue-eyed people from Denmark, Turkey, and Jordan. In addition, point mutations in one of several genes that regulate *OCA2* also are "perfectly associated" with blue eyes (Eiberg et al., 2007). Thus, when we examine any trait, we need to look not only at the genes traditionally associated with them, but also at the DNA sequences that regulate them. Indeed, it's looking more and more like genes don't really do much by themselves; they just follow orders, and if the orders vary, then their effects will also vary.

Polygenic traits actually account for most of the readily observable phenotypic variation in humans, and they've traditionally served as a basis for racial classification (see Chapter 15). Along with skin color, polygenic inheritance in humans is seen in hair color, weight, stature, eye color (see Fig. 4-15), shape of face, shape of nose, and fingerprint pattern. Because they exhibit continuous variation, most polygenic traits can be measured on a scale composed of equal increments. (Incidentally, *all* physical traits discussed in fossils are polygenic.) For example, height (stature) can be measured in feet and inches (or meters and centimeters). If height were measured in a large number of individuals, the distribution of measurements would continue, uninterrupted, from the shortest extreme to the tallest. That's what is meant by *continuous traits*.

Because polygenic traits can usually be measured, scientists treat them statistically. The use of simple summary statistics, such as the *mean* (average) or *standard deviation* (a measure of variation within a group), enables researchers to develop basic descriptions of and comparisons between populations. For example, a physical anthropologist might be interested in average height in two different populations and whether differences between the two are significant, and if so, why.

These particular statistical analyses aren't possible with Mendelian traits simply because those traits can't be measured in the same way. But just because Mendelian

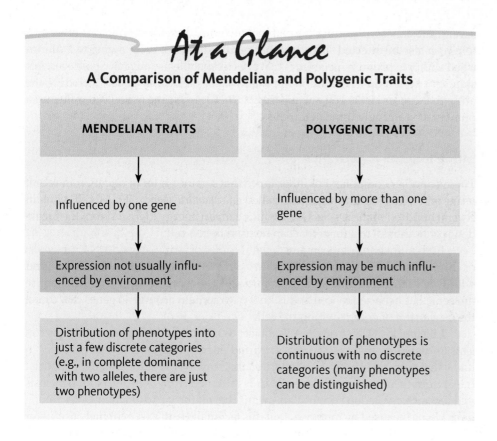

At a Glance

A Comparison of Mendelian and Polygenic Traits

MENDELIAN TRAITS	POLYGENIC TRAITS
Influenced by one gene	Influenced by more than one gene
Expression not usually influenced by environment	Expression may be much influenced by environment
Distribution of phenotypes into just a few discrete categories (e.g., in complete dominance with two alleles, there are just two phenotypes)	Distribution of phenotypes is continuous with no discrete categories (many phenotypes can be distinguished)

traits aren't amenable to the same types of statistical tests that polygenic traits are doesn't mean that they provide less information about genetic processes. Mendelian characteristics can be described in terms of frequency within populations, and this makes it possible to compare groups for differences in prevalence.(For example, one population may have a high frequency of blood type A, while in another group, type A may be almost completely absent.) Also, Mendelian traits can be analyzed for mode of inheritance (dominant or recessive). Finally, for many Mendelian traits, the approximate or exact positions of genetic loci are known, and this makes it possible to examine the mechanisms and patterns of inheritance at these loci. This type of study isn't currently possible for polygenic traits because they're influenced by several genes, most of which haven't been traced to specific loci.

Pleiotropy

While polygenic traits are governed by the actions of several genes, **pleiotropy** is a situation where a single gene influences more than one phenotypic expression. Although this might seem unusual, pleiotropic effects are probably the rule rather than the exception.

The autosomal recessive disorder phenylketonuria (PKU) provides one example of pleiotropy (see Table 4-1). Individuals who are homozygous for the *PKU* allele don't produce the enzyme involved in the initial conversion of the amino acid *phenylalanine* to another amino acid, *tyrosine*. Because of this block in the metabolic pathway, phenylalanine breaks down into substances that accumulate in the central nervous system; and without dietary management, these substances lead to mental deficiencies and several other consequences. Tyrosine is ultimately converted to

pleiotropy A situation that occurs when the action of a single gene influences several seemingly unrelated phenotypic effects.

several substances, including the pigment melanin; therefore, numerous other systems can also be affected. Thus, another manifestation of PKU, owing to a diminished ability to produce melanin, is that affected people usually have blue eyes, fair skin, and light hair. There are many examples of pleiotropic genes, including the allele that causes sickle-cell anemia (see p. 62). Clearly, gene action can influence a number of seemingly unrelated traits.

Mitochondrial Inheritance

There's another component of inheritance that's gained a lot of attention in recent years, and it involves the organelles called *mitochondria* (see p. 50). All cells contain several hundred of these structures, which convert energy (derived from the breakdown of nutrients) to a form that can be used by the cell.

Each mitochondrion contains several copies of a ring-shaped DNA molecule, or chromosome. While *mitochondrial DNA* (*mtDNA*) is distinct from the DNA found within cell nuclei, its molecular structure and functions are the same. The entire molecule has been sequenced and is known to contain around 40 genes that direct the conversion of energy within the cell.

Like nuclear DNA, mtDNA is subject to mutations, and some mutations can lead to disorders that result from impaired energy conversion. It's important to know that animals of both sexes inherit *all* their mtDNA, and thus all mitochondrial traits, from their mothers. Since mtDNA is inherited from only one parent, meiosis and recombination don't occur. This means that all the variation in mtDNA among individuals is caused by mutation, and this fact makes mtDNA extremely useful for studying genetic change over time. So far, geneticists have used mutation rates in mtDNA to investigate evolutionary relationships between species, to trace ancestral relationships within the human lineage, and to study genetic variability among individuals and/or populations. These techniques are still being refined, and it's clear that we have a lot to learn from mtDNA.

Genetic and Environmental Factors

From what we've said so far, you may have the impression that phenotypes are completely determined by genotypes; but that's not true. (Here we use the terms *genotype* and *phenotype* in a broader sense to refer to an individual's *entire* genetic makeup and *all* observable or detectable characteristics.) The genotype sets limits and potentials for development, but it also interacts with the environment; and this genetic-environmental interaction influences many aspects of phenotypic expression.

Many polygenic traits are obviously influenced by environmental conditions. Adult stature is a good example of a trait that's influenced by both genes and the environment. Even though the maximum height a person can achieve is genetically determined, childhood nutrition (an environmental factor) is also very important. One very well-known study showed that children of Japanese immigrants to Hawaii were, on average, 3 to 4 inches taller than their parents. This dramatic difference, seen in one generation, was attributed to environmental factors—specifically to a change in diet (Froelich, 1970). For most traits, however, it's not possible to identify the *specific* environmental components that influence the phenotype.

Other important environmental factors include exposure to sunlight, altitude, temperature, and, unfortunately, increasing levels of exposure to toxic waste and airborne pollutants. These and many other factors contribute in complex ways to the continuous phenotypic variation seen in characteristics governed by several loci.

Mendelian traits are less likely to be influenced by environmental factors. For example, ABO blood type is determined at fertilization and remains fixed throughout the individual's lifetime, regardless of diet, exposure to ultraviolet radiation, temperature, and so forth.

While Mendelian and polygenic inheritance produce different kinds of phenotypic variation, it's important to understand that even for polygenic characteristics, Mendelian principles still apply at individual loci. In other words, if a trait is influenced by six loci, each one of those loci may have two or more alleles, with some perhaps being dominant to others or with the alleles being codominant. It's the combined action of the alleles at all six loci, interacting with the environment, that results in observable phenotypic expression.

Modern Evolutionary Theory

By the beginning of the twentieth century, the foundations for evolutionary theory had already been developed. Darwin and Wallace had described natural selection 40 years earlier, and the rediscovery of Mendelian genetics in 1900 contributed the other major component, namely, a mechanism for inheritance. We might expect that these two basic contributions would have been combined into a comprehensive theory of evolution, but they weren't. For the first 30 years of the twentieth century, some scientists argued that mutation was the main factor in evolution, while others emphasized natural selection. What they really needed was a merger of the two views rather than an either-or situation; but this didn't happen until the mid-1930s (see "A Closer Look," p. 98)

The Modern Synthesis

Biologists working on mathematical models of evolutionary change in the late 1920s and early 1930s realized that mutation and natural selection weren't opposing processes, but that both actually contribute to biological evolution. The two major foundations of the biological sciences had thus been brought together in what is called the Modern Synthesis. From such a "modern" (that is, the middle of the twentieth century onward) perspective, we define evolution as a two-stage process:

1. The production and redistribution of **variation** (inherited differences among individuals)
2. *Natural selection* acting on this variation, whereby inherited differences, or variation, among individuals differentially affect their ability to successfully reproduce

A Current Definition of Evolution

As we discussed in Chapter 2, Charles Darwin saw evolution as the gradual unfolding of new varieties of life from previous forms. This is certainly one result of the evolutionary process. But these long-term effects can come about only through the accumulation of many small genetic changes occurring over the generations. Today, we can demonstrate how evolution works by examining some of these small genetic changes and how they increase or decrease in frequency. From this modern

variation (genetic) Inherited differences among individuals; the basis of all evolutionary change.

A Closer Look

The Development of Modern Evolutionary Theory

Our understanding of the evolutionary process came about through contributions of biologists in the United States, Great Britain, and Russia. While "mutationists" were arguing with "selectionists" about the single primary mechanism in evolution, several population geneticists began to realize that small genetic changes and natural selection were both necessary ingredients in the evolutionary formula.

These population geneticists were largely concerned with mathematical reconstructions of evolution—in particular, they were measuring small accumulations of genetic changes in populations over just a few generations. Central figures in these early theoretical developments included Ronald Fisher and J. B. S. Haldane in Great Britain, Sewall Wright in the United States, and Sergei Chetverikov in Russia.

While these scientists produced brilliant insights, their conclusions were largely unknown to most evolution-

Figure 1

Theodosius Dobzhansky.

Reprinted, with permission, from the *Annual Review of Genetics*, Volume 10 ©1976 by Annual Reviews www.annualreviews.org

ary biologists, especially in North America. Therefore, someone had to merge the mathematical jargon of the population geneticists and the general theories of evolutionary biologists. The scientist who did this was Theodosius Dobzhansky (Fig. 1). In his *Genetics and the Origin of Species* (1937), Dobzhansky integrated the mathematics of population genetics with overall evolutionary theory. His conclusions then became the basis for a period of tremendous activity in evolutionary thinking that directly led to major contributions by George Gaylord Simpson (who brought paleontology into the synthesis), Ernst Mayr, and others. In fact, the Modern Synthesis produced by these scientists stood basically unchallenged for an entire generation as the explanation of the evolutionary process. In recent years, however, some aspects of this theory have been brought under serious question (see Chapter 5).

---

genetic perspective, we define **evolution** as *a change in* **allele frequency** *from one generation to the next.*

Allele frequencies are indicators of the genetic makeup of a **population**, the members of which share a common **gene pool**. To show how allele frequencies change, we'll use a simplified example of an inherited trait, again the ABO blood groups (see p. 87). (*Note*: There are, in fact, several blood groups, all controlled by different loci that determine other properties of the red blood cells.)

Let's assume that the students in your anthropology class represent a population, an interbreeding group of individuals, and that we've identified everyone's ABO blood type. (To be considered a population, individuals must choose mates more often from *within* the group than from outside it. Obviously, your class won't meet this requirement; but we'll overlook this point.) The proportions of the *A*, *B*, and *O* alleles are the allele frequencies for this trait. For example, if 50 percent of all the *ABO* alleles in your class are *A*, 40 percent are *B*, and 10 percent are *O*, then the frequencies of these alleles are *A* = .50, *B* = .40, and *O* = .10.*

Since the frequencies for these alleles represent only proportions, or percentages, of a total, it's obvious that allele frequencies can refer only to groups or populations. Individuals don't have allele frequencies; they have either *A*, *B*, or *O* alleles in any combination of two (see p. 87). Individuals can't change their alleles either.

evolution A change in the frequency of alleles from one generation to the next.

allele frequency In a population, the percentage of all the alleles at a locus accounted for by one specific allele.

population Within a species, a community of individuals where mates are usually found.

gene pool The total complement of genes shared by the reproductive members of a population.

---

*This is a simplified example. Because the ABO system is governed by three alleles, calculating allele frequencies is more complicated than for a two-allele system. In Chapter 15, we'll show how allele frequencies are calculated for a simple two-allele locus.

From conception onward, a person's genetic composition is fixed. If you start out with blood type A, you'll always have type A. And lastly, individuals can't evolve over time; that's something only populations can do.

So, what happens when a population evolves? Assume that 25 years from now, we calculate the frequencies of the ABO alleles in the children of our classroom population and find the following: $A = .30$, $B = .40$, and $O = .30$. We can see that the frequencies, or relative proportions, have changed: A has decreased, O has increased, and B has stayed the same. This apparently minor change doesn't seem very important; still, it's an example of one kind of evolution. Over the short span of just a few generations, such changes in inherited traits may be only very small. But if they continue to happen, and particularly if they go in one direction (for example, the frequency of the O allele continues to increase) because of natural selection, they can produce new adaptations and even new species.

Whether we're talking about the short-term effects (as in our classroom population) from one generation to the next, which is sometimes called **microevolution**, or the long-term effects through time (speciation), also called **macroevolution**, the basic evolutionary mechanisms are similar. But how do allele frequencies change, and what causes evolution? As we've already said, evolution is a two-stage process. Genetic variation must first be produced by mutation, and then it can be acted on by natural selection.

Factors That Produce and Redistribute Variation

Mutation

You've already learned that change in the DNA molecule is one type of mutation and that many genes occur in two or more forms called alleles (A, B, or O, for example). If one allele changes to another—that is, if the gene itself is altered—a mutation has occurred. In fact, alleles are the results of mutations. Even the substitution of just one single DNA base for another, called a **point mutation**, can cause the allele to change. But point mutations have to occur in sex cells if they're going to be important to the evolutionary process. This is because evolution occurs over time, so the mutation has to be passed from one generation to the next. In our classroom example, if a genetic change occurred in the sperm or egg of one of the students (A mutates to B, for example), the offspring's blood type will also be altered, causing a minute shift in allele frequencies of the next generation. In Chapter 3, we showed how a *point mutation* could cause a change in hemoglobin structure from normal to sickle-cell, and we also discussed how transposable elements and microsatellites can change the structure of a gene.

Actually, except in microorganisms, it's rare for evolution to occur solely because of mutation. Mutation rates for any given trait are usually low, so we wouldn't really expect to see a mutation at the ABO locus in so small a population as your class. In larger populations, however, mutations might be observed in, say, 1 individual out of 10,000, but by themselves, they'd have no effect on overall allele frequencies. However, when mutation is combined with natural selection, evolutionary changes not only can occur, but can occur more rapidly.

It's important to remember that mutation is the basic creative force in evolution because it's the *only* way to produce *new* genetic variation. Its key role in the production of variation is the first stage of the evolutionary process.

microevolution Small changes occurring within species, such as a change in allele frequencies.

macroevolution Changes produced only after many generations, such as the appearance of a new species.

point mutation A chemical change in a single base of a DNA sequence.

Gene Flow

The exchange of genes between populations is called **gene flow**. The term *migration* is also sometimes used; but strictly speaking, migration refers to the movement of people. In contrast, gene flow refers to the exchange of genes between groups, which can only occur if the migrants interbreed. Also, even if individuals move temporarily and produce offspring in the new population (thus leaving a genetic contribution), they don't necessarily stay there. For example, the children of U.S. soldiers and Vietnamese women represent gene flow, even though the fathers returned to the United States after the Vietnam War.

In humans, social rules more than any other factor determine mating patterns, and cultural anthropologists can work closely with physical anthropologists to isolate and measure this aspect of evolutionary change. Population movements (particularly in the last 500 years) have reached enormous proportions, and few breeding isolates remain. But migration, on a smaller scale, has been a consistent feature of human evolution since the first dispersal of our genus, and gene flow between populations (even though sometimes limited) helps explain why speciation has been rare during the past million years or so.

An interesting example of how gene flow influences microevolutionary changes in modern human populations is seen in African Americans. African Americans are mostly of West African descent, but there has also been considerable genetic admixture with European Americans. By measuring allele frequencies for specific genetic loci, we can estimate the amount of migration of European alleles into the African American gene pool. Data from northern and western U.S. cities (including New York, Detroit, and Oakland) have shown the migration rate (that is, the proportion of *non*-African genes in the African American gene pool) at 20 to 25 percent (Cummings, 2000). However, more restricted data from the southern United States (Charleston and rural Georgia) have suggested a lower degree of gene flow (4 to 11 percent).

Gene flow occurs for reasons other than large-scale movements of populations. In fact, significant changes in allele frequencies can come about through long-term patterns of mate selection whereby members of a group obtain mates from one or more other groups. This is especially true if mate exchange consistently occurs in one direction over a long period of time. For example, if group A consistently chooses mates from group B but group B doesn't reciprocate, allele frequencies in group A may ultimately be altered.

Today, modern transportation plays a crucial role in determining the potential radius for finding mates. Throughout most of human history, the majority of people found mates within a few miles of their home; but today it's not uncommon to find a partner from another continent. Of course, for most people, actual patterns are somewhat more restricted. For example, data from Ann Arbor, Michigan, indicate a mean marital distance (the average distance between birthplaces of partners) of about 160 miles. This isn't a huge distance, but it's still an area large enough to include a tremendous number of potential marriage partners.

Genetic Drift

Genetic drift is the random factor in evolution, and it's entirely a function of population size. *Drift occurs solely because a population is small.* If an allele is rare in a population composed of, say, a few hundred individuals, then there's a chance it simply may not be passed on to offspring. In this situation, the allele can eventu-

gene flow Exchange of genes between populations.

genetic drift Evolutionary changes—that is, changes in allele frequencies—produced by random factors. Genetic drift is a result of small population size.

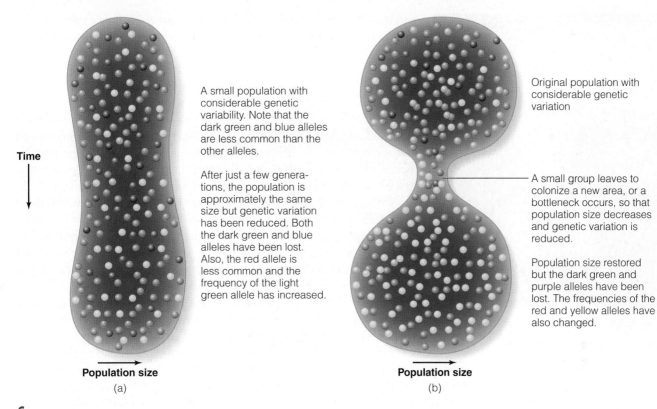

A small population with considerable genetic variability. Note that the dark green and blue alleles are less common than the other alleles.

After just a few generations, the population is approximately the same size but genetic variation has been reduced. Both the dark green and blue alleles have been lost. Also, the red allele is less common and the frequency of the light green allele has increased.

Original population with considerable genetic variation

A small group leaves to colonize a new area, or a bottleneck occurs, so that population size decreases and genetic variation is reduced.

Population size restored but the dark green and purple alleles have been lost. The frequencies of the red and yellow alleles have also changed.

Time

Population size
(a)

Population size
(b)

Figure 4-16

Small populations are subject to genetic drift, where rare alleles can be lost because, just by chance, they weren't passed to offspring. Also, although more common alleles may not be lost, their frequencies may change for the same reason. (a) This diagram represents six alleles (different-colored dots) that occur at one genetic locus in a small population. You can see that in a fairly short period of time (three or four generations), rare alleles can be lost and genetic diversity consequently reduced. (b) This diagram illustrates founder effect, a form of genetic drift where diversity is lost because a large population is drastically reduced in size and it consequently passes through a genetic "bottleneck." Founder effect also happens when a small group leaves the larger group and "founds" a new population elsewhere. (In this case, the group of founders is represented by the bottleneck.) Those individuals that survive (or the founders) and the alleles they carry represent only a sample of the variation that was present in the original population. And future generations, all descended from the survivors (founders), will therefore have less variability.

ally disappear altogether (Fig. 4-16). This may seem like a minor thing; but in effect, genetic variability in this population has been reduced.

One particular kind of genetic drift called **founder effect** is seen in many modern human and nonhuman populations. Founder effect can occur when a small migrant band of "founders" leaves its parent group and forms a colony somewhere else. Over time, a new population will be established, and as long as mates are chosen only from within this population, all of its members will be descended from the small group of founders. In effect, all the genes in the expanding group will have come from the few original colonists. In such a case, an allele that was rare in the founders' parent population but, just by chance, was carried by even one of the founders can eventually become common in that group's descendants. This is because a high proportion of individuals in later generations are all descended from that one founder.

Colonization isn't the only way founder effect can happen. Small founding groups may also consist of a few survivors of a large group that's been mostly wiped

founder effect A type of genetic drift in which allele frequencies are altered in small populations that are taken from, or are remnants of, larger populations.

<figure>Figure **4-17**

Cheetahs, like many other species, have passed through a genetic bottleneck. Consequently, as a species they have little genetic variation.</figure>

out by a disaster of some kind. But like the small group of colonists, the survivors carry only a sample of all the alleles that were present in the original group.

As you can see, just by chance alone, some alleles may be completely lost from a population's gene pool, while other alleles may become "fixed" (that is, the only allele that exists) at a locus where originally there may have been two or more. Whatever the cause, the outcome is a reduction of genetic diversity, and the allele frequencies of succeeding generations may be substantially different from those of the original, larger population. The loss of genetic diversity in this type of situation is called a *genetic bottleneck*, and its effects can be extremely detrimental to a species.

There are many known examples (both human and nonhuman) of species or populations that have passed through genetic bottlenecks. (In fact, right now many species are going through genetic bottlenecks.) For example, cheetahs (Fig. 4-17) are a genetically uniform species, and biologists believe that at some point in the past, these magnificent cats suffered a catastrophic decline in numbers. For reasons we don't know but that are related to the species-wide loss of numerous alleles, male cheetahs produce a high percentage of defective sperm, compared to other cat species. Decreased reproductive potential, greatly reduced genetic diversity, and other factors (especially human hunting) have combined to jeopardize the continued existence of this species. Other species that have passed through genetic bottlenecks include California elephant seals, sea otters, and condors. Indeed, our own species is very uniform genetically, compared to chimpanzees, and it appears that all modern human populations are the descendants of a few small groups (see Chapter 14).

Many examples of founder effect in human populations have been documented in small, usually isolated populations (such as island groups or small agricultural villages in New Guinea or South America). Even larger populations that are descended from fairly small groups of founders can show the effects of genetic drift many generations later. For example, French Canadians in Quebec, who currently number close to 6 million, are all descended from about 8,500 founders who left France during the sixteenth and seventeenth centuries. Because the genes carried by the initial founders represented only a sample of the gene pool from which they were derived, a number of alleles now occur in different frequencies from those of the current population of France. These differences include an increased prevalence of several harmful alleles, including those causing some of the diseases listed in Table 4-1, such as cystic fibrosis, a variety of Tay-Sachs, thalassemia, and PKU (Scriver, 2001).

One other example of genetic drift is provided by a fatal recessive condition called Amish microcephaly, in which a mutation results in abnormally small brains and heads in fetuses. The disorder is found only in the Old Order Amish community of Lancaster County, Pennsylvania, where it occurs in approximately 1 in 500 births (Kelley et al., 2002; Rosenberg et al., 2002). Genealogical research showed that affected families have all been traced back nine generations to a single couple. One member of this couple carried the deleterious recessive allele that, because of customs promoting marriage within (what was then) a small group, has greatly increased in frequency with very serious consequences. Indeed, much insight concerning the evolutionary factors that have acted in the past can be gained by understanding how such mechanisms continue to operate on human populations today. In small populations, drift plays a major evolutionary role because fairly sudden fluctuations in allele frequency can and do occur solely because of small population size. Likewise, throughout a good deal of human evolution, at least the last 4 to 5 million years, hominins probably lived in small groups, and drift probably had a significant impact.

While drift has contributed to evolutionary change in certain circumstances, the effects have been irregular and nondirectional. (Remember, drift is *random* in nature.) Certainly, the pace of evolutionary change could have been accelerated if many small populations were isolated and thus subject to drift. By modifying the genetic makeup of such populations, drift can provide significantly greater opportunities for natural selection, the only truly directional force in evolution.

As we've seen, mutation, gene flow, and genetic drift can produce some evolutionary changes by themselves. These changes are usually *microevolutionary* ones, however; that is, they produce changes within species over the short term. To produce the kind of evolutionary changes that ultimately result in, for example, diversification of the first primates or appearance of the hominins, natural selection is necessary. But natural selection can't operate independently of the other evolutionary factors: mutation, gene flow, and genetic drift.

Additional insight concerning the relative influences of the different evolutionary factors has emerged in recent studies of the early dispersal of modern *Homo sapiens* (discussed in Chapter 14). Evidence suggests that in the last 100,000 to 200,000 years, our species experienced a genetic bottleneck that considerably influenced the pattern of genetic variation seen in all human populations today. In this sense, modern humans can be seen as the fairly recent product of founder effect acting on a somewhat grand scale. Such evolutionary changes could be potentially significant over tens of thousands of years and could cause substantial genetic shifts within species.

Recombination

As we saw earlier in Chapter 3, maternal and paternal chromosomes exchange segments of DNA during meiosis. By itself, recombination doesn't change allele frequencies (that is, it doesn't cause evolution). When paired chromosomes exchange DNA, however, genes sometimes find themselves in altered genetic environments (it's like they've moved to a new neighborhood). This fact can be important because the functions of some genes can be influenced simply by the alleles they're close to. Recombination thus not only changes the composition of parts of chromosomes but also can affect how some genes act, and slight changes of gene function can become material for natural selection to act upon.

Natural Selection Acts on Variation

The evolutionary factors we've just discussed (mutation, gene flow, genetic drift, and recombination) interact to produce variation and then to distribute genes within and between populations. But there's no long-term *direction* to any of these factors, and for adaptation and evolution to occur, a population's gene pool needs to change in a specific direction. This means that some alleles have to consistently become more common, while others become less common, and natural selection is the one factor that can cause directional change in allele frequency relative to *specific environmental factors*. If the environment changes, then the selection pressures also change, and such a shift in allele frequencies is what we mean by *adaptation*. If there are long-term environmental changes in a consistent direction, then allele

Table 4-4 Levels of Organization in the Evolutionary Process

Evolutionary Factor	Level	Evolutionary Process	Technique of Study
Mutation	DNA	Storage of genetic information; ability to replicate; influences phenotype by production of proteins	Biochemistry, electron microscope, recombinant DNA
Mutation	Chromosomes	A vehicle for packaging and transmitting genetic material (DNA)	Light or electron microscope
Recombination (sex cells only)	Cell	The basic unit of life that contains the chromosomes and divides for growth and for production of sex cells	Light or electron microscope
Natural selection	Organism	The unit, composed of cells, that reproduces and which we observe for phenotypic traits	Visual study, biochemistry
Drift, gene flow	Population	A group of interbreeding organisms; changes in allele frequencies between generations; it's the population that evolves	Statistical analysis

frequencies should also shift gradually over time. (The levels of organization in the evolutionary process are summarized in Table 4-4.)

The best-documented example of natural selection in humans involves hemoglobin S (Hb^S), an abnormal form of hemoglobin that results from a point mutation in the gene that produces part of the hemoglobin molecule. As you've

Figure 4-18

The distribution of the sickle-cell allele in the Old World.

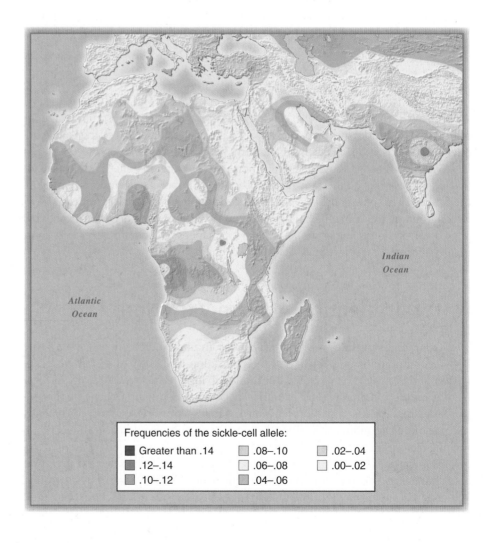

Atlantic Ocean

Indian Ocean

Frequencies of the sickle-cell allele:

■ Greater than .14   □ .08–.10   □ .02–.04
■ .12–.14   □ .06–.08   □ .00–.02
■ .10–.12   ■ .04–.06

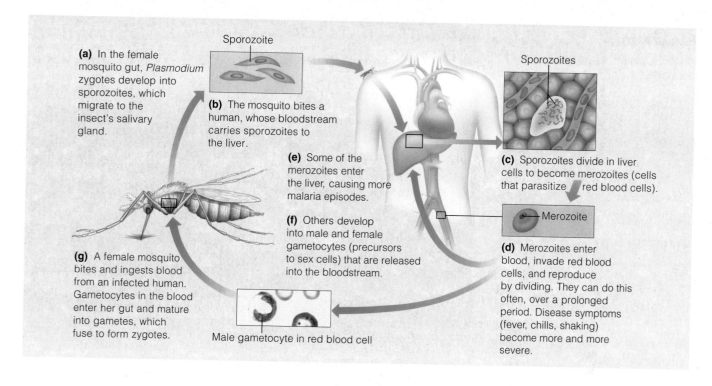

Figure **4-19**
The life cycle of the parasite that causes malaria.

already learned, if an individual inherits this allele (Hb^S) from both parents, he or she will have sickle-cell anemia. Worldwide, sickle-cell anemia causes an estimated 100,000 deaths each year, and in the United States, approximately 40,000 to 50,000 individuals, mostly of African descent, have this disease (Ashley-Koch et al., 2000).

Hb^S is a mutation that occurs occasionally in all human populations, but the allele usually remains rare. In some populations, however, Hb^S is more common; this is especially true in western and central Africa, where its frequency approaches 20 percent. The frequency of the allele is also moderately high in parts of Greece and India (Fig. 4-18). Given the devastating effects of Hb^S in homozygotes, it seems strange that it's fairly common in these populations. One would think natural selection should have acted against it, but it hasn't. In fact, natural selection has actually increased its frequency, and the explanation for this situation can be summed up in one word: malaria.

Malaria is a serious infectious disease caused by a single-celled, parasitic organism referred to as *Plasmodium* (its genus name). This parasite is transmitted to humans by mosquitoes, and it kills an estimated 1 to 3 million people worldwide every year. Very briefly, after an infected mosquito bite, plasmodial parasites invade red blood cells, where they obtain the oxygen they need for reproduction (Fig. 4-19). The consequences of this infection to the human host include fever, chills, headache, nausea, vomiting, and frequently death. In parts of western and central Africa, where malaria is always present, as many as 50 to 75 percent of 2- to 9-year-olds are afflicted.

In the mid-twentieth century, the geographical correlation between malaria and the distribution of the sickle-cell allele (Hb^S) was the only evidence of a biological relationship between the two (Figs. 4-18 and 4-20). Today we know that people with one Hb^S and one Hb^A allele (that is, heterozygotes with sickle-cell trait) have some red blood cells that contain hemoglobin S, and these cells don't provide a suitable environment for the malarial parasite. In other words, having some hemoglobin S is beneficial because it affords some protection from malaria.

Figure 4-20

The distribution of malaria in the Old World.

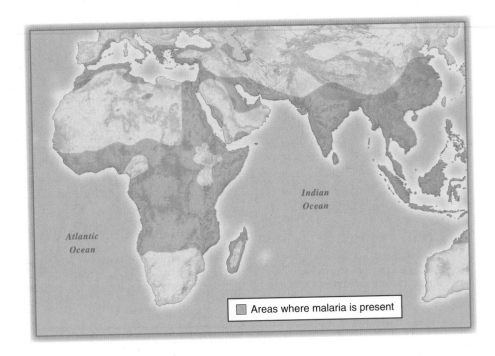

Areas where malaria is present

So, in malarial areas, malaria acts as a selective agent that favors the heterozygous phenotype, since individuals with sickle-cell trait have higher reproductive success than those with normal hemoglobin, who may die of malaria. But selection for heterozygotes means that the Hb^S allele must be maintained in the population and therefore, there will always be some people with sickle-cell anemia. They of course, have the lowest reproductive success of all, since without treatment, most die before reaching adulthood.

The hemoglobin S example illustrates how a deleterious allele can occur in fairly high frequencies in some populations. In this case, natural selection has favored the heterozygous phenotype (sickle-cell trait), which in turn has increased the frequency of the Hb^S allele. The benefit of this kind of selection is that more people in the population have greater resistance to malaria. The cost is that the Hb^S allele isn't being eliminated from the population, which means that there will always be some people with sickle-cell anemia.

Review of Genetics and Evolutionary Factors

In this chapter, we discussed how genetic information is passed from one generation to the next. We also reviewed evolutionary theory, emphasizing the crucial role of natural selection. The various levels—molecular, cellular, individual, and populational—constitute different aspects of the evolutionary process, and they're related to each other in a way that can eventually produce biological change over time. A step-by-step example will make this clear.

In a hypothetical population, everyone has the same hemoglobin type (that is, there's no variation). But in a few individuals of each generation, a substitution of a single base in the DNA sequence changes the genetic code enough to alter the hemoglobin protein and therefore, those individuals' phenotype.

The mutation is carried on chromosomes, and these chromosomes will assort during meiosis to be passed to offspring. The results of this process can be seen by looking at phenotypes (traits) in individuals, and the mode of inheritance is described simply by Mendel's principle of segregation. In other words, if one individual has a mutation in only one member of a pair of alleles on a set of paired chromosomes, there will be a 50 percent chance of passing this chromosome (with the new mutation) to each offspring.

But what does all this have to do with *evolution*? To repeat an earlier definition, evolution is a change in allele frequency in a *population* from one generation to the next. The key point here is that we're considering entire groups of individuals, or populations, and it's populations that may change over time.

We know whether allele frequencies have changed in a population where sickle-cell hemoglobin is found by determining the percentage of individuals with the Hb^S allele versus those with the normal allele (Hb^A). If the relative proportions of these alleles change over time, evolution has occurred. But in addition to knowing that evolution has occurred, it's important to know why; and there are several possible explanations. First, we know that the only way the new Hb^S allele could appear is through mutation, and we've shown how this can happen in a single individual. But this isn't an evolutionary change. For evolutionary change to happen, this new allele must *spread* in the population.

New alleles can spread rather quickly in small populations, and mutations in just a few individuals can alter overall allele frequencies quite rapidly. This would be an example of genetic drift. As we discussed, genetic drift acts in small populations, where random factors may cause significant changes in allele frequencies. Consequently, some alleles may be completely removed from the population, while others may become established as the only allele at that particular locus. (Such alleles are said to be fixed.)

In the course of human evolution, drift has probably played a significant role at times, and it's important to remember that at this microevolutionary level, drift and/or gene flow can (and will) produce evolutionary change, even in the absence of natural selection. However, directional evolutionary trends could only have been sustained by *natural selection*. The way this has worked in the past and still operates today is through differential reproduction. That is, individuals who carry a particular allele or combination of alleles produce more offspring than do other individuals with different alleles. So, the frequency of the new allele in the population increases slowly from generation to generation. When this process is compounded over hundreds of generations for numerous loci, the result is significant evolutionary change. The levels of organization in the evolutionary process are summarized in Table 4-4.

Summary

We've seen how Gregor Mendel discovered the principles of segregation, independent assortment, dominance and recessiveness by doing experiments with pea plants. Even though the field of genetics progressed dramatically during the twentieth century, the concepts first put forth by Gregor Mendel are still the basis of our current knowledge of how traits are inherited.

Basic Mendelian principles are applied to the study of the various modes of inheritance we're familiar with today. We've presented three of these modes in some detail: autosomal dominant, autosomal recessive, and X-linked recessive. The most important factor in all the Mendelian modes of inheritance is the role of segregation of chromosomes, and the alleles they carry, during meiosis.

Building on fundamental nineteenth-century contributions by Charles Darwin and his contemporaries and the rediscovery of Mendel's work in 1900, advances in genetics throughout the twentieth century contributed to contemporary evolutionary thought. In particular, the combination of natural selection with Mendel's principles of inheritance and experimental evidence concerning the nature of mutation have all been synthesized into a modern understanding of evolutionary change, appropriately termed the Modern Synthesis. In this central contemporary theory of evolution, evolutionary change is seen as a two-stage process. The first stage is the production and redistribution of variation. The second stage is the process whereby natural selection acts on the accumulated genetic variation.

Mutation is crucial to all evolutionary change because it's the only source of completely new genetic material (which increases variation). In addition, the factors of recombination, genetic drift, and gene flow redistribute variation within individuals (recombination), within populations (genetic drift), and between populations (gene flow).

Natural selection is the central determining factor that influences the long-term direction of evolutionary change. How natural selection works can best be explained as differential net reproductive success—in other words, how successful individuals are at producing offspring (or passing their genes on to the next generation). For example, in malarial areas, people with sickle-cell trait are more successful at producing offspring than are people with normal hemoglobin or with sickle-cell anemia. Because evolution is an integrated process, we've concluded this chapter with a discussion of how the various evolutionary factors can be integrated into a single, comprehensive view of evolutionary change.

Critical Thinking Questions

1. Has our discussion of dominance and recessiveness changed your understanding of these principles, and did the discussion differ from what you may have learned in the past?
2. Can you think of some examples of how selection, gene flow, genetic drift, and mutation have acted on populations or species in the past? Try to think of at least one human and one nonhuman example we didn't discuss. Why do you think genetic drift might be important today to endangered species?
3. Construct a pedigree chart for your family regarding some Mendelian trait, such as blood type. If possible, include your siblings (if any), your parents, and your grandparents. If you're really ambitious, consider including aunts, uncles, and cousins.

Heredity and Evolution

CHAPTER

5

Macroevolution: Processes of Vertebrate and Mammalian Evolution

Key Question

In what ways do humans fit into a biological continuum (as vertebrates and as mammals)?

Click!

Go to the following media for interactive activities and exercises on topics covered in this chapter:

- Online Virtual Laboratories for Physical Anthropology, Version 4.0

Introduction

Many people think of paleontology as pretty boring and only interesting to overly serious academics. But have you ever been to a natural history museum—or perhaps to one of the larger, more elaborate toy stores? If so, you may have seen a full-size mock-up of *Tyrannosaurus rex*, one that might even have moved its head and arms and screamed threateningly. These displays are usually encircled by enthralled adults, often accompanied by flocks of noisy children, all of whom seem anything but bored.

The study of the history of life on earth is full of mystery and adventure. The bits and pieces of fossils are the remains of once living, breathing animals (some of them extremely large and dangerous). Searching for these fossils in remote corners of the globe is not a task for the faint of heart. Piecing together the tiny clues and ultimately reconstructing what *Tyrannosaurus rex* (or, for that matter, a small, 50-million-year-old primate) looked like and how it might have behaved is really much like detective work. Sure, it can be serious; but it's also a lot of fun.

In this chapter, we review the evolution of vertebrates and, more specifically, mammals. It's important to understand these more general aspects of evolutionary history so that we can place our species in its proper biological context. *Homo sapiens* is only one of millions of species that have evolved. More than that, humans have been around for just an instant in the vast expanse of time that life has existed, and we want to know where we fit in this long and complex story of life on earth. To discover where humans belong in this continuum of evolving life on earth, we also discuss some contemporary issues relating to evolutionary theory. In particular, we emphasize concepts relating to large-scale evolutionary processes, that is, *macroevolution* (in contrast to the microevolutionary focus of Chapters 3 and 4). The fundamental perspectives reviewed here concern geological history, principles of classification, and modes of evolutionary change. These perspectives will serve as a basis for topics covered throughout much of the remainder of this book.

The Human Place in the Organic World

There are millions of species living today; if we were to include microorganisms, the total would likely exceed tens of millions. And if we added in the multitudes of species that are now extinct, the total would be staggering—perhaps *hundreds* of millions!

How do we deal scientifically with all this diversity? As humans, biologists approach complexity by simplifying it. One way to do this is to develop a system of **classification** that organizes diversity into categories and, at the same time, indicates evolutionary relationships.

Multicellular organisms that move about and ingest food (but don't photosynthesize, as do plants) are called animals (Fig. 5-1). Within the kingdom Animalia,

classification In biology, the ordering of organisms into categories, such as orders, families, and genera, to show evolutionary relationships.

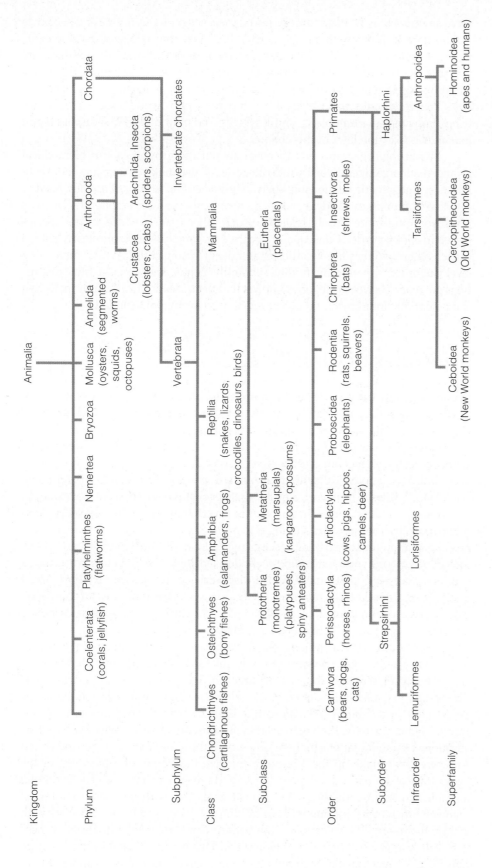

Figure **5-1**

In this classification chart, modified from Linnaeus, all animals are placed in certain categories based on structural similarities. Not all members of categories are shown; for example, there are up to 20 orders of placental mammals (8 are depicted). Chapter 6 presents a more comprehensive classification of the primate order.

there are more than 20 major groups called *phyla* (*sing.,* phylum). One of these phyla is **Chordata**, animals with a nerve cord, gill slits (at some stage of development), and a supporting cord along the back. In turn, most (but not all) chordates are **vertebrates**—so called because they have a vertebral column. Vertebrates also have a developed brain and paired sensory structures for sight, smell, and balance.

The vertebrates themselves are subdivided into five classes: cartilaginous fishes, bony fishes, amphibians, reptiles/birds, and mammals. We'll discuss mammalian classification later in this chapter.

By putting organisms into increasingly narrow groupings, this hierarchical arrangement organizes diversity into categories. It also makes statements about evolutionary and genetic relationships between species and groups of species. Further dividing mammals into orders makes the statement that, for example, all carnivores (Carnivora) are more closely related to each other than they are to any species placed in another order. Consequently, bears, dogs, and cats are more closely related to each other than they are to cattle, pigs, or deer (Artiodactyla). At each succeeding level (suborder, superfamily, family, subfamily, genus, and species), finer distinctions are made between categories until, at the species level, only those animals that can potentially interbreed and produce viable offspring are included.

Principles of Classification

Before we go any further, we need to discuss the basis of animal classification. The field that specializes in establishing the rules of classification is called *taxonomy*. Organisms are classified first, and most traditionally, according to their physical similarities. Such was the basis of the first systematic classification devised by Linnaeus in the eighteenth century (see Chapter 2).

Today, basic physical similarities are still considered a good starting point. But for similarities to be useful, they *must* reflect evolutionary descent. For example, the bones of the forelimb of all air-breathing vertebrates initially adapted to land (terrestrial) environments are so similar in number and form (Fig. 5-2) that the obvious explanation for the striking resemblance is that all four kinds of these "four-footed" (tetrapod) vertebrates ultimately derived their forelimb structure from a common ancestor. What's more, recent discoveries of remarkably well-preserved fossils from Canada have provided exciting new evidence of how the transition from aquatic to land living took place and what the earliest land vertebrates looked like (Daeschler et al., 2006; Shubin et al., 2006).

How could such seemingly major evolutionary modifications in structure occur? They quite likely began with only relatively minor genetic changes. For example, recent research shows that forelimb development in all vertebrates is directed by just a few regulatory genes, called *Hox* genes (see p. 55; Shubin et al., 1997; Riddle and Tabin, 1999). A few mutations in certain *Hox* genes in early vertebrates led to the basic limb plan seen in all subsequent vertebrates. With further additional, small mutations in these genes, or in the genes they regulate, the varied structures that make up the wing of a chicken, the flipper of a porpoise, or the upper limb of a human developed. You should recognize that *basic* genetic regulatory mechanisms are highly conserved in animals; that is, they've been maintained relatively unchanged for hundreds of millions of years. Like a musical score with a basic theme, small variations on the pattern can produce the different "tunes" that differentiate one organism from another. This is the essential genetic foundation for most macroevolutionary change. Large anatomical modifications, there-

Chordata The phylum of the animal kingdom that includes vertebrates.

vertebrates Animals with segmented, bony spinal columns; includes fishes, amphibians, reptiles (including birds), and mammals.

fore, don't always require major genetic rearrangements (see "New Frontiers in Anthropology," pp. 136–138).

Structures that are shared by species on the basis of descent from a common ancestor are called **homologies**. Homologies alone are reliable indicators of evolutionary relationship, but we have to be careful not to draw hasty conclusions from superficial similarities. For example, both birds and butterflies have wings, but they shouldn't be grouped together on the basis of this single characteristic; butterflies (as insects) differ dramatically from birds in several other, even more fundamental ways. (For example, birds have an internal skeleton, central nervous system, and four limbs; insects don't.)

Here's what's happened in evolutionary history: From quite distant ancestors, both butterflies and birds have developed wings *independently*. So their (superficial) similarities are a product of separate evolutionary responses

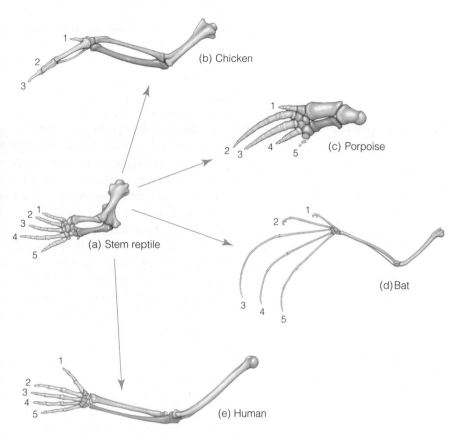

to roughly similar functional demands. Such similarities, based on independent functional adaptation and not on shared evolutionary descent, are called **analogies**. The process that leads to the development of analogies (also called analogous structures) such as wings in birds and butterflies is termed **homoplasy**. In the case of butterflies and birds, the homoplasy has occurred in evolutionary lines that share only very remote ancestry. Here, homoplasy has produced analogous structures separately from any homology. In some cases, however, homoplasy can occur in lineages that are more closely related (and share considerable homology as well). Homoplasy in closely related lineages is evident among the primates; for example, New and Old World monkeys show considerable homoplasy, and so do the great apes (see Chapter 6).

Constructing Classifications and Interpreting Evolutionary Relationships

Evolutionary biologists typically use two major approaches, or "schools," when interpreting evolutionary relationships with the goal of producing classifications. The first approach, called **evolutionary systematics**, is the more traditional. The second approach, called **cladistics**, has emerged primarily in the last three decades. While aspects of both approaches are still used by most evolutionary biologists, in recent years cladistic methodologies have predominated among anthropologists. Indeed, one noted primate evolutionist commented that "virtually all current studies of primate phylogeny involve the methods and terminology" of cladistics (Fleagle, 1999, p. 1).

Before we begin drawing distinctions between these two approaches, it's first helpful to note features shared by both evolutionary systematics and cladis-

Figure **5-2**

Homologies. Similarities in the forelimb bones of these land vertebrates (tetrapods) can be most easily explained by descent from a common ancestor.

homologies Similarities between organisms based on descent from a common ancestor.

analogies Similarities between organisms based strictly on common function, with no assumed common evolutionary descent.

homoplasy (*homo*, meaning "same," and *plasy*, meaning "growth") The separate evolutionary development of similar characteristics in different groups of organisms.

evolutionary systematics A traditional approach to classification (and evolutionary interpretation) in which presumed ancestors and descendants are traced in time by analysis of homologous characters.

cladistics An approach to classification that attempts to make rigorous evolutionary interpretations based solely on analysis of certain types of homologous characters (those considered to be derived characters).

tics. First, both schools are interested in tracing evolutionary relationships and in constructing classifications that reflect these relationships. Second, both schools recognize that organisms must be compared using specific features (called *characters*) and that some of these characters are more informative than others. And third (deriving directly from the previous two points), both approaches focus exclusively on homologies.

But these approaches also have some significant differences—in how characters are chosen, which groups are compared, and how the results are interpreted and eventually incorporated into evolutionary schemes and classifications. The primary difference is that cladistics more explicitly and more rigorously defines the kinds of homologies that yield the most useful information. For example, at a very basic level, all life (except for some viruses) shares DNA as the molecule underlying all organic processes. However, beyond inferring that all life most likely derives from a single origin (a most intriguing point), the mere presence of DNA tells us nothing further regarding more specific relationships among different kinds of life-forms. To draw further conclusions, we need to look at particular characters that certain groups share as the result of more recent ancestry.

This perspective emphasizes an important point: Some homologous characters are much more informative than others. We saw earlier that all terrestrial vertebrates share homologies in the number and basic arrangement of bones in the forelimb. Even though these similarities are broadly useful in showing that these large evolutionary groups (amphibians, reptiles, and mammals) are all related through a distant ancestor, they don't provide information we can use to distinguish one group from another (a reptile from a mammal, for example). These kinds of characters (also called traits) that are shared through such remote ancestry are said to be **ancestral**, or primitive. We prefer the term *ancestral* because it doesn't reflect negatively on the evolutionary value of the character in question. In biological anthropology, the term *primitive* or *ancestral* simply means that a character seen in two organisms is inherited in both of them from a distant ancestor.

In most cases, analyzing ancestral characters doesn't supply enough information to make accurate evolutionary interpretations of relationships between different groups. In fact, misinterpretation of ancestral characters can easily lead to quite inaccurate evolutionary conclusions. Cladistics focuses on traits that distinguish particular evolutionary lineages; such traits are far more informative than ancestral traits. Lineages that share a common ancestor are called a **clade**, giving the name *cladistics* to the field that seeks to identify and interpret these groups. It is perhaps the most fundamental point of cladistics that evolutionary groups (that is, clades) all share one common ancestor and are thus said to be **monophyletic**. If a proposed evolutionary grouping is found to have more than one ancestor (rather than a single one shared by *all* members), it is said to be **polyphyletic**, and it represents neither a well-defined clade nor an evolutionary group actually separate from other ones. We'll encounter problems of exactly this nature in Chapter 6 when we tackle the classification of a small primate called a tarsier as well as that of the great apes.

When we try to identify a clade, the characters of interest are said to be **derived**, or **modified**. Thus, while the general ancestral bony pattern of the forelimb in land vertebrates doesn't allow us to distinguish among them, the further modification of this pattern in certain groups (as hooves, flippers, or wings, for instance) does.

A simplified example might help clarify the basic principles used in cladistic analysis. Figure 5-3a shows a hypothetical "lineage" of passenger vehicles. All of the "descendant" vehicles share a common ancestor, the prototype passenger

ancestral Referring to characters inherited by a group of organisms from a remote ancestor and thus not diagnostic of groups (lineages) that diverged after the character first appeared; also called primitive.

clade A group of organisms sharing a common ancestor. The group includes the common ancestor and all descendants.

monophyletic Referring to an evolutionary group (clade) composed of descendants all sharing a common ancestor.

polyphyletic Referring to an evolutionary group composed of descendants with more than one common ancestor (and thus not a true clade).

derived (modified) Referring to characters that are modified from the ancestral condition and thus diagnostic of particular evolutionary lineages.

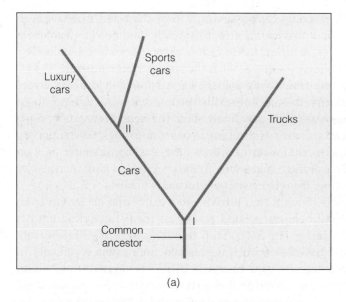

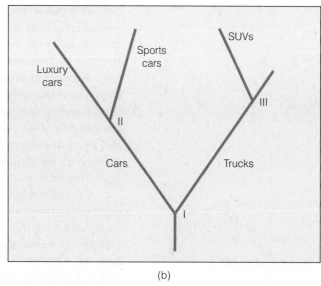

(a)

(b)

From a common ancestor of all passenger vehicles, the first major divergence is that between cars and trucks (I). A later divergence also occurs between luxury cars and sports cars (II). Derived features of each grouping ("lineage") appear only after its divergence from other groups (e.g., cargo beds are found only in trucks, cushioned suspension only in cars; likewise, only sports cars have a decorative racing stripe).

In this "tree," SUVs diverge from trucks, but like sports cars, they have a decorative racing stripe. This feature is a homoplasy and does not make SUVs sports cars. The message is that classifications based on just one characteristic that can appear independently in different groups can lead to an incorrect conclusion. *Note:* In (a), two clades are defined (I and II), while in (b), three clades (I, II, and III) are recognized.

vehicle. The first major division (I) differentiates passenger cars from trucks. The second split (that is, diversification) is between luxury cars and sports cars (you could, of course, imagine many other subcategories). Modified (derived) traits that distinguish trucks from cars might include type of frame, suspension, wheel size, and, in some forms, an open cargo bed. Derived characters that might distinguish sports cars from luxury cars could include engine size and type, wheel base size, and a decorative racing stripe.

Figure **5-3**

Evolutionary "trees" showing development of passenger vehicles.

Now let's assume that you're presented with an "unknown" vehicle (meaning one as yet unclassified). How do you decide what kind of vehicle it is? You might note such features as four wheels, a steering wheel, and a seat for the driver, but these are *ancestral* characters (found in the common ancestor) of all passenger vehicles. If, however, you note that the vehicle lacks a cargo bed and raised suspension (so it's not a truck) but has a racing stripe, you might conclude that it's a car, and more than that, a sports car (since it has a derived feature presumably of *only* that group).

All this seems fairly obvious, and you've probably noticed that this simple type of decision making characterizes much of human mental organization. Still, we frequently deal with complications that aren't so obvious. What if you're presented with a sports utility vehicle (SUV) with a racing stripe (Fig. 5-3b)? SUVs are basically trucks, but the presence of the racing stripe could be seen as a homoplasy with sports cars. The lesson here is that we need to be careful, look at several traits, decide which are ancestral and which are derived, and finally try to recognize the complexity (and confusion) introduced by homoplasy.

Our example of passenger vehicles is useful up to a point. Because it concerns human inventions, the groupings possess characters that humans can add and delete in almost any combination. Naturally occurring organic systems are more limited in this respect. Any species can possess only those characters that have been inherited from its ancestor or that have been subsequently modified (derived) from those shared with the ancestor. So any modification in *any* species is constrained by that species' evolutionary legacy—that is, what the species starts out with.

Another example, one drawn from paleontological (fossil) evidence of actual organisms, can help clarify these points. Most people know something about dinosaur evolution, and some of you may know about the recent controversies surrounding this topic. There are several intriguing issues concerning the evolutionary history of dinosaurs, and recent fossil discoveries have shed considerable light on them. We'll mention some of these issues later in the chapter, but here we consider one of the more fascinating: the relationship of dinosaurs to birds.

Traditionally, it was thought that birds were a quite distinct group from reptiles and not especially closely related to any of them (including extinct forms, such as the dinosaurs; Fig. 5-4a). Still, the early origins of birds were clouded in mystery and have been much debated for more than a century. In fact, the first fossil evidence of a very primitive bird (now known to be about 150 million years old) was discovered in 1861, just two years following Darwin's publication of *Origin of Species*. Despite some initial and quite remarkably accurate interpretations by Thomas Huxley linking these early birds to dinosaurs, most experts concluded that there was no close relationship. This view persisted through most of the twentieth century, but events of the last two decades have swung the consensus back to the hypothesis that birds *are* closely related to some dinosaurs. Two developments in particular have influenced this change of opinion: the remarkable discoveries in the 1990s from China, Madagascar, and elsewhere and the application of cladistic methods to the interpretation of these and other fossils.

Recent finds from Madagascar of chicken-sized, primitive birds dated to 70–65 million years ago (mya) show an elongated second toe (similar, in fact, to that in the dinosaur *Velociraptor*, made infamous in the film *Jurassic Park*). Indeed, these primitive birds from Madagascar show many other similarities to *Velociraptor* and its close cousins, which together comprise a group of small- to medium-sized ground-living, carnivorous dinosaurs called **theropods**. Even more extraordinary finds have been unearthed recently in China, where the traces of what were once

theropods Small- to medium-sized ground-living dinosaurs, dated to approximately 150 mya and thought to be related to birds.

Figure **5-4**

Evolutionary relationships of birds and dinosaurs. (a) Traditional view, showing no close relationship. (b) Revised view, showing common ancestry of birds and dinosaurs.

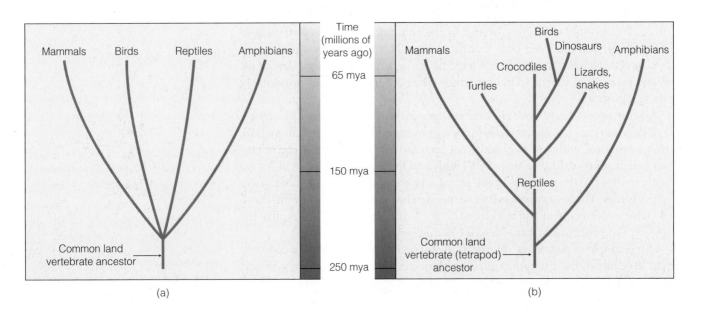

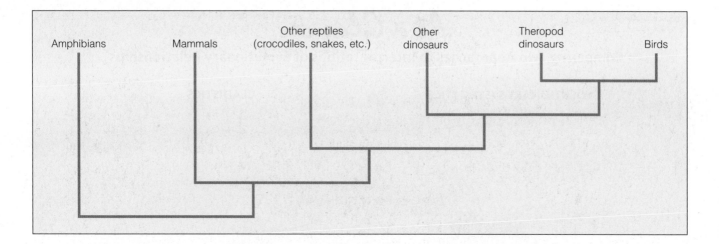

Figure **5-5**

This cladogram shows relationships of birds, dinosaurs, and other terrestrial vertebrates. Notice that there's no time scale, and both living and fossil forms are shown along the same dimension—that is, ancestor-descendant relationships aren't indicated. The chart is slightly simplified, as there are other branches (not shown) within the reptiles (with birds slightly more closely related to crocodiles than to other reptiles, such as snakes and lizards).

feathers have been found embossed in fossilized sediments! For many researchers, these new finds have finally solved the mystery of bird origins (Fig. 5-4b), leading them to conclude that "birds are not only *descended* from dinosaurs, they *are* dinosaurs (and reptiles)—just as humans are mammals, even though people are as different from other mammals as birds are from other reptiles" (Padian and Chiappe, 1998, p. 43).

There are some doubters who remain concerned that the presence of feathers in dinosaurs (145–125 mya) might simply be a homoplasy (that is, these creatures may have developed the trait independently from its appearance in birds). Certainly, the possibility of homoplasy must always be considered, as it can add considerably to the complexity of what seems like a straightforward evolutionary interpretation. Indeed, strict cladistic analysis assumes that homoplasy is not a common occurrence; if it were, perhaps no evolutionary interpretation could be very straightforward! In the case of the proposed relationship between some (theropod) dinosaurs and birds, the presence of feathers looks like an excellent example of a **shared derived** characteristic, which therefore *does* link the forms. What's more, cladistic analysis emphasizes that several characteristics should be examined, since homoplasy might muddle an interpretation based on just one or two shared traits. In the bird/dinosaur case, several other characteristics further suggest their evolutionary relationship.

One last point needs to be mentioned. Traditional evolutionary systematics illustrates the hypothesized evolutionary relationships using a *phylogeny*, more properly called a **phylogenetic tree**. Strict cladistic analysis, however, shows relationships in a **cladogram** (Fig. 5-5). If you examine the charts in Figures 5-4 and 5-5, you'll see some obvious differences. A phylogenetic tree incorporates the dimension of time, as shown in Figure 5-4 (you can find many other examples in this and upcoming chapters). A cladogram doesn't indicate time; all forms (fossil and modern) are shown along one dimension. Phylogenetic trees usually attempt to make some hypotheses regarding ancestor-descendant relationships (for example, theropods are ancestral to modern birds). Cladistic analysis (through cladograms) makes no attempt whatsoever to discern ancestor-descendant relationships. In fact, strict cladists are quite skeptical that the evidence really permits such specific evolutionary hypotheses to be scientifically confirmed (since there are many more extinct species than living ones).

In practice, most physical anthropologists (and other evolutionary biologists) utilize cladistic analysis to identify and assess the utility of traits and to make

shared derived Relating to specific character traits shared in common between two life-forms and considered the most useful for making evolutionary interpretations.

phylogenetic tree A chart showing evolutionary relationships as determined by evolutionary systematics. It contains a time component and implies ancestor-descendant relationships.

cladogram A chart showing evolutionary relationships as determined by cladistic analysis. It's based solely on interpretation of shared derived characters. It contains no time component and does not imply ancestor-descendant relationships.

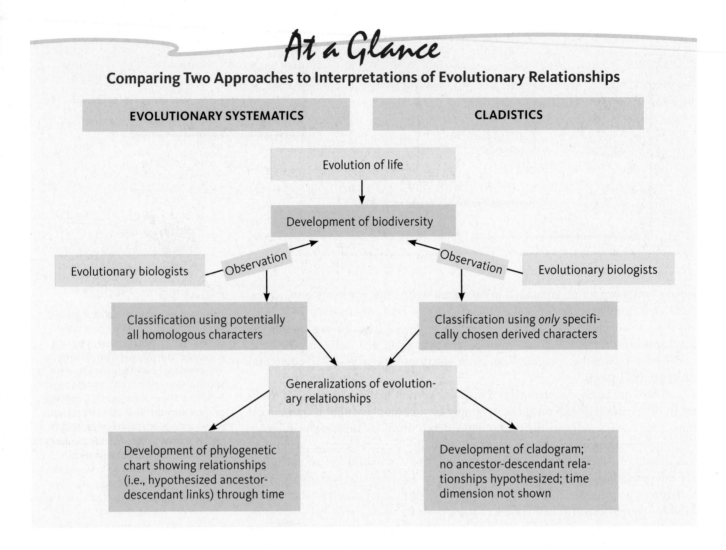

At a Glance

Comparing Two Approaches to Interpretations of Evolutionary Relationships

testable hypotheses regarding the relationships between groups of organisms. They also frequently extend this basic cladistic methodology to further hypothesize likely ancestor-descendant relationships shown relative to a time scale (that is, in a phylogenetic tree). In this way, aspects of both traditional evolutionary systematics and cladistic analysis are combined to produce a more complete picture of evolutionary history.

Definition of Species

Whether biologists are doing a cladistic or more traditional phylogenetic analysis, they're comparing groups of organisms—that is, different species, genera (*sing.,* genus), families, orders, and so forth. Fundamental to all these levels of classification is the most basic, the species. It's appropriate, then, to ask how biologists define species. We addressed this issue briefly in Chapter 1, where we used the most common definition, one that emphasizes interbreeding and reproductive isolation. While it's not the only definition of species (others are discussed shortly), this view, called the **biological species concept** (Mayr, 1970), is the one preferred by most zoologists.

biological species concept A depiction of species as groups of individuals capable of fertile interbreeding but reproductively isolated from other such groups.

To understand what species are, you might consider how they come about in the first place—what Darwin called the "origin of species." This most fundamental of macroevolutionary processes is called **speciation**. According to the biological species concept, the way new species are first produced involves some form of isolation. Picture a single species (baboons, for example) composed of several populations distributed over a wide geographical area. Gene exchange between populations (gene flow) will be limited if a geographical barrier, such as an ocean or mountain range, effectively separates these populations. This extremely important form of isolating mechanism is called *geographical isolation*.

If one baboon population (A) is separated from another baboon population (B) by a mountain range, individual baboons of population A will not mate with individuals from B (Fig. 5-6). As time passes (perhaps hundreds or thousands of generations), genetic differences will accumulate in both populations. If population size is small, we can assume that genetic drift will also cause allele frequencies to change in both populations. And since drift is *random*, we wouldn't expect the effects to be the same. Consequently, the two populations will begin to diverge genetically.

As long as gene exchange is limited, the populations can only become more genetically different over time. What's more, further difference can be expected if the baboon groups are occupying slightly different habitats. These additional genetic differences would be incorporated through the process of natural selection. Certain individuals in population A would be more reproductively fit in their own environment, but they would show less reproductive success in the environment occupied by population B. So allele frequencies will shift further, resulting in even greater divergence between the two groups.

With the cumulative effects of genetic drift and natural selection acting over many generations, the result will be two populations that—even if they were to come back into geographical contact—could no longer interbreed. More than just geographical isolation might now apply. There may, for instance, be behavioral differences that interfere with courtship—what we call *behavioral isolation*. Using our *biological* definition of species, we would now recognize two distinct species where initially only one existed.

Another related process that can contribute to the further differentiation of populations into incipient species concerns mate recognition. This is sometimes called the **recognition species concept**, though the crucial process, again, concerns reproduction (that is, who's mating with whom; Ridley, 1993).

Assume in our baboon example that some isolation has already occurred and that phenotypic (and genotypic) differences are beginning to be established between two populations. In this situation, coloration patterns of faces or the size, location, coloration, or even smell of the female genital swelling might vary from

speciation The process by which a new species evolves from an earlier species. Speciation is the most basic process in macroevolution.

recognition species concept A depiction of species in which the key aspect is the ability of individuals to identify members of their own species for purposes of mating (and to avoid mating with members of other species). In theory, this type of selective mating is a component of a species concept emphasizing mating and is therefore compatible with the biological species concept.

Figure **5-6**

This speciation model illustrates branching evolution, or cladogenesis, which is caused by increasing reproductive isolation.

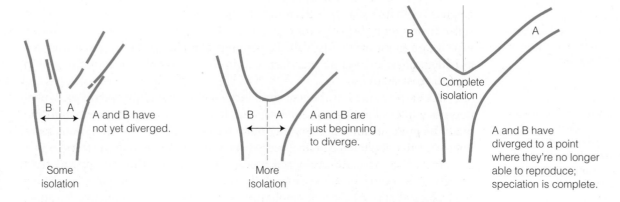

B A — A and B have not yet diverged.

Some isolation

B A — A and B are just beginning to diverge.

More isolation

B A

Complete isolation

A and B have diverged to a point where they're no longer able to reproduce; speciation is complete.

A Closer Look

Small Changes, Big Impact

The phenomenon of island dwarfing, where body size changes can occur quite rapidly, is well recognized but not well understood. What are the precise mechanisms that cause large-bodied creatures to dwarf while many smaller creatures transform to much larger size? This occurrence has been observed and confirmed in a wide variety of animals (reptiles, including birds, and some mammals), but it's only within the past few years that paleoanthropologists have been forced to confront the possibility that humans are not exempt.

The "island rule," as Van Valen (1973) called it, states that due to the unique adaptive pressures of islands, large-bodied vertebrates tend to become smaller over time, and smaller ones become bigger. The effects of the island rule tend to be inversely proportional to the island's size (Heaney, 1978) and positively correlated with the degree of isolation from the mainland (Foster, 1964). So the smaller and more isolated the island, the bigger the size change.

Several mechanisms have been proposed to explain how evolution could produce such physical changes, though the most widely held is the "population and food availability" hypothesis. On islands or in other isolated areas, there's likely to be a decrease in resources due to reduced land area. Fewer animals can be supported by such limited resources, so mammals have fewer young and plants undergo slower growing cycles. Owing to a general absence of large predators, we find

a wider array of responses to the environment both within and between species. This variety is often expressed in complex and much-accelerated patterns of body size evolution (Grant, 1982).

Because larger-bodied individuals use more resources, natural selection favors smaller sizes (Lomolino, 2005). Consider the analogy of the pioneers on the Oregon Trail. Most of the survivors who reached the West were women and children and the smaller-bodied men. The large, burly men who would have been expected to "tough it out" were actually the first to succumb to the effects of dwindling food supplies. In isolated areas with finite resources, the selection for smaller individuals over time gives way to an overall smaller-bodied population. Because of their smaller size, a bigger population of these individuals can be maintained given a constant amount of resources (Anderson and Handley, 2002).

Though just hearing the words *elephant* and *mammoth* makes people think of large size, there are many well-known examples of island dwarfing in these vertebrates. British scientist Dorothea Bate (1879–1951) spent a good deal of her paleontological career studying such curiosities. Since she worked and traveled alone in the early twentieth century, she often dressed like a man while excavating previously unheard-of species, such as pygmy hippos, dwarf elephants, and giant dormice (just like in *Alice in Wonderland*). Among her finds were mainland Mediterranean elephant populations that

group to group. If so, then a female from population A might not recognize a male from population B as an appropriate mate (and vice versa, of course). Natural selection would quickly favor such discrimination if hybrids were less reproductively successful than within-population crosses. Indeed, once such "selective breeding" became established, speciation would be accelerated considerably.

Another definition of species focuses primarily on natural selection and emphasizes that speciation is the result of influences of varied habitats. In this view, called the **ecological species concept**, a species is defined as a group of organisms exploiting a single niche. Also called an **ecological niche**, this is the physical as well as biological position of an organism within the biological world (that is, within the full ecosystem).

For each population, the ecological niche will vary slightly, and different phenotypes will be slightly more advantageous in each. For example, one population might be more arboreal and another more terrestrial; but there would not be an intermediate population equally successful on the ground and in the trees.

In recent years, the ecological species concept has attracted support from several evolutionary biologists, especially among physical anthropologists. While the biological species concept emphasizes gene flow and reproductive isolation,

ecological species concept The concept that a species is a group of organisms exploiting a single niche. This view emphasizes the role of natural selection in separating species from one another.

ecological niche The position of a species within its physical and biological environments. A species' ecological niche is defined by such components as diet, terrain, vegetation, type of predators, relationships with other species, and activity patterns, and each niche is unique to a given species. Together, ecological niches make up an ecosystem.

had become isolated on the islands of Crete and Cyprus, ultimately becoming dwarfed to only 6 feet tall at the shoulder.

Bate had such a gift for discovering island dwarfed species that one of the museum trustees who supported her wrote, "Only imagine the sensation you would make if you could walk down Piccadilly leading by a string your Pigmy [sic] Elephants, Hippopotami, Myotragus, Tortoises, etc. etc. all in one long queue, the little Elephant blowing his trumpet, and the Hippopotamus wagging its tail" (Shindler, 2006 p. 209).

Though she discovered numerous island curiosities, Bate would never see many of these animals appropriately placed in their evolutionary family tree because mainland-to-island body size comparisons make little sense without a detailed phylogeny; it's only within such a framework that any pattern can be discerned. Such phylogenies are constantly under revision, with some evolutionary lineages only coming to light in recent years.

It's crucial to recognize that both natural selection and genetic drift can become more intense in isolated settings, such as islands, thus accelerating the rate of evolutionary change. Such changes begin at a microevolutionary level; but over time, they may lead to macroevolutionary changes within a lineage, leading to speciation. It's within such a phylogenetic/evolutionary framework that we will be forced to confront an interesting variant within our own genus, *Homo*. In Chapter 14, we'll discuss a provocative find from the island of Flores, Indonesia, that brings the island rule shockingly close to home.

Drawing by Robert Greisen

Figure 1

Scaled representation of the relative sizes of a dwarfed elephant, normal hippopotamus, and Indian elephant. Redrawn from Attenborough (1987).

the ecological species concept stresses the role of natural selection. Clearly, our approach in this text has been to focus on the evolutionary contribution of natural selection; thus, the ecological species concept has much to offer here. Nevertheless, our understanding of species need not entail an either-or choice between the biological species concept and the ecological species concept. Some population isolation could indeed *begin* the process of speciation, and at this stage, the influence of genetic drift could be crucial. The process might then be further influenced by mate recognition as well as by natural selection as individuals in different populations adapt to varying environments.

A final approach that biologists use to define species is primarily a practical one. How can species be defined when neither reproductive isolation nor ecological separation can be clearly tested? This type of difficulty plagues the interpretation of fossil organisms but sometimes crops up in discussions of contemporary species as well. For example, Colin Groves, of the Australian National University, has recently advocated splitting many populations of primates into separate species (Groves, 2001b). He utilizes a definition of species called the **phylogenetic species concept**, based on an identifiable pattern of ancestry (that is, who is *clearly* related to whom).

phylogenetic species concept Splitting many populations into separate species based on an identifiable parental pattern of ancestry.

For living species, characteristics that define a phylogenetic species could be phenotypic or more directly genotypic (identifying shared patterns in the karyotype or, as is becoming more widely used, in specific DNA sequences). For extinct groups, with a few notable exceptions (from which ancient DNA has been extracted), the *only* evidence available comes from phenotypic characters that can be identified in fossil forms (see p. 124 for further discussion).

Processes of Speciation

Now that we've seen how species can be defined in somewhat varied ways, what are some of the more explicit theories developed by evolutionary biologists to account for *how* species originate? First, you should recognize that these hypotheses are quite abstract and thus difficult to test doing conventional field biology on contemporary species. Although rates of evolution vary widely among different groups of animals, the process is, by its very nature, a slow one. Some groups, such as fruit flies, members of genus *Drosophila*, seem to speciate especially slowly, taking a million years or more for a new species to be fully separate. The fastest rate of speciation in recent times may have occurred in freshwater fishes. Extreme isolation of cichlid fish populations (of which the angelfish is one of the most familiar forms) has periodically occurred in African lakes, producing "explosive speciation" in just the last few thousand years (Seehausen, 2002). We must emphasize, however, that such extreme isolation has likely never been a factor in the evolution of other vertebrates. Mammals seem to fall somewhere in between the slowly evolving fruit flies and the explosively speciating cichlids. As suggested by fossil evidence, it likely takes tens of thousands of years for speciation to occur in a free-ranging mammalian species.

Given the constraints of field testing in such a slowly occurring phenomenon as macroevolution, biologists have hypothesized that speciation could occur in three different ways: by allopatric speciation, parapatric speciation, or sympatric speciation.

By far, the most widely accepted view of speciation emphasizes an **allopatric** pattern. This model requires complete reproductive isolation within a population, leading to the formation of an incipient species separated (geographically) from its ancestral population.

In parapatric speciation, only *partial* reproductive isolation is required, so that the ranges of the populations may be partially overlapping. In this situation, a hybrid zone would form in an area between the two partially separated populations. More complete separation could then occur through reinforcement of mate recognition and selective breeding.

Interestingly, in some areas of East Africa, there's good evidence that parapatric speciation might be currently (and slowly) taking place between populations of savanna baboons and hamadryas baboons. Long-term research by Jane Phillips-Conroy and Clifford Jolly has carefully documented hybrid individuals produced by the mating of savanna baboons with hamadryas baboons. Traditionally, these two types of baboons have been placed in separate species (savanna as *Papio cynocephalus* and hamadryas as *Papio hamadryas*). Yet, the hybrids appear quite functional and are *fertile* (Phillips-Conroy et al., 1992; Jolly, 1993). So, what we're likely seeing here is speciation in process—and probably following a parapatric pattern. This means that we might regard these two types of baboons as incipient species. It's possible that some mate recognition differentiation may be operating as well, since male-female interactions differ considerably between savanna and hamadryas baboons.

allopatric Living in different areas. This pattern is important in the divergence of closely related species from each other and from their shared ancestral species because it leads to reproductive isolation.

The third type of speciation proposed, sympatric speciation, is theorized to occur completely within one population with *no* necessary reproductive isolation. In other words, two species result from one population that occupies the same geographical locality. However, this form of speciation, while possible, is not well supported by contemporary evidence and is thus considered the least significant of the three models.

A fourth type of speciation, sometimes recognized as a form of sympatric speciation, is called *instantaneous speciation*. In this pattern, chromosomal rearrangements occur (by chromosomal mutation), producing immediate reproductive barriers. This type of speciation, well documented in plants, can be rapid, and varieties can emerge with completely different numbers of chromosomes. Here, the process is one of multiplication of chromosome sets (due to mistakes in meiosis), producing a condition called *polyploidy* (the presence of more than two complete sets of chromosomes in an individual). While common in plants, such drastic reorganization of chromosome number is not a factor in the speciation of animals, where polyploidy is always lethal. However, somewhat less dramatic chromosomal alterations, could accelerate speciation in animals. Certainly, chromosomal alterations may be important in speciation, and some researchers have even suggested that such processes may be a central factor in macroevolution.

Even so, demonstration in animals of the systematic influence of such large-scale mutation has been difficult. In fact, theoretical models suggest that major mutational change could not *by itself* produce speciation in animals, but would require some further mechanism to help "fix" the genetic changes within populations. Inbreeding within small population segments has been suggested by some investigators as a possible mechanism that could reinforce rapid speciation by chromosomal mutation. What's more, some theoretical support for this process has been found in those species divided into small social groupings, such as species of horses and primates.

Interpreting Species and Other Groups in the Fossil Record

Throughout much of this text, we'll be using various taxonomic terms for fossil primates (including fossil hominins). You'll be introduced to such terms as *Proconsul*, *Sivapithecus*, *Australopithecus*, and *Homo*. Of course, *Homo* is still a living primate. But it's especially difficult to make these types of designations from remains of animals that are long dead (and only partially preserved as skeletal remains). In these contexts, what do such names mean in evolutionary terms?

Our goal when applying species, genus, or other taxonomic labels to groups of organisms is to make meaningful biological statements about the variation that's represented. When looking at populations of living or long-extinct animals, we certainly are going to see variation; this happens in *any* sexually reproducing organism due to recombination (see Chapter 3). As a result of recombination, each individual organism is a unique combination of genetic material, and the uniqueness is often reflected to some extent in the phenotype.

Besides such *individual variation*, we see other kinds of systematic variation in all biological populations. *Age changes* alter overall body size, as well as shape, in many mammals. One pertinent example for fossil human and ape studies is the change in number, size, and shape of teeth from deciduous (also known as baby or milk) teeth (only 20 teeth are present) to the permanent dentition (32 are present). It would be an obvious error to differentiate two fossil forms based solely on such age-dependent criteria. If one individual were represented just by milk teeth and another (seemingly very different) individual were represented just by adult teeth, they easily could be different-aged individuals from the *same* population. Variation due to sex also plays an important role in influencing differences among individuals observed in biological populations. Differences in physical characteristics between males and females of the same species, called **sexual dimorphism**, can result in marked variation in body size and proportions in adults of the same species (we'll discuss this important topic in more detail in Chapter 6).

Recognition of Fossil Species Keeping in mind all the types of variation present within interbreeding groups of organisms, the minimum biological category we'd like to define in fossil primate samples is the *species*. As already defined (according to the biological species concept), a species is a group of interbreeding or potentially interbreeding organisms that is reproductively isolated from other such groups. In modern organisms, this concept is theoretically testable by observations of reproductive behavior. In animals long extinct, such observations are obviously impossible. Our only way, then, of getting a handle on the variation we see in fossil groups is to refer to living animals.

When studying a fossil group, we may observe obvious variation, such as some individuals being larger and with bigger teeth than others. The question then becomes: What is the biological significance of this variation? Two possibilities come to mind. Either the variation is accounted for by individual, age, and sex differences seen *within* every biological species (that is, it is **intraspecific**), or the variation represents differences *between* reproductively isolated groups (that is, it is **interspecific**). How do we decide which answer is correct? To do this, we have to look at contemporary species.

If the amount of morphological variation we observe in fossil samples is comparable to that seen today *within species of closely related forms*, then we shouldn't "split" our sample into more than one species. We must, however, be careful in choosing modern analogues, because rates of morphological evolution vary among different groups of mammals. So, for example, when studying extinct fossil primates, we need to compare them with well-known modern primates. Even so, studies of living groups have shown that defining exactly where species boundaries begin and end is often difficult. In dealing with extinct species, the uncertainties are even greater. In addition to the overlapping patterns of variation *spatially* (over space), variation also occurs *temporally* (through time). In other words, even more variation will be seen in **paleospecies**, since individuals may be separated by thousands or even millions of years. Applying strict Linnaean taxonomy to such a situation presents an unavoidable dilemma. Standard Linnaean classification, designed to take account of variation present at any given time, describes a static situation. But when we deal with paleospecies, the time frame is expanded and the situation can be dynamic (that is, later forms might be different from earlier forms). In such a dynamic situation, taxonomic decisions (where to draw species boundaries) are ultimately going to be somewhat arbitrary.

Because the task of interpreting paleospecies is so difficult, paleoanthropologists have sought various solutions. Most researchers today define species using clusters of derived traits (identified cladistically). But owing to the ambiguity of how many derived characters are required to identify a fully distinct species (as opposed to a subspecies), the frequent mixing of characters into novel combinations, and the always difficult problem of homoplasy, there continues to be disagreement. A good deal of the dispute is driven by philosophical orientation. Exactly how much diversity should one expect among fossil primates, especially among fossil hominins?

sexual dimorphism Differences in physical characteristics between males and females of the same species. For example, humans are slightly sexually dimorphic for body size, with males being taller, on average, than females of the same population.

intraspecific Within species; refers to variation seen within the same species.

interspecific Between species; refers to variation beyond that seen within the same species to include additional aspects seen between two different species.

paleospecies Species defined from fossil evidence, often covering a long time span.

Some researchers, called "splitters," claim that speciation occurred frequently during hominin evolution, and they often identify numerous fossil hominin species in a sample being studied. As the nickname suggests, these scientists are inclined to split groups into many species. Others, called "lumpers," assume that speciation was less common and see much variation as being intraspecific. These scientists lump groups together, so that fewer hominin species are identified, named, and eventually plugged into evolutionary schemes. As you'll see in the following chapters, debates of this sort pervade paleoanthropology, perhaps more than in any other branch of evolutionary biology.

Recognition of Fossil Genera The next and broader level of taxonomic classification, the **genus** (*pl.*, genera), presents another problem. To have more than one genus, we obviously must have at least two species (reproductively isolated groups), and the species of one genus must differ in a basic way from the species of another genus. A genus is therefore defined as a group of species composed of members more closely related to each other than they are to species from any other genus.

Grouping species into genera can be quite subjective and is often much debated by biologists. One possible test for contemporary animals is to check for results of hybridization between individuals of different species—rare in nature, but quite common in captivity. If members of two normally separate species interbreed and produce live (though not necessarily fertile) offspring, the two parental species probably are not too different genetically and should therefore be grouped in the same genus. A well-known example of such a cross is horses with donkeys (*Equus caballus* × *Equus asinus*), which normally produces live but sterile offspring (mules).

As previously mentioned, we can't perform breeding experiments with extinct animals, which is why another definition of genus becomes highly relevant. Species that are members of the same genus share the same broad adaptive zone. An adaptive zone represents a general ecological lifestyle more basic than the narrower ecological niches characteristic of individual species. This ecological definition of genus can be an immense aid in interpreting fossil primates. Teeth are the most frequently preserved parts, and they often can provide excellent general ecological inferences. Cladistic analysis also helps scientists to make judgments about evolutionary relationships. That is, members of the same genus should all share derived characters not seen in members of other genera.

As a final comment, we should stress that classification by genus is not always a straightforward decision. For instance, in emphasizing the very close genetic similarities between humans (*Homo sapiens*) and chimpanzees (*Pan troglodytes*), some current researchers (Wildman et al., 2003) place both in the same genus (*Homo sapiens*, *Homo troglodytes*). This philosophy has caused some to advocate for extension of basic human rights to great apes (as proposed by members of the Great Ape Project). Such thinking might startle you. Of course, when it gets this close to home, it's often difficult to remain objective!

Vertebrate Evolutionary History: A Brief Summary

Besides the staggering array of living and extinct life-forms, biologists must also contend with the vast amount of time that life has been evolving on earth. Again, scientists have devised simplified schemes—but in this case to organize *time*, not biological diversity.

genus (*pl.*, genera) A group of closely related species.

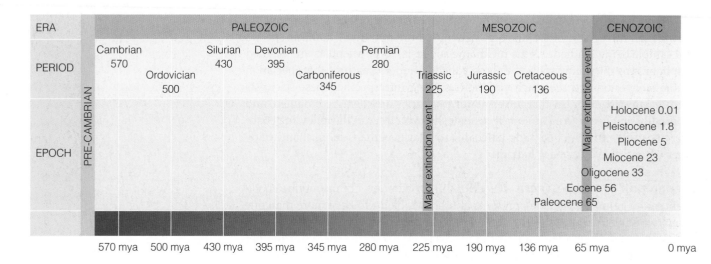

ERA		PALEOZOIC					MESOZOIC			CENOZOIC
PERIOD		Cambrian 570	Silurian 430	Devonian 395	Permian 280	Triassic 225	Jurassic 190	Cretaceous 136	
		Ordovician 500		Carboniferous 345					
EPOCH	PRE-CAMBRIAN								Holocene 0.01 Pleistocene 1.8 Pliocene 5 Miocene 23 Oligocene 33 Eocene 56 Paleocene 65

570 mya   500 mya   430 mya   395 mya   345 mya   280 mya   225 mya   190 mya   136 mya   65 mya   0 mya

Major extinction event (at Permian/Triassic boundary)
Major extinction event (at Cretaceous/Cenozoic boundary)

Figure 5-7

Geological time scale.

Geologists have formulated the **geological time scale** (Fig. 5-7), in which very large time spans are organized into eras that include one or more periods. Periods, in turn, can be broken down into epochs. For the time span encompassing vertebrate evolution, there are three eras: the Paleozoic, the Mesozoic, and the Cenozoic. The first vertebrates are present in the fossil record dating to early in the Paleozoic at 500 mya, and their origins probably go back considerably further. It's the vertebrates' capacity to form bone that accounts for their more complete fossil record *after* 500 mya.

During the Paleozoic, several varieties of fishes (including the ancestors of modern sharks and bony fishes), amphibians, and reptiles appeared. At the end of the Paleozoic, close to 250 mya, several varieties of mammal-like reptiles were also diversifying. It's generally thought that some of these forms ultimately gave rise to the mammals.

The evolutionary history of vertebrates and other organisms during the Paleozoic and Mesozoic was profoundly influenced by geographical events. We know that the positions of the earth's continents have dramatically shifted during the last several hundred million years. This process, called **continental drift**, is explained by the geological theory of *plate tectonics*, which states that the earth's crust is a series of gigantic moving and colliding plates. Such massive geological movements can induce volcanic activity (as, for example, all around the Pacific Rim), mountain building (for example, the Himalayas), and earthquakes. Living on the juncture of the Pacific and North American plates, residents of the Pacific coast of the United States are acutely aware of some of these consequences, as illustrated by the explosive volcanic eruption of Mt. St. Helens and the frequent earthquakes in Alaska and California.

While reconstructing the earth's physical history, geologists have established the prior, much altered, positions of major continental landmasses. During the late Paleozoic, the continents came together to form a single colossal landmass called *Pangea*. (In reality, the continents had been drifting on plates, coming together and separating, long before the end of the Paleozoic around 225 mya.) During the early Mesozoic, the southern continents (South America, Africa, Antarctica, Australia, and India) began to split off from Pangea, forming a large southern continent called *Gondwanaland* (Fig. 5-8a). Similarly, the northern continents (North America, Greenland, Europe, and Asia) were consolidated into a northern landmass called *Laurasia*. During the Mesozoic, Gondwanaland and Laurasia continued to drift apart and to break up into smaller segments. By the end of the Mesozoic (about

geological time scale The organization of earth history into eras, periods, and epochs; commonly used by geologists and paleoanthropologists.

continental drift The movement of continents on sliding plates of the earth's surface. As a result, the positions of large landmasses have shifted drastically during the earth's history.

65 mya), the continents were beginning to assume their current positions (Fig. 5-8b).

The evolutionary ramifications of this long-term continental drift were profound. Groups of animals became effectively isolated from each other by oceans, significantly influencing the distribution of mammals and other land vertebrates. These continental movements continued in the Cenozoic and indeed are still happening, although without such dramatic results.

During most of the Mesozoic, reptiles were the dominant land vertebrates, and they exhibited a broad expansion into a variety of *ecological niches*, which included aerial and marine habitats. The most famous of these highly successful Mesozoic reptiles were the dinosaurs, which themselves evolved into a wide array of sizes and species and adapted to a variety of lifestyles. Dinosaur paleontology, never a boring field, has advanced several startling notions in recent years: that many dinosaurs were "warm-blooded" (see p. 130); that some varieties were quite social and probably also engaged in considerable parental care; that many forms became extinct because of major climatic changes to the earth's atmosphere from collisions with comets or asteroids; and finally, that not all dinosaurs became entirely extinct and have many descendants still living today (that is, all modern birds). (See Fig. 5-9 for a summary of major events in early vertebrate evolutionary history.)

The Cenozoic is divided into two periods, the Tertiary (about 63 million years duration) and the Quaternary, from about 1.8 mya up to and including the present (see Fig. 5-7). Paleontologists often refer to the next, more precise level of subdivision within the Cenozoic as the **epochs**. There are seven epochs within the Cenozoic: the Paleocene, Eocene, Oligocene, Miocene, Pliocene, Pleistocene, and Holocene, the last often referred to as the Recent epoch. As we'll see in Chapter 9, each epoch of the Cenozoic can be roughly assigned to a broad segment of primate evolution.

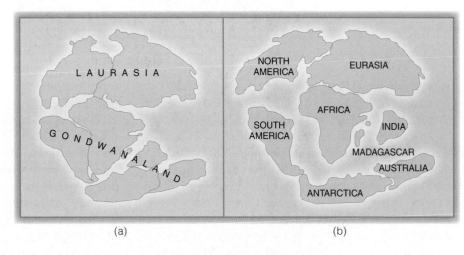

(a)   (b)

Figure 5-8

Continental drift. (a) Positions of the continents during the Mesozoic (ca. 125 mya). Pangea is breaking up into a northern landmass (Laurasia) and a southern landmass (Gondwanaland). (b) Positions of the continents at the beginning of the Cenozoic (ca. 65 mya).

epochs Categories of the geological time scale; subdivisions of periods. In the Cenozoic, epochs include the Paleocene, Eocene, Oligocene, Miocene, and Pliocene (from the Tertiary) and the Pleistocene and Holocene (from the Quaternary).

Figure 5-9

This time line depicts major events in early vertebrate evolution.

PALEOZOIC							MESOZOIC		
Cambrian	Ordovician	Silurian	Devonian	Carbon-iferous	Permian		Triassic	Jurassic	Cretaceous
Trilobites abundant; also brachiopods, jellyfish, worms, and other invertebrates.	First fishes; trilobites still abundant; graptolites and corals become plentiful; possible land plants.	Jawed fishes appear; first air-breathing animals; definite land plants.	Age of Fish; first amphibians and first forests appear.	First reptiles; radiation of amphibians; modern insects diversify.	Reptile radiation; mammal-like reptiles appear.	Major extinction event	Reptiles further radiate; first dinosaurs; egg-laying mammals.	Great Age of Dinosaurs; flying and swimming dinosaurs appear; first toothed birds.	Placental and marsupial mammals appear; first modern birds.

570 mya   500 mya   430 mya   395 mya   345 mya   280 mya   225 mya   190 mya   136 mya   65 mya

A Closer Look

Deep Time

The vast expanse of time during which evolution has occurred on earth staggers the imagination. Indeed, this fundamental notion of what John McPhee has termed "deep time" is not really understood or, in fact, widely believed. Of course, as we've emphasized beginning in Chapter 1, *belief*, as such, is not part of science. But observation, theory building, and testing are. Still, in a world populated mostly by nonscientists, the concept of deep time, crucial as it is to geology and anthropology, is resisted by many people. This situation really isn't surprising; the very notion of deep time is in many ways counterintuitive. Human beings tend to measure their existence in months, years, and the span of human lifetimes.

But what are these durations, measured against geological or galactic phenomena? In a real sense, these vast time expanses are beyond human comprehension. We can reasonably fathom the reaches of human history stretching to about 5,000 years ago. In a leap of imagination, we can perhaps even begin to grasp the stretch of time back to the cave painters of France and Spain, approximately 17,000 to 25,000 years ago. How do we relate, then, to a temporal span that's 10 times this one, back to 250,000 years ago, about the time of the earliest *Homo sapiens*—or to 10 times this span to 2,500,000 years ago (about the time of the appearance of our genus, *Homo*)? And multiply this last duration another 1,000

times (to 2,500,000,000), and we're back to a time of fairly early life-forms. And we'd have to reach still further into earth's past, another 1.5 billion years, to approach the *earliest* documented life.

The dimensions of these intervals are humbling, to say the least. The discovery in the nineteenth century of deep time (see Chapter 2), what the late Stephen Jay Gould called "geology's greatest contribution to human thought," plunged one more dagger into humanity's long-cherished special view of itself. Astronomers had previously established how puny our world was in the physical expanse of space, and then geologists showed that even on our own small planet, we were but residues dwarfed within a river of time "without a vestige of a beginning or prospect of an end" (from James Hutton, a founder of modern geology and one of the discoverers of deep time). It's no wonder that people resist the concept of deep time; it not only stupefies our reason, but implies a sense of collective meaninglessness and reinforces our individual mortality.

Geologists, astronomers, and other scholars have struggled for over a century, with modest success, to translate the tales told in rocks and hurtling stars in terms that everyone can understand. Various analogies have been attempted—metaphors, really—drawn from common experience. Among the most successful of these attempts is a "cosmic calendar"

Mammalian Evolution

We can learn about mammalian evolution from fossils as well as from studying the DNA of living species (Bininda-Emonds et al., 2007). Studies using both of these approaches suggest that all the living groups of mammals (that is, all the orders; see p. 111) had diverged by 75 mya. Later, only after several million years following the beginning of the Cenozoic, did the various current mammalian subgroups (that is, the particular families) begin to diversify.

Today, there are over 4,000 species of mammals, and we could call the Cenozoic the Age of Mammals. It is during this era that, along with birds, mammals replaced earlier reptiles as the dominant land-living vertebrates.

How do we account for the relatively rapid success of the mammals during the late Mesozoic and early Cenozoic? Several characteristics relating to learning and general flexibility of behavior are of prime importance. To process more information, mammals were selected for larger brains than those typically found in reptiles. In particular, the cerebrum became generally enlarged, especially the outer covering, the neocortex, which controls higher brain functions (Fig. 5-10). In some mammals, the cerebrum expanded so much that it came to comprise most of the brain volume; the number of surface convolutions also increased, creating more surface

devised by eminent astronomer Carl Sagan in his book *Dragons of Eden* (1977). In this version of time's immensity, Sagan likens the passage of geological time to that of one calendar year. The year begins on January 1 with the Big Bang, the cosmic explosion marking the beginning of the universe and the beginning of time. In this version, the Big Bang is set at 15 billion years ago,* with some of the major events in the geological past as follows:

Time Unit Conversion Using the Cosmic Calendar

1 year = 15,000,000,000 years   1 hour = 1,740,000 years
1 month = 1,250,000,000 years   1 minute = 29,000 years
1 day = 41,000,000 years   1 second = 475 years

		December 31 Events
Appearance of early hominoids (apes and humans)		12:30 P.M.
Big Bang	January 1	
Formation of the earth	September 14	First hominins	9:30 P.M.
Origin of life on earth (approx.)	September 25	Extensive cave painting in Europe	11:59 P.M.
Significant oxygen atmosphere begins to develop	December 1	Invention of agriculture	11:59:20 P.M.
Precambrian ends; Paleozoic begins; invertebrates flourish	December 17	Renaissance in Europe: Ming Dynasty in China; emergence of scientific method	11:59:59 P.M.
Paleozoic ends and Mesozoic begins	December 25		
Cretaceous period: first flowers; dinosaurs become extinct	December 28	Widespread development of science and technology;	NOW: the first second of the
Mesozoic ends; Cenozoic begins; adaptive radiation of placental mammals	December 29	emergence of a global culture; first steps in space exploration	New Year

---

*Recent evidence gathered by the Hubble Space Telescope has questioned the established date for the Big Bang. However, even the most recent data are somewhat contradictory, suggesting a date from as early as 16 billion years ago (indicated by the age of the oldest stars) to as recent as 8 billion years ago (indicated by the rate of expansion of the universe). Here, we'll follow the conventional dating of 15 billion years; if you apply the most conservative approximation (8 billion years), the calibrations shift as follows: 1 day = 22,000,000 years; 1 hour = 913,000 years; 1 minute = 15,000 years. Using these calculations, for example, the first hominins appear on December 31 at 7:37 P.M., and modern humans (*Homo sapiens*) are on the scene at 11:42 P.M.

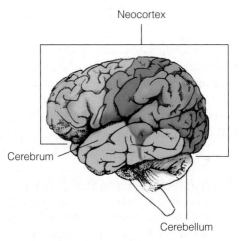

FISH BRAIN

Cortex

Cerebrum   Cerebellum

Olfactory lobe

Neocortex

REPTILE BRAIN

Neocortex

Cerebrum

Cerebellum

PRIMATE BRAIN

Figure **5-10**

Lateral view of the brain in fishes, reptiles, and primates. You can see the increased size of the cerebral cortex (neocortex) of the primate brain. The cerebral cortex integrates sensory information and selects responses.

(a) REPTILIAN (alligator): homodont

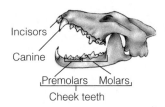

Incisors

Canine

Premolars   Molars

Cheek teeth

(b) MAMMALIAN: heterodont

Figure 5-11

Reptilian and mammalian teeth.

area and thus providing space for even more nerve cells (neurons). As we'll soon see in Chapter 6, this is a trend even further emphasized among the primates.

For such a large and complex organ as the mammalian brain to develop, a longer, more intense period of growth is required. Slower development can occur internally (*in utero*) as well as after birth. Internal fertilization and internal development aren't unique to mammals, but the latter is a major innovation among terrestrial vertebrates. Other forms (most fishes and most reptiles—including birds) incubate their young externally by laying eggs, while mammals, with very few exceptions, give birth to live young. Even among mammals, however, there's considerable variation among the major groups in how mature the young are at birth. As you'll see, it is in mammals like us—the **placental** forms—that *in utero* development goes farthest.

Another distinctive feature of mammals is seen in the dentition. While many living reptiles (such as lizards and snakes) consistently have similarly shaped teeth (called a *homodont* dentition), mammals have differently shaped teeth (Fig. 5-11). This varied pattern, termed a **heterodont** dentition, is reflected in the ancestral (primitive) mammalian array of dental elements, which includes 3 incisors, 1 canine, 4 premolars, and 3 molars in each quarter of the mouth. Since the upper and lower jaws are usually the same and are symmetrical for both sides, the "dental formula" is conventionally illustrated by dental quarter (see p. 149 for a more complete discussion of dental patterns as they apply to primates). So with 11 teeth in each quarter of the mouth, the ancestral mammalian dental complement includes a total of 44 teeth. Such a heterodont arrangement allows mammals to process a wide variety of foods. Incisors can be used for cutting, canines for grasping and piercing, and premolars and molars for crushing and grinding.

A final point regarding teeth relates to their disproportionate representation in the fossil record. As the hardest, most durable portion of a vertebrate skeleton, teeth have the greatest likelihood of becoming fossilized (that is, mineralized), since teeth are predominantly mineral to begin with. As a result, the vast majority of available fossil data (particularly early on) for most vertebrates, including primates, consists of teeth.

Another major adaptive complex that distinguishes contemporary mammals from nonbird reptiles is the maintenance of a constant internal body temperature. Known colloquially (and incorrectly) as warm-bloodedness, this crucial physiological adaptation is also seen in contemporary birds and may have characterized many dinosaurs as well. In fact, many contemporary nonbird reptiles are able to approximate a constant internal body temperature through behavioral means, especially by regulating activity and exposing the body to the sun. In this sense, nonbird reptiles (along with birds and mammals) could be said to be *homeothermic*. So a more useful distinction is to see how the energy to maintain body temperature is produced. In nonbird reptiles, it's obtained directly from exposure to the sun; these reptiles are thus said to be *ectothermic*. In mammals and birds, however, the energy is generated *internally* through metabolic activity (by processing food or by muscle action); for this reason, mammals and birds are said to be **endothermic**.

placental A type (subclass) of mammal. During the Cenozoic, placentals became the most widespread and numerous mammals and today are represented by upward of 20 orders, including the primates.

heterodont Having different kinds of teeth; characteristic of mammals, whose teeth consist of incisors, canines, premolars, and molars.

endothermic (*endo*, meaning "within" or "internal") Able to maintain internal body temperature by producing energy through metabolic processes within cells; characteristic of mammals, birds, and perhaps some dinosaurs.

The Emergence of Major Mammalian Groups

There are three major subgroups of living mammals: the egg-laying mammals, or monotremes; the pouched mammals, or marsupials; and the placental mammals. The monotremes, of which the platypus is one example (Fig. 5-12), are extremely primitive and are considered more distinct from marsupials or placentals than

Figure 5-12

A duck-billed platypus (monotreme).

Figure 5-13

A wallaby with an infant in the pouch (marsupials).

these two subgroups are from each other. The recent sequencing of the full genome of the platypus (Warren et al., 2008) has confirmed monotreme separateness from other mammals and their very ancient origins.

The most notable difference between marsupials and placentals concerns fetal development. In marsupials, the young are born extremely immature and must complete development in an external pouch (Fig. 5-13). But placental mammals develop over a longer period of time *in utero*, made possible by the evolutionary development of a specialized tissue (the placenta) that provides for fetal nourishment.

With a longer gestation period, the central nervous system develops more completely in the placental fetus. What's more, after birth, the "bond of milk" between mother and young allows more time for complex neural structures to form. We should also emphasize that from a *biosocial* perspective, this dependency period not only allows for adequate physiological development but also provides for a wider range of learning stimuli. That is, a vast amount of information is channeled to the young mammalian brain through observation of the mother's behavior and through play with age-mates. It's not enough to have evolved a brain capable of learning. Collateral evolution of mammalian social systems has ensured that young mammal brains are provided with ample learning opportunities and are thus put to good use.

Processes of Macroevolution

As we noted earlier, evolution operates at both microevolutionary and macroevolutionary levels. We discussed evolution primarily from a microevolutionary perspective in Chapters 3 and 4; in this chapter, our focus is on macroevolution. Macroevolutionary mechanisms operate more on the whole species than on individuals or populations, and they take much longer than microevolutionary processes to have a noticeable impact.

Adaptive Radiation

As we mentioned in Chapter 2, the potential capacity of a group of organisms to multiply is practically unlimited, but its ability to increase its numbers is regulated largely by the availability of resources (food, water, shelter, and space). As population size increases, access to resources decreases, and the environment will ultimately prove inadequate. Depleted resources induce some members of a population to seek an environment in which competition is reduced and the opportunities for survival and reproductive success are increased. This evolutionary tendency to exploit unoccupied habitats may eventually produce an abundance of diverse species.

This story has been played out countless times during the history of life, and some groups have expanded extremely rapidly. This evolutionary process, known as **adaptive radiation**, can be seen in the divergence of the stem reptiles into the profusion of different forms of the late Paleozoic and especially those of the Mesozoic. It's a process that takes place when a life-form rapidly takes advantage, so to speak, of the many newly available ecological niches.

The principle of evolution illustrated by adaptive radiation is fairly simple, but important. It may be stated this way: A species, or group of species, will diverge into as many variations as two factors allow. These factors are (1) its adaptive potential and (2) the adaptive opportunities of the available niches.

In the case of reptiles, there was little divergence in the very early stages of evolution, when the ancestral form was little more than one among a variety of amphibian water dwellers. Later, a more efficient egg (one that could incubate out of water) developed in reptiles; this new egg, with a hard, watertight shell, had great adaptive potential, but initially there were few zones to invade. When reptiles became fully terrestrial, however, a wide array of ecological niches became accessible to them. Once freed from their attachment to water, reptiles were able to exploit landmasses with no serious competition from any other animal. They moved into the many different ecological niches on land (and to some extent in the air and sea), and as they adapted to these areas, they diversified into a large number of species. This spectacular radiation burst forth with such evolutionary speed that it may well be termed an adaptive explosion.

Of course, the rapid expansion of placental mammals during the late Mesozoic and throughout the Cenozoic is another excellent example of adaptive radiation.

Generalized and Specialized Characteristics

Another aspect of evolution closely related to adaptive radiation involves the transition from *generalized* characteristics to *specialized* characteristics. These two terms refer to the adaptive potential of a particular trait. A trait that's adapted for many functions is said to be generalized, while one that's limited to a narrow set of functions is said to be specialized.

For example, a generalized mammalian limb has five fairly flexible digits, adapted for many possible functions (grasping, weight support, and digging). In this respect, human hands are still quite generalized. On the other hand (or foot), there have been many structural modifications in our feet to make them suited for the specialized function of stable weight support in an upright posture.

The terms *generalized* and *specialized* are also sometimes used when speaking of the adaptive potential of whole organisms. Consider, for example, the aye-aye of Madagascar, an unusual primate species. The aye-aye is a highly specialized animal, structurally adapted to a narrow, rodent/woodpecker-like econiche—digging holes with prominent incisors and removing insect larvae with an elongated bony finger.

adaptive radiation The relatively rapid expansion and diversification of life-forms into new ecological niches.

It's important to note that only a generalized ancestor can provide the flexible evolutionary basis for rapid diversification. Only a generalized species with potential for adaptation to varied ecological niches can lead to all the later diversification and specialization of forms into particular ecological niches.

An issue that we've already raised also bears on this discussion: the relationship of ancestral and derived characters. It's not always the case, but ancestral characters *usually* tend to be more generalized. And specialized characteristics are nearly always derived ones as well.

Tempos and Modes of Evolutionary Change

For many years, evolutionary biologists generally agreed that microevolutionary mechanisms could be translated directly into the larger-scale macroevolutionary changes, especially the most central of all macroevolutionary processes, speciation. However, three decades ago, this view was seriously challenged. This challenge led to the new view that macroevolution can't be explained solely in terms of slowly accumulated microevolutionary changes. Most evolutionary biologists now recognize that macroevolution is only partly understandable through microevolutionary models and that the process is much more complicated than traditionally assumed.

Gradualism versus Punctuated Equilibrium The conventional view of evolution has emphasized that change accumulates gradually in evolving lineages, an idea called *phyletic gradualism*. According to this view, the complete fossil record of an evolving group (if it could be recovered) would display a series of forms with finely graded transitional differences between each ancestor and its descendant; that is, many "missing links" would be present. The fact that such transitional forms are only rarely found is attributed to the incompleteness of the fossil record, or, as Darwin called it, "a history of the world, imperfectly kept, and written in changing dialect."

For more than a century, this perspective dominated evolutionary biology. But in the last 35 years, some biologists have called the idea into question. The evolutionary mechanisms operating on species over the long run aren't always gradual. In some cases, species persist, basically unchanged, for thousands of generations (stasis). Then, rather suddenly (at least in geological terms), a "spurt" of speciation occurs. This uneven, nongradual process of long stasis and quick spurts has been termed **punctuated equilibrium** (Gould and Eldredge, 1977). In this model, there are no "missing links" between species; the gaps are real, not artifacts of an imperfect fossil record.

What the advocates of punctuated equilibrium dispute are the tempo (rate) and mode (manner) of evolutionary change as commonly understood since Darwin's time. Rather than a slow, steady tempo, this alternate view postulates long periods of no change (that is, equilibrium or stasis) punctuated (interrupted) only occasionally by sudden bursts. From this observation, many researchers concluded that the mode of evolution, too, must be different from that suggested by traditional evolutionary biologists (often called "Darwinists"). Rather than gradual accumulation of small changes in a single lineage, advocates of punctuated equilibrium believe that an additional evolutionary mechanism is required to push the process along. In fact, they postulate *speciation* as the major influence in bringing about rapid evolutionary change (Fig. 5-14).

How well does the paleontological record agree with the predictions of punctuated equilibrium? Some fossil data do, in fact, show long periods of stasis punctuated by occasional quite rapid changes (taking from about 10,000 to 50,000

punctuated equilibrium The concept that evolutionary change proceeds through long periods of stasis punctuated by rapid periods of change.

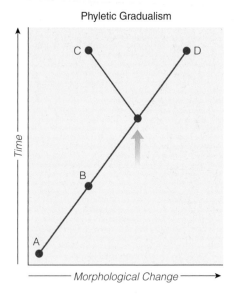

Phyletic Gradualism

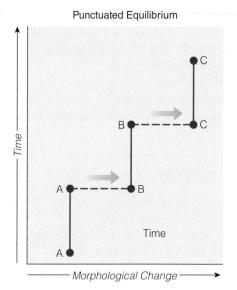

Punctuated Equilibrium

Figure 5-14

Phyletic gradualism compared with punctuated equilibrium. Note that in phyletic gradualism morphological change accumulates gradually with time but occurs in short bursts in punctuated equilibrium. In addition, speciation events (shown by arrows) in phyletic gradualism happen after long and slow accumulated change, but occur rapidly in punctuated equilibrium.

years). The best supporting evidence for punctuated equilibrium has come from marine invertebrate fossils, although not even these data are always clear (Van Bocxlaer et al., 2008). From the perspective of punctuated equilibrium, intermediate forms are rare, not so much because the fossil record is poor, but because the speciation events and longevity of these transitional species were so short that we shouldn't expect to find them very often.

To test these alternative hypotheses, long geological sequences containing well-preserved and well-dated fossils are required. It's important to recognize that in any active scientific discipline (and evolutionary biology is no exception), hypotheses continue to be tested and refined. Some nonscientists, arguing from a creationist perspective, have pointed to this dispute in an attempt to discredit the basis of evolutionary theory. These claims, however, fail to take into account not only the nature of this particular debate, but also the vast accumulation of evidence recognized by evolutionary biologists worldwide. Moreover, as we have already pointed out (see Chapter 2), the creationist perspective fundamentally fails to understand the nature of science itself. Renowned biologist Stephen Jay Gould, a cofounder of punctuated equilibrium, commented on the debate among evolutionary biologists and the popular misunderstanding surrounding it:

> Yet amidst all this turmoil no biologist has been led to doubt the fact that evolution occurred; we are debating *how* it happened. We are all trying to explain the same thing: the tree of evolutionary descent linking all organisms by ties of genealogy (Gould, 1994, p. 256).

In summary, the critical difference between phyletic gradualism and punctuated equilibrium relates to how the timing of speciation events likely occurred in the past. Phyletic gradualism predicts slow accumulation of adaptive differences that finally culminate in a new species, whereas punctuated equilibrium predicts that no changes occur for long periods of time until there is a sudden adaptive change, which results in a new species.

Recent molecular evidence suggests that both gradual change and rapid punctuated change occurred in the evolution of both plants and animals (Pagel et al. 2006). In all lineages, the pace assuredly speeds up and slows down due to factors that influence the size and relative isolation of populations. Environmental changes that influence the pace and direction of natural selection must also be considered. So, in general accordance with the Modern Synthesis and as indicated by molecular evidence, microevolution and macroevolution don't need to be "decoupled," or considered separately, as some evolutionary biologists have suggested; both modes and tempos occur. Some groups of primates, for instance, simply have slower or faster durations of speciation, which is why Old World monkeys typically speciate more slowly than the great apes.

Summary

In this chapter, we've surveyed the basics of vertebrate and mammalian evolution, emphasizing a macroevolutionary perspective. Given the huge amount of organic diversity displayed, as well as the vast amount of time involved, two major organizing perspectives prove indispensable: (1) schemes of formal classification to organize organic diversity and (2) the geological time scale to organize geological time. We reviewed the principles of classification in some detail, contrasting two differing approaches: evolutionary systematics and cladistics. Because primates are vertebrates and, more specifically, mammals, we briefly reviewed these broader groups, emphasizing major evolutionary trends.

Theoretical perspectives relating to contemporary understanding of macroevolutionary processes (especially the concepts of species and speciation) are crucial to any interpretation of long-term aspects of evolutionary history, be it vertebrate, mammalian, or primate.

Since genus and species designation is the common form of reference for both living and extinct organisms (and we use it frequently throughout the text), we discussed its biological significance in depth. From a more general theoretical perspective, evolutionary biologists have postulated two different modes of evolutionary change: gradualism and punctuated equilibrium. Currently, both fossil and molecular data suggest that both evolutionary modes occurred during the evolutionary history of most organisms.

Critical Thinking Questions

1. What are the two goals of classification? What happens when meeting both goals simultaneously becomes difficult or even impossible?
2. Remains of a fossil mammal have been found on your campus. If you adopt a cladistic approach, how would you determine (a) that it's a mammal rather than some other kind of vertebrate (discuss specific characters), (b) what kind of mammal it is (again, discuss specific characters), and (c) how it *might* be related to one or more living mammals (again, discuss specific characters)?
3. For the same fossil find (and your interpretation) in question 2, draw an interpretive figure using cladistic analysis (that is, draw a cladogram). Next, using more traditional evolutionary systematics, construct a phylogeny. Lastly, explain the differences between the cladogram and the phylogeny (be sure to emphasize the fundamental ways the two schemes differ).
4. a. Humans are fairly generalized mammals. What do we mean by this, and what specific features (characters) would you select to illustrate this statement?
   b. More precisely, humans are *placental* mammals. How do humans, and generally all other placental mammals, differ from the other two major groups of mammals?

Evo-Devo: The Evolution Revolution

In Chapter 4, you learned how, in the 1930s, scientists came to a better understanding of evolution once they realized that Mendel's principles and natural selection were both essential components of the process. This merger of ideas, known as the Modern Synthesis, was a major step in evolutionary science, and with the discovery of the structure of DNA in 1953, the foundations of evolutionary biology were firmly established.

Almost half a century after the structure of the DNA molecule was revealed, another merger of disciplines occurred (Goodman and Coughlin, 2000). In 1999, the field of evolutionary developmental biology, or evo-devo, was created by consolidating evolutionary biology with developmental biology. This combination resulted directly from research demonstrating that major evolutionary transformations involve changes in the very same regulatory genes (see p. 58) that direct embryological development. The main goals of evo-devo are to discover how animals are put together and how the genes that control their development can, over time, produce new species.

Right now, there are millions of animal species (including insects and marine life), but they probably represent less than 1 percent of all the species that have ever existed on earth (Carroll et al., 2001). Among these many millions of species the degree of diversity is staggering, even if you only consider the ones you're familiar with (living and extinct), such as earthworms, grasshoppers, snakes, dinosaurs, sharks, frogs, birds, bats, dogs, horses, whales, and even humans. What's so remarkable is that all these animals are ultimately the descendants of a common ancestor that lived more than 600 million years ago.

In spite of how diverse these species are, they share many anatomical similarities. They're all bilaterally symmetrical, meaning that one side is like the other, except for certain aspects of internal organs. Also, and this is important, they all have a modular body plan made up of repeated segments. Arthropods (invertebrates with jointed feet, including all insects, spiders, and crustaceans) have segmented bodies and legs; and many have segmented wings, which are ultimately derived from leg-like appendages (Fig. 1).

Vertebrates have segmented body plans too, initially formed by the developing head and vertebral column. Although the number of vertebrae and the number of each type of vertebra vary among species (see p. 61), the spine is made of repeated segments (Fig. 2).

Individual body parts are also modular. In all tetrapods (including all vertebrates except fishes), limbs follow a modular pattern. In humans, upper arms and thighs

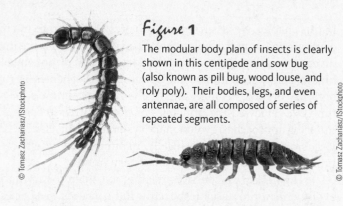

Figure 1

The modular body plan of insects is clearly shown in this centipede and sow bug (also known as pill bug, wood louse, and roly poly). Their bodies, legs, and even antennae, are all composed of series of repeated segments.

have one bone; forearms and lower legs have two; wrists and ankles have eight and seven, respectively; and hands and feet have five digits (see Fig. 5-2, p. 113, and Appendix A, pp. 501–503). (While snakes, whales, and dolphins don't have legs and feet, they're descended from animals that did, and that's why they're considered tetrapods. Moreover, some of these species, such as pythons and whales, have skeletal pelvic remnants.) Although in more derived animals some of the bones in the lower limbs and feet may be reduced and/or modified (see Fig. 6-1a, p. 141), this basic pattern in limb morphology is shared by thousands of species, from sparrows to gorillas. It's the same pattern seen in dinosaur fossils, and its history goes back more than 500 million years.

Anatomical structures that have the same form, even with modifications, are called homologies, meaning that they're shared by species that ultimately inherited them from a common ancestor. Even though the last common

(a)   (b)

Figure 2

Two examples of *Hox* transformations. (a) This sacrum, seen from the front, is composed of 6 vertebrae when there should only be 5. This was caused by the malfunction of one of the *Hox* genes involved in the initial patterning of the sacral vertebrae. (b) Top view of a 6th lumbar vertebra, in itself the result of a *Hox* malfunction. In addition, the left side has the morphology of a first sacral vertebra, and the opening on the right side is typical only of cervical (neck) vertebrae.

ancestor humans share with dinosaurs lived an incomprehensibly long time ago, our limbs are homologous with dinosaur limbs. In fact, all the homologies shared by millions of diverse species (living and extinct) were ultimately inherited from an extremely distant common ancestor.

We know that during embryonic development, bodies are formed according to a pattern that characterizes each species; and that pattern is dictated by that species' genome. Because of advances in comparative genomics, we also now know that the coding sequences of even distantly related species are very similar. For example, around 99 percent of mouse genes have a human counterpart (Mouse Genome Sequencing Consortium, 2002). So, what is it that makes us so different from mice?

Until about 25 years ago, biologists thought that changes in protein-coding genes were the key to evolutionary change, but now it's clear that changes in regulatory genes are the real answer to the question of how macroevolution occurs. DNA sequences of regulatory genes don't differ greatly among species; however (and this is key), these genes do differ when it comes to when, where, and how long they function. And these differences lead to major physical differences, because anatomical development depends on genes turning on and off at different times and in different places. There are many different kinds of regulatory genes, and they all instruct cells to make proteins (and different kinds of RNA) that in turn modulate the activity of yet other genes. Regulatory genes can be thought of as switches that turn other genes on or off at specific times in specific parts of the body (Carroll et al., 2008).

Many evolutionary biologists refer to the group of body-building regulatory genes as the *genetic tool kit*. This genetic tool kit is highly conserved and is shared by all vertebrates and invertebrates. Through the roughly 600 million years of animal evolution, many of the genes that make up the tool kit have been somewhat changed by mutation and many have duplicated to produce families of genes. But given the amount of time and the huge array of descendant species, changes in the DNA sequences of tool kit genes have been extraordinarily minimal, so the roughly 10 percent of your genome that consists of regulatory genes has the same DNA sequences as the regulatory genes of mice. It goes without saying that the tool kit genes serve as the best example of biological continuity among all animals, living and extinct.

The genetic tool kit is composed of genes that make two basic kinds of proteins: *transcription factors* and *signaling molecules*. Here we're focusing on transcription factors, protein molecules that bind to specific DNA segments called *enhancers* or *promoters*. By binding to enhancers, transcription factors switch genes on and off, and they also determine how long those genes produce proteins.

Transcription factors are produced by homeobox genes (see p. 58). These genes contain a highly conserved region of 180 nucleotides called the homeobox, and this sequence codes for the proteins that bind to enhancers. There are several families of genes that contain homeoboxes, but the most familiar one is called *Hox* for short.

As we discussed in Chapter 3, *Hox* genes direct the early stages of embryonic development. Initially, they establish the identity of regions of the body and the pattern of structures along the main body axis that runs lengthwise through the embryo. These structures are actually early precursors to the head and vertebral column. Later in development, these same genes establish where limb buds will form and also determine limb polarity (that is, front, back, and sides). Mutations in these genes cause the transformation of one body part to another, and the most famous of these transformations are results of experiments with fruit flies, in which induced mutations cause all sorts of bizarre phenotypes (such as legs where antennae should be).

Most invertebrates have 10 *Hox* genes, fruit flies have 8, but vertebrates have more. Mammals, for example, have 39, located on four different chromosomes. The reason vertebrates have more *Hox* genes than insects is that, over time, the invertebrate versions have duplicated in vertebrates. Therefore, vertebrate *Hox* genes are descended from invertebrate *Hox* genes. Just to illustrate how conserved these genes are, many experiments have shown them to be interchangeable between species. For example, one study showed that fruit flies can function normally with *Hox* proteins derived from chick embryos (Lutz et al., 1996). This indicates that these genes haven't changed much since fruit flies and chickens last shared a common ancestor some 600 millions years ago (Ayala et al., 1998).

As already stated, mutations in *Hox* genes can lead to transformations where one body segment takes on characteristics of another (like legs instead of antennae, but not so dramatic). Such anatomical changes aren't uncommon in humans, especially in the spine, where the fifth lumbar vertebra (the last one in the lower back) may have certain morphological similarities with the first sacral vertebra. Likewise, the first sacral vertebra may have characteristics of the fifth lumbar (Fig. 2).

The fact that *Hox* transformations in humans tend to occur more frequently between the fifth lumbar and first sacral vertebrae could lead to speculation regarding differences between human and African great ape spines.

Evo-Devo: The Evolution Revolution (continued)

Humans typically have 12 thoracic and 5 lumbar vertebrae, while chimpanzees, gorillas, and bonobos have 13 thoracic and 4 lumbar vertebrae. The shorter lumbar spine in apes has been explained by natural selection favoring a more stable lower back in brachiating animals. Unfortunately, we don't know for certain how many lumbar vertebrae the earliest hominins had. But we do know that the ancestral mammalian pattern is 6 or 7. It's not unreasonable to speculate, although with no supporting evidence at this time, that at some point in chimpanzee and gorilla evolution a *Hox* transformation, or series of transformations, effectively changed the first lumbar vertebra to a 13th thoracic vertebra. Even if this scenario isn't true, it illustrates how anatomical changes can result from *Hox* mutations. Following the evolutionary process, if mutations that produce transformations are advantageous, natural selection can act to increase their frequency in a population or species.

The science of evo-devo allows us, for the first time, to understand how morphological change and macroevolution can occur through the action of the genes that make up the genetic tool kit. This understanding has been made possible through the recently developed techniques of gene cloning and comparative genomics. By adding the evidence provided by evo-devo to comparative anatomy and fossil studies, scientists are on the threshold of demonstrating how evolution has worked to produce the spectacular biological diversity we see today. The key to this great puzzle is to understand that it all derives from simple beginnings with a set of genes that have been shared by all animals for hundreds of millions of years. As Charles Darwin said in the last paragraph of *Origin of Species*, "There is grandeur in this view of life…from so simple a beginning endless forms most beautiful and most wonderful have been, and are being evolved." This quotation has been a favorite of biologists and anthropologists, not only for its eloquence, but also because we've long known that over time, life-forms have become more complex. For 150 years, we've explained this increased complexity in terms of natural selection, and we still do. But now we have the tools we need to reveal the very mechanism that allowed complexity to develop in the first place.

SOURCES

Ayala, F. J., and A. Rzhetskydagger
  1998   Origin of the Metazoan phyla: molecular clocks confirm paleontological estimates. *Proceedings of the National Academy of Sciences* 95(2):606–611.

Carlson, B. M.
  2004   *Human Embryology and Developmental Biology*, 3rd ed. Philadelphia: Moseby.

Carroll, S. B., B. Prud'homme, and N. Gompel
  2008   Regulating evolution. *Scientific American* 298(5):61–67.

Carroll, S. B., J. K. Grenier, and S. D. Weatherbee
  2001   *From DNA to Diversity. Molecular Genetics and the Evolution of Animal Design*. Malden, MA: Blackwell Science.

Goodman, C. S., and B. C. Coughlin
  2000   The evolution of evo-devo biology. *Proceedings of the National Academy of Sciences* 97(9): 4424–4425.

Lutz, B., H. C. Lu, G. Eichele, D. Miller, and T. C. Kaufmann
  1996   Rescue of *Drosophila* labial null mutant by the chicken ortholog *Hoxb-1* demonstrates that the function of Hox genes is phylogenetically conserved. *Genes and Development* 10:176–184.

Mouse Genome Sequencing Consortium
  2002   Initial sequencing and comparative analysis of the mouse genome. *Nature* 420:520–562.

6 Survey of Living Primates

Key Questions

What are the major characteristics of primates? Why are humans considered primates?

Why is it important to study nonhuman primates?

Introduction

Chimpanzees aren't monkeys and neither are gorillas or orangutans. They're apes, and even though most people think they're basically the same, they aren't. Yet, how many times have you seen a greeting card or magazine ad with a picture of a chimpanzee and a phrase that says something like, "Don't monkey around" or "No more monkey business"? Or maybe you've seen people at zoos making fun of primates. While these issues may seem trivial, they aren't, because they show just how little most people know about our closest relatives. This is extremely unfortunate, because by better understanding these relatives, not only can we better know ourselves, but we can also try to preserve the many nonhuman primate species that are critically endangered today. Indeed, many will go extinct in the next 50 years or so if steps aren't taken now to save them.

One way to understand any organism is to compare its anatomy and behavior with that of other, closely related species. This comparative approach helps explain how and why physiological and behavioral systems evolved as adaptive responses to various selective pressures throughout the course of evolution. This statement applies to *Homo sapiens* just as it does to any other species. So, if we want to identify the components that have shaped the evolution of our species, a good starting point is to compare ourselves with our closest living relatives, the approximately 230 species of nonhuman primates (lemurs, lorises, tarsiers, monkeys, and apes).

This chapter describes the physical characteristics that define the order **Primates,** gives a brief overview of the major groups of living primates, and introduces some methods currently used to compare living primates genetically. (For a comparison of human and nonhuman skeletons, see Appendix A.) But before going any further, we again want to call attention to a few common misunderstandings about evolutionary processes.

Evolution isn't a goal-directed process. Therefore, the fact that lemurs evolved before **anthropoids** doesn't mean that lemurs "progressed" or "advanced" to become anthropoids. Living primates aren't in any way "superior" to their evolutionary predecessors or to one another. Consequently, in discussions of major groupings of contemporary nonhuman primates, there's no implied superiority or inferiority of any of these groups. Each lineage or species has come to possess unique qualities that make it better suited to a particular habitat and lifestyle than others. Given that all contemporary organisms are "successful" results of the evolutionary process, it's best to completely avoid using such loaded terms as *superior* and *inferior*. Finally, you shouldn't make the mistake of thinking that contemporary primates (including humans) necessarily represent the final stage or apex of a lineage, because we all continue to evolve as lineages. Actually, the only species that represent final evolutionary stages of particular lineages are the ones that become extinct.

primates Members of the mammalian order Primates (pronounced "pry-may´-tees"), which includes lemurs, lorises, tarsiers, monkeys, apes, and humans.

anthropoids Members of a suborder of Primates, the infraorder Anthropoidea (pronounced "an-throw-poid´-ee-uh"). Traditionally, the suborder includes monkeys, apes, and humans.

Primate Characteristics

All primates share many characteristics with other placental mammals (see Chapter 5). Some of these basic mammalian traits are body hair, a relatively long gestation period followed by live birth, mammary glands (thus the term *mammal*), different types of teeth (incisors, canines, premolars, and molars), the ability to maintain a constant internal body temperature through physiological means or *endothermy* (see Chapter 5), increased brain size, and a considerable capacity for learning and behavioral flexibility. So, to differentiate primates as a distinct group from other mammals, we need to describe those characteristics that, taken together, set primates apart.

Identifying single traits that define the primate order isn't easy because, compared to most mammals, primates have remained quite *generalized*. This means that primates have retained several ancestral mammalian traits that many other mammals have lost over time. In response to particular selective pressures, some mammalian groups have become increasingly specialized, or derived. For example, through the course of evolution, horses and cattle have undergone a reduction in the number of digits (fingers and toes) from the ancestral pattern of five digits to one and two digits, respectively. These species have also developed hard, protective coverings over their feet in the form of hooves (Fig. 6-1a). This limb structure is beneficial in prey species, because their survival depends on speed and stability, but it restricts them to only one type of locomotion. Moreover, limb function is restricted to support and movement, and the ability to manipulate objects is lost completely.

Primates can't be defined by one or even a few traits they share in common because they *aren't* so specialized. Therefore, primatologists have drawn attention to a group of characteristics that, when taken together, more or less characterize the entire primate order. Still, these are a set of *general* tendencies that aren't all equally

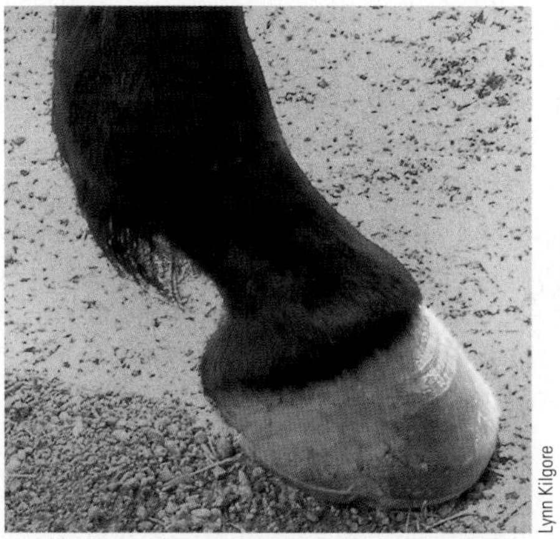

(a)

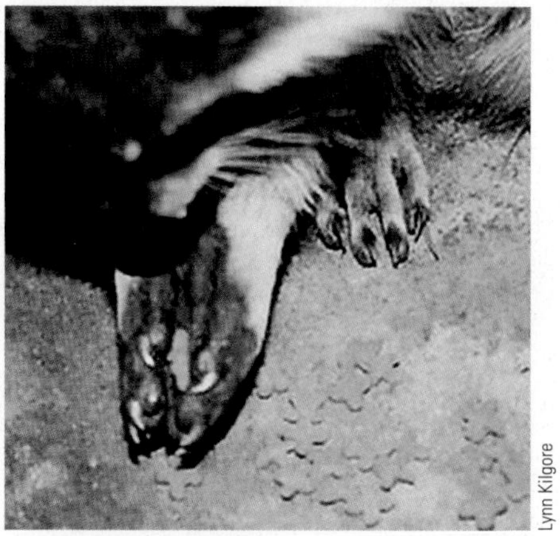

(b)

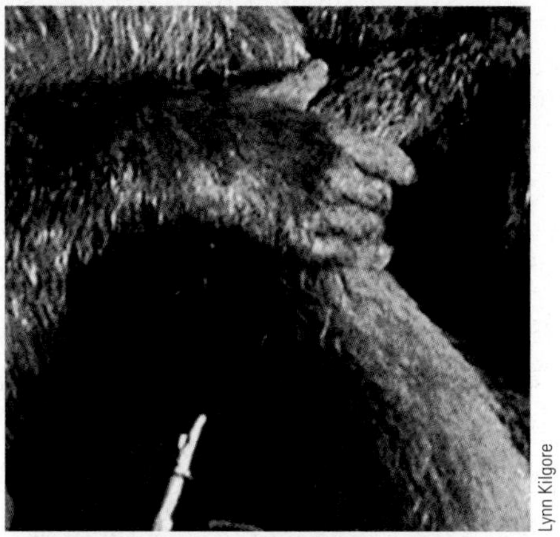

(c)

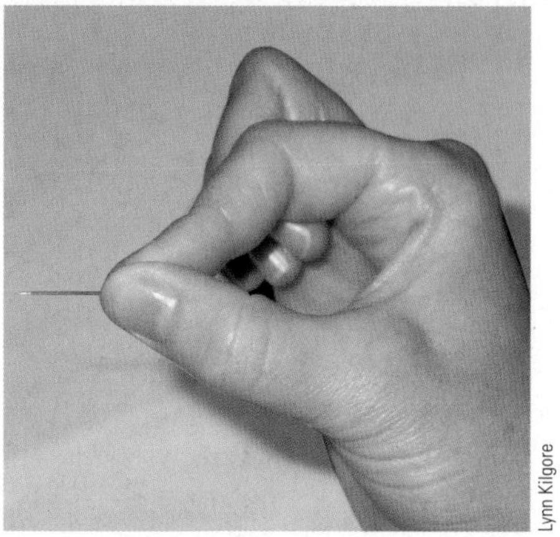

(d)

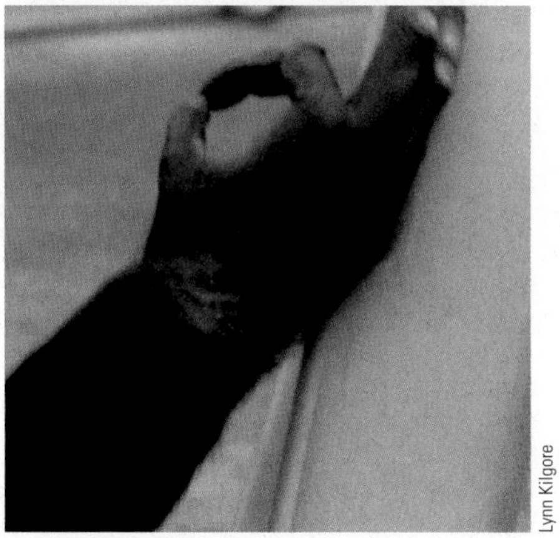

(e)

Figure 6-1

(a) A horse's front foot, homologous with a human hand, has undergone reduction from 5 digits to one. (b) While raccoons are capable of considerable manual dexterity and can readily pick up small objects with one hand, they have no opposable thumb. (c) Many monkeys are able to grasp objects with an opposable thumb, while others have very reduced thumbs. (d) Humans are capable of a "precision grip." (e) Chimpanzees with their reduced thumbs are capable of a precision grip but frequently use a modified form.

expressed in all primates. In addition, while some of these traits are unique to primates, many others are retained ancestral mammalian characteristics shared with other mammals. The following list is meant to give you an overall structural and behavioral picture of the primates in general, focusing on those characteristics that tend to set primates apart from other mammals. Concentrating on certain ancestral mammalian traits along with more specific, derived ones has been the traditional approach of primatologists, and it's still used today. In their limbs and locomotion, teeth, diet, senses, brain, and behavior, primates reflect a common evolutionary history with adaptations to similar environmental challenges, primarily as highly social, arboreal beings.

A. *Limbs and Locomotion*
1. *A tendency toward an erect posture (especially in the upper body).* (Derived trait) All primates show this tendency to some degree, and it's variously associated with sitting, leaping, standing, and, occasionally, bipedal walking.
2. *A flexible, generalized limb structure, which allows most primates to practice various locomotor behaviors.* (Ancestral trait) Primates have retained some bones (such as the clavicle, or collarbone) and certain abilities (like rotation of the forearm) that have been lost in more specialized mammals such as horses. Various aspects of hip and shoulder **morphology** also provide primates with a wide range of limb movement and function. Thus, by maintaining a generalized locomotor anatomy, primates aren't restricted to one form of movement, as are many other mammals. Primates also use their limbs for many activities besides locomotion.
3. *Prehensile hands (and sometimes feet).* (Derived trait) Lots of animals can manipulate objects, but not as skillfully as primates. All primates use their hands, and frequently their feet, to grasp and manipulate objects (Fig. 6-1b). This ability is variably expressed and is enhanced by several characteristics, including these:
    a. *Retention of five digits on the hands and feet.* (Ancestral trait) This trait varies somewhat throughout the order, with some species showing marked reduction of the thumb or of the second digit.
    b. *An opposable thumb, and in most species, a divergent and partially opposable big toe.* (Derived trait) Most primates are capable of moving the thumb so that it opposes or comes in contact with the second digit or with the palm of the hand (Fig. 6-1c through e).
    c. *Nails instead of claws.* (Derived trait) This characteristic is seen in all primates except some highly derived New World monkeys (marmosets and tamarins). All lemurs and lorises also have a claw on one digit.
    d. *Tactile pads enriched with sensory nerve fibers at the ends of digits.* (Derived trait) This characteristic enhances the sense of touch.
B. *Diet and Teeth*
1. Lack of dietary specialization. (Ancestral trait) This characteristic is typical of most primates, who tend to eat a wide assortment of food items. In general, primates are **omnivorous**.
2. *A generalized dentition.* (Ancestral trait) Primate teeth aren't specialized for processing only one type of food, a characteristic related to a general lack of dietary specialization.
C. *The senses and the brain.* Primates (**diurnal** ones in particular) rely heavily on vision and less on **olfaction**, especially when compared to other mammals.

---

morphology The form (shape, size) of anatomical structures; can also refer to the entire organism.

omnivorous Having a diet consisting of many food types, such as plant materials, meat, and insects.

diurnal Active during the day.

olfaction The sense of smell.

nocturnal Active during the night.

stereoscopic vision The condition whereby visual images are, to varying degrees, superimposed. This provides for depth perception, or viewing the external environment in three dimensions. Stereoscopic vision is partly a function of structures in the brain.

binocular vision Vision characterized by overlapping visual fields provided by forward-facing eyes. Binocular vision is essential to depth perception.

hemispheres The two halves of the cerebrum that are connected by a dense mass of fibers. (The cerebrum is the large rounded outer portion of the brain.)

neocortex The more recently evolved portions of the cortex of the brain that are involved with higher mental functions and composed of areas that integrate incoming information from different sensory organs.

sensory modalities Different forms of sensation (e.g., touch, pain, pressure, heat, cold, vision, taste, hearing, and smell).

This emphasis is reflected in evolutionary changes in the skull, eyes, and brain. (Derived trait)

1. *Color vision.* This is a characteristic of all diurnal primates. **Nocturnal** primates don't have color vision.
2. *Depth perception.* Primates have **stereoscopic vision**, or the ability to perceive objects in three dimensions. This is made possible through a variety of mechanisms, including:
   a. *Eyes placed toward the front of the face (not to the sides).* This position provides for overlapping visual fields, or **binocular vision** (Fig. 6-2).
   b. *Visual information from each eye transmitted to visual centers in both **hemispheres** of the brain.* In nonprimate mammals, most optic nerve fibers cross to the opposite hemisphere through a structure at the base of the brain. In primates, about 40 percent of the fibers remain on the same side, so that information is shared.
   c. *Visual information organized into three-dimensional images by specialized structures in the brain itself.* (Derived trait) The capacity for stereoscopic vision depends on each hemisphere of the brain receiving visual information from both eyes and from overlapping visual fields.
3. *Decreased reliance on olfaction.* (Derived trait) This trend is expressed as an overall reduction in the size of olfactory structures in the brain (see p. 212). Corresponding reduction of the entire olfactory apparatus has also resulted in decreased size of the snout in most species. This is related to an increased reliance on vision. In some species, such as baboons, the large muzzle isn't related to olfaction, but to the need to accommodate large canine teeth (see "A Closer Look," p. 145).
4. *Expansion and increased complexity of the brain.* (Derived trait) This is a general trend among placental mammals, but it's especially true of primates. In primates, this expansion is most evident in the visual and association areas of the **neocortex** (portions of the brain where information from different **sensory modalities** is integrated). Expansion in regions involved with the hand (both sensory and motor) is seen in many primate species, particularly humans.

D. Maturation, learning, and behavior
   1. *A more efficient means of fetal nourishment, longer periods of gestation, reduced numbers of offspring (with single births the norm), delayed maturation, and extension of the entire life span.* (Derived trait)
   2. *A greater dependence on flexible, learned behavior.* (Derived trait) This trend is correlated with delayed maturation and subsequently longer periods of infant and child dependency on at least one parent. Because of these trends, parental investment in each offspring is increased, so that although fewer offspring are born, they receive more intense rearing.

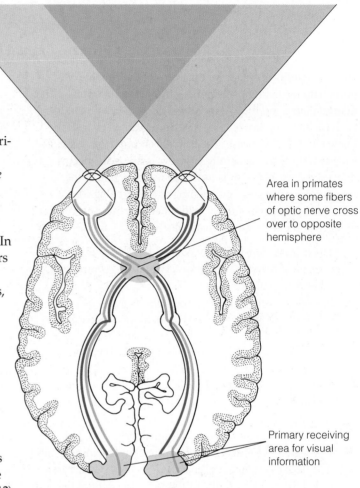

Area in primates where some fibers of optic nerve cross over to opposite hemisphere

Primary receiving area for visual information

Figure 6-2

Simplified diagram showing overlapping visual fields that permit binocular vision in primates with eyes positioned at the front of the face. (The green shaded area represents the area of overlap.) Stereoscopic vision (three-dimensional vision) is provided in part by binocular vision and in part by the transmission of visual stimuli from each eye to both hemispheres of the brain. (In nonprimate mammals, most, if not all, visual information crosses over to the hemisphere opposite the eye in which it was initially received.)

A Closer Look

Primate Cranial Anatomy

Several significant anatomical features of the primate cranium help us distinguish primates from other mammals. The mammalian trend toward increased brain development has been further emphasized in primates, as shown by a relatively enlarged braincase. The primate emphasis on vision is further reflected in generally large eye sockets; the decreased dependence on olfaction is indicated by reduction of the snout and corresponding flattening of the face (Fig. 1).

Here are some of the specific anatomical details seen in modern and most fossil primate crania:

1. The primate face is shortened, and the size of the braincase, relative to that of the face, is enlarged compared to other mammals (see Fig. 1).
2. Eye sockets are enclosed at the sides by a ring of bone called the *postorbital bar* (see Fig. 1). In most other mammals, there is no postorbital bar. Also, in tarsiers, monkeys, apes, and humans, there is a plate of bone at the back of the eye orbit called the *postorbital plate*, a feature that isn't present in lemurs and lorises. The functional significance of these structures hasn't been thoroughly explained, but it may be related to stresses on the eye orbits imposed by chewing (Fleagle, 1999).
3. The region of the skull that contains the structures of the middle ear is completely encircled by a bony structure called the auditory bulla. In primates, the floor of the *auditory bulla* is derived from a segment of the temporal bone (Fig. 2). Of all the skeletal structures, most primate paleontologists consider the postorbital bar and the derivation of the auditory bulla to be the two best diagnostic traits of the primate order.

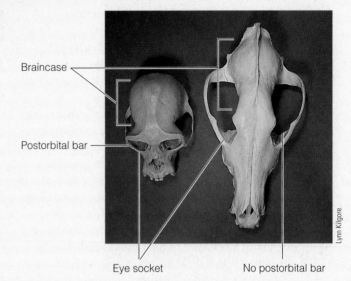

Braincase

Postorbital bar

Eye socket

No postorbital bar

Lynn Kilgore

Figure 1

The skull of a gibbon (left) compared to that of a red wolf (right). Note that the absolute size of the braincase in the gibbon is slightly larger than that of the wolf, even though the wolf (at about 80 to 100 pounds) is six times the size of the gibbon (about 15 pounds).

4. The base of the skull in primates is somewhat flexed, so that the muzzle (mouth and nose) is positioned lower relative to the braincase (Fig. 3). This arrangement provides for the exertion of greater force during chewing, particularly needed for crushing and grinding tough vegetable fibers, seeds, and hard-shelled fruits.

3. *The tendency to live in social groups and the permanent association of adult males with the group.* (Derived trait) Except for some nocturnal species, primates tend to associate with other individuals. Also, the permanent association of adult males with the group is uncommon in most mammals but widespread in primates.
4. *The tendency to diurnal activity patterns.* (Derived trait) This trend is seen in most primates; lorises, tarsiers, one monkey species, and some lemurs are nocturnal; all the rest are diurnal.

Primate Adaptations

In this section, we'll consider how primate anatomical traits evolved as adaptations to environmental circumstances. It's important to remember that when you

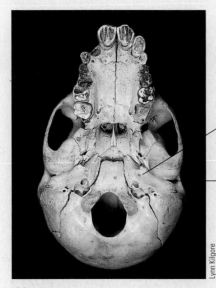

Portion of temporal bone enclosing auditory bulla

External opening to ear (external auditory meatus)

Lynn Kilgore

Figure 2

The base of an adolescent chimpanzee skull. (Note that in an adult animal, the bones of the skull would be fused together and would not appear as separate elements as shown here.)

Figure 3

The skull of a male baboon (a) compared to that of a red wolf (b). The angle at the base of the baboon skull is due to flexion. The corresponding area of the wolf skull is relatively flat. Note the forward-facing position of the eye orbits above the snout in the baboon. Also, note that in the baboon, the enlarged muzzle does *not* reflect a heavy reliance on the sense of smell. Rather, it serves to support very large canine teeth, the roots of which curve back through the bone for as much as 1½ inches.

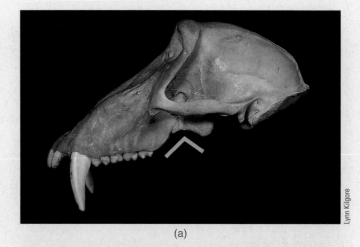

(a)

Lynn Kilgore

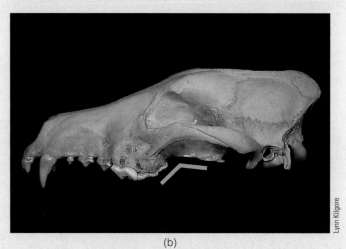

(b)

Lynn Kilgore

see the phrase "environmental circumstances," it refers to several interrelated variables, including climate, diet, habitat (woodland, grassland, forest, and so on), and predation.

Evolutionary Factors

Traditionally, the suite of characteristics shared by primates has been explained as the result of an adaptation to **arboreal** living. While other mammals were adapting to various ground-dwelling lifestyles and even marine environments, the primates found their **adaptive niche** in the trees. A number of other mammals were also adapting to arboreal living; but while many of them nested in the trees, they continued to forage for food on the ground. But throughout the course of evolution, primates increasingly found food (leaves, seeds, fruits, nuts, insects, and small mammals) in the trees themselves. Over time, this dietary shift enhanced a general

arboreal Tree-living; adapted to life in the trees.

adaptive niche An organism's entire way of life: where it lives, what it eats, how it gets food, how it avoids predators, and so on.

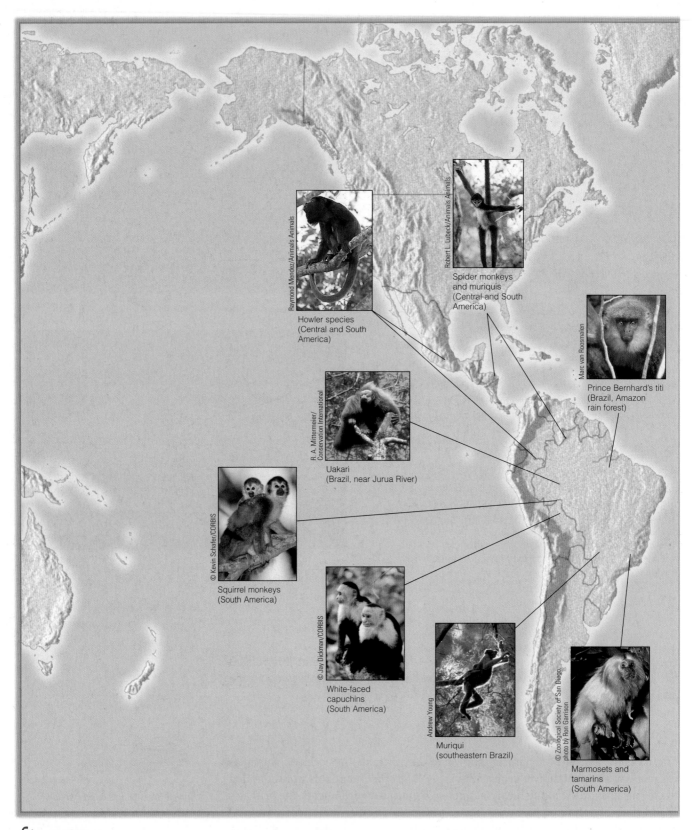

Figure 6-3

Geographical distribution of living nonhuman primates.
Much original habitat is now very fragmented.

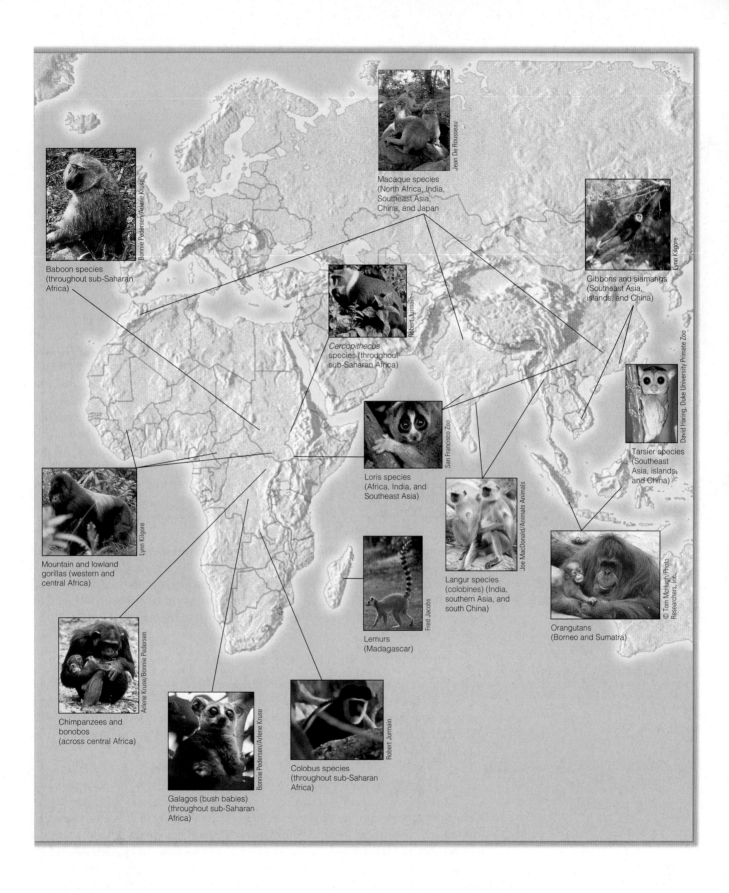

Macaque species
(North Africa, India,
Southeast Asia,
China, and Japan)

Jean De Rousseau

Baboon species
(throughout sub-Saharan
Africa)

Bonnie Pedersen/Arlene Kruse

Gibbons and siamangs
(Southeast Asia,
islands, and China)

Lynn Kilgore

Cercopithecus
species (throughout
sub-Saharan Africa)

Robert Jurmain

Loris species
(Africa, India, and
Southeast Asia)

San Francisco Zoo

Tarsier species
(Southeast
Asia, islands,
and China)

David Haring, Duke University Primate Zoo

Mountain and lowland
gorillas (western and
central Africa)

Lynn Kilgore

Langur species
(colobines) (India,
southern Asia, and
south China)

Joe MacDonald/Animals Animals

Lemurs
(Madagascar)

Fred Jacobs

Orangutans
(Borneo and Sumatra)

© Tom McHugh/Photo
Researchers, Inc.

Chimpanzees and
bonobos
(across central Africa)

Arlene Kruse/Bonnie Pedersen

Galagos (bush babies)
(throughout sub-Saharan
Africa)

Bonnie Pedersen/Arlene Kruse

Colobus species
(throughout sub-Saharan
Africa)

Robert Jurmain

trend toward *omnivory*; and this trend in turn led to the retention of the generalized dentition that's characteristic of primates.

Increased reliance on vision, coupled with grasping hands and feet, are also adaptations to an arboreal lifestyle. In a complex, three-dimensional environment with uncertain footholds, acute color vision with depth perception is, for obvious reasons, extremely beneficial.

An alternative to this traditional *arboreal hypothesis*, called the *visual predation hypothesis* (Cartmill, 1972, 1992), is based on the fact that animals such as squirrels are also arboreal, yet they haven't evolved primate-like adaptations such as prehensile hands or forward-facing eyes. But visual predators, such as cats and owls, do have forward-facing eyes, and this fact may provide insight into an additional factor that could have shaped primate evolution.

Forward-facing eyes (which facilitate binocular vision), grasping hands and feet, and the presence of nails instead of claws may not have come about solely as adaptive advantages in a purely arboreal setting. They may also be the hallmarks of an arboreal visual predator. So, early primates may first have adapted to shrubby forest undergrowth and the lowest tiers of the forest canopy, where they hunted insects and other small prey.

A third scenario, the *angiosperm radiation hypothesis* (Sussman, 1991), suggests that the basic primate traits were developed in conjunction with another major evolutionary occurrence, the rise of the *angiosperms* (flowering plants) that began around 140 mya. Flowering plants provide numerous resources for primates, including nectar, seeds, and fruits. Sussman argues that since visual predation isn't common among modern primates, forward-facing eyes, grasping hands and feet, omnivory, and *color vision* may have arisen in response to the demand for fine visual and tactile discrimination, which is necessary when feeding on small food items such as fruits, berries, and seeds among branches and stems (Dominy and Lucas, 2001).

These hypotheses aren't mutually exclusive. The complex of primate characteristics might well have originated in nonarboreal settings and certainly could have been stimulated by the new econiches provided by evolving angiosperms. But at some point, primates did take to the trees, and that's where most of them still live today. Even if the basic primate structural complexes originally facilitated visual predation and/or omnivory in shrubby undergrowth and terminal branches, they became ideally suited for the arboreal adaptations that followed.

Geographical Distribution and Habitats

With just a couple of exceptions, nonhuman primates are found in tropical or semitropical areas of the New and Old Worlds. In the New World, these areas include southern Mexico, Central America, and parts of South America. Old World primates are found in Africa, India, Southeast Asia (including numerous islands), and Japan (Fig. 6-3 on pp. 146–147).

Diet and Teeth

Omnivory is one example of the overall lack of specialization in primates. Although the majority of primates tend to emphasize some food items over others, most eat a combination of fruit, nuts, seeds, leaves, other plant materials, and insects. Many also get animal protein from birds and amphibians. Some (capuchins, baboons, bonobos, and especially chimpanzees) occasionally kill and eat small mammals, including other primates. Others, such as African colobus monkeys and the leaf-eating mon-

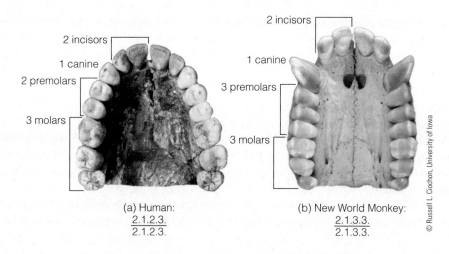

(a) Human:
2.1.2.3.
2.1.2.3.

(b) New World Monkey:
2.1.3.3.
2.1.3.3.

© Russell L. Ciochon, University of Iowa

Figure **6-4**

(a) The human maxilla illustrates a dental formula characteristic of all Old World monkeys, apes, and humans. (b) The New World monkey (Cebus) maxilla shows the dental formula that is typical of most New World monkeys. (Not to scale, the monkey maxilla is actually much smaller than the human.)

keys (langurs) of India and Southeast Asia, have become more specialized and mostly eat leaves.

This wide and varied menu is a good example of the advantages of having a generalized diet, especially in less-predictable environments; if one food source fails (for example, during drought or through human activities), other options may still be available. The downside of being generalized is that there may be competition for some resources with other species, including nonprimates, that eat the same things. Specialization, where a species has a narrow ecological niche and eats only one or two things, can be advantageous in this regard because these species don't have much competition from others; but it can be catastrophic if the food supply disappears.

Like nearly all other mammals, primates have four kinds of teeth: incisors and canines for biting and cutting, and premolars and molars for chewing and grinding. Biologists use what's called a **dental formula** to describe the number of each type of tooth that typifies a species. A dental formula indicates the number of each tooth type in each quadrant of the mouth (Fig. 6-4). For example, all Old World *anthropoids* have two incisors, one canine, two premolars, and three molars on each side of the midline in both the upper and lower jaws, for a total of 32 teeth. This is represented by the following dental formula:

2.1.2.3 (upper)
2.1.2.3 (lower)

The dental formula for a generalized placental mammal is 3.1.4.3 (three incisors, one canine, four premolars, and three molars). Primates have fewer teeth than this ancestral pattern because of a general evolutionary trend toward fewer teeth in many mammal groups. Consequently, the number of each type of tooth varies between lineages. For example, in most New World monkeys, the dental formula is 2.1.3.3 (two incisors, one canine, three premolars, and three molars). In contrast, humans, apes, and all Old World monkeys share a somewhat different dental formula: 2.1.2.3. This formula differs from that of the New World monkeys in that there's one less premolar.

The overall lack of dietary specialization in primates is reflected in the lack of specialization in the size and shape of the teeth, because tooth shape and size are directly related to diet. For example, carnivores typically have premolars and molars with high, pointed **cusps** adapted for tearing meat; but herbivores, such as cattle and horses, have premolars with broad, flat surfaces suited to chewing tough grasses and other plant materials. Most primates have premolars and molars with

dental formula Numerical device that indicates the number of each type of tooth in each side of the upper and lower jaws.

cusps The bumps on the chewing surface of premolars and molars.

low, rounded cusps, a molar morphology that enables them to process most types of foods. So, throughout their evolutionary history, the primates have developed a dentition adapted to a varied diet, and the capacity to exploit many foods has contributed to their overall success during the last 50 million years.

Locomotion

Almost all primates are, at least to some degree, **quadrupedal**, meaning they use all four limbs to support the body during locomotion. However, most primates use more than one form of locomotion, and they're able to do this because of their generalized anatomy.

Most of the quadrupedal primates are primarily arboreal, but terrestrial quadrupedalism is also common. The limbs of terrestrial quadrupeds are approx-

quadrupedal Using all four limbs to support the body during locomotion; the basic mammalian (and primate) form of locomotion.

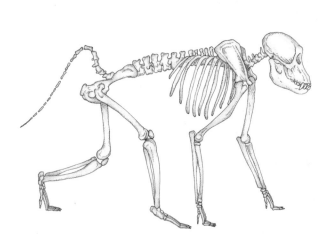

(a) Skeleton of a terrestrial quadruped (savanna baboon).

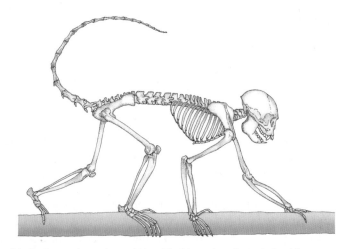

(b) Skeleton of an arboreal New World monkey (bearded saki).

Figure **6-5**

Differences in skeletal anatomy and limb proportions reflect differences in locomotor patterns. (Redrawn by Stephen Nash from original art in John G. Fleagle, *Primate Adaptation and Evolution*, 2nd ed., 1999. Reprinted by permission of publisher and Stephen Nash.)

(c) Skeleton of a vertical clinger and leaper (indri).   (d) Skeleton of a brachiator (gibbon).

imately the same length, with forelimbs being 90 percent (or more) as long as hind limbs (Fig. 6-5a). In arboreal quadrupeds, forelimbs are somewhat shorter (Fig. 6-5b).

Vertical clinging and leaping, another form of locomotion, is characteristic of some lemurs and tarsiers. As the term implies, vertical clingers and leapers support themselves vertically by grasping onto trunks of trees or other large plants while their knees and ankles are tightly flexed (Fig. 6-5c). By forcefully extending their long hind limbs, they can spring powerfully away either forward or backward.

Brachiation, or arm swinging, is a suspensory form of locomotion in which the body moves by being alternatively supported under either forelimb. (You may have brachiated as a child on "monkey bars" in playgrounds.) Because of anatomical modifications at the shoulder joint, apes and humans are capable of true brachiation. However, only the small gibbons and siamangs of Southeast Asia use this form of locomotion almost exclusively (Fig. 6-5d).

Brachiation is seen in species characterized by arms longer than legs, a short, stable **lumbar** spine (lower back), long curved fingers, and reduced thumbs. As these are traits seen in all the apes, it's believed that although none of the great apes (orangutans, gorillas, bonobos, and chimpanzees) habitually brachiates today, they may have inherited these characteristics from brachiating or climbing ancestors.

Some New World monkeys, such as spider monkeys and muriquis (see p. 159), are called *semibrachiators*, since they practice a combination of leaping with some arm swinging. Also, some New World monkeys enhance arm swinging and other suspensory behaviors by using a *prehensile tail*, which in effect serves as an effective grasping fifth hand. It's important to mention here that prehensile tails are exclusively a New World phenomenon; they aren't seen in any Old World primates.

Lastly, all the apes, to varying degrees, have arms that are longer than legs, and some (gorillas, bonobos, and chimpanzees) practice a special form of quadrupedalism called knuckle walking. Because their arms are so long relative to their legs, instead of walking with the palms of their hands flat on the ground like some monkeys do, they support the weight of their upper body on the back surfaces of their bent fingers (Fig. 6-6).

Figure **6-6**

Chimpanzee knuckle walking. Note how the weight of the upper body is supported on the knuckles and not the palm of the hand.

Primate Classification

The living primates are commonly categorized into their respective subgroups, as shown in Figure 6-7. This taxonomy is based on the system originally established by Linnaeus (see Chapter 2). The primate order, which includes a diverse array of approximately 230 species, belongs to a larger group, the class Mammalia.

As you learned in Chapter 5, in any taxonomic system, animals are organized into increasingly specific categories. For example, the order Primates includes *all* primates. But at the next level down, the *suborder*, primates are divided into two smaller categories: **Strepsirhini** (lemurs and lorises) and **Haplorhini** (tarsiers, monkeys, apes and humans). Therefore, the suborder distinction is narrower, or more specific, than that of the order. At the suborder level, the lemurs and lorises are distinct as a group from all the other primates. This classification makes the biological and evolutionary statement that all the lemurs and lorises are more closely related to one another than they are to any of the other primates. Likewise, humans, apes, monkeys, and tarsiers are more closely related to one another than they are to the lorises and lemurs.

The taxonomy shown in Figure 6-7 is a modified version of a similar system that biologists and primatologists have used for decades. The traditional system was

brachiation Arm swinging, a form of locomotion used by some primates. Brachiation involves hanging from a branch and moving by alternately swinging from one arm to the other.

lumbar Pertaining to the lower back. Monkeys have a longer lumbar area than that seen in apes and humans.

Strepsirhini (strep'-sir-in-ee) The primate suborder that includes lemurs and lorises.

Haplorhini (hap'-lo-rin-ee) The primate suborder that includes tarsiers, monkeys, apes, and humans.

Figure 6-7

Primate taxonomic classification. This abbreviated taxonomy illustrates how primates are grouped from broader categories (e.g., the order Primates) into increasingly specific ones (species). Only the more general categories are shown, except for the great apes and humans.

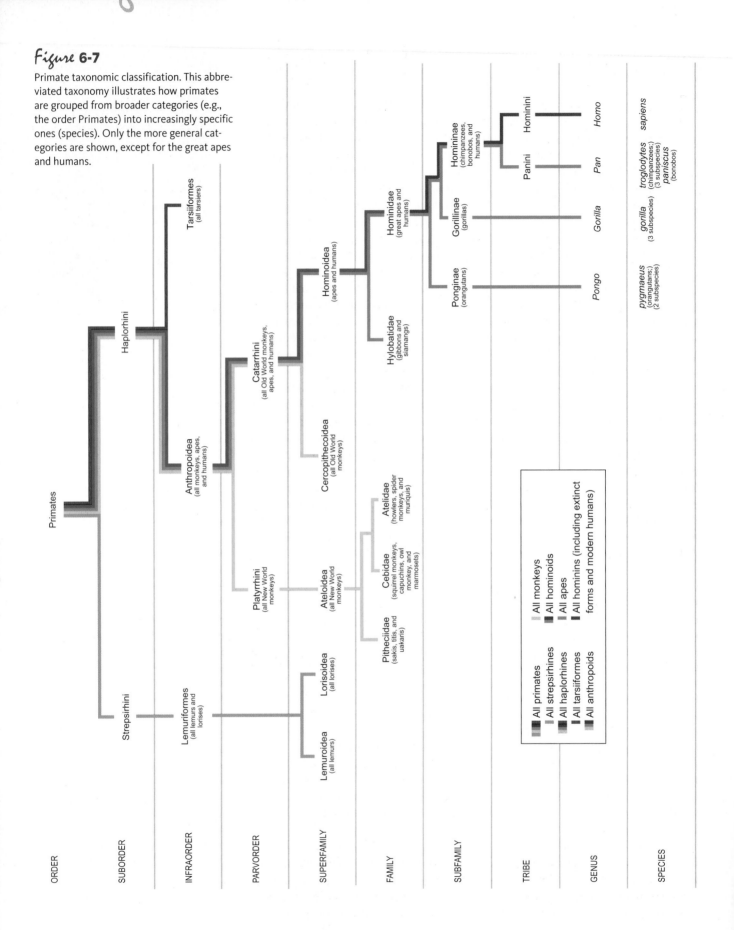

ORDER

SUBORDER

INFRAORDER

PARVORDER

SUPERFAMILY

FAMILY

SUBFAMILY

TRIBE

GENUS

SPECIES

Primates

Haplorhini

Strepsirhini

Tarsiiformes
(all tarsiers)

Anthropoidea
(all monkeys, apes, and humans)

Lemuriformes
(all lemurs and lorises)

Catarrhini
(all Old World monkeys, apes, and humans)

Platyrrhini
(all New World monkeys)

Cercopithecoidea
(all Old World monkeys)

Lorisoidea
(all lorises)

Lemuroidea
(all lemurs)

Hominoidea
(apes and humans)

Ateloidea
(all New World monkeys)

Hominidae
(great apes and humans)

Hylobatidae
(gibbons and siamangs)

Atelidae
(howlers, spider monkeys, and muriquis)

Cebidae
(squirrel monkeys, capuchins, owl monkey, and marmosets)

Pithecidae
(sakis, titis, and uakaris)

Homininae
(chimpanzees, bonobos, and humans)

Gorillinae
(gorillas)

Ponginae
(orangutans)

Hominini

Panini

Homo

Pan

Gorilla

Pongo

sapiens

troglodytes
(chimpanzees)
(3 subspecies)

paniscus
(bonobos)

gorilla
(3 subspecies)

pygmaeus
(orangutans)
(2 subspecies)

All primates
All strepsirhines
All haplorhines
All tarsiiformes
All anthropoids

All monkeys
All hominoids
All apes
All hominins (including extinct forms and modern humans)

based on physical similarities between species and lineages. But that approach isn't foolproof. For instance, some New and Old World monkeys resemble each other anatomically but actually, they aren't closely related at all. In fact, evolutionarily, they're quite distinct from one another, having diverged from a common ancestor perhaps as long ago as 35 mya. By looking only at physical characteristics, it's possible to overlook the unknown effects of separate evolutionary history (see the discussion of homoplasy on p. 113). But, thanks to the rapidly growing number of species whose genomes have been sequenced, geneticists can now make direct comparisons between the genes and indeed the entire genetic makeup of different species. This kind of analysis, called *comparative genomics*, gives us a much more accurate picture of evolutionary and biological relationships between species than was possible even as recently as the late 1990s. So, once again, we see how changing technologies influence the refining of older hypotheses and the development of new ones.

A complete draft sequence of the chimpanzee genome was completed in 2005 (The Chimpanzee Sequencing and Analysis Consortium, 2005). This was a major milestone in human comparative genomics. Comparisons of the genomes of different species are vital because they reveal such differences in DNA as the number of nucleotide substitutions and/or deletions that have occurred since related species last shared a common ancestor. Geneticists estimate the rate at which genes change and then use this information, combined with the amount of change they observe, to estimate when related species diverged from their last common ancestor.

Wildman and colleagues (2003) compared nearly 100 human genes with their chimpanzee, gorilla, and orangutan counterparts and supported some earlier studies that concluded that humans are most closely related to chimpanzees and that the "functional elements" or coding DNA sequences of the two species are 98.4 to 99.4 percent identical. The results of the study also estimated that the chimpanzee and human lineages diverged between 6 and 7 mya. These results are consistent with the molecular findings of several other studies (Chen and Li, 2001; Clark et al., 2003; Steiper and Young, 2006). Other research has substantiated these figures, but it's also revealed more variation in noncoding DNA segments and portions that have been inserted, deleted, or duplicated. So when the *entire* genome is considered, reported DNA differences between chimpanzees and humans range from 2.7 percent (Cheng et al., 2005) to 6.4 percent (Demuth et al., 2006). These aren't substantial differences, but perhaps the most important discovery of all is that humans have much more noncoding DNA than do the other primates that have thus far been studied. Now geneticists are beginning to understand some of the functions of noncoding DNA and hope to explain why humans have so much of it and how it makes us different from our close relatives.

A Survey of the Living Primates

In this section, we discuss the major primate subgroups. Since it's beyond the scope of this book to cover any species in great detail, we present a brief description of each major grouping. Then we take a closer look at the apes.

Lemurs and Lorises

The suborder Strepsirhini includes the lemurs and lorises, the most primitive living primates. Remember that by "primitive" we mean that lemurs and lorises are more similar anatomically to their earlier mammalian ancestors than are the other

Figure 6-8

As you can see, rhinaria come in different shapes and sizes, but they all enhance an animal's sense of smell.

Lynn Kilgore

Lynn Kilgore

Dental comb

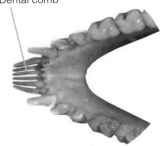

© Viktor Deak, after John G. Fleagle

Figure 6-9

Lemur dental comb, formed by forward-projecting incisors and canines.

Figure 6-10

Geographical distribution of modern lemurs.

rhinarium (rine-air´-ee-um) The moist, hairless pad at the end of the nose seen in most mammalian species. The rhinarium enhances an animal's ability to smell.

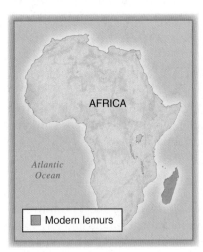

AFRICA

Atlantic
Ocean

■ Modern lemurs

primates (tarsiers, monkeys, apes, and humans). For example, they retain certain ancestral characteristics, such as a more pronounced reliance on *olfaction*. Their greater olfactory capabilities (compared to other primates) are reflected in the presence of a moist, fleshy pad, or **rhinarium**, at the end of the nose and a relatively long snout (Fig. 6-8).

Many other characteristics distinguish lemurs and lorises from the other primates, including eyes placed more to the side of the face, differences in reproductive physiology, and shorter gestation and maturation periods. Lemurs and lorises also have a unique, derived trait called a "dental comb" (Fig. 6-9) formed by forward-projecting lower incisors and canines. These modified teeth are used in both grooming and feeding. One other characteristic that sets lemurs and lorises apart is the retention of a claw (called a "grooming claw") on the second toe.

Lemurs Lemurs are found only on the island of Madagascar and adjacent islands off the east coast of Africa (Fig. 6-10). As the only nonhuman primates on Madagascar, lemurs diversified into numerous and varied ecological niches without competition from monkeys and apes, as we'll see in Chapter 9. Thus, the approximately 60 surviving species of lemurs on Madagascar today represent a kind of *lost world*, an evolutionary pattern that has vanished elsewhere.

Lemurs range in size from the small mouse lemur, with a body length (head and trunk) of only 5 inches, to the indri, with a body length of 2 to 3 feet (Nowak, 1999). Typically, the larger lemurs are diurnal and eat a wide variety of foods, such as leaves, fruit, buds, bark, and shoots, but the tiny mouse and dwarf lemurs are nocturnal and insectivorous.

Lemurs display considerable variation regarding several other aspects of behavior. Some are primarily arboreal, but others, such as ring-tailed lemurs (Fig. 6-11), are more terrestrial. Some arboreal species are quadrupeds, and others (sifakas and indris) are vertical clingers and leapers (Fig. 6-12). Several species (for example, ring-tailed lemurs and sifakas) are gregarious, living in groups of 10 to 25 animals composed of males and females of all ages. However, indris live in "family" units composed of

Figure **6-11**
Ring-tailed lemur.

Figure **6-12**
Sifakas.

a mated pair and dependent offspring. Additionally, several nocturnal forms are mostly solitary.

Lorises Lorises (Fig. 6-13), which resemble lemurs, were able to survive in mainland areas by becoming nocturnal. In this way, they were (and are) able to avoid competition with more recently evolved primates (the diurnal monkeys).

There are at least eight loris species, all of which are found in tropical forest and woodland habitats of India, Sri Lanka, Southeast Asia, and Africa. Also included in the same general category are six to nine galago species (Bearder, 1987; Nowak, 1999), also called bush babies (Fig. 6-14), which are widely distributed throughout most of the forested and woodland savanna areas of sub-Saharan Africa.

Locomotion in some lorises is a slow, cautious, climbing form of quadrupedalism; their flexible hip joints permit suspension by hind limbs while using

Figure **6-13**
Slow loris.

Figure **6-14**
Galago, or "bush baby."

the hands in feeding. All galagos, however, are highly agile vertical clingers and leapers. Some lorises and galagos are almost entirely insectivorous, while others supplement their diet with various combinations of fruits, leaves, gums, and slugs. Lorises and galagos frequently forage alone, but feeding ranges can overlap and two or more females may feed and even nest together. Females also leave young infants behind in nests while they search for food. (This behavior is called infant parking.) While this may seem risky, many mammal mothers leave young infants alone. But lorises take an added precaution of first bathing their young with saliva that can cause an allergic reaction that discourages most predators (Krane et al., 2003).

Lemurs and lorises represent the same general adaptive level. Both groups exhibit good grasping and climbing abilities and a well-developed visual apparatus; however, vision is not completely stereoscopic, and color vision may not be as well developed as in anthropoids. Most lemurs and lorises also have prolonged life spans compared to most other small-bodied mammals, averaging about 14 years for lorises and 19 years for lemurs.

Tarsiers

There are five recognized tarsier species (Nowak, 1999), all of which are restricted to islands of Southeast Asia (Malaysia, Borneo, Sumatra, the Philippines, where they inhabit a wide range of habitats, from tropical forest to backyard gardens (Figs. 6-15 and 6-16). Tarsiers are nocturnal insectivores that use vertical clinging and leaping to surprise prey (which may also include small vertebrates) on lower branches and shrubs. They appear to form stable pair bonds, and the basic tarsier social unit is a mated pair and their young offspring (MacKinnon and MacKinnon, 1980).

Tarsiers are highly specialized (derived) animals that have several unique characteristics. In the past, tarsiers were believed to be more closely related to lemurs and lorises than to other primates because they share several traits with them. Consequently, they were classified in the same suborder as lemurs and lorises. However, tarsiers actually present a complex blend of characteristics not seen in any other primate. One of the most obvious is their enormous eyes, which dominate much of the face and are immobile within their sockets. To compensate for the inability to move their eyes, tarsiers, like owls, can rotate their heads 180°. Interestingly, each eye is about the size of a tarsier's brain (Beard, 2004).

In addition, tarsiers possess certain anthropoid characteristics, and DNA studies have suggested that they are more closely related to monkeys, apes, and humans than to lemurs and lorises. Therefore, although there is still some debate as to the taxonomic status of tarsiers, they are now classified in the suborder Haplorhini, along with the anthropoids (see Fig. 6-7, p. 152 and Appendix A).

Anthropoids: Monkeys, Apes, and Humans

Although there is much variation among anthropoids, they share certain features that, when taken together, distinguish them as a group from lemurs and lorises. Here's a partial list of these traits:

1. A larger average body size
2. Larger brain in absolute terms and relative to body weight
3. Reduced reliance on olfaction, indicated by absence of a rhinarium and other structures

Figure **6-15**

Tarsier.

David Haring

Figure **6-16**

Geographical distribution of tarsiers.

4. Increased reliance on vision, with forward-facing eyes placed more to the front of the face
5. Greater degree of color vision
6. Back of eye socket protected by a bony plate
7. Blood supply to brain different from that of lemurs and lorises
8. Fusion of the two sides of the mandible at the midline to form one bone. (In lemurs and lorises, they're two distinct bones joined by cartilage at the midline)
9. More generalized dentition, as seen in the absence of a dental comb and some other features
10. Differences in female internal reproductive anatomy
11. Longer gestation and maturation periods
12. Increased parental care
13. More mutual grooming

Approximately 85 percent of all primates are monkeys. It's thought that there are about 195 species, but it's impossible to give precise numbers because the taxonomic status of some primates remains in doubt, and primatologists are still making new discoveries. (In fact, between 1990 and 2006, 24 species and subspecies of monkeys were discovered and described.) Monkeys are divided into two groups separated by geographical area (New World and Old World) as well as at least 40 million years of separate evolutionary history (see Chapter 9).

New World Monkeys The approximately 70 New World monkey species can be found in a wide range of arboreal environments throughout most forested areas in southern Mexico and Central and South America (Fig. 6-17). They exhibit a wide range of variation in size, diet, and ecological adaptations (Fig. 6-20, next page). In size, they vary from the tiny marmosets and tamarins (about 12 ounces) to the 20-pound howler monkeys (Figs. 6-18 and 6-19). New World monkeys are almost exclusively arboreal, and some never come to the ground. Like the Old World monkeys, all except one species (the owl monkey) are diurnal.

One characteristic that distinguishes New and Old World monkeys is the shape of the nose. New World monkeys have broad noses with outward-facing

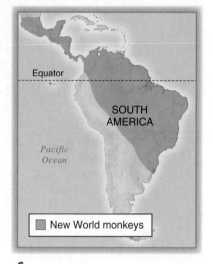

Figure **6-17**

Geographical distribution of New World monkeys.

Figure **6-18**

A pair of golden lion tamarins.

Figure **6-19**

Howler monkeys.

Figure **6-20**

Some New World monkeys.

Squirrel monkeys

© Kevin Schafer/Corbis

Female muriqui with infant

Andrew Young

Prince Bernhard's titi monkey (discovered in 2002)

Marc van Roosmalen

White-faced capuchins

© Jay Dickman/Corbis

Male uakari

R. A. Mittermeier/Conservation International

nostrils; Old World monkeys have narrower noses with downward-facing nostrils. To verify this, compare the white-faced capuchins in Figure 6-20 with the Sykes monkey in Figure 6-23 (p. 160) and with your own downward-facing nostrils. This difference in nose form has given rise to the terms *platyrrhine* (flat-nosed) and *catarrhine* (downward-facing nose) to refer to New and Old World anthropoids, respectively. The more formal terminology used in primate classification is shown in Fig. 6-7 and will be discussed in more detail in Chapter 9.

Marmosets and tamarins are the smallest of the New World monkeys. They have claws instead of nails, and unlike other primates, they usually give birth to twins instead of one infant. They're mostly insectivorous, although the marmoset diet includes gums from trees, and tamarins also eat fruits. Locomotion is quadrupedal, and claws are used for climbing. These small monkeys live in social groups usually composed of a mated pair, or a female and two adult males, and their offspring. This type of mating pattern is rare among mammals. Indeed, marmosets and tamarins are among the few primate species in which males are extensively involved in infant care (a truly progressive society!).

Other New World species range in size from squirrel monkeys (weighing only 1.5 to 2.5 pounds and having a body length of 12 inches) to the larger howlers (as much as 22 pounds in males and around 24 inches long). Diet varies, with most relying on a combination of fruits and leaves supplemented to varying degrees with insects. Most are quadrupedal; but some, such as spider monkeys (Fig. 6-21), are semibrachiators. Howlers, muriquis, and spider monkeys also have prehensile tails that are used not only in locomotion but also for hanging from branches. Socially, most New World monkeys live in mixed-sex groups of all age categories. Some (such as titis) form monogamous pairs and live with their subadult offspring.

Old World Monkeys Except for humans, Old World monkeys are the most widely distributed of all living primates. They're found throughout sub-Saharan Africa and southern Asia, ranging from tropical jungle habitats to semiarid desert and even to seasonally snow-covered areas in northern Japan (Fig. 6-22).

Figure **6-21**

Spider monkey. Note the prehensile tail.

Robert L. Lubeck/Animals Animals

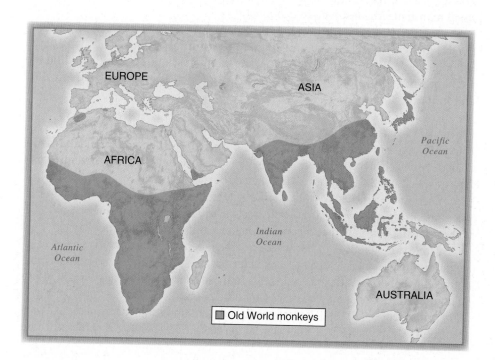

Figure **6-22**

Geographical distribution of living Old World monkeys.

Figure **6-23**

Adult male sykes monkey, one of several guenon species.

Robert Jurmain

Most Old World monkeys are quadrupedal and primarily arboreal, but some (such as baboons) are also adapted to life on the ground. In general, they spend a good deal of time feeding, sleeping, and grooming. Old World monkeys also have areas of hardened skin on the buttocks called **ischial callosities** that serve as sitting pads.

Conveniently, all Old World monkeys are placed in one taxonomic family, **Cercopithecidae**. In turn, this family is divided into two subfamilies: the **cercopithecines** and **colobines**.

The cercopithecines are the more generalized of the two groups, showing a more omnivorous dietary adaptation and cheek pouches for storing food (like hamsters). As a group, they eat almost anything, including fruits, seeds, leaves, grasses, tubers, roots, nuts, insects, birds' eggs, amphibians, small reptiles, and small mammals (the last seen in baboons).

The majority of cercopithecine species, such as the mostly arboreal guenons (Dutch for "clown"; Fig. 6-23) and the more terrestrial savanna and hamadryas baboons (Fig. 6-24), are found in Africa. The many macaque species (including the well-known rhesus monkeys), however, are widely distributed in southern Asia and India.

Colobine species have a narrower range of food preferences and mainly eat mature leaves, which is why they're also called "leaf-eating monkeys." The colobines are found mainly in Asia, but both red colobus and black-and-white colobus are exclusively African (Fig. 6-25). Other colobines include several Asian langur species and the proboscis monkey of Borneo.

Locomotion in Old World monkeys includes arboreal quadrupedalism in guenons, macaques, and langurs; terrestrial quadrupedalism in baboons and macaques; and semibrachiation and acrobatic leaping in colobus monkeys.

Marked differences in body size or shape between the sexes, referred to as **sexual dimorphism**, are typical of some terrestrial species and are especially pronounced in baboons and patas monkeys. In these species, male body weight (up to 80 pounds in baboons) may be twice that of females.

Females of several species (especially baboons and some macaques) have pronounced cyclical changes of the external genitalia. These changes, which include

ischial callosities Patches of tough, hard skin on the buttocks of Old World monkeys and chimpanzees.

Cercopithecidae (serk-oh-pith´-eh-see-dee)

cercopithecines (serk-oh-pith´-eh-seens) The subfamily of Old World monkeys that includes baboons, macaques, and guenons.

colobines (kole´-uh-beans) Common name for members of the subfamily of Old World monkeys that includes the African colobus monkeys and Asian langurs.

sexual dimorphism Differences in physical characteristics between males and females of the same species. For example, humans are slightly sexually dimorphic for body size, with males being taller, on average, than females of the same population.

(a)

(b)

Bonnie Pedersen/Arlene Kruse

swelling and redness, are associated with estrus, a hormonally initiated period of sexual receptivity in female nonhuman mammals correlated with ovulation. They serve as visual cues to males that females are sexually receptive.

Old World monkeys live in a few different kinds of social groups. Colobines tend to live in small groups, with only one or two adult males. Savanna baboons and most macaque species are found in large social units comprising several adults of both sexes and offspring of all ages. Monogamous pairing isn't common in Old World monkeys, but it's seen in a few langurs and possibly one or two guenon species.

Figure 6-24

Savanna baboons. (a) Male. (b) Female. (Note sexual dimorphism.)

Figure 6-25

Black-and-white colobus monkey.

Nelson Ting

Old and New World Monkeys: A Case of Homoplasy We've mentioned several differences between New and Old World monkeys, but the fact remains that they're all monkeys. That is, they're all adapted to a similar (primarily arboreal) way of life. Except for South American owl monkeys, they're all diurnal. All live in social groupings, are omnivorous to varying degrees, and are quadrupedal (though there are variations of this general locomotor pattern).

These similarities are even more striking when you consider that New and Old World monkeys have followed separate evolutionary paths for at least 40 million years. It was once believed that both lineages evolved independently from separate early primate ancestors; but today, the current consensus is that both New and Old World monkeys arose in Africa from a common monkey ancestor. The monkeys that gave rise to today's New World species reached South America by "rafting" over on chunks of land that had broken away from mainland areas (Hoffstetter, 1972; Ciochon and Chiarelli, 1980). This phenomenon, which we'll explain more fully in Chapter 9, probably happened many times over the course of several million years.

Whether the last common ancestor shared by New and Old World monkeys was lemur-like, tarsier-like or, most likely, a monkey-like animal, what's most remarkable is that the two forms haven't become more different from one another than they have. The arboreal adaptations we see in the monkeys of *both* hemispheres are examples of *homoplasy* (see p. 00), resulting from adaptation in geographically distinct populations that have responded to similar selective pressures.

Hominoids: Apes and Humans

Apes and humans are classified together in the same superfamily, the **hominoids**. Apes are found in Asia and Africa. The small-bodied gibbons and siamangs live in Southeast Asia, and the two orangutan subspecies live on the islands of Borneo and Sumatra (Fig. 6-26). In Africa, until the mid-to late twentieth century, gorillas, chimpanzees, and bonobos occupied the forested areas of western, central, and eastern Africa, but their habitat is now extremely fragmented, and all are now threatened or highly endangered (see pp. 169–175). Apes and humans differ from monkeys in numerous ways:

1. Generally larger body size (except for gibbons and siamangs)
2. Absence of a tail
3. Shortened trunk (lumbar area shorter and more stable)
4. Arms longer than legs (only in apes)
5. Anatomical differences in the shoulder joint (related to an adaptation for suspensory feeding and locomotion)
6. More complex behavior
7. More complex brain and enhanced cognitive abilities
8. Increased period of infant development and dependency

Gibbons and Siamangs The eight gibbon species and closely related siamangs are the smallest of the apes, with a long, slender body weighing 13 pounds in gibbons (Fig. 6-27) and around 25 pounds in the larger siamangs. Their most distinctive anatomical features are adaptations to feeding while hanging from tree branches, or brachiation, at which gibbons and siamangs excel. In fact, gibbons and siamangs are more dedicated to brachiation than any other primate, and this fact is reflected in their extremely long arms, long, permanently curved

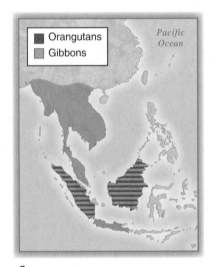

Figure 6-26

Geographical distribution of living Asian apes.

Orangutans
Gibbons
Pacific Ocean

hominoids Members of the primate superfamily (Hominoidea) that includes apes and humans.

fingers, short thumbs, and powerful shoulder muscles. (Their arms are so long that when they're on the ground they have to walk bipedally with their arms raised to the side.) Gibbons and siamangs mostly eat fruits, although both (especially siamangs) also consume a variety of leaves, flowers, and insects.

The basic social unit of gibbons and siamangs is an adult male and female with dependent offspring. Although they've been described as monogamous, in reality, members of a pair do sometimes mate with other individuals. As in marmosets and tamarins, male gibbons and siamangs are very much involved in rearing their young. Both males and females are highly **territorial** and protect their territories with elaborate whoops and siren-like "songs," lending them the name "the singing apes of Asia."

Orangutans Orangutans (*Pongo pygmaeus*) (Fig. 6-28) are represented by two subspecies found today only in heavily forested areas on the Indonesian islands of Borneo and Sumatra. The name *orangutan* (which has no final g and should never be pronounced "o-rang-oo-utang") means "wise man of the forest" in the language of the local people. But despite this somewhat affectionate-sounding label, orangutans are severely threatened with extinction in the wild due to poaching by humans and continuing habitat loss on both islands.

Orangutans are slow, cautious climbers whose locomotor behavior can best be described as four-handed—referring to their tendency to use all four limbs for grasping and support. Although they're almost completely arboreal, orangutans

Figure **6-27**
White-handed gibbon.

(a)

(b)

Figure **6-28**
Orangutans. (a) Female. (b) Male.

territorial Pertaining to the protection of all or a part of the area occupied by an animal or group of animals. Territorial behaviors range from scent marking to outright attacks on intruders.

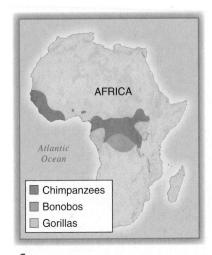

Figure 6-29
Geographical distribution of living African apes.

frugivorous (fru-give´-or-us) Having a diet composed primarily of fruit.

Figure 6-30
Western lowland gorillas. (a) Male. (b) Female.

sometimes travel quadrupedally on the ground. Orangutans exhibit pronounced sexual dimorphism; males are very large and may weigh more than 200 pounds, while females weigh less than 100 pounds. In the wild, orangutans lead largely solitary lives, although adult females are usually accompanied by one or two dependent offspring. They're primarily **frugivorous** but may also eat bark, leaves, insects, and (rarely) meat.

Gorillas The largest of all living primates, gorillas (*Gorilla gorilla*) are today confined to forested areas of western and eastern equatorial Africa (Fig. 6-29). There are four generally recognized subspecies, although molecular data suggest that one of these, the western lowland gorilla (Fig. 6-30), may be genetically distinct enough to be designated as a separate species (Ruvolo et al., 1994; Garner and Ryder, 1996).

Western lowland gorillas, the most numerous of the four subspecies, are found in several countries of west-central Africa. In 1998, Doran and McNeilage estimated their population size at perhaps 110,000, but Walsh and colleagues (2003) suggested that their numbers were far lower. Staggeringly, in August 2008, a report from the International Primatological Society Congress in Edinburgh, Scotland, reported the discovery of an estimated 125,000 western lowland gorillas in the northern region of the Democratic Republic of the Congo (DRC—formerly Zaire)! This is extremely encouraging news, but it doesn't mean that these animals are out of danger. To put this figure into perspective, consider that a large football stadium can hold around 70,000 spectators. So, next time you see a stadium packed with fans, think about the fact that you're perhaps looking at a crowd that numbers around half of all the western lowland gorillas on earth. Unless the DRC government, acting with wildlife conservation groups, can set aside more land as national parks and protect the gorillas, it's likely that due to human hunting and disease, western lowland gorillas may still be facing extinction in the wild.

(a)

(b)

(a)

(b)

Figure **6-31**

Mountain gorillas. (a) Male. (b) Female.

Cross River gorillas, a western lowland gorilla subspecies, were identified in the early 1900s but thought to be extinct until the 1980s when primatologists became aware of a few small populations in areas along the border between Nigeria and Cameroon (Sarmiento and Oates, 2000). Primatologists believe there may be only 250 to 300 of these animals; thus, Cross River gorillas are among the most endangered of all primates. Currently, the International Union for the Conservation of Nature and Natural Resources (IUCN) is developing plans to protect this vulnerable and little-known subspecies (Oates et al., 2007).

Eastern lowland gorillas, which haven't really been studied, live near the eastern border of the DRC. At present their numbers are unknown but suspected to be around 12,000. (You wouldn't need a very large football stadium to hold this many people.) Due to warfare in the region, researchers fear that many of these gorillas have been killed, but it's impossible to know how many.

Mountain gorillas (Fig. 6-31), the most extensively studied of the three subspecies, are restricted to the mountainous areas of central Africa in Rwanda, the DRC (formerly Zaire), and Uganda. There have probably never been many mountain gorillas, and today they're among the more endangered primates, with only about 600 in the wild.

Like all gorillas, Mountain gorillas exhibit marked sexual dimorphism, with males weighing up to 400 pounds and females around 150 to 200 pounds. Adult gorillas, especially males, are primarily terrestrial, and like chimpanzees, they practice a type of quadrupedalism called knuckle walking (refer back to Fig. 6-6, p. 151).

Mountain gorillas live in groups consisting of one, or sometimes two, large silverback males, a variable number of adult females, and their subadult offspring. (The term *silverback* refers to the saddle of white hair across the backs of fully adult males that appears around the age of 12 or 13.) A silverback male may tolerate the presence of one or more young adult "blackback" males (probably his sons) in his group. Typically, but not always, both females and males leave their **natal group** as young adults. Females join other groups; and males, who appear to be less likely to emigrate, may live alone for a while or they may join up with other males before eventually forming their own group.

natal group The group in which animals are born and raised. (*Natal* pertains to birth.)

Systematic studies of free-ranging western lowland gorillas weren't begun until the mid-1980s, so even though they're the only gorillas you'll see in zoos, we don't know as much about them as we do about mountain gorillas. The social structure of western lowland gorillas is similar to that of mountain gorillas, but groups are smaller and somewhat less cohesive.

All gorillas are almost exclusively vegetarian. Mountain and western lowland gorillas concentrate primarily on leaves, pith, and stalks, but western lowland gorillas eat more fruit. Western lowland gorillas, unlike mountain gorillas (which avoid water), also frequently wade through swamps while foraging on aquatic plants (Doran and McNeilage, 1998).

Perhaps because of their large body size and enormous strength, gorillas have long been considered ferocious; in reality, they're usually shy and gentle. But this doesn't mean that gorillas aren't ever aggressive. In fact, among males, competition for females can be extremely violent. As might be expected, males will attack and defend their group from any perceived danger, whether it's another male gorilla or a human hunter. Still, the reputation of gorillas as murderous beasts is the result of uninformed myth making and little else.

Chimpanzees   Chimpanzees are probably the best known of all nonhuman primates, even though many people think they're monkeys (Fig. 6-32). Often misunderstood because of zoo exhibits, circus acts, television shows, and movies, the true nature of chimpanzees didn't become known until years of fieldwork with wild groups provided a more accurate picture. Today, chimpanzees are found in equatorial Africa, in a broad belt from the Atlantic Ocean in the west to Lake Tanganyika in the east. But within this large geographical area, their range is very patchy, and it's becoming even more so with further habitat destruction.

In many ways, chimpanzees are anatomically similar to gorillas, with corresponding limb proportions and upper-body shape. However, the ecological

Figure 6-32

Chimpanzees. (a) Male. (b) Female.

(a)

(b)

166

adaptations and behaviors of chimpanzees and gorillas differ, with chimpanzees spending more time in the trees. Chimpanzees are also frequently excitable, active, and noisy, while gorillas tend to be placid and quiet.

Chimpanzees are smaller than orangutans and gorillas, and although they're sexually dimorphic, sex differences aren't as pronounced as in gorillas and orangutans. A male chimpanzee may weigh 150 pounds, but females can weigh at least 100. In addition to quadrupedal knuckle walking, chimpanzees (particularly youngsters) may brachiate. When on the ground, they frequently walk bipedally for short distances when carrying food or other objects.

Chimpanzees eat a huge variety of foods, including fruits, leaves, insects, nuts, birds' eggs, berries, caterpillars, and small mammals. Moreover, both males and females occasionally take part in group hunting efforts to kill small mammals such as young bushpigs and antelope. Their prey also includes monkeys, especially red colobus (see p. 213). When hunts are successful, the members of the hunting party share the prey.

Chimpanzees live in large, fluid communities ranging in size from 10 to as many as 100 individuals. A group of closely bonded males forms the core of chimpanzee communities in many locations, especially in East Africa (Wrangham and Smuts, 1980; Goodall, 1986; Wrangham et al., 1992). But for some West African groups, females appear to be more central to the community (Boesch, 1996; Boesch and Boesch-Acherman, 2000; Vigilant et al., 2001). Relationships among closely bonded males aren't always peaceful or stable, yet these males cooperatively defend their territory and are highly intolerant of unfamiliar chimpanzees, especially males.

Even though chimpanzees live in communities, it's rare for all members to be together at the same time. Rather, they tend to come and go, so that the individuals they encounter vary from day to day. Adult females usually forage either alone or in the company of their offspring, a grouping that might include several animals, since females with infants sometimes accompany their own mothers and siblings. These associations have been reported for the chimpanzees at Gombe National Park, where about 40 percent of females remain in the group in which they were born (Williams, 1999). But in most other areas, females leave their natal group to join another community. This behavioral pattern may reduce the risk of mating with close male relatives, because males apparently never leave the group in which they were born.

Chimpanzee social behavior is complex, and individuals form lifelong attachments with friends and relatives. If they continue to live in their natal group, the bond between mothers and infants can remain strong until one of them dies. This may be a considerable period, because many wild chimpanzees live well into their 40s and even longer.

Bonobos Bonobos (*Pan paniscus*) are found only in an area south of the Zaire River in the DRC (see Fig. 6-33). Not officially recognized by European scientists until the 1920s, they remain among the least studied of the great apes. Although ongoing field studies have produced much information (Susman, 1984; Kano, 1992), research has been hampered by civil war. There are currently no accurate counts of bonobos, but their numbers are believed to be between 10,000 and 20,000 (IUCN, 1996). These few are highly threatened by human hunting, warfare, and habitat loss.

Since bonobos bear a strong resemblance to chimpanzees, but are slightly smaller, they've been called "pygmy chimpanzees." The differences in body size

Figure **6-33**

Female bonobos with young.

Ellen Ingmanson

aren't very striking, although bonobos are less stocky. They also have longer legs relative to arms, a relatively smaller head, and a dark face from birth.

Bonobos are more arboreal than chimpanzees, and they're less excitable and aggressive. While aggression isn't unknown, it appears that physical violence both within and between groups is uncommon. Like chimpanzees, bonobos live in geographically based, fluid communities, and they eat many of the same foods, including occasional meat derived from small mammals (Badrian and Malinky, 1984). But bonobo communities aren't centered around a group of males. Instead, male-female bonding is more important than in chimpanzees and most other nonhuman primates (Badrian and Badrian, 1984). This may be related to bonobo sexuality, which differs from that of other nonhuman primates in that copulation is frequent and occurs throughout a female's estrous cycle, so sex isn't linked solely to reproduction. In fact, bonobos are famous for their sexual behavior since they copulate frequently and use sex to defuse potentially tense situations. Sexual activity between members of the same sex is also common (Kano, 1992; de Waal and Lanting, 1997). Given this aspect of bonobo behavior, it's perhaps not surprising that they've been called the "make love, not war" primate society.

Humans   Humans are the only living representatives of the habitually bipedal primates (*Homo sapiens*). Our primate heritage is evident in our overall anatomy and genetic makeup and in many behavioral aspects. Except for reduced canine size, human teeth are typical primate (especially ape) teeth. The human dependence on vision and decreased reliance on olfaction, as well as flexible limbs and grasping hands, are rooted in our primate, arboreal past (Fig. 6-34).

Humans in general are omnivorous, although all societies observe certain culturally based dietary restrictions. Even so, as a species with a rather generalized digestive system, we're physiologically adapted to digest an extremely wide assortment of foods. Perhaps to our detriment, we also share with our relatives a fondness for sweets that originates from the importance of high-energy fruits eaten by many nonhuman primates.

But humans are obviously unique among primates and indeed among all animals. For example, no member of any other species has the ability to write or think about issues such as how they differ from other life-forms. This ability is rooted in the fact that during the last 800,000 years of human evolution, brain size increased dramatically, and there were other neurological changes as well (see p. 385).

Humans are also completely dependent on culture. Without cultural innovation, it would never have been possible for us to leave the tropics. As it is, humans inhabit every corner of the planet except for Antarctica, and we've even established outposts there. And, lest we forget, a fortunate few have even walked on the moon! None of the technologies (indeed, none of the other aspects of culture) that humans have developed over the last several thousand years would have been possible without the highly developed cognitive abilities we alone possess. Nevertheless, the neurological basis for **intelligence** is rooted in our evolutionary past, and it's something we share with other primates. Indeed, research has demonstrated that several nonhuman primate species—most notably chimpanzees, bonobos, and gorillas—display a level of problem solving and insight that most people would have considered impossible just 25 years ago (see Chapter 8).

Humans are uniquely predisposed to use spoken language, and for the last 5,000 years or so, we've also used written language. This ability exists because during the course of human evolution, certain neurological and anatomical structures have been modified in ways not observed in any other species. But while nonhuman primates aren't anatomically capable of producing speech, research has shown that to varying degrees, the great apes are able to communicate by using symbols, which is a foundation for language that humans and the great apes (to a limited degree) have in common.

Aside from cognitive abilities, the one other trait that sets humans apart from other primates is our unique (among mammals) form of striding, *habitual* bipedal locomotion. This particular trait appeared early in the evolution of our lineage, and over time, we've become more efficient at it because of related changes in the musculoskeletal anatomy of our pelvis, leg, and foot. But early hominins increasingly adopted bipedalism because they were already *preadapted* for it. That is, as primates, and especially as apelike primates, they were already behaviorally predisposed to, and anatomically capable of, at least short-term bipedal walking before they adopted it wholeheartedly. So, while it's certainly true that human beings are unique intellectually, and in some ways anatomically, we're still primates. As a matter of fact, humans are basically somewhat exaggerated African apes.

Figure **6-34**

Playground equipment frequently allows children to play in ways that reflect their arboreal heritage.

Endangered Primates

In September 2000, scientists announced that a subspecies of red colobus, named Miss Waldron's red colobus, had officially been declared extinct. This announcement came after a 6-year search for the 20-pound monkey that hadn't been seen for 20 years (Oates et al., 2000). Sadly, this species, indigenous to the West African countries of Ghana and the Ivory Coast, has the distinction of being the first nonhuman primate to be declared extinct in the twenty-first century, but it won't be the

intelligence Mental capacity; ability to learn, reason, or comprehend and interpret information, facts, relationships, and meanings; the capacity to solve problems, whether through the application of previously acquired knowledge or through insight.

Table **6-1   African Primates in Danger of Extinction**

Species/Subspecies Common Name	Location	Estimated Size of Remaining Population
Barbary macaque	North Africa	23,000
Tana River mangabey	Tana River, Kenya	800–1,100
Sanje mangabey	Uzungwa Mts., Tanzania	1,800–3,000
Drill	Cameroon, Bioko	?
Preuss' guenon	Cameroon, Bioko	?
White-throated guenon	Southwest Nigeria	?
Pennant's red colobus	Bioko	?
Preuss' red colobus	Cameroon	8,000
Bouvier's red colobus	Congo Republic	?
Tana River red colobus	Tana River, Kenya	200–300
Uhehe red colobus	Uzungwa Mts. Tanzania	10,000
Zanzibar red colobus	Zanzibar	1,500
Mountain gorilla	Virunga Volcanoes (Rwanda, Uganda, and Democratic Republic of the Congo) and Impenetrable Forest (Uganda)	550–650

last. In fact, as of this writing, over half of all nonhuman primate species are now in jeopardy, and some face almost certain extinction in the wild (Table 6-1).

There are three basic reasons for the worldwide depletion of nonhuman primates: habitat destruction, human predation, and live capture for export or local trade. Underlying these three causes is one major factor, unprecedented human population growth, particularly in developing countries, where most nonhuman primates live. The developing nations of Africa, Asia, and Central and South America are home to over 90 percent of all nonhuman primate species; and these countries, aided in no small part by the industrialized countries of Europe and the United States, are cutting their forests at a rate of about 30 million acres per year. Unbelievably, in the year 2002, deforestation of the Amazon increased by 40 percent over that of 2001. This increase was largely due to land clearing for the cultivation of soybeans. In Brazil, the Atlantic rain forest originally covered some 385,000 square miles. Today, an estimated 7 percent is all that remains of what was once home to countless New World monkeys and thousands of other species. Fortunately, in 2008 the Brazilian government announced that in the three preceding years, deforestation decreased by 59 percent. The government also moved to enforce logging restrictions on public lands, but whether they will succeed or not remains to be seen (Tollefson, 2008).

The motivation behind deforestation is, of course, economic: the short-term gains from clearing forests to create immediately available (but poor) farmland or ranchland; the use of trees for lumber and paper products; and large-scale mining operations (with their necessary roads) all causing further habitat destruction. Regionally, the loss of rain forest ranks as a national disaster for some countries. For example, the West African nation of Sierra Leone had an estimated 15,000 square miles of rain forest early in the twentieth century. Today, less than 530

A Closer Look

Aye-Ayes: Victims of Derived Traits and Superstition

The primate order is filled with a variety of fascinating animals, although few seem as unusual as the aye-aye (*Daubentonia madagascariensis*). This is because most primates aren't as derived as aye-ayes are. Today, aye-ayes are the only members of their genus. A second species (a subfossil lemur) was exterminated by humans during the last few centuries, and the aye-aye was unknown (at least to Western science) until 1961. Like all lemurs, aye-ayes are found only on the island of Madagascar, where they occupy a niche similar to that of woodpeckers. Like woodpeckers, which aren't found on Madagascar, aye-ayes feed on insects and grubs that live in tree bark. On the ground they also find these same foods in logs. But instead of using a long beak to drill for hidden prey, this nocturnal primate uses an extremely specialized, elongated, bony middle finger to tap, tap, tap along a tree trunk, listening for hollow spaces (Fig. 1). When an aye-aye finds a hollow space where a grub might be hiding, it tears through the bark with its continuously growing incisor teeth (a rodent trait) and scoops

Figure 1

This nineteenth-century drawing of an aye-aye perfectly illustrates the elongated middle finger used for digging insects and grubs from logs and tree bark.

out the unlucky larva with the long nail at the end of its peculiar middle finger.

Aye-aye dentition is also quite derived and specialized for this particular dietary niche. The aye-aye dental formula of

$$\frac{1.0.1.3}{1.0.0.3}$$

isn't just unique among primates; it's unique among all mammals. As you can see, aye-ayes have no canine teeth and no lower premolars, although there's one upper premolar (Hershkovitz, 1977).

This perhaps strange-looking primate, which seems to have a permanent "bad hair day," is about the size of a small house cat and has little of the appeal of, say, a galago. Unfortunately, many Malagasy (the human inhabitants of Madagascar) find the aye-aye's appearance less than endearing. In fact, many think aye-ayes are bad luck and don't realize that they're simply harmless primates making a living as best they can.

Sadly, human imagination may prove this primate's undoing. Aye-ayes are variously thought to be heralds of evil or killers who creep into thatched huts and puncture their victim's aorta with their frightening middle finger (Goodman and Schütz, 2000). And some Malagasy superstitiously believe that should an aye-aye point its long middle finger at you, you will die. So it seems that cruel fate and humans have pointed their own finger of condemnation at the aye-aye, for only about 2,500 live in the wild and only a dozen or so in captivity.

square miles remain, and most of this destruction has occurred since World War II. People in many developing countries are also short of fuel and frequently use whatever firewood they can get. In addition, the demand for tropical hardwoods (such as mahogany, teak, and rosewood) in the United States, Europe, and Japan continues unabated, creating an enormously profitable market for rain forest products.

Primates are also captured live for zoos, biomedical research, and the exotic pet trade. Live capture has declined since the Convention on International Trade in Endangered Species of Wild Flora and Fauna (CITES) was implemented in 1973. By August 2005, a total of 169 countries had signed this treaty, agreeing not to allow trade in species listed by CITES as being endangered (see CITES Handbook, www.cites.org). However, even some CITES members are still occasionally involved in the illegal primate trade (Japan and Belgium, among others).

Figure 6-35

Red-eared guenons (with red tails) and Preuss' guenons for sale in a bushmeat market, Malabo, Equatorial Guinea.

John Oates

Bushmeat and Ebola: A Deadly Combination

In many areas, habitat loss has been the single greatest cause of declining numbers of nonhuman primates. But in the past few years, human hunting has perhaps posed an even greater threat (Fig. 6-35). During the 1990s, primatologists and conservationists became aware of a rapidly developing trade in *bushmeat*, meat from wild animals, especially in Africa. The current slaughter, which now accounts for the loss of tens of thousands of nonhuman primates (and other animals) annually, has been compared to the near extinction of the American bison in the nineteenth century.

Wherever primates live, people have always hunted them for food. But in the past, subsistence hunting wasn't a serious threat to nonhuman primate populations, and certainly not to entire species. But now, hunters armed with automatic rifles can, and do, wipe out an entire group of monkeys or gorillas in minutes. In fact, it's now possible to buy bushmeat outside the country of origin. In major cities throughout Europe and the United States, illegal bushmeat is readily available to immigrants who want traditional foods or to nonimmigrants who think it's trendy to eat meat from exotic, and frequently endangered, animals.

It's impossible to know how many animals are killed each year, but the estimates are staggering. The Society for Conservation Biology estimates that about 6,000 kg (13,228 pounds) of bushmeat is taken through just seven western cities (New York, London, Toronto, Paris, Montreal, Chicago, and Brussels) every month. No one knows how much of this meat is from primates, but this figure represents only a tiny fraction of all the animals being slaughtered because much smuggled meat isn't detected at ports of entry. Also, the international trade is thought to account for only about 1 percent of the total (Marris, 2006).

Quite clearly, species such as primates, which number only a few hundred or a few thousand animals, cannot and will not survive this onslaught for more than a few years. In addition, hundreds of infants are orphaned and sold in markets as pets. Although a few of these traumatized orphans make it to sanctuaries, most die within days or weeks of capture (Fig. 6-36).

Logging has been a major factor in the development of the bushmeat trade. The construction of logging roads, mainly by French, German, and Belgian lumber companies, has opened up vast tracts of previously inaccessible forest to hunters. What has emerged is a multimillion-dollar trade in bushmeat, a trade in which logging company employees and local government officials participate with hunters, villagers, market vendors, and smugglers who cater to local and overseas markets. In other words, the hunting of wild animals for food, particularly in Africa, has quickly shifted from a subsistence activity to a commercial enterprise of international scope.

Although the slaughter may be best known in Africa, it's by no means limited to that continent. In South America, for example, hunting nonhuman primates for food is common, although it hasn't become a commercial enterprise on the scale seen in Africa and parts of Asia. Nevertheless, one report documented that in less than two years, one family of Brazilian rubber tappers killed almost 500 members of various large-bodied species, including spider monkeys, woolly monkeys, and howlers (Peres, 1990). Moreover, live capture and illegal trade in endangered primate species continue unabated in China and Southeast Asia, where nonhuman primates are not only eaten but also funneled into the exotic pet trade. But just as importantly, primate body parts also figure prominently in traditional medicines, and with increasing human population size, the enormous demand for these products (and products from other, nonprimate species, such as tigers) has placed many species in extreme jeopardy.

As a note of optimism, in November 2007, the DRC government and the Bonobo Conservation Initiative (in Washington, D.C.) created a bonobo reserve consisting of 30,500 km². This amounts to about 10 percent of the land in the DRC, and the government has stated that its goal is to set aside an additional 5 percent for wildlife protection (News in Brief, 2007). This is a huge step forward, but it remains to be seen if protection can be enforced.

But there's yet another threat to West African primates. About 80 percent of the world's remaining gorillas and most chimpanzees are found in two West African countries, Gabon and the Republic of Congo (Walsh et al., 2003; Leroy et al., 2004). Between 1983 and 2000, ape populations in Gabon declined by half, mostly because of hunting, but also due to the viral disease ebola. This devastating disease, first recognized in 1976, is believed to be maintained in wild animals, probably fruit bats (Leroy et al., 2005). Furthermore, ebola is transmitted to humans through contact with infected animals (for example, through butchering). In humans, ebola is frequently fatal, and symptoms include fever, vomiting, diarrhea, and severe hemorrhaging.

Since 1994, there have been four ebola outbreaks in Gabon, and ape carcasses were found near affected settlements in three. In one area of Gabon where large-scale hunting hasn't occurred, ape populations declined by an estimated 90 percent between 1991 and 2000. And Rouguet and colleagues

Figure **6-36**

These orphaned chimpanzee infants are being bottle-fed at a sanctuary near Pointe Noire, Congo. They will probably never be returned to the wild, and they face an uncertain future.

Karl Ammann

(2005) reported that ebola was also the confirmed cause of death in great apes in the Republic of Congo in 2003 and 2004. But the worst news came in 2006, with a report that as many as 5,000 gorillas had died of ebola in that country (Bermejo, 2006). Researchers now think that the disease is spread within and between gorilla groups and not through contact with reservoir species like bats; and this fact offers some slight hope that a vaccination program might be effective. But faced with the combination of ebola and commercial hunting, it's clear that great ape populations in western Africa can't be sustained and are now being diminished to small remnant populations.

Increased Risk to Mountain Gorillas

Mountain gorillas are one of the most endangered nonhuman primate species. All of the approximately 700 mountain gorillas alive today are restricted to a heavily forested area in and around the Virunga Mountains (the Virunga Volcanoes Conservation Area) shared by three countries: Uganda, Rwanda, and the DRC. This entire area is a UNESCO (United Nations Educational, Scientific, and Cultural Organization) World Heritage Site. In addition, there is a separate, noncontiguous park in Uganda—the Bwindi Impenetrable Forest, home to about half of all the remaining mountain gorillas. Tourism has been the only real hope of salvation for these magnificent animals, and for this reason, several gorilla groups have been habituated to humans and are protected by park rangers. Nevertheless, poaching, civil war, and land clearing have continued to take a toll on these small populations.

Between January and late July 2007, 10 mountain gorillas were slaughtered in the park. Two infants orphaned in the attacks were rescued and taken to a veterinary clinic run by the Dian Fossey Gorilla Fund, where they are doing well as of this writing. Six of the victims, including the silverback male (Fig. 6-37), were members of one family group of 12. The remnant of this group consists of 4 immature males and 1 immature female, and without a silverback, their future is uncertain.

The gorillas weren't shot for meat or because they were raiding crops. They were shot because the existence and protection of mountain gorillas in the park is a hindrance to people who would destroy what little remains of the forests that are home to the gorillas. One of the many reasons for cutting the forests is the manufacture of charcoal, a major source of fuel in rural Rwanda and the DRC.

In 2007, paleoanthropologist Richard Leakey and a colleague, Emanuelle de Merode, established WildlifeDirect.org to help support conservationists and especially the rangers who work for little to no pay to protect the mountain gorillas. (It should be pointed out that in the past few years, more than 120 rangers have been killed while protecting wildlife in the Virungas.) You may want to go to their website (www.wildlifedirect.org), where you can read updates and see photographs and videos posted daily by the rangers. These communications offer fascinating insights into their efforts, conditions in the forest, and updates on gorillas and other species.

There are several other conservation groups that work to protect mountain gorillas. Also, in 2000, the United Nations Environmental Program established the Great Ape Survival Project (GRASP). GRASP is an alliance of many of the world's major great ape conservation and research organizations. In 2003, GRASP appealed for $25 million to be used in protecting the great apes from extinction. The money (a paltry sum) would be used to enforce laws that regulate hunting and illegal logging. It goes without saying that GRASP and other organizations must succeed if the great apes are to survive in the wild for even 20 more years!

But GRASP and the various conservation organizations face a formidable task just to save mountain gorillas, not to mention the dozens of other primate species at risk. In early September 2007, rebel forces in the gorilla sector of the DRC attacked a ranger station, where they killed one ranger. Consequently, WildlifeDirect evacuated all rangers from the area, leaving the gorillas unprotected. As of this writing (September, 2008) this situation remains unchanged, and the threat of heavy fighting in the gorilla sector continues to be grave.

If you are in your 20s or 30s, you will certainly live to hear of the extinction of some of our marvelous cousins. Many more will undoubtedly slip away unnoticed. Tragically, this will occur, in most cases, before we've even gotten to know them. Each species on earth is the current result of a unique set of evolutionary events that, over millions of years, has produced a finely adapted component of a diverse ecosystem. When it becomes extinct, that adaptation and that part of biodiversity is lost forever. What a tragedy it will be if, through our own mismanagement and greed, we awaken to a world without chimpanzees, mountain gorillas, or the tiny, exquisite lion tamarin. When this day comes, we truly will have lost a part of ourselves, and we will certainly be the poorer for it.

Figure 6-37

Congolese villagers carrying the body of the silverback gorilla shot and killed in the July 2007 attack. His body was buried with the other members of his group who were also killed.

Summary

In this chapter, we've introduced you to the living primates: the mammalian order that includes lemurs, lorises, tarsiers, monkeys, apes, and humans. We discussed how primates, including humans, have retained some ancestral characteristics that have permitted them, as a group, to be generalized in terms of dietary practices and locomotor patterns. You were also presented with a general outline of traits that differentiate primates from other mammals.

We also discussed primate classification and how primatologists are redefining relationships between some lineages. These changes reflect increasing knowledge of the genetic relationships between primate lineages and, in the case of tarsiers, reconsideration of various anatomical characteristics.

You also became acquainted with the major groups of nonhuman primates, especially regarding their basic social structure, diet, and locomotor patterns. Most primates are diurnal and live in social groups. The only nocturnal primates are lorises, some lemurs, tarsiers, and owl monkeys. Nocturnal species tend to forage for food alone, with offspring, or with one or two other animals. Diurnal primates live in a variety of social groupings, including monogamous pairs; groups consisting of one male with several females and offspring; or groups composed of several males, females, and offspring.

Finally, we talked about the precarious existence of most nonhuman primates today as they face hunting, live capture, and habitat loss. These threats are all imposed by only one primate species (us) that arrived relatively late on the evolutionary stage. In the next two chapters, as we discuss various aspects of human and nonhuman primate behavior, you'll become better acquainted with this fairly recently evolved primate species, *Homo sapiens*, of which you are a member.

Critical Thinking Questions

1. How do you think continued advances in genetic research will influence how we look at our species' relationships with nonhuman primates in 10 years?
2. What factors threaten the existence of nonhuman primates in the wild? How much do you care? What can you do to help save nonhuman primates from extinction?
3. How does a classification scheme reflect biological and evolutionary changes in a lineage? Can you give an example of suggested changes to how primates are classified? What do you think most people's reaction would be to hearing that scientists are placing the great apes into the same taxonomic family as humans?

Primates

7

Primate
Behavior

Robert Jurmain

Key Questions

How can behavior be a product of evolutionary processes?

What are the advantages and disadvantages of living in primate social groups?

 Click!

Go to the following media for interactive activities and exercises on topics covered in this chapter:

- Online Virtual Laboratories for Physical Anthropology, Version 4.0

behavior Anything organisms do that involves action in response to internal or external stimuli; the response of an individual, group, or species to its environment. Such responses may or may not be deliberate, and they aren't necessarily the result of conscious decision making (which is absent in single-celled organisms, insects, and many other species).

Introduction

Do you think cats are cruel when they play with mice? Or if you've ever fallen off a horse when it suddenly jumped sideways for no apparent reason, did you think she deliberately threw you? If you answered yes to either of these questions, you're not alone. To most people, it does seem cruel for a cat to torment a mouse for no obvious reason. And more than one rider has blamed their horse for intentionally throwing them (and admittedly, horses sometimes do). But these views generally demonstrate how little most people really know about nonhuman animal **behavior**.

Especially in mammals and birds, behavior is extremely complex because it's been shaped over evolutionary time by interactions between genetic and environmental factors. But, in general, people don't give this much thought, and even those who do don't necessarily accept this basic premise. For example, many social scientists object to the notion of genetic influences on human behavior because of concerns that behaviors will be seen as fixed and therefore unable to be changed by experience (that is, learning); and such a view could be (and has been) used to support racist and sexist ideologies.

There is also the prevailing notion of a fundamental division between humans and all other animals. In some cultures, this view is fostered by religious views; but even when religion isn't a factor, most people see themselves as uniquely set apart from all other species. But at the same time, and in obvious contradiction, they sometimes judge other species from a strictly human perspective and explain certain behaviors in terms of human motivations (for example, cats are cruel to play with mice). Of course, this isn't a valid thing to do for the simple reason that other animals aren't human. Cats sometimes play with mice before they kill them because that's how, as kittens, they learn to hunt. Cruelty doesn't enter into it because the cat has no concept of cruelty and no idea of what it's like to be the mouse.

Likewise, a horse doesn't deliberately throw you off when it hears leaves rattling in a shrub. It jumps because its behavior has been shaped by thousands of generations of horse ancestors who leaped first and asked questions later. It's important to understand that just as cats evolved as predators, horses evolved as prey animals, and their evolutionary history is littered with unfortunate animals that didn't jump at a sound in a shrub. In many cases, those ancestral horses learned, too late, that the sound wasn't caused by a breeze. This is a mistake that prey animals often don't survive, and those that don't leap first don't leave many descendants.

Obviously, this chapter isn't about cats and horses. It's about what we know and hypothesize about the individual and social behaviors of nonhuman primates. But we begin with the familiar examples of cats and horses because we want to point out that many basic behaviors have been shaped by the evolutionary history of particular species. Likewise, the same factors that have influenced many types of behavior in nonprimate animals also apply to primates. So, if we want to discover the underlying principles of behavioral evolution, we first need to identify the interactions between a number of environmental and physiological variables.

Primate Field Studies

The main goal of primate field studies is to collect information on wild primates whose behavior is unaffected by human activities. Unfortunately, most, if not all primate populations have now been exposed to human activities that influence their behavior (Janson, 2000). What's more, wild primates aren't easy to study until they've been habituated to the presence of humans, whom they generally fear, and the habituation process can take a long time. Also, habituation itself can change primate behavior. Until the last two decades, the most systematic information on free-ranging primates came from species that spend a lot of time on the ground (baboons, macaques, some lemurs, chimpanzees, and gorillas; Fig. 7-1a). This is because it's difficult to identify and observe arboreal primates as they flit through the forest canopy (Fig. 7-1b). Now, however, primatologists have accumulated a great deal of data on many arboreal species. Others have focused on nocturnal lemurs, lorises, and tarsiers. Thanks to these efforts, many of the gaps in our knowledge of nonhuman primates are being filled. But with each new discovery come new questions, so the process will continue as long as there are wild primates to study.

The earliest studies of nonhuman primates in their natural habitats began with an American psychologist named Robert Yerkes, who, in the late 1920s and 1930s, sent students into the field to study gorillas, chimpanzees, and howler monkeys. Japanese scientists began their pioneering work with Japanese macaques in 1948 (Sugiyama, 1965). In 1960, Jane Goodall began her now famous field study of chimpanzees at Gombe National Park, Tanzania. This project was closely followed by Dian Fossey's work with mountain gorillas in Rwanda and by Birute Galdikas' research on orangutans in Borneo.

These initial studies were, of necessity, largely descriptive in nature. However, some early studies of savanna baboons (DeVore and Washburn, 1963), hamadryas

Figure **7-1**

(a) Rhesus macaques spend much of their time on the ground and are much easier to observe than black-and-white colobus. (b) Imagine trying to recognize the colobus monkeys as individuals. What tools and techniques would you use to identify them?

Jean De Rousseau

(a)

John Oates

(b)

baboons (Kummer, 1968), and geladas (Crook and Gartlan, 1966) related aspects of **social structure** and individual behavior to ecological factors. Also, most early work emphasized male behaviors, partly because of the role of males in group defense. But by the late 1970s and early 1980s, primatologists were focusing more attention on females, not only as mothers but also as individuals who have an enormous influence on group dynamics.

Since then, primatologists have studied and continue to study well over 100 nonhuman primate species. Because most primates live in social groups, extensive research is devoted to primate social behavior, the costs and benefits of living in groups, and the advantages and disadvantages of specific behaviors to individuals. Behavioral research is done within an evolutionary framework, so primatologists test hypotheses relating to how behaviors have evolved. And now, the application of genetic techniques to primate behavioral research is beginning to provide answers to many questions, especially those that relate to paternity and reproductive success.

The Evolution of Behavior

Scientists study primates from an ecological and evolutionary perspective, meaning that they focus on the relationship between behaviors (both individual and social), the natural environment, and various physiological traits of the species in question. This approach is called **behavioral ecology**, and it's based on the underlying assumption that all of the biological components of ecological systems (animals, plants, and even microorganisms) evolved together. Behaviors are thus adaptations to environmental circumstances that existed in the past as well as in the present.

Briefly, the cornerstone of this perspective is that *behaviors have evolved through the operation of natural selection.* That is, if behaviors are influenced by genes, then they are subject to natural selection in the same way physical characteristics are. (Remember that within a specific environmental context, natural selection favors traits that provide a reproductive advantage to the individuals who have them.) Therefore, behavior constitutes a phenotype, and individuals whose behavioral phenotypes increase reproductive fitness will pass on their genes at a faster rate than others. But this doesn't mean that primatologists think that genes code for specific behaviors, such as a gene for aggression, another for cooperation, and so on. Studying complex behaviors from an evolutionary viewpoint doesn't imply a one gene–one behavior relationship, nor does it suggest that if behaviors are influenced by genes, they can't be modified through learning.

In insects and other invertebrates, behavior is mostly under genetic control; in other words, most behavioral patterns in these species aren't learned. But in many vertebrates, especially birds and mammals, the proportion of behavior that's due to learning is substantially increased, while the proportion under genetic control is reduced. This is especially true of primates; and in humans, who are so much a product of culture, most behavior is learned. But at the same time, we know that in mammals and birds, some behaviors are at least partly influenced by certain gene products such as hormones. You may have heard about research showing that increased levels of testosterone increase aggression in many species. Also, some conditions, such as depression, schizophrenia, and bipolar disorder, are caused by abnormal levels of certain neurotransmitters. (Neurotransmitters are chemicals produced by brain cells, and they're sent from one cell to another to cause a response (that is, they transmit information from cell to cell). These responses range

social structure The composition, size, and sex ratio of a group of animals. Social structure is the result of natural selection in a specific habitat, and it influences individual interactions and social relationships. In many species, social structure varies, depending on different environmental factors. Thus, in primates, social structure should be viewed as flexible, not fixed.

behavioral ecology The study of the evolution of behavior, emphasizing the role of ecological factors as agents of natural selection. Behaviors and behavioral patterns are favored by natural selection because they increase the reproductive fitness of individuals (i.e., they're adaptive) in specific environmental contexts.

from muscle activity to the release of hormones (such as testosterone) elsewhere in the body.

Brain cells manufacture neurotransmitters as a result of the action of certain genes within them, and in this way, genes can influence aspects of behavior. But *behavioral genetics*, or the study of how genes affect behavior, is a relatively new field. So, we don't currently know the extent to which genes actually influence behavior in humans or other species. What we do know is that behavior must be viewed as the product of complex interactions between genetic and environmental factors. The limits and potentials for learning and for behavioral flexibility vary considerably among species. In some species, such as primates, the potentials are extremely broad; but in others, like insects, they aren't. Ultimately, those limits and potentials are set by genetic factors that have been subjected to natural selection throughout the evolutionary history of every species. That history, in turn, has been shaped by the ecological setting not only of living species *but also of their ancestors.*

One of the main goals of primatology is to determine how behaviors influence reproductive fitness and how ecological factors have shaped the development of these behaviors. While the actual mechanics of behavioral evolution aren't yet fully understood, new technologies and methodologies are beginning to help scientists answer many questions. For example, genetic analysis has recently been used to establish paternity in a few primate groups, and this has helped support hypotheses about some behaviors (see p. 199). But in general, an evolutionary approach to the study of behavior doesn't provide definitive answers to many research questions. Rather, it provides a valuable framework within which primatologists analyze data to generate and test hypotheses concerning behavioral patterns. (Remember, the development and testing of hypotheses is how scientific research is done.)

Because primates are among the most social of animals, social behavior is a major topic in primate research. This is a broad subject that includes all aspects of behavior occurring in social groupings, even some you may not think of as social behaviors, like feeding or mating. To understand the function of one behavioral element, scientists need to determine how it's influenced by numerous interrelated factors. As an example, we'll consider some of the more important variables that influence social structure. But remember that we're discussing complex interactions and that social structure itself influences individual behavior, so in many cases, the distinctions between social and individual behaviors are blurred.

Figure 7-2

Dwarf mouse lemur.

Some Factors That Influence Social Structure

Body Size Among the living primates, body size is extremely diverse, ranging from dwarf mouse lemurs (Fig. 7-2) at about 2.5 ounces to male gorillas at around 260 pounds. As a general rule, larger animals require fewer calories per unit of weight than smaller animals do. This is because larger animals have a smaller ratio of surface area to mass than do smaller animals. Since body heat is lost at the surface, larger animals can retain heat more efficiently, so they require less energy overall. It may seem strange, but two 10-pound monkeys require more food than one 22-pound monkey (Fleagle, 1999).

Lynn Kilgore

Figure **7-3**
This male mountain gorilla has only to reach out to find something to eat.

Basal Metabolic Rate (BMR) The BMR concerns **metabolism**, the rate at which the body uses energy at a resting state to maintain all body functions. Metabolism is closely correlated with body size, so in general, smaller animals have a higher BMR than larger ones do. Consequently, smaller primates, such as galagos, tarsiers, marmosets, and tamarins, require an energy-rich diet high in protein (insects), fats (nuts and seeds), and carbohydrates (fruits and seeds). Some larger primates, which tend to have a lower BMR and reduced energy requirements relative to body size, can do well with less-energy-rich foods such as leaves.

Diet The nutritional requirements of animals are related to the previous two factors, and all three have evolved together. Therefore, when primatologists study the relationships between diet and behavior, they consider the benefits in terms of energy (calories) derived from various food items against the costs (energy expended) of obtaining and digesting them.

As we discussed in Chapter 6, most primates eat a wide variety of foods. But each species concentrates on some kinds of foods more than others; and almost all consume some animal protein, even if it's just in the form of insects and other invertebrates. While small-bodied primates focus on high-energy foods, larger-bodied species don't necessarily need to. For instance, mountain gorillas eat leaves, pith from bamboo stems, and other types of vegetation. Lowland gorillas do likewise, but they also consume a wider variety of items including some water plants. These foods have less caloric value than fruits, nuts, and seeds, but they still serve these animals well because gorillas tend to spend much of the day eating. Besides, gorillas don't use a great deal of energy searching for food, since they're frequently surrounded by it (Fig. 7-3).

Some monkeys, especially colobines (colobus and langur species), are primarily leaf eaters. Compared to many other monkeys, they're fairly large-bodied. They've also evolved elongated intestines and pouched stomachs that enable them, with the assistance of intestinal bacteria, to digest the tough fibers and cellulose in leaves. And in at least two langur species, there's a duplicated gene that produces an enzyme that further helps with digestion. Importantly, this gene duplication isn't found in other primates that have been studied, so the duplication event probably occurred after colobines and cercopithecines last shared a common ancestor (Zhang et al., 2002). Since having a second copy of the gene was advantageous to colobine ancestors who were probably already eating some leaves, natural selection favored it to the point that it was established in the lineage.

Distribution of Resources Different kinds of foods are distributed in different ways. Leaves can be plentiful and dense and will therefore support large groups of animals. Insects, on the other hand, may be widely scattered, so the animals that rely on them usually feed alone or perhaps in the company of one or two others.

Fruits, nuts, and berries in dispersed trees and shrubs occur in clumps. These can most efficiently be exploited by smaller groups of animals, so large groups frequently break up into smaller subunits while feeding. Such subunits may consist of one-male–multifemale groups (some baboons) or **matrilines** (for example,

metabolism The chemical processes within cells that break down nutrients and release energy for the body to use. (When nutrients are broken down into their component parts, such as amino acids, energy is released and made available for the cell to use.)

matrilines Groupings of females who are all descendants of one female (a female, her daughters, granddaughters, and their offspring). Matrilines also include dependent male offspring. Among macaques, some matrilines are dominant to others, so that members of dominant matrilines have greater access to resources than do members of subordinate matrilines.

macaques). Species that subsist on abundantly distributed resources may also live in one-male–multifemale groups, and because food is plentiful, these units are able to join with others to form large, stable communities (for example, howlers and some colobines and baboons). To the casual observer, these communities can look like multimale-multifemale groups.

Some species that depend on foods distributed in small clumps tend to be protective of resources, especially if their feeding area is small enough to be defended. Some of these species live in small groups composed of a mated pair (siamangs) or a female with one or two males (marmosets and tamarins). Naturally, dependent offspring are also included. Lastly, many foods, such as fruits, nuts, seeds, and berries, are only seasonally available, and primates that rely on them must eat a variety of items. This is another factor that tends to favor smaller feeding groups.

The distribution and seasonality of water are also important. Water may be available year-round in continuously flowing rivers and streams or where there's abundant rainfall. But in areas that have a dry season, water may exist only in widely dispersed ponds that primates must share with other animals, including predators.

Predation Primates, depending on their size, are vulnerable to many types of predators, including snakes, birds of prey, leopards, wild dogs, lions, and even other primates. Their responses to predation depend on their body size and social structure and the type of predator. Typically, where predation pressure is high and body size is small, large communities are advantageous. These may be multimale-multifemale groups or congregations of one-male–multifemale groups (see "A Closer Look," next page).

Relationships with Other, Nonpredatory Species Many primate species associate with other primate and nonprimate species for various reasons, including predator avoidance (see p. 188). When they do share habitats with other species, they exploit somewhat different resources (see p. 186).

Dispersal Dispersal is another factor that greatly influences social structure and relationships within groups. As is true of most mammals (and indeed, most vertebrates), members of one sex leave the group in which they were born (their *natal group*) about the time they become sexually mature. Male dispersal is the more common pattern in mammals, and primates are no exception (ring-tailed lemurs, vervets, and macaques, to name a few). But female dispersal is seen in some colobus species, hamadryas baboons, chimpanzees, and mountain gorillas. In species where the basic social structure is a mated pair, offspring of both sexes either leave or are driven away by their parents (gibbons and siamangs).

Dispersal may have more than one outcome. Typically, when females leave, they join another group. Males may do likewise, but in some species they may remain solitary for a time, or they may temporarily join an all-male "bachelor" group until they're able to establish a group of their own. But the common theme is that individuals who disperse usually find mates outside their natal group. This commonality has led primatologists to conclude that the most valid explanations for dispersal are probably related to two major factors: reduced competition for mates (particularly between males) and, perhaps even more important, decreased likelihood of close inbreeding.

Members of the **philopatric** sex enjoy certain advantages. Individuals (of either sex) who remain in their natal group are able to establish long-term bonds

philopatric Remaining in one's natal group or home range as an adult. In most species, members of one sex disperse from their natal group as young adults, and members of the philopatric sex remain. In most non-human primate species, the philopatric sex is female.

A Closer Look

Types of Nonhuman Primate Social Groups

1. *One-male–multifemale*: a single adult male, several adult females, and their offspring. This is the most common primate mating structure, in which only one male actively breeds, and it's typically formed by a male joining a kin group of females. Females usually form the permanent nucleus of the group. Examples: guenons, gorillas, some pottos, some spider monkeys, patas, some langurs, and some colobus. In many species, several one-male groups may form large congregations.

2. *Multimale-multifemale*: several adult males, several adult females, and their young. Many of the males reproduce. The presence of several males in the group may lead to tension and to the formation of a dominance hierarchy. Examples: some lemurs, macaques, mangabeys, savanna baboons, vervets, squirrel monkeys, some spider monkeys, and chimpanzees. In some species (vervets, baboons, and macaques), females are members of matrilines, or groups composed of a female, her female offspring, and their offspring. These kin groups are arranged in a hierarchy, so each matriline is dominant to some other matrilines and subordinate to others.

3. *Monogamous pair*: a mated pair and its young. The term *monogamous* is somewhat misleading because matings with individuals other than partners aren't uncommon.

Species that form pairs are usually arboreal, show minimal sexual dimorphism, and are frequently territorial. Adults don't normally tolerate other adults of the same sex. This grouping isn't found among the great apes, and it's the least common breeding structure among nonhuman primates. Examples: siamangs, gibbons, indris, titis, sakis, owl monkeys, and pottos. Males may directly participate in infant care.

4. *Polyandry*: one female and two males. This social group is seen only in some New World monkeys (marmosets and tamarins). Males participate in infant care.

5. *Solitary*: individual who forages for food alone. This is seen in nocturnal primates such as aye-ayes, lorises, and galagos. In some species, adult females may forage in pairs or may be accompanied by offspring. Also seen in orangutans.

There are also other groupings, such as foraging groups, hunting groups, all-female or all-male groups, and so on. Like humans, nonhuman primates don't always maintain one kind of group; one-male–multifemale groups may sometimes form multimale-multifemale groups, and vice versa. Hamadryas baboons, for example, are described as living in one-male groups; but they form herds of 100 or more at night as they move to the safety of sleeping cliffs.

---

with relatives and other animals, with whom they cooperate to protect resources or enhance their social position. This is well illustrated by chimpanzee males, who permanently reside in their natal groups (see further discussion in Chapter 8). Also, because female macaques are philopatric, they form stable matrilineal subgroups. Larger matrilines can have greater access to foods, and these females support each other in conflict situations.

Because some individuals remain together over a long period of time, members of a primate group get to know each other well. They learn, as they must, how to respond to a variety of actions that may be threatening, friendly, or neutral. In such social groups, individuals must be able to evaluate situations before they act. Evolutionarily speaking, this ability would have placed selective pressure on social intelligence, which in turn would have selected for brains capable of assessing social situations and storing relevant information. One result of such selection would be the evolution of proportionately larger and more complex brains, especially among the anthropoids.

life history traits Characteristics and developmental stages that influence rates of reproduction. Examples include longevity, age at sexual maturity, and length of time between births.

Life Histories **Life history traits** are characteristics or developmental stages that typify members of a given species and therefore influence potential reproductive rates. These traits also influence primate social structure. Examples of life history traits are length of gestation, length of time between pregnancies (interbirth interval), period of infant dependency and age at weaning, age of sexual maturity, and life expectancy.

Life history traits have important consequences for many aspects of social life and social structure. They can also be critical to species survival. In species that live in marginal or unpredictable habitats, shorter life spans can be advantageous. These species mature early and have short interbirth intervals, so reproduction can occur at a relatively fast rate in a habitat that doesn't favor longevity (Strier, 2003). Conversely, species with extended life spans are well suited to stable environmental conditions. The extended life spans of the great apes in particular, characterized by later sexual maturation and long interbirth intervals (three to five years), means that most females will raise only three or four offspring to maturity. Today, this slow rate of reproduction increases the threat of extinction to great ape populations that are now being hunted at a rate that far outpaces their replacement capacities.

Strategies **Strategies** are behaviors that increase individual reproductive success. They also influence the structure and dynamics of primate social groups. We're accustomed to using the word *strategies* to mean deliberate schemes or plans purposefully designed to achieve goals. But in the context of nonhuman behavioral ecology, strategies are seen as products of natural selection, and no conscious planning or motivation is implied (Strier, 2003). Several kinds of strategies are discussed in behavioral studies, including *life history strategies, feeding strategies, social strategies, reproductive strategies, and predator avoidance strategies.*

Distribution and Types of Sleeping Sites Gorillas are the only nonhuman primates that sleep on the ground. Primate sleeping sites can be in trees or on cliff faces, and their spacing can be related to social structure and to predator avoidance.

Activity Patterns Most primates are diurnal, but galagos, lorises, aye-ayes (see p. 171), tarsiers, and one New World monkey (the owl monkey) are nocturnal. Nocturnal species tend to forage for food alone or in groups of two or three, and many avoid predators by hiding.

Human Activities We stated earlier that virtually all nonhuman primate populations are now affected by human hunting and forest clearing (see pp. 169–175). These activities severely disrupt and isolate groups, reduce numbers, reduce resource availability, and eventually can lead to extinction.

Sympatric Species

Another issue that's basic to the behavioral ecology of primates is the differential exploitation of resources by **sympatric** species. This strategy provides a way to maximize access to food while at the same time reducing competition between different species.

Five Monkey Species in the Kibale Forest, Uganda

An early study of sympatric relationships between five monkey species was undertaken in the Kibale Forest (Fig. 7-4) of western Uganda (Struhsaker and Leyland,

strategies Behaviors or behavioral complexes that have been favored by natural selection because they're advantageous to the animals that perform them. Examples include actions that enhance an animal's ability to obtain food, rear infants, or increase one's social status. Ultimately, strategies influence reproductive success.

sympatric Living in the same area; pertaining to two or more species whose habitats partly or largely overlap.

Figure 7-4
Kibale Forest habitat, Uganda.

John Oates

1979). The five species were black-and-white colobus, red colobus, mangabey, blue monkey, and redtail monkey. In addition to these five, the Kibale Forest is home to two other monkey species as well as two galago species and chimpanzees (for a discussion of the latter, see Ghiglieri, 1984). Altogether, 11 different nonhuman primate species coexist at Kibale.

The five species in the study differ in their anatomy, behavior, and dietary preferences. Body weight varies considerably, ranging from 3 to 4 kg for redtail monkeys to as much as 7 to 10 kg for mangabey and colobus species. Diet also differs: The two colobus species mostly eat leaves, and the other three species concentrate more on fruits and insects. These differences are important because for two or more species to share the same habitat and still get enough to eat, they need to exploit somewhat different resources to reduce competition for food.

Several aspects of social organization also vary. For example, red colobus and mangabeys live in multimale-multifemale groups, while only one fully adult male is typically present in the other species. There's so much variability, in fact, that researchers found little correlation between social organization and feeding ecology. The impression one gets from all this is that many primate species are quite flexible regarding group composition, a fact that makes generalizing extremely tentative. Nevertheless, the highly controlled nature of the Kibale study makes some comparisons and provisional generalizations possible:

1. The omnivores (mangabeys, redtail and blue monkeys) move about more than the folivores (the two colobus species).
2. Among the omnivores, there's an inverse relationship between body size and group size (that is, the smaller the body size, the larger the group tends to be). Also among the omnivores, there's a direct relationship between body size and **home range** size.
3. Omnivores are more spatially dispersed than folivores.
4. Female sexual swelling (see p. 195) is obvious only in those species (red colobus) that live in multimale-multifemale groups.
5. Feeding, spacing, dispersal, and **reproductive strategies** may be very different for males and females of the same species. These considerations have become a central focus of ecological and evolutionary research.

Why Be Social?

home range The total area exploited by an animal or social group; usually given for one year or for the entire lifetime of an animal.

reproductive strategies The complex of behavioral patterns that contributes to individual reproductive success. The behaviors need not be deliberate, and they often vary considerably between males and females.

Group living exposes primates to competition with other group members for resources, so why don't they live alone? After all, competition can lead to injury or even death, and it's costly in terms of energy expenditure. One widely accepted answer to the question of why primates live in groups is that the costs of competition are offset by the benefits of predator defense.

Multimale-multifemale groups have traditionally been seen as advantageous in areas where predation pressure is high, particularly in mixed woodlands and open savannas, where there are large predators. Leopards are the most

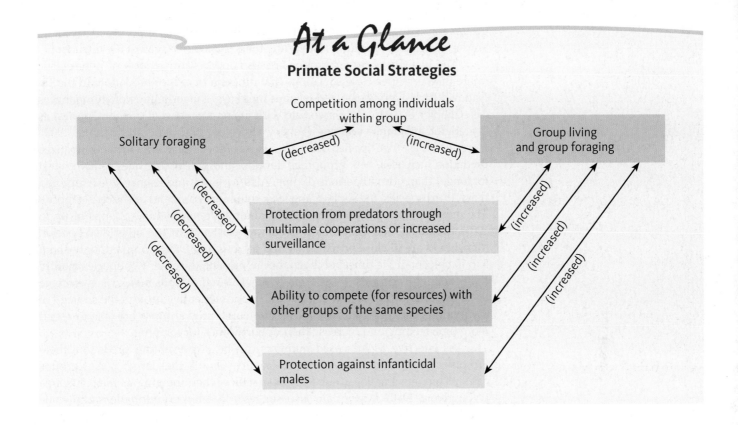

At a Glance
Primate Social Strategies

Competition among individuals within group

| Solitary foraging | ← (decreased) (increased) → | Group living and group foraging |

(decreased) (decreased) (decreased)

Protection from predators through multimale cooperations or increased surveillance

(increased) (increased)

Ability to compete (for resources) with other groups of the same species

(increased) (increased)

(decreased)

Protection against infanticidal males

significant predator of terrestrial primates (Fig. 7-5). When prey animals occur in larger groups, the chances of seeing and escaping a predator are increased simply because more pairs of eyes are looking about. (There really is safety in numbers.) This strategy also has the advantage of giving animals more time to feed because it reduces the amount of time each one spends looking around (Janson, 1990; Isbell and Young, 1993).

Savanna baboons have long been cited as an example of this practice. Savanna baboons live in semiarid grassland and broken woodland habitats throughout sub-Saharan Africa. During the day, they forage in large multimale-multifemale groups, and if they detect nonhuman predators, they flee back into the trees. But if they're at some distance from safety or if the predator is nearby, adult males (and sometimes females) may join forces to chase the intruder away. The effectiveness of male baboons in this regard shouldn't be underestimated, because they've been known to kill domestic dogs and even to attack leopards and lions.

Examples of increased group size as a defense against predators have been reported in vervets (Isbell, 1993) and capuchins (de Ruiter, 1986). In these species, vigilance was seen to increase as group size increased. Hamadryas baboons forage in small

Figure 7-5

When a baboon strays too far from its troop, as this one has done, it's more likely to fall prey to predators. Leopards are the most serious nonhuman threat to terrestrial primates.

Time Life Pictures/Getty Images

groups consisting of one male and a few females and offspring. But when predators are seen, such one-male units join with others to mobilize against the intruder.

The benefits of larger groups are also apparent in reports of polyspecific (more than one species) associations that function to reduce predation. In the Tai National Park, Ivory Coast, red colobus monkeys, a favorite prey of chimpanzees (see Chapter 8), frequently associate with Diana monkeys (a guenon species) as a predator avoidance strategy (Bshary and Noe, 1997; Noe and Bshary, 1997). Normally, these two species don't form close associations. But when chimpanzee predation increases, new groupings develop, and preexisting ones remain intact for longer than normal periods of time. Also, McGraw and Bshary (2002) reported that a third species, the sooty mangabey, sometimes provides additional support. The more terrestrial mangabeys live in multimale-multifemale groups of up to 100 individuals, and they detect predators earlier than the other two species. Mangabeys are in close proximity to red colobus and Diana monkeys only about 5 to 10 percent of the time, but when they're present, the other two species modify their foraging strategies. The normally arboreal red colobus monkeys even come to the ground (McGraw and Bshary, 2002). Consequently, through the strategy of associations between different species, potential prey animals are able to spend more time feeding and increase their opportunities for foraging.

As effective as increased numbers can be in preventing predation, there are other explanations for primate sociality. One is that larger social groups can outcompete smaller groups of **conspecifics** when foraging in the same area (Wrangham, 1980). Wrangham also suggests that large multimale-multifemale groups evolved because males were attracted to related females living in association with one another. And lastly, females may tolerate familiar males, since they can provide protection against other, potentially infanticidal males.

There's probably no single answer to the question of why primates live in groups. More than likely, predator avoidance is a major factor but not the only one. Group living evolved as an adaptive response to a number of ecological variables, and it has served primates well for a very long time.

Primate Social Behavior

Because primates solve their major adaptive problems in a social context, we might expect them to participate in various activities that reinforce the group's integrity. The better known of these activities are described below. As you read about them, remember that all these behaviors evolved as adaptive responses over more than 50 million years of primate evolution.

Dominance

conspecifics Members of the same species.

dominance hierarchies Systems of social organization wherein individuals within a group are ranked relative to one another. Higher-ranking individuals have greater access to preferred food items and mating partners than do lower-ranking individuals. Dominance hierarchies are sometimes referred to as pecking orders.

Many primate societies are organized into **dominance hierarchies**, which impose a certain degree of order by establishing parameters of individual behavior. Although some animals use aggression to increase their status, dominance usually serves to reduce the amount of actual physical violence. Not only are lower-ranking individuals unlikely to attack or even threaten a higher-ranking one, dominant animals can frequently exert control simply by making a threatening gesture. Individual rank or status may be measured by access to resources, including food items and mating partners. Dominant individuals are given priority by others, and they usually don't give way in confrontations.

Many primatologists think that the primary benefit of dominance is the increased reproductive success of high-ranking animals. This may be true in some cases, but there's good evidence that lower-ranking males also successfully mate. For example, subordinate male baboons frequently establish friendships with females, and simply because of this close association, they're able to mate surreptitiously with their female friend when she comes into estrus.

Low-ranking male orangutans also mate frequently. These young males don't develop certain secondary sex characteristics, such as wide cheek pads and heavier musculature, as long as they live near a dominant male (Fig. 7-6). One theory is that this arrested development protects them from the dominant male, who doesn't view them as a threat. Nevertheless, they are a threat in terms of reproductive success because their strategy is to force females to mate with them. In fact, primatologists use the term *rape* to describe the degree of force these young males use.

Increased reproductive success is also hypothesized for high-ranking females, who have greater access to food than subordinate females do. Because they obtain more energy for the production and care of offspring (Fedigan, 1983), their reproductive success is greater. Altmann and colleagues (1988) reported that while dominant female yellow baboons in one study group didn't have higher birthrates than lower-ranking females, they did reach sexual maturity earlier (presumably because of their enhanced nutritional status), thus increasing the potential number of offspring they can produce throughout their lives.

In another example, during a drought in Kenya, dominant female vervets in two groups prevented a third group from gaining access to their water hole. The deprived third group resorted to licking dew from tree trunks; but even in this group, the higher-ranking members denied access to the lower-ranking members. Consequently, over half of this group died, and all of those were either adolescents or low-ranking adults (Cheney et al., 1988).

Pusey and colleagues (1997) showed that the offspring of high-ranking female chimpanzees at Gombe had significantly higher rates of infant survival. Their daughters also matured faster, which meant that they had shorter interbirth intervals and thus produced more offspring.

(a)

(b)

Figure **7-6**

(a) Fully mature, breeding male orangutan with well-developed cheek pads. (b) Suppressed adult male without cheek pads.

An individual's position in the hierarchy isn't permanent, and it changes throughout life. It's influenced by many factors, including sex, age, level of aggression, amount of time spent in the group, intelligence, perhaps motivation, and sometimes the mother's social position (particularly true of macaques).

In species organized into groups containing a number of females associated with one or several adult males, the males are generally dominant to females. Within such groups, males and females have separate hierarchies, although very high-ranking females can dominate the lowest-ranking males (particularly young males). But there are exceptions to this pattern of male dominance. Among many lemur species, females are the dominant sex. Moreover, in species that form bonded pairs (such as indris, gibbons, and siamangs), the sexes are codominant.

All primates *learn* their position in the hierarchy. From birth, an infant is carried by its mother, and it observes how she responds to every member of the group. Just as important, it sees how others react to her. Dominance and subordination are indicated by gestures and behaviors, some of which are universal throughout the primate order (including humans), and this gestural repertoire is part of every youngster's learning experience.

Young primates also acquire social rank through play with age peers. As they spend more time with play groups, their social interactions widen. Competition and rough-and-tumble play allow them to learn the strengths and weaknesses of peers, and they carry this knowledge with them throughout their lives. So, through early contact with the mother and subsequent exposure to peers, young primates learn to negotiate their way through the complex web of social interactions that make up their daily lives.

Communication

Communication is universal among animals and includes scents and unintentional, **autonomic** responses and behaviors that convey meaning. Such things as body posture provide information about an animal's emotional state. For example, crouching indicates submission, insecurity, or fear, and this is true of many nonprimate animals (for example, dogs and cats). At the same time, a purposeful, striding gait implies confidence. Autonomic responses to threatening or novel stimuli, such as raised body hair (most species) or enhanced body odor (gorillas), indicate excitement.

Many intentional behaviors also serve as communication. In primates, these include a wide variety of gestures, facial expressions, and vocalizations, some of which we humans share. Among many primates, an intense stare is a mild threat; and indeed, people find prolonged eye contact with strangers very uncomfortable. (For this reason, people should avoid eye contact with primates in zoos.) Other threat gestures include a quick yawn to expose canine teeth (baboons, macaques; Fig. 7-7); bobbing back and forth in a crouched position (patas monkeys); and branch shaking (many monkey species). High-ranking baboons *mount* the hindquarters of subordinates to express dominance (Fig. 7-8). Mounting may also serve to defuse potentially tense situations by indicating something like, "It's okay" or "Apology accepted."

Primates also use a variety of behaviors to indicate submission, reassurance, or amicable intentions. In addition to crouching to show submission, some primates (baboons) present (turn) their hindquarters to an animal they want to appease. Reassurance takes the form of touching, patting, hugging, and holding hands. **Grooming** also serves in many situations to indicate submission and/or reassurance.

communication Any act that conveys information, in the form of a message, to another individual. Frequently, the result of communication is a change in the recipient's behavior. Communication may not be deliberate, but may instead be the result of involuntary processes or a secondary consequence of an intentional action.

autonomic Pertaining to physiological responses that aren't under voluntary control. An example in chimpanzees would be the erection of body hair during excitement. Blushing is a human example. Both convey information regarding emotional states; but neither behavior is deliberate, and communication is not intended.

grooming Picking through fur to remove dirt, parasites, and other materials that may be present. Social grooming is common among primates and reinforces social relationships.

Lynn Kilgore

Figure 7-7

An adolescent male savanna baboon threatens the photographer with a characteristic "yawn" that shows the canine teeth. Note also that the eyes are closed briefly to expose light, cream-colored eyelids. This has been termed the "eyelid flash."

Lynn Kilgore

Figure 7-8

One young male savanna baboon mounts another as an expression of dominance.

A wide variety of facial expressions indicating emotional state are seen in chimpanzees and, especially, in bonobos (Fig. 7-9). These include the well-known play face (also seen in several other primate and nonprimate species), associated with play behavior, and the fear grin (seen in *all* primates) to indicate fear and submission.

Not surprisingly, vocalizations play a major role in primate communication. Some, such as the bark of a baboon who's just spotted a leopard, are unintentional startled reactions. Others, such as the chimpanzee "food grunt," are heard only in specific contexts. Even so, both vocalizations serve the same function: They inform others, although not always deliberately, of the possible presence of predators or food.

Primates (and other animals) also communicate through **displays**, which are more complicated, frequently elaborate combinations of behaviors. For example, the exaggerated courtship dances of many male birds, often enhanced by colorful plumage, are displays. Common gorilla displays are chest slapping and the tearing of vegetation to indicate threat. Likewise, an angry chimpanzee, with hair on end, may charge an opponent while screaming, waving its arms, and tearing vegetation.

By describing a few communicative behaviors shared by many primates (including humans), we don't mean that these gestures are dictated solely by

displays Sequences of repetitious behaviors that serve to communicate emotional states. Nonhuman primate displays are most frequently associated with reproductive or agonistic behavior.

Figure 7-9

Chimpanzee facial expressions.

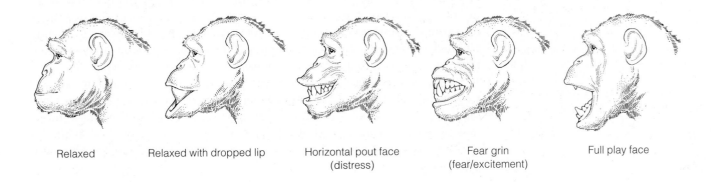

Relaxed   Relaxed with dropped lip   Horizontal pout face (distress)   Fear grin (fear/excitement)   Full play face

genetic factors. Indeed, if primates aren't reared within a relatively normal social context, such behaviors may not be performed appropriately, because the contextual manifestations of communicatory actions are *learned*. But the underlying *predisposition* to learn and use them and the motor patterns involved in their execution are genetically influenced, and these factors do have adaptive significance.

Some theories about how such expressive devices evolved thus focus on motor patterns and the original context in which they occurred. Over time, certain behaviors and motor patterns that originated in specific contexts have assumed increasing importance as communicatory signals. For example, crouching initially helped avoid physical attack. But it also conveyed that the individual was fearful, submissive, and nonaggressive. Crouching thus became valuable not only for its primary function but also for its role in communication, and natural selection increasingly favored it for this secondary role. In this way, over time, the expressions of specific behaviors may thus become elaborated or exaggerated because of their value in enhancing communication. Many complex displays also incorporate various combinations of **ritualized behaviors**.

Mounting, as seen in baboons, is a good example of a ritualized behavior. Higher-ranking individuals mount the hindquarters of more subordinate animals, not to mate but to express dominance. (When mounting serves a communicatory function, mounters and mountees may be members of the same sex.) In most anthropoid species that live in one-male or multimale groups, males (the mounters in the mating context) are socially dominant to females. So, in the context of communication, the mounter assumes the male reproductive role. Likewise, by presenting its hindquarters to solicit mounting, the mountee indicates submission or subordination. As communication, these behavior patterns are entirely removed from their original reproductive context, and they function instead to reinforce and clarify the respective social roles of individuals in specific interactions.

All nonhuman animals use various vocalizations, body postures, and facial expressions that transmit information. But the array of communicative devices is much richer among nonhuman primates, even though they don't use language the way humans do. Communication is important because it's what makes social living possible. Through submissive gestures, aggression is reduced and physical violence is less likely. Likewise, friendly intentions and relationships are reinforced through physical contact and grooming. Indeed, we humans can see ourselves in other primate species most clearly in the familiar uses of nonverbal communication.

Aggressive and Affiliative Interactions

Within primate societies, there's an interplay between **affiliative** behaviors, which promote group cohesion, and aggressive behaviors, which can lead to group disruption. Conflict within a group frequently develops out of competition for resources, including mating partners and food. Instead of actual attacks or fighting, most **intragroup** aggression occurs in the form of various signals and displays, frequently within the context of a dominance hierarchy. Therefore, the majority of tense situations are resolved through various submissive and appeasement behaviors.

But conflicts aren't always resolved peacefully, and they can have serious consequences. For example, as in the previously mentioned vervet example, high-ranking female macaques frequently intimidate, harass, and even attack lower-ranking females in order to restrict their access to food. Eventually, these behaviors can result in weight loss and poorer nutrition in low-ranking females. Moreover,

ritualized behaviors Behaviors removed from their original context and sometimes exaggerated to convey information.

affiliative Pertaining to amicable associations between individuals. Affiliative behaviors, such as grooming, reinforce social bonds and promote group cohesion.

intragroup (*intra*, meaning "within") Within the group, as opposed to between groups (intergroup).

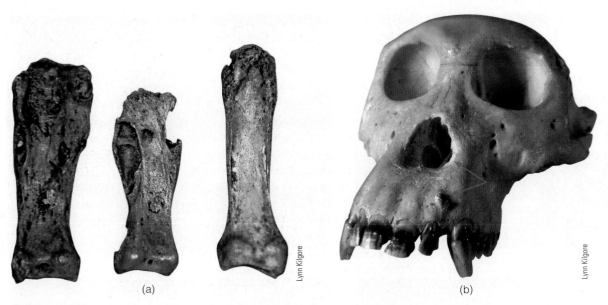

Lynn Kilgore

(a)   (b)

Lynn Kilgore

Figure 7-10

(a) These finger bones are from a female chimpanzee named Gilka, a member of Jane Goodall's study group in Tanzania. On more than one occasion, observers saw another female attack Gilka, and during one attack, Gilka was badly bitten on the hand. Afterwards she suffered periodically from running sores on her hand. The cavities and deformation in these bones indicate severe infection of the marrow cavity, probably resulting from the bite wound. (b) This male chimpanzee cranium from West Africa exhibits a healed bite wound beneath the nose (arrow) most likely inflicted by another chimpanzee. Also the left margin of the nasal opening shows irregularities that may have been caused by an infection, perhaps related to the injury.

subordinate females may have lower reproductive success because they're less able to successfully rear offspring to maturity, partly because they're unable to obtain food (Silk et al., 2003).

Competition between males for mates frequently results in injury and occasionally in death. In species that have a distinct breeding season (such as squirrel monkeys), conflict between males is most common during that time. Male squirrel monkeys form coalitions to compete with other males, and when outright fighting occurs, injuries can be severe. In species not restricted to a mating season, competition between males can be an ongoing occurrence. In one well-known example, Dian Fossey once found the skull of an adult male mountain gorilla with a canine tooth of another male gorilla embedded in it (Fig. 7-10).

Even though conflict can be destructive, a certain amount of aggression is useful in maintaining order within groups and protecting either individual or group resources. Fortunately, to reinforce bonds between individuals, promote group cohesion, minimize actual violence, and defuse potentially dangerous situations, an array of affiliative (friendly) behaviors serve to reinforce bonds between individuals and enhance group stability.

Common affiliative behaviors include reconciliation, consolation, and simple amicable interactions between friends and relatives. Most such behaviors involve various forms of physical contact, such as touching, hand-holding, hugging, and, among chimpanzees, kissing (Fig. 7-11). In fact, physical contact is one of the most important factors in primate development and is crucial in promoting peaceful relationships in many primate social groups.

Lynn Kilgore

Figure 7-11

Adolescent savanna baboons holding hands.

(a)

Robert Jurmain

(b)

Meredith Small

(c)

Arlene Kruse/Bonnie Pedersen

(d)

Arlene Kruse/Bonnie Pedersen

Figure 7-12

Grooming primates. (a) Patas monkeys; female grooming male. (b) Longtail macaques. (c) Savanna baboons. (d) Chimpanzees.

Grooming is one of the most important affiliative behaviors in many primate species, so much so that in 1985, primatologist Allison Jolly called it the "social cement" of primate societies. Although grooming occurs in other animal species, social grooming is mostly a primate activity, and it plays an important role in day-to-day life (Fig. 7-12). Because grooming involves using the fingers to pick through the fur of another individual (or one's own) to remove insects, dirt, and other materials, it serves hygienic functions. But it's also a pleasurable activity that members of some species (especially chimpanzees) engage in for long periods of time.

Grooming occurs in a variety of contexts. Mothers groom infants. Males groom sexually receptive females. Subordinate animals groom dominant ones, sometimes to gain favor. And friends groom friends. In general, grooming is comforting. It restores peaceful relationships after conflict and it provides reassurance during tense situations. In short, grooming reinforces social bonds and consequently helps to maintain and strengthen a group's structure.

Conflict resolution through reconciliation is another important aspect of primate social behavior. Following a conflict, chimpanzee opponents frequently move, within minutes, to reconcile (de Waal, 1982). Reconciliation takes many forms, including hugging, kissing, and grooming. Even uninvolved animals may take part, either grooming one or both participants or forming their own grooming parties. In addition, bonobos are unique in their use of sex to promote group cohesion, restore peace after conflicts, and relieve tension within the group (de Waal, 1987, 1989).

Social relationships are crucial to nonhuman primates, and, as we said earlier, bonds between individuals can last a lifetime. These relationships serve many functions. Individuals of many species form alliances in which one supports another against a third. Alliances, or coalitions, as they're also called, can be used to enhance the status of members. For example, at Gombe, the male chimpanzee Figan achieved alpha status because of his brother's support (Goodall, 1986, p. 424). In fact, chimpanzees so heavily rely on coalitions and are so skillful politically that an entire book, appropriately titled *Chimpanzee Politics: Power and Sex among Chimpanzees* (de Waal, 2007), has been devoted to the topic.

Reproduction and Reproductive Strategies

As is true of most mammals, in most primate species, sexual behavior is tied to the female's reproductive cycle, with females being sexually receptive to males only when they're in estrus. Estrus is characterized by behavioral changes that indicate a female is receptive. In Old World monkeys and apes that live in multimale-multifemale groups, estrus is also accompanied by swelling and changes in color of the skin around the genital area. These changes serve as visual cues of a female's readiness to mate (Fig 7-13).

Permanent bonding between males and females isn't common among nonhuman primates. However, male and female savanna baboons sometimes form mating *consortships*. These temporary relationships last while the female is in estrus, and the two spend most of their time together, mating frequently. Also, as we mentioned earlier, lower-ranking baboon males often form "friendships" (Smuts, 1985) with females and occasionally may mate with them.

Mating consortships are sometimes seen in chimpanzees and are particularly common among bonobos. In fact, a male and female bonobo may spend several weeks mostly in each other's company. During this time, they mate often, even when the female isn't in estrus. These relationships of longer duration aren't typical of chimpanzee males and females.

Such a male-female bond may result in increased reproductive success for both sexes. For the male, there's the increased likelihood that he will be the father of any infant the female conceives. At the same time, the female potentially gains protection from predators or other members of her group and perhaps assistance in caring for offspring she may already have.

Alexander Klemm/iStockphoto

Figure **7-13**

Estrous swelling of genital tissues in a female baboon.

Reproductive Strategies

Reproductive strategies, and especially how they differ between the sexes, have been a primary focus of primate research. The goal of such strategies is to produce and successfully rear to adulthood as many offspring as possible.

reproductive strategies The complex of behavioral patterns that contributes to individual reproductive success. The behaviors need not be deliberate, and they often vary considerably between males and females.

Primates are among the most **K-selected** of mammal species. By this we mean that individuals produce only a few young, in whom they invest a tremendous amount of parental care. Contrast this pattern with that of **r-selected** species, where large numbers of offspring are produced but parents invest little or no energy in infant care. Good examples of r-selected species include insects, most fishes, and, among mammals, mice and rabbits.

Considering the degree of care required by young, dependent primate offspring, it's clear that enormous investment by at least one parent is necessary, and in a majority of species, the mother carries most of the burden certainly before, but also after, birth. Primates are totally helpless at birth, and because they develop slowly, they're exposed to expanded learning opportunities within a *social* environment. This trend has been elaborated most dramatically in great apes and humans, especially the latter. So, what we see in ourselves and our close primate relatives (and presumably in our more recent ancestors as well) is a strategy in which at least one parent, usually the mother, makes an extraordinary investment to produce a few "high-quality," slowly maturing offspring.

Finding food and mates, avoiding predators, and caring for and protecting dependent young are difficult challenges for nonhuman primates. Moreover, in most species, males and females use different strategies to meet these challenges.

Female primates spend almost all their adult lives either pregnant, lactating, and/or caring for offspring, and the resulting metabolic demands are enormous. A pregnant or lactating female, although perhaps only half the size of her male counterpart, may require about the same number of calories per day. Even if these demands are met, her physical resources may be drained. For example, analysis of chimpanzee skeletons from Gombe National Park, in Tanzania, showed significant loss of bone and bone mineral in older females (Sumner et al., 1989).

Given these physiological costs and the fact that her reproductive potential is limited by lengthy intervals between births, a female's best strategy is to maximize the amount of resources available to her and her offspring. Indeed, as we just discussed, females of many primate species (gibbons, marmosets, and macaques, to name a few) are competitive with other females and aggressively protect resources and territories. In other species (for example, chimpanzees), females distance themselves from others to avoid competition. Males, however, face a separate set of challenges. Having little investment in the rearing of offspring, it's to the male's advantage to secure as many mates and produce as many offspring as possible.

Sexual Selection

One outcome of different mating strategies is **sexual selection**, a phenomenon first described by Charles Darwin. Sexual selection is a type of natural selection that operates on only one sex, usually males. The selective agent is male competition for mates and, in some species, mate choice by females. The long-term effect of sexual selection is to increase the frequency of traits that lead to greater success in acquiring mates.

In the animal kingdom, numerous male attributes are the results of sexual selection. For example, female birds of many species are attracted to males with more vividly colored plumage. Selection has thus increased the frequency of alleles that influence brighter coloration in males, and in these species (peacocks may be the best example), males are more colorful than females.

Sexual selection in primates is most important in species in which mating is polygynous and there's considerable male competition for females. In

K-selected Pertaining to K-selection, an adaptive strategy whereby individuals produce relatively few offspring, in whom they invest increased parental care. Although only a few infants are born, chances of survival are increased for each individual because of parental investments in time and energy. Examples of nonprimate K-selected species are birds and canids (e.g., wolves, coyotes, and dogs).

r-selected Pertaining to r-selection, an adaptive strategy that emphasizes relatively large numbers of offspring and reduced parental care (compared to K-selected species). K-selection and r-selection are relative terms (for example, mice are r-selected compared to primates but K-selected compared to most fish).

sexual selection A type of natural selection that operates on only one sex within a species. Sexual selection results from competition for mates, and it can lead to sexual dimorphism regarding one or more traits.

these species, sexual selection produces dimorphism in a number of traits, most noticeably body size (Fig. 7-14). As you've seen, males of many primate species are considerably larger than females, and they have larger canine teeth. Conversely, in species that live in pairs (such as gibbons) or where male competition is reduced, sexual dimorphism in canine and body size is either reduced or nonexistent. For these reasons, the presence or absence of sexually dimorphic traits in a species can be a reasonably good indicator of mating structure.

Infanticide as a Reproductive Strategy?

One way males may increase their chances of reproducing is to kill infants fathered by other males. This explanation was first suggested in an early study of Hanuman langurs in India (Hrdy, 1977). Hanuman langurs (Fig. 7-15) typically live in groups composed of one adult male, several females, and their offspring. Males without mates form "bachelor" groups that frequently for-

Figure 7-14

Mandrills provide an excellent example of sexual dimorphism resulting from sexual selection. Not only are males about twice the size of females, they also are much more brightly colored.

age within sight of the one-male associations. These peripheral males occasionally attack and defeat a reproductive male and drive him from his group. Then, following such a takeover, the new male may kill some or all of the group's infants, who were fathered by the previous male.

At first glance, such behavior would seem to be counterproductive, especially for a species as a whole. However, individual animals behave in ways that maximize their *own* reproductive success, no matter what effect their actions may have on the population or even the species. By killing infants fathered by other animals, male langurs may increase their own chances of fathering offspring, albeit unknowingly. This is because while a female is producing milk and nursing an infant, she doesn't come into estrus and therefore isn't sexually available. But when an infant dies, its mother stops lactating, resumes cycling, and becomes sexually receptive again. So, by killing nursing infants, a new male avoids waiting two to three years for them to be weaned before he can mate with their mothers. This could be advantageous to him, since chances are good that he won't even be in the group for two or three years. He also doesn't expend energy and put himself at risk by defending infants who don't carry his genes.

Hanuman langurs aren't the only primates that practice infanticide. It's been observed (or surmised) in many species, such as redtail monkeys, red colobus, blue monkeys, savanna baboons, howlers, orangutans, gorillas, chimpanzees (Struhsaker and Leyland, 1987), and humans. (It should also be noted that infanticide occurs in many nonprimate species, including rodents, cats, and horses.) In the majority of reported nonhuman primate examples, infanticide coincides with the transfer of a new male into a group or, as in chimpanzees, an encounter with an unfamiliar female and infant.

Numerous objections to this explanation of infanticide have been raised. Alternative hypotheses have included competition for resources (Rudran, 1973), aberrant behaviors related to human-induced overcrowding (Curtin and Dohlinow, 1978), and inadvertent killing during conflict between animals (Bartlett et al., 1993). Sussman and colleagues (1995), as well as others, have questioned the actual prevalence of infanticide, arguing that although it does occur, it's not particularly common. These authors have also suggested that if indeed male reproductive fitness is increased through the killing of infants, such increases are negligible. Yet, others (Struhsaker and Leyland, 1987; Hrdy, 1995) maintain that both the incidence and patterning of infanticide by males are not only significant, but consistent with the assumptions established by theories of behavioral evolution.

Henzi and Barrett (2003) reported that when chacma baboon males migrate into a new group, they "deliberately single out females with young infants and hunt them down" (Fig. 7-16). The importance of these findings is the conclusion that, at least in chacma baboons, newly arrived males consistently try to kill infants, and their attacks are highly aggressive and purposeful. These observations indicate that the incoming males are very motivated and are engaging in a goal-directed behavior, although they most certainly don't understand the possible reproductive advantages they may later gain. Reports like these, however, don't prove that infanticide increases a male's reproductive fitness. To do this, primatologists must demonstrate two crucial facts:

1. Infanticidal males *don't* kill their own offspring.
2. Once a male has killed an infant, he subsequently fathers another infant with the victim's mother.

Figure 7-15

Hanuman langurs.

Figure 7-16

An immigrant male chacma baboon chases a terrified female and her infant (clinging to her back). Resident males interceded to stop the chase.

Borries and colleagues (1999) collected DNA samples from the feces of infanticidal males and their victims in several groups of free-ranging Hanuman langurs, specifically to determine if these males killed their own offspring. Their results showed that in all 16 cases where infant and male DNA was available, the males weren't related to the infants they either attacked or killed. Moreover, DNA analysis also showed that in 4 out of 5 cases where a victim's mother subsequently gave birth, the new infant was fathered by the infanticidal male. Although still more evidence is needed, this study strongly suggests that infanticide may indeed give males an increased chance of fathering offspring.

Mothers, Fathers, and Infants

The basic social unit among all primates is a female and her infants (Fig. 7-17). Except in those species in which **polyandry** occurs or the social group is a bonded pair, males don't directly participate in the rearing of offspring. The mother-infant bond begins at birth. Although the exact nature of the bonding process isn't fully known, there appear to be predisposing innate factors that strongly attract a female to her infant, so long as she herself has had a sufficiently normal experience with her own mother. This doesn't mean that primate mothers have an innate knowledge of how to care for an infant. In fact, they don't. Monkeys and apes raised in captivity without contact with their mothers not only don't know how to care for a newborn infant, but may be afraid of it and attack or even kill it. For this reason, learning is essential to establishing a mother's attraction to her infant.

The role of bonding between primate mothers and infants was clearly demonstrated in a famous series of experiments at the University of Wisconsin. Psychologist Harry Harlow (1959) raised infant rhesus macaques with surrogate mothers made of wire or a combination of wire and cloth. Other infants were raised with no mother at all. Members of the first group retained an attachment to their cloth-covered surrogate mother (Fig. 7-18). But those raised with no mother were incapable of forming lasting attachments with other monkeys; they sat passively in their cages, staring vacantly into space. None of the motherless males ever successfully copulated. Those females who were impregnated either paid little attention to their infants or reacted aggressively toward them (Harlow and Harlow, 1961). The point is that monkeys reared in isolation were denied opportunities to *learn* the rules of social and maternal behavior. Moreover, and just as essential, they were denied the all-important physical contact so necessary for normal primate psychological and emotional development.

The importance of a normal relationship with the mother is demonstrated by field studies as well. From birth, infant primates are able to cling to their mother's fur, and they're in more or less constant physical contact with her for several months. During this critical period, infants develop a closeness with their mothers that doesn't always end with weaning. In fact, especially among some Old World monkeys, mothers and infants may remain close until one or the other dies.

In studies that followed the Harlow research, Suomi and colleagues emphasized that social isolation initiated early in life can have devastating effects on subsequent development and behavior for many primate species. The primate deprivation syndrome that results from early isolation is characterized by displays of abnormal self-directed behavior, such as self-hugging or rocking back and forth, and by deficits in all aspects of social behavior (Suomi et al., 1983, p. 190).

polyandry A mating system characterized by an association between a female and more than one male (usually two or three), with whom she mates. Among nonhuman primates, this pattern is seen only in marmosets and tamarins.

Figure **7-17**
Primate mothers with young.
(a) Mongoose lemur. (b) Chimpanzee.
(c) Patas monkey. (d) Sykes monkey.
(e) Orangutan.

(a)

David Haring

(b)

Arlene Kruse/Bonnie Pedersen

(c)

Robert Jurmain

(d)

Robert Jurmain

(e)

© Tom McHugh/Photo Researchers, Inc.

Although infants are mainly cared for by their mothers, in some species, presumed fathers also participate. Male siamangs actively take care of their offspring, and marmoset and tamarin males provide most of the direct infant care. In fact, marmoset and tamarin offspring (frequently twins) are usually carried on the male's back and are transferred to their mother only for nursing.

Even in species where adult males aren't directly involved in infant care, they may take more than a casual interest in infants, and this is especially true of hamadryas and savanna baboons. But to establish that baboons exhibit paternal care, it's necessary to establish paternity. Buchan and colleagues (2003) did just that by analyzing the DNA of subadults and males. They showed that during disputes, the fathers intervened on behalf of their offspring significantly more often than for unrelated juveniles. Because disputes can lead to severe injury, Buchan and colleagues considered the male intervention an example of true paternal care. Although this study also demonstrates that nonhuman primates can recognize relatives, the exact mechanisms of kin recognition haven't been fully identified. Clues to how nonhuman primates recognize relatives may eventually come from new molecular-based research.

What may be an extension of the mother-infant relationship has been called **alloparenting** (Fig. 7-19). This behavior occurs in many animal species but is most richly expressed in primates, and some researchers believe that it's found among all social primates. Usually, alloparents crowd around an infant and attempt to groom, hold, or touch it. Some species, such as langurs, are well known for their "aunts," and several females may hold an infant during its first day of life. Occasionally, rough treatment by inexperienced or aggressive animals can result in an infant's injury or death. For this reason, mothers may attempt to shield infants from overly attentive individuals.

Several functions are suggested for alloparenting. If the mother dies, the infant stands a chance of being adopted by an alloparent or other individual. Also, it may simply be convenient for the mother to leave her infant occasionally with another female. Finally, alloparenting may help train young females the skills of motherhood.

Because the survival of offspring is the key to individual reproductive success, parenting strategies have evolved throughout the animal kingdom. In many r-selected species, such as fishes, parenting may involve nothing more than laying large numbers of eggs. But in birds and mammals, as you've seen, there's increased care of dependent young. Alloparenting is important in some mammalian species besides primates (for example, elephants), but even so, it's most highly developed in several primate species. Likewise, males provide group defense in many mammal species, but actual paternal care is most common in primates. And with further use of genetic technologies, the role of males and other related individuals in infant care will undoubtedly become clearer.

Figure **7-18**

Infant macaque clinging to cloth mother.

Harlow Primate Laboratory

alloparenting A common behavior in many primate species whereby individuals other than the parent(s) hold, carry, and in general interact with infants.

Figure **7-19**

Male savanna baboon carrying an infant. This is an example of alloparenting—or perhaps parental care.

Lynn Kilgore

Summary

In this chapter, we presented the major theoretical models for the evolution of behavior in primates. We also discussed some of the evidence, including the use of genetic analysis to support these models. The fundamental principle of behavioral evolution is that aspects of behavior (including social behavior) are influenced by genetic factors. And because some behavioral elements are therefore influenced by genes, natural selection can act on them in the same way it acts on physical and anatomical characteristics. We pointed out that in more primitive organisms, such as insects and most other invertebrates, the proportion of behavior that's directly influenced by genes is much greater than in mammals and birds.

Behavioral ecology is the discipline that examines behavior from the perspective of complex ecological relationships and the role of natural selection as it favors behaviors that increase reproductive fitness. This approach generates many models of behavioral evolution that can be applied to all species, including humans. Members of each species inherit a genome that is species-specific, and some part of that genome influences behaviors. But in more complex animals, the genome allows a greater degree of behavioral flexibility and learning. In humans, who rely on cultural adaptations for survival, most behavior is learned.

Life history traits or strategies (developmental stages that characterize a species) are important to the reproductive success of individuals. These traits include length of gestation, number of offspring per birth, interbirth interval, age of sexual maturity, and longevity. Although these characteristics are strongly influenced by the genome of any species, they're also influenced by environmental and social factors, such as nutrition and social status. In turn, nutritional requirements are affected by body size, diet, and basal metabolic rate (BMR).

We also described the various types of primate social groups: one-male–multifemale groups; multimale-multifemale groups; bonded pairs consisting of one male and one female; polyandry; and more or less solitary individuals. In addition, we presented various explanations for why primates live in social groups (for example, predator avoidance and competition for resources with other groups).

There was also discussion of the various strategies primates have adopted to facilitate social living, including affiliative and aggressive interactions. Lastly, we talked about the relationships between mothers and infants and the increasing evidence that male primates provide more parental care than was previously thought.

Critical Thinking Questions

1. Apply some of the topics presented in this chapter to some nonprimate species that you're familiar with. Can you develop some hypotheses to explain the behavior of some domestic species? You might want to speculate on how behavior in domestic animals may differ from that of their wild ancestors.

2. In anticipation of the next chapter, can you speculate on how the behavioral ecology of nonhuman primates may be helpful in explaining human behavior?

3. We used birds as an example of sexual dimorphism resulting from sexual selection. But there are some bird species in which males, not females, sit on the nest to warm and protect the eggs. These males are less colorful than the females. How would you explain this? (*Hint*: Sexual selection may not be the only factor involved in sexual dimorphism in bird coloration.)

Molecular Applications in Primatology

Primatologists have recently used molecular biological techniques to compare the DNA sequences of a wide range of contemporary primates. From these data, new insights have been gained concerning sensory perception, physiology, social relationships, and evolutionary relationships. There is so much interest, in fact, that a conference held in 2006 gave this new field of research its own name—molecular primatology (Molecular Primatology: Progress and Promise, 2006).

At this conference, four different areas of contemporary research were highlighted: (1) *molecular ecology*, "the use of molecular techniques for examining kinship, behavior, dispersal patterns, and social organization in wild primates"; (2) *conservation genetics*, "the application of molecular techniques to primate conservation biology"; (3) *molecular diversity and adaptation*, "the adaptive significance of patterns of molecular diversity within and between primate groups"; and (4) *behavioral genetics and comparative genomics*, "the genetic basis of behavioral variation and intepreting functional patterns revealed in genomic differences seen in different species of primates." Here, we consider some exciting new research relating to aspects of the emerging discipline of molecular primatology.

One crucial source of information concerns the precise identification of kin relationships within primate societies. Recognizing maternity is almost always obvious to primatologists studying primate social groups and probably to all members of these groups. Tracing paternity, however, has always been difficult, and without knowing who fathered whom, it's impossible to test hypotheses that relate to such issues as kin selection, infanticide, and the selective advantage of dominance.

Recently, great strides have been made to overcome these difficulties. Biologist Phillip Morin and anthropologist Jim Moore (of the University of California, San Diego) did the first molecular-based study on the Gombe chimpanzees (Morin et al., 1994). An important advantage of this research was that DNA samples could be obtained *without* interfering with the animals themselves (Fig. 1). Previously, it was necessary to capture the animals (usually by shooting them with a sedative dart), draw a blood sample, and then release them. Clearly, such procedures are dangerous for the animals, and they can seriously disrupt the social group.

What's more, due to the development of PCR techniques (see p. 73), primatologists can use much smaller DNA samples. For example, in this study, DNA was extracted from chimpanzee hairs collected from abandoned sleeping nests. And thanks to even more advanced methods of DNA amplification (PCR), accurate genetic data can now also be obtained from fecal samples. This method provides great advantages because many more samples can be much more easily collected and most primates don't build nests (so finding hair samples isn't usually practical; Bayes et al., 2000; van Horn et al., 2008). In another recent study of chimpanzees in East Africa, in addition to finding DNA in hair and feces, researchers also obtained DNA from urine, from muscle (from a dead animal), from blood from injured animals, and in one case from saliva on twigs that a chimp had sucked on (Inoue et al., 2008).

Researchers from the Max Planck Institute for Evolutionary Anthropology (MPIEA) recently did a more complete study on West African chimpanzees from the Tai Forest. The MPIEA, founded in Leipzig, Germany, in 1997, has quickly become the leading center for a variety of groundbreaking applications within anthropology. Its staff of molecular biologists, primatologists, and molecular anthropologists have contributed significantly to many aspects of molecular research discussed in this text. Led by primatologist Linda Vigilant, the researchers found that most of the chimpanzee offspring within the Tai Forest community were fathered by resident males (Vigilant et al., 2001).

And from Gombe, a study using DNA from both hair and fecal samples found that *all* offspring were fathered by resident males (Constable et al., 2001). Detailed examination of social relationships within the Gombe community also showed that a variety of male strategies, such as dominance, possessiveness, opportunistic mating, and consortships, could lead to reproductive success. DNA can also be used to assess the degree of inbreeding. At Gombe, 13 of 14

Figure 1

Physical anthropologist Jim Moore collecting hair samples from a chimpanzee sleeping nest at Gombe.

Jim Moore/Anthro Photo

offspring weren't closely inbred. But in one case, a male had successfully mated with his mother.

Led by Dr. Leslie Knapp, the Primate Immunogenetics and Molecular Ecology Research Group (PRIME) at the University of Cambridge, is investigating aspects of human and nonhuman primate genetic mechanisms and how these, in turn, might influence immunity, disease, and perhaps even social behavior. The focus of their investigations is a genetic system called the major histocompatibility complex (MHC). The group is currently studying MHC variation in chimpanzees, gorillas, mandrills, several New World monkeys, lemurs, and humans (Fig. 2). Results are used to test hypotheses regarding the effects of natural selection on particular allele combinations, the antiquity of these genes in different primate groups, and the possible influences that different genes may have on kin recognition, mate choice, and inbreeding avoidance (Knapp, 2005).

Primatologists still don't fully understand how non-human primates detect information concerning kin. Some research has proposed that olfactory cues may be crucial. As they test this hypothesis, they're discovering some fascinating genetic patterns that influence olfactory perception in primates, including humans.

Geneticists have identified several genes that directly influence the sense of smell in mammals. One of these, present and active in most mammals and some primates (lemurs, lorises, and New World monkeys), directly influences a particular form of scent perception. However, in all Old World anthropoids (Old World monkeys, apes, and humans), it's completely dysfunctional. These facts were discovered separately by two teams of investigators, one at the University of Southern California (Liman and Innan, 2003) and the other at the University of Michigan (Zhang and Webb, 2003). Moreover, both research teams reached the same conclusions as to *when* in evolution this olfactory capability was lost in Old World anthropoids and *why*. The genetic mutations that led to reduced olfactory capabilities in Old World anthropoids occurred after New and Old World primates diverged from each other but before the divergence of Old World monkeys and hominoids (about 25–20 mya). Furthermore, the reason hypothesized for different selection forces in New and Old World forms is the parallel development of full color vision (which has also recently been investigated in different primates using molecular techniques). The researchers suggest that the advantages provided by full color vision relaxed the selection pressure that favored greater reliance on olfactory cues (such as pheromone detection). Eventually, this relaxed selection pressure led to deactivation of the genes that control this aspect of olfaction.

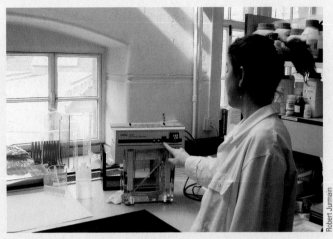

Robert Jurmain

Figure 2

Variation in DNA sequences can be studied using a variety of molecular genetic techniques. A graduate student at the University of Cambridge uses gradient gel electrophoresis to study variability in the chromosomal region involved in immune response (the area of DNA which helps provide protection against infection).

We know that nonhuman primates recognize relatives partly through the sense of smell, but this ability isn't primarily related to pheromone perception (at least not among Old World anthropoids). But it's still quite possible that in many Old World monkeys and apes, other olfactory mechanisms are at work. Indeed, hundreds of other genes have been shown to directly influence olfactory reception. Current research by the PRIME project at Cambridge is currently investigating how genetic differences in indivdiual MHC genes may influence primate behavior (and whether nonhuman primates are using olfaction to detect these differences in each other).

In yet another study, Yoav Gilad has shown that humans have far fewer genes that govern the function of olfactory receptors than any other primate (including our closest African ape cousins; Gilad et al., 2003a, 2003b). But when in hominin evolution this extreme reduction in the sense of smell occurred isn't known. However, at least for modern humans, a reduced sense of smell could be added to the list of characteristics that distinguish us from other primates.

A final area of very exciting new research concerns the identification of specific genes in different primate species that influence brain function. As more genomic data become available for a greater variety of nonhuman primates, we can begin to zero in on those genetic regions that make us most distinct from our closest primate cousins. In other words, we are searching for the very foundations of what makes us human.

Molecular Applications in Primatology (continued)

Several research teams are making the most of these opportunities, and intriguing results are already emerging. Understandably, much of the focus is directed at finding particular genes that influence cognitive function. One research group identified a gene that was repeated an usually high number of times in humans as compared to chimpanzees (Pepesco et al., 2006). This particular gene is potentially crucial because its protein product is expressed in the neocortex.

Another research team surveyed the entire genomes of humans and chimpanzees (as well as other animals) and found several chromosomal regions that have changed unusually quickly (Pollard et al., 2006). A surprising aspect of these regions is that most of them are found in segments of noncoding DNA (that is, these genes don't make protein products—but they still may have important functions).

One of these genes is especially interesting, because it's changed dramatically in the few million years since humans diverged from our common ancestor with chimpanzees. What's more, as in the finding noted previously for the other research group, this gene also appears to influence brain development.

Other studies have also found additional genes that may influence unique human brain capacities. So, despite newspaper headlines suggesting the contrary, there is no *single* gene that gives humans their exceptional mental abilities. Over the last 6 million years or so, several genetic transformations have occurred, but by typical evolutionary standards, they all happened very quickly.

Not surprisingly, researchers are finding it difficult to sort out what these various genes actually *do* in influencing brain development and complex mental functioning (relating to memory, language, and so on). At the moment, we don't know the exact function of any of these "candidate" genes that have been targeted for study. However, in molecular biology, things move very fast.

So, how do we answer that most fundamental of all questions, What is it that makes us human? Understanding how human DNA differs from that of other animals, especially from that of the great apes, provides the most direct information of how we came to be the way we are. And figuring out how a variety of genes interact to produce the human brain and its complex behavioral abilities, not to mention when in the past genetic transformations took place, will help tell us *why* we evolved as we did.

SOURCES

Bayes, M. K., K. L. Smith, C. Alberts, et al.
2000   Testing the reliability of microsatellite typing from faecal DNA in the savannah baboon. *Conservation Genetics* 1:173–176.

Constable, Julie L., Mary V. Ashley, Jane Goodall, and Anne E. Pusey
2001   Noninvasive paternity assignment in Gombe chimpanzees. *Molecular Ecology* 10:1279–1300.

Gagneux, Pascal, Christophe Boesch, and David Woodruff
1999   Female reproductive strategies, paternity, and community structure in wild West African chimpanzees." *Animal Behaviour* 57:19–32.

Gilad, Yoav, Orna Man, Svante Paabo, and Doran Lancet
2003a Human specific loss of receptor genes. *Proceedings of the National Academy of Sciences* 100:3324–3327.

Gilad, Yoav, Carlos D. Bustamante, Doran Lancet, and Svante Pääbo
2003b Natural selection on the olfactory receptor gene family in humans and chimpanzees." *American Journal of Human Genetics* 73:489–501.

Inoue, Eiji, Miho Inoue-Murayama, Linda Vigilant, et al.
2008   Relatedness in wild chimpanzees: Influence of paternity, male philopatry, and demographic factors. *American Journal of Physical Anthropology* 137:256–262.

Knapp, Leslie
2005   The ABCs of MHC. *Evolutionary Anthropology* 14:28–37.

Liman, Emily R. and Hideki Innan
2003   Relaxed selective pressure on an essential component of pheromone transduction in primate evolution. *Proceedings of the National Academy of Sciences* 100:3328–3332.

Max Planck Institute for Evolutionary Anthropology
www.eva.mpg.de

Molecular Primatology: Progress and Promise
2006   March 2–4, 2006 , New York University, New York City. www.nyu.edu/projects/difiore/mpconference/mpoverview.html

Morin, P. A., J. Wallis, J. Moore, and D. S. Woodruff
1994   Paternity exclusion in a community of wild chimpanzees using hypervariable simple sequence repeats. *Molecular Evolution* 3:469–477.

Pollard, K. S., S. R. Salama, B. King, et al.
2006   Forces shaping the fastest evolving regions in the human genome. *PLoS Genetics* 2(10): e168.

Primate Immunogenetics and Molecular Ecology Research Group
www.prime.bioanth.cam.ac.uk.

Popesco, M.C., E.J. Maclaren, J. Hopkins, et al.
2006   Human lineage-specific amplification, selection, and neuronal expression of DUF1220 domains. *Science* 313: 1304–1307.

Primate Immunogenetics and Molecular Ecology Research Group
www.prime.bioanth.cam.ac.uk.

Van Horn, Russell C., Jeanne Altmann, and Susan C. Alberts
2008   Can't get there from here: Inferring kinship from pairwise genetic relatedness. *Animal Behaviour* 75:1173–1180.

Vigilant, Linda, Michael Hofreiter, Heike Siedel, and Christophe Boesch
2001   Paternity and relatedness in wild chimpanzee communities. *Proceedings of the National Academy of Sciences* 98:12890–12895.

Zhang, Jianzhi and David Webb
2003   Evolutionary deterioration of the vomeronasal pheromone transduction pathway in catarrrhine primates. *Proceedings of the National Academy of Sciences* 100:8337–8341.

Primates

CHAPTER

Primate Models for the Evolution of Human Behavior

Key Questions

Which patterns of nonhuman primate behavior are the most important for understanding human evolution?

How are humans unique among primates? In what ways are we not unique?

 Click!

Go to the following media for interactive activities and exercises on topics covered in this chapter:

- Online Virtual Laboratories for Physical Anthropology, Version 4.0

Introduction

In Chapter 1, we said that primates (chimpanzees in particular) are often used as models for early hominin behavior. But once the human and chimpanzee lineages diverged from a common ancestor, they traveled down different evolutionary paths and continued to evolve in response to different environmental pressures. Consequently, no living species, not even chimpanzees, can perfectly serve as a representative of early hominin adaptations.

Anyone who's curious about the beginnings of humankind would like to know more about our early ancestors. Drawings of early hominins, based on fossil remains, may give us a fairly accurate picture of what they looked like; but what did they *really* look like? What were their lives like? Did they have the same diseases people have today? What kinds of social groups did they live in? What did they eat? How long did they live? How did they die? Can we answer these questions? No, not completely. But we can study the complex factors that influence many behaviors in nonhuman primates. We'll also continue to make fossil discoveries, and comparative primate genomics, which has much to tell us, is still in its infancy. By combining what we learn from these approaches, we can at least have a better understanding not only of human biological evolution but also of how certain human behaviors evolved.

In the last chapter, we considered some of the factors that guided the evolutionary history of nonhuman primate behavior. In the past two decades, primatologists have agreed that certain human behavioral predispositions reflect patterns also seen in other primates (Cartmill, 1990; King, 1994, 2004; de Waal, 1996). But just because chimpanzees and humans may both show a particular behavior, we can't say for certain that it's a direct result of shared ancestry. What's important is to closely examine behavioral patterns that have evolved as adaptive responses in nonhuman primates, while keeping in mind the enormous degree of flexibility in primate behavior. Then researchers can look for similar patterns in humans and try to draw conclusions about the ecological and genetic factors that may have produced similarities (and differences) between ourselves and our closest relatives. This approach places the study of human behavior firmly within an evolutionary context.

Certainly, human behavior is predominantly learned. But the ability to learn and behave in complex ways is ultimately rooted in biological factors. Natural selection has consistently favored the increased brain size and neurological complexity that have enhanced learning capacities and behavioral modification in the human lineage. When primatologists approach research questions from this biological perspective, they don't propose that all human abilities and behaviors are genetically determined or unalterable. Rather, it helps explain how certain patterns may have come about and what their adaptive significance might be. Within this framework, the flexibility of human behavior is recognized and emphasized.

Human Origins and Behavior

What does it mean to be human? Clearly, certain aspects of behavior are what set humans apart from other species. Long ago, culture became our strategy for coping with life's challenges. If suddenly stripped of all cultural attributes, modern humans wouldn't be able to survive year-round in many parts of the world.

Although we humans share more than 98 percent of our DNA coding sequences and many anatomical and behavioral characteristics with chimpanzees, we're undeniably quite different from them, both physically and behaviorally. Humans have different limb proportions, flatter faces, smaller teeth, and, most important, relatively and absolutely bigger brains than other primates. These anatomical differences are the results of changes in the behavior of regulatory genes that direct embryonic development. These genes are highly conserved throughout the animal kingdom, and they govern the same developmental processes in all animals. But the length of time they operate to establish patterns and proportions of anatomical structures does vary between species. Indeed, alterations in the activities of these developmental genes through the course of evolution may be the single most important factor in speciation. For example, chimpanzees have longer faces and larger teeth than humans because the genes that control the development of these structures cause them to develop at different rates than they do in humans (Fig. 8-1).

Despite these differences, humans and apes are sufficiently similar anatomically that we can identify many shared derived traits that both species inherited from our last common ancestor. For example, human and ape shoulders are anatomically quite similar, but they're different from monkey shoulders. In humans, as in many species, some systems evolved at different times and rates than others. So, human hands are less derived than ape hands because our thumbs aren't as reduced and our fingers aren't as elongated. In fact, while humans have apelike shoulders, we have the hands of a generalized cercopithecine monkey.

So what does all this mean in terms of behavior? It means that to some extent, we shouldn't limit our behavioral comparisons to chimpanzees, any more than we should limit anatomical comparisons. Rather, we should include many species in our behavioral analogies. The selective pressures that acted on ancestral monkeys have played a role in our evolution, too, and that's something we shouldn't forget.

In the 1970s, the prevailing theory was that early hominins diverged from the apes as they moved out of a forested environment and adapted to a savanna environment. Such a move meant that they were subjected to increased predation pressure, so they adopted bipedality partly out of the need to stand upright while looking for predators (see Chapter 10). But those early hominins were already predisposed to standing upright because that is something many other primates were also able to do. The same principle applies to behavior. Although we now believe that early hominin ancestors probably exploited a more mixed woodland habitat rather than a savanna environment, they still had to have anatomical and behavioral capacities that allowed them to go there in the first place.

As a separate lineage, our own evolutionary story probably began with a behavioral shift to exploiting an econiche different

Figure 8-1

Developmental changes in the skull of (a) chimpanzees and (b) humans illustrate morphological variation between two closely related species. These anatomical differences arise through changes in regulatory genes in one or both species. In turn, regulatory genes determine the timing of development of structures.

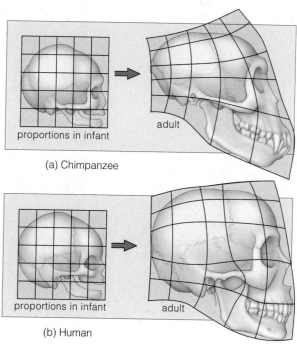

proportions in infant   adult

(a) Chimpanzee

proportions in infant   adult

(b) Human

from that of the great apes, and this new adaptation required spending more time on the ground and exploiting different types of resources. These factors, in turn, selected for additional behavioral and anatomical adaptations, while other hominoids were responding to different environmental pressures.

In what is now a classic study, Washburn and deVore (1961) used savanna baboons as a model of early hominin behavior because they live in open areas and spend much of the day on the ground. Savanna baboons live in large multimale-multifemale groups partly as an adaptive response to predation, and Washburn and deVore proposed that early hominins had a similar social structure (and they probably did). But because we're more closely related to chimpanzees, they, too, were used as an analogue for the development of many human behaviors, including tool use and competition for social rank. Thus, several species have been chosen for comparison based on both behavioral ecology and biological relatedness (Dunbar, 2001).

Today, primatologists still use nonhuman primate behavior to examine the evolution of human behavior, but they also study the relationships between two or more variables. For example, it's important to establish if there's a correlation between body size and basal metabolic rate (see p. 182). Then, having demonstrated a positive correlation, we might add another variable, such as diet. Subsequently, we could add other factors, such as increased brain size and social structure. In other words, we look for correlations between life history traits and sociality. Once positive (or negative) correlations are ascertained, we can propose certain principles to apply to the study of human behavioral evolution.

Brain and Body Size

One predominant characteristic that clearly differentiates humans from other primates is relative brain size, by which we mean the proportion of some measure of body size, such as weight, that's accounted for by the brain. Brain size and body size are closely correlated. Clearly, an animal the size of a chimpanzee (about 100 to 150 pounds) has a larger brain than a squirrel monkey, which weighs about 2 pounds. But in cross-species comparisons, as body weight increases, brain size doesn't necessarily increase at the same rate.

The predictable relationship between body and brain size has been called the "index of **encephalization**" (Jerison, 1973). The degree of encephalization is used to estimate the expected brain size for any given body size. Most primates are close to predicted ratios for brain-body size, but there's one notable exception: ourselves. New World capuchins and squirrel monkeys also show a degree of encephalization that considerably exceeds predictions. Brain size in modern humans is well beyond what would be expected for a primate of similar body weight. It's this degree of encephalization that must be explained as a unique and central component of recent human evolution. Using the same analytical perspectives that are applied to the fossil materials in the next several chapters, we can see that early members of the genus *Homo* as well as more primitive hominins (*Australopithecus*) weren't nearly as encephalized as modern humans are.

Carefully controlled comparisons are essential in making cross-species generalizations about different-sized animals (something to keep in mind when we discuss early hominins). Such controls relate to considerations of what's called scaling, or (more technically) **allometry**. These allometric comparisons have become increasingly important in understanding contemporary primate life history vari-

encephalization The proportional size of the brain relative to some other measure, usually an estimate of overall body size, such as weight. More precisely, the term refers to increases in brain size beyond what would be expected given the body size of a particular species.

allometry Also called scaling; the differential proportion among various anatomical structures (e.g., the size of the brain in proportion to overall body size during the development of an individual). Scaling effects must also be considered when comparing species.

ables and adaptations. Moreover, similar approaches, borrowed from these primate models, are now also routinely applied to the interpretation of the primate/hominin fossil record.

Beyond simple brain size comparisons between different species, it's more appropriate to emphasize the relative size of certain structures in the brain. Primitive (ancestral) brains, such as those of reptiles, are mostly composed of structures related to basic physiological functions, and there's a small **cortex** that receives sensory information (especially olfactory). As discussed in Chapter 5, in mammals, the relative size of the most recently evolved layer of the cortex, called the **neocortex**, has increased. This increase permits a more detailed and precise analysis and interpretation of incoming sensory information and therefore more complex behavior. In primates, expansion of the neocortex has accounted for much of the increase in brain size (Fig. 8-2). The primate neocortex is partly composed of many complicated association areas. It's the part of the brain that, in humans, is associated with cognitive functions related to reasoning, complex problem solving, forethought, and language. In humans, the neocortex accounts for about 80 percent of total brain volume (Dunbar, 1998).

Timing of brain growth is also important. In nonhuman primates, the most rapid period of brain growth occurs shortly before birth; but in humans, it occurs after birth. Human prenatal brain growth is restricted so that the infant can pass through the birth canal. As it is, the size of the head in human newborns makes childbirth more difficult in humans than in any other primate (see p. 478). Thus, in humans, the brain grows rapidly for at least the first five years after birth. Because brain tissue is the most costly of all body tissues in terms of energy consumed, the metabolic costs of such rapid and sustained neurological growth are enormous, requiring more than 50 percent of an infant's metabolic output (Aiello, 1992).

In evolutionary terms, the metabolic costs of a large brain have to be compensated for by benefits. That is, large brains wouldn't have evolved if they didn't offer some advantage (Dunbar, 1998). Various hypotheses have been proposed for the evolution of large brains in primates, and many scientists in the past focused on problems related to food getting and the kinds of foods a species eats. For example, some monkeys (with a smaller relative brain size) primarily eat leaves, which, although plentiful, aren't an energy-rich food. Primates need a complex brain in order to be familiar with their home range; to be aware of when seasonal foods are available; and to solve the problem of extracting foods from shells, hard peels, and even underground roots. But these are problems for all foraging species (including squirrels and raccoons, for example), and yet these other animals haven't evolved such relatively large brains (Fig. 8-3).

Another explanation, the social brain hypothesis, proposes that primate brains increased in relative size and complexity because primates live in social groups. The demands of social living are numerous, and primates must be able to negotiate a complex web of interactions, including competition, alliance formation, forming and maintaining friendships, and avoiding certain individuals. Therefore, Barton and Dunbar (1997) suggested that intelligence evolved not only to solve physical problems (such as finding food and predator avoidance) but also to analyze and use social information, such as which animals are dominant, who forms alliances with whom, and whom to avoid.

In support of the social brain hypothesis, Bergman and colleagues (2003) showed that savanna baboons in a study group in Botswana recognize that the female social hierarchy is divided into matrilines and that the matrilines are ranked relative to one another. These primates also recognize dominance relationships

cortex Layer. In the brain, the cortex is the layer that covers the cerebral hemispheres, which in turn cover more primitive or older structures related to bodily functions and the sense of smell. The cortex is composed of nerve cells called neurons, which communicate with each other and send and receive messages to and from all parts of the body.

neocortex The more recently evolved portions of the cortex of the brain that are involved with higher mental functions and composed of areas that integrate incoming information from different sensory organs.

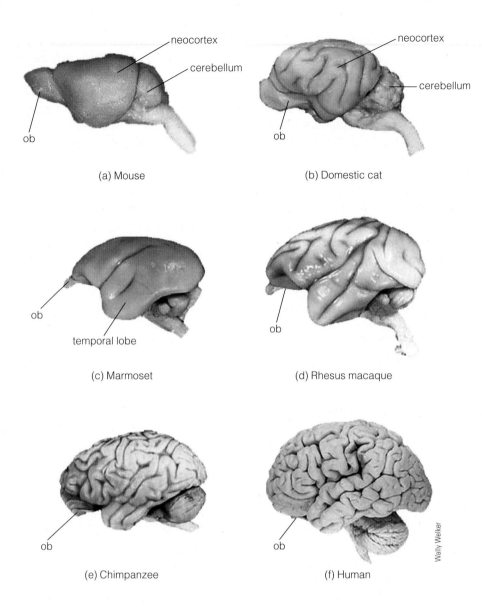

Figure **8-2**

Comparisons of mammalian brains as seen in these left lateral views (front is to left). Expansion of the neocortex, the outer layers of the cerebral hemispheres, has been the most significant trend during the evolution of the mammalian brain. This is especially evident in the size of the neocortex relative to that of the olfactory bulb (ob) at the front of the brain. The olfactory bulb is the termination point of sensory fibers that send olfactory information from the nose to the brain. A relatively large olfactory bulb indicates a greater dependence on the sense of smell. Compare the size of this organ, relative to the neocortex, in these brains. In the mouse and cat, it's particularly large, but it becomes smaller in primates. In humans, it's barely visible. In fact, in chimpanzees and humans, the neocortex is all that's visible from the top and sides except for the cerebellum. Also note the increasingly convoluted surface of the neocortex. This is due to cortical folding, which allows more neurons to be packed into a limited space. Increasing the number of neurons provides more interconnections between areas of the brain, allowing more information to be processed. The marmoset exhibits less cortical folding than the cat, but its temporal lobe (part of the neocortex) is better defined, and brain size compared to body size is greater. As you can see, cortical folding is most pronounced in humans. (Illustrations are shown approximately the same size and not to scale.) (Photos provided by the University of Wisconsin–Madison Comparative Mammalian Brain Collection: http://brainmuseum. org. Preparation of these images and specimens was funded by the National Science Foundation and the National Institutes of Health.)

Lynn Kilgore

Figure 8-3

These young raccoons are extremely intelligent and forage for a wide assortment of foods in a complex environment. However, they don't spend their entire lives in social groups and their relative (and absolute) brain size is smaller than that of similarly sized primates.

within each matriline. In other words, these baboons understand the arrangement of hierarchies within hierarchies. Emphasizing the implications of such behavioral complexity for the evolution of increased intelligence in humans, the authors state, "The selective pressures imposed by complex societies may therefore have favored cognitive skills that constitute an evolutionary precursor to some components of human cognition" (Bergman et al., 2003, p. 1234).

But at the same time, group size is limited by brain size to the extent that a group can't be made up of more animals than individuals can recognize and interact with. Brain and group size therefore probably coevolved (Dunbar, 1998, 2001). Extrapolating from neocortical volume to the size of social groups, as seen in several nonhuman primate species, Dunbar (1998) speculates that large group size in some early members of the genus *Homo* is likely. This isn't to say that early humans always lived in large groups, but they may have formed large congregations by periodic associations of smaller groups.

Stanford (1999, 2001) has proposed that meat eating was also important in the development of increased cognitive abilities in the human lineage. Hunting, especially of big game, was a topic of considerable interest in early hominin studies in the 1960s (Washburn and Lancaster, 1968). But those earlier theories were eventually discounted for various reasons, one of which is that the earliest hominins weren't capable of hunting large prey.

Most nonhuman primates that kill and eat small mammals don't actually hunt them. Chimpanzees, however, do hunt (Fig. 8-4), and their favorite prey is red colobus monkeys. Stanford and others (Aiello and Wells, 2002) argue that if early hominins relied on a diet that increasingly contained a high proportion of meat, rich in protein and fats, such a diet would meet the nutritional demands of a lineage in which relatively large brains were becoming important. But as Stanford also points out, relatively large brain size hasn't developed in social carnivores such as wolves and lions. What's more, the percentage of meat in the chimpanzee diet is small and may be similar to what early hominins obtained.

So, if meat was important in the evolution of large brains in hominins, some factor other than nutrition would have had to be important. Once chimpanzees (usually males) have made a kill, they often share the meat with relatives,

David Bygott, Anthro Photo

Figure 8-4

Male chimpanzees eating a red colobus monkey they have killed.

allies, and females. Negotiating the complexities and strategies involved in the politics of sharing meat might be viewed as one aspect of the social brain hypothesis, which holds that neurological complexity evolved as a response to complicated behavioral challenges.

Compared to most humans, chimpanzees don't really eat much meat, and there's some recent evidence that meat became an important dietary component in human ancestors sometime after chimpanzees and humans went their separate ways. In a preliminary analysis of the chimpanzee genome, Clark and colleagues (2003) discovered that several of the genes responsible for producing enzymes involved in amino acid metabolism have changed over time in both species. (Animal protein is a major source of amino acids.) This finding adds support to theories that increased meat consumption may have been important for increased brain size in early humans (Penny, 2004). At the very least, it indicates that as the two lineages diverged, both responded to different selective pressures; and selection favored enzyme mutations that enabled some hominins to digest meat more efficiently.

Language

One of the most significant events in human evolution was the development of language. In Chapter 7, we described several behaviors and autonomic responses that convey information in nonhuman primates. But although we emphasized the importance of communication to primate social life, we also said that nonhuman primates don't use language the way that humans do.

The view traditionally held by most linguists and behavioral psychologists has been that nonhuman communication consists of mostly involuntary vocalizations and actions that convey information solely about an animal's emotional state (anger, fear, and so on). Nonhuman animals haven't been considered capable of communicating about external events, objects, or other animals, either in close proximity or removed in space or time. For example, when a startled baboon barks, other group members know only that it's startled. But they don't know why it barked, and they can only discover this by looking around to see what provoked it. In general, then, it's been assumed that in nonhuman animals, including primates, vocalizations, facial expressions, body postures, and so on, don't refer to specific external phenomena.

But these views have been challenged for years (Steklis, 1985; King, 1994, 2004). For example, vervet monkeys (Fig. 8-5) use specific vocalizations to refer to particular categories of predators, such as snakes, birds of prey, and leopards (Struhsaker, 1967; Seyfarth, Cheney, and Marler, 1980a, 1980b). When researchers made tape recordings of vervet alarm calls and played them back within hearing distance of wild vervets, they saw different responses to various calls. When the vervets heard leopard-alarm calls, they climbed trees; when they heard eagle-alarm

Figure **8-5**
Group of vervets.

Lynn Kilgore

calls, they looked up; and they responded to snake-alarm calls by looking around at the ground and in nearby grass.

These results show that vervets use distinct vocalizations to refer to specific components of the external environment. Vervet calls aren't involuntary, and they don't refer solely to the individual's emotional state (alarm), although this information is also conveyed. While these findings dispel certain long-held misconceptions about nonhuman communication (at least for some species), they also indicate certain limitations. Vervet communication is restricted to the present; as far as we know, no vervet can communicate about a predator it saw yesterday or one it might see in the future.

Other studies have demonstrated that numerous nonhuman primates, including cottontop tamarins (Cleveland and Snowdon, 1982), Goeldi's monkeys (Masataka, 1983), red colobus (Struhsaker, 1975), and gibbons (Tenaza and Tilson, 1977), produce distinct calls that have specific references. There's also evidence that many birds and some nonprimate mammals use specific predator alarm calls (Seyfarth, 1987).

Humans use *language,* a set of written and/or spoken symbols that refer to concepts, other people, objects, and so on. This set of symbols is said to be arbitrary because the symbol itself has no inherent relationship with whatever it stands for. For example, the English word *flower,* when written or spoken, neither looks, smells, nor feels like the thing it represents. Humans can also recombine their linguistic symbols in an infinite number of ways to create new meanings, and we can use language to refer to events, places, objects, and people far removed in both space and time. For these reasons, language is described as an open system of communication, based on the human ability to think symbolically.

Language, as distinct from other forms of communication, has always been considered a uniquely human achievement, setting humans apart from the rest of the animal kingdom. But work with captive apes has somewhat modified this view. Although many researchers were skeptical about the capacity of nonhuman primates to use language, reports from psychologists, especially those who work with chimpanzees, leave little doubt that apes can learn to interpret visual signs and use them in communication. Other than humans, no mammal can speak. However, the fact that apes can't speak has less to do with lack of intelligence than with differences in the anatomy of the vocal tract and language-related structures in the brain.

Because of unsuccessful attempts by others to teach young chimpanzees to speak, psychologists Beatrice and Allen Gardner designed a study to test language capabilities in chimpanzees by teaching ASL (American Sign Language for the deaf) to an infant female named Washoe. The project began in 1966, and in three years, Washoe acquired at least 132 signs. "She asked for goods and services, and she also asked questions about the world of objects and events around her" (Gardner et al., 1989, p. 6).

Years later, when an infant chimpanzee named Loulis was placed in Washoe's care, she adopted him. Psychologist Roger Fouts and colleagues wanted to know if Loulis would spontaneously acquire signing skills through contact with Washoe and the other chimpanzees in the study group. Within just eight days, Loulis began to imitate signs the other chimps were making. Also, Washoe deliberately *taught* Loulis how to make some signs. For example, when she wanted him to sit down, "Washoe placed a small plastic chair in front of Loulis, and then signed CHAIR/ SIT to him several times in succession, watching him closely throughout" (Fouts et al., 1989, p. 290).

There have been other chimpanzee language experiments. A chimpanzee called Sara was taught to recognize plastic chips as symbols for various objects. Importantly, the chips didn't resemble the objects they represented. For example, the chip that represented an apple was neither round nor red. The fact that Sara was able to use the chips to communicate is significant because her ability to associate chips with concepts and objects to which they bore no similarity implies some degree of symbolic thought. And, at the Yerkes Regional Primate Research Center in Atlanta, Georgia, two male chimpanzees, Sherman and Austin, learned to communicate using a series of lexigrams, or geometric symbols, imprinted on a computer keyboard (Savage-Rumbaugh, 1986).

Other apes have also shown language capabilities. Dr. Francine Patterson, who taught ASL to a female lowland gorilla named Koko, reports that Koko uses more than 500 signs. Furthermore, Michael, an adult male gorilla who was also involved in the same study until his death in 2000, had a considerable vocabulary, and the two gorillas regularly communicated with each other using sign language.

In the late 1970s, a 2-year-old male orangutan named Chantek (also at Yerkes) began to use signs after one month of training. Eventually, he acquired approximately 140 signs, which he sometimes used to refer to objects and people not present. Chantek also invented signs and recombined them in novel ways, and he appeared to understand that his signs were representations of items, actions, and people (Miles, 1990).

Several people questioned this type of experimental work. Do the apes really understand the signs they learn, or are they merely imitating their trainers? Do they learn that a symbol is a name for an object, or do they only understand that making a symbol will produce that object? Other unanswered questions concern the apes' use of grammar, especially when they combine more than just a few "words" to communicate.

Partly in an effort to address some of these questions and criticisms, psychologist Sue Savage-Rumbaugh taught the two chimpanzees Sherman and Austin to use symbols for *categories* of objects, such as "food" or "tool." She did this because in previous studies, apes had been taught symbols only for specific items (such as apple or hammer). Savage-Rumbaugh recognized that using a symbol as a label isn't the same thing as understanding the representational value of the symbol. But if chimpanzees could classify things into groups, it would indicate that they can use symbols referentially.

Sherman and Austin were taught to recognize familiar food items, for which they routinely used symbols, as belonging to a broader category referred to by yet another symbol, "food." They were then introduced to unfamiliar food items, for which they had no symbols, to see if they would place them in the food category. The fact that they both had perfect or nearly perfect scores for this task was further evidence that they could indeed categorize unfamiliar objects. More importantly, it was clear that they could assign symbols to indicate an object's membership in a broad grouping. This ability strongly indicated that the chimpanzees understood that the symbols were being used referentially.

However, subsequent work with a chimpanzee named Lana wasn't as successful. Lana had been involved in an earlier language study and clearly had the ability to use symbols to refer to objects. However, she couldn't assign generic symbols to novel items (Savage-Rumbaugh and Lewin, 1994). It became apparent that the manner in which chimpanzees are introduced to language influences their ability to understand the representational value of symbols.

One criticism of the conclusions drawn from ape language studies has been that young chimpanzees must be *taught* to use symbols, while human children spontaneously acquire language through exposure, without being deliberately taught. Therefore, it was significant when Savage-Rumbaugh and her colleagues reported that Kanzi, an infant male bonobo, was spontaneously acquiring and using symbols at the age of 2½ years (Savage-Rumbaugh et al., 1986; Fig. 8-6). In the same way, Kanzi's younger half sister began to use symbols spontaneously when she was only 11 months old. Both animals had been exposed to the use of lexigrams, or symbols that represent words, when they accompanied their mother to training sessions; but neither had been directly involved in these sessions, nor had they been taught the various symbols.

While Kanzi and his sister showed a remarkable degree of cognitive complexity, it's still clear that apes don't acquire and use language in the same way humans do. It also appears that not all signing apes understand the referential relationship between symbols and objects, individuals, or actions. Nonetheless, we now have abundant evidence that humans aren't the only species capable of some degree of symbolic thought and complex communication.

Figure 8-6

The bonobo Kanzi, as a youngster, using lexigrams to communicate with human observers.

(a)

Lynn Kilgore

(b)

Manoj Shah/The Image Bank

Figure 8-8

(a) This little girl is learning basic computer skills by watching her older sister. (b) A chimpanzee learns the art of termiting through intense observation.

them. Within three years, several other monkeys were also washing their potatoes, though instead of the stream, they were using the ocean nearby. Maybe they liked the salt!

The researchers suggested that dietary habits and food preferences are learned and that potato washing was an example of nonhuman culture. Because the practice arose as an innovative solution to a problem (removing dirt) and gradually spread through the troop until it became a tradition, it was seen as containing elements of human culture.

A study of orangutans in six areas (four Bornean and two Sumatran) listed 19 behaviors that showed sufficient regional variation to be classed as "very likely cultural variants" (van Schaik et al., 2003). Four activities in the "very likely" category involved the use of nests. In five locations, nests were built exclusively for play activities and not for resting or sleeping. There was also variation in the building of nests or roofs above resting nests to provide shelter from bright sun or rain. Lastly, while tool use isn't as elaborate as in chimpanzees, in one Bornean locality, orangutans used sticks to scratch themselves and leaves as "napkins." And in one Sumatran area, they pushed sticks into tree holes to obtain insects.

Using tools or objects to accomplish tasks has always been considered one of the hallmarks of being human. In fact, tool use and language have traditionally been said to set humans apart from other animals. However, we now know that humans aren't the only animals that use tools. A few nonhuman primates also use tools, with chimpanzees being the most notable example. And what's more, tool use isn't even restricted to primates. New Caledonian crows modify and use leaf stems to probe for insect larvae, and in captivity, they've bent wire to make "hooks" to obtain food (Hunt, 1996, Weir et al., 2008); some bottlenose dolphins tear off chunks of sponges to wear on their noses as protection while foraging for fish on the ocean floor (Krützen et al., 2005); and sea otters use rocks to crack open abalone shells (Fig. 8-9). Nevertheless, tool use is most elaborate among primates, and needless to say, no other species even comes close to developing tools to the degree that humans have. But human technology had to begin somewhere, so we briefly discuss some of the many examples of tool use in nonhuman primates and how these behaviors may have come about in our own lineage.

Reports of tool use in gorillas aren't common, but Breuer and colleagues (2005) reported seeing two female lowland gorillas in the DRC using branches as tools. In one case, a gorilla used a branch to test the depth of a pool of water. Then, as she waded bipedally through the pool, she used the branch again, this time as a walking stick (Fig. 8-10).

Chimpanzees exhibit more complex forms of tool use than any other nonhuman primate. They routinely insert twigs and grass blades into termite mounds in a practice primatologists call "termite fishing" (refer back to Fig. 8-8). The termites seize the twig in an attempt to protect their nest; but unfortunately for them, they become a light snack once the chimpanzee pulls the twig out of the mound. Importantly, chimpanzees frequently modify some of their stems and twigs by stripping the leaves—in effect, making a tool. For example, chimpanzees often choose a particular piece of vine, twig, or palm frond, remove leaves or other extraneous material, and then break off portions until it's the proper length. Chimpanzees have also been seen making these tools even before the termite mound is in sight.

The modification of natural objects for use as tools has several implications for nonhuman primate intelligence. First, the chimpanzees are engaged in an activity that prepares them for a future (not immediate) task at a somewhat distant location, and this action implies planning and forethought. Second, attention to the shape

Figure **8-9**

This California sea otter is eating a clam it has opened with a rock. It's common for sea otters to put their shell-cracking rocks on their stomachs as they eat just in case they need them again.

Figure **8-10**

A female lowland gorilla using a "wading stick" (in her right hand) for support.

and size of the raw material indicates that chimpanzees have a preconceived idea of what the finished product needs to be in order to be useful. To produce a tool, even a simple tool, based on a concept is an extremely complex behavior that, as we now know, isn't the exclusive domain of humans.

Primatologists have been aware of termite fishing and similar behaviors since the 1960s, but they were surprised by the discovery that chimpanzees also use tools to catch small prey. Preutz and Bertolani (2007) report that savanna chimpanzees at Fongoli in Senegal, West Africa, sharpen small branches to use as thrusting spears for capturing galagos. Prior to this study, there was no evidence that any nonhuman primate actually hunted with what is basically a manufactured (albeit simple) weapon.

Yet on 22 occasions, 10 different animals repeatedly and forcefully jabbed sharpened sticks into cavities in branches and trunks to extract galagos from their sleeping nests. In much the same way they modify termiting sticks, these chimpanzees had stripped off side twigs and leaves. But they'd also chewed the ends to sharpen them, in effect producing small thrusting spears.

The spears weren't necessarily used to impale victims so much as to injure or immobilize them, because galagos are extremely agile, fast, and hard to catch. Thus, after several thrusts, the chimpanzee would reach into the opening to see if there was anything to be had. Only one galago was actually seen to be retrieved and eaten, and although it wasn't moving or vocalizing, it was unclear if it had actually been killed by the "spear" (Preutz and Bertolani, 2007).

It's important to mention that hunting tools were used by two adults, one male and one female. All the other tool users were subadults of both sexes. Also, the animal that was observed retrieving and eating a galago was an adolescent female. Until now, all evidence suggested that while termite fishing was largely done by females and subadults, hunting was largely done by adult males, sometimes accompanied by one or two females. The fact that females and subadults were involved in tool use, tool manufacture, and hunting may imply an increased role for females in the development of these behaviors in our own species, and this will be an important topic in future research.

There are other examples of tool use, although they don't involve modification of materials. For example, chimpanzees crumple and chew handfuls of leaves, which they dip into tree hollows where water accumulates. Then they suck the water that would otherwise be inaccessible from their newly made "leaf sponges." They also use leaves to wipe substances from fur; twigs as toothpicks; and stones as weapons. They may drag or roll various objects, such as branches and stones, to enhance displays. Lastly, in some populations, chimpanzees use sticks or leaves to help process (but not obtain) mammalian prey. In the Tai Forest (Ivory Coast), for example, chimpanzees use sticks to extract marrow from long bones (Boesch and Boesch, 1989).

Hernandez-Aguilar and colleagues (2007) report compelling evidence that savanna chimpanzees in western Tanzania use sticks and pieces of tree bark to dig for roots and tubers. These authors describe 11 digging sites, consisting of more than 200 holes. These sites were in an area inhabited by chimpanzees and in close proximity to trees containing chimpanzee sleeping nests. Although chimpanzees weren't actually seen digging the holes, there were portions of digging sticks and tree bark with adhering dirt, uneaten portions of roots, chewed wads of fibrous root remains, and chimpanzee feces and knuckle prints, all associated with the holes. Moreover, at that time, there was no evidence of other mammals in the digging areas.

Prior to this report, digging with tools had not been reported for chimpanzees. Since the digging occurred in a savanna habitat (and most chimpanzees live in forested areas), this behavior may be an example of regional variation in food-getting behavior due to different environmental circumstances. In a somewhat marginal habitat for chimpanzees, digging makes it possible to exploit roots and tubers, which are an energy-rich food source. But the fact that the chimpanzees dug for roots during the rainy season, when other foods were also abundant, contradicts the hypothesis that roots are eaten as a fallback food during times of scarcity. Because the extremely hard soil may be too difficult to dig during the dry season, Hernandez and colleagues (2007) suggest that chimpanzees may simply be exploiting a difficult-to-obtain resource whenever they can get it.

In several West African study groups, chimpanzees use unmodified stones as hammers and **anvils** (Fig. 8-11) to crack nuts and hard-shelled fruits (Boesch et al., 1994). Interestingly, stone hammers and platforms are used only in West African groups and not in East Africa. Likewise, termite fishing is seen in central and East Africa, but apparently it's not done in West African groups (McGrew, 1992).

The fact that chimpanzees show regional variation in their types and methods of tool use is significant because these differences, in effect, represent cultural variation from one area to another. Chimpanzees also show regional dietary preferences (Nishida et al., 1983; McGrew, 1992, 1998). For example, oil palm fruits and nuts are eaten at many locations, including Gombe. But even though oil palms also grow in the Mahale Mountains (only about 90 miles from Gombe), the chimpanzees there seem to ignore them. Such regional patterns in tool use and food preferences that aren't related to environmental variation are reminiscent of the cultural variations characteristic of humans. Therefore, it's likely that this kind of variation probably existed in early hominins too.

So far, we've mainly discussed tool use and culture in great apes, but these aren't the only nonhuman primates that consistently use tools and exhibit elements of cultural behavior. Primatologists have been studying tool use in capuchin (cebus) monkeys for over 30 years (although indigenous human groups have been aware of the capuchin propensity for tool use long before this). Capuchins are found in South America, from Colombia and Venezuela, through Brazil, and as far south as northern Argentina. They are the most encephalized of all the monkeys, and while forest-dwelling species are arboreal, several species live in a more savanna-like habitat and these spend a fair amount of time on the ground.

Many of the capuchin tool-using behaviors parallel those we've discussed for chimpanzees. Capuchins use leaves to extract water from cavities in trees (Phillips, 1998); they use small branches, which they modify, to probe into holes in trees and logs for invertebrates (Westergaard and Fragaszy, 1987); and they smash hard-shelled palm nuts against stones and tree trunks (Izawa and Mizuno, 1977). But what they've really become known for is using stones in a number of ways to obtain food. They use stones to smash foods into smaller pieces and crack palm nuts; to break open hollow tree branches and logs; and to dig for tubers and insects. In fact, capuchins are the only monkeys known to use stones as tools and the only nonhuman primate to dig with stones (Visalberghi, 1990; Moura and Lee, 2004; Ottoni and Izar, 2008).

anvils Surfaces on which an object such as a palm nut, root, or seed is placed before being struck with another object such as a stone.

Figure 8-11

Chimpanzees in Bossou, Guinea, West Africa, use a pair of stones as hammer and anvil to crack oil palm nuts. Although the youngster isn't being taught to use stone tools, it's learning about them through observation.

Tetsuro Matsuzawa

Figure 8-12

This capuchin monkey is going to considerable effort, walking bipedally and carrying a heavy stone to a palm-nut cracking location.

Figure 8-13

A capuchin monkey using a stone as a digging tool.

When processing foods such as hard-shelled palm nuts, capuchins use stones as hammers. The anvils on which they place the nuts may be logs, flat stones, or any hard, relatively flat surface. The importance of this food source is revealed by the enormous effort expended to obtain it. Adult female capuchins weigh around 6 pounds, and the males weigh around 8 pounds, and yet they walk bipedally carrying stones that weigh as much as 2 pounds, or 25 to 40 percent of their own body weight (Fragaszy et al., 2004; Visalberghi et al., 2007) (Fig. 8-12)! Because the stones are heavy, it's difficult for capuchins to sit while cracking nuts with one hand, as humans and frequently chimpanzees do; and when they do sit, they use both hands. More often, they stand bipedally, raise the hammer stone with both hands, and then pound the nut, basically using their entire body (Fragaszy et al., 2004; see book cover photo).

Unlike subadult chimpanzees (especially females) who learn about termite fishing by watching their mothers, capuchin subadults tend to spend more time watching adult males, who allow youngsters to sit next to them and "scrounge" for bits of food. Even with the close attention young capuchins pay to nut cracking, it's not a skill they master until they're around 3 years old.

In addition to nut cracking, capuchins in a dry forest area of Brazil use stones to dig for roots and tubers (Moura and Lee, 2004) (Fig. 8-13). This is quite significant because until now, no nonhuman primate has been observed using stones for digging.

Capuchins who use stones to crack nuts and dig for roots have one extremely important thing in common with chimpanzees who dig with sticks and hunt galagos with small sharpened branches: they all live in seasonally dry, open woodland, savanna-like environments and not in forests. In general, this is much the same habitat occupied by early hominins. Of course, capuchins and chimpanzees aren't hominins, but those populations that live in more marginal environmental settings face many of the same challenges encountered by early hominins. Moreover, chimpanzees and capuchins are among the most encephalized nonhuman primates and have manipulative abilities similar to those of early hominins. By further studying these behaviors, researchers hope to better understand how savanna-like habitats, where resources are somewhat reduced and unpredictable (compared to forest environments), may have been the context that stimulated the use of tools as a means of obtaining foods that otherwise would have been inaccessible.

Primatologist William McGrew (1992) presented eight criteria for cultural behaviors in nonhuman species (Table 8-1). Of these, the first six were established by the pioneering cultural anthropologist Alfred Kroeber (1928). McGrew (1992) demonstrated that Japanese macaques meet the first six criteria. However, all the macaque examples developed within

Table 8-1 Criteria for Cultural Acts in Other Species

Innovation	New pattern is invented or modified.
Dissemination	Pattern is acquired (through imitation) by another from an innovator.
Standardization	Form of pattern is consistent and stylized.
Durability	Pattern is performed without presence of demonstrator.
Diffusion	Pattern spreads from one group to another.
Tradition	Pattern persists from innovator's generation to the next.
Nonsubsistence	Pattern transcends subsistence.
Naturalness	Pattern is shown in absence of direct human influence.

Source: Adapted from Kroeber (1928) and McGrew and Tutin (1978). In McGrew (1992).

the context of human interference (which isn't to say they all resulted directly from human intervention). To avoid this difficulty, the last two criteria were added later (McGrew and Tutin, 1978).

Capuchins and chimpanzees unambiguously meet the first six criteria, although not all groups meet the last two because most study groups have been at least minimally provisioned. However, all criteria are met by at least some chimpanzees in some instances (McGrew, 1992). While it's obvious that chimpanzees don't possess human culture, we can't overlook the possibility that human culture probably originated in exactly the same kinds of behaviors we've just described in several nonhuman primates. In fact, it's quite possible that these behaviors had already developed before the chimpanzee and human lineages diverged. While sticks and unmodified stones don't remain to tell tales, our early ancestors surely used these same objects as tools in much the same ways as chimpanzees and capuchins do today.

We've made it clear that even though chimpanzees and capuchins modify sticks to make tools, they haven't been observed modifying the stones they use. However, Kanzi, the signing bonobo (see p. 217), learned to strike two stones together to produce sharp-edged flakes. In a study conducted by Sue Savage-Rumbaugh and archaeologist Nicholas Toth, Kanzi was allowed to watch as Toth produced stone flakes, which were then used to open a transparent plastic food container (Savage-Rumbaugh and Lewin, 1994).

Bonobos don't commonly use objects as tools in the wild, and as far as we know, they don't use stones. But Kanzi readily appreciated the usefulness of the flakes in getting food. What's more, he was able to master the basic technique of producing flakes without having been taught the various components of the process, although at first his progress was slow. But eventually, Kanzi realized that if he threw the stone onto a hard floor, it would shatter and he would have an abundance of cutting tools. Although his solution wasn't necessarily the one that Savage-Rumbaugh and Toth expected, it more importantly provided an excellent example of bonobo insight and problem-solving ability. Kanzi did eventually learn to strike two stones together to make flakes, and then he used them to obtain food. This behavior is not only an example of tool manufacture and tool use, albeit in a captive situation; it's also a very sophisticated, goal-directed activity and provides a wonderful example of bonobo problem-solving abilities.

As we said earlier, culture has become the environment in which modern humans live. Quite clearly, catching termites with sticks and cracking nuts with stones are hardly comparable to modern human technology. Even so, modern human technology had its beginnings in these very sorts of behaviors. But this doesn't mean that nonhuman primates are "on their way" to becoming human. Remember, evolution is not goal directed, and if it were, there's nothing to dictate that modern humans necessarily constitute an evolutionary goal. Such a conclusion is a purely **anthropocentric** view, and it has no validity in discussions of evolutionary processes.

Aggression

For many primate species, especially those whose ranges are small, contact with one or more other groups of their own species is a daily occurrence; and the nature of these encounters can vary from one species to another. Primate groups are associated with a *home range*, where they remain permanently. (Although individuals may leave their home range and join another community, the group itself remains in a particular area.) Within the home range is a portion called the **core area**. This area contains the highest concentration of predictable resources, and it's where the group is most likely to be found. Although portions of the home range may overlap with that of one or more other groups, core areas of adjacent groups don't overlap. The core area can also be said to be a group's **territory**, and it's the portion of the home range defended against intrusion. In some species, however, other areas of the home range may also be defended.

Not all primates are territorial. In general, territoriality is associated with species (such as gibbons and vervets) whose ranges are sufficiently small to permit patrolling and protection. But male chimpanzees are highly intolerant of unfamiliar chimpanzees, especially other males, and fiercely defend their territories and resources. Therefore, chimpanzee intergroup interactions almost always include aggressive displays, chasing, and sometimes fighting.

In recent years, a good deal of attention has been focused on coalitionary attacks on conspecifics. Such attacks occur when a number of individuals attack and sometimes kill one or two others who may or may not be members of the same group. Lethal aggression is relatively common between groups of chimpanzees, and it's also been reported for red colobus monkeys (Starin, 1994); spider monkeys, although no actual killings have been observed (Aureli et al., 2006; Campbell, 2006); and capuchin monkeys (Gros-Louis et al., 2003).

Chimpanzees frequently travel to areas where their group's home range borders or overlaps that of another community, and they also occasionally enter another group's territory (Wrangham, 1999; Wilson et al., 2004). These peripheral areas aren't safe, so before they enter them, chimpanzees usually hoot and display to determine if other animals are present. They then become silent and listen for a response. If members of another community appear, some form of aggression occurs until one group retreats. But if the intruding group encounters a lone individual or a female with an infant, they will almost certainly attack it, and if there is an infant, chances are good that it will be killed.

Male chimpanzees (sometimes accompanied by one or two females) also patrol their borders (Fig. 8-14). When patrolling, chimpanzees travel silently in compact groupings. They stop frequently to sniff, look around, or climb tall trees, where they may sit for an hour or more surveying the region. During such times, individuals are tense; a sudden sound, such as a snapping twig, causes them to touch or embrace each other for reassurance (Goodall, 1986). It's apparent

anthropocentric Viewing nonhuman organisms in terms of human experience and capabilities; emphasizing the importance of humans over everything else.

core area The portion of a home range containing the highest concentration and most reliable supplies of food and water. The core area is frequently the area that will be most aggressively defended.

territory The portions of an individual's or group's home range actively defended against intrusion, particularly by conspecifics.

Figure **8-14**

Members of a chimpanzee "border patrol" at Gombe survey their territory from a tree.

from their nervous behavior and uncharacteristic silence that they know they're venturing into a potentially dangerous situation. If a border patrol comes across only one or two strangers, they usually attack. However, if they encounter a group larger than their own, they themselves may be attacked or at least chased as they retreat.

Beginning in 1974, Jane Goodall and her colleagues witnessed at least five unprovoked and extremely brutal attacks by groups of chimpanzees (usually, but not always, males) upon lone individuals. To explain these attacks, we must point out that by 1973, the original Gombe chimpanzee community had split into two distinct groups, one in the north and the other in the south of what was once the original group's home range. In effect, the southern splinter group had denied the others access to part of their former home range.

By 1977, all seven males and one female of the splinter group were either known or suspected to have been killed. All observed incidents involved several animals, usually adult males, who brutally attacked lone individuals (Fig. 8-15). It's impossible to know exactly what motivated the attacks, but it was clear that the attackers intended to incapacitate their victims (Goodall, 1986). Whether chimpanzees intend to actually kill their victims is difficult to know, since, at most, they have a limited concept of death.

The violence at Gombe has continued over the years, although the actual number of observed attacks is low. Wilson and colleagues (2004) have described four cases of aggression between groups at Gombe between 1993 and 2002. In these incidents, two infants were killed and eaten, and two young adult males

Figure **8-15**

The right ulna (the long bone on the little finger side of the forearm) of a female Gombe chimpanzee called Madam Bee. Madam Bee was one of the 1970s attack victims. The enlarged area of the shaft is the site of a healing fracture near the wrist. Apparently the bone was broken in one attack, then rebroken in a subsequent episode. (As her left arm had been paralyzed by polio, she only had her right arm to defend herself.) Madam Bee died within a few days of this last attack.

were severely injured and presumed dead, as they weren't seen again. In all these attacks, the victims were either lone males or mothers with dependent young. And there were always at least four attackers; thus, the risk of injuries to attackers was minimal.

A situation similar to the one at Gombe was also reported for a group of chimpanzees in the Mahale Mountains south of Gombe. Over a 17-year period, all the males of a small community disappeared. Although no attacks were actually observed, there was circumstantial evidence that most of these males met the same fate as the Gombe attack victims (Nishida et al., 1985, 1990).

Even though chimpanzees clearly engage in lethal attacks, the actual number of observed incidents is low. In the period between 1966 and 1999 at Mahale, aggression accounted for 16 percent of known (not presumed) deaths. In all, 18 individuals were known to have been killed by adult males, and all but one were infants. Actually, the major cause of death among the Mahale chimpanzees was disease (48 percent) (Nishida et al., 2003), and this is probably typical of most chimpanzee populations and even early hominin populations. Certainly, in preindustrial modern humans, infant childhood and adolescent mortality was at least 50 percent for most groups.

In chimpanzees and most traditional human cultures, males are philopatric and form lifelong bonds within their social group. Indeed, the core of a chimpanzee community is a group of closely bonded males who, because of their long-term association, act cooperatively in various endeavors, including hunting and attack. In most other primate species, females are the philopatric sex; and in some species (notably macaques and baboons), females may cooperate in aggressive encounters against females from other groups. (Usually these conflicts develop as contests for resources, and they don't result in fatalities.) Generally, then, conflicts between groups of conspecifics may tend to involve members of the philopatric sex. In fact, Manson and Wrangham (1991) suggest that in chimpanzees, lethal aggression is a male activity because males are the philopatric sex. The fact that males are also the philopatric sex in spider monkeys supports this hypothesis. However, this explanation doesn't account for lethal attacks by males in capuchins, in which females are philopatric.

Efforts to identify the social and ecological factors that predispose males of some species to engage in lethal attacks have led to hypotheses that attempt to explain the function and adaptive value of these activities (Cheney, 1987; Manson and Wrangham, 1991; Nishida, 1991). In this context, the benefits and costs of extreme aggression must be identified. The principal benefits to aggressors are protection of territory (and reduced competition for resources) and acquisition of mating partners, especially in cases of infanticide. Costs include risk of injury or death and loss of energy expended in performing aggressive acts, but these risks tend to be reduced, since attacks occur only when the attackers considerably outnumber their victim.

Although we may never have a precise explanation for lethal raiding, it appears that resource acquisition and protection are of major importance (Nishida et al., 1985, 1990; Goodall, 1986; Manson and Wrangham, 1991; Nishida, 1991; Aureli et al., 2006). Through careful examination of shared aspects of human and nonhuman primate social life, we can develop hypotheses regarding how intergroup conflict may have arisen in our own lineage.

Early hominins and chimpanzees may have inherited from a common ancestor the predispositions that have resulted in shared patterns of strife between populations. It's impossible to draw direct comparisons between conflict in nonhuman primates and modern human warfare, owing to later human elaborations of culture, symbols (such as national flags), and language. But it's important to speculate on the fundamental issues that may have led to the development of similar patterns in different species.

Affiliation, Altruism, and Cooperation

In Chapter 7, we briefly discussed affiliative behaviors and the role they play in maintaining group cohesion by reinforcing bonds between individuals. There are also behaviors that indicate just how important such bonds are, and some of them can perhaps be said to be examples of care giving, or compassion.

It's somewhat risky to use the term *compassion* because in humans, compassion is motivated by empathy for another individual. We don't know whether nonhuman primates can empathize with another's suffering or misfortune, but laboratory research has indicated that some of them do. Certainly, there are many examples, mostly from chimpanzee studies, of actions that resemble compassionate behavior in humans. Examples include protecting victims during attacks, helping younger siblings, and remaining near ill or dying relatives or friends.

In a poignant example from Gombe, the young adult female Little Bee brought food to her mother (Madam Bee, see Fig. 8-15 caption) at least twice while the latter lay dying of wounds inflicted by attacking males (Goodall, 1986). When chimpanzees have been observed sitting near a dying relative, they were seen occasionally to shoo flies away or groom the other, as if trying to help in some way.

Altruism

Altruism is behavior that benefits another individual while involving some risk or sacrifice to the performer. It's common in many primate species, and altruistic acts sometimes contain elements of compassion and cooperation. The most fundamental of altruistic behaviors, protecting dependent offspring, is ubiquitous among mammals and birds; and in most species, altruistic acts are confined to this context. However, among primates, recipients of altruistic acts may include individuals who aren't offspring and who may not even be closely related to the performer.

Chimpanzees routinely come to the aid of relatives and friends; female langurs join forces to protect infants from infanticidal males; and male baboons protect infants and cooperate to chase predators. In fact, the primate literature abounds with examples of altruistic acts, when individuals place themselves at some risk to protect others from attacks by conspecifics or predators.

One very intriguing report concerns the attempted rescue of a young adult male baboon who, at some distance from his group, was being chased by a hyena. Suddenly, observers saw an adult female racing toward the hyena in what turned out to be a vain attempt to rescue the male (Stelzner and Strier, 1981; Strier, 2003). The female wasn't the victim's mother, and a female baboon is no match for a hyena. So why would she place herself in serious danger to help an animal to whom, as far as we know, she wasn't closely related?

Adopting orphans is a form of altruism that has been reported for capuchins, macaques, and baboons, and it's common in chimpanzees. When chimpanzee youngsters are orphaned, they're routinely adopted, usually by older siblings who are solicitous and highly protective. Adoption is crucial to the survival of orphans,

altruism Behavior that benefits another individual at some potential risk or cost to oneself.

who certainly wouldn't survive on their own. In fact, it's extremely rare for a chimpanzee orphan less than 3 years old to survive, even if it is adopted.

Evolutionary explanations of altruism are based on the premise that individuals are more likely to perform risky or self-sacrificing behaviors for the benefit of a relative, who shares genes with the performer. According to this hypothesis, known as kin selection, an individual may enhance his or her reproductive success by saving the life of a relative. Even if the performer's life is lost because of the act, the relative may survive to reproduce and pass on genes that both individuals shared.

There's also the idea of reciprocal altruism, where the recipient of an altruistic act (that is, the one who benefits) may later return the favor (the debt to be paid in the future). Coalitions, or alliances, between two or more individuals is an often-cited example of reciprocal altruism, and it's common in baboons and chimpanzees. As we mentioned in Chapter 7, members of alliances support and defend one another in conflicts with others and may use the alliance to increase their status within the group hierarchy. In chimpanzees, members of coalitions are sometimes related, but this isn't always the case. Even though reciprocal altruism may occur, we still haven't explained it, so it's a hypothesis that needs further testing.

Group selection is another hypothesis that some primatologists have supported over the years. According to this model, an individual may act altruistically to benefit other group members because ultimately it's to the performer's benefit that the group be maintained. If the altruist dies, genes he or she shares with other group members may still be passed on (as in kin selection).

But there's a problem with group selection theory: According to natural selection theory, individual reproductive success is enhanced by acting selfishly, and the individual is the object of natural selection. Therefore, supporters of group selection theory argue that natural selection acts not only at the level of the individual, but at the species level as well. But this is a point on which there is much disagreement.

Although the group selection issue hasn't been resolved, we do know that for many reasons discussed in Chapter 7, primates, including humans, have a better chance of surviving and reproducing if they live in groups. Given this important fact, any behavioral mechanism that reinforces the integrity and cohesion of social groupings is to the advantage of individual group members. These mechanisms include altruism, perhaps a form of compassion, and a certain degree of empathy (de Waal, 2005), even if we don't accept all the premises of group selection. And we also know that even though it isn't always obvious, people succeed better when using their highly developed communication skills to solve problems through cooperation instead of aggression.

The Primate Continuum

It's unfortunate that humans generally view themselves as separate from the rest of the animal kingdom. This perspective is, in no small measure, due to a prevailing lack of knowledge about other species' behaviors and abilities. To make matters worse, we're exposed to advertising, movies, and television programs that continuously reinforce these notions.

For decades, behavioral psychology taught that animal behavior represents nothing more than a series of conditioned responses to specific stimuli. (This perspective is convenient for those who exploit nonhuman animals, for whatever purposes, and remain free of guilt.) Fortunately, this attitude has been changing in recent years to reflect a growing awareness that humans, although in many ways unquestionably unique, are nevertheless part of a biological continuum. Indeed, we're also a part of a behavioral continuum.

Where do humans fit, then, in this biological continuum? Are we at the top? The answer depends on the criteria used. Certainly, we're the most intelligent species if we define intelligence in terms of problem-solving abilities and abstract thought. But if we look more closely, we recognize that the differences between ourselves and our primate relatives, especially chimpanzees and bonobos, are primarily quantitative and not qualitative.

Although the human brain is absolutely and relatively larger than those of other primates, neurological processes are functionally the same. The need for close bonding with at least one parent and the need for physical contact are essentially the same. Developmental stages and dependence on learning are strikingly similar. Indeed, even in the capacity for cruelty and aggression combined with compassion, tenderness, and altruism exhibited especially by chimpanzees, we see a close parallel to the dichotomy between "evil" and "good" so long recognized in ourselves. The main difference between how chimpanzees and humans express these qualities (and thus the dichotomy) is one of degree. Humans are much more adept at cruelty and compassion, and we can reflect on our behavior in ways that chimpanzees can't. Like the cat in Chapter 7 that plays with a mouse, chimpanzees don't seem to understand the suffering they inflict on others; but humans do. Likewise, while an adult chimpanzee may sit next to and protect a dying relative or friend, it doesn't seem to feel intense grief and a sense of loss to the extent a human normally does.

To arrive at any understanding of what it is to be human, it's important to recognize that many of our behaviors are but elaborate extensions of those of our hominin ancestors and close primate relatives. The fact that so many of us prefer to bask in the warmth of the "sun belt" with literally thousands of other people reflects our heritage as social animals adapted to life in the tropics. Likewise, the "sweet tooth" seen in so many humans is a direct result of our earlier primate ancestors' predilection for high-energy sugar contained in desirably sweet, ripe fruit. Recognizing our primate heritage is a significant aspect in our exploration of how humans came to be and how we continue to adapt.

Summary

In this chapter, we discussed how biological anthropologists (including primatologists) apply what they've learned about nonhuman primate evolution, life history traits, and behavior to the study of early hominin behavior and adaptations. Although we humans share a common ancestry with all nonhuman primates, our complex behavior and use of language are unique. This uniqueness is related to expansion of the neocortex of the brain since the divergence of the hominin lineage from that of the African great apes.

Because of the importance of neocortical expansion in human evolution, we emphasized some of the evolutionary changes that have occurred in the brain, particularly as they relate to language. Because the brain is such a metabolically expensive organ to maintain, selective pressures favoring increased behavioral complexity would have been enormous. An important source of these pressures may have been living in social groups.

We also described some of the evidence for cultural behavior in nonhuman primates, particularly regarding tool use in various populations. For example, while West African chimpanzees use stones to crack palm nuts, East African populations don't. Some savanna chimpanzees use sharpened sticks to hunt for galagos, and others use sticks to dig for roots. But neither of these behaviors has been seen in forest-dwelling chimpanzees. Likewise, capuchins that inhabit savanna-like environments crack nuts and dig for roots with stones, but forest-dwelling capuchins don't. Variation in cultural behavior and the transmission of these behaviors from one individual to another through observation and learning are hallmarks of human culture. Nonhuman primates exhibit certain aspects of culture, and so do several nonprimate species, although none of these species have adopted culture as an adaptive strategy the way humans have.

Critical Thinking Questions

1. Do you think that knowing about aggression between groups of chimpanzees is useful in understanding conflicts between human societies? Why or why not?
2. What are some examples of cultural behavior in nonprimate species that weren't mentioned in this chapter? Have you personally witnessed such behaviors?
3. Knowing what you currently know, how would you explain the presence of tool-using behaviors in chimpanzees and capuchin monkeys who live in savanna-like environments, while these activities aren't seen in forest-dwelling chimpanzees and capuchins?

Primates

CHAPTER

Overview of the Fossil Primates

Natural History Museum, London

235

Key Questions

What were the oldest primates like, and how do they compare with the most primitive of the living primates (the lemurs and lorises)?

Who are the oldest members of Hominoidea (apes and humans), and how do they compare with their modern counterparts? How do they fit into the primate family tree?

 Click!

Go to the following media for interactive activities and exercises on topics covered in this chapter:

- Online Virtual Laboratories for Physical Anthropology, Version 4.0

strepsirhines (strep-sir´-rines) Members of the primate suborder Strepsirhini, which includes lemurs and lorises.

haplorhines (hap-lore´-ines) Members of the primate suborder Haplorhini, which includes tarsiers, monkeys, apes, and humans.

orthograde An upright body position. This term relates to the position of the head and torso during sitting, climbing, etc., and doesn't necessarily mean that an animal is bipedal.

Introduction

When gazing into the eyes of a great ape, we see in them something unique that we feel inside ourselves. Often, however, when looking into the eyes of a galago ("bush baby"), we see nothing but a cuddly animal that we might like to take home as a pet (see Fig. 6-14, p. 155). When most of us think back to the origins of our own species, we generally stop once we've evoked the idea of an upright-walking ape ancestor. But have you ever considered extending your family tree to the baboons you may see in a wildlife park or to the lemurs or bush babies you see in the zoo? You might think, "How can a creature so small and, well, *animal*-like have anything to do with us or our evolutionary background?" In this chapter, we focus on bridging the gap between these creatures and ourselves—between **strepsirhines** and **haplorhines**—to help us better understand our own evolutionary history.

As we've seen in Chapters 6 through 8, some of our primate cousins share many of the traits we generally think of as uniquely human. Many of these similarities can be traced to shared origins in highly social groups living in the trees. We see these origins in the structure of our body and in the retention of many primitive features, such as pentadactyly (five fingers and toes) and unfused lower arm bones, but also in more "derived" skeletal traits that came later. Among the most important of these derived primate traits are a more **orthograde** (upright) body position and forward-facing eyes. Distinguishing these uniquely primate features in the fossil record, as being different from those traits found in more distantly related mammalian cousins, is the first step in recognizing our own beginnings. As we move in time through the Cenozoic era (see Figure 5-7 in Chapter 5) we see in rough form the recapitulation of our own (Primate) order from "primitive" to highly derived. We'll also trace the development of mammals that resemble us more and more over time until we conclude this chapter in the Miocene, 23 to 5 million years ago (mya), with the emergence of the first hominoids (apes) and then the first possible hominins (humans). As you'll see, our ability to recognize primate families in the fossil record not only uses the same skills that allow us to discover our later human origins, but also allows us to organize these creatures into meaningful groups.

This organization means that you'll face a multitude of taxonomic designations (Fig. 9-2 on p. 238). These names aren't meant to scare you, but they should impress upon you how successful past lineages of primates have been—in fact, much more so than they are now. As you'll see, learning about the earliest beginnings and recent past of our primate order can lend powerful perspective and meaning to our own origins, even though most of the fossil groups discussed in this chapter never led to any living forms, and even fewer are related to our own hominin ancestors.

Background to Primate Evolution: Late Mesozoic

The exact origins of the earliest primates aren't well understood; in fact, they're shrouded in some amount of mystery. We *do* know that following the extinction of the dinosaurs at the end of the Mesozoic, the reign of the giant reptiles was over and the Age of Mammals had begun. Primates were just one of the many groups of small mammals that were left to diversify and explore the many niches left vacant with the passing of the dinosaurs.

It was during the last period of the Mesozoic era (the Cretaceous) that primates began to diverge from closely related mammalian lineages. Some scientists place these closely related ("sister") lineages into a group known as **Euarchonta**. Euarchonta is the **superorder** designated for the sister orders of tree shrews, flying lemurs (also known as the colugos, which don't fly and aren't lemurs), and primates (Fig. 9-1). This diversification of early mammals took place in a global, tropical climate that accompanied the emergence of modern plants—although neither the exact region where primates first evolved nor the precise pressures that molded their adaptations are known. These uncertainties continue to intrigue scientists even today.

With respect to the taxonomic position of many of these early groups, we must introduce a few new concepts. A **stem group** is all of the taxa in a clade *before* a major speciation event. For this reason, stem taxa are often difficult to recognize in the fossil record, since they don't often have the shared derived traits found in the

Euarchonta The superorder designated for the sister (closely related) orders of tree shrews, flying lemurs, and primates.

superorder A taxonomic group ranking above an order and below a class or subclass.

stem group All of the taxa in a clade before a major speciation event. Stem groups are often difficult to recognize in the fossil record, since they don't often have the shared derived traits found in the crown group.

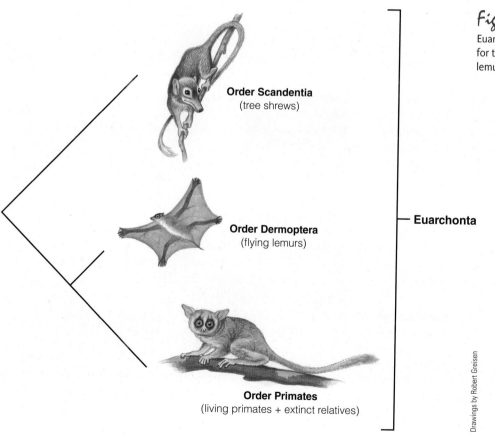

Figure 9-1

Euarchonta. The superorder designated for the sister orders of tree shrews, flying lemurs, and primates.

Order Scandentia
(tree shrews)

Order Dermoptera
(flying lemurs)

Order Primates
(living primates + extinct relatives)

— Euarchonta

Drawings by Robert Greisen

237

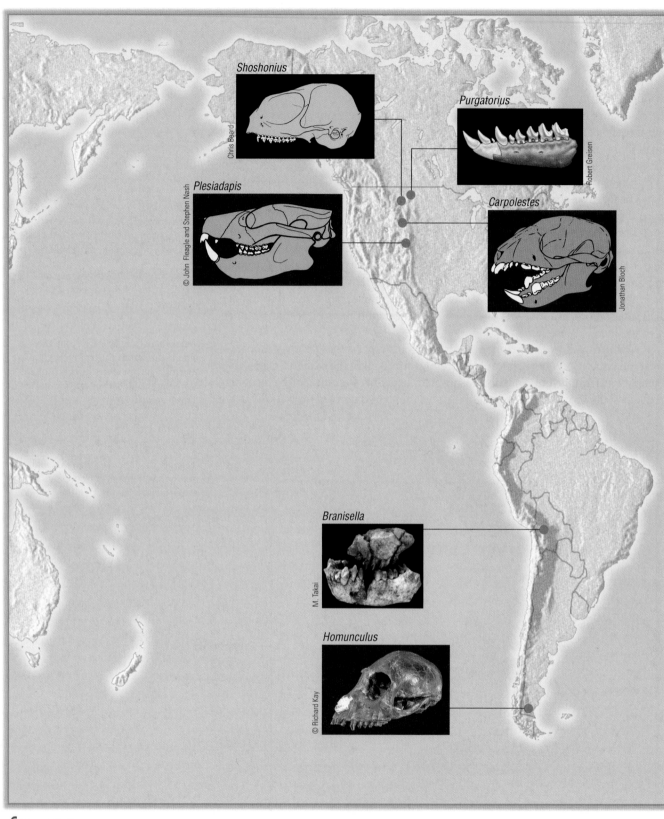

Figure 9-2

A map showing the location of the fossil
primates discussed in this chapter.

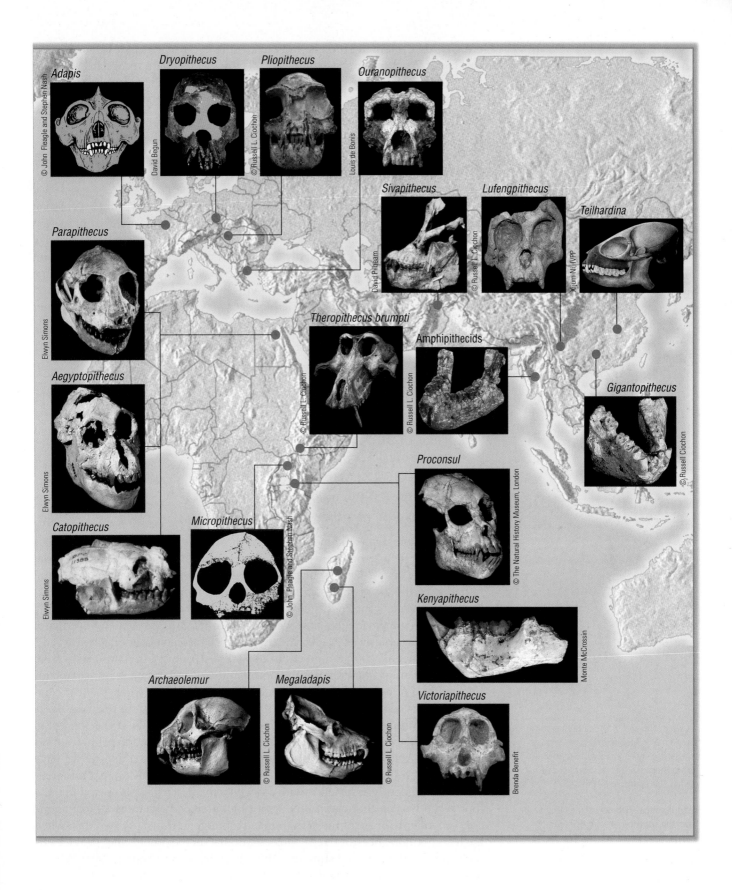

Adapis
© John Fleagle and Stephen Nash

Dryopithecus
David Begun

Pliopithecus
© Russell L. Ciochon

Ouranopithecus
Louis de Bonis

Sivapithecus
David Pilbeam

Lufengpithecus
© Russell L. Ciochon

Teilhardina
Xijum Ni, IVPP

Parapithecus
Elwyn Simons

Aegyptopithecus
Elwyn Simons

Catopithecus
Elwyn Simons

Micropithecus
© John Fleagle and Stephen Nash

Theropithecus brumpti
© Russell L. Ciochon

Amphipithecids
© Russell L. Ciochon

Gigantopithecus
© Russell Ciochon

Proconsul
© The Natural History Museum, London

Kenyapithecus
Monte McCrossin

Victoriapithecus
Brenda Benefit

Archaeolemur
© Russell L. Ciochon

Megaladapis
© Russell L. Ciochon

crown group. A **crown group** is easier to identify because it includes all of the taxa that come *after* a major speciation event. These members are recognized because they possess the clade's shared derived traits. Related to both of these groups is the concept of **sister groups**, two new clades that result from the splitting of a single common lineage.

Primate Origins

The Cenozoic era is the broad time period during which most of primate evolution has unfolded (and continues to unfold). This time period is divided into seven epochs, the oldest of which is called the Paleocene (beginning 65 mya). For each of these broad epochs, we can roughly attribute a particular phase of primate evolution and development. However, evolution knows no temporal bounds, so the time line for these phases will always be imperfectly defined (more precise dates and particular fossil primate groups listed for each epoch will be discussed fully later in this chapter):

- Paleocene (65–55.8 mya; first archaic primates, plesiadapiforms)
- Eocene (55.8–33 mya; first euprimates, early strepsirhines and haplorhines)
- Oligocene (33–23 mya; early catarrhines, precursors to monkeys and apes, emerge)
- Miocene (23–5.3 mya; monkeys and apes emerge; the first humanlike creatures appear)
- Pliocene (5.3–1.8 mya; early hominins diversify)
- Pleistocene (1.8–0.01 mya; early *Homo* develops)
- Holocene (0.01 mya–present; modern humans)

Paleontological evidence indicates that the first indisputable primates emerged just before the Eocene epoch (56 mya). Given that this is the first fossil occurrence, it has led many primate biologists to hypothesize that the initial radiation of archaic primates must have occurred long before this, perhaps during the early Paleocene epoch (65–55.8 mya; Miller et al., 2005; Bloch et al., 2007). Recent molecular evidence, however, has been used to predict the origins of primates to be as early as 90–80 mya, during the Cretaceous period (Tavaré et al., 2002; Martin et al., 2007; Soligo et al., 2007). This disparity in dates arises from the difficulty in reconciling morphological and molecular data in our search for the key time of evolutionary divergence—that is, the time when the last common ancestor between primates and their closest (euarchontan) relatives lived. The **last common ancestor (LCA)** is the hypothetical species that was the last to exist before it speciated into the myriad of sister orders related to primates. This critical species is difficult to pinpoint morphologically, since it doesn't yet have well-defined traits that we can identify as primate, which means that researchers can't confidently associate it with any given fossil. It's for this reason that the time when we can first *confidently* identify an archaic primate is almost assuredly an underestimate of the actual time of divergence (the assumed date when the last common ancestor lived). Molecular data, on the other hand, provides us with what is often an overestimate of this time (Steiper and Young, 2008). What is important to realize, however, is that since molecular estimates are calibrated by using known fossil dates, the two approaches are inextricably linked. Together,

crown group All of the taxa that come after a major speciation event. Crown groups are easier to identify than stem groups because the members possess the clade's shared derived traits.

sister groups Two new clades that result from the splitting of a single common lineage.

last common ancestor (LCA) The final evolutionary link between two related groups.

these two approaches (morphological and molecular) enable us to bracket the origins of indisputable primates at sometime between 90 mya and 65 mya (Steiper and Young, 2008)—a very large swath of time, indeed! However, until more fossil evidence emerges in support of the more ancient genetically predicted date of 90 mya, 65 mya remains the conservative estimate—although there are important implications related to which of the two dates one accepts with regard to what characteristics most properly define our order (see "Evolution of True Lemurs and Lorises," pp. 246–247).

Made to Order: Archaic Primates

Fossil evidence indicates that between 65 and 52 mya, a major radiation of archaic primates, known as the plesiadapiforms, occurred. Plesiadapiforms are members of an extinct group that occupies a controversial position in primate phylogeny. When first discovered, these creatures were considered early members of the primate order, but in the 1960s, this conclusion was reversed and they were treated as their own order, Plesiadapiformes. In recent years, however, the careful analysis of an amazing array of recently discovered fossils has once again placed plesiadapiforms back within Primates (Bloch and Silcox, 2001; Silcox, 2001; Bloch and Boyer, 2002; Bloch et al., 2007). They are now gaining acceptance as a **semiorder** within Primates that is separate from the later **euprimates** (Silcox, 2007).

Plesiadapiforms are best known from a large number of fossil finds from the American West (especially Montana and Wyoming). Some of the more recent finds of these Paleocene mammals, particularly those from Clarks Fork Basin in Wyoming, have yielded a variety of nearly complete skeletons. Some members of this group exhibit a striking continuity of traits with some of the earliest strepsirhines from the later Eocene epoch. Although as many as six families are commonly recognized within this group, we'll concentrate on the three families that are most pertinent for this discussion.

The first family, Purgatoriidae, counts among their numbers the oldest-recognized archaic primate, *Purgatorius* (Clemens, 1974; Fig. 9.3). Members of this extinct genus are believed to have been about the size of modern rats, and at least two (and perhaps as many as four) species lived in the American Northwest during the earliest Paleocene about 65 mya (Lofgren, 1995; Clemens, 2004; Bloch et al., 2007). Evidence of a radiation of this kind, however, most likely indicates an origin in the late Cretaceous. Based on its placement at the base of Euarchonta lineages (think "stem group"), one can hypothesize that unpublished **postcranial** material from the Bug Creek Anthills site (rich in Purgatoriidae) in Montana will include evidence for nails; only time will tell.

Another family, Plesiadapidae, was among the more successful plesiadapiform groups. They were chipmunk- to marmot-sized mammals with large incisors similar to those of a rodent. However, unlike rodents, the plesiadapids had incisors that weren't continuously growing and didn't self-sharpen, suggesting that they used their incisors for a purpose other than gnawing. Some have suggested that this family subsisted on a vegetative diet of leaves supplemented with fruits. The best-known of this family is the genus *Plesiadapis*, which probably originated in North America but went on to colonize Europe via a land bridge across Greenland before eventually dying out.

The last family we'll look at, Carpolestidae (whose name means "fruit stealer"), was quite common during the Paleocene in North America and Asia, although its

semiorder The taxonomic category above suborder and below order.

euprimates "True primates." This term was coined by Elwyn Simons in 1972.

postcranial Referring to all or part of the skeleton not including the skull. The term originates from the fact that in quadrupeds, the body is posterior to the head; the term literally means "behind the head."

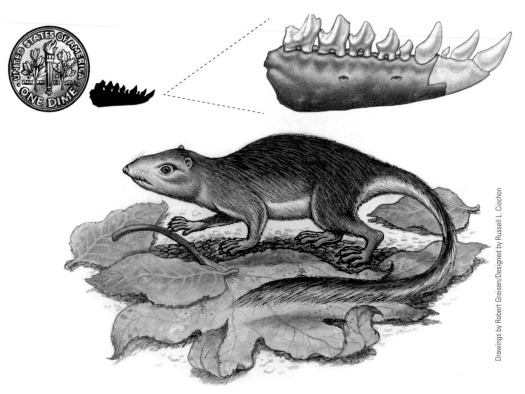

Drawings by Robert Greiser/Designed by Russell L. Ciochon

Figure **9-3**

Artist's representations of *Purgatorius*. (a) Rendering of the best-preserved jaw of *Purgatorius* with the front portion reconstructed. The dime is present to indicate the small scale of the specimen. (b) An artist's depiction of *Purgatorius* based on our current knowledge of the groups to which it belongs. Note in particular, the feet as they tread over the Paleocene sycamore and hackberry leaf litter.

members were never as successful as the plesiadapids. These creatures were much smaller, generally mouse- to rat-sized, though they exhibit the typical enlarged incisors. They also have specialized dental traits that allowed them to efficiently process fibrous vegetation as well as nuts and insects. For a long time, carpolestids were known only from fossil teeth and jaws, but our knowledge of them changed recently when a nearly complete skeleton of *Carpolestes* (Fig. 9-4) was discovered in the Clarks Fork Basin in Wyoming (Bloch and Boyer, 2002). This specimen is estimated at about 3.5 ounces, the size of the average hamster, and its postcranial anatomy reveals many traits adapted to a highly arboreal environment (particularly since it had opposable, grasping big toes with nails instead of claws). But unlike later euprimates that were fully adapted to living in the trees, *Carpolestes* displays no adaptations for leaping, though it was almost certainly a terminal branch feeder (Sargis et al., 2007).

Eocene Euprimates

During the Eocene epoch (55.8–33 mya), we see the gradual extinction of the plesiadapiforms and their replacement by the so-called "primates of modern aspect" (Simons, 1972, p. 174), or the euprimates (Fig. 9-5). These mammals, unlike the plesiadapiforms, have definite recognizable and modern derived primate traits, such as forward-facing eyes, greater encephalization, a postorbital bar, nails instead of claws at the ends of their fingers and toes, and an opposable big toe (see pp. 141–144 for a discussion of basic primate characteristics). These features suggest an adaptation to environmental conditions that were fundamentally different from those experienced by the plesiadapiforms: a warmer climate with year-round rainfall and lush, broad-leaved evergreen forests.

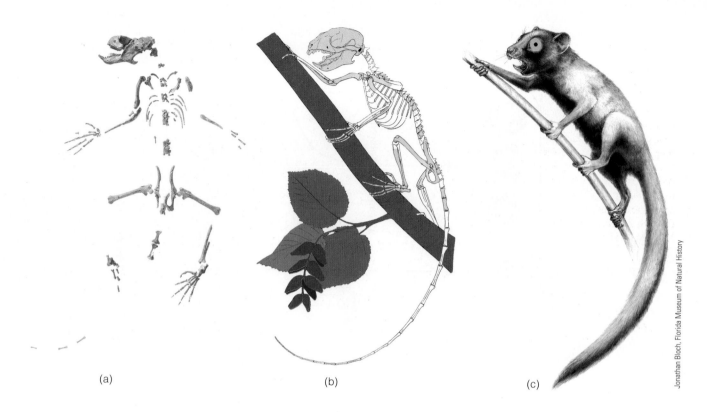

(a) (b) (c)

Jonathan Bloch, Florida Museum of Natural History

Figure **9-4**

Nearly complete skeleton of *Carpolestes* discovered in the Clarks Fork Basin of Wyoming. (a) *Carpolestes* as it was discovered. (b) Reconstructed skeleton of *Carpolestes*. (c) Artist's rendering of *Carpolestes* as it might have looked in life.

At the beginning of the Eocene epoch, North America and Europe were connected; they didn't split apart until the middle Eocene. Meanwhile, during the middle to late Eocene, North America was sporadically connected to Asia via the Bering land bridge. These early connections between these three continents meant that they shared many species in common. In contrast, the continents of Africa, Antarctica, Australia, and South America remained isolated by large bodies of water. These connections and isolations led to a variety of animals of very different characters. In fact, coming at the end of the reign of dinosaurs, the Eocene is a time of rapid diversification for *all* mammals, not just the primates. As a result, the variety of animals known from this time period is much greater than that known from the earlier Paleocene.

Euprimates are part of this wave of diversification. They came on the scene around 56 mya—nearly simultaneously, it seems—in North America, Europe, and Asia. There are two main branches of euprimates, grouped into different superfamilies (Adapoidea and Omomyoidea). These two superfamilies include primitive primates that are described as being either more lemur-like (adapoid) or tarsier- or galago-like (omomyoid). Both groups are well known from cranial, dental, and postcranial remains from North America, Europe, and, increasingly, Asia and Africa.

Lemur-like Adapoids

The adapoids are the best known of the Eocene stem strepsirhines and include more than 35 genera. These are the most primitive of any known primate group, living or dead, as recognized by their dental anatomy. Their primitive dental formula (2.1.4.3; see Chapter 6) provided a generalized ancestral baseline from which many later, more derived varieties of dental specializations could evolve. The adapoids

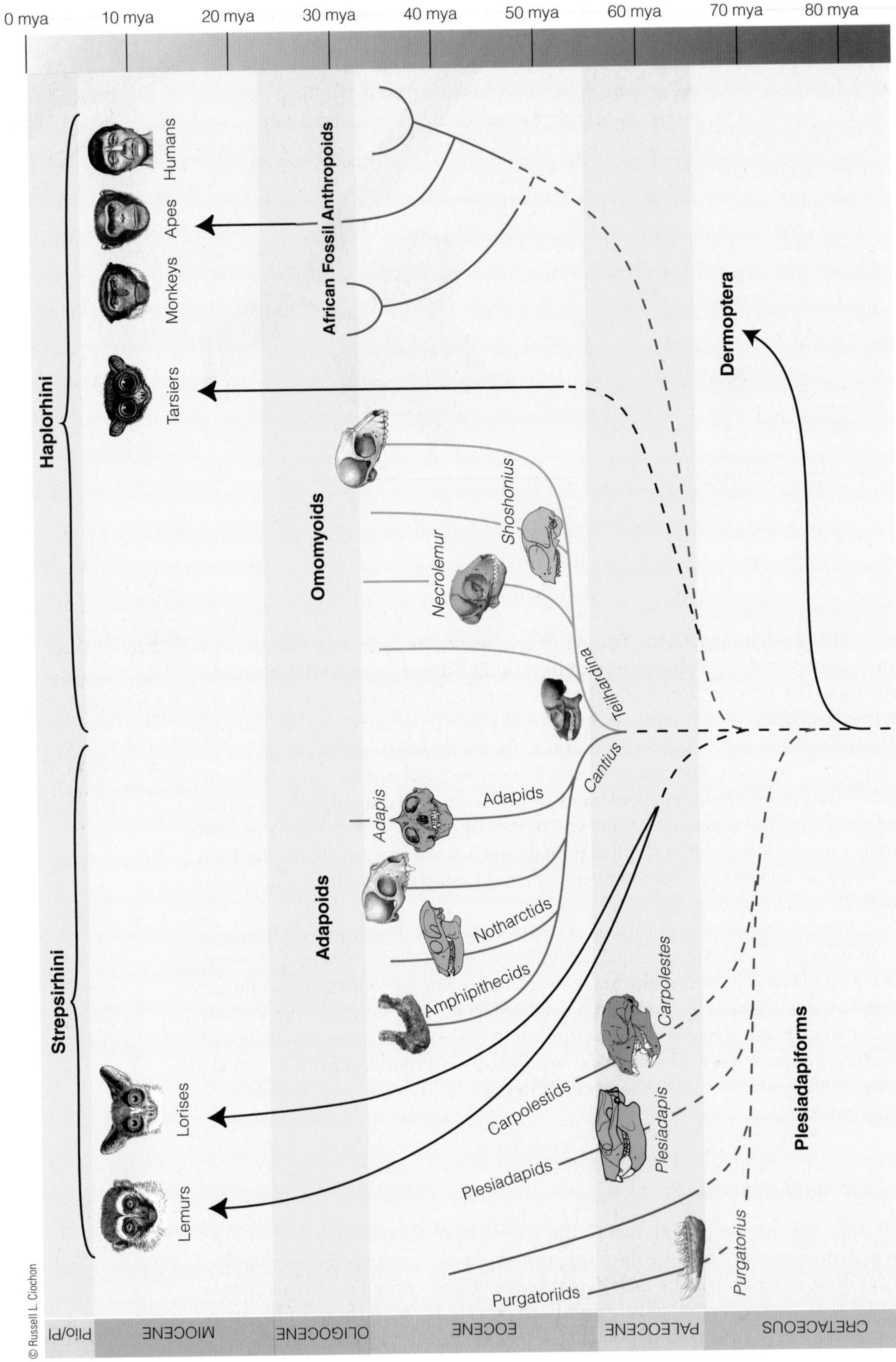

Figure **9-5**

Family tree of euprimates and their relationships to modern strepsirhine and haplorhine groups. Colors represent major groupings within Primates. Red is for the lemur-like adapoids; green is for the tarsier-like omomyoids; purple is for the plesiadapiforms; and blue represents the Fayum early anthropoid radiation. For a taxonomy of living and extinct primates, see Appendix B, pages 514–516.

244

are divided into five families, based mostly on biogeographical distinctions. The most prominent are the notharctids of North America (predominantly), the adapids of Europe, and the amphipithecids of Asia.

Cantius was the earliest notharctid and one of the earliest adapoids in general. This small- to medium-sized animal is known primarily from North America, with just two species from Europe. Cranial and skeletal remains indicate that it was a diurnal creature, foraging during the day. It also probably traveled very rapidly through the trees, leaping quadrupedally. Traits of its mandible and its primitive dental formula of 2.1.4.3 indicate that it was probably a fruit eater.

The second prominent family of adapoids, the adapids, abruptly appeared in Europe near the end of the Eocene and just as quickly became extinct. For this reason, phylogenetic relations for this group are not well understood, although they probably emigrated from another continent, most likely Asia. Perhaps the best known of this group is *Adapis*. Not only was it the first nonhuman fossil primate named, but it was also first described by the well-known nineteenth-century naturalist Georges Cuvier. As you may remember from Chapter 2, Cuvier didn't believe in evolving lineages, even going so far as to state in 1812, "*l'homme fossile n'existe pas*" ("fossil man does not exist"; by this he also meant fossil primates). So it's ironic that in 1822, it was Cuvier who described and named the first fossil primate. Unfortunately for him, he confused the remains for that of an ungulate (a hoofed mammal); shortly after his death in 1837, the fossil was correctly identified as a primate. *Adapis'* dental formula remains primitive (2.1.4.3), and some have argued that an incipient dental comb (a lemur feature; see p. 154) can be recognized in this fossil genus. (You may recall from Chapter 6 that a dental comb is a specialization of the front teeth in the lower jaw; the teeth are elongated and project forward like a small comb.) A slow, arboreal quadruped, *Adapis* most likely spent its time foraging for leaves during the daytime hours.

The third major adapoid family, the amphipithecids from Myanmar (Burma) and Thailand, doesn't fit neatly into any of the preconceived notions about early primates. Amphipithecids had generally been accepted as a dead-end lineage that had its heyday in the Eocene with no Oligocene relations, though recently, just such a primate has been found in Pakistan (Marivaux et al., 2005). Still, even with the new material, this curious family of animals from Asia has many challenging features that are difficult to interpret, with hazy evolutionary affiliations. Some say these creatures are stem anthropoids of some kind (Marivaux et al., 2005); others say they're adapoids. Why the disagreement?

Remember that in Chapter 5 we introduced the terms *homology* (similar traits based on descent) and *homoplasy* (similar traits that evolve independently in different groups) and talked about the example of theropod dinosaurs and birds sharing derived traits. Unlike dinosaurs and birds, however, the amphipithecids are a textbook example of convergent evolution: Their seemingly "anthropoid" traits are actually homoplasies, not shared derived traits. Their teeth in particular can be somewhat deceiving. Since both early anthropoids and amphipithecids were exploiting the same dietary niche, they developed similar dental patterns. On the other hand, the postcranial skeleton and mandibles (Fig. 9-6) of amphipithecids betray their true affiliation as more primitive but specialized adapoids that exploited a slow-moving arboreal niche (Ciochon and Gunnell, 2002). For many years, the amphipithecid dental pattern confounded researchers; but with the discovery of more complete specimens, this mystery has now been solved. It seems that these remarkable adapoids, alone in Asia and in the absence of anthropoids, converged on the anthropoid dental pattern.

Figure **9-6**

The teeth of the amphipithecids are misleading, but their mandibles betray their true phylogenetic affinity as lower primates.

© Russell L. Ciochon

Evolution of True Lemurs and Lorises

As we've mentioned, the adapoids were fairly lemur-like in their overall pattern, and they show distinctive primate tendencies. Although the ancient adapoids do resemble lemurs in overall anatomical body plan, this is mostly due to modern lemurs retaining some ancestral traits. The adapoid fossils don't show the same specializations seen in crown members of lemurs, galagos, and lorises, such as development of the dental comb. For this reason, we may say that modern-day lemurs, galagos, and lorises have retained many "primitive" aspects of anatomy, but there's no clear evolutionary relationship between the Eocene adapoids and these latter-day creatures (but see Kay et al., 2004; Ross et al., 2004).

It's important to note that the evolution of lemurs and other strepsirhines is of great interest to researchers because of their basal position as the sister group to all other primate lineages (Horvath and Willard, 2008; Horvath et al., 2008). Accordingly, information related to their initial emergence and dispersal can be used to time subsequent primate divergence dates.

Lorisoids (lorises and galagos) are the earliest examples of strepsirhine primates in the fossil record. These small, primitive creatures have been found in late Eocene deposits of the Fayum Depression in Egypt, an area that we'll discuss in more detail next. A late Eocene (~34 mya) fossil find from Egypt appears to have had a dental comb (Stevens and Heesy, 2006). This and other features have led to the conclusion that it's a stem galagid. When combined with molecular evidence (Seiffert et al., 2003), it can be inferred that lorises and galagos likely diverged by the close of the middle Eocene.

The existence of an early African bush baby in Egypt during this time indicates that stem strepsirhines were from the African mainland. These primates likely colonized Madagascar to give rise to crown lemuriforms. This would mean that lemurs have *never* existed outside of this tiny island (Seiffert et al., 2005a). The colonization itself most likely occurred by crossing the Mozambique Channel, perhaps by unintentionally rafting over on drifting debris (Yoder et al., 1996, 2003; Kappeler, 2000), though other biogeographical mechanisms have been suggested (McCall, 1997; Arnason et al., 2000). This phenomenon of migration on drifting debris is described in "A Closer Look," on page 257. As we'll see, this is also the suggested explanation for how monkeys originally colonized South America.

There are few, if any, truly fossilized lemur remains in Madagascar; but there are numerous **subfossil** lemurs. These unfossilized skeletal remains are too recent to have become completely mineralized into fossils. Many of these extinct subfossil lemurs were colossal compared to the lemurs of today—some of them were up to five times as big! Despite their large size, they were mostly tree-dwelling and possibly even diurnal. Most interesting of all, many filled unusual ecological niches not shared by any living lemurs. Many of these peculiar adaptations provide examples of convergence with higher primate niches found elsewhere in the Old World. For instance, the extinct *Archaeolemur* (Fig. 9-7), with its fused mandible and **bilophodont** molars, in many ways more closely resembled a monkey than the 37-pound lemur that it was (Fleagle, 1999). What's more, the sulcal (grooved) pattern of *Archaeolemur's* brain was similar to that seen in higher primates (Martin, 1990). Based on this evidence, we can see this group as converging on a monkey-like role on a monkey-less island.

The best known of the giant lemurs, however, was the 170-pound *Megaladapis*. Built more like a gorilla than a lemur (another incident of convergence), this specialized forest dweller lost its livelihood when the trees were cleared for farmland with the appearance of humans on the island. Sadly, the *Megaladapis* story isn't unusual; most of the 16 subfossil species discovered went extinct within the last 2,000 years—at the same time that humans began colonizing the island. Many believe that the predation and deforestation carried out by these early peoples caused the extinction of these massive forms. Unfortunately, the remaining lemurs of Madagascar will meet the same fate unless the continued destruction to their habitat ceases.

subfossil Bone not old enough to have become completely mineralized as a fossil.

bilophodont Referring to molars that have four cusps oriented in two parallel rows, resembling ridges, or "lophs." This trait is characteristic of Old World monkeys.

Figure **9-7**

Comparison of the skull of *Archaeolemur* (left) and a macaque monkey. Note how the lemur resembles the monkey in the shape of the jaw, teeth, and overall cranial form. This is an excellent example of convergent evolution.

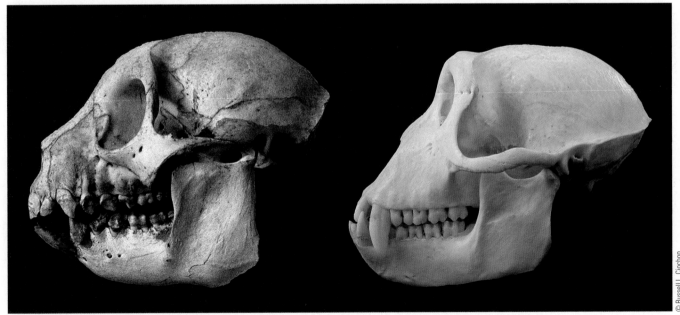

© Russell L. Ciochon

A Closer Look

The Lost World

In many ways, Madagascar is the island that time left behind. Just off the eastern coast of the African nation of Mozambique, Madagascar has proved an incubator for all manner of curious creatures. Over 70 percent of the 250,000 species native to Madagascar are found nowhere else in the world! Among its living menagerie are the brookesia chameleon—at just over an inch long, one of the world's smallest reptiles; the fossa, perhaps best described as a mongoose on steroids; and the strange hedgehog- and shrew-like tenrecs. Absent are the standard African fare of apes, monkeys, elephants, giraffes, lions, and rhinoceroses, among many others. Now vanished from the island are the giant tortoises, pygmy hippopotamuses, and flightless elephant birds (the world's largest birds, over 10 feet tall!) of the past, as well as fully one-third of all identified lemur species that are known to have ever existed, including all species over 22 pounds (Goodman and Benstead, 2003).

Unlocking the key to Madagascar's diversity has long been a holy grail of biologists. The insular nature of island environments is known to have dramatic effects on the animals within their bounds (see "A Closer Look," p. 120). The microclimates found within this Texas-sized island contribute to the differences seen; highland areas are hot and humid, while low-lying regions are arid. Among living lemurs, larger species tend to inhabit the higher, wetter regions, whereas smaller species tend to inhabit the lower, arid regions (Godfrey et al., 1990). This phenomenon has led to limited distribution of many species within Madagascar, a condition known as "micro-endemism" (Goodman, 2008).

The subfossil lemurs are in many ways even more fantastic than their already amazing living relatives. Coupled with the effects of island gigantism and the general super-sizing of animals toward the Ice Age, subfossil lemurs are known to have grown to gargantuan proportions! But for a long time, it was questioned just how lemur-like these ancient forms were, given that their body size more closely resembles that of living anthropoids, such as baboons and gorillas. The "sloth," "koala," and "monkey" lemurs, while un-lemur-like in their size, actually had much in common

Figure 1

Paleoanthropologist, Laurie Godfrey, measures subfossil lemur limb bones in Madagascar. Many of these creatures were significantly larger than their modern-day counterparts.

with their latter-day forms. Like living lemurs, the subfossils are found in forested environments and may have exhibited female dominance in their social structure—an extraordinary display of "girl power," where females win the majority of aggressive confrontations with males. Their victories, however, are not related to their superior size or strength, so the pattern of sexual dimorphism in these species is not reversed, but neither is it marked. The resulting lack of big canines relative to body size makes the subfossil and living lemurs very different from most living anthropoids (Godfrey et al., 2006).

Subfossil lemurs, because of their size and reconstructed positional and locomotor behavior, also likely shared a relatively energy-conserving lifestyle with their modern counterparts. This means that they probably lived in small groups exploiting only locally available resources that were subject to Madagascar's notorious extreme seasonality. This seasonality of resources has been present for thousands of years, precipitating many unique adaptations in the island's animal inhabitants. Unlike many living lemurs, omnivorous forms were more prevalent in the past, often eating hard seeds and other fibrous foods along with the ubiquitous leaves. Additionally, all ancient forms were diurnal, unusual for many strepsirhines, though their eyesight was unlikely to have been as sharp as that of anthropoids of the same size. In all, the picture of subfossil lemurs emerges as a group similar in size to anthropoids, but with great affinity to their more petite strepsirhine relatives in daily life and behavior (Godfrey et al., 2006).

Unfortunately, the large size, slow locomotion, and diurnality of subfossil lemurs may have contributed to their destruction by humans. Evidence abounds of lemur bones scarred with cut marks like those associated with skinning, disarticulation, and filleting. This evidence of megafaunal butchery coincides with the earliest period of human colonization of the island around 2,300 years ago (Perez et al., 2005). The same constrained island bounds that led to the subfossil lemurs' diversity and success likely had a role in their annihilation. Hunting them was probably like "shooting monkeys in a barrel."

Tarsier-like Omomyoids

The tarsier-like omomyoids, the earliest haplorhine group, are more taxonomically diverse than the adapoids. They're often called tarsier-like because the European specimens of this group more closely resemble the tarsier, though no specific phylogenetic connection has yet been made. They have a similar dental formula (1.1.3.3), large orbits, and small snouts. Earlier members of this group are somewhat more generalized than later ones, and some researchers believe they represent the stock for all later haplorhines—that is, tarsiers, New World monkeys, Old World monkeys, apes, and humans (Ross, 2000). **Paleoprimatologists** have recognized this successful radiation from primarily the Eocene and early Oligocene of North America and Europe, with a small number known from Asia.

Members of the genus *Teilhardina* (Fig. 9-8) are found on three continents (although a new analysis disputes whether all the attributed material belongs in the same genus; see Tornow, 2008). The fossil record appears to show that the earliest euprimates (including all adapoids and omomyoids) engaged in a rapid westward dispersal with evidence pointing to Asia as the euprimates' starting point. In fact, analysis of related species of *Teilhardina* has shown that the oldest and most primitive members were from Asia, while the youngest were from North America. This evidence would tend to support a westward migration of euprimates from Asia, through Europe, and eventually to North America (Smith et al., 2006; Fig. 9-9). A brand new species of *Teilhardina* recently unearthed in Mississippi, however, has challenged this view. If the fossils of this coastal dweller are as old as they are purported to be, it would predate those in Europe, meaning that the genus actually moved from Asia to North America before finally moving into western Europe (Beard, 2008). It is important to recognize, however, that standard carbon isotope evidence has been notably omitted from the published study (Gingerich et al., 2008). Without this evidence, it's difficult to accept the early date of the Mississippi *Teilhardina* on face value.

Other Eocene fossils, of the family Omomyidae, from North America (*Shoshonius*) and Europe (*Necrolemur*) are also thought to be closely related to the tarsier. Like modern tarsiers, these animals apparently possessed large convergent eye orbits as well as details of the ear region that unite them to the tarsier group. In addition, there is some evidence that *Necrolemur* may have had a fused tibia

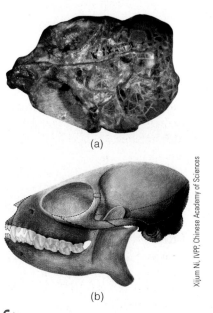

(a)

(b)

Xijun Ni, IVPP, Chinese Academy of Sciences

Figure **9-8**

Teilhardina. (a) View of the skull of *Teilhardina* from the top. (b) An artist's reconstruction of *Teilhardina*, with areas in gray representing missing fragments.

paleoprimatologists Anthropologists specializing in the study of the nonhuman primate fossil record.

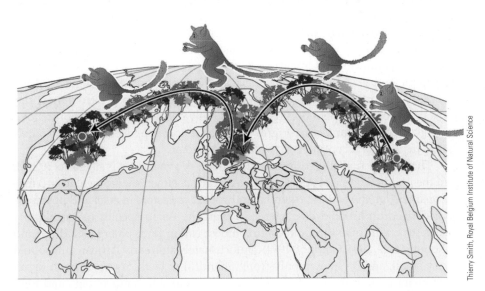

Thierry Smith, Royal Belgium Institute of Natural Science

Figure **9-9**

The rapid westward dispersal of euprimates of the genus *Teilhardina*. Analysis of related species of *Teilhardina* shows that the oldest and most primitive members were from Asia, while the youngest were from North America.

and fibula as well as an elongated calcaneus, a lever-like construction (much like that seen in a jackrabbit) that gives modern tarsiers their fantastic leaping abilities. However, many researchers believe that these similarities are superficial ones, not necessarily indicating any unique (that is, shared derived) relationship. Even so, at least one feature, the position of the olfactory portion of the brain that processes scent, links these Eocene forms with later tarsiers, though not with anthropoids (Fleagle, 1999).

Evolution of True Tarsiers

For many years, "the 'living fossil' [had] no fossil record!" (Schwartz, 1984, p. 47). However, the situation has recently improved. Fragmentary remains of fossil tarsiers (a single jaw and isolated teeth) are now known from Egypt, China, and Thailand. In addition, the first cranial remains of an early tarsier have been described. Amazingly enough, these remains are "virtually identical to the corresponding anatomy in living tarsiers" (Rossie et al., 2006, p. 4381). From these fossils it's been generally concluded that modern tarsiers have retained essentially the same body plan that they had in the Eocene. Biomolecular evidence has shown that the five extant (currently existing) species of tarsiers diverged in the Miocene (Wright et al., 2003); and as you learned in Chapter 6, all living tarsiers are now limited to a few islands in Southeast Asia.

Toward the end of the Eocene, there was a shift from tropical to drier and more seasonal climates. This change led to more diverse landscapes, opening many niches for the highly adaptable primates to exploit. This backdrop sets the stage for our next saga in primate origins—that of our own infraorder, Anthropoidea. Of course, tarsiers and strepsirhine primates have continued to evolve since the Eocene, but we'll now focus on those primates most directly related to our own evolution as humans.

Eocene and Oligocene Early Anthropoids

It's important to realize that when we're trying to interpret the past, things aren't as straightforward as they first seem. In addition to the debate about the earliest emergence of strepsirhines and tarsiers (and therefore the most "primitive" members of Primates), we're equally unsure about the origins of anthropoid primates—the ones that eventually led to apes and monkeys, as well as to our own lineage.

In recent years, new discoveries have led scientists to dispute an adapoid or even omomyoid origin of anthropoids. Instead, some recent molecular evidence indicates that anthropoid primates probably emerged *separately* from either of these two groups; and at 77 mya, they may have a time depth as ancient as either (Miller et al., 2005). Unfortunately, fossil anthropoid remains aren't known from that time, so the cradle of anthropoid origins remains hotly debated. Some paleoprimatologists have suggested an Asian origin, while most now support an African source, which was an island continent in the late Cretaceous.

The earliest undisputed fossil anthropoid, *Algeripithecus*, is dated to 50 mya from the middle Eocene of Algeria. This African specimen shows up at least 3 million years before the earliest potential anthropoid ancestors in Asia and possesses more derived anthropoid characteristics than the Asian specimens, precluding Asia as the cradle of anthropoid origins unless earlier finds emerge (Godinot and Mahboubi, 1992, 1994; Godinot, 1994). Unfortunately, this early African anthropoid is very small, and it's known only from a handful of teeth. So it's difficult to say much about it other than that its teeth are unmistakably "anthropoid" and foreshadow other early anthropoids from the late Eocene of Egypt.

The Fayum Depression in Egypt (see "A Closer Look," p. 252), an arid region today, provides most of our early anthropoid record for the Eocene and Oligocene. Over the last five decades, paleoprimatologist Elwyn Simons and colleagues have excavated this rich area and found a remarkable array of fossil primates. One of the most recent discoveries, a new species of *Biretia*, is precisely dated to 37 mya and represents the most complete remains of an early African anthropoid. This small primate, weighing just under a pound, exhibits dental morphology typical of that expected for a basal (most primitive) anthropoid. Surprisingly, though, the structure of the upper molar tooth roots points to large orbits, implying that *Biretia* was nocturnal (Seiffert et al., 2005b). This is interesting because as discussed in Chapter 6 (see p. 142), the general trend for Anthropoidea is toward a diurnal activity pattern. Simons has placed these fossils, based on their dental characters, into the extinct superfamily Parapithecoidea. This superfamily is significant as the root stock from which the entire New World anthropoid evolutionary group (that is, clade; see p. 114) evolved.

Its later Oligocene evolution (Seiffert et al., 2005b) is discussed in the next section. Somewhat younger (35 mya) Fayum primate genera from the family Oligopithecidae, including *Catopithecus* (Fig. 9-10), clearly possessed anthropoid

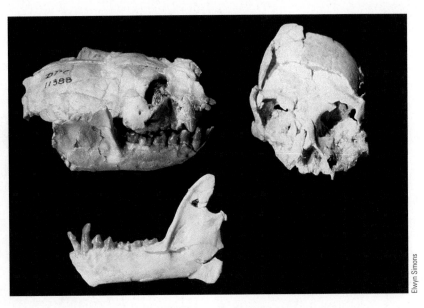

Elwyn Simons

Figure 9-10

Three specimens of *Catopithecus*, the earliest anthropoid genus to preserve a skull. These elements give us our first view of early catarrhine cranial anatomy, including fully enclosed orbits.

At a Glance

Lemuriform vs. Anthropoid Characteristics

GENERAL LEMURIFORM CHARACTERISTICS	GENERAL ANTHROPOID CHARACTERISTICS
1. Smaller body size	1. Generally larger body size
2. Longer snouts with greater emphasis on smell	2. Shorter snouts with greater emphasis on vision
3. Eye sockets not completely enclosed in bone	3. Back of eye socket formed by bony plate
4. Dental comb	4. Less specialized dentition, as seen in absence of dental comb and some other features
5. Small, simple premolars	5. Larger and more complex premolars
6. Primitive triangle-shaped molars	6. Derived square-shaped molars with new cusp
7. Grooming claw	7. Nails instead of claws on all digits
8. Artery running through the bone of the middle ear	8. Loss of the artery running through the bone of the middle ear
9. Unfused mandible	9. Fusion of the two sides of the mandible to form one bone
10. Unfused frontal bone	10. Fusion of the two sides of the frontal bone
11. Smaller brain size relative to body size	11. Larger brain (in absolute terms and relative to body weight)

See Appendix A, Fig. A-9A and A-9B for illustrations of these differences.

A Closer Look

Primate Diversity in the Fayum

Today El-Fayuom, or the Fayum, is an Egyptian province about 40 miles southwest of Cairo. In the Eocene and Oligocene epochs, it was a swampy forest playground for primates. Now all that's left of that primate Eden is chunks of petrified wood, flotsam adrift in the vast desert of the Sahara. The name Fayum probably comes from the ancient Egyptian word *Baym*, meaning "lake or sea" and referring to the area's proximity to a large lake near the Nile. Nowadays, though, the last thing anyone would associate with this arid region is a body of water.

In 1906, the first primate ever discovered in Egypt was unearthed and later identified as *Apidium*. Many considered this discovery, hailed as a "dawn ape," to be the earliest relative of apes and monkeys. Though several primate fossils were discovered in the early 1900s, it wasn't until 1961 that the dogged persistence of Elwyn Simons led to the unearthing of the Fayum's true fossil primate abundance. Fifty years later, Simons still coaxes dry bones from the sand of the Fayum. Through the efforts of Simons and colleagues (Fig. 1), the Fayum primates are the best-studied fossils in the region and far and away the most abundant late Eocene and Oligocene finds from anywhere in the world, and they shape many of our views regarding the diversification of strepsirhines, tarsiers, monkeys, and apes. These fossils are often referred to as the "lower sequence primates" and "upper sequence primates," according to their placement in the stratigraphic section. From these Eocene (lower) and Oligocene (upper) sediments, over 17 genera are known, presenting us with a wide variety of dietary niches. What's most surprising, however, is that the strepsirhines and some anthropoids exploit a frugivorous (fruit-eating) lifestyle, challenging the idea that ecological changes might account for the emergence of the latter group (Kirk and Simons, 2001). So, for the time being, anthropoid origins remain as enigmatic as the sphinx.

Figure 1

Elwyn Simons and colleagues toil in the harsh heat of the Fayum in Egypt while collecting fossils of the earliest anthropoids. These fossils are so small that workers must excavate with their faces pressed close to the ground.

features (such as complete postorbital closure) and some derived **catarrhine** features (such as a 2.1.2.3 dental formula).

These Fayum discoveries help fill in the gap between later anthropoids and the middle Eocene anthropoids of Algeria. The earliest fossil anthropoids are known from Africa, and current molecular and biogeographical data agree that anthropoids had an African origin, much like the African origin of our own genus, *Homo* (Miller et al., 2005).

Oligocene Primates

The vast majority of Old World primate fossils of the Oligocene epoch (33–23mya) come from just one region, the Fayum Depression in Egypt—the same area that has yielded abundant late Eocene remains. Altogether, well over 1,000 specimens have been retrieved from the Fayum, representing a paleontological record of what was once an extremely rich primate ecosystem.

True Anthropoids

The early stem primates of the Oligocene are generally placed into three families: the oligopithecids, parapithecids, and propliopithecids. Members of the oligopithecid family are among the earliest anthropoid primates, and they're known from key fossil discoveries from the late Eocene of the Fayum in Egypt. One of these early taxa, *Catopithecus* (mentioned earlier), is represented by several crushed crania. Analyses of these fragmentary remains, with their complete postorbital closure and derived 2.1.2.3 dental formula, have led paleoprimatologists to conclude that *Catopithecus* is the earliest catarrhine.

The most abundant of the Oligocene fossils from the Fayum are from the parapithecid family, and they belong to the genus *Apidium*. About the size of a squirrel, *Apidium* had several anthropoid-like features, but it also possessed some unusual dental features. *Apidium* fossils exhibit a dental formula of 2.1.3.3, indicating that *Apidium* probably appeared before the Old and New World anthropoids diverged. As noted, this makes it a candidate as an early ancestor of New World anthropoids (that is, **platyrrhines**; Fig. 9-11). The teeth also suggest a diet composed of fruits and probably some seeds. Another interesting feature suggests something about this animal's social behavior; an unusually large degree of sexual dimorphism in canine size may indicate that *Apidium* lived in polygynous social groups of a single male and multiple females and offspring. Limb remains show that this creature was a small arboreal quadruped, adept at leaping and springing. We now know much more about the cranial anatomy of the parapithecids

catarrhine Member of Catarrhini, a parvorder of Primates, one of the three major divisions of the suborder Haplorhini. It contains the Old World monkeys and the apes.

platyrrhines Members of Platyrrhini, a parvorder of Primates, one of the three major divisions of the suborder Haplorhini. It contains only the New World monkeys.

Figure **9-11**

Diagram of the phyletic relationships (cladogram) of Fayum early anthropoids and living catarrhines (monkeys, apes, and humans). (Adapted from Fig. 13-18 in Fleagle, 1999, p. 418.)

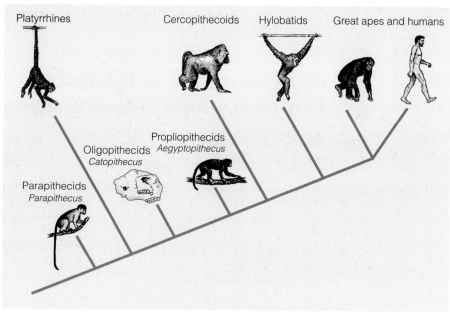

Figure 9-12

Parapithecus belongs to the group of Fayum anthropoids that are most closely related to the ancestry of New World monkeys.

Figure 9-13

Skull of *Aegyptopithecus*. This genus has been proposed as the ancestor of *both* Old World monkeys and hominoids.

thanks to the discovery of a complete skull of the genus *Parapithecus* (Fig. 9-12), a close relative of *Apidium*.

The third major family, the propliopithecids, includes the most significant fossil genus from the Fayum, *Aegyptopithecus* (Fig. 9-13). This genus has been proposed as the ancestor of both later Old World monkeys and hominoids. *Aegyptopithecus* is known from several well-preserved crania, numerous jaw fragments, and a fair number of limb bones. The largest of the Fayum anthropoids, *Aegyptopithecus* was roughly the size of a modern howler monkey at 13 to 18 pounds, with considerable sexual dimorphism. With a dental formula of 2.1.2.3, *Aegyptopithecus* shares the derived catarrhine (Old World anthropoid) dental formula. The skull was small and resembles a modern monkey skull in certain details, while the brain size appears to have been at best strepsirhine-like and at worst non-primate-like. In fact, a reappraisal of intracranial size has determined that given the small brain size of this genus, greater encephalization must have evolved independently within the two anthropoid parvorders, Platyrrhini and Catarrhini (Simons, 2007). Postcranial evidence reveals that *Aegyptopithecus* was likely a short-limbed, heavily muscled, slow-moving arboreal quadruped. So in most respects, *Aegyptopithecus* represents a primitive catarrhine; this makes it the best candidate from the Fayum to have given rise to Old World monkeys, apes, and humans.

Early Platyrrhines: New World Anthropoids

The first primates found in the New World date to around 27 mya, about 10 million years after fossil evidence for the first anthropoids appears in the Fayum of Egypt. However, they probably evolved from ancestors similar to those seen within the parapithecids of the Fayum primate radiation. The earliest platyrrhine, or New World anthropoid, fossils are found in the late Oligocene of Bolivia and have been placed into the genus *Branisella*. Members of this genus appear to have been small monkeys (about 2 pounds), with diets comprised primarily of fruit. The evolutionary relationships of these first fossil platyrrhines are still greatly debated. *Branisella* is thought to be so primitive that it's not placed in any living platyrrhine lineage; it may represent a remnant of the first platyrrhine radiation. Molecular evidence supports this view, as living platyrrhines converge on a shared ancestor that is only 20 million years old (Hodgson et al., 2009a). Another member of this

At a Glance

New World Monkey vs. Old World Monkey Characteristics

GENERAL NEW WORLD MONKEY CHARACTERISTICS	GENERAL OLD WORLD MONKEY CHARACTERISTICS
1. Sideways-facing nostrils 2. Ringlike ear hole with no tube 3. Dental formula of 2.1.3.3 4. Grasping tail 5. Distribution: Mexico and South America See Appendix A, Fig. A-10 for illustrations of these differences.	1. Downward-facing nostrils 2. Tubelike ear hole 3. Dental formula of 2.1.2.3 4. Ischial callosities 5. Distribution: Africa, southern Asia, and Japan

mysterious early radiation—*Homunculus* (meaning "miniature human")—appears in the middle Miocene. A cranium of this creature was found in Argentina in 2004 embedded in volcanic ash dated to 16.5 mya (Fig. 9-14). *Branisella* and *Homunculus* represent different side branches from the clade of living New World monkeys that includes the last common ancestor of extant platyrrhines (Fig. 9-15). But this doesn't mean that they have nothing to tell us about modern platyrrhines. As remnants of the earliest New World radiation, these fossils open a window through which we can begin to view the first primate colonizers of South America.

Based on the presence of the first platyrrhines in South America at 27 mya, it's likely that the very first anthropoids arrived in the New World somewhat earlier, probably during the late Eocene (45–35 mya). In fact, recent molecular data indicate that the platyrrhine-catarrhine (New World–Old World anthropoid) lineages diverged approximately between 50 and 35 mya, with a conservative estimate of 43 mya (Steiper and Young, 2006). This early transatlantic migration would have

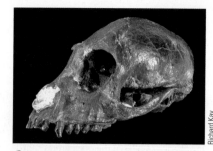

Richard Kay

Figure **9-14**

Skull of *Homunculus*, a middle Miocene descendant of the earliest platyrrhine radiation.

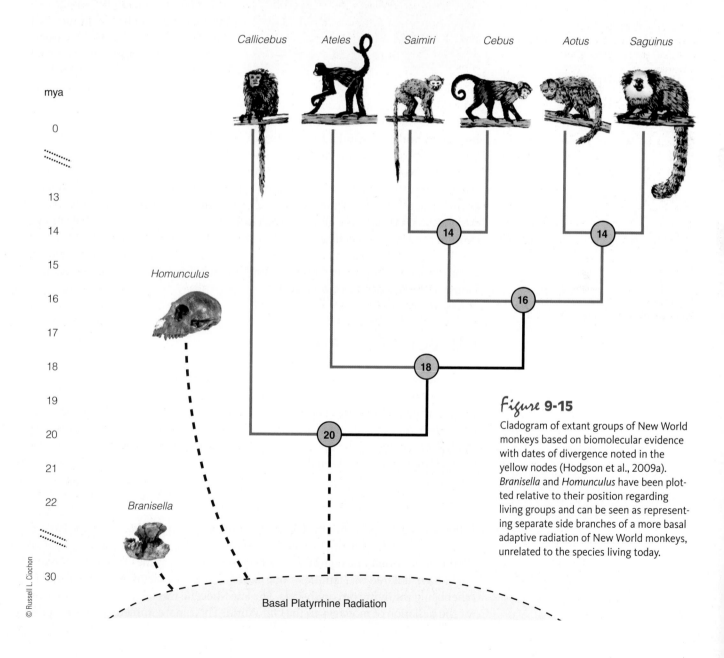

© Russell L. Ciochon

Figure **9-15**

Cladogram of extant groups of New World monkeys based on biomolecular evidence with dates of divergence noted in the yellow nodes (Hodgson et al., 2009a). *Branisella* and *Homunculus* have been plotted relative to their position regarding living groups and can be seen as representing separate side branches of a more basal adaptive radiation of New World monkeys, unrelated to the species living today.

Overview of the Fossil Primates

Figure 9-16

Here are the continental relationships during the late Eocene. Several competing theories have been proposed in an attempt to explain the arrival of platyrrhines in South America: North American migration, Antarctic migration, and South Atlantic migration (by way of rafting or island hopping). The broken white line and surrounding shades of blue in the ocean represent seafloor spreading, which caused the continents to drift apart.

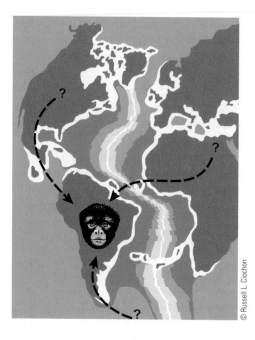

© Russell L. Ciochon

involved the crossing of some sort of oceanic barrier, since South America was an island continent until 5 mya. How platyrrhines arrived in the New World in general, and in South America in particular, remains one of the most fascinating questions in primate evolution (Fig. 9-16). Several competing theories have been proposed in an attempt to explain the mysterious arrival of platyrrhines in South America: North American migration, Antarctic migration, and Atlantic "rafting."

The scenario for a North American migration route argues that one of the North American tarsier-like omomyoids journeyed down to South America, giving rise to the later platyrrhines. An alternative scenario contends that migration could have been accomplished by passing through the Antarctic—first crossing by water from Africa south to Antarctica and then crossing a land bridge that linked Antarctica to South America.

The most likely scenario for the arrival of platyrrhines to South America, however, involves their floating across the Atlantic Ocean from Africa to South America on rafts made of naturally formed mats of vegetation (see "A Closer Look," p. 257). The rafting scenario is supported by the fact that during the Eocene, South America and Africa were closer to each other than they are today. An additional drop in sea level would have further decreased the distance between Africa and South America and may have exposed mid-Atlantic islands, allowing early platyrrhines to **island-hop** their way to South America (Ciochon and Chiarelli, 1980a; Houle, 1999; Poux and Douzery, 2004).

Miocene Primates

Throughout the Miocene, we see diversification of the anthropoids into the groups we're familiar with today. The cercopithecoid monkeys and the hominoids competed for the dominant position on the primate landscape in the Old World, with the former finally emerging victorious. Today, the number of ape groups is very limited, compared to the diversity they enjoyed in the Miocene, while cercopithecoids remain relatively varied.

Monkeying Around

Following the emergence of the Oligocene anthropoid *Aegyptopithecus* in the Fayum, we have evidence of further diversification of later catarrhines—namely, the Old World monkeys and the hominoids. The cercopithecoids, as the Old World monkeys are known, fall into two families—one extinct (called the victoriapithecids) and the other being the living cercopithecids. The late Miocene was a highly successful time for the radiation of monkeys in the Old World. Their more immediate descendants

island-hop To travel from one island to the next.

A Closer Look

Rafting and Primate Evolution

Despite the peculiar images this statement might conjure, rafting is actually a well-recognized method of animal migration for some vertebrates. In fact, there's documented evidence of a natural raft carrying a crocodile 685 miles from Java to the Cocos Islands in 1930 (Ciochon and Chiarelli, 1980b). Admittedly, such instances of natural rafting are rare; but given the geological span of time, even unlikely events (such as you winning the lottery or monkeys floating to South America) become likely. This idea is known as the sweepstakes model, and it was popularized by evolutionist G. G. Simpson (contributor to the Modern Synthesis, discussed in Chapter 4).

As better information regarding the rare availability of land bridges and the implausibility of lost continents has been absorbed, scientists are relying more and more on sweepstakes models such as rafting to explain events that are otherwise impossible to explain. Such is the case for the lemur population of Madagascar and the New World monkeys. In both circumstances, we have the relatively sudden appearance of primates in areas where no ancestor is present and for which migration could only have been over a large body of water. Coincidentally, Africa is the apparent source of both the lemur and platyrrhine root stock.

The scenario goes like this: A female primate and her mate live on the edge of a river. During one particularly nasty storm, their home is disconnected from the mainland, becoming a natural houseboat of sorts. The storm rages, and the entire raft is carried out to sea. Days later, the bedraggled primates wash ashore at their new home (Fig. 1). The rest is history. Or is it?

Recently, scientists reevaluated this sweepstakes model, exposing some serious flaws. To be a lucky ticket holder, the primates would have to actually survive the voyage, or the whole model is useless. In 1976, Simons calculated that it would take only 4 to 6 days for most small primates to succumb to the combined effects of lacking food and water and experiencing salt imbalance and exposure (Simons, 1976). The shortest distance today from the African mainland to Madagascar is 249 miles. Even with a stiff continuous wind, it would take 10 days to make the journey, so the migrant lemurs would be comatose days before. The first platyrrhines would

have had to cross 870 miles—that's an intolerable amount of time for a thirsty primate.

Despite these shortcomings, rafting is still viewed by many to be the best explanation that we have for these dispersals—short of some even more obscure method of transportation. Combined with the probable existence of islands intermediate to Madagascar and the New World during the times of these voyages, it's quite possible that the primates were first washed up on one of these isles and only later rafted to their current residences. This would mean that they would not have to cross the entire span in one daunting voyage, but would instead engage in "island-hopping." In addition, Alain Houle (1998) has researched the idea of "floating islands" as a mode of distant dispersal of small- to medium-sized vertebrates. These vegetation rafts could have supported microhabitats that would have permitted small vertebrates, such as primates, to cross ocean barriers reaching far-distant islands. Additional random dispersals on vegetation rafts from these distant islands ultimately would have allowed primates to colonize the New World.

Drawing by Robert Greisen/Design by Russell L. Ciochon

Figure 1

An artist's rendering of the South Atlantic populating scenario called rafting. The scene depicts a natural raft with primate passengers being swept into the sea. This raft might ultimately drift to the New World in one voyage but would more likely beach on a closer island. The latter scenario, called island-hopping, would allow primates to take their time in moving from one island to another before finally reaching South America.

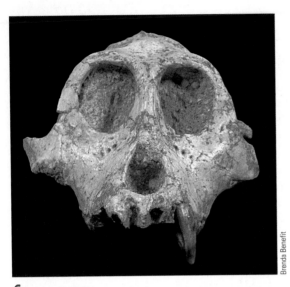

Figure 9-17

Skull of *Victoriapithecus*, the first Old World monkey.

from the Pliocene and the Pleistocene were much more varied in size, locomotion, and diet than their counterparts today.

The extinct family Victoriapithecidae represents the earliest members of the lineage leading to present-day Old World monkeys. The victoriapithecids were found throughout northern and eastern Africa as early as 19 mya, predating the split between the two extant subfamilies of Old World monkeys—the colobines (leaf-eating monkeys) and the cercopithecines (cheek-pouch monkeys)—which occurred around 15 mya (Sterner et al., 2006). Since they're more "primitive" in many features than either colobines or cercopithecines, the victoriapithecids may represent the last common ancestors of all living Old World monkeys; but it's also possible that they represent an extinct sister group. The best known of the victoriapithecids is *Victoriapithecus* (Fig. 9-17), a small monkey whose cranium exhibits a mosaic of later colobine and cercopithecine features that place it close to the root of both subfamilies. The molars of *Victoriapithecus* exhibit bilophodonty, like all living Old World monkeys, indicating a diet of hard fruits and seeds. Meanwhile, postcranial skeletal features demonstrate similarities to living terrestrial monkeys (Benefit and McCrossin, 1997).

By 12 mya, the victoriapithecids had been replaced by Old World forms whose direct descendants are still alive today—that is, cercopithecines and colobines (see Chapter 6, p. 160). Fossils of the first true colobine are found in African deposits dating to approximately 9 mya. This form was smaller than most living forms, though at 8 to 9 pounds, it was no lightweight. The colobines quickly radiated into Europe and Asia following their first appearance in Africa. As we'll see, this was when Eurasian ape groups also began reentering Africa.

You may not know it, but you're probably already familiar with members of Cercopithecinae, a subfamily of the family Cercopithecidae. This subfamily includes monkeys such as today's macaques (for example, the rhesus monkeys used in labs) and baboons. Most fossil macaques appear remarkably similar to each other and to living forms, indicating that ancestral macaque morphology has been retained for more than 5 million years. This is bolstered by biomolecular evidence

At a Glance

Old World Monkey vs. Ape Characteristics

GENERAL OLD WORLD MONKEY CHARACTERISTICS	GENERAL APE CHARACTERISTICS
1. Narrow nose and palate	1. Broad nose and palate
2. Smaller brain (in absolute terms and relative to body weight)	2. Larger brain (in absolute terms and relative to body weight)
3. Bilophodont molars	3. Y-5 molars
4. Smaller average body size	4. Larger average body size
5. Longer torso	5. Shorter torso
6. Shorter arms	6. Longer arms
7. Tail	7. No tail

See Appendix A, Fig. A-11 for illustrations of these differences.

indicating that *Macaca* diverged from *Papio* (the modern baboon) about 10 mya (Raaum et al., 2005).

In East Africa, the baboon-like *Theropithecus* was the dominant cercopith-ecine genus of the Plio-Pleistocene (Fig. 9-18). Adaptations of the hands and teeth indicate that all species of *Theropithecus* exploited a dietary niche consisting almost exclusively of grasses—a unique diet among primates that feed on small objects. This group contains some notable fossil specimens, among them the largest mon-key that ever lived (225 pounds). *Theropithecus* was an incredibly successful genus throughout much of the Pliocene and Early Pleistocene; but sometime during the Middle Pleistocene, most of its members went extinct, leaving a single remaining species—the gelada (*Theropithecus gelada*). While we don't completely understand exactly what caused these extinctions, many researchers hypothesize that competi-tion with the closely related *Papio* baboons of today was a major factor. Today, the living gelada is confined to the high, wet grasslands of the Amhara Plateau, in Ethiopia, an ecological zone where no *Papio* baboons are found.

Aping Monkeys

By the end of the Oligocene, the world's major continents were located about where they are today. During the Miocene (23–5.3 mya), however, the drifting of South America and Australia away from Antarctica significantly altered ocean currents. At the same time, the South Asian Plate continued to ram into Asia, producing the

Figure 9-18

Skull of *Theropithecus brumpti*, the most bizarre fossil monkey (inset). An artist's rendering of *Theropithecus* on the land-scape in the Omo Basin of Ethiopia about 3 mya.

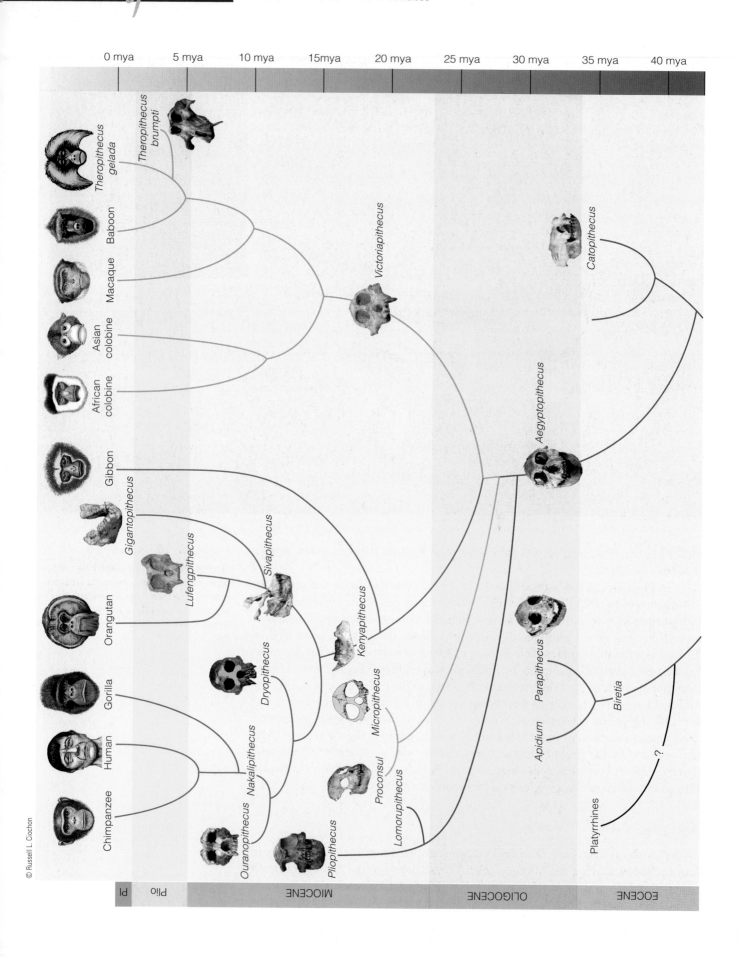

Himalayan Plateau. Together, these major paleogeographical modifications significantly affected the climate, causing the early Miocene to be considerably warmer and wetter than the Oligocene. As a result, rain forests and dense woodlands became the dominant environments of Africa during the early Miocene. It was in this forested environment of Africa that the first apelike primates evolved.

Molecular evidence suggests that the evolutionary lineages leading to monkeys and apes diverged approximately 27 mya (Janečka et al., 2007; Fig. 9-19). Not surprisingly, the first apelike fossils share many anatomical characteristics with monkeys. In fact, in many of these early forms of the superfamily Proconsuloidea, the only apelike feature is the presence of the **Y-5 molar** pattern. As shown in Figure 9-20, the ape molars have five cusps separated by a "Y" groove, as opposed to the monkey's typical four bilophodont cusps. Consequently, proconsuloids are commonly called **dental apes**, reflecting their apelike teeth but monkey-like postcranial skeleton.

Nearly all of the proconsuloid fossils come from East Africa, although some fossils have been recovered as far south and west as Namibia, on the southern coast of Africa. The fossil record shows that these early apes were a highly diverse group, varying greatly in both size and locomotor patterns. They ranged in size from 22 to 110 pounds in *Proconsul* to the tiny *Micropithecus*, which probably weighed no more than 6 to 8 pounds, making it the smallest ape ever known to have lived (Ruff et al., 1989; Rafferty et al., 1995; Fig. 9-21). The fossil record suggests a considerable diversity of locomotor patterns among the dental apes, including suspensory locomotion (swinging from their arms) as well as quadrupedalism either in trees or on the ground (Gebo et al., 1997; Fleagle, 1999).

The best known of the proconsuloids is the genus *Proconsul*, which lived in Africa 20–17 mya. The first example of *Proconsul*, a skull, was discovered on Rusinga Island, Kenya, in 1948 by esteemed fossil hunter Mary Leakey. For a long time, it was considered the first ape, but that position has been recently challenged. This fruit-eating, apelike creature roamed a wide range of environments from rain forest to open woodlands. Though generally considered small-bodied, various *Proconsul*

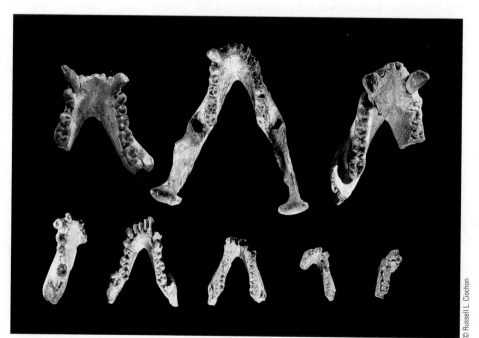

Figure 9-19 (opposite)

Family tree of early catarrhines and their relationships to modern Old World monkeys and apes. Red is for living apes and their immediate ancestors (Hominoidea); green is for the Old World monkeys and their immediate ancestors (Cercopithecoidea); orange is for dental apes (Proconsuloidea); purple is for the primitive catarrhines (Pliopithecoidea); and blue represents the Fayum early anthropoid radiation.

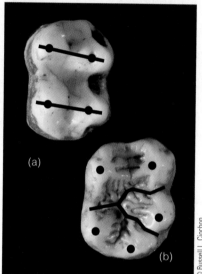

(a)

(b)

Figure 9-20

Comparison of bilophodont molars as found in cercopithecoids and Y-5 molars as seen in hominoids. (a) Notice that the four cusps are positioned in two parallel rows or lobes. (b) See how the five cusps are arranged so that a Y-shaped valley runs between them.

Y-5 molar Molar that has five cusps with grooves running between them, forming a Y shape. This is characteristic of hominoids.

dental apes Early apes that postcranially resemble monkeys but dentally are hominoids (i.e., they have a Y-5 molar configuration).

Figure 9-21

Diversity of early Miocene ape mandibles. The shapes and sizes of these mandibles and teeth illustrate the adaptive diversity of apes during this time. The apes ranged in size from that of a male orangutan to half the size of a modern gibbon and ate foods as varied as hard roots and soft fruit.

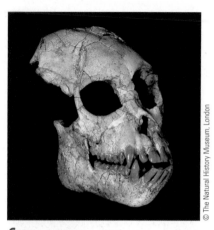

Figure 9-22

Skull of *Proconsul*, the best known of the early Miocene dental apes.

Figure 9-23

Pliopithecus, from the middle Miocene of Europe. The pliopithecoids were the first catarrhines to leave Africa.

© The Natural History Museum, London

© Russell L. Ciochon

species actually ranged in size from 10 to 150 pounds (Harrison, 2002). A typical dental ape, *Proconsul* exhibits a generalized cranium (Fig. 9-22) and an apelike Y-5 dental pattern, but postcranial remains show that *Proconsul's* limbs and long torso retained adaptations for quadrupedal locomotion similar to that of monkeys. Curiously enough, some scientists hypothesize that *Proconsul* might not have had a tail, which could indicate that this particular hominoid characteristic had a relatively ancient origin (Begun, 2003; Nakatsukasa et al., 2004; Ward, 2005). However, the proconsuloids' position as mere dental apes has caused many researchers to place them outside of Hominoidea (in Proconsuloidea), just prior to the divergence of hominoids and cercopithecoids. This would mean not only that *Proconsul's* lack of tail was due to convergence, but also that the time depth of taillessness within Hominoidea itself is still unknown.

Members of the superfamily Pliopithecoidea, like the proconsuloids, also date to the early Miocene of Africa, though they're more primitive than all other catarrhines. Most evidence indicates that the pliopithecoids were an early, small-bodied offshoot of the ape family tree; but they appear to have been a highly successful group, undergoing a rapid adaptive radiation in the Miocene.

Toward the end of the early Miocene, around 19 mya, the Arabian Plate moved to its current location, forming a land bridge between Africa and Eurasia. Major animal migrations could then take place between the two previously separated landmasses. It's thought that African pliopithecoids were among the first transcontinental migrants and, importantly, represent the first anthropoids to colonize both Asia and Europe. Researchers thus commonly agree that the pliopithecoids were the first catarrhines to leave Africa. Until recently, however, this migration was only assumed, since pliopithecoid fossil remains were known only from Eurasia. However, a newly discovered genus of pliopithecoid, *Lomorupithecus*, has proved to be the earliest member of this group, dating to the early Miocene (nearly 20 mya), and (as predicted) it's from Uganda, in Africa (Rossie and MacLatchy, 2006)! This find provides the proof that pliopithecoids had their roots in Africa, bringing this idea from the realm of conjecture into reality.

Dating to the middle Miocene, *Pliopithecus* is the best-known pliopithecoid from Europe. Robust features of the mandible indicate that *Pliopithecus* probably ate a diet consisting of relatively tough foods, most likely leaves (Fig. 9-23). Postcranially, it appears that *Pliopithecus* possessed some features for suspensory locomotion (arm hanging) similar to that of some large platyrrhines, although it clearly lacked the grasping prehensile tail of New World monkeys. There are some indications that *Pliopithecus* may have possessed a short tail (decidedly un-apelike), but this feature is still greatly debated (Ankel, 1965).

Despite the intensity of their radiation early on, it appears that later, during the Pliocene, the success of the pliopithecoids ended. All forms went extinct with no living descendants.

True Apes

The first true apes, those belonging to the superfamily Hominoidea, appear in Africa during the middle Miocene, approximately 16 mya. Probably the best known of these early African hominoids is *Kenyapithecus*. Anatomical evidence indicates that *Kenyapithecus* was a large-bodied terrestrial quadruped, possibly the first hominoid to adapt to life on the ground, with specialized adaptations in the humerus, wrist, and hands (McCrossin et al., 1998). In particular, the hand bones indicate that *Kenyapithecus* may have employed a form of locomotion similar to the knuckle-walking gait typical of living gorillas and chimpanzees. The jaw and dentition of *Kenyapithecus* also exhibit greater similarities to extant great apes than to earlier Miocene forms such as *Proconsul*.

Soon after the pliopithecoids became the first anthropoids to leave Africa, the hominoids also began to migrate out of Africa. Like the pliopithecoids, the hominoids rapidly colonized the Old World and quickly experienced two highly successful adaptive radiations in Europe and Asia.

West Side Story: European Radiation Europe was likely the first stop on the hominoid radiation outside of Africa at around 16 mya; the colonization of Asia actually occurred later, at around 15 mya (Heizmann and Begun, 2001). Although this radiation was widespread geographically, so far we've found only scant evidence of it from scattered localities in France, Spain, Italy, Greece, Austria, Germany, and Hungary.

The best-known middle Miocene (~12–9 mya) hominoid from Europe is *Dryopithecus*, from southern France and northern Spain (Fig. 9-24). *Dryopithecus* resembles modern hominoids in many cranial and postcranial features, including long arms, large hands, and long fingers—all signifying an ability to brachiate, or swing through the trees. The teeth of *Dryopithecus* imply an unusual diet of both fruits and leaves (Begun, 1994). The skeletal and dental remains suggest that *Dryopithecus* was a highly arboreal species, rarely descending from its high-canopy forested habitat.

One late Miocene (9.6–8.7 mya) European fossil hominoid is *Ouranopithecus*, unique in that the first fossils were discovered in Greece during World War I when Allied soldiers dug trenches to protect themselves from enemy troops. The abundance of the fossils found within these trenches led Camille Arambourg, a French commander (and paleontologist), to order his machine-gun-toting soldiers to unearth fossils until they were redeployed elsewhere (de Bonis and Koufos, 1994).

The result of this amateur excavation (and, the professional excavation that followed) was an abundance of *Ouranopithecus* fossils that appear to have been deposited when a flood drowned a large local population. The face of *Ouranopithecus* shares many features with living African great apes, including large browridges and a wide distance between the eye orbits (Fig. 9-25). Some of these traits are even shared by some early fossil hominins. *Ouranopithecus'* powerful jaws, with small canines and extremely thick molar enamel, led some researchers to postulate that these hominoids subsisted on a diet consisting of relatively hard foods, such as nuts (Ungar and Kay, 1995). The variation in both body and canine size indicates a range of sexual dimorphism comparable to that of the modern gorilla, which they resemble in size.

East Side Story: Asian Radiation The hominoids of the middle and late Miocene of Asia represent one of the most varied Miocene fossil ape assemblages. These Asian fossil apes are geographically dispersed from Turkey in the west to China in the east.

Sivapithecus dates to the middle and late Miocene and has been recovered from southern Asia, in the Siwalik Hills of India and Pakistan. Over the last 30 years, paleoanthropologists led by David Pilbeam have recovered numerous specimens from the Potwar Plateau of Pakistan. Included in this large collection are a multitude of mandibles, many postcranial remains, and a partial cranium, including most of the face. *Sivapithecus* was a large hominoid, ranging from 70 to

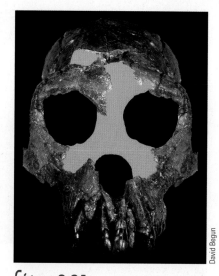

David Begun

Figure **9-24**

Skull of *Dryopithecus*, the earliest European ape. The left side is reconstructed as a mirror image of the complete right side.

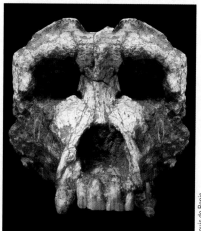

Louis de Bonis

Figure **9-25**

Ouranopithecus, possible extinct relative of the African apes. Notice that the face shares many features with living African great apes, including large browridges and a wide distance between the eye orbits. The upper left side is reconstructed as a mirror image of the complete right side.

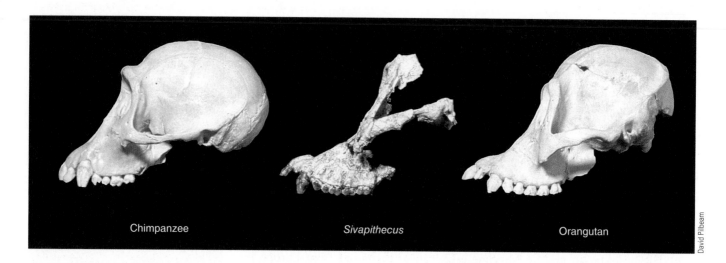

Chimpanzee   *Sivapithecus*   Orangutan

David Pilbeam

Figure **9-26**

Comparison of a modern chimpanzee (left), *Sivapithecus* (middle), and a modern orangutan (right). Notice that both *Sivapithecus* and the orangutan exhibit a dished face, broad cheekbones, and projecting maxilla and incisors.

zygomatics Cheekbones.

150 pounds, and probably inhabited a mostly arboreal niche. The most characteristic anatomical aspects of *Sivapithecus* are seen in the face, which exhibits a concave profile (dished face), broad **zygomatics** (cheekbones), and procumbent (projecting) maxilla and incisors, remarkably resembling that of the modern orangutan (Pilbeam, 1982; Fig. 9-26). It's important to note that the body of *Sivapithecus* is distinctly unlike living orangutans or any other known hominoid, for that matter. For example, the forelimb exhibits a unique mixture of traits, probably indicating some mode of arboreal quadrupedalism with no ability for brachiation (Pilbeam et al., 1990).

One of *Sivapithecus'* descendants from the late Miocene through the Pleistocene, *Gigantopithecus* ("Giganto"), was discovered in a rather unconventional way. For thousands of years, Chinese pharmacists have used fossils as ingredients in potions intended to cure ailments ranging from backache to sexual impotence. In 1935, Dutch paleoanthropologist Ralph von Koenigswald came across a large fossil primate molar in a Hong Kong apothecary shop. He named the fossil tooth *Gigantopithecus*, meaning "gigantic ape," and the species *blacki*, in honor of his late friend and colleague Davidson Black (the discoverer of "Peking Man").

Figure **9-27**

Comparison of the mandibles and teeth of *Gigantopithecus* and *Homo sapiens*. Notice that Giganto's jaw is almost three times the size of the human's, as are the teeth.

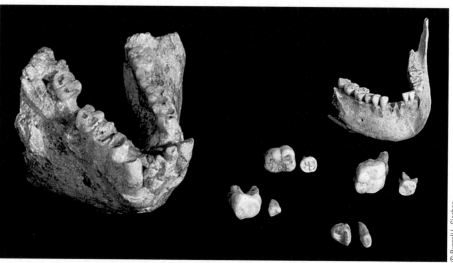

© Russell L. Ciochon

Subsequent researchers were able to source the teeth to China's southernmost Guangxi Province, a karstic (eroded limestone) region of great rock towers riddled with caves.

While four lower jaws and 1,500 isolated teeth of the extinct ape have been found, no other bones have turned up (Fig. 9-27). Based only on the jaws and teeth, however, researchers can attempt to reconstruct both the animal and its way of life. Estimates based on their massive mandibles indicate that the Chinese species of Giganto likely weighed more than 800 pounds and was possibly 9 feet tall when standing erect on its hind legs (though it was most likely a terrestrial fist walker). This makes *Gigantopithecus* the largest primate that ever lived. But Giganto wasn't always the king of apes that it became in later years. Evidence shows that this great ape increased in size as the genus evolved, which follows a trend seen in other large Pleistocene mammals, such as the mammoth. The earlier Indian and Pakistani *Gigantopithecus giganteus* (8.5 mya), despite its specific name, was about half the size of the later Chinese and Southeast Asian *Gigantopithecus blacki* (around 2 mya).

The small incisors and canines, very thick enamel on the cheek teeth, and massive, robust jaws lead to the inevitable conclusion that the animal was adapted to the consumption of tough, fibrous foods by cutting, crushing, and grinding them. Some researchers have argued that Giganto's huge mandible and dentition were an adaptation for a diet consisting primarily of bamboo, much like that of the giant panda. More current research has supported this claim and also concludes that its diet may have included the durian, a tropical fruit with a tough outer skin (Ciochon et al., 1990; Fig. 9-28).

Sadly, sometime near the end of the Middle Pleistocene, around 200,000 years ago (ya), Giganto went extinct. The animal had flourished for more than 8.5 million years, but human predation or environmental change may have proved too much for the vegetarian giant.

A final ape from Asia, *Lufengpithecus*, has been recovered from localities in southern China and dated to the late Miocene/early Pliocene (9–5 mya). This medium-sized ape, with an estimated adult body weight of about 110 pounds, is known from one of the most complete fossil ape assemblages: 5 crania, 41 mandibles, over 650 isolated teeth, and, most recently, postcrania including finger bones and a femur (Xu and Lu, 2007). With its narrow intraorbital distance, ovoid orbits, and procumbent incisors (Fig. 9-29), some researchers have argued that *Lufengpithecus* is related to the modern orangutan, while others believe that it is related to the European *Dryopithecus*. If not for its location in southern China, *Lufengpithecus* would just be another of the many apes that faced extinction at the end of the Miocene. However, this, in conjunction with its newly described curved phalanges, has catapulted this genus to prominence. It now appears that *Lufengpithecus* is most properly considered a stem orangutan (Harrison et al., 2008).

Lufengpithecus is also noted for its existence within a protected area created by the uplift of the Tibetan Plateau—the result of Himalayan mountain building (Harrison et al., 2002). Within this refuge, a sort of "lost world," *Lufengpithecus* survived until at least 5 mya—or at least that's what conventional wisdom leads us to believe. In recent years, however, Pleistocene cave sites in southern China that have long yielded teeth belonging to *Gigantopithecus* have now also produced more diminutive teeth initially identified as belonging to an early human. These

Figure **9-28**

An artist's rendering of *Gigantopithecus* enjoying a meal of the tasty, but tough, tropical fruit known as durian.

Figure 9-29

Skull of a *Lufengpithecus* juvenile from the late Miocene of Yunnan Province, China. Note the orangutan-like oval eye orbits and narrow distance between the eyes.

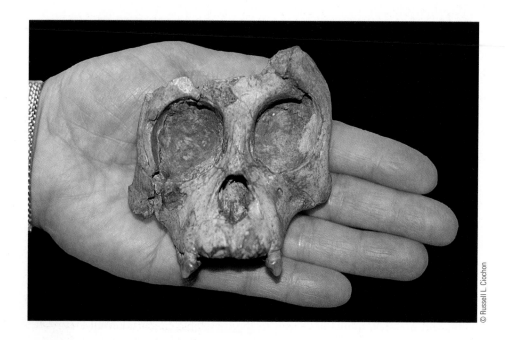

© Russell L. Ciochon

same teeth, following more rigorous analysis, are now thought to be those of a previously unknown, medium-sized Pleistocene ape. The teeth are too small to be those of either Giganto or the orangutan, *Pongo*. Could these mystery ape teeth be a descendant of *Lufengpithecus*? In fact, the strongest evidence points to the existence of three distinct great ape lineages in Asia: the massive *Gigantopithecus*, the large-bodied *Pongo*, and the medium-sized *Lufengpithecus* descendant. But as you've seen in Chapter 6, this Asian hominoid diversity has dwindled, just as it has in Africa and elsewhere in the world.

Evolution of Extant Hominoids

Hylobatids: The Lesser Apes Biomolecular evidence indicates that the gibbon–great ape split occurred approximately 15–18 mya. This would place their divergence around the time that migration into Eurasia from Africa would have first become geographically possible (Pilbeam, 1996; Raaum et al., 2005). The molecular evidence also shows that the radiation of the current hylobatids (lesser apes, such as gibbons) occurred only 10.5 mya (Chatterjee, 2006), with newly discovered 9 mya *Yuanmoupithecus* supporting that date (Harrison et al., 2008). Before this new find, various researchers had previously considered pliopithecoids as a possible gibbon ancestor due to similarities in the shape of their face. But pliopithecoids and Oligocene catarrhines actually share numerous primitive features, including the lack of a tubelike middle ear, the presence of a small tail, and an elbow joint that's strikingly similar to those of various Fayum primates. These features, as well as their monkey-like limb proportions, clearly remove pliopithecoids from consideration as the ancestors of modern gibbons. From molecular evidence and from fossil remains of the small-bodied Chinese stem hylobatid *Yuanmoupithecus* (Harrison et al., 2008), however, we can determine that the gibbon radiation began 10.5–9 mya in China before dispersing southward to Malaysia and Sumatra. Once in Sumatra, gibbons differentiated into two taxa, including the modern *Hylobates*, which eventually made its way into Borneo and Java around 5–3 mya (Chatterjee, 2006; Harrison et al., 2008).

The African Great Apes Recent molecular studies suggest that gorillas diverged from humans and chimpanzees between 9 and 8 mya (Kumar et al., 2005), with the divergence between humans and chimpanzees occurring between 6 and 5 mya (Steiper and Young, 2006, 2008). If these estimates are right, then the late Miocene (11–5 mya) becomes a crucial period for understanding African great apes and human origins. Strangely, after beginning their migration into Asia and Europe, hominoids disappear from the African fossil record around 13 mya, not to reappear until the late Miocene, around 10.5–10 mya (in the form of *Chororapithecus*). Since there is no evidence of a mass extinction of hominoids in the middle Miocene, this "ape gap" (Hill, 2007) in the fossil record has led some researchers to hypothesize that the reappearance of hominoids in Africa during the late Miocene was the result of Eurasian fossil apes migrating back into Africa at the same time the colobine monkeys were leaving. This has been the prevailing paradigm for the past decade or so.

For this reason, *Ouranopithecus* (9.6–8.7 mya), the large-bodied hominoid from Greece, was long thought to be a stem African ape/human ancestor. This argument is based primarily on the facial similarities discussed earlier. This would make an ape similar to *Ouranopithecus* a kind of prodigal son who returned to Africa from a long stay (and evolution) in Europe. This out-of-Europe ape line would then later diverge in the late Miocene, producing the human line (see Chapter 11).

However, given some provocative finds from Kenya, many researchers are shifting from an out-of-Europe scenario to a plausible African origin for the living African apes (Bernor, 2007). The oldest of these African specimens is the recently described 10.5–10 mya Ethiopian *Chororapithecus*. This genus is notable as the first representative of a large-bodied Miocene ape in eastern Africa following the "ape gap," in an important intersection between Africa and Eurasia. Its dental morphology and apparent adaptation to a hard, fibrous diet have caused some to believe that it represents the basal stock for the modern gorilla (Suwa et al., 2007). In fact, its discoverers have gone so far as to say that the eight molars and one canine "are collectively indistinguishable from modern gorilla subspecies" (Dalton, 2007, p. 844; Fig. 9-30). If this genus represents a gorilla ancestor to the exclusion of humans, this would place the divergence of the two groups at 11–10 mya, more than 2 million years earlier than generally believed. Additional fossils of this exciting new genus are greatly anticipated to further determine its true phylogenetic affinities.

Another newly described genus is the 9.9–9.8 mya *Nakalipithecus* from Kenya, thought by some to be close to the last common ancestor of the African great apes and humans (but see previous discussion of *Chororapithecus*). Though slightly older than *Ouranopithecus* (9.9–9.8 mya versus 9.6–8.7 mya), *Nakalipithecus* shares many features with *Ouranopithecus*, as they both lived in similar environments. *Nakalipithecus*' size is reconstructed as comparable to that of a female gorilla, with dental features that indicate a hard-object diet. Both of these features are suggestive of a **terrestrial** lifestyle (substantial ground living; Kunimatsu et al., 2007).

Nakalipithecus' and *Ouranopithecus*' morphological similarities have led some to propose a possible ancestor-descendant relationship between the two. Coupled with *Nakalipithecus*' and *Chororapithecus*' East African origins and earlier ages when compared to *Ouranopithecus*, this would appear to indicate an African rather than Eurasian origin for the living African apes (Fig. 9-31).

In 2005, researchers discovered several teeth of a fossil chimpanzee at a site near Lake Baringo, in Kenya. This discovery adds some fossil time depth to at least the *Pan* lineage. These fossil chimpanzee teeth date to approximately 500,000 ya and represent the first and only fossils belonging to the genus *Pan* (such fossils are

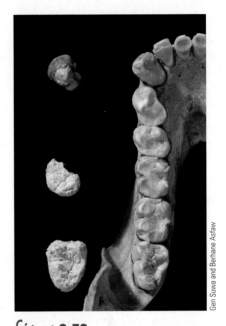

Gen Suwa and Berhane Asfaw

Figure **9-30**

Comparison of three mandibular teeth belonging to *Chororapithecus* (left) with a modern gorilla mandible (right).

terrestrial Living and locomoting primarily on the ground.

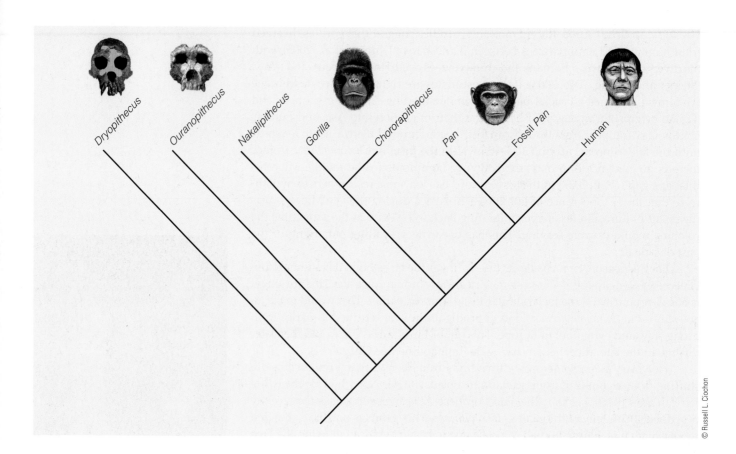

Figure 9-31

Cladogram of Homininae showing the relationships of gorillas, chimpanzees, and humans with their fossil ape relatives.

rare because tropical forest environments aren't conducive to preserving organic remains). Also note that these fossils are quite late, several million years after the chimpanzee lineage diverged from hominins. Although currently not placed in a particular chimpanzee species, the fossil teeth exhibit greater similarities to the common chimpanzee (*Pan troglodytes*) than to bonobos (*Pan paniscus*) (McBrearty and Jablonski, 2005).

Asia's Lone Great Ape Of all the living apes, the orangutan's ancestry is probably the best documented. Current evidence indicates that *Sivapithecus* gave rise to *Gigantopithecus* (sometime before 9 mya) as well as to *Lufengpithecus* and then finally to the orangutans (*Pongo*) sometime in the late Miocene. Since the earliest *Sivapithecus* fossils date to more than 12 mya, it's clear that the branching event separating orangutans and the lineage leading to the African great apes and humans must have occurred before then. In fact, biomolecular evidence indicates that this divergence took place approximately 14 mya (Raaum et al., 2005). The relationship between *Sivapithecus* and *Pongo* is based primarily on cranial similarities, though their vastly differing postcranial anatomies raise questions regarding their evolutionary proximity to each another. As mentioned earlier, the face of *Lufengpithecus* is also very similar to that of the modern orangutan. However, it's the postcrania of *Lufengpithecus* (particularly its curved phalanges) that indicate its closer relationship to *Pongo* than to *Sivapithecus* (Harrison et al., 2008). Several other Asian hominoids have been suggested as more recent orangutan ancestors, but there's little evidence to support these assertions (Fig. 9-32).

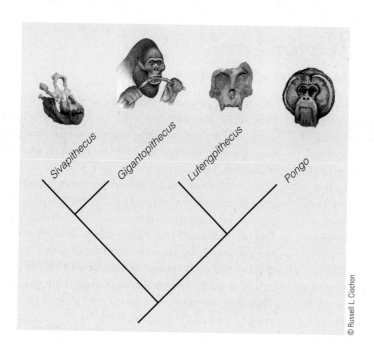

© Russell L. Ciochon

Figure 9-32

Cladogram of Ponginae showing the relationships of of the orangutan with its fossil ape relatives.

Summary

In this chapter, we've traced the evolutionary history of our primate origins from as early as 65 mya down to a few thousand years ago. Beginning in the late Cretaceous, the earliest primate ancestors were probably little more than arboreally adapted insectivores, much like the modern tree shrews. In the Paleocene, no indisputable euprimates are yet apparent, despite claims to the contrary. In the following epoch, the Eocene, we begin to see an abundant diversification of primates that are readily identifiable. During this epoch, the lemur-like adapoids and the tarsier-like omomyoids begin their evolutionary radiations. As demonstrated by recent evidence from the Fayum and other locations in Africa, early anthropoid origins also date to sometime in the middle Eocene. In addition, Old and New World anthropoids apparently shared their last common ancestry in the Eocene or early Oligocene and have gone their separate evolutionary pathways ever since.

In the Old World, the Oligocene reveals numerous possible early anthropoid ancestors, again at the Fayum, but none of the modern lineages (Old World monkeys, gibbons, large-bodied apes) can definitely be traced to this time. The Miocene reveals the first Old World monkeys and a highly complex array of ape forms, many of large-bodied varieties. More than 30 different genera and probably dozens of species of fossil apes are represented in those remains discovered in Africa, Asia, and Europe. Some early forms from Kenya and Uganda (the proconsuloids) are more primitive than all of the hominoids from Eurasia. Though there's little firm evidence tying these fossil forms to living apes or humans, morphological evidence suggests that *Yuanmoupithecus* may be related to the gibbon and *Lufengpithecus* is probably the most closely related to the orangutan. Are the newly discovered *Chororapithecus* and *Nakalipithecus* really the ancestors of the African apes? If these aren't our distant relatives, where *do* we come from? In the next part of your text, we'll seek answers to this question.

A Closer Look

Building Family Trees from Genes

Molecular anthropology is the branch of anthropology that uses genetics to investigate the evolution of humans and our closest relatives—the nonhuman primates. One area of specialization for molecular anthropologists is in testing hypotheses regarding the relationships within the primate order. The use of molecular methods in this manner has revolutionized our knowledge of primate systematics and has revealed evolutionary relationships that have been difficult to resolve using other methods. This family tree is compiled from the research of a number of molecular anthropologists (Raaum et al., 2005; Sterner et al., 2006; Steiper and Young, 2006; Janečka et al., 2007; Hodgson et al., 2008; Hodgson et al., 2009b).

Phylogenetic hypotheses can be tested by comparing DNA (nucleotide) sequences from various primate species to infer a gene tree of primate family relationships. When using DNA to test phylogenetic hypotheses, it's important to construct gene trees from various loci because different parts of the genome can have unique evolutionary histories. For example, studies on macaques and colobines have shown that mitochondrial, sex-linked, and autosomal gene trees from the same individuals can show very different relationships. Determining the cause behind these different evolutionary histories across the genome, as well as which gene trees most accurately reflect the relationships among primate species, requires careful interpretation.

Molecular anthropologists can also use sequences of DNA to infer how long it has been since primate species last shared a common ancestor. Because mutations in DNA occur at a relatively constant rate of change, the amount of difference between two samples is proportional to the amount of time elapsed since their last common ancestor existed. This is often referred to as the "molecular clock." The fossil record is used to calibrate this "clock" by telling us how long ago two or more species on a tree diverged from one another and thus how long it takes for a certain number of mutations to occur. This information can then be used to infer when in time other primate species across the tree last shared a common ancestor. As with the construction of gene trees, molecular divergence dates are best inferred from various parts of the genome in order to ensure that divergences calculated from one region are consistent with those calculated from

others. In many cases, primate divergence dates inferred from molecular data are much farther back in time than expected, which leaves the exciting possibility that we are missing even more of the primate fossil record than previously thought.

A relatively recent molecular method for the inference of primate evolutionary relationships is the use of transposable genomic elements. These are regions of DNA that are replicated and inserted into different areas across the genome. They have therefore been called "jumping genes," and each "jump" to a different part of the genome can be used as a character for phylogenetic analysis. Therefore, the presence of a transposable element in a specific part of the genome in two species could represent a shared derived trait that reveals a close evolutionary relationship. One type of transposable element, called an *Alu*, is particularly common in primate genomes. In fact, there are over 1 million copies of this repetitive element in humans, making up approximately 10 percent of our genome. Because their mode of evolution is unidirectional and free of homoplasy, transposable elements, and *Alus* in particular, are becoming prominent in phylogenetic analyses. However, because their replication and jumping do not follow a "clock," they cannot be used to infer divergence dates among primate species.

Advances in technology now allow for the collection of an unprecedented amount of molecular data. The same time and money used to collect 500 base pairs of DNA 10 years ago can now be used to collect tens of thousands of base pairs. This large amount of data provides us with increasing confidence that the gene trees and divergence dates we infer are accurate representations of primate evolutionary history. Furthermore, following the draft sequence of the human genome in 2001, molecular anthropology has quickly moved into the age of genomics, and many additional primate genome projects have since been initiated. Genomic data are now being collected so rapidly that we are having a difficult time keeping up in the development of new analytical methods. At the time of this printing, draft assemblies of the rhesus macaque and common chimpanzee have already been completed, while the baboon, small-eared galago, white-tufted-ear marmoset, orangutan, and Philippine tarsier are all in progress. Smaller portions of the gray mouse lemur and squirrel monkey genomes are both finished and moving into draft phase, while other projects on the bonobo, long-tailed macaque, squirrel monkey, and vervet monkey are all planned for the immediate future (see www.genome.gov/10002154 for the most up-to-date information regarding ongoing projects). The merging of computer programming and biology has become essential to sort through all of this data, thus making the field of bioinformatics extremely important.

Even though the field of molecular anthropology has made significant contributions to our understanding of primate evolutionary history, it's likely that even greater revelations lie ahead. The age of genomics is still in its infancy, and as it grows, so will our understanding of human and primate evolution.

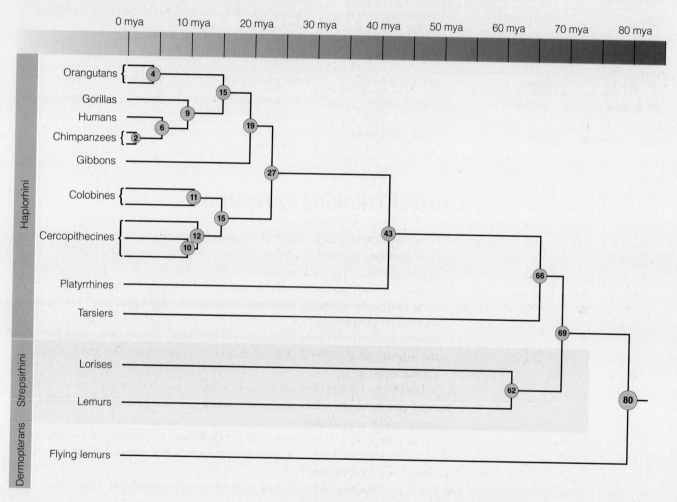

Figure 1

Biomolecular primate family tree based on the works of various researchers (see text). Dates of divergence are noted in the gold-colored nodes.

What's Important **Key Discoveries of Fossil Primates**

Epoch	Genus or Superfamily Name	Sites/Regions	The Big Picture
Paleocene	*Purgatorius*	American Northwest; Bug Creek Anthills (Montana)	Plesiadapiform; first known archaic primate
Mainly Eocene	Adapoidea	North America and Europe	Lemur-like stem strepsirhines; one of the two main branches of euprimates; may or may not have had a tooth comb
Mainly Eocene	Omomyoidea	North America, Europe, and (more rarely) Africa and Asia	Tarsier- or galago-like stem haplorhines; one of the two main branches of euprimates
Middle Eocene	*Algeripithecus*	North Africa; Algeria	First undisputed anthropoid primate
Oligocene	*Aegyptopithecus*	North Africa; the Fayum (Egypt)	Has 2.1.2.3 dental formula; ancestor of both later catarrhines and hominoids
Middle Miocene	*Victoriapithecus*	East Africa	Has bilophodont molar pattern; ancestor of all Old World monkeys
Late Miocene	*Lufengpithecus*	China, East Asia	Fossil great ape closely related to the modern orangutan
Late Miocene	*Ouranopithecus*	Greece, Europe	Fossil great ape; believed to be connected to the origins of the chimpanzee and gorilla
Miocene-Pleistocene	*Gigantopithecus*	China, India, Pakistan, Vietnam, and Burma	The largest ape that ever lived; only great ape to go extinct in the Pleistocene

Critical Thinking Questions

1. How do biomolecular and direct estimates of dating fossil lineages differ? How can they be used to give us a more complete view of the past?

2. Why is it difficult to distinguish the earliest members of the primate order from other placental mammals? If you found a nearly complete skeleton of an early Paleocene mammal, what structural traits might lead you to determine that it was a euprimate?

3. Compare and contrast the adapoids and omomyoids with living members of the primate order. Why do we call them lemur- or tarsier-like and not lemurs and tarsiers?

4. Where is the Fayum Depression, and why is it significant in primate evolution? Are there any other sites where so many fossil primates have been found? Why or why not?

5. What is meant by dental apes as opposed to true hominoids? If you were given a jaw to study of a supposed dental ape, what particular features would you look for first?

6. Compare *Gigantopithecus* in Asia with the modern gorilla in Africa. How do their dietary niches differ?

CHAPTER

10

Paleoanthropology: Reconstructing Early Hominin Behavior and Ecology

Key Questions

What are the central aspects of paleoanthropology?

Why, from a biocultural perspective, do we want to learn about both the behavior and the anatomy of ancient hominins?

 Click!

Introduction

A portion of a pig's tusk, a small sample of volcanic sediment, a battered rock, a primate's molar: What do these seemingly unremarkable remains have in common, and more to the point, why are they of interest to paleoanthropologists? First of all, if they're all discovered at sites in Africa or Eurasia, they *may* be quite ancient—indeed, perhaps millions of years old. Further, some of these materials actually inform scientists directly of quite precise dating of the finds. Last, and most exciting, some of these finds may have been modified, used, and discarded by bipedal creatures who looked and behaved in some ways like ourselves (but were in other respects very different). And what of that molar? Is it a fossilized remnant of an ancient hominin? These are the kinds of questions asked by paleoanthropologists, and to answer them, these researchers travel to remote locales across the Old World.

How do we distinguish possible hominins from other types of animals (most notably, from other primates), especially when all we have are fragmentary fossil remains from just a small portion of a skeleton? How do humans and our most distant ancestors compare with other animals? In the last four chapters, we've seen how humans are classified as primates, both structurally and behaviorally, and how our evolutionary history coincides with that of other mammals and, specifically, other primates. Even so, we're a unique kind of primate, and our ancestors have been adapted to a particular lifestyle for several million years. Some late Miocene fossil apes probably began this process close to 7 mya, though better-preserved fossil discoveries reveal more definitive evidence of hominins shortly after 5 mya.

We're able to determine the hominin nature of these remains by more than the structure of teeth and bones; we know that these animals are hominins also because of the way they behaved—emphasizing once again the *biocultural* nature of human evolution. In this chapter, we'll discuss the methods scientists use to explore the secrets of early hominin behavior and ecology, and we'll demonstrate these methods through the example of the best-known early hominin site in the world: Olduvai Gorge, in East Africa.

Definition of Hominin

The earliest evidence of hominins that has been found dates to the end of the Miocene and mainly includes dental and cranial pieces. But dental features alone don't describe the special features of hominins, and they certainly aren't distinctive of the later stages of human evolution. Modern humans, as well as our most immediate hominin ancestors, are distinguished from the great apes by more obvious features than tooth and jaw dimensions. For example, various scientists have

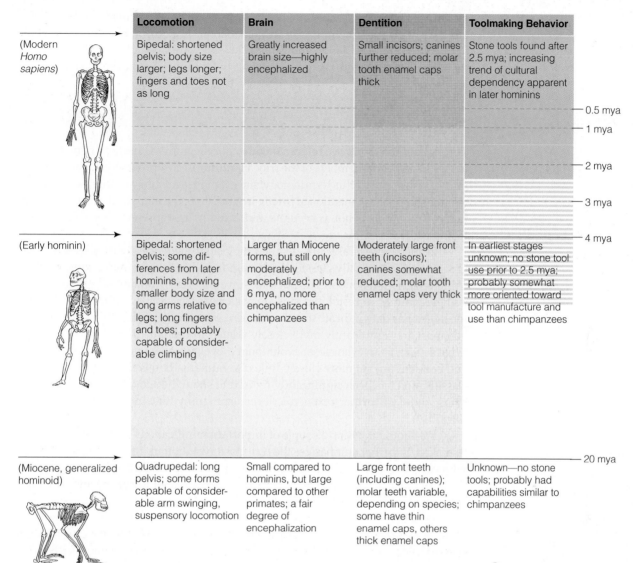

	Locomotion	Brain	Dentition	Toolmaking Behavior
(Modern *Homo sapiens*)	Bipedal: shortened pelvis; body size larger; legs longer; fingers and toes not as long	Greatly increased brain size—highly encephalized	Small incisors; canines further reduced; molar tooth enamel caps thick	Stone tools found after 2.5 mya; increasing trend of cultural dependency apparent in later hominins
(Early hominin)	Bipedal: shortened pelvis; some differences from later hominins, showing smaller body size and long arms relative to legs; long fingers and toes; probably capable of considerable climbing	Larger than Miocene forms, but still only moderately encephalized; prior to 6 mya, no more encephalized than chimpanzees	Moderately large front teeth (incisors); canines somewhat reduced; molar tooth enamel caps very thick	In earliest stages unknown; no stone tool use prior to 2.5 mya; probably somewhat more oriented toward tool manufacture and use than chimpanzees
(Miocene, generalized hominoid)	Quadrupedal: long pelvis; some forms capable of considerable arm swinging, suspensory locomotion	Small compared to hominins, but large compared to other primates; a fair degree of encephalization	Large front teeth (including canines); molar teeth variable, depending on species; some have thin enamel caps, others thick enamel caps	Unknown—no stone tools; probably had capabilities similar to chimpanzees

Time line (right of table): 0.5 mya, 1 mya, 2 mya, 3 mya, 4 mya, 20 mya

Figure 10-1

Mosaic evolution of hominin characteristics: a postulated time line.

pointed to such distinctive hominin characteristics as bipedal locomotion, large brain size, and toolmaking behavior as being significant (at some stage) in defining what makes a hominin a hominin.

It's important to recognize that not all these characteristics developed simultaneously or at the same pace. In fact, over the last several million years of hominin evolution, quite a different pattern has been evident, in which the various components (dentition, locomotion, brain size, and toolmaking) have developed at quite different rates. This pattern, in which physiological and behavioral systems evolve at different rates, is called **mosaic evolution**. As we first pointed out in Chapter 1 and will emphasize in this and the next chapter, the single most important defining characteristic for the full course of hominin evolution is bipedal locomotion. In the earliest stages of hominin emergence, skeletal evidence indicating bipedal locomotion is the only truly reliable indicator that these fossils were indeed hominins. But in later stages of hominin evolution, other features, especially those relating to brain development and behavior, become highly significant (Fig. 10-1).

mosaic evolution A pattern of evolution in which the rate of evolution in one functional system varies from that in other systems. For example, in hominin evolution, the dental system, locomotor system, and neurological system (especially the brain) all evolved at markedly different rates.

These behavioral aspects of hominin emergence—particularly toolmaking—are what we'd like to emphasize in this chapter. Important structural attributes of the hominin brain, teeth, and especially locomotor apparatus are discussed in the next chapter, where we investigate early hominin anatomical adaptations in greater detail.

What's in a Name?

Throughout this book, we refer to members of the human family as hominins (the technical name for members of the tribe Hominini). Most professional paleoanthropologists now prefer this terminology, since it more accurately reflects evolutionary relationships. As we mentioned briefly in Chapter 6, the more traditional classification of hominoids is not as accurate and actually misrepresents key evolutionary relationships.

In the last several years, detailed molecular evidence clearly shows that the great apes (traditionally classified as pongids and including orangutans, gorillas, chimpanzees, and bonobos) do not make up a coherent evolutionary group sharing a single common ancestor and thus are not a *monophyletic* group (see p. 114). Indeed, the molecular data indicate that the African great apes (gorillas, chimpanzees, and bonobos) are significantly more closely related to humans than is the orangutan. What's more, at an even closer evolutionary level, we now know that chimpanzees and bonobos are yet more closely linked to humans than is the gorilla. Hominoid classification has been significantly revised to show these more complete relationships, and two further taxonomic levels (subfamily and tribe) have been added (Fig. 10-2).

We should mention a couple of important ramifications of this new classification. First, it further emphasizes the *very* close evolutionary relationship of humans with African apes and most especially that with chimpanzees and bonobos. Second, the term *hominid*, which has been used for decades to refer to our specific evolutionary lineage, has a quite different meaning in the revised classification; now it refers to *all* great apes and humans together.

Unfortunately, during the period of transition to the newer classification scheme, confusion is bound to result. For this reason, we won't use the term *hominid* in this book except where absolutely necessary (for example, in a formal classification; see Fig. 6-6 and Appendix B). To avoid confusion, we'll simply refer to the

Figure **10-2**

(a) Traditional classification of hominoids. (b) Revised classification of hominoids. Note that two additional levels of classification are added (subfamily and tribe) to show more precisely and more accurately the evolutionary relationships among the apes and humans. In this classification, "hominin" is synonymous with the use of "hominid" in [A].

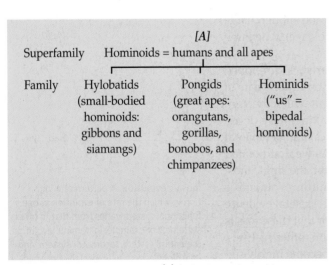

(a)

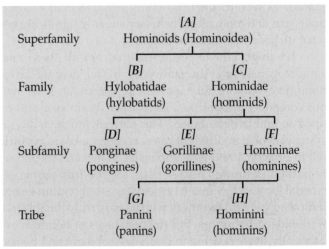

(b)

grouping of great apes and humans as "large-bodied hominoids." And when you see the term *hominid* in earlier publications (including earlier editions of this text), simply regard it as synonomous with *hominin*, the term we use in this book.

Biocultural Evolution: The Human Capacity for Culture

One of the most distinctive behavioral features of humans is our extraordinary elaboration of and dependence on **culture**. Certainly other primates, and many other animals, for that matter, modify their environments. As we saw in Chapter 8, chimpanzees especially are known for such behaviors as using termite sticks, and some chimpanzees as well as capuchin monkeys even carry rocks to use for crushing nuts. Because of such observations, we're on shaky ground when it comes to drawing sharp lines between early hominin toolmaking behavior and that exhibited by other animals.

Another point to remember is that human culture, at least as it's defined in contemporary contexts, involves much more than toolmaking capacity. For humans, culture integrates an entire adaptive strategy involving cognitive, political, social, and economic components. *Material culture*—or the tools humans use—is but a small portion of this cultural complex.

Still, when we examine the archaeological record of earlier hominins, what's available for study is almost exclusively limited to material culture, especially the bits and pieces of broken stone left over from tool manufacture. This is why it's extremely difficult to learn anything about the earliest stages of hominin cultural development before the regular manufacture of stone tools. As you'll see, this most crucial cultural development has been traced to approximately 2.6 mya (Semaw et al., 2003). Yet because of our contemporary primate models, we can assume that hominins were undoubtedly using other kinds of tools (made of perishable materials) and displaying a whole array of other cultural behaviors long before then. But with no "hard" evidence preserved in the archaeological record, our understanding of the early development of these nonmaterial cultural components remains elusive.

The fundamental basis for human cultural success relates directly to our cognitive abilities. Again, we're not dealing with an absolute distinction, but a relative one. As you've already learned, other primates, as documented in the great apes, have some of the language capabilities exhibited by humans. Even so, modern humans display these abilities in a complexity several orders of magnitude beyond that of any other animal. And only humans are so completely dependent on symbolic communication and its cultural by-products that contemporary *Homo sapiens* could not survive without them.

At this point you may be wondering when the unique combination of cognitive, social, and material cultural adaptations became prominent in human evolution. In answering that question, we must be careful to recognize the manifold nature of culture; we can't expect it to always contain the same elements across species (as when comparing ourselves to nonhuman primates) or through time (when trying to reconstruct ancient hominin behavior). Richard Potts (1993) has critiqued such overly simplistic perspectives and suggests instead a more dynamic approach, one that incorporates many subcomponents (including aspects of behavior, cognition, and social interaction).

We know that the earliest hominins almost certainly didn't regularly manufacture stone tools (at least, none that have been found and identified as such). These earliest members of the hominin lineage, dating back to approximately 7–5 mya, may have carried objects such as naturally sharp stones or stone flakes, parts

culture Extrasomatic (nonbody) adaptations to the environment. This includes systematic learned behaviors that can be communicated to others. Aspects of this capacity have been identified among our closest ape relatives.

A Closer Look

Who Was Doing What at Olduvai and the Other Plio-Pleistocene Sites?

The long-held interpretation of the bone refuse and stone tools discovered at Olduvai has been that most, if not all, of these materials result from hominin activities. More recently, however, a comprehensive reanalysis of the bone remains from Olduvai localities has challenged this view (Binford, 1981, 1983). Archaeologist Lewis Binford criticizes those drawn too quickly to concluding that these bone scatters are the remnants of hominin behavior patterns while simultaneously ignoring the possibility of other explanations.

From information concerning the kinds of animals present, which body parts were found, and the differences in preservation among these skeletal elements, Binford has concluded that much of what's preserved can be explained by carnivore activity. This conclusion has been reinforced by certain details observed by Binford himself in Alaska—details on animal kills, scavenging, the transportation of elements, and preservation that are the result of wolf and dog behaviors. Binford describes his approach:

> I took as "known," then, the structure of bone assemblages produced in various settings by animal predators and scavengers; and as "unknown" the bone deposits excavated by the Leakeys at Olduvai Gorge. Using mathematical and statistical techniques I considered to what degree the finds from Olduvai Gorge could be accounted for in terms of the results of predator behavior and how much was "left over." (Binford, 1983, pp. 56–57)

Binford isn't arguing that all of the remains found at Olduvai resulted from nonhominin activity. In fact, he recognizes that "residual material" was consistently found on surfaces with high tool concentration "which could not be explained by what we know about African animals" (Binford, 1983).

Support for the idea that early hominins utilized at least some of the bone refuse has come from a totally different perspective. Researchers have analyzed (both macroscopically and microscopically) the cut marks left on fossilized bones. By experimenting with modern materials, they've been able to delineate more clearly the differences between marks left by stone tools and those left by animal teeth or other factors (Bunn, 1981; Potts and Shipman, 1981). Analyses of bones from several early localities at Olduvai have shown unambiguously that hominins used these specimens and left telltale cut marks from their stone tools. The sites investigated so far reveal a somewhat haphazard cutting and chopping, apparently unrelated to deliberate disarticulation. So the conclusion (Shipman, 1983) is that hominins scavenged carcasses, probably of carnivore kills, and did *not* hunt large animals themselves.

Following and expanding on the experimental approaches pioneered by Binford, Bunn, and others, Robert Blumenschine, of Rutgers University, has more recently conducted a more detailed analysis of the Olduvai material. Like his predecessors, Blumenschine has also concluded that the cut marks on animal bones are the result of hominin processing (Blumenschine, 1995). Blumenschine and colleagues further surmise that most meat acquisition (virtually all from large animals) was the result of scavenging (from remains of carnivore kills or from animals

of carcasses, and pieces of wood around their home ranges. At the very least, we would expect them to have displayed these behaviors to at least the same degree as that exhibited in living chimpanzees.

Also, as you'll see in the next chapter, by 6 mya—and perhaps as early as 7 mya—hominins had developed one crucial advantage: They were bipedal and so could more easily carry all kinds of objects from place to place. Ultimately, the efficient exploitation of resources widely distributed in time and space would most likely have led to using "central" spots where key components—especially stone objects—were cached, or collected (Potts, 1991; see "A Closer Look," above).

What we know for sure is that over a period of several million years, during the formative stages of hominin emergence, many components interacted, but not all of them developed simultaneously. As cognitive abilities developed, more efficient means of communication and learning resulted. Largely because of consequent neurological reorganization, more elaborate tools and social relationships also emerged.

that died from natural causes). In fact, these researchers suggest that scavenging was a crucial adaptive strategy for early hominins and considerably influenced their habitat usage, diet, and stone tool utilization (Blumenschine and Cavallo, 1992; Blumenschine and Peters, 1998). What's more, Blumenschine and colleagues have developed a model detailing how scavenging and other early hominin adaptive strategies integrate into patterns of land use (that is, differential utilization of various niches in and around Olduvai). From this model, they formulated specific hypotheses concerning the predicted distribution of artifacts and animal remains in different areas at Olduvai. Ongoing excavations at Olduvai are now aimed specifically at testing these hypotheses.

If early hominins (close to 2 mya) weren't hunting consistently, what did they obtain from scavenging the kills of other animals? One obvious answer is, whatever meat was left behind. However, the position of the cut marks suggests that early hominins were often hacking at non-meat-bearing portions of the skeletons. Perhaps they were after bone marrow and brain, substances not fully exploited by other predators and scavengers (Binford, 1981; Blumenschine and Cavallo, 1992).

Exciting new discoveries from the Bouri Peninsula of the Middle Awash of Ethiopia provide the best evidence yet for meat and marrow exploitation by early hominins. Dated to 2.5 mya (that is, as old as the oldest known artifacts), antelope and horse fossils from Bouri show telltale incisions and breaks, indicating that bones were not only smashed to extract marrow but also cut, ostensibly to retrieve meat (de

Heinzelin et al., 1999). The researchers who analyzed these materials have suggested that the greater dietary reliance on animal products may have been important in stimulating brain enlargement in the lineage leading to genus *Homo*.

Another new research twist relating to the reconstruction of early hominin diets has come from biochemical analysis of hominin teeth from South Africa (dating to about the same time range as hominins from Olduvai—or perhaps slightly earlier). In an innovative application of stable carbon isotope analysis (see p. 294), Matt Sponheimer and Julia Lee-Thorp found that these early hominin teeth revealed telltale chemical signatures relating to diet (Sponheimer and Lee-Thorp, 1999). In particular, the proportions of stable carbon isotopes indicated that these early hominins either ate grass products (such as seeds) or ate meat/marrow from animals that in turn had eaten grass products (that is, the hominins might well have derived a significant portion of their diet from meat or other animal products). This evidence comes from an exciting new perspective that provides a more direct indicator of early hominin diets. While it's not clear how much meat these early hominins consumed, these new data do suggest that they were consistently exploiting more open regions of their environment. Moreover, a new laser technology makes it possible to detect, from a single tooth, what sorts of foods were eaten from year to year and even seasonally within the same year. Sponheimer, Thorpe, and colleagues have used this exciting new approach to show that some early hominins were able to flexibly move between different environments and exploit seasonally available foods (Sponheimer et al., 2006).

These, in turn, selected for greater intelligence, which in turn selected for further neural elaboration. Quite clearly, these mutual dynamic interactions are at the very heart of what we call hominin *biocultural* evolution.

The Strategy of Paleoanthropology

To adequately understand human evolution, we obviously need a broad base of information. It's the paleoanthropologist's task to recover and interpret all the clues left by early hominins. *Paleoanthropology* is defined as "the study of ancient humans." As such, it's a diverse **multidisciplinary** pursuit seeking to reconstruct every possible bit of information concerning the dating, anatomy, behavior, and ecology of our hominin ancestors. In the past few decades, the study of early humans has marshaled the specialized skills of many different kinds of scientists.

multidisciplinary Pertaining to research involving mutual contributions and cooperation of experts from various scientific fields (i.e., disciplines).

Table **10-1   Subdisciplines of Paleoanthropology**

Physical Sciences	Biological Sciences	Social Sciences
Geology	Physical anthropology	Archaeology
Stratigraphy	Paleoecology	Ethnoarchaeology
Petrology	Paleontology	Cultural anthropology
(rocks, minerals)	(fossil animals)	Ethnography
Pedology (soils)	Palynology (fossil pollen)	Psychology
Geomorphology	Primatology	
Geophysics		
Chemistry		
Taphonomy		

This growing and exciting adventure includes, but is not limited to, geologists, vertebrate paleontologists, archaeologists, physical anthropologists, and paleo-ecologists (Table 10-1).

Geologists, usually working with other paleoanthropologists, do the initial surveys to locate potential early hominin sites. Many sophisticated techniques aid in this search, including the analysis of aerial and satellite imagery, though the most common way to find these sites is simply to trip over fossil remains. Vertebrate paleontologists are usually involved in this early survey work, helping find fossil beds containing faunal (animal) remains, because where conditions are favorable for the preservation of bone from such species as pigs and elephants, hominin remains may also be preserved. Paleontologists also can (through comparison with known faunal sequences) give quick and dirty approximate age estimates of fossil sites in the field without having to wait for the results of more time-consuming (though more accurate) analyses that will later be performed in a lab.

Once identified, fossil beds likely to contain hominin finds are subjected to extensive field surveying. For some sites, generally those postdating 2.6 mya (roughly the age of the oldest identified human artifacts), archaeologists take over in the search for hominin material traces. We don't necessarily have to find remains of early hominins themselves to know that they consistently occupied a particular area. Such material clues as **artifacts** inform us directly about early hominin activities. Modifying rocks according to a consistent plan or simply carrying them around from one place to another over fairly long distances (to be later discovered by archaeologists distributed in a manner not explicable by natural means, like streams or glaciers) is characteristic of no other animal but a hominin. So, when we see such material evidence at a site, we know without a doubt that hominins were present.

Because organic materials such as wood or fiber aren't usually preserved in the archaeological record of the oldest hominins, we have no solid evidence of the earliest stages of hominin cultural modifications. On the other hand, our ancestors at some point around 2.6 mya started showing a veritable fascination with stones, partly because they could be used as convenient objects for throwing or for holding down other objects, such as skins and windbreaks. Even more crucially, they also provided the most durable and sharpest cutting edges available at that time. Luckily for us, stone is almost indestructible, and some early hominin sites are strewn with thousands of stone artifacts. The earliest artifact sites now documented are from the Gona and Bouri areas in northeastern Ethiopia, dating to 2.6 mya (de Heinzelin et al., 1999; Semaw et al., 2003). Other contenders for the "earliest" stone assemblage come from the adjacent Hadar and Middle Awash areas, immediately to the south in Ethiopia, dated 2.5–2.0 mya.

artifacts Objects or materials made or modified for use by hominins. The earliest artifacts are usually made of stone or, occasionally, bone.

If an area is clearly demonstrated to be a hominin site, much more concentrated research will then begin. We should point out that a more mundane but significant aspect of paleoanthropology not reflected in Table 10-1 is the financial one. Just the initial survey work in usually remote areas costs many thousands of dollars, and mounting a concentrated research project costs several hundred thousand dollars more. This is why many projects are engaged in areas where promising surface finds have been made; massive financial support is required from government agencies and private donations, and it's unrealistic to simply dig at random. A great deal of a paleoanthropologist's effort and time is necessarily devoted to writing grant proposals or speaking on the lecture circuit to raise the required funds for this work.

Once the financial hurdle has been cleared, a coordinated research project can begin. Usually headed by an archaeologist or physical anthropologist, the field crew continues to survey and map the target area in great detail. In addition, field crew members begin searching carefully for bones and artifacts eroding out of the soil, taking pollen and soil samples for ecological analysis, and carefully collecting rock and other samples for use in various dating techniques. If, in this early stage of exploration, members of the field crew find fossil hominin remains, they will feel very lucky indeed. The international press usually considers human fossils the most exciting kind of discovery, a fortunate circumstance that produces wide publicity and often ensures future financial support. More likely, the crew will accumulate much information on geological setting, ecological data (particularly faunal remains), and, with some luck, artifacts and other archaeological traces.

Although paleoanthropological fieldwork is typically a long and arduous process, the detailed analyses of collected samples and other data back in the laboratory are even more time-consuming. Archaeologists must clean, sort, label, and identify all artifacts, and vertebrate paleontologists must do the same for all faunal remains. Knowing the kinds of animals represented—whether forest browsers, woodland species, or open-country forms—greatly helps in reconstructing the local *paleoecological* settings in which early hominins lived. Analyzing the fossil pollen collected from hominin sites by a scientist called a palynologist further aids in developing a detailed environmental reconstruction. All these paleoecological analyses can assist in reconstructing the diet of early humans. Also, the **taphonomy** of the site must be worked out in order to understand its depositional history—that is, how the site formed over time and if its present state is in a *primary* or *secondary* **context**.

In the concluding stages of interpretation, the paleoanthropologist draws together these essentials:

1. *Dating*: geological, paleontological, geophysical
2. *Paleoecology*: paleontology, palynology, geomorphology, taphonomy
3. *Archaeological traces of behavior*
4. *Anatomical evidence from hominin remains*

By analyzing all this information, scientists try to "flesh out" the kind of creature that may have been our direct ancestor (or at least a very close relative). Primatologists may assist here by showing the detailed relationships between the anatomical structure and behavior of humans and that of contemporary nonhuman primates (see Chapters 6 through 8). Cultural anthropologists and ethnoarchaeologists (who study the "archaeology" of living groups by examining their material remains) may contribute ethnographic information concerning the varied nature of modern human behavior, particularly ecological adaptations of those contemporary hunter-gatherer groups exploiting roughly similar environmental settings as those reconstructed for a hominin site.

taphonomy (*taphos*, meaning "tomb") The study of how bones and other materials came to be buried in the earth and preserved as fossils. Taphonomists study the processes of sedimentation, the action of streams, preservation properties of bone, and carnivore disturbance factors.

context The environmental setting where an archaeological trace is found. Primary context is the setting in which the archaeological trace was originally deposited. A secondary context is one to which it has been moved (such as by the action of a stream).

The end result of years of research by dozens of scientists will (we hope) produce a more complete and accurate understanding of human evolution—how we came to be the way we are. Both biological and cultural aspects of our ancestors contribute to this investigation, each process developing in relation to the other.

Paleoanthropology in Action—Olduvai Gorge

Several paleoanthropological projects of the scope just discussed have recently been pursued in diverse places in the Old World, including East and South Africa, Indonesia, and the Republic of Georgia in eastern Europe. Of all these localities, the one that has yielded the finest quality and greatest abundance of paleoanthropological information concerning early hominin behavior has been Olduvai Gorge.

First "discovered" in the early twentieth century by a German butterfly collector, Olduvai was soon scientifically surveyed and its wealth of paleontological evidence recognized. In 1931, Louis Leakey made his first trip to Olduvai Gorge and almost immediately realized its significance for studying early humans. From 1935, when she first worked there, until she retired in 1984, Mary Leakey directed the archaeological excavations at Olduvai.

Located in the Serengeti Plain of northern Tanzania, Olduvai is a steep-sided valley resembling a miniature version of the Grand Canyon. A deep ravine cut into an almost mile-high grassland plateau of East Africa, Olduvai extends more than 25 miles in total length. Climatically, the semiarid pattern of present-day Olduvai is believed to be similar to what it has been for the last 2 million years. The surrounding countryside is a grassland savanna broken occasionally by scrub bushes and acacia trees.

Geographically, Olduvai is located on the eastern branch of the Great Rift Valley of Africa. The geological processes associated with the formation of the Rift Valley make Olduvai (and other East African sites) extremely important to paleoanthropological investigation. Three of these processes of geological rifting are most significant:

1. Faulting, or earth movement, exposes geological beds near the surface that are normally hidden by hundreds of feet of accumulated sediment called overburden.
2. Active volcanic processes cause rapid sedimentation, which often yields excellent preservation of bone and artifacts that normally would be scattered by carnivore activity and erosion forces.
3. Volcanic activity provides a wealth of radiometrically datable material.

As a result, Olduvai is a site of superb preservation of ancient hominins, portions of their environment, and their behavioral patterns in datable contexts, all of which are readily accessible.

The greatest contribution Olduvai has made to paleoanthropological research is the establishment of an extremely well-documented and correlated sequence of geological, paleontological, archaeological, and hominin remains over the last 2 million years. At the very foundation of all paleoanthropological research is a well-established geological context. At Olduvai, the geological and paleogeographical context is known in minute detail. Today, Olduvai is a geologist's delight, containing sediments in some places 350 feet thick, accumulated from lava flows (basalts), tuffs (windblown or waterborne fine deposits from nearby volcanoes), sandstones, claystones, and limestone conglomerates, all neatly stratified like a layer cake

(Fig. 10-3). A hominin site can therefore be accurately dated relative to other sites in the Olduvai Gorge by cross-correlating known marker beds that have already been dated and can be quite quickly identified by geologists in the field. At the most general geological level, the stratigraphic sequence at Olduvai is broken down into four major geological strata called beds (Beds I–IV).

Paleontological evidence of fossilized animal bones also has come from Olduvai in great abundance. More than 150 species of extinct animals have been recognized, including fish, turtles, crocodiles, pigs, giraffes, horses, and many birds, rodents, and antelopes. Careful analysis of such remains has yielded voluminous information concerning the ecological conditions of early human habitats. What's more, the precise analysis of bones directly associated with artifacts can sometimes tell us about the diet as well as the various ways bone was handled and modified by early hominins. (There are some reservations, however; see "A Closer Look," pp. 278–279.)

The archaeological sequence is also well documented for the last 2 million years. Beginning at the earliest hominin site in Olduvai (circa 1.85 mya), there is already a well-developed stone tool kit, consisting primarily of numerous small flake tools (Leakey, 1971). Such a tool industry is called *Oldowan* (after Olduvai), and it continues into later beds with some small modifications.

Finally, partial remains of several fossilized hominins have been found at Olduvai, ranging in time from the earliest occupation levels to fairly recent *Homo sapiens*. Of the more than 40 individuals represented, many are quite fragmentary, but a few are excellently preserved. While the center of hominin discoveries has now shifted to other areas of East Africa, it was the initial discovery by Mary Leakey of the *Zinjanthropus* (nicknamed "Zinj") skull at Olduvai in July 1959 that focused the world's attention on this remarkably rich area (Fig. 10-4; also see "A Closer Look," p. 284).

Dating Methods

An essential objective of paleoanthropology is to place sites and fossils into a time frame. In other words, we want to know how old they are. How, then, do we date sites—or more precisely, the geological strata, or layers, in which sites are found? The question is both reasonable and important, so let's examine the dating techniques used by paleontologists, archaeologists, and other scientists involved in paleoanthropological research.

Scientists use two kinds of dating for this purpose: relative dating and **chronometric dating** (also known as *absolute dating*). Relative dating methods tell us that something is older or younger than something else, but not by how much. If, for example, a cranium is found at a depth of 50 feet and another cranium at 70 feet at the same site, we usually assume that the specimen discovered at 70 feet is older. We may not know the date (in years) of either one, but we'd know that one is older

Robert Jurmain

Figure 10-3

View of the main gorge at Olduvai. Note the clear sequence of geological beds. The discontinuity in the stratigraphic layers (to the right of the red arrow) is a major fault line.

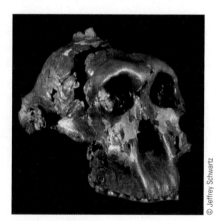

© Jeffrey Schwartz

Figure 10-4

Zinjanthropus cranium, discovered by Mary Leakey at Olduvai Gorge in 1959. As we will see in Chapter 11, this fossil is now included as part of the genus *Paranthropus*.

chronometric dating (*chrono*, meaning "time," and *metric*, meaning "measure") A dating technique that gives an estimate in actual numbers of years; also known as absolute dating.

A Closer Look

Discovery of *Zinjanthropus* and the Beginnings of Modern Paleoanthropology

On a typically hot and dry East African summer's day 50 years ago, paleoanthropology changed forever. Really, it was more than that. On July 17, 1959, with Mary Leakey's discovery of the "Zinj" skull at Olduvai Gorge, modern paleoanthropology was born. This was the first truly ancient hominin to be found in East Africa, and its discovery pointed the way to all the further remarkable finds made since. It also catapulted the Leakeys onto the world stage, where they became perhaps the most famous anthropological couple ever. Through the allure of their personalities and the publication of their work in *National Geographic* as well as their many television specials, millions of people learned about and became fascinated with the story of early hominins and the scientists who study them.

Looking back at that extraordinary July day 50 years ago, the magic of the moment is best captured in Louis Leakey's own words, published the next year in *National Geographic*:

That morning I woke with a headache and a slight fever. Reluctantly I agreed to spend the day in camp.

With one of us out of commission, it was even more vital for the other to continue the work, for our precious seven-week season was running out. So Mary departed for the diggings with Sally and Toots [two of their dalmatians] in the Land-Rover, and I settled back to a restless day off.

Some time later—perhaps I dozed off—I heard the Land-Rover coming up fast to camp. I had a momentary vision of Mary stung by one of our hundreds of resident scorpions or bitten by a snake that had slipped past the dogs.

The Land-Rover rattled to a stop, and I heard Mary's voice calling over and over: "I've got him! I've got him! I've got him!"

Still groggy from the headache. I couldn't make her out. "Got what? Are you hurt?" I asked.

"Him, the man! *Our* man," Mary said. "The one we've been looking for [for more than 20 years]. Come quick, I've found his teeth!"

Magically, the headache departed. I somehow fumbled into my work clothes while Mary waited.

As we bounced down the trail in the car, she described the dramatic moment of discovery. She had been searching the slope where I had found the first Oldowan tools in 1931, when suddenly her eye caught a piece of bone lodged in a rock slide. Instantly, she recognized it as part of a skull—almost certainly not that of an animal.

Her glance wandered higher, and there in the rock were two immense teeth, side by side. This time there was no question: They were undeniably human. Carefully, she marked the spot with a cairn of stones, rushed to the Land-Rover, and sped back to camp with the news.

The gorge trail ended half a mile from the site, and we left the car at a dead run. Mary led the way to the cairn, and we knelt to examine the treasure.

I saw at once that she was right. The teeth were premolars, and they had belonged to a human. I was sure they were larger than anything similar ever found, nearly twice the width of modern man's.

I turned to look at Mary, and we almost cried with sheer joy, each seized by that terrific emotion that comes rarely in life. After all our hoping and hardship and sacrifice, at last we had reached our goal—we had discovered the world's earliest known human.

Figure 1

Louis and Mary Leakey, shown holding a cast of the *"Zinj"* skull compared to a modern human skull.

© Bettmann/Corbis

(or younger) than the other. Although this may not satisfy our curiosity about the actual number of years involved, it would give some idea of the evolutionary changes in cranial morphology (structure), especially if we found several crania at different levels and compared them.

This method of relative dating is based on **stratigraphy** and was one of the first techniques to be used by scientists working with the vast period of geological time. Stratigraphy, in turn, is based on the **principle of superposition**, which states that a lower stratum (layer) is older than a higher stratum. Because much of the earth's crust has been laid down by layer after layer of sedimentary rock, much like the layers of a cake, stratigraphy has been a valuable aid in reconstructing the history of the earth and the life upon it.

Stratigraphic dating does, however, have some problems. Earth disturbances, such as volcanic activity, river activity, and mountain building, may shift strata and the objects within them, and the chronology of the material may be difficult or even impossible to reconstruct. What's more, it's impossible to accurately determine the time period of a particular stratum—that is, how long it took to accumulate.

Another method of relative dating is *fluorine analysis*, which applies only to bones (Oakley, 1963). Bones in the earth are exposed to the seepage of groundwater that usually contains fluorine. The longer a bone lies in the earth, the more fluorine it will incorporate during the fossilization process. Bones deposited at the same time in the same location thus should contain the same amount of fluorine. Professor Kenneth Oakley, of the British Museum, used this technique in the early 1950s to expose the Piltdown (England) hoax by demonstrating that a human skull was considerably older than the jaw (ostensibly also human) found with it (Weiner, 1955). When a discrepancy in fluorine content led Oakley and others to more closely examine the bones, they found that the jaw was not that of a hominin at all but of a young adult orangutan!

Unfortunately, fluorine analysis is useful only with bones found at the same location. Because the amount of fluorine in groundwater is based on local conditions, it varies from place to place. Also, some groundwater may not contain any fluorine. For these reasons, it's impossible to use fluorine analysis when comparing bones from different localities.

In both stratigraphy and fluorine analysis, it's impossible to calculate the actual age of the rock stratum and the objects in it. To determine the age in years, scientists have developed various chronometric techniques based on the phenomenon of radioactive decay. Actually, the theory is pretty simple: Certain radioactive isotopes of elements are unstable, causing them to decay and form an isotopic variation of another element. Since the rate of decay follows a definite mathematical pattern, the radioactive material forms an accurate geological time clock of sorts. By measuring the amount of decay in a particular sample, scientists can calculate the number of years it took for that amount of decay to accumulate. Chronometric techniques have been used for dating the immense age of the earth as well as artifacts less than 1,000 years old. Several techniques have been employed for a number of years and are now quite well known.

The most important chronometric technique used to date early hominins involves potassium-40 (^{40}K), which has a **half-life** of 1.25 billion years and produces argon-40 (^{40}Ar). Known as the K/Ar or potassium-argon method, this procedure has been extensively used by paleoanthropologists in dating materials in the 1- to 5-million-year range, especially in East Africa where past volcanic activity makes this dating technique possible. A variant of this technique, the ^{40}Ar/^{39}Ar method, also has recently been used to date several hominin localities. The ^{40}Ar/^{39}Ar

stratigraphy Study of the sequential layering of deposits.

principle of superposition In a stratigraphic sequence, the lower layers were deposited before the upper layers. Or, simply put, the stuff on top of a heap was put there last.

half-life The time period in which one-half the amount of a radioactive isotope is converted chemically to a daughter product. For example, after 1.25 billion years, half the ^{40}K remains; after 2.5 billion years, one-fourth remains.

method allows analysis of smaller samples (even single crystals), reduces experimental error, and is more precise than standard K/Ar dating. Consequently, it can be used to date a wide chronological range—indeed, the entire hominin record, even up to modern times. Recent applications have provided excellent dates for several early hominin sites in East Africa (discussed in Chapter 11) as well as somewhat later sites in Java (discussed in Chapter 12). In fact, the technique was recently used to date the famous Mt. Vesuvius eruption of A.D. 79, which destroyed the city of Pompeii as documented by ancient historians. Remarkably, the midrange date obtained by the $^{40}Ar/^{39}Ar$ technique was A.D. 73, just 6 years from the known date (Renne et al., 1997)! Organic material, such as bone, can't be measured by these techniques; but the rock matrix in which the bone is found can be. Scientists used K/Ar dating to obtain a minimum date for the deposit containing the *Zinjanthropus* cranium by dating a volcanic layer above the fossil.

Rocks that provide the best samples for K/Ar and $^{40}Ar/^{39}Ar$ are those heated to an extremely high temperature, such as that generated by volcanic activity. When the rock is in a molten state, argon, a gas, is driven off. As the rock cools and solidifies, potassium-40 continues to break down to argon; but now the gas is physically trapped in the cooled rock. To obtain the date of the rock, scientists reheat it and measure the escaping gas. Because the rock must in the past have been exposed to extreme heat, this limits these techniques to areas where sediments have been superheated, such as regions of past volcanic activity or meteorite falls.

A well-known radiometric method popular with archaeologists makes use of carbon-14 (^{14}C), with a half-life of 5,730 years. Carbon-14 has been used to date organic materials (such as wood, bone, cloth, and plant remains) from less than 1,000 years to as old as 75,000 years, although accuracy is reduced for materials more than 40,000 years old. Since this technique applies to the latter stages of hominin evolution, its applications relate to material discussed in Chapters 13 and 14.

Some inorganic artifacts can be directly dated through the use of **thermoluminescence** (TL). This method, too, relies on the principle of radiometric decay. Stone material used in manufacturing tools invariably contains trace amounts of radioactive elements, such as uranium or thorium. As the rock gets heated (perhaps by accidentally falling into a campfire or by deliberately being heated to help in its production), the rapid heating releases displaced beta particles trapped within the rock. As the particles escape, they emit a dull glow known as thermoluminescence. After that, radioactive decay resumes within the fired stone, again building up electrons at a steady rate. To determine the age of an archaeological sample, the researcher must heat the sample to 500°C and measure its thermoluminescence; from that, the date can be calculated. Used especially by archaeologists to date ceramic pots from recent sites, TL can also be used to date burned flint tools from earlier hominin sites.

Like TL, two other techniques used to date sites from the latter phases of hominin evolution (where neither K/Ar nor radiocarbon dating is possible) are uranium series dating and electron spin resonance (ESR) dating. Uranium series dating relies on radioactive decay of short-lived uranium isotopes, and ESR is similar to TL because it's based on measuring trapped electrons. However, while TL is used on heated materials such as clay or stone tools, ESR is used on the dental enamel of animals. All three of these dating methods have been used to provide key dating controls for hominin sites discussed in Chapters 12 through 14.

You should realize that none of these methods is precise. Each one has problems that must be carefully considered during laboratory measurement and when

thermoluminiscence (TL) (ther-mo-loo-min-ess´-ence) Technique for dating certain archaeological materials (such as stone tools) that were heated in the past and that release stored energy of radioactive decay as light upon reheating.

A Closer Look

Chronometric Dating Estimates

Chronometric dates are usually determined after testing several geological samples. The dates that result from such testing are combined and expressed statistically. For example, say that five different samples are used to give the K/Ar date 1.75 ± 0.2 mya for a particular geological bed. The individual results from all five samples are totaled together to give an average date (here, 1.75 mya), and the standard deviation is calculated (here, 0.2 million years; that is, 200,000 years). The dating estimate is then reported as the mean plus or minus (±) one standard deviation. Those of you who have taken statistics will realize that (assuming a normal distribution) 67 percent of a distribution of dates is included within 1 standard deviation (±) of the mean. Thus, the chronometric result, as shown in the reported range, is simply a probability statement that 67 percent of the dates from all the samples tested fell within the range of dates from 1.55 to 1.95 mya. You should carefully read chronometric dates and study the reported ranges. It's likely that the smaller the range, the more samples were analyzed. Smaller ranges mean more precise estimates; better laboratory controls will also increase precision.

collecting material to be analyzed. Because the methods aren't perfectly accurate, approximate dates are given as probability statements with an error range. For example, a date given as 1.75 ± 0.2 mya should be read as having a 67 percent chance that the actual date lies somewhere between 1.55 and 1.95 mya (see "A Closer Look," above).

To sum up, there are two ways of answering the question of age. We can say that a particular fossil is *x* number of years old, a date usually determined by chronometric dating. Or we can say that fossil X lived before or after fossil Y, as determined by relative dating.

At a Glance

Relative and Chronometric Dating

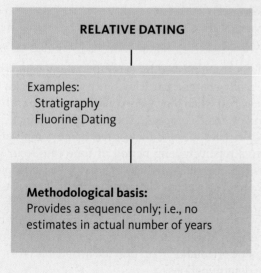

RELATIVE DATING

Examples:
  Stratigraphy
  Fluorine Dating

Methodological basis:
Provides a sequence only; i.e., no estimates in actual number of years

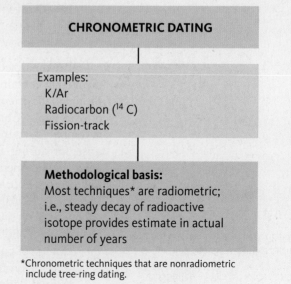

CHRONOMETRIC DATING

Examples:
  K/Ar
  Radiocarbon (^{14}C)
  Fission-track

Methodological basis:
Most techniques* are radiometric; i.e., steady decay of radioactive isotope provides estimate in actual number of years

*Chronometric techniques that are nonradiometric include tree-ring dating.

Applications of Dating Methods: Examples from Olduvai

Olduvai has been a rich proving ground for numerous dating techniques. As a result, it has some of the best-documented chronology for any hominin site in the Early or Middle Pleistocene.

As we've noted, the potassium-argon (K/Ar) method is an extremely valuable tool for dating early hominin sites and has been widely used in areas containing suitable volcanic deposits (mainly in East Africa) or superheated debris from meteorites (mainly in Indonesia). At Olduvai, K/Ar has given several reliable dates of the underlying basalt and several tuffs in Bed I, including the one associated with the "Zinj" find (now dated at 1.79 ± 0.03 mya).

Due to several potential sources of error, K/Ar dating must be cross-checked using other independent methods. Once again, the sediments at Olduvai provide some excellent examples of the use of many of these other dating techniques.

Fission-track dating is one of the most important techniques for cross-checking K/Ar determinations. The key to fission-track dating is that uranium-238 (^{238}U) decays regularly by spontaneous fission. By counting the proportion of uranium atoms that have fissioned, or split apart (shown as microscopic tracks caused by explosive fission of ^{238}U nuclei), researchers can estimate the age of a mineral or natural glass sample. One of the earliest applications of this technique was on volcanic pumice from Olduvai, giving a date of 2.30 ($\pm$ 0.28) mya—in good agreement with K/Ar dates. Fission-track dating has also been used to date baked earth and pottery from contexts as recently as 5,000 years ago from a site in Iran (Wagner, 1996).

Another important means of cross-checking dates is called **paleomagnetism**. This technique is based on the constantly shifting nature of the earth's magnetic pole. Of course, the earth's magnetic pole is now oriented in a northerly direction, but this hasn't always been so. In fact, the orientation and intensity of the geomagnetic field have undergone numerous documented changes in the last few million years. From our current viewpoint, we call a northern orientation "normal" and a southern one "reversed." Here are the major epochs (also called "chrons") of recent geomagnetic time for the last few million years:

0.7 mya–present	Normal
2.6–0.7 mya	Reversed
3.4–2.6 mya	Normal
?–3.4 mya	Reversed

Paleomagnetic dating is accomplished by carefully taking samples of sediments that contain magnetically charged particles. Since these particles maintain the magnetic orientation they had when they were consolidated into rock (millions of years ago), we have a kind of "fossil compass." Then the paleomagnetic sequence is compared against the K/Ar dates to see if they agree. Some complications may arise, for during an epoch, a relatively long period of time can occur when the geomagnetic orientation is the opposite of what's expected. For example, during the reversed epoch from 2.6 to 0.7 mya (the Matuyama epoch), there was an event lasting about 210,000 years when orientations were normal. (Because this phenomenon was first conclusively demonstrated at Olduvai, it's appropriately called the *Olduvai event.*) But once these oscillations in the geomagnetic pole are worked out, the sequence of paleomagnetic orientations can provide a valuable cross-check for K/Ar and fission-track age determinations.

A final dating technique used at Olduvai and other African sites is based on the regular evolutionary changes in well-known groups of mammals. This technique, called *faunal correlation* or **biostratigraphy**, provides yet another means

paleomagnetism Dating method based on the earth's shifting magnetic pole.

biostratigraphy A relative dating technique based on regular changes seen in evolving groups of animals as well as presence or absence of particular species.

of cross-checking the other methods. This technique employs some of the same methods used in relative stratigraphic dating, but it incorporates information on sequences of faunal remains from different sites. For instance, the presence of particular fossil pigs, elephants, antelopes, rodents, and carnivores in areas where dates are known (by K/Ar, for example) can be used to extrapolate an approximate age for other, more hard-to-date sites by noting which genera and species are present at those sites.

All these methods—K/Ar dating, fission-track dating, paleomagnetism, and biostratigraphy—have been used in dating sites at Olduvai. So many different dating techniques are necessary because no single method is perfectly reliable by itself. Sampling error, contamination, and experimental error can all introduce ambiguities into our so-called absolute dates. Because the sources of error are different for each technique, however, cross-checking among several independent methods is the most reliable way of authenticating the chronology for early hominin sites.

Excavations at Olduvai

Because the vertical cut of the Olduvai Gorge provides a cross section of 2 million years of earth history, sites can be excavated by digging "straight in" rather than first having to remove tons of overlying dirt (Fig. 10-5). In fact, as mentioned before, sites are usually discovered by merely walking the exposures and observing what bones, stones, and so forth, are eroding out.

Several dozen hominin sites (at a minimum, they are bone and tool scatters) have been surveyed at Olduvai, and Mary Leakey extensively excavated close to 20 of these. An incredible amount of paleoanthropological information has come from these excavated areas.

There has been much controversy regarding how to interpret the types of activities early hominins carried out at these sites (Fig. 10-6). Archaeologists had thought, as suggested by Mary Leakey and others, that many of the sites functioned as "campsites." Lewis Binford has forcefully critiqued this view and has alternatively suggested that much of the refuse accumulated is the result of nonhominin

Robert Jurmain

Figure 10-5

Excavations in progress at Olduvai. This site, more than 1 million years old, was located when a hominin ulna (arm bone) was found eroding out of the side of the gorge.

Robert Jurmain

Figure 10-6

A dense scatter of stone and some fossilized animal bone from a site at Olduvai, dated at approximately 1.6 mya. Some of these remains are the result of hominin activities.

blanks In archaeology, stones suitably sized and shaped to be further worked into tools.

flake Thin-edged fragment removed from a core.

core Stone reduced by flake removal. A core may or may not itself be used as a tool.

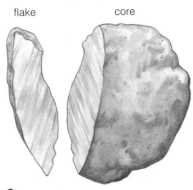

flake   core

Figure 10-7

Flake and core.

290

(that is, predator) activities. Another possibility, suggested by Richard Potts (1984), is that these areas served as collecting points (caches) for some tools. This last interpretation has received considerable support from other archaeologists in recent years.

A final interpretation, incorporating aspects of the hypotheses proposed by Binford and Potts, has been suggested by Robert Blumenschine. He argues that early hominins were gatherers and scavengers, and the bone and stone scatters reflect these activities (Blumenschine, 1986; Blumenschine and Cavallo, 1992; see "A Closer Look," pp. 278–279).

Experimental Archaeology

Simply classifying artifacts into categories and types is not enough. We can learn considerably more about our ancestors by understanding how they made and used their tools. It is, after all, the artifactual traces of prehistoric tools of stone (and, to a lesser degree, bone) that provide much of our information concerning early human behavior. Tons of stone debris litter archaeological sites worldwide. A casual walk along the bottom of Olduvai Gorge could well be interrupted every few seconds by tripping over prehistoric tools!

So, archaeologists are presented with a wealth of information revealing at least one part of human material culture. What do these artifacts tell us about our ancestors? How were these tools made, and how were they used? To answer these questions, contemporary archaeologists have tried to reconstruct prehistoric techniques of stone toolmaking, butchering, and so forth. In this way, experimental archaeologists are, in a sense, trying to re-create the past.

Stone Tool (Lithic) Technology

Stone is by far the most common residue of prehistoric cultural behavior. For this reason, archaeologists have long been keenly interested in this material.

When struck properly, certain types of stone will fracture in a controlled way; these nodules are called **blanks**. The smaller piece that comes off is called a **flake**, while the larger remaining chunk is called a **core** (Fig. 10-7). Both core and flake have sharp edges useful for cutting, sawing, or scraping. The earliest hominin cultural inventions probably used nondurable materials that didn't survive archaeologically (such as a digging stick or an ostrich eggshell used as a watertight container). Still, a basic human invention was the recognition that stone can be fractured to produce sharp edges.

For many years, it's been assumed that in the earliest known stone tool industry (that is, the Oldowan), both core and flake tools were deliberately manufactured as final, desired products. Such core implements as "choppers" were thought to be central artifactual components of these early **lithic** assemblages (in fact, the Oldowan is often depicted as a "chopping tool industry"). However, detailed reevaluation of these artifacts has thrown these traditional assumptions into doubt. By carefully analyzing the attributes of Oldowan artifacts from Olduvai, Potts (1991, 1993) concluded that the so-called core tools really weren't tools after all. He suggests instead that early hominins were deliberately producing flake tools, and the various stone choppers were simply "incidental stopping points in the process of removing flakes from cores" (Potts, 1993, p. 60). As Potts concludes, "The flaked stones of the Oldowan thus cannot be demonstrated to constitute discrete target designs, but can be shown to represent simple by-products of the repetitive act of producing sharp flakes" (Potts, 1993, pp. 60–61).

Breaking rocks by bashing them together is one thing. Producing consistent results, even apparently simple flakes, is quite another. You might want to give it a try, just to appreciate how difficult making a stone tool can be. It takes years of practice before modern stone **knappers** learn the intricacies—the type of rock to choose, the kind of hammer to employ, the angle and velocity with which to strike, and so on. Such experience allows us to appreciate how skilled in stoneworking our ancestors truly were.

Flakes can be removed from cores in various ways. The object in making a tool, however, is to produce a usable cutting surface. By reproducing results similar to those of earlier stoneworkers, experimental archaeologists can infer which kinds of techniques *might* have been employed.

For example, the nodules (now thought to be blanks) found in sites in Bed I at Olduvai (circa 1.85–1.2 mya) are flaked on one side only (that is, *unifacially*). It's possible, but by no means easy, to produce such implements by hitting one stone—the hammerstone—against another—the core—in a method called **direct percussion** (Fig. 10-8).

In Bed IV sites (circa 400,000 ya*), however, most of the tools are flaked on both sides (that is, *bifacially*) and have long rippled edges. Such a result can't be reproduced by direct percussion with just a hammerstone. The edges must have been straightened ("retouched") with a "soft" hammer, such as bone or antler.

Reproducing implements similar to those found in later stages of human cultural development calls for even more sophisticated techniques. Tools such as the delicate **microliths** found in the uppermost beds at Olduvai (circa 17,000 ya), the superb Solutrean blades from Europe (circa 20,000 ya), and the expertly crafted Folsom projectile points from the New World (circa 10,000 ya) all require a mastery of stone matched by few knappers today.

To reproduce implements like those just mentioned, the knapper must remove extremely thin flakes. This can be done only through **pressure flaking**—for example, using a pointed piece of bone, antler, or hard wood and pressing firmly against the stone (Fig. 10-9).

Once the tools were manufactured, our ancestors used them in ways that we can infer through further experimentation. For example, archaeologists from the Smithsonian Institution successfully butchered an entire elephant (which had died in a zoo) using stone tools they had made for that purpose (Park, 1978). Other archaeologists have cut down (small) trees using stone axes they had made.

Ancient tools themselves may carry telltale signs of how they were used. Lawrence Keeley performed a series of experiments in which he manufactured

*ya = years ago.

Figure **10-8**
Direct percussion.

Figure **10-9**
Pressure flaking.

lithic (*lith*, meaning "stone") Referring to stone tools.

knappers People (frequently archaeologists) who make stone tools.

direct percussion Striking a core or flake with a hammerstone.

microliths (*micro*, meaning "small," and *lith*, meaning "stone") Small stone tools usually produced from narrow blades punched from a core; found especially in Africa during the latter part of the Pleistocene.

pressure flaking A method of removing flakes from a core by pressing a pointed implement (e.g., bone or antler) against the stone.

Figure **10-10**

Photomicrograph (200x) showing bone working polish on a 9,050 year old stone tool excavated from the O.V. Clary Site in Nebraska by Dr. M.G. Hill of Iowa State University.

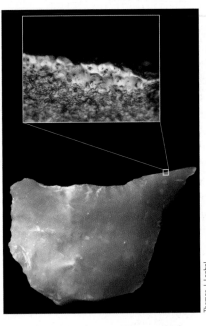

Thomas J. Loebel

flint tools and then used them in diverse ways—whittling wood, cutting bone, cutting meat, and scraping skins. Viewing these implements under a microscope at fairly high magnification revealed patterns of polishes, striations, and other kinds of **microwear**. What's most intriguing is that these patterns varied, depending on how the tool was used and which material was worked. For example, Keeley was able to distinguish among tools used on bone, antler, meat, plant materials, and hides. In the latter case, he was even able to determine if the hides were fresh or dried! Orientations of microwear markings also give some indication of how the tool was used (such as for cutting or scraping). Because these experiments into stone tool manufacture and use reveal valuable information about variations in microwear morphology, researchers are able to use the experimentally produced data to infer about specific stone tool usage in the past—such as for the 9,000-year-old paleo-Indian flake from Nebraska shown in Figure 10-10, which shows microwear polish from cutting antler or bone. Evidence of microwear polish has been examined on even the extremely early hominin stone tools from Koobi Fora (East Lake Turkana), in Kenya (Keeley and Toth, 1981).

Recent advances in tool use studies include the application of scanning electron microscopy (SEM). Working at 10,000× magnification, researchers have found that the edges of stone implements sometimes retain plant fibers and amino acids, as well as nonorganic residues, including **phytoliths**. Because phytoliths produced by different plant species are morphologically distinctive, there is good potential for identifying the botanical materials that came in contact with the tool during use (Rovner, 1983). Such work is most exciting; for the first time, we may be able to make definite statements concerning the uses of ancient tools.

Analysis of Bone

Experimental archaeologists are also interested in the ways bone is altered by human and natural forces. Other scientists are vitally concerned with this process as well; in fact, it has produced an entire new branch of paleoecology—taphonomy. Taphonomists have carried out comprehensive research on how natural factors influence bone deposition and preservation. In South Africa, C. K. Brain collected data on contemporary African butchering practices, carnivore (dog) disturbances, and so forth, and then correlated these factors with the kinds and numbers of elements usually found in bone accumulations (Brain, 1981). In this way, he was able to account for the accumulation of most (if not all) of the bones in South African cave sites. Likewise, in East African game parks, observations have been made on decaying animals to measure the effects of weathering, predator chewing, and trampling (Behrensmeyer et al., 1979; Perkins, 2003).

Further insight into the many ways bone is altered by natural factors has come from experimental work in the laboratory (Boaz and Behrensmeyer, 1976). In an experiment conducted at the University of California, Berkeley, human bones

microwear Polishes, striations, and other diagnostic microscopic changes on the edges of stone tools.

phytoliths (*phyto*, meaning "hidden," and *lith*, meaning "stone") Microscopic silica structures formed in the cells of many plants, particularly grasses.

were put into a running-water trough. Researchers observed how far the water carried different pieces and recorded how much and what kind of damage was done. Such information is extremely useful in interpreting early hominin sites. For example, the distribution of hominin fossils at Olduvai suggests that active water transport was less prevalent there than in the Omo River Valley in southern Ethiopia (another area from which hominin fossils have been found; discussed in Chapter 11).

Detailed examination of bones may also provide evidence of butchering and bone breakage by hominins, including cut marks and percussion marks left by stone tools. Great care must be taken to distinguish marks left on bone by carnivore or rodent gnawing, weathering processes, hoof marks, or even normal growth. High magnification of a cut made by a stone tool may reveal a minutely striated and roughened groove scored into the bone's surface. Many such finds have been recognized at early hominin sites, including Olduvai Gorge (Bunn, 1981; Potts and Shipman, 1981; see "A Closer Look," pp. 278–279).

Reconstruction of Early Hominin Environments and Behavior

Now that we've reviewed the various methods used by paleoanthropologists to collect their varied data, we can look at the intriguing ways this information is *interpreted*. Be aware that much of this interpretation is quite speculative and less amenable to scientific verification than more concrete sources of data (for example, that relating to dating, geology, or hominin anatomy). (In Chapter 1, we discussed how hypotheses are developed and tested by scientists, noting the requirement that *scientific* explanations be falsifiable.)

Paleoanthropologists are keenly interested not just in *how* early hominins evolved but also in *why* the process occurred the way it did. Accordingly, they frequently use the data available as a basis for broad, speculative scenarios that try to explain both early hominin adaptations to a changing environment and the new behaviors that these hominins adopted. Such scenarios are fascinating, and paleoanthropologists enjoy constructing them (and certainly many in the general public enjoy reading them). Without doubt, for scientists and laypersons alike, our curiosity inevitably leads to intriguing and sweeping generalizations. Still, in the following discussion, we'll focus on what is *known* from the paleoanthropological record itself and separate that from the more speculative conclusions. You, too, should evaluate these explanations with a critical eye and try to identify the empirical basis for each type of reconstruction. It's important not to accept a scenario merely because it's appealing (often because it's simple) or just because it seems plausible. We always need to ask ourselves what kinds of evidence support a particular contention, how generally the explanation fits the evidence (that is, how consistent it is with different types of data from varied sources), and what types of new evidence might either help to verify or potentially falsify the interpretation.

Environmental Explanations for Hominin Origins

As we'll discuss in the next chapter, the earliest hominins evolved late in the Miocene or very early in the Pliocene (7–5 mya). What were the environmental conditions at that time? Can these general ecological patterns help explain the origins of the first hominins (as they diversified from other kinds of hominoids)?

Before continuing, we'll give you one more word of caution. Many students have the common misconception that a single large environmental change is related clearly to a major adaptive change in a type of organism (in other words, environmental change X produced adaptation Y in a particular life-form). This oversimplification is a form of **environmental determinism**, and it grossly underestimates the true complexity of the evolutionary process. It's clear that the environment influences evolutionary change, as seen in the process of natural selection; but organisms are highly complex systems, composed of thousands of genes, and any adaptive shift to changing environmental circumstances is likely to be a compromise, balancing several selective factors simultaneously (such as temperature requirements, amount and distribution of food and water, predators, and safe sleeping sites). In our discussion of the socioecological dynamics of nonhuman primate adaptations in Chapter 7, we made this same point.

There's some evidence that at about the same time the earliest hominins were diverging, some major ecological changes *may* have been occurring in Africa. Could these ecological and evolutionary changes be related to each other? As we'll see, such a sweeping generalization has produced much debate. For most of the Miocene, Africa was generally tropical, with heavy rainfall persisting for most of the year; consequently, most of the continent was heavily forested. However, beginning later in the Miocene and intensifying up to the end of the epoch (about 5 mya), the climate became cooler, drier, and more seasonal.

We should also mention that in other regions of the world, paleoecological evidence reveals a distinct cooling trend at the end of the Miocene. But our focus is on Africa, particularly eastern and central Africa, for it's from these regions that we have the earliest evidence of hominin diversification. We've already noted that one method paleoanthropologists use to reconstruct environments is to analyze animal remains and fossilized pollen. Using another innovative technique, scientists study the chemical pathways utilized by different plants. In particular, **stable carbon isotopes** are produced by plants in differing proportions, depending partly on temperature and aridity (plants adapted to warmer, wetter climates—such as most trees, shrubs, and tubers—versus plants requiring hotter, drier conditions, as typified by many types of grasses). Animals eat the plants, and the differing concentrations of the stable isotopes of carbon are incorporated into their bones and teeth, thus providing a "signature" of the general type of environment in which they lived.

Through a combination of these analytical techniques, paleoecologists have gained a reasonably good handle on worldwide and continent-wide environmental patterns of the past. For example, one model postulates that as climates grew cooler in East Africa 12–5 mya, forests became less continuous. As a result, forest "fringe" habitats and transitional zones between forests and grasslands became more widespread. It's hypothesized that in such transitional environments, some of the late Miocene hominoids may have more intensively exploited the drier grassland portions of the fringe (these would be the earliest hominins); conversely, other hominoids concentrated more on the wetter portions of the fringe (these presumably were the ancestors of African great apes). In the incipient hominins, further adaptive strategies would have followed, including bipedalism, increased tool use, dietary specialization (perhaps with an emphasis on hard items such as seeds and nuts), and changes in social organization.

Such assertions concerning interactions of habitat, locomotion, dietary changes, and social organization are not really testable (since we don't know which

environmental determinism An interpretation that links simple environmental changes directly to a major evolutionary shift in an organism. Such explanations tend to oversimplify the evolutionary process.

stable carbon isotopes Isotopes of carbon that are produced in plants in differing proportions, depending on environmental conditions. By analyzing the proportions of the isotopes contained in fossil remains of animals (who ate the plants), it's possible to reconstruct aspects of ancient environments (particularly temperature and aridity).

changes came first). Still, some of the more restricted contentions of this "climatic forcing" theory are amenable to testing, though some of the model's more basic predictions haven't been confirmed. Most notably, further analyses using stable carbon isotopes from several East African localities suggest that during the late Miocene, environments across the area were consistently quite densely forested (that is, grasslands never predominated, except perhaps at a local level).

You should be aware that at the local level, there can be wide fluctuations in temperature, rainfall, and vegetation as well as in the animals exploiting the vegetation. For example, local uplift, like a mountain, can produce a rain shadow, dramatically altering rainfall and temperature in a region. River and related lake drainages also have major impacts in some areas, and these topographical features are often influenced by highly localized geological factors. To generalize about climates in Africa, good data from several regions are required.

So it would seem, given current evidence and available analytical techniques, that our knowledge of the factors influencing the appearance of the *earliest* hominins is very limited. Considering the constraints, most hypotheses relating to potential factors are best kept restricted in scope and directly related to actual data. In this way, scientists can more easily evaluate the usefulness of these hypotheses, and the hypotheses themselves can be modified and built upon.

Other environmentally oriented hypotheses have been proposed for somewhat later stages of hominin evolution in Africa. Analysis of faunal remains from South African sites led Elizabeth Vrba, of Yale University, to suggest an *evolutionary pulse theory*. In this view, at various times during the Pliocene and Early Pleistocene, the environment all across Africa became notably more arid. Vrba hypothesized that these major climatic shifts may have played a central role in stimulating hominin evolutionary development at key stages.

At one group of later hominin sites in Java, Indonesia, researchers are seeking to discover something about the plants and animals that they believe may have *enticed* our ancestors away from Africa, rather than thinking that harsh environments drove them out. The long sedimentary sequence of this region, known as the Sangiran Dome, allows for stable isotope analyses of the large and varied fossil assemblage—everything from mammals to clams and snails to fossil pollen and other plant remains. It's here, in these favorable circumstances, that nearly 100 fossils of the extinct human *Homo erectus* have been found, spanning a 700,000-year time span from 1.6 to 0.9 mya. This unique co-occurrence makes Sangiran an outstanding locality to test the effects of climate change on the evolving human lineage. The surrounding sites provide a wealth of information about climatic conditions and the environment that attracted and sustained *H. erectus* in Central Java. This region offers scientists a rare opportunity to determine just how flexible the adaptations of our hominin cousins might have been.

This new view of humans—as just one of many animals lured out of Africa by the promise of open niches—is more in line with additional data derived from thousands of animal fossils from various sites East Africa (Behrensmeyer et al., 1997). Analysis of these remains have failed to show that the environmental transitions that Vrba (1992) and others suggested were as widespread as initially proposed. Further detailed analysis by Richard Potts, of the Smithsonian Institution, has in fact shown that ecosystems changed rapidly and often unpredictably throughout various areas of Africa (Bower, 2003; Potts, 2003). Rather than large-scale environmental changes "forcing" hominins into new adaptive strategies, perhaps our ancestors flourished and evolved because they were flexible opportunists.

Why Did Hominins Become Bipedal?

As we've noted several times, the adaptation of hominins to bipedal locomotion was *the* most fundamental adaptive shift among the early members of our lineage. But what were the factors that initiated this crucial change? Ecological theories similar to some of those just discussed have long been thought to be central to the development of bipedalism. Clearly, however, environmental influences would have to occur *before* documented evidence of well-adapted bipedal behavior. In other words, the major shift would have been at the end of the Miocene. Although the evidence indicates that no *sudden* wide ecological change took place at that time, locally forests probably did become patchier as rainfall became more seasonal. Given the changing environmental conditions, did hominins come to the ground to seize the opportunities offered in these more open habitats? Did bipedalism quickly ensue, stimulated somehow by this new way of life? At a very general level, the answer to these questions is yes. Obviously, hominins did at some point become bipedal, and this adaptation took place on the ground. Likewise, hominins are more adapted to mixed and open-country habitats than are our closest modern ape cousins. Successful terrestrial bipedalism probably made possible the further adaptation to more arid, open-country terrain. Still, this rendition simply tells us *where* hominins found their niche, not *why*.

As always, it's wise to be cautious when speculating about causation in evolution. It is all too easy to draw superficial conclusions. For example, scientists often surmise that the mere fact that ground niches were available (and perhaps lacked direct competitors) inevitably led the earliest hominins to terrestrial bipedalism. But consider this: Plenty of mammalian species, including some nonhuman primates, also live mostly on the ground in open country—and they aren't bipedal. Clearly, beyond such simplistic environmental determinism, some more complex explanation for hominin bipedalism is required. There must have been something more than just an environmental opportunity to explain this adaptation to such a unique lifestyle.

Another issue sometimes overlooked in the discussion of early hominin bipedal adaptation is that these creatures did not suddenly become completely terrestrial; but they also didn't slouch about, as illustrations of a linear progression of human evolution would suggest. As Tim White has pointed out, "You don't gradually go from being a quadruped to being a biped. What would the intermediate stage be—a triped? I've never seen one of those." His joke rings true, for the gradual transition would not be to a hunched-over, lolloping thing—a creature like that would be quickly eaten on the savanna—but would occur more as a time-sharing arrangement where early hominins spent some of their time as competent bipeds on the ground and some of their time safely concealed in the trees. We know, for example, that all terrestrial species of nonhuman primates (including savanna baboons, hamadryas baboons, and patas monkeys; see Chapter 7) regularly seek out safe sleeping sites off the ground. These safe havens help protect against predation and are usually found in trees or on cliff faces. Likewise, early hominins almost certainly sought safety at night in the trees, even after they became well adapted to terrestrial bipedalism during daytime foraging. What's more, the continued opportunities for feeding in the trees would most likely have remained significant to early hominins, well after they were also utilizing ground-based resources.

Various hypotheses explaining why hominins initially became bipedal have been suggested and are summarized in Table 10-2. The primary influences claimed to have stimulated the shift to bipedalism include acquiring the ability to carry

Table **10-2** **Possible Factors Influencing the Initial Evolution of Bipedal Locomotion in Hominins**

Factor	Speculated Influence	Comments
Carrying (objects, tools, weapons, infants)	Upright posture freed the arms to carry various objects (including offspring).	Charles Darwin emphasized this view, particularly relating to tools and weapons; however, evidence of stone tools is found much later in the record than first evidence of bipedalism.
Hunting	Bipedalism allowed carrying of weapons, more accurate throwing of certain weapons, and improved long-distance walking.	Systematic hunting is now thought not to have been practiced until after the origin of bipedal hominins (see Issue, Chapter 12).
Seed and nut gathering	Feeding on seeds and nuts occurred while standing upright.	Model initially drawn from analogy with gelada baboons (see text).
Feeding from bushes	Upright posture provided access to seeds, berries, etc., in lower branches; analogous to adaptation seen in some specialized antelope.	Climbing adaptation already existed as prior ancestral trait in earliest hominins (i.e., bush and tree feeding already was established prior to bipedal adaptation).
Thermoregulation (cooling)	Vertical posture exposes less of the body to direct sun; increased distance from ground facilitates cooling by increased exposure to breezes.	Works best for animals active midday on savanna; moreover, adaptation to bipedalism may have initially occurred in woodlands, not on savanna.
Visual surveillance	Standing up provided better view of surrounding countryside (view of potential predators as well as other group members).	Behavior seen occasionally in terrestrial primates (e.g., baboons); probably a contributing factor, but unlikely as "prime mover."
Long-distance walking	Covering long distances was more efficient for a biped than for a quadruped (during hunting or foraging); mechanical reconstructions show that bipedal walking is less energetically costly than quadrupedalism (this is not the case for bipedal *running*).	Same difficulties as with hunting explanation; long-distance foraging on ground also appears unlikely adaptation in earliest hominins.
Male provisioning	Males carried back resources to dependent females and young.	Monogamous bond suggested; however, most skeletal data appear to falsify this part of the hypothesis (see text).

297

objects (and offspring); hunting on the ground; gathering of seeds and nuts; feeding from bushes; improved thermoregulation (that is, keeping cooler on the open savanna); having a better view of open country (to spot predators); walking long distances; and provisioning by males of females with dependent offspring.

These are all creative scenarios, but once again they're not very conducive to rigorous testing and verification. Still, two of the more ambitious scenarios proposed by Clifford Jolly (1970) and Owen Lovejoy (1981) deserve further mention. Both of these views sought to link several aspects of early hominin ecology, feeding, and social behavior, and both utilized models derived from studies of contemporary nonhuman primates.

Jolly's seed-eating hypothesis used the feeding behavior and ecology of gelada baboons as an analogy for very early hominins. Seed eating is an activity that requires keen hand-eye coordination, with bipedal shuffling improving efficiency of foraging. In this view, early hominins are hypothesized to have adapted to open country and bipedalism as a result of their primary adaptation to eating seeds and nuts (found on the ground). The key assumption is that early hominins were eating seeds acquired in similar ecological conditions to those of contemporary gelada baboons.

Lovejoy, meanwhile, has combined presumed aspects of early hominin ecology, feeding, pair bonding, infant care, and food sharing to devise his creative scenario. This view hinges on these assumptions: (1) that the earliest hominins had offspring at least as K-selected (see p. 196) as other large-bodied hominoids; (2) that hominin males ranged widely and provisioned females and their young, who remained more tied to a "home base"; and (3) that males were paired monogamously with females.

As we've noted, while not strictly testable, such scenarios do make certain predictions (which can be potentially falsified or upheld). Accordingly, aspects of each scenario can be evaluated in light of more specific data (obtained from the paleoanthropological record). Regarding the seed-eating hypothesis, predictions relating to size of the back teeth in most early hominins are met, but the proportions of the front teeth in many forms aren't what we'd expect to see in a committed seed eater. Besides, the analogy with gelada baboons is not as informative as once thought; these animals actually don't eat that many seeds and certainly aren't habitual bipeds. Finally, many of the characteristics that Jolly suggested were restricted to hominins (and geladas) are also found in several late Miocene hominoids (who weren't hominins—nor obviously bipeds). Thus, regarding the seed-eating hypothesis, the proposed dental and dietary adaptations don't appear to be linked specifically to hominin origins or bipedalism.

Further detailed analyses of data have also questioned crucial elements of Lovejoy's male-provisioning scenario. The evidence that appears to most contradict this view is that all early hominins were quite sexually dimorphic (McHenry, 1992). According to Lovejoy's model (and analogies with contemporary monogamous nonhuman primates such as gibbons), there shouldn't be such dramatic differences in body size between males and females. Recent studies (Reno et al., 2003, 2005) have questioned this conclusion regarding sexual dimoprhism, suggesting, at least for one species (*Australopithecus afarensis*), that sexual dimorphism was only very moderate. This conclusion appears at odds with most of the evidence regarding early hominins. What's more, the notions of food sharing (presumably including considerable meat), home bases, and long-distance provisioning are questioned by more controlled interpretations of the archaeological record (see "A Closer Look," pp. 278–279).

Another imaginative view is also relevant to this discussion of early hominin evolution, since it relates the adaptation to bipedalism (which was first) to increased brain expansion (which came later). This interpretation, proposed by Dean Falk, suggests that an upright posture put severe constraints on brain size (since blood circulation and drainage would have been altered and cooling would consequently have been more limited than in quadrupeds). Falk thus hypothesizes that new brain-cooling mechanisms must have coevolved with bipedalism, articulated in what she calls the "radiator theory" (Falk, 1990). Falk further surmises that the requirements for better brain cooling would have been particularly marked as hominins adapted to open-country ground living on the hot African savanna. Another interesting pattern observed by Falk concerns two different cooling adaptations found in different early hominin species. She thus suggests that the type of "radiator" adapted in the genus *Homo* was particularly significant in reducing constraints on brain size—which presumably limited some other early hominins. The radiator theory works well, since it not only helps explain the relationship of bipedalism to later brain expansion but also explains why only some hominins became dramatically encephalized.

The radiator theory, too, has been criticized by some paleoanthropologists. Most notably, the presumed species distinction concerning varying cooling mechanisms is not as obvious as suggested by the hypothesis. Both types of venous drainage systems can be found in contemporary *Homo sapiens* as well as within various early hominin species (that is, the variation is intraspecific, not just interspecific). Indeed, in some early hominin specimens, both systems can be found in the same individual (expressed on either side of the skull). Besides, as Falk herself has noted, the radiator itself didn't lead to larger brains; it simply helped reduce constraints on increased encephalization among hominins. It thus requires some further mechanism (prime mover) to explain why, in some hominin species, brain size increased the way it did.

As with any such ambitious effort, it's all too easy to find holes. Falk aptly reminds us that "the search for such 'prime movers' is highly speculative, and these theories do not lend themselves to hypothesis testing" (Falk, 1990, p. 334). Even so, the attempt to interrelate various lines of evidence, the use of contemporary primate models, and predictions concerning further evidence obtained from paleoanthropological contexts all conform to sound scientific methodology. All the views discussed here have contributed to this venture—one not just aimed at understanding our early ancestors but also seeking to refine its methodologies and scientific foundation.

Summary

The biocultural nature of human evolution requires that any meaningful study of human origins examine both biological and cultural information. The multidisciplinary approach of paleoanthropology is designed to bring together varied scientific specializations to reconstruct the anatomy, behavior, and environments of early hominins. Such a task centers on the skills of the geologist, paleontologist, paleoecologist, archaeologist, and physical anthropologist.

Much of what we know about the origins of human culture between 2 and 1 mya comes from archaeological excavations by Mary Leakey at Olduvai Gorge, in East Africa. Olduvai's well-documented stratigraphic sequence, its superior preservation of remains, and the varied dating techniques possible there have made it an information bonanza for paleoanthropologists. Excavated sites have yielded many bones of fossil animals as well as artifact traces of hominin behavior. These findings have enabled us to make ecological reconstructions of habitat and dietary preferences that inform us in great detail about crucial evolutionary processes affecting early hominin populations.

Archaeologists are better able to interpret these "bones and stones" of earlier populations through experimentation. In recent years, much new light has been shed on the techniques of making stone tools as well as the factors affecting preservation of bone.

Broader interpretations, leading to several speculative scenarios, have also been attempted to help us understand the environmental influences and behavioral adaptations exhibited by early hominins. Most notably, attempts have been made to link the earliest origins of hominins as well as somewhat later diversifications to general ecological changes in Africa and Asia. Finally, many researchers have speculated about the factors influencing that most fundamental of all early hominin adaptations, the development of bipedal locomotion. In the next chapter, we'll survey the fossil hominin evidence in central, South, and East Africa that informs us directly about human origins.

Critical Thinking Questions

1. You are leading a paleoanthropological expedition aimed at discovering an early hominin site dating to the Pliocene. In what part of the world will you pick your site, and why? After selecting a particular region, how will you identify which area(s) to survey on foot?

2. Refer to the expedition proposed in question 1. Once you've settled on a particular area to investigate intensively, what types of experts will you include on your team for the initial survey? Let's assume that your team is very lucky (as well as skilled), and you discover a hominin fossil in the first year of exploration. How will you alter your research strategy for your second season, and which further experts will you include in the field (as well as in laboratory phases of the work)?

3. Why is it important to have accurate dates for paleoanthropological localities? Why is it necessary to use more than one kind of dating technique?

4. What do we mean when we say that early hominins displayed *cultural behavior*? What types of behavior do you think this would have included? (Imagine that you've transported yourself back by time machine, and you're sitting in a tree watching a group of hominins at Olduvai Gorge 1.5 mya.)

5. Now put yourself in the same place, this time leading an archaeological excavation. What would be left for you to detect of the cultural behavior you observed in question 4? What happened to the remainder of this behavioral repertoire?

6. What do we mean when we say that human evolution is biocultural? How do paleoanthropologists investigate early hominins using such a biocultural perspective?

7. Devise a scenario to explain why bipedal locomotion first evolved in hominins. First do it as though you were presenting your scenario to classmates. Then redo the scenario in a form to present to a group of professional paleoanthropologists. How will you go about making your scenario more "scientific"?

Hominin Origins in Africa

John Hodgkiss

301

Key Questions

 Click!

Go to the following media for interactive activities and exercises on topics covered in this chapter:

- Online Virtual Laboratories for Physical Anthropology, Version 4.0
- Hominid Fossils: An Interactive Atlas CD-ROM

Introduction

Our species today dominates our planet as we use our brains and cultural inventions to invade every corner of the earth. Yet, 5 million years ago, our ancestors were little more than bipedal apes, confined to a few regions in Africa. What were these creatures like? When and how did they begin their evolutionary journey?

In Chapter 10, we discussed the techniques paleoanthropologists use to locate and excavate sites, as well as the multidisciplinary approaches used to interpret discoveries. In this chapter, we turn to the physical evidence of the hominin fossils themselves. The earliest fossils identifiable as hominins are all from Africa. They date from as early as 7 mya, and after 4 mya, varieties of these early hominins become more plentiful and widely distributed in Africa. It's fascinating to think about all these quite primitive early members of our family tree living side by side for millions of years, especially when we also try to figure out how they managed to coexist with their different adaptations. Most of these species became extinct. But why? What's more, were some of these apelike animals possibly our direct ancestors?

Hominins, of course, evolved from earlier primates (dating from the Eocene to late Miocene), and in Chapter 9 we discussed the fossil evidence of prehominin primates. These fossils provide us with a context within which to understand the subsequent evolution of the human lineage. In recent years, paleoanthropologists from several countries have been excavating sites in Africa, and many exciting new finds have been uncovered. However, because many finds have been made so recently, detailed evaluations are still in progress, and conclusions must remain tentative.

One thing is certain, however. The earliest members of the human lineage were confined to Africa. Only much later did their descendants disperse from the African continent to other areas of the Old World. (This "out of Africa" saga will be the topic of the next chapter.)

The Bipedal Adaptation

In our overview in Chapter 10 of behavioral reconstructions of early hominins, we highlighted several hypotheses that attempt to explain *why* bipedal locomotion first evolved in the hominins. Here we turn to the specific anatomical (that is, **morphological**) evidence that shows us when, where, and how hominin bipedal locomotion evolved. From a broader perspective in Chapter 6, we noted a tendency in all primates for erect body posture and some bipedalism. Of all living primates, however, efficient bipedalism as the primary (habitual) form of locomotion is seen *only* in hominins. Functionally, the human mode of locomotion is most clearly shown in our striding gait, where weight is alternately placed on a single fully extended hind limb. This specialized form of locomotion has developed to a point where energy levels are used to near peak efficiency. Our manner of bipedal locomotion is a far

morphological Pertaining to the form and structure of organisms.

cry from what we see in nonhuman primates, who move bipedally with hips and knees bent and maintain balance clumsily and inefficiently, tottering along rather than striding.

From a survey of our close primate relatives, it is apparent that while still in the trees, our ancestors were adapted to a fair amount of upper-body erectness. Prosimians, monkeys, and apes all spend considerable time sitting erect while feeding, grooming, or sleeping. Presumably, our early ancestors displayed similar behavior. What caused these forms to come to the ground and embark on the unique way of life that would eventually lead to humans is still a mystery. Perhaps natural selection favored some Miocene hominoids coming occasionally to the ground to forage for food on the forest floor and forest fringe. In any case, once they were on the ground and away from the immediate safety offered by trees, bipedal locomotion could become a tremendous advantage (for a discussion of some specific hypotheses that have tried to explain the early evolution of bipedal locomotion, see pp. 295–298).

Our mode of locomotion is indeed extraordinary, involving, as it does, a unique kind of activity in which "the body, step by step, teeters on the edge of catastrophe" (Napier, 1967, p. 56). In this way, the act of human walking is the act of *almost falling* repeatedly! The problem is to maintain balance on the "stance" leg while the "swing" leg is off the ground. In fact, during normal walking, both feet are simultaneously on the ground only about 25 percent of the time, and this figure becomes even less as we walk (or run) faster.

Maintaining a stable center of balance in this complex form of locomotion calls for many drastic structural/anatomical alterations in the basic primate quadrupedal pattern. The most dramatic changes are seen in the pelvis. The pelvis is composed of three elements: two hip bones, or ossa coxae (*sing.*, os coxae), joined at the back to the sacrum (Fig. 11-1). In a quadruped, the ossa coxae are vertically elongated bones positioned along each side of the lower portion of the spine and oriented more or less parallel to it. In hominins, the pelvis is comparatively much shorter and broader and extends around to the side (Fig. 11-2). This configuration helps to stabilize the line of weight transmission in a bipedal posture from the lower back to the hip joint (Fig. 11-3).

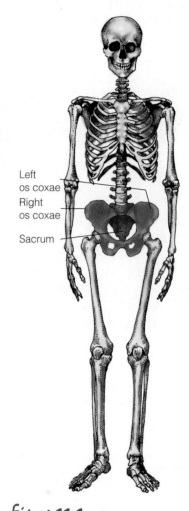

Left os coxae
Right os coxae
Sacrum

Figure 11-1

The human pelvis: various elements shown on a modern skeleton.

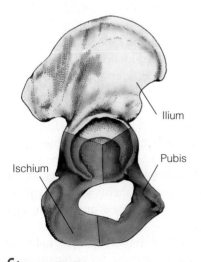

Ilium
Ischium
Pubis

Figure 11-2

The human os coxae, composed of three bones (right side shown).

Figure 11-3

Ossa coxae. (a) *Homo sapiens*. (b) Early hominin (australopith) from South Africa. (c) Great ape. Note especially the length and breadth of the iliac blade (boxed) and the line of weight transmission (shown in red).

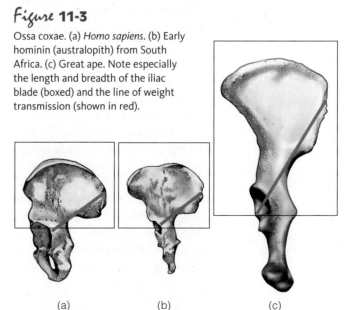

(a)   (b)   (c)

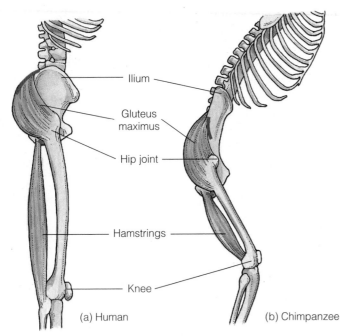

- Ilium
- Gluteus maximus
- Hip joint
- Hamstrings
- Knee

(a) Human   (b) Chimpanzee

Figure 11-4

Comparisons of important muscles that act to extend the hip. Note that the attachment surface (origin, shown in red) of the gluteus maximus in humans (a) is farther in back of the hip joint than in a chimpanzee standing bipedally (b). Conversely, in chimpanzees, the hamstrings are farther in back of the knee.

habitual bipedalism Bipedal locomotion as the form of locomotion shown by hominins most of the time.

Several consequences resulted from the remodeling of the pelvis during early hominin evolution. Broadening the two sides and extending them around to the side and front of the body produced a basin-shaped structure that helps support the abdominal organs (*pelvis* means "basin" in Latin). These alterations also repositioned the attachments of several key muscles that act on the hip and leg, changing their mechanical function. Probably the most important of these altered relationships is that involving the gluteus maximus, the largest muscle in the body, which in humans forms the bulk of the buttocks. In quadrupeds, the gluteus maximus is positioned to the side of the hip and functions to pull the thigh to the side and away from the body. In humans, this muscle is positioned behind the hip; this arrangement allows it, along with the hamstrings, to extend the thigh, pulling it to the rear during walking and running (Fig. 11-4). The gluteus maximus is a truly powerful extensor of the thigh and provides additional force, particularly during running and climbing.

Modifications also occurred in other parts of the skeleton because of the shift to bipedalism. The most significant of these, summarized in "A Closer Look" on pages 306–307, include (1) repositioning of the foramen magnum, the opening at the base of the skull through which the spinal cord emerges; (2) the addition of spinal curves that help to transmit the weight of the upper body to the hips in an upright posture; (3) shortening and broadening of the pelvis and the stabilization of weight transmission (discussed earlier); (4) lengthening of the hind limb, thus increasing stride length; (5) angling of the femur (thighbone) inward to bring the knees and feet closer together under the body; and (6) several structural changes in the foot, including the development of a longitudinal arch and realignment of the big toe in parallel with the other toes (that is, it was no longer divergent).

As you can appreciate, the evolution of hominin bipedalism required complex anatomical reorganization. For natural selection to produce anatomical change of the magnitude seen in hominins, the benefits of bipedal locomotion must have been significant indeed! We mentioned in Chapter 10 several possible adaptive advantages that bipedal locomotion may have conferred upon early hominins. But these all remain hypotheses (even more accurately, they could be called scenarios), and we have inadequate data for testing the various proposed models.

Still, given the anatomical alterations required for efficient bipedalism, some major behavioral stimuli must have been influencing its development. When interpreting evolutionary history, biologists are fond of saying that form follows function. In other words, during evolution, organisms don't undergo significant reorganization in structure *unless* these changes—over many generations—assist individuals in some functional capacity (and in so doing increase their reproductive success). Such changes didn't necessarily occur all at once, but probably evolved over a fairly long period of time. Even so, once behavioral influences initiated certain structural modifications, the process gained momentum and proceeded irreversibly.

We say that hominin bipedalism is both habitual and obligate. By **habitual bipedalism**, we mean that hominins, unlike any other primate, move bipedally as their standard and most efficient mode of locomotion. By **obligate bipedalism**, we mean that hominins are committed to bipedalism and cannot locomote efficiently in any other way. For example, the loss of grasping ability in the foot makes climbing much more difficult for humans (although by no means impossible). The central task, then, in trying to understand the earliest members of the hominin lineage is to identify anatomical features that indicate bipedalism and to interpret to what degree these organisms were committed to this form of locomotion (that is, was it habitual and was it obligate?).

What structural patterns are observable in early hominins, and what do they imply regarding locomotor function? By at least 4 mya, all the major structural changes required for bipedalism are seen in early hominins from Africa (at least as far as the evidence permits conclusions to be made). In particular, the pelvis, as clearly documented by several excellently preserved specimens, was dramatically remodeled to support weight in a bipedal stance (see Fig. 11-3b).

Other structural changes shown after 4 mya in the earliest relatively complete hominin postcranial remains further confirm the pattern seen in the pelvis. For example, the vertebral column (as known from specimens in East and South Africa) shows the same curves as in modern hominins. The lower limbs are also elongated, and they seem to be proportionately about as long as in modern humans (although the arms are longer in these early hominins). Further, the carrying angle of weight support from the hip to the knee is very similar to that seen in *Homo sapiens*.

Fossil evidence of early hominin foot structure has come from two sites in South Africa; especially important are some recently announced new fossils from **Sterkfontein** (Clarke and Tobias, 1995). These specimens, consisting of four articulating elements from the ankle and big toe, indicate that the heel and longitudinal arch were both well adapted for a bipedal gait. But the paleoanthropologists (Ron Clarke and Phillip Tobias) who analyzed these remains also suggest that the large toe was *divergent*, unlike the hominin pattern shown in "A Closer Look" on pages 306–307. If the large toe really did possess this anatomical position (and this is disputed), it most likely would have aided the foot in grasping. In turn, this grasping ability (as in other primates) would have enabled early hominins to more effectively exploit arboreal habitats. Finally, since anatomical remodeling is always constrained by a set of complex functional compromises, a foot highly capable of grasping and climbing is less capable as a stable platform during bipedal locomotion. Some researchers therefore see early hominins as perhaps not quite as fully committed to bipedal locomotion as were later hominins.

Further evidence for evolutionary changes in the foot comes from two sites in East Africa where numerous fossilized elements have been recovered (Fig. 11-5). As in the remains from South Africa, the East African fossils suggest a well-adapted bipedal gait. The arches are developed, but some differences in the ankle also imply that considerable flexibility was possible (again, probably indicating some continued adaptation to climbing). From this evidence, some researchers have recently concluded that many forms of early hominins probably spent considerable time in the trees. What's more, they may not have been quite as efficient bipedally, as has previously been suggested. Nevertheless, most researchers maintain that *all* the early hominins identified from Africa displayed both habitual and obligate bipedalism (despite the new evidence from South Africa and the earliest traces from central and East Africa, all of which will require further study).

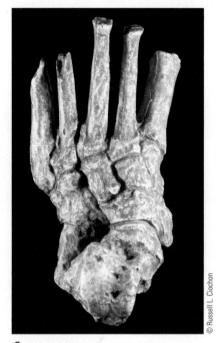

Figure **11-5**

A nearly complete hominin foot (OH 8) from Olduvai Gorge, Tanzania. (See Appendix C for an explanation of how specimen numbers such as OH 8 are assigned.)

© Russell L. Ciochon

obligate bipedalism Bipedalism as the *only* form of hominin terrestrial locomotion. Since major anatomical changes in the spine, pelvis, and lower limb are required for bipedal locomotion, once hominins adapted this mode of locomotion, other forms of locomotion on the ground became impossible.

Sterkfontein (sterk´-fawn-tane)

Finding Early Hominin Fossils

As we've discussed, paleoanthropology is a multidisciplinary science, and the finding, surveying, and eventual excavation of hominin sites is a time-consuming and expensive undertaking. What's more, since hominin fossils are never common anywhere and are usually at least partially buried under sediment, finding them also requires no small portion of good luck.

In Africa, most fossil discoveries have come from either East or South Africa. As we'll soon see, a few extremely important discoveries have recently come from

A Closer Look

Major Features of Bipedal Locomotion

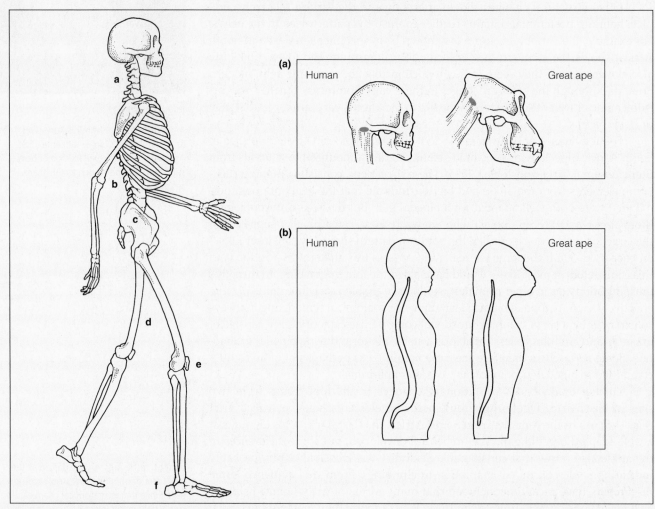

During hominin evolution, several major structural features throughout the body have been reorganized (from that seen in other primates) to facilitate efficient bipedal locomotion. These are illustrated here, beginning with the head and progressing to the foot: (a) The foramen magnum (shown in red) is repositioned farther underneath the skull, so that the head is more or less balanced on the spine (and thus requires less-robust neck muscles to hold the head upright). (b) The spine has two distinctive curves—a backward (thoracic) one and a forward (lumbar) one—that keep the trunk (and weight) centered above the pelvis. (c) The pelvis is shaped more in the form of a basin

central Africa. Nevertheless, more than 99 percent of the early African hominin fossils so far discovered come from the eastern and southern portions of the continent.

In East Africa, early hominin sites are located along the Great Rift Valley. Stretching over more than 2,000 miles, the Rift Valley was formed by geological shifting (actually separation, producing the "rift") between two of the earth's tectonic plates. That is, it's the same geological process as that leading to "continental drift" (discussed in Chapter 5, p. 127). The outcome of these geological upheavals leads to faulting (with earthquakes), volcanoes, and sometimes rapid

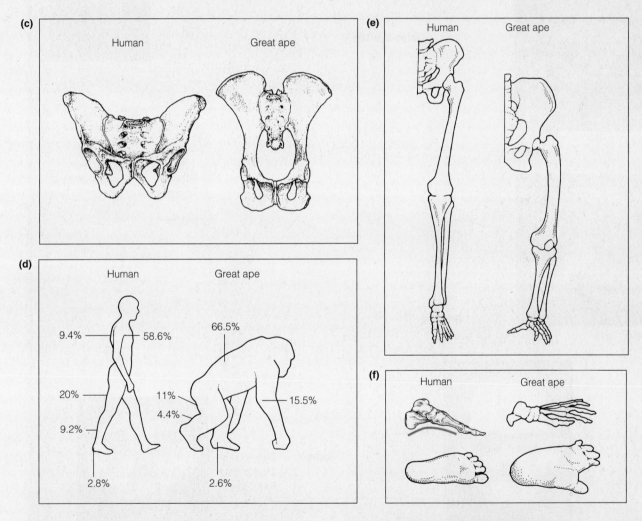

to support internal organs; the ossa coxae (specifically, iliac blades) are also shorter and broader, thus stabilizing weight transmission. (d) Lower limbs are elongated, as shown by the proportional lengths of various body segments (for example, in humans the thigh comprises 20 percent of body height, while in gorillas it comprises only 11 percent. (e) The femur is angled inward, keeping the legs more directly under the body; modified knee anatomy also permits full extension of this joint. (f) The big toe is enlarged and brought in line with the other toes; a distinctive longitudinal arch also forms, helping absorb shock and adding propulsive spring.

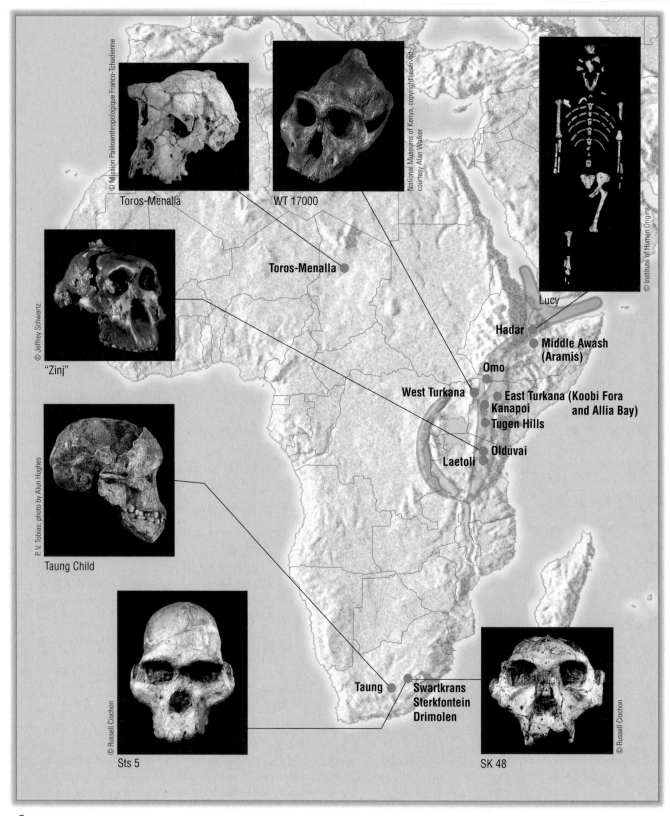

Toros-Menalla

WT 17000

Lucy

"Zinj"

Toros-Menalla

Hadar

Middle Awash
(Aramis)

Omo

West Turkana

East Turkana (Koobi Fora
and Allia Bay)

Kanapoi

Tugen Hills

Olduvai

Laetoli

Taung Child

Taung

Swartkrans
Sterkfontein
Drimolen

Sts 5

SK 48

Figure **11-6**

Early hominin fossil finds (pre-australopith and australopith localities).
The Rift Valley in East Africa is shown in gold.

sedimentation. Paleoanthropologists see all this as a major plus, since it produces a landscape that has many geological exposures revealing at surface level ancient beds that just might contain fossils of all sorts—including hominins. What's more, the chemical makeup of the volcanic sediments makes accurate chronometric dating much more possible.

Paleoanthropological discoveries along the East African branch of the Rift Valley extend from northern Ethiopia, through Kenya, and finally into northern Tanzania (Fig. 11-6). Key locales within the Rift Valley where in total more than 2,000 hominin fossils have been found include the extremely productive Middle Awash area of northeastern Ethiopia (containing Aramis, Hadar, and Dikika). In Kenya, crucial discoveries have come from the east and west sides of Lake Turkana and just a bit to the south from the Tugen Hills. Lastly, in northern Tanzania, the remarkably informative paleoanthropological site of Olduvai Gorge has been explored for several decades, and nearby, the Laetoli site has yielded other key fossils as well as extraordinarily well-preserved hominin footprints.

South Africa has also been a very productive area for early hominin discoveries. Over the last 80 years, paleoanthropologists have explored numerous sites, which together have yielded several hundred hominin specimens. The most important South African hominin sites are Taung, Sterkfontein, and Swartkrans.

It's important to recognize that the geological context of all the South African sites is quite different from that in East Africa. The Rift Valley does not extend into southernmost Africa, where, instead, the sediments are composed of layer upon convoluted layer of accumulated limestones. As a result, the geological layers are extremely complex and do not form into such recognizable strata as seen in sites along the East African Rift Valley. In the South African landscape, caves and fissures form, into which animals fall or perhaps are dragged by predators. Consequently, the hominins accumulated in these caverns and fissures, where they eventually became encased in a rock matrix. Decades ago, the hominins were removed by dynamite. Today, they are retrieved using small hand tools, and only then with extraordinarily painstaking effort (Fig 11-7).

John Hodgkiss

Figure 11-7

Paleoanthropologist Ronald Clarke carefully excavates a 2-million-year-old skeleton from the limestone matrix at Sterkfontein Cave. Clearly seen are the cranium (with articulated mandible) and the upper arm bone.

Because the geological setting is so much more complicated in South Africa than in East Africa, the fossils are generally more difficult to locate and usually not as well preserved, and chronometric dating is far more difficult. Still, there are some exceptions, as exemplified by an extraordinarily well-preserved skeleton still being excavated at Sterkfontein (see Fig. 11-7).

Early Hominins from Africa

As you are now well aware, a variety of early hominins lived in Africa, and we'll cover their comings and goings over a 6-million-year period, from 7 to 1 mya. It's also important to keep in mind that these hominins were geographically widely distributed, with fossil discoveries coming from central, East, and South Africa. Paleoanthropologists generally agree that among these early African hominins, there were at least 6 different genera, which in turn comprised upward of 12 different species. At no time, nor in any other place, were hominins ever as diverse as were these very ancient members of our family tree.

As you've already guessed, there are quite a few different hominins from many sites, and you'll find that their formal naming can be difficult to pronounce and not easy to remember. So we'll try to discuss these fossil groups in a way that's easy to understand. Our primary focus will be to organize them by time and by major evolutionary trends. In so doing, we recognize three major groups:

- Pre-australopiths— the earliest and most primitive hominins (7.0–4.4 mya)
- Australopiths—diverse forms, some more primitive, others highly derived (4.2–1.2 mya)
- Early *Homo*—the first members of our genus (2.4–1.4 mya)

Pre-Australopiths (7.0–4.4 mya)

The oldest and most surprising of these earliest hominins is represented by a cranium discovered at a central African site called Toros-Menalla in the modern nation of Chad (Brunet et al., 2002; Fig. 11-8). Provisional dating using faunal correlation (biostratigraphy; see p. 288) suggests a date of nearly 7 mya (Vignaud et al., 2002). However, the estimated date for this fossil is quite early and places it at almost 1 million years before *any* other proposed early hominin. Closer examination of the evidence used in obtaining this biostratigraphic date now has led many paleoanthropologists to suggest that the later date (6 mya) is more likely.

The morphology of the fossil is unusual, with a combination of characteristics unlike that found in other early hominins. The braincase is small, estimated at no larger than a modern chimpanzee's (preliminary estimate in the range of 320 to 380 cm^3), but it is massively built, with huge browridges in front, a crest on top, and large muscle attachments in the rear. Yet, combined with these apelike features is a smallish vertical face containing front teeth very unlike an ape's. In fact, the lower face, being more tucked in under the brain vault (and not protruding, as in most other early hominins), is more of a *derived* feature more commonly expressed in much later hominins (especially members of genus *Homo*). What's more, unlike the dentition seen in apes (and some early hominins), the upper canine is reduced and is worn down from the tip (rather than shearing along its side against the first lower premolar).

Figure **11-8**

A nearly complete cranium of *Sahelanthropus* from Chad, dating to 7–6 mya.

In recognition of this unique combination of characteristics, paleoanthropologists have placed the Toros-Menalla remains into a new genus and species of hominin, *Sahelanthropus tchadensis* (Sahel being the region of the southern Sahara in North Africa). These new finds from Chad have forced an immediate and significant reassessment of early hominin evolution. Two cautionary comments, however, are in order. First, as we noted, the dating is only approximate, based, as it is, on biostratigraphic correlation with sites in Kenya (1,500 miles to the east). Second, and perhaps more serious, is the hominin status of the Chad fossil. Given the facial structure and dentition, it's difficult to see how *Sahelanthropus* could be anything but a hominin. However, the position of its foramen magnum is intermediate between that of a quadrupedal ape and that of a bipedal hominin (Fig. 11-9); for this and other reasons, some researchers (Wolpoff et al., 2002) suggest that at this time "ape" may be a better classification for *Sahelanthropus*. As we have previously said, the best-defining anatomical characteristics of hominins relate to bipedal locomotion. Unfortunately, no postcranial elements have been recovered from Chad—at least not yet. Consequently, we do not yet know the locomotor behavior of *Sahelanthropus*, and this raises even more fundamental questions: What if further finds show this form not to be bipedal? Should we still consider it a hominin? What, then, are the defining characteristics of our lineage?

About a million years later than *Sahelanthropus*, two other very early hominins have been found at sites in central Kenya in the Tugen Hills and from the Middle Awash area of northeastern Ethiopia. The earlier of these finds (dated by radiometric methods to about 6 mya) comes from the Tugen Hills and includes mostly dental remains, but also some quite complete lower limb bones. The fossils have been placed in a separate early hominin genus called *Orrorin*. The postcranial remains are especially important, since they clearly indicate bipedal locomotion (Pickford and Senut, 2001; Senut et al., 2001; Galik et al., 2004; Richmond and Jungers, 2008). As a result of these further analyses, *Orrorin* is now widely recognized as the earliest firmly established hominin.

The last group of fossil hominins thought to date to the late Miocene (that is, earlier than 5 mya) comes from the Middle Awash in the Afar Triangle of Ethiopia. Radiometric dating places the age of these fossils in the very late Miocene, 5.8–5.2 mya. The fossil remains themselves are very fragmentary. Some of the dental remains resemble some later fossils from the Middle Awash (discussed shortly), and Yohannes Haile-Selassie, the researcher who first found and described these earlier materials, has provisionally assigned them to the genus *Ardipithecus* (Haile-Selassie et al., 2004; see "At a Glance," p. 312). In addition, some postcranial elements have been preserved, most informatively a toe bone, a phalanx from the middle of the foot (see Appendix A, Fig. A-8). From clues in this bone, Haile-Selassie concludes that this primate was a well-adapted biped (once again, the best-supporting evidence of hominin status).

From another million years or so later in the geological record in the Middle Awash region, along the banks of the Awash River, a very large and significant assemblage of fossil hominins has been discovered at the **Aramis** site. Radiometric dating firmly places these remains at about 4.4 mya. The site, represented by a 6-foot-thick bed of bones, has yielded more than 6,000 fossils. This abundant find reveals both large and small vertebrates—reptiles (including birds) and even very small mammals. Additionally, fossil wood and pollen samples have been recovered from this rich bone bed, which are important for the paleoenvironmental studies discussed shortly.

Hominin fossil remains from Aramis include several individuals, with the most noteworthy being one nearly complete skeleton and a second individual

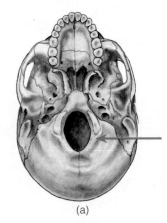

(a)

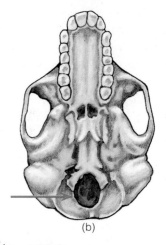

(b)

Figure **11-9**

Position of the foramen magnum in (a) a human and (b) a chimpanzee. Note the more forward position in the human cranium.

Aramis (air-ah-miss)

Table 11-1 Estimated Body Weights and Stature in Plio-Pleistocene Hominins

| | Body Weight | | Stature | |
	Male	Female	Male	Female
A. afarensis	45 kg (99 lb)	29 kg (64 lb)	151 cm (59 in.)	105 cm (41 in.)
A. africanus	41 kg (90 lb)	30 kg (65 lb)	138 cm (54 in.)	115 cm (45 in.)
A. robustus	40 kg (88 lb)	32 kg (70 lb)	132 cm (52 in.)	110 cm (43 in.)
A. boisei	49 kg (108 lb)	34 kg (75 lb)	137 cm (54 in.)	124 cm (49 in.)
H. habilis	52 kg (114 lb)	32 kg (70 lb)	157 cm (62 in.)	125 cm (49 in.)

Source: After McHenry, 1992. *Note:* Reno et al. (2003) conclude that sexual dimorphism in *A. afarensis* was considerably less than shown here.

represented by an upper forelimb skeleton. Other hominins are represented by isolated teeth and cranial bones. In all cases, the bones are encased in limestone matrix, thus requiring a long and tedious process to remove the fossils intact from the cement-like material surrounding them. The results of this long and time-consuming process will be published in an upcoming monograph that will provide a full description of this exciting paleoanthropological find.

These were clearly quite primitive hominins, displaying an array of characteristics quite distinct from other members of our lineage. These primitive characteristics include flattening of the cranial base and relatively thin enamel caps on the molar teeth. From measurements of the humerus, body weight for one of the individuals is estimated at 42 kg (93 pounds); if this bone comes from a male individual, this weight estimate is very similar to that hypothesized for other early hominins (Table 11-1).

Thus, current conclusions (which will be either unambiguously confirmed or falsified as the skeleton is fully cleaned and studied) interpret the Aramis remains as among the earliest hominins yet known. These individuals, while very primitive hominins, may or may not have been bipedal—we will have to await the publication of the results on the Aramis fossils.

At a Glance
Key Pre-Australopith Discoveries

DATES	REGION	HOMININS	SITES	EVOLUTIONARY SIGNIFICANCE
4.4 mya	East Africa	*Ardipithecus ramidus*	Aramis	Large collection of fossils, including partial skeletons; bipedal, but derived
5.8–5.2 mya		*Ardipithecus*	Middle Awash	Fragmentary, but probably bipedal
~6.0 mya		*Orrorin tugenensis*	Tugen Hills	First hominin with postcranial remains; probably bipedal
~7.0–6.0 mya	Central Africa	*Sahelanthropus tchadensis*	Toros-Menalla	Oldest hominin; well-preserved cranium; very small-brained; bipedal?

Tim White and colleagues have argued that the fossil hominins from Aramis are so primitive and so different from other early hominins that they should be assigned to a new genus (and, necessarily, a new species as well): *Ardipithecus ramidus* (White et al., 1995). Most especially, the thin enamel caps on the molars are in dramatic contrast to all other early hominins, who show quite thick enamel.

Another intriguing aspect of all these late Miocene/early Pliocene locales (that is, Tugen Hills, early Middle Awash sites, and Aramis) relates to the ancient environments associated with these earliest hominins. Rather than the more open grassland savanna habitats so characteristic of most later hominin sites, the environment at all these early locales is more heavily forested. Perhaps we are seeing at Aramis and these other ancient sites the very beginnings of hominin divergence, not long after the division from the African apes.

Australopiths (4.2–1.2 mya)

The best-known, most widely distributed, and most diverse of the early African hominins are colloquially called **australopiths**. In fact, this diverse and very successful group of hominins is made up of two closely related genera, *Australopithecus* and *Paranthropus*. These hominins have an established time range of over 3 million years, stretching back as early as 4.2 mya and not becoming extinct until apparently close to 1 mya—making them the longest-enduring hominin yet documented. In addition, these hominins have been found in all the major geographical areas of Africa that have, to date, produced early hominin finds, namely, South Africa, central Africa (Chad), and East Africa. From all these areas combined, there appears to have been considerable complexity in terms of evolutionary diversity, with numerous species now recognized by most paleoanthropologists.

There are two major subgroups of australopiths, an earlier one that is more anatomically primitive and a later one that is much more derived. These earlier australopiths, dated 4.2–3.0 mya, show several more primitive (ancestral) hominin characteristics than the later australopith group, whose members are more derived, some extremely so. These more derived hominins lived after 2.5 mya and are composed of two different genera, together represented by at least four different species (see Appendix C for a complete listing and more information about early hominin fossil finds).

Given the 3-million-year time range as well as quite varied ecological niches, there are numerous intriguing adaptive differences among these varied australopith species. We'll discuss the major adaptations of the various species in a moment. But first let's emphasize the major features that all australopiths share:

1. They are all clearly bipedal (although not necessarily identical to *Homo* in this regard).
2. They all have relatively small brains (at least compared to *Homo*).
3. They all have large teeth, particularly the back teeth, with thick to very thick enamel on the molars.

In short, then, all these australopith species are relatively small-brained, big-toothed bipeds.

The earliest australopiths, dating to 4.2–3.0 mya, come from East Africa from a couple of sites in northern Kenya. Among the fossil finds of these earliest australopiths so far discovered, a few postcranial pieces clearly indicate that locomotion was *bipedal*. There are, however, a few primitive features in the dentition, including a large canine and a **sectorial** lower first premolar (Fig. 11-10).

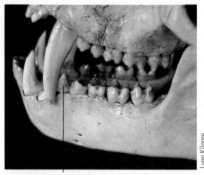

Sectorial lower first premolar

Figure **11-10**

Sectorial lower first premolar. Left lateral view of the teeth of a male patas monkey. Note how the large upper canine shears against the elongated surface of the sectorial lower first premolar.

australopiths A colloquial name referring to a diverse group of Plio-Pleistocene African hominins. Australopiths are the most abundant and widely distributed of all early hominins and are also the most completely studied.

sectorial Adapted for cutting or shearing; among primates, refers to the compressed (side-to-side) first lower premolar, which functions as a shearing surface with the upper canine.

Figure 11-11

Hominin footprint from Laetoli, Tanzania. Note the deep impression of the heel and the large toe (arrow) in line (adducted) with the other toes.

Peter Jones

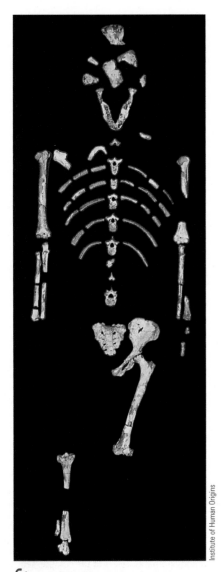

Institute of Human Origins

Figure 11-12

"Lucy," a partial hominin skeleton, discovered at Hadar in 1974. This individual is assigned to *Australopithecus afarensis*.

Since these particular fossils have initially been interpreted as more primitive than all the later members of the genus *Australopithecus*, paleoanthropologists have provisionally assigned them to a separate species. This important fossil species is now called *Australopithecus anamensis*, and some researchers suggest that it is a potential ancestor for many later australopiths as well as perhaps early members of the genus *Homo* (White et al., 2006).

Australopithecus afarensis Slightly later and much more complete remains of *Australopithecus* have come from the sites of Hadar (in Ethiopia) and Laetoli (in Tanzania). Much of this material has been known for three decades, and the fossils have been very well studied; indeed, in certain instances, they are quite famous. For example, the Lucy skeleton was discovered at Hadar in 1974, and the Laetoli footprints were first found in 1978. These hominins are classified as members of the species *Australopithecus afarensis*.

Literally thousands of footprints have been found at Laetoli, representing more than 20 different kinds of animals (Pliocene elephants, horses, pigs, giraffes, antelopes, hyenas, and an abundance of hares). Several hominin footprints have also been found, including a trail more than 75 feet long made by at least two—and perhaps three—individuals (Leakey and Hay, 1979; Fig. 11-11). Such discoveries of well-preserved hominin footprints are extremely important in furthering our understanding of human evolution. For the first time, we can make *definite* statements regarding the locomotor pattern and stature of early hominins.

Studies of these impression patterns clearly show that the mode of locomotion of these hominins was bipedal (Day and Wickens, 1980). As we have emphasized, the development of bipedal locomotion is the most important defining characteristic of early hominin evolution. Some researchers, however, have concluded that *A. afarensis* was not bipedal in quite the same way that modern humans are. From detailed comparisons with modern humans, estimates of stride length, cadence, and speed of walking have been ascertained, indicating that the Laetoli hominins moved in a slow-moving ("strolling") fashion with a rather short stride.

One extraordinary discovery at Hadar is the Lucy skeleton (Fig. 11-12), found by Don Johanson eroding out of a hillside. This fossil is scientifically designated

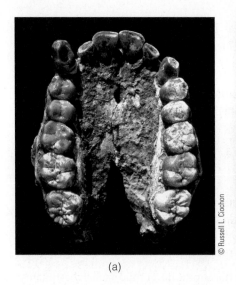
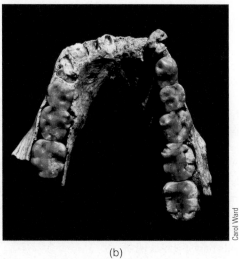

© Russell L. Ciochon

Carol Ward

(a)　　　　　　　　　　　　(b)

Figure **11-13**

Jaws of *Australopithecus afarensis*.
(a) Maxilla, AL 200-1a, from Hadar,
Ethiopia. (Note the parallel tooth rows and
large canines.) (b) Mandible, LH 4, from
Laetoli, Tanzania. This fossil is the type
specimen for the species *Australopithecus
afarensis*.

as Afar Locality (AL) 288-1, but is usually just called Lucy (after the Beatles song "Lucy in the Sky with Diamonds"). Representing almost 40 percent of a skeleton, this is one of the most complete individuals from anywhere in the world for the entire period before about 100,000 years ago.

Because the Laetoli area was covered periodically by ashfalls from nearby volcanic eruptions, accurate dating is possible and has provided dates of 3.7–3.5 mya. Dating from the Hadar region hasn't proved as straightforward; however, more complete dating calibration using a variety of techniques has determined a range of 3.9–3.0 mya for the hominin discoveries from this area.

Several hundred *A. afarensis* specimens, representing a minimum of 60 individuals (and perhaps as many as 100), have been removed from Laetoli and Hadar. At present, these materials represent the largest *well-studied* collection of early hominins and as such are among the most significant of the hominins discussed in this chapter.

Without question, *A. afarensis* is more primitive than any of the other later australopith fossils from South or East Africa (discussed shortly). By "primitive" we mean that *A. afarensis* is less evolved in any particular direction than are later-occurring hominin species. That is, *A. afarensis* shares more primitive features with other late Miocene apes and with living great apes than do later hominins, who display more derived characteristics.

For example, the teeth of *A. afarensis* are quite primitive. The canines are often large, pointed teeth. Moreover, the lower first premolar is semisectorial (that is, it provides a shearing surface for the upper canine), and the tooth rows are parallel, even converging somewhat toward the back of the mouth (Fig. 11-13).

The cranial portions that are preserved also display several primitive hominoid characteristics, including a crest in the back as well as several primitive features of the cranial base. Cranial capacity estimates for *A. afarensis* show a mixed pattern when compared with later hominins. A provisional estimate for the one partially complete cranium—apparently a large individual—gives a figure of 500 cm^3, but another, even more fragmentary cranium is apparently quite a bit smaller and has been estimated at about 375 cm^3 (Holloway, 1983). Thus, for some individuals (males?), *A. afarensis* is well within the range of other australopith species (see "A Closer Look," p. 316), but others (females?) may have a significantly smaller cranial capacity. However, a detailed depiction of cranial size for *A. afarensis* is not possible at this time; this part of the skeleton is unfortunately too poorly

A Closer Look

Cranial Capacity

Cranial capacity, usually reported in cubic centimeters, is a measure of brain size, or volume. The brain itself, of course, doesn't fossilize. However, the space once occupied by brain tissue (the inside of the cranial vault) does sometimes preserve, at least in those cases where fairly complete crania are recovered.

For purposes of comparison, it's easy to obtain cranial capacity estimates for contemporary species (including humans) from analyses of skeletonized specimens in museum collections. From studies of this nature, estimated cranial capacities for modern hominoids have been determined as follows (Tobias, 1971, 1983):

	Range (cm³)	Average (cm³)
Human	1150–1750*	1325
Chimpanzee	285–500	395
Gorilla	340–752	506
Orangutan	276–540	411
Bonobo	—	350

---

*The range of cranial capacity for modern humans is very large—in fact, even greater than that shown (which approximates cranial capacity for the majority of contemporary *H. sapiens* populations).

These data for living hominoids can then be compared with those obtained from early hominins:

	Average (cm³)
Sahelanthropus	~350
Orrorin	Not currently known
Ardipithecus	Not currently known
Australopithecus anamensis	Not currently known
Australopithecus afarensis	438
Later australopiths	410–530
Early members of genus *Homo*	631

As the tabulations indicate, cranial capacity estimates for australopiths fall within the range of most modern great apes, and gorillas actually average slightly greater cranial capacity than *A. afarensis*. It's important to remember, however, that gorillas are very large animals, whereas australopiths probably weighed on the order of 100 pounds (see Table 11-1, p. 312). Since brain size is partially correlated with body size, comparing such different-sized animals can't be justified. Compared to living chimpanzees (most of which are slightly larger than early hominins) and bonobos (which are somewhat smaller), australopiths had *proportionately* about 10 percent bigger brains, and so we would say that these early hominins were more *encephalized*.

represented. One thing is clear: *A. afarensis* had a small brain, probably averaging for the whole species not much over 420 cm³.

On the other hand, a large assortment of postcranial pieces representing almost all portions of the body of *A. afarensis* have been found. Initial impressions suggest that relative to lower limbs, the upper limbs are longer than in modern humans (also a primitive Miocene ape condition). (This statement does not mean that the arms of *A. afarensis* were longer than the legs.) In addition, the wrist, hand, and foot bones show several differences from modern humans (Susman et al., 1985). From such excellent postcranial evidence, stature can now be confidently estimated: *A. afarensis* was a short hominin. From her partial skeleton, Lucy is estimated to be only 3 to 4 feet tall (see Fig. 11-12). However, Lucy—as demonstrated by her pelvis—was probably a female, and there is evidence of larger individuals as well. The most economical hypothesis explaining this variation is that *A. afarensis* was quite sexually dimorphic: The larger individuals are male, and the smaller ones, such as Lucy, are female. Estimates of male stature can be approximated from the larger footprints at Laetoli, inferring a height of not quite 5 feet. If we accept this interpretation, *A. afarensis* was a very sexually dimorphic form indeed. In fact, for overall body size, this species may have been as dimorphic as *any* living primate (that is, as much as gorillas, orangutans, or baboons).

An important new find of a mostly complete skeleton of an *A. afarensis* infant was announced in 2006 (Fig. 11-14). The discovery was made at the Dikika locale in northeastern Ethiopia, very near the Hadar sites mentioned earlier. What's more, the infant comes from the same geological horizon as Hadar, with the same dating (3.3 mya). Although the initial discovery of the fossil was back in 2000, it has taken several years and thousands of hours of preparation to remove portions of the skeleton from the surrounding cemented matrix (full preparation will likely take several more years; Alemseged et al., 2006).

This find of a 3-year-old infant is remarkable because it's the first example of a very well-preserved immature hominin prior to about 100,000 years ago. From the infant's extremely well-preserved teeth, scientists hypothesize that she was female. A comprehensive study of her developmental biology has already begun, and many more revelations are surely in store as the Dikika infant is more completely cleaned and studied. For now, and accounting for her immature age, the skeletal pattern appears to be quite similar to an *A. afarensis* adult. What's more, the limb proportions, anatomy of the hands and feet, and shape of the scapula (shoulder blade) reveal a similar "mixed" pattern of locomotion. The foot and lower limb indicate that this infant would have been a terrestrial biped; yet, the shoulder and (curved) fingers suggest that she was also capable of climbing about quite ably in the trees.

What makes *A. afarensis* a hominin? The answer is revealed by its manner of locomotion. From the abundant limb bones recovered from Hadar and those beautiful footprints from Laetoli, we know unequivocally that *A. afarensis* walked bipedally when on the ground. (At present, we do not have nearly such good evidence concerning locomotion for *any* of the earlier hominin finds.) Whether Lucy and her contemporaries still spent considerable time in the trees and just how efficiently they walked have become topics of some controversy. Most researchers, however, agree that *A. afarensis* was an efficient habitual biped while on the ground. These hominins were also clearly *obligate* bipeds, which would have hampered their climbing abilities but would not necessarily have precluded arboreal behavior altogether.

Australopithecus afarensis is a crucial hominin group. Since it comes after the earliest, poorly known group of pre-australopith hominins, but prior to all later australopiths as well as *Homo*, it is an evolutionary bridge, linking together much of what we assume are the major patterns of early hominin evolution. The fact that there are many well-preserved fossils and that they have been so well studied also adds to the paleoanthropological significance of *A. afarensis*. The consensus among most experts over the last several years has been that *A. afarensis* is a potentially strong candidate as the ancestor of *all* later hominins. Some ongoing analysis has recently challenged this hypothesis (Rak et al., 2007), but at least for the moment, this new interpretation has not been widely accepted. Still, it reminds us that science is an intellectual pursuit that constantly reevaluates older views and seeks to provide more systematic explanations about the world around us. When it comes to understanding human evolution, we should always be aware that things might change. So stay tuned.

Later More Derived Australopiths (2.5–1.2 mya) Following 2.5 mya, hominins became more diverse in Africa. As they adapted to varied niches, australopiths became considerably more derived. In other words, they show physical changes making them quite distinct from their immediate ancestors.

In fact, there were at least three separate lineages of hominins living (in some cases side by side) between 2.5 and 1.2 mya. One of these is a later form of *Australopithecus*; another is represented by the highly derived three species that

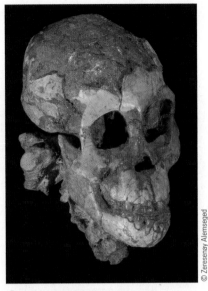

© Zeresenay Alemseged

Figure **11-14**

Complete skull with attached vertebral column of the infant skeleton from Dikika, Ethiopia (estimated age, 3.3 mya).

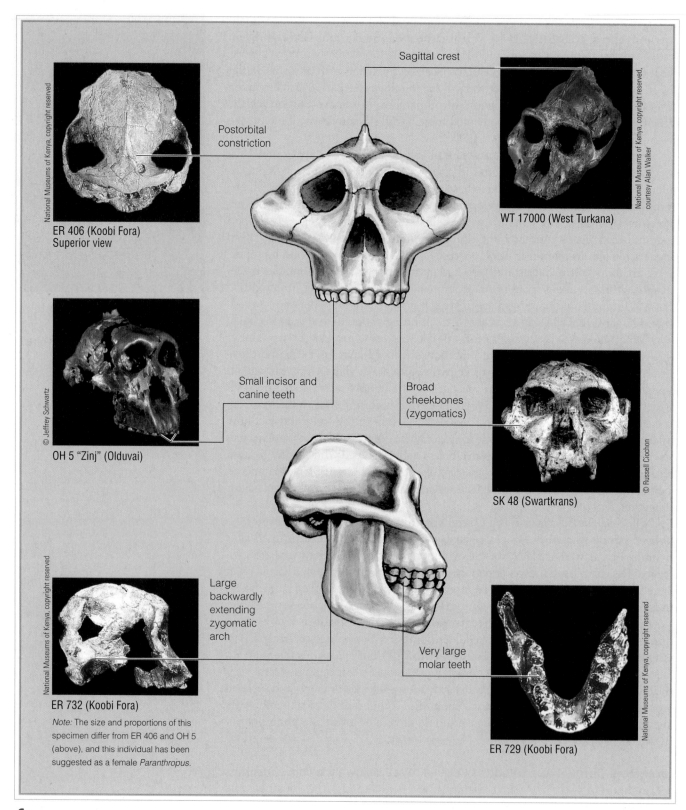

Figure **11-15**

Morphology and variation in *Paranthropus*.
(Note both typical features and range of
variation as shown in different specimens.)

belong to the genus *Paranthropus*; and the last consists of early members of the genus *Homo*. Here we'll discuss *Paranthropus* and *Australopithecus*. *Homo* will be discussed in the next section.

The most derived australopiths are the various members of *Paranthropus*. While all australopiths are big-toothed, *Paranthropus* has the biggest teeth of all, especially as seen in its huge premolars and molars. Along with these massive back teeth, these hominins show a variety of other specializations related to powerful chewing (Fig. 11-15). For example, they all have large, deep lower jaws and large attachments for muscles associated with chewing. In fact, these chewing muscles are so prominent that major anatomical alterations evolved in the architecture of their face and skull vault. In particular, the *Paranthropus* face is flatter than that of any other australopith; the broad cheekbones (to which the masseter muscle attaches) flare out; and a ridge develops on top of the skull (this is called a **sagittal crest**, and it's where the temporal muscle attaches).

All these morphological features suggest that *Paranthropus* was adapted for a diet emphasizing rough vegetable foods. However, this does not mean that these very big-toothed hominins did not also eat a variety of other foods, perhaps including some meat. In fact, sophisticated new chemical analyses of *Paranthropus* teeth suggest that their diet may have been quite varied (Sponheimer et al., 2006).

The first member of the *Paranthropus* evolutionary group (clade) comes from a site in northern Kenya on the west side of Lake Turkana. This key find is that of a nearly complete skull, called the "Black Skull" (owing to chemical staining during fossilization), and it dates to approximately 2.5 mya (Fig. 11-16). This skull, with a cranial capacity of only 410 cm^3, is among the smallest for any hominin known, and it has other primitive traits reminiscent of *A. afarensis*. For example, there's a compound crest in the back of the skull, the upper face projects considerably, and the upper dental row converges in back (Kimbel et al., 1988).

But here's what makes the Black Skull so fascinating: Mixed into this array of distinctively primitive traits are a host of derived ones that link it to other, later *Paranthropus* species (including a broad face, a very large palate, and a large area for the back teeth). This mosaic of features seems to place this individual between earlier *A. afarensis* on the one hand and the later *Paranthropus* species on the other. Because of its unique position in hominin evolution, the Black Skull (and the population it represents) has been placed in a new species, *Paranthropus aethiopicus*.

Around 2 mya, different varieties of even more derived members of the *Paranthropus* lineage were on the scene in East Africa. As well documented by finds dated after 2 mya from Olduvai and East Turkana, *Paranthropus* continues to have relatively small cranial capacities (ranging from 510 to 530 cm^3) and very large, broad faces with massive back teeth and lower jaws. The larger (probably male) individuals also show that characteristic raised ridge (sagittal crest) along the midline of the cranium. Females are not as large or as robust as the males, indicating a fair degree of sexual dimorphism. In any case, the East African *Paranthropus* individuals are all extremely robust in terms of their teeth and jaws—although in overall body size they are much like other australopiths (see Table 11-1). Since these somewhat later East African *Paranthropus** fossils are so robust, they are usually placed in their own separate species, *Paranthropus boisei*.

---

*Note that these later East African *Paranthropus* finds are at least 500,000 years later than the earlier species (*P. aethiopicus*, exemplified by the Black Skull).

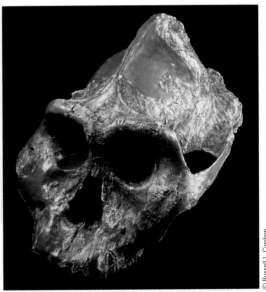

© Russell L. Ciochon

Figure 11-16

The "Black Skull," discovered at West Lake Turkana. This specimen is usually assigned to *Paranthropus aethiopicus*. It's called the Black Skull due to its dark color from the fossilization (mineralization) process.

sagittal crest A ridge of bone that runs down the middle of the cranium like a short Mohawk. This serves as the attachment for the large temporal muscles, indicating strong chewing.

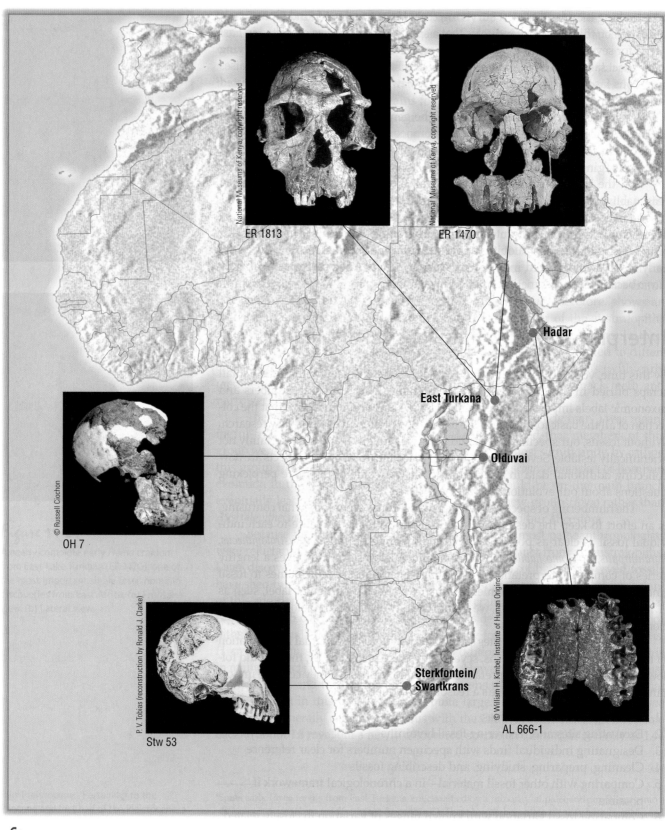

Figure 11-22

Early *Homo* fossil finds.

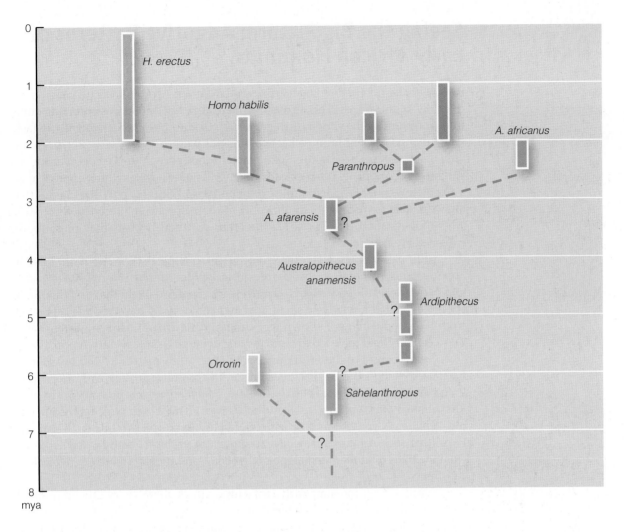

0
1
2
3
4
5
6
7
8
mya

H. erectus

Homo habilis

A. africanus

Paranthropus

A. afarensis ?

Australopithecus anamensis

Ardipithecus
?

Orrorin
?

Sahelanthropus

?

Figure **11-23**

A tentative early hominin phylogeny. Note the numerous question marks, indicating continuing uncertainty regarding evolutionary relationships.

But the task of interpretation still isn't complete, for what we really want to know in the long run is what happened to the populations represented by the fossil remains. In looking at the fossil hominin record, we're actually looking for our ancestors. In the process of eventually determining those populations that are our most likely antecedents, we may conclude that some hominins are on evolutionary side branches. If this conclusion is accurate, those hominins necessarily must have become extinct. It's both interesting and relevant to us as hominins to try to find out what influenced some earlier members of our family tree to continue evolving while others died out.

Although a clear evolutionary picture is not yet possible for organizing all the early hominins discussed in this chapter, there are some general patterns that for now make good sense (Fig. 11-23). New finds may of course require serious alterations to this scheme. Science can be exciting but can also be frustrating to many in the general public looking for simple answers to complex questions. For well-informed students of human evolution, it's most important to grasp the basic principles of paleoanthropology and *how* interpretations are made and *why* they sometimes must be revised. This way you'll be prepared for whatever shows up tomorrow.

Seeing the Big Picture: Adaptive Patterns of Early African Hominins

As you are by now aware, there are several different African hominin genera and certainly lots of species. This, in itself, is interesting. Speciation was occurring quite frequently among the various lineages of early hominins—more frequently, in fact, than among later hominins. What explains this pattern?

Evidence has been accumulating at a furious pace in the last decade, but it's still far from complete. What's clear is that we'll never have anything approaching a complete record of early hominin evolution, so significant gaps will remain. After all, we're able to discover hominins only in those special environmental contexts where fossilization was likely. All the other potential habitats they might have exploited are now invisible to us.

Still, patterns are emerging from the fascinating data we do have. First, it appears that early hominin species (pre-australopiths, *Australopithecus*, *Paranthropus*, and early *Homo*) all had restricted ranges. It's therefore likely that each hominin species exploited a relatively small area and could easily have become separated from other populations of its own species. So genetic drift (and to some extent natural selection) could have led to rapid genetic divergence and eventual speciation.

Second, most of these species appear to be at least partially tied to arboreal habitats, although there's disagreement on this point regarding early *Homo* (see Wood and Collard, 1999b; Foley 2002). Also, *Paranthropus* was probably somewhat less arboreal than *Ardipithecus* or *Australopithecus*. These very large-toothed hominins apparently concentrated on a diet of coarse, fibrous plant foods, such as roots. Exploiting such resources may have routinely taken these hominins farther away from the trees than their dentally more gracile—and perhaps more omnivorous—cousins.

Third, except for some early *Homo* individuals, there's very little in the way of an evolutionary trend of increased body size or of markedly greater encephalization. Beginning with *Sahelanthropus*, brain size was no more than that in chimpanzees—although when controlling for body size, this earliest of all known hominins may have had a proportionately larger brain than any living ape. Close to 6 million years later (that is, the time of the last surviving australopith species), relative brain size increased by no more than 10 to 15 percent. Perhaps tied to this relative stasis in brain capacity, there's no absolute association of any of these hominins with patterned stone tool manufacture (see Chapter 10).

Although conclusions are becoming increasingly controversial, for the moment, early *Homo* appears to be a partial exception. This group shows both increased encephalization and numerous occurrences of likely association with stone tools (though at many of the sites, australopith fossils were *also* found).

Lastly, all of these early African hominins show an accelerated developmental pattern (similar to that seen in African apes), one quite different from the *delayed* developmental pattern characteristic of *Homo sapiens* (and our immediate precursors). This apelike development is also seen in some early *Homo* individuals (Wood and Collard, 1999a). Rates of development can be accurately reconstructed by examining dental growth markers (Bromage and Dean, 1985), and these data may provide a crucial window into understanding this early stage of hominin evolution.

These African hominin predecessors were rather small, able bipeds, but still closely tied to arboreal and/or climbing niches. They had fairly small brains and, compared to later *Homo*, matured rapidly. It would take a major evolutionary jump to push one of their descendants in a more human direction. For the next chapter in this more human saga, read on.

Summary

The earliest members of our lineage date as far back as 7 mya. For the next 5 million years, they stayed geographically restricted to Africa, where they diversified into many different forms. During this 5-million-year span, at least 6 different hominin genera and upward of 12 species have been identified from the available fossil record. We have organized these fascinating early African hominins into three major groupings:

Pre-australopiths (7.0–4.4 mya)
> Including three genera of very early, and still primitive, hominins (*Sahelanthropus*, *Orrorin*, and *Ardipithecus*)

Australopiths (4.2–1.2 mya)
> Early, more primitive australopith species (4.2–3.0 mya), including *Australopithecus anamensis* and *Australopithecus afarensis*

> Later, more derived australopith species (2.5–1.2 mya), including two genera (*Paranthropus* and a later species of *Australopithecus*)

Early *Homo* (2.4–1.4 mya)
> The first members of our genus, who around 2 mya likely diverged into more than one species

What's Important Key Early Hominin Fossil Discoveries from Africa

Dates	Hominins	Sites/Regions	The Big Picture
1.8–1.4 mya	Early *Homo*	Olduvai; E. Turkana (E. Africa)	Bigger-brained; possible ancestor of later *Homo*
2.5–2.0 mya	Later *Australopithecus* (*A. africanus*)	Taung; Sterkfontein (S. Africa)	Quite derived; likely evolutionary dead end
2.0–1.0 mya	Later *Paranthropus*	Several sites (E. and S. Africa)	Highly derived; very likely evolutionary dead end
2.4 mya	*Paranthropus aethiopicus*	W. Turkana (E. Africa)	Earliest robust australopith; likely ancestor of later *Paranthropus*
3.6–3.0 mya	*Australopithecus afarensis*	Laetoli; Hadar (E. Africa)	Many fossils; very well studied; earliest well-documented biped; possible ancestor of all later hominins
4.4 mya	*Ardipithecus ramidus*	Aramis (E. Africa)	Many fossils; not yet well studied; bipedal, but likely quite derived; any likely ancestral relationship to later hominins not yet possible to say
~7.0 mya	*Sahelanthropus*	Toros-Menalla (Central Africa)	The earliest hominin; bipedal?

Critical Thinking Questions

1. In what ways are the remains of *Sahelanthropus* and *Ardipithecus* primitive? How do we know that these forms are hominins? How sure are we?

2. Assume that you are in the laboratory analyzing the "Lucy" *A. afarensis* skeleton. You also have complete skeletons from a chimpanzee and a modern human. (a) Which parts of the Lucy skeleton are more similar to the chimpanzee? Which are more similar to the human? (b) Which parts of the Lucy skeleton are *most informative*?

3. Discuss the first thing you would do if you found an early hominin fossil and were responsible for its formal description and publication. What would you include in your publication?

4. Discuss two current disputes regarding taxonomic issues concerning early hominins. Try to give support for alternative positions.

5. What is a phylogeny? Construct one for early hominins (7.0–1.0 mya). Make sure you can describe what conclusions your scheme makes. Also, try to defend it.

Hominin Evolution

CHAPTER

12

The Earliest Dispersal of the Genus *Homo*: *Homo erectus* and Contemporaries

David Lordkipanidze

Key Question

Who were the first members of the human lineage to disperse from Africa, and what were they like (behaviorally and anatomically)?

 Click!

Go to the following media for interactive activities and exercises on topics covered in this chapter:

- Online Virtual Laboratories for Physical Anthropology, Version 4.0

- Hominid Fossils: An Interactive Atlas CD-ROM

Introduction

Today it's estimated that upward of 1 million people daily cross national borders. Some individuals travel for business, others for pleasure. Refugees fleeing their homes may feel an urgent need to find safety elsewhere. Regardless, it seems that modern humans have wanderlust—a desire to see distant places. Our most distant hominin ancestors were essentially homebodies, staying in fairly restricted areas, exploiting the local resources, and trying to stay out of harm's way. In this respect, they were much like other primate species.

One thing's for sure: All these early hominins were restricted to Africa. When did the first hominins leave Africa? What were they like, and why did they leave their ancient homeland? Did they differ physically from their australopith and early *Homo* forebearers, and did they have new behavioral and cultural capabilities that helped them successfully exploit new environments?

It would be a romantic misconception to think of these first hominin transcontinental emigrants as "brave pioneers, boldly going where no one had gone before." They weren't deliberately striking out to go someplace in particular. It's not as though they had a map! Still, for what they did, deliberate or not, we owe them a lot.

Sometime close to 2 mya, something decisive occurred in human evolution. As the title of this chapter suggests, for the first time, hominins expanded widely out of Africa into other areas of the Old World. Since all the early hominin fossils have been found *only* in Africa, it seems that hominins were restricted to this continent for perhaps as long as 5 million years. The later, more widely dispersed hominins were quite different both anatomically and behaviorally from their African ancestors. They were much larger, were more committed to a completely terrestrial habitat, used more elaborate stone tools, and perhaps ate meat.

There is some variation among the different geographical groups of these highly successful hominins, and anthropologists still debate how to classify them. Discoveries continue as well. In particular, new finds from Europe are forcing a major reevaluation of exactly which were the first to leave Africa (Fig. 12-1).

Nevertheless, after 2 mya, there's less diversity in these hominins than is apparent in their pre-australopith and australopith predecessors. Consequently, there is universal agreement that the hominins found outside of Africa are all members of genus *Homo*. Thus, taxonomic debates focus solely on how many species are represented. The species for which we have the most evidence is called *Homo erectus*. Furthermore, this is the one group that most paleoanthropologists have recognized for decades and still agree on. Thus, in this chapter we'll focus our discussion on *Homo erectus*. We will, however, also discuss alternative interpretations that "split" the fossil sample into more species.

A New Kind of Hominin

The discovery of fossils now referred to as *Homo erectus* began in the nineteenth century. Later in this chapter, we'll discuss the historical background of these earliest discoveries in Java and the somewhat later discoveries in China. From this work, as well as presumably related finds in Europe and North Africa, a variety of taxonomic names were suggested.

It's important to realize that such taxonomic *splitting* was quite common in the early years of paleoanthropology. More systematic biological thinking came to the fore only after World War II and with the incorporation of the Modern Synthesis into paleontology (see p. 97). Most of the fossils that were given these varied names are now placed in the species *Homo erectus*—or at least they've all been lumped into one genus (*Homo*).

In the last few decades, discoveries from East Africa of firmly dated finds have established the clear presence of *Homo erectus* by 1.8 mya. Some researchers see several anatomical differences between these African representatives of an *erectus*-like hominin and their Asian cousins (hominins that almost everybody refers to as *Homo erectus*). Thus, they place the African fossils into a separate species, one they call *Homo ergaster* (Andrews, 1984; Wood, 1991).

While there are some anatomical differences between the African specimens and those from Asia, they are all clearly *closely* related and quite possibly represent geographical varieties of a single species. We'll thus refer to these hominins as *Homo erectus*.

All analyses have shown that *H. erectus* hominins represent a different **grade** of evolution than their more ancient African predecessors. A grade is an evolutionary grouping of organisms showing a similar adaptive pattern. Increase in body size and robustness, changes in limb proportions, and greater encephalization all indicate that these hominins were more like modern humans in their adaptive pattern than their African ancestors were.* We should point out that a grade only implies general adaptive aspects of a group of animals; it implies nothing directly about shared ancestry. Organisms that share common ancestry are said to be in the same *clade* (see p. 114). For example, orangutans and African great apes could be said to be in the same grade, but they are not in the same clade (see p. 269).

The hominins discussed in this chapter are not only members of a new and distinct grade of human evolution; they're also closely related to each other. It's clear from these fossils that a major adaptive shift had taken place—one setting hominin evolution in a distinctly more human direction.

We mentioned that there is considerable variation in different regional populations of hominins broadly defined as *Homo erectus*. New discoveries are showing even more dramatic variation, suggesting that some of these hominins may not fit closely at all with this general adaptive pattern (more on this presently). For the moment, however, let's review what most of these fossils look like.

The Morphology of *Homo erectus*

Homo erectus populations lived in very different environments over much of the Old World. They all, however, shared several common physical traits that we'll now summarize briefly.

grade A grouping of organisms sharing a similar adaptive pattern. Grade isn't necessarily based on closeness of evolutionary relationship, but it does contrast organisms in a useful way (e.g., *Homo erectus* with *Homo sapiens*).

---

*We did note in Chapter 11 that early *Homo* is a partial exception, being transitional in some respects.

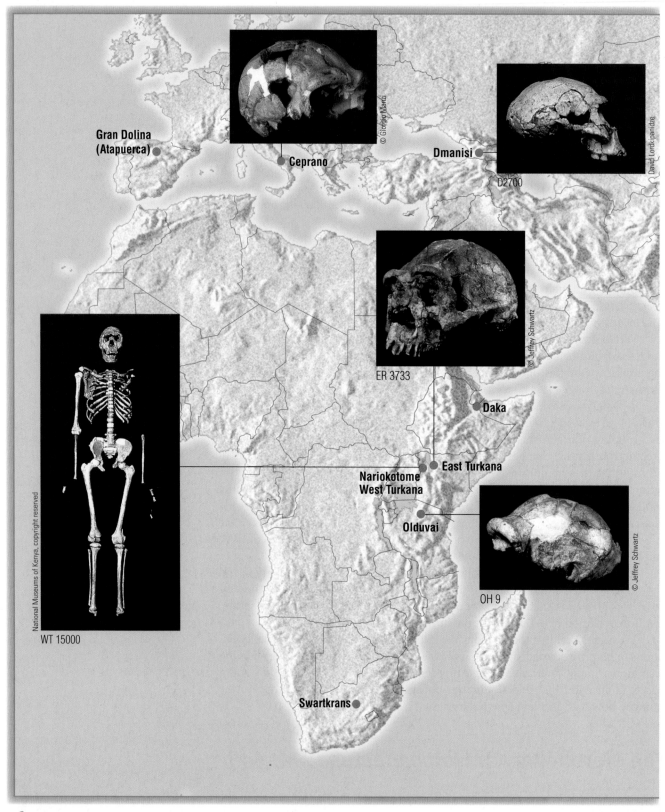

Figure **12-1**

Major *Homo erectus* sites and localities of other contemporaneous hominins.

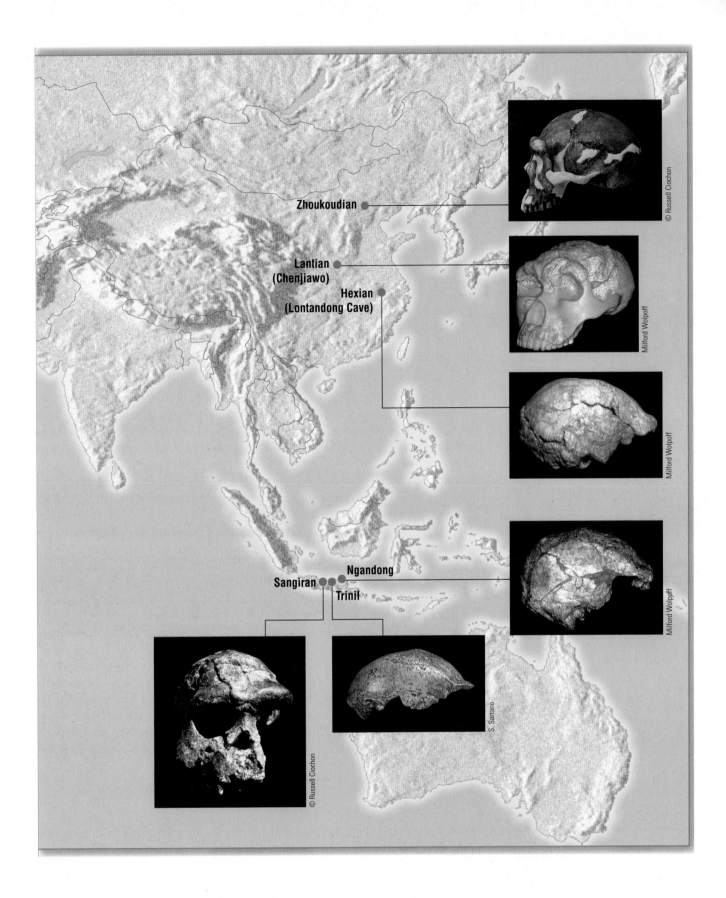

Zhoukoudian

Lantian
(Chenjiawo)

Hexian
(Lontandong Cave)

Ngandong

Sangiran

Trinil

© Russell Ciochon

Milford Wolpoff

Milford Wolpoff

Milford Wolpoff

© Russell Ciochon

S. Sartano

Body Size

As conclusively shown by the discovery of the nearly complete skeleton of "Nariokotome Boy" (from **Nariokotome**, on the west side of Lake Turkana, in Kenya), we know that *H. erectus* was larger than earlier hominins. From this and other less-complete specimens, anthropologists estimate that some *H. erectus* adults weighed well over 100 pounds, with an average adult height of about 5 feet 6 inches (McHenry, 1992; Ruff and Walker, 1993; Walker and Leakey, 1993). Another point to keep in mind is that *H. erectus* was quite sexually dimorphic—at least as indicated by the East African specimens. Some adult males may have weighed considerably more than 100 pounds. And if the Nariokotome Boy had lived to adulthood, he probably would have grown to an adult height of over 6 feet (Walker, 1993).

Increased height and weight in *H. erectus* are also associated with a dramatic increase in robusticity. In fact, a heavily built body was to dominate hominin evolution not just during *H. erectus* times, but through the long transitional era of premodern forms as well. Only with the appearance of anatomically modern *H. sapiens* did a more gracile skeletal structure emerge, and it still characterizes most modern populations.

Brain Size

While *Homo erectus* differs in several respects from both early *Homo* and *Homo sapiens*, the most obvious feature is its cranial size—which is closely related to brain size. Early *Homo* had cranial capacities ranging from as small as 500 cm^3 to as large as 800 cm^3. *H. erectus*, on the other hand, shows considerable brain enlargement, with a cranial capacity of about 700* to 1,250 cm^3 (and a mean of approximately 900 cm^3). However, in making such comparisons, we must bear in mind two key questions: What is the comparative sample, and what were the overall body sizes of the species being compared?

As for the first question, you may recall that many anthropologists are now convinced that more than one species of early *Homo* existed in East Africa around 2 mya. If so, only one of them could have been the ancestor of *H. erectus*. If we choose the smaller-bodied sample of early *Homo* as our presumed ancestral group, then *H. erectus* shows as much as a 40 percent increase in average cranial capacity. But if the comparative sample we use is the larger-bodied group of early *Homo* (for example, skull 1470, from East Turkana), then *H. erectus* shows a 25 percent increase in cranial capacity.

As we've discussed, brain size is closely linked to overall body size. We've focused on the increase in *H. erectus* brain size, but *H. erectus* was also considerably larger overall than earlier members of the genus *Homo*. In fact, when we compare *H. erectus* with the larger-bodied early *Homo* sample, their *relative* brain size is about the same (Walker, 1991). What's more, when we compare the relative brain size of *H. erectus* with that of *H. sapiens*, we see that *H. erectus* was considerably less encephalized than later members of the genus *Homo*.

Cranial Shape

Homo erectus crania display a highly distinctive shape, partly because of increased brain size, but probably more correlated with increased body size. The ramifica-

Nariokotome (nar´-ee-oh-koh´-tow-may)

nuchal torus (nuke´-ul) (*nucha*, meaning "neck") A projection of bone in the back of the cranium where neck muscles attach. These muscles hold up the head.

_____

*Even smaller cranial capacities are seen in recently discovered fossils from the Caucasus region of southeastern Europe at a site called Dmanisi. We'll discuss these fossils in a moment.

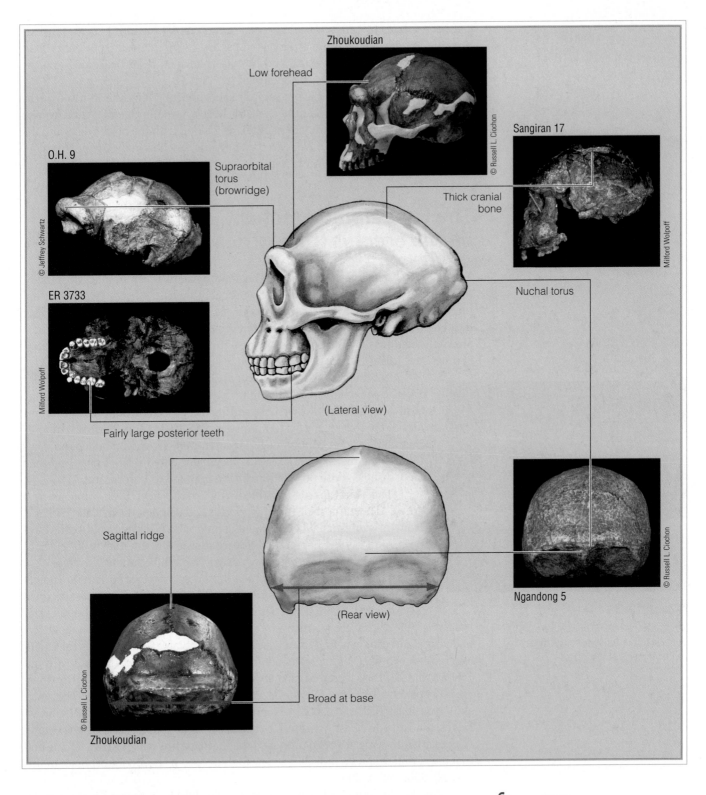

Zhoukoudian

Low forehead

© Russell L. Ciochon

Sangiran 17

O.H. 9

Supraorbital torus (browridge)

© Jeffrey Schwartz

Thick cranial bone

Milford Wolpoff

ER 3733

Nuchal torus

Milford Wolpoff

(Lateral view)

Fairly large posterior teeth

Sagittal ridge

Ngandong 5

© Russell L. Ciochon

(Rear view)

© Russell L. Ciochon

Broad at base

Zhoukoudian

Figure **12-2**

Morphology and variation in *Homo erectus*.

tions of this heavily built cranium are reflected in thick cranial bone, large brow-ridges (supraorbital tori) above the eyes, and a projecting **nuchal torus** at the rear of the skull (Fig. 12-2).

The braincase is long and low, receding from the large browridges with little forehead development. Also, the cranium is wider at the base compared with earlier *and* later species of genus *Homo*. The maximum cranial breadth is below the ear opening, giving the cranium a pentagonal shape (when viewed from behind). In contrast, the skulls of early *Homo* and *H. sapiens* have more vertical sides, and the maximum width is *above* the ear openings.

Most specimens also have a sagittal keel running along the midline of the skull. Very different from a sagittal crest, the keel is a small ridge that runs front to back along the sagittal suture. The sagittal keel, along with the browridges and the nuchal torus, don't seem to have served an obvious function in the life of *H. erectus*, but most likely reflect bone buttressing in a very robust skull.

The First *Homo erectus*: *Homo erectus* from Africa

Where did *Homo erectus* first appear? The answer seems fairly simple: Most likely, this species initially evolved in Africa, probably in East Africa. Two important pieces of evidence help confirm this hypothesis. First, *all* the earlier hominins prior to the appearance of *H. erectus* come from Africa. What's more, by 1.8 mya, there are well-dated fossils of this species at East Turkana, in Kenya, and not long after at other sites in East Africa.

Still, there's a small wrinkle in this neat view. At 1.75 mya, similar populations were already living far away in southeastern Europe, and by 1.6 mya, in Indonesia as well. So, adding these pieces to our puzzle, it seems very likely that *H. erectus* first arose in East Africa and then very quickly migrated to other continents far away from their African homeland. Let's first review the African *H. erectus* specimens dated at 1.8–1 mya, and then we'll discuss those populations that emigrated to Europe and Asia.

The oldest fossils identified as *H. erectus* have been found in East Africa. The earliest of these *H. erectus* fossils come from East Turkana, from the same area where earlier australopith and early *Homo* fossils have been found (see Chapter 11). Indeed, it seems likely that in East Africa around 2–1.8 mya, some form of early *Homo* evolved into *H. erectus*.

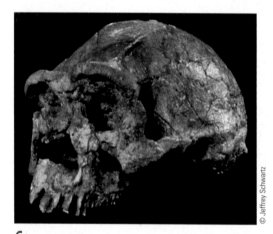

Figure **12-3**

Nearly complete skull of *Homo erectus* from East Lake Turkana, Kenya, dated to approximately 1.8 mya.

© Jeffrey Schwartz

The most significant *H. erectus* discovery from East Turkana is a nearly complete skull (Fig. 12-3). Dated at 1.8 mya, this is the oldest *H. erectus* specimen ever found. The cranial capacity is estimated at 848 cm^3, in the lower range for *H. erectus* (700 to 1,250 cm^3), which isn't surprising considering its early date. A second very significant new find from East Turkana is notable because it has the smallest cranium of any *H. erectus* specimen from anywhere in Africa. Dated to around 1.5 mya, the skull has a cranial capacity of only 691 cm^3. As we'll see shortly, there are a couple of crania from southeastern Europe that are even smaller. The small skull from East Turkana also shows more gracile features (such as smaller browridges) than do other East African *H. erectus* individuals, but it preserves the overall *H. erectus* vault shape. It's been proposed that perhaps this new find is a female and that the variation shown indicates a very high degree of sexual dimorphism in this species (Spoor et al., 2007).

Another remarkable discovery was made in 1984 by Kamoya Kimeu, a member of Richard Leakey's team known widely as an outstanding fossil hunter. Kimeu discovered a small piece of skull on the west side of Lake Turkana at the site known as Nariokotome. Excavations produced the most complete *H. erectus* skeleton ever found (Fig. 12-4). Known properly as WT 15000, the almost complete skeleton includes facial bones, a pelvis, and most of the limb bones, ribs, and vertebrae and

At a Glance

Key *Homo erectus* Discoveries from Africa

DATES	SITE	EVOLUTIONARY SIGNIFICANCE
1.4 mya	**Olduvai**	Large individual, very robust (male?) *H. erectus*
1.6 mya	**Nariokotome W. Turkana**	Nearly complete skeleton; young male
1.8 mya	**E. Turkana**	Oldest well-dated *H. erectus*; great amount of variation seen among individuals, possibly due to sexual dimorphism

is chronometrically dated to about 1.6 mya. Such well-preserved postcranial elements make for a very unusual and highly useful discovery, because these elements are scarce at other *H. erectus* sites. The skeleton is that of a boy about 8 years of age with an estimated height of about 5 feet 3 inches (Walker and Leakey, 1993; Dean and Smith, quoted in Gibbons, 2008). Had he reached maturity, it's estimated that he would have grown quite tall, perhaps close to 6 feet. The postcranial bones look very similar, though not quite identical, to those of modern humans. The cranial capacity of WT 15000 is estimated at 880 cm^3; brain growth was nearly complete, and the boy's adult cranial capacity would have been approximately 909 cm^3 (Begun and Walker, 1993).

Other important *H. erectus* finds have come from Olduvai Gorge, in Tanzania, and they include a very robust skull discovered there by Louis Leakey back in 1960. The skull is dated at 1.4 mya and has a well-preserved cranial vault with just a small part of the upper face. Estimated at 1,067 cm^3, the cranial capacity is the largest of all the African *H. erectus* specimens. The browridge is huge, the largest known for any hominin, but the walls of the braincase are thin. This latter characteristic is seen in most East African *H. erectus* specimens; in this respect, they differ from Asian *H. erectus*, in which cranial bones are thick.

Three other sites from Ethiopia have yielded *H. erectus* fossils, the most noteworthy coming from the Gona area and the Daka locale, both in the Awash River region. As you've seen, numerous remains of earlier hominins have come from this area (see Chapter 11 and Appendix C).

A recently discovered nearly complete female *H. erectus* pelvis comes from the Gona area and is dated to approximately 1.3 mya (Simpson et al., 2008). This find is particularly interesting because *H. erectus* postcranial remains are so rare and this is the first *H. erectus* female pelvis yet found. This fossil also reveals some tantalizing glimpses of likely *H. erectus* development. The pelvis has a very wide birth canal, indicating that quite large-brained babies could have developed *in utero* (before birth); in fact it's possible that a newborn *H. erectus* infant's brain could have been almost as large as that seen in a typical modern *H. sapiens* newborn.

This evidence has led Scott Simpson and his colleagues to suggest that *H. erectus* prenatal brain growth was more like later humans' and quite different from that found in apes *or* in australopiths such as Lucy. However, it is also evident that *H. erectus* brain growth after birth was more rapid than in modern humans. This new pelvis is very different from that of the Nariokotome boy's pelvis and,

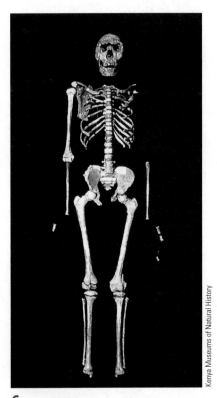

Kenya Museums of Natural History

Figure **12-4**

WT 15000 from Nariokotome, Kenya: the most complete *H. erectus* specimen yet found.

taken together, may reflect considerable sexual dimorphism in skeletal anatomy linked to reproduction as well as in body size. The female pelvis provides new evidence that *H. erectus* brain development was different from that seen in apes (and australopiths) as well as from that seen in modern humans. It thus looks like a unique developmental strategy, different from all known hominoids (living and extinct). More discoveries will help confirm this intriguing hypothesis.

Another recent discovery from the Middle Awash of Ethiopia of a mostly complete cranium from Daka is also important because this individual (dated at approximately 1 mya) is more like Asian *H. erectus* than are most of the earlier East African remains we've discussed (Asfaw et al., 2002). Consequently, the suggestion by several researchers that East African fossils are a different species from (Asian) *H. erectus* isn't supported by the morphology of the Daka cranium.

Who Were the Earliest African Emigrants?

The fossils from East Africa imply that a new grade of human evolution appeared in Africa not long after 2 mya. Thus, the hominins who migrated to Asia and Europe are generally assumed to be their immediate descendants because the dates of all hominins outside of Africa start after the oldest African *H. erectus* material and because these travelers look like *Homo*, with longer limbs and bigger brains. Since *H. erectus* began in East Africa, these hominins were close to land links to Eurasia (through the Middle East) and thus were probably the first to leave the continent. We can't be sure of why these hominins left—whether they were following animal migrations or maybe it was simply population growth and expansion. What we do know is that we're seeing a greater range of physical variation in the specimens outside of Africa and that the emigration out of Africa happened earlier than we had previously thought. *H. erectus* appears in East Africa at about 1.8 mya, and soon after similar hominins are living in the Caucasus region (now in the country of Georgia) at about 1.75 mya. Eventually, hominins make it all the way to the island of Java, Indonesia, by 1.6 mya! It took *H. erectus* less than 200,000 years to travel from East Africa to Southeast Asia. Let's review the evidence.

The site of **Dmanisi**, now in the Republic of Georgia, has produced several individuals, giving us a unique look at these first travelers. The Dmanisi crania are similar to those of *H. erectus* (for example, the long, low braincase, wide base, and sagittal keeling; see especially Fig. 12-5b, and compare with Fig. 12-2). However, other characteristics of the Dmanisi individuals are different from other hominin finds outside of Africa. In particular, the most complete specimen (specimen 2700;

Dmanisi (dim´-an-eese´-ee)

Figure **12-5**

Dmanisi crania discovered in 1999 and 2001 and dated to 1.8–1.7 mya.
(a) Specimen 2282.
(b) Specimen 2280.
(c) Specimen 2700.

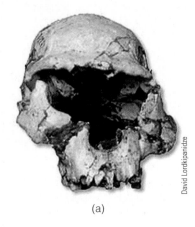

(a)

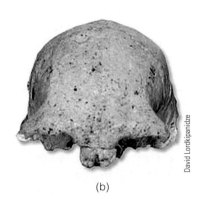

(b)

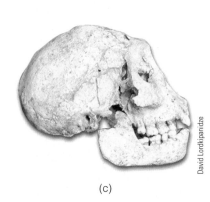

(c)

see Fig. 12-5c) has a less-robust and thinner browridge, a projecting lower face, and a relatively large upper canine. At least when viewed from the front, this skull is more reminiscent of the smaller early *Homo* specimens from East Africa than it is of *H. erectus*. Also, specimen 2700's cranial capacity is very small—estimated at only 600 cm^3, well within the range of early *Homo*. In fact, all four Dmanisi crania so far described have relatively small cranial capacities—the other three estimated at 630 cm^3, 650 cm^3, and 780 cm^3.

Probably the most remarkable find from Dmanisi is the most recently discovered of these skulls, excavated by researchers in 2002 (and published in 2005). This nearly complete cranium is of an older adult male; and surprisingly for such an ancient find, he died with only one tooth remaining in his jaws (Lordkipanidze et al., 2006). Because his jawbones show advanced resorption of bone, it seems that he lived for several years without being able to chew his food (Fig. 12-6). David Lordkipanidze, who leads the excavations at Dmanisi, and his colleagues have suggested that this individual required a fair amount of assistance to survive in an era when the only way to process food was to use your teeth (Lordkipanidze et al., 2005, 2006). However, this contention requires more detailed investigation before it can be confirmed.

Researchers have also recovered some stone tools at Dmanisi. The tools are similar to the Oldowan industry from Africa, as would be expected for a site dated earlier than the beginning of the **Acheulian** industry broadly associated with African *H. erectus* after 1.4 mya (see p. 350).

The newest evidence from Dmanisi includes several postcranial bones, coming from at least four individuals (Lordkipanidze et al., 2007). This new evidence is especially important because it allows us to make comparisons with what is known of *H. erectus* from other areas. The Dmanisi fossils have an unusual combination of traits. These hominins were not especially tall, with an estimated height ranging from about 4 feet 9 inches to 5 feet 5 inches. Certainly, based on this evidence, they seem much smaller than the full *H. erectus* specimens from East Africa or Asia. Yet, although very short in stature, they still show body proportions (such as leg length) like that of *H. erectus* (and *H. sapiens*) and quite different from that seen in earlier hominins.

Based on these startling new revelations from Dmanisi, we can ask several questions:

1. Was *Homo erectus* the first hominin to leave Africa—or did an earlier form of *Homo* migrate even earlier?
2. Did hominins require a large brain and sophisticated stone tool culture to disperse out of Africa?
3. Was the large, robust body build of *H. erectus* a necessary adaptation for the initial occupation of Eurasia?

Based on very recent interpretations, here are the most current answers to these questions:

1. While the Dmanisi specimens are small in both stature and cranial capacity, they have specific characteristics that identify them as *H. erectus* (for example, a sagittal keel and low braincase). So, for now, the Dmanisi hominins are thought to be *H. erectus*, although an early and quite different variety from that found almost anywhere else.
2. Now that these small hominins have been found outside of Africa at 1.75 mya, we realize that travel didn't require big brains or having an Acheulian culture (as previously thought).

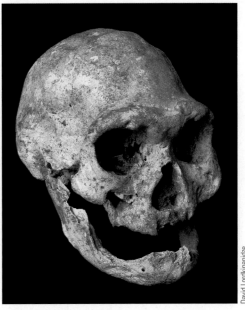

David Lordkipanidze

Figure **12-6**

Most recently discovered cranium from Dmanisi, almost totally lacking in teeth (with both upper and lower jaws showing advanced bone resorption).

Acheulian (ash´-oo-lay-en) Pertaining to a stone tool industry from the Early and Middle Pleistocene; characterized by a large proportion of bifacial tools (flaked on both sides). Acheulian tool kits are common in Africa, Southwest Asia, and western Europe, but they're thought to be less common elsewhere. Also spelled Acheulean.

A Closer Look

In Search of Ancient Human Ancestors—and a Little Shade

"Whoops!" Upon hearing this exclamation, my colleagues halt their progress along the narrow earthen walkways that outline the flooded rice paddies and make an emerald patchwork quilt on the Java landscape. They turn around and see that I've slipped. Again. Each misstep comes with some good-hearted ribbing as my comrades heave me back onto dry land. Each day we traverse the paddies by way of the thin dikes en route to our research site in central Java. Around us rise great cliffs of ancient soil, striated like an intricately layered cake. Rich green jewel tones dazzle the eye as we pass by peasants laboring in the fields under the hot sun. We, too, are in Java to work, but we toil for a different kind of produce—we seek answers about our early ancestor, Homo erectus. *As we tread across the paddies to a dusty oxcart path, our eyes comb the adjacent outcrops for darkened silhouettes of fossils—carefully, we note their locations. By the time we reach our destination, our backpacks are filled with curious remains— this one a tooth of a fossil deer, that one a piece of ancient crocodile bone—but no humans. All the fossils are stained crimson or black by the very soils in which they have lain for nearly a million years. As we begin to examine the exposed sediments, we resume our search for more fossils, our sweat-soaked shirts sticking to our skin. It's 9 A.M. and we're already tired and hot, but we quickly brush these distractions away. Our search has just begun.*

For the past eight years, my colleagues and I have been conducting fieldwork in the rice paddies of central Java. You might think it unusual to conduct scientific research in a rice paddy, but you have to "follow the fossils." Ancient sediments in our field area, the Sangiran Dome, were forced to the surface by the pressure of subterranean

mud volcanoes about 120,000 years ago. What attracts us to the Sangiran Dome? It's the 1- to 2-million-year-old fossils and sediments that have been unearthed by erosion and other natural processes. This special series of events means that the Sangiran Dome is prime for both discovering the fossils of early humans in their original environmental context and for radiometrically dating them using volcanic sediments—a common occurrence in Java, an island formed by volcanoes.

If the cradle of human origins is Africa, then Asia was one of the playgrounds where our species grew and matured. Around 2 mya, *Homo erectus*, our first widely traveled ancestor, left the African savanna homeland to expand its horizons in the larger world. The first stop on this species' journey was in what is now the Republic of Georgia in southeastern Europe, where four skulls and a partial skeleton have been found. From here, we know that *Homo erectus* ventured onward to East Asia and eventually Java. We know little about the features that attracted these hominins to the Javanese landscape or when the first migration to this island occurred. We do know that over time, the descendants of original *Homo erectus* immigrants evolved, giving us both full-sized primitive peoples with thick skulls and projecting browridges and later the diminutive "Hobbits" on the island of Flores (you'll meet them in Chapter 14).

Every good realtor will tell you that it's "location, location, location!" What was it about this Asian setting— particularly the island of Java—that drew these ancient

3. It seems that *Homo* was built to travel regardless of height, having attained long leg proportions.

While new and thus tentative, the recent evidence raises important and exciting possibilities. The Dmanisi findings suggest that the first hominins to leave Africa were quite possibly a small-bodied very early form of *H. erectus*, possessing smaller brains than later *H. erectus* and carrying with them a typical African Oldowan stone tool culture.

So, from the evidence to date, the Dmanisi hominins can be seen as generally short and small-brained, having none of the adaptations hypothesized to be essential to hominin migration—that is, being tall and having relatively large brains. Another explanation may be that we will find that there were *two* migrations out of Africa at this time: one consisting of the small-brained, diminutive Dmanisi hominins and an almost immediate second one that founded the well-recognized *H. erectus* populations of Java and China. All this evidence is so new, however, that it's too soon even to predict what further revisions may be required.

immigrants to colonize, as evidenced by the nearly 100 fossils of *Homo erectus* that have been unearthed there over the past 70 years? Was it, perhaps, the rich volcanic soils and the vegetation they fostered that attracted our distant relatives to the Sangiran Dome, or did *Homo erectus* simply follow land-loving animals to the newly emergent environment of central Java? Our research centers on this very issue, using visual and geochemical clues from soils and plant and animal fossils to reconstruct the landscape of Java when *Homo erectus* first arrived millions of years ago.

As the sun dips low on the horizon, the valley of the Sangiran Dome dims. At the end of the day, our team reassembles for the trek back to our van, joking and chatting about the day's finds. Our packs are heavy with samples of ancient soils, fossil shells and teeth, and rocks from ancient volcanic eruptions, all being hauled back for analysis. We watch our shadowy likenesses in the murky water of the paddies as we trudge out of the mists of time. In an hour we'll return to the hustle and bustle of Solo and wash away the dirt of ages. But before reentering civilization, we cast one last look into the past and wonder—"What was this place like during the time of our very ancient ancestors?" Was the landscape dominated by palms, mahogany, and cashew-bearing trees, as it is today, or was the countryside completely foreign? The full answers are just beyond our grasp. Perhaps today we carry in our backpacks the answers to these questions. Some day soon we'll be able to look at this landscape as our ancestors did, linking our common histories with modern technology.

—*Russell L. Ciochon*

Figure 1

The Sangiran Dome Team, composed of researchers from the University of Iowa and the Bandung Institute of Technology, shown here doing a paleoecological analysis of the ancient strata of the dome.

Homo erectus from Indonesia

After the publication of *On the Origin of Species*, debates about evolution were prevalent throughout Europe. While many theorists simply stayed home and debated the merits of natural selection and the likely course of human evolution, one young Dutch anatomist decided to go find evidence of it. Eugene Dubois (1858–1940) enlisted in the Dutch East Indian Army and was shipped to the island of Sumatra, Indonesia, to look for what he called "the missing link."

In October 1891, after moving his search to the neighboring island of Java, Dubois' field crew unearthed a skullcap along the Solo River near the town of Trinil—a fossil that was to become internationally famous as the first recognized human ancestor (Fig. 12-7). The following year, a human femur was recovered about 15 yards upstream in what Dubois claimed was the same level as the skullcap, and he assumed that the skullcap (with a cranial capacity of slightly over 900 cm^3) and the femur belonged to the same individual.

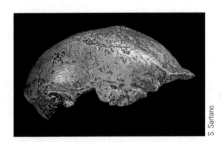

Figure 12-7

The famous Trinil skullcap discovered by Eugene Dubois near the Solo River in Java. Discovered in 1891, this was the first fossil human found outside of Europe or Africa.

Six sites in eastern Java have yielded all the *H. erectus* fossil remains found to date on that island. The dating of these fossils has been hampered by the complex nature of Javanese geology, but it's been generally accepted that most of the fossils belong to the Early to Middle **Pleistocene** and are between 1.6 and 1 million years old. What's more, there was also a very late surviving *H. erectus* group in Java at the Ngandong site, where the fossils are dated to just 27,000 years ago.

The earliest *H. erectus* fossils from Java come from the central part of the island. Beginning with Dubois' famous discovery at Trinil, over 80 different specimens have been located, with many coming from an area called the "Sangiran Dome," located just west of Trinil. Several crania have been found, although only one preserves the face. Cranial capacities range between 813 cm^3 and 1,059 cm^3, with an average slightly larger than that of African *H. erectus*. These specimens have thick cranial vaults, sagittal keels, browridges, and nuchal tori, and often these traits are a bit more pronounced than in African *H. erectus*. Sangiran Dome gives us a picture of a sustained population of H. erectus from 1.6 to 1 mya living on the banks of rivers, in the shadows of erupting volcanoes. This environment doesn't seem so different from that of Lake Turkana at that time: water, grassland, and roaming animals.

By far, the most recent group of *H. erectus* fossils from Java come from Ngandong, in an area to the east of the other finds already mentioned. At Ngandong, an excavation along an ancient river terrace produced 11 mostly complete hominin skulls. Two specialized dating techniques, discussed in Chapter 10, have determined that animal bones found at the site—and presumably associated with the hominins—are only about 50,000–25,000 years old (Swisher et al., 1996). These dates are controversial, but further evidence is now establishing a *very* late survival of *H. erectus* in Java, long after the species had disappeared elsewhere. So these individuals would be contemporary with *H. sapiens*—which, by this time, had expanded widely throughout the Old World and into Australia around 60,000–40,000 years ago (ya). Recent work on the old excavation site of Ngandong (first excavated in the early 1930s) has led to a rediscovery of the fossil bed where the 14 individuals had been found (Ciochon et al., 2009). New dating techniques and fossil identification will be undertaken to better understand site formation and taphonomy. As we'll see in Chapter 14, even later—and very unusual—hominins have been found not far away, apparently evolving while isolated on another Indonesian island.

Very few artifacts have been found, and those have come mainly from river terraces, not from primary sites: "On Java there is still not a single site where artifacts can be associated with *H. erectus*" (Bartstra, 1982, p. 319).

Homo erectus from China

The story of the first discoveries of Chinese *H. erectus* is another saga filled with excitement, hard work, luck, and misfortune. Europeans had known for a long time that "dragon bones," used by the Chinese as medicine and aphrodisiacs, were actually ancient mammal bones. Scientists eventually located one of the sources of these bones near Beijing at a site called **Zhoukoudian**. Serious excavations were begun there in the 1920s, and in 1929, a fossil skull was discovered. The skull turned out to be a juvenile's, and although it was thick, low, and relatively small, there was no doubt that it belonged to an early hominin.

Pleistocene The epoch of the Cenozoic from 1.8 mya until 10,000 ya. Frequently referred to as the Ice Age, this epoch is associated with continental glaciations in northern latitudes.

Zhoukoudian (Zhoh´-koh-dee´-en)

Zhoukoudian *Homo erectus*

The fossil remains of *H. erectus* discovered in the 1920s and 1930s, as well as some more recent excavations at Zhoukoudian (Fig. 12-8), are by far the largest collection of *H. erectus* material found anywhere. This excellent sample includes 14 skull-caps (Fig. 12-9), other cranial pieces, and more than 100 isolated teeth, but only a scattering of postcranial elements (Jia and Huang, 1990). Various interpretations to account for this unusual pattern of preservation have been offered, ranging from ritualistic treatment or cannibalism to the more mundane suggestion that the *H. erectus* remains are simply the leftovers of the meals of giant hyenas. The hominin remains were studied and casts were made immediately, which proved invaluable, since the specimens were lost during the American evacuation of China at the start of World War II.

The hominin remains belong to upward of 40 adults and children and together provide a good overall picture of Chinese *H. erectus.* Like the materials from Java, they have typical *H. erectus* features, including a large browridge and nuchal torus. Also, the skull has thick bones, a sagittal keel, and a protruding face and is broadest near the bottom. This site has been dated at various times to between 670,000 and 410,000 years old.

Figure 12-8

Zhoukoudian cave.

Cultural Remains More than 100,000 artifacts have been recovered from this vast site, which was occupied intermittently for many thousands of years. Early on, tools are generally crude and shapeless, but they become more refined over time. Common tools at the site are choppers and chopping tools, but retouched flakes were fashioned into scrapers, points, burins, and awls (Fig. 12-10).

The way of life at Zhoukoudian has traditionally been described as that of hunter-gatherers who killed deer, horses, and other animals and gathered fruits, berries, and ostrich eggs. Fragments of charred ostrich eggshells and abundant deposits of hackberry seeds unearthed in the cave suggest that these hominins supplemented their diet of meat by gathering herbs, wild fruits, tubers, and eggs. Layers of what has long been thought to be ash in the cave (over 18 feet deep at one point) have been interpreted as indicating the use of fire by *H. erectus.*

More recently, several researchers have challenged this picture of Zhoukoudian life. Lewis Binford and colleagues (Binford and Ho, 1985; Binford and Stone, 1986a, 1986b) reject the description of *H. erectus* as hunters and argue that the evidence clearly points more accurately to scavenging. Using advanced archaeological analyses, Noel Boaz and colleagues have even questioned whether the *H. erectus* remains at Zhoukoudian represent evidence of hominin habitation of the cave. By comparing the types of bones, as well as the damage to the bones, with that seen in contemporary carnivore dens, Boaz and Ciochon (2001) have suggested that much of the material in the cave likely accumulated through the activities of giant extinct hyenas. In fact, they hypothesize that most of the *H. erectus* remains, too, are the food refuse of hyena meals.

Boaz and his colleagues do recognize that the tools in the cave, and possibly the cut marks on some of the animal bones, provide evidence of hominin activities at Zhoukoudian. They also recognize that more detailed analysis is required to test their hypotheses and

Figure 12-9

Composite cranium of Zhoukoudian *Homo erectus*, reconstructed by Ian Tattersall and Gary Sawyer, of the American Museum of Natural History in New York.

A Closer Look

Dragon Bone Hill: Cave Home or Hyena Den?

About 30 miles southwest of Beijing, near Zhoukoudian, is the locality known as Dragon Bone Hill. In the 1920s and 1930s, this cave site yielded the first (and still the largest) cache of fossils of *Homo erectus*, historically known as Peking Man. The remains of about 45 individuals, along with thousands of stone tools, debris from tool manufacture, and thousands of animal bones, were contained within the 100-foot-thick deposits that once completely filled the original cave. Some evidence unearthed at the site suggests to many researchers that these creatures, who lived from about 670,000 to 410,000 ya, had mastered the use of fire and practiced cannibalism. Still, despite years of excavation and analysis, little is certain about what occurred here long ago.

To most of the early excavators, the likely scenario was that these particular early humans lived in the cave where

their bones and stone tools were found. The animal bones were likely the remains of meals—proof of their hunting expertise. A more sensational view, first advanced in 1929, was that the cave contained evidence of cannibalism. Skulls were conspicuous among the remains, suggesting to Chinese paleoanthropologist Jia Lanpo that these might be the trophies of headhunters.

But another Chinese paleoanthropologist—Pei Wenzhong, who codirected the early Zhoukoudian excavations—believed that the skulls and accompanying damage were due to hyena chewing, not human killers. In 1939, his views were bolstered by the emerging science of taphonomy, which is the study of how, after death, animal and plant remains become modified, moved, buried, and fossilized (see Chapter 10, p. 281). Published observations on the way hyenas at the Vienna zoo fed on cow bones led later

(a)

(b)

Figure 1

These illustrations demonstrate the two interpretations of the remains from Dragon Bone Hill: (a) the more traditional cave home model and (b) the newer, and probably more accurate, hyena den model.

Zhoukoudian Museum, China and © Russell L. Ciochon

Figure 12-10

Chinese tools from Middle Pleistocene sites. (Adapted from Wu and Olsen, 1985.)

Graver, or burin

Flint awl

Flint point

Quartzite chopper

scientists to reject the idea of cannibalism, although they continued to look upon the cave as a shelter used by early humans equipped with stone tools and fire (as reflected in the title of *The Cave Home of Peking Man,* published in 1975).

In the mid- to late 1970s, however, Western scientists began to better appreciate and develop the field of taphonomy. One assumption of taphonomy is that the most common species at a fossil site and/or the best-preserved animal remains at the site are most likely the ones to have inhabited the area in life. Of all the mammal fossils from the cave, very few belonged to *H. erectus*—perhaps only 0.5 percent, suggesting that most of the time, this species did not live in the cave. What's more, none of the *H. erectus* skeletons are complete. There's a lack of limb bones—especially of forearms, hands, lower leg bones, and feet—indicating that these individuals died somewhere else and that their partial remains were later carried to the cave. But how?

The answer is suggested by the remains of the most common and complete animal skeletons in the cave deposit—those of the giant hyena, *Pachycrocuta brevirostris.* Had *H. erectus,* instead of being the mighty hunter of anthropological lore, simply met the same unhappy fate as the deer and other prey species in the cave? To test the giant hyena hypothesis, scientists reexamined the fossil casts and a few actual fossils of *H. erectus* from Zhoukoudian for evidence of carnivore damage. Surprisingly, two-thirds of the *H. erectus* fossils displayed puncture marks from a carnivore's large, pointed front teeth, most likely the canines of a hyena. What's more, there were long, scraping bite marks, typified by U-shaped grooves along the bone, and fracture patterns comparable to those modern hyenas make when they chew bone. One of the *H. erectus* bones, part of a femur,

even reveals telltale surface etchings from stomach acid, indicating it was swallowed and then regurgitated.

Cut marks (made by stone tools) observed on several mammal bones from the cave suggest that early humans did sometimes make use of Zhoukoudian, even if they weren't responsible for accumulating most of the bones. Stone tools left near the cave entrance also attest to their presence. Given its long history, the cave may have served a variety of occupants or at times have been configured as several separate, smaller shelters. Another possibility is that, in a form of time sharing, early humans ventured partway into the cave during the day to scavenge on what the hyenas had not eaten and to find temporary shelter. They might not have realized that the animals, which roamed at twilight and at night, were sleeping in the dark recesses a couple of hundred feet away.

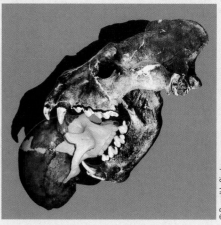

Figure 2

A composite image of the skulls of *Pachycrocruta* and *Homo erectus* that shows how the giant hyena may have attacked the face. Recent studies have shown that many of the *Homo erectus* remains from Zhoukoudian show hyena damage.

© Russell L. Ciochon

to "determine the nature and scope" of the *H. erectus* presence at Zhoukoudian (see "A Closer Look," above).

Probably the most intriguing archaeological aspect of the presumed hominin behavior at Zhoukoudian has been the long-held assumption that *H. erectus* deliberately used fire inside the cave. Controlling fire was one of the major cultural breakthroughs of all prehistory. By providing warmth, a means of cooking, light to further modify tools, and protection, controlled fire would have been a giant technological innovation. While some potential early African sites have yielded evidence that to some have suggested hominin control of fire, it's long been concluded that the first *definite* evidence of hominin fire use comes from Zhoukoudian.

Now, more recent evidence has also radically altered this assumption. Much more detailed excavations at Zhoukoudian were carried out in the 1990s. During these excavations, the researchers also carefully collected and analyzed soil samples for distinctive chemical signatures that would show whether fire had occurred in the cave (Weiner et al., 1998). They found that burnt bone was only rarely found in association with tools. And in most cases, the burning appeared to have taken place *after* fossilization—that is, the bones were not cooked. In fact, it turns out that the "ash" layers mentioned earlier aren't actually ash, but naturally accumulated organic sediment. This last conclusion was derived from chemical testing that showed absolutely no sign of wood having been burnt inside the cave. Finally, the "hearths" that have figured so prominently in archaeological reconstructions of presumed fire control at this site are apparently not hearths at all. They are simply round depressions formed in the past by water.

Another provisional interpretation of the cave's geology suggests that the cave wasn't open to the outside like a habitation site, but was accessed only through a vertical shaft. This theory has led archaeologist Alison Brooks to remark, "It wouldn't have been a shelter, it would have been a trap" (quoted in Wuethrich, 1998). These serious doubts about control of fire, coupled with the suggestive evidence of bone accumulation by carnivores, have led anthropologists Boaz and Ciochon to conclude that "Zhoukoudian cave was neither hearth nor home" (Boaz and Ciochon, 2001).

Other Chinese Sites

More work has been done at Zhoukoudian than at any other Chinese site. Even so, there are other paleoanthropological sites worth mentioning. Three of the more important regions outside of Zhoukoudian are Lantian County (including two sites, often simply referred to as Lantian), Yunxian County, and several discoveries in Hexian County (usually referred to as the Hexian finds).

Before the excavation of two sites in Lantian County, Shaanxi Province, in the mid-1960s, Zhoukoudian was widely believed to be the oldest hominin site in China. Dated to 1.15 mya, Lantian is older than Zhoukoudian (Zhu et al., 2003). From the Lantian sites, the cranial remains of two adult *H. erectus* females have been found in association with fire-treated pebbles and flakes as well as ash (Woo, 1966; Fig. 12-11a). One of the specimens, an almost complete mandible containing several teeth, is quite similar to those from Zhoukoudian.

Two badly distorted crania were discovered in Yunxian County, Hubei Province, in 1989 and 1990 (Li and Etler, 1992). A combination of ESR and paleomagnetism dating methods gives us an average dating estimate of 800,000–580,000 ya. If the dates are correct, this would place Yunxian between Lantian and Zhoukoudian in the Chinese sequence. Due to extensive distortion of the crania from ground pressure, it was very difficult to compare these crania with other *H. erectus* fossils; recently, however, French paleoanthropologist Amélie Vialet has restored the crania using sophisticated imaging techniques (Vialet et al., 2005). And from a recent analysis of the fauna and paleoenvironment at Yunxian, the H. erectus inhabitants are thought to have had limited hunting capabilities, since they appear to have been restricted to the most vulnerable prey, namely, the young and old animals.

In 1980 and 1981, the remains of several individuals, all bearing some resemblance to similar fossils from Zhoukoudian, were recovered from Hexian County, in southern China (Wu and Poirier, 1995; see Fig. 12-11b). A close relationship has been postulated between the *H. erectus* specimens from the Hexian finds and from Zhoukoudian (Wu and Dong, 1985). Indeed, some date the Hexian remains to 400,000 ya (Wu et al., 2006), making it contemporaneous with Zhoukoudian; these dates are disputed, and other experts place the Homo age at only 190,000 ya.

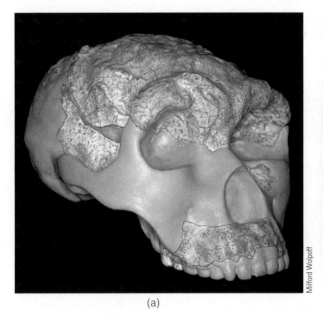

(a)

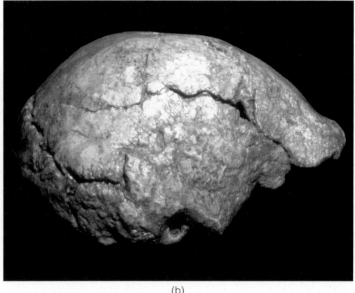

(b)

The Asian crania from Java and China share many similar features, which may be explained by *H. erectus* migration from Java to China perhaps around 1 mya. Asia has a much longer *H. erectus* habitation than Africa (1.6 mya–50,000 ya versus 1.8–1 mya), and it's important to understand the variation seen in this geographically dispersed species.

Figure **12-11**

(a) Reconstructed cranium of *Homo erectus* from Lantian, China, dated to approximately 1.15 mya. (b) Hexian cranium.

Asian and African *Homo erectus*: A Comparison

The *Homo erectus* remains from East Africa show several differences from the Javanese and Chinese fossils. Some African cranial specimens—particularly ER 3733, presumably a female, and WT 15000, presumably a male—aren't as strongly buttressed at the browridge and nuchal torus, and their cranial bones aren't as thick. Indeed, some researchers are so impressed by these differences, as well as others in the postcranial skeleton, that they're arguing for a *separate* species status for the African material, to distinguish it from the Asian samples. Bernard Wood, the leading proponent of this view, has suggested that the name *Homo ergaster* be used for the African remains and that *H. erectus* be reserved solely for the Asian material (Wood, 1991). In addition, the very early dates now postulated for the dispersal of *H. erectus* into Asia (Java) would argue for a more than 1-million-year separate history for Asian and African populations.

With the discovery of Daka and continued comparison of these specimens, this species division has not been fully accepted, and the current consensus (and the one we prefer) is to continue referring to all these hominins as *Homo erectus* (Kramer, 1993; Conroy, 1997; Rightmire, 1998; Asfaw et al., 2002). So, as with some earlier hominins, we'll have to accommodate a considerable degree of intraspecific variation within this species. Wood has concluded, regarding variation within such a broadly defined *H. erectus* species, that "it is a species which manifestly embraces an unusually wide degree of variation in both the cranium and postcranial skeleton" (Wood, 1992a, p. 329).

At a Glance

Key *Homo erectus* Discoveries from Asia

DATES	SITE	EVOLUTIONARY SIGNIFICANCE
50,000–25,000 ya	**Ngandong** (Java)	Very late survival of *H. erectus* in Java
670,000–410,000 ya	**Zhoukoudian** (China)	Large sample; most famous *H. erectus* site; shows some *H. erectus* populations well adapted to temperate (cold) environments
1.6 mya	**Sangiran** (Java)	First discovery of *H. erectus* from anywhere; shows dispersal out of Africa by 1.6 mya

Later *Homo erectus* from Europe

We've talked about *H. erectus* in Africa, the Caucasus region, and Asia, but there are European specimens as well, found in Spain and Italy. While not as old as the Dmanisi material, fossils from the Atapuerca region in northern Spain are significantly extending the antiquity of hominins in western Europe. There are several caves in the Atapuerca region, two of which (Sima del Elefante and Gran Dolina) have yielded hominin fossils contemporaneous with *H. erectus*.

The earliest find from Atapuerca (from Sima del Elefante) has been recently discovered and dates to 1.2 mya, making it clearly the oldest hominin yet found in western Europe (Carbonell et al., 2008). So far, just one specimen has been found here, a partial jaw with a few teeth. Very provisional analysis suggests that it most closely resembles the Dmanisi fossils. There are also tools and animal bones from the site. As at the Dmanisi site, the implements are simple flake tools similar to that of the Oldowan. Some of the animal bones also bear the scars of hominin activity. with cut marks indicating butchering (similar to what we discussed in Chapter 10 for Olduvai).

Gran Dolina is a later site, and based on specialized techniques discussed in Chapter 10 (see p. 286), it is dated to approximately 850,000–780,000 ya (Parés and Pérez-González, 1995; Falguéres et al., 1999). Because all the remains so far identified from both these caves at Atapuerca are fragmentary, assigning these fossils to particular species poses something of a problem. Spanish paleoanthropologists who have studied the Atapuerca fossils have decided to place these hominins into another (separate) species, one they call *Homo antecessor* (Bermúdez de Castro et al., 1997; Arsuaga et al., 1999). However, it remains to be seen whether this newly proposed species will prove to be distinct from other species of *Homo* (see p. 352 for further discussion).

Finally, the southern European discovery of a well-preserved cranium from the Ceprano site in central Italy may be the best evidence yet of *H. erectus* in Europe (Ascenzi et al., 1996). Provisional dating of a partial cranium from this important site suggests a date

Figure **12-12**

The Ceprano *Homo erectus* cranium from central Italy, provisionally dated between 800,000 and 900,000 ya. This is the best evidence for *Homo erectus* in Europe.

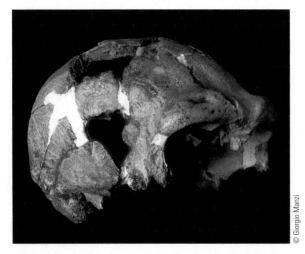

© Giorgio Manzi

between 900,000 and 800,000 ya (Fig. 12-12). Phillip Rightmire (1998) has concluded that cranial morphology places this specimen quite close to *H. erectus*. Italian researchers have proposed a different interpretation that classifies the Ceprano hominin as a species separate from *H. erectus*. For the moment, the exact relationship of the Ceprano find to *H. erectus* remains to be fully determined.

After about 400,000 ya, the European fossil hominin record becomes increasingly abundant. More fossils mean more variation, so it's not surprising that interpretations regarding the proper taxonomic assessment of many of these remains have been debated, in some cases for decades. In recent years, several of these somewhat later "premodern" specimens have been regarded either as early representatives of *H. sapiens* or as a separate species, one immediately preceding *H. sapiens*. These enigmatic premodern humans are discussed in Chapter 13. A time line for the *H. erectus* discoveries discussed in this chapter as well as other finds of more uncertain status is shown in Figure 12-13.

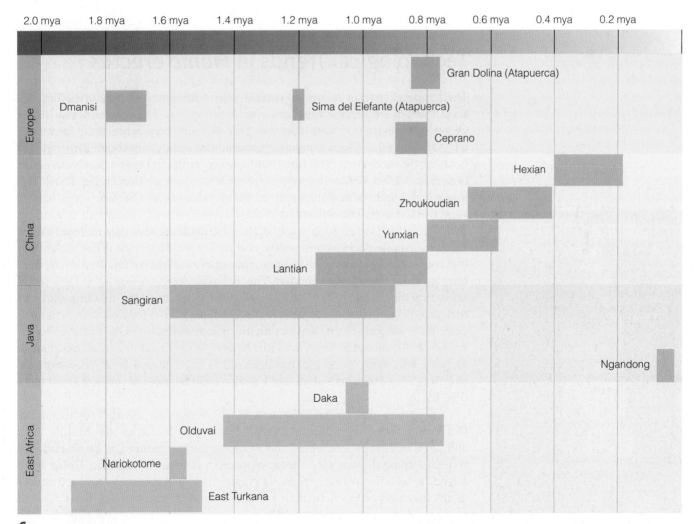

Figure 12-13

Time line for *Homo erectus* discoveries and other contemporary hominins.

(*Note*: Most dates are only imprecise estimates. However, the dates from East African sites are chronometrically determined and are thus much more secure. The early dates from Java are also radiometric and are gaining wide acceptance.)

At a Glance

Key *Homo erectus* and Contemporaneous Discoveries from Europe

DATES	SITE	EVOLUTIONARY SIGNIFICANCE
900,000–800,000 ya	**Ceprano** (Italy)	Well-preserved cranium; best evidence of full *H. erectus* morphology from any site in Europe
850,000–780,000 ya	**Gran Dolina** (Atapuerca, Spain)	Oldest evidence of hominins in western Europe; likely not *H. erectus*
1.75 mya	**Dmanisi** (Republic of Georgia)	Oldest well-dated hominins outside of Africa; not like full *H. erectus* morphology, but are small-bodied and small-brained

Technological Trends in *Homo erectus*

The temporal span of *H. erectus* straddles two different tool industries, the second of which we suggest was developed by *H. erectus*. The species begins using Oldowan tools, which were taken to Dmanisi and Java, since these hominins left Africa around 1.4 mya, before the newer industry came about. This new kit is called the Acheulian. The important change in this kit was a core worked on both sides, called a *biface* (known widely as a hand axe or cleaver; Fig. 12-14). The biface had a flatter shape than seen in the rounder earlier Oldowan cores (which were worked to make quick and easy flakes and were soon discarded). Beginning with the Acheulian culture, we find the first evidence that raw materials were being transported more consistently and for longer distances. When Acheulian tool users found a good piece of stone, they often would take it with them as they traveled from one place to another. This behavior suggests foresight: They likely knew that they might need to use a stone tool in the future and that this chunk of rock could later prove useful. This is a major change from the Oldowan, where all stone tools are found very close to their raw-material sources. With the biface as a kind of "Acheulian Swiss army knife," these tools served to cut, scrape, pound, and dig. This most useful tool has been found in Africa, parts of Asia, and later in Europe. Note that Acheulian tool kits also included several types of small tools (Fig. 12-15).

For many years, scientists thought that a cultural "divide" separated the Old World, with Acheulian technology made *only* in Africa, the Middle East, and parts of Europe (elsewhere, the Acheulian was presumed to be absent). But recently reported excavations from more than 20 sites in southern China have forced reevaluation of this hypothesis (Yamei et al., 2000). As we've noted, the most distinctive tools of the Acheulian are bifaces, and they're the very tools thought lacking throughout most of the Pleistocene in eastern Europe and most of Asia. The new archaeological assemblages from southern China are securely dated at about 800,000 ya and contain numerous bifaces, very similar to contemporaneous Acheulian bifaces from Africa (see Fig. 12-14). It now appears likely that cultural

William Turnbaugh

Figure **12-14**

Acheulian biface ("hand axe"), a basic tool of the Acheulian tradition.

traditions relating to stone tool technology were largely equivalent over the *full* geographical range of *H. erectus* and its contemporaries (see "A Closer Look," p. 352).

Evidence of butchering is widespread at *H. erectus* sites, and in the past, such evidence has been cited in arguments for consistent hunting. Researchers formerly interpreted any association of bones and tools as evidence of hunting, but many studies now suggest that cut marks on bones from the *H. erectus* time period often overlay carnivore tooth marks. This means that hominins were gaining access to the carcasses after the carnivores and were therefore scavenging the meat, not hunting the animals. It's also crucial to mention that these hominins were gaining a large amount of their daily calories from gathering wild plants, tubers, and fruits. Like hunter-gatherers of modern times, *H. erectus* individuals were most likely consuming 80 percent of their daily calories from plant materials.

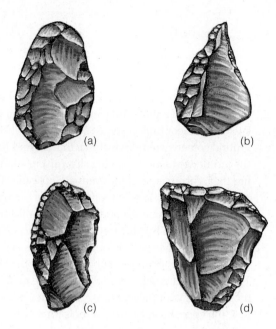

Figure 12-15

Small tools of the Acheulian industry. (a) Side scraper. (b) Point. (c) End scraper. (d) Burin.

Seeing the Big Picture: Interpretations of *Homo erectus*

Several aspects of the geographical, physical, and behavioral patterns shown by *H. erectus* seem clear. But new discoveries and more in-depth analyses are helping us to reevaluate our prior ideas. The fascinating fossil hominins discovered at Dmanisi are perhaps the most challenging piece of this puzzle.

Past theories suggest that *Homo erectus* was able to emigrate from Africa owing to more advanced tools and a more modern anatomy (longer legs, larger brains) compared to earlier African predecessors. Yet, the Dmanisi cranial remains show that these very early Europeans still had small brains; and both the Dmanisi and Javan *H. erectus* were still using Oldowan-style tools.

So it seems that some key parts of earlier hypotheses are not fully accurate. At least some of the earliest emigrants from Africa didn't yet show the entire suite of *H. erectus* physical and behavioral traits. How different the Dmanisi hominids are from the full *H. erectus* pattern remains to be seen, and the discovery of more complete postcranial remains will be most illuminating.

Going a step further, the four crania from Dmanisi are extremely variable; one of them, in fact, does look more like *H. erectus*. It would be tempting to conclude that more than one type of hominin is represented here, but they're all found in the same geological context. The archaeologists who excavated the site conclude that all the fossils are closely associated with each other. The simplest hypothesis is that they all are members of the *same* species. This degree of apparent intraspecific variation is biologically noteworthy, and it's influencing how paleoanthropologists interpret all of these fossil samples.

This growing awareness of the broad intraspecific variation among some hominins brings us to our second consideration: Is *Homo ergaster* in Africa a separate species from *Homo erectus*, as strictly defined in Asia? While this interpretation was popular in the last decade, it now is losing support. The finds from Dmanisi raise fundamental issues of interpretation. Among these four crania from one locality (see Fig. 12-5), we see more variation than between the African and Asian forms, which many researchers have interpreted as different species. Also, the new

A Closer Look

The Sky Is Falling

The blazing red soil of Guangxi, in southwest China, is all that remains of a powerful conflagration in the wake of a violent meteor impact some 800,000 ya. As it struck the ground somewhere in Indochina, the asteroid liquefied the terrain and sent it spewing skyward in a hailstorm of fire that scarred land as far south as Australia. The remnants of this event can be found scattered across China, Indonesia, and Australia and are known collectively as the Australasian Tektite Strewn Field (Paine, 2001). The tektites themselves are the fragments of ejecta fused in the furnace of the impact and flung across the landscape. These onyx spheroids resemble miniature meteorites; and, most crucially for paleoanthropology, they allow us to date the appearance of bifacial tools (that is, the Acheulian industry) in China. Because tektites are superheated, as in volcanic eruptions, they can be radiometrically dated using the potassium-argon technique (see Chapter 10, p. 285). Consequently, we can also get a date for the stone tools lying alongside them in the Bose Basin of China.

The "Movius Line" (named after Harvard archaeologist Hallum Movius) was long believed to represent an imaginary, though very real, technological barrier separating the primitive residents of Asia from the western makers of bifacial hand axes. Underlying this dichotomy was the implicit conviction that a lack of Acheulian-type tools throughout eastern Eurasia was more a function of reduced intelligence than resource scarcity. Recent excavations in the Bose Basin, in Guangxi, have thrown this scheme into doubt with the revelation that at least some Asian *H. erectus* populations were fully capable of making bifacial tools and were doing so as early as 800,000 ya (Yamei et al., 2000).

More important still, the tektites represent an underlying reason that these tools exist at all. As molten earth showered the region, it scoured the landscape of the dense and impenetrable forest that had long excluded habitation by *H. erectus* populations, previously restricting them to more open river valleys. A cataclysmic natural event opened a new world for human hands to exploit. Outcroppings of

discovery from Daka (Ethiopia) of a young African specimen with Asian traits further weakens the separate-species interpretation of *H. ergaster*.

The separate-species status of the early European fossils from Spain (Sima del Elefante and Gran Dolina) is also not yet clearly established. We still don't have much good fossil evidence from these two sites; but early dates going back to 1.2 mya for the earlier site are well confirmed. Recall also that no other western European hominin fossils are known until at least 500,000 years later, and a 900,000–800,000 ya find from Italy looks like *H. erectus* (Bischoff et al., 2007). It remains to be seen if any of these European hominins dating prior to 500,000 ya are ancestors of any later hominin species. Nevertheless, it's quite apparent that later in the Pleistocene, there are well-established hominin populations widely dispersed in both Africa and in Europe. These later premodern humans are the topic of the next chapter.

When looking back at the evolution of *H. erectus*, we realize how significant this early human was. *H. erectus* had greater limb length and thus more efficient bipedalism; showed evidence of forethought about surroundings and needs; was the first species with a cranial capacity approaching the range of *H. sapiens*; became a more efficient scavenger and exploited a new range of nutrients in the form of meat; and ranged across the Old World, from Spain to Indonesia. In short, it was *H. erectus* who transformed hominin evolution to human evolution. As Richard Foley states, "The appearance and expansion of *H. erectus* represented a major change in adaptive strategy that influenced the subsequent process and pattern of human evolution" (1991, p. 425).

stone materials ideal for biface manufacture were left bare and steaming. An event that so nearly ended life in the region—a small-scale version of the asteroid impact that ended the reign of dinosaurs—became a reason for it to prosper. Far from dim-witted country cousins, *Homo erectus* in Asia represents a population of savvy opportunists who turned a potential doomsday into the heyday of stone tool manufacture in the region.

Figure 1

The red laterite soils of Guangxi in southwest China, from which many important Acheulian-style hand axes have been discovered alongside tektites used to date the site to 800,000 ya.

Summary

Homo erectus remains have been found in Africa, Europe, and Asia dating from about 1.8 mya to at least 200,000 ya—and probably much later—and spanning a period of more than 1.5 million years. While the nature and timing of these emigrations are uncertain, it's likely that *H. erectus* first appeared in East Africa and later migrated to other areas. This widespread and highly successful hominin defines a new and more modern grade of human evolution.

Historically, the first finds were made by Dubois in Java, and later discoveries came from China and Africa. Differences from early *Homo* are notable in *H. erectus'* larger brain, taller stature, robust build, and changes in facial structure and cranial buttressing.

The long period of *H. erectus* existence was marked by a major change in the tool kit around 1.4 mya. *H. erectus* and contemporaries introduced more sophisticated tools and probably ate novel foods processed in new ways. By using these new tools and—at later sites—possibly fire as well, they were also able to move into different environments and successfully adapt to new conditions.

It's generally assumed that certain *H. erectus* populations evolved into later premodern humans, some of which, in turn, evolved into *Homo sapiens*. Evidence supporting such a series of transitions is seen in the Ngandong fossils (and others discussed in Chapter 13), which display both *H. erectus* and *H. sapiens* features. There are still many questions about *H. erectus* behavior. For example, did they regularly hunt, and did they control fire? We also wonder about their relationship

to later hominins. Was the mode of evolution gradual or rapid, and which *H. erectus* populations contributed genes? The search for answers continues.

In "What's Important," you'll find a useful summary of the most significant hominin fossils discussed in this chapter.

What's Important Key Fossil Discoveries of *Homo erectus*

Dates	Region	Site	The Big Picture
1.6 mya–25,000 ya	**Asia** (Indonesia)	Java (Sangiran and other sites)	Shows *H. erectus* early on (by 1.6 mya) in tropical areas of Southeast Asia; *H. erectus* persisted here for more than 1 million years
600,000–400,000 ya	China	Zhoukoudian	Largest, most famous sample of *H. erectus*; shows adaptation to colder environments; conclusions regarding behavior at this site have been exaggerated and are now questioned
900,000–800,000 ya	**Europe** (Italy)	Ceprano	Likely best evidence of full-blown *H. erectus* morphology in Europe
1.8–1.7 mya	(Republic of Georgia)	Dmanisi	Very early dispersal to southeastern Europe (by 1.8 mya) of small-bodied, small-brained *H. erectus* population; may represent an earlier dispersal from Africa than one that led to wider occupation of Eurasia
1.6 mya	**Africa** (Kenya)	Nariokotome	Beautifully preserved nearly complete skeleton; best postcranial evidence of *H. erectus* from anywhere
1.8 mya		East Turkana	Earliest *H. erectus* from Africa; some individuals more robust, others smaller and more gracile; variation suggested to represent sexual dimorphism

Critical Thinking Questions

1 Why is the nearly complete skeleton from Nariokotome so important? What kinds of evidence does it provide?

2 Assume that you're in the laboratory and have the Nariokotome skeleton, as well as a skeleton of a modern human. First, given a choice, what age and sex would you choose for the comparative human skeleton, and why? Second, what similarities and differences do the two skeletons show?

3 What fundamental questions of interpretation do the fossil hominins from Dmanisi raise? Does this evidence completely overturn the hypothesis concerning *H. erectus* dispersal from Africa? Explain why or why not.

4 How has the interpretation of *H. erectus* behavior at Zhoukoudian been revised in recent years? What kinds of new evidence from this site have been used in this reevaluation, and what does that tell you about modern archaeological techniques and approaches?

5 You're interpreting the hominin fossils from three sites in East Africa (Nariokotome, Olduvai, and Daka)—all considered possible members of *H. erectus*. What sorts of evidence would lead you to conclude that there was more than one species? What would convince you that there was just one species? Why do you think some paleoanthropologists (splitters) would tend to see more than one species, while others (lumpers) would generally not? What kind of approach would you take, and why?

Hominin Evolution

CHAPTER

13 Premodern Humans

Robert Franciscus

Key Question

Who were the immediate precursors to modern *Homo sapiens*, and how do they compare with modern humans?

 Click!

Go to the following media for interactive activities and exercises on topics covered in this chapter:

- Online Virtual Laboratories for Physical Anthropology, Version 4.0
- Hominid Fossils: An Interactive Atlas CD-ROM

Introduction

What do you think of when you hear the term *Neandertal*? Most people think of imbecilic, hunched-over brutes. Yet, Neandertals were quite advanced; they had brains at least as large as ours, and they showed many sophisticated cultural capabilities. What's more, they definitely weren't hunched over, but fully erect (as hominins had been for millions of years previously). In fact, Neandertals and their immediate predecessors could easily be called human.

That brings us to possibly the most basic of all questions: What does it mean to be human? The meaning of this term is highly varied, encompassing religious, philosophical, and biological considerations. As you know, physical anthropologists primarily concentrate on the biological aspects of the human organism. All living people today are members of one species, sharing a common anatomical pattern and similar behavioral potentials. We call hominins like us "modern *Homo sapiens*," and in the next chapter we'll discuss the origin of forms that were essentially identical to living people.

When in our evolutionary past can we say that our predecessors were obviously human? Certainly, the further back we go in time, the less hominins look like modern *Homo sapiens*. This is, of course, exactly what we'd expect in an evolutionary sequence.

We saw in Chapter 12 that *Homo erectus* took crucial steps in the human direction and defined a new *grade* of human evolution. In this chapter, we'll discuss the hominins who continued this journey. Both physically and behaviorally, they're much like modern *Homo sapiens*, though they still show several significant differences. So while most paleoanthropologists are comfortable referring to these hominins as "human," we need to qualify this recognition a bit to set them apart from fully modern people. Thus, in this text, we'll refer to these fascinating immediate predecessors as "premodern humans."

When, Where, and What

Most of the hominins discussed in this chapter lived during the **Middle Pleistocene**, a period beginning 780,000 ya and ending 125,000 ya. In addition, some of the later premodern humans, especially the Neandertals, lived well into the **Late Pleistocene** (125,000–10,000 ya).

The Pleistocene

The Pleistocene has been called the Ice Age because, as had occurred before in geological history, it was marked by periodic advances and retreats of massive

Middle Pleistocene The portion of the Pleistocene epoch beginning 780,000 ya and ending 125,000 ya.

Late Pleistocene The portion of the Pleistocene epoch beginning 125,000 ya and ending approximately 10,000 ya.

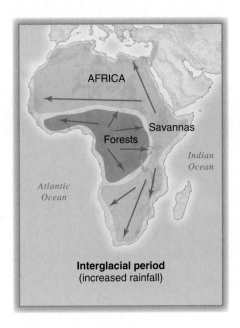

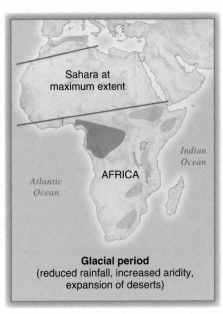

Interglacial period
(increased rainfall)

Glacial period
(reduced rainfall, increased aridity,
expansion of deserts)

Figure **13-1**

Changing Pleistocene environments in Africa.

continental **glaciations**. During glacial periods, when temperatures dropped dramatically, ice accumulated as a result of more snow falling each year than melting, causing the advance of massive glaciers. As the climate fluctuated, at times it became much warmer. During these **interglacials**, the ice that had built up during the glacial periods melted, and the glaciers retreated back toward the earth's polar regions. The Pleistocene was characterized by numerous advances and retreats of ice, with at least 15 major and 50 minor glacial advances documented in Europe alone (Tattersall et al., 1988).

These glaciations, which enveloped huge swaths of Europe, Asia, and North America as well as Antarctica, were mostly confined to northern latitudes. Hominins living at this time—all still restricted to the Old World—were severely affected as the climate, flora, and animal life shifted during these Pleistocene oscillations. The most dramatic of these effects were in Europe and northern Asia—less so in southern Asia and in Africa.

Still, the climate also fluctuated in the south. In Africa, the main effects were related to changing rainfall patterns. During glacial periods, the climate in Africa became more arid, while during interglacials, rainfall increased. The changing availability of food resources certainly affected hominins in Africa; but probably even more importantly, migration routes also swung back and forth. For example, during glacial periods (Fig. 13-1), the Sahara Desert expanded, blocking migration in and out of sub-Saharan Africa (Lahr and Foley, 1998).

In Eurasia, glacial advances also greatly affected migration routes. As the ice sheets expanded, sea levels dropped, more northern regions became uninhabitable, and some key passages between areas became blocked by glaciers. For example, during glacial peaks, much of western Europe would have been cut off from the rest of Eurasia (Fig. 13-2).

During the warmer—and, in the south, wetter—interglacials, the ice sheets shrank, sea levels rose, and certain migration routes reopened (for example, from central into western Europe). Clearly, to understand Middle Pleistocene hominins, it's crucial to view them within their shifting Pleistocene world.

glaciations Climatic intervals when continental ice sheets cover much of the northern continents. Glaciations are associated with colder temperatures in northern latitudes and more arid conditions in southern latitudes, most notably in Africa.

interglacials Climatic intervals when continental ice sheets are retreating, eventually becoming much reduced in size. Interglacials in northern latitudes are associated with warmer temperatures, while in southern latitudes the climate becomes wetter.

Figure **13-2**

Changing Pleistocene environments in Eurasia. Green areas show regions of likely hominin occupation. White areas are major glaciers. Arrows indicate likely migration routes.

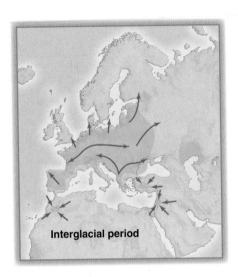

Interglacial period

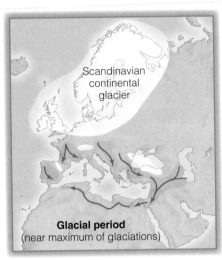

Scandinavian continental glacier

Glacial period
(near maximum of glaciations)

Dispersal of Middle Pleistocene Hominins

Like their *Homo erectus* predecessors, later hominins were widely distributed in the Old World, with discoveries coming from three continents—Africa, Asia, and Europe. For the first time, Europe became more permanently and densely occupied, as Middle Pleistocene hominins have been discovered widely from England, France, Spain, Germany, Italy, Hungary, and Greece. Africa, as well, probably continued as a central area of hominin occupation, and finds have come from North, East, and South Africa. Finally, Asia has yielded several important finds, most especially from China (see Fig. 13-6 on pp. 362–363). We should point out, though, that these Middle Pleistocene premodern humans didn't vastly extend the geographical range of *Homo erectus,* but largely replaced the earlier hominins in previously exploited habitats. One exception appears to be the more successful occupation of Europe, a region where earlier hominins have only sporadically been found.

Middle Pleistocene Hominins: Terminology

The premodern humans of the Middle Pleistocene (that is, after 780,000 ya) generally succeeded *H. erectus.* Still, in some areas—especially in Southeast Asia—there apparently was a long period of coexistence, lasting 300,000 years or longer; you'll recall the very late dates for the Javanese Ngandong *H. erectus* (see p. 342).

The earliest premodern humans exhibit several *H. erectus* characteristics: The face is large, the brows are projected, the forehead is low, and in some cases the cranial vault is still thick. Even so, some of their other features show that they were more derived toward the modern condition than were their *Homo erectus* predecessors. Compared to *H. erectus,* these premodern humans possessed an increased brain size, a more rounded braincase (that is, maximum breadth is higher up on the sides), a more vertical nose, and a less-angled back of the skull (occipital). We should note that the time span encompassed by Middle Pleistocene premodern humans is at least 500,000 years, so it's no surprise that over time we can observe certain trends. Later Middle Pleistocene hominins, for example, show even more brain expansion and an even less-angled occipital than do earlier forms.

We know that premodern humans were a diverse group dispersed over three continents. Deciding how to classify them has been in dispute for decades, and anthropologists still have disagreements. However, a growing consensus has recently emerged. Beginning perhaps as early as 850,000 ya and extending to about 200,000 ya, the fossils from Africa and Europe are placed within *Homo heidelbergensis*, named after a fossil found in Germany in 1907. What's more, some Asian specimens possibly represent a regional variant of *H. heidelbergensis*.

Until recently, many researchers regarded these fossils as early, but more primitive, members of *Homo sapiens*. In recognition of this somewhat transitional status, the fossils were called "archaic *Homo sapiens*," with all later humans also belonging to the species *Homo sapiens*. However, most paleoanthropologists now find this terminology unsatisfactory. For example, Phillip Rightmire concludes that "simply lumping diverse ancient groups with living populations obscures their differences" (1998, p. 226). In our own discussion, we recognize *Homo heidelbergensis* as a transitional species between *Homo erectus* and later hominins (that is, primarily *Homo sapiens*). Keep in mind, however, that this species was probably an ancestor of both modern humans and Neandertals. It's debatable whether *H. heidelbergensis* actually represents a fully separate species in the *biological* sense, that is, following the *biological* species concept (see p. 110). Still, it's useful to give this group of premodern humans a separate name to make this important stage of human evolution more easily identifiable. (We'll return to this issue later in the chapter when we discuss the theoretical implications in more detail.)

Premodern Humans of the Middle Pleistocene

Africa

In Africa, premodern fossils have been found at several sites. One of the best known is Kabwe (Broken Hill). At this site in Zambia, fieldworkers discovered a complete cranium (Fig. 13-3), together with other cranial and postcranial elements belonging to several individuals. In this and other African premodern specimens, we can see a mixture of older and more recent traits. The skull's massive browridge (one of the largest of any hominin), low vault, and prominent occipital torus recall those of *H. erectus*. On the other hand, the occipital region is less angulated, the cranial vault bones are thinner, and the cranial base is essentially modern. Dating estimates of Kabwe and most of the other premodern fossils from Africa have ranged throughout the Middle and Late Pleistocene, but recent estimates have given dates for most of the sites in the range of 600,000–125,000 ya.

Bodo is another significant African premodern fossil (Fig. 13-4). A nearly complete cranium, Bodo has been dated to relatively early in the Middle Pleistocene (estimated at 600,000 ya), making it one of the oldest specimens of *Homo heidelbergensis* from the African continent. The Bodo cranium is particularly interesting because it shows a distinctive pattern of cut marks, similar to modifications seen in butchered animal bones. Researchers have thus hypothesized that the Bodo individual was defleshed by other hominins, but for what purpose is not clear. The defleshing may have been related to cannibalism, though it also may have been for some other purpose, such as ritual. In any case, this is the earliest evidence of deliberate bone processing of hominins *by* hominins (White, 1986).

A number of other crania from South and East Africa also show a combination of retained ancestral with more derived

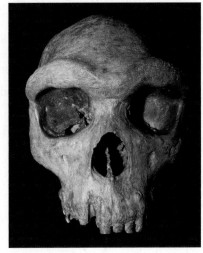

Milford Wolpoff

Figure 13-3

The Kabwe (Broken Hill) *Homo heidelbergensis* skull from Zambia. Note the very robust browridges.

Figure 13-4

Bodo cranium, the earliest evidence of *Homo heidelbergensis* in Africa.

© Robert Franciscus

At a Glance

Key Premodern Human (*H. heidelbergensis*) Fossils from Africa

DATE	SITE	EVOLUTIONARY SIGNIFICANCE
130,000+ ya	**Kabwe** (Broken Hill, (Zambia)	Nearly complete skull; mosaic of features (brow-ridge very robust, but braincase expanded)
600,000 ya	**Bodo** (Ethiopia)	Earliest example of African *H. heidelbergensis*; likely evidence of butchering

(modern) characteristics, and they're all mentioned in the literature as being similar to Kabwe. The most important of these African finds come from the sites of Florisbad and Elandsfontein in South Africa, and Laetoli in Tanzania.

The general similarities in all these African premodern fossils indicate a close relationship between them, almost certainly representing a single species (most commonly referred to as *H. heidelbergensis*). These African premodern humans also are quite similar to those found in Europe.

Europe

More fossil hominins of Middle Pleistocene age have been found in Europe than in any other region. Maybe it's because more archaeologists have been searching longer in Europe than anywhere else. In any case, during the Middle Pleistocene, Europe was more widely and consistently occupied than it was earlier in human evolution.

The time range of European premodern humans extends the full length of the Middle Pleistocene and beyond. At the earlier end, the Gran Dolina finds from northern Spain (discussed in Chapter 12; see p. 348) are definitely not *Homo erectus*. The Gran Dolina remains may, as proposed by Spanish researchers, be members of a new hominin species. However, Rightmire (1998) has suggested that the Gran Dolina hominins may simply represent the earliest well-dated occurrence of *H. heidelbergensis*, possibly dating as early as 850,000 ya.

More recent and more completely studied *H. heidelbergensis* fossils have been found throughout much of Europe. Examples of these finds come from Steinheim (Germany), Petralona (Greece), Swanscombe (England), Arago (France), and another cave site at Atapuerca (Spain) known as Sima de los Huesos. Like their African counterparts, these European premoderns have retained certain *H. erectus* traits, but they're mixed with more derived ones—for example, increased cranial capacity, less-angled occiput, parietal expansion, and reduced tooth size (Figs. 13-5 and 13-6).

Figure **13-5**

Steinheim cranium, a representative of *Homo heidelbergensis* from Germany.

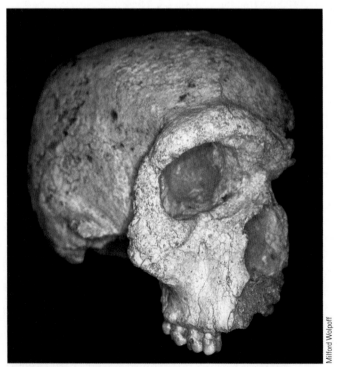

Milford Wolpoff

At a Glance

Key Premodern Human (*H. heidelbergensis*) Fossils from Europe

DATES	SITE	EVOLUTIONARY SIGNIFICANCE
300,000?–259,000? ya	**Swanscombe** (England)	Partial skull, but shows considerable brain expansion
600,000–530,000 ya	**Atapuerca** (Sima de los Huesos, northern Spain)	Large sample; very early evidence of Neandertal ancestry (>500,000 ya); earliest evidence of deliberate body disposal

The hominins from the Atapuerca site of Sima de los Huesos are especially interesting. These finds come from another cave in the same area as the Gran Dolina discoveries, but are slightly younger, dating to between 600,000 and 530,000 ya (Bischoff et al., 2007). A total of at least 28 individuals have been recovered from Sima de los Huesos, which literally means "pit of bones." In fact, with more than 4,000 fossil fragments recovered, Sima de los Huesos contains more than 80 percent of all Middle Pleistocene hominin remains in the world (Bermudez de Castro et al., 2004). Excavations continue at this remarkable site, where bones have somehow accumulated within a deep chamber inside a cave. From initial descriptions, paleoanthropologists interpret the hominin morphology as showing several indications of an early Neandertal-like pattern, with arching browridges, projecting midface, and other features (Rightmire, 1998).

Asia

Like their contemporaries in Europe and Africa, Asian premodern specimens discovered in China also display both earlier and later characteristics. Chinese paleoanthropologists suggest that the more ancestral traits, such as a sagittal ridge (see p. 335) and flattened nasal bones, are shared with *H. erectus* fossils from Zhoukoudian. They also point out that some of these features can be found in modern *H. sapiens* in China today, indicating substantial genetic continuity. That is, some Chinese researchers have argued that anatomically, modern Chinese didn't evolve from *H. sapiens* in either Europe or Africa; instead, they evolved locally in China from a separate *H. erectus* lineage. Whether such regional evolution occurred or whether anatomically modern migrants from Africa displaced local populations is the subject of a major ongoing debate in paleoanthropology. This important controversy will be the central focus of the next chapter.

Dali, the most complete skull of the later Middle or early Late Pleistocene fossils in China, displays *H. erectus* and *H. sapiens* traits, with a cranial capacity of 1,120 cm^3 (Fig. 13-7). Like Dali, several other Chinese specimens combine both earlier and later traits. In addition, a partial skeleton from Jinniushan, in northeast China, has been given a provisional date of 200,000 ya (Tiemel et al., 1994). The cranial capacity is fairly large (approximately 1,260 cm^3), and the walls of the braincase are thin. These are both modern features, and they're somewhat

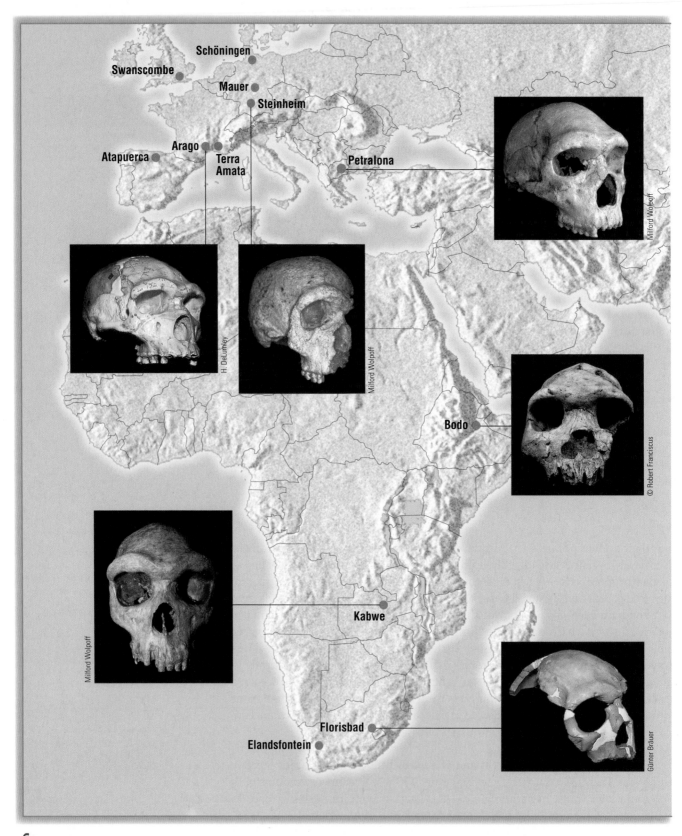

Figure **13-6**

Fossil discoveries and archaeological localities of
Middle Pleistocene premodern hominins.

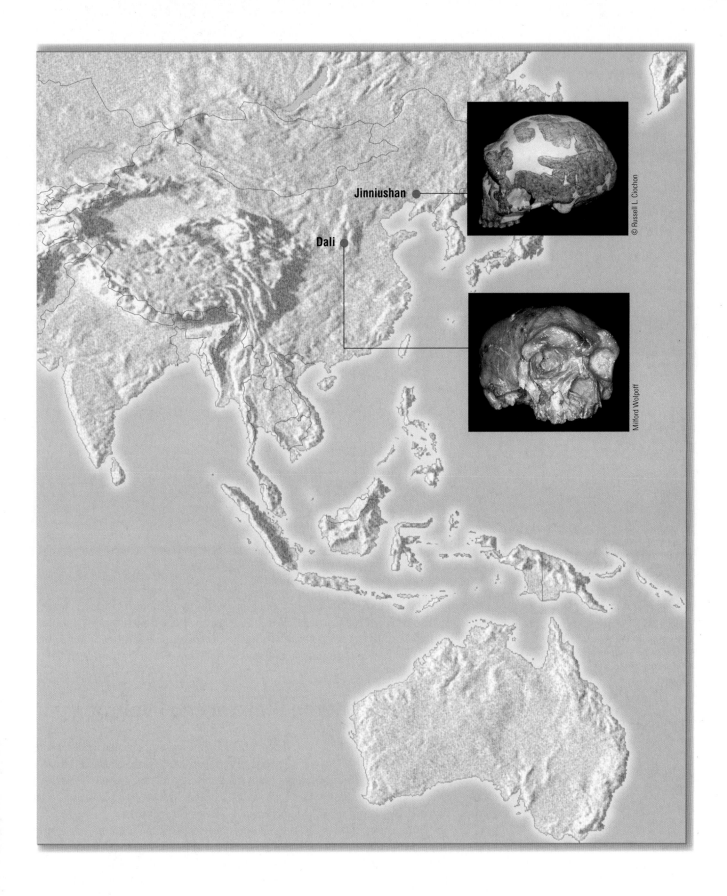

Jinniushan

Dali

© Russell L. Ciochon

Milford Wolpoff

At a Glance

Key Premodern Human (*H. heidelbergensis*) Fossils from Asia

DATES	SITE	EVOLUTIONARY SIGNIFICANCE
230,000–180,000 ya	**Dali** (China)	Nearly complete skull; best evidence of *H. heidelbergensis* in Asia
200,000 ya	**Jinniushan** (China)	Partial skeleton with cranium showing relatively large brain size; some Chinese scholars suggest it as possible ancestor of early Chinese *H. sapiens*

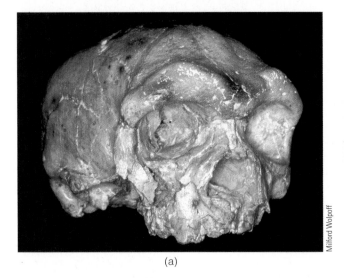

(a)

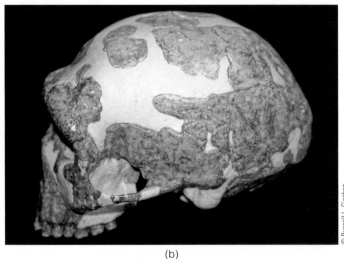

(b)

Figure 13-7

(a) Dali skull and (b) Jinniushan skull, both from China. These two crania are considered by some to be Asian representatives of *Homo heidelbergensis*.

unexpected in an individual this ancient—if the dating estimate is indeed correct. Just how to classify these Chinese Middle Pleistocene hominins has been a subject of debate and controversy. Recently, though, a leading paleoanthropologist has concluded that they're regional variants of *H. heidelbergensis* (Rightmire, 2004).

A Review of Middle Pleistocene Evolution

Premodern human fossils from Africa and Europe resemble each other more than they do the hominins from Asia. The mix of some ancestral characteristics—retained from *Homo erectus* ancestors—with more derived features gives the African and European fossils a distinctive look; thus, Middle Pleistocene hominins from these two continents are usually referred to as *H. heidelbergensis*.

The situation in Asia isn't so tidy. To some researchers, the remains, especially those from Jinniushan, seem more modern than do contemporary fossils from either Europe or Africa. This observation explains why Chinese paleoanthropologists and some American colleagues conclude that the Jinniushan remains are early

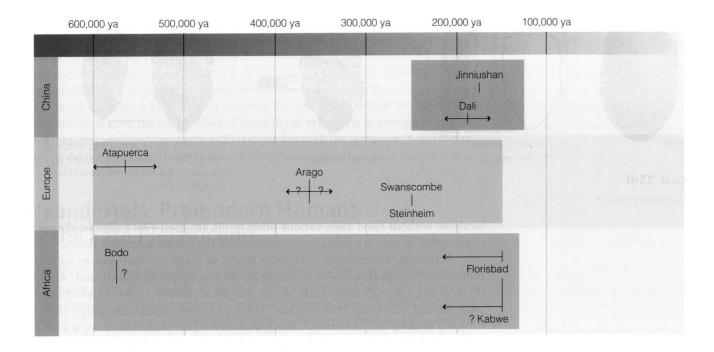

Figure 13-8

Time line of Middle Pleistocene hominins. Note that most dates are approximations. Question marks indicate those estimates that are most tentative.

members of *H. sapiens*. Other researchers (for example, Rightmire, 1998, 2004) suggest that they represent a regional branch of *H. heidelbergensis*.

The Pleistocene world forced many small populations into geographical isolation. Most of these regional populations no doubt died out. Some, however, did evolve, and their descendants are likely a major part of the later hominin fossil record. In Africa, *H. heidelbergensis* is hypothesized to have evolved into modern *H. sapiens*. In Europe, *H. heidelbergensis* evolved into Neandertals. Meanwhile, the Chinese premodern populations may all have met with extinction. Right now, though, there's no consensus on the status or the likely fate of these enigmatic Asian Middle Pleistocene hominins (Fig. 13-8).

Middle Pleistocene Culture

The Acheulian technology of *H. erectus* carried over into the Middle Pleistocene with relatively little change until near the end of the period, when it became slightly more sophisticated. Bone, a high-quality tool material, remained practically unused during this time. Stone flake tools similar to those of the earlier era persisted, possibly in greater variety. Some of the later premodern humans in Africa and Europe invented a method—the Levallois technique (Fig. 13-9)—for controlling flake size and shape. The Levallois technique required several complex and coordinated steps, suggesting increased cognitive abilities in later premodern populations.

Interpreting the distribution of artifacts during the later Middle Pleistocene has generated considerable discussion among archaeologists. As we noted in Chapter 12, a general geographical distribution characterizes the Early Pleistocene, with bifaces (mostly hand axes) found quite often at sites in Africa, at several sites in parts of Asia, but not at all among the rich assemblage at Zhoukoudian. Also, where hand axes proliferate, the stone tool industry is referred to as Acheulian. At

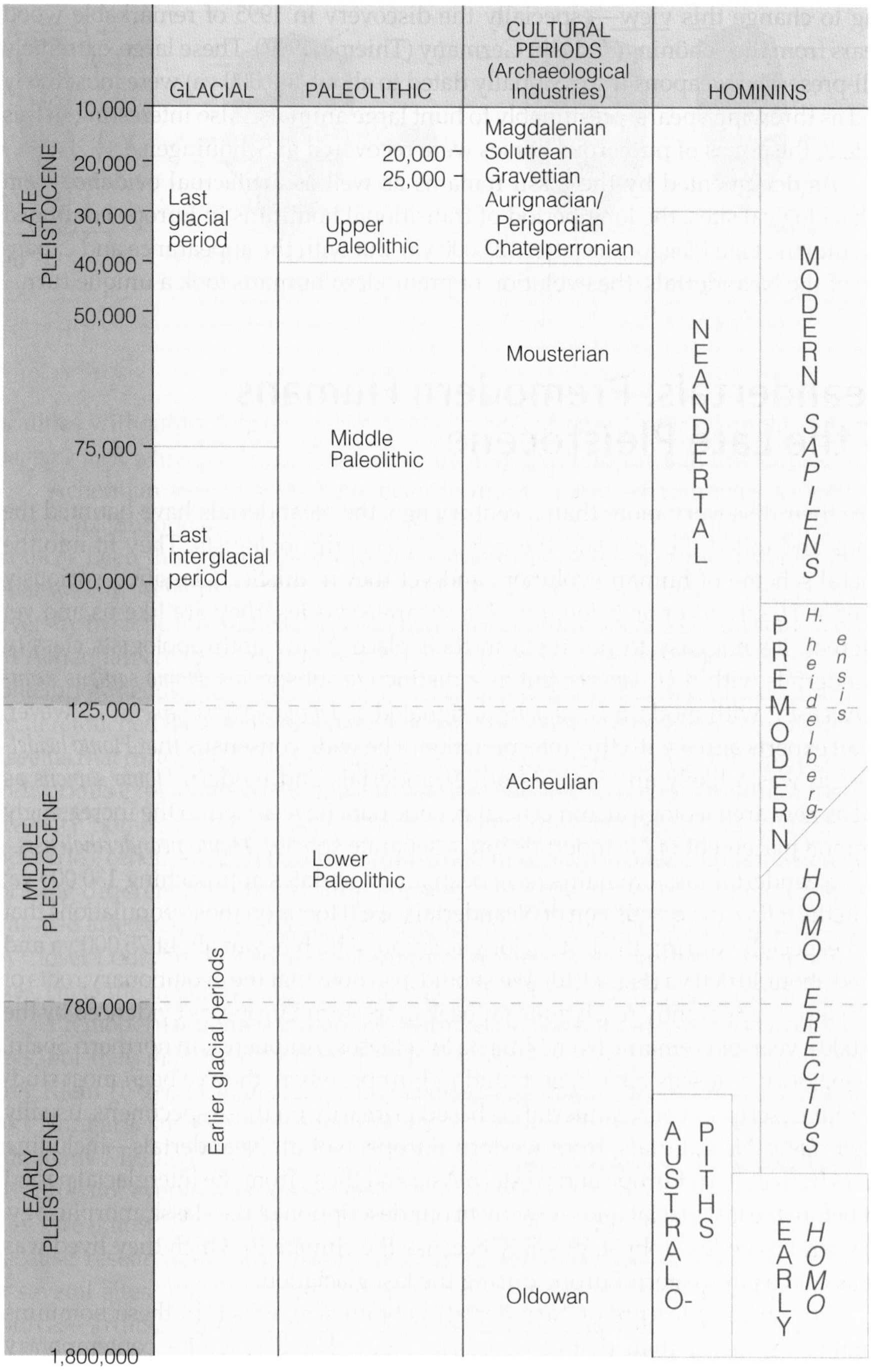

Figure 13-10

Correlation of Pleistocene subdivisions with archaeological industries and hominins. Note that the geological divisions are separate and different from the archaeological stages (e.g., Late Pleistocene is not synonymous with Upper Paleolithic).

		GLACIAL	PALEOLITHIC	CULTURAL PERIODS (Archaeological Industries)	HOMININS
LATE PLEISTOCENE	10,000 20,000 30,000 40,000 50,000 75,000	Last glacial period	Upper Paleolithic 20,000 – 25,000 –	Magdalenian Solutrean Gravettian Aurignacian/ Perigordian Chatelperronian	NEANDERTAL / MODERN SAPIENS
				Mousterian	
			Middle Paleolithic		
	100,000	Last interglacial period			PREMODERN H. heidelberg-ensis
MIDDLE PLEISTOCENE	125,000 780,000	Earlier glacial periods	Lower Paleolithic	Acheulian	HOMO ERECTUS
EARLY PLEISTOCENE	1,800,000			Oldowan	AUSTRALO-PITHS / EARLY HOMO

point out that the larger brain size in both premodern and contemporary human populations adapted to *cold* climates is partially correlated with larger body size, which has also evolved among these groups (see Chapter 16).

The classic Neandertal cranium is large, long, low, and bulging at the sides. Viewed from the side, the occipital bone is somewhat bun-shaped, but the marked occipital angle typical of many *H. erectus* crania is absent. The forehead rises more vertically than that of *H. erectus*, and the browridges arch over the orbits instead of forming a straight bar (Fig. 13-11).

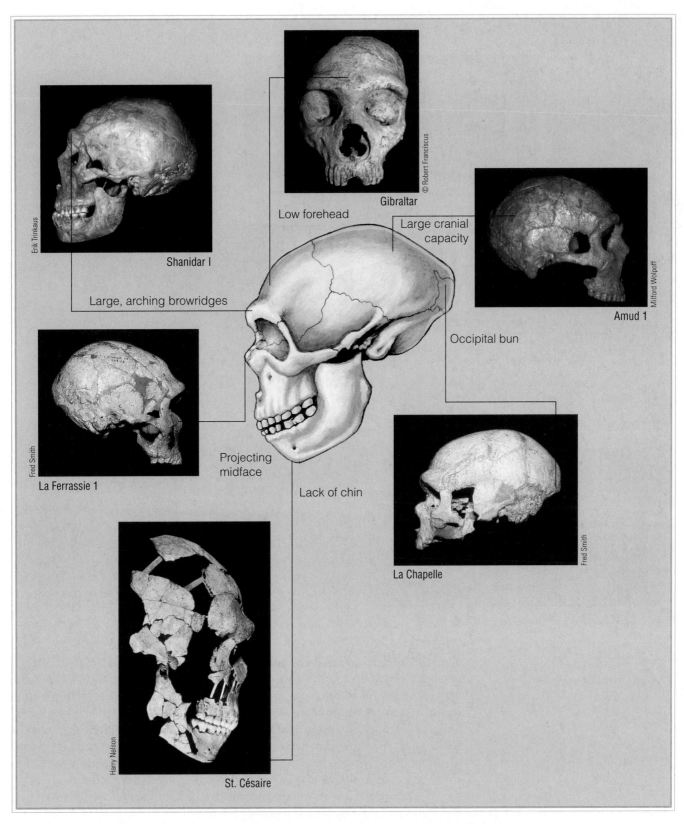

Shanidar I

Gibraltar

Low forehead

Large cranial capacity

Large, arching browridges

Amud 1

Occipital bun

La Ferrassie 1

Projecting midface

Lack of chin

La Chapelle

St. Césaire

Figure **13-11**

Morphology and variation in Neandertal crania.

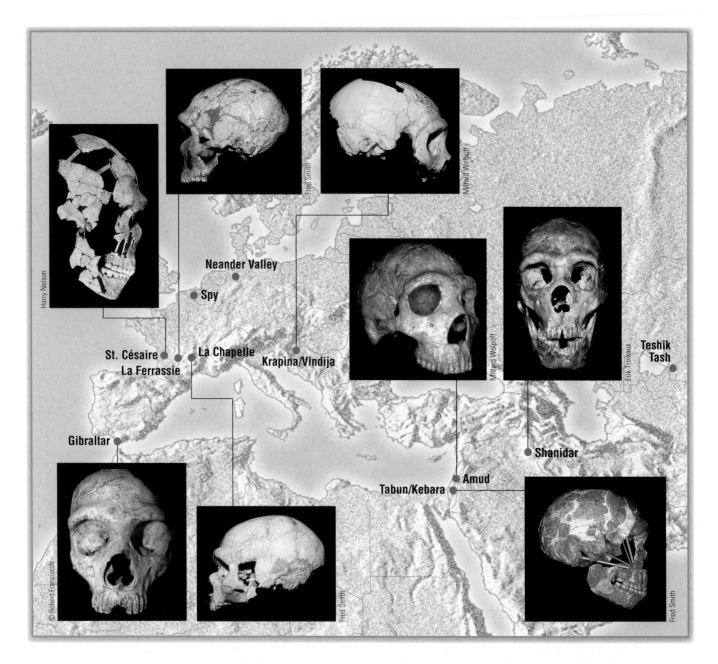

Neander Valley

Spy

St. Césaire
La Ferrassie

La Chapelle

Krapina/Vindija

Gibraltar

Tabun/Kebara

Amud

Shanidar

Teshik
Tash

Figure **13-12**

Fossil discoveries of Neandertals.

Compared with anatomically modern humans, the Neandertal face stands out. It projects almost as if it were pulled forward. Postcranially, Neandertals were very robust, barrel-chested, and powerfully muscled. This robust skeletal structure, in fact, dominates hominin evolution from *H. erectus* through all premodern forms. Still, the Neandertals appear particularly robust, with shorter limbs than seen in most modern *H. sapiens* populations. Both the facial anatomy and the robust postcranial structure of Neandertals have been interpreted by Erik Trinkaus, of Washington University in St. Louis, as adaptations to rigorous living in a cold climate.

For about 100,000 years, Neandertals lived in Europe and western Asia (see Fig. 13-12), and their coming and going have raised more questions and controversies than for any other hominin group. As we've noted, Neandertal forebears were transitional forms dating to the later Middle Pleistocene. However, it's not until the Late Pleistocene that Neandertals become fully recognizable.

Western Europe

One of the most important Neandertal discoveries was made in 1908 at La Chapelle-aux-Saints, in southwestern France. A nearly complete skeleton was found buried in a shallow grave in a **flexed** position. Several fragments of nonhuman long bones had been placed over the head, and over them, a bison leg. Around the body were flint tools and broken animal bones.

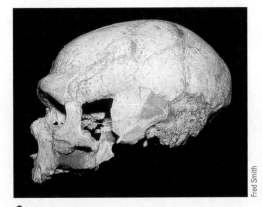

Figure **13-13**

La Chapelle-aux-Saints. Note the occipital bun, projecting face, and low vault.

The skeleton was turned over for study to a well-known French paleontologist, Marcellin Boule, who depicted the La Chapelle Neandertal as a brutish, bent-kneed, not fully erect biped. Because of this exaggerated interpretation, some scholars, and certainly the general public, concluded that all Neandertals were highly primitive creatures.

Why did Boule draw these conclusions from the La Chapelle skeleton? Today, we think he misjudged the Neandertal posture because this adult male skeleton had osteoarthritis of the spine. Also, and probably more important, Boule and his contemporaries found it difficult to fully accept as a human ancestor an individual who appeared in any way to depart from the modern pattern.

The skull of this male, who was possibly at least 40 years of age when he died, is very large, with a cranial capacity of 1,620 cm^3. Typical of western European classic forms, the vault is low and long; the browridges are immense, with the typical Neandertal arched shape; the forehead is low and retreating; and the face is long and projecting. The back of the skull is protuberant and bun-shaped (Figs. 13-11 and 13-13).

The La Chapelle skeleton isn't a typical Neandertal, but an unusually robust male who "evidently represents an extreme in the Neandertal range of variation" (Brace et al., 1979, p. 117). Unfortunately, this skeleton, which Boule claimed didn't even walk completely erect, was widely accepted as "Mr. Neandertal." But few other Neandertal individuals possess such exaggerated expression of Neandertal traits as the "Old Man of La Chapelle-aux-Saints" (see Figs. 13-11 and 3-13).

Another Neandertal site excavated recently in southern France has revealed further fascinating details about Neandertal behavior. From the 100,000- to 120,000-year-old Moula-Guercy Cave site, Alban Defleur, Tim White, and colleagues have analyzed 78 broken skeletal fragments from probably six individuals (Defleur et al., 1999). The intriguing aspect of these remains concerns *how* they were broken. Detailed analysis of cut marks, pits, scars, and other features clearly suggests that these individuals were *processed*—that is, they "were defleshed and disarticulated. After this, the marrow cavity was exposed by a hammer-on-anvil technique" (Defleur et al., 1999, p. 131). What's more, the nonhuman bones at this site, especially the deer remains, were processed in an identical way. In other words, the Moula-Guercy Neandertals provide the best-documented evidence thus far of Neandertal *cannibalism*.

Some of the most recent of the western European Neandertals come from St. Césaire, in southwestern France, and are dated at about 35,000 ya (Fig. 13-14). At St. Césaire, Neandertal remains were recovered from an archaeological level

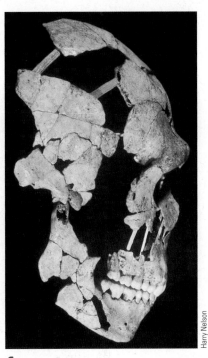

Figure **13-14**

St. Césaire, among the "last" Neandertals.

flexed The position of the body in a bent orientation, with arms and legs drawn up to the chest.

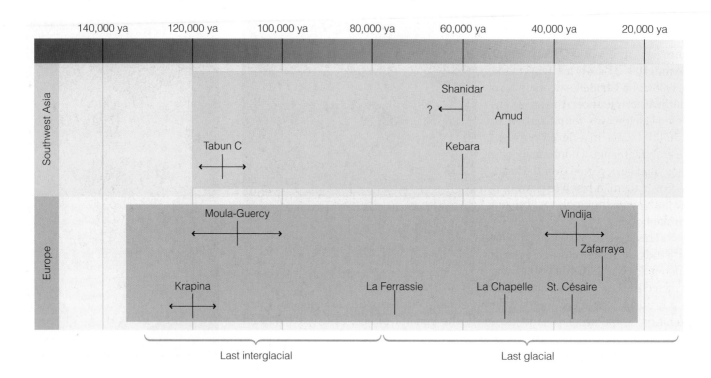

Figure 13-15

Time line for Neandertal fossil discoveries.

that also included discarded chipped blades, hand axes, and other stone tools of an **Upper Paleolithic** tool industry associated with Neandertals. Perhaps the most recent Neandertal remains yet recovered come from central Europe, at the site of Vindija, in Croatia. Radiocarbon dating suggests that the Vindija remains may date as late as 33,000–32,000 ya (Smith et al., 1999).

The St. Césaire and Vindija sites are important for several reasons. Anatomically modern humans were living in both western and central Europe by about 35,000 ya or a bit earlier. So it's possible that Neandertals and modern *H. sapiens* were living quite close to each other for several thousand years (Fig. 13-15). How did these two groups interact? Evidence from a number of French sites indicates that Neandertals may have borrowed technological methods and tools (such as blades) from the anatomically modern populations and thereby modified their own tools, creating a new industry, the **Chatelperronian.**

Central Europe

There are quite a few other European classic Neandertals, including significant finds in central Europe (see Fig. 13-12). At Krapina, Croatia, researchers have recovered an abundance of bones—1,000 fragments representing up to 70 individuals—and 1,000 stone tools or flakes (Trinkaus and Shipman, 1992). Krapina is an old site, possibly the earliest showing the full classic Neandertal morphology, dating back to the beginning of the Late Pleistocene (estimated at 130,000–110,000 ya). And despite the relatively early date, the characteristic Neandertal features of the Krapina specimens, although less robust, are similar to the western European finds (Fig. 13-16). Krapina is also important as an intentional burial site—one of the oldest on record.

About 30 miles from Krapina, Neandertal fossils have also been discovered at Vindija. The site is an excellent source of faunal, cultural, and hominin materials stratified in *sequence* throughout much of the Late Pleistocene. Neandertal fossils

Upper Paleolithic A cultural period usually associated with modern humans, but also found with some Neandertals, and distinguished by technological innovation in various stone tool industries. Best known from western Europe, similar industries are also known from central and eastern Europe and Africa.

Chatelperronian Pertaining to an Upper Paleolithic industry found in France and Spain, containing blade tools and associated with Neandertals.

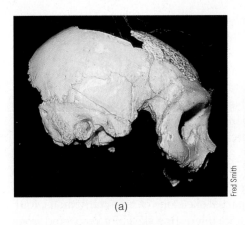
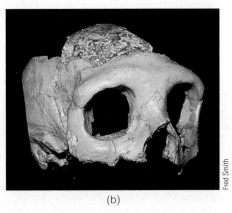

(a)   (b)

Fred Smith
Fred Smith

Figure **13-16**

Krapina cranium. (a) Lateral view showing characteristic Neandertal traits. (b) Three-quarters view.

from Vindija consist of some 35 specimens, dated to between 42,000 and 32,000 ya—making them some of the most recent Neandertals ever discovered (Higham et al., 2006.) While the overall anatomical pattern is definitely Neandertal, some features of the Vindija individuals, such as smaller browridges and slight chin development, approach the morphology seen in early modern south-central European *H. sapiens*. These similarities have led some researchers to suggest a possible evolutionary link between the late Vindija Neandertals and modern *H. sapiens*.

Western Asia

Israel In addition to European Neandertals, many important discoveries have been made in southwest Asia. Neandertal specimens from Israel are less robustly built than the classic Neandertals of Europe, though again, the overall pattern is clearly Neandertal. One of the best known of these discoveries is from Tabun—short for Mugharet-et-Tabun, meaning "cave of the oven"—at Mt. Carmel, a short drive south from Haifa (Fig. 13-17). Tabun, excavated in the early 1930s, yielded a female

Harry Nelson

Figure **13-17**

Excavation of the Tabun Cave, Mt. Carmel, Israel.

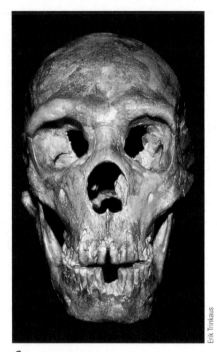

Figure **13-18**

Shanidar 1. Does he represent Neandertal compassion for the disabled?

skeleton, recently dated by thermoluminescence (TL) at about 120,000–110,000 ya. If this dating is accurate, Neandertals at Tabun were generally contemporary with early modern *H. sapiens* found in nearby caves. (TL dating is discussed on p. 286.)

A more recent Neandertal burial, a male discovered in 1983, comes from Kebara, a neighboring cave of Tabun at Mt. Carmel. A partial skeleton, dated to 60,000 ya, contains the most complete Neandertal pelvis so far recovered. Also recovered at Kebara is a hyoid—a small bone located in the throat, and the first ever found from a Neandertal; this bone is especially important because of its usefulness in reconstructing language capabilities.*

Iraq A most remarkable site is Shanidar Cave, in the Zagros Mountains of northeastern Iraq, where fieldworkers found partial skeletons of nine individuals, four of them deliberately buried. One of the more interesting skeletons recovered from Shanidar is that of a male (Shanidar 1) who lived to be approximately 30 to 45 years old, a considerable age for a prehistoric human (Fig. 13-18). He is estimated to have stood 5 feet 7 inches tall, with a cranial capacity of 1,600 cm³. The skeletal remains of Shanidar 1 also exhibit several other fascinating features:

> There had been a crushing blow to the left side of the head, fracturing the eye socket, displacing the left eye, and probably causing blindness on that side. He also sustained a massive blow to the right side of the body that so badly damaged the right arm that it became withered and useless; the bones of the shoulder blade, collar bone, and upper arm are much smaller and thinner than those on the left. The right lower arm and hand are missing, probably not because of poor preservation . . . but because they either atrophied and dropped off or because they were amputated. (Trinkaus and Shipman, 1992, p. 340)

Besides these injuries, the man had further trauma to both legs, and he probably limped. It's hard to imagine how he could have performed day-to-day activities. This is why Erik Trinkaus, who has studied the Shanidar remains, suggests that to survive, Shanidar 1 must have been helped by others: "A one-armed, partially blind, crippled man could have made no pretense of hunting or gathering his own food. That he survived for years after his trauma was a testament to Neandertal compassion and humanity" (Trinkaus and Shipman, 1992, p. 341).

Central Asia

Neandertals extended their range even farther to the east, far into central Asia. A discovery made in the 1930s at the Teshik-Tash site in Uzbekistan of a Neandertal child associated with tools of the Mousterian industry suggested that this species had dispersed a long way into Asia. However, owing to poor archaeological control during excavation and the young age of the individual, the find was not considered by all paleoanthropologists as clearly that of a Neandertal. New finds and molecular evaluation have provided crucial evidence that Neandertals did in fact extend their geographical range far into central Asia and perhaps even farther east.

DNA analysis of the Teshik-Tash remains shows that they are clearly Neandertal. What's more, other fragments from southern Siberia also show a

---

*The Kebara hyoid is identical to that of modern humans, suggesting that Neandertals did not differ from modern *H. sapiens* in this key element.

At a Glance

Key Neandertal Fossil Discoveries

DATES	SITE	EVOLUTIONARY SIGNIFICANCE
42,000–28,000 ya	**Vindija** (Croatia)	Large sample (best evidence of Neandertals in eastern Europe); latest well-dated Neandertal site
50,000 ya	**La Chapelle** (France)	Most famous Neandertal site; historically provided early, but distorted, interpretation of Neandertals
70,000–60,000 ya	**Shanidar** (Iraq)	Several well-preserved skeletons; good example of Neandertals from southwestern Asia; one individual with multiple injuries
110,000 ya; date uncertain	**Tabun** (Israel)	Well-preserved and very well-studied fossils showing early evidence of Neandertals in southwestern Asia

distinctively Neandertal genetic pattern (Krause et al., 2007). As we'll see shortly (see p. 379), researchers have recently been able to identify and analyze DNA from several Neandertal specimens. It's been shown that Neandertals and modern humans differ in both their mitochondrial DNA (mtDNA) and nuclear DNA, and these results are extremely significant in determining the evolutionary uniqueness of the Neandertal lineage. Moreover, in the case of the fragmentary remains from southern Siberia, it was the DNA findings that provided the key evidence in determining whether the hominin was even a Neandertal. In a sense, this is analogous to doing forensic analysis on our ancient hominin predecessors.

Culture of Neandertals

Anthropologists almost always associate Neandertals, who lived in the cultural period known as the Middle Paleolithic, with the **Mousterian** industry—although they don't always associate the Mousterian industry with Neandertals. Early in the last glacial period, Mousterian culture extended across Europe and North Africa into the former Soviet Union, Israel, Iran, and as far east as central Asia and possibly even China. Also, in sub-Saharan Africa, the contemporaneous Middle Stone Age industry is broadly similar to the Mousterian.

Technology

Neandertals improved on previous prepared-core techniques—that is, the Levallois—by inventing a new variation. They trimmed a flint nodule around the edges to form a disk-shaped core. Each time they struck the edge, they produced a flake, and they kept at it until the core became too small and was discarded. In this way, they produced more flakes per core than their predecessors did. They then reworked the flakes into various forms, including scrapers, points, and knives (Fig. 13-19).

Mousterian Pertaining to the stone tool industry associated with Neandertals and some modern *H. sapiens* groups; also called Middle Paleolithic. This industry is characterized by a larger proportion of flake tools than found in Acheulian tool kits.

Figure **13-19**

Examples of the Mousterian tool kit, including (from left to right), a Levallois point, a perforator, and a side scraper.

© Randall White

Neandertal craftspeople elaborated and diversified traditional methods, and there's some indication that they developed specialized tools for skinning and preparing meat, hunting, woodworking, and hafting. Even so, in strong contrast to the next cultural period, the Upper Paleolithic, there's almost no evidence that they used bone tools. Still, Neandertals advanced their technology well beyond that of earlier hominins. It's possible that their technological advances helped provide part of the basis for the remarkable changes of the Upper Paleolithic, which we'll discuss in the next chapter.

Subsistence

We know, from the abundant remains of animal bones at their sites, that Neandertals were successful hunters. But while it's clear that Neandertals could hunt large mammals, they may not have been as efficient at this task as Upper Paleolithic modern humans. For example, it wasn't until the beginning of the Upper Paleolithic that the spear-thrower, or atlatl, came into use (see p. 413). Soon after that, in Upper Paleolithic groups, the bow and arrow greatly increased efficiency (and safety) in hunting large mammals. Because Neandertals had no long-distance weaponry and were mostly limited to thrusting spears, they may have been more prone to serious injury—a hypothesis supported by paleoanthropologists Thomas Berger and Erik Trinkaus. Berger and Trinkaus (1995) analyzed the pattern of trauma, particularly fractures, in Neandertals and compared it with that seen in contemporary human samples. Interestingly, the pattern in Neandertals, especially the relatively high proportion of head and neck injuries, was most similar to that seen in contemporary rodeo performers. Berger and Trinkaus concluded that "the similarity to the rodeo distribution suggests frequent close encounters with large ungulates unkindly disposed to the humans involved" (Berger and Trinkaus, 1995, p. 841).

We know much more about European Middle Paleolithic culture than any earlier period because it's been studied longer and by more scholars. Recently, however, Africa has been a target not only of physical anthropologists but also of archaeologists, who have added considerably to our knowledge of African Pleistocene hominin prehistory. In many cases, the technology and assumed cultural adaptations in Africa were similar to those in Europe and southwest Asia.

We'll see in the next chapter that the African technological achievements also kept pace with, or even preceded, those in western Europe.

Speech and Symbolic Behavior

There are a variety of hypotheses concerning the speech capacities of Neandertals, and many of these views are contradictory. While some researchers argue that Neandertals were incapable of human speech, the prevailing consensus has been that they *were* capable of articulate speech and possibly capable of producing the same range of sounds as modern humans.

Recent genetic evidence is providing further evidence that likely will help us determine when fully human language first emerged (Enard et al., 2002). In humans today, mutations in a particular gene (locus) are known to produce serious language impairments. From an evolutionary perspective, what is perhaps most significant is the greater variability seen in the alleles at this locus in modern humans as compared to other primates. One explanation for this increased variation is intensified selection acting on human populations, and as we'll see shortly, DNA evidence from Neandertal fossils shows that they had already made this transformation.

But even if we conclude that Neandertals *could* speak, it doesn't necessarily mean that their abilities were at the level of modern *Homo sapiens*. Today, paleoanthropologists are quite interested in the apparently sudden population and geographical expansion of modern *H. sapiens* (discussed in Chapter 14), and they've proposed various explanations for this group's rapid success. Also, as we attempt to explain how and why modern *H. sapiens* expanded its geographical range, we're left with the problem of explaining what happened to the Neandertals. In making these types of interpretations, a growing number of paleoanthropologists suggest that *behavioral* differences are the key.

Researchers believe that Upper Paleolithic *H. sapiens* had some significant behavioral advantages over Neandertals and other premodern humans. Was it some kind of new and expanded ability to symbolize, communicate, organize social activities, elaborate technology, obtain a wider range of food resources, or care for the sick or injured—or was it some other factor? Compared with modern *H. sapiens*, were the Neandertals limited by neurological differences that may have contributed to their demise?

The direct anatomical evidence derived from Neandertal fossils isn't much help in answering these questions. Ralph Holloway (1985) has maintained that Neandertal brains—at least as far as the fossil evidence suggests—aren't significantly different from those of modern *H. sapiens*. What's more, as we've seen, Neandertal vocal tracts (as well as other morphological features), compared with our own, don't appear to have seriously limited them.

Most of the reservations about advanced cognitive abilities in Neandertals are based on archaeological data. Interpretation of Neandertal sites, when compared with succeeding Upper Paleolithic sites—especially those documented in western Europe—have led to several intriguing contrasts, as shown in Table 13-1.

From this type of behavioral and anatomical evidence, Neandertals have increasingly been viewed as an evolutionary dead end. Right now, we can't say whether their disappearance and ultimate replacement by anatomically modern Upper Paleolithic peoples—with their presumably "superior" culture—was the result of cultural differences alone or whether it was also influenced by biological variation.

CHAPTER 13

Table **13-1**   **Cultural Contrasts* Between Neandertals and Upper Paleolithic Modern Humans**

Neandertals	Upper Paleolithic Modern Humans
Tool Technology Numerous flake tools; few, however, apparently for highly specialized functions; use of bone, antler, or ivory very rare; relatively few tools with more than one or two parts	Many more varieties of stone tools; many apparently for specialized functions; frequent use of bone, antler, and ivory; many more tools comprised of two or more component parts
Hunting Efficiency and Weapons No long-distance hunting weapons; close-proximity weapons used (thus, more likelihood of injury)	Use of spear-thrower and bow and arrow; wider range of social contacts, perhaps permitting larger, more organized hunting parties (including game drives)
Stone Material Transport Stone materials transported only short distances— just "a few kilometers" (Klein, 1989)	Stone tool raw materials transported over much longer distances, implying wider social networks and perhaps trade
Art Artwork uncommon; usually small; probably mostly of a personal nature; some items perhaps misinterpreted as "art"; others may be intrusive from overlying Upper Paleolithic contexts; cave art absent	Artwork much more common, including transportable objects as well as elaborate cave art; well executed, using a variety of materials and techniques; stylistic sophistication
Burial Deliberate burial at several sites; graves unelaborated; graves frequently lack artifacts	Burials much more complex, frequently including both tools and remains of animals

**Note:* The contrasts are more apparent in some areas (particularly western Europe) than others (eastern Europe, Near East). Elsewhere (Africa, eastern Asia), where there were no Neandertals, the cultural situation is quite different. Even in western Europe, the cultural transformations weren't necessarily abrupt but may have developed more gradually from Mousterian to Upper Paleolithic times. For example, Straus (1995) argues that many of the Upper Paleolithic features weren't consistently manifested until after 20,000 ya.

Burials

Anthropologists have known for some time that Neandertals deliberately buried their dead. Undeniably, the spectacular discoveries at La Chapelle, Shanidar, and elsewhere were the direct results of ancient burial, which permits preservation that's much more complete. Such deliberate burial treatment goes back at least 90,000 years at Tabun. From a much older site, some form of consistent "disposal" of the dead—not necessarily belowground burial—is evidenced: As previously discussed, at the Sima de los Huesos site in Spain, thousands of fossilized bone fragments were found in a cave at the end of a deep vertical shaft. From the nature of the site and the accumulation of hominin remains, Spanish researchers are convinced that the site demonstrates some form of human activity involving deliberate disposal of the dead (Arsuaga et al., 1997).

The recent dating of Sima de los Huesos to more than 500,000 ya suggests that Neandertal precursors were already handling their dead in special ways during the Middle Pleistocene. Such behavior was previously thought to have emerged only much later, in the Late Pleistocene. As far as current data indicate, this practice is seen in western European contexts well before it appears in Africa or eastern Asia. For example, in the premodern sites at Kabwe and Florisbad (discussed earlier), deliberate disposal of the dead is not documented. Nor is it seen in African early modern sites—for example, the Klasies River Mouth, dated at 120,000–100,000 ya (see Chapter 14, p. 397).

Yet, in later contexts (after 35,000 ya), where modern *H. sapiens* remains are found in clear burial contexts, their treatment is considerably more complex than in Neandertal burials. In these later (Upper Paleolithic) sites, grave goods, including bone and stone tools as well as animal bones, are found more consistently and in greater concentrations. Because many Neandertal sites were excavated in the nineteenth or early twentieth century, before more rigorous archaeological methods were developed, many of these supposed burials are now in question. Still, the evidence seems quite clear that deliberate burial was practiced not only at La Chapelle, La Ferrassie (eight graves), Tabun, Amud, Kebara, Shanidar, and Teshik Tash, but also at several other localities, especially in France. In many cases, the body's *position* was deliberately modified and placed in the grave in a flexed posture (see p. 371). This flexed position has been found in 16 of the 20 best-documented Neandertal burial contexts (Klein, 1999).

Finally, as further evidence of Neandertal symbolic behavior, researchers point to the placement of supposed grave goods in burials, including stone tools, animal bones (such as cave bear), and even arrangements of flowers, together with stone slabs on top of the burials. Unfortunately, in many instances, again due to poorly documented excavation, these finds are questionable. Placement of stone tools, for example, is occasionally seen, but wasn't done consistently. In those 33 Neandertal burials for which we have adequate data, only 14 show definite association of stone tools and/or animal bones with the deceased (Klein, 1989). It's not until the next cultural period, the Upper Paleolithic, that we see a major behavioral shift, as demonstrated in more elaborate burials and development of art.

Genetic Evidence

With the revolutionary advances in molecular biology (discussed in Chapter 3), fascinating new avenues of research have become possible in the study of earlier hominins. It's becoming fairly commonplace to extract, amplify, and sequence ancient DNA from contexts spanning the last 10,000 years or so. For example, researchers have analyzed DNA from the 5,000-year-old "Iceman" found in the Italian Alps.

It's much harder to find usable DNA in even more ancient remains, since the organic components, often including the DNA, have been destroyed during the mineralization process. Still, in the past few years, exciting results have been announced about DNA found in more than a dozen different Neandertal fossils dated between 50,000 and 32,000 ya. These fossils come from sites in France (including La Chapelle), Germany (from the original Neander Valley locality), Belgium, Italy, Spain, Croatia, and Russia (Krings et al., 1997, 2000; Ovchinnikov et al., 2000; Schmitz et al., 2002; Serre et al., 2004; Green et al., 2006). Newly ascertained ancient DNA evidence strongly suggests that other fossils from central Asia (Uzbekistan and southern Siberia) dated at 38,000–30,000 ya are also Neandertals (Pennisi, 2007).

The technique most often used in studying the Neandertal fossils involves extracting mitochondrial DNA (mtDNA), amplifying it through polymerase chain reaction (PCR; see p. 73), and sequencing nucleotides in parts of the molecule. Results from the Neandertal specimens show that these individuals are genetically more different from contemporary *Homo sapiens* populations than modern human populations are from each other—in fact, about three times as much. Consequently, Krings and colleagues (1997) have hypothesized that the Neandertal lineage separated from that of our modern *H. sapiens* ancestors sometime between 690,000 and 550,000 ya.

Major advances in molecular biology have allowed much more of the Neandertal genetic pattern to be determined with the ability to now sequence big chunks of the *nuclear* DNA (which, as you may recall, contains more than

A Closer Look

The Evolution of Language

One of the most distinctive behavioral attributes of all modern humans is our advanced ability to use highly sophisticated symbolic language. Indeed, it would be impossible to imagine human social relationships or human culture without language.

When did language evolve? First, we should define what we mean by full human language. As we discussed in Chapter 8 (see p. 214), nonhuman primates have shown some elements of language. For example, some chimpanzees, gorillas, and bonobos display the ability to manipulate symbols and a rudimentary understanding of grammar. Still, the full complement of skills displayed by humans includes the extensive use of arbitrary symbols; sophisticated grammar; and a complex, open system of communication.

Most scholars are comfortable attributing such equivalent skills to early members of *H. sapiens*, as early as 200,000–100,000 ya. In fact, several researchers hypothesize that the elaborate technology and artistic achievements, as well as the rapid dispersal, of modern humans were a direct result of behavioral advantages—particularly full language capabilities. This rapid expansion of presumably culturally sophisticated modern *H. sapiens* (and the consequent disappearance of other hominins) has sometimes been called "the human revolution."

Of course, this hypothesis doesn't deny that earlier hominins had some form of complex communication; almost everyone agrees that even the earliest hominins did communicate (and the form was at least as complex as that seen in living apes). What's not generally agreed upon is just when the full complement of human language capacity first

emerged. Indeed, the controversy relating to this process will continue to ferment, since there's no clear answer to the question. There's not enough evidence available to establish clearly the language capabilities of any fossil hominin. We said in Chapter 8 that there are neurological foundations for language and that these features relate more to brain reorganization than to simple increase in brain size. Also, as far as spoken language is concerned, during hominin evolution crucial physiological consequences came about due to alterations within several anatomical structures, including the brain and the vocal tract.

Yet, we have no complete record of fossil hominin brains or their vocal tracts. We do have endocasts, which preserve a few external features of the brain. For example, there are several preserved endocasts of australopiths from South Africa. However, the information is incomplete and thus subject to varying interpretations. (For example, did these hominins possess language? If not, what form of communication did they display?) Evidence from the vocal tract has been even more elusive, although some new finds are helping fill in at least some gaps.

In such an atmosphere of fragmentary data, a variety of conflicting hypotheses have been proposed. Some paleoanthropologists argue that early australopiths (3 mya) had language. Others think that such capabilities were first displayed by early *Homo* (perhaps 2 mya). Still others suggest that language didn't emerge fully until the time of *Homo erectus* (2–1 mya), or perhaps it was premodern humans (such as the Neandertals) who first displayed such skills. And finally, some researchers assert that language first developed only with the appearance of fully modern *H. sapiens*.

99 percent of the human genome). In fact, one group of researchers in Germany has already sequenced more than 1 million bases and will likely complete the sequencing for the entire Neandertal genome within the next few years (Green et al. 2006)! Just a couple of years ago, this sort of achievement would have seemed like science fiction.

One immediate application of these remarkable new data is further confirmation of the suggested divergence dates derived from mitochondrial DNA. From the studies reported in 2006 and 2007 (Green et al. 2006; Noonan et al., 2006; Pennisi, 2007), the origins of the Neandertals have been traced to approximately 800,000–500,000 ya. Moreover, the early date (>500,000 ya) of the transitional Neandertal fossils at Atapuerca, Spain (Bischoff et al., 2007), further

Because the question of language evolution is so fundamental to understanding human evolution (indeed, what it means *to be* human), a variety of creative techniques have been applied to assess the (limited) evidence that's available. We've already mentioned the analysis of endocasts.

To reconstruct speech capabilities in fossil hominins, the physiology of the vocal tract also can provide some crucial hints, especially the position of the voice box (larynx) within the throat. In adult modern humans, the larynx is placed low in the throat, where it can better act as a resonating chamber. Unfortunately, since all the crucial structures within the vocal tract are soft tissue, they decompose after death, leaving paleoanthropologists to their own imagination to speculate about their relative positions in life. One way to determine the position of the larynx in long-dead hominins is to look at the degree of flexion at the base of the cranium. This flexion can be directly linked to the placement of the larynx in life, since "it shapes the roof of the voice box" (Klein 1999). In comparisons of fossil hominin crania, it's been determined that full cranial base flexion similar to that found in modern *sapiens* is not found before *Homo heidelbergensis*.

The tongue is, of course, another crucial structure influencing speech. Because it's a site of attachment for one of the muscles of the tongue, the shape and position of the hyoid bone (Fig. 1) can tell us a lot about speech capabilities in earlier hominins. A hyoid located higher up and farther back in the throat allows modern humans to control their tongue much more efficiently and precisely. In the *Australopithecus afarensis* child's skeleton (from Dikika, Ethiopia; see p. 317), the hyoid is shaped more like that in

a chimpanzee than in a modern human. So, it seems most likely that these early hominins weren't able to fully articulate human speech. The only other hyoid found in a fossil hominin comes from the Neandertal skeleton found at Kebara (Israel), and quite unlike the australopith condition, it resembles modern hyoids in all respects. We thus have some basis for concluding that the tongue musculature of Neandertals may have been much like our own.

Also potentially informative are possible genetic differences between humans and apes in regard to language (see p. 220). As the human genome is fully mapped (especially identifying functional regions and their specific actions) and compared with ape DNA (the chimpanzee genome is now also completely sequenced at a structural level), we might at long last begin to find a key to solving this great mystery.

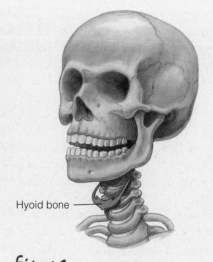

Hyoid bone

Figure 1

The position of the hyoid bone in the throat, shown in a modern human skeleton.

confirms this early divergence date. Lastly, the much more extensive Neandertal nuclear DNA patterns are as distinct from those of modern humans as are the differences seen in mtDNA. Considering the length of time that Neandertals were likely separate from the lineage of modern humans as well as their distinct genetic patterning, it seems reasonable that they should be considered a separate species—or at least a population well on its way to becoming separate (see p. 385).

As more specific areas of the Neandertal nuclear genome are investigated, even more significant information is surely forthcoming, and some of it already is proving surprising (see "New Frontiers in Research," pp. 388–390, for further discussion.

Trends in Human Evolution: Understanding Premodern Humans

As you can see, the Middle Pleistocene hominins are a very diverse group, broadly dispersed through time and space. There is considerable variation among them, and it's not easy to get a clear evolutionary picture. We know that regional populations were small and frequently isolated, and many of them probably died out and left no descendants. So it's a mistake to see an "ancestor" in every fossil find.

Still, as a group, these Middle Pleistocene premoderns do reveal some general trends. In many ways, for example, it seems that they were *transitional* between the hominins that came before them (*H. erectus*) and the one that followed them (modern *H. sapiens*). It's not a stretch to say that all the Middle Pleistocene premoderns derived from *H. erectus* forebears and that some of them, in turn, were probably ancestors of the earliest fully modern humans.

Paleoanthropologists are certainly concerned with such broad generalities as these, but they also want to focus on meaningful anatomical, environmental, and behavioral details as well as underlying processes. So they consider the regional variability displayed by particular fossil samples as significant—but just *how* significant is up for debate. In addition, increasingly sophisticated theoretical approaches are being used to better understand the processes that shaped the evolution of later *Homo*, at both macroevolutionary and microevolutionary levels.

Scientists, like all humans, assign names or labels to phenomena, a point we addressed in discussing classification in Chapter 5. Paleoanthropologists are certainly no exception. Yet, working from a common evolutionary foundation, paleoanthropologists still come to different conclusions about the most appropriate way to interpret the Middle/Late Pleistocene hominins. Consequently, a variety of species names have been proposed in recent years.

Paleoanthropologists who advocate an extreme lumping approach recognize only one species for all the premodern humans discussed in this chapter. These premoderns are classified as *Homo sapiens* and are thus lumped together with modern humans, although they're partly distinguished by such terminology as "archaic *H. sapiens*." As we've noted, this degree of lumping is no longer supported by most researchers. Alternatively, a second, less extreme view postulates modest species diversity and labels the earlier premoderns as *H. heidelbergensis* (Fig. 13-20a).

At the other end of the spectrum, more enthusiastic paleontological splitters have identified at least two (or more) species distinct from *H. sapiens*. The most important of these, *H. heidelbergensis* and *H. neanderthalensis*, have been discussed earlier. This more complex evolutionary interpretation is shown in Figure 13-20b.

We addressed similar differences of interpretation in Chapters 11 and 12, and we know that disparities like these can be frustrating to students who are new to paleoanthropology. The proliferation of new names is confusing, and it might seem that experts in the field are endlessly arguing about what to call the fossils.

Fortunately, it's not quite that bad. There's actually more agreement than you might think. No one doubts that all these hominins are closely related to each other as well as to modern humans. And everyone agrees that only some of the fossil samples represent populations that left descendants. Where paleoanthropologists disagree is when they start discussing which hominins are the most likely to be closely related to later hominins. The grouping of hominins into evolutionary clusters (clades) and assigning of different names to them is a reflection of differing interpretations—and, more fundamentally, of somewhat differing philosophies.

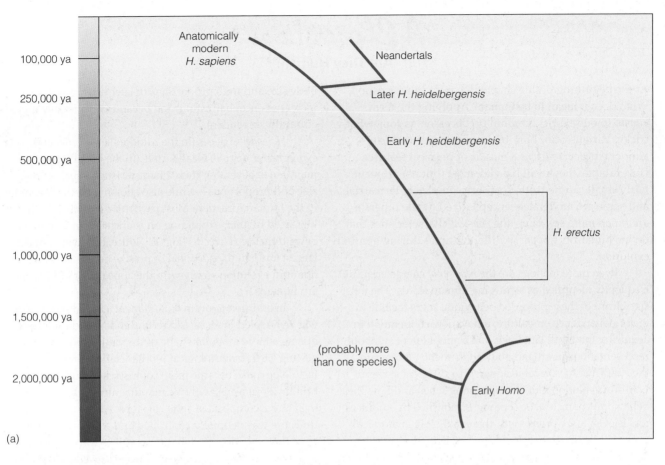

(a)

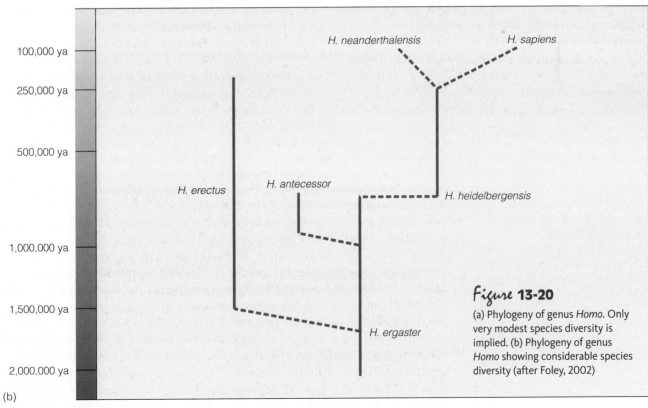

(b)

Figure **13-20**

(a) Phylogeny of genus *Homo*. Only very modest species diversity is implied. (b) Phylogeny of genus *Homo* showing considerable species diversity (after Foley, 2002)

A Closer Look

Are They Human?

At the beginning of this chapter we posed the question, What does it mean to be human? Applying the term *human* to our extinct hominin predecessors is somewhat tricky. Various prior hominin species share with contemporary *Homo sapiens* a mosaic of physical features. For example, they're all bipedal, most (but not all) have fairly small canine teeth, some are completely terrestrial, and some are moderately encephalized (while others are much more so). Thus, the *physical* characteristics that define humanity appear at different times during hominin evolution.

Even more tenuous are the *behavioral* characteristics frequently identified as signifying human status. The most significant of these proposed behavioral traits include major dependence on culture, innovation, cooperation in acquiring food, full language, and elaboration of symbolic representations in art and body adornment. Once again, the characteristics become apparent at different stages of hominin evolution. But distinguishing when and how these behavioral characteristics became established in our ancestors is even more problematic than analyzing anatomical traits. While the archaeological record provides considerable information regarding stone tool technology, it's mostly silent on other aspects of material culture. The social organization and language capabilities of earlier hominins are as yet almost completely invisible.

From the available evidence, we can conclude that *H. erectus* took significant steps in the human direction—well beyond that of earlier hominins. *H. erectus* vastly expanded hominin geographical ranges, achieved the full body size and limb proportions of later hominins, had increased encephalization, and became considerably more culturally dependent.

H. heidelbergensis (in the Middle Pleistocene) and, to an even greater degree, Neandertals (in the Late Pleistocene) maintained several of these characteristics—such as body size and proportions—while also showing further evolution in the human direction. Most particularly, relative brain size increased further, expanding on average about 22 percent beyond that of *H. erectus* (Fig. 1). Notice, however, that the largest jump in proportional brain size occurs very late in hominin evolution—only with the appearance of fully modern humans.

In addition to brain enlargement, cranial shape also was remodeled in *H. heidelbergensis* and Neandertals, producing a more globular shape of the vault as well as suggesting further neurological reorganization. Stone tool technology also became more sophisticated during the Middle Pleistocene, with the manufacture of tools requiring a more complicated series of steps. Also, for the first time, fire was definitely controlled and widely used; caves were routinely occupied; hominin ranges were successfully expanded throughout much of Europe as well as into northern Asia (that is, colder habitats were more fully exploited); structures were built; the dead were deliberately buried; and more systematic hunting took place.

Some premoderns also were like modern humans in another significant way. Analysis of teeth from a Neandertal shows that these hominins had the same *delayed maturation* found in modern *H. sapiens* (Dean et al., 2001). We don't yet

But we shouldn't emphasize these naming and classification debates too much. Most paleoanthropologists recognize that a great deal of these disagreements result from simple, practical considerations. Even the most enthusiastic splitters acknowledge that the fossil "species" are not true species as defined by the biological species concept (see p. 110). As prominent paleoanthropologist Robert Foley puts it, "It is unlikely they are all biological species. . . . These are probably a mixture of real biological species and evolving lineages of subspecies. In other words, they could potentially have interbred, but owing to allopatry [that is, geographical separation] were unlikely to have had the opportunity" (Foley, 2002, p. 33).

Even so, Foley, along with an increasing number of other professionals, distinguishes these different fossil samples with species names to highlight their distinct position in hominin evolution. That is, these hominin groups are more loosely defined as a type of paleospecies (see p. 115) rather than as fully biological species. Giving distinct hominin samples a separate (species) name makes

have similar data for earlier *H. heidelbergensis* individuals, but it's possible that they, too, showed this distinctively human pattern of development.

Did these Middle and Late Pleistocene hominins have the full language capabilities and other symbolic and social skills of living peoples? It's impossible to answer this question completely, given the types of fossil and archaeological evidence available. Yet, it does seem probable that neither *H. heidelbergensis* nor the Neandertals had this entire array of *fully* human attributes. That's why we call them premodern humans.

So, to rephrase our initial question, Were these hominins human? We could answer conditionally: They were human—at least, mostly so.

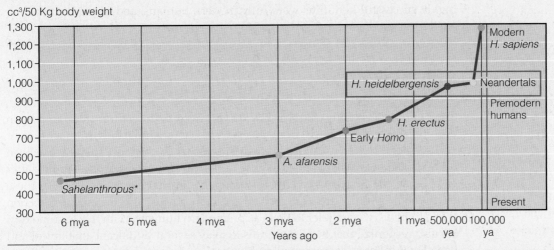

cc³/50 Kg body weight

*There are no direct current data for body size in *Sahelanthropus*. Body size is estimated from tooth size in comparison with *A. afarensis*. Data abstracted from McHenry (1992), Wood and Collard (1999), Brunet (2002), and Carroll (2003).

Figure 1

Relative brain size in hominins. The scale shows brain size as cm³ per 50 kg of body weight. Premodern humans have a more than 20 percent increase in relative brain size compared to *H. erectus*, but modern humans show another 30 percent expansion beyond that seen in premodern humans.

them more easily identifiable to other researchers and makes various cladistic hypotheses more explicit—and equally important, more directly testable. Eminent paleoanthropologist F. Clark Howell, of the University of California, Berkeley, also recognized these advantages but was less emphatic about species designations. Howell recommended the term *paleo-deme* for referring to either a species or subspecies classification (Howell, 1999).

The hominins that best illustrate these issues are the Neandertals. Fortunately, they're also the best known, represented by dozens of well-preserved individuals. With all this evidence, researchers can systematically test and evaluate many of the differing hypotheses.

Are Neandertals very closely related to modern *H. sapiens*? Certainly. Are they physically and behaviorally distinct from both ancient and fully modern humans? Yes. Does this mean that Neandertals are a fully separate biological species from modern humans and therefore theoretically incapable of fertilely interbreeding with modern people? Probably not. Finally, then, should Neandertals really be placed in a separate species from *H. sapiens*? For most purposes, it doesn't matter, since the distinction at some point is arbitrary. Speciation is, after all, a *dynamic* process. Fossil groups like the Neandertals represent just one point in this process (see Fig. 5-6, p. 111).

We can view Neandertals as a distinctive side branch of later hominin evolution. It is not unreasonable to say that Neandertals were likely an incipient species. Given enough time and enough isolation, they likely would have separated completely from their modern human contemporaries. The new DNA evidence suggests that they were well on their way, very likely approaching full speciation from *Homo sapiens*. However, some fossil and archaeological data continue to suggest that Neandertals perhaps never quite got that far. Their fate, in a sense, was decided for them as more successful competitors expanded into Neandertal habitats. These highly successful hominins were fully modern humans, and in the next chapter we'll focus on their story.

Summary

The Middle Pleistocene (780,000–125,000 ya) was a period of transition in human evolution. Fossil hominins from this period show similarities both with their predecessors (*H. erectus*) and with their successors (*H. sapiens*). They've also been found in many areas of the Old World, in Africa, Asia, and Europe—in the latter case, being the first truly successful occupants of that continent. Because these transitional hominins are more derived and more advanced in the human direction than *H. erectus*, we can refer to them as premodern humans. With this terminology, we also recognize that these hominins display several significant anatomical and behavioral differences from modern humans.

Although there's some dispute about the best way to formally classify the majority of Middle Pleistocene hominins, most paleoanthropologists now prefer to call them *H. heidelbergensis*. Similarities between the African and European Middle Pleistocene hominin samples suggest that they all can be reasonably seen as part of this same species. The contemporaneous Asian fossils, however, don't fit as neatly into this model, and conclusions regarding these premodern humans remain less definite.

Some of the later *H. heidelbergensis* populations in Europe likely evolved into Neandertals. Abundant Neandertal fossil and archaeological evidence has been collected from the Late Pleistocene time span of Neandertal existence, about 130,000–30,000 ya. But unlike their Middle Pleistocene (*H. heidelbergensis*) predecessors, Neandertals are more geographically restricted; they're found in Europe, southwest Asia, and central Asia. Various lines of evidence—anatomical, archaeological, and genetic—also suggest that they were isolated and distinct from other hominins.

These observations have led to a growing consensus among paleoanthropologists that the Neandertals were largely a side branch of later hominin evolution. Still, there remain significant differences in theoretical approaches regarding how best to deal with the Neandertals; that is, should they be considered a separate species or a subspecies of *H. sapiens*? We suggest that the best way to view the Neandertals is within a dynamic process of speciation. Neandertals can thus be interpreted as an incipient species—one in the process of splitting from early *H. sapiens* populations.

In "What's Important," you'll find a useful summary of the most significant premodern human fossils discussed in this chapter.

What's Important Key Fossil Discoveries of Premodern Humans

Dates	Region	Site	Hominin	The Big Picture
50,000 ya	Western Europe	La Chapelle (France)	Neandertal	Most famous Neandertal discovery; led to false interpretation of primitive, bent-over creature
110,000 ya	Southwestern Asia	Tabun (Israel)	Neandertal	Best evidence of early Neandertal morphology in S. W. Asia
130,000 ya	South Africa	Kabwe (Broken Hill, Zambia)	*H. heidelbergensis*	Transitional-looking fossil; perhaps a close ancestor of early *H. sapiens* in Africa
600,000–530,000 ya	Western Europe	Atapuerca (Sima de los Huesos)	*H. heidelbergensis* (early Neandertal)	Very early evidence of Neandertal ancestry; suggests Neandertals likely are a different species from *H. sapiens*
600,000 ya	East Africa	Bodo (Ethiopia)	*H. heidelbergensis*	Earliest evidencce of *H. heidelbergensis* in Africa—and possibly ancestral to later *H. sapiens*

Critical Thinking Questions

1. Why are the Middle Pleistocene hominins called premodern humans? In what ways are they human?
2. What is the general popular conception of Neandertals? Do you agree with this view? (Cite both anatomical and archaeological evidence to support your conclusion.)
3. Compare the skeleton of a Neandertal with that of a modern human. In which ways are they most alike? In which ways are they most different?
4. What evidence suggests that Neandertals deliberately buried their dead? Do you think the fact that they buried their dead is important? Why? How would you interpret this behavior (remembering that Neandertals were not identical to us)?
5. How are species defined, both for living animals and for extinct ones? Use the Neandertals to illustrate the problems encountered in distinguishing species among extinct hominins. Contrast specifically the interpretation of Neandertals as a distinct species with the interpretation of Neandertals as a subspecies of *H. sapiens*.

Ancient DNA

An exciting and potentially highly informative new direction of research has focused on extracting and analyzing DNA samples from ancient remains. Some of these finds can be extremely ancient, most notably insect tissue embedded in amber (that is, fossilized tree resin). Some of the insect DNA derived from these sources is upward of 120 million years old, and these discoveries, first reported in 1992, were the inspiration for Michael Crichton's *Jurassic Park*.

Amber provides an unusual and favorable environment for long-term preservation of small organisms—a situation, unfortunately, not applicable to larger organisms such as vertebrates. Even so, following the introduction of PCR technology, scientists were able to look for *very* small amounts of DNA that just might still linger in ancient human remains.

In 1986, researchers reported results of sequenced brain DNA obtained from mummified remains found in a Florida bog and dated at 7,000–8,000 years ago (Doran et al., 1986). The famous "Iceman" mummy discovered in the Alps in 1991 also yielded widely publicized DNA information about his population origins, shown to be not far from where he died (Fig. 1).

More recently, a group of Italian biologists led by Franco Rollo of the Molecular Anthropology/Ancient DNA Laboratory of the University of Camerino has analyzed the Iceman's intestinal contents using molecular techniques. Their results show that the Iceman's last meal was composed of red deer and possibly cereal grains and that his preceding meal contained ibex, cereals, and other plant food (Rollo et al., 2002). He apparently ate his next-to-last meal at a lower altitude than the 10,500-foot locale where he died. This observation is supported by other DNA studies of pollen found in his lungs, showing that he had recently passed through a lower-altitude forest.

No nuclear DNA was identified in any of the examples just discussed, so researchers used the more plentiful mitochondrial DNA. Their successes gave hope that they could analyze even more ancient remains containing preserved human DNA. And indeed, in 1997, Matthias Krings and associates from the University of Munich and the Max Planck Institute of Evolutionary Anthropology (see p. 204) made a startling breakthrough. They successfully extracted, amplified, and sequenced DNA from a Neandertal skeleton. As discussed in Chapter 13 (see p. 379), more than a dozen Neandertals ranging in date from 100,000 ya to 32,000 ya have since yielded enough mtDNA for analysis.

As we've noted, the place of Neandertals in human evolution has been and continues to be a topic of fascination and contention. This is why the Neandertal DNA evidence is so important. Besides, comparing Neandertal DNA patterns with those of early modern humans would be extremely illuminating.

Certainly, numerous early *H. sapiens* skeletons from Europe and elsewhere are still likely to contain some DNA. And indeed, as we'll see in Chapter 14, in just the last five years, several early modern *H. sapiens* individuals have had their DNA sequenced (Caramelli et al., 2003; Kulikov et al., 2004; Serre et al., 2004). These new finds, all coming from Europe or easternmost Asia, extending from France in the west to Russia in the east, support the view that Neandertal DNA is quite distinct from living people *as well as* from the first modern *H. sapiens* finds in Europe. But questions remain concerning possible contamination of the ancient samples. With PCR, even the tiniest amounts of extraneous DNA (even a single molecule) can be replicated millions of times; so there's always a chance of contamination from handling by excavators or lab investigators. In fact, one researcher has estimated that the few skin cells shed by researchers in the lab contain more DNA than most fossils do! Even with the best attempts at contamination control, inadvertent contamination can never be ruled out. Difficulties of this sort have surrounded the analysis of a potentially older early modern

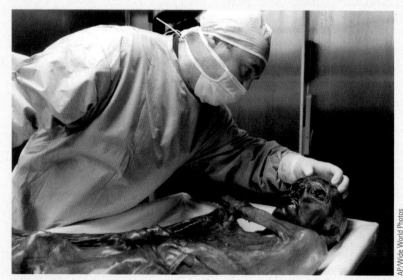

AP/Wide World Photos

Figure 1

Iceman.

human from the Lake Mungo site in Australia (see Chapter 14, p. 404, for further discussion).

Significant technological advances in 2005 allowed much faster analysis of small fragments of ancient DNA and allow for the first time accurate evaluation of *nuclear* DNA; with these powerful new molecular tools teams of researchers obtained considerable nuclear DNA sequence information from an ancient mammoth (Poinar et al., 2005) and from a cave bear (Noonan et al., 2005). But, by far the most startling breakthrough came in late 2006 when two teams of researchers simultaneously announced remarkably successful nuclear DNA sequencing of a 38,000-year-old Neandertal. One group of researchers from California (Noonan et al., 2006) was the same as one as that which had analyzed the mammoth DNA and the other (from the Max Planck Institute) used a com-

Figure 2

The Max Planck Institute of Evolutionary Anthropology in Leipzig, Germany. Many of the ancient DNA analyses of Neandertals and early modern *H. sapiens* are done here.

pletely new method to obtain amazing results (Green et al., 2006). The California researchers sequenced an impressive 65,000 Neandertal base pairs, and the Max Planck team, led by Svante Pääbo, sequenced approximately one million Neandertal base pairs! (Fig. 2).

With further refinements, the Max Planck team is predicting a complete genome sequence for Neandertals within two years; that is, they are confident they can determine all 3 billion base pairs from a tiny sample from one bone of this 38,000-year-old hominin. Just two years ago, this would have seemed more like science fiction than an attainable scientific goal.

These results will be extraordinarily important because they'll provide a data base from which to learn a vast amount about Neandertal biology and behavior. For example, are there particular gene differences between Neandertals and modern humans that can help explain alterations in brain organization? And, even more intriguing, will genetic changes be discovered that help account for the development of particular fully human behaviors, such as language?

With these new tools and data available, researchers have begun to answer some of these fascinating but difficult questions. As more specific areas of the Neandertal nuclear genome are investigated, even more significant information is surely forthcoming, and some of it might prove surprising. For example, one of the first two nuclear loci identified in Neandertals influences skin and hair pigmentation, and

the other is thought to be a crucial locus influencing speech and language.

The pigmentation locus indicates that at least some Neandertals were redheaded and also were likely light-skinned (Lalueza-Fox et al., 2007). These new data help confirm earlier hypotheses suggesting that Neandertals quite likely had light skin.

The second finding relates to the *FOXP2* locus, a genetic region thought to influence speech and language function in modern humans. Interestingly, two distinctive changes in this gene (point mutations) distinguish humans from all other living primates, and these exact same genetic modifications have also been identified in Neandertals (Krause et al., 2007). So it appears that this evolutionary change is quite ancient, going back perhaps as far as 500,000 ya. Moreover, it shows that Neandertals did not differ genetically from us in this crucial respect. Did they, then, have full human language? Given that this highly complex behavior is controlled by dozens of genes, we can't really answer this question just yet. For now, the very limited genetic information relating to language doesn't yet show any differences from us. Anthropologists have wondered for more than a century just how different the Neandertals were from modern people and exactly what became of them. The extraordinary new window that the DNA evidence provides will go a long way toward answering these questions (for more discussion, see the next chapter).

Ancient DNA (continued)

SOURCES

Abbott, Alison
    2003   Anthropologists cast doubt on human DNA evidence. *Nature* (News) 423:468.

Caramelli, David, Carlos Lalueza-Fox, Cristano Vernesi, et al.
    2003   Evidence for a genetic discontinuity between Neandertals and 24,000-year-old anatomically modern Europeans. *Proceedings of the National Academy of Sciences* 100:6593–6597.

Doran, G. H., D. N. Dickel, W.E. Ballinger, Jr., et al.
    1986   Anatomical, cellular, and molecular analysis of 8,000-yr-old human brain tissue from the Windover archaeological site. *Nature* 323:803–806.

Green, Richard E., Johannes Krause, Susan E. Ptak, et al.
    2006   Analysis of one million base pairs of Neanderthal DNA. *Nature* 444:330–336.

Krause, Johannes, Carlos Lalueza-Fox, Ludavic Orlando, et al.
    2007   "The derived *FOXP2* variant of modern humans was shared with Neandertals. *Current Biology* 17:1908–1912.

Krings, M., A. Stone, R. W. Schmitz, et al.
    1997   Neandertal DNA sequences and the origin of modern humans. *Cell* 90:19–30.

Kulikov, Eugene E., Audrey B. Poltaraus, and Irina A. Lebedeva
    2004   DNA analysis of Sunghir remains. Poster presentation, European Paleopathology Association Meetings, Durham, U.K., August 2004.

Lalueza-Fox, Carles, Hogler Römpler, David Caramelli, et al.
    2007   A melanocortin receptor allele suggests varying pigmentation among Neanderthals. *Science Express*, Oct 25, 2007.

Noonan, James P. M., Graham Coop, Sridhar Kudaravalli, et al.
    2006   Sequencing and analysis of Neanderthal genomic DNA. *Science* 314:1113–1118.

Noonan, James P., Michael Hofreiter, Doug Smith, et al.
    2005   Genomic sequencing of Pleistocene cave bears." *Science* 309:597–600.

O'Rourke, Dennis H., M. Geoffrey Hayes, and Shawn W. Carlyle
    2000   Ancient DNA studies in physical anthropology. *Annual Reviews of Anthropology* 29:217–242.

Poinar, Hendrik N., Carsten Schwarz, Ji Qi, et al.
    2005   Metagenomics to paleogenomics: Large-scale sequencing of mammoth DNA. *Science Express*, December 20, 2005. www.scienceexpress.org/20 December 2005/

Rollo, Franco, Massimo Ubaldi, Lucca Ermini, and Isolina Marota
    2002   Otzi's last meals: DNA analysis of the intestinal content of the Neolithic glacier mummy from the Alps. *Proceedings of the National Academy of Sciences* 99:12594–12599.

Schmitz, Ralf W., David Serre, Georges Bonani, et al.
    2002   The Neandertal type site revisited: Interdisciplinary investigations of skeletal remains from the Neander Valley, Germany. *Proceedings of the National Academy of Sciences* 99:13342–13347.

Hominin Evolution

CHAPTER

14

The Origin and Dispersal of Modern Humans

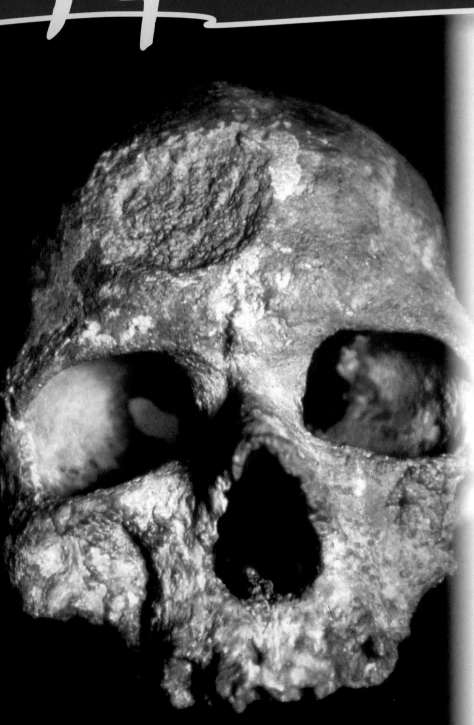

Milford Wolpoff

Key Question

Is it possible to determine when and where modern humans first appeared?

 Click!

Go to the following media for interactive activities and exercises on topics covered in this chapter:

- Online Virtual Laboratories for Physical Anthropology, Version 4.0
- Hominid Fossils: An Interactive Atlas CD-ROM

Introduction

Today, our species numbers more than 6 billion individuals, scattered all over the globe, but there are no other living hominins but us. Our last hominin cousin disappeared several thousand years ago. But about 30,000 years ago, modern peoples in Europe may have encountered beings that walked on two legs, hunted large animals, made fire, lived in caves, and fashioned complex tools. These beings were the Neandertals, and imagine what it would have been like to be among a band of modern peoples following game into what is now Croatia and coming across these other *humans*, so like yourself in some ways, yet so disturbingly odd in others. It's almost certain that such encounters took place, perhaps many times. How strange would it have been to look into the face of a being sharing so much with you, yet being a total stranger both culturally and, to some degree, biologically as well? What would you think seeing a Neandertal for the first time? What do you imagine a Neadertal would think seeing you?

Sometime, probably close to 200,000 ya, the first modern *Homo sapiens* evolved in Africa. Within 150,000 years or so, their descendants had spread across most of the Old World, even expanding as far as Australia (and somewhat later to the Americas).

Who were they, and why were these early modern people so successful? What was the fate of the other hominins, such as the Neandertals, who were already long established in areas outside Africa? Did they evolve as well, leaving descendants among some living human populations? Or were they completely swept aside and replaced by African emigrants?

In this chapter, we'll discuss the origin and dispersal of modern *H. sapiens*. All contemporary populations are placed within this species (and the same subspecies as well). Most paleoanthropologists agree that several fossil forms, dating back as far as 100,000 ya, should also be included in the same fully modern group as us. In addition, some recently discovered fossils from Africa also are clearly *H. sapiens*, but they show some (minor) differences from living people and could thus be described as near-modern. Still, we can think of these early African humans as well as their somewhat later relatives as "us."

These first modern humans, who evolved by 195,000 ya, are probably descendants of some of the premodern humans we discussed in Chapter 13. In particular, African populations of *H. heidelbergensis* are the most likely ancestors of the earliest modern *H. sapiens*. The evolutionary events that took place as modern humans made the transition from more ancient premodern forms and then dispersed throughout most of the Old World were relatively rapid, and they raise several basic questions:

1. When (approximately) did modern humans first appear?
2. Where did the transition take place? Did it occur in just one region or in several?

3. What was the pace of evolutionary change? How quickly did the transition occur?
4. How did the dispersal of modern humans to other areas of the Old World (outside their area of origin) take place?

These questions concerning the origins and early dispersal of modern *Homo sapiens* continue to fuel much controversy among paleoanthropologists. And it's no wonder, for members of early *H. sapiens* are the direct ancestors of all contemporary humans. They were much like us skeletally, genetically, and (most likely) behaviorally, too. In fact, it's the various hypotheses regarding the behaviors and abilities of our most immediate predecessors that have most fired the imaginations of scientists and laypeople alike. In every major respect, these are the first hominins that we can confidently refer to as *fully* human.

In this chapter, we'll also discuss archaeological evidence from the Upper Paleolithic (see p. 372). This evidence will give us a better understanding of the technological and social developments during the period when modern humans arose and quickly came to dominate the planet.

The evolutionary story of *Homo sapiens* is really the biological autobiography of all of us. It's a story that still has many unanswered questions; but several theories can help us organize the diverse information that's now available.

Approaches to Understanding Modern Human Origins

In attempting to organize and explain modern human origins, paleoanthropologists have developed two major theories: the complete replacement model and the regional continuity model. These two views are quite distinct, and in some ways they're completely opposed to each other. What's more, the popular press has further contributed to a wide and incorrect perception of irreconcilable argument on these points by "opposing" scientists. In fact, there's a third theory, which we call the partial replacement model, that's a kind of compromise, incorporating some aspects of the two major theories. Since so much of our contemporary view of modern human origins is influenced by the debates linked to these differing theories, let's start by briefly reviewing each one. Then we'll turn to the fossil evidence itself to see what it can contribute to answering the four questions we've posed.

The Complete Replacement Model: Recent African Evolution

The *complete replacement model* was developed by British paleoanthropologists Christopher Stringer and Peter Andrews (1988). It's based on the origin of modern humans in Africa and later replacement of populations in Europe and Asia (Fig. 14-1). This theory proposes that anatomically modern populations arose in Africa within the last 200,000 years and then migrated from Africa, *completely replacing* populations in Europe and Asia. It's important to note that this model doesn't account for a transition from premodern forms to modern *H. sapiens* anywhere in the world except Africa. A critical deduction of the Stringer and Andrews theory is that anatomically modern humans appeared as the result of a biological speciation event. So in this view, migrating African modern *H. sapiens* could not have interbred with local non-African populations, because the African modern humans were a *biologically* different species. Taxonomically, all of the premodern

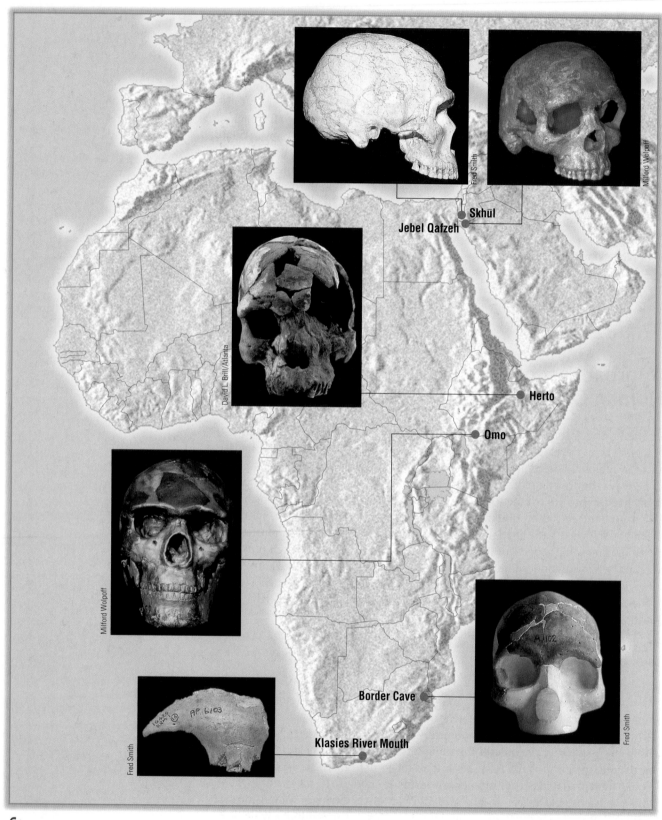

Figure **14-1**

Modern humans from Africa and the Near East.

populations outside Africa would, in this view, be classified as belonging to different species of *Homo*. For example, the Neandertals would be classified as *H. neanderthalensis* (see p. 382 for further discussion). This speciation explanation fits nicely with, and in fact helps explain, *complete* replacement; but Stringer has more recently stated that he isn't dogmatic on this issue. He does suggest that even though there may have been potential for interbreeding, apparently very little actually took place.

Interpretations of the latter phases of human evolution have recently been greatly extended by newly available genetic techniques. As we emphasized elsewhere, advances in molecular biology have revolutionized the biological sciences, including physical anthropology, and they've recently been applied to the question of modern human origins. Using numerous contemporary human populations as a data source, geneticists have precisely determined and compared a wide variety of DNA sequences. The theoretical basis of this approach assumes that at least some of the genetic patterning seen today can act as a kind of window on the past. In particular, the genetic patterns observed today between geographically widely dispersed humans are thought to partly reflect migrations occurring in the Late Pleistocene. This hypothesis can be further tested as various types of contemporary population genetic patterning are better documented.

To get a clearer picture of these genetic patterns, geneticists have studied both nuclear and mitochondrial DNA (mtDNA; see p. 50). They consider Y chromosome and mtDNA patterns particularly informative, since neither is significantly recombined during sexual reproduction. As a result, mitochondrial inheritance follows a strictly maternal pattern (inherited through females), while the Y chromosome follows a paternal pattern (transmitted only from father to son).

As these new data have accumulated, consistent relationships are emerging, especially in showing that indigenous African populations have far greater diversity than do populations from elsewhere in the world. The consistency of the results is highly significant, because it strongly supports an African origin for modern humans and some mode of replacement elsewhere. What's more, as we'll discuss in Chapter 15, new, even more complete data on contemporary population patterning of large portions of nuclear DNA further confirm these conclusions.

Certainly, most molecular data come from contemporary species, since DNA is not *usually* preserved in long-dead individuals. Even so, exceptions do occur, and these cases open another genetic window—one that can directly illuminate the past. As discussed in Chapter 13, DNA has been recovered from more than a dozen Neandertal fossils.

In addition, nine ancient fully modern *H. sapiens* skeletons from sites in Italy, France, the Czech Republic, and Russia have recently had their mtDNA sequenced (Caramelli et al., 2003, 2006; Kulikov et al., 2004; Serre et al., 2004). The results show mtDNA sequence patterns very similar to the patterns seen in living humans—and thus significantly different from the mtDNA patterns found in the Neandertals so far analyzed.

If these results are further confirmed, they provide strong *direct* evidence of a genetic discontinuity between Neandertals and these early fully modern humans. In other words, these data suggest that no—or very little—interbreeding took place between Neandertals and anatomically modern humans.

Still, there's a potentially serious problem with these latest DNA results from the early modern skeletons. The mtDNA sequences are so similar to those of modern humans that they could, in fact, be the result of contamination. That is, the amplified and sequenced DNA could belong to some person who recently handled the fossil. The molecular biologists who did this research took many experimental precautions, following standard practices used by other laboratories. But there's currently no way to rule out such contamination, which would likely have occurred during excavation. Still, the results do fit with an emerging overall agreement on the likely distinctions between Neandertals and modern humans.

Partial Replacement Models

Various alternative perspectives also suggest that modern humans originated in Africa and then, when their population increased, expanded out of Africa into other areas of the Old World. But unlike those who subscribe to the complete replacement hypothesis, supporters of these partial replacement models claim that some inter-breeding occurred between emigrating Africans and resident premodern populations elsewhere. So, partial replacement assumes that no speciation event occurred, and all these hominins should be considered members of *H. sapiens*. Günter Bräuer, of the University of Hamburg, suggests that very little interbreeding occurred—a view supported recently by John Relethford (2001) in what he describes as "mostly out of Africa." Fred Smith, of Loyola University, also favors an African origin of modern humans; but his "assimilation" model hypothesizes that in some regions, more interbreeding took place (Smith, 2002).

The Regional Continuity Model: Multiregional Evolution

The regional continuity model is most closely associated with paleoanthropologist Milford Wolpoff, of the University of Michigan, and his associates (Wolpoff et al., 1994, 2001). They suggest that local populations—not all, of course—in Europe, Asia, and Africa continued their indigenous evolutionary development from premodern Middle Pleistocene forms to anatomically modern humans. But if that's true, then we have to ask how so many different local populations around the globe happened to evolve with such similar morphology. In other words, how could anatomically modern humans arise separately in different continents and end up so much alike, both physically and genetically? The multiregional model answers this question by (1) denying that the earliest modern *H. sapiens* populations originated *exclusively* in Africa, challenging the notion of complete replacement; and (2) asserting that significant levels of gene flow (migration) between various geographically dispersed premodern populations were extremely likely throughout the Pleistocene.

Through gene flow and natural selection, according to the multiregional hypothesis, local populations would *not* have evolved totally independently from one another, and such mixing would have "prevented speciation between the regional lineages and thus maintained human beings as a *single*, although obviously *polytypic* (see p. 425), species throughout the Pleistocene" (Smith et al., 1989). Thus, under a multiregional model, there are no taxonomic distinctions between modern and premodern hominins. That is, all hominins following *H. erectus* are classified as a single species: *H. sapiens*.

Advocates of the multiregional model aren't dogmatic about the degree of regional continuity. They recognize that a likely strong influence of African migrants existed throughout the world and is still detectable today. Agreeing with Smith's assimilation model, this modified multiregionalism suggests that perhaps only minimal gene continuity existed in several regions (for example, western Europe) and that most modern genes are the result of large African migrations and/or more incremental gene flow (Relethford, 2001; Wolpoff et al., 2001).

Seeing the Big Picture

Looking beyond the arguments concerning modern human origins—which the popular media often overstate and overdramatize—most paleoanthropologists now recognize an emerging consensus view. In fact, new evidence from fossils and especially from molecular comparisons is providing even more clarity. Data from sequenced ancient DNA, various patterns of contemporary human DNA, and the newest fossil finds from Ethiopia all suggest that a "strong" multiregional model is extremely unlikely. Supporters of this more extreme form of multiregionalism claim that modern human populations in Asia and Europe evolved *mostly* from local premodern ancestors—with only minor influence coming from African population expansion. But with the breadth and consistency of the latest research, this strong version of multiregionalism is falsified.

Also, as various investigators integrate these new data, views are beginning to converge even further. Several researchers suggest an out-of-Africa model that leads to virtually complete replacement elsewhere. At the moment, this complete replacement rendition can't be falsified. Still, even devoted advocates of this strong replacement version recognize the potential for at least *some* interbreeding, although they believe it was likely very minor. We can conclude, then, that during the later Pleistocene, one or more major migrations from Africa fueled the worldwide dispersal of modern humans. However, the African migrants might well have interbred with resident populations outside Africa. In a sense, it's all the same, whether we see this process either as weak multiregional continuity or as "incomplete" replacement.

The Earliest Discoveries of Modern Humans

Africa

In Africa, several early fossil finds have been interpreted as fully anatomically modern forms (see Fig. 14-1). The earliest of these specimens comes from Omo Kibish, in southernmost Ethiopia. Using radiometric techniques, recent redating of a fragmentary skull (Omo 1) demonstrates that, coming from 195,000 ya, this is the earliest modern human yet found in Africa—or, for that matter, anywhere (McDougall et al., 2005). An interesting aspect of fossil finds at this site concerns the variation shown between the two individuals discovered there. Omo 1 (Fig. 14-2) is essentially modern in most respects (note the presence of a chin; Fig. 14-3), but another ostensibly contemporary cranium (Omo 2) is much more robust and less modern in morphology.

Somewhat later modern human fossils come from the Klasies River Mouth on the south coast of Africa and Border Cave, just slightly to the north. Using relatively new techniques, paleoanthropologists have dated both sites to about 120,000–80,000 ya. The original geological context at Border Cave is uncertain, and the fossils may be younger than those at Klasies River Mouth. Although recent reevaluation of the Omo site has provided much more dependable dating, there are still questions remaining about some of the other early African modern fossils. Nevertheless, it now seems very likely that early modern humans

Figure **14-2**

Reconstructed skull of Omo 1, an early modern human from Ethiopia, dated to 195,000 ya. Note the clear presence of a chin.

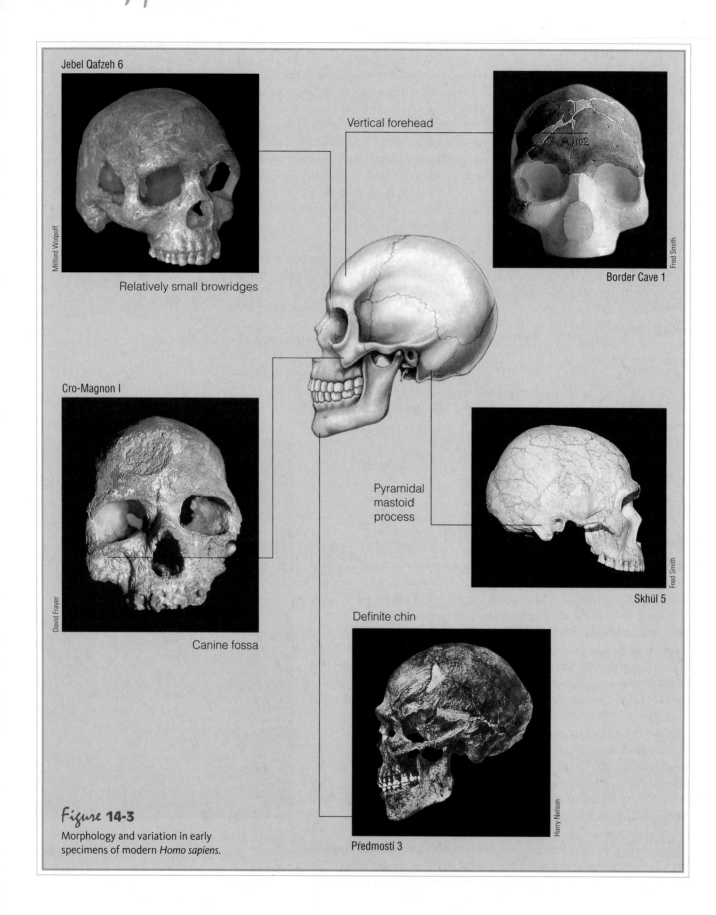

Jebel Qafzeh 6

Milford Wolpoff

Relatively small browridges

Vertical forehead

Border Cave 1

Fred Smith

Cro-Magnon I

David Frayer

Canine fossa

Pyramidal mastoid process

Skhūl 5

Fred Smith

Definite chin

Předmostí 3

Harry Nelson

Figure **14-3**

Morphology and variation in early specimens of modern *Homo sapiens*.

appeared in East Africa by shortly after 200,000 ya and had migrated to southern Africa by approximately 100,000 ya. New fossil finds are helping confirm this view.

Herto The announcement in June 2003 of well-preserved *and* well-dated *H. sapiens* fossils from Ethiopia has now gone a long way toward filling gaps in the African fossil record. As a result, these fossils are helping to resolve key issues regarding modern human origins. Tim White, of the University of California, Berkeley, and his colleagues have been working for three decades in the Middle Awash area of Ethiopia. They've discovered a remarkable array of early fossil hominins (*Ardipithecus* and *Australopithecus anamensis*) as well as somewhat later forms (*H. erectus*). From this same area in the Middle Awash—in the Herto member of the Bouri formation—highly significant new discoveries came to light in 1997. For simplicity, these new hominins are referred to as the Herto remains.

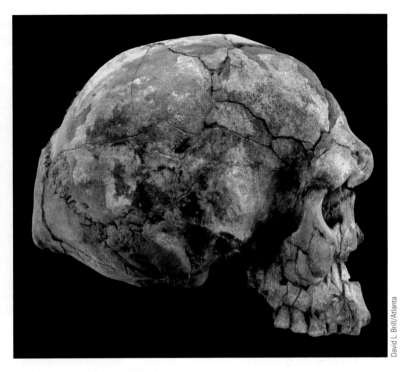

David L. Brill/Atlanta

Figure **14-4**

Herto cranium from Ethiopia, dated 160,000–154,000 ya. This is the best-preserved early modern *H. sapiens* cranium yet found.

These exciting new Herto fossils include a mostly complete adult cranium, a fairly complete (but heavily reconstructed) child's cranium, another adult incomplete cranium, and a few other cranial fragments. Following lengthy reconstruction and detailed comparative studies, White and colleagues were prepared to announce their findings in 2003.

What they found caused quite a sensation among paleoanthropologists, and it was reported in the popular press as well. First, well-controlled radiometric dating ($^{40}Ar/^{39}Ar$) securely places the remains at between 160,000 and 154,000 ya, making these the best-dated hominin fossils from this time period from anywhere in the world. And note, especially, that this date is clearly *older* than for any other equally modern *H. sapiens* from anywhere else in the world. Moreover, the preservation and morphology of the remains leave little doubt about their relationship to modern humans. The mostly complete adult cranium (Fig. 14-4) is very large, with an extremely long cranial vault. The cranial capacity is 1,450 cm^3, well within the range of contemporary *H. sapiens* populations. The skull is also in some respects heavily built, with a large, arching browridge in front and a large, projecting occipital protuberance in back. The face does not project, in stark contrast to Eurasian Neandertals.

The overall impression is that this individual is clearly *Homo sapiens*—as is the child, aged 6 to 7 years, and the other incomplete adult cranium. White and his team performed comprehensive statistical studies, comparing these fossils with other early *H. sapiens* remains as well as with a large series (over 3,000 crania) from modern populations. They concluded that while not identical to modern people, the Herto fossils are near-modern. That is, these fossils "sample a population that is on the verge of anatomical modernity but not yet fully modern." (White et al., 2003, p. 745). To distinguish these individuals from fully modern humans (*H. sapiens sapiens*), the researchers have placed them in a newly defined subspecies: *Homo sapiens idaltu*. The word *idaltu*, from the Afar language, means "elder."

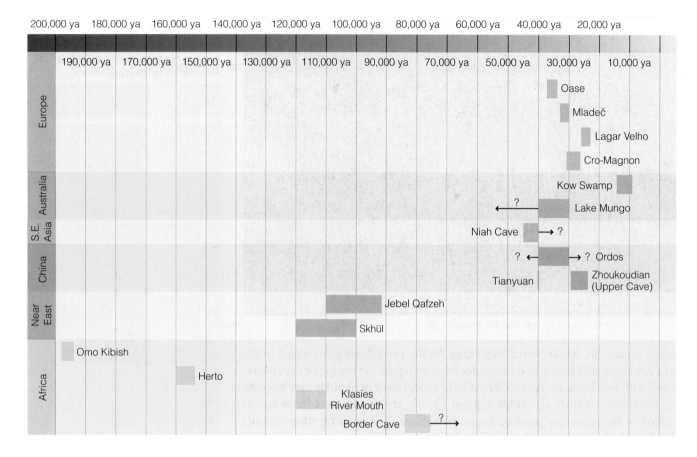

Figure 14-7

Time line of modern *Homo sapiens* discoveries. Note that most dates are approximations. Question marks indicate those estimates that are most tentative.

skull and partial skeleton from Liujang Cave (in Guangxi Province) are also considered to be from the Late Pleistocene (although an older date has also been suggested). However, local farmers digging up some of the cave's limestone deposits for fertilizer originally found the remains, so it's no longer possible to determine their original context. It's thus unlikely that firm dates will ever be established, and Liujiang can't be regarded as the oldest anatomically modern material from China. Great antiquity has also been proposed for the Mongolian Ordos skull (Etler, personal communication), but this dating is not very secure and has therefore been questioned (Trinkaus, 2005).

In addition, some researchers (Tiemel et al., 1994) have suggested that the Jinniushan skeleton discussed in Chapter 13 (see p. 361) hints at modern features in China as early as 200,000 ya. If this date—as early as that proposed for direct antecedents of modern *H. sapiens* in Africa—should prove accurate, it would cast doubt on the complete replacement model. This position, however, is a minority view and is not supported by more recent and more detailed analyses. Still, many Chinese paleoanthropologists take a position quite contrary to the complete replacement model and more in support of regional continuity. They thus see a continuous evolution first from Chinese *H. erectus* to premodern forms and finally to anatomically modern humans. This view is supported by Wolpoff, who mentions that materials from Upper Cave at Zhoukoudian "have a number of features that are characteristically regional" and that these features "are definitely not African" (1989, p. 83)*.

---

*Wolpoff's statement supports his multiregional hypothesis. His reference to Africa is a criticism of the complete replacement hypothesis.

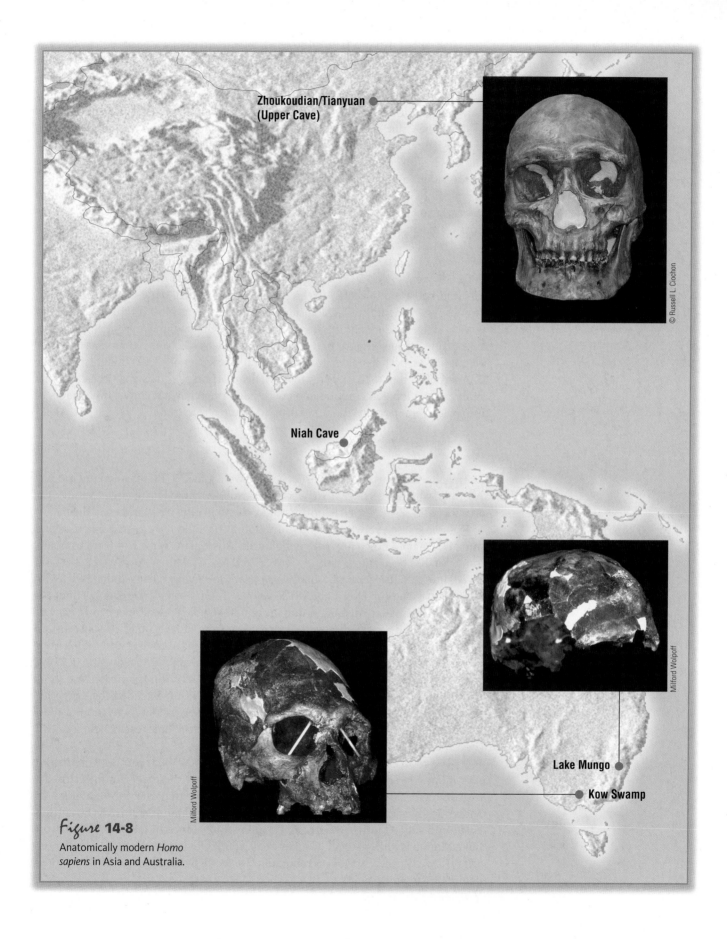

Zhoukoudian/Tianyuan
(Upper Cave)

© Russell L. Ciochon

Niah Cave

Milford Wolpoff

Milford Wolpoff

Lake Mungo

Kow Swamp

figure **14-8**

Anatomically modern *Homo sapiens* in Asia and Australia.

Just about 4 miles down the road from the famous Zhoukoudian Cave is another cave called Tianyuan, the source of an important find in 2003. Consisting of a fragmentary skull, a few teeth, and several postcranial bones, this fossil is accurately dated by radiocarbon at close to 40,000 ya (Shang et al., 2007). The individual shows mostly modern skeletal features, but also has a few archaic characteristics as well. The Chinese and American team of researchers who have analyzed the remains from Tianyuan suggest that they indicate an African origin of modern humans but also show a good possibility of at least some interbreeding in China with resident archaic populations. More complete analysis and (with some luck) further finds at this new site will help provide a better picture of early modern *H. sapiens* in China. For the moment, this is the best-dated early modern *H. sapiens* from China and one of the two earliest from anywhere in Asia.

The other early find is a partial skull from Niah Cave, on the north coast of the Indonesian island of Borneo (see Fig. 14-8). This is actually not a new find and was, in fact, first excavated 50 years ago. However, until recent more extensive analysis, this find had been relegated to the paleoanthropological back shelf due to uncertainties regarding its archaeological context and dating. Now all this has changed with a better understanding of the geology of the site and new dates strongly supporting an age of more than 35,000 ya and most likely as old as 45,000–40,000 ya, making it perhaps older than Tianyuan (Barker et al., 2007). Like its Chinese counterparts, the Niah skull is modern in morphology. It is hypothesized that some population contemporaneous with Niah or somewhat earlier inhabitants of Indonesia were perhaps the first group to colonize Australia.

Australia

During glacial times, the Indonesian islands were joined to the Asian mainland, but Australia was not. It's likely that by 50,000 ya, modern humans inhabited Sahul—the area including New Guinea and Australia. Bamboo rafts may have been the means of crossing the sea between islands, and doing so would have been dangerous and difficult. It's not known just where the future Australians came from, but as noted, Indonesia has been suggested.

Human occupation of Australia appears to have occurred quite early, with some archaeological sites dating to 55,000 ya. There's some controversy about the dating of the earliest Australian human remains, which are all modern *H. sapiens*. The earliest finds so far discovered have come from Lake Mungo, in southeastern Australia (see Fig. 14-8). In agreement with archaeological context and radiocarbon dates, the hominins from this site have been dated at approximately 30,000–25,000 ya. However, newly determined age estimates using electron spin resonance (ESR) and uranium series dating (see p. 286) have dramatically extended the suggested time depth to about 60,000 ya (Thorne et al., 1999). The lack of correlation of these more ancient age estimates with other data, however, has some researchers seriously concerned (Gillespie and Roberts, 2000).

The recovery and sequencing of mitochondrial DNA from these prehistoric Australians is as intriguing—and controversial—as the early dating estimates (Adcock et al., 2001). The primary researchers are confident that these samples are authentically ancient, but the nagging possibility of contamination can't be entirely ruled out. Indeed, other researchers remain unconvinced that the mtDNA from Lake Mungo is ancient at all (Cooper et al., 2001). Obviously, because of the uncertainties, we'll need further corroboration for both the dating and DNA findings before passing judgment.

Unlike the more gracile early Australian forms from Lake Mungo are the Kow Swamp people, who are thought to have lived between about 14,000 and 9,000 ya (see Fig. 14-8). These fossils display certain archaic traits—such as receding foreheads, heavy supraorbital tori, and thick bones—that are difficult to explain, since these features contrast with the postcranial anatomy, which matches that of recent native Australians. Regardless of the differing morphology of these later Australians, new genetic evidence indicates that all native Australians are descendants of a *single* migration dating back to about 50,000 ya (Hudjashov et al., 2007).

Central Europe

Central Europe has been a source of many fossil finds, including the earliest anatomically modern *H. sapiens* yet discovered anywhere in Europe. Dated to 35,000 ya, the best dated of these early *H. sapiens* fossils come from recent discoveries at the Oase Cave, in Romania (Fig 14-11 on p. 407). Here, cranial remains of three individuals were recovered, including a complete mandible and a partial skull (Fig. 14-9). While quite robust, these individuals are quite similar to later modern specimens, as seen in the clear presence of both a chin and a canine fossa (see Fig. 14-3, p. 398; Trinkaus et al., 2003).

Another early modern human site in central Europe is Mladeč, in the Czech Republic. Several individuals have been excavated here and are dated to

Figure **14-9**

Excavators at work within the spectacular cave at Oase, in Romania. The floor is littered with the remains of fossil animals, including the earliest dated cranial remains of *Homo sapiens* in Europe.

© Mircea Gerase

Figure **14-10**

The Mladeč (a) and Dolní Věstonice (b) crania, both from the Czech Republic, represent good examples of early modern *Homo sapiens* in central Europe. Along with Oase, in Romania, the evidence for early modern *Homo sapiens* appears first in central Europe before the later finds in western Europe.

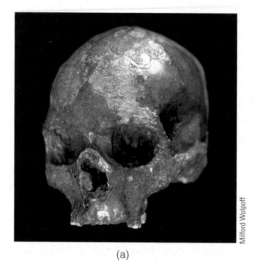

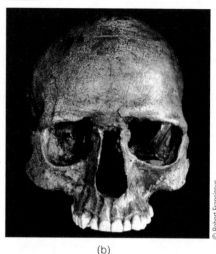

Milford Wolpoff

© Robert Franciscus

(a)   (b)

approximately 31,000 ya. While there's some variation among the crania, including some with big browridges, Fred Smith (1984) is confident that they're all best classified as modern *H. sapiens* (Fig 14-10). It's clear that by 28,000 ya, modern humans are widely dispersed in central Europe and into western Europe (Trinkaus, 2005). Also from the Czech Republic and dated at about 26,000 ya, Dolní Věstonice provides another example of a central European early modern (see Fig. 14-10b).

Western Europe

For several reasons, one of them probably serendipity, western Europe and its fossils have received the most attention. Over the last 150 years, many of the scholars interested in this kind of research happened to live in western Europe, and the southern region of France happened to be a fossil treasure trove. Also, early on, discovering and learning about human ancestors caught the curiosity and pride of the local population.

As a result of this scholarly interest, a great deal of data accumulated beginning back in the nineteenth century, with little reliable comparative information available from elsewhere in the world. Consequently, theories of human evolution were based almost exclusively on the western European material. It's only been in recent years, with growing evidence from other areas of the world and with the application of new dating techniques, that recent human evolutionary dynamics are being seriously considered from a worldwide perspective.

Western Europe has yielded many anatomically modern human fossils, but by far the best-known sample of western European *H. sapiens* is from the **Cro-Magnon** site. From a rock shelter in southern France, remains of eight individuals were discovered here in 1868.

The Cro-Magnon materials are associated with an **Aurignacian** tool assemblage, an Upper Paleolithic industry. Dated at about 28,000 ya, these individuals represent the earliest of France's anatomically modern humans. The so-called Old Man (Cro-Magnon 1) became the original model for what was once termed the Cro-Magnon, or Upper Paleolithic, "race" of Europe (Fig. 14-12). Actually, of course, there's no such valid biological category, and Cro-Magnon 1 is not typical of Upper Paleolithic western Europeans—and not even all that similar to the other two male skulls found at the site.

Cro-Magnon (crow-man´-yon)

Aurignacian Pertaining to an Upper Paleolithic stone tool industry in Europe beginning at about 40,000 ya.

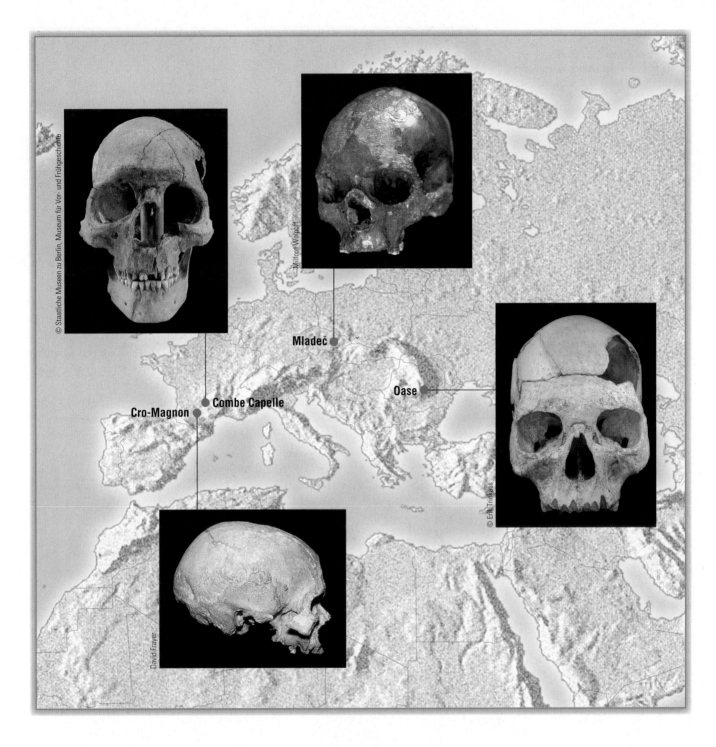

Figure **14-11**

Anatomically modern humans in Europe.

Most of the genetic evidence, as well as the newest fossil evidence, from Africa argues against continuous local evolution producing modern groups directly from any Eurasian premodern population (in Europe, these would be Neandertals). Still, for some researchers, the issue isn't completely settled. With all the latest evidence, there's no longer much debate that a *large* genetic contribution from migrating early modern Africans influenced other groups throughout the Old World. What's being debated is just how much admixture might have

Figure 14-12

Cro-Magnon 1 (France). In this specimen, modern traits are quite clear. (a) Lateral view. (b) Frontal view.

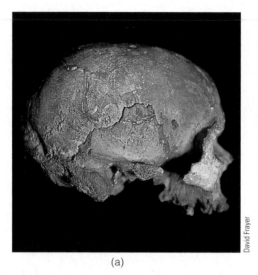

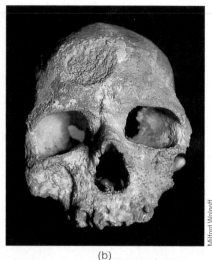

(a)   (b)

David Frayer

Milford Wolpoff

occurred between these migrating Africans and the resident premodern groups. One group of researchers that has evaluated genetic evidence from living populations (Eswaran et al., 2005) suggests that significant admixture occurred in much of the Old World. What's more, for those paleoanthropologists who also hypothesize that significant admixture (assimilation) occurred in western Europe as well as elsewhere (for example, Trinkaus, 2005), a recently discovered child's skeleton from Portugal provides some of the best evidence of ostensible interbreeding between Neandertals and anatomically modern *H. sapiens*. This important new discovery from the Abrigo do Lagar Velho site (see "A Closer Look," p. 409) was excavated in late 1998 and is dated to 24,500 ya—that's at least 5,000 years later than the last clearly Neandertal find. Associated with an Upper Paleolithic

At a Glance

Key Early Modern *Homo sapiens* Discoveries from Europe and Asia

DATES	SITE	HOMININ	EVOLUTIONARY SIGNIFICANCE
24,500 ya	**Abrigo do Lagar Velho** (Portugal)	*H. sapiens sapiens*	Child's skeleton; some suggestion of possible hybrid between Neandertal and modern human—but is controversial
30,000 ya	**Cro-Magnon** (France)	*H. sapiens sapiens*	Most famous early modern human find in world; earliest evidence of modern humans in France
40,000 ya	**Tianyuan Cave** (China)	*H. sapiens sapiens*	Partial skull and a few postcranial bones; oldest modern human find from China
45,000– 40,000 ya	**Niah Cave** (Borneo, Indonesia)	*H. sapiens sapiens*	Partial skull recently redated more accurately; oldest modern human find from Asia

A Closer Look

Hybridization in the Fossil Record: What Exactly Were Those Hominins Doing at Lagar Velho?

In 1999, researchers from Portugal announced an exciting discovery from the Lapedo Valley, in central Portugal (Duarte et al., 1999). At the site of Lagar Velho, researchers excavated a burial containing the largely complete skeleton of a 4-year-old child dated to around 24,500 ya (Fig. 1). What made this discovery particularly interesting was that the researchers claimed that the Lagar Velho child, as it's been called, represented a hybrid between Neandertals and modern humans: a Paleolithic lovechild of sorts. That is, the Lagar Velho child's anatomy was suggestive of generations of genetic admixture between indigenous Neandertal populations and modern humans who had migrated into Europe. Researchers looked to several morphological features as evidence of hybridization. For example, the mandible clearly exhibits a chin, which is a telltale sign of modernity. At the same time, though, this region recedes, as in Neandertals. In addition, aspects of the postcrania—such as limb proportions and robusticity of the skeleton—indicate the possible influence of Neandertal genes.

This interpretation of the Lagar Velho skeleton as a combination of both Neandertal and modern human morphology (which resulted from genetic admixture) is highly controversial. Adding to the controversy is the fact that the remains are those of a small child. Most anatomical characteristics used to define fossil species are normally based on adult skeletons, and there's no way to tell what this individual would have looked like once fully grown; we can only make predictions.

This isn't the first time that researchers have interpreted the morphology of hominin fossils as the result of hybridization. Later Neandertals, such as those found at the sites of St. Césaire, in France, and from the upper levels at the site of Vindija, in Croatia, have also been regarded as the result of genetic admixture. While there's no consensus

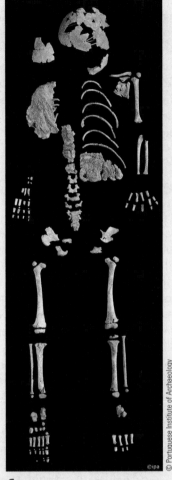

Figure 1

The skeleton of the Lagar Velho child thought by some to be a Neandertal–modern human hybrid.

on whether or not these fossils are *actually* the product of hybridization, what makes the interpretation of the Lagar Velho remains so important is that they have stimulated significant discussion and research into the concept of genetic admixture in the fossil record. This discussion led paleoanthropologists to ask some important questions regarding the nature of population hybridization.

All of the proposed models of modern human origins must deal with, to some extent, the question of hybridization between Neandertals and modern humans. This is particularly true of the assimilation model, since it's based on significant levels of genetic exchange between Neandertal and modern human populations. Thus, the ability for Neandertals and modern humans to hybridize speaks directly to one of the most frequently asked questions in paleoanthropology: What happened to the Neandertals? Did they go extinct due to competition with modern humans, or were they genetically assimilated by these new European inhabitants?

Looking for signs of hybridization in the fossil record is a challenging endeavor for the obvious reason that we can't directly observe the breeding habits of fossil hominins. Researchers must therefore turn to other areas of inquiry to begin to understand the nature of genetic barriers that define a species. One type of study that's shedding new light on this issue is exemplified by the research of Trent Holliday, of Tulane University. He and his colleagues have comprehensively investigated hybridization among extant species of primates as well as among other mammals. In particular, Holliday's study of genetic admixture in living animals has allowed researchers to understand not only the genetic markers associated with hybridization but also the morphological differences that result from the pairing of different species. By applying this type of research to the study of modern human origins, we can begin to address and test hypotheses regarding hybridization between Neandertals and modern humans.

industry and buried with red ocher and pierced shell is a fairly complete skeleton of a 4-year-old child (Duarte et al., 1999). In studying the remains, Cidália Duarte, Erik Trinkaus, and colleagues found a highly mixed set of anatomical features. Many characteristics, especially of the teeth, lower jaw, and pelvis, were like those seen in anatomically modern humans. Yet, several other features—including lack of chin, limb proportions, and muscle insertions—were more similar to Neandertal traits. The authors thus conclude that "the presence of such admixture suggests the hypothesis of variable admixture between early modern humans dispersing into Europe and local Neandertal populations" (Duarte et al., 1999, p. 7608). They suggest that this new evidence strongly supports the partial replacement model while seriously weakening the complete replacement model. Of course, the evidence from one child's skeleton—while intriguing—certainly isn't going to convince everyone.

Something New and Different: The "Little People"

As we've seen, by 25,000 years ago, modern humans had dispersed to all major areas of the Old World, and they would soon journey to the New World as well. But at about the same time, remnant populations of earlier hominins still survived in a few remote and isolated corners. We mentioned in Chapter 12 that populations of *Homo erectus* in Java managed to survive on this island long after their cousins had disappeared from other areas, for example, China and East Africa. What's more, even though they persisted well into the Late Pleistocene, physically these Javanese hominins were still very similar to other *H. erectus* individuals.

Even more surprising, it seems that other populations branched off from some of these early inhabitants of Indonesia and either intentionally or accidentally found their way to other, smaller islands to the east. There, under even more extreme isolation pressures, they evolved in an astonishing direction. In late 2004, the world awoke to the startling announcement that an extremely small-bodied, small-brained hominin had been discovered in Liang Bua Cave, on the island of Flores, east of Java (see Fig. 14-13). Dubbed the "Little Lady of Flores" or simply "Flo," the remains consist of an incomplete skeleton of an adult female (LB1) as well as additional pieces from nine other individuals, which the press have collectively nicknamed "hobbits." The female skeleton is remarkable in several ways (Fig. 14-14), though surprisingly similar to the Dmanisi hominins. First, she stood barely 3 feet tall—as short as the smallest australopith—and her brain, estimated at a mere 417 cm^3 (Falk et al., 2005), was no larger than that of a chimpanzee (Brown et al., 2004). Possibly most startling of all, these extraordinary hominins were still living on Flores just 13,000 ya (Morwood et al., 2004, 2005)!

Where did they come from? As we said, their predecessors were probably *H. erectus* populations like those found on Java. How they got to Flores—some 400 miles away, partly over open ocean—is a mystery. There are several connecting islands, and to get between them, these hominins may have drifted across on rafts; but there's no way to be sure of this.

How did they get to be so physically different from all other known hominins? Here we're a little more certain of the answer. Isolated island populations can quite rapidly diverge from their relatives elsewhere, as we noted in "A Closer Look" in Chapter 5 (see p. 120). Among such isolated animals, natural selection frequently favors reduced body size. For example, populations of dwarf elephants are

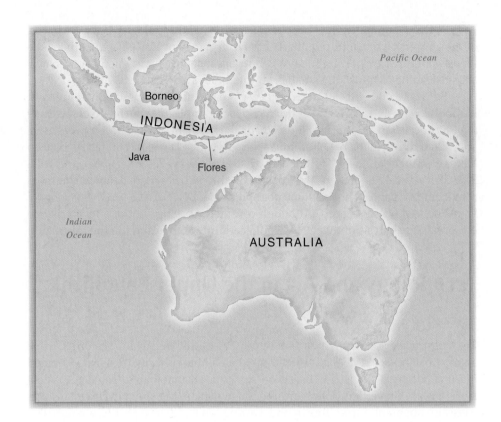

Figure 14-13
Location of the Flores site in Indonesia.

found on islands in the Mediterranean as well as on some channel islands off the coast of southern California. And perhaps most interesting of all, dwarf elephants *also* evolved on Flores; they were found in the same geological beds with the little hominins. The evolutionary mechanism (called "insular dwarfing") thought to explain such extreme body size reduction in both the elephants and the hominins is an adaptation to reduced resources, leading through selection to smaller size (Schauber and Falk, 2008).

Other than short stature, what did the Flores hominins look like? In their cranial shape, thickness of cranial bone, and dentition, they most resemble *H. erectus*, and specifically those from Dmanisi. Still, they have some derived features that also set them apart from all other hominins. For that reason, many researchers have placed them in a separate species, *Homo floresiensis*.

Immediately following the first publication of the Flores remains, intense controversy arose regarding their interpretation (Jacob et al., 2006; Martin et al., 2006). Some researchers have argued that the small-brained find (LB1) is actually a pathological modern *H. sapiens* afflicted with a severe growth disorder called microcephaly. The researchers who did most of the initial work reject this conclusion and provide some further details to support their original interpretation (for example, Dean Falk's further analysis of microcephalic endocasts, as reported in Bower, 2006).

The conclusion that among this already small-bodied island population the one individual found with a preserved cranium happened to be afflicted with a severe (and rare) growth defect is highly unlikely. Yet, it must also be recognized that long-term, extreme isolation of hominins on Flores leading to a new species showing dramatic body size dwarfing and even more dramatic brain size reduction is also quite unusual.

Figure 14-14
Cranium of adult female *Homo floresiensis* from Flores, Indonesia, dated 18,000 ya.

411

A third possibility has been suggested by anthropologist Gary Richards, of the University of California, Berkeley. He argues that LB1 (and the other little Flores hominins) are normal *H. sapiens*, but ones that have had a microevolutionary change leading to unusually small body and brain size (Richards, 2006).

So where does this leave us? Because a particular interpretation is unlikely, it's not necessarily incorrect. We do know, for example, that such "insular dwarfing" has occurred in other mammals. For the moment, the most comprehensive analyses indicate that a new hominin species (*H. floresiensis*) did, in fact, evolve on Flores (Nevell et al., 2007; Tocheri et al., 2007; Falk et al., 2008; Schauber and Falk, 2008). For several researchers, this conclusion still requires more detailed and more convincing evidence. There is some possibility that DNA can be retrieved from the Flores bones and sequenced. Although considered a long shot due to poor bone preservation, analysis of this DNA would certainly help in solving the mystery.

Technology and Art in the Upper Paleolithic

Europe

The cultural period known as the Upper Paleolithic began in western Europe approximately 40,000 ya (Fig. 14-15). Upper Paleolithic cultures are usually divided into five different industries, based on stone tool technologies: Chatelperronian, Aurignacian, Gravettian, Solutrean, and Magdalenian. Major environmental shifts were also apparent during this period. During the last glacial period, about 30,000 ya, a warming trend lasting several thousand years partially melted the glacial ice. The result was that much of Eurasia was covered by tundra and steppe, a vast area of treeless country dotted with lakes and marshes. In many areas in the north, permafrost prevented the growth of trees but permitted the growth, in the short summers, of flowering plants, mosses, and other kinds of vegetation. This vegetation served as an enormous pasture for herbivorous animals, large and small, and carnivorous animals fed off the herbivores. It was a hunter's paradise, with millions of animals dispersed across expanses of tundra and grassland, from Spain through Europe and into the Russian steppes.

Large herds of reindeer roamed the tundra and steppes, along with mammoths, bison, horses, and a host of smaller animals that served as a bountiful source of food. In addition, humans exploited fish and fowl systematically for the first time, especially along the southern tier of Europe. It was a time of relative abundance, and ultimately Upper Paleolithic people spread out over Europe, living in caves and open-air camps and building large shelters. Far more elaborate burials are also found, most spectacularly at the 24,000-year-old Sungir site near Moscow (Fig. 14-16), where grave goods included a bed of red ocher, thousands of ivory beads, long spears made of straightened mammoth tusks, ivory engravings, and jewelry (Formicola and Buzhilova, 2004). During this period, either western Europe or perhaps portions of Africa achieved the highest population density in human history up to that time (see "A Closer Look," p. 414).

Humans and other animals in the midlatitudes of Eurasia had to cope with shifts in climatic conditions, some of them quite rapid. For example, at 20,000 ya, another climatic "pulse" caused the weather to become noticeably colder in Europe and Asia as the continental glaciations reached their maximum extent for this entire glacial period, which is called the Würm in Eurasia.

GLACIAL	UPPER PALEOLITHIC (beginnings)	CULTURAL PERIODS
W Ü R M	17,000 – 21,000 – 27,000 – 40,000 –	Magdalenian Solutrean Gravettian Aurignacian Chatelperronian
	Middle Paleolithic	Mousterian

Figure **14-15**

Cultural periods of the European Upper Paleolithic and their approximate beginning dates.

As a variety of organisms attempted to adapt to these changing conditions, *Homo sapiens* had a major advantage: the elaboration of an increasingly sophisticated technology and most likely other components of culture as well. In fact, probably one of the greatest challenges facing numerous Late Pleistocene mammals was the ever more dangerously equipped humans—a trend that has continued to modern times.

The Upper Paleolithic was an age of technological innovation that can be compared to the past few hundred years in our recent history of amazing technological change after centuries of relative inertia. Anatomically modern humans of the Upper Paleolithic not only invented new and specialized tools (Fig. 14-17) but, as we've seen, also experimented with and greatly increased the use of new materials, such as bone, ivory, and antler.

Solutrean tools are good examples of Upper Paleolithic skill and perhaps aesthetic appreciation as well (see Fig. 14-17b). In this lithic (stone) tradition, stoneknapping developed to the finest degree ever known. Using specialized flaking techniques, the artist/technicians made beautiful parallel-flaked lance heads, expertly flaked on both surfaces. The lance points are so delicate that they can be considered works of art that quite possibly never served, nor were they intended to serve, a utilitarian purpose.

The last stage of the Upper Paleolithic, known as the **Magdalenian**, saw even more advances in technology. The spear-thrower, or atlatl, was a wooden or bone hooked rod that extended the hunter's arm, enhancing the force and distance of a spear throw (Fig. 14-18). For catching salmon and other fish, the barbed harpoon is a clever example of the craftsperson's skill. There's also evidence that the bow and arrow may have been used for the first time during this period. The introduction of much more efficient manufacturing methods, such as the punch blade technique (Fig. 14-19), provided an abundance of standardized stone blades. These could be fashioned into **burins** (see Fig. 14-17a) for working wood, bone, and antler; borers for drilling holes in skins, bones, and shells; and knives with serrated or notched edges for scraping wooden shafts into a variety of tools.

By producing many more specialized tools, Upper Paleolithic peoples probably had more resources available to them; moreover, these more effective tools may also have had an impact on the biology of these populations. Emphasizing a biocultural interpretation, C. Loring Brace, of the University of Michigan, has suggested that with more effective tools as well as the use of fire allowing for more efficient

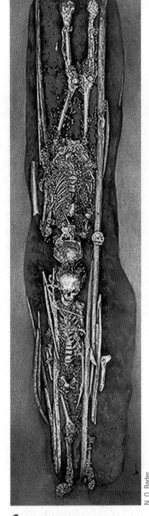

N. O. Bader

Figure 14-16

Skeleton of two teenagers, a male and a female, from Sungir, Russia. Dated 24,000 ya, this is the richest find of any Upper Paleolithic grave.

Magdalenian Pertaining to the final phase of the Upper Paleolithic stone tool industry in Europe.

burins Small, chisel-like tools with a pointed end; thought to have been used to engrave bone, antler, ivory, or wood.

(a)   (b)

Figure 14-17

(a) A burin, a very common Upper Paleolithic tool.
(b) A solutrean blade. This is the best-known work of the Solutrean tradition. Solutrean stonework is considered the most highly developed of any Upper Paleolithic industry.

Figure 14-18

Spear-thrower (atlatl). Note the carving.

A Closer Look

Maybe, You Can Take It with You

The practice of deliberately burying the dead is an important and distinctive aspect of later human biocultural evolution. We saw in Chapter 13 that Neandertals buried their dead at a number of sites; but we also noted that the assortment of grave goods found in Neandertal burials was pretty sparse.

Something remarkable happened with the appearance and dispersal of modern humans. Suddenly—at least in archaeological terms—graves became much more elaborate. And it wasn't just that many more items were placed with the deceased; it was also the kinds of objects. Neandertal graves sometimes contain a few stone tools and some unmodified animal bones, such as cave bear. But fully modern humans seem to have had more specialized and far more intensive cultural capacities. For example, from 40,000 years ago at Twilight Cave, in Kenya, researchers have found 600 fragments of carefully drilled ostrich eggshell beads (Klein and Edgar, 2002). These beads aren't directly associated with a human burial, but they do show us an intensification of craft specialization and possibly a much greater interest in personal adornment.

A locale where such elaborate grave goods (including beads) have been found in association with Upper Paleolithic modern human burials is the famous Cro-Magnon site in southwestern France. Likewise, numerous elaborate grave goods were found with human burials at Grimaldi, in Italy.

No doubt, the richest Upper Paleolithic burial sites are those at Sungir, in Russia. Parts of several individuals have been recovered there, dating to about 24,000 ya. However, three individuals were found in direct association with thousands of ivory beads and other elaborate grave goods. Two of the individuals, a girl about 9 or 10 years of age and a boy about 12 or 13 years of age, were buried together head to head in a spectacular grave (see Fig. 14-16). The more than 10,000 beads excavated here were probably woven into clothing, a task that would have been extraordinarily time-consuming.

The two individuals were placed directly on a bed of red ocher, and with them were two magnificent spears made of straightened mammoth tusks—one of them more than 6 feet (240 cm) long! What's more, there were hundreds of drilled fox canine teeth, pierced antlers, and ivory carvings of animals, as well as ivory pins and pendants (Formicola and Buzhilova, 2004).

Producing all of these items that were so carefully placed with these two young individuals took thousands of hours of labor. Indeed, one estimate suggests that it took 10,000 hours just to make the beads (Klein and Edgar, 2002). What were the Magdalenian people who went to all this trouble thinking? The double burial is certainly the most extravagant of any from the Upper Paleolithic, but another at Sungir is almost as remarkable. Here, the body of an adult male—perhaps about 40 years old when he died—was also found with thousands of beads, and he, too, was carefully laid out on a bed of red ocher.

Sungir is likely a somewhat extraordinary exception; still, far more elaborate graves are often found associated with early modern humans than was ever the case in earlier cultures. At Sungir, and to a lesser extent at other sites, it took hundreds or even thousands of hours to produce the varied and intricate objects.

The individuals who were buried with these valuable goods must have been seen as special. Did they have unique talents? Were they leaders or the children of leaders? Or did they have some special religious or ritual standing? To be sure, this evidence is the earliest we have from human history revealing highly defined social status. Thousands of years later, the graves of the Egyptian pharaohs express the same thing—as do the elaborate monuments seen in most contemporary cemeteries. The Magdalenians and other Upper Paleolithic cultures were indeed much like us. They, too, may have tried to defy death and take it with them!

---

food processing, anatomically modern *H. sapiens* wouldn't have required the large teeth and facial skeletons seen in earlier populations.

In addition to their reputation as hunters, western Europeans of the Upper Paleolithic are even better known for their symbolic representation, or what has commonly been called art. Given uncertainties about what actually should be called "art," archaeologist Margaret Conkey, of the University of California, Berkeley, refers to Upper Paleolithic cave paintings, sculptures, engravings, and so forth, as "visual and material imagery" (Conkey, 1987, p. 423). We'll continue using the term

(a) A large core is selected and the top portion removed by use of a hammerstone.

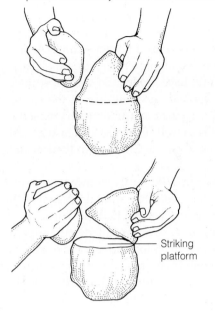

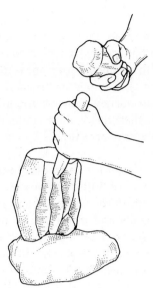

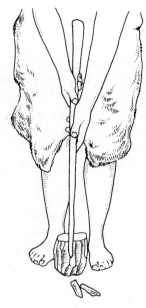

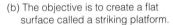
Striking platform

(b) The objective is to create a flat surface called a striking platform.

(c) Next, the core is struck by use of a hammer and punch (made of bone or antler) to remove the long narrow flakes (called blades).

(d) Or the blades can be removed by pressure flaking.

(e) The result is the production of highly consistent sharp blades, which can be used, as is, as knives; or they can be further modified (retouched) to make a variety of other tools (such as burins, scrapers, and awls).

Figure **14-19**
The punch blade technique.

art to describe many of these prehistoric representations, but you should recognize that we do so mainly as a cultural convention—and perhaps a limiting one.

It's also important to remember that there is an extremely wide geographical distribution of symbolic images, best known from many parts of Europe, but now also well documented from Siberia, North Africa, South Africa, and Australia. Given a 25,000-year time depth of what we call Paleolithic art, and its nearly world-wide distribution, we can indeed observe marked variability in expression.

Besides cave art, there are many examples of small sculptures excavated from sites in western, central, and eastern Europe. Perhaps the most famous of these are the female figurines, popularly known as "Venuses," found at such sites as Brassempouy, France, and Grimaldi, Italy. Some of these figures were realistically carved, and the faces appear to be modeled after actual women. Other figurines may seem grotesque, with sexual characteristics exaggerated, perhaps for fertility or other ritual purposes.

Beyond these quite well-known figurines, there are numerous other examples of what's frequently called portable art, including elaborate engravings on tools and tool handles (see Fig. 14-18). Such symbolism can be found in many parts of Europe and was already well established early in the Aurignacian, by 33,000 ya. Innovations in symbolic representations also benefited from, and probably further stimulated, technological advances. New methods of mixing pigments and applying them were important in rendering painted or drawn images. Bone and ivory carving and engraving were made easier with the use of special stone tools (see Fig. 14-17). At two sites in the Czech Republic, Dolní Věstonice and Předmostí (both dated at approximately 27,000–26,000 ya), small animal figures were fashioned from fired clay. This is the first documented use of ceramic technology anywhere; in fact, it precedes later pottery invention by more than 15,000 years.

But it wasn't until the final phases of the Upper Paleolithic, particularly during the Magdalenian, that European prehistoric art reached its climax. Cave art is now known from more than 150 separate sites, the vast majority from southwestern France and northern Spain. Apparently, in other areas the rendering of such images did not take place in deep caves. Peoples in central Europe, China, Africa, and elsewhere certainly may have painted or carved representations on rock faces in the open, but these images long since would have eroded. So we're fortunate that the people of at least one of the many sophisticated cultures of the Upper Paleolithic chose to journey belowground to create their artwork, preserving it not just for their immediate descendants, but for us as well. The most spectacular and most famous of the cave art sites are Lascaux and Grotte Chauvet (in France) and Altamira (in Spain).

In Lascaux Cave, for example, immense wild bulls dominate what's called the Great Hall of Bulls; and horses, deer, and other animals drawn with remarkable skill adorn the walls in black, red, and yellow. Equally impressive, at Altamira the walls and ceiling of an immense cave are filled with superb portrayals of bison in red and black. The "artist" even took advantage of bulges in the walls to create a sense of relief in the paintings. The cave is a treasure of beautiful art whose meaning has never been satisfactorily explained. It could have been religious or magical, a form of visual communication, or simply art for the sake of beauty.

Inside the cave called Grotte Chauvet, preserved unseen for perhaps 30,000 years, are a multitude of images, including dots, stenciled human handprints, and, most dramatically, hundreds of animal representations. Radiocarbon dating has placed the paintings during the Aurignacian, likely more than 35,000 ya, making Grotte Chauvet considerably earlier than the Magdalenian sites of Lascaux and Altamira (Balter, 2006).

Africa

Early accomplishments in rock art, possibly as early as in Europe, are seen in southern Africa (Namibia) at the Apollo 11 rock shelter site, where painted slabs have been identified dating to between 28,000 and 26,000 ya (Wendt, 1976; Freundlich et al., 1980; Vogelsang, 1998). In addition, incised ostrich eggshell fragments from the site may be much older (Kokis, 1988; Miller et al., 1999). Similarly, the Blombos Cave site is revealing amazing artifacts, including incised ocher fragments and various bone tools that are dated to 77,000 ya. In addition, more than 40 tick shell beads have been found at Blombos Cave that are dated to this same early time (Henshilwood and Sealey, 1997; Henshilwood et al., 2002; Henshilwood et al., 2004). In terms of stone tool technology, microliths (thumbnail-sized stone flakes hafted to make knives, saws, and so on) and blades characterize Late Stone Age* African industries.

The most recent and highly notable discovery from South Africa comes from another cave located at Pinnacle Point, not far from Blombos. At Pinnacle Point, ocher has been found (perhaps used for personal adornment) as well as clear evidence of systematic exploitation of shellfish and use of microliths. What is both important and surprising is that the site is dated to approximately 165,000 ya, providing the earliest evidence from anywhere of these behaviors, thought by many as characteristic of modern humans (Marean et al., 2007).

In central Africa, there was also considerable use of bone, some of it possibly quite old. Excavations in the Katanda area of the eastern portion of the Democratic Republic of the Congo (Fig. 14-20) have shown remarkable development of bone craftwork. Dating of the site is potentially quite early. Initial results using ESR and

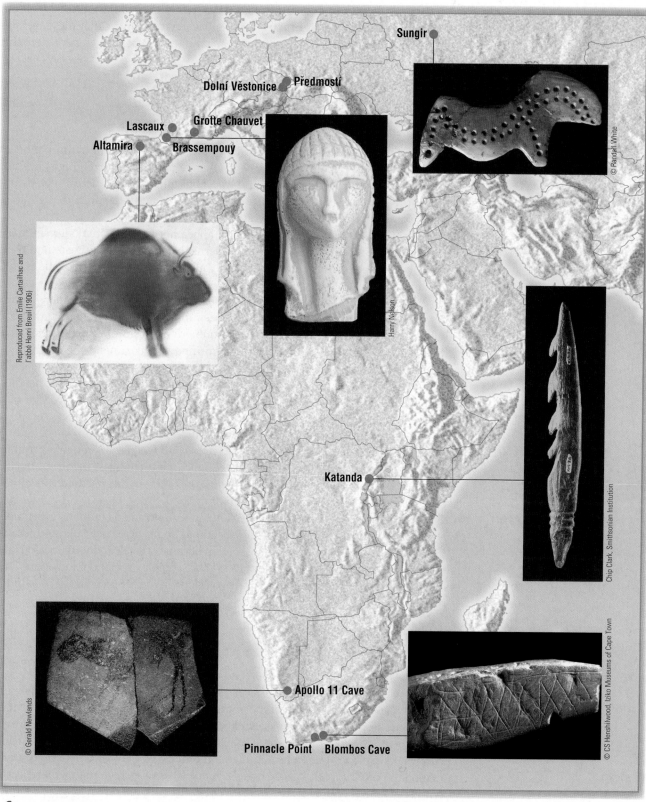

Figure 14-20

Symbolic artifacts from the Middle Stone Age of Africa and the Upper Paleolithic in Europe. It is notable that evidence of symbolism is found in Blombos Cave (77,000 ya) and Katanda (80,000 ya), both in Africa, about 45,000 years before any comparable evidence is known from Europe.

TL dating indicate an age as early as 80,000 ya (Feathers and Migliorini, 2001). From these intriguing data, preliminary reports have demonstrated that these technological achievements rival those of the more renowned European Upper Paleolithic (Yellen et al., 1995).

Summary of Upper Paleolithic Culture

In looking back at the Upper Paleolithic, we can see it as the culmination of 2 million years of cultural development. Change proceeded incredibly slowly for most of the Pleistocene; but as cultural traditions and materials accumulated, and the brain—and, we assume, intelligence—expanded and reorganized, the rate of change quickened.

Cultural evolution continued with the appearance of early premodern humans and moved a bit faster with later premoderns. Neandertals in Eurasia and their contemporaries elsewhere added deliberate burials, technological innovations, and much more.

Building on existing cultures, Late Pleistocene populations attained sophisticated cultural and material heights in a seemingly short (by previous standards) burst of exciting activity. In Europe and southern and central Africa particularly, there seem to have been dramatic cultural innovations, among them big game hunting with powerful new weapons, such as harpoons, spear-throwers, and eventually the bow and arrow. Other innovations included body ornaments, needles, "tailored" clothing, and burials with elaborate grave goods—a practice that may indicate some sort of status hierarchy.

This dynamic age was doomed, or so it seems, by the climatic changes of about 10,000 ya. As the temperature slowly rose and the glaciers retreated, animal and plant species were seriously affected, and these changes, in turn, affected humans. As traditional prey animals were depleted or disappeared altogether, humans had to seek other means of obtaining food.

Grinding hard seeds or roots became important, and as humans grew more familiar with propagating plants, they began to domesticate both plants and animals. Human dependence on domestication became critical, and with it came permanent settlements, new technology, and more complex social organization. This continuing story of human biocultural evolution will be the topic of the remainder of this text.

Summary

For the past two decades, and there's no end in sight, researchers have fiercely debated the date and location of the origin of anatomically modern human beings. One hypothesis (complete replacement) claims that anatomically modern forms first evolved in Africa more than 100,000 ya and then, migrating out of Africa, completely replaced premodern humans in the rest of the world. Another school (regional continuity) takes a completely opposite view and maintains that in various geographical regions of the world, local groups of premodern *H. sapiens* simultaneously evolved into anatomically modern humans by maintaining constant genetic contact. A third hypothesis (partial replacement) takes a somewhat middle position, suggesting an African origin but also accepting some later hybridization outside of Africa.

Recent research coming from several sources is beginning to clarify the origins of modern humans. Molecular evidence, as well as the dramatic new fossil finds from Herto, in Ethiopia, suggests that a multiregional origin of modern humans is unlikely. Sometime, soon after 150,000 ya, complete replacement of all hominins outside Africa may have occurred when migrating Africans displaced the populations in other regions. However, such absolutely *complete* replacement will be very difficult to prove, and it's not really what we'd expect. More than likely, at least some interbreeding probably did take place. Still, it's looking more and more like there wasn't very much intermixing of migrating African populations with other Old World groups.

Archaeological evidence of early modern humans also paints a fascinating picture of our most immediate ancestors. The Upper Paleolithic was an age of extraordinary innovation and achievement in technology and art. Many new and complex tools were introduced, and their production indicates fine skill in working wood, bone, and antler. Cave art in France and Spain displays the masterful ability of Upper Paleolithic painters, and beautiful sculptures have been found at many European sites. Sophisticated symbolic representations have also been found in Africa and elsewhere. Upper Paleolithic *H. sapiens* displayed amazing development in a relatively short period of time. The culture produced during this period led the way to still newer and more complex cultural techniques and methods.

In "What's Important," you'll find a useful summary of the most significant fossil discoveries discussed in this chapter.

What's Important Key Fossil Discoveries of Early Modern Humans and *Homo floresiensis*

Dates	Region	Site	Hominin	The Big Picture
95,000–13,000 ya	Southeast Asia	Flores (Indonesia)	*H. floresiensis*	Late survival of very small-bodied and small-brained hominin on island of Flores; designated as different species (*H. floresiensis*) from modern humans
30,000 ya	Europe	Cro-Magnon(France)	*H. sapiens sapiens*	Famous site historically; good example of early modern humans from France
35,000 ya	Europe	Oase Cave(Romania)	*H. sapiens sapiens*	Earliest well-dated modern human from Europe
110,000 ya	Southwest Asia	Qafzeh (Israel)	*H. sapiens sapiens*	Early site; shows considerable variation
115,000 ya	Southwest Asia	Skhūl (Israel)	*H. sapiens sapiens*	Earliest well-dated modern human outside of Africa; perhaps contemporaneous with neighboring Tabun Neandertal site
160,000–154,000 ya	Africa	Herto (Ethiopia)	*H. sapiens idaltu*	Best-preserved and best-dated early modern human from anywhere; placed in separate subspecies from living *H. sapiens*

Critical Thinking Questions

1. What anatomical characteristics define *modern* as compared to *premodern* humans? Assume that you're analyzing an incomplete skeleton that may be early modern *H. sapiens*. Which portions of the skeleton would be most informative, and why?

2. Go through the chapter and list all the forms of evidence that you think support the complete replacement model. Now, do the same for the regional continuity model. What evidence do you find most convincing, and why?

3. Why are the fossils recently discovered from Herto so important? How does this evidence influence your conclusions in question 2?

4. What archaeological evidence shows that modern human behavior during the Upper Paleolithic was significantly different from that of earlier hominins? Do you think that early modern *H. sapiens* populations were behaviorally superior to the Neandertals? Be careful to define what you mean by "superior."

5. Why do you think some Upper Paleolithic people painted in caves? Why don't we find such evidence of cave painting from a wider geographical area?

15

Modern Human Biology: Patterns of Variation

NASA/James Steidl (DNA)

Key Questions

Is evolution still occurring in modern humans?

What is meant by race, and how useful is this concept in understanding the biology and evolution of our species?

 Click!

Go to the following media for interactive activities and exercises on topics covered in this chapter:

- Online Virtual Laboratories for Physical Anthropology, Version 4.0
- Genetics in Anthropology: Principles and Applications CD-ROM, Version 2.0

Introduction

At some time or other, you've probably been asked to specify your "race" or "ethnicity" on an application or census form. Did that bother you, and if so, why? Usually, you can choose from a few racial/ethnic categories. Was it easy to pick one? Where would your parents and grandparents fit in?

Notions about human diversity have played an extremely important role in human relations for at least a few thousand years, and they still influence political and social perceptions. While we'd like to believe that informed views have become almost universal, the gruesome tally of genocidal/ethnic cleansing atrocities in recent years tells us tragically that worldwide, we have a long way to go before tolerance becomes the norm.

Unfortunately, there are probably hundreds (if not thousands) of popular misconceptions regarding human diversity, and to make matters worse, many people seem unwilling to accept what science has to say on the subject. Many misconceptions, especially those regarding how race is defined and categorized, are rooted in cultural history over the last few centuries.

In Chapters 3 and 4, we saw how physical characteristics are influenced by the DNA in our cells. We discussed how people inherit genes from their parents and how variations in those genes (alleles) can produce different expressions of traits. We also focused on how the basic principles of inheritance are related to evolutionary change.

In this chapter, we'll continue to deal with topics that directly relate to genetics, namely, biological diversity in humans and how humans adapt physically to environmental challenges. After discussing historical attempts to explain human phenotypic variation and racial classification, we'll examine contemporary methods of interpreting diversity. In recent years, several new techniques have emerged that permit direct examination of the DNA molecule, revealing differences among people even at the level of single nucleotides. But as discoveries of different levels of diversity emerge, geneticists have also shown that our species is remarkably uniform genetically, particularly when compared with other species.

Historical Views of Human Variation

The first step toward understanding diversity in nature is to organize it into categories that can then be named, discussed, and perhaps studied. Historically, when different groups of people came into contact with each other, they tried to account for the physical differences they saw. Because skin color was so noticeable, it was one of the more frequently explained characteristics, and most systems of racial classification were based on it.

As early as 1350 B.C., the ancient Egyptians had classified humans based on their skin color: red for Egyptian, yellow for people to the east, white for those to the north, and black for sub-Saharan Africans (Gossett, 1963). In the sixteenth century, after the discovery of the New World, several European countries embarked on a period of intense exploration and colonization in both the New and Old Worlds. One result of this contact was an increased awareness of human diversity.

Throughout the eighteenth and nineteenth centuries, European and American scientists concentrated on describing and classifying biological variation in humans and also in nonhuman species. The first scientific attempt to describe the newly discovered variation among human populations was Linnaeus' taxonomic classification (see p. 28), which placed humans into four separate categories (Linnaeus, 1758). Linnaeus assigned behavioral and intellectual qualities to each group, with the least complimentary descriptions going to sub-Saharan Africans. This ranking system was typical of the period and reflected the almost universal European view that Europeans were superior to everyone else.

Johann Friedrich Blumenbach (1752–1840), a German anatomist, classified humans into five races. Although Blumenbach's categories came to be described simply as white, yellow, red, black, and brown, he also used criteria other than skin color. What's more, he emphasized that racial categories based on skin color were arbitrary and that many traits, including skin color, weren't discrete phenomena. Blumenbach pointed out that classifying all humans using such a system would completely omit everyone who didn't fall into a specific category. Blumenbach and others also recognized that traits such as skin color showed overlapping expression between groups.

By the mid-nineteenth century, populations were ranked on a scale based primarily on skin color (along with size and shape of the head), again with sub-Saharan Africans at the bottom. The Europeans themselves were also ranked, so that northern, light-skinned populations were considered superior to their southern, somewhat darker-skinned neighbors in Italy and Greece.

To many Europeans, the fact that non-Europeans weren't Christian suggested that they were "uncivilized" and implied an even more basic inferiority of character and intellect. This view was rooted in a concept called **biological determinism**, which in part holds that there is an association between physical characteristics and such attributes as intelligence, morals, values, abilities, and even social and economic condition. In other words, cultural variations were thought to be *inherited* in the same way that biological variations are. It followed, then, that there are inherent behavioral and cognitive differences between groups and that some groups are by nature superior to others. Unfortunately, many people still hold these views, and following this logic, it's a simple matter to justify the persecution and even enslavement of other peoples simply because their outward appearance differs from what is familiar.

After 1850, biological determinism was a constant theme underlying common thinking as well as scientific research in Europe and the United States. Most people, including such notables as Thomas Jefferson, Georges Cuvier, Benjamin Franklin, Charles Lyell, Abraham Lincoln, Charles Darwin, and Supreme Court justice Oliver Wendell Holmes, held deterministic (and what today we'd call racist) views. Commenting on this usually de-emphasized characteristic of more respected historical figures, the late evolutionary biologist Stephen J. Gould (1981, p. 32) remarked that "all American culture heroes embraced racial attitudes that would embarrass public-school mythmakers."

Francis Galton (1822–1911), Charles Darwin's cousin, shared a growing fear among nineteenth-century Europeans that "civilized society" was being weakened by the

biological determinism The concept that phenomena, including various aspects of behavior (e.g., intelligence, values, morals) are governed by biological (genetic) factors; the inaccurate association of various behavioral attributes with certain biological traits, such as skin color.

A Closer Look
Racial Purity: A False and Dangerous Ideology

During the late nineteenth and early twentieth centuries, a growing sense of nationalism swept Europe and the United States. At the same time, an increased emphasis on racial purity had been coupled with the more dangerous aspects of what's known as biological determinism (see p. 423). The concept of pure races is based, in part, on the notion that in the past, races were composed of people who conformed to idealized types and who were similar in appearance and intellect. According to this concept, over time some variation had been introduced into these pure races through interbreeding with other groups, and increasingly, this type of "contamination" was seen as a threat to be avoided.

In today's terminology, pure races would be said to be genetically homogenous, or to possess little genetic variation. Therefore, everyone would have the same alleles at most of their loci. Actually, we do see this situation in "pure breeds" of domesticated animals and plants, developed deliberately by humans through selective breeding. We also see many of the detrimental consequences of such genetic uniformity in various congenital abnormalities, such as hip dysplasia in some breeds of dogs.

With our current understanding of genetic principles, we're able to appreciate the potentially negative outcomes of matings between genetically similar individuals. For example, we know that inbreeding increases the likelihood of offspring who are homozygous for certain deleterious recessive alleles. We also know that decreased genetic variation in a species diminishes the potential for natural selection to act, thus compromising that species' ability to adapt to certain environmental fluctuations. What's more, in genetically uniform populations, individual fertility can be seriously reduced, potentially with disastrous consequences for the entire species. So, even if pure human races did exist at one time (and they didn't), theirs would not have been a genetically desirable condition, and they most certainly would have been at an evolutionary disadvantage.

In northern Europe, particularly Germany, and in the United States, racial superiority was increasingly embodied in the so-called Aryan race. *Aryan* is a term that's still widely used, albeit erroneously, with biological connotations. Actually, Aryan doesn't refer to a biological population, as most people who use the term intend it. Rather, it's a linguistic term that refers to an ancient language group that was ancestral to the Indo-European family of languages, and it's the word from which the name Iran is derived.

By the early twentieth century, the "Aryans" had been transformed into a mythical super race of people whose noble traits were embodied in an extremely idealized "Nordic type." The true Aryan was held to be tall, blond, blue-eyed, strong, industrious, and "pure in spirit." Nordics were extolled as the developers of all ancient "high" civilizations and as the founders of modern industrialized nations. (It would appear that the ancient cultures of the Indus Valley, China, Arabia, Mexico, Greece, and Rome were unknown.) In Europe, there was growing emphasis on the superiority of northwestern Europeans as the modern representatives of "true Nordic stock," while southern and eastern Europeans were viewed as inferior.

eugenics The philosophy of "race improvement" through the forced sterilization of members of some groups and increased reproduction among others; an overly simplified, often racist view that's now discredited.

failure of natural selection to completely eliminate unfit and inferior members (Greene, 1981, p. 107). Galton wrote and lectured on the necessity of "race improvement" and suggested government regulation of marriage and family size, an approach he called **eugenics**. Although eugenics had its share of critics, its popularity flourished throughout the 1930s. Nowhere was it more attractive than in Germany, where the viewpoint took a horrifying turn. The false idea of pure races was increasingly extolled as a means of reestablishing a strong and prosperous state. Eugenics was seen as scientific justification for purging Germany of its "unfit," and many of Germany's scientists continued to support the policies of racial purity and eugenics during the Nazi period (Proctor, 1988, p. 143), when these policies served as justification for condemning millions of people to death.

But at the same time, many scientists were turning away from racial typologies and classification in favor of a more evolutionary approach. No doubt for some, this shift in direction was motivated by their growing concerns over the goals of the eugenics movement. Probably more important, however, was the synthesis of

In the United States, there prevailed the strongly held opinion that America was originally settled by Christian Nordics. Before about 1890, most newcomers to the United States had come from Germany, Scandinavia, Great Britain, and Ireland. But by the 1890s, the pattern of immigration had changed. The arrival of increasing numbers of Italians, Turks, Greeks, and Jews among the thousands of newcomers raised fears that society was being contaminated by immigration from southern and eastern Europe.

Also, in the United States, there were concerns about the large population of former slaves and their descendants. As African Americans left the South to work in the factories of the North, many unskilled white workers felt economically threatened by competition. It was no coincidence that the Ku Klux Klan, which had been inactive for some years, was revived in 1915 and by the 1920s was preaching vehement opposition to African Americans, Jews, and Catholics in support of the supremacy of the white, Protestant "Nordic race." These sentiments were widespread in the general population, although they didn't always take the extreme form advocated by the Klan. One result of these views was the Immigration Restriction Act of 1924, which was aimed at curtailing the immigration of non-Nordics, including Italians, Jews, and eastern Europeans, in order to preserve "America's Nordic heritage."

To avoid the further "decline of the superior race," many states practiced policies of racial segregation until the mid-1950s. Particularly in the South, segregation laws resulted in an almost total separation of whites and blacks, except where blacks were employed as servants or laborers. There were also laws against marriage between whites and blacks in over half the states, and unions between whites and Asians were frequently illegal. In several states, marriage between whites and blacks was punishable as either a misdemeanor or a felony, and astonishingly, some of these laws weren't repealed until the late 1950s or early 1960s. Likewise, in Germany by 1935, the newly instituted Nuremberg Laws forbade marriage or sexual intercourse between so-called Aryan Germans and Jews.

The fact that belief in racial purity and superiority led ultimately to the Nazi death camps in World War II is undisputed (except for continuing efforts by certain white supremacist and neo-Nazi organizations). It's one of the great tragedies of the twentieth century that some of history's most glaring examples of discrimination and brutality were perpetrated by people who believed their actions to be based in scientific principles. In reality, there's absolutely no evidence to suggest that "pure" human races ever existed. Indeed, such an idea flies in the face of everything we know about natural selection, recombination, and gene flow. The degree of genetic uniformity throughout our species (compared to some other species), as evidenced by mounting data from mitochondrial and nuclear DNA analysis, argues strongly that there has always been gene flow between human populations and that genetically homogenous races are nothing more than fabrication.

genetics and Darwin's theories of natural selection during the 1930s. As discussed in Chapter 4, this breakthrough influenced all the biological sciences, and some physical anthropologists soon began applying evolutionary principles to the study of human variation.

The Concept of Race

All contemporary humans are members of the same **polytypic** species, *Homo sapiens*. A polytypic species is composed of local populations that differ in the expression of one or more traits. Even *within* local populations, there's a great deal of genotypic and phenotypic variation between individuals.

In discussions of human variation, people have traditionally clumped together various characteristics, such as skin color, face shape, nose shape, hair color, hair form (curly or straight), and eye color. People who have particular combinations

polytypic Referring to species composed of populations that differ in the expression of one or more traits.

of these and other traits have been placed together in categories associated with specific geographical localities. Such categories are called *races*.

We all think we know what we mean by the word *race*, but in reality, the term has had various meanings since the 1500s, when it first appeared in the English language. Race has been used synonymously with *species*, as in "the human race." Since the 1600s, race has also referred to various culturally defined groups, and this meaning is still common. For example, you'll hear people say, "the English race" or "the Japanese race," when they actually mean nationality. Another phrase you've probably heard is "the Jewish race," when the speaker is really talking about a particular ethnic and religious identity.

So, even though *race* is usually a term with biological connotations, it also has enormous social significance. And there's still a widespread perception that certain physical traits (skin color, in particular) are associated with numerous cultural attributes (such as occupational preferences or even morality). As a result, in many cultural contexts a person's social identity is strongly influenced by the way he or she expresses those physical traits traditionally used to define "racial groups." Characteristics such as skin color are highly visible, and they make it easy to immediately and superficially place people into socially defined categories. However, so-called racial traits aren't the only phenotypic expressions that contribute to social identity. Sex and age are also critically important. But aside from these two variables, an individual's biological and/or ethnic background is still inevitably a factor that influences how he or she is initially perceived and judged by others.

References to national origin (for example, African, Asian) as substitutes for racial labels have become more common in recent years, both within and outside anthropology. Within anthropology, the term *ethnicity* was proposed in the early 1950s to avoid the more emotionally charged term *race*. Strictly speaking, ethnicity refers to cultural factors, but the fact that the words *ethnicity* and *race* are used interchangeably reflects the social importance of phenotypic expression and demonstrates once again how phenotype is mistakenly associated with culturally defined variables.

In its most common biological usage, the term *race* refers to geographically patterned phenotypic variation within a species. By the seventeenth century, naturalists were beginning to describe races in plants and nonhuman animals. They had recognized that when populations of a species occupied different regions, they sometimes differed from one another in the expression of one or more traits. But even today, there are no established criteria for assessing races of plants and animals, including humans.

Before World War II, most studies of human variation focused on visible phenotypic variation between large, geographically defined populations, and these studies were largely descriptive. But in the last 60 years or so, the emphasis has shifted to examining the differences in allele frequencies within and between populations, as well as considering the adaptive significance of phenotypic and genotypic variation. This shift in focus occurred partly because of the Modern Synthesis in biology and partly because of further advances in genetics.

In the twenty-first century, the application of evolutionary principles to the study of modern human variation has replaced the superficial nineteenth-century view of *race based solely on observed phenotype*. Additionally, the genetic emphasis has dispelled previously held misconceptions that races are fixed biological entities that don't change over time and that are composed of individuals who all conform to a particular *type*.

Clearly, there are visible phenotypic differences between humans, and some of these differences roughly correspond to particular geographical locations. But we need to ask if there's any adaptive significance attached to these differences. Is genetic drift a factor? What is the degree of underlying genetic variation that influences phenotypic variation? These questions place considerations of human variation within a contemporary evolutionary framework.

Although, as a discipline, physical anthropology is rooted in attempts to explain human diversity, no contemporary scholar subscribes to pre–Modern Synthesis concepts of races (human or nonhuman) as fixed biological entities. Also, anthropologists recognize that race isn't a valid concept, especially from a genetic perspective, because the amount of genetic variation accounted for by differences *between* groups is vastly exceeded by the variation that exists *within* groups. Many physical anthropologists also argue that race is an outdated creation of the human mind that attempts to simplify biological complexity by organizing it into categories. So, human races are a product of the human tendency to impose order on complex natural phenomena. In this view, simplistic classification may have been an acceptable approach 100 years ago, but given the current state of genetic and evolutionary science, it's meaningless.

However, even though racial categories based on outwardly expressed variations are invalid, many biological anthropologists continue to study differences in such traits as skin or eye color because these characteristics, and the genes that influence them, can yield information about population adaptation, genetic drift, mutation, and gene flow. Forensic anthropologists, in particular, find the phenotypic criteria associated with race (especially in the skeleton) to have practical applications. Law enforcement agencies frequently call on these scientists to help identify human skeletal remains. Because unidentified human remains are often those of crime victims, identification must be as accurate as possible. The most important variables in such identification are the individual's sex, age, stature, and ancestry ("racial" and ethnic background). Using metric and nonmetric criteria, forensic anthropologists employ various techniques for establishing broad population affinity (that is, a likely relationship) for that individual, and their findings are accurate about 80 percent of the time.

Some people also object to racial taxonomies because traditional classification schemes are *typological*, meaning that categories are distinct and based on stereotypes or ideals that comprise a specific set of traits. So in general, typologies are inherently misleading because any grouping always includes many individuals who don't conform to all aspects of a particular type. In any so-called racial group, there are individuals who fall into the normal range of variation for another group based on one or several characteristics. For example, two people of different ancestry might differ in skin color, but they could share any number of other traits, including height, shape of head, hair color, eye color, and ABO blood type. In fact, they could easily share more similarities with each other than they do with many members of their own populations (Fig. 15-1).

To blur this picture further, the characteristics that have traditionally been used to define races are *polygenic;* that is, they're influenced by more than one gene and therefore exhibit a continuous range of expression. So it's difficult, if not impossible, to draw distinct boundaries between populations with regard to many traits. This limitation becomes clear if you ask yourself, At what point is hair color no longer dark brown but medium brown, or no longer light brown but dark blond? (Look back at Fig. 4-15, p. 94, for an illustration showing variability in eye color.)

Figure 15-1

Some examples of phenotypic variation among Africans. (a) San (South African). (b) West African (Bantu). (c) Ethiopian. (d) Ituri (Central African). (e) North African (Tunisia).

(a)

(b)

(c)

(d)

(e)

The scientific controversy over race will fade as we increase our understanding of the genetic diversity (and uniformity) of our species. Given the rapid changes in genome studies, and because very few genes actually contribute to outward expressions of phenotype, dividing the human species into racial categories isn't a biologically meaningful way to look at human variation. But among the general public, variations on the theme of race will undoubtedly continue to be the most common view of human biological and cultural variation. Keeping all this in mind, it's up to anthropologists and biologists to continue exploring the issue so that, to the best of our abilities, accurate information about human variation is available to anyone who seeks informed explanations of complex phenomena.

Racism

Racism is based on the previously mentioned false belief that along with our physical characteristics, humans inherit such factors as intellect and various cultural attributes. Such beliefs also commonly rest on the assumption that one's own group is superior to other groups.

Since we've already alluded to certain aspects of racism, such as the eugenics movement and persecution of people based on racial or ethnic misconceptions, we won't belabor the point here. Even though enormous progress has been made, racism is hardly a thing of the past, and it's not restricted to Europeans and

Americans of European descent (Fig. 15-2). Racism is a cultural phenomenon, and it's found worldwide.

We end this brief discussion of racism with an excerpt from an article, "The Study of Race," by the late Sherwood Washburn, a well-known physical anthropologist who taught at the University of California, Berkeley. Although written many years ago, the statement is as fresh and applicable today as it was then:

> Races are products of the past. They are relics of times and conditions which have long ceased to exist. Racism is equally a relic supported by no phase of modern science. We may not know how to interpret the form of the Mongoloid face, or why Rh is of high incidence in Africa, but we do know the benefits of education and of economic progress. We know that the roots of happiness lie in the biology of the whole species and that the potential of the species can only be realized in a culture, in a social system. It is knowledge and the social system which give life or take it away, and in so doing change the gene frequencies and continue the million-year-old interaction of culture and biology. Human biology finds its realization in a culturally determined way of life, and the infinite variety of genetic combinations can only express themselves efficiently in a free and open society. (Washburn, 1963, p. 531)

Figure 15-2

Barack Obama and his family after he was elected president of the United States November 4, 2008. The significance of electing the first African American president cannot be overstated. It was a watershed event that powerfully signalled a monumental shift in attitudes toward race in the United States.

Intelligence

As we've shown, belief in the relationship between physical characteristics and specific behavioral attributes is common even today, but there's no scientific evidence to show that personality or any other behavioral trait differs genetically between human populations. Most scientists would agree with this last statement, but one question that produces controversy inside scientific circles and among the general public is whether population affinity and intelligence are associated.

Genetic and environmental factors contribute to intelligence, although it's not possible to accurately measure the percentage each contributes. What can be said is that IQ scores and intelligence aren't the same thing. IQ scores, which result from standardized testing, can change during a person's lifetime, and average IQ scores of different populations overlap. Such differences in average IQ scores that do exist between groups are difficult to interpret, given the problems inherent in the design of the IQ tests. What's more, complex cognitive abilities, however they're measured, are influenced by multiple loci and are therefore polygenic.

Innate factors set limits and define potentials for behavior and cognitive ability in any species. In humans, the limits are broad and the potentials aren't fully known. Individual abilities result from complex interactions between genetic and environmental factors. One product of this interaction is learning, and the ability to learn is influenced by genetic and other biological components. Undeniably, there are differences between individuals regarding these biological components. It's probably impossible, though, to determine what proportion of the variation in test scores is due to biological factors. Besides, innate differences in abilities reflect individual variation *within* populations, not inherent differences *between* groups. Comparing populations based on the results of IQ tests is a complete misuse of testing procedures. There's no convincing evidence

whatsoever that populations vary with regard to cognitive abilities, regardless of what some popular books may suggest. Unfortunately, racist attitudes toward intelligence continue to flourish, despite the questionable validity of intelligence tests and the complete lack of evidence of mental inferiority of some populations and mental superiority of others.

Contemporary Interpretations of Human Variation

Because the physical characteristics (such as skin color and hair form) that are used to define race are *polygenic,* precisely measuring the genetic influence on them hasn't been possible (although geneticists are getting closer; see p. 93). Physical anthropologists and other biologists who study modern human variation have largely abandoned the traditional perspective of describing superficial phenotypic characteristics in favor of examining differences in various allele frequencies.

Beginning in the 1950s, studies of modern human variation focused on the various components of blood as well as other aspects of body chemistry. Such traits as the ABO blood types are phenotypes, but they're also direct products of the genotype. (Recall that protein-coding genes direct cells to make proteins, and the antigens on blood cells and many constituents of blood serum are partly composed of proteins; Fig.15-3.) During the twentieth century, this perspective met with a great deal of success, as eventually dozens of loci were identified and the frequencies of many specific alleles were obtained from numerous human populations. Even so, in all these cases, it was the phenotype that was observed, and information about the underlying genotype remained largely unobtainable. But beginning in the 1990s, with the advent of genomic studies, new techniques were developed. Now that we can directly sequence DNA, we can actually identify entire genes and even larger DNA segments and make comparisons between individuals and populations. A decade ago, only a small portion of the human genome was accessible to physical anthropologists, but now we have the capacity to obtain DNA profiles for virtually every human population on earth. And we can expect that in the next decade, our understanding and knowledge of human biological variation and adaptation will dramatically increase.

Figure **15-3**

Blood typing. (a) A blood sample is drawn. (b) To determine an individual's blood type, a few drops of blood are treated with specific chemicals. Presence of A and B blood type, as well as Rh, can be detected by using commercially available chemicals. The glass slides below the blue- and yellow-labeled bottles show reactions for the ABO system. The blood on the top slide (at left) is type AB; the middle is type B; and the bottom is type A. The two samples to the right depict Rh-negative blood (top) and Rh-positive blood (bottom).

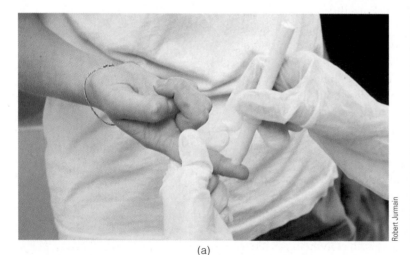

(a)

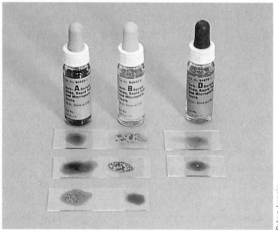

(b)

Robert Jurmain

Robert Jurmain

Human Polymorphisms

Traits that differ in expression between populations and individuals are called **polymorphisms**, and they're the main focus of human variation studies. A genetic trait is *polymorphic* if the locus that governs it has two or more alleles. (Refer to p. 87 for a discussion of the ABO blood group system governed by three alleles at one locus.)

Understanding polymorphisms requires evolutionary explanations, and geneticists use polymorphisms as a principal tool to understand evolutionary processes in modern populations. By using these polymorphisms to compare allele frequencies between different populations, we can begin to reconstruct the evolutionary events that link human populations with one another.

By the 1960s, the study of *clinal distributions* of individual polymorphisms had become a popular alternative to the racial approach to human diversity. A **cline** is a gradual change in the frequency of a trait or allele in populations dispersed over geographical space. In humans, the various expressions of many polymorphic characteristics exhibit a more or less continuous distribution from one region to another, and most traits that show a clinal distribution are Mendelian. The distribution of the B allele in the Old World provides a good example of a clinal distribution (Fig. 15-4). Since clinal distributions are generally thought to reflect microevolutionary influences of natural selection and/or gene flow, they're explained in evolutionary terms.

The ABO system is interesting from an anthropological perspective because the frequencies of the *A*, *B*, and *O* alleles vary tremendously among humans. In most groups, *A* and *B* are rarely found in frequencies greater than 50 percent, and usually their frequencies are much lower. Still, most human groups are polymorphic for all three alleles, but there are exceptions. For example, in native South

polymorphisms Loci with more than one allele. Polymorphisms can be expressed in the phenotype as the result of gene action (as in ABO), or they can exist solely at the DNA level within noncoding regions.

cline A gradual change in the frequency of genotypes and phenotypes from one geographical region to another.

Figure 15-4

ABO blood group system. Distribution of the B allele in the indigenous populations of the world. (After Mourant et al., 1976.)

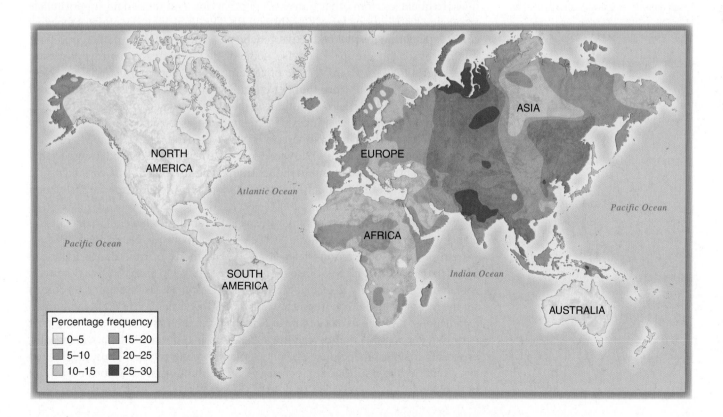

Percentage frequency
0–5	15–20
5–10	20–25
10–15	25–30

© Peter Turnley/Corbis

Figure 15-5

People in Sardinia, a large island off the west coast of Italy, differ from other European populations in allele frequencies at some loci.

American Indians, frequencies of the *O* allele reach 100 percent. Exceptionally high frequencies of *O* are also found in northern Australia, and some islands off the Australian coast show frequencies exceeding 90 percent. In these populations, the high frequencies of the *O* allele are probably due to genetic drift (founder effect), although the influence of natural selection can't be entirely ruled out.

Besides ABO, there are many other red blood cell phenotypes, each under the control of a different genetic locus. These include the well-known Rh blood group as well as the less familiar Duffy and MN blood groups. Some antigens on white blood cells are also polymorphic. Called human leukocyte antigens (HLA) in humans, these are crucial to the immune response because they allow the body to recognize and resist potentially dangerous infections. But unlike simple polymorphisms such as ABO (one locus with three alleles) or MN (one locus with only two alleles), the HLA system is governed by perhaps hundreds of alleles at six different loci. Therefore, the HLA system is by far the most polymorphic genetic system known in humans (Knapp, 2002).

Because there are so many HLA alleles, they're useful in showing patterns of human population diversity. For example, Lapps, Sardinians, and Basques differ in allele frequencies from other European populations, and these data support allele frequency distributions for ABO, MN, and Rh (Fig. 15-5). Founder effect is the most likely explanation for the distinctive genetic patterning in these smaller, traditionally more isolated groups. Likewise, some of the atypical frequencies of certain HLA alleles that are characteristic of certain populations in Australia and New Guinea probably result from founder effect. Natural selection also has influenced the evolution of HLA alleles in humans, especially as related to infectious disease. For example, certain HLA antigens appear to be associated with resistance to malaria and hepatitis B and perhaps to HIV as well. And finally, one physiological and evolutionary influence of HLA concerns male fertility. Recent data suggest that some HLA antigens are found in higher frequencies in infertile males, suggesting that there may be some influence of two or more HLA loci on sperm production and function (van der Ven et al., 2000).

Another well-studied polymorphism is the ability to taste an artificial substance called phenylthiocarbamide (PTC). While many people perceive PTC as extremely bitter, others don't taste it at all. The mode of inheritance follows a Mendelian pattern, with two alleles (*T* and *t*). The ability to taste PTC is a dominant trait, while the inability to taste it is recessive. So, "nontasters" are homozygous (*tt*) for the recessive allele. The frequency of PTC tasting varies considerably in human populations, and the evolutionary explanation for the patterns of variation isn't clear. But it's possible that perceiving substances as bitter could be advantageous, especially in children, because poisonous plants are often bitter. Thus, heightened sensitivity to bitter substances increases the likelihood that toxic substances will be avoided.

Patterns of Polymorphic Variation

Examining single traits can give us information about potential influences of natural selection or gene flow. But this approach is limited when we try to sort out relationships between populations. Studying single traits, by themselves, can yield confusing interpretations; studying several traits simultaneously is a more meaningful approach.

An early example of this approach to human diversity was undertaken by Harvard population geneticist R. D. Lewontin (1972). Lewontin calculated population differences in allele frequency for 17 polymorphic characteristics. To do this, he divided his sample into seven geographical areas and included several population samples within each region (Table 15-1). These large geographical population groupings are roughly equivalent to traditional definitions of major (geographical) races, and Lewontin examined the genetic differences both among individuals within a particular group and between different populations. Next he calculated how much of the total genetic variability within our species could be accounted for by these large population subdivisions, and the results were surprising. Only 6.3 percent of the total genetic variation was explained by differences between major population groups (Lewontin's seven geographical units). In other words, close to 94 percent of human genetic diversity occurs *within* these groups, not between them. This means that most of the genetic differences among human beings can be explained in terms of differences from one village to another, one family to another, and, to a significant degree, one person to another, even within the same family. More recent data from genome studies even more strongly reinforce these findings. Indeed, the protein-coding DNA sequences in all humans, regardless of where their ancestors are from, are about 99 percent identical (Stix, 2008)*. In fact, humans are much more genetically uniform than are our closest ape cousins.

As you can see, and as we mentioned earlier, the visible traits most often used to make racial distinctions (skin color, hair form, nose shape, and so on) don't provide an accurate picture of the actual pattern of genetic variation. Simple polymorphic traits provide a more objective basis for accurate biological comparisons of human groups. Indeed, Lewontin concluded his analysis with a ringing

Table **15-1 Population Groupings Used by Lewontin in Population Genetics Study (1972)**

Geographic Group	Examples of Populations Included
Caucasians	Arabs, Armenians, Tristan da Cunhans
Black Africans	Bantu, San, U.S. blacks
Asians	Ainu, Chinese, Turks
South Asians	Andamanese, Tamils
Amerinds	Aleuts, Navaho, Yanomama
Oceanians	Easter Islanders, Micronesians
Australians	All treated as a single group

* For the noncoding portions of DNA, humans show considerably more variability between individuals than is found for coding regions.

condemnation of traditional studies: "Human racial classification is of no social value and is positively destructive of social and human relations. Since such racial classification is now seen to be of virtually no genetic or taxonomic significance either, no justification can be offered for its continuance" (Lewontin, 1972, p. 397).

Polymorphisms at the DNA Level

The Human Genome Project has provided considerable insight regarding human variation at the DNA level, and molecular biologists have discovered many previously unknown variations in the human genome. For example, there are hundreds of sites where DNA segments are repeated, in some cases just a few times and in other cases hundreds of times. Segments that are repeated only a few times are called *microsatellites*, and they vary tremendously from person to person. In fact, every person has their own unique arrangement that defines their distinctive "DNA fingerprint."

Researchers are expanding their approach to map patterns of variation for individual nucleotides. As you know, point mutations have been recognized for some time. But what's only been recently appreciated is that such single-nucleotide changes also frequently occur in *noncoding* portions of DNA. These point mutations, together with those in coding regions of DNA, are all referred to as *single-nucleotide polymorphisms (SNPs)*. Already, about 3 million SNPs have been recognized. SNPs are dispersed throughout the human genome (96 percent of them are in noncoding DNA), and they're extraordinarily variable (International SNP Map Working Group, 2001). So, at the beginning of the twenty-first century, geneticists have gained access to a vast biological "library" that documents the genetic history of our species.

The field of **population genetics** is taking advantage of these new discoveries. While traditional polymorphic traits, such as ABO, are still being studied, researchers are directing more and more attention to the remarkably variable DNA polymorphisms. These molecular applications are now being widely used to evaluate human variation at a microevolutionary level, and this information provides far more accurate measures of within-group and between-group variation than was previously possible. Besides that, we can now use the vast amount of new data to more fully understand very recent events in human population history, including the many roles of natural selection, genetic drift, gene flow, and mutation. As an example of how far the study of human variation has moved toward a molecularly based approach, more than 95 percent of the papers presented at a recent anthropology conference on population variation concerned DNA polymorphisms in populations from all over the world.

The most recent and most comprehensive population data regarding worldwide patterns of variation come from analysis of extremely large portions of DNA, in what are called "whole-genome" analyses. Two recent studies used newly compiled molecular information for the entire genome of over 900 individuals from widely distributed modern populations. One analysis investigated the population patterning shown in 650,000 SNPs in 51 populations (Li et al., 2008). The other focused on more than 500,000 SNPs in 29 populations (Jakobsson et al., 2008). Just goes to show what you can do with computers!

The results of these new studies are highly significant because they confirm earlier findings from more restricted molecular data and they provide new insights. The higher degree of genetic variation seen in African populations as compared to any other geographical group was once again clearly seen. All human populations outside Africa have much less genetic variation than is seen in Africa. These

population genetics The study of the frequency of alleles, genotypes, and phenotypes in populations from a microevolutionary perspective.

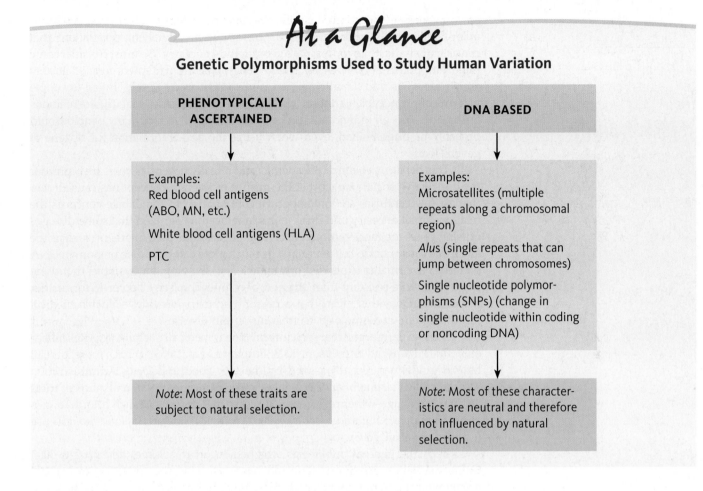

At a Glance

Genetic Polymorphisms Used to Study Human Variation

PHENOTYPICALLY ASCERTAINED

Examples:
Red blood cell antigens (ABO, MN, etc.)

White blood cell antigens (HLA)

PTC

Note: Most of these traits are subject to natural selection.

DNA BASED

Examples:
Microsatellites (multiple repeats along a chromosomal region)

Alus (single repeats that can jump between chromosomes)

Single nucleotide polymorphisms (SNPs) (change in single nucleotide within coding or noncoding DNA)

Note: Most of these characteristics are neutral and therefore not influenced by natural selection.

findings further verify the earlier genetic studies (as well as fossil discoveries) that suggest a fairly recent African origin of all modern humans (as discussed in Chapter 14). Moreover, these new data also shed light on the genetic relationships between populations worldwide and the nature of human migrations out of Africa. They also provide evidence of the role of genetic drift (founder effect) in recent human evolution as successively smaller populations split off from larger ones (see "New Frontiers in Research," pp. 447–448). Finally, preliminary results suggest that the patterning of human variation at the global level may help scientists identify genetic risk factors that influence how susceptible different populations are to various diseases. Specifically, the relative genetic uniformity in non-African populations (for example, European Americans) as compared to those of more recent African descent (for example, African Americans) exposes them to a greater risk of developing disease (Lohmueller et al., 2008). How such information might be put to use, however, is controversial.

All these genetic data, including the more traditional polymorphisms (such as blood groups) and the vast new DNA-based evidence, point in the same direction: Genetically, humans differ individually within populations far more than large geographical groups ("races") differ from each other. Does this mean, as Richard Lewontin suggested more than 30 years ago (see p. 433), that there's no biological value in further study and scientific understanding of geographical populations? Even with all our new information, the answer isn't entirely clear. Some of the

newest genetic evidence from patterns of *Alu* segments (Bamshad et al., 2003) and microsatellites (Rosenberg et al., 2002) has found broad genetic correlations that consistently indicate an individual's geographical ancestry. We must consider some important points here, however. These geographically patterned genetic clusters aren't "races" as traditionally defined, and so they aren't closely linked to simple patterns of phenotypic variation (such as skin color). Besides that, the correlations are broad, so not all individuals can be easily classified. In fact, many people would probably be misclassified, even when using the best information for dozens of genetic loci.

This debate isn't entirely academic, and it really never has been. Just consider the destructive social impact that the misuse of the race concept has caused over the last few centuries. A contemporary continuation of the debate concerns the relationship of ancestry and disease. It's long been recognized that some disease-causing genes are more common in certain populations than in others (such as the allele that causes sickle-cell anemia). The much more complete data on human DNA patterns have further expanded our knowledge, showing, for example, that some people are more resistant than others to HIV infection (see Chapter 16 for further discussion). Does this mean that a person's ancestry provides valuable medical information in screening or even treating certain diseases?

Some experts argue that such information is medically helpful (e.g., Rosenberg et al., 2002; Bamshad and Olson, 2003; Burchard et al., 2003). What's more, official federal guidelines recently issued by the U.S. Food and Drug Administration recommend collection of ancestry data ("race/ethnic identity") in all clinical trials testing new drugs. Other researchers disagree and argue that such information is at best tenuous (King and Motulsky, 2002) or that it has no obvious medical use (e.g., Cooper et al., 2003).

Even the general public has weighed in on this issue, defeating a 2003 California ballot measure that would have restricted the collection of "racial" (ethnic) information on medical records. There are no easy answers to the questions we've raised, and this is an even stronger argument for an informed public. The subject of race has been contentious, and anthropology and other disciplines have struggled to come to grips with it. Our new genetic tools have allowed us to expand our knowledge at a rate far beyond anything seen previously. But increased information alone doesn't permit us to fully address all human concerns. How we address diversity, individually and collectively, must balance the potential scientific benefits against a history of social costs.

Population Genetics

As we defined it in Chapter 4, a *population* is a group of interbreeding individuals. More precisely, a population is the group within which an individual is most likely to find a mate. As such, a population is marked by a degree of genetic relatedness and shares a common **gene pool**.

In theory, this is a straightforward concept. In every generation, the genes (alleles) are mixed by recombination and rejoined through mating. What emerges in the next generation is a direct product of the genes going into the pool, which in turn is a product of who is mating with whom.

In practice, however, describing human populations is difficult. The largest human population that can be described is our entire species. All members of a

gene pool The total complement of genes shared by the reproductive members of a population.

species are *potentially* capable of interbreeding, but are incapable of producing fertile offspring with members of other species. Our species, like any other, is thus a *genetically closed system*. The problem arises not in describing who can potentially mate with whom, but in determining the exact pattern of those individuals who are doing so.

Factors that determine mate choice are geographical, ecological, and social. If individuals are isolated on a remote island in the middle of the Pacific Ocean, there isn't much chance that they'll find a mate outside the immediate vicinity. Such **breeding isolates** are fairly easily defined and are a favorite focus of microevolutionary studies. Geography plays a dominant role in producing these isolates by severely limiting the range of available mates. But even within these limits, cultural rules can easily play a deciding role by stipulating who is most appropriate among those who are potentially available.

Human population segments are defined as groups with relative degrees of **endogamy** (marrying/mating within the group). But these aren't totally closed systems. Gene flow often occurs between groups, and individuals may choose mates from distant locations. With the advent of modern transportation, the rate of **exogamy** (marrying/mating outside the group) has dramatically increased.

Today, most humans aren't clearly defined as members of particular populations because they don't belong to a breeding isolate. Inhabitants of large cities may appear to be members of a single population; but within the city, there's a complex system of social, ethnic, and religious boundaries that are crosscut to form smaller population segments. Besides being members of these highly open local population groupings, we're simultaneously members of overlapping gradations of larger populations—the immediate geographical region (a metropolitan area or perhaps an entire state), a section of the country, the entire nation, and ultimately the whole species.

After identifying specific human populations, the next step is to find out what evolutionary forces, if any, are operating on them. To determine whether evolution is taking place at a given genetic locus, we measure allele frequencies for specific traits. We then compare these observed frequencies with those predicted by a mathematical model called the **Hardy-Weinberg theory of genetic equilibrium**. This model gives us a baseline set of evolutionary expectations under known conditions.

The Hardy-Weinberg theory establishes a set of conditions in a hypothetical population where no evolution occurs. In other words, no evolutionary forces are acting, and all genes have an equal chance of recombining in each generation (that is, there's random mating of individuals). More precisely, the conditions that such a population would be *assumed* to meet are as follows:

1. The population is infinitely large. This condition eliminates the possibility of random genetic drift or changes in allele frequencies due to chance.
2. There's no mutation; thus, no new alleles are being added by changes in genes.
3. There's no gene flow; thus, there's no exchange of genes with other populations that could alter allele frequencies.
4. Natural selection isn't operating; thus, specific alleles offer no advantage over others that might influence reproductive success.
5. Mating is random; therefore, there's nothing to influence who mates with whom, and all females are assumed to have an equal chance of mating with any male and vice versa.

breeding isolates Populations that are clearly isolated geographically and/or socially from other breeding groups.

endogamy Mating with individuals from the same group.

exogamy Mating pattern whereby individuals obtain mates from groups other than their own.

Hardy-Weinberg theory of genetic equilibrium The mathematical relationship expressing—under conditions in which no evolution is occurring—the predicted distribution of alleles in populations; the central theorem of population genetics.

If all these conditions are met, allele frequencies won't change from one generation to the next (that is, no evolution will take place), and as long as these conditions prevail, the population maintains a permanent equilibrium. This equilibrium model provides population geneticists a standard against which they can compare actual circumstances. Notice that the idealized conditions defining the Hardy-Weinberg equilibrium are an idealized, hypothetical state. In the real world, no actual population would fully meet any of these conditions. But don't be confused by this distinction. By explicitly defining the allele frequencies that would be expected if no evolutionary change were occurring (that is, in equilibrium), we establish a baseline with which to compare the allele frequencies we actually observe in real human populations.

If the observed frequencies differ from those of the expected model, we can then say that evolution is taking place at the locus in question. The alternative, of course, is that the observed and expected frequencies don't differ enough that we can confidently say that evolution is occurring at a particular locus in a population. In fact, this is often what happens; in such cases, population geneticists aren't able to clearly define evolutionary change at the particular locus under study.

The simplest way to do a microevolutionary study is to use a genetic trait that follows a simple Mendelian pattern and has only two alleles (*A* and *a*). Remember that there are only three possible genotypes: *AA*, *Aa*, and *aa*. Proportions of these genotypes (*AA:Aa:aa*) are a function of the allele frequencies themselves (percentage of *A* and percentage of *a*). To provide uniformity for all genetic loci, a standard notation is employed to refer to these frequencies:

Frequency of dominant allele (*A*) = *p*
Frequency of recessive allele (*a*) = *q*

Since in this case there are only two alleles, their combined total frequency must represent all possibilities. In other words, the sum of their separate frequencies must be 1:

$$p \quad + \quad q \quad = \quad 1 \text{ (100\% of alleles at the locus in question)}$$

(Frequency of *A alleles*)   (Frequency of *a* alleles)

To determine the expected proportions of genotypes, we compute the chances of the alleles combining with one another into all possible combinations. Remember, they all have an equal chance of combining, and no new alleles are being added. These probabilities are a direct function of the frequency of the two alleles. The chances of all possible combinations occurring randomly can be simply shown as

$$
\begin{array}{rcccc}
 & p & + & q & \\
 & p & + & q & \\
\hline
 & pq & + & q^2 & \\
p^2 & + & pq & & \\
\hline
p^2 & + & 2pq & + & q^2
\end{array}
$$

Mathematically, this is known as a binomial expansion and can also be shown as:

$$(p + q)(p + q) = p^2 + 2pq + q^2$$

What we have just calculated is simply:

Allele Combination	Genotype Produced	Expected Proportion in Population
Chances of A combining with A	AA	$p \times p = p^2$
Chances of A combining with a;	Aa	$p \times q =$
a combining with A	aA	$p \times q = {}^{2pq}$
Chances of a combining with a	aa	$q \times q = q^2$

Thus, p^2 is the frequency of the AA genotype, $2pq$ is the frequency of the Aa genotype, and q^2 is the frequency of the aa genotype, where p is the frequency of the dominant allele and q is the frequency of the recessive allele in a population.

Calculating Allele Frequencies

We can best demonstrate how geneticists use the Hardy-Weinberg formula by giving an example. Let's assume that a population contains 200 individuals, and we'll use the MN blood group locus as the gene to be measured. The two alleles of the MN locus produce two antigens (M and N) that are similar to the ABO antigens and are also located on red blood cells. Because the M and N alleles are codominant, we can ascertain everyone's phenotype by taking blood samples and testing them in a process very similar to that for ABO (see Fig. 15-3). From the phenotypes, we can then directly calculate the observed allele frequencies. So let's see what we can determine.

All 200 individuals are tested, and the observed data for the three phenotypes are as follows:

Genotype	Number of individuals*	Percent	Number of Alleles M	N
MM	80	40	160	0
MN	80	40	80	80
NN	40	20	0	80
Totals	200	100	240 + 160 = 400	
		Proportion	.6 + .4 = 1	

From these observed results, we can count the number of M and N alleles and thus calculate the observed allele frequencies:

p = frequency of M = .6

q = frequency of N = .4

The total frequency of the two alleles combined should always equal 1. As you can see, they do.

Next, we need to calculate the expected genotypic proportions. This calculation comes directly from the Hardy-Weinberg equilibrium formula: $p^2 + 2pq + q^2$.

$$p^2 = (.6)(.6) = .36$$
$$2pq = 2(.6)(.4) = 2(.24) = .48$$
$$q^2 = (.4)(.4) = .16$$
Total $\quad$ 1.00

---

*Each individual has two alleles, so a person who's MM contributes two M alleles to the total gene pool. A person who's MN contributes one M and one N. For the MN locus, then, 200 individuals have 400 alleles.

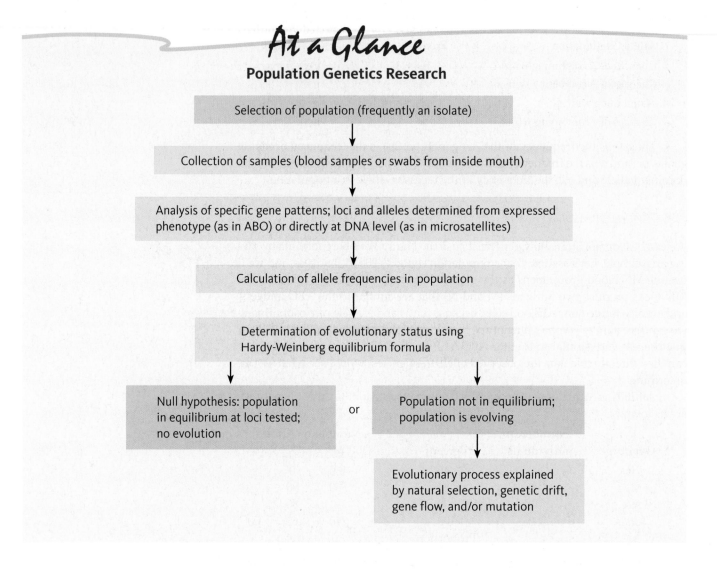

At a Glance

Population Genetics Research

Selection of population (frequently an isolate)

Collection of samples (blood samples or swabs from inside mouth)

Analysis of specific gene patterns; loci and alleles determined from expressed phenotype (as in ABO) or directly at DNA level (as in microsatellites)

Calculation of allele frequencies in population

Determination of evolutionary status using Hardy-Weinberg equilibrium formula

Null hypothesis: population in equilibrium at loci tested; no evolution

or

Population not in equilibrium; population is evolving

Evolutionary process explained by natural selection, genetic drift, gene flow, and/or mutation

There are only three possible genotypes: *MM, MN, NN*. The total of the relative proportions should equal 1. Again, as you can see, they do.

Finally, we need to compare the two sets of data, that is, the observed frequencies (what we actually found in the population) with the expected frequencies (those predicted by Hardy-Weinberg under conditions of genetic equilibrium). How do these two sets of data compare?

	Expected Frequency	Expected Number of Individuals	Observed Frequency	Actual Number of Individuals with Each Genotype
MM	.36	72	.40	80
MN	.48	96	.40	80
NN	.16	32	.20	40

We can see that although the match between observed and expected frequencies isn't perfect, it's close enough statistically to satisfy equilibrium conditions. Since our population isn't a large one, sampling may easily account for the small observed differences. Our population is therefore probably in equilibrium (that is, it's not evolving at this locus).

Of course, the observed allele frequencies do sometimes vary enough from equilibrium predictions to suggest that the population isn't in equilibrium; that is, it's evolving. For example, consider the locus influencing PTC tasting (see p. 432). What makes PTC tasting such a useful characteristic is how easy it is to identify. Unlike blood antigens such as ABO or MN, PTC tasting can be tested by simply having subjects place a thin paper strip on their tongues. This paper contains concentrated PTC, and people either taste it or they don't. So testing is quick, inexpensive, and doesn't involve a blood test. With such an efficient means of screening subjects, we now consider a sample population of 500 individuals. The results from observing the phenotypes and calculations of expected genotypic proportions are shown in "A Closer Look," on page 442. You'll find additional examples of population genetics calculations in Appendix D.

Evolution in Action: Modern Human Populations

Once a population has been defined, it's possible to determine whether allele frequencies are stable (that is, in genetic equilibrium) or changing. As we've seen, the Hardy-Weinberg formula provides the tool to establish whether allele frequencies are indeed changing. But what factors cause changes in allele frequencies? There are a number of factors, including:

1. Production of new variation (that is, mutation)
2. Redistribution of variation through gene flow or genetic drift
3. Selection of "advantageous" allele combinations that promote reproductive success (that is, natural selection)

Notice that factors 1 and 2 constitute the first stage of the evolutionary process, as first emphasized by the Modern Synthesis, while factor 3 is the second stage (see p. 97). There's also another factor, as implied by the condition of genetic equilibrium that under idealized conditions all matings are random. Thus, the evolutionary alteration (that is, deviation from equilibrium) is called **nonrandom mating**.

Nonrandom Mating

Although sexual recombination doesn't itself alter allele frequencies, any consistent bias in mating patterns can change the genotypic proportions. By affecting genotype frequencies, nonrandom mating causes deviations from Hardy-Weinberg expectations of the proportions p^2, $2pq$, and q^2. It therefore sets the stage for the action of other evolutionary factors, particularly natural selection.

A form of nonrandom mating, called assortative mating, occurs when individuals of either similar phenotypes (positive assortative mating) or dissimilar phenotypes (negative assortative mating) mate more often than expected by Hardy-Weinberg predictions. However, in the vast majority of human populations, neither factor appears to have much influence.

Inbreeding is a second type of nonrandom mating, and it can have important medical and evolutionary consequences. Inbreeding occurs when relatives mate more often than expected. Such matings will increase homozygosity, since relatives who share close ancestors will probably also share more alleles than two unrelated people would. When relatives mate, their offspring have an increased

nonrandom mating Pattern of mating in which individuals choose mates preferentially. That is, mate choice is based on different criteria such as social status, ethnicity, or biological relationship. An individual doesn't have an equal chance of mating with all other individuals in their group.

inbreeding A type of nonrandom mating in which relatives mate more often than predicted under random mating conditions.

A Closer Look

Calculating Allele Frequencies: PTC Tasting in a Hypothetical Population

For the PTC tasting trait, it's assumed there are two alleles, *T* and *t*. Also, while dominance is displayed, it's incomplete. So it's theoretically possible to ascertain the phenotypes of heterozygotes. To simplify calculations for this example, we assume that all heterozygotes can be ascertained.

In our population of 500 individuals, we find the following observed phenotypic frequencies:

Genotype	Number of Individuals	Percent	Number of Alleles *T*	*t*
TT	125	25	250	0
Tt	325	65	325	325
tt	50	10	0	100
Totals	500	100	575	425

Thus, the observed allele frequencies are

$T(p) = .575$

$t(q) = .425$

The expected genotypic proportions are

p^2	=	(.575)(.575)	= .33
$2pq$	=	2(.575)(.425)	= .49
q^2	=	(.425)(.425)	= .18

Now we compare the observed and expected genotypic frequencies:

	Expected Frequency	Expected Number of Individuals	Observed Frequency	Actual Number of Individuals with Each Genotype
TT	.33	165	.25	125
Tt	.49	245	.65	325
tt	.18	90	.10	50

These results show considerable departures of the observed genotypic proportions from those predicted under equilibrium conditions. Both types of homozygotes (*TT* and *tt*) are less commonly observed than expected, while the heterozygote (*Tt*) is more common than expected.

A statistical test (called a chi-square) can be performed to test the statistical significance of this difference. The results of this test are shown in Appendix C.

---

probability of inheriting two copies of potentially harmful recessive alleles from a relative (perhaps a grandparent) they share in common. Many potentially deleterious genes that are normally "masked" in heterozygous carriers, may be expressed in homozygous offspring of inbred matings and therefore "exposed" to the action of natural selection. Among offspring of first-cousin matings in the United States, the risk of congenital disorders is 2.3 times greater than it is for the overall population. Matings between especially close relatives (incest) often lead to multiple genetic defects.

All societies have incest taboos that ban matings between close relatives, such as between parent and child or brother and sister. Thus, these matings usually occur less frequently than predicted under random mating conditions. Whether biological factors also interact to inhibit such behavior has long been a topic of debate among anthropologists. For many social, economic, and ecological reasons, exogamy is an advantageous strategy for hunting and gathering bands. Selective pressures may also play a part, since highly inbred offspring have a greater chance of expressing a recessive genetic disorder and thereby lowering their reproductive fitness. What's more, inbreeding reduces genetic variability among offspring, potentially reducing reproductive success (Murray, 1980). In this regard, it's interesting to note that **incest avoidance** is widespread among

incest avoidance   In animals, the tendency not to mate with close relatives. This tendency may be due to various social and ecological factors that keep the individuals apart. There may also be innate factors that lead to incest avoidance but these aren't well understood.

vertebrates. Detailed studies of free-ranging chimpanzees indicate that they usually avoid incestuous matings within their family group, although exceptions do occur (Constable et al., 2001). In fact, in most primate species, adults of one sex consistently find mates from groups other than the one in which they were reared (see p. 205). As we've seen, recognition of close kin apparently is an ability displayed by several (perhaps all) primates. Primatologists are currently investigating this aspect of our primate cousins. Apparently, both biological factors (in common with other primates) and uniquely human cultural factors have interacted during hominin evolution to produce this universal behavior pattern among contemporary societies.

Human Biocultural Evolution

We've defined *culture* as the human strategy of adaptation. Human beings live in cultural environments that are continually modified by human activity; thus, evolutionary processes are understandable only within this cultural context. We've discussed at length how natural selection operates within specific environmental settings. For humans and many of our hominin ancestors, this means an environment dominated by culture. For example, the sickle-cell allele hasn't always been an important genetic factor in human populations. Before the development of agriculture, humans rarely, if ever, lived close to mosquito-breeding areas. With the spread in Africa of **slash-and-burn agriculture**, perhaps in just the last 2,000 years, penetration and clearing of tropical rain forests occurred. This deforestation created open, stagnant pools that provided prime mosquito-breeding areas in close proximity to human settlements. DNA analyses have further confirmed such a recent origin and spread of the sickle-cell allele in West Africa. A recent study of a population from Senegal has estimated the origin of the Hb^S mutation in this group at between 2,100 and 1,250 ya (Currat et al., 2002).

So quite recently, and for the first time, malaria struck human populations with its full impact; and it became a powerful selective force. No doubt, humans attempted to adjust culturally to these circumstances, and many biological adaptations also probably came into play. The sickle-cell trait is one of these biological adaptations. But there's a definite cost involved with such an adaptation. Carriers have increased resistance to malaria and presumably higher reproductive success, though some of their offspring may be lost through the genetic disease sickle-cell anemia. So there's a counterbalancing of selective forces with an advantage for carriers only in malarial environments. (The genetic patterns of recessive traits such as sickle-cell anemia were discussed in Chapter 4.)

Following World War II, extensive DDT spraying by the World Health Organization began systematic control of mosquito-breeding areas in the tropics. Forty years of DDT spraying killed millions of mosquitoes; but at the same time, natural selection acted to produce several strains of DDT-resistant mosquitoes (Fig. 15-6). Accordingly, malaria is again on the rise, with several hundred thousand new cases reported annually in India, Africa, and Central America.

A genetic characteristic (such as sickle-cell trait) that provides a reproductive advantage to heterozygotes in certain environments is a clear example of natural selection in action among human populations. The precise evolutionary mechanism in the sickle-cell example is termed

slash-and-burn agriculture A traditional land-clearing practice involving the cutting and burning of trees and vegetation. In many areas, fields are abandoned after a few years and clearing occurs elsewhere.

Figure **15-6**

Evolutionary interactions affecting the frequency of the sickle-cell allele.

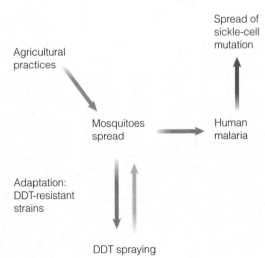

CHAPTER 15

Table 15-2 Frequencies of Lactase Persistence

Population Group	Percent
U.S. whites	81–98
Swedes and Danes	>90
Swiss	12
U.S. blacks	70–77
Ibos	99
Bantu	10
Fulani	50
Chinese	1
Thais	1
Asian Americans	<5
Native Australians	85

Source: Lerner and Libby, 1976, Tishkoff et al., 2007.

balanced polymorphism The maintenance of two or more alleles in a population due to the selective advantage of the heterozygote.

lactase persistence In adults, the continued production of lactase, the enzyme that breaks down lactose (milk sugar). This allows adults in some human populations to digest fresh milk products. The discontinued production of lactase in adults leads to lactose intolerance and the inability to digest fresh milk.

a **balanced polymorphism**. A polymorphism, as we've defined it, is a trait with more than one allele at a locus in a population. But when a harmful allele (such as the sickle-cell allele) has a higher frequency than can be accounted for by mutation alone, a more detailed evolutionary explanation is required. In this case, the additional mechanism is natural selection.

This brings us to the second part of the term *balanced polymorphism*. By "balanced" we mean the interaction of selective pressures operating on specific alleles in a particular environment (in this case, the sickle-cell alleles in malarial areas). Some individuals (mainly homozygous normals) will die of the infectious disease malaria. Others (homozygous recessives) will die of the inherited disease sickle-cell anemia. Thus, the individuals with the highest reproductive success are the heterozygotes who have sickle-cell trait. These heterozygotes pass both the normal allele (Hb^A) and the sickle-cell allele (Hb^S) to offspring, thus maintaining both alleles at fairly high frequencies. Since one allele in this population won't significantly increase in frequency over the other allele, this situation will become "balanced" and will persist as long as malaria continues to be a selective factor.

Lactose intolerance, which involves an individual's ability to digest milk, is another example of human biocultural evolution. In all human populations, infants and young children are able to digest milk, an obvious necessity for any young mammal. One ingredient of milk is *lactose*, a sugar that's broken down by the enzyme lactase. In most mammals, including many humans, the gene that codes for lactase production "switches off" in adolescence. Once this happens, if a person drinks fresh milk, the lactose ferments in the large intestine, leading to diarrhea and severe gastrointestinal upset. So, as you might expect, adults stop drinking fresh milk. Among many African and Asian populations (a majority of humankind today), most adults are lactose-intolerant (Table 15-2). But in other populations, including some Africans and Europeans, adults continue to produce lactase and are able to digest fresh milk. This continued production of lactase is called **lactase persistence**.

Evidence has suggested a simple dominant mode of inheritance for lactase persistence in adults. The environment also plays a role in expression of the trait—that is, whether a person will be lactose-intolerant—since intestinal bacteria can somewhat buffer the adverse effects of drinking fresh milk. Because these bacteria increase with previous exposure, some tolerance can be acquired, even in individuals who genetically are not lactase-persistent.

Throughout most of hominin evolution, milk was unavailable after weaning, so there *may* be a selective advantage to switching off the gene that codes for lactase production. So why can some adults (the majority in some populations) tolerate milk? The distribution of lactose-tolerant populations may provide an answer to this question, and it suggests a powerful cultural influence on this trait.

Europeans, who are generally lactose-tolerant, are partly descended from Middle Eastern populations. Often economically dependent on pastoralism, these groups raised cows and/or goats and probably drank considerable quantities of milk. In such a cultural environment, strong selection pressures apparently favored lactose tolerance, a trait that has been retained in modern Europeans. Genetic evidence from north-central Europe supports this interpretation. DNA analysis of both cattle and humans suggests that these species have, to some extent, influenced each other genetically. The interaction between humans and cattle resulted in cattle that produce high-quality milk and humans with the ability to digest it (Beja-Pereira et al., 2003). In other words, more than 5,000 ya, populations of north-central Europe were selectively breeding cattle for higher milk yields. And as these populations were increasing their dependence on fresh milk, they were inadvertently selecting for the gene that produces lactase persistence in themselves.

But perhaps even more informative is the distribution of lactose tolerance in Africa, where the majority of people are lactose-intolerant. Groups such as the Fulani and Tutsi have been pastoralists for perhaps thousands of years and have much higher rates of lactose persistence than nonpastoralists (Fig. 15-7). Presumably, like their European counterparts, they've retained the ability to produce lactase because of their continued consumption of fresh milk (Powell et al., 2003).

Recent molecular evidence has supported this hypothesis, showing a similar coevolution of humans and cattle in East Africa (Tishkoff et al., 2007). The pattern of DNA mutations (SNPs) in Africa is different from that seen in Europe, strongly suggesting that lactase persistence has evolved independently in the two regions. In fact, the data show that lactase persistence has evolved several times just in East Africa. The importance of cattle domestication in providing milk for human groups was clearly a cultural and dietary shift of major importance. As humans selectively bred cattle to produce more and higher-quality milk, they promoted fairly rapid evolution in these animals. At the same time, humans in different areas coevolved through natural selection as allele frequencies shifted to produce higher frequencies of lactase persistence.

As we've seen, the geographical distribution of lactase persistence is related to a history of cultural dependence on fresh milk products. There are, however, some populations that rely on dairying but don't have high rates of lactase persistence (Fig. 15-8). It's been suggested that such groups have traditionally consumed their milk in the form of cheese and yogurt, in which the lactose has been broken down by bacterial action.

The interaction of human cultural environments and changes in lactose tolerance in human populations is another example of biocultural evolution. In the last few thousand years, cultural factors have initiated specific evolutionary changes in human groups. Such cultural factors have probably influenced the course of human evolution for at least 3 million years, and today they are of paramount importance.

Figure **15-7**

Fulani cattle herder with his cattle.

Figure **15-8**

Natives of Mongolia rely heavily on milk products from goats and sheep, but mostly consume these foods in the form of cheese and yogurt.

Molecular Applications in Modern Human Biology (continued)

more than 15 million men have this same (or nearly identical) Y chromosome. How did it spread so quickly, and from where did it originate? Allele frequency distribution strongly points to Mongolia as the area of origin. Moreover, today's broader geographical pattern of this genotype nearly exactly coincides with the extent of the Mongol empire at the time of Genghis Khan's death (Fig. 1).

SOURCES

Stix, Gary
2008   Traces of a distant past. *Scientific American*
        299(July):56–63.
Zerjel, Tatiana, Yali Xue, Giorgio Bertorelle, et al.
2003   The genetic legacy of the Monguls. *American Journal of
        Human Genetics* 72:717–721.

Figure **1**

The extent of the empire of Genghis Khan at the time of this death.

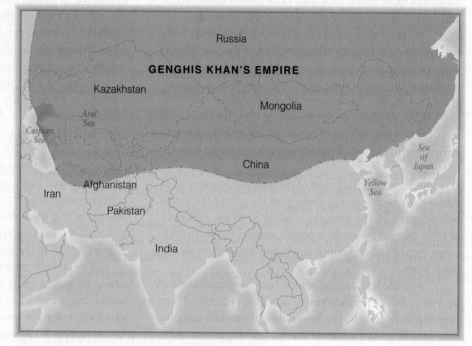

Source: Adapted from *Science News*, 163(6), February 8, 2003, p. 91.

CHAPTER

16

Modern Human Biology:
Patterns of Adaptation

NASA

Key Question

Can patterns of evolution in contemporary human populations be linked to the role of natural selection?

 Click!

Go to the following media for interactive activities and exercises on topics covered in this chapter:

- Online Virtual Laboratories for Physical Anthropology, Version 4.0

- Genetics in Anthropology: Principles and Applications CD-ROM, Version 2.0

stress In a physiological context, any factor that acts to disrupt homeostasis; more precisely, the body's response to any factor that threatens its ability to maintain homeostasis.

homeostasis A condition of balance, or stability, within a biological system, maintained by the interaction of physiological mechanisms that compensate for changes (both external and internal).

Introduction

We've all heard it said: "No two people are alike." It's an old expression, but like so many old expressions, it's true; and now that we're approaching the end of this book, you should know why. One exception to this old adage is identical twins, who are genetically the same; but even *they* don't look exactly alike, and they also have personality differences. You should also know why this is true, even if we haven't addressed this issue specifically.

In previous chapters, we explored the genetic bases for biological variation within and between human populations. We discussed how, as a species, humans are remarkably genetically uniform compared with our closest primate relatives. We've also placed these discussions within an evolutionary framework, emphasizing the roles of natural selection and genetic drift in human evolution.

With this foundation, we can turn our attention to some of the factors that have challenged us through our evolutionary journey and consider how we've met these challenges as a species, as populations, and as individuals. Except for the oceans, the highest mountain peaks, and Antarctica, we now inhabit the entire planet. But during this process, we've had to cope with ultraviolet (UV) radiation, altitude differences, temperature extremes, and infectious diseases. All of these factors, plus the fact that populations were separated from one another, have produced many kinds of variation in our species.

The Adaptive Significance of Human Variation

Today, biological anthropologists view human variation as the result of such evolutionary factors as genetic drift, founder effect, gene flow, and adaptations to environmental conditions, both past and present. Cultural adaptations have certainly played a critical role in the evolution of our species, and although in this discussion we're primarily concerned with biological issues, we must still consider the influence of cultural practices on human adaptive responses.

To survive, all organisms need to maintain the normal functions of internal organs, tissues, and cells. What's more, they must accomplish this task in the context of an ever-changing environment. Even during the course of a single, seemingly uneventful day, there are numerous fluctuations in temperature, wind, solar radiation, humidity, and so on. Physical activity also places **stress** on physiological mechanisms. The body must accommodate all these changes by compensating in some way to maintain internal constancy, or **homeostasis**, and all life-forms have evolved physiological mechanisms that, within limits, achieve this goal.

Physiological response to environmental change is influenced by genetic factors. We've already defined adaptation as a response to environmental conditions in populations and individuals. In a narrower sense, adaptation refers to long-term evolutionary (that is, genetic) changes that characterize all individuals within a population or species.

Examples of long-term adaptations in humans include some physiological responses to heat (sweating) or excessive levels of UV light (deeply pigmented skin near the equator). These characteristics are the results of evolutionary change in our species or in populations, and they don't vary because of short-term environmental change. For example, the ability to sweat isn't lost in people who spend their lives in predominantly cool areas. Likewise, individuals born with dark skin wouldn't become pale, even if they were never exposed to sunlight.

Acclimatization is another kind of physiological response to environmental conditions, and it can be short-term, long-term, or even permanent. The physiological responses to environmental stressors are at least partially influenced by genetic factors, but some can also be affected by the duration and severity of the exposure, technological buffers (such as shelter or clothing), individual behavior, weight, and overall body size.

The simplest form of acclimatization is a temporary and rapid adjustment to an environmental change (for example, tanning). Another example is one you may not know about, although you've probably experienced it: the rapid increase in hemoglobin production that occurs in people who live at lower elevations but travel to higher ones (see p. 462). (It's happened in your own body if you've spent a few days at a ski resort.) In both these examples, the physiological changes are temporary. Tans fade when exposure to sunlight is reduced, and hemoglobin production drops to original levels after returning to lower elevations.

Another type of acclimatization, called developmental acclimatization, results from exposure to an environmental challenge during growth and development. Because this kind of acclimatization is incorporated into an individual's physiology, it isn't reversible. An example of developmental acclimatization is the physiological responses we see in lifelong residents of high altitude (see p. 463).

In the next section, we present some of the many examples of how humans respond to environmental challenges. Some of these examples describe adaptations that characterize our entire species. Others are shared by most or all members of only certain populations. And a few illustrate acclimatization in individuals.

Solar Radiation and Skin Color

Deeply Pigmented Skin For many years, skin color has been cited as an example of adaptation through natural selection in humans. In general, pigmentation in indigenous populations prior to European contact (beginning around 1500) followed a particular geographical distribution, especially in the Old World. This pattern pretty much holds true today, and Figure 16-1 shows that populations with the most pigmentation are found in the tropics, while lighter skin color is associated with more northern latitudes, especially the long-term inhabitants of northwestern Europe.

Three substances influence skin color: hemoglobin, the protein carotene, and, most important, the pigment melanin. Melanin is a granular substance produced by cells called melanocytes, located in the outer layer of the skin (Fig. 16-2). Melanin is extremely important because it acts as a built-in sunscreen by absorbing potentially dangerous ultraviolet (UV) rays that are present, but not visible, in sunlight. So

acclimatization Physiological responses to changes in the environment that occur during an individual's lifetime. Such responses may be temporary or permanent, depending on the duration of the environmental change and when in the individual's life it occurs. The capacity for acclimatization may typify an entire species or population, and because it's under genetic influence, it's subject to evolutionary factors such as natural selection and genetic drift.

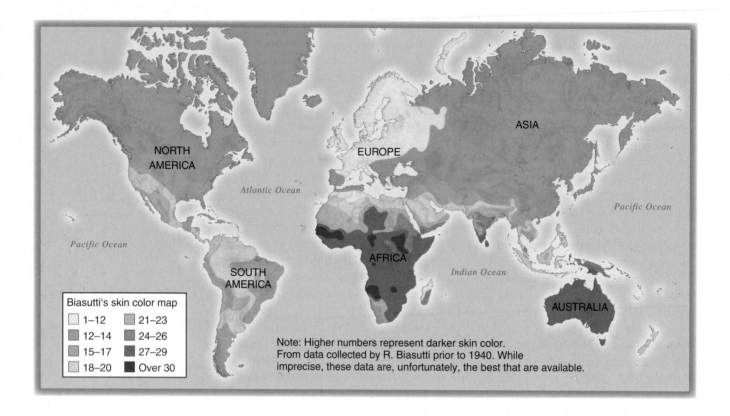

Note: Higher numbers represent darker skin color.
From data collected by R. Biasutti prior to 1940. While imprecise, these data are, unfortunately, the best that are available.

Biasutti's skin color map

1–12	21–23
12–14	24–26
15–17	27–29
18–20	Over 30

Figure **16-1**

Geographical distribution of skin color in indigenous human populations. (After Biasutti, 1959.)

melanin protects us from overexposure to UV radiation, which frequently causes genetic mutations in skin cells. These mutations can lead to skin cancer, which, if left untreated, can eventually spread to other organs and even result in death (see "A Closer Look," pp. 458–459).

As we mentioned earlier, exposure to sunlight triggers a protective mechanism in the form of tanning, the result of temporarily increased melanin production (acclimatization). This response occurs in all humans except albinos, who carry a genetic mutation that prevents their melanocytes from producing melanin (see Fig. 4-11, p. 00). But even people who do produce melanin differ in their ability to tan. For instance, many people of northern European descent tend to have very fair skin, blue eyes, and light hair. Their cells produce small amounts of melanin, but when exposed to sunlight, they have almost no ability to increase production. And in all populations, women tend not to tan as deeply as men.

Natural selection has favored dark skin in areas closest to the equator, where the sun's rays are most direct and where exposure to UV light is most intense and constant. In considering the cancer-causing effects of UV radiation from an evolutionary perspective, keep in mind these three points:

1. Early hominins lived in the tropics, where solar radiation is more intense than in temperate areas to the north and south.
2. Unlike most modern city dwellers, early hominins spent their days outdoors.
3. Early hominins didn't wear clothing that would have protected them from the sun.

Under these conditions, UV radiation was a powerful agent selecting for maximum levels of melanin production in early hominins. There's an important objection to this hypothesis, however. As we mentioned in Chapter 4, natural selec-

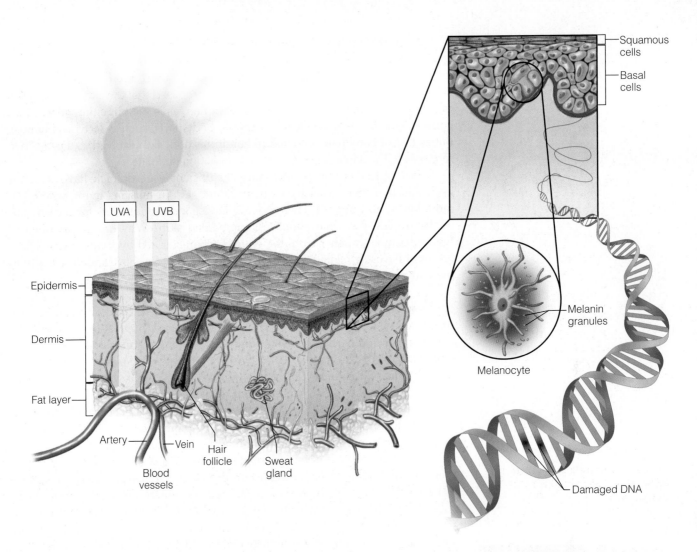

Squamous cells

Basal cells

Melanin granules

Melanocyte

Damaged DNA

UVA UVB

Epidermis

Dermis

Fat layer

Artery Vein

Blood vessels

Hair follicle

Sweat gland

tion can act only on traits that affect reproduction. Because cancers tend to occur later in life, after the reproductive years, it should theoretically be difficult for selection to act effectively against any factor that might predispose people to cancer. But in one African study, it was shown that all albinos in dark-skinned populations of Nigeria and Tanzania had either precancerous lesions or skin cancer by the age of 20 (Robins, 1991). This evidence suggests that even in early hominins of reproductive age, less-pigmented skin could have reduced individual reproductive fitness in regions of intense sunlight.

Jablonski (1992) and Jablonski and Chaplin (2000) have provided substantial evidence for an additional explanation for deeply pigmented skin in the tropics. This research concerns the degradation of folate by UV radiation. Folate is a B vitamin that isn't stored in the body and must be replenished through dietary sources. Adequate levels of folate are required for many developmental processes. In pregnant women, insufficient levels of folate are associated with numerous fetal developmental disorders, including **neural tube** defects such as **spina bifida**. The consequences of severe neural tube defects can include pain, infection, paralysis, and failure of the brain to develop. Given the importance of folate to many processes related to reproduction, it's clear that maintaining adequate levels of this vitamin contributes to individual reproductive fitness.

Figure **16-2**

Ultraviolet rays penetrate the skin and can eventually damage DNA within skin cells. The three major types of cells that can be affected are squamous cells, basal cells, and melanocytes. (See also "A Closer Look," pp. 458–459.)

neural tube In early embryonic development, the anatomical structure that develops to form the brain and spinal cord.

spina bifida A condition in which the arch of one or more vertebrae fails to fuse and form a protective barrier around the spinal cord.

Some studies have shown that UV radiation rapidly depletes folate serum levels both in laboratory experiments and in light-skinned individuals. These findings have implications for pregnant women, for children, and for the evolution of dark skin in early hominins. Jablonski (1992) proposed that the earliest hominins may have had light skin covered with dark hair, as is seen in chimpanzees and gorillas (who have darker skin on exposed body parts, such as faces and hands). But as loss of body hair occurred in hominins, dark skin evolved as a protective response to the damaging effects of UV radiation on folate.

Skin cancer and the maintenance of sufficient levels of folate have no doubt been selective agents that have favored dark skin in humans living where UV radiation is most intense. Therefore, we have good explanations for darker skin in the tropics. But what about less-pigmented skin? Why are populations in higher latitudes, farther from the equator, characterized by lighter skin? There are several closely related hypotheses, and recent studies have added strength to these arguments.

Less-Pigmented Skin As hominins migrated out of Africa into Asia and Europe, they faced new selective pressures. In particular, those populations that eventually occupied northern Europe encountered cold temperatures and cloudy skies, frequently during summer as well as in winter. Winter also meant fewer hours of daylight, and with the sun well to the south, solar radiation is very indirect. What's more, people in these areas wore animal skins and other types of clothing, which blocked the sun's rays. For some time researchers proposed that because of reduced exposure to sunlight, the advantages of deeply pigmented skin in the tropics no longer applied, and selection for melanin production may have been relaxed.

However, relaxed selection for dark skin doesn't explain the very depigmented skin seen in some northern Europeans. In fact, natural selection appears to have acted very rapidly in favor of fair skin as humans moved to northern latitudes. This is because the need for a physiological UV filter conflicted with another extremely important biological necessity, and that necessity was almost certainly the production of vitamin D. The theory concerning the role of vitamin D is called the vitamin D hypothesis.

Since the early twentieth century, scientists have known that vitamin D is essential for the mineralization and normal growth of bones during infancy and childhood because it enables the body to absorb calcium (the major source of bone mineral) from dietary sources. (Vitamin D is also required for the continued mineralization of bones in adults.) Many foods, including fish oils, egg yolk, butter, cream, and liver, are good sources of vitamin D. But the body's primary source of vitamin D is its own ability to synthesize it through the interaction of UV light and a form of cholesterol found in skin cells. Therefore, adequate exposure to sunlight is essential to normal bone growth.

Insufficient amounts of vitamin D during childhood result in rickets, a condition that leads to bone deformities throughout the skeleton, especially the weight-bearing bones of the legs and pelvis. Thus, people with rickets frequently have bowed legs and pelvic deformities (Fig. 16-3). Pelvic deformities are of particular concern for women, since they can lead to a narrowing of the birth canal. Without surgical intervention, this deformity can result in the death of both mother and infant during childbirth.

In addition to its role in bone mineralization, vitamin D plays many other critical roles in biological function. In the body, vitamin D is converted to a different molecule called 1,25D, and this molecule can attach directly to DNA, after which it

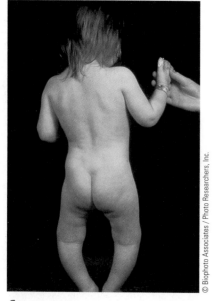

Figure **16-3**
A child with rickets.

acts as a regulator of more than 1,000 different genes (Tavera-Mendoza and White, 2007). Some of these genes are involved in cell replication, and because 1,25D acts to regulate this activity, it appears to provide some protection against certain cancers, especially prostate and colon cancer (Lin and White, 2004). (Cancer is caused by uncontrolled cell replication.) Other genes influenced by 1,25D produce proteins that act as natural antibiotics to kill certain bacteria and viruses, one of which is the bacterium that causes tuberculosis. (This may explain why, in the early twentieth century, tuberculosis patients often improved after being sent to sanitariums in sunny locations.) And lastly, 1,25D reduces inflammation and may eventually be used as a basis for treating certain diseases, including multiple sclerosis (Tavera-Mendoza and White, 2007).

The influence of latitude and skin pigmentation on levels of 1,25D in the body has been shown by epidemiological studies of modern populations. For example, one study revealed that 92 percent of a sample of more than 400 girls in several northern European countries were severely deficient in 1,25D during the winter months. Also, the fact that African Americans appear to have about half the amount of 1,25D seen in European Americans illustrates the role of increased pigmentation in reducing vitamin D levels in more northern latitudes (Tavera-Mendoza and White, 2007).

As you can see, vitamin D is an immensely important factor in the body's response to a number of conditions, many of which influence reproductive success. This evidence substantially supports the vitamin D hypothesis and argues for strong and rapid positive selection for depigmented skin in northern latitudes. Furthermore, the vitamin D evidence is strongly supported by recent genetic studies.

More than 100 genetic loci are thought to be involved in pigmentation in vertebrates, and one of the more important ones is *MC1R*, which affects coloration in all mammals. In fact, work with DNA from an approximately 43,000-year-old mammoth bone revealed that coat color in mammoths varied from dark to lighter brown (Römpler et al., 2006). The human version of this gene has at least 30 alleles, some of which are associated with red hair combined with fair skin and a tendency to freckle (Lin and Fisher, 2007). As we mentioned in Chapter 13, research on Neandertal DNA has revealed that some Neandertals probably had red hair and fair skin. This research demonstrates the presence of an *MC1R* allele that reduces the amount of pigment in skin and hair, but it's not an allele that's present in modern humans. The fact that less-pigmented skin developed in two hominin species, but through different mutations in the same gene, strongly reinforces the theory that there is a significant selective advantage to lighter skin in higher latitudes.
Lastly, evidence for the importance of vitamin D is provided by the recent discovery of yet another gene, called *SCL24A5*, which we'll refer to simply as *SCL* (Lamason et al., 2005). This gene and its effects on pigmentation were first discovered in zebrafish, and just to emphasize (yet again) the concept of biological continuity between species, we'll point out that approximately 68 percent of the sequences of DNA bases in the human and Zebrafish *SCL* genes are the same (Balter, 2007).

Like *MC1R*, the *SCL* gene is involved in melanin production. This gene has two primary alleles that differ by one single base substitution; that is, one allele arose as a point mutation. The original form (allele) of the gene is present in 93 to 100 percent of Africans, Native Americans. and East Asians. However, and most importantly, virtually 100 percent of Europeans and European Americans have the more recent (mutated) allele that inhibits melanin production! These frequencies make a very compelling case for very strong selection for lighter skin in northern

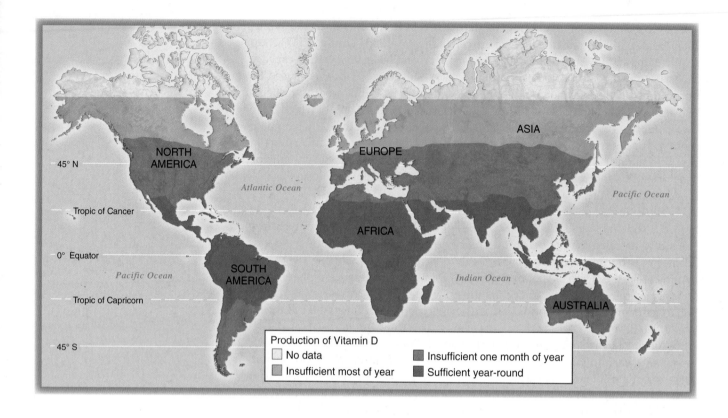

45° N

Tropic of Cancer

0° Equator

Tropic of Capricorn

45° S

NORTH AMERICA

SOUTH AMERICA

EUROPE

ASIA

AFRICA

AUSTRALIA

Atlantic Ocean

Pacific Ocean

Pacific Ocean

Indian Ocean

Production of Vitamin D

No data

Insufficient most of year

Insufficient one month of year

Sufficient year-round

Figure 16-4

Populations indigenous to the tropics (brown band) receive enough UV radiation for vitamin D synthesis year-round. The dark orange band shows areas where people with moderately melanized skin don't receive enough UV light for vitamin D synthesis for one month of the year. The light orange band shows areas where even light skin doesn't receive enough UV light for vitamin D synthesis during most of the year. (Adapted from Jablonski and Chaplin, 2000, 2002.)

latitudes. In fact, it appears that natural selection favored the mutated allele to the point that it became the only *SCL* allele in Northern European populations.

But there's a question that has yet to be answered. (Actually, there are several questions, but we'll mention only one.) In East Asians, the frequency of the original, melanin-producing allele is the same as in sub-Saharan Africans, yet on average, skin color in East Asians is fairly light. Lamason and colleagues (2005) contend that this means that there are other, as yet unidentified genes that interact with the *SCL* locus in East Asian populations to reduce skin pigmentation. Certainly, several other genes that contribute to skin pigmentation have been identified, but none has yet been shown to have the same degree of variation between populations.

Jablonski and Chaplin (2000) have looked at the potential for vitamin D synthesis in people of different skin color based on the yearly average UV radiation at various latitudes (Fig. 16-4). Their conclusions support the vitamin D hypothesis to the point of stating that the requirement of vitamin D synthesis in northern latitudes was as important to natural selection as the need for protection from UV radiation in tropical regions.

Except for a person's sex, more social importance has been attached to skin color than to any other single human biological trait. But there's absolutely no reason this should be so. Aside from its probable adaptive significance relative to UV radiation, skin color is no more important physiologically than many other biological characteristics. But from an evolutionary perspective, skin color provides an outstanding example of how the forces of natural selection have produced geographically patterned variation as the result of two conflicting selective forces: the need for protection from overexposure to UV radiation, on the one hand, and the need for adequate UV exposure for vitamin D synthesis on the other.

The Thermal Environment

Mammals and birds have evolved complex mechanisms to maintain a constant internal body temperature. While reptiles must rely on exposure to external heat sources to raise body temperature and energy levels, mammals and birds have physiological mechanisms that, within certain limits, increase or reduce the loss of body heat. The optimum body temperature for normal cellular functions is species-specific, and for humans it's approximately 98.6°F.

People are found in a wide variety of habitats, with thermal environments ranging from exceedingly hot (in excess of 120°F) to bitter cold (less than −60°F). In such extremes, particularly cold, human life wouldn't be possible without cultural innovations. But even accounting for the artificial environments we live in, such external conditions place the human body under enormous stress.

Response to Heat All available evidence suggests that the earliest hominins evolved in the warm-to-hot woodlands and savannas of East Africa. The fact that humans cope better with heat (especially dry heat) than they do with cold is testimony to the long-term adaptations to heat that evolved in our ancestors.

In humans, as well as some other species, such as horses, sweat glands are distributed throughout the skin. This wide distribution of sweat glands makes it possible to lose heat at the body's surface through **evaporative cooling**, a mechanism that has evolved to the greatest degree in humans. In fact, perspiration is the most important factor in heat dissipation in humans.

The capacity to dissipate heat by sweating is seen in all human populations to an almost equal degree, with the average number of sweat glands per individual (approximately 1.6 million) being fairly constant. However, there's some variation, since people who aren't generally exposed to hot conditions do experience a period of acclimatization that initially involves significantly increased perspiration rates (Frisancho, 1993). An additional factor that enhances the cooling effects of sweating is increased exposure of the skin through reduced amounts of body hair. We don't know when in our evolutionary history the loss of body hair occurred, but it represents a species-wide adaptation.

Heat reduction through evaporation can be expensive, and indeed dangerous, in terms of water and sodium loss. For example, a person engaged in heavy work in high heat can lose up to 3 liters of water per hour. To appreciate the importance of this fact, consider that losing 1 liter of water is approximately equivalent to losing 1.5 percent of total body weight, and losing 10 percent of body weight can be life threatening. So, water must be continuously replaced during exercise in heat.

Basically, there are two types of heat, arid and humid. Arid environments, such as those of the southwestern United States, the Middle East, and much of Africa, are characterized by high temperatures, wind, and low water vapor. Humid heat is associated with increased water vapor and is found in regions with a great deal of vegetation and precipitation, conditions found in the eastern and southern United States, parts of Europe, and much of the tropics. Because the increased water vapor in humid climates inhibits the evaporation of sweat on the skin's surface, humans adjust much more readily to dry heat. In fact, people exercising in dry heat may be unaware that they're sweating because the perspiration evaporates as soon as it reaches the skin's surface. While rapid evaporation increases comfort, it can lead to dehydration. Therefore, in dry heat it's important to keep drinking water, even if you aren't particularly thirsty.

evaporative cooling A physiological mechanism that helps prevent the body from overheating. It occurs when perspiration is produced from sweat glands and then evaporates from the surface of the skin.

A Closer Look
Skin Cancer and UV Radiation

Even though we know we can't live without it, most people tend to take their skin for granted. The many functions of this complex organ (and skin *is* an organ) are vital to life. Yet most of us thoughtlessly expose our skin to any number of environmental assaults and especially abuse it with overexposure to the sun, practically to the point of charbroiling. For these reasons, we think it's appropriate here to examine a little more closely this watertight, evolutionary achievement that permits us to live on land, just as it allowed some vertebrates to leave the oceans several hundred million years ago.

Skin is composed of two layers, the epidermis and, just beneath it, the dermis (see Fig. 16-2, p. 453). The upper portion of the epidermis is made up of flattened, somewhat overlapping squamous (scale-like) cells. Beneath these cells, near the base of the epidermis, are several layers of round basal cells. Interspersed within the basal cells are still two other cell types: melanocytes, which produce melanin, and keratinocytes, which are involved in vitamin D synthesis.

Skin cells are continuously produced at the base of the epidermis through mitosis. As they mature, they migrate to the surface, becoming flattened and avascular; that is, they have no direct blood supply. Approximately one month after forming, skin cells die in a process of genetically directed cellular suicide. The results of this suicidal act are the little white flakes people with dry skin are uncomfortably aware of. (Incidentally, dead skin cells are a major component of common household dust.)

The dermis is composed of connective tissue and many structures, including blood vessels, lymphatic vessels, sweat glands, oil glands, and hair follicles. Together, the epidermis and dermis allow the body to retain fluid, help regulate body temperature, synthesize a number of essential substances, and provide protection from ultraviolet (UV) radiation.

There are three main types of UV radiation, but here we're concerned with only two: UVA and UVB. UVA has the longest wavelength and can penetrate through to the bottom of the dermis, while the medium-length UVB waves usually penetrate only to the basal layer of the epidermis (see Fig. 16-2).

The stimulation of vitamin D production by UVB waves is the only benefit we get from exposure to UV radiation. Following a sunburn, both UVB and UVA rays cause short-term suppression of the immune system. But because UVB is directly absorbed by the DNA within cells, it can potentially cause genetic damage, and this damage can lead to skin cancer.

You know that cancers are tumorous growths that invade organs, a process that often results in death, even after treatment. But you may not know that a cell becomes cancerous when a carcinogenic agent, such as UV radiation, damages its DNA, and some DNA segments are more susceptible than others. The damage allows the affected cell to divide uncontrollably. Each subsequent generation of cells receives the mutant DNA, and with it, the potential to divide indefinitely. Eventually, cancer cells form a mass that invades other tissues. They can also break away from the original tumor and travel through the circulatory or lymphatic system to other parts of the body, where they establish themselves and continue to divide. For example, cells from lung tumors (frequently caused by carcinogenic agents in tobacco) can travel to the brain or parts of the skeleton and develop tumors in these new sites before the lung tumor is even detectable. (The former Beatle, George Harrison, died of brain cancer that had spread from the lungs. It's probably no coincidence that he was a heavy smoker when he was young.)

All three types of cells in the epidermis are susceptible to cancerous changes. The most common form of skin cancer is basal cell carcinoma (BCC), which affects about 800,000 people per year in the United States. Fortunately, BCCs are slow growing and, if detected early, can be successfully removed before they spread. They can appear as a raised lump and be uncolored, red-brown, or black (Fig.1a).

vasodilation Expansion of blood vessels, permitting increased blood flow to the skin. Vasodilation permits warming of the skin and facilitates radiation of warmth as a means of cooling. Vasodilation is an involuntary response to warm temperatures, various drugs, and even emotional states (blushing).

Another mechanism for radiating body heat is vasodilation, which occurs when capillaries near the skin's surface widen to increase blood flow to the skin. The visible effect of **vasodilation** is flushing, or increased redness and warming of the skin, particularly of the face. But the physiological effect is to permit heat, carried by the blood from the interior of the body, to be emitted from the skin's surface to the surrounding air. (Some drugs, including alcohol, also produce vasodilation; this accounts for the increased redness and warmth of the face in some people after a couple of drinks.)

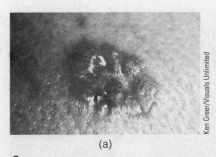

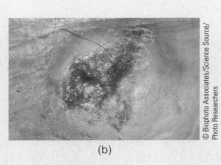

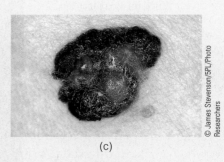

(a) (b) (c)

Figure 1

(a) Basal cell carcinoma. (b) Squamous cell carcinoma. (c) Malignant melanoma.

Squamous cell carcinoma (SCC) is the second most common skin cancer (Fig. 1b). These cancers grow faster than BCCs, but they're also amenable to treatment if detected reasonably early. They usually appear as firm pinkish lesions and may spread rapidly on skin exposed to sunlight.

The third form is malignant melanoma, a cancer of the melanocytes. Melanoma is thought to be caused by UVA radiation, and it accounts for only about 4 percent of all skin cancers. But while it's the least common of the three, melanoma is the fastest growing and the deadliest, killing 30 to 40 percent of affected people. Melanoma looks like an irregularly shaped, very dark or black mole (Fig. 1c). In fact, it may be a mole that has changed because some of its cells have been damaged. It's extremely important to notice any changes in a mole or the appearance of a new dark, perhaps roughened spot on the skin and to have it examined as soon as possible. If a melanoma is less than a millimeter deep, it can be removed before it spreads. But if it has progressed into the dermis, it's likely that it's already spread to other tissues.

Brash and colleagues (1991) and Ziegler and colleagues (1994) determined that the underlying genetic factor in most nonmelanoma skin cancers is a mutation of a gene called *p53* located on chromosome 17. This gene produces a protein, also called p53, which prevents any cell (not just skin cells) with damaged DNA from dividing until the damage is repaired. In addition, if the damage to a cell's DNA is too severe to repair, the p53 protein can cause the cell to die. Thus, *p53* is what's known as a tumor suppressor gene (Vogelstein et al., 2000).

Unfortunately, the *p53* gene is itself susceptible to mutation, and when certain mutations occur, it can no longer prevent cancer cells from dividing. Luckily, there are other tumor suppressor genes. In fact, damaged *p53* genes don't appear to be involved in melanoma. Instead, a UV-induced mutation in another tumor suppressor gene on chromosome 9 appears to be the culprit (NCBI, 2003).

BCCs and SCCs tend to appear in middle age, long after the underlying genetic damage occurred during childhood and adolescence. If you've had even one serious sunburn in your life, your odds of developing one of the nonmelanoma skin cancers have increased dramatically. Malignant melanomas can occur at any age, although the DNA damage can precede the development of cancer by several years. The best advice is don't take the threat of skin cancer lightly, and don't overexpose your skin to the sun. Wear a hat and a broad-based sunblock that will filter out both UVA and UVB rays. In other words, do your best to keep your tumor suppressor genes happy.

Body size and proportions are also important in regulating body temperature. In fact, there seems to be a general relationship between climate and body size and shape in birds and mammals. In general, within a species, body size (weight) increases as distance from the equator increases. In humans, this relationship holds up fairly well, but there are many exceptions.

Two rules that pertain to the relationship between body size, body proportions, and climate are *Bergmann's rule* and *Allen's rule*.

Figure 16-5

(a) This African woman has the linear proportions characteristic of many inhabitants of sub-Saharan Africa. (b) By comparison, the Inuit woman is short and stocky. Although these two individuals don't typify everyone in their populations, they do serve as good examples of Bergmann's and Allen's rules.

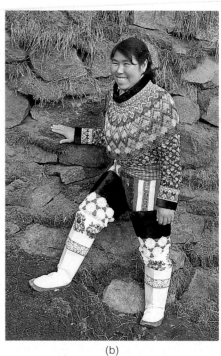

(a)   (b)

1. *Bergmann's rule concerns the relationship of body mass or volume to surface area.* Among mammals, body size tends to be greater in populations that live in colder climates. This is because as mass increases, the relative amount of surface area decreases proportionately. Because heat is lost at the surface, it follows that increased mass allows for greater heat retention and reduced heat loss. (Remember our discussion of basal metabolic rate and body size in Chapter 7.)

2. *Allen's rule concerns shape of body, especially appendages.* In colder climates, shorter appendages, with increased mass-to-surface ratios, are adaptive because they're more effective at preventing heat loss. Conversely, longer appendages, with increased surface area relative to mass, are more adaptive in warmer climates because they promote heat loss.

According to these rules, the most suitable body shape in hot climates is linear with long arms and legs. In a cold climate, a more suitable body type is stocky with shorter limbs. Considerable data gathered from several human populations generally conform to these principles. In colder climates, body mass tends, on average, to be greater and characterized by a larger trunk relative to arms and legs. People living in the Arctic tend to be short and stocky, while many sub-Saharan Africans, especially the East African pastoralists, are tall and linear (Fig. 16-5). But there's a lot of human variability regarding body proportions, and not all populations conform so obviously to Bergmann's and Allen's rules.

Response to Cold Human physiological responses to cold increase heat production and enhance heat retention. Of the two, heat retention is more efficient because less energy is required. This is an important point because energy is obtained from dietary sources. Unless food is abundant, and in winter it frequently isn't, any factor that conserves energy can be beneficial.

Short-term responses to cold include increased metabolic rate and shivering, both of which generate body heat, at least for a short time. **Vasoconstriction,**

vasoconstriction Narrowing of blood vessels to reduce blood flow to the skin. Vasoconstriction is an involuntary response to cold and reduces heat loss at the skin's surface.

another short-term response, restricts heat loss and conserves energy. Humans also have a subcutaneous (beneath the skin) fat layer that provides insulation throughout the body. Behavioral modifications include increased activity, increased food consumption, and even curling up into a ball.

Increases in metabolic rate (the rate at which cells break up nutrients into their components) release energy in the form of heat. Shivering also generates muscle heat, as does voluntary exercise. But these methods of heat production are costly because they require an increased intake of nutrients to provide needed energy. (Perhaps this explains why we tend to have a heartier appetite during the winter and why we also tend to eat more fats and carbohydrates, the very sources of energy we require.)

In general, people exposed to chronic cold (meaning much or most of the year) maintain higher metabolic rates than do those living in warmer climates. The Inuit (Eskimo) people living in the Arctic maintain metabolic rates between 13 and 45 percent higher than observed in non-Inuit control subjects (Frisancho, 1993). What's more, the highest metabolic rates are seen in inland Inuit, who are exposed to even greater cold stress than coastal populations. Traditionally, the Inuit had the highest animal protein and fat diet of any population in the world. Their diet was dictated by the available resource base, and it served to maintain the high metabolic rates required by exposure to chronic cold.

Vasoconstriction restricts capillary blood flow to the surface of the skin, thus reducing heat loss at the body surface. Because retaining body heat is more economical than creating it, vasoconstriction is very efficient, provided temperatures don't drop below freezing. However, if temperatures do fall below freezing, continued vasoconstriction can allow skin temperature to decrease to the point of frostbite or worse.

Long-term responses to cold vary among human groups. For example, in the past, desert-dwelling native Australian populations were subjected to wide temperature fluctuations from day to night. Since they wore no clothing and didn't build shelters, they built sleeping fires to protect themselves from nighttime temperatures that hovered only a few degrees above freezing. Also, they experienced continuous vasoconstriction throughout the night that permitted a degree of skin cooling most people would find extremely uncomfortable. But since there was no threat of frostbite, continued vasoconstriction helped prevent excessive internal heat loss.

By contrast, the Inuit experience intermittent periods of vasoconstriction and vasodilation. This compromise provides periodic warmth to the skin that helps prevent frostbite in below-freezing temperatures. At the same time, because vasodilation is intermittent, energy loss is restricted to retain more heat at the body's core.

These examples illustrate two of the ways adaptations to cold vary among human populations. Obviously, winter conditions exceed our ability to adapt physiologically in many parts of the world. So if they hadn't developed cultural innovations, our ancestors would have remained in the tropics.

High Altitude

Studies of high-altitude residents have greatly contributed to our understanding of physiological adaptation. As you'd expect, altitude studies have focused on inhabited mountainous regions, particularly in the Himalayas, Andes, and Rocky Mountains. Of these three areas, permanent human habitation probably has the longest history in the Himalayas (Moore et al., 1998). Today, perhaps as many as 25 million people live at altitudes above 10,000 feet. In Tibet, permanent

(a)

(b)

L.G. Moore

William Pratt

Figure **16-6**

(a) A household in northern Tibet, situated at an elevation of over 15,000 feet above sea level. (b) La Paz, Bolivia, at just over 12,000 feet above sea level, is home to well over 1 million people.

settlements exist above 15,000 feet; in the Andes, they can be found as high as 17,000 feet (Fig. 16-6).

Because the mechanisms that maintain homeostasis in humans evolved at lower altitudes, we're compromised by the conditions at higher elevations. At high altitudes, many factors produce stress on the human body. These include hypoxia (reduced available oxygen), more intense solar radiation, cold, low humidity, wind (which amplifies cold stress), a reduced nutritional base, and rough terrain. Of these, hypoxia exerts the greatest amount of stress on human physiological systems, especially the heart, lungs, and brain.

Hypoxia is caused by reduced barometric pressure. It's not that there's less oxygen in the atmosphere at high altitudes; rather, it's less concentrated. Therefore, to obtain the same amount of oxygen at 9,000 feet as at sea level, people must make certain physiological alterations that increase the body's ability to transport and efficiently use the oxygen that's available.

Reproduction, in particular, is affected through increased infant mortality rates, miscarriage, low birth weights, and premature birth. An early study (Moore and Regensteiner, 1983) reported that in Colorado, infant deaths are almost twice as common above 8,200 feet (2,500 meters) as at lower elevations. One cause of fetal and maternal death is preeclampsia, a severe elevation of blood pressure in pregnant women after the twentieth gestational week. In another study of Colorado residents, Palmer and colleagues (1999) reported that among pregnant women living at elevations over 10,000 feet, the prevalence of preeclampsia was 16 percent, compared to 3 percent at around 4,000 feet. In general, the problems related to childbearing are attributed to issues that compromise the vascular supply (and thus oxygen transport) to the fetus.

People born at lower altitudes and high-altitude natives differ somewhat in how they adapt to hypoxia. When people born at low elevations travel to higher ones, the process of acclimatization begins within a day or two. These changes include an increase in respiration rate, heart rate, and production of red blood cells. (Red blood cells contain hemoglobin, the protein responsible for transporting oxygen to organs and tissues.)

In high-altitude natives acclimatization occurs during growth and development. This type of developmental acclimatization is present only in people who grow up in high-altitude areas, not in those who moved there as adults. Compared to populations at lower elevations, lifelong residents of high altitude grow somewhat more slowly and mature later. Other differences include larger chest size, associated, in turn, with greater lung volume and larger heart. In addition to greater lung capacity, people born at high altitudes are more efficient than migrants at diffusing oxygen from blood to body tissues. Developmental acclimatization to high-altitude hypoxia serves as a good example of physiological flexibility by illustrating how, within the limits set by genetic factors, development can be influenced by environmental factors.

There's evidence that entire populations may have genetically adapted to high altitudes. Indigenous peoples of Tibet who have inhabited regions higher than 12,000 feet for around 25,000 years may have made genetic (that is, evolutionary) accommodations to hypoxia. Altitude doesn't appear to affect reproduction in these people to the degree it does in other populations. Infants have birth weights as high as those of lowland Tibetan groups and higher than those of recent (20 to 30 years) Chinese immigrants. This fact may be the result of alterations in maternal blood flow to the uterus during pregnancy (Moore et al., 2006).

Another line of evidence concerns how the body processes glucose (blood sugar). Glucose is critical because it's the only source of energy used by the brain, and it's also used, although not exclusively, by the heart. Both highland Tibetans and the Quechua (inhabitants of high-altitude regions of the Peruvian Andes) burn glucose in a way that permits more efficient oxygen use. This implies the presence of genetic mutations in the mitochondrial DNA because mtDNA directs how cells process glucose. It also indicates that natural selection has acted to increase the frequency of these advantageous mutations in these groups.

There's no certain evidence that Tibetans and Quechua have made evolutionary changes to accommodate high-altitude hypoxia. As yet, the genetic mechanisms underlying these populations' unique abilities haven't been identified. But the data strongly suggest that selection has operated to produce evolutionary change in these two groups. If further study supports these findings, we have an excellent example of evolution in action producing long-term adaptation at the population level.

Infectious Disease

Infection, as opposed to other disease categories, such as degenerative or genetic disease, includes those pathological conditions caused by microorganisms (viruses, bacteria, and fungi). Throughout the course of human evolution, infectious disease has exerted enormous selective pressures on populations, influencing the frequency of alleles that affect the immune response. Indeed, the importance of infectious disease as an agent of natural selection in human populations cannot be overemphasized. But as important as infectious disease has been, its role in this regard isn't very well documented.

The effects of infectious disease on humans are mediated culturally as well as biologically. Innumerable cultural factors, such as architectural styles, subsistence techniques, exposure to domesticated animals, transportation, and even religious practices, affect how infectious disease develops and persists within and between populations.

Until about 10,000 to 12,000 years ago, all humans lived in small nomadic hunting and gathering groups. These groups rarely stayed in one location more than a few days or weeks at a time, so they had little contact with refuse heaps that house disease **vectors**. But with the domestication of plants and animals, people became more sedentary and began living in small villages. Gradually, villages became towns; and towns, in turn, developed into densely crowded, unsanitary cities.

As long as humans lived in small bands, there wasn't much opportunity for infectious disease to affect large numbers of people. Even if an entire local group or band were wiped out, the effect on the overall population in a given area would have been negligible. Moreover, for a disease to become **endemic** in a population, there must be enough people to sustain it. Therefore, small bands of hunter-gatherers weren't faced with continuous exposure to endemic disease.

But with the advent of settled living and association with domesticated animals, opportunities for disease increased. As sedentary life permitted larger group size, it became possible for several diseases to become permanently established in some populations. In addition, exposure to domestic animals, such as cattle and fowl, provided an opportune environment for the spread of several **zoonotic** diseases, such as tuberculosis. Close association with nonhuman animals has always been a source of disease for humans. But with the domestication of animals, humans greatly increased the spread of zoonoses, infectious conditions that spread to humans through contact with nonhuman animals. The crowded, unsanitary conditions that characterized parts of all cities until the late nineteenth century and that still persist in much of the world today further added to the disease burden borne by human populations.

Malaria provides perhaps the best-documented example of how disease can act to change allele frequencies in human populations. In Chapter 4, you saw how, in some African and Mediterranean populations, malaria has altered allele frequencies at the locus that governs hemoglobin formation, leading to increased prevalence of sickle-cell anemia. Despite extensive long-term eradication programs, malaria still poses a serious threat to human health. Indeed, the World Health Organization estimates the number of people currently infected with malaria to be between 300 and 500 million worldwide. And this number is increasing as drug-resistant strains of the disease-causing microorganism become more common (Olliaro et al., 1995).

Another example of the selective role of infectious disease is indirectly provided by AIDS (acquired immunodeficiency syndrome). In the United States, the first cases of AIDS were reported in 1981. Since then, perhaps as many as 1.5 million Americans have been infected by HIV (human immunodeficiency virus), the agent that causes AIDS. However, most of the burden of AIDS is borne by developing countries, where 95 percent of all HIV-infected people live (Fig. 16-7). According to World Health Organization estimates, between 30 and 36 million people worldwide were living with HIV infection as of January 2008, and more than 25 million have died since 1981 (UNAIDS/WHO 2007 AIDS Epidemic Updates).

HIV is transmitted from person to person through the exchange of bodily fluids, usually blood or semen. It's not spread through casual contact with an infected person. Within six months of infection, most infected people test positive for anti-HIV **antibodies**, meaning that their immune system has recognized the presence of foreign antigens and is attempting to fight the infection. However, HIV is a "slow virus," and it may be present for years before the onset of severe illness. This asymptomatic state is called a "latency period," and the average latency period in the United States is more than 11 years.

vectors Agents that serve to transmit disease from one carrier to another. Mosquitoes are vectors for malaria, just as fleas are vectors for bubonic plague.

endemic Continuously present in a population.

zoonotic (zoh-oh-no´-tic) Pertaining to a zoonosis (*pl.*, zoonoses), a disease that's transmitted to humans through contact with nonhuman animals.

antibodies Proteins that are produced by some types of immune cells and that serve as major components of the immune system. Antibodies recognize and attach to foreign antigens on bacteria, viruses, and other pathogens. Then other immune cells destroy the invading organism.

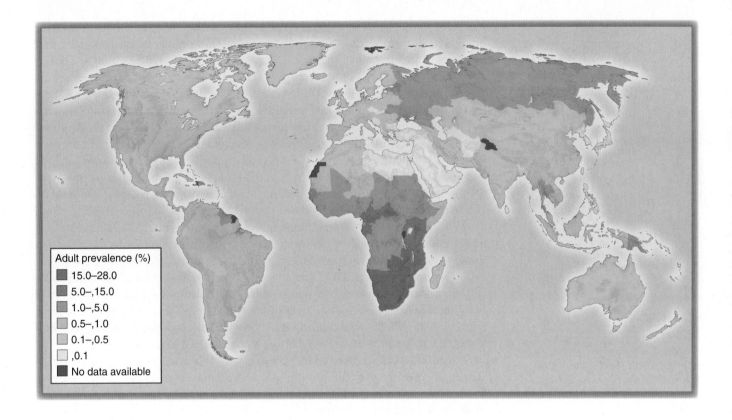

Geographic distribution of HIV infection as of the end of 2004.

Like all viruses, HIV must invade certain types of cells and alter the functions of those cells to produce more virus particles in a process that eventually leads to cell destruction. HIV can attack various types of cells, but it especially targets so-called T4 helper cells, which are major components of the immune system. As HIV infection spreads and T4 cells are destroyed, the patient's immune system begins to fail. Consequently, he or she begins to show symptoms caused by various **pathogens** that are commonly present but usually kept in check by a normal immune response. When an HIV-infected person's T cell count drops to a level indicating that immunity has been suppressed, and when symptoms of "opportunistic" infections appear, the patient is said to have AIDS.

By the early 1990s, scientists were aware of some patients who had been HIV positive for 10 to 15 years but continued to show few if any symptoms. This fact led researchers to suspect that some individuals are naturally resistant to HIV. This was shown to be true in late 1996 with the publication of two different studies (Dean et al., 1996; Samson et al., 1996) that demonstrated a mechanism for HIV resistance.

These two reports describe a genetic mutation that involves a major protein "receptor site" on the surface of certain immune cells, including T4 cells. (Receptor sites are protein molecules that enable HIV and other viruses to invade cells.) In this particular situation, the mutant allele results in a malfunctioning receptor site to which HIV is unable to bind, and current evidence strongly suggests that people who are homozygous for this allele may be completely resistant to many types of HIV infection. In heterozygotes, infection may still occur; but the course of HIV disease is markedly slowed.

For unknown reasons, the mutant allele occurs mainly in people of European descent, among whom its frequency is about 10 percent. Samson and colleagues (1996) reported that in the Japanese and West African samples they studied, the

pathogens Substances or microorganisms, such as bacteria, fungi, or viruses, that cause disease.

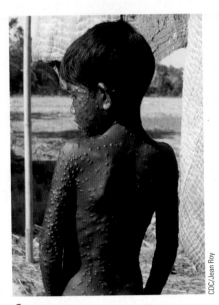

CDC/Jean Roy

Figure 16-8

This 1974 photo shows a young boy in Bangladesh with smallpox. His body is covered with the painful pustules that are typical of the disease. These lesions frequently leave severe scarring on the skin of survivors.

mutation was absent; but Dean and colleagues (1996) reported an allele frequency of about 2 percent among African Americans. These researchers speculated that the presence of the allele in African Americans may be entirely due to genetic admixture (gene flow) with European Americans. They further suggest that this polymorphism exists in Europeans because of selective pressures favoring an allele that originally occurred as a rare mutation. But it's important to understand that the original selective agent wasn't HIV. Instead, it was some other, as yet unidentified pathogen that requires the same receptor site as HIV. One possibility is bubonic plague, but it's largely been ruled out. Another, perhaps more likely suggestion is smallpox. In December 1999, Lalanie and colleagues (1999) reported that a poxvirus, related to the virus that causes smallpox, can use the same receptor site as HIV. While this conclusion hasn't yet been proved or even really investigated, it offers an exciting avenue of research. It may reveal how a mutation that has been favored by selection because it provides protection against one type of infection can also increase resistance to another (AIDS).

Examples such as AIDS and the relationship between malaria and sickle-cell anemia are continuously revealing new insights into the complex interactions between disease organisms and their host populations. These insights in turn form a growing basis for understanding the many variations between individuals and populations that have arisen as adaptive responses to infectious disease.

Smallpox, once a deadly viral disease, may be a good example of how exposure to infectious agents can produce polymorphisms in host populations. During the eighteenth century, smallpox is estimated to have accounted for 10 to 15 percent of all deaths in parts of Europe. But today, this once devastating killer is the only condition to have been successfully eliminated by modern medical technology. By 1977, through massive vaccination programs, the World Health Organization was able to declare the smallpox virus extinct, except for a few colonies in research labs in the United States and Russia (Fig. 16-8).*

Smallpox had a higher incidence in people with either blood type A or AB than in type O individuals, a fact that may be explained by the presence of an antigen on the smallpox virus that's similar to the A antigen. It follows that when some type A individuals were exposed to smallpox, their immune systems failed to recognize the virus as foreign and didn't mount an adequate immune response. So, in regions where smallpox was common in the past, it could have altered allele frequencies at the ABO locus by selecting against the *A* allele.

The Continuing Impact of Infectious Disease

It's important to understand that humans and pathogens exert selective pressures on each other, creating a dynamic relationship between disease organisms and their human (and nonhuman) hosts. Just as disease exerts selective pressures on host populations to adapt, microorganisms also evolve and adapt to various pressures exerted on them by their hosts.

---

*Concern over the potential use of the smallpox virus by bioterrorists relates to these laboratory colonies. Although the virus is extinct outside these labs, some officials fear the possibility that samples of the virus could be stolen. Also, there are apparently some concerns that unknown colonies of the virus may exist in labs in countries other than Russia and the United States. Using disease organisms against enemies isn't new. In the Middle Ages, armies catapulted the corpses of smallpox and plague victims into towns under siege, and during the U.S. colonial period, British soldiers knowingly gave Native Americans blankets used by smallpox victims.

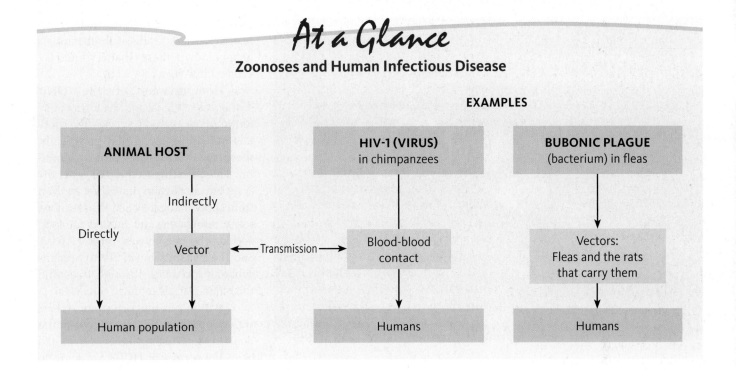

At a Glance

Zoonoses and Human Infectious Disease

EXAMPLES

| ANIMAL HOST | HIV-1 (VIRUS) in chimpanzees | BUBONIC PLAGUE (bacterium) in fleas |

Directly / Indirectly → Vector ←— Transmission —→ Blood-blood contact

Vectors: Fleas and the rats that carry them

Human population / Humans / Humans

Evolutionarily speaking, it's to the advantage of any pathogen not to be so virulent that it kills its host too quickly. If the host dies shortly after becoming infected, the viral or bacterial agent may not have time to reproduce and infect other hosts. Thus, selection sometimes acts to produce resistance in host populations and/or to reduce the virulence of disease organisms, to the benefit of both. However, members of populations exposed for the first time to a new disease frequently die in huge numbers. This type of exposure was a major factor in the decimation of indigenous New World populations after Europeans introduced smallpox into Native American groups. And this has also been the case with the current worldwide spread of HIV.

Of the known disease-causing organisms, HIV provides the best-documented example of evolution and adaptation in a pathogen. It's also one of several examples of interspecies transfer of infection. For these reasons, we focus much of this discussion of evolutionary factors and infectious disease on HIV and AIDS.

The type of HIV responsible for the AIDS epidemic is HIV-1, which in turn is divided into three major subtypes comprising at least 10 different varieties (Hu et al., 1996; Gao, 1999). Another far less common type is HIV-2, which is present only in populations of West Africa. HIV-2 also exhibits a wide range of genetic diversity, and while some strains cause AIDS, others are less virulent.

Since the late 1980s, researchers have been comparing the DNA sequences of HIV and a closely related retrovirus called simian immunodeficiency virus (SIV). SIV is found in chimpanzees and several African monkey species. Like HIV, SIV is genetically variable, and each strain appears to be specific to a given species and even subspecies of primate. SIV produces no symptoms in the African monkeys and chimpanzees that are its traditional hosts, but when injected into Asian monkeys, it eventually causes immune suppression, AIDS-like symptoms, and death. These findings indicate that the various forms of SIV have shared a long evolutionary history (perhaps several hundred thousand years) with a number of African primate species and that these primates have developed ways of accommodating this

Figure **16-9**

These people selling butchered chimpanzees may not realize that, by handling this meat, they could be exposing themselves to HIV.

virus, which is deadly to their Asian relatives. These results also substantiate long-held hypotheses that SIV and HIV evolved in Africa.

Comparisons of the DNA sequences of HIV-2 and the form of SIV found in one monkey species (the sooty mangabey) revealed that genetically, these two viruses are almost identical. These findings led to the generally accepted conclusion that HIV-2 evolved from sooty mangabey SIV. What's more, sooty mangabeys are hunted for food and kept as pets in west-central Africa, and the transmission of SIV to humans probably occurred through bites and the butchering of monkey carcasses.

Although the origin of HIV-2 was established, there was continuing debate over which primate species had been the source of HIV-1. So, a group of medical researchers (Gao et al., 1999) compared DNA sequences of HIV-1 and the form of SIV found in chimpanzees indigenous to west-central Africa. Their results showed that HIV-1 almost certainly evolved from the strain of chimpanzee SIV that infects the subspecies *Pan troglodytes troglodytes*, which is indigenous to central Africa.

Unfortunately for both species, chimpanzees are routinely hunted by humans for food in parts of West Africa (see pp. 172–173). So the most probable explanation for the transmission of SIV from chimpanzees to humans is, as with sooty mangabeys, the hunting and butchering of chimpanzees (Gao et al., 1999; Weiss and Wrangham, 1999; Fig. 16-9).

For these reasons, HIV/AIDS is considered to be a zoonotic disease. The DNA evidence further suggests that there were at least three separate human exposures to chimpanzee SIV, and at some point the virus was altered to the form we call HIV. Exactly when chimpanzee SIV was transmitted to humans is unknown. The oldest evidence of human infection is a frozen HIV-positive blood sample taken from a West African patient in 1959. There are also a few documented cases of AIDS infection by the late 1960s and early 1970s. Therefore, although human exposure to SIV/HIV probably occurred many times in the past, the virus didn't become firmly established in humans until the latter half of the twentieth century.

From this SIV/HIV example, you can appreciate how, through the adoption of various cultural practices, humans have radically altered patterns of infectious disease. The interaction of cultural and biological factors has influenced microevolutionary change in humans, as in the example of sickle-cell anemia (see p. 61), to accommodate altered relationships with disease organisms.

Until the twentieth century, infectious disease was the number one cause of death in all human populations. Even today, in many developing countries, as much as half of all mortality is due to infectious disease, compared to only about 10 percent in the United States. For example, malaria is a disease of the poor in developing nations. Annually, there are an estimated 1 million deaths due to malaria.

That figure computes to one malaria-related death every 30 seconds (Weiss, 2002)! Ninety percent of these deaths occur in sub-Saharan Africa, where 5 percent of children die of malaria before age 5 (Greenwood and Mutabingwa, 2002; Weiss, 2002). In the United States and other industrialized nations, with improved sanitation, and (especially) the widespread use of antibiotics and pesticides beginning in the late 1940s, infectious disease has given way to heart disease and cancer as the leading causes of death.

Optimistic predictions held that infectious disease would be a thing of the past in developed countries and, with the introduction of antibiotics and better living standards, in developing nations, too. But between 1980 and 1992, the number of deaths in the United States in which infectious disease was the underlying cause rose from 41 to 65 per 100,000, an increase of 58 percent (Pinner et al., 1996).

Obviously, AIDS contributed substantially to the increase in mortality due to infectious disease in the United States between 1980 and 1992. By 1992, AIDS was the leading cause of death in men aged 25 to 44 years. As of 1998, mortality due to AIDS had decreased significantly; still, even when subtracting the effect of AIDS in mortality rates, there was a 22 percent increase in mortality rates due to infectious disease between 1980 and 1992 (Pinner et al., 1996).

This increase may partly be due to the overuse of antibiotics. It's estimated that half of all antibiotics prescribed in the United States are used to treat viral conditions, such as colds and flu. Because antibiotics are completely ineffective against viruses, such therapy is not only useless, but may also have dangerous long-term consequences. There's considerable concern in the biomedical community over the indiscriminate use of antibiotics since the 1950s. Antibiotics have exerted selective pressures on bacterial species that have, over time, developed antibiotic-resistant strains (an excellent example of natural selection). So, in the past few years, there's been a *reemergence* of many bacterial diseases, including influenza, pneumonia, cholera, and tuberculosis (TB), in forms that are less responsive to treatment.

The World Health Organization now lists tuberculosis as the world's leading killer of adults (Colwell, 1996). In fact, the number of tuberculosis cases has risen 28 percent worldwide since the mid-1980s, with an estimated 10 million people infected in the United States alone. Although not all infected people develop active disease, in the 1990s an estimated 30 million persons worldwide are believed to have died from TB. One very troubling aspect of the increase in tuberculosis infection is that newly developed strains of *Mycobacterium tuberculosis*, the bacterium that causes TB, are resistant to antibiotics and other treatments.

Various treatments for nonbacterial conditions have also become ineffective. One such example is the appearance of chloroquin-resistant malaria, which has rendered chloroquin (the traditional preventive medication) virtually useless in some parts of Africa. And many insect species have also developed resistance to commonly used pesticides.

Fundamental to all these factors is human population growth (see pp. 491–493); as it continues to soar, it causes more environmental disturbance and, through additional human activity, adds further to global warming. Moreover, in developing countries, where as much as 50 percent of mortality is due to infectious disease, overcrowding and unsanitary conditions increasingly contribute to increased rates of communicable illness. It's hard to conceive of a better set of circumstances for the appearance and spread of communicable disease, and it remains to be seen if scientific innovation and medical technology will be able to meet the challenge.

Summary

In this chapter, we've explored some of the many ways humans have adapted to environmental challenges as they evolved and migrated out of Africa to eventually inhabit most of the planet. We began with a brief discussion of acclimatization as a form of adaptation and the various ways it can occur.

We considered skin color and its adaptive value in response to conflicting selective pressures, all having to do with ultraviolet (UV) radiation. One reason we focused on skin color is that so much importance has been placed on it in the past, particularly in racial classification schemes. Also, skin color is an excellent example of how variations in a characteristic can develop rapidly in response to strong selective pressures. Heavily pigmented skin is adaptive in the tropics because it provides protection from UV radiation, which can cause skin cancer and degrade folate. But as people moved away from the tropics, dark skin became disadvantageous, because a decrease in sunlight meant insufficient exposure to UV radiation for the adequate production of vitamin D. We discussed recent research that documents how two genes (*MC1R* and *SCL24A5*) in particular have been responsible for the geographical patterning of human skin color. These studies are of crucial importance to biological anthropologists.

We also dealt with the various forms of acclimatization that have evolved in humans to deal with environmental stressors like heat, cold, and high altitude. And we emphasized the role of infectious disease in human evolution. We're still coping with infectious disease as we alter the environment and as global climate change facilitates the spread of disease vectors. Cultural innovations also have altered disease patterns and have increased the rate of spread of infectious conditions. Examples of this type of spread are HIV/AIDS and malaria.

Certainly, without cultural adaptations, our species never would have left the tropics. But as in the case of sickle-cell anemia, HIV, and many bacterial diseases, some of our cultural innovations themselves have become selective agents. Many of our practices have had a nasty way of turning on us, and they continue doing so, often with devastating consequences. More than ever, we need to examine our biocultural interactions if we want to explain our past and perhaps predict our future.

Critical Thinking Questions

1. Why can we say that variations in human skin color are the result of natural selection in different environments? Why is less-pigmented skin a result of conflicting selective factors?
2. How has infectious disease played an important role in human evolution? Do you think it plays a current role in human adaptation? How have human cultural practices influenced the patterns of infectious disease seen today? List as many examples as you can, including some not discussed in this chapter.

CHAPTER

17

Legacies of Human Evolutionary History

Michael S. Yamashita/Corbis

Key Questions

How are humans part of a biological continuum that includes all living things?

Given that humans are part of a biological continuum, how does culture make us different from other species?

 Click!

Go to the following media for interactive activities and exercises on topics covered in this chapter:

- Online Virtual Laboratories for Physical Anthropology, Version 4.0

Introduction

By now, you've read 16 chapters that have emphasized human biological evolution and adaptation. You have followed along as we've talked about genetics, evolutionary factors, nonhuman primates, fossil hominins, and how humans vary from one another. But you have also learned that we are remarkably genetically uniform when compared to other primate species that have been studied.

You have accompanied us through geological time to the development of *Homo sapiens:* 225 million years of mammalian evolution, 65 million years of primate evolution, 6 million years of hominin evolution, and 2 million years of evolution of the genus *Homo.* So, what do you think now? Are we just another mammal—or just another primate? In most ways, of course, we are like other mammals and primates. But as we have emphasized throughout the text, modern human beings are the result of *biocultural evolution.* In other words, modern human biology and behavior have been shaped by the biological and cultural forces that operated on our ancestors. In fact, it would be fruitless to attempt an understanding of modern human biology and diversity without considering that humans have evolved in the context of culture. It would be like trying to understand the biology of fish without considering that they live in water.

In the two previous chapters, we have seen that modern human beings are a highly generalized species. This means that we can live in a great variety of climates, eat a wide variety of foods, and respond to most environmental challenges in myriad ways. For example, as human populations moved into cold northern climates, they were able to respond both physiologically and behaviorally to the environmental challenges they faced. As noted in Chapter 16, adaptations to cold include physiological responses to conserve or increase heat such as vasoconstriction of the capillaries, increased metabolic rate, and shivering. Considering these responses from an evolutionary perspective, we can assume that among the earliest human populations inhabiting cold regions of the world, those individuals who had genotypes and phenotypes enabling them to respond physiologically had more surviving offspring to pass along these characteristics. Behavioral and cultural adaptations to cold climates probably included fire, house structures, warm clothing, and hunting for foods that provided energy to withstand the cold. In these examples, we see evidence of human adaptations to cold that are both biological and cultural and that are rooted in evolution.

In this chapter, we'll explore ways in which the legacies of human evolution continue to have profound impact on our behavior throughout our lives and on the planet we inhabit. We begin with a view of the legacies of human evolution that impact each of us as individuals throughout our life course. Later we will discuss how the legacies of our evolutionary history impact the earth and other life-forms.

Human Behavioral Ecology and Evolutionary Psychology

Examining human social behavior in an evolutionary framework is known as *behavioral ecology,* which we discussed in Chapter 7 in the context of primate behavior. Of course, humans are primates, and many biological anthropologists are interested in the extent to which evolution can explain contemporary human behaviors. Behavioral ecologists suggest that humans, like other animals, behave in ways that increase their fitness, or reproductive success. This includes behaviors affecting mating and parenting success. Finding mates and taking care of offspring require time and energy, and as we know all too well, both of these commodities exist in finite amounts. Thus, reproductive efforts require trade-offs in time, energy, and resources invested in mating and parenting. When we read about these concepts as they pertain to monkeys and apes, most of us probably find little to disagree with. But to suggest that evolutionary processes have an impact on human behavior today raises a lot of issues, some of which aren't so easily resolved.

For example, this view argues that natural selection is not limited to physical and physiological responses, but has had an effect on the way humans think—in other words, on human cognition, perception, and memory. An example of the argument goes something like this: The ability to remember a dangerous event that may have resulted in loss of life would be favorably selected if it prevented a person from being caught in a similar situation. The ability to distinguish a wildebeest (food) from a lion (danger) would be selectively favored. Likewise, economic behaviors involved in the allocation of resources to increase survival and reproductive success would be favored.

The study of how natural selection has influenced the way humans and other primates think is often called *evolutionary psychology.* Among the topics explored by evolutionary psychologists are mate attraction, sexuality, aggression, and violence. As you might guess, all of these are hot topics, and there is no end in sight to the controversy that surrounds them.

Because it implies that our behavior is constrained in ways that we may not be able to overcome, many people are uncomfortable with such an explicit evolutionary perspective on contemporary human behavior and thought. For example, it can be argued that individual males can increase their reproductive success by increasing the number of women with whom they mate. Women, meanwhile, are thought to best increase the health of their offspring (and thus their reproductive success) if they can find mates and other people who will supply resources to them and their children. At first glance, these two recipes for reproductive success seem to conflict. Further examination, however, reveals that the optimal route to reproductive success for males and females represents a compromise between what is argued to be the best strategy for each sex. Males who "love 'em and leave 'em" usually end up with fewer surviving offspring than males who take on the role of provider.

Aggression and violence, particularly on the part of males, is the subject of a number of books and papers in evolutionary psychology. A common approach is to contrast the behaviors of our two closest living relatives, the chimpanzees and bonobos (de Waal, 2006). Most striking is that chimpanzee society seems to be based on male-male competition and aggression, occasionally leading to violence both within and between troops, whereas bonobo society is described as a female-dominated community based on cooperation and peaceful interaction (Fig. 17-1). To Wrangham and Peterson (1996), these two behavior patterns represent the extremes

(a)

(b)

Figure **17-1**

(a) These chimpanzees exhibit an aggressive reaction when confronted by others. (b) The bonobos show more relaxed expressions.

of human societies and also show potentials for both violence and peace that may be rooted in human evolutionary history. On the other hand, these and other authors acknowledge the role of culture and society in fostering aggression and violence in males. Mirroring some of the discussions of terrorism today, Wrangham and Peterson point out that chimpanzee communities with abundant resources have far fewer incidents of violence than communities with limited resources; in general, bonobos live in areas of relative resource abundance. But whatever their roots, it appears to many observers that war, genocide, rape, rioting, and terrorism are unwelcome legacies of human evolutionary history. Unfortunately, because of recent events, like the 2001 terrorist attacks and the wars in Afghanistan and Iraq, the argument that violence and agression are rooted in human evolutionary history resonate more profoundly and convincingly than they did when the first edition of this textbook was written. Perhaps by the next edition, the pendulum of thinking about world events will have swung toward the idea that peaceful cooperation is more fundamental to human behavior, a view held by primatologist Frans de Waal (1989, 1996, 1998) and many others.

In suggesting that some of our behaviors reflect our evolutionary history, we aren't saying that there are "genes for" such behaviors (see p. 180). No matter how you cut it, human behavior is an extremely complex phenomenon, and its expression depends on a combination of myriad genes, environmental context, and individual experience. There's really no way of predicting how an individual mother or father will allocate resources in the task of child rearing, but behavioral ecologists argue that patterns can be seen when populations (or even the entire species) are examined for allocation of parenting resources.

One aspect of behavioral ecology that may have less emotional baggage than reproductive and parenting strategies is how people make decisions about food acquisition. For example, when a behavioral ecologist examines the hunting strategy on a given day for a band of foragers, the prediction would be that the hunters would pursue a strategy that would maximize return and minimize time and energy invested (Fig. 17-2). In other words, they predict that the hunters would pursue an "optimal foraging strategy." But if the analysis considers only the calories in the food obtained weighed against the calories expended in pursuit of the

© Peter Johnson/Corbis

Figure **17-2**
When these G/wi hunters plan their hunting strategy, they consider many factors in addition to calories expended and acquired.

food item, the theory will always come up short, because other important factors are left out of the model. What dangers were between the foragers and the foods that may have led them to take an alternate route or avoid a food patch or prey animal altogether? Does pursuit of a particular prey animal take them too far away from home when night falls? Does a smaller food or prey item provide additional resources, such as a pelt that's useful for clothing? And have the people been eating this food for several days, so that they desire a bit of variety? All of these factors could explain why a band of hunters and gatherers might choose to pursue a food item of less caloric value and thus deviate from the prediction. To return to the idea of an optimal reproductive strategy, wouldn't similar complicating factors apply? Certainly, contemporary humans choose mates based on many more factors besides how many offspring they can produce or raise together.

Biocultural Evolution and the Life Cycle

Despite its limitations and challenges, examining human behavior as a product of evolution helps us explain and understand some aspects of our lives. It also allows predictions that can be examined and tested through field observations, demographic studies, and other methods. Examples from the human life cycle further illustrate how evolution has influenced human reproductive behavior and how reproduction is embedded in culture. In other words, we view the life cycle as a biocultural process. If we consider how a human develops from an embryo into an adult and examine the forces that operate on that process, then we will have a better perspective of how both biology and culture influence our own lives and how our evolutionary history creates opportunities and sets limitations.

Of course, cultural factors interact with genetically based biological characteristics to widely varying degrees; these variable interactions influence how characteristics are expressed in individuals. Some genetically based characteristics will be exhibited no matter what the cultural context of a person's life happens to be. If a person inherits two alleles for albinism, for example (see Chapter 4), she will

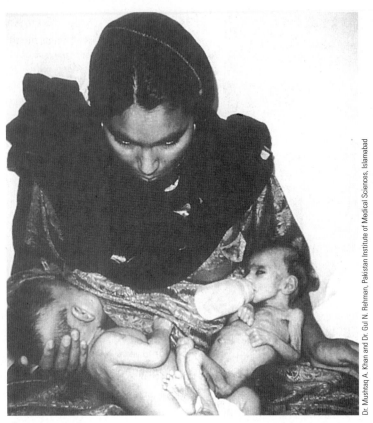

Figure **17-3**

This is a mother with her twin children. The one on the left is a boy and is breast-fed. The girl, on the right, is bottle-fed. This illustrates both differential treatment of boys and girls in many societies and the potential negative effects of bottle-feeding.

Dr. Mushtaq A. Khan and Dr. Gul N. Rehman, Pakistan Institute of Medical Sciences, Islamabad

be deficient in the production of the pigment melanin, resulting in lightly colored skin, hair, and eyes. This phenotype will emerge regardless of the woman's cultural environment. Likewise, the sex-linked trait for hemophilia (also described in Chapter 4) will be exhibited by all males who inherit it, no matter where they live.

Other characteristics, such as intelligence, body shape, and growth reflect the interaction of environment and genes. We know, for example, that each of us is born with a genetic makeup that influences the maximum stature we can achieve in adulthood. But to reach that maximum stature, we must be properly nourished during growth (including when we were *in utero*), and we must avoid many childhood diseases and other stresses that inhibit growth. What factors determine whether we are well fed and receive good medical care? In the United States, socioeconomic status is probably the primary factor that determines nutrition and health. Socioeconomic status is thus an example of a cultural factor that affects growth. But in another culture, diet and health status might be influenced by whether the individual is male or female. In some cultures, males receive the best care in infancy and childhood and are thus often larger and healthier as adults than are females (Fig. 17-3). If there's a cultural value on slimness in women, young girls may try to restrict their food intake in ways that affect their growth; but if the culture values plumpness, the effect on diet in adolescence will likely be different. These are all examples of how cultural values affect growth and development.

Life History Theory

As noted in earlier chapters, primatologists and other physical anthropologists view primate and human growth and development from an evolutionary perspective, with an interest in how natural selection has operated on the life cycle from conception to death, a perspective known as *life history theory* (see pp. 184–185). Why, for example, do humans have longer periods of infancy and childhood compared with other primates? What accounts for differences seen in the life cycles of such closely related species as humans and chimpanzees? Life history research seeks to answer such questions (e.g., Mace, 2000; Hawkes and Paine, 2006).

Life history theory begins with the premise that an organism has only a certain amount of energy available for growing, maintaining life, and reproducing. Energy invested in one of these processes is not available for another. So, the entire life course is a series of trade-offs among life history traits, such as length of gestation, age at weaning, time spent in growth to adulthood, adult body size, and length of life span. For example, life history theory provides the basis for understanding how fast an organism will grow and to what size, how many offspring can be produced, how long gestation will last, and how long an individual will live. Crucial to understanding life history theory is its link to the evolutionary process: It is the action of natural selection that shapes life history traits, determining which traits

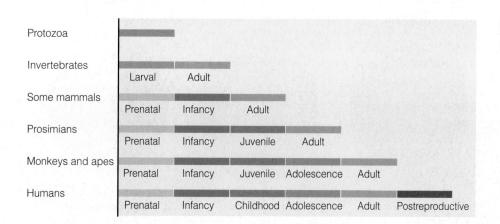

Figure **17-4**
Life cycle stages for various animal species.

will succeed or fail in a given environment. It's not clear whether life history theory works in contemporary human populations (Strassman and Gillespie, 2002), but it's a useful guide for examining the various life cycle phases from evolutionary and ecological perspectives.

Not all animals have clearly demarcated phases in their lives; moreover, among mammals, humans have more such phases than do other species (Fig. 17-4). Protozoa, among the simplest of animals, have only one phase; many invertebrates have two: larval and adult. Most primates have four phases: gestation, infancy, juvenile (usually called childhood in humans), and adult. Apes, humans, and perhaps monkeys have a phase between the juvenile, or childhood, phase and adulthood that is referred to as adolescence (the teenage years, in humans). Finally, for humans there is the addition of a sixth phase in women, the postreproductive years following **menopause**. One could argue that during the course of primate evolution, more recently evolved forms have longer life spans and more divisions of the life span into phases, or stages.

Most of these life cycle stages are well marked by biological transitions. The prenatal phase begins with conception and ends with birth; infancy is the period of nursing; childhood, or the juvenile phase, is the period from weaning to sexual maturity (puberty in humans); adolescence is the period from puberty to the end of growth; adulthood is marked by the birth of the first child and/or the completion of growth; and menopause is recognized as having occurred one full year after the last menstrual cycle. These biological markers are similar among higher primates, but for humans, there is an added complexity: They occur in cultural contexts that define and characterize them. Puberty, for example, has very different meanings in different cultures. A girl's first menstruation (**menarche**) is often marked with ritual and celebration, and a change in social status typically occurs with this biological transition. Likewise, menopause is often associated with a rise in status for women in non-Western societies, but it's commonly seen as a negative transition for women in many Western societies. As we'll see, collective and individual attitudes toward these life cycle transitions affect an individual's growth and development.

Birth, Infancy, and Childhood

A characteristic that humans share with most other primates is a relatively large brain compared with body size (see p. 210). In fact, the delivery of a large newborn head through a somewhat small pelvis is a challenge that modern humans share

menopause The end of menstruation in women, usually occurring at around age 50.

menarche The first menstruation in girls, usually occurring in the early to mid-teens.

Figure **17-5**
The relationship between the average diameter of the birth canal of adult females and average head length and breadth of newborns of the same species. (After Jolly, 1985.)

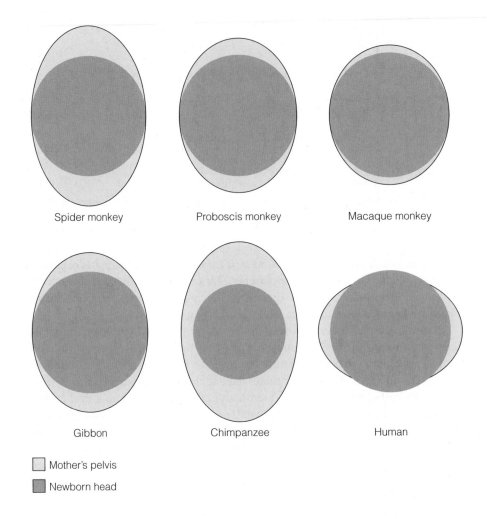

Spider monkey Proboscis monkey Macaque monkey

Gibbon Chimpanzee Human

☐ Mother's pelvis
☐ Newborn head

with many other primates, including most monkeys (Fig. 17-5). A further challenge for modern humans, however, is that human brains are somewhat undeveloped at birth, so the babies are more helpless and dependent on their caretakers than are most monkey infants. After a human infant is born, the brain continues growing much faster than any other part of the body except the eyeball. At birth, the human brain is about 25 percent of its adult size. By 6 months of age, the brain has doubled in size, reaching 50 percent of adult size, and it reaches near-adult size by age 10 years. At adolescence, the brain displays only a very small growth spurt, making it an exception to the growth curves for most other parts of the body. This pattern of brain growth, including the relatively small amount of growth before birth, is unusual among primates and other mammals. By contrast, most mammalian species have typically achieved at least 50 percent of adult brain size before birth. For humans, however, the narrow pelvis that evolved for walking bipedally limits the size of the fetal head that can be delivered through it. That limitation, along with the value of having most brain growth occur in the more stimulating environment outside the womb, has resulted in human infants being born with far less of their total adult brain size than most other mammals. (As we saw in Chapter 12, this pattern of delayed maturation was probably already established in hominin evolution by 1.5 mya.)

Delayed brain growth may be particularly important for a species dependent on language. The human brain's language centers develop in the first three years of life, when the brain is rapidly expanding; these three years are considered a critical period for the development of language in the human child. In fact, children who aren't exposed to speech during this period never develop fully normal language skills.

The narrow human pelvis adapted for bipedalism and the large newborn head offer another challenge in human development. Most primate infants are born head first, facing the front of the birth canal, making it easy for the mother to reach down and guide the infant out. Because of some modifications to the human pelvis, the infant is typically born facing the back of the birth canal. This means that the mother must reach behind her to pull the infant into the world. This added difficulty may explain why humans routinely seek assistance at birth, rather than delivering an infant alone as most mammals do. Although it's certainly possible for a woman to deliver an infant alone (Walrath, 2003), having someone else to guide the baby out, wipe its face so it can breathe, and prevent the umbilical cord from choking the infant, can significantly reduce mortality associated with birth (Rosenberg and Trevathan, 2001). In fact, a survey of world cultures reveals that it's unusual to give birth alone, particularly to a first child. So for humans, birth is a life cycle event that typically takes place in the context of culture; it's a social rather than a solitary event, unlike that for most other mammals.

Infancy is defined for mammals as the period when breast-feeding takes place, typically lasting about three to four years in humans. When we consider how unusual it is for a mother to breastfeed her child for even a year in the United States or Canada, this figure may surprise us. But considering that four or five years of breast-feeding is the norm for chimpanzees, gorillas, orangutans, and for women in foraging societies, most anthropologists conclude that four years was the norm for most humans in the evolutionary past (Stuart-Macadam and Dettwyler, 1995). Other lines of evidence confirm this pattern, including the lack of other foods that infants could consume until the origin of agriculture and the domestication of milk-producing animals. In fact, if the mother died during childbirth in preagricultural populations, it's very likely that the child died also, unless there was another woman available who could nurse the child. Jane Goodall has noted that this is also true for chimpanzees: Infants who are orphaned before they are weaned do not usually survive. Even those orphaned after weaning are still emotionally dependent on their mothers and exhibit clinical signs of depression for a few months or years after the mother's death, assuming they survive the trauma (Goodall, 1986).

Human milk, like that of other primates, is extremely low in fats and protein. Such a low nutrient content is typical for species in which mothers are seldom or never separated from their infants and nurse in short, frequent bouts. Not coincidentally, prolonged, frequent nursing suppresses ovulation in marginally nourished women (Konner and Worthman, 1980), especially when coupled with high activity levels and few calorie reserves (Ellison, 2001). Under these circumstances, breast-feeding can help maintain a four-year birth interval, during which infants have no nutritional competition from siblings. Thus, nursing served as a natural birth control mechanism in the evolutionary past, as it does in some populations today. The importance of adequate nutrients during the period of rapid brain growth cannot be overestimated, so it's not surprising that there are many cultural practices designed to ensure successful nursing.

Breast milk also provides important antibodies that contribute to infant survival. Throughout the world, breast-fed infants have far greater survival rates than those who are not breast-fed or who are weaned too early. The only exception is in societies where scientifically developed milk substitutes are readily available and appropriately used, and even then, important antibodies and other immune

Table **17-1 Providing for Juveniles**

	Percent of Those Who Survive	
	Weaning	Adolescence
Lion	28	15
Baboon	45	33
Macaque	42	13
Chimpanzee	48	38
Provisioned macaques	82	58
Human Populations		
!Kung*	80	58
Yanomamo†	73	50
Paleoindian‡	86	50

*Hunting and gathering population of southern Africa.
†Horticultural population of South America.
‡ Preagricultural people of the Americas.

Source: Adapted from Lancaster and Lancaster, 1983.

factors are not passed to the infants. Furthermore, there is increasing evidence that breast-feeding may be protective against later-life obesity, types 1 and 2 diabetes, and hypertension (Pollard, 2008).

Humans have unusually long childhoods and a slowed growth process, reflecting the importance of learning for our species (Bogin, 2006). Childhood is the time between weaning and puberty; it is a time when growth in stature is occurring, the brain is completing its growth, and technical and social skills are being acquired. For most other mammals, once weaning has occurred, getting food is left to individual effort. Humans may be unique in the practice of providing food for juveniles (Lancaster and Lancaster, 1983). Such sustained care requires much extra effort by parents, but the survival rate of offspring is a great deal higher than in other primates (Table 17-1). During childhood, the roles of fathers, older siblings, grandmothers, and other kin become very significant. While mothers are highly involved with caring for new infants, the socialization and child care of other children often fall to other family or community members. Clearly, family environment, stress, and other biosocial factors have a major impact on children's health (Flinn, 1999, 2008).

Before continuing to examine the life cycle from the vantage point of life history theory, let's take a look at factors that affect growth and development throughout the growing years.

Nutritional Effects on Growth and Development

Nutrition has an impact on human growth at every stage of the life cycle. During pregnancy, for example, a woman's diet can have a profound effect on the development of her fetus and the eventual health of the child. Moreover, the effects are transgenerational, because a woman's own supply of eggs is developed while she herself is *in utero*. So, if a woman is malnourished during pregnancy, the eggs that develop in her female fetus may be damaged in a way that affects her future grandchildren's health. And even if a baby girl whose mother was malnourished during pregnancy is well nourished from birth on (as often happens in adoptions), her growth, health, and future pregnancies appear to be compromised—a legacy that may even extend for several generations (Kuzawa, 2005). Furthermore, nutritional stress during pregancy commonly results in low-birth-weight babies that are at great risk for developing hypertension, cardiovascular disease, and diabetes later in life (Barker, 1994; Gluckman and Hanson, 2005). Low-birth-weight babies are particularly at risk if they are born into a world of abundant food resources (especially cheap fast food) and gain weight rapidly in childhood (Kuzawa, 2005, 2008).These findings have clear implications for public health efforts that attempt to provide adequate nutritional support to pregnant women and infants throughout the world.

Nutrients needed for growth, development, and body maintenance include proteins, carbohydrates, lipids (fats), vitamins, and minerals. The specific amount that we need of each of these nutrients coevolved with the types of foods that were available to human ancestors throughout our evolutionary history. For example, the specific pattern of amino acids required in human nutrition (the essential amino acids) reflects an ancestral diet high in animal protein. Unfortunately for modern humans, these coevolved nutritional requirements are often incompatible with the foods that are available and typically consumed today.

The ancestral diet, while perhaps high in animal protein, was probably lower in fats, particularly saturated fats. The diet was also most likely high in complex carbohydrates (including fiber), low in salt, and high in calcium. We don't need to be reminded that the contemporary diet typically seen in many industrialized societies is just the opposite of the ancestral one. It's high in saturated fats and salt and low in complex carbohydrates, fiber, and calcium (Table 17-2). There's very good evidence that many of today's diseases in industrialized countries are related to the lack of fit between our diet today and the one with which we evolved (Eaton, Shostak, and Konner, 1988; Eaton, Eaton, and Konner, 1999; Cordain, 2002).

Table 17-2 Preagricultural, Contemporary American, and Recently Recommended Dietary Composition

	Preagricultural Diet	Contemporary Diet	Recent Recommendations
Total dietary energy (%)			
Protein	33	12	12
Carbohydrate	46	46	58
Fat	21	42	30
Alcohol	~0	(7–10)	—
P:S ratio*	1.41	0.44	1
Cholesterol (mg)	520	300–500	300
Fiber (g)	100–150	19.7	30–60
Sodium (mg)	690	2,300–6,900	1,000–3,300
Calcium (mg)	1,500–2,000	740	800–1,500
Ascorbic acid (mg)	440	90	60

*Polyunsaturated: saturated fat ratio.

Source: From *The Paleolithic Prescription*, by S. Boyd Eaton, Marjorie Shostak, and Melvin Konner (New York: Harper & Row, 1988).

A Closer Look
Diabetes

What is diabetes? There are actually two different diseases that are referred to as diabetes. One, the less common, is type 1 diabetes (also called insulin-dependent diabetes mellitus or IDDM and juvenile-onset diabetes), which occurs when the immune system interferes with the body's ability to produce the insulin that converts sugars (glucose) into energy. This type of diabetes is usually first recognized in childhood and requires lifelong insulin injections to avoid cell damage and death. It is unlikely that children with type 1 diabetes lived very long in the past. Type 2 diabetes, far more common today, is a problem with the way insulin is used in the body. Sometimes this is described as "insulin resistance" in that there may be sufficient insulin produced, but the cells are not able to utilize it, resulting in a buildup of glucose in the bloodstream that can result in a number of complications of the cardiovascular system, kidneys, and nervous system. If untreated, usually with diet modifications, weight control, and exercise, type 2 diabetes can also result in early death.

A few years ago, type 2 diabetes was something that happened to older people living primarily in the developed world. Sadly, this is no longer true. The World Diabetes Foundation estimates that 80% of the new cases of type 2 diabetes that appear between now and 2025 will be in developing nations and the World Health Organization (WHO) predicts that more than 70% of *all* diabetes cases in the world will be in developing nations in 2025. Furthermore, type 2 diabetes is occurring in children as young as 4 (Pavkov et al., 2006) and the mean age of diagnosis in the United States dropped from 52 to 46 between 1988 and 2000 (Koopman, et al., 2005). In fact, we predict that almost everyone reading this book has a friend or family member who has diabetes. What's happened to make this former "disease of old age" and "disease of civilization" reach what some have described as epidemic proportions?

Although there appears to be a genetic link (type 2 diabetes tends to run in families), most fingers point to lifestyle factors. Two that have been implicated in the emergence of this epidemic are bad diets and no exercise. Noting that our current diets and low levels of activity are very different from those of our ancestors, proponents of evolutionary medicine suggest that diabetes is the price we pay for novel lifestyles that find people of all ages consuming diets high in sugars and other refined carbohydrates while they spend their days in front of TVs and computer monitors. The reason that diabetes incidence is increasing in developing nations is that these bad habits are also spreading to those nations.

Several decades ago, geneticist James Neel (1962) proposed that people who develop diabetes have "thrifty genotypes" that served their ancestors well when they lived under alternating feast and famine conditions and engaged in high levels of physical activity, but that today are nothing but trouble for people living under conditions of constant food availability and relative inactivity. Thus, what was formerly an asset (i.e., the ability to be thrifty and "save" calories for future use) is now a liability. Recent reviews, however, find the thrifty genotype hypothesis to be an oversimplification and a "thrifty phenotype hypothesis" has emerged to take its place. According to this view, poor fetal and early post-natal nutrition impose mechanisms of nutritional thrift upon the growing individual resulting in impaired glucose resistance throughout life (Hales and Barker, 2001). The long-term consequences of early malnutrition are thus impaired development of glucose metabolism and a far greater susceptibility to type 2 diabetes. Recognition of the role of early nutrition in predisposing to diabetes suggests that by improving maternal and prenatal health worldwide, we may be able to reduce the incidence of type 2 diabetes in a far more effective way than we can by urging people to change their diets and other aspects of their lifestyles.

Many of our biological and behavioral characteristics evolved because in the past they contributed to survival and reproductive success, but today these same characteristics may be maladaptive. An example is our ability to store fat. This capability was an advantage in the past, when food availability often alternated between abundance and scarcity. Those who could store fat during the times of abundance could draw on those stores during times of scarcity and remain healthy, resist disease, and, for women, maintain the ability to reproduce. Today, people with adequate economic resources spend much of their lives with a relative abundance of foods. Considering the number of disorders associated with obesity, the formerly positive ability to store extra fat has now turned into a liability. Our "feast or famine" biology is now incompatible with the constant feast many of us indulge in today.

Perhaps no disorder is as clearly linked with dietary and lifestyle behaviors as the form of diabetes mellitus that typically begins in later life. This form is referred to either as type 2 diabetes or NIDDM (non-insulin-dependent diabetes mellitus). In 1900, diabetes ranked twenty-seventh among the leading causes of death in the United States; today it ranks seventh. And the threat to world health from this disease is growing, with projections of an increase in incidence between 2000 and 2010 of 57 percent in Asia, 50 percent in Africa, 44 percent in South America, and 23 percent in North America (Zimmet, Alberti, and Shaw, 2001). Part of this projected increase will be due to decreases in other causes of death (or example, infectious diseases), but much of it has to do with lifestyle and dietary changes associated with modernization and globalization, especially the decrease in levels of daily activity and increase in dietary intake of fats and refined carbohydrates (Lieberman, 2003).

Rates for obesity and diabetes in the United States and throughout the world have grown over the last decade, and some fear that the increase is accelerating. In fact, medical and popular news reports refer to increases in obesity and diabetes as epidemics (Mokdad et al., 2001). It used to be that only affuent countries had to worry about obesity, but recent years have seen dramatic increases in overweight and obesity in less affluent and even poor countries. Although it is not the best measure for scientific studies, body mass index (BMI—weight in kg/height in m^2) is easily obtained and is useful for population-level assessments. According to the World Health Organization (WHO), overweight is a BMI of 25–29, and obesity is marked by a BMI of 30 or greater. By these measures, 1.6 billion adults in the world were overweight and 400 million were obese in 2006. Furthermore, obesity in childhood is of increasing concern because of what it forebodes for future health challenges, especially diabetes (Lieberman, 2008). Unlike many scourges that threaten

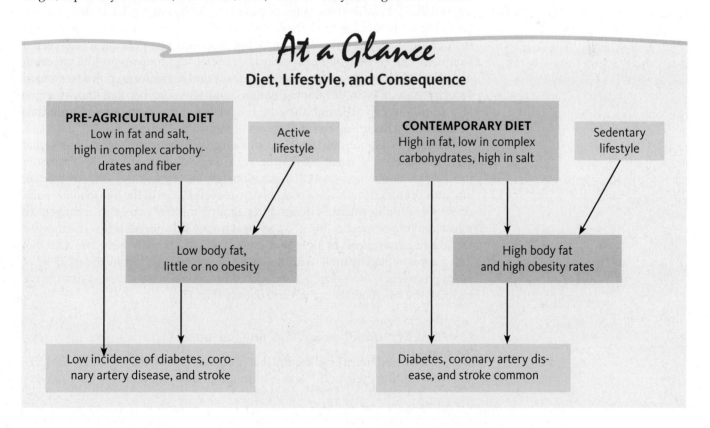

At a Glance

Diet, Lifestyle, and Consequence

| PRE-AGRICULTURAL DIET Low in fat and salt, high in complex carbohydrates and fiber | Active lifestyle | CONTEMPORARY DIET High in fat, low in complex carbohydrates, high in salt | Sedentary lifestyle |

Low body fat, little or no obesity

High body fat and high obesity rates

Low incidence of diabetes, coronary artery disease, and stroke

Diabetes, coronary artery disease, and stroke common

© Digital Vision/Getty Images

© Peter Turnley/Corbis

Figure **17-6**

Some people suffer from an overabundance of food (left), while others suffer from tragically insufficient amounts of food.

our health, though, obesity and diabetes can usually be prevented by modifying diet and activity.

It's clear that both deficiencies and excesses of nutrients can cause health problems and interfere with childhood growth (see pp. 454–455). Certainly, many people in all parts of the world, both industrialized and developing, suffer from inadequate supplies of food of any quality. We read daily of thousands dying from starvation due to drought, warfare, or political instability. The blame must be placed not only on the narrowed food base that resulted from the emergence of agriculture, but also on the increase in human population that occurred when people began settling in permanent villages and having more children. Today, the crush of billions of humans almost completely dependent on cereal grains (Cordain, 1999) means that millions face undernutrition, malnutrition, and even starvation. Even with these huge populations, however, food scarcity may not be as big a problem as food inequality. In other words, there may be enough food produced for all people on earth, but economic and political forces keep it from reaching those who need it most. Of increasing concern are the effects of globalization (including liberalization of trade and agricultural policies) on food security, especially in developing nations, and what has become known as the "global south." In particular, the adoption of "Western" diets and lifestyles has contributed to declining health in much of the world (Young, 2004).

In summary, our nutritional adaptations were shaped in environments that included times of scarcity alternating with times of abundance. The variety of foods consumed was so great that nutritional deficiency diseases were rare. Small amounts of animal foods were probably an important part of the diet in many parts of the world. In northern latitudes, after about 1 million years ago, meat was an important part of the diet. But because meat from wild animals is low in saturated fats, the negative effects of high meat intake that we see today were rare. Our diet today is often incompatible with the adaptations that evolved in the millions of years preceding the development of agriculture. The consequences of that incompatibility include both starvation and obesity (Fig. 17-6).

Onset of Reproductive Functioning in Humans

Having reviewed nutritional factors that influence growth during childhood, let's return to the life cycle and follow it through until the end of life. Take another look at Figure 17–4 and you'll see that for most animals, the juvenile, or child-hood, stage ends when adulthood begins. For humans and apes, and possibly some monkeys, there's an additional life cycle stage called adolescence. This is a period of extremely rapid growth in humans (the "adolescent growth spurt") that is not seen in other primates (Bogin, 1999). A number of biological events mark the transition to adolescence for both males and females. These include increase in body size, change in body shape, and the development of testes and penes in boys, and breasts in girls. Hormonal changes are the driving forces behind all these physical alterations, especially increased testosterone production in boys and increased estrogen production in girls. During this time after reproductive functioning begins, individuals may be mature in some ways but immature in others. For example, an adolescent girl of 14 may be capable of bearing children, but she is not yet fully grown herself and is often too immature socially and economically to successfully raise a child.

The onset of menarche in girls is affected by several factors, including genetic patterns (girls tend to become mature at about the same age as their mothers), nutrition, stress, and disease. You'll remember from our discussion of life history theory that energy must be allocated among growth, body maintenance, and reproduction. During childhood, most resources are directed toward growth; but at some point, the body switches to allocating more energy to reproduction, and for girls, this shift is somewhat abrupt. What "tells" the body that it's time to direct more energy to reproduction and less (or none) to growth? An early hypothesis was that the switch occurred when a girl had accumulated a certain amount of body fat (Frisch, 1988). This proposal made sense because of a trend toward lower age of menarche that has been noted in affluent human populations in the last hundred years (Fig. 17-7) and the tendency for girls who are very active and thin to mature later than those who are heavier and less active. An alternative view that seems to fit the data better is Ellison's (2001) proposal that the criti-

cal growth parameter is not body fat but skeletal growth, specifically growth of the pelvis. We've already seen what a tight squeeze it is for the human infant to pass through the birth canal; just imagine what it would be like for an 8-year-old girl to try to give birth! Thus, it's not only fat that's important for reproduction, but completion of skeletal growth as well.

Life history theory provides ways of predicting the timing of reproduction under favorable circumstances. For example, if early maturity results in higher numbers of surviving offspring, then it is predicted that natural selection would favor those members of a population who mature earlier. Until the advent of settled living, it's likely that females became pregnant as soon as they were biologically able to do so,

Figure 17-7

The declining age of menarche in Europe.

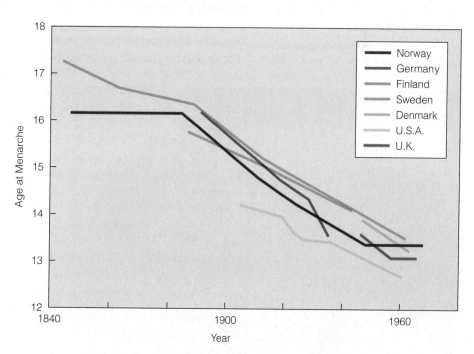

Source: Wood, James W., 1994 *Dynamics of Human Reproduction*, New York: Aldine de Gruyter, original redrawn from Eveleth, P. B. and J. M. Tanner, 1976. *Worldwide Variation in Human Growth*, Cambridge: Cambridge University Press.)

that is, as soon as they had finished growing. This would be an advantage because individual life expectancy would have been low. Paleodemographic studies indicate a mortality rate of at least 50 percent in subadults in preindustrial populations; and of the half that survived to adulthood, most did not survive to age 50. Considering the reality of short life spans combined with the long period of infant dependency, producing offspring as early as possible may have contributed to the reproductive success of females, particularly early hominin females. By giving birth as soon as she reached sexual maturity, an early hominin female enhanced her chances of rearing even one offspring to the point it could survive without her.

The high rates of adolescent pregnancy seen in the United States and some other countries today reflect this ancient biological heritage. Today, however, there may be disadvantages to early maturity, including its effect on health in later life (Worthman, 1999). If delayed maturity is associated with higher-quality care of the offspring, then offspring survival may improve, resulting in a net increase in fitness for those who mature a few years later. Unfortunately, all too frequently today in many parts of the world, young girls become reproductively mature long before they're socially mature. And if they're also sexually active, they may become pregnant before finishing school or obtaining the skills necessary for economic self-sufficiency. This means that the quality of care that they can provide their offspring may be compromised. We know that the infant mortality rate in humans rises rapidly as the mother's age at first birth decreases (Stearns, 1992). In most contemporary societies, it's likely that those who delay reproducing until they're emotionally, socially, and economically mature will have more surviving offspring than those who begin their parenting careers before they themselves have matured. But if the young, maturing parents have sufficient help from their extended families, social and religious organizations, or government agencies, early childbearing may not compromise their reproductive fitness. Clearly, the road to reproductive success is more complicated than most early theories of behavioral ecology suggested, although they're useful models for predicting behavior.

What about the number of offspring produced at each birth? Primates such as monkeys, apes, and humans typically give birth to one infant at a time. Twins occur in apes and humans at about the same frequency, but the survival rate of twins (or triplets) is far lower than the survival rate of singletons. So, we can argue that humans are somewhat limited in the number of offspring resulting from each conception. Because we are mammals, we're also physiologically constrained regarding the dependency of our offspring in the first few years of life, as discussed earlier in this chapter (Fig. 17-8). Apes (and, we assume, ancestral humans) breast-feed their infants for three to four years, resulting in approximately a four-year birth interval. That interval can be reduced with earlier weaning or, in the case of formula feeding, by not breast-feeding at all. This means that contemporary humans can easily reduce the birth interval to less than two years, potentially doubling the number of offspring produced. But again, in most cases, the quality of parental care is compromised when there are too many dependent offspring. If the number of offspring reaching

Figure **17-8**

Human infants require extensive parental care, especially in the first few years of life.

© Alan Abraham/Corbis

reproductive maturity is lower with two-year birth intervals than with four-year birth intervals, then natural selection will favor the latter.

While an evolutionary perspective can help us understand how natural selection has impacted offspring numbers, it can also help us understand parenting behaviors that may, at first glance, seem counter to the goal of increasing reproductive success. For example, in Chapter 7, we discussed infanticide in langurs and other species, noting that it seems counterproductive to the supposed goal of increasing reproductive success. The evolutionary perspective argues that when a male commits infanticide against the offspring of another male, the first male can be interpreted as increasing his own reproductive success at the other male's expense. But what about situations in which a mother kills her own offspring? Can this contribute to her reproductive success in any way? Sarah Hrdy tackles such challenging questions in her book *Mother Nature: A History of Mothers, Infants, and Natural Selection* (1999). Hrdy points out that in many situations, maternal behavior defies the claim that mammals have a natural "instinct" for mother love. But if we place the behaviors in an evolutionary context, the discrepancies can often be resolved. For example, consider a mother who abandons her newborn infant when social and economic conditions are so dire that the chances of the child surviving very long are slim. She may have an older child whose life would be placed in jeopardy if the mother allocated her meager resources to two children. It may be better (in an evolutionary sense, not in a moral sense) to let the younger child die so that the mother can bear another as soon as conditions and chances for child survival are improved or so that she can focus her resources on the older child. This example illustrates the concept that for most measures of reproductive success, quality of offspring produced is more important than quantity. This is not to say that all maternal behaviors are adaptive. But a behavior that at first glance seems maladaptive may actually serve to increase reproductive success for the mother in the long run.

Grandmothers

Can behavioral ecology explain the long period of reproductive sterility in human females following menopause? If increasing reproductive success is what it's all about, then how could natural selection favor cessation of reproductive functioning relatively early in a woman's lifetime?

For women, menopause, or the end of menstruation, is a sign that they're entering a new life cycle phase. Estrogen and progesterone production begin to decline toward the end of the reproductive years until ovulation (and thus menstruation) ceases altogether. This occurs at about age 50 in all parts of the world. Throughout human evolution, most females (and males) didn't survive to age 50; thus, few women lived much past menopause. But today, this event occurs when women have as much as one-third of their active and healthy lives ahead of them. No other female primates have such a long postreproductive period. Female chimpanzees and monkeys experience decreased fertility in their later years, but most continue to have reproductive cycles until their deaths. Occasional reports of menopause in apes and monkeys have been noted, but it's far from a routine and expected event.

Why do human females cease reproducing and then live such a long time when they can no longer reproduce? There are two questions here, one about cessation and one about living for so long after cessation. A theory regarding cessation of ovulation (menopause) suggests that it wasn't itself favored by natural selection; rather, it is an artifact of the extension of the human life span. It's been suggested

James F. O'Connell

Figure **17-9**

Senior Hadza woman and grandchild.

that the maximum life span of the mammalian egg is 50 years (you'll recall that all the ova are already present before birth; see p. 480). Thus, although the human life span has increased in the last several hundred years, the reproductive life span has not. To put it another way, the long postreproductive years and associated menopause in women have been "uncovered" by our extended life expectancy resulting from the reduction in many causes of death (Sievert, 2006). Another proposal to explain menopause is that so much energy is needed "up front" for reproduction in the early years that there's nothing left over by the time a woman reaches 50.

One theory for a long postreproductive life relates to parenting. Because it takes about 12 to 15 years before a child becomes independent, it's argued that females are biologically "programmed" to live 12 to 15 years beyond the birth of their last child (Mayer, 1982). This suggests that the maximum human life span for preagricultural humans was about 65 years, a figure that corresponds to what's known for contemporary hunter-gatherers and for prehistoric populations. One final explanation for the long postreproductive period in human females has been proposed by behavioral ecologists and is known as the "grandmother hypothesis." This proposal argues that natural selection may have favored this long period in women's lives because by ceasing to bear and raise their own children, postmenopausal women are freed to provide high-quality care for their grandchildren (Fig. 17-9). In other words, an older woman would do more to increase her lifetime fitness by enhancing the survival of her older grandchildren (who share one-quarter of her genes) through provisioning and direct child care than by having her own, possibly low-quality, infants (Hawkes, O'Connell, and Blurton Jones, 1997; but see Peccei, 2001). This is an example of the trade-offs considered by life history theory.

Human Longevity

Compared to most other animals, humans have a long life span (Table 17-3). The maximum life span potential, estimated to be about 120 years, probably hasn't changed in the last several thousand years. But life expectancy at birth (the average length of life) has increased significantly in the last 100 years, owing to advances in standards of living, hygiene, and medical care. The most important advance is likely treatment and prevention of infectious diseases, which typically take their toll on the young (Crews and Harper, 1998).

To some extent, aging is something we do throughout our lives. But we usually think of aging as **senescence**, the process of physiological decline in all systems of the body that occurs toward the end of the life course. Actually, throughout adulthood, there's a gradual decline in our cells' ability to synthesize proteins, in immune system function, in muscle mass (with a corresponding increase in fat mass) and strength, and in bone mineral density (Lamberts et al., 1997). This decline is associated with an increased risk for the chronic degenerative diseases usually listed as the causes of death in industrialized nations.

As you know, most causes of death that have their effects after the reproductive years won't be subjected to the forces of natural selection. What's more, in evolutionary terms, reproductive success isn't measured by how long we live.

senescence Decline in physiological function usually associated with aging.

Instead, as we have emphasized throughout this textbook, it's measured by how many offspring we produce. So organisms need to survive only long enough to produce offspring and rear them to maturity. Most wild animals die young of infection, starvation, predation, injury, and cold. Obviously, there are exceptions to this statement, especially in larger-bodied animals. Elephants, for example, may live over 50 years, and we know of several chimpanzees at Gombe that have survived into their 40s.

Here's one explanation for why humans age and are affected by chronic degenerative diseases like atherosclerosis, cancers, and hypertension: Genes that enhance reproductive success in earlier years (and thus were favored by natural selection) may have detrimental effects in later years. These are referred to as **pleiotropic genes**, meaning that they have multiple effects at different times in the life span or under different conditions (Williams, 1957). For example, genes that enhance the function of the immune system in the early years may also damage tissue so that cancer susceptibility increases in later life (Nesse and Williams, 1994). Alternatively, in later life, cancer-protecting genes may override genes for organ and tissue renewal.

Pleiotropy may help us understand evolutionary reasons for aging, but what are the causes of senescence in the individual? Much attention has been focused recently on free radicals, highly reactive molecules that can damage cells. These by-products of normal metabolism can be protected against by antioxidants such as vitamins A, C, and E and by a number of enzymes (Kirkwood, 1997). Ultimately, damage to DNA can occur, which in turn contributes to the aging of cells, the immune system, and other functional systems of the body. Additionally, there is evidence that programmed cell death is also a part of the normal processes of development that can obviously contribute to senescence.

Another hypothesis for senescence is known as the "telomere hypothesis." In this view, the DNA sequence at the end of each chromosome, known as the telomere, is shortened each time a cell divides (Fig. 17-10). Cells that have divided many times throughout the life course have short telomeres, eventually reaching the point at which they can no longer divide and are unable to maintain healthy tissues and organs. Changes in telomere length have also been implicated in cancers. In the laboratory, the enzyme telomerase can lengthen telomeres, allowing the cell to continue to divide. For this reason, the gene for telomerase has been called the "immortalizing gene." But this may not be a good thing, since the only cells that can divide indefinitely are cancer cells. Although this research isn't likely to lead to a lengthening of the life span, it may contribute to a better understanding of cellular functions and cancer.

Far more important than genes in the aging process, however, are lifestyle factors, such as smoking, physical activity, diet, and medical care. Life expectancy at birth varies considerably from country to country and among socioeconomic classes within a country. Throughout the world, women have higher life expectancies than men. A Japanese girl born in 2006, for example, can expect to live to age 86, a boy to age 79. Girls and boys born in that same year in the United States have life expectancies of 80 and 75, respectively. In contrast to these children in industrialized nations, girls and boys in Mali have life expectancies of only 47 and 44, respectively (data from World Health Organization). Many African nations have seen life expectancy drop below 40 due to deaths from AIDS. For example, before the AIDS epidemic, Zimbabweans had a life expectancy of 65 years; today,

Table 17-3 Maximum Life Spans for Selected Species

Organism	Approximate Maximum Life Span (in Years)
Bristlecone pine	5,000
Tortoise	170
Rockfish	140
Human	120
Blue whale	80
Indian elephant	70
Gorilla	39
Domestic dog	34
Rabbit	13
Rat	5

Source: From "The Biology of Human Aging," by William A. Stini; in C. G. N. Mascie-Taylor and G. W. Lasker (eds.), *Applications of Biological Anthropology to Human Affairs* (Cambridge, UK: Cambridge University Press, 1991, p. 215).

Figure 17-10

Telomeres are repeated sequences of DNA at the ends of chromosomes, and the sequences appear to be the same in all animals. They stabilize and protect the ends of chromosomes, and as they shorten with each cell division, the chromosomes eventually become unstable.

pleiotropic genes Genes that have more than one effect; genes that have different effects at different times in the life cycle.

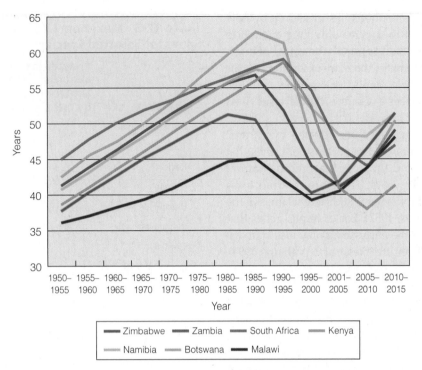

Figure **17-11**

Changes in life expectancy due to AIDS in seven African nations. (From United Nations, 1998.)

life expectancy in Zimbabwe is less than 37 (Fig 17-11). Unfortunately, some scholars are now predicting a leveling off or even a decline in life expectancy in nations like the United States because of rising rates of obesity and related health problems (Oshansky et al., 2005).

Evolutionary Medicine

A few years ago, scholars in evolutionary theory, biological anthropology, and medicine joined forces to develop what many saw as a new field, referred to variously as evolutionary or Darwinian medicine (Williams and Nesse, 1991; Nesse and Williams, 1994; Trevathan, Smith, and McKenna, 1999, 2008). There are several ways in which an evolutionary view can contribute to understanding contemporary health challenges. One is the recognition that the inevitible outcome of more and more aggressive interventions to fight pathogens that cause disease in humans will be stronger pathogens that eventually evolve resistance to therapies such as antibiotics.

Because most of the viruses and bacteria that cause disease have very short generation times, it doesn't take long for strains that are resistant to antibiotics to emerge victorious. We've seen this occur with staphylococcal infections, some strains of tuberculosis, and *E. coli*. The pathogens that cause HIV and malaria mutate so fast that all attempts to develop a vaccine against them have failed so far.

For the most part, the antibiotic-pathogen arms race has led to the development of more and more lethal strains of disease, but the evolutionary process doesn't have to lead in that direction. In fact, one suggestion for beating deadly pathogens like HIV and malaria is to turn the evolutionary process around by directing the process toward less and less virulence (Ewald, 1994, 1999). Ewald has called this procedure "domesticating" pathogens and cites as an example diphtheria, which has apparently evolved toward milder strains with vaccination. The primary argument is that medical interventions capable of responding to the *processes* of disease emergence and evolution are much more likely to be successful in the long run than those that target specific disease variants and their manifestations. Consider, for example, the influenza virus that appears every fall. Medical researchers work hard to predict which strain will be the problem and target a vaccine against that strain. If their prediction is wrong, an influenza epidemic could emerge.

The latest developments in assessing the complete genetic sequences of chimpanzees and humans have confirmed how few differences there are. But they've also pointed to tiny differences that may explain why humans are susceptible to diseases like cholera, malaria, and influenza, while chimpanzees are not. For example, a molecule known as sialic acid differs in humans and chimpanzees by a single oxygen atom (Varki, 2000). The chimpanzee version of the sialic acid gene is the one found in other mammals, so it's been suggested that the human form is derived and most likely evolved after the chimpanzee and human lines split (see Chapter 9). Sialic acid serves as a binding site for organisms that cause diseases such as cholera, malaria, and some forms of influenza (Muchmore, Diaz, and Varki, 1998), and the discovery may lead to treatments for these diseases. It's also an important reminder that even one genetic difference between humans and chimpanzees can have extensive and as yet unforeseen consequences.

Evolutionary medicine proponents also argue that knowing about the conditions under which humans evolved can contribute to understanding health problems and may point to potential solutions or interventions. As already noted, the human diet, activity levels, and other aspects of our lives evolved under very different conditions from the way we live today. This "mismatch" of evolved bodies (sometimes referred to as "paleolithic bodies") and twenty-first century lifestyles may account for diseases and disorders such as type 2 diabetes, atherosclerosis, hypertension, some cancers, diverticular disease, and osteoporosis. Many popular books argue that by adopting some aspects of our ancestral diet (lower fat, more complex carbohydrates, lower sodium, frequent small meals) and lifestyles (more exercise, less alcohol, no smoking, lower stress), we'll lose weight, feel better, and live longer (e.g., Cordain, 2002).

Evolutionary medicine also helps to distinguish traits that may have evolved because they enhanced survival and reproductive success in the past or are beneficial in one form while detrimental in another. For example, as discussed in Chapters 3 and 4, the allele for sickle cell is harmful in homozygotes, but protects heterozygotes against malaria. As another example, Tay-Sachs disease, found most commonly among Ashkenazi Jews, is a progressively deteriorating neurological disorder that usually results in death by age 4. One hypothesis is that the allele is maintained in somewhat high frequencies in this population because in the past it conferred survival advantages for the heterozygotes in the face of tuberculosis or influenza, which were common diseases in the ghettos of Europe where Jews were forced to live (Motulsky 1995). And while the allele for cystic fibrosis is usually lethal in the homozygous form, it may be protective against cholera in heterozygotes (Hill and Motulsky 1999). With the addition of evolutionary theory to epidemiology and human genetics, populations that may be vulnerable to disease outbreaks may be identified in advance and appropriate preventive measures taken.

Human Impact on the Planet and Other Life-Forms

The figures cited earlier for life expectancy in various nations of the world remind us of the importance of diet, health care, and social environment for lifelong health and survival. Clearly, the data indicate that living conditions in Japan are more supportive of good health for the general population than those in Mali. At some level, we can measure a nation's success by indicators such as infant mortality rates and life expectancy. But how do we measure the success of a species?

By most standards, *Homo sapiens* is a successful species. There are currently more than 6 billion human beings living on this planet. Each one of these individuals comprises upward of 20 trillion cells. Even so, we and all other multicellular organisms contribute but a small fraction of all the cells on the planet—most of which are bacteria. So if we see life ultimately as a competition among reproducing organisms, bacteria are the winners, hands down.

Evolutionary success can also be gauged by species longevity. As we have seen, fossil evidence indicates that *Homo sapiens* has been on the scene for at least 200,000 years and possibly as long as 400,000 years. Such time spans, seen through the perspective of a human lifetime, may seem enormous. But consider this: Our immediate predecessor, *Homo erectus*, had a species longevity of about 1.5 million years. In other words, we as a species would need to exist another million years simply to match *Homo erectus*! If such considerations as these are not humbling enough, remember that some sharks and turtles have thrived basically unchanged structurally for 400 million years (although many of these species are now seriously threatened).

No matter what criterion for success is used, there's no question that *Homo sapiens* has had an inordinate impact on the earth and all other forms of life. In the past, humans had to respond primarily to challenges in the natural world; today the greatest challenges for our species (and all others) are environments of our own making. Increasing population size is one reason that human impact has been so great. As human population pressure increases, more and more land is converted to crops, pasture, and construction, providing more opportunities for still more humans and fewer (or no) habitats for most other species.

Scientists estimate that around 10,000 years ago, only about 5 million people inhabited the earth (not even half as many as live in Los Angeles County or New York City today). By the year 1650, there were perhaps 500 million, and by 1800, around 1 billion (Fig. 17-12). In other words, between 10,000 years ago and 1650 (a period of 9,650 years), population size doubled 7½ times. On average, then, the doubling time between 10,000 years ago and 1650 was about 1,287 years. But from 1650 to 1800, it doubled again, which means that doubling time had been reduced to 150 years (Ehrlich and Ehrlich, 1990). And in the 37 years between 1950 and 1987, world population doubled from 2 billion to 4 billion. To state this problem in terms we can appreciate, we add 1 billion people to the world's population approximately every 11 years. That comes out to 90 to 95 million every year and roughly a quarter of a million every day—or more than 10,000 an hour.

Figure **17-12**

Growth curve (orange) depicting the exponential growth of the human population. The vertical axis shows the world population in billions. It wasn't until 1804 that the population reached 1 billion, but the numbers went from 5 to 6 billion in 12 short years. Population increase occurs as a function of some percentage (in developing countries, the annual rate is over 3 percent). With advances in food production and medical technologies, humans are undergoing a population explosion, as this figure illustrates.

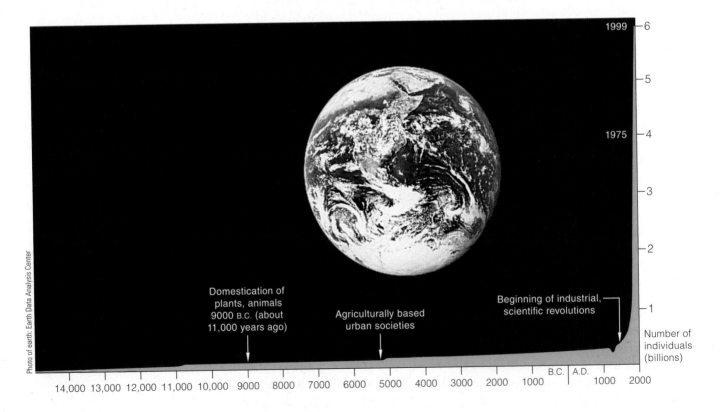

The rate of growth is not equally distributed among all nations. The most recent United Nations report on world population notes that 95 percent of population growth is occurring in the developing world. Likewise, resources are not distributed equally among all nations. Only a small percentage of the world's population, located in a few industrialized nations, control and consume most of the world's resources.

Efforts to slow the rate of world population growth have focused on improving women's education, health, and rights throughout the world, based on the idea that if women are educated, they choose to have fewer children and are able to achieve better health for the ones they do have. Despite resistance to this strategy in parts of the world, there's evidence of success; fertility rates have declined from 4.5 children per woman in 1970–1975 to 2.65 today (United Nations population 2004 revised). As with resources, however, most of the decline in fertility rates has been in the developed world. Realistic projections from the United Nations are that total fertility in all countries will reach 1.85 children per woman in 2050, with a total world population of slightly more than 9 billion people. These projections are based on continuing success at educating women and improving maternal and child health worldwide.

Global Warming

Consider for a moment the fact that much of the energy used for human activities is derived from the burning of fossil fuels, such as oil and coal. The burning of fossil fuels releases carbon dioxide into the atmosphere, and this, in turn, traps heat. Increased production of carbon dioxide and other *greenhouse gases*, such as methane and chlorofluorocarbons (CFCs), is of great concern to many in the scientific community, who anticipate dramatic climate change in the form of global warming.

Deforestation, particularly in the tropics, also contributes to global warming, since we're reducing the number of trees available to absorb carbon dioxide. Moreover, in the tropics, trees are burned as land is cleared, a practice that releases yet more carbon dioxide. In fact, an estimated 20 percent of all carbon dioxide emissions are accounted for by the burning of the Amazon rain forest alone. Because these fires also destroyed peat deposits (layers of ancient, decayed vegetation that serve as storehouses of carbon), an estimated 810 million to 2.6 billion metric tons (2,240 pounds) of carbon were released into the atmosphere. This amounts to between 13 to 40 percent of the world's annual carbon emissions from the burning of fossil fuels (Page et al., 2002).

The scientific community is now in almost complete agreement that we are seeing the effects of global warming. Scientists from numerous fields (including climatology, paleoclimatology, geophysics, and geology) are justifiably concerned, and most agree that the buildup of greenhouse gases results from human activity. Unfortunately, until recently, the general public and many politicians seemed to believe that the obvious warming we are experiencing is part of a "normal" cyclical trend. Certainly, there have been dramatic climatic fluctuations throughout earth's history that had nothing to do with human activity. And many of these fluctuations were sudden and had devastating consequences. But even if the current warming trend (which, incidentally, began during the early years of the industrial revolution and increased use of coal) is part of a general cycle, scientists are concerned that human-produced greenhouse gases could tip the balance toward a catastrophic global climate change. Recent weather-related events such as hurricanes, typhoons, floods, melting polar ice, droughts, and fires have begun to convince doubters that we are indeed seeing the effects of at least some degree of human activity on climate change.

Global warming is the result of the interactions of many factors, and the consequences of these interactions aren't possible to predict with accuracy. But the consensus among scientists is that we can anticipate dramatic fluctuations in weather patterns along with alterations in precipitation levels. The results of changing temperatures and rainfall include loss of agricultural lands due to desertification in some regions and flooding in others; increased human hunger; extinction of numerous plant and animal species; and altered patterns of infectious disease. Regarding the latter, health officials are particularly concerned about the spread of mosquito-borne diseases such as malaria, dengue fever, and yellow fever as warmer temperatures increase the geographical range of mosquitoes. And in addition to altering the geographical distribution of insect and vertebrate disease vectors, changing climate conditions can also increase the range and reproductive rates of the very microbes that are the direct causes of infectious diseases. Reversing these trends will be enormously expensive and will require individual sacrifice and huge changes in business and industrial practices, but the consequences of ignoring them are even greater.

Impact on Biodiversity

According to biologist Stephen Palumbi (2001), humans are the "world's greatest evolutionary force." What Palumbi means is that we humans, like no other species before us, have a profound effect on the evolutionary histories of almost all forms of life, including the potential to alter global ecology and destroy ourselves and virtually all life on earth. Even massive evolutionary catastrophes and mass extinctions did not wreak the havoc that may result from modern human technology.

Two major extinction events have occurred in the last 250 million years. A third major extinction event, perhaps of the same magnitude, is occurring now, and according to some scientists, it may have begun in the Late Pleistocene or early **Holocene** (Ward, 1994). Unlike all other mass extinctions, the current one hasn't been caused by continental drift, climate change (so far), or collisions with asteroids. Rather, these recent and ongoing extinctions are due to the activities of a single species—*Homo sapiens*.

Many scientists, in fact, believe that several large mammalian species were pushed toward extinction as a result of overhunting by earlier human populations, particularly near the end of the Pleistocene, some 10,000 ya. In North America, at least 57 mammalian species became extinct, including the mammoth, mastodon, giant ground sloth, saber-toothed cat, several large rodents, and numerous ungulates (hooved mammals), or grazing animals. Climate change was undoubtedly a factor in these Pleistocene extinctions, but hunting and other human activities may also have been important (Worthy and Holdaway, 2002; Guthrie, 2006). Although there is some dispute as to when humans first entered North America from Asia, it's certain that they were firmly established by at least 12,000 ya (and probably earlier).

We have no direct evidence that early American big game hunters contributed to extinctions; but we do have evidence of what can happen to indigenous species when new areas are colonized by humans for the first time. Within just a few decades of human occupation of New Zealand, the moa, a large flightless bird, was exterminated. Madagascar serves as a similar example (Perez et al., 2005). In the past

Holocene The most recent epoch of the Cenozoic. Following the Pleistocene, it's estimated to have begun 10,000 years ago.

1,000 years, after the arrival of permanent human settlement, 14 species of lemurs, in addition to other mammalian and bird species, have become extinct (Napier and Napier, 1985). One such species was *Megaladapis*, a lemur that weighed an estimated 300 pounds (Fleagle, 1999)! Lastly, scientists have debated for years whether the extinction of all large-bodied animals (some 60 species) in Australia during the Late Pleistocene was due to human hunting and other activities or to climate change.

Since the end of the Pleistocene, human activities have continued to take their toll on nonhuman species. Today, however, species are disappearing at an unprecedented rate. Hunting, which occurs for reasons other than acquiring food, continues to be a major factor. Competition with introduced nonnative species, such as pigs, goats, and rats, has also contributed to the problem. But in many cases, the most important single cause of extinction is habitat reduction. We're all aware of the risk to such visible species as the elephant, panda, rhinoceros, tiger, and mountain gorilla, to name a few. These risks are real, and within your lifetime some of these species will certainly become extinct, at least in the wild. But the greatest threat to biodiversity is to the countless unknown species that live in the world's rain forests (Fig. 17-13). By the year 2022, half the world's remaining rain forests will be gone if destruction continues at its current rate. This will result in a loss of between 10 and 22 percent of all rain forest species, or 5 to 10 percent of all plant and animal species on earth (Wilson, 1992).

Should we care about the loss of biodiversity? If so, why? In truth, many people don't seem very concerned. What's more, in explaining why we should care, we usually point out the benefits (known and unknown) that humans may derive from wild species of plants and animals. An example of such a benefit is the chemical taxol (derived from the Pacific yew tree), which may be an effective treatment for ovarian and breast cancer.

Undeniably, humans stand to benefit from continued research into potentially useful rain forest products. Still, such anthropocentric reasons are not the sole justification for preserving the earth's biodiversity. Each species the earth loses is the product of millions of years of evolution, and each one fills a specific econiche. Quite simply, the destruction of so many of the planet's life-forms is within our power. But, we must ask ourselves, is it our right?

Joseph Luoman/iStockphoto

Figure **17-13**

Stumps of recently felled forest trees are still visible in this newly cleared field in the Amazon.

Acceleration of Evolutionary Processes

Another major impact of human activities is the acceleratation of the evolutionary process for hundreds of life-forms. Many of these changes have occurred over one human generation—not the millions of years usually associated with evolution. As noted earlier and in Chapter 16, our use of antibiotics has directed the course of evolution of several infectious diseases to the point that many have become resistant to our antibiotics. Human-invented antibiotics have become the agents of natural selection directing the course of evolution of many bacteria to a more virulent state. It's even likely that human technology and lifestyles are responsible for the deadly nature of some of the so-called new diseases that have arisen in recent decades, such as HIV-AIDS (see p. 464), dengue hemorrhagic fever, Legionnaires' disease, Lyme disease, and resistant strains of tuberculosis, *Staphylococcus*, and *E coli*. A few years ago, the fear of anthrax drove thousands of people to use antibiotics such as ciprofloxacin in the extremely unlikely event that they would be exposed to the deadly bacterium. Certainly, we understand the desire for preventive action on the part of those at heightened risk. But if more harmful bacteria become resistant as a by-product of this practice, the risk to society from the overuse and improper use of this powerful class of antibiotics is potentially far greater. We could reach a point where we have no antibiotics strong enough to overpower dangerous bacteria that live and mutate in our midst.

A similar phenomenon has occurred with the overuse and misuse of insecticides and pesticides on agricultural crops (Palumbi, 2001). Insects evolve resistance to each new generation of toxic agents, eventually reaching a point where they're no longer affected by most of the insecticides used on the fields. Bt toxin (*Bacillus thuringiensis*) has been highly touted as an "organic" and environmentally friendly agent because it is naturally produced (often by the crops it protects), targets specific insect larvae, and isn't toxic to humans. Genes for producing Bt toxin have been engineered into millions of acres of plants; unfortunately, recent evidence suggests that some insects are evolving resistance to it.

As mentioned in Chapter 15, perhaps the best-known insecticide to have altered the course of evolution of a species is DDT. When this insecticide was first developed, it was hailed as the best way to reduce malaria, eliminating the mosquitoes that transmit the disease. DDT was highly effective when it was first applied to mosquito-ridden areas; but soon, mosquitoes had evolved resistance to the powerful agent, rendering it almost useless in the fight against malaria. Moreover, the use of DDT proved disastrous to many bird species, including the bald eagle. Its use was curtailed, even banned in some countries, in the 1970s, but the failure of other efforts to treat malaria has led to a recent call to begin using DDT again.

From these examples, it's clear that the process of evolution is something that can result in great harm for our species and planet. Certainly, none of the scientists working to develop antibiotics, insecticides, pesticides, and other biological tools intend to cause harm. But they may lack the understanding of the evolutionary process necessary to foresee long-term consequences of their work. As the great geneticist Theodosius Dobzhansky (1973) said, "Nothing in biology makes sense except in the light of evolution." Indeed, we can't afford even a single generation of scientists who lack knowledge about the process of evolution, which is responsible for the life-forms around us, both helpful and harmful. If human actions can cause an organism to evolve from a relatively benign state to a dangerously virulent state, then there is no reason why we can't turn that process around. In other words, as noted earlier, it is theoretically possible to direct the course of evolution of a dangerous organism like HIV to a more benign, less harmful state (Ewald, 1999). But using evolution to solve health problems requires that medical researchers have a very sophisticated understanding of the evolutionary process, and evolutionary theory isn't usually offered as part of medical training (Nesse and Williams, 1994; Nesse, Stearns, and Omenn, 2006).

Is There Any Good News?

Now that you are thoroughly depressed about the potentially gloomy future of the earth and our species, is there any good news? In 2000, heads of state from almost 150 countries agreed to support a set of Millennium Development Goals that would help to reduce human misery throughout the world. Here are the eight goals:

1. Eradicate extreme poverty and hunger.
2. Achieve universal primary education.
3. Promote gender equity and empower women.
4. Reduce child mortality.
5. Improve maternal health.
6. Combat HIV/AIDS, malaria, and other diseases.
7. Ensure environmental sustainability.
8. Build a global partnership for development.

These goals set measurable targets that can be examined year after year to see how close we come to meeting them. There will be immense and expensive challenges, but this international agreement seems a good start toward concerted cooperative effort to solve the major problems of the world today, and it goes a long way toward encouraging partnerships between rich and poor nations. Unfortunately (and this is *not* good news), the world economic slowdown and increasing food insecurity have slowed progress toward meeting the goals and, in some cases, reversed progress (Millennium Development Goals Report 2008).

Although world population growth continues, it appears that the rate of growth has slowed somewhat. It's common knowledge among economists that as income and education increase, family size decreases, and as infant and child mortality rates decrease, families are having fewer children. In fact, as noted earlier, one of the best strategies for reducing family size and thus world population is to educate girls and women. Educated women are more likely to be in the labor force and are better able to provide food for their families, seek health care for themselves and their children, delay marriage, and use family planning. In 1990, the international community adopted the World Declaration on Education for All, and it remains one of the Millennium Development Goals. Since then, there have been steady increases in efforts to educate all segments of society. In fact, in some parts of the world, there have been so many efforts to improve education for girls that they're now favored by the gender gap in education.

With decreases in family size and improvements in education and employment opportunities for both men and women throughout the world, we are also likely to see improvements in environmental conservation and habitat preservation. A generally recognized phenomenon is that habitat destruction and poverty often go hand in hand. Although successes in Costa Rica can't be replicated everywhere, this small nation has been a model for making environmental concerns integral to social and economic development. Ecotourism, built on preserving the nation's abundant and beautiful natural resources, has now become its primary industry. Today, Costa Rica's poverty levels are the lowest in Central America.

Recently, several international agreements designed to preserve endangered species and habitats have been signed. These often mean the development of national parks and preserves. Figure 17-14 shows the increase in protected sites during the past 30 years.

There are also a number of international efforts to preserve primates, most notably the United Nation's Great Apes Survival Project (GRASP). This project

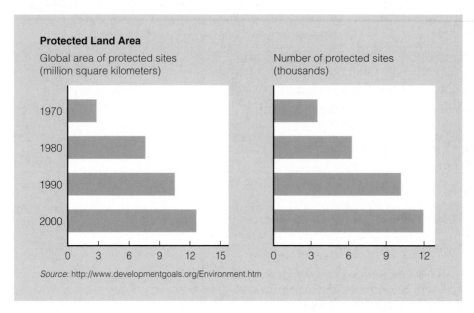

Protected Land Area

Global area of protected sites
(million square kilometers)

Number of protected sites
(thousands)

Source: http://www.developmentgoals.org/Environment.htm

Figure **17-14**

There has been a steady increase in the number and total area of protected sites in the world in the past few decades.

brings together great ape research and conservation organizations that have struggled to save the animals they care about with varying degrees of success and failure. Five GRASP Patrons have been appointed: Russell Mittermeier (Director of Conservation International), Jane Goodall (see p. 179), Toshisada Nishida (see p. 225), Richard Leakey (see p. 336) and Richard Wrangham (see p. 188). By combining efforts and targeting resources, they hope to have the political and financial clout to halt the decline of great ape species (see also p. 174).

Finally, annually since 2005, leaders from both developing and developed countries have come together to discuss new ways of reducing global poverty, especially in sub-Saharan Africa. The developed countries, including the European Union, the United States, Canada, and Australia, have renewed commitments to double aid for Africa by 2010. Countries in Latin America and the Caribbean have made significant progress in meeting some of the goals, but countries in sub-Saharan Africa have fallen further behind than when earlier agreements were made. Aid from some countries hasn't come as quickly as originally hoped. Fortunately, some of the wealthiest individuals in the world (including Bill and Melinda Gates, George Soros, Warren Buffet, Richard Branson, and Ted Turner) have begun to invest their personal fortunes (or in the case of former U.S. presidents Carter and Clinton, their diplomatic talents and charisma) in reducing poverty and poor health and in trying to achieve global peace and prosperity

What should be obvious is that only by working together can nations and individuals of the world hope to bring about solutions to the world's problems. As we argued earlier in this chapter and in Chapter 8, despite occasional evidence to the contrary, cooperation may have been more important in human evolution than conflict. These international efforts illustrate how strongly we believe that to be the case. The question now is whether or not we have the collective will to see that our admirable goals are met. Many people believe that it's our only hope.

Are We Still Evolving?

In many ways, it seems that culture has enabled us to transcend most of the limitations our biology imposes on us. But that biology was shaped during millions of years of evolution in environments very different from those in which most of us live today. There is, to a great extent, a lack of fit between our biology and our twenty-first-century cultural environments. Our expectations that scientists can easily and quickly discover a "magic bullet" to enable us to resist any disease that arises have been painfully dashed as death tolls from AIDS reach catastrophic levels in many parts of the world.

Socioeconomic and political concerns also have powerful effects on our species today. Whether you die of starvation or succumb to disorders associated with overconsumption depends a great deal on where you live, what your socioeconomic status is, and how much power and control you have over your life. These are all factors that are not likely related to biology. They also affect whether you'll be killed in a war or spend most of your life in a safe, comfortable community. Your chances of being exposed to one of the "new" pathogens such as HIV, SARS, or tuberculosis has a lot to do with your lifestyle and other cultural factors. But your chances of dying from the disease or failing to reproduce because of it still have a lot to do with your biology. The 4.3 million children dying annually from respiratory infections are primarily those in the developing world, with limited access to adequate medical care—clearly a cultural factor. But in those same areas, lacking that same medical care, are millions of other children who aren't getting the infections or aren't dying from them. Presumably, among the factors affecting this difference is resistance afforded by genes. By considering this simple example, we can see that human gene frequencies are still changing from one generation to the next in response to selective agents such as disease; thus, our species is still evolving.

We can't predict whether we will become a different species or become extinct as a species (remember, that is the fate of almost every species that has ever lived on earth). Will our brains get larger, or will our hands evolve solely to push buttons? Or will we change genetically so that we no longer have to eat food? This is the stuff of science fiction, not anthropology. But as long as new pathogens appear or new environments are introduced by technology, there's little doubt that just like every other species on earth, the human species will either continue to evolve or become extinct.

Culture has enabled us to transcend many limits imposed by our biology. Today, people who never would have been able to do so in the past are surviving and having children. This in itself means that we are evolving. How many of you would be reading this text if you had been born under the health and economic conditions prevalent 500 years ago?

Summary

In this chapter, we've discussed legacies of human evolutionary history that leave their marks on us today. For the individual, these legacies include patterns of growth and nutritional requirements that result from millions of years of biological evolution and thousands of years of cultural evolution. Our evolutionary history also means that human infants are relatively undeveloped at birth, especially in brain size, and require intense parental investment to reach adulthood and independence. For humans in society, legacies from evolutionary history include thought processes and behaviors that reflect natural selection operating on individuals to increase reproductive success, or fitness. A review of behavioral ecology summarizes the ways in which genes, environment, and culture have interacted to produce complex adaptations to equally complex challenges. Critical review of hypotheses for such human behaviors as aggression, violence, nurturance, and reproduction reveals the complexity of this interrelationship. Infusion of evolutionary theory into medicine may lead to improvements in human health. The final set of legacies reviewed in this chapter concerns the impact of the human species on the planet and other life-forms. Thanks to our amazing reproductive "success," the human population has reached more than 6 billion from an estimated base of about 5 million people 10,000 years ago. These numbers, coupled with technological developments, have turned humans into what Stephen Palumbi has called "the world's greatest evolutionary force." *Homo sapiens* has become a powerful agent of natural selection, influencing virtually every life-form on earth, causing the extinction of many species, and accelerating evolutionary change in others. Increasing global warming, due in part to human activities, is also of considerable concern.

Studies of human evolution have much to contribute to our understanding of how we, as a single species, came to exert such control over the destiny of our planet. It's a truly phenomenal story of how a small apelike creature walking on two feet across the African savanna challenged nature by learning to make stone tools. From these humble beginnings came large-brained humans who, instead of stone tools, have telecommunications satellites, computers, and nuclear arsenals at their fingertips. The human story is indeed unique and wonderful. Our two feet have carried us not only across the plains of Africa, but onto the polar caps, the ocean floor, and even across the surface of the moon! Surely, if we can accomplish so much in so short a time, we can act responsibly to preserve our home and the wondrous creatures who share it with us.

Critical Thinking Questions

1. What is meant by the analogy, "Water is to fish as culture is to humans"? Do you think it's possible to study humans without studying culture? Can we study humans only as cultural animals, or do we need to know something about human biology to understand behavior?

2. Compare and contrast the human preagricultural diet with that seen today in places like the United States. Discuss at least one major health consequence of what has been termed the "lack of fit" between the diet to which humans have evolved and the one many people now consume.

3. How natural selection might act on such behaviors as mate selection, parenting, and aggression is controversial. Choose one of these and first argue how natural selection *could* have shaped the way the behavior is expressed in humans. Then critique your first argument, suggesting, instead, some alternatives.

4. Do you think that teenage pregancy is a "problem"? Describe circumstances under which adolescent pregnancy might be advantageous, in an evolutionary sense. What are some of the disadvantages of adolescent pregnancy for reproductive success?

5 Why do the authors of this text claim that human overpopulation is a major challenge facing our planet today? Do you agree or disagree? Why?

6. What is evolutionary medicine? Briefly discuss two ways in which understanding evolutionary theory or human evolutionary history may lead to improvements in human health. Do you think it's possible to do good medical research without knowing anything about evolutionary processes? Why or why not?

7. The authors of this text claim that humans are still subjected to the forces of evolution. Do you agree? What is the evidence for or against that claim?

8. Does an understanding of the human species within a broad, evolutionary framework help us predict (and even determine, if we so choose) the future of our species?

Appendix A

Atlas of Primate Skeletal Anatomy

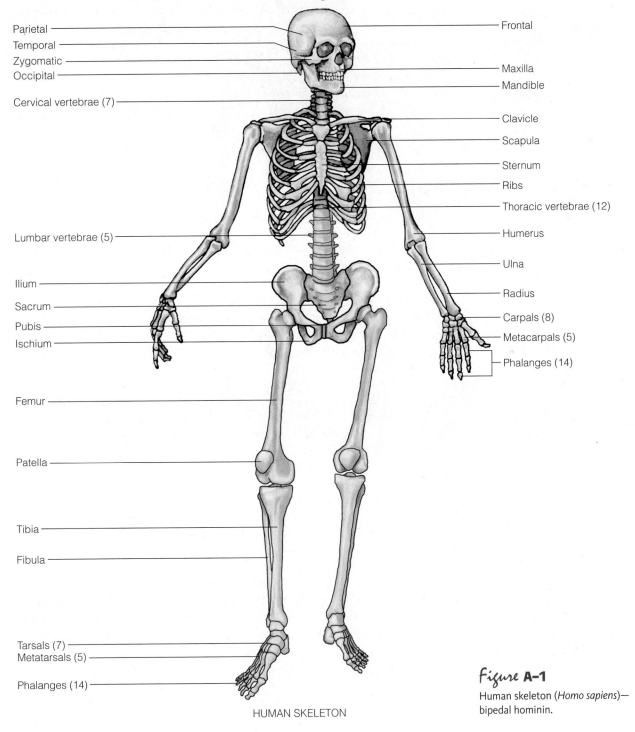

Parietal
Temporal
Zygomatic
Occipital
Cervical vertebrae (7)
Lumbar vertebrae (5)
Ilium
Sacrum
Pubis
Ischium
Femur
Patella
Tibia
Fibula
Tarsals (7)
Metatarsals (5)
Phalanges (14)

Frontal
Maxilla
Mandible
Clavicle
Scapula
Sternum
Ribs
Thoracic vertebrae (12)
Humerus
Ulna
Radius
Carpals (8)
Metacarpals (5)
Phalanges (14)

HUMAN SKELETON

Figure **A–1**
Human skeleton (*Homo sapiens*)—
bipedal hominin.

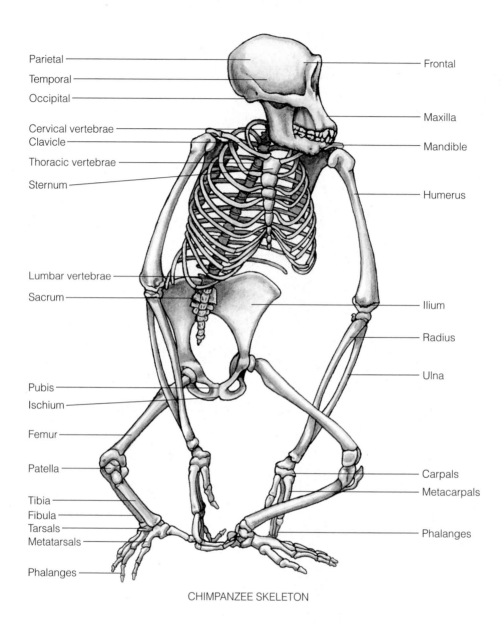

Parietal

Temporal

Occipital

Cervical vertebrae

Clavicle

Thoracic vertebrae

Sternum

Lumbar vertebrae

Sacrum

Pubis

Ischium

Femur

Patella

Tibia

Fibula

Tarsals

Metatarsals

Phalanges

Frontal

Maxilla

Mandible

Humerus

Ilium

Radius

Ulna

Carpals

Metacarpals

Phalanges

CHIMPANZEE SKELETON

Figure **A-2**

Chimpanzee skelton (*Pan troglodytes*)—
knuckle-walking pongid.

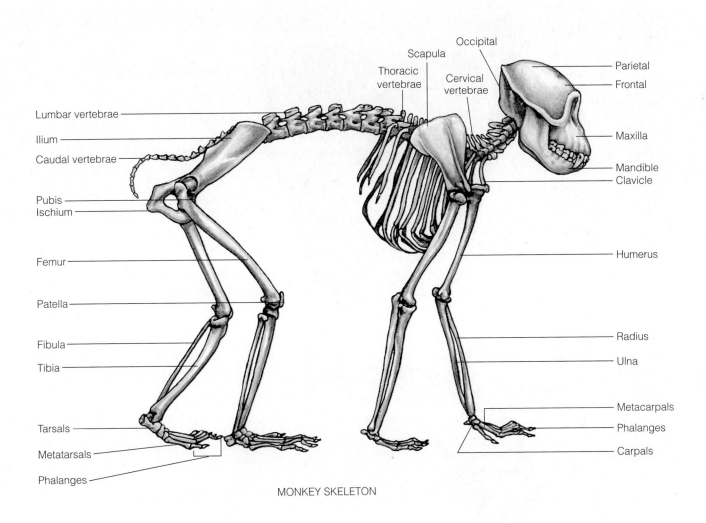

MONKEY SKELETON

Figure **A-3**

Monkey skeleton (rhesus macaque; *Macaca mulatta*)—a typical quadrupedal primate.

Figure **A-4**

Human cranium.
(continued on next page)

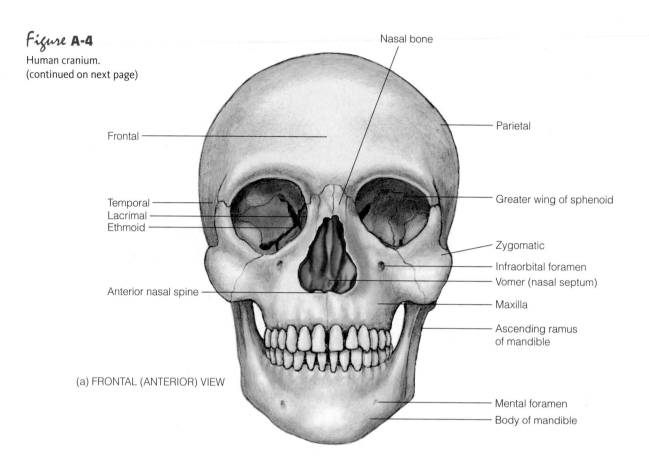

Nasal bone

Frontal

Parietal

Temporal
Lacrimal
Ethmoid

Greater wing of sphenoid

Zygomatic

Infraorbital foramen

Vomer (nasal septum)

Anterior nasal spine

Maxilla

Ascending ramus
of mandible

(a) FRONTAL (ANTERIOR) VIEW

Mental foramen

Body of mandible

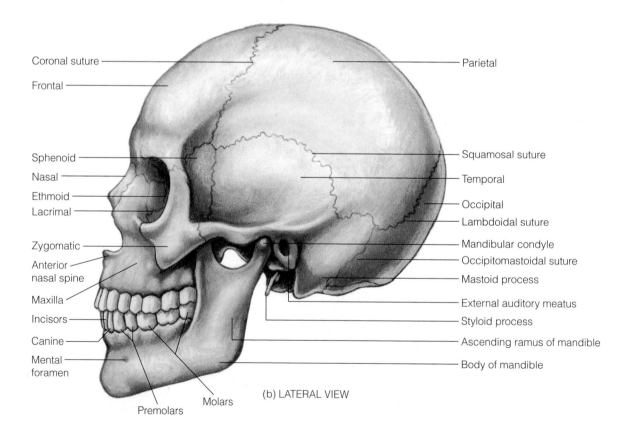

Coronal suture

Parietal

Frontal

Sphenoid

Squamosal suture

Nasal

Temporal

Ethmoid

Occipital

Lacrimal

Lambdoidal suture

Zygomatic

Mandibular condyle

Anterior
nasal spine

Occipitomastoidal suture

Mastoid process

Maxilla

External auditory meatus

Incisors

Styloid process

Canine

Ascending ramus of mandible

Mental
foramen

Body of mandible

(b) LATERAL VIEW

Premolars

Molars

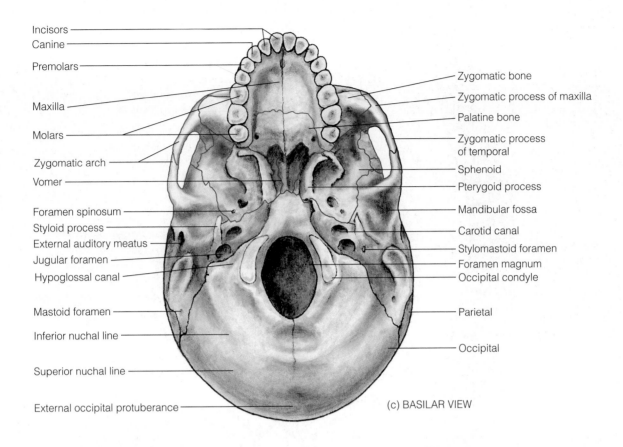

Incisors
Canine
Premolars
Maxilla
Molars
Zygomatic arch
Vomer
Foramen spinosum
Styloid process
External auditory meatus
Jugular foramen
Hypoglossal canal
Mastoid foramen
Inferior nuchal line
Superior nuchal line
External occipital protuberance

Zygomatic bone
Zygomatic process of maxilla
Palatine bone
Zygomatic process of temporal
Sphenoid
Pterygoid process
Mandibular fossa
Carotid canal
Stylomastoid foramen
Foramen magnum
Occipital condyle
Parietal
Occipital

(c) BASILAR VIEW

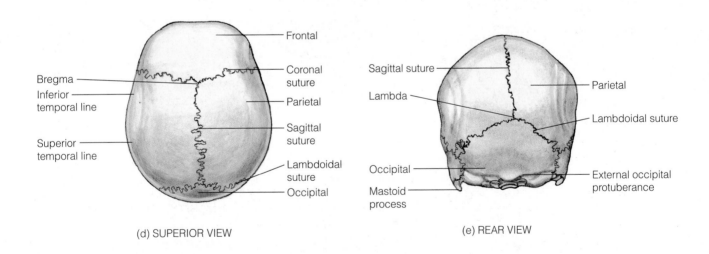

Frontal
Coronal suture
Bregma
Inferior temporal line
Parietal
Superior temporal line
Sagittal suture
Lambdoidal suture
Occipital

(d) SUPERIOR VIEW

Sagittal suture
Lambda
Occipital
Mastoid process
Parietal
Lambdoidal suture
External occipital protuberance

(e) REAR VIEW

Figure A-4
Human cranium.
(continued)

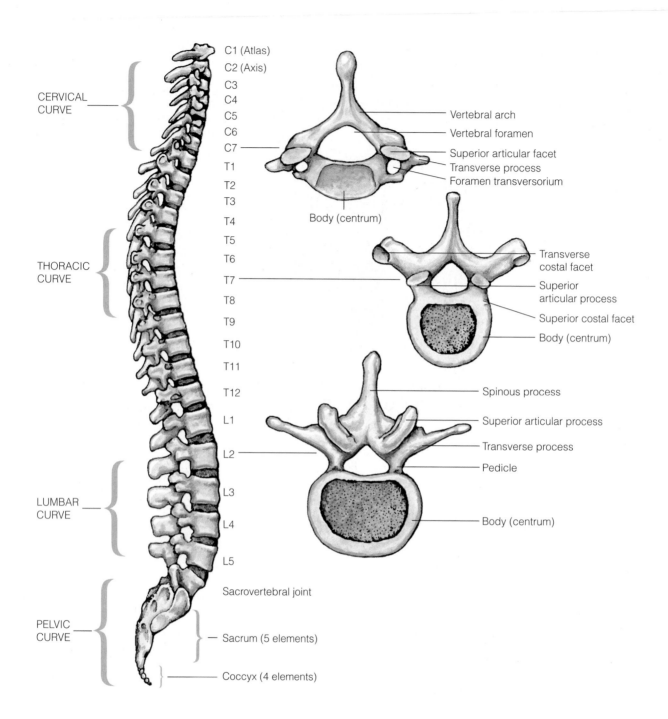

Cervical Curve

C1 (Atlas)
C2 (Axis)
C3
C4
C5
C6
C7

Thoracic Curve

T1
T2
T3
T4
T5
T6
T7
T8
T9
T10
T11
T12

Lumbar Curve

L1
L2
L3
L4
L5

Pelvic Curve

Vertebral arch
Vertebral foramen
Superior articular facet
Transverse process
Foramen transversorium
Body (centrum)

Transverse costal facet
Superior articular process
Superior costal facet
Body (centrum)

Spinous process
Superior articular process
Transverse process
Pedicle
Body (centrum)

Sacrovertebral joint
Sacrum (5 elements)
Coccyx (4 elements)

Figure **A-5**

Human vertebral column (lateral view) and representative cervical, thoracic, and lumbar vertebrae (superior views).

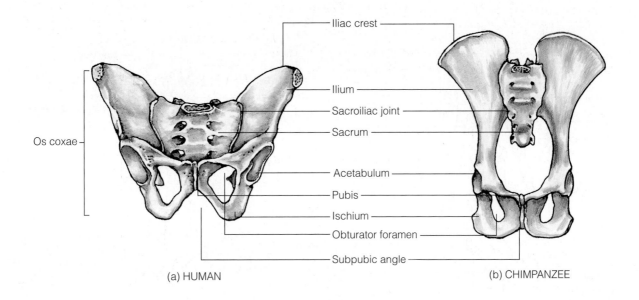

Iliac crest

Ilium

Sacroiliac joint

Sacrum

Os coxae

Acetabulum

Pubis

Ischium

Obturator foramen

Subpubic angle

(a) HUMAN

(b) CHIMPANZEE

Figure **A-6**
Pelvic girdles.

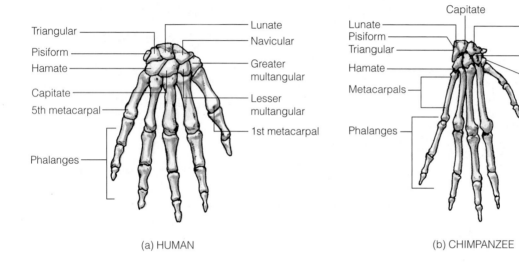

Triangular
Pisiform
Hamate
Capitate
5th metacarpal

Phalanges

Lunate
Navicular
Greater multangular
Lesser multangular
1st metacarpal

(a) HUMAN

Capitate

Lunate
Pisiform
Triangular
Hamate
Metacarpals

Phalanges

Navicular
Lesser multangular
Greater multangular

(b) CHIMPANZEE

Figure **A-7**
Hand anatomy.

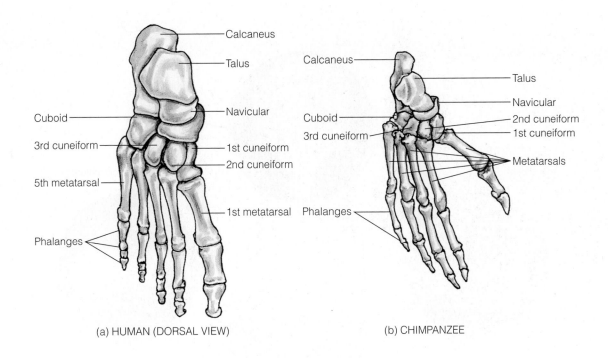

(a) HUMAN (DORSAL VIEW)

(b) CHIMPANZEE

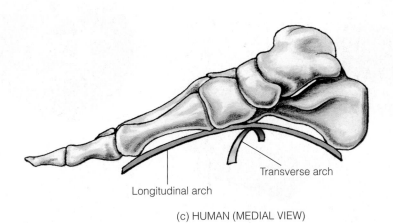

(c) HUMAN (MEDIAL VIEW)

Figure **A-8**
Foot (pedal) anatomy.

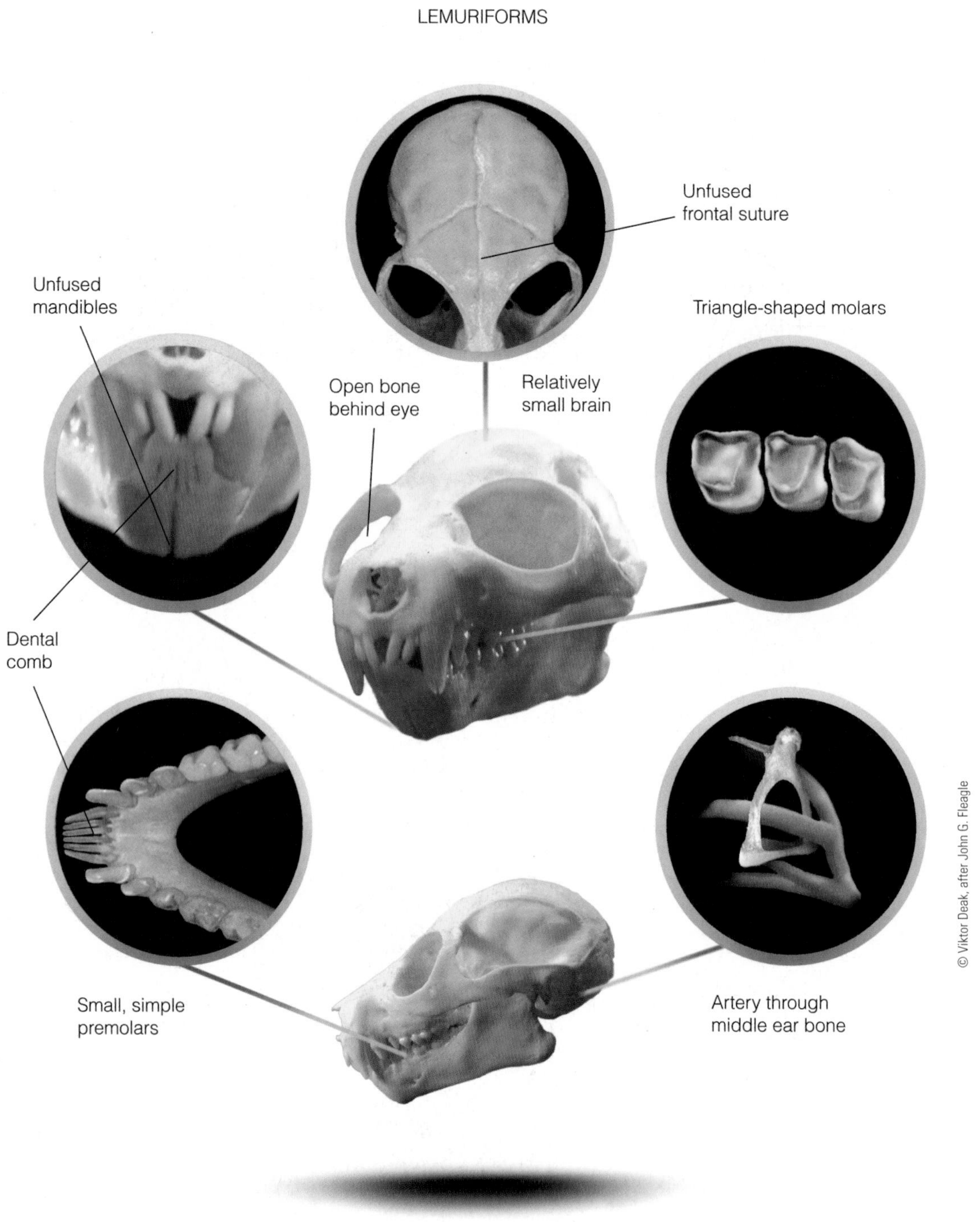

LEMURIFORMS

Unfused
frontal suture

Unfused
mandibles

Triangle-shaped molars

Open bone
behind eye

Relatively
small brain

Dental
comb

Artery through
middle ear bone

Small, simple
premolars

© Viktor Deak, after John G. Fleagle

Figure **A-9A**

Lemuriform anatomy. Refer to At a Glance:
Lemuriforms vs. Anthropoids, Chapter 9,
p. 251.

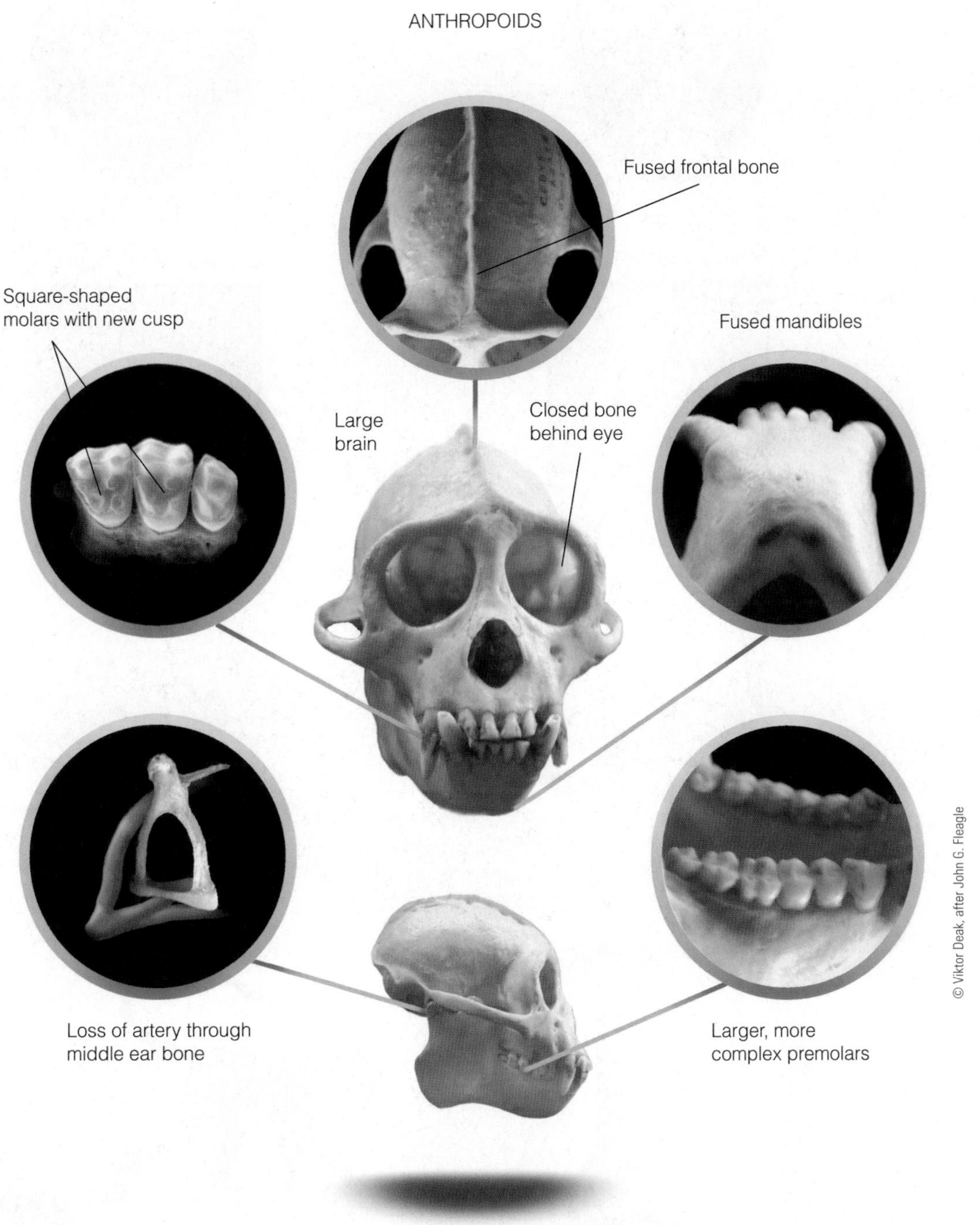

ANTHROPOIDS

Fused frontal bone

Square-shaped
molars with new cusp

Fused mandibles

Large
brain

Closed bone
behind eye

Loss of artery through
middle ear bone

Larger, more
complex premolars

© Viktor Deak, after John G. Fleagle

Figure **A-9B**

Anthropoid anatomy. Refer to At a Glance:
Lemuriforms vs. Anthropoids, Chapter 9,
p. 251.

Figure **A-10**

Comparison of New World Monkey and Old World Monkey anatomy. Refer to At a Glance: New World Monkeys vs. Old World Monkeys, Chapter 9, p. 254.

New World Monkeys

Old World Monkeys

Sideways-facing nostrils

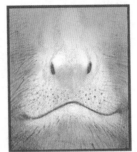

Downward-facing nostrils

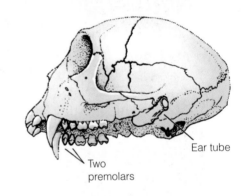

Three premolars

No ear tube

Two premolars

Ear tube

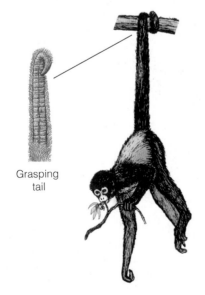

Grasping tail

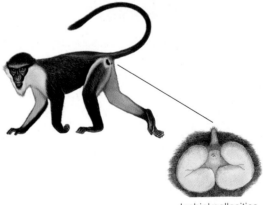

Ischial callosities

Old World Monkeys

Apes

Figure **A-11**

Comparison of Old World Monkey and ape anatomy. Refer to At a Glance: Old World Monkeys vs. Apes, Chapter 9, p. 258.

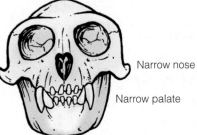

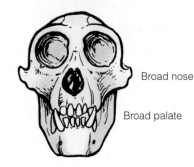

Narrow nose

Broad nose

Narrow palate

Broad palate

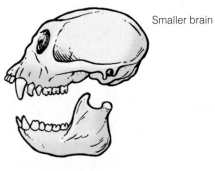

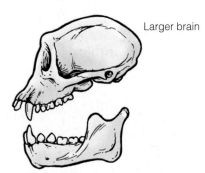

Smaller brain

Larger brain

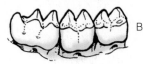

Bilophodont molars

Simple molars with Y-5 pattern

Tail

Longer torso

Shorter torso

No tail

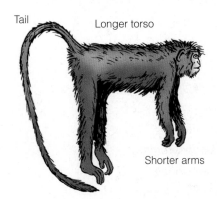

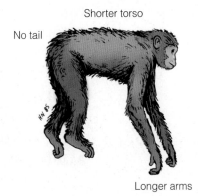

Shorter arms

Longer arms

Adapted from John G. Fleagle and Stephen Nash, Stony Brook University, New York

Appendix B

Taxonomy of Living and Selected Extinct Primates

ORDER: Primates

    SEMIORDER: Plesiadapiformes

                SUPERFAMILY: Plesiadapoidea

                FAMILY: Plesiadapidae

                    GENUS: *Plesiadapis*

                FAMILY: Carpolestidae

                    GENUS: *Carpolestes*

                FAMILY: Purgatoriidae

                    GENUS: *Purgatorius*

    SEMIORDER: Euprimates

        SUBORDER: Strepsirhini

            INFRAORDER: Adapiformes

                SUPERFAMILY: Adapoidea

                FAMILY: Notharctidae

                    GENUS: *Cantius*

                FAMILY: Adapidae

                    GENUS: *Adapis*

                FAMILY: Amphipithecidae

            INFRAORDER: Lemuriformes

                SUPERFAMILY: Lemuroidea

                FAMILY: Cheirogaleidae

                FAMILY: Lemuridae

                FAMILY: Lepilemuridae

                    GENUS: *Megaladapis*

                FAMILY: Indriidae

                FAMILY: Daubentoniidae

                    GENUS: *Daubentonia*

                FAMILY: Archaeolemuridae

                    GENUS: *Archaeolemur*

                SUPERFAMILY: Lorisoidea

                FAMILY: Galagidae

                FAMILY: Lorisidae

SUBORDER: **Haplorhini**

  INFRAORDER: **Omomyiformes**

    SUPERFAMILY: **Omomyoidea**

      FAMILY: Omomyidae

        SUBFAMILY: Anaptomorphinae

          GENUS: *Teilhardina*

        SUBFAMILY: Microchoerinae

          GENUS: *Necrolemur*

        SUBFAMILY: Omomyinae

          GENUS: *Shoshonius*

  INFRAORDER: **Tarsiiformes**

    SUPERFAMILY: **Tarsioidea**

      FAMILY: Tarsiidae

  INFRAORDER: **Anthropoidea**

    SUPERFAMILY: **Parapithecoidea**

      FAMILY: *Incertae sedis**

        GENUS: *Algeripithecus*

      FAMILY: Parapithecidae

        GENUS: *Apidium*

        GENUS: *Parapithecus*

        GENUS: *Biretia*

    PARVORDER: **Platyrrhini**

    SUPERFAMILY: **Ateloidea**

      FAMILY: Pitheciidae

      FAMILY: Atelidae

      FAMILY: Cebidae

        GENUS: *Cebus*

      FAMILY: *Incertae sedis*

        GENUS: *Branisella*

        GENUS: *Homunculus*

    PARVORDER: **Catarrhini**

    SUPERFAMILY: **Propliopithecoidea**

      FAMILY: Oligopithecidae

        GENUS: *Catopithecus*

      FAMILY: Propliopithecidae

        GENUS: *Aegyptopithecus*

    SUPERFAMILY: **Cercopithecoidea**

      FAMILY: Victoriapithecidae

      GENUS: *Victoriapithecus*

*Latin phrase meaning "of uncertain placement"; this designation is used for a taxonomic group where its broader relationships are unknown or undefined, meaning it cannot be reliably assigned to a recognized group at this time.

FAMILY: Cercopithecidae
  SUBFAMILY: Cercopithecinae
    GENUS: *Macaca*
    GENUS: *Papio*
    GENUS: *Theropithecus*
  SUBFAMILY: Colobinae
    GENUS: *Colobus*
    GENUS: *Presbytis*
    GENUS: *Nasalis*
SUPERFAMILY: **Pliopithecoidea**
  FAMILY: *Incertae sedis*
    GENUS: *Lomorupithecus*
  FAMILY: Pliopithecidae
    GENUS: *Pliopithecus*
SUPERFAMILY: **Proconsuloidea**
  FAMILY: Proconsulidae
    GENUS: *Proconsul*
    GENUS: *Micropithecus*
SUPERFAMILY: **Hominoidea**
  FAMILY: Hylobatidae
    GENUS: *Yuanmoupithecus*
    GENUS: *Hylobates*
  FAMILY: Hominidae
    SUBFAMILY: Kenyapithecinae
      GENUS: *Kenyapithecus*
    SUBFAMILY: Ponginae
      GENUS: *Sivapithecus*
      GENUS: *Gigantopithecus*
      GENUS: *Lufengpithecus*
      GENUS: *Pongo*
    SUBFAMILY: Homininae
      GENUS: *Dryopithecus*
      GENUS: *Ouranopithecus*
      GENUS: *Nakalipithecus*
      GENUS: *Chororapithecus*
      GENUS: *Gorilla*
      GENUS: *Pan*
      GENUS: *Homo*

Appendix C

Summary of Early Hominin Fossil Finds from Africa

Ardipithecus

Taxonomic designation:
Ardipithecus ramidus

Year of first discovery: 1992

Dating: Earlier sites, 5.8–5.6 mya; Aramis, 4.4 mya

Fossil material: Earlier materials: 1 jaw fragment, 4 isolated teeth, postcranial remains (foot phalanx, 2 hand phalanges, 2 humerus fragments, ulna). Later sample (Aramis) represented by many fossils, including up to 50 individuals (many postcranial elements, including at least 1 partial skeleton). Considerable fossil material retrieved from Aramis but not yet published; no reasonably complete cranial remains yet published.

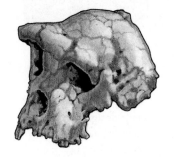

Sahelanthropus

Taxonomic designation:
Sahelanthropus tchadensis

Year of first discovery: 2001

Dating: ~7–6 mya

Fossil material: Nearly complete cranium, 2 jaw fragments, 3 isolated teeth

Orrorin

Taxonomic designation:
Orrorin tugenensis

Year of first discovery: 2000

Dating: ~6 mya

Fossil material: 2 jaw fragments, 6 isolated teeth, postcranial remains (femoral pieces, partial humerus, hand phalanx). No reasonably complete cranial remains yet discovered.

Location of finds: Toros-Menalla, Chad, central Africa

Location of finds: Middle Awash region, including Aramis (as well as earlier localities), Ethiopia, East Africa

Location of finds: Lukeino Formation, Tugen Hills, Baringo District, Kenya, East Africa

517

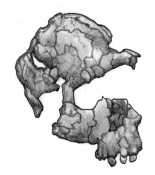

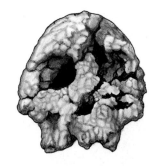

Australopithecus anamensis

Taxonomic designation:
   Australopithecus anamensis

Year of first discovery: 1965 (but not recognized as separate species at that time); more remains found in 1994 and 1995

Dating: 4.2–3.9 mya

Fossil material: Total of 22 specimens, including cranial fragments, jaw fragments, and postcranial pieces (humerus, tibia, radius). No reasonably complete cranial remains yet discovered.

Australopithecus afarensis

Taxonomic designation:
   Australopithecus afarensis

Year of first discovery: 1973

Dating: 3.6–3.0 mya

Fossil material: Large sample, with up to 65 individuals represented: 1 partial cranium, numerous cranial pieces and jaws, many teeth, numerous postcranial remains, including partial skeleton. Fossil finds from Laetoli also include dozens of fossilized footprints.

Kenyanthropus

Taxonomic designation:
   Kenyanthropus platyops

Year of first discovery: 1999

Dating: 3.5 mya

Fossil material: Partial cranium, temporal fragment, partial maxilla, 2 partial mandibles

Location of finds: Kanapoi, Allia Bay, Kenya, East Africa

Location of finds: Laetoli (Tanzania), Hadar/Dikika (Ethiopia), also likely found at East Turkana (Kenya) and Omo (Ethiopia), East Africa

Location of finds: Lomekwi, West Lake Turkana, Kenya, East Africa

Australopithecus garhi

Taxonomic designation:
Australopithecus garhi
Year of first discovery: 1997
Dating: 2.5 mya
Fossil material: Partial cranium, numerous limb bones

Paranthropus aethiopicus

Taxonomic designation:
Paranthropus aethiopicus (also called *Australopithecus aethiopicus*)
Year of first discovery: 1985
Dating: 2.4 mya
Fossil material: Nearly complete cranium

Paranthropus boisei

Taxonomic designation:
Paranthropus boisei (also called *Australopithecus boisei*)
Year of first discovery: 1959
Dating: 2.2–1.0 mya
Fossil material: 2 nearly complete crania, several partial crania, many jaw fragments, dozens of teeth. Postcrania less represented, but parts of several long bones recovered.

Location of finds: Bouri, Middle Awash, Ethiopia, East Africa

Location of finds: West Lake Turkana, Kenya

Location of finds: Olduvai Gorge and Peninj (Tanzania), East Lake Turkana (Koobi Fora), Chesowanja (Kenya), Omo (Ethiopia)

Australopithecus africanus

Taxonomic designation:
Australopithecus africanus
Year of first discovery: 1924
Dating: ~3.0?–2.0 mya
Fossil material: 1 mostly complete cranium, several partial crania, dozens of jaws/partial jaws, hundreds of teeth, 4 partial skeletons representing significant parts of the postcranium

Paranthropus robustus

Taxonomic designation:
Paranthropus robustus
(also called *Australopithecus robustus*)
Year of first discovery: 1938
Dating: ~2–1 mya
Fossil material: 1 complete cranium, several partial crania, many jaw fragments, hundreds of teeth, numerous postcranial elements

Early *Homo*

Taxonomic designation:
Homo habilis
Year of first discovery: 1959/1960
Dating: 2.4–1.8 mya
Fossil material: 2 partial crania, other cranial pieces, jaw fragments, several limb bones, partial hand, partial foot, partial skeleton

Location of finds: Taung, Sterkfontein, Makapansgat, Gladysvale (all from South Africa)

Location of finds: Kromdraai, Swartkrans, Drimolen, Cooper's Cave, possibly Gondolin (all from South Africa)

Location of finds: Olduvai Gorge (Tanzania), Lake Baringo (Kenya), Omo (Ethiopia), Sterkfontein (?) (South Africa)

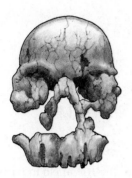

Early *Homo*

Taxonomic designation:
Homo rudolfensis

Year of first discovery: 1972

Dating: 1.8–1.4 mya

Fossil material: 4 partial crania, 1 mostly complete mandible, other jaw pieces, numerous teeth, a few postcranial elements (none directly associated with crania)

Location of finds: East Lake Turkana (Koobi Fora), Kenya, East Africa

Abbreviations Used for Fossil Hominin Specimens

For those hominin sites where a number of specimens have been recovered, standard abbreviations are used to designate the site as well as the specimen number (and occasionally museum accession information as well).

Abbreviation	Explanation	Example
AL	Afar locality	AL-288-1
LH	Laetoli hominin	LH 4
OH	Olduvai hominin	OH 5
KNM-ER (or simply ER)	Kenya National Museums, East Rudolf *	ER 1470
KNM-WT (or simply WT)	Kenya National Museums, West Turkana	WT 17000
Sts	Sterkfontein, main site	Sts 5
Stw	Sterkfontein, west extension	Stw 53
SK	Swartkrans	SK 48

* East Rudolf is the former name for Lake Turkana; the abbreviation was first used before the lake's name was changed. All these fossils (as well as others from sites throughout Kenya) are housed in Nairobi at the National Museums of Kenya.

Appendix D

Population Genetics: The Math of Microevolution

Part A. Further Examples Using the Hardy-Weinberg Equilibrium Formula

Example 1. Hemoglobin Beta Locus In West Africa

As discussed in Chapter 15, there is a high frequency of the Hb^S allele in parts of West Africa. One study (see p. 443) in a Senegalese group found a frequency of the Hb^S allele at 12 percent.

What follows is a hypothetical example for a Senegalese population of 4,000 individuals. Ascertainment is done on all individuals at 6 months of age. Because of incomplete dominance, all three phenotypes (and therefore all three genotypes) can be determined.

Observed frequencies:

	Number of Individuals	Hb^A Alleles	Hb^S Alleles
Hb^AHb^A	3,070	6,140	——
Hb^AHb^S	905	905	905
Hb^SHb^S	25	——	50
Totals	4,000	7,045	955

Allele frequencies:

$Hb^A = p = 7{,}045/8{,}000 = .881$

$Hb^S = q = 955/8{,}000 = .119$

Expected genotypic frequencies:

$Hb^AHb^A = p^2 = (.881)(.881) = .776$

$Hb^AHb^S = 2pq = 2(.881)(.119) = .210$

$Hb^SHb^S = q^2 = (.119)(.119) = .014$

Comparison of expected and observed frequencies:

	Expected Frequency	Expected No. Individuals	Observed Frequency	Observed No. Individuals
Hb^AHb^A	.776	3,105	.767	3,070
Hb^AHb^S	.210	839	.227	905
Hb^SHb^S	.014	57	.006	25

As you can see, there is a noticeable difference between the expected and observed frequencies. There are fewer actual (observed) individuals of both homozygotes than expected and more heterozygotes than expected. Indeed, when performing a statistical test (see Part 2 of this appendix), the difference is statistically significant.

We can extend the example further. Let us assume that we again ascertain allele frequencies in this same population 30 years later, at which point there are 3,000 survivors.

Observed phenotypic frequencies:

	Number of Individuals	Hb^A Alleles	Hb^S Alleles
Hb^AHb^A	2,123	4,246	——
Hb^AHb^S	875	875	875
Hb^SHb^S	2	——	4
Totals	3,000	5,121	879

Allele frequencies:

$Hb^A = p = 5,121/6,000 = .854$

$Hb^S = q = 879/6,000 = .146$

Expected genotypic frequencies:

$Hb^AHb^A = p^2 = (.854)(.854) = .729$

$Hb^AHb^S = 2pq = 2(.854)(.146) = .249$

$Hb^SHb^S = q^2 = (.146)(.146) = .021$

Comparison of expected and observed frequencies:

	Expected Frequency	Expected No. Individuals	Observed Frequency	Observed No. Individuals
Hb^AHb^A	.729	2,188	.708	2,123
Hb^AHb^S	.249	748	.292	875
Hb^SHb^S	.021	64	.001	2

In this adult sample, the differences between the expected and observed frequencies are even greater than they were for the infant sample (and are even more highly statistically significant; see Part 2). Moreover, these differences are in the same direction as before: There are fewer homozygotes and more heterozygotes than expected under equilibrium conditions. A likely explanation for this pattern of allele frequencies would focus on natural selection. At age 6 months, there are slightly fewer Hb^AHb^A homozygotes than expected and considerably fewer Hb^SHb^S homozygotes than expected. Correspondingly, there are many more heterozygotes (Hb^AHb^S) than expected. These differences could arise from differential mortality of Hb^AHb^A individuals due to malaria (likely in early infancy) and Hb^SHb^S individuals due to sickle-cell anemia occurring both *in utero* and during early infancy.

These same factors would continue throughout childhood and early adulthood, so that by age 30, the effects of differential mortality due to both malaria and sickle-cell anemia are even more dramatic. While hypothetical, these figures represent a good example of how natural selection could operate on this population.

Example 2. Adenosine Deaminase (ADA) in a Sri Lankan Population

ADA is an enzyme present in many types of cells. The locus producing this enzyme has two common codominant alleles, A^1 and A^2. There are also very rare mutant alleles that can cause a fatal form of inherited immune deficiency.

From actual data derived from a polymorphic population in Sri Lanka,* the following observed frequencies were found. (*Note:* Because the alleles are codominant, the three phenotypes correspond directly to the three genotypes.)

Observed frequencies:

	Number of Individuals	A^1 Alleles	A^2 Alleles
A^1A^1	113	226	——
A^1A^2	38	38	38
A^2A^2	3	——	6
Totals	154	264	44

Allele frequencies:

$A^1 = p = 264/308 = .857$

$A^2 = q = 44/308 = .143$

Expected genotypic frequencies:

$A^1A^1 = p^2 = (.857)(.857) = .734$

$A^1A^2 = 2pq = 2(.857)(.143) = .249$

$A^2A^2 = q^2 = (.143)(.143) = .020$

Comparison of expected and observed frequencies:

	Expected Frequency	Expected No. Individuals	Observed Frequency	Observed No. Individuals
A^1A^1	.734	113	.734	113
A^1A^2	.245	38	.247	38
A^2A^2	.020	3	.019	3

As you can clearly see, the expected and observed frequencies are nearly identical (in fact, the raw frequencies are identical). There is thus a probability of 1.0 that the null hypothesis is correct and a 0 percent confidence limit in rejecting the null hypothesis. This population at this locus thus appears to be in equilibrium. Such is often the case in actual population genetics studies, especially when the sample size is small.

Example 3. Determining the Number of Heterozygous Carriers for PKU in a Hypothetical Population

Another way to apply the Hardy-Weinberg formula is to first *assume* equilibrium and then work the formula in reverse. For example, for many recessive traits where there is complete dominance (or nearly complete dominance), traditionally it has been impossible to ascertain the heterozygotes directly. However, if we make certain assumptions, we can use the formula to estimate the number of heterozygotes (that is, carriers) in a population.

Let us assume that we are studying PKU in a group of 20,000 students at a university. PKU is an autosomal recessive disorder with an overall frequency in the

United States of approximately 1/10,000 (see p. 95). In some subgroups (for example, individuals of European descent), the frequency of PKU is higher.

In our hypothetical student population, we find two individuals with PKU (which was treated when the individuals were children). Because PKU is an autosomal recessive, the number of PKU homozygotes (2/20,000, or .0001) is equal to q^2.

If $q^2 = .0001$, then
$q = .01$ and $p = .99$

The frequency of the heterozygote is $2pq$:

$2(.99)(.01) = .0198$

The estimated number of carriers for PKU in the university student sample is

$(.0198)(20,000) = 198$

An interesting pattern is evident here. In the entire population, there is a total of 200 individuals who possess at least one PKU allele. Of these, the vast majority (99 percent) are carriers.

Example 4. Applying the Hardy-Weinberg Formula to ABO, a More Complex Genetic System

In Chapter 15 and in the three examples given so far in this appendix, we have used examples of loci with only two alleles (and therefore just three possible genotypes). However, many loci are more complex, having three or more alleles. For example, ABO has three alleles and six genotypes (see p. 87)

How do we utilize the Hardy-Weinberg equilibrium formula for a locus like ABO? First, there are three alleles, so the allele frequencies are designated as:

Frequency of $A = p$
Frequency of $B = q$
Frequency of $O = r$

Under equilibrium conditions, the genotypic frequencies would be calculated as follows:

$(p + q + r)^2 = 1$

This is an expansion of a trinomial (rather than the binomial used in a two-allele system). With a three-allele system like ABO, the genotypic frequency formula is

$p^2 + 2pq + 2pr + 2qr + q^2 = r^2 = 1$

There are six terms in this formula, each one representing a different genotype:

Term	Genotype Represented
p^2	AA
$2pq$	AB
$2pr$	AO
$2qr$	BO
q^2	BB
r^2	OO

We will not include actual numbers here. We simply wish to illustrate that population genetics calculations can be considerably more complex than implied by our earlier examples.

Part B. Statistical Evaluation: Testing Hardy-Weinberg Results

Following are the results using statistical tests comparing the expected and observed frequencies for the relevant examples shown in Chapter 15 as well as those discussed in this appendix. The test used is the chi-square (χ^2), which assumes that two variables are independent. In our examples, this independence is tested against a null hypothesis stating that there is equilibrium (in other words, the expected and observed frequencies do not differ any more than would be the case strictly as a result of chance). Further details concerning statistical approaches can be found in any introductory statistics text.

In the data tables that follow, all figures are shown as *raw* frequencies.

MN Data (from Chapter 15, p. 439) Contingency Table:

Observed frequencies	80	80	40
Expected frequencies	72	96	32

$\chi^2 = 2.76, p = .251$

The generally accepted confidence limit for rejection of the null hypothesis is less than or equal to .05. Thus, in this case, we cannot confidently reject the null hypothesis.

PTC Tasting Data (from Chapter 15, p. 442) Contingency Table:

Observed frequencies	125	325	50
Expected frequencies	165	245	90

$\chi^2 = 28.17, p < .0000$

This result is highly significant and allows us to reject the null hypothesis with a great deal of confidence. We are able to say there is less than 1 chance in 10,000 that the null hypothesis applies to these data.

Hemoglobin Beta Locus (Example 1, this appendix) Contingency Tables:

At 6 months:

Observed frequencies	3,070	905	25
Expected frequencies	3,105	839	57

$\chi^2 = 15.18, p = .0005$

This is a highly significant result that allows us to reject the null hypothesis with high confidence.

At Age 30:

Observed frequencies	2,123	875	2
Expected frequencies	2,188	748	64

$\chi^2 = 69.16, p < .0000$

This result is even more highly significant than at age 6 months, as there has been further disruption of equilibrium expectations (that is, greater evidence of evolutionary shifts in allele frequencies).

Glossary

Acheulian (ash´-oo-lay-en) Pertaining to a stone tool industry from the Early and Middle Pleistocene; characterized by a large proportion of bifacial tools (flaked on both sides). Acheulian tool kits are common in Africa, Southwest Asia, and western Europe, but they're thought to be less common elsewhere. Also spelled Acheulean.

acclimatization Physiological responses to changes in the environment that occur during an individual's lifetime. Such responses may be temporary or permanent, depending on the duration of the environmental change and when in the individual's life it occurs. The capacity for acclimatization may typify an entire species or population, and because it's under genetic influence, it's subject to evolutionary factors such as natural selection and genetic drift.

adaptation An anatomical, physiological, or behavioral response of organisms or populations to the environment. Adaptations result from evolutionary change (specifically, as a result of natural selection).

adaptive niche An organism's entire way of life: where it lives, what it eats, how it gets food, how it avoids predators, and so on.

adaptive radiation The relatively rapid expansion and diversification of life-forms into new ecological niches.

affiliative Pertaining to amicable associations between individuals. Affiliative behaviors, such as grooming, reinforce social bonds and promote group cohesion.

allele frequency In a population, the percentage of all the alleles at a locus accounted for by one specific allele.

alleles Alternate forms of a gene. Alleles occur at the same locus on paired chromosomes and thus govern the same trait. But because they're different, their action may result in different expressions of that trait. The term *allele* is sometimes used synonymously with *gene*.

allometry Also called scaling; the differential proportion among various anatomical structures (e.g., the size of the brain in proportion to overall body size during the development of an individual). Scaling effects must also be considered when comparing species.

alloparenting A common behavior in many primate species whereby individuals other than the parent(s) hold, carry, and in general interact with infants.

allopatric Living in different areas. This pattern is important in the divergence of closely related species from each other and from their shared ancestral species because it leads to reproductive isolation.

altruism Behavior that benefits another individual at some potential risk or cost to oneself.

amino acids Small molecules that are the components of proteins.

analogies Similarities between organisms based strictly on common function, with no assumed common evolutionary descent.

ancestral Referring to characters inherited by a group of organisms from a remote ancestor and thus not diagnostic of groups (lineages) that diverged after the character first appeared; also called primitive.

anthropocentric Viewing nonhuman organisms in terms of human experience and capabilities; emphasizing the importance of humans over everything else.

anthropoids Members of a suborder of Primates, the infraorder Anthropoidea (pronounced "an-throw-poid´-ee-uh"). Traditionally, the suborder includes monkeys, apes, and humans.

anthropology The field of inquiry that studies human culture and evolutionary aspects of human biology; includes cultural anthropology, archaeology, linguistics, and physical, or biological, anthropology.

anthropometry Measurement of human body parts. When osteologists measure skeletal elements, the term *osteometry* is often used.

antibodies Proteins that are produced by some types of immune cells and that serve as major components of the immune system. Antibodies recognize and attach to foreign antigens on bacteria, viruses, and other pathogens. Then other immune cells destroy the invading organism.

antigens Large molecules found on the surface of cells. Several different loci govern various antigens on red and white blood cells. (Foreign antigens provoke an immune response.)

anvils Surfaces on which an object such as a palm nut, root, or seed is placed before being struck with another object such as a stone.

applied anthropology The practical application of anthropological and archaeological theories and techniques. For example, many biological anthropologists work in the public health sector.

arboreal Tree-living; adapted to life in the trees.

artifacts Objects or materials made or modified for use by hominins. The earliest artifacts are usually made of stone or, occasionally, bone.

assort To sort out or separate.

Aurignacian Pertaining to an Upper Paleolithic stone tool industry in Europe beginning at about 40,000 ya.

australopiths A colloquial name referring to a diverse group of Plio-Pleistocene African hominins. Australopiths are the most abundant and widely distributed of all early hominins and are also the most completely studied.

autonomic Pertaining to physiological responses that aren't under voluntary control. An example in chimpanzees would be the erection of body hair during excitement. Blushing is a human example. Both convey information regarding emotional states; but neither behavior is deliberate, and communication is not intended.

autosomes All chromosomes except the sex chromosomes.

balanced polymorphism The maintenance of two or more alleles in a population due to the selective advantage of the heterozygote.

behavior Anything organisms do that involves action in response to internal or external stimuli; the response of an individual, group, or species to its environment. Such responses may or may not be deliberate, and they aren't necessarily the result of conscious decision making (which is absent in single-celled organisms, insects, and many other species).

behavioral ecology The study of the evolution of behavior, emphasizing the role of ecological factors as agents of natural selection. Behaviors and behavioral patterns are favored by natural selection because they increase the reproductive fitness of individuals (i.e., they're adaptive) in specific environmental contexts.

bilophodont Referring to molars that have four cusps oriented in two parallel rows, resembling ridges, or "lophs." This trait is characteristic of Old World monkeys.

binocular vision Vision characterized by overlapping visual fields provided by forward-facing eyes. Binocular vision is essential to depth perception.

binomial nomenclature (*binomial*, meaning "two names") In taxonomy, the convention established by Carolus Linnaeus whereby genus and species names are used to refer to species. For example, *Homo sapiens* refers to human beings.

biocultural evolution The mutual, interactive evolution of human biology and culture; the concept that biology makes culture possible and that developing culture further influences the direction of biological evolution; a basic concept in understanding the unique components of human evolution.

biological continuity Refers to a biological continuum. When expressions of a phenomenon continuously grade into one another so that there are no discrete categories, they exist on a continuum. Color is one such phenomenon, and life-forms are another.

biological determinism The concept that phenomena, including various aspects of behavior (e.g., intelligence, values, morals) are governed by biological (genetic) factors; the inaccurate association of various behavioral attributes with certain biological traits, such as skin color.

biological species concept A depiction of species as groups of individuals capable of fertile interbreeding but reproductively isolated from other such groups.

biostratigraphy A relative dating technique based on regular changes seen in evolving groups of animals as well as presence or absence of particular species.

bipedally On two feet. Walking habitually on two legs.

blanks In archaeology, stones suitably sized and shaped to be further worked into tools.

brachiation Arm swinging, a form of locomotion used by some primates. Brachiation involves hanging from a branch and moving by alternately swinging from one arm to the other.

breeding isolates Populations that are clearly isolated geographically and/or socially from other breeding groups.

burins Small, chisel-like tools with a pointed end; thought to have been used to engrave bone, antler, ivory, or wood.

catarrhine Member of Catarrhini, a parvorder of Primates, one of the three major divisions of the suborder Haplorhini. It contains the Old World monkeys and the apes.

catastrophism The view that the earth's geological landscape is the result of violent cataclysmic events. Cuvier promoted this view, especially in opposition to Lamarck.

centromere The constricted portion of a chromosome. After replication, the two strands of a double-stranded chromosome are joined at the centromere.

cercopithecines (serk-oh-pith´-eh-seens) The subfamily of Old World monkeys that includes baboons, macaques, and guenons.

Chatelperronian Pertaining to an Upper Paleolithic industry found in France and Spain, containing blade tools and associated with Neandertals.

Chordata The phylum of the animal kingdom that includes vertebrates.

Christian fundamentalists Adherents to a movement in American Protestantism that began in the early twentieth century. This group holds that the teachings of the Bible are infallible and the scriptures are to be taken literally.

chromatin The loose, diffuse form of DNA seen when a cell isn't dividing. When it condenses, chromatin forms into chromosomes.

chromosomes Discrete structures composed of DNA and protein found only in the nuclei of cells. Chromosomes are visible under magnification only during certain phases of cell division.

chronometric dating (*chrono*, meaning "time," and *metric*, meaning "measure") A dating technique that gives an estimate in actual numbers of years; also known as absolute dating.

clade A group of organisms sharing a common ancestor. The group includes the common ancestor and all descendants.

cladistics An approach to classification that attempts to make rigorous evolutionary interpretations based solely on analysis of certain types of homologous characters (those considered to be derived characters).

cladogram A chart showing evolutionary relationships as determined by cladistic analysis. It's based solely on interpretation of shared derived characters. It contains no time component and does not imply ancestor-descendant relationships.

cline A gradual change in the frequency of genotypes and phenotypes from one geographical region to another.

clones Organisms that are genetically identical to another organism. The term may also be used to refer to genetically identical DNA segments, molecules, or cells.

codominance The expression of two alleles in heterozygotes. In this situation, neither allele is dominant or recessive so they both influence the phenotype.

colobines (kole´-uh-beans) Common name for members of the subfamily of Old World monkeys that includes the African colobus monkeys and Asian langurs.

communication Any act that conveys information, in the form of a message, to another individual. Frequently, the result of communication is a change in the recipient's behavior. Communication may not be deliberate, but may instead be the result of involuntary processes or a secondary consequence of an intentional action.

complementary In genetics, referring to the fact that DNA bases form pairs (called base pairs) in a precise manner. For example, adenine can bond only to thymine. These two bases are said to be complementary because one requires the other to form a complete DNA base pair.

conspecifics Members of the same species.

context The environmental setting where an archaeological trace is found. Primary context is the setting in which the archaeological trace was originally deposited. A secondary context is one to which it has been moved (such as by the action of a stream).

continental drift The movement of continents on sliding plates of the earth's surface. As a result, the positions of large landmasses have shifted drastically during the earth's history.

continuum A set of relationships in which all components fall along a single integrated spectrum. All life reflects a single biological continuum.

core Stone reduced by flake removal. A core may or may not itself be used as a tool.

core area The portion of a home range containing the highest concentration and most reliable supplies of food and water. The core area is frequently the area that will be most aggressively defended.

cortex Layer. In the brain, the cortex is the layer that covers the cerebral hemispheres, which in turn cover more primitive or older structures related to bodily functions and the sense of smell. The cortex is composed of nerve cells called neurons, which communicate with each other and send and receive messages to and from all parts of the body.

crown group All of the taxa that come after a major speciation event. Crown groups are easier to identify than stem groups because the members possess the clade's shared derived traits.

culture Behavioral aspects of human adaptation, including technology, traditions, language, religion, marriage patterns, and social roles. Culture is a set of learned behaviors transmitted from one generation to the next by nonbiological (i.e., nongenetic) means.

cusps The bumps on the chewing surface of premolars and molars.

cytoplasm The portion of the cell contained within the cell membrane, excluding the nucleus. The cytoplasm consists of a semifluid material and contains numerous structures involved with cell function.

data (sing., datum) Facts from which conclusions can be drawn; scientific information.

dental apes Early apes that postcranially resemble monkeys but dentally are hominoids (i.e., they have a Y-5 molar configuration).

dental formula Numerical device that indicates the number of each type of tooth in each side of the upper and lower jaws.

derived (modified) Referring to characters that are modified from the ancestral condition and thus diagnostic of particular evolutionary lineages.

direct percussion Striking a core or flake with a hammerstone.

displays Sequences of repetitious behaviors that serve to communicate emotional states. Nonhuman primate displays are most frequently associated with reproductive or agonistic behavior.

DNA (deoxyribonucleic acid) The double-stranded molecule that contains the genetic code. DNA is a main component of chromosomes.

dominance hierarchies Systems of social organization wherein individuals within a group are ranked relative to one another. Higher-ranking individuals have greater access to preferred food items and mating partners than do lower-ranking individuals. Dominance hierarchies are sometimes referred to as pecking orders.

dominant Describing a trait governed by an allele that's expressed in the presence of another allele (i.e., in heterozygotes). Dominant alleles prevent the expression of recessive alleles in heterozygotes. (This is the definition of complete dominance.)

ecological niche The position of a species within its physical and biological environments. A species' ecological niche is defined by such components as diet, terrain, vegetation, type of predators, relationships with other species, and activity patterns, and each niche is unique to a given species. Together, ecological niches make up an ecosystem.

ecological species concept The concept that a species is a group of organisms exploiting a single niche. This view emphasizes the role of natural selection in separating species from one another.

empirical Relying on experiment or observation; from the Latin *empiricus*, meaning "experienced."

encephalization The proportional size of the brain relative to some other measure, usually an estimate of overall body size, such as weight. More precisely, the term refers to increases in brain size beyond what would be expected given the body size of a particular species.

endemic Continuously present in a population.

endogamy Mating with individuals from the same group.

endothermic (*endo*, meaning "within" or "internal") Able to maintain internal body temperature by producing energy through metabolic processes within cells; characteristic of mammals, birds, and perhaps some dinosaurs.

environmental determinism An interpretation that links simple environmental changes directly to a major evolutionary shift in an organism. Such explanations tend to oversimplify the evolutionary process.

enzymes Specialized proteins that initiate and direct chemical reactions in the body.

epochs Categories of the geological time scale; subdivisions of periods. In the Cenozoic, epochs include the Paleocene, Eocene, Oligocene, Miocene, and Pliocene (from the Tertiary) and the Pleistocene and Holocene (from the Quaternary).

ethnocentric Viewing other cultures from the inherently biased perspective of one's own culture. Ethnocentrism often results in other cultures being seen as inferior to one's own.

ethnographies Detailed descriptive studies of human societies. In cultural anthropology, an ethnography is traditionally the study of a non-Western society.

Euarchonta The superorder designated for the sister (closely related) orders of tree shrews, flying lemurs, and primates.

eugenics The philosophy of "race improvement" through the forced sterilization of members of some groups and increased reproduction among others; an overly simplified, often racist view that's now discredited.

euprimates "True primates." This term was coined by Elwyn Simons in 1972.

evaporative cooling A physiological mechanism that helps prevent the body from overheating. It occurs when perspiration is produced from sweat glands and then evaporates from the surface of the skin.

evolution A change in the genetic structure of a population. The term is also frequently used to refer to the appearance of a new species.

evolutionary systematics A traditional approach to classification (and evolutionary interpretation) in which presumed ancestors and descendants are traced in time by analysis of homologous characters.

exogamy Mating pattern whereby individuals obtain mates from groups other than their own.

exons Segments of genes that are transcribed and are involved in protein synthesis. (The prefix "ex" denotes that these segments are expressed.)

fertility The ability to conceive and produce healthy offspring.

fitness Pertaining to natural selection, a measure of the relative reproductive success of individuals. Fitness can be measured by an individual's genetic contribution to the next generation compared to that of other individuals. The terms *genetic fitness*, *reproductive fitness*, and *differential reproductive success* are also used.

fixity of species The notion that species, once created, can never change; an idea diametrically opposed to theories of biological evolution.

flake Thin-edged fragment removed from a core.

flexed The position of the body in a bent orientation, with arms and legs drawn up to the chest.

forensic anthropology An applied anthropological approach dealing with legal matters. Forensic anthropologists work with coroners and others in identifying and analyzing human remains.

founder effect A type of genetic drift in which allele frequencies are altered in small populations that are taken from, or are remnants of, larger populations.

frugivorous (fru-give´-or-us) Having a diet composed primarily of fruit.

gametes Reproductive cells (eggs and sperm in animals) developed from precursor cells in ovaries and testes.

gene flow Exchange of genes between populations.

gene pool The total complement of genes shared by the reproductive members of a population.

genes Sequences of DNA bases that specify the order of amino acids in an entire protein, a portion of a protein, or any functional product. A gene may be made up of hundreds or thousands of DNA bases organized into coding and noncoding segments.

genetic Having to do with the study of gene structure and action and the patterns of inheritance of traits from parent to offspring. Genetic mechanisms are the foundation for evolutionary change.

genetic drift Evolutionary changes—that is, changes in allele frequencies—produced by random factors. Genetic drift is a result of small population size.

genome The entire genetic makeup of an individual or species. In humans, it's estimated that each individual possesses approximately 3 billion DNA nucleotides.

genotype The genetic makeup of an individual. Genotype can refer to an organism's entire genetic makeup or to the alleles at a particular locus.

genus (*pl.*, genera) A group of closely related species.

geological time scale The organization of earth history into eras, periods, and epochs; commonly used by geologists and paleoanthropologists.

glaciations Climatic intervals when continental ice sheets cover much of the northern continents. Glaciations are associated with colder temperatures in northern latitudes and more arid conditions in southern latitudes, most notably in Africa.

grade A grouping of organisms sharing a similar adaptive pattern. Grade isn't necessarily based on closeness of evolutionary relationship, but it does contrast organisms in a useful way (e.g., *Homo erectus* with *Homo sapiens*).

grooming Picking through fur to remove dirt, parasites, and other materials that may be present. Social grooming is common among primates and reinforces social relationships.

habitual bipedalism Bipedal locomotion as the form of locomotion shown by hominins most of the time.

half-life The time period in which one-half the amount of a radioactive isotope is converted chemically to a daughter product. For example, after 1.25 billion years, half the ^{40}K remains; after 2.5 billion years, one-fourth remains.

haplorhines (hap-lore´-ines) Members of the primate suborder Haplorhini, which includes tarsiers, monkeys, apes, and humans.

Haplorhini (hap´-lo-rin-ee) The primate suborder that includes tarsiers, monkeys, apes, and humans.

Hardy-Weinberg theory of genetic equilibrium The mathematical relationship expressing—under conditions in which no evolution is occurring—the predicted distribution of alleles in populations; the central theorem of population genetics.

hemispheres The two halves of the cerebrum that are connected by a dense mass of fibers. (The cerebrum is the large rounded outer portion of the brain.)

hemoglobin A protein molecule that occurs in red blood cells and binds to oxygen molecules.

heterodont Having different kinds of teeth; characteristic of mammals, whose teeth consist of incisors, canines, premolars, and molars.

heterozygous Having different alleles at the same locus on members of a pair of chromosomes.

Holocene The most recent epoch of the Cenozoic. Following the Pleistocene, it's estimated to have begun 10,000 years ago.

home range The total area exploited by an animal or social group; usually given for one year or for the entire lifetime of an animal.

homeobox genes An evolutionarily ancient family of regulatory genes that directs the development of the overall body plan and the segmentation of body tissues.

homeostasis A condition of balance, or stability, within a biological system, maintained by the interaction of physiological mechanisms that compensate for changes (both external and internal).

hominins Colloquial term for members of the evolutionary group that includes modern humans and now extinct bipedal relatives.

hominoids Members of the primate superfamily (Hominoidea) that includes apes and humans.

homologies Similarities between organisms based on descent from a common ancestor.

homoplasy (*homo*, meaning "same," and *plasy*, meaning "growth") The separate evolutionary development of similar characteristics in different groups of organisms.

homozygous Having the same allele at the same locus on both members of a pair of chromosomes.

hormones Substances (usually proteins) that are produced by specialized cells and that travel to other parts of the body, where they influence chemical reactions and regulate various cellular functions.

Human Genome Project An international effort aimed at sequencing and mapping the entire human genome, completed in 2003.

hybrids Offspring of parents that differ from each other with regard to certain traits or certain aspects of genetic makeup; heterozygotes.

hypotheses (*sing.*, hypothesis) A provisional explanation of a phenomenon. Hypotheses require verification or falsification through testing.

inbreeding A type of nonrandom mating in which relatives mate more often than predicted under random mating conditions.

incest avoidance In animals, the tendency not to mate with close relatives. This tendency may be due to various social and ecological factors that keep the individuals apart. There may also be innate factors that lead to incest avoidance but these aren't well understood.

intelligence Mental capacity; ability to learn, reason, or comprehend and interpret information, facts, relationships, and meanings; the capacity to solve problems, whether through the application of previously acquired knowledge or through insight.

interglacials Climatic intervals when continental ice sheets are retreating, eventually becoming much reduced in size. Interglacials in northern latitudes are associated with warmer temperatures, while in southern latitudes the climate becomes wetter.

interspecific Between species; refers to variation beyond that seen within the same species to include additional aspects seen between two different species.

intragroup (*intra*, meaning "within") Within the group, as opposed to between groups (intergroup).

intraspecific Within species; refers to variation seen within the same species.

introns Segments of genes that are initially transcribed and then deleted. Because they aren't expressed, they aren't involved in protein synthesis.

ischial callosities Patches of tough, hard skin on the buttocks of Old World monkeys and chimpanzees.

island-hop To travel from one island to the next.

karyotype The chromosomal complement of an individual, or what is typical for a species. Usually displayed in a photo micrograph, the chromosomes are arranged in pairs and according to size and position of the centromere.

knappers People (frequently archaeologists) who make stone tools.

K-selected Pertaining to K-selection, an adaptive strategy whereby individuals produce relatively few offspring, in whom they invest increased parental care. Although only a few infants are born, chances of survival are increased for each individual because of parental investments in time and energy. Examples of nonprimate K-selected species are birds and canids (e.g., wolves, coyotes, and dogs).

lactase persistence In adults, the continued production of lactase, the enzyme that breaks down lactose (milk sugar). This allows adults in some human populations to digest fresh milk products. The discontinued production of lactase in adults leads to lactose intolerance and the inability to digest fresh milk.

last common ancestor (LCA) The final evolutionary link between two related groups.

Late Pleistocene The portion of the Pleistocene epoch beginning 125,000 ya and ending approximately 10,000 ya.

lateralized Localized to one side of the brain. Lateralization is the functional specialization of the hemispheres of the brain for specific activities.

life history traits Characteristics and developmental stages that influence rates of reproduction. Examples include longevity, age at sexual maturity, and length of time between births.

lithic (*lith*, meaning "stone") Referring to stone tools.

locus (*pl.*, loci) (lo´-kus, lo-sigh´) The position on a chromosome where a given gene occurs. The term is sometimes used interchangeably with *gene*.

lumbar Pertaining to the lower back. Monkeys have a longer lumbar area than that seen in apes and humans.

macroevolution Changes produced only after many generations, such as the appearance of a new species.

Magdalenian Pertaining to the final phase of the Upper Paleolithic stone tool industry in Europe.

matrilines Groupings of females who are all descendants of one female (a female, her daughters, granddaughters, and their offspring). Matrilines also include dependent male offspring. Among macaques, some matrilines are dominant to others, so that members of dominant matrilines have greater access to resources than do members of subordinate matrilines.

meiosis Cell division in specialized cells in ovaries and testes. Meiosis involves two divisions and results in four daughter cells, each containing only half the original number of chromosomes. These cells can develop into gametes.

menarche The first menstruation in girls, usually occurring in the early to mid-teens.

Mendelian traits Characteristics that are influenced by alleles at only one genetic locus. Examples include many blood types, such as ABO. Many genetic disorders, including sickle-cell anemia and Tay-Sachs disease, are also Mendelian traits.

menopause The end of menstruation in women, usually occurring at around age 50.

messenger RNA (mRNA) A form of RNA that's assembled on a sequence of DNA bases. It carries the DNA code to the ribosome during protein synthesis.

metabolism The chemical processes within cells that break down nutrients and release energy for the body to use. (When nutrients are broken down into their component parts, such as amino acids, energy is released and made available for the cell to use.)

microevolution Small changes occurring within species, such as a change in allele frequencies.

microliths (*micro*, meaning "small," and *lith*, meaning "stone") Small stone tools usually produced from narrow blades punched from a core; found especially in Africa during the latter part of the Pleistocene.

microwear Polishes, striations, and other diagnostic microscopic changes on the edges of stone tools.

Middle Pleistocene The portion of the Pleistocene epoch beginning 780,000 ya and ending 125,000 ya.

mitochondria (*sing.*, mitochondrion) Structures contained within the cytoplasm of eukaryotic cells that convert energy, derived from nutrients, to a form that can be used by the cell.

mitochondrial DNA (mtDNA) DNA found in the mitochondria; mtDNA is inherited only from the mother.

mitosis Simple cell division; the process by which somatic cells divide to produce two identical daughter cells.

molecules Structures made up of two or more atoms. Molecules can combine with other molecules to form more complex structures.

monophyletic Referring to an evolutionary group (clade) composed of descendants all sharing a common ancestor.

morphological Pertaining to the form and structure of organisms.

morphology The form (shape, size) of anatomical structures; can also refer to the entire organism.

motor cortex The areas of the brain's cortex involved with movement. The motor cortex is located just behind the frontal lobe and is composed of cells that send information to muscle cells throughout the body.

Mousterian Pertaining to the stone tool industry associated with Neandertals and some modern *H. sapiens* groups; also called Middle Paleolithic. This industry is characterized by a larger proportion of flake tools than found in Acheulian tool kits.

multidisciplinary Pertaining to research involving mutual contributions and cooperation of experts from various scientific fields (i.e., disciplines).

mutation A change in DNA. The term can refer to changes in DNA bases (specifically called point mutations) as well as to changes in chromosome number and/or structure.

natal group The group in which animals are born and raised. (*Natal* pertains to birth.)

natural selection The most critical mechanism of evolutionary change, first described by Charles Darwin; refers to genetic change or changes in the frequencies of certain traits in populations due to differential reproductive success between individuals.

neocortex The more recently evolved portions of the cortex of the brain that are involved with higher mental functions and composed of areas that integrate incoming information from different sensory organs.

neural tube In early embryonic development, the anatomical structure that develops to form the brain and spinal cord.

nocturnal Active during the night.

nondisjunction The failure of partner chromosomes or chromosome strands to separate during cell division.

nonrandom mating Pattern of mating in which individuals choose mates preferentially. That is, mate choice is based on different criteria such as social status, ethnicity, or biological relationship. An individual doesn't have an equal chance of mating with all other individuals in their group.

nuchal torus (nuke´-ul) (*nucha*, meaning "neck") A projection of bone in the back of the cranium where neck muscles attach. These muscles hold up the head.

nucleotides Basic units of the DNA molecule, composed of a sugar, a phosphate, and one of four DNA bases.

nucleus A structure (organelle) found in all eukaryotic cells. The nucleus contains chromosomes (nuclear DNA).

obligate bipedalism Bipedalism as the *only* form of hominin terrestrial locomotion. Since major anatomical changes in the spine, pelvis, and lower limb are required for bipedal locomotion, once hominins adapted this mode of locomotion, other forms of locomotion on the ground became impossible.

olfaction The sense of smell.

omnivorous Having a diet consisting of many food types, such as plant materials, meat, and insects.

orthograde An upright body position. This term relates to the position of the head and torso during sitting, climbing, etc., and doesn't necessarily mean that an animal is bipedal.

osteology The study of skeletal material. Human osteology focuses on the interpretation of the skeletal remains from archaeological sites, skeletal anatomy, bone physiology, and growth and development. Some of the same techniques are used in paleoanthropology to study early hominins.

paleoanthropology The interdisciplinary approach to the study of earlier hominins—their chronology, physical structure, archaeological remains, habitats, and so on.

paleomagnetism Dating method based on the earth's shifting magnetic pole.

paleopathology The branch of osteology that studies the evidence of disease and injury in human skeletal (or, occasionally, mummified) remains from archaeological sites.

paleoprimatologists Anthropologists specializing in the study of the nonhuman primate fossil record.

paleospecies Species defined from fossil evidence, often covering a long time span.

pathogens Substances or microorganisms, such as bacteria, fungi, or viruses, that cause disease.

pedigree chart A diagram showing family relationships. It's used to trace the hereditary pattern of particular genetic (usually Mendelian) traits.

phenotypes The observable or detectable physical characteristics of an organism; the detectable expressions of genotypes, frequently influenced by environmental factors.

philopatric Remaining in one's natal group or home range as an adult. In most species, members of one sex disperse from their natal group as young adults, and members of the philopatric sex remain. In most nonhuman primate species, the philopatric sex is female.

phylogenetic species concept Splitting many populations into separate species based on an identifiable parental pattern of ancestry.

phylogenetic tree A chart showing evolutionary relationships as determined by evolutionary systematics. It contains a time component and implies ancestor-descendant relationships.

phytoliths (*phyto*, meaning "hidden," and *lith*, meaning "stone") Microscopic silica structures formed in the cells of many plants, particularly grasses.

placental A type (subclass) of mammal. During the Cenozoic, placentals became the most widespread and numerous mammals and today are represented by upward of 20 orders, including the primates.

platyrrhines Members of Platyrrhini, a parvorder of Primates, one of the three major divisions of the suborder Haplorhini. It contains only the New World monkeys.

pleiotropic genes Genes that have more than one effect; genes that have different effects at different times in the life cycle.

pleiotropy A situation that occurs when the action of a single gene influences several seemingly unrelated phenotypic effects.

Pleistocene The epoch of the Cenozoic from 1.8 mya until 10,000 ya. Frequently referred to as the Ice Age, this epoch is associated with continental glaciations in northern latitudes.

Plio-Pleistocene Pertaining to the Pliocene and first half of the Pleistocene, a time range of 5–1 mya. For this time period, numerous fossil hominins have been found in Africa.

point mutation A chemical change in a single base of a DNA sequence.

polyandry A mating system characterized by an association between a female and more than one male (usually two or three), with whom she mates. Among nonhuman primates, this pattern is seen only in marmosets and tamarins.

polygenic Referring to traits that are influenced by genes at two or more loci. Examples include stature, skin color, eye color, and hair color. Many, but not all (eye color, for example), polygenic traits are influenced by environmental factors such as nutrition.

polymerase chain reaction (PCR) A method of producing thousands of copies of a DNA sample.

polymorphisms Loci with more than one allele. Polymorphisms can be expressed in the phenotype as the result of gene action (as in ABO), or they can exist solely at the DNA level within noncoding regions.

polyphyletic Referring to an evolutionary group composed of descendants with more than one common ancestor (and thus not a true clade).

polytypic Referring to species composed of populations that differ in the expression of one or more traits.

population Within a species, a community of individuals where mates are usually found.

population genetics The study of the frequency of alleles, genotypes, and phe-notypes in populations from a microevolutionary perspective.

postcranial Referring to all or part of the skeleton not including the skull. The term originates from the fact that in quadrupeds, the body is posterior to the head; the term literally means "behind the head."

pressure flaking A method of removing flakes from a core by pressing a pointed implement (e.g., bone or antler) against the stone.

primate paleontology The study of fossil primates, especially those that lived before the appearance of hominins.

primates Members of the mammalian order Primates (pronounced "pry-may´-tees"), which includes lemurs, lorises, tarsiers, monkeys, apes, and humans.

primatology The study of the biology and behavior of nonhuman primates (lemurs, lorises, tarsiers, monkeys, and apes).

principle of independent assortment The distribution of one pair of alleles into gametes does not influence the distribution of another pair. The genes controlling different traits are inherited independently of one another.

principle of segregation Genes (alleles) occur in pairs because chromosomes occur in pairs. During gamete formation, the members of each pair of alleles separate, so that each gamete contains one member of each pair. During fertilization, the full number of chromosomes is restored, and members of gene or allele pairs are reunited.

principle of superposition In a stratigraphic sequence, the lower layers were deposited before the upper layers. Or, simply put, the stuff on top of a heap was put there last.

protein synthesis The assembly of chains of amino acids into functional protein molecules. The process is directed by DNA.

proteins Three-dimensional molecules that serve a wide variety of functions through their ability to bind to other molecules.

punctuated equilibrium The concept that evolutionary change proceeds through long periods of stasis punctuated by rapid periods of change.

quadrupedal Using all four limbs to support the body during locomotion; the basic mammalian (and primate) form of locomotion.

quantitatively Pertaining to measurements of quantity and including such properties as size, number, and capacity. When data are quantified, they're expressed numerically and can be tested statistically.

random assortment The chance distribution of chromosomes to daughter cells during meiosis; along with recombination, a source of genetic variation (but not new alleles) from meiosis.

recessive Describing a trait that isn't expressed in heterozygotes; also refers to the allele that governs the trait. For a recessive allele to be expressed, an individual must have two copies of it (i.e., the individual must be homozygous).

recognition species concept A depiction of species in which the key aspect is the ability of individuals to identify members of their own species for purposes of mating (and to avoid mating with members of other species). In theory, this type of selective mating is a component of a species concept emphasizing mating and is therefore compatible with the biological species concept.

recombinant DNA technology A process in which genes from the cell of one species are transferred to somatic cells or gametes of another species.

recombination The exchange of genetic material between homologous chromosomes during meiosis; also sometimes called *crossing over*.

regulatory proteins Proteins that can bind to certain DNA segments and modify the action of genes. Many are active only during certain stages of development.

reproductive strategies The complex of behavioral patterns that contributes to individual reproductive success. The behaviors need not be deliberate, and they often vary considerably between males and females.

reproductive success The number of off-spring an individual produces and rears to reproductive age; an individual's genetic contribution to the next generation.

reproductively isolated pertaining to groups of organisms that, mainly because of genetic differences, are prevented from mating and producing offspring with members of other groups.

rhinarium (rine-air´-ee-um) The moist, hairless pad at the end of the nose seen in most mammalian species. The rhinarium enhances an animal's ability to smell.

ribosomes Structures composed of a form of RNA called ribosomal RNA (rRNA) and protein. Ribosomes are found in a cell's cytoplasm and are essential to the manufacture of proteins.

ritualized behaviors Behaviors removed from their original context and sometimes exaggerated to convey information.

RNA (ribonucleic acid) A single-stranded molecule, similar in structure to DNA. Three forms of RNA are essential to protein synthesis: messenger RNA (mRNA), transfer RNA (tRNA), and ribosomal RNA (rRNA).

r-selected Pertaining to r-selection, an adaptive strategy that emphasizes relatively large numbers of offspring and reduced parental care (compared to K-selected species). K-selection and r-selection are relative terms (for example, mice are r-selected compared to primates but K-selected compared to most fish).

sagittal crest A ridge of bone that runs down the middle of the cranium like a short Mohawk. This serves as the attachment for the large temporal muscles, indicating strong chewing.

science A body of knowledge gained through observation and experimentation; from the Latin *scientia*, meaning "knowledge."

scientific method An approach to research whereby a problem is identified, a hypothesis (provisional explanation) is

stated, and that hypothesis is tested by collecting and analyzing data.

scientific testing The precise repetition of an experiment or expansion of observed data to provide verification; the procedure by which hypotheses and theories are verified, modified, or discarded.

sectorial Adapted for cutting or shearing; among primates, refers to the compressed (side-to-side) first lower premolar, which functions as a shearing surface with the upper canine.

selective breeding A practice whereby animal or plant breeders choose which individual animals or plants will be allowed to mate based on the traits (such as coat color or body size) they hope to produce in offspring. Animals or plants that don't have the desirable traits aren't allowed to breed.

selective pressures Forces in the environment that influence reproductive success in individuals.

semiorder The taxonomic category above suborder and below order.

senescence Decline in physiological function usually associated with aging.

sensory modalities Different forms of sensation (e.g., touch, pain, pressure, heat, cold, vision, taste, hearing, and smell).

sex chromosomes In mammals, the X and Y chromosomes.

sexual dimorphism Differences in physical characteristics between males and females of the same species. For example, humans are slightly sexually dimorphic for body size, with males being taller, on average, than females of the same population.

sexual selection A type of natural selection that operates on only one sex within a species. Sexual selection results from competition for mates, and it can lead to sexual dimorphism regarding one or more traits.

shared derived Relating to specific character traits shared in common between two life-forms and considered

the most useful for making evolutionary interpretations.

sickle-cell anemia A severe inherited hemoglobin disorder in which red blood cells collapse when deprived of oxygen. It results from inheriting two copies of a mutant allele. This allele is caused by a single base substitution in the DNA.

sister groups Two new clades that result from the splitting of a single common lineage.

slash-and-burn agriculture A traditional land-clearing practice involving the cutting and burning of trees and vegetation. In many areas, fields are abandoned after a few years and clearing occurs elsewhere.

social structure The composition, size, and sex ratio of a group of animals. Social structure is the result of natural selection in a specific habitat, and it influences individual interactions and social relationships. In many species, social structure varies, depending on different environmental factors. Thus, in primates, social structure should be viewed as flexible, not fixed.

somatic cells Basically, all the cells in the body except those involved with reproduction.

speciation The process by which a new species evolves from an earlier species. Speciation is the most basic process in macroevolution.

species A group of organisms that can interbreed to produce fertile offspring. Members of one species are reproductively isolated from members of all other species (i.e., they cannot mate with them to produce fertile offspring).

spina bifida A condition in which the arch of one or more vertebrae fails to fuse and form a protective barrier around the spinal cord.

stable carbon isotopes Isotopes of carbon that are produced in plants in differing proportions, depending on environmental conditions. By analyzing the proportions of the isotopes contained in fossil remains of animals (who ate the plants), it's possible to reconstruct aspects of ancient environments (particularly temperature and aridity).

stem group All of the taxa in a clade before a major speciation event. Stem groups are often difficult to recognize in the fossil record, since they don't often have the shared derived traits found in the crown group.

stereoscopic vision The condition whereby visual images are, to varying degrees, superimposed. This provides for depth perception, or viewing the external environment in three dimensions. Stereoscopic vision is partly a function of structures in the brain.

strategies Behaviors or behavioral complexes that have been favored by natural selection because they're advantageous to the animals that perform them. Examples include actions that enhance an animal's ability to obtain food, rear infants, or increase one's social status. Ultimately, strategies influence reproductive success.

stratigraphy Study of the sequential layering of deposits.

strepsirhines (strep-sir´-rines) Members of the primate suborder Strepsirhini, which includes lemurs and lorises.

stress In a physiological context, any factor that acts to disrupt homeostasis; more precisely, the body's response to any factor that threatens its ability to maintain homeostasis.

subfossil Bone not old enough to have become completely mineralized as a fossil.

subsistence strategies Activities and behavioral patterns aimed at obtaining food. These can include hunting, gathering wild plant foods, agriculture, and raising domesticated animals for meat and other products.

superorder A taxonomic group ranking above an order and below a class or subclass.

sympatric Living in the same area; pertaining to two or more species whose habitats partly or largely overlap.

taphonomy (*taphos*, meaning "tomb") The study of how bones and other materials came to be buried in the earth and preserved as fossils. Taphonomists study the processes of sedimentation, the action of streams, preservation properties of bone, and carnivore disturbance factors.

taxonomy The branch of science concerned with the rules of classifying organisms on the basis of evolutionary relationships.

terrestrial Living and locomoting primarily on the ground.

territorial Pertaining to the protection of all or a part of the area occupied by an animal or group of animals. Territorial behaviors range from scent marking to outright attacks on intruders.

territory The portions of an individual's or group's home range actively defended against intrusion, particularly by conspecifics.

theory A broad statement of scientific relationships or underlying principles that has been substantially verified through the testing of hypotheses.

thermoluminiscence (TL) (ther-mo-loo-min-ess´-ence) Technique for dating certain archaeological materials (such as stone tools) that were heated in the past and that release stored energy of radioactive decay as light upon reheating.

theropods Small- to medium-sized ground-living dinosaurs, dated to approximately 150 mya and thought to be related to birds.

transfer RNA (tRNA) The type of RNA that binds to specific amino acids and transports them to the ribosome during protein synthesis.

uniformitarianism The theory that the earth's features are the result of long-term processes that continue to operate in the present as they did in the past. Elaborated on by Lyell, this theory opposed catastrophism and contributed strongly to the concept of immense geological time.

Upper Paleolithic A cultural period usually associated with modern humans, but

also found with some Neandertals, and distinguished by technological innovation in various stone tool industries. Best known from western Europe, similar industries are also known from central and eastern Europe and Africa.

variation (genetic) Inherited differences among individuals; the basis of all evolutionary change.

vasoconstriction Narrowing of blood vessels to reduce blood flow to the skin. Vasoconstriction is an involuntary response to cold and reduces heat loss at the skin's surface.

vasodilation Expansion of blood vessels, permitting increased blood flow to the skin. Vasodilation permits warming of the skin and facilitates radiation of warmth as a means of cooling. Vasodilation is an involuntary response to warm temperatures, various drugs, and even emotional states (blushing).

vectors Agents that serve to transmit disease from one carrier to another. Mosquitoes are vectors for malaria, just as fleas are vectors for bubonic plague.

vertebrates Animals with segmented, bony spinal columns; includes fishes, amphibians, reptiles (including birds), and mammals.

worldview General cultural orientation or perspective shared by members of a society.

Y-5 molar Molar that has five cusps with grooves running between them, forming a Y shape. This is characteristic of hominoids.

zoonotic (zoh-oh-no´-tic) Pertaining to a zoonosis (*pl.*, zoonoses), a disease that's transmitted to humans through contact with nonhuman animals.

zygomatics Cheekbones.

zygote A cell formed by the union of an egg cell and a sperm cell. It contains the full complement of chromosomes (in humans, 46) and has the potential of developing into an entire organism.

Bibliography

Adcock, G. J., E. S. Snow, and D. Simon
2001　Mitochondrial DNA sequences in ancient Australians: Implications for modern human origins. *Proceedings of the National Academy of Sciences, USA* 98: 537–542.

Aiello, L. C.
1992　Body size and energy requirements. In: *The Cambridge Encyclopedia of Human Evolution*, J. Jones, R. Martin, and D. Pilbeam (eds.), pp. 41–45. Cambridge, England: Cambridge University Press.

Aiello, L. C. and J. C. K. Wells
2002　Energetics and the evolution of the genus *Homo*. *Annual Review of Anthropology* 31: 323–338.

Altmann, J., G. Hausfater, and S. A. Altmann
1988　Determinants of reproductive success in savannah baboons, *Papio cynocephalus*. In: *Reproductive Success*, T. H. Clutton-Brock (ed.), pp. 403–418. Chicago: University of Chicago Press.

Anderson, R. P. and C. O. Handley
2002　Dwarfism in insular sloths: Biogeography, selection, and evolutionary rate. *Evolution* 56(5): 1045–1058.

Andrews, P.
1984　An alternative interpretation of the characters used to define *Homo erectus*. *Cour Forschungist Senckenb* 69: 167–175.

Ankel, F.
1965　Der canalis sacralis als indikator für die lange der caudelregion der primaten. *Folia Primatologica* 3: 263–276.

Arnason, U., A. Gullberg, et al.
2000　Molecular estimates of primate divergences and new hypotheses for primate dispersal and the origin of modern humans. *Hereditas* 133(3): 217–228.

Arsuaga, J. L., I. Martinez, et al.
1997　Sima de los Huesos (Sierra de Atapuerca, Spain): the site. *Journal of Human Evolution* 33(2-3): 109–127.

Arsuaga, J. L., I. Martinez, et al.
1999　The human cranial remains from Gran Dolina Lower Pleistocene site (Sierra de Atapuerca, Spain). *Journal of Human Evolution* 37(3–4): 431–457.

Ascenzi, A., I. Biddittu, et al.
1996　A calvarium of late *Homo erectus* from Ceprano, Italy. *Journal of Human Evolution* 31(5): 409–423.

Asfaw, B., W. H. Gilbert, et al.
2002　Remains of *Homo erectus* from Bouri, Middle Awash, Ethiopia. *Nature* 416(6878): 317–320.

Ashley-Koch, A., Q. Yang, et al.
2000　Sickle hemoglobin (HbS) alleles and sickle cell disease. *American Journal of Genetics* 151(9): 839–845.

Aureli, F., C. M. Schaffner, et al.
2006　Raiding parties of male spider monkeys: Insights into human warfare? *American Journal of Physical Anthropology* 131(4): 486–497.

Badrian, A. and N. Badrian
1984　Social organization of *Pan paniscus* in the Lomako Forest, Zaire. In: *The Pygmy Chimpanzee*, R. L. Susman (ed.), pp. 325–346. New York: Plenum Press.

Badrian, N. and R. K. Malenky
1984　Feeding ecology of *Pan paniscus* in the Lomako Forest, Zaire. In: *The Pygmy Chimpanzee*, R. L. Susman (ed.), pp. 275–299. New York: Plenum Press.

Balter, M.
2006　Radiocarbon dating's final frontier. *Science* 313: 1560–1563.

Balter, M.
2007　Zebrafish researchers hook gene for human skin color. *Science* 310: 1754–1755.

Bamshad, M. J. and S. E. Olson
2003　Does race exist? *Scientific American* 289: 78–85.

Bamshad, M. J., S. Wooding, et al.
2003　Human population genetic structure and inference of group membership. *American Journal of Human Genetics* 72(3): 578–589.

Barker, D.
1994　*Mothers, Babies, and Disease in Later Life*. London: BMJ Publishing.

Barker, G., Huw Barton, et al.
2007　The human revolution in lowland tropical Southeast Asia: The antiquity and behavior of anatomically modern humans at Niah Cave (Sarawak, Borneo). *Journal of Human Evolution* 52: 243–261.

Bartlett, T. Q., R. W. Sussman, and J. M. Cheverud
1993　Infant killing in primates: A review of observed cases with specific references to the sexual selection hypothesis. *American Anthropologist* 95(4): 958–990.

Barton, R. A. and R. L. M. Dunbar
1997　Evolution of the social brain. In: *Machiavellian Intelligence*, A. Whiten and R. Byrne (eds.). Cambridge, England: Cambridge University Press.

Bartstra, G. J.
1982　*Homo erectus erectus*: the search for his artifacts. *Current Anthropology* 23: 318–320.

Beard, C.
2004　*The Hunt for the Dawn Monkey: Unearthing the Origins of Monkeys, Apes, and Humans*. Berkeley, CA: University of California Press.

Beard, K. C.
2008   The oldest North American primate and mammalian biogeography during the Paleocene-Eocene Thermal Maximum. *Proceedings of the National Academy of Sciences, USA* 105: 3815–3818.

Bearder, S. K.
1987   Lorises, bush babies & tarsiers: Diverse societies in solitary foragers. In: *Primate Societies*, B. B. Smuts, D. L. Cheney, and R. M. Seyfath (eds.), pp. 11–24. Chicago, IL: University of Chicago Press.

Begun, D. and A. Walker
1993   The Endocast. In: *The Nariokotome Homo erectus Skeleton*, A. Walker and R. E. Leakey (eds.), pp. 326–358. New York, NY: Springer.

Begun, D. R.
1994   Relations among the great apes and humans: New interpretations based on the fossil great ape *Dryopithecus. Yearbook of Physical Anthropology* 37: 11–63.

Begun, D. R.
2003   Planet of the Apes. *Scientific American* 289: 74–83.

Behrensmeyer, A. K., N. E. Todd, et al.
1997   Late Pliocene faunal turnover in the Turkana Basin, Kenya and Ethiopia. *Science* 278: 1589–1594.

Behrensmeyer, A. K., D. Western, et al.
1979   New perspectives in vertebrate paleoecology from a recent bone assemblage. *Paleobiology* 5(1): 12–21.

Beja-Pereira, A., G. Luikart, et al.
2003   Gene-culture coevolution between cattle milk protein genes and human lactase genes. *Nature Genetics* 35: 311–313.

Benefit, B. R. and M. L. McCrossin
1997   Earliest known Old World monkey skull. *Nature* 388(6640): 368–371.

Berger, T. D. and E. Trinkaus
1995   Patterns of trauma among the Neandertals. *Journal of Archaeological Science* 22(6): 841–852.

Bergman, T. J., J. C. Beehner, et al.
2003   Hierarchical classification by rank and kinship in baboons. *Science* 302(5648): 1234–1236.

Bermijo, M., J. Rodriguez, et al.
2006   Ebola outbreak killed 5000 gorillas. *Science* 314: 1564.

Bermudez de Castro, J. M., J. Arsuaga, et al.
1997   A hominid from the Lower Pleistocene of Atapuerca, Spain. Possible ancestor to Neandertals and modern humans. *Science* 276: 1392–1395.

Bermudez de Castro, J. M., M. Martinon-Torres, et al.
2004   The Atapuerca sites and their contribution to the knowledge of human evolution in Europe. *Evolutionary Anthropology* 13: 25–41.

Bernor, R. L.
2007   New apes fill the gap. *Proceedings of the National Academy of Sciences* 104(50): 19661–19662.

Biasutti, R.
1959   Razze e Popoli della Terra. *Turin: Unione-Tipografico-Editrice.*

Binford, L. R.
1981   *Bones. Ancient Men and Modern Myths.* New York, NY: Academic Press.

Binford, L. R.
1983   *In Pursuit of the Past.* New York, NY: Thames and Hudson.

Binford, L. R. and C. K. Ho
1985   Taphonomy at a distance: Zhoukoudian, the cave home of Beijing Man. *Current Anthropology* 26(4): 413–442.

Binford, L. R. and N. M. Stone
1986a   The Chinese Paleolithic: An outsider's view. *AnthroQuest* 1: 14–20.

Binford, L. R. and N. M. Stone
1986b   Zhoukoudian: A closer look. *Current Anthropology* 27(5): 453–475.

Bininda-Emonds, R. P. O., Marcel Cordillo, et al.
2007   The delayed rise of present-day mammals. *Nature* 446: 507–512.

Bischoff, J. L., R. W. Williams, R. J. Rosebauer, et al.
2007   High-resolution U-series dates from the Sima de los Huesos hominids yields 600+/–66 kyrs: Implications for the evolution of the early Neanderthal lineage. *Journal of Archaeological Science* 34: 763–770.

Bloch, J. I. and D. M. Boyer
2002   Grasping primate origins. *Science* 298(5598): 1606–1610.

Bloch, J. I. and M. T. Silcox
2001   New basicrania of Paleocene-Eocene Ignacius: Re-evaluation of the plesiadapiform-dermopteran link. *American Journal of Physical Anthropology* 116(3): 184–198.

Bloch, J. I., M. T. Silcox, et al.
2007   New Paleocene skeletons and the relationship of plesiadapiforms to crown-clade primates. *Proceedings of the National Academy of Sciences, USA* 104(4): 1159–1164.

Blumenschine, R. J.
1986   *Early Hominid Scavenging Opportunities.* Oxford, Bar International Series 283.

Blumenschine, R. J.
1995   Percussion marks, tooth marks, and experimental determinants of the timing of hominid and carnivore access to long bones at FLK *Zinjanthropus*, Olduvai Gorge, Tanzania. *Journal of Human Evolution* 29: 21–51.

Blumenschine, R. J. and J. A. Cavallo
1992   Scavenging and human evolution. *Scientific American* 267: 90–96.

Blumenschine, R. J. and C. R. Peters
1998   Archaeological predictions for hominid land use in the paleo-Olduvai Basin, Tanzania, during lowermost Bed II times. *Journal of Human Evolution* 34(6): 565–607.

Boaz, N. T. and A.K. Behrensmeyer
1976   Hominid taphonomy: Transport of human skeletal parts in an artificial fluviatile environment. *American Journal of Physical Anthropology* 45: 56–60.

Boaz, N. T. and R. L. Ciochon
  2001   The scavenging of *Homo erectus pekinensis*. *Natural History* 110(2): 46–51.
Boesch, C.
  1996   Social grouping Tai chimpanzees. In: *Great Ape Societies*, W. C. McGrew, L. Marchant and T. Nishida (eds.), pp. 101–113. Cambridge, England: Cambridge University Press.
Boesch, C. and H. Boesch
  1989   Hunting behavior of wild chimpanzees in the Tai National Park. *American Journal of Physical Anthropology* 78(4): 547–573.
Boesch, C. and H. Boesch-Achermann
  2000   *The Chimpanzees of the Tai Forest*. Oxford, England: Oxford University Press.
Boesch, C., P. Marchesi, et al.
  1994   Is nut cracking in wild chimpanzees a cultural behaviour? *Journal of Human Evolution* 26: 325–338.
Bogin, B.
  1999   *Patterns of Human Growth*. Cambridge, England: Cambridge University Press.
Bogin, B.
  2006   Modern human life history: the evolution of human childhood and fertility. In: *The Evolution of Human Life History*, K. Hawkes and R. R. Paine (eds.). Santa Fe, NM: SAR Press.
Borries, C., K. Launhardt, et al.
  1999   DNA analyses support the hypothesis that infanticide is adaptive in langur monkeys. *Proceedings of the Royal Society of London Series B-Biological Sciences* 266(1422): 901–904.
Bower, B.
  2003   The ultimate colonists. *Science News* 164: 10–12.
Bower, B.
  2006   Evolution's mystery woman. *Science News* 170: 330–332.
Brace, C. L., H. Nelson, and N. Korn
  1979   *Atlas of Human Evolution (2nd Ed.)*. New York, NY: Holt, Rinehart & Winston.
Brain, C. K.
  1981   *The Hunters or the Hunted? An Introduction to African Cave Taphonomy*. Chicago, IL: University of Chicago Press.
Brash, D. E., J. A. Rudolph, et al.
  1991   A role for sunlight in skin cancer: UV-induced P53 mutations in squamous cell carcinoma. *Proceedings of the National Academy of Sciences, USA* 88(22): 10124–10128.
Breuer, T., M. Ndoundou-Hockemba, et al.
  2005   First observations of tool use in wild gorillas. *PloS Biology* 3(11): e380.
Brown, P., T. Sutikna, et al.
  2004   A new small-bodied hominin from the Late Pleistocene of Flores, Indonesia. *Nature* 431(7012): 1055–1061.

Brunet, M., F. Guy, et al.
  2002   A new hominid from the Upper Miocene of Chad, Central Africa. *Nature* 418(6894): 145–151.
Bshary, R. and R. Noe
  1997   Red colobus and diana monkeys provide mutual protection against predators. *Animal Behavior* 54: 1461–1474.
Buchan, J. C., S. C. Alberts, et al.
  2003   True paternal care in a multi-male primate society. *Nature* 425: 179–180.
Bunn, H. T.
  1981   Archaeological evidence for meat-eating by Plio-Pleistocene hominids from Koobi Fora and Olduvai Gorge. *Nature* 291(5816): 574–577.
Burchard, E. G., E. Ziv, et al.
  2003   The importance of race and ethnic background in biomedical research and clinical practice. *New England Journal of Medicine* 348(12): 1170–1175.
Campbell, C. J.
  2006   Lethal intragroup aggression by adult male spider monkeys (*Ateles geoffroyi*). *American Journal of Physical Anthropology* 68(1197–1201).
Cantalupo, C. and W. D. Hopkins
  2001   Asymmetric Broca's area in great apes: A region of the ape brain is uncannily similar to one linked with speech in humans. *Nature* 414(6863): 505–505.
Caramelli, D., C. Lalueza-Fox, et al.
  2003   Evidence for genetic discontinuity between Neandertals and 24,000-year-old anatomically modern humans. *Proceedings of the National Academy of Sciences* 100: 6593–6597.
Caramelli, D., C. Lalueza-Fox, et al.
  2006   A highly divergent mtDNA sequence in a Neandertal individual from Italy. *Current Biology* 16(16): R630–R632.
Carbonell, E., Jose M. Bermuda de Castro, et al.
  2008   The first hominin of Europe. *Nature* 452: 465–469.
Carroll, S. B.
  2003   Genetics and the making of *Homo sapiens*. *Nature* 422(6934): 849–857.
Cartmill, M.
  1972   Arboreal adaptations and the origin of the order primates. In: *The Functional and Evolutionary Biology of Primates*, R. H. Tuttle (ed.), pp. 97–122. Chicago: Aldine-Atherton.
Cartmill, M.
  1990   Human uniqueness and theoretical content in paleoanthropology. *International Journal of Primatology* 11(3): 173–192.
Cartmill, M.
  1992   New views on primate origins. *Evolutionary Anthropology* 1: 105–111.
Chatterjee, H. J.
  2006   Phylogeny and biogeography of gibbons: A dispersal-vicariance analysis. *International Journal of Primatology* 27(3): 699–712.

Chen, F. C. and W. H. Li
2001   Genomic divergences between humans and other hominoids and the effective population size of the common ancestor of humans and chimpanzees. *American Journal of Human Genetics* 68(2): 444–456.

Cheney, D. L.
1987   Interaction and relationships between groups. In: *Primate Societies*, B. B. Smuts, D. L. Cheney, R. M. Seyfarth, R. W. Wrangham, and T. T. Struhsaker (eds.), pp. 267–281. Chicago: University of Chicago Press.

Cheney, D. L., R. M. Seyfarth, et al.
1988   Reproductive success in vervet monkeys. In: *Reproductive Success*, T. H. Clutton-Brock (ed.), pp. 384–402. Chicago: University of Chicago Press.

Cheng, Z., M. Ventura, et al.
2005   A Genome-wide comparison of recent chimpanzee and human segmental duplications. *Nature* 437: 88–93.

Chin, S. Y.
2008   Personal Communication, Ascension Health.

Ciochon, R. L. and A. B. Chiarelli
1980a   *Evolutionary Biology of the New World Monkeys and Continental Drift*. New York, NY: Plenum Press.

Ciochon, R. L. and A. B. Chiarelli
1980b   Paleobiogeographic perspectives on the origin of Platyrrhini. In: *Evolutionary Biology of the New World Monkeys and Continental Drift*, R. L. Ciochon and A. B. Chiarelli (eds.), pp 459–493. New York: Plenum Press.

Ciochon, R. L. and G. F. Gunnell
2002   Eocene primates from Myanmar: Historical perspectives on the origin of Anthropoidea. *Evolutionary Anthropology* 11(4): 156–168.

Ciochon, R. L., F. Huffman, et al.
2009   Rediscovery of the *Homo erectus* bed at Ngandong: Site formation of a Late Pleistocene hominin site in Asia. *American Journal of Physical Anthropology, in press* 138(S48): 154.

Ciochon, R. L., J. J. Olsen, and J. James
1990   *Other Origins: The Search for the Giant Ape in Human Prehistory*. New York, NY: Bantam.

Clark, A. G., S. Glanowski, et al.
2003   Inferring nonneutral evolution from human-chimp-mouse orthologous gene trios. *Science* 302(5652): 1960–1963.

Clemens, W.
1974   *Purgatorius*, an Early Paromomyid Primate (Mammalia). *Science* 184(4139): 903–905.

Clemens, W. A.
2004   *Purgatorius* (Plesiadapiformes, Primates?, Mammalia), A Paleocene immigrant into Northeastern Montana: Stratigraphic occurrences and incisor proportions. *Bulletin of Carnegie Museum of Natural History* 36.

Cleveland, J. and C. T. Snowdon
1982   The complex vocal repertoire of the adult cotton-top tamarin (*Saguinus oedipus oedipus*). *Zeitschrift Fur Tierpsychologie-Journal of Comparative Ethology* 58(3): 231–270.

Colwell, R. R.
1996   Global climate and infectious disease: The cholera paradigm. *Science* 274(5295): 2025–2031.

Conkey, M.
1987   New approaches in the search for meaning? A review of the research in "Paleolithic art." *Journal of Field Archaeology* 14: 413–430.

Conroy, G. C.
1997   *Reconstructing Human Origins. A Modern Synthesis*. New York, NY: Norton.

The Chimpanzee Sequencing and Analysis Consortium
2005   Initial sequence of the chimpanzee genome and comparison with the human genome. *Nature* 437: 69–87.

Constable, J. L., M. V. Ashley, et al.
2001   Noninvasive paternity assignment in Gombe chimpanzees. *Molecular Ecology* 10(5): 1279–1300.

Cooper, A., A. Rambaut, et al.
2001   Human origins and ancient human DNA. *Science* 292(5522): 1655–1656.

Cooper, R. S., J. S. Kaufman, et al.
2003   Race and genomics. *New England Journal of Medicine* 348(12): 1166–1170.

Cordain, L.
1999   Cereal grains: Humanity's double-edged sword. *World Review of Nutrition and Diet* 84: 19–73.

Cordain, L.
2002   *The Paleo Diet: Lose Weight and Get Healthy by Eating the Food You Were Designed to Eat*. New York, NY: John Wiley and Sons, Inc.

Crews, D. E. and G. J. Harper
1998   Ageing as part of the developmental process. In: *The Cambridge Encyclopedia of Human Growth and Development*, S. J. Ulijaszek (ed.), pp. 425–427. Cambridge, England: Cambridge University Press.

Crook, J. H. and J. S. Gartlan
1966   Evolution of primate societies. *Nature* 210: 1200–1203.

Cummings, M.
2000   *Human Heredity. Principles and Issues (5th Ed.)*. St. Paul, MN: Wadsworth/West Publishing Co.

Currat, M., G. Trabuchet, et al.
2002   Molecular analysis of the beta-globin gene cluster in the Niokholo Mandenka population reveals a recent origin of the beta(S) senegal mutation. *American Journal of Human Genetics* 70(1): 207–223.

Curtin, R. and P. Dolhinow
1978   Primate social behavior in a changing world. *American Scientist* 66: 468–475.

Daeschler, E. B., N. H. Shubin, and F. A. Jenkins Jr.
2006   A Darwinian tetrapod-like fish and the evolution of the tetrapod body plan. *Nature* 440: 757–763.

Dalton, R.
2007   Oldest gorilla ages our joint ancestor. *Nature News* 448: 844–845.

Darwin, C.
1859   *On the Origin of Species. A Facsimile of the First Edition.* Cambridge: Harvard University Press (1964).

Darwin, F.
1950   *The Life and Letters of Charles Darwin.* New York, NY: Henry Schuman.

De Bonis, L. and G. D. Koufos
1994   Our ancestors' ancestor: *Ouranopithecus* is a Greek link in human ancestry. *Evolutionary Anthropology* 3: 75–83.

de Heinzelin, J., J. D. Clark, et al.
1999   Environment and behavior of 2.5-million-year-old Bouri hominids. *Science* 284(5414): 625–629.

de Lumley, H. and M. de Lumley
1973   Pre-Neanderthal human remains from Arago Cave in southeastern France. *Yearbook of Physical Anthropology* 16: 162–168.

de Reuter, J. R.
1986   The influence of group size on predator scanning and foraging behavior of wedge-capped capuchin monkeys (*Cebus olivaceus*). *Behaviour* 98: 240–258.

de Waal, F.
1982   *Chimpanzee Politics.* London: Jonathan Cape.

de Waal, F. B. M.
1987   Tension regulation and nonreproductive functions of sex in captive bonobos (*Pan paniscus*). *National Geographic Research* 3(3): 318–335.

de Waal, F.
1998   No imitation without identification. *Behavioral and Brain Sciences* 21(5): 689.

de Waal, F.
1999   Cultural primatology comes of age. *Nature* 399(6737): 635–636.

de Waal, F. B. M.
2006   *Our Inner Ape.* New York, NY: Penguin.

de Waal, F. B. M.
2007   With a little help from a friend. *PloS Biology* 5(7): 1406–1408.

de Waal, F. and F. Lanting
1989   *Peacemaking Among Primates.* Cambridge: Harvard University Press.

de Waal, F. and F. Lanting
1996   *Good Natured. The Origins of Right and Wrong in Humans and Other Animals.* Cambridge, MA: Harvard University Press.

de Waal, F. and F. Lanting
1997   *Bonobo: The Forgotten Ape.* Berkeley, CA: University of California Press.

de Waal, F. and F. Lanting
2005   *Our Inner Ape.* New York, NY: Penguin Group.

Deacon, T. W.
1992   The human brain. In: *The Cambridge Encyclopedia of Human Evolution*, S. Jones, R. Martin and D. Pilbeam (eds.), pp. 115–123. Cambridge, England: Cambridge University Press

Dean, C., M. G. Leakey, D. Reid, et al.
2001   Growth processes in teeth distinguishing modern humans from *Homo erectus* and earlier hominins. *Nature* 414: 628–631.

Dean, M., M. Carrington, et al.
1996   Genetic restriction of HIV-1 infection and progression to AIDS by a deletion allele of the CKR5 structural gene. *Science* 273(5283): 1856–1862.

Defleur, A., T. White, et al.
1999   Neanderthal cannibalism at Moula-Guercy, Ardèche, France. *Science* 286: 128–131.

Demuth, J. P., T. D. Bie, et al.
2006   The evolution of mammalian gene families. *PloS ONE* 1(1): e85.

Desmond, A. and J. Moore
1991   *Darwin.* New York, NY: Warner Books.

DeVore, I. and S. L. Washburn
1963   Baboon ecology and human evolution. In: *African Ecology and Human Evolution*, F. C. Howell and F. Bourlière (eds.), pp. 335–367. New York, NY: Viking Fund Publication.

Dobzhansky, T.
1973   Nothing in Biology Makes Sense Except in the Light of Evolution. *American Biology Teacher* 35: 125–129.

Dominy, N. J. and P. W. Lucas
2001   Ecological importance of trichromatic vision to primates. *Nature* 410(6826): 363–366.

Doran, D. M. and A. McNeilage
1998   Gorilla ecology and behavior. *Evolutionary Anthropology* 6(4): 120–131.

Duarte, C., J. Mauricio, et al.
1999   The early Upper Paleolithic human skeleton from the Abrigo do Lagar Velho (Portugal) and modern human emergence in Iberia. *Proceedings of the National Academy of Sciences, USA* 96(13): 7604–7609.

Dumas, F., R. Stanyon, et al.
2007   Phylogenomics of species from four genera of New World monkeys by flow sorting and reciprocal chromosome painting. *BMC Evolutionary Biology* 7(Suppl 2): S11.

Dunbar, R.
2001   Brains on two legs: Group size and the evolution of intelligence. In: *Tree of Origin: What Primate Behavior Can Tell Us about Human Social Evolution*, pp. 173–191. Cambridge: Harvard University Press.

Dunbar, R. I. M.
1998   The social brain hypothesis. *Evolutionary Anthropology* 6(5): 178–190.

Eaton, S. B., S. B. Eaton III, and M. J. Konner
1999   Paleolithic nutrition revisited. In: *Evolutionary Medicine*, W. Trevathan, J. J. McKenna and E. O. Smith (eds.), pp. 313–332. New York, NY: Oxford University Press.

Eaton, S. B., M. Shostak, and M. Konner
1988   *The Paleolithic Prescription*. New York, NY: Harper and Row.

Ehret, G.
1987   Left-hemisphere advantage in the mouse-brain for recognizing ultrasonic communication calls. *Nature* 325(6101): 249–251.

Ehrlich, P. R. and A. H. Ehrlich
1990   *The Population Explosion*. New York, NY: Simon & Schuster.

Ellison, P. T.
2001   *On Fertile Ground: A Natural History of Human Reproduction*. Cambridge, MA: Harvard University Press.

Enard, W., M. Przeworski, et al.
2002   Molecular evolution of FOXP2, a gene involved in speech and language. *Nature* 418(6900): 869–872.

Eswaran, V., H. Harpending, et al.
2005   Genomics refutes an exclusively African origin of humans. *Journal of Human Evolution* 49(1): 1–18.

Ewald, P. W.
1994   *Evolution of Infectious Disease*. New York, NY: Oxford University Press.

Ewald, P. W.
1999   Evolutionary control of HIV and other sexually transmitted viruses. In: *Evolutionary Medicine*, W. R. Trevathan, E. O. Smith, and J. J. McKenna (eds.). New York, NY: Oxford University Press.

Falgueres, C., J. J. Bahain, et al.
1999   Earliest humans in Europe: The age of TD6 Gran Dolina, Atapuerca, Spain. *Journal of Human Evolution* 37(3-4): 343–352.

Falk, D.
1990   Brain evolution in *Homo*: The 'Radiator' Theory. *Behavioral and Brain Sciences* 13: 333–344.

Falk, D., C. Hildebolt, et al.
2005   The brain of LB1, *Homo floresiensis*. *Science* 308(5719): 242–245.

Falk, D., C. Hildebolt, et al.
2008   LB1 did not have Laron Syndrome. *American Journal of Physical Anthropology, Supplement* 43: 95.

Feathers, J. K. and E. Migliorini
2001   Luminescence dating at Katanda: A reassessment. *Quaternary Science Reviews* 20: 961–966.

Fedigan, L. M.
1983   Dominance and reproductive success in primates. *Yearbook of Physical Anthropology* 26: 91–129.

Fleagle, J.
1988/   *Primate Adaptation and Evolution*. New York, NY:
1999   Academic Press.

Flinn, M.
2008   Why words can hurt us: social relationships, stress and health. In: *Evolutionary Medicine and Health*, W. R. Trevathan, E. O. Smith, and J. J. McKenna (eds.), pp. 242–258. New York, NY: Oxford University Press.

Flinn, M. V.
1999   Family environment, stress, and health during childhood. In: *Hormones, health, and behavior*, C. Panter-Brick and C. M. Worthman (eds.), pp. 105–138. Cambridge, UK: Cambridge University Press.

Foley, R.
2002   Adaptive radiations and dispersals in hominin evolutionary ecology. *Evolutionary Anthropology* 11: 32–37.

Foley, R. A.
1991   How many hominid species should there be? *Journal of Human Evolution* 20(5): 413–427.

Formicola, V. and A. P. Buzhilova
2004   Double child burial from Sunghir (Russia): Pathology and inferences for Upper Paleolithic funerary practices. *American Journal of Physical Anthropology* 124(3): 189–198.

Foster, J. B.
1964   Evolution of mammals on islands. *Nature* 202: 234–235.

Fouts, R. S., D. H. Fouts, and T. T. van Cantfort
1989   The infant Loulis learns signs from cross-fostered chimpanzees. In: *Teaching Sign Language to Chimpanzees*, R. A. Gardner (ed.) pp. 280–292. Albany, NY: State University of New York Press.

Fragaszy, D., P. Izar, et al.
2004   Wild Capuchin Monkeys (*Cebus libidinosus*) use anvils and stone pounding tools. *American Journal of Primatology* 64: 359–366.

Freundlich, J. C., H. Schwabedissen, and E. Wendt
1980   Köln radiocarbon measurements II. *Radiocarbon* 22: 68–81.

Frisancho, R. A.
1996   *Human Adaptation and Accommodation*. Ann Arbor, MI: The University of Michigan Press.

Frisch, R. E.
1988   Fatness and fertility. *Scientific American* 258(3): 88–95.

Froelich, J. W.
1970   Migration and plasticity physique in the Japanese-Americans of Hawaii. *American Journal of Physical Anthropology* 32: 429.

Gao, F., E. Bailes, et al.
1999   Origin of HIV-1 in the chimpanzee *Pan troglodytes troglodytes*. *Nature* 397: 436–441.

Gardner, R. A., B. T. Gardner, and T. T. van Cantfort (eds.)
1989   *Teaching Sign Language to Chimpanzees*. Albany, NY: State University of New York Press.

Garner, K. J. and O. A. Ryder
1996   Mitochondrial DNA diversity in gorillas. *Molecular Phylogenetics and Evolution* 6(1): 39–48.

Gebo, D. L., L. MacLatchy, et al.
1997   A hominoid genus from the early Miocene of Uganda. *Science* 276(5311): 401–404.

George, I., H. Cousillas, H. Richard, et al.
2002   Song perception in the European starling: Hemispheric specialization and individual variations. *C.R. Biol.* 325: 197–204.

Ghiglieri, M. P.
1984   *The Chimpanzees of Kibale Forest.* New York, NY: Columbia University Press.

Gillespie, B. and R. G. Roberts
2000   On the reliability of age estimate for human remains at Lake Mungo. *Journal of Human Evolution* 38: 727–732.

Gingerich, P. D., K. D. Rose, et al.
2008   Oldest North American primate. *Proceedings of the National Academy of Sciences, USA* 105(23): E30–E31.

Gluckman, P. D. and M. Hanson
2005   *The Fetal Matrix: Evolution, Development, and Disease.* New York, NY: Cambridge University Press.

Godfrey, L. R., W. L. Jungers, et al.
2006   Ecology and extinction of Madagascar's subfossil lemurs. In: *Lemurs Ecology and Adaptation*, L. Gould and M. L. Sauther (eds.), pp. 41–64. New York, Springer.

Godfrey, L. R., M. R. Sutherland, et al.
1990   Size, space, and adaptation in some subfossil lemurs from Madagascar. *American Journal of Physical Anthropology* 81(1): 45–66.

Godinot, M.
1994   Early North African primates and their significance for the origin of Simiiformes (= Anthropoidea). In: *Anthropoid Origins*, J. G. Fleagle and R. F. Kay (eds.), pp. 235–95. New York, NY: Plenum.

Godinot, M. and M. Mahboubi
1992   Earliest known simian primate found in Algeria. *Nature* 357: 324–326.

Godinot, M. and M. Mahboubi
1994   Small simiiform primates from Glib-Zegdou (Early to Middle Eocene, Algeria). *Comptes Rendus De L'Académie Des Sciences Serie II* 319(3): 357–364.

Goodall, J.
1986   *The Chimpanzees of Gombe.* Cambridge, MA: Harvard University Press.

Goodman, S. and H. Schütz
2000   The lemurs of the northeastern slopes of the Réserve Spéciale de Manongarivo. *Lemur News* 5(32).

Goodman, S. M.
2008   Conservation priorities on Madagascar: Synergy between surveys and geological history in understanding patterns. *South African Journal of Botany* 74: 358.

Goodman, S. M., J. P. Benstead, H. Schutz (Eds.)
2003   *The Natural History of Madagascar.* Chicago, IL: University of Chicago Press.

Gossett, T. F.
1963   *Race, the History of an Idea in America.* Dallas, TX: Southern Methodist University Press.

Gould, S. J.
1981   *The Mismeasures of Man.* New York, NY: W.W. Norton.

Gould, S. J.
1985   Darwin at sea—and the virtues of port. In: *The Flamingo's Smile. Reflections in Natural History.* S. J. Gould (ed.), pp. 347–359. New York, NY: W.W. Norton.

Gould, S. J.
1994   *Hen's Teeth and Horse's Toes.* New York, NY: W.W. Norton.

Gould, S. J. and N. Eldredge
1977   Punctuated equilibria: The tempo and mode of evolution reconsidered. *Paleobiology* 3: 115–151.

Grant, P. R.
1982   Variation in the size and shape of Darwin's finch eggs. *Auk* 99: 5–23.

Green, R. E., J. Krause, et al.
2006   Analysis of one million base pairs of Neanderthal DNA. *Nature* 444(7117): 330–336.

Greene, J. C.
1981   *Science, Ideology, and World View.* Berkeley, CA: University of California Press.

Greenwood, B. and T. Mutabingwa
2002   Malaria in 2000. *Nature* 415: 670–672.

Gregory, J. M., P. Huybrechts, et al.
2004   Threatened loss of the Greenland Ice-sheet. *Nature* 428: 616.

Gros-Louis, J., H. Perry, et al.
2003   Violent coalitionary attacks and intraspecific killing in wild White-faced Capuchin Monkeys (*Cebus capucinus*). *Primates* 44: 341–346.

Gross, L.
2006   Scientific illiteracy and the partisan takeover of biology. *PLoS Biology* 4(5): 206.

Groves, C. P.
2001b   Why taxonomic stability is a bad idea, or why are there so few species of primates (or are there?). *Evolutionary Anthropology* 10: 191–197.

Grün, R. and C. B. Stringer
1991   ESR dating and the evolution of modern humans. *Archaeometry* 33: 153–199.

Grün, R., C. B. Stringer, et al.
2005   U-series and ESR analysis of bones and teeth relating to the human burials from Skhūl. *Journal of Human Evolution* 49: 316–334.

Hales, C. N. and D. J. P. Barker
2001   The thrifty phenotype hypothesis. *British Medical Bulletin* 60: 5–20.

Harlow, H. F.
1959   Love in infant monkeys. *Scientific American* 200: 68–74.

Harlow, H. F. and M. K. Harlow
1961   A study of animal affection. *Natural History* 70: 48–55.

543

Harrison, T.
2002   Late Oligocene to middle Miocene catarrhines from Afro-Arabia. In: *Primate Fossil Record*. W. Hartwig (ed.), pp. 311–338. Cambridge: Cambridge University Press.

Harrison, T., X. Ji, et al.
2008   Renewed investigations at the late Miocene hominoid locality of Leilao, Yunnan, China. *American Journal of Physical Anthropology* 135(S46): 113.

Harrison, T., X. Ji, and D. Su
2002   On the systematic status of the late Neogene hominoids from Yunnan Province, China. *Journal of Human Evolution* 43: 207–227.

Hawkes, K., J. F. O'Connell, and N. G. Blurton Jones
1997   Hadza women's time allocation, offspring provisioning, and the evolution of long postmenopausal life spans. *Current Anthropology* 38: 551–577.

Hawkes, K. and R. R. Paine
2006   *The Evolution of Human Life History*. SAR Press.

Heaney, L. R.
1978   Island area and body size of insular mammals: Evidence from the tri-colored squirrel (*Callosciurus prevosti*) of Southeast Asia. *Evolution* 32: 29–44.

Heizmann, E. and D. R. Begun
2001   The oldest European hominoid. *Journal of Human Evolution* 41: 465–481.

Henshilwood, C. S., F. d'Errico, et al.
2002   Emergence of modern human behavior: Middle Stone Age engravings from South Africa. *Science* 295(5558): 1278–1280.

Henshilwood, C. S., F. d'Errico, et al.
2004   Middle stone age shell beads from South Africa. *Science* 304: 404.

Henshilwood, C. and J. Sealy
1997   Bone artefacts from the Middle Stone Age at Blombos Cave, Southern Cape, South Africa. *Current Anthropology* 38(5): 890–895.

Henzi, P. and L. Barrett
2003   Evolutionary ecology, sexual conflict, and behavioral differentiation among baboon populations. *Evolutionary Anthropology* 12(5): 217–230.

Hernandez-Aguilar, R. A., J. Moore, et al.
2007   Savanna chimpanzees use tools to harvest the underground storage organs of plants. *Proceedings of the National Academy of Sciences* 104(49): 19210–19213.

Hershkovitz, P.
1977   *Living New World Monkeys (Platyrrhini): With an Introduction to Primates*. Chicago and London: University of Chicago Press.

Higham, T., C. B. Ramsey, et al.
2006   Revised direct radiocarbon dating of the Vindija G_1 Upper Paleolithic Neandertals. *Proceedings of the National Academy of Sciences* 103: 553–557.

Hill, A.
2007   Introduction. In: *Hominin Environments in the East African Pliocene: An Assessment of the Faunal Evidence*, R. Bobe, Z. Alemseged, and A. K. Behrensmeyer (eds.), pp. xvii–xx. Dordrecht, The Netherlands: Springer.

Hill, A. V. S. and A. G. Motulsky
1999   Genetic variation and human disease: The role of natural selection. In: *Evolution in Health and Disease*, S. Stearns (ed.), pp. 50–61. New York, NY: Oxford University Press.

Hodgson, J., K. Sterner, et al.
2009a   Successive radiations, not stasis, in the South American primate fauna. *Proceedings of the National Academy of Sciences USA* in press.

Hodgson, J. A., L. Pozzi, et al.
2009b   Molecular divergence dates suggest an origin of crown primates near the K/T boundary. *American Journal of Physical Anthropology* 138(S48): 227

Hodgson, J. A., K. N. Sterner, et al.
2008   Phylogenetic relationship of the Platyrrhini inferred from complete mitochondrial genome sequences. *American Journal of Physical Anthropology* S46: 118–119.

Hoffstetter, R.
1972   Relationships, origins, and history of the ceboid monkeys and the caviomorph rodents: A modern reinterpretation. In: *Evolutionary Biology*, T. Dobzhansky, T. M. K. Hecht, and W. C. Steere (eds.), pp. 323–347. New York, NY: Appleton-Century-Crofts.

Holloway, R. L.
1985   The poor brain of *Homo sapiens neanderthalensis*. In: *Ancestors, The Hard Evidence*, E. Delson (ed.), pp. 319–324. New York, NY: Alan R. Liss.

Horvath, J. E., D. W. Weisrock, et al.
2008   Development and application of a phylogenetic toolkit: Resolving the evolutionary history of Madagascar's lemurs. *Genome Research* 18: 489–499.

Horvath, J. E. and H. F. Willard
2007   Primate comparative genomics: Lemur biology and evolution. *Trends in Genetics* 23: 173–182.

Houle, A.
1998   Floating islands: A mode of long-distance dispersal for small and medium-sized terrestrial vertebrates. *Diversity and Distribution* 4: 201–219.

Houle, A.
1999   The origin of platyrrhines: An evaluation of the Antarctic scenario and the floating island model. *American Journal of Physical Anthropology* 109(4): 541–559.

Howell, F. C.
1999   Paleo-demes, species clades, and extinctions in the Pleistocene hominin record. *Journal of Anthropological Research* 55(2): 191–243.

Hrdy, S. B.
1977   *The Langurs of Abu*. Cambridge, MA: Harvard University Press.

Hrdy, S. B.
1999   *Mother Nature: A History of Mothers, Infants, and Natural Selection.* New York, NY: Pantheon Books.

Hrdy, S. B., C. Janson, and C. van Schaik
1995   Infanticide: Let's not throw out the baby with the bath water. *Evolutionary Anthropology* 3: 151–154.

Hu, D. J., T. J. Dondero, et al.
1996   The emerging genetic diversity of HIV: The importance of global surveillance for diagnostics, research, and prevention. *Journal of the American Medical Association* 275(3): 210–216.

Hudjashou Georgi, T. K., Peter A. Underhill, et al.
2007   Revealing the prehistoric settlement of Australia by Y Chromosome and mtDNA Analysis. *Proceedings of the National Academy of Sciences, USA* 104: 8726–8730.

Hunt, G. R.
1996   Manufacture and use of hook-tools by New Caledonian crows. *Nature* 379: 249–251.

Isbell, L. A. and T. P. Young
1993   Social and ecological influences on activity budgets of vervet monkeys, and their implications for group living. *Behavioral Ecology and Sociobiology* 32(6): 377–385.

Izawa, K. and A. Mizuno
1977   Palm-fruit cracking behaviour of wild black-capped capuchin (*Cebus apella*). *Primates* 18: 773–793.

Jablonski, N. G.
1992   Sun, skin colour, and spina bifida: An exploration of the relationship between ultraviolet light and neural tube defects. *Proceedings of the Australian Society of Human Biology* 5: 455–462.

Jablonski, N. G. and G. Chaplin
2000   The evolution of human skin coloration. *Journal of Human Evolution* 39: 57–106.

Jablonski, N. G. and G. Chaplin
2002   Skin deep. *Scientific American* 287(4): 74–81.

Jacob, T., E. Indriati, et al.
2006   Pygmoid Australomelonesian *Homo sapiens* skeletal remains from Liang Bua, Flores: Population affinities and pathological anomalies. *Proceedings of the National Academy of Sciences, USA* 103: 13421–13426.

Jakobsson, M., Sonja W. Scholz, et al.
2008   Genotype, haplotype and copy-number variation in worldwide human populations. *Nature* 451: 998–1003.

Janečka, J. E., W. Miller, et al.
2007   Molecular and genomic data identify the closest living relative of primates. *Science* 318: 792–794.

Janson, C. H.
1990   Ecological consequences of individual spatial choice in foraging groups of brown capuchin monkeys, *Cebus apella*. *Animal Behaviour* 40: 922–934.

Janson, C. H.
2000   Primate socio-ecology: The end of a golden age. *Evolutionary Anthropology* 9(2): 73–86.

Jerison, H. J.
1973   *Evolution of the Brain and Behavior.* New York, NY: Academic Press.

Jia, L.
1975   *The Cave Home of Peking Man.* Peking: Foreign Language Press.

Jia, L. and W. Huang
1990   *The Story of Peking Man.* New York, NY: Oxford University Press.

Jolly, A.
1985   *The Evolution of Primate Behavior (2nd. Ed.).* New York, NY: Macmillan.

Jolly, C. J.
1970   The seed-eaters: A new model of hominid differentiation based on a baboon analogy. *Man, New Series* 5: 5–26.

Jolly, C. J.
1993   Species, subspecies, and baboon systematics. In: *Species, Species Concepts, and Primate Evolution*, W. H. Kimbel and L. B. Martin (eds.), pp. 67–107. New York, NY: Plenum Press.

Kano, T.
1992   *The Last Ape. Pygmy Chimpanzee Behavior and Ecology.* Stanford, CA: Stanford University Press.

Kappeler, P. M.
2000   Lemur origins: Rafting by groups of hibernators? *Folia Primatologica* 71(6): 422–425.

Kappleman, J., M. Alçiçek, et al.
2008   Brief communication: First *Homo erectus* from Turkey and implications for migrations into temperate Eurasia. *American Journal of Physical Anthropology* 135: 110–116.

Kay, R. F., C. Schmitt, et al.
2004   The paleobiology of Amphipithecidae, South Asian late Eocene primates. *Journal of Human Evolution* 46: 3–25.

Keeley, L. H. and N. Toth
1981   Microwear polishes on early stone tools from Koobi-Fora, Kenya. *Nature* 293(5832): 464–465.

Kelley, R. I., D. Robinson, et al.
2002   Amish lethal microcephaly: A new metabolic disorder with severe congenital microcephaly and 2-ketoglutaric aciduria. *American Journal of Medical Genetics* 112(4): 318–326.

Kettlewell, H. B. D.
1956   Further selection experiments on industrial melanism in the Lepidoptera. *Heredity* 10: 287–301.

Keynes, R.
2002   *Darwin, His Daughter and Human Evolution.* New York, NY: Riverhead Books.

King, B. J.
1994   *The Information Continuum.* Santa Fe, NM: School of American Research.

King, B. J.
2004   *Dynamic Dance: Nonvocal Communication in the African Great Apes.* Cambridge, MA: Harvard University Press.

King, M. C. and A. G. Motulsky
2002   Mapping human history. *Science* 298(5602): 2342–2343.

Kirk, E. C. and E. L. Simons
2001   Diets of fossil primates from the Fayum Depression of Egypt: A quantitative analysis of molar shearing. *Journal of Human Evolution* 40(3): 203–229.

Kirkwood, T. B. L.
1997   The origins of human ageing. *Philosophical Transactions of the Royal Society of London B* 352: 1765–1772.

Klein, R. G.
1989/   *The Human Career. Human Biological and Cultural*
1999   *Origins (2nd Ed.).* Chicago, IL: University of Chicago Press.

Klein, R. G. and B. Edgar
2002   *The Dawn of Human Culture.* New York, NY: John Wiley & Sons.

Knapp, L. A.
2002   Evolution and immunology. *Evolutionary Anthropology* 11: 140–144.

Kokis, J. E.
1988   Protein Diagensis Dating of (*Struthio camelus*) Eggshell: An Upper Pleistocene Dating Technique. Unpublished M.Sc. thesis, George Washington University, Washington, 154 pp.

Konner, M. J. and C. M. Worthman
1980   Nursing frequency, gonadal functioning, and birth spacing among !Kung hunter-gartherers. *Science* 207(4432): 768–770.

Koopman, R. J., A. G. Mainous, et al.
2005   Changes in age at diagnosis of type 2 diabetes mellitus in the United States, 1988 to 2000. *Annals of Family Medicine* 3(1): 60–69.

Kramer, A.
1993   Human taxonomic diversity in the Pleistocene: Does *Homo erectus* represent multiple hominid species? *American Journal of Physical Anthropology* 91: 161–171.

Krane, S., Y. Itagaki, et al.
2003   "Venom" of the slow loris: Sequence similarity of prosimian skin gland protein and Fel d 1 cat allergen. *Naturwissenschaften* 90(2): 60–62.

Krause, J., C. Lalueza-Fox, et al.
2007   The derived FOXP2 variant of modern humans was shared with Neandertals. *Current Biology* 17: 1908–1912.

Krings, M., C. Capelli, et al.
2000   A view of Neandertal genetic diversity. *Nature Genetics* 26(2): 144–146.

Krings, M., A. Stone, et al.
1997   Neandertal DNA sequences and the origin of modern humans. *Cell* 90(1): 19–30.

Kroeber, A. L.
1928   Sub-human cultural beginning. *Quarterly Review of Biology* 3: 325–342.

Krützen, M., J. Mann, M. R. Heithaus, et al.
2005   Cultural transmission of tool use in bottlenose dolphins. *Proceedings of the National Academy of Sciences, USA* 102(25): 8939–8943.

Kulikov, E. E., Audrey B. Poltaraus, and Irina A. Lebedeva
2004   DNA Analysis of Sunghir Remains: Problems and Perspectives. Durham, U.K, European Paleopathology Association Meetings.

Kumar, S., A. Filipski, et al.
2005   Placing confidence limits on the molecular age of the human–chimpanzee divergence. *Proceedings of the National Academy of Sciences, USA* 102(52): 18842–18847

Kummer, H.
1968   *Social Organization of Hamadryas Baboons.* Chicago, IL: University of Chicago Press.

Kunimatsu, Y., M. Nakatsukasa, et al.
2007   A new Late Miocene great ape from Kenya and its implications for the origins of African great apes and humans. *Proceedings of the National Academy of Sciences* 104(49): 19220–19225.

Kuzawa, C.
2008   The developmental origins of adult health: intergenerational inertia in adaptation and disease. *Evolutionary Medicine and Health: New Perspectives,* W. Trevathan, E. O. Smith, and J. J. McKenna (eds.). New York, NY: Oxford University Press.

Kuzawa, C. W.
2005   Fetal origins of developmental plasticity: Are fetal cues reliable predictors of future nutritional environments? *American Journal of Human Biology* 17: 5–21.

Lahr, M. M. and R. A. Foley
1998   Towards a theory of modern human origins: Geography, demography, and diversity in recent human evolution. *Yearbook of Physical Anthropology.* XLI: 137–176.

Lai, C. S. L., S. E. Fisher, et al.
2001   A forkhead-domain gene is mutated in a severe speech and language disorder. *Nature* 413(6855): 519–523.

Lalani, A. S., J. Masters, et al.
1999   Use of chemokine receptors by poxviruses. *Science* 286(5446): 1968–1971.

Lamason, R. L., M-A. P.K. Mohideen, et al.
2005   SCL24A5, a putative cation exchanger, affects pigmentation in zebrafish and humans. *Science* 310: 1782–1786.

Lamberts, S. W. J., A. W. van den Beld, et al.
1997   The endocrinology of aging. *Science* 278(5337): 419–424.

Lancaster, J. B. and C. S. Lancaster
1983   Parental investment: the hominid adaptations. In: *How Humans Adapt: A Biocultural Odyssey,* D. J. Ortner (ed.) pp. 33–66. Washington, D.C.: Smithsonian Institution Press.

Leakey, L. S. B.
1960   Finding the world's earliest man. *National Geographic* 118: 431.

Leakey, M. D.
1971   Remains of *Homo erectus* and associated artifacts in Bed IV at Olduvai Gorge, Tanzania. *Nature* 232: 380–383.

Leroy, E. M., B. Kumulungui, et al.
2005   Fruit bats as reservoirs of Ebola virus. *Nature* 438(7068): 575–576.

Leroy, E. M., P. Rouquet, et al.
2004   Multiple Ebola virus transmission events and rapid decline of central African wildlife. *Science* 303(5656): 387–390.

Lewontin, R. C.
1972   The apportionment of human diversity. In: *Evolutionary Biology*, T. Dobzhansky (ed.), pp. 381–398. New York, NY: Plenum.

Li, J. Z., Devin M. Absher, et al.
2008   Worldwide human relationships inferred from genome-wide patterns of variation. *Science* 319: 1100–1104.

Li, T. Y. and D. A. Etler
1992   New middle Pleistocene hominid crania from Yunxian in China. *Nature* 357(6377): 404–407.

Lieberman, L. S.
2003   Dietary, evolutionary, and modernizing influences on the prevalence of type 2 diabetes. *Annual Review of Nutrition* 23: 345–377.

Lieberman, L. S.
2008   Diabesity and Darwinian medicine: the evolution of an epidemic. In: *Evolutionary Medicine and Health: New Perspectives*, W. R. Trevathan, E. O. Smith, and J. J. McKenna (eds.), pp. 72–95. New York, NY: Oxford University Press.

Lin, D. R. and J. H. White
2004   Pleiotropic Actions of Vitamin D. *BioEssays* 26(1): 21–28.

Lin, J. Y. and D. E. Fisher
2007   Melanocyte biology and skin pigmentation. *Nature* 445: 843–850.

Linnaeus, C.
1758   *Systema Naturae*. Holmiae: Laurentii Salvii.

Lofgren, D. L.
1995   The bug creek problem and the Cretaceous-Tertiary transition at McGuire Creek, Montana. *University of California Publications in Geological Sciences* 140: 1–185.

Lohmueller, K. E., Amit R. Indap, et al.
2008   Proportionally more deleterious genetic variation in European than in African populations. *Nature* 451: 994–997.

Lomolino, M. V.
2005   Body size evolution in insular vertebrates: Generality of the island rule. *Journal of Biogeography* 32(10): 1683–1699.

Lordkipandize, D., Tea Jashashuil, et al.
2007   Postcranial evidence from early *Homo* from Dmanisi, Georgia. *Nature* 449: 305–310.

Lordkipanidze, D., A. Vekua, et al.
2005   The earliest toothless hominin skull. *Nature* 434(7034): 717–718.

Lordkipanidze, D., A. Vekua, et al.
2006   A fourth hominid skull from Dmanisi, Georgia. *The Anatomical Record: Part A* 288: 1146–1157.

Lovejoy, C. O.
1981   The origin of man. *Science* 211(4480): 341–350.

Mace, R.
2000   Evolutionary ecology of human life history. *Animal Behaviour* 59: 1–10.

MacKinnon, J. and K. MacKinnon
1980   The behavior of wild spectral tarsiers. *International Journal of Primatology* 1: 361–379.

Manson, J. H. and R. W. Wrangham
1991   Intergroup aggression in chimpanzees and humans. *Current Anthropology* 32(4): 369–390.

Marean, C. W., Miryam Bar-Matthews, et al.
2007   Early human use of marine resources and pigment in South Africa during the Middle Pleistocene. *Nature* 449(905–908).

Marivaux, L., P.-O. Antoine, et al.
2005   Anthropoid primates from the Oligocene of Pakistan (Bugti Hills): Data on early anthropoid evolution and biogeography. *Proceedings of the National Academy of Sciences, USA* 102(24): 8436–8441.

Marris, E.
2006   Bushmeat surveyed in western cities. Illegally hunted animals turn up in markets from New York to London. *Nature* Volume, DOI: 10.1038/news060626-10

Martin, R. D.
1990   *Primate Origins and Evolution: A Phylogenetic Reconstruction*. Princeton, NJ: Princeton University Press.

Martin, R. D., A. M. Maclarnon, et al.
2006   Flores hominid: New species or microcephalic dwarf? *Anatomical Record Part A-Discoveries in Molecular Cellular and Evolutionary Biology* 288A(11): 1123–1145.

Martin, R. D., C. Soligo, et al.
2007   Primate origins: Implications of a Cretaceous ancestry. *Folia Primatologica* 78(5-6): 277–296.

Masataka, N.
1983   Categorical responses to natural and synthesized alarm calls in Goeldi's monkeys (*Callimico goeldi*). *Primates* 24: 40–51.

Mayer, P.
1982   Evolutionary advantages of menopause. *Human Ecology* 10: 477–494.

McBrearty, S. and N. G. Jablonski
2005   First fossil chimpanzee. *Nature* 437(7055): 105–108.

McCall, R. A.
1997   Implications of recent geological investigations of the Mozambique channel for the mammalian colonization of Madagascar. *Proceedings of the Royal Society of London Series B-Biological Sciences* 264(1382): 663–665.

McCrossin, M. L., B. R. Benefit, et al.
1998   Fossil evidence for the origins of terrestriality among Old World monkeys and apes. In: *Primate Locomotion: Recent Advances*, E. Strasser, J. G. Fleagle, H. M. McHenry, and A. L. Rosenberger (eds.), pp. 353–396. New York, NY: Plenum.

McDougall, I., F. H. Brown, et al.
2005   Stratigraphic placement and age of modern humans from Kibish, Ethiopia. *Nature* 433(7027): 733–736.

McGraw, W. S. and R. Bshary
2002   Association of terrestrial mangabeys (*Cercocebus atys*) with arboreal monkeys: Experimental evidence for the effects of reduced ground predator pressure on habitat use. *International Journal of Primatology* 23(2): 311–325.

McGrew, W. C.
1992   *Chimpanzee Material Culture. Implications for Human Evolution.* Cambridge, England: Cambridge University Press.

McGrew, W. C.
1998   Culture in nonhuman primates? *Annual Review of Anthropology* 27: 301–328.

McGrew, W. C. and E. G. Tutin
1978   Evidence for a social custom in wild chimpanzees? *Man, New Series* 13: 234–251.

McHenry, H.
1992   Body size and proportions in early hominids. *American Journal of Physical Anthropology* 87: 407–431.

McKusick, V. A., S. E. Antonarakis, et al.
1998   *Mendelian Inheritance in Man.* Baltimore, MD: Johns Hopkins University Press.

Miles, H. L. W.
1990   The cognitive foundations for reference in a signing orangutan. In: *Language and Intelligence in Monkeys and Apes: Comparative Developmental Perspectives,* S. T. Parker and K. R. Gibson (eds.), pp. 511–539. New York, NY: Cambridge University Press.

Miller, E. R., G. F. Gunnell, et al.
2005   Deep time and the search for anthropoid origins. *Yearbook of Physical Anthropology.* 48: 60–95.

Miller, G. H., P. B. Beaumont, et al.
1999a   Earliest modern humans in southern Africa dated by isoleucine epimerization in ostrich eggshell. *Quaternary Science Reviews* 18(13): 1537–1548.

Miller, G. H., J. W. Magee, et al.
1999b   Pleistocene extinction of *Genyornis newtoni*: Human impact on Australian megafauna. *Science* 283(5399): 205–208.

Mokdad, A. H., B. A. Bowman, et al.
2001   The continuing epidemics of obesity and diabetes in the United States. *Journal of the American Medical Association* 286(10): 1195–1200.

Moore, L. G., S. Niermeyer, et al.
1998   Human adaptation to high altitude: Regional and life-cycle perspectives. *Yearbook of Physical Anthropology.* 41: 25–64.

Moore, L. G. and J. G. Regensteiner
1983   Adaptation to high altitude. *Annual Review of Anthropology* 12: 285–304.

Moore, L. G., M. Shriver, et al.
2006   An evolutionary model for identifying genetic adaptation to high altitude. *Advances in Experimental Medicine and Biology* 588: 101–118.

Morwood, M. J., P. Brown, et al.
2005   Further evidence for small-bodied hominins from the Late Pleistocene of Flores, Indonesia. *Nature* 437(7061): 1012–1017.

Morwood, M. J., R. P. Soejono, et al.
2004   Archaeology and age of a new hominin from Flores in eastern Indonesia. *Nature* 431(7012): 1087–1091.

Motulsky, A. G.
1995   Jewish diseases and origins. *Nature Genetics* 9(2): 99–101.

Moura, A. C. A. and P. C. Lee
2004   Capuchin tool use in Caatinga dry forest. *Science* 306(5703): 1909.

Mourant, A. E., A. C. Kopec, et al.
1976   *The Distribution of Human Blood Groups and other Polymorprhisms.* Oxford: Oxford University Press.

Muchmore, E. A., S. Diaz, et al.
1998   A structural difference between the cell surfaces of humans and the great apes. *American Journal of Physical Anthropology* 107(2): 187–198.

Murray, R. D.
1980   The evolution and functional significance of incest avoidance. *Journal of Human Evolution* 9(3): 173–178.

Nakatsukasa, M., C. V. Ward, et al.
2004   Tail loss in *Proconsul heselonsi. Journal of Human Evolution* 46: 777–784.

Neal, J. V.
1962   Diabetes mellitus: A thrifty genotype rendered detrimental by "progress"? *American Journal of Human Genetics* 14: 353–362.

Nesse, R. M., S. C. Stearns, et al.
2006   Medicine needs evolution. *Science* 311(5764): 1071.

Nesse, R. M. and G. C. Williams
1994   *Why We Get Sick. The New Science of Darwinian Medicine.* New York, NY: Vintage Books.

Nevell, L., A. Gordon, et al.
2007   *Homo floresiensis* and *Homo sapiens* size-adjusted cranial shape variations. *American Journal of Physical Anthropology, Supplement* 14: 177–178.

News in Brief
2007   Congolese government creates bonobo reserve. *Nature* 450: 470.

Nishida, T.
1991   Comments: Intergroup aggression in chimpanzees and humans by J. H. Manson and R. Wrangham. *Current Anthropology* 32: 369–390, 381–382.

Nishida, T., N. Corp, M. Hamai, et al.
2003   Demography, female life history, and reproductive profiles among the chimpanzees of Mahale. *American Journal of Primatology* 59: 99–121.

Nishida, T., M. Hiraiwahasegawa, et al.
1985   Group extinction and female transfer in wild chimpanzees in the Mahale National-Park, Tanzania. *Zeitschrift Fur Tierpsychologie-Journal of Comparative Ethology* 67(1–4): 284–301.

Nishida, T., H. Takasaki, and Y. Takahata
1990   Demography and reproductive profiles. In: *The Chimpanzees of the Mahale Mountains*, T. Nishida (ed.), pp. 63–97. Tokyo: University of Tokyo Press.

Nishida, T., R. W. Wrangham, et al.
1983   Local differences in plant-feeding habits of chimpanzees between the Mahale Mountains and Gombe National Park, Tanzania. *Journal of Human Evolution* 12(5): 467–480.

Noe, R. and R. Bshary
1997   The formation of red colobus-diana monkey associations under predation pressure from chimpanzees. *Proceedings of the Royal Society of London Series B-Biological Sciences* 264(1379): 253–259.

Noonan, J. P., G. Coop, et al.
2006   Sequencing and analysis of Neanderthal genomic DNA. *Science* 314(5802): 1113–1118.

Nowak, R. M.
1999   *Walker's Primates of the World*. Baltimore, MD: Johns Hopkins University Press.

Oakley, K.
1963   Analytical methods of dating bones. In: *Science in Archaeology*. D. Brothwell and E. Higgs (eds.). New York, NY: Basic Books, Inc.

Oates, J. F., M. Abedi-Lartey, et al.
2000   Extinction of a West African red colobus monkey. *Conservation Biology* 14(5): 1526–1532.

Oates, J. F., R. A. Bergl, et al.
2007   *Gorilla gorilla* ssp. Diehli. *IUCN Red List of Threatened Species*.

Olliaro, P., J. Cattani, et al.
1995   Malaria, the submerged disease. *Journal of the American Medical Association* 275(3): 230–233.

Olshansky, S. J., D. J. Passaro, et al.
2005   A potential decline in life expectancy in the United States in the 21st Century. *New England Journal of Medicine* 352: 1138–1145.

Ottoni, E. B. and P. Izar
2008   Capuchin monkey tool use: Overview and implications. *Evolutionary Anthropology* 17: 171–178.

Ovchinnikov, I. V., A. Gotherstrom, et al.
2000   Molecular analysis of Neanderthal DNA from the northern Caucasus. *Nature* 404(6777): 490–493.

Padian, K. and L. M. Chiappe
1998   The origin of birds and their flight. *Scientific American* 278(2): 38–47.

Page, S. E., F. Siegert, et al.
2002   The amount of carbon released from peat and forest fires in Indonesia during 1997. *Nature* 420: 61–65.

Pagel, M., C. Venditti, et al.
2006   Large punctuational contribution of speciation to evolutionary divergence at the molecular level. *Science* 314(5796): 119–121.

Paine, M.
2001   Source of the Australasian tektites? *Meteorite*, from http//www.meteor.co.nz/.

Palmer, S. K., L. G. Moore, et al.
1999   Altered blood pressure course during normal pregnancy and increased preeclampsia at high altitude (3100 meters) in Colorado. *American Journal of Obstetrics and Gynecology* 180(5): 1161–1168.

Palumbi, S. R.
2001   *The Evolution Explosion: How Humans Cause Rapid Evolutionary Change*. New York, NY: W.W. Norton.

Pares, J. M. and A. Perez-Gonzalez
1995   Paleomagnetic age for hominid fossils at Atapuerca Archaeological Site, Spain. *Science* 269(5225): 830–832.

Park, E.
1978   The Ginsberg Caper: Hacking it as in Stone Age. *Smithsonian* 9: 85–96.

Pavkov, M. E., P. H. Bennett, et al.
2006   Effect of young-onset type 2 diabetes mellitus on incidence of end-stage renal disease and mortality in young and middle-aged Pima Indians. *Journal of the American Medical Association* 296(4): 421–426.

Pavkov, M. E., R. L. Hanson, et al.
2006   Secular trends in the prevalence and incidence rate of type 2 diabetes. *Diabetes* 55: A224-A224.

Peccei, J. S.
2001   Menopause: Adaptation or epiphenomenon? *Evolutionary Anthropology* 10(2): 43–57.

Pennisi, E.
2007   No sex please, we're Neandertals. *Science* 316(967).

Penny, D.
2004   Our relative genetics. *Nature* 427(6971): 208–209.

Peres, C. A.
1990   Effects of hunting on western Amazonian primate communities. *Biological Conservation* 54(1): 47–59.

Perez, V. R., L. R. Godfrey, et al.
2005   Evidence of early butchery of giant lemurs in Madagascar. *Journal of Human Evolution* 49(6): 722–742.

Perkins, S.
2003   Learning from the present. *Science News* 164: 42–44.

Phillips, K. A.
1998   Tool use in wild capuchin monkeys (*Cebus albifrons trinitatis*). *American Journal of Primatology* 46(3): 259–261.

Phillips-Conroy, J. E., C. J. Jolly, P. Nystrom, and H. A. Hemmalin
1992   Migration of male hamadryas baboons into anubis groups in the Awash National Park, Ethiopia. *International Journal of Primatology* 13: 455–476.

Pilbeam, D.
1982   New hominoid skull material from the Miocene of Pakistan. *Nature* 295(5846): 232–234.

Pilbeam, D.
1996   Genetic and morphological records of the Hominoidea and hominid origins: A synthesis. *Molecular Phylogenetics and Evolution* 5(1): 155–168.

Pilbeam, D., M. D. Rose, et al.
1990   New *Sivapithecus* humeri from Pakistan and the relationship of *Sivapithecus* and *Pongo*. *Nature* 348(6298): 237–239.

Pinner, R. W., S. M. Teutsch, et al.
1996   Trends in infectious diseases mortality in the United States. *Journal of the American Medical Association* 275(3): 189–193.

Pollard, T. and N. Unwin
2008   Impaired reproductive function in women in Western and "Westernizing" populations: An evolutionary approach. In: *Evolutionary Medicine and Health: New Perspectives*, W. R. Trevathan, E. O. Smith, and J. J. McKenna (eds.). New York, NY: Oxford University Press.

Poremba, A., M. Malloy, et al.
2004   Species-specific calls evoke asymmetric activity in the monkey's temporal poles. *Nature* 427: 448–451.

Potts, R.
1984   Home bases and early hominids. *American Scientist* 72(4): 338–347.

Potts, R.
1991   Why the Oldowan? Plio-Pleistocene toolmaking and the transport of resources. *Journal of Anthropological Research* 47: 153–176.

Potts, R.
1993   Archeological interpretations of early hominid behavior and ecology. In: *The Origin and Evolution of Humans and Humanness*, D. T. Rasmussen (ed.), pp. 49–74. Boston, MA: Jones and Bartlett.

Potts, R. and P. Shipman
1981   Cutmarks made by stone tools on bones from Olduvai Gorge, Tanzania. *Nature* 291(5816): 577–580.

Potts, R. and R. Teague
2003   Heterogeneity in large-mammal paleocommunities and hominin activities in the southern Kenya rift valley during the mid-Pleistocene (1.2–0.4 Ma). *Abstracts, Paleoanthropology Society Annual Meetings.* Tempe, AZ.

Poux, C. and E. J. Douzery
2004   Primate phylogeny, evolutionary rate variations, and divergence times: a contribution from the nuclear gene IRBP. *American Journal of Physical Anthropology* 124(1): 1–16.

Powell, K. B.
2003   The evolution or lactase persistence in African populations. *American Journal of Physical Anthropology* Supplement 36: 170.

Proctor, R.
1988   From anthropologie to Rassenkunde. In: *Bones, Bodies, Behavior. History of Anthropology*, W. J. Stocking (ed.), pp. 138–179. Madison, WI: University of Wisconsin Press.

Pruetz, J. D. and P. Bertolani
2007   Savanna chimpanzees, *Pan troglodytes verus*, hunt with tools. *Current Biology* 17: 412–417.

Pusey, A., J. Williams, et al.
1997   The influence of dominance rank on the reproductive success of female chimpanzees. *Science* 277(5327): 828–831.

Qinghua, X. and L. Qingwu
2007   *Series monograph III: Lufengpithecus - An Early Member of Hominidae*. Bejing: Science Press.

Raaum, R. L., K. N. Sterner, et al.
2005   Catarrhine primate divergence dates estimated from complete mitochondrial genomes: Concordance with fossil and nuclear DNA evidence. *Journal of Human Evolution* 48(3): 237–257.

Rafferty, K. L., A. Walker, et al.
1995   Postcranial estimates of body weight in *Proconsul*, with a note on a distal tibia of *P. major* from Napak, Uganda. *American Journal of Physical Anthropology* 97: 391–402.

Relethford, J. H.
2001   *Genetics and the Search for Modern Human Origins*. New York, NY: Wiley-Liss.

Renne, P. R., W. D. Sharp, et al.
1997 ^{40}Ar/^{39}Ar dating into the historic realm: Calibration against Pliny the younger. *Science* 277: 1279–1280.

Reno, P. L., R. S. Meindl, et al.
2003   Sexual dimorphism in *Australopithecus afarensis* was similar to that of modern humans. *Proceedings of the National Academy of Sciences of the United States of America* 100(16): 9404–9409.

Reno, P. L., R. S. Meindl, et al.
2005   The case is unchanged and remains robust: *Australopithecus afarensis* exhibits only moderate skeletal dimorphism: A reply to Plavcan et al., 2005. *Journal of Human Evolution* 49: 279–288.

Richards, G. D.
2006   Genetic, physiologic and ecogeographic factors contributing to variation in *Homo sapiens: Homo floresiensis* reconsidered. *Journal of Evolutionary Biology* 19(6): 1744–1767.

Riddle, R. D. and C. J. Tabin
1999   How limbs develop. *Scientific American* 280(2): 74–79.

Ridley, M.
1993   *Evolution*. Boston, MA: Blackwell Scientific Publications.

Rightmire, G. P.
1998   Human evolution in the Middle Pleistocene: The role of *Homo heidelbergensis*. *Evolutionary Anthropology* 6(6): 218–227.

Rightmire, G. P.
2004   Affinities of the Middle Pleistocene cranium from Dali and Jinniushan. *American Journal of Physical Anthropology* Supplement 38: 167.

Robins, A. H.
1991   *Biological Perspectives on Human Pigmentation*. Cambridge: Cambridge University Press.

Römpler, H., N. Rohland, et al.
2006   Nuclear gene indicates coat-color polymorphism in mammoths. *Science* 313: 62–64.

Rosenberg, N. A., J. K. Pritchard, et al.
2002   Genetic structure of human populations. *Science* 298(5602): 2381–2385.

Ross, C. F.
2000   Into the light: The origin of Anthropoidea. *Annual Review of Anthropology* 29: 147–194.

Ross, C. F., M. Henneberg, et al.
2004   Curvilinear, geometric and phylogenetic modeling of basicranial flexion: Is it adaptive, is it constrained? *Journal of Human Evolution* 46: 185–213.

Rossie, J. B. and L. MacLatchy
2006   A new pliopithecoid genus from the early Miocene of Uganda. *Journal of Human Evolution* 50(5): 568–586.

Rouquet, P., J. Froment, et al.
2005   Wild animal mortality monitoring and human Ebola outbreaks, Gabon and Republic of Congo. *Emerging Infectious Diseases* 11(2): 283–290.

Rovner, I.
1983   Plant opal phytolith analysis: Major advances in archaeobotanical research. In: *Advances in Archaeological Method and Theory*, M. B. Schiffer (ed.), pp. 225–266. New York, NY: Academic Press.

Rudran, R.
1973   Adult male replacement in one-male troops of purple-faced langurs (*Presbytis senex senex*) and its effect on population structure. *Folia Primatologica* 19: 166–192.

Ruff, C. B. and A. Walker
1993   The body size and shape of KNM-WT 15000. In: *The Nariokotome* Homo erectus *Skeleton*, A. Walker and R. E. Leakey (eds.), pp. 234–265. Cambridge, MA: Harvard University Press.

Ruff, C. B., A. Walker, et al.
1989   Body mass, sexual dimorphism and femoral proportions of *Proconsul* from Rusinga and Mfangano Islands, Kenya. *Journal of Human Evolution* 18: 515–536.

Rukang, W. and J. W. Olsen
1985   *Palaeoanthropology and Palaeolithic Archaeology in the People's Republic of China*. Orlando: Academic Press.

Ruvolo, M., D. Pan, et al.
1994   Gene trees and hominoid phylogeny. *Proceedings of the National Academy of Sciences of the United States of America* 91(19): 8900–8904.

Sagan, C.
1977   *The Dragons of Eden: Speculations on the Evolution of Human Intelligence*. Random House.

Samson, M., F. Libert, et al.
1996   Resistance to HIV-1 infection in Caucasian individuals bearing mutant alleles of the CCR-5 chemokine receptor gene. *Nature* 382(6593): 722–725.

Sargis, E. J., D. M. Boyer, et al.
2007   Evolution of pedal grasping in Primates. *Journal of Human Evolution* 53(1): 103–107

Sarmiento, E. E. and J. F. Oates
2000   The Cross River gorilla: A distinct subspecies *Gorilla gorilla diehli* Matschie 1904. *American Museum Novitates* 3304: 1–55.

Savage-Rumbaugh, S.
1986   *Ape Language: From Conditioned Responses to Symbols*. New York, NY: Columbia University Press.

Savage-Rumbaugh, S. and R. Lewin
1994   *Kanzi: The Ape at the Brink of the Human Mind*. New York, NY: John Wiley and Sons.

Savage-Rumbaugh, S., K. McDonald, et al.
1986   Spontaneous symbol acquisition and communicative use by pygmychimpanzees (*Pan paniscus*). *Journal of Experimental Psychology General* 115(3): 211–235.

Schauber, A. D. and D. Falk
2008   Proportional dwarfism in foxes, mice, and humans: Implications for relative brain size in *Homo floresiensis* [abstract]. *American Journal of Physical Anthropology, Supplement* 43: 185.

Schmitz, R. W., D. Serre, et al.
2002   The Neandertal type site revisited: Interdisciplinary investigations of skeletal remains from the Neander Valley, Germany. *Proceedings of the National Academy of Sciences, USA* 99(20): 13342–13347.

Schwartz, J. H.
1984   What Is a Tarsier? In: *Living Fossils*. Niles and Steven M. Stanley Eldridge (eds.). New York, NY: Springer Verlag: 38–49.

Scriver, C. R.
2001   *The Metabolic and Molecular Bases of Inherited Disease*. New York, NY: McGraw Hill.

Seehausen, O.
2002   Patterns of fish radiation are compatible with Pliestocene dessication of Lake Victoria and 14,600 year history for its cichlid species flock. *Proceedings of the Royal Society of London (Biological Science)* 269: 491–497.

Seiffert, E. R., E. L. Simons, et al.
2003   Fossil evidence for an ancient divergence of lorises and galagos. *Nature* 422: 421–424.

Seiffert, E. R., E. L. Simons, et al.
2005a   Additional remains of *Wadilemur elegans*, a primitive stem galagid from the late Eocene of Egypt. *Proceedings of the National Academy of Science, USA* 102(32): 11396–11401.

Seiffert , E., Elwyn Simons, et al.
2005b   Basil anthropoids from Egypt and the antiquity of Africa's higher primate radiation. *Science* 310: 300–304.

Semaw, S., M. J. Rogers, et al.
2003   2.6-million-year-old stone tools and associated bones from OGS-6 and OGS-7, Gona, Afar, Ethiopia. *Journal of Human Evolution* 45: 169–177.

Serre, D., A. Langaney, et al.
2004   No evidence of Neandertal mtDNA contribution to early modern humans. *Plos Biology* 2(3): 313–317.

Seyfarth, R. M.
1987   Vocal communication and its relation to language. In: *Primate Societies*. B. Smuts, D. L. Cheney, R. M. Seyfarth, et al. (eds.) Chicago, IL, University of Chicago Press: 440–451.

Seyfarth, R. M., Dorothy L. Cheney, and Peter Marler
1980a   Monkey responses to three different alarm calls. *Science* 210: 801–803.

Seyfarth, R. M., D. L. Cheney, and P. Marler
1980b   Vervet monkey alarm calls: semantic communication in a free-ranging primate. *Animal Behaviour* 28:1070–1094.

Shang, H., Haowen Tong, et al.
2007   An early modern human from Tianyuan Cave, Zhoukoudian, China. *Proceedings of the National Academy of Sciences, USA* 104(6573–6578).

Shea, J. J.
1998   Neandertal and early modern human behavioral variability—A regional-scale approach to lithic evidence for hunting in the Levantine Mousterian. *Current Anthropology* 39: S45–S78.

Shindler, K.
2006   *Discovering Dorothea: The Life of the Pioneering Fossil-Hunter Dorothea Bate.* London: Harper Collins Ltd.

Shipman, P.
1983   Early hominid lifestyle. hunting and gathering or foraging and scavenging? In: *Animals and Archaeology.* J. Clutton-Brock and C. Grigson (eds.), pp. 31–51. Vol. I: Hunters and Their Prey. Brit. Arch. Rpts.: London.

Shubin, N., Cliff Tabin, and Sean Carroll
1997   Fossils, genes, and the evolution of animal limbs. *Nature* 388: 639–648.

Shubin, N. H., E. B. Daeschler, et al.
2006   The pectoral fin of *Tiktaalik roseae* and the origin of the tetrapod limb. *Nature* 440(7085): 764–771.

Silcox, M. T.
2001   A Phylogenetic Analysis of Plesiadapiformes and Their Relationship to Euprimates and Other Archontans, Unpublished PhD dissertation, Johns Hopkins University School of Medicine, Baltimore, MD.

Silcox, M. T.
2007   Primate taxonomy, plesiadapiforms, and approaches to primate origins. In: *Primate Origins: Adaptations and Evolution.* M. J. Ravosa and M. Dagosto (eds.), pp. 143–178. New York, NY: Plenum Press.

Silk, J. B., S. C. Alberts, et al.
2003   Social bonds of female baboons enhance infant survival. *Science* 302(5648): 1231–1234.

Simons, E. L.
1972   *Primate Evolution: An Introduction to Man's Place in Nature.* New York, NY: MacMillan Company.

Simons, E. L.
1976   The fossil record of primate phylogeny. In: *Molecular Anthropology: Genes and Proteins in the Evolutionary Ascent of the Primates.* M. Goodman (ed.), pp. 35–62. New York, NY: Plenum Press.

Simons, E. L., E. R. Seiffert, et al.
2007   A remarkable female cranium of the early Oligocene anthropoid *Aegyptopithecus zeuxis* (Catarrhini, Propliopithecidae). *Proceedings of the National Academy of Sciences, USA* 104(21): 8731–8736.

Simpson, S. W., J. Quade, et al.
2008   A female *Homo erectus* pelvis from Gona, Ethiopia. *Science* 322: 1089–1092.

Skaletsky, H., T. Kuroda-Kawaguchi, et al.
2003   The male-specific region of the human Y chromosome is a mosaic of discrete sequence classes. *Nature* 423(6942): 825-U2.

Smith, F. H.
2002   Migrations, radiations and continuity: Patterns in the evolution of Late Pleistocene humans. In: *The Primate Fossil Record*, W. Hartwig (ed.), pp. 437–456. Cambridge: Cambridge University Press.

Smith, F. H., A. B. Falsetti, et al.
1989   Modern human origins. *Yearbook of Physical Anthropology* 32: 35–68.

Smith, F. H., E. Trinkaus, et al.
1999   Direct radiocarbon dates for Vindija G1 and Velika Pécina Late Pleistocene hominid remains. *Proceedings of the National Academy of Sciences* 96: 12281–12286.

Smith, T., K. D. Rose, and P. Gingerich
2006   Rapid Asia-Europe-North America geographic dispersal of earliest Eocene primate *Teilhardina* during the Paleocene-Eocene thermal maximum. *Proceedings of the National Academy of Sciences, USA* 103: 11223–11227.

Smuts, B.
1985   *Sex and Friendship in Baboons.* Hawthorne, NY: Aldine de Gruyter.

Soligo, C. and R. D. Martin
2007   The first primates: A reply to Silcox et al. (2007). *Journal of Human Evolution* 53(3): 325–328

Sponheimer, M., B. H. Passey, et al.
2006   Isotopic evidence for dietary variability in the early hominin *Paranthropus robustus*. *Science* 314(5801): 980–982.

Spoor, F., M. G. Leakey, et al.
2007   Implications of new early *Homo* fossils from Ileret, east of Lake Turkana, Kenya. *Nature* 448: 688–691.

Stanford, C.
1999   *The Hunting Apes: Meat Eating and the Origins of Human Behavior.* Princeton, NJ: Princeton University Press.

Stanford, C.
2001   The ape's gift: Meat-eating, meat-sharing, and human evolution. In: *Tree of Origin*, F. deWaal (ed.), pp. 95-117. Cambridge, MA: Harvard University Press.

Starin, E. D.
1994   Philopatry and affiliation among red colobus. *Behaviour* 130: 253–270.

Stearns, S. C.
1992   *The Evolution of Life Histories.* Oxford: Oxford University Press.

Steiper, M. E. and N. M. Young
2006   Primate molecular divergence dates. *Molecular Phylogenetics and Evolution* 41(2): 384–394.

Steiper, M. E. and N. M. Young
2008   Timing primate evolution: lessons from the discordance between molecular and paleontological estimates. *Evolutionary Anthropology* 17 (4): 179–188

Steklis, H. D.
1985   Primate communication, comparative neurology, and the origin of language reexamined. *Journal of Human Evolution* 14: 157–173.

Stelzner, J. and K. Strier
1981   Hyena predation on an adult male baboon. *Mammalia* 45: 259–260.

Sterner, K. N., R. L. Raaum, et al.
2006   Mitochondrial data support an odd-nosed colobine clade. *Molecular Phylogenetics and Evolution* 40(1): 1–7.

Stevens, N. J. and C. P. Heesy
2006   Malagasy primate origins: Phylogenies, fossils, and biogeographic reconstructions. *Folia Primatologica* 77(6): 419–433

Stix, G.
2008   Traces of a distant past. *Scientific American* 299: 56–63.

Strassmann, B. I. and B. Gillespie
2002   Life-history theory, fertility and reproductive success in humans. *Proceedings of the Royal Society of London Series B-Biological Sciences* 269(1491): 553–562.

Strier, K. B.
2003   *Primate Behavioral Ecology*. Boston, MA: Allyn and Bacon.

Stringer, C. B. and P. Andrews
1988   Genetic and fossil evidence for the origin of modern humans. *Science* 239(4845): 1263–1268.

Struhsaker, T. T.
1967   Auditory communication among vervet monkeys (*Cercopithecus aethiops*). In: *Social Communication Among Primates*, S. A. Altmann (ed.). Chicago, IL: University of Chicago Press.

Struhsaker, T. T.
1975   *The Red Colobus Monkey*. Chicago, IL: University of Chicago Press.

Struhsaker, T. T. and L. Leland
1979   Socioecology of five sympatric monkey species in the Kibale forest, Uganda. In: *Advances in the Study of Behavior*. J.S. Rosenblatt, R.A. Hinde, C. Beer, and M.C. Busnel (eds.). New York, NY, Academic Press: 9: 159–229.

Struhsaker, T. T. and L. Leland
1987   Colobines: Infanticide by adult males. In: *Primate Societies*. B. Smuts, D. L. Cheney, R. M. Seyfarth, et al. (eds.). Chicago, IL, University of Chicago Press: 83–97.

Stuart-Macadam, P. and K. A. Dettwyler
1995   *Breastfeeding: Biocultural Perspectives*. Hawthorne, NY: Aldine de Gruyter.

Sturm, R. A., D. L. Duffy, et al.
2008   A single SNP in an evolutionary conserved region within intron 86 of the HERC2 gene determines human blue-brown eye color. *American Journal of Human Genetics* 82: 424–431.

Sugiyama, Y.
1965   Short history of the ecological and sociological studies on non-human primates in Japan. *Primates* 6: 457–460.

Sumner, D. R., M. E. Morbeck, et al.
1989   Age-related bone loss in female Gombe chimpanzees. *American Journal of Physical Anthropology* 72: 259.

Suomi, S. J., Susan Mineka, and Roberta D. DeLizio
1983   Short-and long-term effects of repetitive mother-infant separation on social development in rhesus monkeys. *Developmental Psychology* 19: 710–786.

Susman, R. L. (Ed.)
1984   *The Pygmy Chimpanzee: Evolutionary Biology and Behavior*. New York, NY: Plenum.

Sussman, R. W.
1991   Primate origins and the evolution of angiosperms. *American Journal of Primatology* 23(4): 209–223.

Sussman, R. W., J. M. Cheverud, and T. Q. Bartlett
1995   Infant killing as an evolutionary strategy: reality or myth? *Evolutionary Anthropology* 3: 149–151.

Suwa, G., R. T. Kono, et al.
2007   A new species of great ape from the Late Miocene epoch in Ethiopia. *Nature* 448: 921–924.

Swisher, C. C., W. J. Rink, et al.
1996   Latest *Homo erectus* of Java: Potential contemporaneity with *Homo sapiens* in Southwest Java. *Science* 274: 1870–1874.

Tattersall, I., E. Delson, and J. Van Couvering
1988   *Encyclopedia of Human Evolution and Prehistory*. New York, NY: Garland Publishing.

Tavaré, S., C. R. Marshall, et al.
2002   Using the fossil record to estimate the age of the last common ancestor of extant primates. *Nature* 416(6882): 726–729.

Tavera-Mendoza, L. E. and J. H. White
2007   Cell defenses and the sunshine vitamin. *Scientific American* 297(5): 62–72.

Tenaza, R. and T. Tilson
1977   Evolution of long-distance alarm calls in Kloss' gibbon. *Nature* 268: 233–235.

Teresi, D.
2002   *Lost Discoveries. The Ancient Roots of Modern Science—from the Babylonians to the Maya*. New York, NY: Simon and Schuster.

Thieme, H.
1997   Lower Palaeolithic hunting spears from Germany. *Nature* 385(6619): 807–810.

Thorne, A., R. Grün, et al.
1999   Australia's oldest human remains: Age of the Lake Mungo 3 skeleton. *Journal of Human Evolution* 36: 591–612.

Tiemel, C., Y. Quan, and W. En
1994   Antiquity of *Homo sapiens* in China. *Nature* 368(6466): 55–56.

Tishkoff, S. A., F. A. Reed, et al.
2007   Convergent adaptation of human lactase persistence in Africa and Europe. *Nature Genetics* 39(1): 31–40.

Tocheri, M. W., Caley M. Orr, et al.
2007   The primitive wrist of *Homo floresiensis* and its implications for hominin evolution. *Science*: 1743–1745.

Tollefson, J.
2008   Brazil goes to war against logging. *Nature* 452: 134–135.

Tornow, M. A.
2008   Systematic analysis of the Eocene primate family Omomyidae using gnathic and postcranial data. *Bulletin of the Peabody Museum of Natural History*: 43–129

Trevathan, W. R., E. O. Smith, et al.
1999   *Evolutionary Medicine*. New York, NY: Oxford University Press.

Trevathan, W. R., E. O. Smith, et al.
2008   *Evolutionary Medicine and Health: New Perspectives*. New York, NY: Oxford University Press.

Trinkaus, E.
2005   Early modern humans. *Annual Review of Anthropology* 34: 207–230.

Trinkaus, E., S. Milota, et al.
2003   Early modern human cranial remains from the Pestera cu Oase, Romania. *Journal of Human Evolution* 45(3): 245–253.

Trinkaus, E. and P. Shipman
1992   *The Neandertals*. New York, NY: Alfred A. Knopf.

Ungar, P. S. and R. F. Kay
1995   The dietary adaptations of European Miocene catarrhines. *Proceedings of the National Academy of Sciences, USA* 92(12): 5479–5481.

Van Bocxlaer, B., D. Van Damme, et al.
2007   Gradual versus punctuated equilibrium evolution in the Turkana Basin mollusks: Evolutionary events or biological invasion? *Evolution*: 511–520.

van der Ven, K., R. Fimmers, et al.
2000   Evidence for major histocompatability complex-mediated effects on spermatogenesis in humans. *Human Reproduction* 15: 189–196.

van Schaik, C. P., M. Ancrenaz, et al.
2003   Orangutan cultures and the evolution of material culture. *Science* 299(5603): 102–105.

Van Valen, L.
1973   Pattern and the balance of nature. *Evolutionary Theory* 1: 31–49.

Varki, A.
2000   A chimpanzee genome project is a biomedical imperative. *Genome Research* 10(8): 1065–1070.

Vialet, A., L. Tianyuan, et al.
2005   Proposition de reconstitution du deuxième crâne d'*Homo erectus* de Yunxian (Chine). *Comptes rendus. Palévol* 4: 265–274.

Vigilant, L., M. Hofreiter, et al.
2001   Paternity and relatedness in wild chimpanzee communities. *Proceedings of the National Academy of Sciences, USA* 98(23): 12890–12895.

Villa, P.
1983   *Terra Amata and the Middle Pleistocene Archaeological Record of Southern France*. Berkeley, CA: University of California Press.

Visalberghi, E.
1990   Tool use in cebus. *Folia Primatologica* 54(3–4): 146–154.

Visalberghi, E. D. F., E. Ottoni, et al.
2007   Characteristics of hammer stones and anvils used by wild bearded capuchin monkeys (*Cebus libidinosus*) to crack open palm nuts. *American Journal of Physical Anthropology* 132: 426–444.

Vogelsang, R.
1998   *The Middle Stone Age Fundstellen in Süd-west Namibia*. Köln: Heinrich Barth Institut.

Vogelstein, B., D. Lane, et al.
2000   Surfing the p53 network. *Nature* 408(6810): 307–310.

Vrba, E. S.
1992   Mammals as a key to evolutionary theory. *Journal of Mammalogy* 73(1): 1–28.

Wagner, G. A.
1996   Fission-track dating in paleoanthropology. *Evolutionary Anthropology* 5: 165–171.

Walker, A.
1991   The origin of the genus *Homo*. *Evolution of Life*. S. Osawa and T. Honjo (eds.). Tokyo, Springer-Verlag: 379–389.

Walker, A.
1993   The origin of the genus *Homo*. In: *The Origin and Evolution of Humans and Humanness*, D. T. Rasmussen (ed.), pp. 29–47. Boston, MA: Jones and Bartlett.

Walker, A. and R. E. Leakey
1993   *The Nariokotome* Homo erectus *Skeleton*. Cambridge, MA: Harvard University Press.

Walker, A. and P. Shipman
2005   *The Ape in the Tree. An Intellectual and Natural History of* Proconsul. Cambridge, MA: Belknap Press.

Walrath, D.
2003   Rethinking pelvic typologies and the human birth mechanism. *Current Anthropology* 44(1): 5–31.

Walsh, P. D., K. A. Abernethy, et al.
2003   Catastrophic ape decline in western equatorial Africa. *Nature* 422(6932): 611–614.

Ward, C. V.
2005   Torso morphology and locomotion in *Proconsul nyanzae*. *American Journal of Physical Anthropology* 92: 321–328.

Ward, P.
1994   *The End of Evolution*. New York, NY: Bantam.

Warren W. C., LaDeana W. Hillier, et al.
2008   Genome analysis of the platypus reveals unique signatures of evolution. *Nature* 453: 175–183.

Washburn, S. L.
1963   The study of race. *American Anthropologist* 65(3): 521–531.

Washburn, S. L. and Irven DeVore
1961   The social life of baboons. *Scientific American* 204: 62–71.

Washburn, S. L. and C. S. Lancaster
1968   The evolution of hunting. In: *Man the Hunter*. R. B. Lee and I. DeVore (eds.). Chicago, IL, Aldine de Gruyter: 293–303.

Weiner, J. S.
1955   *The Piltdown Forgery*. London: Oxford University Press.

Weiner, S., Q. Q. Xu, et al.
1998   Evidence for the use of fire at Zhoukoudian, China. *Science* 281(5374): 251–253.

Weir, A., J. Chappell, et al.
2008   Shaping of hooks in New Caledonian crows. *Science* 297: 981.

Weiss, K.
2003   Come to me, my melancholic baby! *Evolutionary Anthropology* 12(1): 3–6.

Weiss, R. A. and R. W. Wrangham
1999   From *Pan* to pandemic. *Nature* 397(6718): 385–386.

Weiss, U.
2002   Nature insight: Malaria. *Nature* 415: 669.

Wendt, W. E.
1976   Art Mobilier' from the Apollo 11 Cave, South West Africa: Africa's oldest dated works of art. *South African Archaeological Bulletin* 31: 5–11.

Westergaard, G. C. and D. M. Fragaszy
1987   The manufacture and use of tools by capuchin monkeys (*Cebus apella*). *Journal of Comparative Psychology* 101: 159–168.

White, T. D.
1986   Cut marks on the Bodo cranium: a case of prehistoric defleshing. *American Journal of Physical Anthropology* 69(4): 503–509.

White, T. D., B. Asfaw, et al.
2003   Pleistocene *Homo sapiens* from Middle Awash, Ethiopia. *Nature* 423(6941): 742–747.

Whiten, A., J. Goodall, et al.
1999   Cultures in chimpanzees. *Nature* 399(6737): 682–685.

Wildman, D. E., M. Uddin, et al.
2003   Implications of natural selection in shaping 99.4% nonsynonymous DNA identity between humans and chimpanzees: Enlarging genus *Homo*. *Proceedings of the National Academy of Sciences, USA* 100(12): 7181–7188.

Williams, G. C.
1957   Pleiotropy, natural selection, and the evolution of senescence. *Evolution* 11(4): 398–411.

Williams, G. C. and R. M. Nesse
1991   The dawn of Darwinian medicine. *The Quarterly Review of Biology* 66: 1–22.

Williams, J. M.
1999   Female Strategies and the Reasons for Territoriality in Chimpanzees. Lessons from Three Decades of Research at Gombe. Unpublished Ph.D. Thesis, University of Minnesota.

Wilson, E. O.
1992   *The Diversity of Life*. Cambridge, MA: The Belknap Press of Harvard University Press.

Wilson, M. L., W. R. Wallauer, et al.
2004   New cases of intergroup violence among Chimpanzees in Gombe National Park, Tanzania. *International Journal of Primatology* 25(3): 523–549.

Wolpoff, M. H.
1989   Multiregional evolution: The fossil alternative to Eden. In: *The Human Revolution*. P. Mellars and C. B. Stringer (eds.), pp. 62–108. Princeton, NJ: Princeton University Press

Wolpoff, M. H., J. Hawks, et al.
2001   Modern human ancestry at the peripheries: A test of the replacement theory. *Science* 291(5502): 293–297.

Wolpoff, M., A. G. Thorne, et al.
1994   Multiregional evolutions: A world-wide source for modern human populations. In: *Origins of Anatomically Modern Humans*. M. H. Nitecki and D. V. Nitecki (eds.), pp. 175–199. New York, NY: Plenum Press

Woo, J. K.
1966   Skull of Lantian Man. *Current Anthropology* 7(1): 83–86.

Wood, B.
1991   *Koobi Fora Research Project IV: Hominid Cranial Remains from Koobi Fora*. Oxford: Clarendon Press.

Wood, B.
1992   Origin and evolution of the genus *Homo*. *Nature* 355(6363): 783–790.

Wood, B. and M. Collard
1999a   The human genus. *Science* 284(5411): 65–71.

Wood, B. and M. Collard
1999b   The changing face of genus *Homo*. *Evolutionary Anthropology* 8(6): 195–207.

Worthy, T. W. and R. N. Holdaway
2002   *The Lost World of the Moa: Prehistoric Life of New Zealand*. Bloomington, IN: Indiana University Press.

Wrangham, R., A. Clark, and G. Isabiryre-Basita
1992   Female social relationships and social organization of Kibale forest chimps. In: *Topics in Primatology*. W. McGrew T. Nishida, P. Marler, et al. (eds.), pp. 81–98. Tokyo: Tokyo University Press.

Wrangham, R. and D. Peterson
1996   *Demonic Males: Apes and the Origins of Human Violence*. New York, NY: Houghton Mifflin.

Wrangham, R. W.
1999   The evolution of coalitionary killing. *Yearbook of Physical Anthropology* 42: 1–30.

Wrangham, R. W. and B. B. Smuts
1980   Sex differences in the behavioural ecology of chimpanzees in Gombe National Park, Tanzania. *Journal of Reproduction and Fertility* 28: 13–31.

Wright, P. C., E. L. Simons, et al.
2003   *Tarsiers: Past, Present, and Future*. Rutgers University Press.

Wu, R. and X. Dong
1985   *Homo erectus* in China. In: *Palaeoanthropology and Palaeolithic Archaeology in the People's Republic of China*. R. Wu and J. W. Olsen (eds.). New York, NY, Academic Press: 79–89.

Wu, X. and F. E. Poirier
1995   *Human Evolution in China*. Oxford: Oxford University Press.

Wu, X. J., L. A. Schepartz, et al.
2006   Endocranial cast of Hexian *Homo erectus* from South China. *American Journal of Physical Anthropology* 130(4): 445–454.

Wuethrich, B.
1998   Geological analysis damps ancient Chinese fires. *Science* 281(5374): 165–166.

Xu, Q. and Q. Lu
2007   *Series monograph III: Lufengpithecus—An Early Member of Hominidae*. Beijing: Science Press.

Yamei, H., R. Potts, et al.
2000   Mid-Pleistocene Acheulean-like stone technology of the Bose basin, South China. *Science* 287(5458): 1622–1626.

Yellen, J. E., A. S. Brooks, et al.
1995   A Middle Stone-Age worked bone industry from Katanda, Upper Semliki Valley, Zaire. *Science* 268(5210): 553–556.

Yoder, A. D., M. M. Burns, et al.
2003   Single origin of Malagasy carnivora from an African ancestor. *Nature* 421: 734–737.

Yoder, A. D., M. Cartmill, et al.
1996   Ancient single origin for Malagasy primates. *Proceedings of the National Academy of Sciences* 93(10): 5122–5126.

Young, D.
1992   *The Discovery of Evolution*. Cambridge: Natural History Museum Publications, Cambridge University Press.

Young, E. M.
2004   Globalization and food security: novel questions in a novel context? *Progress in Development Studies* 4: 1–21.

Zhang, J. Z., Y. P. Zhang, et al.
2002   Adaptive evolution of a duplicated pancreatic ribonuclease gene in a leaf-eating monkey. *Nature Genetics* 30(4): 411–415.

Zhu, R. X., Z. S. An, et al.
2003   Magnetostratigraphic dating of early humans in China. *Earth-Science Reviews* 61(3-4): 341–359.

Ziegler, A., A. S. Jonason, et al.
1994   Sunburn and P53 in the onset of skin-cancer. *Nature* 372(6508): 773–776.

Zimmet, P., K. Alberti, et al.
2001   Global and societal implications of the diabetes epidemic. *Nature* 414(6865): 782–787.

Photo Credits

iv, Lynn Kilgore; **v**, Drawing by Robert Greisen; **vi**, top, Courtesy, Nelson Ting; bottom, Courtesy, San Francisco Zoo; **vii**, top, bottom, © Russell L. Ciochon, University of Iowa; **viii**, top, Courtesy, David Lordkipanidze; bottom, Courtesy, Institute of Human Origins; **ix**, top, Courtesy, Milford Wolpoff; bottom, Courtesy, Fred Smith; **x**, Joseph Luoman/iStockphoto; **1**, Penny Tweedie/Corbis; **2**, Courtesy, Peter Jones; **3**, © Bettmann/Corbis; **5**, top left, Lynn Kilgore; top right, NASA/Space Telescope Science Institute; bottom left, Lynn Kilgore; bottom right, Justin Horocks/iStockphoto; **9**, top, © Kenneth Garrett/NGS Image Collection; bottom, © Russell L. Ciochon, University of Iowa; **10**, Lynn Kilgore; **11**, top, Courtesy, Judith Regensteiner; bottom, Courtesy, Kathleen Galvin; **12**, top left, Robert Jurmain; top right, Courtesy, Nelson Ting; bottom left and right, Lynn Kilgore; **13**, bottom left, Courtesy, D. France; bottom right, Courtesy, Lorna Pierce/Judy Suchey; **14**, top, Courtesy, Linda Levitch; bottom, Courtesy, Julie Lesnik; **17**, top, bottom, Nanette Barkey; **23**, George Richmond/The Gallery Collection/Corbis; **26**, © Wikipedia; **27**, J. van (Johannes) Loon/Wikimedia Commons; **23**, top, American Museum of Natural History; **30**, Wikipedia; **31**, top left, With permission from the Master of Haileybury; top right, © National Portrait Gallery, London; **32**, top left and right, Lynn Kilgore; **33**, top, The Natural History Museum, London; bottom, © Bettmann/Corbis; **35**, bottom, Dogs surrounding wolf: Lynn Kilgore and Lin Marshall; wolf: John Giustina/Getty Images; **36**, © National Portrait Gallery, London; **37**, © Russell L. Ciochon, University of Iowa; **39**, top, Michael Tweedie/Photo Researchers; bottom, Breck P. Kent/Animals Animals; **43**, © Gordon Chancellor; **45**, © Bettmann/Corbis; **49**, Courtesy, Dr. Michael S. Donnenberg; **50**, top, Professors P. Motta and T. Naguro/SPL/Photo Researchers, Inc.; bottom, A. Barrington Brown/Photo Researchers, Inc.; **51**, The Novartis Foundation; **61**, Lynn Kilgore; **62**, top left and right, © Dr. Stanley Flegler/Visuals Unlimited; **64**, © Biophoto Associates/Science Source/Photo Researchers; **67**, CNRI/Photo Researchers, Inc; **73**, Cellmark Diagnostics, Abingdon, UK; **74**, Courtesy, Advanced Cell Technology, Inc., Worcester, Massachusetts; **76**, Courtesy, Margaret Maples; inset, © Bettmann/Corbis; **78**, Craig King, Armed Forces DNA Identification Laboratory; **79**, CNRI/Photo Researchers; **80**, bottom left and right, Wikipedia; **81**, Raychel Ciemma and Precision Graphics; **90**, Norman Lightfoot/Photo Researchers; **93**, Courtesy, Ray Carson, University of Florida News and Public Affairs; **94**, a–f, Lynn Kilgore; g, Robert Jurmain; **98**, Reprinted, with permission, from the *Annual Review of Genetics*, Volume 10 ©1976 by Annual Reviews www.annualreviews.org; **102**, Lynn Kilgore; **109**, Louie Psihoyos/Corbis; **121**, Drawing by Robert Greisen; **131**, Tom McHugh, Photo Researchers; **132**, J. C. Stevenson/Animals Animals; **136**, top left and right, © Tomasz Zachariasz/iStockphoto; bottom left and right, Lynn Kilgore; **139**, Nature Expressions/Getty Images; **141**, a–e, Lynn Kilgore; **144**, Lynn Kilgore; **145**, Lynn Kilgore; **146**, Howler species: Raymond Mendez/Animals Animals; Spider monkey: Robert L. Lubeck/Animals Animals; Prince Bernhard's titi: Marc van Roosmalen; Tamarin: © Zoological Society of San Diego, photo by Ron Garrison; Muriqui: Andrew Young; White-faced capuchins: © Jay Dickman/Corbis; Squirrel monkey: © Kevin Schafer/Corbis; Uakari: R. A. Mittermeier/Conservation International; **147**, Baboon: Courtesy, Bonnie Pedersen/Arlene Kruse; Macaque: Courtesy, Jean De Rousseau; Gibbon: Lynn Kilgore; Tarsier: Courtesy, David Haring, Duke University Primate Zoo; Orangutan: © Tom McHugh/Photo Researchers, Inc.; Langur: Joe MacDonald/Animals Animals; Lemur: Courtesy, Fred Jacobs; Loris: Courtesy, San Francisco Zoo; Cercopithecus: Robert Jurmain; Colobus: Robert Jurmain; Galagos: Courtesy, Bonnie Pedersen/Arlene Kruse; Chimpanzee: Courtesy, Arlene Kruse/Bonnie Pedersen; Mountain gorilla: Lynn Kilgore; **149**, © Russell L. Ciochon, University of Iowa; **151**, Lynn Kilgore; **154**, top left and right, Lynn Kilgore; left, © Viktor Deak, after John G. Fleagle; **137**, top left and right, Courtesy, Fred Jacobs; bottom left, Courtesy, San Francisco Zoo; bottom right, Courtesy, Bonnie Pedersen/Arlene Kruse; **156**, David Haring, Duke University Primate Zoo; **157**, bottom left, © Zoological Society of San Diego, photo by Ron Garrison; bottom right, Raymond Mendez/Animals Animals; **158**, top left, © Andrew Young; top right, © Kevin Schafer/Corbis; center right, Marc van Roosmalen; bottom right, R. A. Mittermeier/Conservation International; bottom left, © Jay Dickman/Corbis; **159**, top, Robert L. Lubeck/Animals Animals; **160**, Robert Jurmain; **161**, top left and right, Courtesy, Bonnie Pedersen/Arlene Kruse; bottom, Courtesy, Nelson Ting; **163**, top, Lynn Kilgore; bottom left, Noel Rowe; bottom right, Lynn Kilgore; **164**, left, right, Lynn Kilgore; **165**, left, right, Lynn Kilgore; **166**, left, Lynn Kilgore; right, Robert Jurmain, photo by Jill Matsumoto/Jim Anderson; **168**, Courtesy, Ellen Ingmanson; **169**, Lynn Kilgore; **172**, John Oates; **173**, Karl Ammann; **175**, WildlifeDirect.org; **177**, Robert Jurmain; **179**, bottom left, Courtesy, Jean De Rousseau; bottom right, John Oates; **181**, Russ Mittermeir; **182**, Lynn Kilgore; **186**, John Oates; **187**, Time Life Pictures/Getty Images; **189**, left, © Chris Hellier/Corbis; right, © Theo Allofs/Corbis; **190**, Lynn Kilgore; **191**, Lynn Kilgore; **193**, top left and right, Lynn Kilgore; bottom, Lynn Kilgore; **194**, top left, Robert Jurmain; top right, Courtesy, Meredith Small; bottom left and right, Courtesy, Arlene Kruse/Bonnie Pedersen; **195**, Alexander Klemm/iStockphoto; **197**, whozoo.org; **198**, top, Joe MacDonald/Animals Animals; bottom, © Peter Henzi; **200**, top left, Courtesy, David Haring , Duke University

Index

World Political Map